INTRODUCTORY FOODS

FIFTEENTH EDITION

Barbara Scheule PHD, RD
Kent State University

Amanda Frye
MS, RDN

Vice President, Portfolio Management: Andrew Gilfillan
Portfolio Manager: Pamela Chirls
Editorial Assistant: Lara Dimmick
Product Marketing Manager: Heather Taylor
Director, Digital Studio and Content Production: Brian Hyland
Managing Producer: Cynthia Zonneveld
Content Producer: Rinki Kaur
Manager, Rights Management: Johanna Burke

Manufacturing Buyer: Deidra Headlee
Full-Service Management and Composition: Integra Software Services, Ltd.
Full-Service Project Manager: Abinaya Rajendran
Cover Design: Studio Montage
Cover Photo: Nadki/Shutterstock
Printer/Binder: LSC Communications, Inc.
Cover Printer: LSC Communications, Inc.
Text Font: Helvetica Neue LT W1G

Library of Congress Cataloging-in-Publication Data

Names: Frye, Amanda, author | Scheule, Barbara, author.
Title: Introductory foods / Barbara Scheule, Kent State University, Amanda Frye.
Description: Fifteenth edition. | Boston : Pearson, [2020] | Includes bibliographical references and index.
Identifiers: LCCN 2019041387| ISBN 9780134552767 | ISBN 0134552768
Subjects: LCSH: Food. | Cooking.
Classification: LCC TX354 .B46 2020 | DDC 641.3—dc23
    LC record available at https://lccn.loc.gov/2018041387

1 2019

ISBN-10:   0-13-455276-8
ISBN-13: 978-0-13-455276-7

contents

Preface

The fifteenth edition of *Introductory Foods* has been written and revised to introduce the reader to the world of food and associated scientific principles. This edition focuses on food that surrounds the modern and diverse college student studying food- and nutrition-related fields such as food science, nutrition, dietetics, hospitality management, family and consumer science education, and culinary arts. The book is written to engage the reader and expand understanding of the science, laws, and issues involving food.

The science behind food is discussed with applications extending beyond the home kitchen into global and commercial food worlds. The science discussions in the fifteenth edition are more in-depth and applied for greater understanding of food and interactions in food products. This edition extends food science to commercial and processed foods demonstrating how basic food science principles are used by food manufacturers. New topics draw in readers by emphasizing foods and beverages commonly consumed. Furthermore, this edition expands food science principles to variations in food found throughout the world.

Real scientists are featured throughout the book, demonstrating how scientific research is improving our understanding of food, safety, and the development of new food products. Historical food highlights are included in many chapters. Maps are used to explore where and how food is produced in the United States today. Graphs and charts are used to provide quick glimpses into food trends in the United States and the global food market.

The fifteenth edition replaces the previous black-and-white format with vibrant colors and colored photographs to bring concepts to life. Fun facts and discussion are included to provide an exciting twist into the science behind the foods we eat. A new chapter on alternative proteins has been added to reflect the growing interest in vegan and other nontraditional protein foods. New sections on olives and vinegar are also added. Sections on commercially prepared snack foods, fermented foods and beverages, modern food, and globally diverse food products are aimed at connecting readers with today's food world.

This edition bridges the understanding of foods from farm to table. The reader will gain an appreciation of how food is produced with explanations of how a cow produces milk and how a hen produces an egg. The role of biotechnology in food production and protection of our food supply are examined. Discussions of organic and GMO foods are also included.

Nutrition and consumption trends focusing on how each food product fits into current dietary patterns and guidelines are provided in each food-focused chapter. This edition helps to connect food and nutrition concepts. Chapters examine the basic food systems as well as the physical, biological, and chemical science-based interactions. Discussions on Halal and Kosher laws will enrich understanding food requirements for specific foods among these important growing consumer segments.

Highlights of New Content in This Edition

- Baking chapters extensively revised
- New chapter added on alternative proteins (Chapter 19), including legumes, grains, nuts, seaweed, and insects
- Discussion of cultural and world foods extended with historical aspects of our food supply
- Maps and charts to show location of where our food supply originates
- Food science principles presented for home as well as commercial and manufacturing applications
- Nutritional considerations of food updated throughout
- An overview of large commercial equipment added to the newly titled "Equipment and Recipe Basics" (Chapter 4)
- 2015 Dietary Guidelines for Americans included, along with proposed new nutrition labeling
- Chapter 8 extended to include more kinds of fats, their processing, and use in food systems
- Crackers included in Chapter 16
- Olives, vinegars, and a broader variety of greens added in Chapter 21
- Extensive references are included and updated with hundreds of new sources.

Acknowledgments

I am pleased to introduce Amanda Frye, MS, RDN, as a new author in this book. Amanda Frye brings her knowledge and experience as a dietitian, with a master's in Food Science, post MS nutrition graduate coursework, and her passion for food, health, and science to this book.

This book continues to build on the many years when Marion Bennion was the sole author. She passed away in 2018 and is greatly missed. I thank her for patiently mentoring me during both the eleventh and twelfth editions. Her kind notes of encouragement during the revision phase, or congratulations when later editions of *Introductory Foods* were published, were appreciated and now are missed.

My parents, Emaline and Lamoine Einspahr, are recognized for the value they always placed on the quest for knowledge and a quality education. Finally, my husband, Doug, and sons, Colin and Nathan, have been supportive through many editions of this book, including the fifteenth. I appreciate their understanding, patience, and encouragement. My sincere thanks to Doug especially for the many hours he spent alphabetizing and numbering hundreds of references to enable my energies to be directed toward chapter revisions, and his assistance with photographs over the years.

–Barbara Einspahr Scheule

I appreciate Barbara Scheule for giving me the opportunity to coauthor this edition. Thanks to my family and friends for their help and support during the process of working on the book. I would like to recognize and thank my husband and cartographer, Charlie Frye, for sharing his talents in producing wonderful maps for the book. I am extremely grateful for my ecologist/botanist son, Henry Frye, who so willingly shared his knowledge and assisted in research even when we were on separate continents. Special thanks go to my son, Sam Frye, for taking time at the end of busy workdays to create graphs and charts needed for the book. Tommy Frye, your sincere kindness, support, and willingness to help your mom is always noticed and appreciated, especially when it means going back to a store in Berlin just to find a Springerele rolling pin so I could have a photograph for the book. Sophia Frye, your patience, kind suggestions, and publishing experiences were so helpful. I am so lucky to have such a wonderful daughter who supported me during the entire process. Thanks go to the Pearson Education Team and everyone who helped to make this book a reality. A special appreciation goes to everyone who allowed their works to be used in this edition.

–Amanda Frye

Appreciation is extended to all of the reviewers of this edition for their insightful and constructive comments:

Beverley Demetrius, Life University; Margaret Galvin, Cincinnati State Technical and Community College; Dallas Hoover, University of Delaware; Sarah Murray, Missouri State University; Kathryn Rowberg, Purdue University Calumet; Terra Smith, The University of Memphis; Sherri Stastny, North Dakota State University; and Diane Withrow, Cape Fear Community College.

Instructor Supplements

Instructor's Manual with Test Bank. Includes content outlines for classroom discussion, teaching suggestions, and answers to selected end-of-chapter questions from the text. This also contains a Word document version of the test bank.

TestGen. This computerized test generation system gives you maximum flexibility in creating and administering tests on paper, electronically, or online. It provides state-of-the-art features for viewing and editing test bank questions, dragging a selected question into a test you are creating, and printing sleek, formatted tests in a variety of layouts. Select test items from test banks included with TestGen for quick test creation, or write your own questions from scratch. TestGen's random generator provides the option to display different text or calculated number values each time questions are used.

PowerPoint Presentations. Our presentations offer clear, straightforward. Photos, illustrations, charts, and tables from the book are included in the presentations when applicable.

To access supplementary materials online, instructors need to request an instructor access code. Go to **www.pearsonhighered.com/irc**, where you can register for an instructor access code. Within 48 hours after registering, you will receive a confirming email, including an instructor access code. Once you have received your code, go to the site and log on for full instructions on downloading the materials you wish to use.

Alternate Versions

eBooks. This text is also available in multiple eBook formats. These are an exciting new choice for students looking to save money. As an alternative to purchasing the printed textbook, students can purchase an electronic version of the same content. With an eTextbook, students can search the text, make notes online, print out reading assignments that incorporate lecture notes, and bookmark important passages for later review. For more information, visit your favorite online eBook reseller or visit **www .mypearsonstore.com**.

About the Authors

Barbara Scheule has been an author of *Introductory Foods*, since the 11th edition. She is a registered dietitian with a career spanning 16 years as a food service manager at Kansas State University where "from scratch" was emphasized, followed by 21 years as an educator of nutrition/dietetics and hospitality management students at Kent State University in Ohio. She recently retired from Kent State University. Her interest in food, food science, and nutrition took root during her upbringing on a farm and her undergraduate education at University of Nebraska.

A registered dietitian and food scientist, Amanda Frye has a multi-decade history as an educator, food service manager, small business owner, and a social and political activist. She has campaigned for environmental and agriculture awareness in Southern California and has written for various publications. Over the last two decades, she has raised four children on a hobby farm where she resides with her husband in Redlands, California.

1
Factors Influencing Food Choices

This book provides an introductory scientific understanding of food. This scientific perspective is applied to food prepared and consumed within homes, in various food service outlets, or by food manufacturers. This food knowledge can then serve as a building block for understanding our food supply, and for further study in the areas of food science, nutrition, culinary, or food service management. In this chapter, many intersecting concerns that influence the choices we make when selecting food to prepare and consume will be discussed to offer a broader perspective on our food and food supply as we move forward to the specific study of individual foods. Some of the ideas discussed in this chapter, such as nutrition and consumer food trends, will be highlighted briefly in many of the chapters that follow.

People are biological beings who require food to sustain life. We eat to satisfy hunger and to meet a basic drive for food. The decision of what and when to eat is not solely driven by biological needs, however. Food consumption patterns are influenced by family and friends, cultural traditions, religious beliefs, psychological influences, health and nutrition factors, economic and income concerns, sensory quality, and more. Foods must be **palatable** or have **appetite** appeal if they are to be eaten. A palatable food is one that is both acceptable to an individual and agreeable to his or her taste. Various **sensory** impressions or sensations, including odor, appearance, taste, and **mouthfeel** or touch, are involved in our judgment of palatability and food quality.

Technological developments also influence our food choices. Consider the food choices available during each season of the year before various current-day food preservation and storage methods such as refrigeration, frozen storage, and canning were available. Cooking methods have also changed with temperature-controlled gas, electric, and induction ranges. Microwave cooking is another relatively recent technological development. Think about how cooking and baking would be very different if your heat source is an open flame fed with wood, corn cobs, or other combustible materials.

Finally, what we choose to purchase when grocery shopping to prepare at home or foods we order

in a restaurant may be additionally influenced by current trends. There are a variety of ways that what people eat is measured, and several of these data sources will be discussed.

In this chapter, the following topics will be discussed:

- Family, social, and personal influences on food choices
- Nutrition and health
- Economic and marketplace
- Technological development and convenience
- Sensory and objective evaluation of food
- Measurement of food trends

FAMILY, SOCIAL, AND PERSONAL INFLUENCES ON FOOD CHOICES

Family and Social

The family structure and interactions among family members are important influences on the development of our food habits. Children learn that food provides comfort when they are hungry and is a pleasurable dimension of family activities, celebrations, and time with friends (**Figure 1–1**). Several studies have shown an association between children's food preferences, the food practices of their parents, and parenting

Figure 1–1

Two children enjoy each other's company while enjoying a healthy snack. (Keith Weller, U.S. Department of Agriculture)

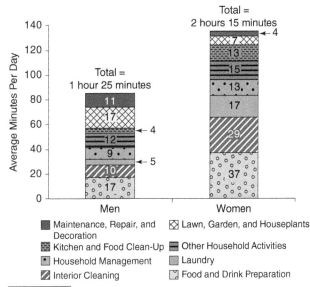

Figure 1–2

Average minutes per day men and women spend in household activities. (U.S. Bureau of Labor Statistics, American Time Use Survey)

styles [1, 8, 34, 82]. Peers, schools, day-care providers, and the media also influence eating patterns of children and adolescents [1, 4, 34, 37]. Adults share meals with friends, family, and coworkers as part of their social interactions.

The food patterns of families in the twenty-first century are being influenced by time restraints. Seventy percent of mothers with children under 18 work outside the home, and of these, 75 percent work full-time. Furthermore, in 40 percent of households, mothers are the primary or sole earners [31]. Women spend 50 minutes per day on food preparation and clean-up as compared to 21 minutes by men [116], and overall spend more time daily in household activities than men (**Figure 1–2**). Food preparation time is impacted by work and further limited by a variety of extracurricular family activities. Families are coping with time challenges and preparation skill by purchasing takeout foods, ready-to-eat prepared foods, and purchase and heat foods as **home meal replacements** [45, 93, 94, 95]. Drive-through food from a quick-service restaurant or "desktop" brown-bag or microwave meals when at work are all additional timesaving strategies. Meals purchased outside the home accounted for 48 percent of total food expenditures in 2017 [72].

Regular, shared meals have been declining under the pressures of modern society. Nevertheless, the family meal plays an important role in human communication—communicating love, values, and information (**Figure 1–3**). It can be especially effective in increasing the well-being of children. Even in our changing society, ideals about the importance of family meals have persisted [8]. Five nights out of seven, Americans prepare dinner at home [90, 96].

Figure 1–3

Children, adults, and elders enjoy time together during a meal. (Mark Bowden/123RF)

Cultural

Cultural forces shape our food behaviors. The **culture** in which we develop determines, to a large extent, our food patterns or habits. Foods are eaten in combination with other foods in ways that are determined and perpetuated by our culture. Food patterns differ markedly from one culture to another. Not everyone in a cultural group eats exactly alike, however, because of individual and family preferences.

The influence of **ethnic** groups is also seen in geographical areas where individuals from these cultures represent a large percentage of the population. Food habits learned in other areas of the world tend to continue, when possible, as individuals or groups move to new locations. In the United States, some regional food preferences can be traced to the influx of immigrants into the region. Each culture passes on its unique food habits and patterns to their children (**Figure 1–4**) [28, 41]. In the United States, cultural food habits are modified as **acculturation** with the "American" diet occurs [5, 120, 122].

Figure 1–4

Families have different traditions surrounding food and how they eat it. This family is using chopsticks. (Sirtravelalot/Shutterstock)

MULTICULTURAL CUISINE
AMERICA—SO WHAT IS THE TYPICAL MEAL?

Throughout America there are regional cuisines that evolved in light of the foods available in the nearby area and also influenced by the people living in the area preparing and consuming these foods. Thus, in some areas we see foods such as Bierocks or Runzas, originating with immigrants with German-Russian roots. Fried Sauerkraut Balls, Pierogies, and Walleye are found in yet other areas of the United States. Think also about Po'Boys, Gumbo, Grits, Jambalaya, Collard Greens, SheCrab Soup, Boiled Peanuts, and Red Beans and Rice. We also have New England Clam Chowder, Boiled Lobster, Crab Cakes, Philadelphia Cheese Steaks, Scrapple, Blueberry Cobbler, Shoofly Pie, and Woopie Pies. In other areas, Indian Fry Bread, Burritos, Enchiladas, Mexican Mole Sauce, Flan, and Sopaipillas are favorites. Barbeque, Chili, and Pizza seem to have their own regional twists. There are so many more foods to mention, including Hamburgers and Hot Dogs!

Italian, Mexican, and Chinese cuisines, like many foods served in America, found a home in the United States by traveling with immigrants from these countries. These ethnic cuisines are the "big three" that three-fourths of Americans eat periodically [91]. Also popular are Mediterranean, Japanese, German, French, Greek, Middle Eastern, Thai, Caribbean, Latin American, Indian, Vietnamese, and Korean foods. Featured in some areas of the United States, but relatively unknown in other areas, are Brazilian, Argentinian, and Peruvian cuisines [91]. Chefs are taking these international cuisines and further blending them with regional American food for new concepts [69]. Cookbooks such as *The Soul of a New Cuisine: A discovery of the Foods and Flavors of Africa* [83] and many others offer additional insight into world foods.

Take time to explore food by learning from your friends, neighbors, international classmates, and guests. Try "street" food and food trucks! Also travel—not only in the United States but globally, and enjoy dining with your hosts as you try and enjoy food previously unknown to you. ■

The study of foods should help you understand and appreciate the food patterns of other cultures or ethnic groups as well as different taste preferences among various regions of the United States [51]. America is becoming increasingly more global in its tastes for food, resulting from a more diverse population, increased travel, and rapid communication [87]. Each ethnic group has developed a **cuisine** with its distinctive combination of flavorings for basic foodstuffs. When eating out, many people choose a culinary experience involving different and sometimes exotic foods. The food industry is accepting the challenges presented by **demographic** changes with new menu items featuring Japanese, Thai, Vietnamese, Korean, Indian, Middle Eastern, Caribbean, Jamaican, and Mediterranean foods [84, 87].

Religious Beliefs

Food has significance in relation to many religious beliefs. Food laws within religious life may set strict guidelines dictating the types of food to be consumed, the procedures for processing and preparing foods, the complete omission of certain foods, and the frequency of eating other foods. To take advantage of the large markets available in religious communities, the food industry must serve the needs of these various groups.

Christian. The foods consumed (or not consumed) vary by the church denomination, although few dietary restrictions are common in most Christian denominations. Some churches, such as Catholic, may encourage members to avoid meat consumption during specific days in Lent.

Judaism. The kosher dietary laws, *kashruth*, are observed to varying degrees by members of the Jewish faith [51, 80]. Reform Jews are generally more flexible in observance of dietary laws as compared to Orthodox or Conservative Jews [80].

Kosher laws include a prohibition against eating blood and thus dictate rules concerning the slaughter of animals and their further processing [49]. Milk products and meat products must be kept separate. Only certain species of animals are considered to be suitable for consumption. Pork and shellfish, among others, are prohibited. Only seafood with scales or fins is acceptable [80]. Most insects are also not allowed; thus, natural red pigments derived from insects would be unacceptable. Additional restrictions occur during the observance of Passover to include the prohibition of usual grain products, such as various breads, pasta, breaded coatings, and so forth, produced from wheat, rye, oats, barley and spelt, as well as unleavened bread. Matzo is produced from wheat and other grains with rabbinical inspection [80].

Kosher laws also extend to ingredients that are used in food processing. Even many non-Jewish individuals choose kosher products because they are regarded as clean, high-quality foods that may additionally help in meeting their individual dietary needs and preferences. An estimated 7,500 products in the United States are kosher [80].

Islam. Islam also prescribes a set of food laws [51, 80]. Foods that are lawful for Muslims to consume are called *halal* [51]. Most of the estimated eight million

Muslims in North America follow halal laws, especially with regard to pork.

Prohibited foods include swine and all their by-products, intoxicants of all types, birds of prey, land animals without ears, such as snakes, flowing or congealed blood, and animals killed in a manner that prevents their blood from being fully drained from their bodies. Thus, there are strict requirements for the slaughtering of animals. Furthermore, gelatin, often derived as a by-product of pork, is unacceptable.

Fish from the sea is controversial among various Muslim groups. The Shia accept only fish with scales as halal [80]. Alcohol used in cooking is prohibited in part because more than 5 percent of the alcohol can remain after over two hours of cooking. In food processing, the use of alcohol as a carrier for food flavorings such as vanilla should be noted. Alcohol used in processing can be allowed if less than 0.1 percent alcohol remains in the final product [80]. Food products may be certified by the Islamic Food and Nutrition Council of America.

Hinduism. Hindu dietary practices emphasize the avoidance of foods that may interfere with the development of the body or mind [51]. Although not required, many Hindus are vegetarian, and of these, many are vegan. The consumption of cows is prohibited because cows are considered sacred. Pork is also frequently avoided by Hindus. Fish or meat must first be sanctified before it is consumed.

Vegetarianism and Religious Belief. Several religions advocate vegetarianism, although vegetarianism may be chosen for ecological, health, or other reasons as well. Chinese Buddhists advocate vegetarianism because they believe in compassion [46]. A vegetarian diet is recommended by the Seventh-Day Adventist Church but is not required for membership [12]. In the United States, more than 3 percent of the population are vegetarians. Additionally, about 36 percent of Americans eat vegetarian meals at least once weekly [33]. Twelve percent of millennials are vegetarians [33], thus the trend toward meatless as well as vegan meals may continue to grow.

The majority of vegetarians consume dairy and eggs and are classified as **lacto-ovo vegetarians**. About half of American vegetarians are strict vegetarians or **vegans** [33] and do not consume any animal products or honey. More will be discussed about vegetarian food choices and other alternative proteins in Chapter 19.

Personal Beliefs and Preferences

Consumers are also influenced in their food choice by personal beliefs and preferences. The environment, sustainability, carbon foot print, organic, genetic modification, animal and employee welfare, personal ethical consideration, locally produced, Fair Trade, and a wide host of other issues also impact our food choices

[32, 73, 92]. Food responsibility and sustainability are identified as having a "great impact" on purchase decisions by one-third of consumers [92]. The purchase of organic foods increased by more than 15 percent during the 2000s, and in 2016 was estimated to be up by 9 percent from 2015 [52].

The media, in all of its many forms and including social media, can also have an impact on our food choices. As consumers, we need to be mindful of our sources of information and the accuracy of the information we consume. Our interpretation of media messages can impact healthy eating [121]. Throughout this text, great effort has been taken to provide a scientific perspective.

Emotional and Psychological Effects

With all of today's technological influences, it is important that the meanings of food, other than the biological and economic ones, be considered (**Figure 1–5**). Food means security, hospitality, and even status. Infants learn about security when given food (**Figure 1–6**). Familiar foods bring back memories

Figure 1–5

This couple shares a joyful moment while eating ice-cream cones. (Tony Bowler/Shutterstock)

Figure 1–6

Babies learn security and comfort when hungry and being fed. (Mariusz S. Jurgielewicz/Shutterstock)

of home and family and make one feel secure. Feeling full and physically satisfied and knowing that there is more food available for other meals bring security. Food is a symbol of hospitality and is used to show that one cares about others and is a friend. Gifts of food are given in times of both happiness and sorrow.

NUTRITION AND HEALTH

An interest in healthful lifestyles, including recognition of nutrition as an important part of the health improvement process, is flourishing among Americans. At the same time, obesity rates for adults and children have increased dramatically since 1990 (**Figure 1–7**) [103]. Seventy-three percent of men, 65 percent of women, and nearly 33 percent of children are overweight or obese [114]. Data indicate most Americans struggle with consistently eating healthy and engaging in physical activity [114]. National nutrition objectives are included in the broad-based initiative *Healthy People 2020* [75] and are supported through the U.S. Dietary Guidelines, MyPlate, and Nutrition Facts labeling on food products. How Americans respond to government health and dietary recommendations by adjusting their dietary habits will become more apparent in the years ahead (**Figure 1–8**). An increased interest in healthy choices is evident in some segments of the food marketplace [22, 85, 88].

Dietary Guidelines

The *Dietary Guidelines for Americans* was first published in 1980 by the U.S. Department of Agriculture (USDA) and the Department of Health and Human Services (HHS). Under the 1990 National Nutrition Monitoring and Research Act, USDA and HHS must jointly publish updated guidelines every five years using "current scientific and medical knowledge" [114]. The eighth edition of the *Dietary Guidelines* is for years 2015–2020, whereas the ninth edition will be in effect for 2020–2025. The eighth edition emphasizes five points: (a) "follow a healthy eating pattern across the lifespan," (b) "focus on variety, nutrient density, and amount," (c) "limit calories from added sugars and saturated fats, and reduce sodium intake," (d) "shift to healthier food and beverages choices," and (e) "support healthy eating patterns for all" [114]. The 2020 guidelines will be expanded to include recommendations for infants and toddlers (birth to 2 years old) and pregnant women.

As in the 2000–2015 *Dietary Guidelines for Americans*, the 2015–2020 guidelines continue to encourage the consumption of less sodium (less than 2,300 milligrams per day for those older than 14 years of age), saturated fats (less than 10 percent of calories per day), trans fats (to be avoided), and added sugar (less than 10 percent of calories per day) [114]. Saturated fats are often described as solid fats. Coconut oil, palm oil, and cream are considered to be solid fats because of their high saturated fat content (**Figure 1–9**).

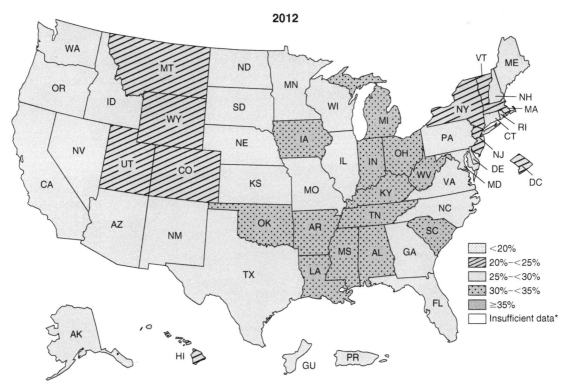

*Sample size <50 or the relative standard error (dividing the standard error by the prevalence) ≥ 30%.

Figure 1–7

Obesity trends among U.S. adults. (U.S. Centers for Disease Control)

2014

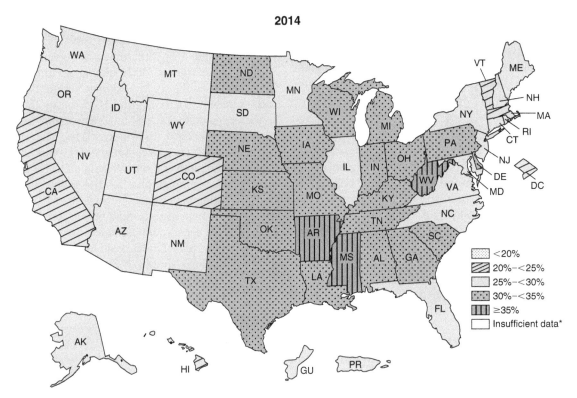

*Sample size <50 or the relative standard error (dividing the standard error by the prevalence) ≥ 30%.

2016

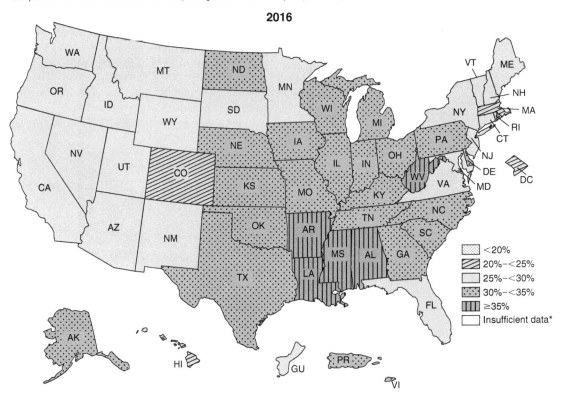

*Sample size <50 or the relative standard error (dividing the standard error by the prevalence) ≥ 30%.

Figure 1-7 *(Continued)*

Many foods include natural sugar as a component of the food found in nature. Fruit is an example of a food that is sweet without added sugar. Thus, added sugar is defined as sugar, honey, brown sugar, molasses, corn syrup, and other forms of sugar that have been "added" to the foods. It is foods with "added" sugar that Americans are encouraged to consume less of when choosing foods and beverages. Many beverages included a surprising amount

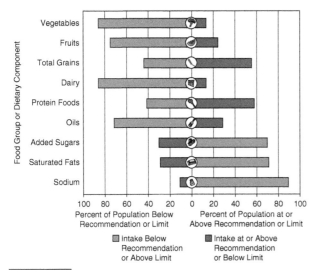

Figure 1–8

Americans eat too little of some foods and too much of other foods to meet USDA *Dietary Guidelines*. The percent of consumers represented by orange bars need to be changing their consumption to more closely align with the center. For example, about 85 percent of consumers (orange) are eating less vegetables than recommended for health, and about 15 percent (blue) are eating more vegetables than the minimum suggested amounts. (U.S. Department of Agriculture)

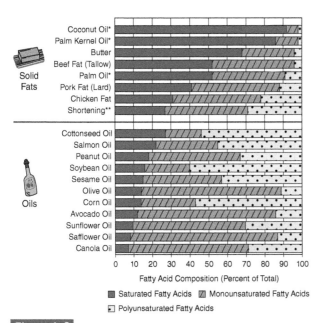

Figure 1–9

The fatty acid profiles of several common dietary fats and oils are provided on this chart. USDA *Dietary Guidelines* recommend less than 10 percent of our calories daily come from saturated fats. Coconut, palm kernel, and palm oils are called oils because they are from plants, but they are solid or semi-solid at room temperature and also contain a very high percentage of saturated fats. Therefore, nutritionally they are considered solid fats along with butter, shortening, and animal fats. (U.S. Department of Agriculture)

of added sugar. About 47 percent of the added sugar consumed by Americans is found in beverages such as soft drinks, fruit drinks, and other sugar-sweetened drinks [114]. For a 2,000-calorie diet, the *Dietary Guidelines* suggest the following amounts or equivalent amounts:

- 2½ cups daily to include a variety of vegetables during the week
- 2 cups daily to emphasize whole fruits
- 6 ounces daily with half of the grains consumed as whole grains
- 3 cups daily of dairy (substitutions for vegans with nutritional similarities)
- 5½ ounces of protein daily
- 27 grams per day of oils

Within each week, the vegetable choices should include dark green, red and orange vegetables, legumes, and starchy vegetables. Protein foods should also reflect variety with eight ounces of seafood consumed weekly, and lean meats should be selected over higher fat counterparts. Legumes, nuts, seeds, and soy products also offer valuable nutrients within the protein choices. Additionally, the *Dietary Guidelines* offer specific suggestions for those following a vegan or vegetarian diet or a Mediterranean Diet pattern [114]. The DASH diet is another healthy option and is associated with lowering blood pressure.

ChooseMyPlate

In 2011, the Food Guide Pyramid was replaced by MyPlate, also called Choose MyPlate. The MyPlate was designed to simplify the message to the public to encourage Americans to proportionally have half of their plate composed fruits and vegetables (**Figure 1–10**)

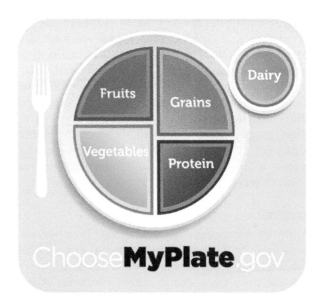

Figure 1–10

Choose MyPlate. The majority of our plate should be composed of fruits, vegetables, and whole grains. (USDA, Center for Nutrition Policy and Promotion)

[106]. Individualized dietary recommendations and a "SuperTracker" tool were also created to help consumers monitor their nutritional intake. This tool was discontinued in June 2018 because there are many mobile apps in the marketplace that perform this same function, thus enabling USDA to focus on other healthy eating initiatives.

Food Labeling

In 1990, the Nutrition Labeling and Education Act resulted in the provision of standardized nutrition labels on nearly all processed foods. The Nutrition Facts labels are used by consumers seeking to make informed choices about the foods purchased [76]. Nutrition labeling is discussed further in Chapter 3.

ECONOMIC AND MARKETPLACE FACTORS

Consumers also make food choices because of economic and marketplace factors. The size of the household budget impacts how much can realistically be spent on food selections. Furthermore, when foods are obtained, the options available, and the various outlets (near or far) will influence the food ultimately prepared and served.

Geographical Food Availability

The geography of an area and variations in climate influence the types of food that can be—and usually are—grown. Historically, this fact has had a profound influence on the availability of particular foods and, in turn, on the eating patterns of people in the area. Examples are the widespread use of pinto beans and chili peppers in the southwestern United States and the extensive use of seafood in coastal areas. With the development of rapid transportation and modern food-handling facilities, the influence of geography and climate on our food habits has decreased. For example, 95 percent of coffee, cocoa, spices, fish, and shellfish and about 50 percent of fruits and fruit juices consumed by Americans are imported, greatly impacting food selection (**Figure 1–11**) [105].

Economics

We are all consumers. Throughout our lives, we exchange money for goods and services. The cost of food is usually a significant expenditure for a household [25]; thus, using our resources effectively is important to obtain acceptable, enjoyable, and healthful foods. Food purchasing is an important responsibility. The decisions we make regarding our food impact our health and well-being. Choices made with regard to convenience foods and the types of foods purchased

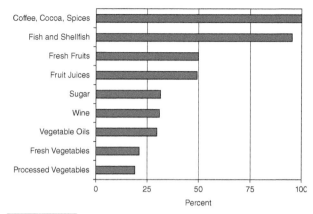

Figure 1–11

Import share of U.S. food consumption, 2011–2013. (USDA, Economic Research Service)

for the home or for a food service organization also have a significant impact on resources available for other expenses. The use of our available resources is further impacted by economic and marketplace conditions.

Share of Expenditures for Food. In countries such as the United States, Singapore, the United Kingdom, Switzerland, and Canada, a small percent of the consumer expenditures are spent for food consumed at home (less than 10 percent). Forty to 60 percent of consumer expenditures were used for food consumed at home in less affluent countries such as Guatemala, Pakistan, Philippines, Kazakhstan, Cameroon, Kenya, and Nigeria [110].

Likewise, among U.S. families, the highest income families in the top quintile of income spend more money for food than do low-income families. The U.S. households in the lowest income quintile (20 percent) spent 29 to 43 percent of their before-tax income (including earnings and public assistance) on food as compared to the highest quintile who spent 7 to 9 percent [102]. **Figure 1–12** provides the average household spending for food in the United States. Lowest income quintile households spend less on food overall and eat out less than those in the highest income quintile [115].

Income also has an impact on what foods are purchased and consumed. Globally, consumers in lower-income countries consume a higher proportion of cereals, roots, and tubers [64]. Among U.S. consumers, low-income households spend less of their food dollar away from home and consume a less healthy diet as compared to high-income consumers [62]. However, U.S. consumers regardless of income level fail to consume a healthy diet as measured with the Healthy Eating Index [62].

Food Insecurity. Food insecurity, or the inability to afford food for a healthy life, as indicated by the inability to provide enough food because of lack

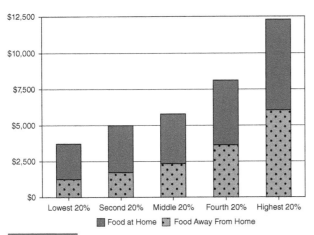

Figure 1–12

Average household spending at home and away from home by income group, 2015. (U.S. Bureau of Labor Statistics)

of resources [2], was experienced by 12 percent U.S. households in 2016. Nearly 4 percent of the U.S. households in 2016 experienced very low food insecurity and as a result experienced reduced food intake or skipped meals because of the lack of resources [79]. Households experiencing food insecurity are often single-parent households and households with children. In 2016, the federal poverty line was $24,339 for a household with two adults and two children. Most food-insecure households (59 percent) are low-income households. Additional leading predictors of food insecurity are households with a disabled or mentally ill member of the home [18, 26].

Globally, food insecurity is also an important concern in many other countries. In an examination of countries receiving U.S. food aid, Sub-Saharan Africa had the greater percent of food insecure at 32 percent. An estimated 15 percent of people in Latin America and the Caribbean and 14 percent in Asia were also food insecure. Famine, an extreme form of food insecurity, is declared when starvation deaths have occurred. A famine was declared in South Sudan in 2017. Overall projections are for improvement in food security in many of these areas the coming decade [64].

Within the United States, there are 15 nutrition assistance programs found within the Farm Bill to help families. These programs include the Supplemental Nutrition Assistance Program (SNAP), National School Lunch Program, and Special Supplemental Nutrition Program for Women, Infants, and Children. Additionally, community resources such as food banks and food pantries help to fill the gap. The USDA calculates costs for four levels of food plans (thrifty, low cost, moderate, and liberal) to obtain a nutritious diet [107]. All Americans, including those with and without income constraints, need to reallocate spending to purchase less miscellaneous foods (soft drinks, snacks), and more fruits and vegetables, thereby allocating more for healthy foods [23].

Factors Influencing Food Costs

Our food choices and where we live can impact our food costs. Food prices also generally modestly rise overtime along with the cost of many other consumer goods (**Figure 1–13**) [113]. In addition to the general effects of inflation, a number of other factors, such as marketing, crop production, trade policies, processing, geographical location, and purchasing practices, affect the cost of food and therefore household expenditures.

Marketing Costs. The USDA calculates marketing costs for food purchased by consumers in the United States, including food purchased both in retail markets and in food service establishments. In 2016, marketing expenses accounted for 85 percent of the cost of a food product (**Figure 1–14**). These marketing expenses include the cost of all post-farm activities in the food supply chain, including food processing, packaging, transportation, advertising, energy use, and other costs incurred in bringing food from the farmer to the consumer [111]. The **farm-value share** of food purchased in grocery stores was 15 percent. Thus, for every dollar consumers spent on food grown in the United States, the farmer received 15 cents for the sale of raw food commodities.

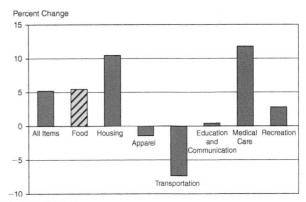

Figure 1–13

Percent of change in major consumer price index (CPI) categories, 2013–2017. (USDA, Economic Research Service)

Figure 1–14

The Food Dollar. 85.2 percent of a typical dollar spent on food goes to pay for marketing costs, including all of the steps that result in the farm commodity being sold as food to the consumer. (USDA)

HEALTHY EATING
FOOD DESERTS AND FOOD SWAMPS

"Food deserts" or "low-income and low-supermarket access" areas are places where low-income residents do not have nearby access to supermarkets and other retailers that sell healthy, affordable foods [81, 119]. Many households in these low-access and food desert neighborhoods do not have access to a vehicle, so traveling to a supermarket may be difficult. Although smaller grocery stores and convenience stores are located in these areas, prices at these stores are often higher than supermarkets. Food swamps address a companion issue to food deserts. In food swamps, less healthy, energy-dense, convenient, and inexpensive foods are readily available [119].

Researchers exploring healthy food options in two rural Texas counties found that the widest selection of healthy food items was available in supermarkets [20]. There were two supermarkets in each of the two counties studied; thus, many residents of these counties would need to travel several miles to one of these stores. ■

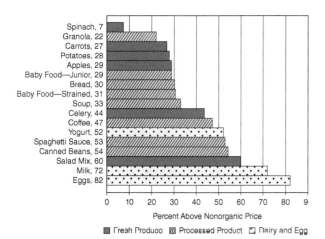

Figure 1-15

Eggs and milk have the highest premiums of the organic products included in the data. (USDA, Economic Research Service)

Crop Production. Food production is costly, yet farmers receive a relatively small percentage of the consumer food dollar. Substantial initial investments must be made by farmers in property and equipment. Farmers have become increasingly dependent on fuel to operate their equipment and on the fertilizers, herbicides, and insecticides purchased to promote high crop yields. Additionally, some crops in particular are very labor intensive, and prices for these crops are therefore influenced by the cost of wages. Organic corn and soybeans have been found to have higher costs of production than those conventionally produced, with much of this added expense in labor [38].

Poor weather conditions often reduce the size of crops of fruits, vegetables, and grains. Droughts, floods, and unexpected freezes all have a significant impact on crops. The weather is not controllable, and efficient management of commodity production thus becomes quite difficult. Crop shortages translate into higher prices in the marketplace when demand exceeds the supply.

Organic foods represent a small share of the total food sales; however, they have grown rapidly since 2000. Because of the costs associated with organic food production, price premiums for these foods exist in the marketplace. As shown in **Figure 1-15**, milk and eggs cost much more than the conventionally produced milk and eggs as compared to other organic foods [38].

Trade Policies. The United States presently enjoys a competitive advantage for a number of products in world agricultural trade. American agricultural exports forecast for 2018 is $139.5 billion per year as compared to $118.5 billion in agricultural imports [108, 112]. Top agricultural commodities exported and imported are provided in **Figures 1-11** and **1-16**. Abundant natural resources and technological developments have contributed to the United States becoming a net exporter of agricultural products. Sound policy decisions help to promote export sales.

Geographic Food Price Variation. Where you live will have an impact on how much you pay for food. The cost of foods such as eggs, milk, fruit (canned,

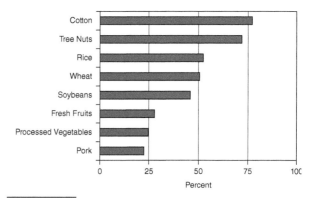

Figure 1-16

Export share of U.S. farm production, 2011–2013. Exports account for a large share of the total volume of U.S. production for select agricultural products. For example, over 70 percent of the volume of U.S. production of tree nuts (largely almonds) and cotton were exported in 2011–2013, as was more than 50 percent of rice and wheat production. (USDA, Economic Research Service)

fresh, or frozen), lettuce, and carbonated beverages can be 40 to 93 percent higher in price depending on where in the United States the food was purchased [100]. The cost of food, as measured by the average prices of 11 grocery items, was 8 percent higher in the Northeast and 6 percent lower in the Midwest compared to the national average [59].

Food Waste. Food waste also impacts food costs. When food is purchased but not consumed, additional food is purchased, adding to costs. An estimated 31 percent of food (133 billion pounds annually or 789 calories per capita daily) that was available at the retail and consumer levels in the United States is uneaten and therefore wasted [21]. One-third of global food production has also been estimated as wasted. In the United States, a greater percentage of waste occurs at the retail or consumer level, whereas globally the food loss is more likely to occur at the farm or retail levels with very little waste by consumers [21].

What is food waste? Different definitions may be used. In a broad sense, however, any food that was once usable but has since been discarded and not eaten by humans may be considered waste. Food eaten by household pets may be counted as waste if this food was originally prepared for human consumption.

Trends toward increasing food prices, coupled with growing concerns about conservation of resources, have focused attention on food loss or waste. Discarded food has associated expenses; thus, practices to avoid food waste are suggested from an economic perspective. The impact of food and packaging waste on the environment is another important consideration [3].

Storage Loss. Food loss may occur at different stages of handling and preparation. As food is taken home from the market and transferred to cabinets, refrigerators, and freezers, it should be handled to minimize loss. While food is in storage, even on a very temporary basis, waste may result from microbial spoilage, contamination by insects and rodents, and spilling as a result of broken or open containers. If food is held or stored too long, particularly with improper packaging or temperature control, it may be discarded simply because it is not fresh.

Preparation Loss. Additional waste may occur during preparation as a result of discarding edible portions of the food before cooking, improper cooking procedures such as scorching or overcooking, preparing too much for the number of people to be served, and spoilage because of inappropriate holding of the food before service. Not serving leftovers also creates waste.

Plate Waste. Food may be left on plates at home or in the food service setting. This plate waste accounts for a significant portion of total food loss (**Figure 1–17**). In a

study of a university dining hall serving 850 male and 490 female students who were on board plans, an average of 17 percent of the food items selected was wasted [74].

There may be various reasons for food waste in food service settings. For example, overall plate waste was reduced from 40 percent to 27 percent when elementary students in grades 3, 4, and 5 had recess before rather than after lunch [10]. In another study, plate waste decreased from 43 to 27 percent when elementary students in grades 3, 4, and 5 had 30 minutes for lunch as opposed to 20 minutes [9]. Children waste more food if hurried when eating lunch, either because of a short meal period or a desire to go out to recess. In a continuing-care retirement community, there was less food waste when residents received family-style service or waitstaff service than when they were served trays [40].

Food Purchasing Practices

Consumers have many options to consider when purchasing foods. Perhaps the first decision is where to buy food and in what form the food will be purchased. Price, quality, and convenience are all factors to be taken into account. Food preparation skills for some consumers may be a significant concern. Slightly more than half of Americans describe themselves as "experienced" cooks [90]. Others enjoy new culinary challenges and experiences and therefore may seek out exotic ingredients without regard to cost.

Eating Out or Cooking at Home. U.S. households on average spent 57 percent of their total food expenditures on food consumed at home [115]. Higher-income Americans spend closer to 50 percent of their food expenditure eating out [115]. Millennials also appear to have a greater preference for eating out as compared to other generational groups [56].

American consumers spend about 43 percent of their food expenditures eating out. Food purchased

Figure 1–17

Food is wasted in a variety of ways. Plate waste, or food on our plates but not consumed, is one source of waste. (Simez78/Shutterstock)

from a food service includes the cost of labor, entertainment, service, and ambiance and therefore is more expensive. The menu price reflects a food cost mark-up, which may be four times the food cost, to cover these additional expenses when providing service. Thus, although eating-out expenditures are nearly half of the overall food expenditures, consumers are not eating half of their meals outside of the home.

Food Processing and Packaging. An increasing number of today's foods have built-in "maid service," with partial or complete preparation before the food is purchased. How much do **convenience foods** cost? In assessing costs, the cost of the food itself and your time are considerations. Furthermore, the purchase of convenience foods is likely to be less expensive as compared to "takeout" or "eating out." Thus, the costs are relative to your alternatives. The cost of convenience can also vary greatly with the product or the season the year. For example, out-of-season fruits and vegetables are likely to be more economical if purchased either canned or frozen.

Today's millennials, as compared to other generations, spend a greater proportion of their home food purchases on prepared foods [56]. These prepared and processed convenience foods may include minimal processing, such as the trimming of retail meat cuts, shredding of cheese, or packing of fresh vegetables. Alternatively, foods may be highly processed foods. Breakfast cereals, meat substitutes produced from textured vegetable proteins, frozen ready-to-eat entrees, and pre-prepared packaged salads are examples of foods generally perceived as highly processed.

Types of Food Stores. Where food is purchased impacts not only our choices but also our costs. There are a number of different types of stores through which food is marketed on a retail basis. For food service institutions, a variety of vendors supply different types of food products, generally on a wholesale basis. In the retail sector, consumers can purchase foods from grocery stores, supermarkets, specialty food stores, food cooperatives, farmers' markets, convenience stores, warehouses, wholesale markets, pharmacies, and a variety of other store formats, including online sales (**Table 1–1**).

Supermarkets are the leading choice of consumers, with 65 percent of the retail food sales in the United States. Supercenters and warehouse stores are now capturing nearly 17 percent of at-home sales [55]. Between 1998 and 2017, the number of farmers' markets grew by more than 200 percent, and resulted in consumers purchasing more fruits and vegetables [97]. Online ordering is predicted to account for 20 percent of grocery sales by 2025 [19].

Meanwhile, supermarkets are continuing to expand their services to attract consumers. Fresh and local foods are being increasingly featured in grocery stores, along with dine-in restaurant sales and "hang-out" opportunities through wine bars or cooking classes [7]. Sales of prepared foods or *home meal replacement* options in supermarkets are also continuing to grow as a way for supermarkets to compete for consumer's dollar [53]. *Home meal replacements* are ready-made meals, such as rotisserie chickens, that can be taken home for immediate consumption. Furthermore, with men doing 40 percent of the primary grocery shopping in household, stores also need to cater to the specific interests and preferences of men, who tend to like bolder flavors and are more likely to make impulse purchases as compared to women [89].

Prices are influenced by services offered and can vary between stores by as much as 5 to 15 percent [58, 59, 119]. Consumers should evaluate the various kinds of markets in terms of the services and benefits desired and the price they are willing to pay. The availability of organic, local, or sustainable foods; prepared foods; and quality and variety of fresh produce may be additional considerations. Services such as online ordering, drive-up lanes, bagging of groceries, or in-store restaurants are important to some shoppers [53].

Shopping Aids. Food manufacturers and retailers offer the consumer several conveniences to facilitate efficient shopping for food. These include unit pricing, open-date labeling, and nutrition labeling. Computerized checkout systems are the norm in supermarkets. Many of today's stores use self-checkout.

Unit Pricing. The cost per pound or ounce for products sold by weight or the cost per quart, pint, or fluid ounce for products sold by volume may be printed

Table 1-1
TYPES OF FOOD STORES OR OTHER OUTLETS

Store or Other Outlet	Key Characteristics
Supermarkets	Stock thousands of food items and, usually, other merchandise, including beauty aids, pharmaceutical supplies, kitchen tools, flowers, and plants. May include florist shops, bakeries, ethnic food takeout services, catering, delicatessens, sushi bars, pharmacies, photo-finishing shops, branch banks, and post offices. May offer cooking classes, home delivery, and valet parking [44].
Specialty stores	Bakeries and fish markets are examples of specialty stores. Usually offer only one type of food.
Food cooperatives, or co-ops	Organized by groups of consumers to purchase food on a wholesale basis.
Fresh format stores	Emphasize fresh foods that are organic, natural, and ethnic.
Convenience stores or C-stores	Carry a limited stock of merchandise that has high turnover. May be associated with a gas station. Usually are open 24 hours a day. Prices are usually higher than other stores, such as grocery and supermarkets [119].
Warehouse or discount markets	May not provide some consumer services, such as bagging of groceries. Generally buy in very large quantities and pass some of their cost savings on to the customer. Costco and Sam's Club are examples of warehouse clubs.
Supercenters	Giant stores that include a wide range of merchandise from clothing to groceries. Walmart, Kmart, Target, and other major retailers are transitioning their stores to supercenters as a way to corner the market on consumers seeking to purchase multiple products including food in one stop [29, 44]. Prices are often lower than at traditional supermarkets.
Direct sales to consumers	Internet and catalog sales of food.
Meal kit deliveries	Food is delivered to the home in "meal kits." Recipes are provided along with the correct amounts of ingredients as needed in the recipe.
Farmers' markets	Open seasonally as outlets for local farm produce. Consumers purchase foods directly from the farmer.
Community-supported agriculture	Consumers purchase shares in a farmer's expected harvest. Weekly deliveries or pick up from the farm throughout the growing season.

on a label attached to the edge of the shelf where the products are displayed. The most economical size to buy can thus be readily determined. Generally, the smaller package sizes and individual-size convenience items are more expensive per unit because of the basic package cost.

Open-Date Labeling. A date code is on each packaged food product for the customer to read and interpret. The date may appear in different forms on different packages. It may represent the last recommended day of retail sale, the end of the period of optimum quality, or the date of processing or final packaging. Open-date labeling provides some information for the shopper, but the conditions, such as temperature, under which the products are handled and stored will also affect the quality.

Some consumers have found the product dates confusing and have unnecessarily discarded food, resulting in waste. The "sell by" date indicates the product should not be sold after that date so the buyer has a quality product after purchase. The "use by" or "best by" dates indicate the processors' estimate of how long the product will be at its best quality, but are not dates when the product must be discarded. Foods, when stored properly, can be expected to be safe and of good quality after the "best by" and "use by" dates [117].

Food Labeling. The basic requirements for all food labels include net weight of contents, manufacturer's or distributor's name and address, and ingredient declaration. Regulations governing the labeling of most food products are prepared by the U.S. Food and Drug Administration (FDA), but the labeling of meat and poultry products is under the jurisdiction of the USDA. Current food labeling regulations including nutrition labeling, when foods may be labeled as organic or with health claims, and more product attributes are discussed in Chapter 3.

Computerized Checkout Systems. The first item marked with the Universal Product Code (UPC) was scanned at a grocery store in Troy, Ohio, in 1974. This bar code with different width black lines enables a scanner to scan the code, thereby providing product information and pricing to a computer. Today, nearly all stores in America use bar code labeling to scan products at sale to the consumer.

Price-Conscious Buying. Several strategies are recommended for price-conscious buying: (1) making a complete list before shopping, (2) stocking up when preferred brands are on sale, (3) comparison shopping, and (4) redeeming coupons. Many additional suggestions may be made for the food shopper:

1. Compare prices for specified quality items; use unit pricing; consider cost of packaging; watch advertised specials; choose stores with reasonable pricing.
2. Assess price per serving, as well as the cost for the nutrition being provided. Some foods may be less per pound or less as packaged but are actually more expensive per serving, and other foods offer little in terms of nutrients to support health.
3. Purchase less expensive cuts of meat, or use less expensive alternative protein sources such as legumes, and use appropriate cooking techniques for high-quality meals.
4. Buy the fruits and vegetables in season when their prices are lower.
5. Buy only quantities that can be utilized well; do not overbuy.
6. Buy in-store brands or generic items when the quality is acceptable for a particular use.
7. Factor in the cost of convenience products. Compare cost of frozen juice to refrigerated-prepared or the cost of a frozen entree as compared

to preparing the item "from scratch" using basic ingredients.
8. Plan ahead and purchase on a regular basis; avoid impulse buying.

TECHNOLOGICAL DEVELOPMENTS AND CONVENIENCE FOODS

Food science and technology have helped to promote a safe, nutritious, and abundant food supply. Our access to foods has changed over the centuries because of technological developments associated with food preservation and crops grown. Our patterns of eating and cooking have also been influenced by different types of cooking equipment (**Figure 1–18**), including the microwave oven (see Chapter 5).

Perhaps the earliest form of food processing was basic cooking over two million years ago. In the years that followed, fermentation, drying, smoking, and preservation with salt enabled people to store foods for later consumption. Even in ancient Greece, food processing was used to produce bread, olive oil, and wine [35]. Food preservation and processing became more sophisticated with the development of canning techniques by Appert and Durand in the early nineteenth century (see Chapter 28 for more information on food preservation, canning, and freezing). Foods previously available only during the summer months became available throughout the year as canned foods. Aseptic processing and retort pouches (**Figure 1–19**) are more recent developments utilizing canning concepts.

Chilling of foods to extend storage was initially accomplished by taking advantage of winter weather. Later, ice from rivers and lakes was stored for use in "iceboxes" during warm seasons. In the 1920s, Clarence Birdseye perfected frozen foods and

---

HOT TOPICS
LOCAL FOODS

"Local foods" is a popular marketing phrase and for good reason consumers appear to be willing to pay a premium for foods identified as local. So what is local? It turns out that it depends on who you ask.

- *The New Oxford American Dictionary* identifies a "locavore" as an individual consuming food within a 100-mile radius.
- Some stores define local as within state borders, but others use a 250-mile radius or indicate that local foods must travel seven or fewer hours by car or truck.
- The U.S. Congress has defined local in the 2008 Food, Conservation, and Energy Act as food that traveled less

than 400 miles from its origin or from within the state produced.

- In Virginia some farmers' markets define local as food grown within 75 miles, but other Virginia markets use a 100-mile standard.
- Vermont law defines local as items that originate within 30 miles of the sale.

Regardless of the definition, consumers buy local food because of perceived freshness, support for the local economy, and knowledge of product source [63]. ∎

Figure 1–18

Cooking food under the sky over an open flame was routine throughout the world before the development of technology to allow the wide choices in food storage, cooking, and products available today. (AAR Studio/Shutterstock)

Figure 1–19

Starkist provides consumers with convenient kind of retort packaging for tuna. (Starkist Seafood)

Figure 1–20

Ready-made salads in modified atmosphere packaging.
(U.S. Department of Agriculture)

launched the frozen food industry. Today, refrigerators and freezers simplify the storage of perishable foods.

Consumers have access to a wide variety of foods year around, in large part because of the food processing and preservation methods developed by the food industry. Many of these foods offer convenience that our ancestors could have only imagined. Shelf-stable fruit boxes, tuna in retort pouches, fruit packaged in multilayer barrier plastic cups with peelable closures, and fresh-cut produce and salad ingredients (**Figure 1–20**) are some of the products available to today's consumers. Relatively recent food processing developments are described in **Table 1–2**.

Processed Foods and Clean Labels

Processed foods can range from simply blanching and freezing a vegetable to a fully prepared packaged food. As much as consumers may enjoy the convenience of processed foods, some consumers are also seeking whole, fresh foods without processing. One reason for this trend is the desire for clean labeling—or labels

that do not have ingredients described as artificial on the ingredient list [70]. Some of these ingredients serve as preservatives, and therefore removing these ingredients can create challenges for processors seeking to maintain the quality and food safety of the product. Some consumers may define any ingredient they do not recognize as an unacceptable ingredient; however, not all "chemical sounding" names are artificial ingredients. Consider, for example, ascorbic acid that is often known as Vitamin C. Additionally, processed foods can contain high levels of sodium, thereby running counter to current dietary recommendations. Manufacturers are seeking ways to reduce sodium in their products; however, sodium serves as not only a flavor enhancer but may also impact the food safety, preservation, or texture of the final product [68]. Food additives, and their functions, are discussed further in Chapter 6.

Technological Developments in Crops

Conventional breeding and selection of plants and animals over the centuries has been used to improve food supplies. Utilizing a group of genetic tools that falls under the heading of **biotechnology**, the variety, productivity, and efficiency of food production can be targeted in less time and with greater predictability and control than was possible with traditional methods [35, 42]. Genetic engineering may be used to increase crop yields and disease resistance and to produce faster-maturing, drought-resistant varieties. Biotechnology could be used to improve the nutritional quality of the food supply and reduce the use of chemicals [11]. However, in spite of the benefits, biotechnology has not been without controversy [48].

Technological Developments for Space and Military Foods

Space travel and military training and operations have necessitated the ultimate in convenience foods. The development of convenience foods for these specialized

Table 1–2
FOOD PROCESSING AND PRESERVATION DEVELOPMENTS

Aseptic processing/aseptic packaging	The food and package are sterilized separately, therefore requiring less heat. The food is placed in the package within a sterile environment and sealed [35]. Juice boxes are an example of an aseptically processed product.
Retort pouches and trays	Retort processing follows the same regulatory requirements as low-acid canned foods. However, because flexible retort pouches and trays have a high surface-to-volume ratio, heat transfers more quickly than with traditional metals cans. Consequently, retort foods have a higher quality because they are less "overcooked" as compared to canned foods. Retort processing uses steam or hot water with steam as the heating method [14, 16]. Meal, Ready-to-Eat (MRE) and tuna in pouches are examples of retort processed foods.
Modified/controlled atmosphere	The shelf life of fruits and vegetables may be extended by storage in a modified atmosphere. The atmosphere in either a storage area or a package is modified by reducing or eliminating the oxygen. Other modifications can be used to control ethylene gas, a natural fruit-ripening gas [35].
High-pressure processing	The use of high pressures (100,000 pounds per square inch) will reduce microbial populations with minimal heat [35]. Foods with similar taste, color, and textures to fresh can be produced without the need for preservative ingredients.
Irradiation	Ionizing radiation has been used for more than 40 years to destroy bacteria and insects on foods. Electron beams, X-rays, or gamma rays are sources of ionizing radiation that may be used [35]. Irradiation does not heat the food and therefore is a nonthermal method of destroying microorganisms. Irradiation can decrease bacterial contamination on poultry and meat, increase the shelf life of fresh fruits, and kill pests on imported fruits that would otherwise need to be fumigated.

FOCUS ON SCIENCE
MODIFIED ATMOSPHERE PACKAGING

The atmosphere within modified atmosphere packaging (MAP) is changed so that the composition is different than air. Air is composed of oxygen (O_2), carbon dioxide (CO_2), and nitrogen (N_2). The choice of the gas for MAP depends on the food product being packed and may be used alone or in combination with other gases. Storage of foods in a modified gaseous atmosphere can maintain quality and extend product shelf life by slowing chemical and biochemical deteriorative reactions. The growth of some spoilage organisms also can be slowed because of their inability to grow in low oxygen environments.

In addition to maintaining quality, MAP can improve product presentation. Foods packaged in MAP can include the following:

- Dairy products such as whole milk powder and cheddar cheese—to improve shelf life.
- Red meat—to maintain bright red color (oxymyoglobin pigment).
- Raw poultry—to prevent growth of spoilage bacteria.
- Cooked, cured, and processed meat—to prevent microbial growth, color changes, and rancidity.
- Fish and fish products—to prevent microbial contamination, reduce oxidation reactions, or reduce deterioration by enzymes found in the fish.
- Fruit and vegetables—to reduce respiration (senescence), thereby slowing ripening and maturing. Also to prevent or reduce bacterial contamination and mold growth.

environments and circumstances has resulted in new products and food processing technologies.

Space-Age Convenience. Travel into space brought special requirements with regard to food for the astronauts. The demanding specifications for weight, volume, and ease of preparation are met by convenience-type foods [13, 71]. Because the astronauts have much work and experimentation to do in space, the time required to prepare and eat must be kept to a minimum. Foods must be stable to store at temperatures up to 100°F (38°C). Packaging must be flexible and able to withstand extremes of pressure, humidity, temperature, and vibration that could cause breakage or cracking. Food packages also must be convenient to handle (**Figure 1–21**).

Food developed for space travel is researched at the Food Systems Engineering Facility (FSEF) at

Figure 1-21a

NASA astronaut Sunita Williams, Expedition 32 flight engineer, is consuming a snack near the galley on the International Space Station.

Figure 1-21b

Typical space foods are shown in this photo taken by an Expedition 32 crew member on the International Space Station.

Figure 1-21c

The Expedition 40 commander, NASA astronaut Steve Swanson, harvests a crop of red romaine lettuce plants grown from seed inside the station's Veggie facility.

the National Aeronautics and Space Administration (NASA) Johnson Space Center. Food scientists, dietitians, and engineers analyze the foods for nutritional,

sensory, and packaging quality. Before foods are used on space flights, FSEF personnel test the foods on NASA's Zero-Gravity KC-135 airplane [71]. The challenges associated with maintaining the quality of food from a sensory as well as nutritional perspective are being explored to enable long-duration missions [6, 17, 27]. Additionally, growing food in space, such as lettuce and other vegetables, is also currently being studied on the space station.

Military Convenience Foods. Military rations for battlefield food service have also undergone many changes over the years. During World War II, canned meats such as Spam® were common. The basic combat ration used today is the Meal, Ready-to-Eat (MRE). MREs provide a full meal consisting of 9 or 10 components that provide about 1,300 kcal. The packaging consists of retort pouches (flexible packaging) in a meal bag (**Figure 1-22**).

(a)

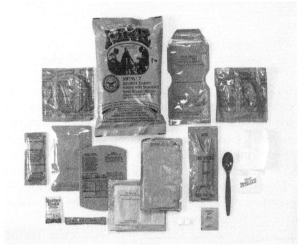

(b)

Figure 1-22

(a) Foods, such as Meal, Ready-to-Eat (MRE), for the military must offer special conveniences as well as high quality.
(b) The components of a MRE, are shown here and may also be used for humanitarian purposes following natural disasters. (Defense Logistics Agency, @ Pfc. Rachel Wilridge photographer)

UP CLOSE
THE EVOLUTION OF FOOD IN SPACE

Mercury flights	It was learned a person could chew and swallow while weightless. Early space foods were either pureed to be forced into the mouth through tubes or compressed into compact, bite-sized pieces that were coated to avoid any loose crumbs that would float in zero gravity.
Apollo flights	A spoon, rather than a tube, was used to eat moist foods, and hot water was available for the first time to make the rehydration of foods easier.
Skylab program	Space was available for a dining room with tables and a refrigerator and freezer. Astronauts had knives and forks available to them and ate from a food tray with cavities to hold containers of food.
Space Shuttle	A galley has been designed on the shuttle for astronauts' food service needs. The galley has hot and cold water, an oven, and a small refrigeration unit but no freezer. The food includes (1) rehydratable foods such as macaroni and cheese; (2) thermostabilized foods in cans, plastic cups, or flexible retort packages such as puddings, fruits, and tuna; (3) intermediate-moisture foods such as dried peaches; (4) natural form foods such as granola bars; and (5) irradiated meat. Condiments such as salt and pepper are packaged with liquid so that these seasonings can be used without floating into equipment on the shuttle. Many foods are dehydrated to reduce weight at takeoff, but water produced onboard as a by-product of the spacecraft's fuel cells was readily available for use in space.
Space station	Foods are frozen, refrigerated, or thermostabilized, then heated to serving temperatures with an onboard microwave/forced air convection oven. Few dehydrated foods are used on the space station because the solar panels used to provide electricity do not produce water. In 2005, the space station crew enjoyed some gourmet creations of chef Emeril Lagasse.
Future space travel	Future space travel is likely to involve manned flights of longer duration. NASA is cooperating with universities and the food industry in the research and development of controlled ecological life-support systems. Such a system includes biomass production, food processing, waste treatment, atmosphere regeneration, and water purification. Imagine the challenge to food scientists and engineers as they discover how to produce nutritious, safe, palatable foods from a limited amount of biomass materials, with serious constraints in space and facilities for food processing and preparation.

Source: References 15, 17, 27, 36, 71.

The MRE must be able to be dropped out of aircraft, to withstand environmental extremes from −60°F to +120°F, to be shelf stable for 3 years at 80°F, to be resistant to wildlife, and to taste good. MREs may be eaten cold or heated by a variety of ways, including with a flameless heating device provided in the meal bag. MREs have improved considerably since they were used during Operation Desert Storm in the Persian Gulf War of 1991. Product developers go into the field with soldiers to assess performance of the MREs and interview the soldiers. This approach has increased soldiers' satisfaction [65].

Other rations include the First Strike Ration, a more compact ration designed to be light and small in volume for missions in mobile operations. Another ration, called Meal, Cold Weather and Food Packet, Long Range Patrol is used for long-range missions in cold weather conditions. Additional kinds of rations have been developed for other special needs.

SENSORY AND OBJECTIVE EVALUATION OF FOOD

Sensory Characteristics of Food

Sensory characteristics are important factors in determining whether we will first taste, then eat, and enjoy the food. Those involved in food preparation, both in homes and in commercial establishments, must take into careful account the appearance, flavor, and texture of the dishes prepared. Humans assess their food using the five senses: taste, smell, sight, touch, and hearing. For example, consider how the sounds of crisp foods such as raw carrots and the sizzle of fajitas when brought to the table influence the total experience with these foods. Understanding these sensory characteristics is essential in the study of food.

Appearance. Appearance often creates the first impression of food. Such qualities as color, form, consistency, size, and design or arrangement contribute to what may be called "eye appeal" of foods. Without a pleasing appearance, foods may be rejected without being tasted. For the commercial vendors, the appearance of food is extremely important because it is the first opportunity to impress the potential buyer.

Color is an especially important attribute. Try eating a jelly bean and guessing the flavor without prior knowledge of the color. Not only does color influence the expectation of flavor, but it provides a perception of quality. Olive-green broccoli or a fruit tray with slices of apples and pears that have turned brown on the surface would not be favorably received.

Taste. Although *flavor* and *taste* are used synonymously, in a strict sense, taste is only one part of flavor. Taste involves the sensations produced through stimulation of the **taste buds** on the tongue, as well as the roof of the mouth and the throat [54]. There are five primary taste sensations: sweet, sour, bitter, salty, and umami, also called savory. All of these tastes are sensed within the same taste bud within a complex system [54].

Sweet tastes are primarily associated with hydroxyl (-OH) groups, whereas salty tastes occur due to the ions of salts. Sour substances are generally the result of hydrogen ions (H^+) found in acids. A number of compounds taste bitter, including, in part, caffeine and theobromine. Umami is a taste associated with amino acid–based substances and is often described as "savory," "meaty," or "brothy." Monosodium glutamate is one example of a substance providing an umami taste. Other foods contributing umami include tomatoes, eggs, seafoods, cheese, and soy sauce.

The transmission of taste-related messages is also provided by the trigeminal nerve. This nerve transmits sensations such as heat or burning, cooling, or tingling. Foods causing these sensations include those with capsaicin found in hot peppers, menthol, or carbonated drinks [54].

Taste Buds. Taste buds are found in small elevations, called **papillae**, on the surface of the tongue (**Figure 1–23**). Taste sensations are produced when bitter, salty, sweet, or acid substances in a solution contact **taste receptors** in the **taste pore** leading to the taste bud. Sensation of bitter tastes is generally delayed rather than immediate. A message is sent to the brain from the taste cells via nerve fibers with endings in the taste cells. The brain interprets and identifies the specific taste as well as associated emotions and memories [54].

Influence of Temperature and Sound. Temperature may affect the blending of primary tastes and other factors contributing to flavor. The temperature of foods when eaten, from ice cream to hot chocolate, affects the apparent intensity of some tastes. Sugar seems sweeter at higher temperatures than at lower temperatures. Just the reverse seems to be true of salt. Noise appears to reduce the perception of sweetness, but does not impact the sensation of salty, bitter, and sour. The umami taste is more intense in noisy environments, however [54].

Genetics. Our genetics and the genes we inherent can impact our taste preferences. The hypersensitivity to bitterness is inherited. Furthermore, researchers have found about 30 percent of our sweetness perception is genetically influenced [54].

Odor. An odor may be pleasing or offensive. The term *aroma* is usually applied to a pleasant odor. The

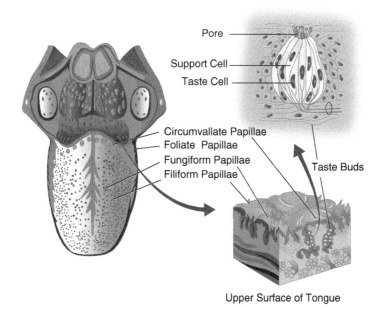

Figure 1–23

The tongue, taste bud, and surface of the tongue are shown in these diagrams.

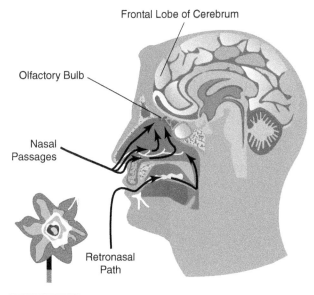

Frontal Lobe of Cerebrum

Olfactory Bulb

Nasal Passages

Retronasal Path

Figure 1–24

The olfactory system is shown here. What we describe as flavor is composed of both aromas and taste.

smell of fresh baked bread, hot apple cider, freshly cut cantaloupe, and many other foods is considered appealing and, when experienced, encourages tasting of the food. In contrast, the odor resulting from burnt food is offensive. Some foods, especially those that are cold, have a limited odor. Ice cream is an example of this.

The olfactory center is found at the top of the nasal cavity, as shown in **Figure 1–24**. To stimulate the olfactory center, substances must be in gaseous

form. The gaseous molecules enter the nose as food is placed in the mouth and are drawn toward the olfactory center, where they stimulate nerve endings. These aromas can be experienced "orthonasally" through the nose, or "retronasally" when vaporizing chemicals released when chewing stimulate the nose from the back [54]. Nerve impulses are thus sent to the brain to be interpreted. The sense of smell is estimated to be about 10,000 times as sensitive as the sense of taste in detecting minute concentrations, and it can differentiate hundreds or possibly thousands of distinct odors.

Flavor. Flavor is a blending of **taste** and **odor**. Millions of flavor sensations are experienced in a lifetime. For most, the perceived pleasantness of the flavor will determine if the food will be consumed. Flavor perceptions change over time, and foods not liked when one is young may become favorites later in life. Older adults may have less sensitivity to some flavors and therefore are inclined to add more sugar, salt, or other flavoring substances to enhance eating enjoyment [77].

Perceived flavor results from an integrated response to a complex mixture of stimuli or sensations from the **olfactory** center in the nasal cavity, the taste buds on the tongue, **tactile** receptors in the mouth, and the perception of **pungency**, heat, cooling, and so on when a food is placed in the mouth [47]. The flavor of food can be affected by every step in the production process, from selection of ingredients to processing to packaging and storage of the final product [57].

FOCUS ON SCIENCE
SENSORY CHARACTERISTICS OF FOOD

Flavor

Flavor is a complex mixture of taste, smell, texture, and temperature. The nose and mouth work together to deliver signals that the brain translates into the flavor of food. Some other facts about taste:

- Salt can hide bitter flavors.
- The heat of chili peppers is actually not a flavor but a response of pain receptors on the tongue.
- Aging tends to cause a loss of taste buds and sensitivity to food decreases—food tastes more bland to older people.

"The nose knows." How does the nose participate in tasting food?

Most of what is called "flavor" actually comes from odors that reach nerves via nasal passages at the back of the throat. A person could detect 10,000 odors, but how one could be detected from the other is still unknown. Scientists think that a person has many different receptors that "light up" in various combinations in response to different scents.

Scientists also have found a strong link between smell and memory. Consider how a dinner experience could be enhanced if guests could enjoy the food with a smell associated with a pleasant experience.

Umami—What is it?

Umami is a Japanese word meaning "savory" or "meaty" and thus applies to the sensation of savoriness—specifically to the detection of glutamates which are especially common in meats, cheese (Parmesan, Roquefort), soy sauce, fish sauce, walnuts, grapes, broccoli, tomatoes, and mushrooms. The action of umami receptors explains why foods treated with monosodium glutamate (MSG) often taste fuller or better.

The glutamate taste sensation is most intense in combination with sodium. This is one reason why tomatoes exhibit a strong taste after adding salt. Sauces with savory and salty tastes are very popular for cooking, such as tomato sauces and ketchup for Western cuisines, and soy sauce and fish sauce for East-Asian and South-Asian cuisines.

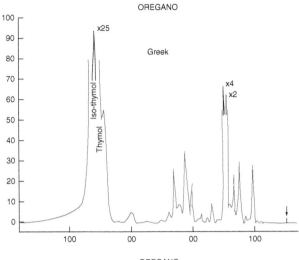

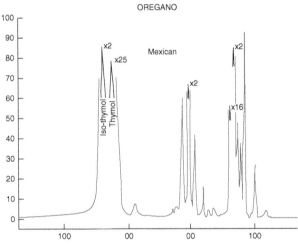

Figure 1–25

The geographic origin of a spice may be identified by examining the gas chromatographic tracing of its flavor components. Each peak on the tracing represents a different flavor substance. Oregano grown in Greece contains various flavor components in different amounts than oregano grown in Mexico. (Reckitt Benckiser LLC, French's Food Division)

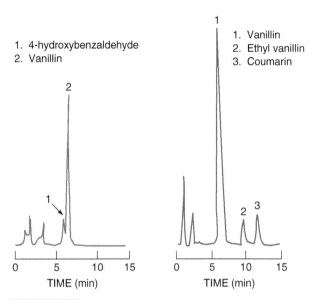

Figure 1–26

High-performance liquid chromatography (HPLC) may be used in testing vanilla for adulteration. The tracing on the left is from a true vanilla-bean extract, and the one on the right is from a sample that has been adulterated with coumarin, a substance banned as a flavor source in the United States. (Based on Kenney, B. F. "Applications of high-performance liquid chromatography for the flavor research and quality control laboratories in the 1990s." Food Technology 44(9), 80, 1990. Copyright © Institute of Food Technologists)

Analysis of Flavor. Countless numbers of molecules contribute to our perception of odor or aroma and taste. One single flavor may be produced from the interaction of many different chemical molecules. Did you know, for example, that more than 200 different compounds are used to make artificial banana flavor? Many of the odorous substances in foods occur in such vanishingly small concentrations that it is difficult to show that they are even present. With the development of analytical tools such as the gas chromatograph, tracings from which are shown in **Figure 1–25**, the chemist has been able to separate, isolate, and identify many of the molecules that are responsible for aroma and taste in such foods as onions, strawberries, and beef.

Analytical tools used to great advantage by the flavor researcher are high-performance liquid chromatography (HPLC), the electronic nose, and the electronic tongue [50, 61, 101]. HPLC is especially useful for studying **nonvolatile** and/or **labile** (unstable) flavor components (**Figure 1–26**). Among other things, it can be used to test for adulteration of flavoring materials from natural sources. The electronic nose is a chemical sensing system that offers the advantage of the rapid detection of volatiles.

Impact of Heat on Flavor Development. The flavors of some foods are readily perceivable in the raw "natural" state, whereas cooking other foods produces flavors from nonflavor substances called flavor **precursors**. The method of cooking also has an impact on flavor development. For example, flavors produced when meat is cooked in water are different from those produced when it is roasted in an oven surrounded by dry heat. The tantalizing odors that develop during the baking of bread are additional examples of flavor substances produced by heating. Many of the volatile substances that waft from the oven where bread is baking are initially the products of **yeast fermentation**. The browning of the bread crust in a hot oven contributes to a pleasant flavor as well as an attractive appearance.

Natural Flavors. Flavors also may be produced during processing by **enzymatic reactions**, such as cheese flavors, or by microbial fermentation, such as butter flavors. Flavor substances that occur naturally or that are generated during heating, processing, or fermentation are considered to be "natural" flavors [47].

Artificial or Synthetic Flavors. Biotechnology can be used to generate natural flavor substances from enzymatic or microbial reactions. Natural flavors are simulated as closely as possible through the production of **synthetic compounds**. Synthetic compounds added to foods either individually or as part of a mixture are considered in the United States to be "artificial" or "synthetic" flavors. Both natural and artificial flavorings are combined in many foods.

Flavor Researchers. Knowledge of flavor chemistry and ways of simulating natural flavors are especially important as the world population increases and global markets expand. Foods must be flavored so that they are accepted by consumers in their unique cultural environment. To apply the science of flavor successfully to the development of new products and the improvement of old ones, the flavor researcher must first identify the substances that are responsible for the acceptable flavor and the mechanism by which people eating the food experience flavor. New food-flavor ingredients can then be developed, and foods can be prepared in a manner that results in the most desirable flavors [43, 57].

Texture. The physical properties of foods, including **texture**, consistency, and shape, involve the sense of touch or feeling, also called the *tactile* sense. When food is contacted, pressure and movement receptors on the skin and muscles of the mouth and tongue are stimulated. Sensations of smoothness, stickiness, graininess, brittleness, fibrous qualities, or lumpy characteristics may be detected [98]. The tingling feeling that comes from drinking a carbonated beverage is an attribute of texture. Terms describing extremes of texture and consistency may include dry or moist, solid or fluid, thick or thin, rough or smooth, coarse or fine, tough or tender, hard or soft, and compact or porous.

Texture includes those qualities that can be felt with the fingers, the tongue, the palate, or the teeth. Textural characteristics of food influence consumer preferences both positively and negatively [99]. Those textures that are universally liked are crisp, crunchy, tender, juicy, and firm. Those generally disliked are tough, soggy, crumbly, lumpy, watery, and slimy. Texturizing agents are often used by the food processor to impart body, to improve consistency or texture of a food, or to stabilize an **emulsion** [78]. Such agents, of which there are many, optimize the quality of a food product so that consumers will find it acceptable.

Sound. The sound made when a food is eaten is also part of palatability and the enjoyment of eating. We often evaluate crispness by the sound it makes and by its tactile sensations in the mouth. Try to imagine how crisp carrot and celery sticks would "taste" without the accompanying sound of crunching. When microwave popcorn was introduced, one of the significant sensory concerns was the squeaky, rather than crunchy, sound audible when eating.

Sensory Evaluation of Food

When the quality of a food is judged or evaluated by the senses (taste, smell, sight, touch, and hearing), it is said to be a sensory evaluation. Because food is prepared for the primary purpose of being eaten and enjoyed through the senses, sensory evaluation is most appropriate. No machine has yet been devised that can totally substitute for the human senses in evaluating the quality of human food. However, the human instrument used in sensory evaluation is complex, and many issues need to be managed when collecting and analyzing data.

Flavor perceptions are difficult to characterize verbally. For example, think about how a strawberry tastes, then try to describe it to someone else. The character of a taste or aroma may be described using a wide variety of terms. Often the terms used to describe the flavor of a food indicate that the flavor is similar to that of some other familiar food product. For example, prepared cereal may be described as being nutty, starchy, haylike, floury, oily, or buttery. The primary tastes—sweet, sour, salty, and bitter—are relatively easy to describe. Other terms used to describe flavors in foods include caramel, stale, rancid, metallic, cardboardlike, musty, fragrant, flowery, fruity, sharp, pungent, tart, chalky, branny, burnt, spicy, astringent, sulfury, diacetyl (butterlike), malty, effervescent, earthy, chemical, putrid, yeasty, fishy, grassy, bland, toasted, and **aftertaste**. You may enjoy the challenge of finding new descriptive words for flavor evaluation.

Trained Sensory Panels. In food research, small groups of trained individuals, called judging panels or sensory panels, are commonly used to determine differences among food samples. These panels often consist of 5 to 15 individuals who have had training and experience in testing the particular food products being evaluated.

A variety of scoring, ranking, or difference tests are used by sensory panels. It may sometimes be desirable to do a complete analysis of all flavor components, such as sweet, buttery, burnt, fragrant, grainy, and metallic, in a particular food. Such a **flavor profile** of the food, giving a picture of its palatability, may be determined by a panel of trained judges working together. Aroma and taste are studied separately to complete the total flavor analysis.

Because any food product will likely contain many flavor components of differing degrees of volatility, these flavor components will impact the olfactory center at different times. Thus, aroma, taste, and texture may change as we eat and drink, especially for foods, such as chocolate, that melt in the mouth. These dynamic aspects of taste may be examined by using a time–intensity curve. The intensity of the

FOCUS ON SCIENCE
GAS CHROMATOGRAPHY—HOW AND WHY IS IT USED?

Gas chromatography is used as a means of identification and for quantification determination. The procedure is relatively simple. A small quantity of sample is introduced, typically by a micrometer syringe through a self-sealing diaphragm onto a column. The sample is vaporized on being injected onto the head of the column by striking a heated plate. Inert gas carries the sample along. The sample travels at various speeds depending on solubility, volatility, and gas pressure. Various components present in the sample will emerge at different times from the discharge end of the column. The time between injection of the test sample and the peak maxima shown on the chart printout is known as the retention time for the component.

FOCUS ON SCIENCE
SENSORY TESTING—CAN YOU IDENTIFY THE FOOD THAT IS DIFFERENT?

Discrimination testing is a class of tests that represents one of the most useful tools available to the sensory professional. All of these methods are intended to answer a seemingly simple question: "Are these samples perceived as different?" It is on the basis of perceived differences between two products that can lead to a descriptive evaluation in order to identify the basis for the difference.

The identification of the samples is an important aspect of testing. Perhaps the researcher wants to know if a low-fat product can be identified as different from the standard product. If the product is labeled as low fat, bias would be introduced. Therefore, food and beverage samples used in sensory testing are usually identified with a numerical or alphabetic code.

Three types of discrimination tests are the following:

- *Paired Comparison*. Sensory panelists are asked to distinguish between two samples by identifying the sample that has more of a designated characteristic. For example, panelists may be asked to identify the spicier or sweeter sample.
- *Triangle Test*. Three samples are presented to the panelists for testing. The sensory panelists are asked to pick the two samples that are the same, thereby identifying one sample as different.
- *Duo-Trio Test*. Three samples are provided to the panelists for tasting. One of the samples is designated as the reference or control sample. From the remaining two samples, panelists are asked to identify the sample that matches the reference or control sample.

flavor may be weak, moderate, strong, or someplace in between. Using a computer, the taster may record the changing intensity of a particular flavor attribute over a 30-second to two- or three-minute period [118]. Combining time–intensity curves for the various flavor components in a particular food may produce what has been called a dynamic flavor profile [30].

Consumer Panels. As new food products are developed, food manufacturers need to know if they can capture a large enough share of the market to warrant the cost of development and marketing. Many new products are introduced and fail each year. Sensory-evaluation professionals and marketing personnel may conduct consumer tests to obtain information on product quality and preference. Consumers and producers may not always agree on quality or preference. Both trained sensory panels and consumer panels involve people. However, trained panels are usually more objective than consumer panels. By correlating the two panels, the consumer can be better understood and the likelihood of product success enhanced. Consumer input is important from the very beginning of the development process.

In some cases, particularly in consumer preference testing that involves large groups of people, a **hedonic** scale is used without a description of the flavor components. A hedonic scale for children is shown in **Figure 1–27**. An example of a scale for adults follows:

____Like extremely well   ____Dislike slightly
____Like very much   ____Dislike moderately
____Like moderately well   ____Dislike very much
____Like slightly   ____Dislike extremely
____Neither like nor dislike

Figure 1–27
A hedonic scale for children provides easy to interpret faces.

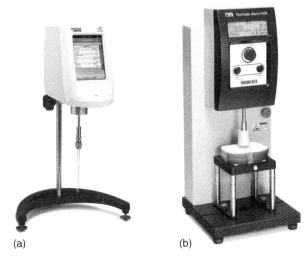

(a)   (b)

Figure 1-28

A variety of instruments are used in the objective measurement of food quality. (a) A Brookfield viscometer. (b) A Brookfield texture analysis instrument. (Brookfield Engineering Laboratories, Inc.)

Objective Evaluation of Food

Objective evaluation of food involves the use of laboratory instruments to determine certain characteristics that may be related to eating quality. Devices and the objective measurements that may be made in the laboratory include a viscometer to measure viscosity (thickness or consistency) of a tomato paste or a starch-thickened pudding, a gelometer to measure the firmness or strength of a gelatin gel or a fruit jelly, a pH meter to measure the acidity of lemon juice, a colorimeter to measure the color of red apples, a compressimeter to measure the compressibility or softness of a slice of bread, and a shear or cutting apparatus to measure the tenderness of a sample of meat (**Figure 1–28**). These types of tests do not directly involve the human senses and thus are not part of a sensory evaluation.

The use of judging panels to evaluate food is often time consuming and expensive. Therefore, the use of laboratory instruments that give useful information with less time and expense is desirable when the information thus collected correlates well with sensory characteristics. Objective tests can usually be reproduced with reasonable precision. In the overall evaluation of the quality of a food product, sensory and objective methods complement each other.

MEASUREMENT OF FOOD TRENDS

What do people eat? And how much? Answers to these questions are important to those who work in the various fields of food, food service management, and nutrition. Information on food consumption by populations and individuals may be collected in different ways using various sources.

Food Availability Data

The U.S. Department of Agriculture (USDA) obtains information on the food consumption or food use of populations by measuring directly (or estimating through sampling and statistical procedures) the quantities of food that "disappear" into the nation's food distribution system. The total available food supply is measured using three components: total food production, total imports of food, and beginning-of-the-year inventories. From this total of available food is subtracted food that was exported, used by nonfood industries, used for seed by farmers, and year-end inventories. Food consumption calculated in this manner is called a *residual component*—what is left over when other uses are subtracted from the available total supply. The Economic Research Service of the USDA has periodically collected data since 1909 for up to 350 commodities, such as beef, eggs, wheat, and various fruits and vegetables. *Loss-adjusted food availability* data have been further adjusted to account for spoilage and other losses in efforts to more closely approximate actual consumption. The loss-adjusted data are used to compare the consumption of food to the *Dietary Guidelines for Americans* [66].

Food availability or food disappearance data, as a method of measuring food consumption, should be interpreted with an understanding of data collection strengths and limitations. The method of sampling, incomplete reporting, and estimation techniques all may contribute to errors. Strengths of these data are that they provide an independent measurement of food consumption without the errors inherent in consumer survey data.

The Economic Research Service, under the USDA, provides online access to food availability or food supply data. Go to www.ers.usda.gov or visit www.usda.gov and search using the key term "Food Availability" or "Food Consumption." Spreadsheets or tables and charts may be obtained for the foods and dates you specify.

Using this data source, the food quantities per capita on an annual basis were obtained to highlight changes in food consumption since 1970 [109] (**Table 1–3**).

Food Consumption Surveys

USDA and HHS Food Consumption Data. The USDA's Continuing Survey of Food Intakes by Individuals (CSFII) and the Health and Human Services' (HHS) National Health and Nutrition Examination Survey (NHANES) provided information about food consumption and health prior to 2002. Beginning in 2002, these two surveys were conducted jointly under the NHANES/CSFII survey [24]. This new integrated survey is called "What We Eat in America" [67, 104].

Unlike the information about food consumption obtained from the food disappearance studies, the data for "What We Eat in America" are obtained from a nationally representative sample of Americans over

Table 1–3
CHANGE IN FOOD AVAILABILITY IN THE UNITED STATES USING USDA FOOD AVAILABILITY (PER CAPITA) DATA

	1970	2016	Percent Change
Meat (includes red meat, poultry, fish, and shellfish)	178 #	192 #	+8%
Eggs	302 eggs	268 eggs	–11%
Fruits	238 #	256 #	+8%
Vegetables	336 #	385 #	+15%
Flour and Cereal Products	137 #	172 #	+26%
Cheese	11 #	36 #	+227%
Beverage Milk	21 gallons	12 gallons	–42%
Caloric Sweeteners, Added	119 #	131 #	+10%
Total Fat and Oils, Added	55 #	84 #	+52%

a two-day period. In the 2013–2014 data set, 8,661 individuals participated in interviews and a physical examination at a mobile exam center, and 7,574 completed a dietary phone interview [104].

As with the food disappearance data, these data should be interpreted with an understanding of their strengths and limitations. Survey data of Americans provide insight into Americans' food consumption patterns and allow a check on the accuracy of the USDA food disappearance data. Furthermore, these survey data allow an analysis of food patterns by age, region of the country, and other variables. However, individuals may not clearly recall exact consumption of foods or may be uncomfortable being entirely candid about the foods consumed. Researchers have developed the survey method to minimize these potential inaccuracies.

National Eating Trends Data. The NPD Group provides consumer and retail market research. NPD national eating trends data are obtained through consumer report of consumption in two-week diaries [66]. Self-reported diaries are considered a less reliable method of data collection.

Consumer Purchases and Store Sales Data. Food consumption is also tracked through the collection of data on consumer purchases using self-reported diaries or scanned data. Three major sources for this information include the (1) Consumer Expenditure Survey by the Bureau of Labor Statistics, (2) Consumer Report on Eating Share Trends by the NPD group, and (3) Homescan Consumer Panel by Nielson. The Consumer Report of Eating Share only includes food-away-from-home, whereas the Homescan Consumer Panel data include retail store sales only and therefore do not include food-away-from-home [66]. Because not all sources of food are captured by these data sources, an incomplete understanding of overall food consumption is provided.

Point-of-sale data are used for the Infoscan by the Information Resources, Inc., and the Scantrack Services by Nielsen. These data are used primarily as an analysis of sales, prices, and quantities. These point-of-sale data sources do not include items without UPC codes or sales from Walmart [66].

Changes in Food Consumption
Although food habits may be quite firmly established, people are receptive to change with sufficiently compelling reasons. Diet and health concerns, as well as changing prices and increasing or decreasing real disposable income, contribute to changes seen in U.S. food consumption. Other factors influencing these changes are the plethora of new products on the market (especially convenience items), the global food market, smaller households, and more two-earner households [66]. An increasing proportion of ethnic minorities in the U.S. population also is having an impact on foods consumed [86].

STUDY QUESTIONS

Family, Social, and Personal Influences on Food Choices

1. Explain what "palatable" food means to you, and identify ways that others may have different ways of describing palatable foods.

2. Discuss how family, society, culture, and religious practices may affect the eating patterns that an individual develops.

3. Define acculturation in regard to food habits and offer examples.

4. Identify several regional or ethnic food patterns, and then discuss how these foods are becoming integrated into home and restaurant menus.

5. Discuss several ways in which people may identify themselves as vegetarian or alternatively consume vegetarian meals?

6. Discuss ways in which personal beliefs about food may influence healthy or unhealthy eating patterns.

Nutrition and Health

7. Discuss the primary focus of the USDA *Dietary Guidelines for Americans* and on what basis these guidelines are established.

8. Explain how Americans either consume too much or too little of food and food groups as recommended by the USDA *Dietary Guidelines for Americans*.

9. Create an education plan using "MyPlate" to help Americans select their foods.

Economic and Marketplace Factors

10. Identify multiple ways that economic and marketplace factors may impact what people eat.

11. Prepare a food budget, meeting the USDA *Dietary Guidelines for Americans*, for a family of four at 200 percent of the poverty line. Discuss the challenges of planning this menu, the choices made, and how other household expenses would be handled.

12. Define food insecurity, food deserts, food swamps, and famine.

13. Identify several food assistance programs for Americans found within the Farm Bill.

14. Explain various factors that impact food costs (marketing/farm-value share, crop production, trade, geographical location, food waste, home versus eating out, convenience foods, choice of stores, and other.

15. Discuss why food waste is a major concern, and its impact on food cost, health, and the environment,

Technological Developments and Convenience Foods

16. Explain the wide range of what may be considered a "processed food."

17. Discuss how the availability of technological developments has influenced what foods you consume.

18. Define the following, and provide food examples for each: aseptic processing, retort pouches, modified and controlled atmosphere, high-pressure processing, and irradiation.

19. Explain what is meant by a "clean food label," and discuss reasons why consumers may be seeking clean labeled foods.

20. Identify several unique issues associated with military foods and foods consumed in space travel.

Sensory and Objective Evaluation of Food

21. Discuss how the appearance, aroma, or texture of a food may influence your evaluation of its flavor or other quality characteristics.

22. Define and distinguish among the terms *flavor, taste, odor,* and *aroma*.

23. List the five primary tastes.

24. Explain how food temperature, noise, and aging influence sensations of taste and smell in humans.

25. Discuss your ideas on the practical importance to humanity of research on flavor chemistry.

26. Identify the human sense(s) that perceives the texture and consistency of a food.

27. Food quality may be evaluated by sensory or objective methods. (a) Provide examples of each type of evaluation, and (b) describe several situations or conditions under which quality evaluation of specific food products may be desirable or necessary.

Measurement of Food Trends

28. Compare and contrast several ways that the food consumption of Americans is tracked.

29. Explain why from health and economic perspectives, it can be helpful to know the trends in food consumption within a population.

2

Food Safety

Food safety is everyone's responsibility. From the farmer to the processor, packager, wholesaler, retailer, food service operator, and consumer, everyone should recognize potential health hazards related to food and know how to control them. Why is food safety so important? Foodborne microbes remain one of the most common causes of illness in the United States. Young children, pregnant women, elderly people, and people with weakened immune systems or chronic health conditions (e.g., patients with diabetes, HIV/AIDS, cancer, or autoimmune diseases) are at the highest risk for foodborne illness [75, 100].

Exactly how many people become sick each year from foodborne illness is not known because not every illness is reported. Estimates from the Centers for Disease Control and Prevention (CDC) suggest that annually 3,000 deaths, 48 million illnesses (1 out of 6 Americans), and 128,000 hospitalizations in the United States are caused by foodborne illness [84, 85]. In 2016, surveillance data documented 24,029 laboratory-diagnosed cases of foodborne illness, 5,512 hospitalizations, and 98 deaths [26, 63]. The CDC collected these surveillance data from 10 states, covering 49 million people (15 percent of the U.S. population). Although the number of foodborne illnesses reported by this system provides useful data about the prevalence of foodborne illness, it reflects only a fraction of the cases nationwide. National foodborne illness outbreaks (two or more related illness) are also tracked and reported by the CDC using data from local and state health departments [19]. In this chapter, the following topics will be discussed:

- Preventing foodborne illness, including (1) the role of government, consumers, and others; (2) four keys to safe food handling; (3) the Hazard Analysis and Critical Control Points (HACCP) system; and (4) technologies to improve food safety
- Microorganisms and other causes of foodborne illness, such as animal parasites, prions, natural toxins, chemical or physical contaminants, and food allergies and intolerances
- Additional potential food-safety issues such as biotechnology and bioterrorism

PREVENTING FOODBORNE ILLNESS

Who Has a Role in Preventing Foodborne Illness?

The concept of food safety from farm to table was emphasized in a report to President Clinton prepared by the Food and Drug Administration (FDA), the U.S. Department of Agriculture (USDA), the Environmental Protection Agency (EPA), and the CDC [57]. Foodborne illness is prevented through the multifaceted efforts of all who have a role in producing, processing, regulating, and preparing food.

Government. The government promotes food safety through oversight, regulations, and monitoring by the FDA, USDA, EPA, CDC, and other selected agencies. The Food Safety Modernization Act, signed into law in 2011, was a comprehensive reform of food-safety laws that emphasized prevention [47]. The USDA for many years has required safe handling instructions on packages of all raw or partially cooked meat and poultry (**Figure 2–1**). Both the FDA and the USDA regulate as well as inspect processors. Local health departments inspect food service establishments to enforce safe food-handling

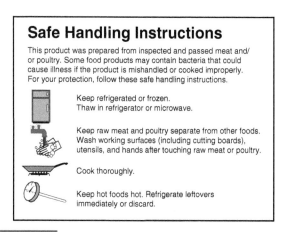

Safe Handling Instructions

This product was prepared from inspected and passed meat and/or poultry. Some food products may contain bacteria that could cause illness if the product is mishandled or cooked improperly. For your protection, follow these safe handling instructions.

Keep refrigerated or frozen. Thaw in refrigerator or microwave.

Keep raw meat and poultry separate from other foods. Wash working surfaces (including cutting boards), utensils, and hands after touching raw meat or poultry.

Cook thoroughly.

Keep hot foods hot. Refrigerate leftovers immediately or discard.

Figure 2–1

The USDA requires safe handling instructions on packages of all raw or partially cooked meat and poultry products. (U.S. Department of Agriculture, Food Safety Inspection Service)

practices in the commercial sector. (Regulations are discussed further in Chapter 3.) All of these components help to provide safe and wholesome food.

Producers, Processors, and Retailers.   On the farm, good agricultural practices help to prevent or reduce contamination of produce foods and promote healthy herds and flocks. The food-processing industry utilizes a variety of measures to limit potential food hazards. It **pasteurizes**, **sterilizes**, uses specialized packaging, freezes, refrigerates, dehydrates, and applies approved antimicrobial preservatives to various food products. Food retailers have a responsibility to store food at recommended temperatures and to turn over inventory so that consumers have access to fresh foods. With the many fresh and takeout food choices in today's grocery stores, it must be ensured that these foods are prepared and held properly to prevent food-safety hazards.

Food Service Establishments.   Over 1 million restaurants and many other food service establishments serve the American public [74]. Workers in the food service industry—including those employed in fast-food and carryout restaurants, delicatessens, self-service food counters, mobile refreshment stands, family and gourmet restaurants, schools, hospitals, and other establishments—must be educated about potential food-safety hazards. The ServSafe program developed by the Educational Foundation of the National Restaurant Association has been widely used by the industry to provide education and food-safety certification [75]. Some states mandate that commercial food service operations have a food-safety-certified employee or manager on premise during all hours of operation. Food service managers and dietetic practitioners have a responsibility to supply consumers with safe products that are as free as possible from **pathogenic** microorganisms and other health hazards [1, 75].

Consumers.   Consumers have important responsibilities for food safety through the selection, preparation, and proper storage of foods. They, however, may lack the necessary information to prepare food safely. Consumers in one study erroneously believed that contaminated food could be identified by taste or smell; they did not refrigerate hot foods quickly as recommended, but instead left foods to cool slowly at room temperature before refrigeration [66]. A multistate survey of consumer food-handling practices found nearly 20 percent did not adequately wash hands or cutting boards after contact with raw meat or chicken [2]. A number of food-handling errors were observed by researchers at Utah State University who concluded that consumers report safer food-handling practices on surveys than observations of actual food preparation reveals [4, 5]. In general, many consumers

Food Safety and Inspection Service, USDA

Figure 2–2

Thermy, the cartoon thermometer, promotes the use of thermometers in the home. (U.S. Department of Agriculture)

do not appear to be acting on the messages concerning food safety that have been disseminated for years by both government and industry groups, as evidenced by the consumption of undercooked eggs and other risky behaviors [13, 37, 60, 80, 87]. Men tend to engage in more risky food-safety behaviors as compared to women [13, 80]. Consumer food-safety education campaigns are listed in **Table 2–1** and include the USDA's cartoon thermometer called "Thermy" (**Figure 2–2**).

Four Keys to Safe Food Handling

The consumer education campaign of the Partnership for Food Safety Education (**Figure 2–3**) focuses on four critical messages:

1. Wash hands and surfaces often.
2. Don't cross-contaminate.
3. Cook to proper temperatures.
4. Refrigerate promptly.

Wash Hands and Surfaces.   Following simple rules of sanitation, such as washing hands before handling food, putting clean bandages on cuts and sores before

Table 2–1
FOOD-SAFETY EDUCATION RESOURCES

There are a wide range of web pages, brochures, and flyers to use in educating consumers about safe food handling. A few of these food-safety education resources are provided below. Please note that Internet content changes rapidly, and the web addresses may change over time.

Food-Safety Education Sources	Type of Information Available
Partnership for Food Safety Education http://www.fightbac.org	A wide variety of consumer education resources focus on four key messages: Clean, Separate, Cook, Chill.
Home Food Safety: It's in Your Hands Academy of Nutrition and Dietetics and ConAgra Foods Foundation https://www.eatright.org/homefoodsafety	Home food-safety statistics, information about foodborne illness, and safe food-handling information are provided.
National Science Teachers Association FDA/NSTA Partnership in Food Science http://www.teachfoodscience.org/i_food_science_program.asp	Middle and High School Science Curriculum Teacher guides contain hands-on experiments and activities focusing on food and food safety.
Health Educators: Food Safety and Education Campaigns Food and Drug Administration https://www.fda.gov/Food/ResourcesForYou/HealthEducators/default.htm	Materials, including PowerPoint slides, to use in providing food-safety education for pregnant women, food labeling, Hispanic community bilingual materials, science and our food supply with educational materials for middle and high school classes, and more.
Food-Safety Education U.S. Department of Agriculture, Food Safety, and Inspection Service https://www.fsis.usda.gov/wps/portal/fsis/topics/food-safety-education	Information is provided for consumers on a variety of timely food-safety concerns. Some of the links include: • Get answers including links to the "Ask Karen" for your questions about food safety • Links to the USDA Food Safety Fact Sheets with content targeted for at risk populations (cancer, transplant, and HIV/AIDS patients, pregnant women, older adults, and diabetes patients), emergency preparedness, and general food safety • "Thermy" and "Is It Done Yet" education programs about safe cooking temperatures • Links for kids and teens including games and quizzes
Government Food-Safety Gateway Page https://www.foodsafety.gov/	This webpage provides a gateway to a wide variety of U.S. federal government food-safety information and educational resources.
State Cooperative Extension	Food-safety materials are available through the State Cooperative Extension Service in many states across the United States.

working with food, and wearing plastic gloves, can prevent numerous outbreaks of illness. In 2015, norovirus was the leading cause of foodborne illness outbreaks, accounting for 37 percent of such outbreaks [24]. Norovirus is primarily spread because of poor personal hygiene. Although 96 percent of Americans say they wash their hands after using a public restroom, researchers observed hand-washing practices in six U.S. public attractions in four metropolitan areas and found that only 85 percent washed their hands after using the restroom [34]. Another group of researchers observed hand-washing practices after using the restroom in a college town. They found men were significantly less likely to wash their hands as compared to women, and

hand-washing compliance was lower later in the day. Overall, only 68 percent of the nearly 4,000 observed people used soap, 10 percent made no attempt to wash their hands, and only 5 percent spent more than 15 seconds washing their hands [10]. In a study where the food preparation practices of consumers were videotaped, researchers found that the average length of hand washing was only 4.4 seconds and that 34 percent of the hand-washing attempts were without soap [5]. When working with food, hand washing is necessary before food preparation and multiple times during food preparation. Additionally, hands must be washed properly. Hands should be washed in hot running water with soap and scrubbed for at least 20 seconds,

Figure 2–3

An eye-catching Fight BAC™ character is used to attract attention of the public in a campaign to teach consumers about food safety. (Fight Bac! Partnership for Food Safety Education)

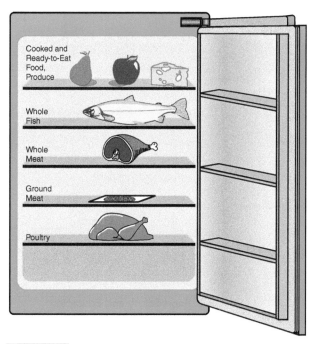

Figure 2–4

Proper placement of food in the refrigerator helps to reduce chances of contracting a foodborne illness by preventing cross-contamination of harmful bacteria into foods that may not be cooked before consumption.

with care taken to clean under the fingernails. Hands should be rinsed under clean running water and then dried with a single-use towel [75]. Saying the "ABCs" or singing "Happy Birthday" twice is a way to see that hands are washed for the appropriate length of time. Surfaces in kitchens need to be cleaned thoroughly as well. Fight BAC recommends the use of paper towels. If cloth towels are used, they must be clean and not left damp for extended periods of time, such as between meals. A damp dish towel or a sponge contaminated with even small amounts of food soil is a perfect growing medium for bacteria that will cross-contaminate the surfaces later being "cleaned." In commercial food service operations, towels used are clean from the laundry, or, if to be used again a short while later, the towels are stored in a solution of a food-safe chemical sanitizer.

All dishes and equipment used in food preparation should be carefully cleaned. Machine-washed dishes, both in homes and in commercial food service establishments, may have a very low, if not almost nonexistent, bacteria count because hot water and sanitizing agents are used in machine washing. A solution of one tablespoon of unscented liquid chlorine bleach per gallon of water may be used to sanitize countertops, dishcloths, cutting boards, and dishes [43].

Don't Cross-Contaminate. Cross-contamination can occur because of a dirty cloth, unclean surfaces, contaminated cutting boards, dirty hands, or poor storage

techniques. In the Utah State University study, dirty hands accounted for 51 percent of the cross-contamination cases observed. Another key problem was the storage of raw meat on the middle or top shelf of the refrigerator that could drip into other foods, such as lettuce or fruit to be consumed raw [5]. Another group of researchers found only 17 percent of consumers reported proper storage of raw poultry in their refrigerators [37]. Foods should be stored in the refrigerator so that potentially hazardous raw foods are stored low in the refrigerator in containers to prevent any dripping of juices into ready-to-eat foods such as produce, deli meats, or cheese (**Figure 2–4**).

Cross-contamination during shopping can also occur. Raw meats, poultry, and fish should not be bagged with lettuce, fruit, and deli meats to be consumed without cooking. Reusable grocery bags should be washed, especially if used to bring home hazardous foods, to prevent cross-contamination with other grocery items.

Cook to Proper Temperatures. Foods such as poultry, eggs, ground beef, pork, and seafood must be cooked to specified temperatures to enhance sensory qualities and also to kill pathogenic organisms such as *Salmonella*, *Escherichia coli*, *Listeria monocytogenes*, *Staphylococcus aureus*, *Trichinella spiralis*, *Anisakis simplex*, *Vibrio parahaemolyticus*, *Vibrio vulnificus*, and others that may be present. The USDA food cooking temperature guidelines provided as part of the "Is it done yet?" consumer

Figure 2–5

USDA-recommended temperatures for the safe cooking of meats, poultry, eggs, and fish are presented on this consumer-friendly flyer. (USDA, Food Safety and Inspection Service)

FOCUS ON SCIENCE
HOW DOES BLEACH INACTIVATE BACTERIA?

Clorox™, a sodium hypochlorite bleach, inactivates bacteria by breaking down proteins in cell walls. Sodium hypochlorite breaks down into little more than saltwater once it completes killing microorganisms. It should be noted that when a solution of bleach becomes "dirty," it becomes inactive. Thus, a bleach solution must be periodically re-mixed fresh, or it will be ineffective as a sanitizer.

Different concentrations of bleach are recommended depending on the task or purpose. For example, one concentration may be recommended for water to be sanitized for drinking and another level for the cleaning of surfaces and food contact equipment.

---

education materials are shown in **Figure 2–5** [97], and the FDA Food Code temperatures for food service operators are provided in **Table 2–2** [41, 75].

More consumer education about food temperatures and the use of thermometers is needed. For example, ground beef is not guaranteed safe to consume when it is brown throughout. Browned ground beef may be cooked to a temperature less than the recommended minimum temperature of 155 to 160°F (68 to 71°C), which is needed to destroy potential pathogenic organisms [59, 83]. Consequently, color alone as a measure of doneness is ineffective as a safety measure. Many consumers in the Utah State University study undercooked chicken, meatloaf, or fish. Only 5 percent of the consumers in the Utah study used a thermometer, but many of the consumers who used a thermometer did not know the recommended temperatures [5]. Researchers exploring consumers' preparation practices for poultry items found less than 25 percent used a thermometer to check for a safe cooking temperature,

with many deciding on doneness by the exterior color of the chicken or turkey [37].

First, consumers need to own a thermometer. Food-safety advocates suggest instant-read and refrigerator thermometers can make great "stocking stuffers" or housewarming and wedding gifts. Accurate temperature readings when using a thermometer depend on proper use and maintenance. Most thermometers used to check cooking temperatures must be calibrated periodically to provide accurate measurements. Thermometers may be calibrated in ice water to 32°F (0°C) or in boiling water to 212°F (100°C) (**Figure 2–6c**). However, as discussed in Chapter 5, water boils at 212°F (100°C) at sea level. For those living at higher elevations, water boils at a temperature below 212°F (100°C), and therefore the use of ice water to calibrate to 32°F (0°C) is the preferable technique.

A stem thermometer (**Figure 2–6a**) must be inserted up to the dimple on the stem (typically about

Table 2–2
COOKING TEMPERATURES RECOMMENDED IN THE 2013 FDA FOOD CODE

Product	Temperature
Poultry	165°F (74°C) for 15 seconds
Stuffing (prepared with poultry, meat, or fish); stuffed meat, seafood, poultry, or pasta; and dishes combining raw and cooked food (including soups and casseroles)	
Ground meats (beef, pork, and other meat); injected meats (including brined ham and flavor-injected roasts); mechanically tenderized meat, ratites (ostrich and emu); ground, chopped, or minced seafood	155°F (68°C) for 15 seconds
Steaks or chops of pork, beef, veal, lamb; seafood (including fish, shellfish, and crustaceans); commercially raised game	145°F (63°C) for 15 seconds
Fresh shell eggs for immediate service	145°F (63°C) for 15 seconds
Roasts of pork, beef, veal, and lamb. Lower endpoint cooking temperatures are an option if the holding time is extended; for example, 130°F (54°C) for 112 minutes	145°F (63°C) for 4 minutes
Any potentially hazardous food cooked in a microwave oven	165°F (74°C) let food stand for 2 minutes after cooking

Source: References 41, 75.

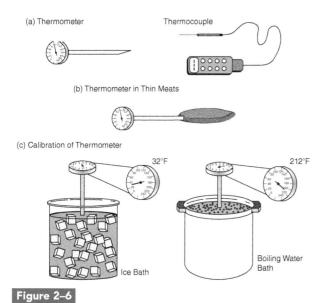

(a) Thermometer
Thermocouple
(b) Thermometer in Thin Meats
(c) Calibration of Thermometer
32°F
212°F
Ice Bath
Boiling Water Bath

Figure 2–6

(a) Stem thermometer and thermocouple. (b) Proper use of thermometer in thin meats. (c) Method of thermometer calibration.

2 inches) and sufficient time allowed for the temperature to register (usually 15 seconds). When taking the temperature of a thin food such as a hamburger or chicken breast, the thermometer should be inserted from the side (**Figure 2–6b**) to obtain the internal temperature. The stacking of thin foods to measure temperatures is not recommended as this will result in inaccurate measurement of the internal temperature. Thermocouples often are used in food service operations. Thermocouples record the temperature quickly and often require only one-fourth inch of food contact

to provide an accurate reading; however, because the cost is high, home use is not common.

Refrigerate Promptly. High-risk, hazardous foods must be held hot or cold. The **temperature danger zone** is between 41 and 135°F (5 and 57°C). Pathogenic bacteria grow rapidly when in the temperature danger zone (**Figure 2–7**). Food preparers need to be aware of and minimize the total time the food is exposed to the danger zone, including preparation, service, and cooling times.

Improper holding and inadequate cooling are a common risk factor for foodborne illness [75]. More than one researcher has documented that a significant number of consumers leave perishable foods at room temperature to cool before refrigeration [4, 5, 66]. Bacteria grow most rapidly between 70°F (21°C) and 125°F (52°C) therefore, keeping food at room temperatures is very hazardous.

Even when foods are placed under refrigeration quickly following a meal, the food may still not cool quickly. Tips for cooling of hot foods and thawing of frozen foods are provided in **Table 2–3**. Foods should not be in the temperature danger zone for more than 4 hours, or for a total of 6 hours if the food is cooled to 70°F (21°C) within 2 hours and then to 41°F (5°C) within an additional 4 hours. Many consumers may have the refrigerator temperature regulator set too high [5, 13] and may not know the temperature of their refrigerator. Refrigerators must be at or below 41°F (5°C). Refrigerator and freezer thermometers need to be used and checked regularly. Placement of the thermometers on a shelf within the refrigerator or freezer (not on the door) is recommended.

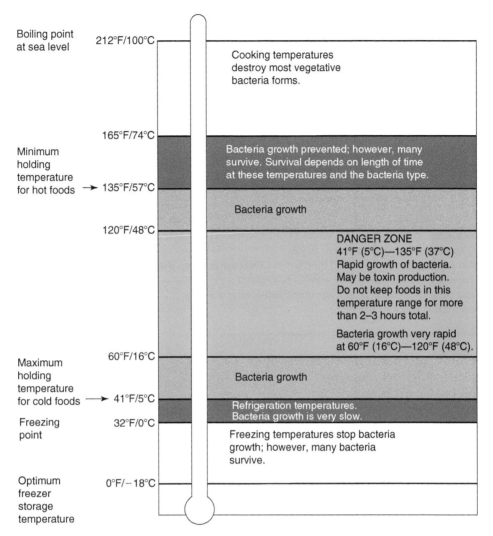

Figure 2–7

Effect of temperature on growth of bacteria.

Hazard Analysis and Critical Control Points—A Systematic Approach

The HACCP system was developed by Pillsbury Company for the NASA space program. HACCP is a systematic process to identify and control food-safety hazards that may be microbiological, physical, or chemical. Thus, HACCP is a preventive system designed to build safety into the entire process of food preparation or manufacture. It is a quality control tool that focuses on critical factors directly affecting the **microbiology** of foods. HACCP operates on a set of basic procedures and involves the following steps (**Table 2–4**):

1. Analyze **hazards** and assess **risks**.
2. Identify **critical control points** in the process for each hazard where loss of control may result in an unacceptable health risk.
3. Establish preventative measures with critical limits for each control point.
4. Establish procedures to monitor the control points.
5. Establish corrective action to be taken if a deviation occurs at a critical control point.
6. Establish procedures for verifying the HACCP system.
7. Establish record-keeping procedures that document the hazard analysis so that the problems can be effectively traced.

The HACCP system is an important part of food processors' overall quality assurance programs and helps to ensure the safety of their products. The FDA and the USDA require the adoption of HACCP systems by juice, meat, seafood, and other food processors [36]. In addition to HACCP systems, slaughter plants must test for generic *Escherichia coli* bacteria to verify that their control systems are preventing fecal contamination, the primary source of these organisms in the plant. The USDA also requires plants to adopt and follow written **standard operating procedures** for sanitation as part of good manufacturing practices [36].

Table 2–3
TIPS FOR RAPID CHILLING OF HOT FOODS AND FOR SAFE THAWING OF FROZEN FOODS

Rapid Chilling of Hot Foods

- Keep refrigerator at 41°F (5°C) or lower and monitor with a refrigerator thermometer.
- Put hot foods in small, shallow, cool containers. Less than 2 inches in depth is preferable. Use multiple containers if necessary.
- Cut large roasts into smaller portions.
- Cook soups or other foods by placing in a larger container of ice water and stirring to lower the temperature. Divide into smaller containers and then refrigerate promptly.
- *DO NOT* leave foods at room temperature "to cool" before placing in the refrigerator.
- *DO NOT* store foods such as stews or casseroles in large, deep (4- to 6-inch) containers.

Safe Thawing of Frozen Foods

- Take from the freezer to the refrigerator. Allow 24 or more hours for thawing. Put the food in a container that will prevent any juices from dripping into other foods.
- Put the food in a moisture-proof bag and then put in *COLD* water. Keep the water cold. Depending on the volume of food to be thawed, food will thaw safely within a few hours.
- Use the defrost setting on microwave. Cook immediately after thawing.
- *DO NOT* thaw food at room temperature.

After the product leaves the plant, it is the responsibility of the wholesaler, retailer, and consumer to handle, store, and cook the product properly to ensure safety.

Many restaurants and other food service operations are required to use the HACCP system as part of their quality assurance program [74]. The following safeguards are essential for safe food service: control time and temperature through appropriate heating and cooling of **high-risk or potentially hazardous foods**, good personal hygiene, and prevention of contamination and **cross-contamination** in preparation and storage [74]. At each of these critical control points in production, a schedule for monitoring should be established and followed precisely. If monitoring reveals a potential hazard, a clearly defined corrective action must be taken and documented.

In homes, food preparers can also benefit by being aware of HACCP. For example, knowing what foods are perishable and then addressing how to protect against foodborne illness are the first steps in a HACCP plan. Table 2–4 provides examples of how the steps in HACCP can be used to guide food handling in the home setting.

Technologies to Improve Food Safety

Pasteurization. A number of foods including milk, fruit juices, and eggs may be pasteurized to reduce the risk of foodborne illness. Pasteurized foods have been heated to kill pathogenic bacteria. The heat process may be very brief (161°F/72°C for 15 seconds) or a longer process (145°F/63°C for 30 minutes). Foods that have been ultra-pasteurized have been heated to a higher temperature (280°F/138°C for 2 seconds) and as a result have a longer shelf life, even though refrigeration is still necessary.

Milk and egg products such as liquid or dried eggs must be pasteurized because the risk of foodborne illness from these products is significant. Fruit juices must include a warning label if not pasteurized or otherwise treated to cause a 5-log (i.e., 100,000-fold) reduction in foodborne pathogens.

Irradiation. Irradiation has been found to be a safe and effective method of reducing foodborne pathogens through more than 50 years of research [89]. It is approved for use on several foods by the FDA and the USDA. Irradiation has also been referred to as cold pasteurization because it destroys harmful bacteria without heating the food. The sources of radiation energy allowed for food processing include gamma rays (produced from cobalt 60 and cesium 137), electron accelerators, and machine-generated X-rays [32, 89]. The electron-beam (E-beam) system uses commercial electricity to accelerate electrons that kill harmful bacteria in frozen beef patties and other thin foods [64, 68]. E-beams require only a few seconds of exposure and can replace the need to fumigate for insects on fruits, vegetables, and grains being imported or exported [64]. Food irradiated using gamma rays, E-beams, or X-rays does not become radioactive [89].

The improved microbiological quality of the food is an important benefit from the use of ionization radiation. Consumers can prepare foods such as ground beef and chicken with greater confidence, if these are irradiated, because 99.9 percent of any *E. coli* 0157:H7 or *salmonella* is destroyed while maintaining sensory qualities of the food. Irradiated foods are labeled "Radura" and the words "treated by irradiation" or "treated with radiation" (**Figure 2–8**). Consumers have been reluctant to purchase and use irradiated foods. Consumer education

Table 2–4
WHAT DO THE SEVEN HACCP STEPS REALLY MEAN?

HACCP Steps	What Should Be Considered
1. Analyze hazards.	What potential hazards exist with the food being prepared? For example, chicken and ground beef are high-protein foods that will readily support the growth of microorganisms, and both of these foods could be contaminated.
2. Identify critical control points.	How will the hazards be controlled? Storage at appropriate temperatures, cooking, sanitation, methods to avoid cross-contamination, or other measures?
3. Establish preventative measures.	Highly perishable foods such as meat, poultry, fish, and dairy must be refrigerated to safeguard against rapid microbial growth. Ground beef must be cooked to 160°F (71°C) and chicken must be cooked to 165°F (74°C) to kill any pathogenic organisms that may be present. Foods such as meat, potato, and pasta salads, generally served cold, must be kept out of the temperature danger zone. If taking a salad to a picnic, it must be kept cold.
4. Establish procedures to monitor critical control points.	How will you know if food is kept cold or cooked to proper temperatures? Thermometers in the refrigerator and thermometers used to check cooking temperatures are needed to allow accurate monitoring of the critical controls.
5. Establish corrective action.	If ground beef is only at 140°F (40°C), the corrective action would be to continue cooking. When monitoring cold foods, if a salad has been in the danger zone for longer than the recommended time period, the corrective action is to discard the salad.
6. Establish procedures to verify the system is working.	Especially in food service organizations, procedures must be in place to establish how the organization will know the system is working. In homes, methods of making sure your system is working may include checking your thermometers regularly to be sure the readings are correct. Is your refrigerator thermometer in a location where it is checked on a daily basis?
7. Establish record keeping.	In homes, you may be unlikely to record the temperature of your refrigerator on a log; however, in food service organizations, this record keeping is an important way of keeping the HACCP system on track.

HOT TOPICS
RAW MILK? IS IT SAFE?

Milk has been pasteurized since the early 1920s, and as a result illness and death caused by contaminated milk have been dramatically reduced. Today, a renewed interest in raw milk (milk not pasteurized) is occurring. What are the issues?

Pasteurization is a heat process used to destroy harmful bacteria. It does not significantly change the nutritional value of the milk. Federal law, enforced by the FDA, prohibits the sale of raw milk across state lines. Sale of raw milk within a state is governed by the laws within the state and therefore may be different from state to state.

Why is the sale of raw milk prohibited in many jurisdictions? Consider that from 2007 through 2012, 979 illnesses and 73 hospitalizations occurred because of the consumption of raw milk or raw milk products such as Queso Panela, Asadero, Blanco, and Ranchero soft cheeses. These illnesses have been caused by *Campylobacter, Shigella* toxin-producing *E. coli, Salmonella*, and other microorganisms found in raw milk. Nearly 60 percent of these foodborne illness outbreaks involved a child less than 5 years of age.

Foodborne outbreaks associated with raw milk are higher in states where the sale of raw milk is legal. In 2007–2012, the number of raw-milk foodborne illness outbreaks was four times higher than in 1993–2006 when fewer states allowed the sale of raw milk.

Proponents of raw milk suggest it is healthier. Research, however, does not support the argument that significant amounts of nutrients are destroyed or that changes in enzymes have an impact on health. Cases of serious illness, however, are well documented. ■

Source: References 11, 28, 30, 42, 70.

FOCUS ON FOOD SCIENCE
PASTEURIZATION AND STERILIZATION: WHAT IS THE DIFFERENCE?

Pasteurization is a heat process with temperatures usually between 140 and 180°F (60 and 82°C). Pasteurization is used to destroy pathogenic bacteria. Milk, fruit juices, and other foods are pasteurized to destroy pathogens such as *Salmonella, Listeria monocytogenes, Escherichia coli*, and *Campylobacter jejuni*. However, some (~1 percent) of the nonpathogenic bacteria remain, and thus pasteurized foods need to be refrigerated.

Sterilization includes boiling (212°F/100°C), steaming, heating, and canning of low-acid foods at temperatures above boiling to completely destroy microorganisms. Canned foods may be stored at room temperature until opened. Once opened, canned foods are contaminated by microorganisms in the environment and must therefore be refrigerated.

Figure 2–8

An irradiated food on the retail market should bear the international symbol along with either of the statements "treated with radiation" or "treated by irradiation." (U.S. Department of Agriculture)

about this method of processing has been shown to increase consumer acceptance [53, 61, 76].

High-Pressure Processing. High-pressure processing is the application of high pressures to reduce vegetative bacteria cells without impacting enzymes or nutrients [33]. Raw fruit and vegetable juices, ready-to-eat meats, and some shellfish may be processed using high-pressure processing. High-pressure processing offers the advantage of providing foods that taste fresh and have reduced bacteria levels without the use of preservatives [6]. Because high-pressure processing does not destroy spores as found with *Clostridium botulinum*, heat in addition to high-pressure processing may be used for low-acid foods [6, 33].

MICROORGANISMS AND OTHER CAUSES OF FOODBORNE ILLNESS

Food provides nutrients needed to maintain health yet may include harmful microorganisms or toxins that may cause foodborne illness. Bacteria, viruses, parasites, and fungi are examples of some microorganisms. Together, viruses and bacteria are responsible for 92 percent of foodborne illness outbreaks from all causes [24].

There are three general types of foodborne illness: infections, intoxications, and toxin-mediated infections.

Food infection results when food containing live pathogenic microorganisms is consumed. Illness does not appear immediately. **Food intoxication** can occur due to the consumption of a food contaminated with toxin-producing microorganisms or a food contaminated with a biological or chemical toxin. Symptoms of food intoxication usually occur within a few hours. **Toxin-mediated infections** occur when a food contaminated with microorganisms is consumed, and these microorganisms then produce toxins in the intestine [75].

Although this chapter will focus on microorganisms that may result in foodborne illness, not all microorganisms are **pathogenic** and may perform some extremely useful functions in food preparation and processing. For example, the delightful flavors and characteristic textures of a variety of cheeses result from the activity of various bacteria or molds. Cultured dairy products such as yogurt, buttermilk, and sour cream depend on bacteria. Sauerkraut and pickles are made by using bacterial **fermentation**. Yeast leavens bread by producing carbon dioxide; it also produces alcohol through the fermentation process for beverages such as beer and wine. Those who enjoy soy sauce and blue cheese are indebted to molds used in their production.

Bacteria

Bacteria are tiny one-celled microbes smaller than either molds or yeasts and may be rod shaped (bacilli) or round (cocci). Generally, bacteria require more moisture than either molds or yeasts and grow best where concentrations of sugar or salt are low and where the pH is about neutral (neither acid nor alkaline). The pH scale runs from 0 (very acidic) to 14 (very basic or alkaline). A neutral pH is rated 7. Some bacteria love the cold; these are called *psychrophilic* and thrive at refrigerator temperatures. Others are heat loving (*thermophilic*) and may create particular hazards in cooked foods. Many others, however, are *mesophilic*, meaning that they do best at moderate temperatures. Bacteria also vary in their need for oxygen or air. *Aerobic* bacteria must have oxygen, *anaerobic* bacteria can grow only in the absence of oxygen, and *facultative* bacteria can grow either with or without free oxygen.

Table 2-5
FOOD INFECTIONS AND INTOXICATIONS

Organism	Type of Illness	Time until Onset of Symptoms	Nature of Illness	Foods Involved	Control Measures
Salmonella	Infection. May be toxin mediated.	6–72 hours.	Nausea, diarrhea, abdominal pain, fever, headache. May be life-threatening in infants, the elderly, and the immunocompromised. May cause arthritic symptoms 3–4 weeks later.	Eggs, poultry, meat, fish, milk products, cantaloupe, and other fresh produce.	Cook all animal foods to recommended temperatures. Cook poultry to 165°F (74°C). Do not consume raw or undercooked eggs. No cross-contamination. Thoroughly wash melons and other produce. Refrigerate promptly after cutting fruit.
Campylobacter jejuni	Infection. Even with low numbers of bacteria.	2–5 days is common.	Diarrhea (watery or bloody), fever, nausea and vomiting, headache, and muscle pain. Severe complications are rare but can occur.	Raw and undercooked poultry and meat, raw milk, eggs, contaminated water.	Handle raw poultry and meat to prevent cross-contamination. Cook all animal foods properly. Cook poultry to 165°F (74°C). Consume pasteurized milk and cheese. Avoid raw, unpasteurized milk.
Listeria monocytogenes	Infection.	3 days to 3 months.	Nausea, vomiting, diarrhea, headache, fever, backache. Meningitis, septicemia, miscarriage. High fatality rate in immunocompromised.	Unpasteurized milk, cheese prepared from unpasteurized milk, soft-ripened cheese, Queso fresco, deli meats and uncooked hot dogs, poultry, seafood, and vegetables.	Consume pasteurized milk and pasteurized milk products. Cook foods to recommended temperatures. Thoroughly wash vegetables. If pregnant or immunocompromised, heat deli meats and hot dogs to 165°F (74°C) before consumption.
Yersinia enterocolitica and *Yersinia pseudotuberculosis*	Infection.	1–11 days.	Fever, diarrhea, vomiting. Severe abdominal pain; may mimic acute appendicitis.	Meats (pork, beef, lamb, etc.), oysters, fish, and raw milk.	Cook foods to recommended temperatures. Consume pasteurized milk and cheese. Avoid cross-contamination with careful sanitation and hand washing.
Vibrio parahaemolyticus and *Vibrio vulnificus*	Infection.	*V. parahaemolyticus* 4–90 hours; often 17 hours. *V. vulnificus* 12 hours to 21 days; septicemia may occur within 4 days.	Diarrhea, abdominal cramps, nausea, vomiting, headache, fever, and chills. Severe cases of *V. vulnificus* can include decreased blood pressure and septicemia. Fatality from *V. vulnificus* infection occurs in about 35 percent of those who develop septicemia. Those most likely to experience severe illness are individuals with underlying illnesses (diabetes, cirrhosis, immunocompromised, insufficient gastric acid).	Raw, improperly cooked, or cooked cross-contaminated fish and shellfish. More common in warmer months. *V. vulnificus* commonly in raw oysters, clams, and crabs.	Consume properly cooked fish and seafood. Avoid cross-contamination with good sanitation practices. Individuals with underlying medical conditions should not consume raw oysters, or other undercooked seafood

(Continued)

Table 2-5
FOOD INFECTIONS AND INTOXICATIONS (CONTINUED)

Organism	Type of Illness	Time until Onset of Symptoms	Nature of Illness	Foods Involved	Control Measures
Escherichia coli 0157:H7	Toxin-mediated infection.	3–4 days, most commonly, but 1–9 days is also possible.	Hemorrhagic colitis. Severe cramping; watery or bloody diarrhea. Hemolytic uremic syndrome characterized by kidney failure.	Raw and undercooked ground beef. Raw milk, unpasteurized apple cider, and juice. Contaminated produce and water.	Thoroughly cook ground beef to a minimum of 155–160°F (68–71°C) throughout. Use pasteurized milk and pasteurized juices. Avoid cross-contamination and use good sanitary practices.
Clostridium perfringens	Toxin-mediated infection.	8–16 hours.	Abdominal cramps, diarrhea, and nausea.	Temperature-abused foods. Generally meat and meat containing foods such as gravy are cooled improperly, then heated insufficiently before consumption.	Cool foods to below 41°F (5°C) rapidly after cooking (see food cooling guidelines). Hold hot foods above 135°F (57°C). Reheat leftovers to a minimum of 165°F (74°C).
Shigella spp.	Toxin-mediated infection.	8–50 hours.	Abdominal pain; cramps; diarrhea; fever; vomiting; blood, pus, or mucus in stools.	Meat, poultry, and fish salads and products. Tofu and other protein foods. Sliced melons and other fresh produce. Tolerates low pH.	Good personal hygiene practices. Avoid cross-contamination from hands and working surfaces. Properly cook foods to recommended temperatures.
Staphylococcus aureus	Toxin.	1–7 hours.	Severe vomiting, diarrhea, abdominal cramping. In severe cases, headache, muscle cramping, changes in blood pressure and pulse rate.	Reheated meat and other protein foods. Custard- or cream-filled baked goods. Salads such as egg, potato, meat, or pasta.	Good personal hygiene practices. Avoid cross-contamination from hands and working surfaces. Rapidly cool prepared foods under refrigeration.
Clostridium botulinum	Toxin.	4 hours to 8 days; usually 18–36 hours.	Fatigue, headache, dry mouth, double vision, muscle paralysis, respiratory failure. High mortality rate if not treated promptly.	Low-acid canned foods, meats, sausage, fish. Improperly processed or preserved garlic-in-oil.	If canning foods in the home, proper procedures must be followed. Rapidly cool leftover foods. Infant botulism: Infants should not consume honey until more than 12 months of age.
Bacillus cereus	Toxin (emetic) or toxin-mediated (diarrheal).	30 minutes–6 hours (vomiting); 6–15 hours (diarrhea).	Nausea and vomiting. Abdominal cramps or diarrhea.	Rice products; starchy foods; food mixtures such as sauces, puddings, soups, and casseroles. Meats, milk, vegetables, and fish.	Careful time and temperature control of foods. Cook foods to recommended temperatures. Cool food quickly.

Source: References 40, 75.

HOT TOPICS
PROBIOTICS—FRIENDLY BACTERIA?

The Nobel Prize–winning Russian scientist Elie Metchnikoff suggested in the early 1900s that the long, healthy lives of Bulgarian peasants resulted from their regular consumption of Bulgarian milk—now known as yogurt. He claimed that live friendly bacteria, such as lactic acid bacteria, needed to be ingested regularly through fermented dairy products [88]. This concept now goes by the name *probiotics*.

Probiotic foods are those containing live microorganisms that, when consumed in sufficient numbers, actively enhance health by improving intestinal microbial balance [38, 86]. Research regarding probiotics is still emerging; however, the scientific literature has reported enhanced gastrointestinal tolerance to antibiotic therapy, control of lactose intolerance symptoms, and enhanced immune response in select situations [38]. Foods with live and active cultures in the United States include kefir, yogurt, and cheeses. Many of these foods have live *Lactobacillus* or *Bifidobacterium* bacteria cultures.

Challenges exist because probiotics are sensitive to heat, moisture, oxygen, and acid [38, 88]. Microencapsulation or enteric coatings have been developed to promote survival of the probiotics in the acidic stomach. Although the research is promising, at this time no health claims have been approved by the FDA for the emerging market of probiotic foods. ∎

Some bacteria are able to form spores or endospores that have special protective coatings, making them highly resistant to destruction by heating. These spores are especially resistant in low-acid environments, such as many vegetable and meat dishes. **Table 2–5** identifies common foodborne infections, toxin-mediated infections, and intoxications.

Salmonella. *Salmonella* bacteria cause the most deaths and hospitalizations because of foodborne illness [85]. An estimated 1 million cases of **salmonellosis**, including 378 deaths and 19,336 hospitalizations, occur annually in the United States [85]. Children under five, older adults, and those with weakened immune systems are most likely to develop serious complications.

Of the approximately many different strains of *salmonella*, four types (Enteritidis, Typhimurium, Newport, and Javiana) are responsible for most illnesses [29]. The organisms, which appear under the microscope as short rods (**Figure 2–9**), usually enter the body orally through contaminated food or water and may produce a food-poisoning syndrome as they multiply in the intestinal tract. Even relatively small numbers of bacteria can result in infection.

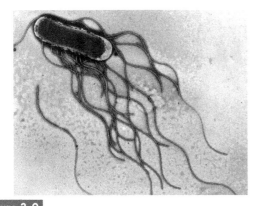

Figure 2–9

Salmonella is a rod-shaped bacterium with multiple flagellum. (Science History Images/Alamy Stock Photo)

Food Sources. A variety of foods have been associated with the outbreak of salmonellosis. Eggs and poultry, however, are frequently implicated. Eggs must be properly refrigerated from the time they are laid. Governmental regulations require retail establishments to hold eggs at or below 45°F (7°C). Chicken has also commonly been associated with *salmonella*. It is not unusual to find that a significant percent of broiler chickens are carrying *salmonella*. Melons, especially cantaloupe, and other kinds of produce may be contaminated with *salmonella* as well.

Prevention of Foodborne Illness. Foodborne illness caused by *salmonella* can be significantly reduced by producers, processors, and food preparers who adhere to recommended practices. In homes and food services, those preparing food should avoid cross-contamination, control the time and temperature of foods, cook to recommended temperatures, and use good personal hygiene. At present, processing methods cannot ensure that raw meat, poultry, and eggs are free of *salmonella* unless the food has been irradiated; thus, these foods should be handled with potential contamination in mind. New food-safety regulations adopted in 2009 for egg producers were enacted to reduce *salmonella*-contaminated eggs [81].

Salmonella are sensitive to heat and are destroyed by cooking of foods and pasteurization of milk. Poultry should be cooked to a minimum of 165°F (74°C) throughout. Cutting boards used for cutting up raw poultry or meat should be disinfected (one to three tablespoons of chlorine bleach per gallon of water) before use for other foods to prevent cross-contamination of microorganisms.

Many of the outbreaks of illness traced to this organism have been associated with eggs. Raw eggs should not be used in foods, such as ice cream, eggnog, and mayonnaise, when a heating process is not applied to kill *salmonella*. Pasteurized eggs are a good option to permit the safe preparation of products such as eggnog. Food services use pasteurized eggs to avoid the pooling of several dozen shell eggs. Eggs are "pooled" when a large number of eggs are cracked into a bowl. This practice is not allowed in food services because one infected egg will contaminate the entire mixture, and if the eggs are undercooked when served, foodborne illness can occur. Cantaloupe has also been implicated in outbreaks of salmonellosis. Cantaloupe must be washed using water and scrubbed with a vegetable brush to remove bacteria on the rind before cutting and then storing under refrigeration.

Good personal hygiene and thorough hand washing are essential. People who have had salmonellosis may carry the infecting organisms in their digestive tracts for some time after the symptoms of the disease have disappeared and thus may contaminate foods that they handle improperly. Hand washing after handling household pets (especially turtles, iguanas, lizards, and snakes) is also critical because these pets can carry *salmonella* [29].

Campylobacter jejuni.   *C. jejuni* is the most common cause of bacterial diarrhea in the United States [15], where it is estimated to cause 845,024 illnesses, 8,463 hospitalizations, and 76 deaths annually [85]. The infectious dose of *C. jejuni* can be quite low; illness can result from the ingestion of only a few hundred cells. The organisms are gram-negative rods with a curved to S-shape and have a requirement for reduced levels of oxygen [40]. *Campylobacter* is a relatively fragile organism and is sensitive to drying, normal atmospheric concentrations of oxygen, storage at room temperature, acidic conditions, and high heat. It grows at temperatures between 86 and 117°F (30 and 47°C) and is preserved by refrigeration, but it is readily destroyed by heat sufficient to cook foods. Therefore, *C. jejuni* is not likely to be a problem in properly cooked foods or in processed foods that have been pasteurized or dehydrated.

Food Sources.   *C. jejuni* is often found in the intestinal tract of cattle, swine, sheep, chickens, and turkeys. Therefore, the most likely sources of human infection are raw or inadequately cooked foods of animal origin and foods that are contaminated after cooking through contact with *C. jejuni*–infected materials. Research has shown that the majority (71 percent) of retail chickens are contaminated with *C. jejuni* [102]. Undercooked poultry, ground beef, raw milk, and non-chlorinated water have been implicated in several outbreaks.

Prevention of Foodborne Illness.   Illness can be prevented by thorough cooking of poultry and meat, pasteurization of milk, and proper handling of foods both before and after preparation for service. Care must be taken when storing and handling potentially contaminated foods such as poultry to prevent

cross-contamination. Raw poultry should be stored so liquids cannot drip into other foods, especially foods that will not be cooked before consumption.

Listeria monocytogenes.   Although the occurrence of *Listeria*-related illnesses has declined since the late 1990s, there are still an estimated 1,591 illnesses, 1,455 hospitalizations, and 255 deaths annually [85]. This organism can be responsible for a variety of health problems, including meningitis, **septicemia**, and miscarriage. Listeria is salt tolerant and will grow under refrigeration. Compared to the general population, pregnant women are about 10 times more likely and pregnant Hispanic women are 24 times more likely to get listeriosis [23]. In addition to pregnant women, illness occurs principally in individuals whose immune system is compromised in some way by such conditions as cancer, cirrhosis, AIDS, or transplantation of organs. In these cases, the mortality rate is high. Healthy individuals are usually able to overcome the infection with considerably fewer problems.

Food Sources.   Soil is a common reservoir of *L. monocytogenes*, which may be carried in the intestinal tracts of a variety of animals, including humans. Home environments may be contaminated with *L. monocytogenes*. This organism is found most often in raw milk or cheese prepared using raw milk, soft-ripened cheeses, Mexican-style soft cheese such as Queso fresco, ice cream, raw vegetables, hot dogs, deli meats, fermented raw sausages, raw and undercooked poultry and meat, and seafood products [40]. It may also be present in some vegetables. Listeriosis was in the national spotlight in 1998, when 21 deaths and 80 illnesses were traced to a single plant producing deli meat and hot dogs [101].

Prevention of Foodborne Illness.   Six of the 21 deaths in 1998 from contaminated hot dogs and deli meats were because of miscarriages or stillbirths. Therefore, pregnant women must thoroughly cook hot dogs; avoid prepared deli salads and soft cheeses such as feta, Brie, Camembert, blue-veined, and Mexican-style cheeses; and are advised to avoid deli meats or heat deli meats before consumption [23, 44, 94].

Listeria grows well in the manufacturing environment that is usually cool and moist. Many methods to reduce the possibility of contamination of products in manufacturing are being implemented and researched [39]. Refrigerator storage temperatures must be carefully controlled because fluctuations in temperature are likely to affect the growth of this and other organisms. *L. monocytogenes* can grow well at temperatures as low as 32°F (0°C) but is sensitive to heat and is destroyed by pasteurization.

Yersinia enterocolitica.   An infection caused by *Y. enterocolitica*, known as yersiniosis, may cause **gastroenteritis** with symptoms that may mimic appendicitis. *Y. enterocolitica* is psychotropic and can grow under refrigeration temperatures [40]. It is a relatively infrequent cause of foodborne illness. Raw or undercooked pork products are a common source, although other meats, fish, and raw milk may also be implicated [22]. Care should be taken to cook pork thoroughly; to clean hands and surfaces thoroughly when preparing chitlins; to avoid cross-contamination of ready-to-eat foods with pork and porcine wastes; and to practice good hygiene and hand-washing practices.

Vibrio parahaemolyticus and Vibrio vulnificus. These bacteria are associated with the consumption of raw or improperly cooked fish and shellfish [40]. The growth of *V. parahaemolyticus* is slowed or arrested at refrigeration temperatures. Most important with respect to human infections is prevention of bacterial growth in uncooked seafoods and avoidance of the contamination of cooked foods. Consumption of raw seafoods should be avoided. Although the risk of illness is higher during the warmer months of the year when the *Vibrio* organisms tend to increase in numbers, illness can occur whenever raw oysters or other undercooked seafood are consumed [40]. It is important that the elderly and those whose immune systems are compromised because of diabetes, cancer, HIV, renal disease, and so on be informed of the dangers associated with eating raw shellfish. *V. vulnificus* infections that result in septicemia have a 35 percent mortality rate. Limb amputations may also be necessary.

Escherichia coli. *E. coli* is a normal inhabitant of the human intestinal tract. However, certain strains of *E. coli* have caused serious foodborne illness outbreaks (**Figure 2–10**). It is estimated to be one of the top five pathogens resulting in hospitalization [85], and the most common cause of hemolytic uremic syndrome in children [73]. Each year in the United States, 63,153 cases of infection, 2,138 hospitalizations, and 20 deaths are estimated to occur because of *E. coli* 0157:H7 [85].

E. coli 0157:H7 produces the Shiga toxin leading to **hemorrhagic colitis** with bloody diarrhea and severe abdominal pain. Children, the elderly, and those with weak immune systems are most likely to develop a complication of this foodborne illness called *hemolytic uremic syndrome*, which is characterized by renal injury and

can lead to permanent kidney damage or death. Damage to the central nervous system can be another complication. As few as 10 organisms may result in illness.

Food Sources. *E. coli* 0157:H7 is not only associated with cattle and their products—beef and raw milk, but also produce. Ground beef is especially of concern because the bacteria, if present, are spread throughout the meat when it is ground. *E. coli* foodborne illness has also been associated with water, unpasteurized apple cider and apple juice, and produce foods such as lettuce that have been cross-contaminated either in the field or in the kitchen.

Prevention of Foodborne Illness. To avoid illness caused by *E. coli*, foods should be adequately cooked and post-cooking contamination avoided through careful hand washing and cleaning of surfaces and equipment that have come in contact with raw meat. Consumers should use a calibrated thermometer to be sure that ground meat has been safely cooked to an internal temperature of 155 to 160°F (68 to 71°C). In the 1990s, consumers were told to look for a brown color throughout when preparing ground beef [67], but research has shown that ground beef may be light gray or brown even when at an unsafe temperature below 155 to 160°F (68 to 71°C) [59, 83]. Consumer education efforts are now directed at encouraging the use of thermometers.

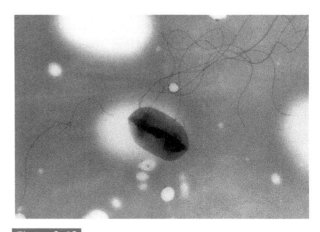

Figure 2–10

Transmission electron micrograph of *E. coli*. (Mediscan/Alamy Stock Photo)

Fresh fruits and vegetables should be washed thoroughly before eating. The FDA recommends that children, older adults, and people with weakened immune systems drink *only* pasteurized cider and juice. *E. coli* 0157:H7 can survive freezer storage as well as refrigeration.

The USDA requires that the HACCP system be used by livestock slaughter operations and meat-processing plants operating under federal inspection. The plants must also test for generic *E. coli* bacteria to verify that fecal contamination is not occurring. Processing methods such as steam pasteurization of the carcass, sprays, and organic washes help reduce contamination during processing [69]. In 1999, irradiation of meat products was approved by the Food Safety and Inspection Service as another method to assure the safety of meat products [69].

Clostridium perfringens. *C. perfringens* is estimated to be the third most common foodborne illness in the United States [85]. The mechanism causing illness seems to involve the ingestion of large numbers of live vegetative cells of *C. perfringens*. These cells then form encapsulating spores in the intestinal tract and release an enterotoxin. The toxin produces the characteristic symptoms [25, 40].

Foods responsible include beef, chicken, turkey, stews, meat pies, and gravy that have been mishandled. These foods may have been cooled too slowly after cooking or kept several hours without refrigeration, then improperly reheated. Because *C. perfingens* will grow at relatively warm temperatures, foods that have been held at a temperature below 130°F (55°C) for an extended period are another common cause of illness. *C. perfringens* organisms multiply rapidly under these conditions of poor temperature control during cooling, heating, or hot holding. Leftovers should be cooled rapidly and then reheated to a minimum of 165°F (74°C).

Shigella. The major cause of shigellosis is infected food handlers who are carrying the organism in their intestinal tracts and who practice poor personal

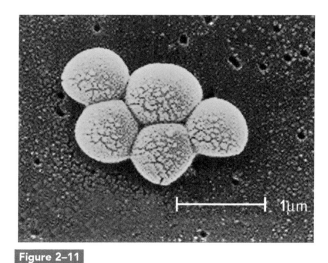

Figure 2–11

Scanning electron micrograph of *S. aureus*. (Scott Camazine/ Alamy Stock Photo)

hygiene. Most outbreaks result from contamination of raw or previously cooked foods during preparation in homes or in food service establishments. The best preventive measure is education of the food handler, with an emphasis on good personal hygiene. In homes and day cares, careful hand washing is a necessity after changing diapers. Relatively small numbers of the organisms can cause disease [40].

Staphylococcus aureus. Certain strains of *S. aureus* produce a potent toxin that is estimated to be the fifth most common cause of foodborne illness in the United States [85]. The toxin produced by *S. aureus* is called an *enterotoxin* because it produces gastroenteritis or inflammation of the lining of the stomach and intestines. *S. aureus* are present in the nasal passages and skin of 25 percent of healthy people [21]. Cuts may also be infected [75]. Food may be contaminated with these potentially dangerous organisms when transfer occurs from the nasal passage or a cut on the hands of the food handler to the food being prepared. *Staphylococcus* organisms are shown in **Figure 2–11**.

KEEP IT SAFE

THE WORLD IS CHANGING, AND SO ARE FOODBORNE PATHOGENS

One key to understanding food safety is to appreciate that what we have done safely in the past may not continue to be safe in the future.

The consumption of rare ground beef at one time was common. What changed? *E. coli* 0157:H7 was identified as a relatively new pathogen. In 1993, more than 700 people in the northwestern United States became seriously ill after eating undercooked hamburger at a chain of fast-food restaurants. Four children subsequently died.

Likewise, recipes in many older cookbooks include raw eggs. The recommendation used to be that if an egg was "intact," meaning the shell was not cracked, then it was safe to consume raw. What changed? In the early 1980s, it was found that ovarian tissues of some hens were contaminated with *Salmonella enteritidis*, and these hens produced eggs with contaminated yolks in the intact egg. Current recommendations are that no eggs should be consumed raw or undercooked unless irradiated or pasteurized. ■

Food Sources. A wide variety of foods may provide excellent media for the growth of staphylococcal bacteria. Cooked poultry, baked ham, tuna, egg products, potato salad, and custard- or cream-filled baked goods are often involved. These foods, in particular, should be refrigerated at 35 to 40°F (2 to 4°C). Failure to refrigerate and quickly cook foods that have been contaminated with the microorganisms, thus allowing the toxin to form, is the usual reason for an outbreak of the disease. The toxin does not necessarily affect the taste of the product, so individuals consuming such foods are not aware that they are eating "spoiled" food.

Prevention of Foodborne Illness. Prevention is accomplished by the sanitary handling of food during preparation and by proper refrigeration of prepared foods. Because staphylococci usually get into food by way of human handlers, contamination can be controlled by such simple rules as washing hands before preparing food and rewashing hands after sneezing, coughing, or contact with other sources of contamination. Rubber or plastic gloves should be worn if cuts or sores are present on the hands.

Rapid cooling and refrigeration of foods at or below 41°F (5°C) are critical. Foods contaminated with staphylococcal organisms that are cooled very slowly or are held without refrigeration will provide favorable conditions for the growth of organisms and production of the toxin responsible for illness. Once the toxin has formed in the food, the staphylococcal toxin is not easily inactivated or destroyed; thus, prevention is critical. The toxin is stable to heat and may withstand boiling for 20 to 60 minutes.

Clostridium botulinum.
Botulism is a condition that results from the action of a potent toxin on the neurological system of the body, causing paralysis. The toxin is produced by the bacterium *C. botulinum*, which is readily found in soil. Symptoms include nausea, vomiting, diarrhea, double vision, drooping eyelids, slurred speech, difficulty in swallowing, inability to talk, and, finally, respiratory paralysis and death. Infants with botulism are lethargic, feed poorly, are constipated, and have a weak cry and poor muscle tone [40].

C. botulinum is able to form spores (**Figure 2–12**) that are very resistant to destruction by heat in a low-acid environment. It is also *anaerobic*, meaning that it can grow and produce toxin only in the absence of free oxygen. The organism itself and its spores are not pathogenic or disease producing in adult humans, but the toxin that it produces is one of the most potent known.

Food Sources. Inadequate processing of home-canned foods that are low in acid—particularly vegetables, low-acid varieties of tomatoes, and meats—creates the greatest problem with respect to botulism. Toxin production has also occurred in such foods as fresh mushrooms kept in tight plastic bags, baked potatoes wrapped in foil and left at room temperature

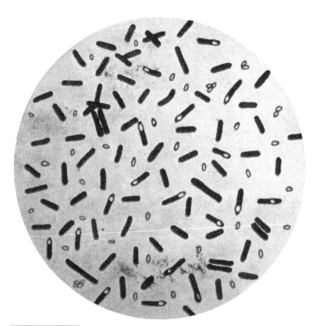

Figure 2–12

Gram-positive *Clostridium botulinum* bacteria and spores are shown here. (Centers for Disease Control)

for several days before being consumed, seasoned cooked onions that were kept warm for extended periods of service, and homemade garlic-infused oil held at room temperature [75].

C. botulinum spores may be found in honey, which has been implicated in some cases of infant botulism. Although adults can consume the *C. botulinum* cells that may be present in honey without ill effect, infants up to 1 year of age should not be fed honey. Out of 161 cases of botulism reported in the United States in 2014, 128 (80 percent) were infant botulism [18]. *C. botulinum* is able to colonize, grow, and produce toxin in the colons of infants, causing typical signs of neurological distress.

Prevention of Foodborne Illness. When home-canning foods, procedures recommended by the USDA or by established companies that manufacture home-canning equipment should always be carefully followed for low-acid foods to guard against any possibility of toxins development [7, 72]. Various strains of the organism vary in their temperature resistance, but low-acid foods are never safely processed unless they are heated at temperatures considerably above the boiling point of water, 212°F (100°C). It is recommended that temperatures no lower than 240°F (115°C) are used for low-acid foods. These temperatures can be achieved by processing in a pressure cooker at 10 to 15 pounds pressure. Canning procedures are discussed further in Chapter 28.

Spoiled foods containing the botulinum toxin may have off-odors and gas and appear to be soft and disintegrated. However, cases of botulism have been reported from eating foods that had little or no abnormal appearance or odor. Commercially canned foods should be discarded if the can is damaged or the food appears suspect. Garlic-in-oil should be used immediately after preparation, or commercially prepared garlic-in-oil mixtures should be used. Honey should not be served to infants less than 12 months of age.

Viruses

Viruses are responsible for the majority of foodborne illnesses in the United States [26]. Essentially all foodborne viruses are transmitted to humans enterically, that is, by the fecal–oral route. They are shed in feces and infect by being ingested. Infection may come directly by person-to-person contact or indirectly via the vehicles of food and water. Infection often results from mishandling of food by infected persons. Thus, sanitary personal hygiene habits and the avoidance of cross-contamination of ready-to-eat foods are critical. Viruses cannot multiply in foods and can usually be inactivated by cooking; however, they survive refrigeration and freezer temperatures [75].

Hepatitis A.   Foodborne illness due to the hepatitis A virus usually presents as a mild illness characterized by sudden onset of fever, malaise, nausea, anorexia, and abdominal discomfort, followed in several days by **jaundice**. The onset of symptoms occurs in two to four weeks. The infectious dose is presumed to be 10 to 100 virus particles [40]. Water, **mollusks** such as clams and oysters, and salads are frequently implicated in outbreaks. Other foods involved include sandwiches, fruits and fruit juices, milk and milk products, vegetables, salads, shellfish, and iced drinks.

Norovirus or Calicivirus.   Norovirus is estimated to be the leading cause of foodborne illness in the United States. Annually, 5,461,731 (58 percent) of illnesses, 14,663 hospitalizations, and 149 deaths are estimated to be the result of norovirus [85]. It spreads easily and quickly in groups of people [40]. Gastroenteritis, characterized by severe vomiting and diarrhea, may be caused by Norwalk-like viruses that are shed in the feces. Norwalk viruses, also called *noroviruses*, have been implicated in outbreaks of gastroenteritis on cruise ships, often a result of cross-contamination of food or surfaces from an ill guest or employee. Shellfish and salad ingredients are foods often implicated in Norwalk outbreaks. The Norwalk virus is notable in that it has been spread through ice contaminated by unsanitary water or the poor personal hygiene of those who handled the ice. Hand washing is critically important; alcohol-based hand gels are not effective in protecting people from norovirus [40].

Fungi

Fungi include molds, yeasts, and mushrooms. Fungi may be microscopic single-celled organisms to large multicellular organisms. Molds and yeasts have many beneficial functions in foods. Molds develop the characteristic flavors of some varieties of cheese, and yeast plays an important role in the leavening of yeast breads and the production of alcoholic beverages such as wine. Food spoilage or foodborne illness can also result from these organisms.

Molds.   Molds are multicellular, filamentous microbes that appear fuzzy or cotton-like when they grow on the surface of foods. The growth may be white, dark, or various colors, such as green or orange. Mold **spores**, by which molds reproduce, are small, light, and resistant to drying. They easily spread through the air and can contaminate any food on which they settle. Molds may grow readily on relatively dry foods such as bread or stored cereal grains because they require less moisture than most other microorganisms. They thrive at ordinary room temperatures but may also grow under cool conditions in refrigerators or at relatively high temperatures.

Mycotoxins are toxins produced by molds that can contaminate foods such as grains, nuts, and fruits. *Asperillus, Fusarium,* and *Penicillium* species are three fungi naturally associated with foods that can produce mycotoxins. Several mycotoxins of concern include aflatoxins, patulin, ochractixin, zearalenone, trichothecenes, and fumonisins. When present in foods in sufficiently high levels, mycotoxins can cause liver or kidney deterioration, liver cancer, skin irritation, immunosuppression, birth defects, and death [71, 77].

Mycotoxins may be produced by *Fusarium* molds when adverse weather conditions, including both unusually wet spring and summer months and certain drought environments, occur during the growth of cereal crops (**Figure 2–13**). Contamination of the harvested grains by the toxin is a problem because the toxins survive most processing methods. Fortunately,

Figure 2–13

A healthy wheat head (left) and one with *Fusarium* head blight disease (right). *Fusarium* can produce mycotoxins. (USDA)

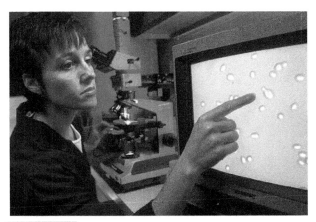

This technician is using a video monitor and light microscope to study yeast cells. Some of the cells are budding to form new cells. (Photo by Keith Weller. USDA)

accumulation of mycotoxins on cereal crops is not a significant problem during normal growing seasons [8]. The FDA has established regulatory limits for aflatoxins on both human and animal food. Monitoring programs are important in controlling the levels of mycotoxins in foods [51, 96].

In homes, foods that develop mold growth should be discarded; however, solid cheeses may be trimmed of mold and the non-moldy portion used if the cheese has been kept under refrigeration. Studies indicate that aflatoxins do not develop under refrigeration and that other toxins may be produced only in very small amounts or not at all. In the holding or storing of foods, precautions should always be taken to minimize mold growth by such practices as adequate refrigeration and use of foods within a reasonable time [96].

Yeast. Yeasts are one-celled organisms that are often spherical in shape. They usually reproduce asexually through budding, during which new daughter cells are pinched off from the parent cell (**Figure 2–14**). Unlike molds, most yeasts grow best with a generous supply of moisture. They also grow in the presence of greater concentrations of sugar than do most bacteria. The growth of many yeasts is favored by an acidic reaction (**pH** 4.0 to 4.5), and they grow best in the presence of oxygen. Thus, yeasts thrive particularly in acidic fruit juices, where they can ferment the sugar, producing alcohol. The range of temperature for the growth of most yeasts is, in general, similar to that for molds, with the optimum around 77 to 86°F (25 to 30°C). Foods spoiled by yeast should be discarded [96].

Animal Parasites

The globalization of the world's food supply is causing exposure to parasites not previously common in a given geographical area. Consequently, the risk to American consumers of parasites has increased significantly. Only 13 species of parasitic animals were of

concern in the United States in the 1990s. In 10 years that number has increased to over 100 species [78]. Current estimates suggest that up to 232,705 cases of illness annually in the United States are because of foodborne and beverage-borne parasites [85].

In some parts of the world, infestation by such parasites as roundworms, flatworms, and certain species of **protozoa** may be common problems, and food or water may be carriers of these infecting agents. Protozoa include *Entamoeba histolytica,* the cause of amoebic dysentery, which is spread principally by fecal contamination of water, food, and diverse objects. Food handlers can spread this parasite. *Ascaris lumbricoides* is a roundworm or nematode that is spread fecally and is resistant to sewage treatment. It may survive for years in the soil and contaminate vegetables. *Trichinella spiralis*, another nematode, becomes encysted in meat and may be spread by this route. Certain tapeworms (flatworms) may also be encysted in meat, while other types may be acquired by eating raw or insufficiently cooked fish [78].

Trichinella spiralis. There is a continuing though small risk in the United States from the tiny roundworm *T. spiralis.* Legislation controlling hog feed, the increased freezing of pork, and public understanding of the need to cook pork products properly have all promoted a reduction in cases.

Trichinella now is most often associated with the consumption of meats other than pork, including undercooked game meats such as bear, boar, deer, rabbit, and others. When meat from these animals is consumed before it has been sufficiently cooked to destroy the larvae in it, trichinosis results. The larvae are freed in the digestive tract after consumption of the meat and enter the small intestine, where they develop into mature worms. Their offspring (newborn larvae) migrate throughout the body via the circulatory system and invade striated muscles. Here they become encysted and may persist for years. In the first few weeks after ingestion of trichinae, symptoms include nausea, vomiting, diarrhea, sweating, and loss of appetite. Later, after the larvae reach muscles in the body, muscular pains, facial edema, and fever may occur. Several medications are available to treat trichinosis.

The USDA has recommended a procedure for processing cured pork products so that any trichinae present are destroyed. Therefore, these pork products should be free of trichinae. Poultry products that contain pork are subject to the same requirements concerning treatment for trichinae as are meat products containing pork. Thorough cooking of fresh pork to an internal temperature of at least 137°F (58°C) should ensure the destruction of any trichinae that may be present; however, a minimum of 145°F (63°C) is generally recommended for pork products. Pork cuts that are less than 6 inches thick can be frozen for 20 days at 5°F (−15°C) to destroy any trichinae present. However, the freezing of game does not consistently protect against trichinosis; thus, game meats must be thoroughly cooked regardless of freezing [14, 40]. Precautions must be taken when cooking pork or game meats by microwaves to ensure that a final temperature sufficient to destroy any trichinae is achieved throughout the meat.

Anisakis simplex. *A. simplex* is a roundworm that can be found in cod, haddock, fluke, Pacific salmon, herring, flounder, monkfish, and fish used in sushi and sashimi. Fish must be cooked properly; if consumed raw, the fish must have been previously frozen. To protect against anisakiasis by freezing, the fish must be maintained at −4°F (−20°C) for 7 days. Marinades are not protective, and marinated fish must still be properly cooked or previously frozen [40].

Toxoplasma gondii. This single-celled parasite causes a disease called *toxoplasmosis*. Toxoplasmosis infection is of concern for pregnant women because infants infected in the womb may develop serious eye or brain damage. Immunocompromised individuals also have a higher risk of complications. This pathogen is estimated as the second highest cause of death from a foodborne illness in the United States [85]. This parasite is frequently associated with cat feces and thus may be found in cat litter or contaminated soil. Raw and undercooked meat, however, can also be a source of *T. gondii*. Therefore, those at highest risk should be advised to wash hands carefully after gardening, when preparing food, and to cook all meat to recommended endpoint temperatures by using a thermometer [40]. Raw meats should be handled in storage and during preparation to avoid cross-contamination of other foods and surfaces.

Cyclospora cayetanensis. In the United States, the protozoa *C. cayetanensis* became a focus of public attention in the summer of 1996 [58]. This organism was recovered in multiple, clustered cases of prolonged diarrhea in the United States and Canada. More than 1,400 cases appeared from the Rocky Mountains eastward and were associated with the eating of fresh raspberries. The implicated raspberries were grown in Guatemala, but the *Cyclospora* was not actually found on the fruit. None of the available standardized tests for protozoan contamination of raw products was specifically intended for use on raspberries, creating difficulties in analysis. Although these cases are rare, foods most often implicated are fresh produce imported from the tropics [40].

Prions

Prions are normal proteins found in animal tissue that can become infectious. It is believed these misfolded, infectious proteins transform normally shaped proteins into abnormally shaped prions through contact. Prions are associated with bovine spongiform encephalopathy (BSE),

often called "mad cow" disease. BSE and the human illness variant Creutzfeldt–Jakob disease (vCJD) appear to be caused by the same agent. These diseases result in irreversible damage of the central nervous system after an extended incubation period of several years [16].

The concern for consumers is the potential contamination of meat products. Worldwide, there have been 229 confirmed or probable cases of vCJD [62]. In the United States, four reported cases of vCJD have occurred. Two are believed to be related to consumption of potentially contaminated BSE meat while living in the United Kingdom, where BSE was first reported in 1986. The third case most likely resulted from contact with contaminated meat in Saudi Arabia. In 2014, the fourth case was confirmed in a U.S. citizen who was born and lived outside of the United States [27]. The infection is believed to have been acquired outside of the United States [62]. High-risk tissues include the cattle's skull, brain, eyes, tonsils, spinal cord, and part of the small intestine. As of 2017, four classical and one atypical BSE-infected cows have been confirmed in the United States by the USDA [17]. The FDA and the USDA have regulations in place to prevent BSE among U.S. cattle and to protect consumers through active testing and surveillance. See Chapter 24 for more information on BSE.

Natural Toxins and Sources of Contamination

Although the term *natural* is generally associated with safety, certain plants and animals may contain natural constituents that are toxic, thereby producing gastrointestinal disturbances or even death when they are consumed in sufficient quantities.

Plant Toxins. Many toxic substances are found in tiny amounts in plant foods as normal components. Poisonous varieties of mushrooms, mistaken for edible kinds, are a well-known example of toxic plants. Poisonous mushrooms can cause death or severe acute illnesses from various toxins depending on the mushroom variety [40]. Oxalic acid is a constituent of plants such as spinach and beet greens. In large amounts, these may be responsible for oxalic acid poisoning in certain individuals. A very high content of oxalic acid is found in the leaves of the rhubarb plant, which is why the leaves are not consumed.

Solanine is a water-soluble toxin that may be present in potatoes and increases during sprouting or exposure to light. This toxin is found principally in green skin and the green surface of the potato underneath the skin. It may be removed by paring. However, solanine, oxalic acid, and several other natural toxins in foods have not been shown to be toxic in the amounts usually eaten. These toxins, therefore, represent only minor hazards [35].

Vegetables of the cabbage family contain substances called **goitrogens** that can depress the activity of the thyroid gland. Legumes contain **protease** inhibitors that may interfere with the digestion of proteins. These inhibitors are destroyed by cooking. Substances called hemagglutinins, which cause **agglutination** of red blood cells, are found in soybeans, peanuts, kidney beans, and wax beans. Kidney beans that are raw, undercooked, or cooked at a low temperature (slow cooker) should not be consumed. A toxin, believed to be phytohaemagglutinin, is destroyed when kidney beans are fully cooked, but will cause severe illness if not destroyed by high heat cooking [40]. The *Senecio* genus is poisonous to livestock and people.

Marine Toxins. Toxins have been associated with seafood. Marine toxins are naturally occurring chemicals that generally do not affect the appearance, flavor, or smell of the seafood.

Ciguatoxin. Consuming predatory tropical reef fish, such as barracuda, contaminated by microscopic sea plants (dinoflagellates) causes ciguatera poisoning. Although barracuda is the fish most commonly associated with this toxin, grouper, sea bass, snapper, and mullet also have caused illness. Cooking and freezing do not reduce the toxin, and it is not detectable by taste, sight, or smell [40]. Symptoms occur usually within six hours after consumption of the contaminated seafood. Nausea, vomiting, diarrhea, sweating, headache, and muscle aches are common. A sensation of burning or "pins and needles" may occur in some cases [40].

Scombrotoxins. Scombrotoxic fish poisoning can occur when fish such as tuna, mahi-mahi, mackerel, bluefish, sardines, amberjack, anchovies, and others have begun to spoil, resulting in high histamine levels in the fish. Symptoms of scombroid poisoning include flushing, rash, sweating, a burning or peppery taste in the mouth, dizziness, nausea, and headache. These symptoms occur within few minutes to few hours of consumption. Seafood must be kept cold; if temperature abused, it should not be purchased or consumed. This toxin is not affected by cooking, freezing, or canning, and cannot be detected by appearance or odor [40].

Shellfish Toxins. There are several shellfish toxins associated with shellfish harvested from areas with algae called "dinoflagellates." Some of these, but not all, may cause a "red tide" because of the red-brown color of one of the offending types of algae. Paralytic, diarrhetic, neurotoxic, and amnesic shellfish poisoning result in different symptoms, and none may be destroyed by cooking, freezing, or other types of preparation. Paralytic shellfish poisoning can be deadly in only three to four hours after consumption. Symptoms of shellfish poisoning include numbness, tingling, and gastrointestinal upset, neurologic effects, dizziness, and muscle aches [40].

Shellfish such as mussels, cockles, clams, scallops, oysters, crabs, and lobsters typically from the colder coastal waters of the Pacific and New England states are most often affected. Purchasing fish from reliable suppliers is important. Seafood harvest areas are closed when toxin-producing algae numbers are high.

Chemical and Physical Contaminants

Toxic substances may contaminate the environment in which people, plants, and animals live. These substances include both inorganic elements—such as arsenic, cadmium, mercury, and lead—and organic substances—such as various chemicals used in pesticides. When contaminants persist in the environment, they may accumulate along the food chain in amounts that are toxic to humans when various animals and plants are consumed.

Mercury. Fish taken from water contaminated by mercury contain high levels of mercury, which may cause illness in humans if consumed in large amounts. Pregnant women, nursing women, and young children have been advised by the FDA to avoid king mackerel, marlin, orange roughy, shark, swordfish, tilefish (Gulf of Mexico), and bigeye tuna [46]. The EPA also provides water advisories to inform sport fishermen of the areas where fish may be contaminated [99].

Other Metals. Metals may enter foods from certain utensils. Galvanized containers are not suitable for foods because the zinc used for galvanizing is toxic. Cadmium and brass are also undesirable metals for use as food containers. Tin-coated cans are used in food processing, but only very small amounts of tin are generally found in most foods. Acid fruits and fruit juices packed in **lacquered tin-coated cans** and stored in opened cans in the refrigerator contain increased amounts of both tin and iron [55]. Food stored in opened tin-coated cans may also change in color or develop a metallic taste. Although these changes are undesirable, illness will not result from the canning materials currently used in the food-processing industry.

Small quantities of aluminum are dissolved from utensils in many cooking processes. This is apparently not harmful, but scientists are continuing to study the effects of aluminum in the diet. The element copper is nutritionally essential, yet certain salts of copper are toxic. Cooking green vegetables in copper containers to get a bright green color is no longer practiced because of the danger of toxicity. Foods cooked in iron utensils, steel woks, and stainless steel cookware show increases in iron content [79], adding to the dietary intake of iron.

Packaging. Foods are packaged in various types of containers from which certain chemical molecules may migrate to the food contained inside. The FDA is responsible for approving food-grade packaging materials to ensure that the type and amount of material that may migrate into the food will not be harmful to the consumer. Chapter 28 provides more information about packaging.

Pesticide Residues. Consumer concern about pesticide residues has varied over the years. Food scientists and some consumers consider the predominant risk in the food supply to be microbiological, not chemical. At the same time, some consumers choose organic foods, in part because of a desire to avoid pesticides. Organic foods are discussed in Chapter 3.

To protect the safety of our food supply, the FDA regularly monitors pesticide residues on foods, including in its program the completion of a yearly Total Diet Study [45]. Representative foods that might be consumed by various age and sex groups are purchased from grocery stores across the United States and analyzed in FDA laboratories for pesticide residues as well as for other contaminants and some nutrients. In 2014, the FDA tested a total of 6,272 samples of domestic and imported foods for pesticide residues. Nearly 99 percent of the domestic foods were within regulatory limits, and 71 percent had no detectable residuals of pesticides. Among the import samples, 88 percent were in compliance, and 53 percent had no detectable pesticide residuals. Overall, 1.4 percent of the domestic samples and 11.8 percent of the import samples had residual levels in violation of standards [49].

Food Allergies and Intolerances

Foods safe for the general population may be unsafe for selected individuals who are allergic to specified foods. True allergies are characterized by abnormal immune system response to naturally occurring proteins in foods [90, 91]. **Food allergy** symptoms are varied and can include gastrointestinal, cutaneous, respiratory, or other symptoms. Some individuals experience **anaphylactic shock** that can result in death within minutes of consuming an offending food unless prompt medical attention is received [50]. Each year, approximately 150 Americans die from a severe allergic reaction, and 30,000 require emergency room treatment [48].

Prevalence of allergies in the U.S. population is estimated to be 2 to 2.5 percent of the population overall. Comparatively, children exhibit a higher rate of allergies, ranging from 5 to 8 percent [91]. Children will often grow out of their allergies, whereas adults tend to remain allergic throughout their lives. The "Big Eight" causes of food allergy are wheat, crustacea such as shrimp and crabs, eggs, fish, peanuts, milk, tree nuts, and soybeans [91]. These eight foods are responsible for 90 percent of food allergic reactions [48]. Individuals who experience the most severe symptoms must carefully avoid even traces of the food responsible for the allergic reaction.

The Food Allergen Labeling and Consumer Protection Act of 2004 mandates that effective January 1, 2006, the "Big Eight" allergenic foods must be declared in plain language in the ingredient statement or a separate statement indicating "contains ———" [48, 93]. Understandable and accurate food labels are essential if allergic individuals are to avoid

THINKING GREEN
MERCURY AND OUR ENVIRONMENT

Mercury occurs naturally in our environment. However, our actions also contribute to the pollution of air, soil, lakes, and rivers with mercury. Waterways polluted with mercury result in fish contaminated with methylmercury, and therefore the EPA and FDA have provided fish advisories for pregnant women and young children who are most at risk.

In 2011, the EPA proposed new standards for emissions to reduce mercury in the air that then pollutes water and the soil [98]. Current estimates indicate that 50 percent of the human-caused mercury emissions in the United States are from coal-burning plants [98].

Consumers play a role in mercury pollution through our use of energy and also how we handle our trash. Compact fluorescent lightbulbs (CFLs) use less energy. However, these bulbs contain small amounts of mercury and therefore should be recycled. Simply putting CFLs into the trash contributes to mercury pollution. ∎

FOCUS ON SCIENCE
SULFITES—WHY ARE THEY USED?

Some individuals may become ill when exposed to sulfites. As a result of this risk, the use of sulfite in food has been limited, yet it is still used for some purposes. Sulfites are strong antioxidants that will prevent the darkening of light fruit such as apples, apricots, and bananas when dried. Because fruits cannot be blanched when dried, the enzyme polyphenoloxidase is still active. Sulfur dioxide will inhibit the activity of the enzyme and keep the fruit looking light.

offending foods. Good manufacturing practices to reduce cross-contamination of products during processing are another important strategy in the effort to provide safe food to those who are allergic [31, 92].

Food intolerances are different from allergies because food intolerances occur through non-immunological means. Three categories of intolerances include **anaphylactoid reactions**, **metabolic food disorders**, and **idiosyncratic illnesses**. Sensitivity to strawberries is an example of an anaphylactoid reaction. Metabolic disorders include the intolerance of lactose or fava beans. Lactose-intolerant individuals have an impaired ability to digest lactose, the principal sugar in milk. Sulfite-induced asthma has been well documented and represents an idiosyncratic illness because the mechanism for this reaction is not understood [91].

ADDITIONAL POTENTIAL FOOD-SAFETY ISSUES

Biotechnology

Biotechnology provides an important tool for growth and progress in the area of food and agriculture. The breeding of plants using cross-pollination has been a common, acceptable practice for many years in developing new plant varieties. With increased understanding of deoxyribonucleic acid (DNA) and genetics, beginning during the 1950s, a technology was developed by which DNA material (i.e., genes) could be taken from an unrelated plant, bacterium, or animal and inserted into the genetic material of the plant being modified. Thus, this new **biotechnology**, called **genetic engineering**, offered the ability to introduce new and desirable traits more efficiently [52].

The main crops produced from biotechnology are corn, soybeans, cotton, potatoes, and rapeseed (grown for canola oil). These crops have been modified to resist insects or increase herbicide tolerance [3]. Biotechnology may also be used to improve the eating quality of a fruit or vegetable. In 1994, the "Flavr Savr" tomato was the first genetically altered food to be sold to U.S. consumers [52]. These tomatoes have increased resistance to softening so that they can be vine ripened, with consequent increased flavor.

The first food-processing aid produced by a genetically engineered microorganism was approved by the FDA in March 1990—the enzyme *rennin* or *chymosin*. Other enzymes, processing aids, and food ingredients are being developed.

The safety of biotechnology products is regulated by the FDA, and potentially negative consequences to the environment are scrutinized by the USDA. Biotechnology, however, may cause safety concerns for some people. Most in the scientific community endorse the safety of genetic engineering stating that the risks are no different than the risks posed by traditional breeding methods [1, 3, 56]. Biotechnology has the potential to ensure safe, abundant, affordable, and highly nutritious foods [54]. Plants can be made resistant to insects and viruses, thus reducing crop losses and the use of chemical insecticides [9]. The public's concerns must therefore be addressed and satisfied by the scientific community. Consumers have been found to be more favorable toward biotechnology when educational information is provided [12].

Bioterrorism

Since 2001, the FDA has conducted food supply vulnerability assessments, established with the CDC and the USDA. The Food Emergency Response Network hired more than 655 new field inspectors to monitor imports and updated labs to handle an increased number of food samples as efforts to protect the food supply from terrorism [65]. In 2002, the Public Health Security and Bioterrorism Preparedness and Response Act of 2002 was passed to "improve the ability of the United States to prevent, prepare for, and respond to bioterrorism and other public health emergencies" [82]. Under this new law, four major regulations with implications for food safety have been implemented. These include (1) registration of facilities that manufacture, process, pack, or hold food for animal or human consumption; (2) prior notification of imported food shipments to the FDA; (3) manufacturers, processors, packers, importers, and others are required to keep records identifying the source of food and where it is being shipped; and (4) the FDA has new authority to detain any food for 30 days if credible evidence exists that the food may be dangerous [65].

STYDY QUESTIONS

Preventing Foodborne Illness

1. Why is food safety important, and who is most at risk for foodborne illness?
2. Discuss the role of the government; producers, processors, and retailers; food service establishments; and consumers in the prevention of foodborne illness.
3. Create a safe food-handling educational session that incorporates the four keys to safe food handling (clean, separate, chill, cook) for (a) college students living on or off campus, (b) new parents, (c) older adults, (d) clients or patients with health challenges, or (e) first-time food service employees.
4. Discuss the importance of clean hands and other food preparation contact surfaces.

(a) Explain the process for washing hands thoroughly.

(b) Identify multiple times before, during, and after food preparation that hands should be washed.

(c) Explain recommendations for cleaning and sanitizing cutting boards, food preparation surfaces, dishes, and utensils.

5. Create an educational plan to promote the use of thermometers in food storage and food preparation for home food preparers, inexperienced food service employees, and experienced food service employees.

(a) Explain how your plan should be modified for home food preparers as compared to inexperienced and experienced food service employees.

(b) In your plan, include
   (i) methods to educate food preparers about the proper temperatures and methods for storing, cooking, and cooling multiple types of foods;
   (ii) calibration of thermometers; and
   (iii) how to obtain temperatures on thin foods such as hamburger patties.

6. Discuss the proper refrigeration of foods.

(a) How should food be stored in the refrigerator to prevent cross-contamination?

(b) Describe storage methods for foods so that cooling is rapid.

7. Identify the correct endpoint cooking temperatures for beef, pork, lamb, chicken, turkey, fish, ground meat, stuffing (e.g., turkey stuffing), and eggs.

8. Explain why the endpoint temperatures are not the same for all protein-based foods.

9. Explain each of the HAACP steps, and discuss how HACCP principles are used to prevent foodborne illness.

10. Discuss the process of pasteurization, sterilization, and irradiation, and how each protects food safety.

11. Debate the food-safety and health implications of consuming raw milk by utilizing information obtained from refereed research journals.

Microorganisms and Other Causes of Foodborne Illness

12. Explain the difference between *food infection, food intoxication,* and *toxin-mediated infection.*

13. Discuss the conditions that are favorable for the growth of pathogenic bacteria in foods.

14. Explain the importance of water activity and pH in relationship to bacterial growth.

15. For each type of food poisoning listed below, (a) indicate if it is an infection, intoxication, or toxin-mediated infection; (b) list the usual symptoms; (c) list the types of food most likely to be involved; and (d) suggest how to prevent foodborne illness.

(a) Salmonellosis

(b) *C. jejuni* poisoning

(c) *E. coli* 0157:H7 poisoning

(d) Yersiniosis

(e) Listeriosis

(f) Staphylococcal poisoning

(g) *C. perfringens* poisoning

(h) Botulism

16. Identify and discuss bacteria in food that may be beneficial to our health.

17. Discuss how the viruses hepatitis A and norovirus are often transmitted. Identify the implications of

(a) Proper hand washing

(b) Healthy food handlers

18. Compare and contrast the optimum growth conditions for molds and yeasts as compared to bacteria.

19. Discuss for each of the parasites below the (a) foodborne illnesses associated with it, (b) the foods that are typically involved, and (c) recommended safe food practices.

(a) *Trichinella spiralis*

(b) *Anisakis simplex*

(c) *Toxoplasma gondii*

20. Explain how prions are associated with food safety.

21. Discuss each of the natural toxins found in plants and marine environments

(a) Plant toxins, including those found in select mushrooms, oxalic acid, solanine, and raw or undercooked navy beans.

(b) Marine toxins, including ciguatoxin, scombro-toxins, and shellfish poisoning.

22. Identify several ways that chemical or physical contaminates may result in a foodborne health hazard.

23. Compare and contrast food allergies and food intolerances; then discuss why food allergies and intolerances may be a food-safety issue for some individuals.

24. Identify the big eight causes of food allergy.

Additional Potential Food-Safety Issues

25. Discuss the potential food-safety implications of biotechnology and bioterrorism.

3
Food Regulations and Standards

The government, through legislation and regulation, helps to ensure the quality and safety of the foods we purchase. Historically, as well as today, the regulation of food safety has been regarded as an important function of government. The Food and Drug Administration (FDA) and the United States Department of Agriculture (USDA) provide the primary oversight for our food supply. Various federal agencies also have responsibilities to regulate the food supply—including the setting of standards, control of adulteration and misbranding, promotion of **good manufacturing practices**, and approval of **food additives**, **inspection**, and **grading**. By promulgating regulations and setting standards, the government is attempting to implement the constitutional mandate to "promote the general welfare."

In this chapter, the role of U.S. government agencies in assuring the quality and safety of the food supply; key laws and regulations that impact on the food supply; and some specific areas of government oversight, including quality standards, food labels, food additives, biotechnology, pesticides, irradiation, inspection, quality grading, and organic foods, will be examined through a discussion of the following topics:

- Food and Drug Administration (FDA)
- The United States Department of Agriculture (USDA)
- The Environmental Protection Agency (EPA)
- Centers for Disease Control and Prevention (CDC)
- The Federal Trade Commission (FTC)
- Other Federal Agencies
- State and Local Agencies
- International Standards

FDA

The FDA is part of the U.S. Department of Health and Human Services and includes the Center for Food Safety and Applied Nutrition (CFSAN). The FDA regulates 75 percent of the food supply, including all foods except red meats, poultry, and some egg products. Products regulated by the FDA account for 20 cents of each dollar consumers spend [63]. The FDA budget is composed of industry user fees and funds from the U.S. Treasury.

In overseeing our food supply, the FDA performs several key roles to ensure food is safe, sanitary, wholesome, and accurately labeled. Regulations and laws, including the Federal Food, Drug, and Cosmetic Act of 1938 and its several amendments, are administered by the FDA (**Table 3–1**). The safety of food additives, colorings, and foods developed through biotechnology is investigated and regulated. Scientific assessment of nutrition claims has led to nutrition labeling and health claims laws. Food industry surveillance and compliance is achieved in part through the efforts of FDA investigators and inspectors who oversee sanitation in food-processing plants, food service sanitation, and interstate travel facilities. Both domestic and imported foods are inspected. Products identified as unsafe are prevented from coming to the market. Products already in the marketplace may be detained or subject to voluntary or court-ordered recalls. The FDA through the CFSAN also takes an active role in educating consumers about safe food handling.

History

The FDA grew out of the Division of Chemistry within the USDA. Dr. Harvey Wiley, the chief chemist in the USDA, was an early pioneer involved in the struggle for adequate laws to protect the public's food supply (**Figure 3–1**). During the late 1800s and early 1900s, Dr. Wiley tried various tactics, including feeding measured amounts of chemical preservatives to 12 young volunteers in a so-called Poison Squad experiment, to increase understanding of food additive safety and highlight food-safety concerns. The Poison Squad experiment gained the attention of citizens and helped to convince Congress and the president of the need for pure food legislation. In 1906, the Pure Food and Drugs Act and the Meat Inspection Act were passed [18, 22].

The passage of the Pure Food and Drugs Act essentially marks the beginning of what is today known as the FDA, even though named the Division of Chemistry at the time. After a series of name changes, it became the Food and Drug Administration in the 1930s.

To reflect an emphasis on health and not agriculture, in 1940, the FDA was transferred out

Table 3–1

FOOD AND DRUG ADMINISTRATION: FOOD REGULATIONS TO PROTECT THE HEALTH AND SAFETY OF THE PUBLIC

Laws, Statutes, and Regulations	Overview of Basic Provisions
1906 Pure Food and Drug Act	Prohibited misbranded and adulterated foods, drinks, and drugs in interstate commerce; addition of color additives to conceal poor quality; and use of "poisonous" colors in confections. • Authorized factory inspections. • 1913 Gould Amendment requires contents be plainly labeled on the outside of the food package with weight, measure, or count. Some manufacturers use "distinctive" names to market products that would have otherwise been illegal. For example, "Bred-Spread," a product that had no strawberries yet was marketed as an alternative to jam and jelly. The 1938 act closed this "loophole."
1938 Federal Food, Drug, and Cosmetic Act	Food must be labeled by its common or usual name. Distinctive name provision in the 1906 act was removed. • Three kinds of food standards were authorized—identity, quality, and fill of container. • Colors had to be approved *before* use in foods, drugs, and cosmetics.
1954 Miller Pesticide Amendment	Defines procedures for setting safety limits for pesticide residues on agricultural commodities.
1958 Food Additives Amendment	Required manufacturers to establish safety before marketing. The generally recognized as safe (GRAS) list was published in 1958. Includes Delaney clause prohibiting approval of any additive shown to induce cancer in humans or animals.
1960 Color Additives Amendment	Defined "color additive" and required manufacturers to establish safety before use in food.
1966 Fair Packaging and Labeling Act	All consumer products involved in interstate commerce must be honestly and informatively labeled. FDA enforces foods, drugs, cosmetics, and medical devices affected by this act.
1973 Low-Acid Processing Regulations Issued	Adequate heat treatment of low-acid foods is further regulated to prevent botulism resulting from commercially canned foods.
1980 Infant Formula Act	Required additional quality control procedures to assure nutritional content and safety.
1990 Nutrition Labeling and Education Act	Requires most foods to include nutrition labeling. • Starting in 1993, the "Nutrition Facts" label was required. • Health claims were regulated. • Use of terms "light," "low," "reduced," and others was legally defined. • Effective 2006, "Nutrition Facts" labels must include the trans fat content.
1996 Food Quality Protection Act	Amends the 1938 Food, Drug, and Cosmetic Act with regard to pesticides.
Hazard Analysis and Critical Control Points (HACCP) Regulations	In 1997, seafood processors were required to use HACCP to ensure food safety. In 2001, HACCP regulations for fruit juice were established.
2002 Public Health Security and Bioterrorism Preparedness and Response Act	Four regulations to address provision of the act were developed by the FDA: • Food facility registration. • Prior notice of import foods. • Record keeping of food received and shipped by all shippers, manufacturers, and others. • Procedures for FDA to detain suspect foods.
2004 Food Allergen Labeling and Consumer Protection Act	Starting in 2006, the major food allergens (peanuts, soybeans, cow's milk, eggs, fish, crustacean shellfish, tree nuts, and wheat) must be clearly labeled. In 2013, new rules were added to define the term "gluten-free" as less than 20 parts per million (ppm) for voluntary use in food labels.
2011 FDA Food Safety Modernization Act	Updates and strengthens FDA oversight in five key areas: (1) *prevention* with greater science-based preventive controls, (2) *inspection and compliance* with more frequent inspections, (3) *response* with FDA authority for mandatory recalls and greater product traceability systems, (4) *imports* with greater FDA authority to ensure safety, and (5) *enhanced partnerships* with other government agencies. Food defense oversight is also included to protect food from intentional adulteration.

Source: References 11, 22, 33, 50, 64, 65.

(a)

(b)

Figure 3–1

(a) Members of the Poison Squad dine together consuming wholesome meals containing potentially harmful substances. This scientific investigation, conducted by Dr. Harvey W. Wiley, dramatized the need for pure food legislation. (b) William R. Carter was hired as the chef for the Poison Squad experiments. He later earned a degree in pharmaceutical chemistry and worked in FDA laboratories for 43 years. (U.S. Food and Drug Administration)

of the USDA into the Federal Security Agency. In 1953, the FDA was moved again to the Department of Health, Education, and Welfare, which became the Department of Health and Human Services in 1979 [35].

The original 1906 Pure Food and Drug Act was completely revised in 1938 and renamed the Federal Food, Drug, and Cosmetic Act. Among other things, the 1938 law required truthful labeling of additives. Several amendments to the Federal Food, Drug, and Cosmetic Act have been passed to strengthen the law and keep up with changes in food technology and medical science. The FDA Food Safety Modernization Act of 2011 represents one of the most significant recent changes to the role of the FDA by enabling the FDA to have a greater focus on prevention while providing new enforcement authorities. This new act allows the FDA to issue mandatory food recalls, increase food facility inspections, develop mandatory produce safety standards, establish a system of food traceability, and have greater authority over imported food safety [50].

Federal Food, Drug, and Cosmetic Act of 1938

Under the Federal Food, Drug, and Cosmetic Act, the FDA sets three kinds of mandatory standards for products being shipped across state lines: identity, minimum quality, and fill of container. The public also is protected from food that may be unclean, decomposed, or contaminated.

Standards of Identity. The basic purpose for setting standards of identity for food products is to "promote honesty and fair dealing in the interest of consumers." Standards of identity define what a food product must be or must contain if it is to be legally labeled and sold by its common or usual name. The standard also lists optional ingredients that may be used but are not required. For example, the standard of identity for mayonnaise specifies the ingredients it must contain—oil, egg, and an acid component—and requires that at least 65 percent oil be included in the finished dressing. Prior to the establishment of standards of identity, consumers could not be assured that products, such as mayonnaise, ice cream, fruit jams, or jellies, were composed of the generally expected ingredients. In fact, prior to these standards, jam or jelly-like products were sold that did not contain fruit.

Standards of identity have been established for a large number of food products, including bakery and cereal products, cacao products, canned fruits and vegetables, fruit butters and preserves, fish and shellfish, eggs and egg products, margarine, nut products, dressings for foods, cheeses and cheese products, milk and cream, frozen desserts, macaroni and noodle products, and tomato products. Standards are finalized only after public hearings and input from food industry representatives and consumers.

Many of the standards of identity for food were established in the early years following passage of the Federal Food, Drug, and Cosmetic Act in 1938.

The FDA has promulgated few new standards of identity since 1970. In 1998, the standards of identity for several enriched grain products were amended to require fortification with folic acid [14], and in 2002 a new standard of identity was established for white chocolate [69]. Essentially, all foods, including those with a standard of identity, are subject to nutrition labeling under the 1990 Nutrition Labeling and Education Act.

Standards of Minimum Quality. Standards of minimum quality have been set for several canned fruits and vegetables, specifying minimum requirements for such characteristics as tenderness, color, and freedom from defects. If a food does not meet the minimum standard, it must be labeled "below standard in quality; good food—not high grade." Other words may be substituted for the second part of the statement to show in what respect the product is substandard, such as "below standard in quality; excessively broken." The consumer seldom sees a product with a substandard label at retail stores. Standards of minimum quality, as well as other grade standards, are indications of quality characteristics and are not concerned specifically with safety. Both lower- and higher-grade products are safe to eat.

Standards of Fill of Container. Standards of fill of container state how full a food container must be for certain processed foods. These standards aim to avoid deception by preventing the sale of air or water in place of food. They are needed especially for products that consist of a number of pieces packed in a liquid, such as various canned vegetables, or for products, such as nuts and ready-to-eat cereals, that shake down after filling.

Sanitation Requirements.   One basic purpose of the Federal Food, Drug, and Cosmetic Act is the protection of the public from foods that are unclean or decomposed or exposed to unsanitary conditions. The law requires foods to be (1) protected from contamination at all stages of production and (2) produced in sanitary facilities. Foods may not be distributed if they contain repulsive or offensive matter considered to be filth, whether or not it poses actual physical danger to an individual. Filth includes rodent hair and excreta, insects or insect parts and excreta, maggots, larvae, pollution from the excrement of humans and animals, or other materials that, because of their repulsiveness, would not be eaten knowingly.

The Federal Food, Drug, and Cosmetic Act declared any food prepared, packed, or held under unsanitary conditions to be adulterated. Therefore, the FDA has produced directives called *current good manufacturing practices*. These directives establish regulations regarding many facets of the food-manufacturing process and include requirements for cleanliness; education, training, and supervision of workers; design and ease of cleaning and maintenance of buildings, facilities, and equipment; and adequate record keeping to ensure quality control.

Food Additives and Colorings

What is a food additive? Under a broad definition, it is any substance that becomes part of a food product either when it is added intentionally or when it incidentally becomes part of the food. Examples of incidental additives are substances that may migrate from the packaging material into a food [19]. The Federal Food, Drug, and Cosmetic Act governs the use of additives in food entering interstate commerce.

The legal definition of *food additive* extends only to those substances that must receive special approval from the FDA after they have been thoroughly tested for safety and before they can be used in food. In addition to tested and approved additives, the FDA maintains an official list of other substances added to foods that are "generally recognized as safe" (GRAS)

IN DEPTH
FOOD STANDARDS AND THE NUTRITION LABELING AND EDUCATION ACT

When many of the food standards were developed, "recipes" for these products were based on the ingredients typically expected for a high-quality food product. With an increasing emphasis on lower-calorie and lower-fat foods over the years, processors have developed foods to meet the public's desire for foods with a particular nutritional profile. Prior to the 1990 Nutrition Labeling and Education Act, reduced-fat foods that did not meet the standards of identity were labeled as *imitation* or with completely different names.

Today, reduced-fat versions of foods such as sour cream, mayonnaise, and ice cream may still be called by their respective names even if the traditional standard of identity has not been met. For example, prior to 1990, "low-fat" or "reduced-fat" ice cream was called ice milk and by law could not be called ice cream because the standard of identity was not met. To maintain the standard name, reduced-fat versions of foods must (1) be labeled "low fat" or "light" as appropriate, (2) not be nutritionally inferior (vitamin A must be added to reduced-fat products to replace the vitamin A lost when the fat was removed), (3) perform like the standard product, and (4) contain a significant amount of any mandatory ingredients [48]. ■

IN DEPTH
WHAT ARE JUSTIFIABLE USES FOR FOOD ADDITIVES?

Approved additives must serve a useful purpose. Additives may not be used to conceal damage or spoilage or to deceive the consumer. An additive may be intentionally used for one or more of the following general purposes:

1. To maintain or improve nutritional value. Vitamins and minerals are used to fortify some foods when these nutrients may have been lost in processing or when they might be otherwise lacking in the usual diet.

2. To maintain or improve safety and freshness. Freshness may be maintained by the use of additives to prevent or slow spoilage caused by mold, bacteria, fungi, or yeast.

Antioxidants prevent the development of rancidity in oils and fats.

3. Improve taste, texture, and appearance. Many additives will make food look and taste better. Natural and synthetic flavoring agents, colors, and flavor enhancers serve this purpose. Other additives are used to give body and texture to foods as stabilizers or thickeners, distribute water-soluble and fat-soluble particles evenly together as emulsifiers, control the acidity or alkalinity, retain moisture as humectants, leaven baked products, and prevent caking or lumping [19]. ■

for human consumption by experts in the field. Salt, sugar, and spices are examples of GRAS ingredients [19]. GRAS substances do not require the detailed clearance for safety and premarket approval that is specified for legally defined food additives. FDA amended their voluntary affirmation process and provided criteria for GRAS substances in 2016 as explained in the final rule in the *Federal Register* [34]. Ongoing industry assessment of GRAS substances is conducted [26]. A Flavor and Extract Manufacturers' Association Expert Panel has completed a comprehensive assessment of the GRAS flavoring substances, with the most recent assessment in 2015 [8]. Occasionally, substances may be removed from the GRAS list as more sophisticated analytical tools and methodologies for evaluation of safety are developed. Partially hydrogenated fats that contain trans fats were removed from the GRAS list by the FDA because of research associating trans fats with heart disease [9]. It should be emphasized that there is an ongoing process of reassessment and evaluation by the FDA on all issues of food safety, including additives and GRAS substances.

Food Additives Amendment. The 1958 Food Additives Amendment was designed to protect the public by requiring approval of new additives before they can be used in foods. The responsibility for proving the safety of additives rests with the manufacturer, who must file a petition with the FDA showing the results of extensive tests for safety. The FDA approves additives before marketing of products. The FDA also determines the types of foods in which the additive can be used and specifies labeling directions. Additives in meat and poultry products are under the jurisdiction of the USDA.

Color Additives Amendment. A color additive may be a dye, pigment, or other substance that imparts color to foods. Colors may be used to (1) offset color loss due to light, air, temperature, moisture, and other conditions; (2) enhance natural colors; (3) correct natural variations in color; or (4) provide color. Colors may not be used to hide inferior or defective foods. **Certified colors** are synthetically produced and have historically been called "coal-tar" colors even though today most are made from raw materials obtained from petroleum [1]. Certification of colors applies to domestic and foreign manufacturers with a sample of each "lot" submitted to the FDA for analysis prior to use in food [17, 27]. Colors that may be exempt from certification include pigments from natural sources, such as red or green from grape skin extract [19]. Colors exempt from certification must still comply with other FDA specifications for use [1].

All coloring substances added to foods are regulated under the Color Additives Amendment, passed in 1960. Rules regarding color additives were made stronger under this amendment, and previously approved certified colors were retested. An FDA batch certification of all synthetic colors is required. No color additives may be considered to be GRAS [1].

Labeling of Additives and Colors. Food additives must be listed as ingredients on food labels. Spices and flavors may be simply mentioned as such, without each specific item being named. The presence of any artificial colors or flavors must be indicated. Certified colors, such as FD&C Yellow #5, commonly known as tartrazine, must be listed by name. Color additives, exempt from certification, may be listed as "artificial color" even if derived from natural sources [27].

FOCUS ON SCIENCE
MORE FACTS ON FOOD COLORS

Why use artificial instead of natural colorings in food?

The artificial water-solvent colorants used in a variety of foods are quite stable to heat, light, acid, and alkaline conditions. Natural colorants such as annatto extract (orange color), beet powder, and cochineal extract (red-blue color similar to beet powder) are unstable. Certain conditions, such as heat, pH of the food, and storage, will have a negative effect on the color brilliance of these natural colors.

What are "lake" colorants?

Water-soluble FD&C colorants can be transformed to an insoluble powder (lake) by precipitation with aluminum, calcium, or magnesium salts on a substrate of aluminum hydroxide. These colorants are more stable to heat and light and do not "bleed" or migrate. Lake colorants are used extensively in confectionery products, bakery products, salad dressings, and chocolate substitutes in which the presence of water is undesirable. They are also used in the packaging industry, when films and inks are in contact with food, and in pharmaceutical tablets.

Can people be allergic to artificial colors?

Yes, tartrazine, also known as FD&C Yellow #5, is one such color. Tartrazine is a synthetic lemon azo dye that is derived from coal tar. Tartrazine appears to cause the most allergic and intolerance reactions of the azo dyes, particularly among those with aspirin intolerance and asthmatics. Because of tartrazine intolerance, the FDA requires the presence of tartrazine to be declared on food and drug products. In drug products, the colorant is declared as tartrazine, but in food products, it is declared on the label as FD&C Yellow #5.

Source: Reference 15.

Delaney Clause and Safety. Included in the 1958 Food Additives and 1960 Color Additives Amendments is a special clause named after Congressman James J. Delaney, who was chairman of the congressional committee that investigated the use of chemicals in foods. The Delaney clause provides "that no additive shall be deemed to be safe if it is found to induce cancer when ingested by man or animal, or if it is found, after tests which are appropriate for the evaluation of the safety of food additives, to induce cancer in man or animals" [70].

The Delaney clause has created much discussion and disagreement in the years since the legislation was passed [1, 70, 71]. Science, in relation to the study of cancer and carcinogenesis (cancer development), has changed, and the causes and nature of cancer have become better understood. The Delaney clause makes no distinction between cancer in humans and experimental animals, nor is there a specification on the amount of the substance to be consumed in testing.

Irradiation

Irradiation is used to destroy bacteria, pathogens, and pests in food [32]. Over 50 years of research point to the safety of this process. The FDA has primary responsibility for the regulation and approval of irradiation of foods as part of the Food Additives Act. The inclusion of irradiation under the food additive regulations has been controversial because irradiating food is a process that does not add ingredients to the food.

Food irradiation is a recognized method for reducing postharvest food losses and ensuring hygienic quality. Irradiation is not a substitution for sanitary practices but does provide an added measure of safety because *E. coli* and other pathogenic organisms may be destroyed. Approval has been granted for the production and marketing of several irradiated food products, including herbs and spices, wheat flour, white potatoes, fruits and vegetables, poultry, and red meat [39, 36]. Irradiated food must be labeled with the Radura symbol and "treated by irradiation" or "treated with radiation." See Chapter 2 for more information on irradiation and its role in food safety.

Pesticide Regulation

In the 1950s, as well as today, growers use pesticides to increase yields and produce foods with little if any insect damage. The Miller Pesticide Amendment of 1954 was passed to establish a procedure for setting safe levels or tolerances for pesticide residues on fresh fruits, vegetables, and other raw agricultural commodities.

Pesticide safety standards were further modified by the Food Quality Protection Act signed into law in 1996. This act amended both the Federal Food, Drug, and Cosmetic Act and the Federal Insecticide, Fungicide, and Rodenticide Act to (1) include a new pesticide safety standard, (2) resolve inconsistencies in the regulation of pesticide residues on raw and processed commodities,

(3) provide special protection for children and infants, and (4) require periodic reevaluation of pesticides [16]. The safety standard for pesticides is currently defined as "a reasonable certainty that no harm will result from aggregate exposure to the pesticide chemical residue, including all anticipated dietary exposures and all other exposures for which there is reliable information." Tolerance limits for all pesticide residues, whether carcinogens or not, are set by the Environmental Protection Agency (EPA) at "safe" levels. The maximum allowable levels for pesticide residues are established after careful consideration of the risks and benefits for all consumers, with special attention to children. These tolerances are monitored and enforced by the FDA and the USDA [16]. Of note is that 71 percent of the domestically grown foods tested by the FDA, as part of the Total Diet Study, contained no pesticide residues [61]. See Chapters 2 and 18 for more information about pesticides and safety monitoring.

Prior to the 1996 Food Quality Protection Act, when a pesticide residue was found to concentrate higher levels in a processed food than in the original agricultural product before processing (e.g., grapes dried for raisins), the EPA was required to treat the residue as a food additive. As food additives, these pesticide residues were subject to the Delaney clause in the Food Additives Amendment that was passed in 1958. Thus, under the law, pesticide residues on raw and processed commodities had to be treated differently, causing confusion. The 1996 legislation provides for a single, health-based standard for all pesticides in foods.

What Must Be on a Food Label?

The FDA shares with the Federal Trade Commission (FTC) the responsibility for enforcing fair packaging and labeling laws. The USDA also is involved in labeling of selected foods.

If a food is packaged, the following must appear on the label:

1. Name and address of the manufacturer, packer, or distributor
2. Accurate statement of the net amount of food in the package—weight, measure, or count
3. Common or usual name of the product (i.e., peaches) and the form (i.e., sliced, whole, or chopped)
4. Ingredients listed by their common names in order of their predominance by weight
5. Nutrition information, with few exceptions, as mandated by the 1990 Nutrition Labeling and Education Act

Nutrition Labeling

The Nutrition Labeling and Education Act was signed into law in 1990 and took effect in 1994. The USDA Food Safety and Inspection Service established similar regulations for meat and poultry products. Nutrition labeling was designed to help consumers choose diets that are well balanced, health promoting, and at the lowest cost. This legislation established the Nutrition Facts label, nutrient content descriptors, and allowed health claims.

In 2016, the first major revision of the Nutrition Facts label was finalized to change the label format and content, as well as the portion sizes given on labels [12, 13]. The date for manufacturers to comply with the changes will be after 2020 [62]. The key changes to the label are shown in **Figure 3–2** and explained in **Table 3–2**.

The 1990 Nutrition Labeling and Education Act provided exemptions for food sold in food service establishments. The Patient Protection and Affordable Health Care Act of 2010 requires chain restaurants and companies with 20 or more vending machines to post the number of calories for standard

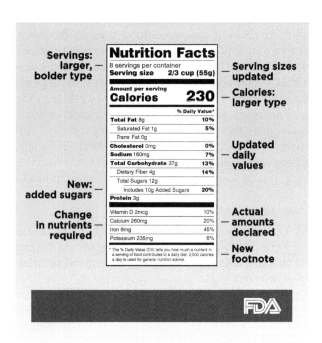

Figure 3–2

This is an example of the proposed revision of the Nutrition Facts label scheduled for adoption in 2020–2021. Read the label to take note of the serving size and calories per serving. A serving may or may not be the entire package. Next the percent of daily value is provided for several nutrients. The daily values are based on a 2,000-calorie diet, which means that if you eat 2,000 calories in one day, then this product in the serving size indicated (shown above) will provide 7 percent of the sodium and 20 percent calcium suggested for consumption in one day. Americans in general consume too much sodium on a daily basis and too little calcium. Added sugars is new to this revised label, and represents sugar "added" to the food and not sugar found naturally in the food. (U.S. Food and Drug Administration)

menu items on menus, menu boards, or vending machines. The date for compliance was May 7, 2018 [60]. The complete Nutrition Facts label, found on packaged foods, is not required. Additional nutrition information must be provided in writing to customers requesting it.

In 2012, the USDA started to require nutrition labeling on major cuts of meat and poultry products [2]. This nutrition information may be presented on package labels or on signage near the meat counter. These single-ingredient meat and poultry foods were previously exempt from nutritional labeling requirements.

Nutrition Facts Label. As previously noted, the Nutrition Facts label will be updated starting in 2020 (Figure 3–2 and Table 3–2). As required under the 1990 Nutrition Labeling and Education Act, nutrition information will continue to be presented as a percent of **daily values**. Daily values are dietary standards used for labeling purposes and include two types: **Daily Reference Values** (DRVs) and **Reference Daily Intakes** (RDIs). DRVs refer to fat, carbohydrates (including fiber), protein, cholesterol, sodium, and potassium. RDIs are for other nutrients such as vitamin D, calcium, iron, and potassium. RDIs replace the U.S. Recommended Daily Allowances that were previously used. Selected RDIs are listed in **Table 3–3**. Starting in 2006, trans fats were also added to the Nutrition Facts label [67] and will remain on the new label. Consumption of trans fats is associated with an increased risk of heart disease.

Labeling Claims. FDA provides guidance for claims that may be made on food packages. Four types of claims are allowed and regulated: (a) nutrient content, (b) health, (c) qualified health, and (d) structure/function.

Nutrient Content Claims. Prior to the 1990 Nutrition Labeling and Education Act, a consumer did not know how "light" or "low fat" a product was, even if labeled with these terms. These nutrient content claims are now standardized and thus, when used on a food label, have specific, legal definitions. Some of these nutrient content claim terms and their definitions are given in **Table 3–4**.

Health Claims. Health claims describe a relationship between the food and reduced risk of a health-related condition [48]. The FDA regulates health claims based on scientific evidence. Currently approved health claims are provided in **Table 3–5**. The health claims labeling oversight includes not only words but also symbols such as a heart. These health claims, when approved, can identify relationships between the nutrient and food or the risk of

Table 3–2
KEY CHANGES IN THE NUTRITION FACTS LABEL

Change	Rational and Implications
Servings	The print size of the servings will be larger and in bold. The serving sizes will also now reflect the amount that consumers most likely consume. With the previous labels, consumers may have not understood the amount of calories they were consuming if they did not notice the portion size as being smaller than their actual consumption. For example, if you purchase a 16-ounce beverage, you are likely to consume all of it and not only 8 ounces or half.
Calories	The print size of calories is larger and bolder. As the percent of Americans who are overweight or obese continues to be a concern, this change will make caloric value easier to see on food packages.
Added Sugars	Scientific evidence suggests it can be difficult to maintain a healthy calorie intake if consuming excess added sugar. No more than 10 percent of your total daily intake from added sugar is suggested. Sugar contains calories without other nutrients needed for health. Added sugar in a product is sugar that is added and not found naturally in the food. This added sugar could be listed on the ingredient label as sugar, honey, sucrose, dextrose, and other forms of sugar. Many foods have sugar found naturally within them. Fruits such as apples, oranges, and more all contain sugar, but it is not "added sugar." Milk likewise contains sugar naturally. Thus, milk would contain no added sugars, but some flavored milks, such as chocolate milk, may have "added sugar."
Nutrients	The required nutrients on the label reflect those nutrients most likely to be deficient in the American diet. Vitamin A and C will no longer be required on the label, and instead the new label will include Vitamin D and potassium. Calcium and iron will remain on the label. As before, manufacturers may list additional nutrients found in their product. The revised label will include percent daily value for these nutrients, but now will also include amounts.
Footnote	The footnote explaining percent daily value has been revised to better explain how to use the daily value percentages on the label.
Calories from Fat	This information was in the previous label and is removed in the new label. Current research suggests the type of fat consumed is more important than the amount.

Source: Reference 56, 62.

disease. There are additional specific requirements, such as other allowed ingredients, that govern the use of these claims.

Qualified Health Claims and Structure/Function Claims. Two additional claims may be found on food labels. Qualified health claims may be used, following FDA authorization, when there is emerging scientific evidence for a relationship between the food and reduction of a health risk [48]. For example, in 2003, the FDA approved a qualified health claim for almonds stating "scientific evidence suggests, but does not prove that eating 1.5 ounces per day of most nuts, as part of a diet low in saturated fat and cholesterol may reduce the risk of heart disease" [30].

Structure and function claims may also be found on labels and include statements such as "calcium builds strong bones." The structure and function claims do not address the relationship to disease. These claims must be truthful, but are not prereviewed by the FDA [48].

Food Allergen Labeling

As a result of the Food Allergen Labeling and Consumer Protection Act of 2004, the "Big Eight" allergenic foods must be clearly labeled on the package [57]. The "Big Eight" causes of food allergy are wheat, crustacean shellfish, eggs, fish, peanuts, milk, tree nuts, and soybeans. Previously, some of these ingredients could be labeled as "natural flavorings" or with terms such as "casein." Casein is a milk protein, and those allergic to milk must often avoid products containing casein. Using this example, labels now need to specifically list "casein (milk)" under the ingredients or state "contains milk."

In 2014, rules for the voluntary gluten-free labeling of foods were established and included as a rule under the Food Allergen Labeling and Consumer Protection Act of 2004 [11]. These rules were created to legally define the terms "gluten-free," "no gluten," and "without gluten" as being less than 20 parts per million. About 1 percent of the population has Celiac disease and needs to avoid the consumption of gluten [25]. See Chapter 2 for additional information about food allergies and intolerances in relation to food safety.

Table 3–3
REFERENCE DAILY INTAKES (RDIs)

Nutrient	RDI Value
Vitamin A	5,000 IU
Vitamin C	60 mg
Thiamin (B₁)	1.5 mg
Riboflavin (B₂)	1.7 mg
Niacin	20 mg
Calcium	1,000 mg
Iron	18 mg
Vitamin D	400 IU
Vitamin E	30 IU
Vitamin B₆	2.0 mg
Folic acid	0.4 mg
Vitamin B₁₂	6 mcg
Phosphorus	1,000 mg
Iodine	150 mcg
Magnesium	400 mg
Zinc	15 mg
Copper	2 mg
Biotin	0.3 mg
Pantothenic acid	10 mg

Table 3–4
NUTRIENT CONTENT DESCRIPTORS USED ON FOOD LABELS*

Descriptor	Definition
Free	No amount or an amount that is of no physiological consequence based on serving size
Calorie free	Less than 5 calories
Sodium free	Less than 5 milligrams
Fat free	Less than 0.5 gram of fat and no added fat
Cholesterol free	Less than 2 milligrams
Sugar free	Less than 0.5 gram
Low	Would allow frequent consumption of a food low in a nutrient without exceeding the dietary guidelines
Low calorie	Less than 40 calories
Low sodium	Less than 140 milligrams
Very low sodium	Less than 35 milligrams
Low fat	Less than 3 grams
Low in saturated fat	Less than 1 gram and less than 15 percent of calories from saturated fat
Low in cholesterol	20 milligrams or less, with less than 2 grams of saturated fat
Reduced	Nutritionally altered product containing 25 percent less of a nutrient or 25 percent fewer calories than a reference food
Less	Contains 25 percent less of a nutrient or 25 percent fewer calories than a reference food
Light	33 percent fewer calories or 50 percent of the fat in a reference food; if 50 percent or more of the calories comes from fat, reduction must be 50 percent of the fat; or sodium content of a low-calorie, low-fat food has been reduced by 50 percent; thus, the term "light in sodium" may be used; or describes such properties as texture and color, as "light brown sugar" or "light and fluffy"
High	20 percent or more of the DRV for a nutrient
Good source	Contains 10 to 19 percent of the DRV for a particular nutrient

Source: References 23, 49.

* Per serving basis.

Food Biotechnology

The term biotechnology includes a range of methods, including traditional plant or animal breeding, to alter the characteristics of plants or animals. Genetic engineering is a type of biotechnology that makes changes by introducing, rearranging, or removing genes through scientific methods, including those referred to as recombinant DNA. Genetic modification is another term that some may use synonymously with genetic engineering, whereas others may use genetic modification to include changes made by traditional breeding as well as foods produced through the use of biotechnology [41, 47, 52]. The first substance produced by genetic engineering to be approved by the FDA was an enzyme, *chymosin* or *rennin,* used in cheese-making. This approval was given in 1990. The first genetically engineered vegetable approved was a tomato that ripens on the vine without undue softening, thus increasing its natural flavor while allowing normal shipping procedures.

The FDA, USDA, and EPA together oversee the regulation of genetically engineered foods. Genetically engineered foods must adhere to the FDA food laws that require safe and lawful foods [42, 52]. Through the voluntary plant biotechnology consultation program, FDA works with developers to see their

Table 3–5
HEALTH CLAIMS ALLOWED FOR CONVENTIONAL FOODS

- Calcium, vitamin D, and osteoporosis
- Dietary lipids (fat) and cancer
- Dietary saturated fat and cholesterol and risk of coronary heart disease
- Dietary noncarcinogenic carbohydrate sweeteners and dental caries
- Fiber-containing grain products, fruits, and vegetables and cancer
- Folic acid and neural tube defects
- Fruits and vegetables and cancer
- Fruits, vegetables, and grain products that contain fiber, particularly soluble fiber, and risk of coronary heart disease
- Sodium and hypertension
- Soluble fiber from certain foods (e.g., whole oats) and risk of coronary heart disease
- Soy protein and risk of coronary heart disease
- Stanols/sterols and risk of coronary heart disease

Source: References 3, 48.

foods are safe and lawful [58]. Multiple agencies under USDA oversee biotechnology. The USDA Animal and Plant Health Inspection Service oversees safe development and the potential environmental impact. The USDA Food Safety Inspection Service is responsible for safe, wholesome, and correctly labeled animal foods, including those involved with biotechnology [43]. EPA has responsibility for genetically engineered biological pesticides [47].

Although genetically modified organisms (GMOs) have not been found to present a food safety or health risk, and are considered safe by a number of scientific and world organizations, including the World Health Organization, American Association for the Advancement of Science, American Medical Association, Britain's Royal Society of Medicine, and the European Commission [7], some consumers prefer to avoid foods produced using GMOs or other forms of biotechnology. Historically, the FDA required labeling of genetically engineered plants only if the food was "materially" different than the non-engineered food. In 2016, the National Bioengineered Food Disclosure Standard (Public Law No. 114-216) was signed by the president; it requires the establishment of a national standard for the labeling of bioengineered foods [59]. As of 2017, USDA is continuing to seek input on proposed rules for biotechnology labeling [40]. FDA has provided voluntary guidelines to manufacturers with acceptable terminology that includes "not bioengineered," "not genetically engineered," "not genetically modified through the use of modern biotechnology," and similar phrases [55].

IN DEPTH
HOW CAN YOU HAVE INPUT INTO GOVERNMENT REGULATIONS?

By law, anyone may participate in the rule-making process by sending comments on FDA proposals to FDA online, or through e-mail and standard mail on the FDA proposals [54]. When the FDA, USDA, or other government agencies plan to issue a new regulation or revise an existing one, an announcement is placed in the *Federal Register*, which also provides background on the issue and gives the address for submitting written comments by a specified deadline. The *Federal Register* is available on the Internet.

Contacting your state representative or senator offers another opportunity for involvement with the government. In fact, public input was a significant factor in the passage of the 1906 Pure Food and Drug Act, the 1906 Federal Meat Inspection Act, the 1938 Federal Food, Drug, and Cosmetic Act, and the 2004 Food Allergen Labeling and Consumer Protection Act.

Here are some ways to keep in touch with the government. ∎

Internet Web Address	Information Available
www.usa.gov	Gateway to the U.S. government. Links are provided to help you get the information you need.
https://www.usa.gov/elected-officials	Contact your elected officials. This page provides links for the president, U.S. senators, U.S. representatives, state governors, and state legislators.
https://www.govinfo.gov/	Federal Digital System. A variety of government documents may be located here from the budget of the U.S. government to the constitution, and congressional or presidential documents.
https://www.federalregister.gov/	Federal register, the daily journal of the U.S. government is found here.
https://www.ecfr.gov	Electronic code of federal regulations.
https://www.congress.gov/	Legislative information from the Library of Congress is provided. You may search for a bill by text or bill number or by the senator or representative sponsoring the bill.
www.regulations.gov	U.S. government regulations for all federal agencies may be found. Comments on regulations may be submitted on this website.

IN DEPTH
DIETARY SUPPLEMENTS

Dietary supplements are regulated by the FDA under the Dietary Supplement Health and Education Act of 1994. Under the provisions of this act, the manufacturer is responsible for safety of the supplement. The FDA does not preapprove supplements but by law may take action against unsafe supplements *after* they are sold [53]. In 2004, ephedra, found naturally in plants, was banned from supplements. Ephedra in dietary supplements was associated with cardiovascular complications, including strokes, that resulted in death [22].

Dietary supplements are not regulated in the same way as food or food additives. Food additives must be approved by the FDA *before* use in foods after a review of scientific data. Dietary supplements, however, are *not reviewed* by the FDA for safety or effectiveness before being sold to consumers. ■

(a)

(b)

Figure 3–3

(a) USDA meat inspectors, under regulation of the Federal Meat Inspection Act, will examine cattle, raised on a farm as shown here, before slaughter and (b) beef carcasses for wholesomeness and freedom from disease. (USDA, (a) photographer Alice Welch (b) photographer Preston Keres)

FDA Food Code

In yet another food oversight role, the FDA publishes an updated Food Code every four years. The FDA Food Code provides food-safety guidelines for all retail food service operations [51]. Because local restaurants and food service establishments are inspected and regulated by state and local governments, local food codes may be different from the FDA Food Code. Nevertheless, the FDA Food Code provides guidance to state and local governments when developing and updating their food-safety regulations.

THE USDA

The USDA is involved with food processing and marketing in several different ways. Under the auspices of the Food Safety and Inspection Service, the USDA inspects meat and poultry products for wholesomeness and truthful labeling, administering the Federal Meat Inspection Act and the Poultry Products Inspection Act (**Figure 3–3**). The USDA Agricultural Marketing Service is responsible for administering the Egg Products Inspection Act, which requires inspection of all plants that process liquid, dried, or frozen egg products. It also offers grading services for meat, poultry, fruits, vegetables, eggs, and dairy products. Selected regulations and laws administered by the USDA are provided in **Table 3–6**.

History

Legislation creating the USDA was signed by President Abraham Lincoln in 1862 [46]. In the early years, the primary focus of the department was to promote food production by providing information for farmers. With the growth of the meatpacking industry after the Civil War, the Bureau of Animal Industry, a forerunner to the USDA Food Safety and Inspection Service, was created to prevent diseased animals from being used as food. Upton Sinclair's book *The Jungle,* which described filthy conditions in the Chicago meatpacking industry, led to the passage of the 1906 Federal Meat Inspection Act. Under this act, continuous government inspection of meatpacking plants was started and continues today. Over the years, new legislation has been passed to strengthen the role of the USDA.

Inspection

The USDA administers a mandatory continuous inspection program for meat and poultry that is sold in interstate commerce and in those states that do not have an inspection program of their own that is equal to the federal program. This inspection is for wholesomeness (safety) and proper labeling. The meat and poultry must be (1) from healthy animals or birds, (2) processed under strict sanitary conditions using good manufacturing practices and an HACCP system, (3) tested for the

Table 3–6
USDA: FOOD REGULATIONS TO PROTECT THE HEALTH AND SAFETY OF THE PUBLIC

Laws, Statutes, and Regulations	Basic Provisions
1906 Federal Meat Inspection Act	Mandates inspection of live animals, carcasses, and processed products. Also requires improved sanitary conditions for slaughter and processing.
1957 Poultry Products Inspection Act	Requires inspection of poultry products.
1967–1968 Wholesome Meat and Wholesome Poultry Products Acts	Meat Inspection and Poultry Product Inspection Acts were amended. The USDA gained authority to control unfit meat and meat products. Poultry products involved in interstate and foreign commerce must meet federal inspection standards.
1970 The Egg Products Inspection Act	Mandatory continuous inspection of liquid, frozen, and dried egg product processing.
1993 Nutrition Labeling of Meat and Poultry Products	Voluntary nutrition labeling guidelines established for single-ingredient raw meat and poultry products. Mandatory nutrition labeling for all other meat and poultry products.
1994 Testing for *E. coli* 0157:H7	*E. coli* 0157:H7 declared to be an adulterant. Testing program for ground beef started.
1996–2000 HACCP Systems	Meat and poultry plants must develop and use HACCP plans to ensure safety of their products.
1999 Testing for *Listeria monocytogenes*	Testing for this pathogen implemented at plants processing high- and medium-risk ready-to-eat products (deli meats and other products).
2010 Nutrition Labeling of Single Ingredient Products and Ground or Chopped Meat and Poultry Products	Final rule to establish mandatory nutrition labeling on major cuts of meat and poultry at point of sale.

presence of some microorganisms, and (4) truthfully labeled. Meat and poultry slaughter and processing plants must test for generic *E. coli* to verify that the process is under control with respect to preventing and removing fecal contamination. The Food Safety and Inspection Service tests for salmonella on raw meat and poultry products to verify that pathogen reduction standards are being met for this organism. Prior to the USDA modernization of the inspection service with the implementation of HACCP, the USDA meat inspection was done by using sight, touch, and smell [3,46].

USDA Grades

All meat and poultry must be inspected for wholesomeness before it can be graded for quality. The inspection determines wholesomeness; the grading determines quality. Official USDA grading services are generally voluntarily requested but may be required on a local level or for a particular industry program. The USDA grading service is paid for by the manufacturer requesting the service. Grading is performed by USDA inspectors who use standardized quality criteria. Grading may be done for meat, poultry, eggs, dairy products, some fish, nuts, rice, and fresh fruits and vegetables.

Grade standards were originally established to aid in wholesale food trading; however, USDA grades may also be found on retail food packages. The grade reflects the quality of the food at the time it was graded. No allowance is made for changes in quality that may occur during the handling and storage involved in the marketing process. The quality of some foods is more variable than others, and therefore more grades may be needed. For example, there are eight grades for beef but only three for chicken. Foods that are officially graded may be labeled with one of the shield-shaped marks shown in **Figure 3–4**. Even though a product may have been officially graded, the law still does not require that a designation of grade appear on the label.

Because the grade standards for various products were developed at different times, the naming systems vary. For instance, the top-quality grade for cantaloupes is U.S. Fancy; for beets, it is U.S. No. 1; for carrots, it is U.S. Grade A; and for celery, it is U.S. Extra No. 1. U.S. Grades A, B, and C are used on poultry and on canned fruits and vegetables. To help achieve a more uniform grading system, the USDA has issued a policy statement that when future standards

for fresh fruits, vegetables, and nuts are issued, revised, or amended, only the classifications U.S. Fancy and Grades 1, 2, and 3 may be used.

Food grading aids food service managers as they write **specifications** for the purchasing of various food products. The required quality of the product being ordered can be easily specified by grade because the grade standards are known to both purchasers and vendors. Food grading is also useful for consumers to help them meet their needs and desires more effectively.

Organic Foods

The Organic Foods Production Act was passed by Congress in 1990 [44]. This act required that the USDA develop national standards for organically produced agricultural products to provide consumers with products consistently and uniformly identified as "organic." Regulations developed through the Organic Foods Production Act and the National Organic Program established an organic certification program and labeling standards. These regulations prohibit the use of conventional pesticides, petroleum-based fertilizers, sewage sludge–based fertilizers, genetic engineering, and ionizing radiation. Animals to be marketed as organic must be fed organic feed, given access to the outdoors, and not be given antibiotics or growth hormones [44].

Starting in 2002, the USDA labeling rules for organic foods were implemented. Certified foods labeled as "100 percent organic" or "95 percent organic" may include the USDA organic seal (**Figure 3–5**). Foods containing 70 to 95 percent organic ingredients may be labeled "made with organic ingredients." Products with less than 70 percent organic ingredients may not include organic claims on the front of the package but may list specific organically produced ingredients on the side panel (**Figure 3–6**). These labeling standards will help consumers to decide whether they want to pay a premium price for these products. With estimated annual sales of over $43 billion 2016, the organic food industry has become an important component of the U.S. food system, accounting for more than 5 percent of the food sales in the United States [68]. Organic foods are generally more expensive than their conventional counterparts by 7 percent or more [6].

"Natural" has been appearing on product labels with greater frequency, in large part because consumers

Figure 3–4

A variety of different shield-shape marks are used by the USDA in grading food products. (U.S. Department of Agriculture)

like this term. However, "natural" and "organic" are not interchangeable terms; only "organic" foods have been certified by USDA [28, 37, 44]. A USDA policy memo describes natural foods as those that are minimally

Figure 3–5

Government-certified organic symbol that can be placed on foods only after they meet government guidelines. (U.S. Department of Agriculture)

processed and do not contain artificial colors, flavors, or preservatives. The FDA informally defines "natural" as meaning that nothing artificial or synthetic is included in the food [10]. The FDA invited public comments on the use of "natural" in labeling, and will be reviewing this issue.

Some consumers may be purchasing foods labeled "natural" when they actually want an organic food or because they believe the product has other benefits in spite of the limited oversight by FDA or USDA of this terminology. Researchers have found consumers perceive products identified as "natural" have a higher quality and greater nutritional content, and furthermore are willing to pay more for these products [20].

Other Areas of USDA Influence

Like the FDA, the USDA has an impact on the regulation of irradiation, biotechnology, additives, and labeling of foods. Specifically, the USDA oversees these related concerns with regard to foods regulated by the USDA, including meat, poultry, egg products, and foods containing meat or poultry. The USDA has approved the irradiation of meat and poultry to increase food safety. In the area of biotechnology, the USDA specifically oversees biotechnology applications with impact on foods regulated by the USDA and ensures that plants developed through genetic engineering do not have an adverse impact on the agricultural environment.

Specific labeling regulations of the USDA include the safe food-handling labels found on eggs and meat

Figure 3–6

These sample cereal boxes show the four organic labeling categories. From left: 100 percent organic ingredients, 95–100 percent organic ingredients, at least 70 percent organic ingredients, and less than 70 percent regnic ingredients. (U.S. Department of Agriculture)

packages as well as the organic labeling program and nutrition labeling of meat and poultry. Country of origin labeling has been recently implemented. Cuts of meat and poultry, ground meats, fish, shellfish, perishable agricultural commodities, peanuts, pecans, macadamia nuts, and ginseng must all be labeled to identify the country of origin [45]. These additional roles of the USDA will be addressed in greater depth in chapters focusing on USDA-regulated foods.

THE EPA

The EPA protects the public health through the oversight of environmental risks from pesticides. It administers the 1947 Federal Insecticide, Fungicide, and Rodenticide Act that was amended by the 1996 Food Quality Protection Act. The EPA establishes maximum legally permissible levels for pesticide residues in food. Genetically engineered foods also may fall under EPA oversight if the alteration includes a component that functions as a natural pesticide.

CENTERS FOR DISEASE CONTROL AND PREVENTION

The Centers for Disease Control and Prevention (CDC) promotes health by preventing and controlling disease. The CDC collaborates with the FDA and the USDA in the FoodNet system to measure the incidence and sources of bacterial foodborne diseases. The CDC manages the PulseNet system, which is another collaborative effort with the FDA and USDA. PulseNet helps to control foodborne outbreaks through a national laboratory and computer database. Through this database, distinctive DNA "fingerprint" patterns for microorganisms may be identified, thereby permitting the tracing of foodborne illnesses

that may be linked by one common food. Early identification of the source of foodborne illness helps the FDA and USDA prevent further illnesses from the same food.

THE FTC

The FTC is an independent law enforcement agency charged with promoting free and fair competition in the marketplace. One major activity of the FTC is ensuring that fair and honest competition is allowed in the marketing of food products. The FTC attempts to protect the consumer from false or misleading advertising and misbranding, and shares with the FDA responsibility for enforcing labeling laws.

OTHER FEDERAL AGENCIES

The National Oceanic and Atmospheric Administration (NOAA) of the U.S. Department of Commerce oversees the management of fisheries in the United States. The Seafood Inspection Program of NOAA operates under the 1946 Agricultural Marketing Act. The voluntary inspection service provides product grading, facility inspection, product lot inspection, process and product inspection, laboratory analysis, training, and consultation. The FDA, however, oversees the mandatory HACCP regulations and inspections for seafood processors through the FDA Seafood Regulatory Program [66]. The NOAA Seafood Inspection Program provides additional services for processors that include product grading.

The Bureau of Alcohol, Tobacco, Firearms, and Explosives in the Department of the Treasury regulates most alcoholic beverages. The qualifications and operations of distilleries, wineries, and breweries are controlled. New products coming into the market are

IN DEPTH
A SINGLE FOOD-SAFETY AGENCY—IS THIS THE ANSWER?

There are about 12 different federal agencies and 35 different federal laws governing food safety [21, 24]. Although a number of these organizations—including the Bureau of Alcohol, Tobacco, and Firearms (ATF)—are only peripherally involved in assuring food safety, several agencies play key roles that call for close coordination and collaboration with others. The FDA and the USDA are primary among these. The need for close working relationships among agencies became even more apparent when terrorism struck the United States on September 11, 2001. What is the answer to this problem?

The consolidation of all federal food-safety responsibilities into a single, independent agency has been proposed.

Others, however, believe such a reorganization of food-safety responsibility would cause more problems than it solved [31]. Most agreed on two principles—first, that the United States now has the safest food supply in the world, and, second, that there are problems to be fixed in order to maintain that position.

Although discussion about a single food agency continues periodically, the respective agencies have developed new areas of collaboration and have continued existing partnerships such as **Foodborne Disease Active Surveillance Network (FOODNET), PULSENET**, and **FORC-G**. The FDA Food Safety Modernization Act directs the FDA to enhance partnerships with other domestic and foreign agencies [50]. ∎

tested to ensure that alcoholic ingredients are within legal limits. Labels are examined to see that legal requirements have been met.

STATE AND LOCAL AGENCIES

The legislation and regulations previously discussed in this chapter are federal and apply only in interstate commerce. Within each state and within cities are many laws and regulations dealing with food processing, quality, and marketing. Each state has its own unique problems and attempts to solve them in individual ways, but federal laws and regulations are often used as models. States are usually organized with their own departments of agriculture and health and their own food and drug commissions. Assurance of sanitation, milk quality, inspection of meat and poultry, and protection of vegetable crops are some of the activities conducted by state organizations.

State and local governments provide for the inspection of food service establishments to protect the public who eat in restaurants, cafeterias, and other places where food service is offered. This service is usually the responsibility of state, county, and city health departments, which assess cleanliness and sanitary practices. In many cases, those working with food served to the public are required to obtain food-handling permits, sometimes involving both a physical examination and educational certification.

INTERNATIONAL STANDARDS

In our rapidly shrinking world, international trade in food is accelerating. The U.S. food industry plays a major role in international food marketing, and the world demand for fresh and processed foods continues to rise.

Increased international trade in foods has created an even greater need for international standards to safeguard the consumer's health and ensure fair food-trade practices. The Codex Alimentarius Commission was established in 1963 by a joint effort of the UN Food and Agriculture Organization and the World Health Organization to meet this need. Any nation that is a member of either of these organizations may become a member of the commission. The international standards are quite comprehensive and include a description of the product; composition requirements; additives that may be allowed, if any; sanitary handling practices; fill of container, weight, and measure or count of units; labeling provisions; and methods of analysis and sampling necessary to determine that the standard is being met [38].

After the commission develops a recommended international standard, it is sent to the member nations for consideration of adoption. Individual members may adopt the standard for themselves. The World Trade Organization accepts Codex food standards, guidelines, and recommendations as representing international consensus in this area [29].

STUDY QUESTIONS

Food and Drug Administration

1. Identify the foods regulated by the Food and Drug Administration and the impact on the U.S. food supply.

2. Discuss the historical or current impact of each of the following on the food supply and consumers
   (a) 1906 Pure Food and Drug Act
   (b) 1938 Federal Food, Drug, and Cosmetic Act
   (c) 1954 Miller Pesticide Amendment
   (d) 1958 Food Additives Amendment
   (e) 1960 Color Additives Amendment
   (f) 1966 Fair Packaging and Labeling Act
   (g) 1973 Low-Acid Processing Regulations
   (h) 1980 Nutrition Labeling and Education Act
   (i) 1996 Food Quality Protection Act
   (j) Hazard Analysis and Critical Control Points (HACCP) regulations
   (k) 2002 Public Health Security and Bioterrorism Preparedness and Response Act
   (l) 2004 Food Allergen Labeling and Consumer Protection Act
   (m) 2011 FDA Food Safety Modernization Act

3. Explain how each of the following protects consumers and food manufacturers?
   (a) Standards of identity
   (b) Standards of fill of container
   (c) Standards of minimum quality
   (d) Sanitation requirements

4. Explain in both general and legal terminology the definition of a food additive.

5. Explain when a food additive is "intentional" and when it may be "incidental."

6. Identify GRAS substances, and explain how the regulation of GRAS substances is different than food additives.

7. Describe three justifiable uses for food additives.

8. Explain the intent of the Delaney clause.

9. Discuss the regulation of irradiation, and identify the agencies or departments in the U.S. government that are most involved with the oversight of pesticides in our food.

10. Explain the Total Diet Study, and discuss the implications of this study to understanding pesticide residuals in our food supply.

11. Identify the five items that must appear on a food package label.

12. Develop a presentation to teach consumers how to read the Nutrition Facts label to select food to fit within a healthy daily diet.

13. Discuss the regulatory aspects of claims on packages. Include
    (a) nutrient content claims—what terms are legally regulated?
    (b) health claims—how are allowed claims determined?
    (c) qualified health claims—difference between qualified health claims and health claims.
    (d) structure and function claims—how do these differ from other claims in relationship to legal oversight?

14. Develop a presentation for individuals with food allergies or celiac disease on the Food Allergen Labeling, including gluten-free labeling. Include in your presentation discussion about the regulations and what may or may not be found on the label.

15. Explain some differences in the FDA regulation of dietary supplements as compared to foods and food additives.

16. Discuss the regulation of food biotechnology, and identify the agencies or departments in the U.S. government that are most involved with the oversight of genetically engineered food.

17. Identify the purpose of the FDA Food Code.

18. Explain how you can have input into government regulations.

The United States Department of Agriculture (USDA)

19. Identify the importance and impact of the USDA with regard to consumers and the U.S. food supply.

20. Identify the foods that USDA inspects and significant laws, statutes, and regulations under the oversight of USDA.

21. Identify the foods that USDA grades, and discuss how grading is different than inspection.

22. Discuss how the grading of food products is useful to the wholesaler, the retailer, and the consumer.

23. Discuss the USDA standards for organic foods. How can consumers know that they are truly getting organic food?

24. Compare and contrast the meaning of USDA organic foods and those foods labeled "natural."

25. Identify additional areas of USDA influence and areas of collaboration between USDA, FDA, EPA, and other government agencies or departments.

The Environmental Protection Agency (EPA)

26. Identify key areas of EPA oversight that impact our food supply.

Centers for Disease Control and Prevention (CDC)

27. Explain ways that the CDC collaborates with other government agencies and departments for safe food.

The Federal Trade Commission (FTC)

28. Identify an important area of food oversight of FTC.

Other Federal Agencies

29. Discuss the role of the following in food regulation and oversight:
    (a) National Oceanic and Atmospheric Administration
    (b) Bureau of Alcohol, Tobacco, Firearms, and Explosives

State and Local Agencies

30. Identify several of the ways that state and local agencies oversee our food supply.

International Standards

31. Discuss the Codex Alimentarius Commission, and what functions it performs.

4
Equipment and Recipe Basics

The preparation of high-quality foods, whether at home or in a commercial kitchen, involves the use of small and large equipment, as well as trustworthy, standardized recipes. Some equipment and tools may be considered essential, whereas others may make the preparation task easier or faster to accomplish. Measuring utensils for both dry ingredients and liquids are needed to allow for the correct amount of ingredients to be used in a recipe. Standardized recipes are designed to consistently produce a specified yield and quality. Standardized recipes also enable the control of food costs, and ensure nutrient content is accurate when the recipe is prepared according to specific instructions.

In this chapter, the following topics will be discussed:

- Knives, hand tools, and small equipment
- Large equipment
- Weights, volume measures, and measurement techniques used in food preparation
- Metric as compared to U.S. customary measures and weights
- Recipes and recipe standardization

KNIVES, HAND TOOLS, AND SMALL EQUIPMENT

Many different types of tools are used when preparing foods. Knives are one of the most important. Understanding the best knife for each task and the development of good knife skills will enable you to prepare high-quality foods efficiently and safely. In addition to the measuring cups and scales to be discussed later in the chapter, whisks, spatulas, scoops, ladles, and multiple other tools and types of small equipment each have an important purpose in food preparation.

Knives

A variety of knives are available, each with a specific purpose. In food services, a number of different knives are used because using the proper knife for a given task is safer and more efficient. The same is true in the home. In addition to using the proper knife for the task, a cutting board is a must to protect you, the work surface, and the knife. Cutting on surfaces other than cutting boards will dull the knife and holding foods in the hands will increase the risk of cuts. Sharp knives reduce effort and reduce the risk of cuts caused by a dull knife requiring excessive pressure followed by a sudden cutting action. For this reason, knives should be sharpened regularly and knives with high-quality blades should be purchased.

Matching Knife to Task. A chef's or French knife is used for chopping, slicing, and mincing vegetables, such as onions, or meats, such as diced ham or turkey. This knife should be held with the thumb and index finger gripping the blade. The other three fingers hold the handle (**Figure 4–1**). This method of gripping the knife provides added stability and control. Although in food services 10- to 14-inch blades are common, a 6- to 8-inch knife may be best in home use or preferred by those with smaller hands.

When cutting foods, the product should be held with all the fingers, including the thumb, curled back. The blade of the chef's knife is guided by the flat surface of the fingers between the first and second knuckles (**Figure 4–2**). With the fingertips tucked back, cuts are much less likely than when the food is held with the fingertips pointed outward. Initially, gripping the chef's knife and food as described may feel awkward. However, with added practice, these positions will become natural and will permit the rapid and safe dicing, mincing, and chopping of foods.

Figure 4–1

The most common grip: Hold the handle with three fingers while gripping the blade between the thumb and index finger. (Richard Embery/Pearson Education)

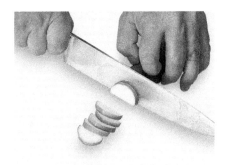

Figure 4–2

The proper cutting method shown with fingers and thumb curled back with blade of the chef's knife guided against the knuckles. (Richard Embery/Pearson Education)

Several other kinds of knives are used for specific tasks (**Figure 4–3**). The utility knife is an all-purpose knife that may be used for cutting fruits and vegetables or carving poultry. A paring knife is usually 2 to 4 inches in length and is used for very detailed work. Although used by some for many tasks in the kitchen, it is not the best choice for most products that are to be sliced, chopped, or diced. The French knife is more efficient for these types of jobs. A slicer is used for carving cooked meat, whereas a serrated knife is typically used for slicing bread or pastry products. The butcher's knife is usually used to cut raw meats [5].

Knife Quality and Blade Material. A knife should be balanced and made from high-quality materials for both the blade and the handle. The parts of the knife are shown in **Figure 4–4**. A full tang and bolster result in a well-balanced, durable knife. Handles may be made from wood or molded polypropylene. However, regardless of the material, the handle should be comfortable to hold and easily cleanable.

Knife blades are generally made from carbon steel, stainless steel, or high-carbon stainless steel. Carbon steel is an alloy of carbon and iron that sharpens easily, but also corrodes and discolors. Stainless steel blades do not corrode or discolor, but these blades are difficult to sharpen. High-carbon stainless steel blades are generally preferred because they share advantages of carbon steel and stainless steel by sharpening to a desirable sharp edge and not corroding [5].

Sharpening. A sharp knife is easier to use and reduces fatigue and, more importantly, the risk of injury. Sharp knives cut through food products more easily, thereby reducing the risk of dangerous slips. Knives should be sharpened regularly as the edge becomes dull. A sharpening stone or whetstone is used to place an edge on a dull blade (**Figure 4–5**). To use a stone, the blade is

Figure 4–3

Knife varieties: (a) French or chef's knife, an all-purpose knife for chopping, slicing, and mincing. (b) Utility knife used for cutting fruits, vegetables, and poultry. (c) Rigid boning knife is useful for separating meat from bone. (d) Paring knife is short for detailed work such as fruit or vegetable work. (e) Cleavers are used for chopping through bones. (f) Slicer is primarily used for cutting cooked meats. (g) Serrated slicer is used for cutting bread or pastry. (h) Butcher's knife is used to prepare raw meats. (i) Oyster and clam knives effectively open oyster and clam shells.

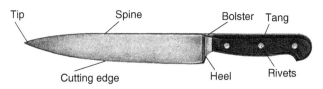

Figure 4–4

The parts of a chef's or French knife.

(a) Three-Sided Sharpening or Whetstone

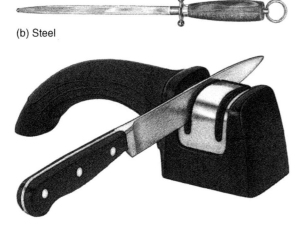

(b) Steel

(c) Knife Sharpeners

Figure 4-5

(a) A whetstone is used to sharpen knives. (b) A steel is used to straighten the knife blade between sharpenings. (c) Knife sharpeners such as this one are easy to use and are a good choice for the home setting. The knife is simply pulled through the slot for sharpening of the blade.

pressed evenly against the stone at a 20-degree angle as if slicing the stone. This step is repeated on both sides of the blade until sharp. Generally, the stone is lubricated with water or mineral oil. Vegetable oil is not recommended because it will become gummy. The final step in sharpening is to hone the blade with a steel. A steel

is a long, thin, cylindrical metal tool that hones and straightens the blade immediately after sharpening and between occasions of sharpening (Figure 4–5). As with the sharpening process, a 20-degree angle is maintained.

There are other methods of sharpening knives, including sharpeners available through local kitchen supply stores that may be used by simply drawing the knife blade through the sharpener. Other types of sharpeners are electric, but if not used with care, excessive wear to the blade may occur.

Hand Tools

Many hand tools are used in the kitchen to stir, whip, flip, peel, or grasp foods (**Figure 4–6**). Spoons may be solid, perforated, or slotted. Perforated spoons have round holes to drain away liquid from small foods such as peas, whereas slotted spoons have large slots to drain liquid from larger, more coarse foods. Whisks can be used to whip eggs, egg whites, or heavy cream by hand. Although whisks may be used to mix some bakery products, they may not be the best choice for delicate products that need to be mixed lightly.

Portioning and Measuring Tools

Scales and measuring cups will be discussed later; however, there are other tools that may be used to measure or portion foods. Ladles come in ounce sizes and may be used to measure liquids in the kitchen or for portioning food when served (**Figure 4–7**). Portion scoops or dishers are sized by a number that corresponds to the number of level scoops per quart [5]. For example, a number 12 scoop is equivalent to 1/3 cup because there are 12 portions of 1/3 cup per quart. Scoops not only measure the amount of food but also are the most efficient way to portion cookies onto a cookie tray or muffins into muffin tins for baking.

Thermometers are an essential item to have in the kitchen. Thermometers are used to measure the end-point cooking temperatures and to

---

FOCUS ON SCIENCE
CARBON STEEL, STAINLESS STEEL, AND HIGH-CARBON STAINLESS STEEL—WHAT IS THE DIFFERENCE IN COMPOSITION?

Carbon Steel

Carbon steel is an alloy of iron that is approximately 1 percent carbon. It is easier to sharpen than stainless steel, holds its edge longer, but is vulnerable to rusts and stains.

Stainless Steel

Stainless steel is an alloy of iron, approximately 10 to 15 percent chromium, possibly nickel, and molybdenum with only a small amount of carbon. Lower grades of stainless steel are not able to take as sharp an edge as carbon steel, but they

are resistant to corrosion, do not taint food, and are inexpensive. Expensive knives are the "exotic" stainless steel (mostly from Japan), are extremely sharp with excellent edge retention, and equal or outperform carbon steel blades.

High-Carbon Stainless Steel

High-carbon stainless steel contains a certain amount of carbon arbitrarily deemed "high." It is intended to combine the best attributes of carbon steel and ordinary stainless steel. High-carbon stainless steel blades maintain a sharp edge and do not discolor.

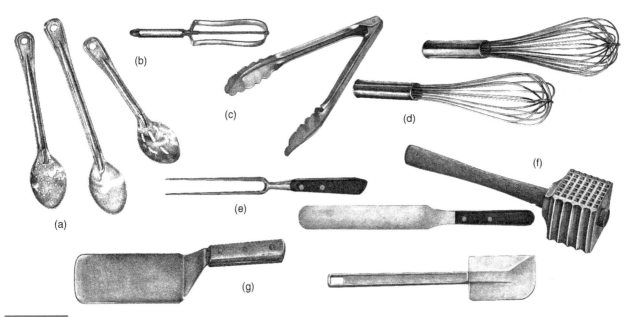

Figure 4–6

Variety of hand tools: (a) Perforated, plain, and slotted spoons. (b) Vegetable peeler. (c) Straight tongs. (d) Balloon and rigid whisks. (e) Chef's fork. (f) Meat mallet. (g) Grill, rubber, and straight or cake spatulas.

monitor proper refrigeration and freezer temperatures, thereby promoting food safety (see Chapter 2). Food preparation can be better controlled by measuring the temperature of the oven, of oils when deep-fat frying, and of the point at which a candy mixture should be removed from the heat (see Chapter 9).

Other Small Equipment

For draining liquid from large quantities of food, a colander, strainer, china cap, or chinois all have specific intended purposes (**Figure 4–8**). For example, both a colander and a china cap usually are constructed of metal bodies, whereas chinois and strainers are composed of fine mesh screens. The piece of equipment chosen will depend on the type of product being prepared.

Foods may be mixed using different hand tools depending on whether the product is to be stirred, folded, or whipped. Likewise, mixers have different attachments such as flat paddles, whips, or dough hooks. Each performs the mixing function in a specified way (**Figure 4–9**). The science behind food preparation provides an understanding of why a flat paddle is more

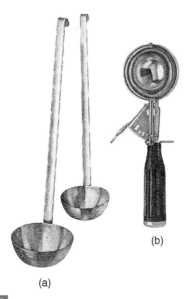

Figure 4–7

(a) Two ladle sizes used for portioning liquids. (b) Portion scoops are used for dishing cookie dough onto cookie sheets or ice cream into a dish.

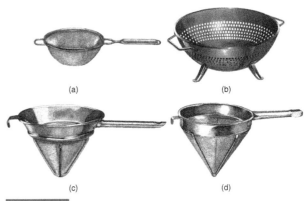

Figure 4–8

(a) Round mesh strainer. (b) Colander. (c) Chinois. (d) China cap.

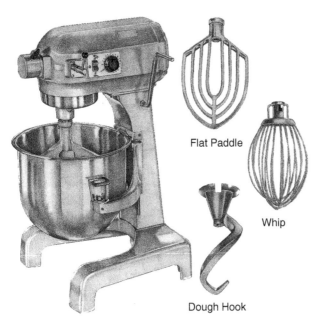

Flat Paddle

Whip

Dough Hook

20-Quart Mixer and Attachments

Figure 4–9

Mixer and three attachments: the flat paddle, the whip, and the dough hook.

appropriate for muffins than a whip, even though a whip is necessary for making angel food cake. Food processors, food choppers, and food blenders are additional pieces of small equipment that can make food preparation quicker and easier. Food processors can chop vegetables, such as onions, but will not result in the consistency of size possible when chopped or diced by hand using a chef's knife. Blenders are used to puree ingredients and otherwise blend to generally a fine consistency depending on the length of blending.

LARGE EQUIPMENT

Many kinds of large equipment are used in the home and commercial settings to cook food with moist, dry, or combination (both dry and moist) cooking methods. Heat transfer including dry, moist, and combination methods

of cooking will be discussed further in Chapter 5. In brief, dry-heat methods include baking, roasting, sautéing, and frying—all cooking methods that do not use water. Moist-heat cooking methods involve water and include boiling, simmering, and steaming.

Cooking Equipment

In the commercial setting and in the home there are a variety of choices for equipment used to cook food. Each type of equipment offers certain advantages in relation to how it cooks and the quality or characteristics of the food produced. These aspects related to food quality will be discussed further in the chapters that follow.

Ranges and Stoves.   Ranges, also called stoves, may be gas or electric. Induction ranges are also available in both the home and commercial setting. The surface of an induction range does not heat up; instead it heats an iron-containing pan by the magnetic friction produced by the induction cooktop (see Chapter 5). Gas ranges offer the advantage of quick responsiveness; they are hot when turned on and fully off when turned off. In contrast, electric ranges must heat up after being turned on and, when turned off, remain hot until fully cooled down. Both home and commercial ranges may include an oven and other cooking options such as a broiler (also called a salamander), or flattop that can provide even heat as shown in **Figure 4–10**.

Grills.   In the home kitchen, a griddle or other flat pan is used on range-top for pancakes or similar items, and a steak may be sautéed in a skillet. In commercial kitchens, a large freestanding grill holds 30 or more steaks or pancakes at one time. Grills, also called griddles, are metal plates that will heat to moderate temperatures for fried eggs and pancakes or higher temperatures to sear steaks and other cuts of meat, producing browning and the associated flavors (**Figure 4–11**).

Tilt Fry Pans.   A tilt fry pan, as implied by the name, is a large tilting fry pan used in commercial kitchens. It is a large, freestanding flat-bottom skillet that will tilt

---

KEEP IT SAFE
FIRE EXTINGUISHERS

All kitchens, not only commercial kitchens where it is required, should have a basic fire extinguisher in case of a kitchen fire. Although exiting the kitchen or home for safety is always a top consideration, small fires may be quickly extinguished with fire extinguisher. Fire extinguishers should be UL rated and designed for one or more of the following types of fires.

A—Combustible materials, such as paper, wood, cloth, or cardboard
B—Flammable liquids, such as grease, oil, kerosene, or gasoline
C—Electrical fires ■

Figure 4–10
A food service range with gas burners, ovens below cooking surfaces, and a salamander (also called a broiler) above the range.

Figure 4–11
A griddle, also called a grill, is a hot surface that may be used for cooking pancakes, frying eggs, and grilling meats.

to enable the removal of sauces or stews cooked in the skillet. An attached lid allows the skillet contents to be cooked, covered or open. These tilt fry pans are similar to small electric fry pans used in the home, however, much larger. Both have a heating element below the pan's bottom.

A tilt skillet offers a great deal of flexibility by heating to temperatures that are high enough to sear and brown meats, yet can cook at lower temperatures to simmer a sauce. Although a flattop grill is preferable for cooking pancakes, the tilt fry pan may also be used for this purpose in spite of the approximately 6-inch deep side walls. The tilt skillet can also heat water and then hold pans of food placed in the skillet to hold the food hot, or heat the food in the hot water bath (**Figure 4–12**).

Figure 4–12
A tilt skillet can tilt to pour out sauces or stews as shown here.

Ovens. In the home kitchen, ovens may be powered by gas or electricity. Convection ovens are an available option known for even heating because of a fan in the oven circulating the air. Ovens, conventional or convection, may be part of a range with a cooktop or a separate wall oven. In commercial kitchens, ovens may also be gas or electric; however, wood-fired ovens are another option found in some restaurants.

Commercial ovens may be located under a range (Figure 4–10) or, more frequently, are a separate piece of equipment. Stack ovens are so named because essentially more than one oven is stacked on top of another (**Figure 4–13**). Each oven can be controlled to its own temperature and usually contains space for two shelves. Reel ovens are ovens with a "reel" inside the oven that rotates trays of food through the oven in a motion similar to a ferrous wheel. Because the food moves continuously in the oven, except when pans are loaded or unloaded, these ovens cook evenly.

Convection ovens have a fan on the back of the oven that automatically turns off when the oven door is opened (**Figure 4–14**). The fans in commercial convection ovens are generally much more powerful than those found in home ovens. Because convection ovens cook food more quickly, it is recommended that the temperature is reduced by 25°F (10°C) and the length of cooking is reduced. Convection ovens cook evenly, minimizing or eliminating the need for pans to be rotated. Furthermore, cookie or muffin trays may be placed closely together with little concern about evenness of the heat. Thus, especially in a high-volume commercial kitchen, more food can be cooked in these ovens than a similarly sized non-convection oven.

Deep-Fat Fryers. Deep-fat frying is a form of dry heat where food is submerged in hot oil for cooking. Crisp coatings and tender interiors are common characteristics of many fried foods. Small home-sized

Figure 4–13

Stack ovens are stacked. In this figure there are three ovens stacked on top of each other. Each may be set to its own temperature offering flexibility in preparation of large quantities of food in a food service.

Figure 4–14

Convection ovens may be a single oven as shown here or a larger unit with an oven on top and another on the bottom. Convection ovens have a large fan in the back of the oven that circulates the hot air. Convection ovens cook more quickly and promote even temperatures throughout the oven, even when trays of food are placed on oven racks close to each other.

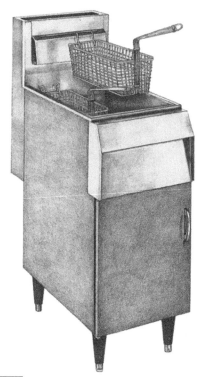

Figure 4–15

This deep-fat fryer cooks food submerged in the frying oil.

deep-fat fryers are available that will automatically control the temperature of the oil. Alternatively, food can be fried on a range top using a deep pan and deep-fat frying thermometer to monitor the correct temperature. In commercial kitchens, deep-fat fryers are large (**Figure 4–15**) and placed under a hood system with an automatic fire suppression system that is activated by high temperatures that are experienced in a fire.

Temperatures often used for frying are 350°F (177°C) to 375°F (191°C) [10]. An oil at a temperature that is too high can burn resulting in a kitchen fire. See Chapter 8 for more information on deep-fat frying and acceptable oils.

Steam Jacketed Kettles. Steam jacketed kettles are often used in commercial food services to cook sauces (cheese sauce, spaghetti sauce, or gravy), soups (chicken noodle, chili), pasta, puddings, or pie fillings (**Figure 4–16**). These kettles have a "jacket" of steam that envelops the sides and usually rounded bottom. The steam may be supplied directly from a facility providing steam line, or produced via electricity or gas power.

These kettles cook more evenly and quickly than a stockpot on the range top, especially when cooking in large quantities because the heat is not only at the bottom of the kettle but also usually about half way up the side of the kettle. Additionally, because the heat is supplied by steam, while scorching can occur, it is less likely as compared to a pot directly on the range top where the electric or gas flame burner can get very hot. Some of these kettles have an automatic stirrer to keep the contents moving in the kettle without a cook's constant attention.

Figure 4–16
Steam jacketed kettles heat kettle contents with steam trapped "in jackets" between the interior and exterior of the kettle. These steam jackets generally surround the bottom of the kettle and go about one-third or one-half up the side of the kettle. On many kettles, the end of the jacketed area can be seen by the line around the mid-section of the kettle. Steam jacketed kettles can hold 5 gallons (19 liters) or 80 gallons (302 liters) and more.

Kettles that are smaller (5 or 10 gallon or 19 to 38 liters) can be tilted manually to pour out the contents, or, if larger (60 or more gallons or 227 liters), can be tilted with a crank system to pour out the ingredients. Most large kettles also have a large spigot that can be opened to drain the contents into another container.

Steamers. Home cooks may cook using steam by using a perforated pan insert (pan with small holes) above a pan of boiling water. Two types of steamers may be found in food services, a high-pressure steamer or a convection steamer. Both heat hotel-sized pans with foods, such as vegetables and rice, rapidly. High-pressure steamers may cook at 5 pounds per square inch (PSI) of pressure and are manually cranked closed so that the steamer door is secure and does not leak. The pressure level must return to 0 PSI before the door is opened. High-pressure steamers may cook a hotel-size half pan of vegetables to tender crisp in as little as 3 to 5 minutes using a temperature of about 250°F (121°C).

Convection steamers cook with steam, but do not cook under pressure (**Figure 4–17**). Thus, the door can be opened and closed during cooking. Convection steamers cook at 212°F (100°C). Although they do not cook as rapidly as high-pressure steamers, they still provide a relatively rapid means of cooking vegetables and other steamed foods. Like steam jacketed kettles, the steam in convection or high-pressure steamers can be provided with a clean source of

Figure 4–17
Convection steamers cook pans of food with steam within the closed steamer. Convection steams do not cook under pressure, and therefore can be opened anytime during the cooking process. This convection steamer is shown with three perforated hotel pans of food. Full-size hotel pans are 12 by 20 inches (30.5 by 50.8 centimeters). The perforations in the pans enable steam to pass through the pan to the cooking food.

facility steam, or may generate their own steam using gas or electricity to heat water and produce steam.

Refrigeration

Cold storage is necessary in the kitchen to hold foods below the danger zone (41°F/5°C) to promote food safety (see Chapter 2) and extend food storage (see Chapter 28). Freezers are colder than refrigerators and are able to store food for longer periods of time at a temperature usually of 0°F (−18°C).

In food services, refrigerators may be similar in size to a home refrigerator. These smaller units are commonly called "reach ins." Walk-in refrigerators and freezers are common to accommodate large amounts of food. These cold-storage units are called walk-ins because they are large enough to "walk-in." Walk-in cold-storage units can be a 10 feet by 10 feet (or approximately 3 meters by 3 meters) room or considerably larger depending on the size of the food service and need for cold storage.

Dishwashing

Dishes may be washed in a sink by hand, or in a dishwasher. In food services, dishes washed by hand must be washed in three sinks—wash, rinse, sanitize. Frequently, dishes in both food services and the home are washed with dishwashers. In food services, dishwashers vary greatly in size depending on the number of guests served and dishes to be washed. These dishwashers may be a rack-style, where one or two racks of dishes pass through the dishwasher at a time, or a "conveyer" machine. A conveyer dishwasher may be continuously loaded with dishes on the conveyer pegs. Racks of glasses and other types of items can also be placed on top of the conveyer to pass through the machine. Dishwashers in food services have mandated rinse temperatures (180°F/82°C) to sanitize the dishes or use chemicals in the final rinse to disinfect the dishes.

Using Tools and Equipment

As you develop skill in food preparation and an understanding of food science, knowing the most appropriate knife, tool, or piece of equipment will come naturally. There are many more pieces of equipment available for use in the home and commercially that have not been discussed in this chapter (see Chapter 5 for cookware). You are encouraged to learn how to use equipment to the best advantage to prepare high-quality food. In some cases, you may find that some functions are best done by hand, even though using a mixer or processor would complete the task quicker. Safe and efficient work in a kitchen includes knowing how to use tools and equipment.

WEIGHTS AND MEASURES

In the United States, recipes usually call for volume measurements. Tablespoons, cups, pints, and gallons are the units commonly used. In some food service operations and in other countries, however, ingredients may be more commonly weighed than measured. Weighing is generally more accurate than measuring. Consequently, weights are often used in bakeries because the need for accuracy is especially critical in baked goods. Some ingredients, such as flour, may pack down in the container [7], thereby resulting in inconsistent and thus inaccurate measurements. Weight per a specific volume can also vary with certain chopped foods, such as onions, depending on the fineness and uniformity of chopping before measuring.

Knowing measurement equivalents is beneficial so that recipes may be increased or decreased in size; or ingredients may be converted from measures to weights or vice versa. Some of the most frequently used U.S. customary measures are provided in **Table 4–1**. Additional measures, weights, and metric equivalencies may be found in Appendix A. It is important to realize that dry ingredients do not have the same **density** as liquids. For example, in U.S. standard weights, 1 cup of water equals 8 ounces. However, one cup of white flour equals only 4 ounces, and 1 cup of leaf tarragon is only 1 ounce [8]. Thus, if the recipe calls for weights, these units cannot be changed into measures or vice versa unless the appropriate conversion factor is known. Conversions are provided in books such as *Food for Fifty* [8].

Table 4–1
U.S. Customary Measurements and Fluid Weights

3 teaspoons (t. or tsp.) = ½ *fluid* ounce	
	= 1 tablespoon (T. or Tbsp.)
4 tablespoon = 2 *fluid* ounces = ¼ cup (c.)	
16 tablespoon = 1 cup (c.)	
1 cup = 8 *fluid* ounces = ½ pint	
2 cups = 16 *fluid* ounces = 1 pint	
4 cups = 32 *fluid* ounces = 1 quart	
16 cups = 128 *fluid ounces* = 4 quarts = 1 gallon	

Note: A fluid, such as water, will weigh 8 ounces per cup. These conversions cannot be used for dry ingredients, such as flour, spices, diced vegetables, and other similar ingredients.

Measuring Equipment

Liquid and Dry Measurements. Liquid measuring cups are designed with space above the liquid being measured. In contrast, a dry-measuring cup is designed for the dry ingredient to be filled completely to the top and then leveled off (**Figure 4–18**). For the best accuracy, the measuring cup (for liquid or dry) should be chosen based on the ingredient being measured. It is difficult to accurately measure dry ingredients in a liquid-measuring cup because leveling off is not possible.

In quantity food preparation, gallon measures (4-quart or 16-cup capacity) 1/2-gallon or 2-quart measures, and quart measures are commonly used. A glass liquid-measuring cup (1/2 pint or 8 fluid ounce) is usually used in home food preparation. Fractional dry-measuring cups and 1- and 2-cup measures are available in addition to measuring spoons.

Accuracy of Measuring Equipment. The American Association of Family and Consumer Sciences (previously called American Home Economics Association)

(a)　　　　(b)　　　　(c)

Figure 4–18

Household measuring utensils can be labeled with metric or U.S. customary units. (a) Measuring spoons. (b) Liquid-measuring cups are best for liquids such as milk, water, or vegetable oil. (c) Dry-measuring cups should be used for dry ingredients such as flour or sugar. The flat surface on dry-measuring cups enables the dry ingredient to be leveled with a straight knife or spatula.

Figure 4–19

Two types of scales, portion and balance, used to weigh ingredients accurately.

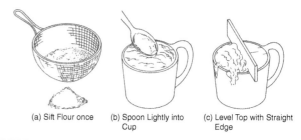

(a) Sift Flour once   (b) Spoon Lightly into Cup   (c) Level Top with Straight Edge

Figure 4–20

A recommended procedure for measuring white flour.

and the American National Standards Institute (previously called American Standards Association) published a set of standards and tolerances for household measuring utensils in 1963 [2]. These standards allow for a deviation of 5 percent from the precise measure indicated on the measuring utensil. Not all measuring utensils on the market meet the tolerance of 5 percent, however. The teaspoons and tablespoons that are part of flatware or silverware sets should not be trusted as accurate measurements.

A scale or balance can be used to weigh foods (**Figure 4–19**). To be accurate, the scale must be of good quality and may need to be periodically oiled and calibrated. Weighing is often more practical than measuring, in terms of time and convenience, when large quantities are involved. Weighing also is generally more accurate than measuring volumes, particularly for foods that tend to pack down, such as flours and chopped ingredients. However, scales are not routinely used in U.S. homes, and home-sized recipes are typically printed with measures.

Measurement of Staple Foods

Accurate and consistent measurement of ingredients is important in producing uniform products of high quality time after time [1]. Most recipes allow small deviations in the amounts of ingredients used, and acceptable products are still produced. However, the quality of some products, such as shortened cakes, may be adversely affected by different methods of measuring the flour [3].

Flour. To measure flour, sift, then spoon tablespoons of the flour lightly into a dry-measuring cup until the cup is heaping full. Then level the top of the filled cup with the straight edge of a spatula (**Figure 4–20**). Do not pack the flour by shaking the cup while filling or hitting it with the spoon. Quantities of less than 1 cup should be measured in the smaller fractional cups, such as 1/4, 1/3, or 1/2 cup. Likewise, when using measuring tablespoons or teaspoons, the spoon should be heaped full by dipping into the flour and then leveled with the straight edge of a spatula. Fractional measuring spoons should be used to measure half and quarter spoonfuls.

Solid Fats. Sticks of butter or margarine are typically measured by using the markings on the wrapper and cutting on the desired line with a sharp knife. To measure **plastic** fats, such as shortening, press the fat into a dry-measuring cup or measuring spoon with a spatula or knife so that air spaces are forced out. Then level the cup or fractional cup with a straight edge.

As an alternative, a water displacement method may be used if the water that clings to the fat does not affect the product. Pour cold water into a liquid-measuring cup up to the measure that will equal 1 cup when added to the amount of fat to be measured. Then add enough fat to bring the water up to 1 cup when the fat is completely submerged in the water. Finally, drain off the water.

Sugar. Granulated sugar is simply spooned into a dry-measuring cup and then leveled with the straight edge of a spatula. For brown sugar, any lumps should first be rolled out before the sugar is pressed into the cup firmly enough that it holds its shape when turned out of the cup. Measured in this way, 1 cup of brown sugar is approximately equal in mass to 1 cup of granulated sugar.

For the measurement of confectioners' or powdered sugar, sifting is followed by spooning the sugar into a cup, as for flour. Sifting the powdered sugar will remove any lumps. One cup of confectioners' sugar is slightly heavier than 1/2 cup of granulated sugar. About 1-3/4 cups of confectioners' sugar is equal in weight to 1 cup of granulated sugar.

Syrups. To measure syrups or molasses, place the cup or fractional cup on a flat surface and fill completely. Because syrups are thick, the liquid may tend to round up higher than full level on measuring cups or spoons. It should be leveled by cutting off with the straight edge of a spatula. To keep the syrup from sticking to the measuring cup or spoon, the empty measuring utensil may be lightly sprayed with a non-stick vegetable spray, provided that minute amounts of fat will not compromise the recipe.

Liquids. A liquid-measuring cup with a lip for pouring should be used for measuring liquids. Place the cup on a flat surface and fill to the desired measure mark. The eye should be at the level of the measure mark, when

---

UP CLOSE
WHY SIFT FLOUR?

In brief, flour is sifted to ensure accurate measurement and enable easy blending into the other ingredients.

Because most recipes are standardized for sifted flour, failure to sift flour will result in too much flour in the recipe. Unsifted flour is more tightly packed into the cup, and therefore more flour is in each cup. Flour is a difficult ingredient to measure consistently because it is composed of tiny particles of different sizes that tend to pack [3]. If unsifted white flour is substituted for sifted flour in a recipe standardized for sifted flour, the amount of flour may be adjusted by removing 2 level tablespoons from each cup of unsifted flour measured [7]. If weighing flour, 1 pound of flour will weigh 1 pound, regardless of whether it is sifted. When measuring other types of flour, issues to consider include the following:

- Graham or whole-wheat flours are usually not sifted before they are measured because the bran particles may be sifted out. Finely milled whole-wheat flour, however, may be sifted.

- Instantized flour, which contains agglomerated particles of quite uniform size, does not require sifting before being measured.

- The mass or weight of equal measures of white and whole-wheat flour also are not the same. One cup of whole-wheat flour weighs approximately 132 grams (4.4 ounces), whereas 1 cup of white flour weighs approximately 115 grams (3.8 ounces). ∎

---

reading the contents. In clear liquids, a **meniscus** can be seen at the upper surface as a curved concave line. The eye should read the lowest point of this meniscus (**Figure 4–21**). Some liquids, such as milk, honey, and corn syrup, do not form a meniscus and should therefore be measured at eye level where the liquid matches the desired measurement line. Liquid measuring cups are designed to accurately measure liquids and should not be used to measure dry ingredients.

The Metric System

During the French Revolution, France's lawmakers asked their scientists to develop a system of measurement based on science rather than custom. The result was the metric system, which has since been adopted by most of the nations of the world. The metric system is a decimal system based on multiples of 10. The basic unit of length is the meter, which is slightly longer than

a yard. Each unit of measure may be divided by 10 for the next smaller unit of measurement. Thus, 1 meter equals 1,000 millimeters, or 100 centimeters or 10 decimeters. The same prefixes are combined with the basic unit of **mass** or weight (gram) and the basic unit of volume or capacity (liter) to indicate designated amounts. Prefixes and symbols for mass, volume, and length are shown in **Table 4–2**. Other units and symbols associated with the metric system are given in **Table 4–3**.

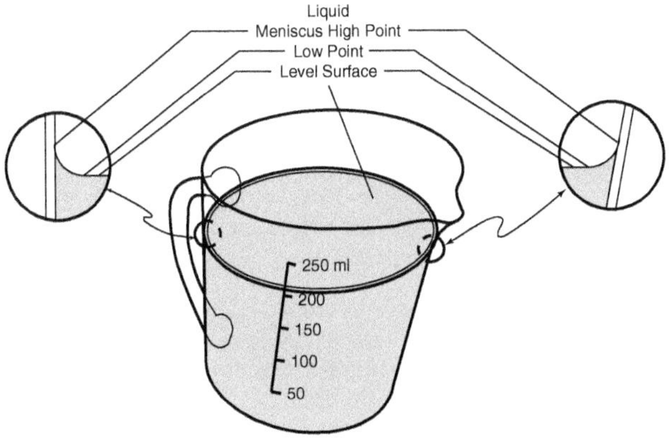

Conversion to Metric

The United States is one of the very few nations in the world that has not fully converted to metric [9]. A change in the United States from the U.S. customary system of weights and measures to the metric system was recommended and became public policy with passage of the Metric Conversion Act of 1975. The change to metric was to be voluntary; however, the conversion process moved slowly. In 1988, an amendment to the 1967 Fair Packaging and Labeling Act required that manufacturers show both U.S. customary and metric designations on most consumer products. Some metric containers, such as 1-liter soft drink bottles, are being used, but most food packages are labeled with the U.S. customary weight first and then the metric weight.

Metric and Recipes

The conversion of recipes using U.S. customary measures to metric measurements will require recipe testing and standardization to accommodate metric measuring cups and spoons. Metric measures are available in various equivalents of 1-liter and 500- and 250-milliliter capacities. Metric measuring spoons are available in 1 milliliter, 2 milliliters, 5 milliliters, and 15 milliliters. One cup converts to 237 milliliters; however,

Figure 4–21

When measuring clear liquids, read the meniscus at the lowest point.

Table 4–2
THE METRIC SYSTEM—PREFIXES AND SYMBOLS

	Prefix	Mass	Symbol	Volume	Symbol	Length	Symbol
0.000001	micro-	microgram	μg	microliter	μL	micrometer	μm
0.001	milli-	milligram	mg	milliliter	mL	millimeter	mm
0.01	centi-	centigram	cg	centiliter	cL	centimeter	cm
0.1	deci-	decigram	dg	deciliter	dL	decimeter	dm
1.0		gram	g	liter	L	meter	m
10	deka-	dekagram	dag	dekaliter	daL	dekameter	dam
100	hecto-	hectogram	hg	hectoliter	hL	hectometer	hm
1,000	kilo-	kilogram	kg	kiloliter	kL	kilometer	km

Table 4–3
SOME METRIC UNITS AND SYMBOLS

	Unit	Symbol
Energy	Joule	J
Temperature	Degree Celsius	°C
Pressure	Pascal	Pa
Frequency	Hertz	Hz
Power	Watt	W

Table 4–4
SELECTED U.S. CUSTOMARY AND METRIC EQUIVALENT WEIGHTS AND MEASURES

U.S. Customary	Metric
Measures	
1 teaspoon	4.9 milliliters
1 tablespoon	14.8 milliliters
1 cup	237 milliliters
1 quart	946 milliliters, or 0.946 liter
1.06 quarts	1 liter, or 1,000 milliliters
Weights	
0.035 ounce	1 gram
1 ounce	28.35 grams
1 pound	0.454 kilogram
2.2 pounds	1 kilogram

it would be more practical to use the 250-milliliter measure. Depending on the recipe, the small differences in amount from 237 milliliters (1 cup) to 250 milliliters could affect the final product. Therefore, standardization of each converted recipe is necessary.

Although the change to metric initially would offer some challenges, a strong benefit will be greater ease when adjusting recipes to smaller or larger sizes. Compared to the U.S. customary units, the conversions from ounces to pounds, tablespoons to cups, cups to gallons, and so forth will no longer be necessary because the metric system is based on multiples of 10. Selected equivalent weights or measurements between U.S. customary units and metrics are found in **Table 4–4**. A more comprehensive listing of conversions is found in Appendix A. Charts for changing Fahrenheit and Celsius temperatures and formulas for these conversions are given in Appendix B.

UP CLOSE
METRIC IN THE U.S. MARKETPLACE

Metric measurements may be found on packages sold in the U.S. marketplace. The metric measurement labeling may be a *soft conversion* or a *hard conversion*.

Soft Conversion

When the container is sized and labeled in U.S. customary units followed by metric, this is a soft conversion. For example, the label on a 1.5-quart bottle of fruit juice may read "48 fl. oz. (1-1/2 qts.) 1.42 L." Home measuring cups also often provide both U.S. customary and metric units of measurement and are another example of a soft conversion. The U.S. cups, quarter cups, and so forth are provided on one side of the measuring cup with the metric units provided on the other side.

Hard Conversion

When containers and packages are actually designed for the metric system with the U.S. customary units provided after the metric measurement as a conversion quantity, this is a hard conversion. For example, many soft drinks are now being marketed in 1-, 2-, or 3-liter bottles. ■

RECIPES

A recipe lists the ingredients and the procedure for preparing a food product. Recipes may be found from a variety of sources, such as cookbooks, friends and family, or the Internet. Comparing a recipe to other similar recipes will help to predict if the recipe is likely to provide good results. When using recipes from the Internet, you should assess the credibility of the source. You also may develop your own special dishes over time through experimentation in the kitchen. The study of food science will provide a foundation of knowledge on the ingredient functions that will enable you to adjust recipe ingredients successfully to suit your particular tastes or nutritional preferences.

Recipe Styles

To be effective, the recipe must be written simply and clearly so that it is easily understood. Four general styles of written recipes [1] are common. These styles include the following:

- *Standard Style.* Ingredients are listed in the order used. Following the ingredient listing, the method of combining ingredients is provided in either step or paragraph form.
- *Action Style.* The narrative describing the action or method is interspersed with the listing of ingredients. The action or method and ingredients are provided in the order to be followed when preparing the recipe.
- *Descriptive Style.* These recipes are presented in a column format. Ingredients, ingredient quantity, and procedure are each in a column. The ingredient listing includes a description of any modification necessary such as *sifted* flour or *sliced* carrots.
- *Narrative Style.* The amounts of ingredients and the method are combined in narrative. This recipe style is best for very short recipes with few ingredients and brief instructions.

Regardless of the recipe style, a few key points in presenting recipes need to be followed:

1. Ingredients, as well as instructions, should be provided in the order of preparation. Do not list an ingredient first that is to be used at the very end of the recipe preparation.
2. Ingredients must be clearly described. For example, if an onion is needed, should it be white, yellow, or another variety of onion? Is it to be sliced, diced, or coarsely chopped? Are ingredients such as meats and vegetables to be prepared before or after measuring? For example, does it use 1 pound of cooked ground beef or 1 pound of raw ground beef? Likewise with vegetables, is it a purchased quantity (1 pound of potatoes) or prepared quantity (1 pound of peeled potatoes)? Food service recipes will often designate an ingredient as AP (as purchased) to indicate the meat is raw, the potatoes are unpeeled, and so forth. If the ingredient amount is a prepared or cooked quantity, the recipe may state EP (edible portion).
3. Instructions should be clearly understood by another person unfamiliar with the recipe. The audience for the recipe should be considered. Many will understand culinary terminology, whereas others may need an explanation for cooking terms, such as fold, blanch, and poach.
4. Provide food safety recommendations, such as "Cook chicken to a minimum internal temperature of 165°F (74°C) throughout."
5. Provide the recipe yield. For example, four 1/2-cup servings.
6. Pan sizes, oven temperatures, and cooking times should be given.

Standardization and Recipe Adjustment

A recipe is considered standardized only after it has been tried and evaluated for quality and any necessary adaptations or adjustments have been made. Equipment, types of ingredients available, and skill of the person preparing the recipe differ from one situation to another. Therefore, each recipe must be adapted and standardized for use in a particular situation. Once a recipe has been standardized, it is useful for making grocery and purchase orders and calculating food costs or nutritional content. Recipes that are standardized for inclusion in cookbooks generally use the methods for measuring ingredients outlined earlier in this chapter. Recipes with eggs are generally standardized using large eggs.

Factor Method of Recipe Adjustment. Recipe yields may need to be adjusted to meet individual situations. In enlarging home-size recipes for quantity use, it is best to first prepare the recipe and evaluate the result to be sure that it produces an acceptable product. Then the recipe may be adjusted for a larger or smaller yield by using the *factor method*. Many restaurant and home cooks increase or decrease recipe yields by the factor method. However, when the recipe yield is changed by a large factor, inaccuracies can occur because the relative proportions of the ingredients change, and therefore product failure can occur [6].

The steps in adjusting a recipe using the factor method are as follows:

1. Divide the *desired* number of portions by the *current* recipe yield to obtain a factor to use for the increase or decrease of the recipe. When decreasing a recipe, the factor is less than one; when increasing, the factor is greater than one.

   If desired portions = 32 and current portions = 8, then 32/8 = 4.

FOUR BASIC STANDARDIZED RECIPE STYLES

Standard Recipe Style

1 cup sifted all-purpose flour
2 Tbsp granulated sugar
1 tsp baking powder
1/4 tsp salt
1/4 cup shortening (at room temperature)
(And so on).

1. Preheat oven to 350°F (177°C).
2. Sift dry ingredients together into mixing bowl.
3. Add shortening (And so on).

Action Recipe Style

Measure and sift together in a mixing bowl:
1 cup sifted flour
2 Tbsp sugar
1 tsp baking powder
1/4 tsp salt

Add:
1/4 cup shortening (And so on).

Descriptive Recipe Style

Flour, all-purpose, sifted	1 cup	Sift dry ingredients together in mixing bowl.
Sugar, granulated	2 Tbsp	
Baking powder	1 tsp	
Salt	1/4 tsp	
Shortening	1/4 cup	Add to dry ingredients.

(And so on).

Narrative Style

Sift all-purpose flour once. Measure 1 cup sifted flour, 2 Tbsp granulated sugar, 1 tsp baking powder, and 1/4 tsp salt. Sift all dry ingredients together in a mixing bowl. Add 1/4 cup shortening. (And so on).

Narrative style is best used with a recipe with few ingredients such as this recipe:

Thaw 2 pounds of frozen fish fillets. Cut into serving-size pieces. Place on broiler rack. Brush with melted butter or margarine. (And so on). ■

---

2. Multiply each ingredient measurement by the factor and convert to appropriate units of measure.
   4×1 cup = 4 cups or 1 quart
   4×1 tablespoon = 4 tablespoons or 1/4 cup
3. Check your calculations for accuracy.

Percentage Method of Recipe Adjustment. Probably the most accurate method for yield adjustment, particularly when large volumes are involved, is called the *percentage method* [8]. When using the percentage method, if an ingredient, for example, is 25 percent of the recipe by weight, it will always be 25 percent by weight regardless of the amount of increase or decrease of the recipe. The steps in adjusting a recipe using the percentage method are as follows:

1. All ingredient measurements must be in weights.
2. Add weight of each ingredient and total to obtain a total recipe weight.

Ingredient A	8 ounces (or 0.5 pound)
Ingredient B	+1 pound
Ingredient C	+4 ounces (or .25 pound)
Total recipe weight	= 1 pound and 12 ounces (or 1.75 pounds)

3. Calculate the percentage of each ingredient weight in relation to the total recipe weight by dividing the ingredient weight by the total recipe weight.

Ingredient A   0.5 pound/1.75 pounds = 28.6 percent

4. Recipe increases and decreases can be made by multiplying the *desired* total recipe weight (yield) by the percentage of each ingredient.

If a total recipe weight of 5 pounds is desired, then

Ingredient A   5 pounds $\times$ 28.6 percent = 1.43 pounds

5. To check accuracy of calculations, total the new weight of each ingredient. This total should equal the new recipe weight, which in this example is 5 pounds.
6. The use of the percentage method is best used with digital scales, so conversions of fractions of pounds do not need to be recalculated into pounds and ounces.

Baker's Percentage. Professional bakers use a baker's percentage in the calculation of recipes. Baker's percentages for ingredients are based on the total weight of flour in the recipe instead of the total weight of all ingredients. As a first step in determining the baker's percentages, the weight of all flour in the recipe is set at 100 percent. Next, the weight of each ingredient is divided by the weight of the flour and multiplied by 100 percent to provide the baker's percentage [4].

STUDY QUESTIONS

Knives, Hand Tools, and Small Equipment

1. Identify the purpose for which each of the following knives is best used: French/chef's, utility, paring, slicer, serrated, and butcher's.

2. Explain how to grasp a knife and how to hold food when cutting or slicing.

3. Identify the advantages and disadvantages of the three materials commonly used for knife blades.

4. Explain how to sharpen a knife and describe the tools that are used.

5. Identify the purpose for each of the following tools: (a) perforated, slotted, and solid spoons; (b) whisks; (c) ladles; and (d) portion scoops or dishers.

6. Create a brief public service announcement to encourage households to have a fire extinguisher available, and explain the difference in type A, B, and C extinguishers.

7. Compare and contrast colander, strainer, china cap, and chinois.

Large Equipment

8. Discuss differences between gas and electric ranges.

9. Explain how each of the following ovens are similar to or different from others: (a) traditional electric or gas oven, (b) convection oven, (c) stack oven, or (d) reel oven.

10. Provide specific recommendations for cooking time and temperatures when using a convection oven.

11. Explain how a deep-fat fryer cooks food and identify if this is a "dry" or "moist" method of cooking.

12. Explain how steam jacket kettles heat food, and identify reasons why these kettles can be advantageous in a food service.

13. Discuss the differences between the two types of steamers that may be used in food services.

14. Describe a food service walk-in refrigerator and a reach-in refrigerator.

15. Explain two ways that dishwashers may sanitize dishes.

Weights, Volume Measures, and Measurement Techniques Used in Food Preparation

16. Discuss why accurate measurements are important in the preparation of quality food products.

17. Identify the type of measuring cups to be used to measure liquids. What type of measuring cup should be used to measure dry ingredients? Explain.

18. Identify the measurement equivalencies.
    (a) 1 cup equals ____ tablespoons
    (b) 3 teaspoons equals ____ tablespoon(s)
    (c) 1 cup equals ____ fluid ounces
    (d) 1 quart equals ____ cups ____ fluid ounces
    (e) 1 gallon equals ____ quarts ____ pints ____ cups ____ fluid ounces

19. Explain how to measure a dry ingredient such as flour in a recipe that states 8 ounces of flour, if you do not have a scale to weigh the flour.
    (a) State if the weight of 1 cup of flour is equal to the weight of 1 cup of water.
    (b) Discuss why you can or cannot convert the weight of any dry ingredient (such as flour) to measures using the conversion of 1 cup is equal to 8 fluid ounces.

20. Describe appropriate procedures for measuring flour, liquid, solid fat, sugar, and syrups.

Metric as Compared to U.S. Customary Measures and Weights

21. (a) Describe the metric system of measurement.
    (b) Identify advantages as well as challenges to a change from U.S. customary measurements to the metric system in the United States.
    (c) Name the basic metric units for length, volume or capacity, and weight or mass. Identify what is indicated by the prefixes *deci-*, *centi-*, *milli-*, and *micro*.
    (d) Explain *soft conversion* and *hard conversion* to the metric system by using examples of foods available for purchase.

Recipes and Recipe Standardization

22. Describe what is necessary for a recipe to be standardized, and discuss why standardized recipes are important.

23. Identify three methods of recipe yield adjustment and explain how they are used. Identify which method is most accurate when large changes in yield are to be calculated.

24. Describe several styles of written recipes and discuss the advantages of each.

5
Heat Transfer in Cooking

Cooking or heating foods causes changes that impact sensory qualities as well as other characteristics. Many foods are more palatable when cooked. Cooking results when heat is transferred to or produced in a food and then distributed throughout.

Heat is a form of energy that results from the rapid movement or vibration of **molecules** within a substance. This movement of molecules is called *kinetic energy*. With the use of a thermometer, we can measure the average intensity of the heat resulting from the molecular movement within a substance. We record heat as *temperature*.

As the molecules move, they constantly collide with other molecules in the same substance or with molecules of another substance with which they come into contact. As molecules collide, their speed of movement may be changed. Rapidly moving molecules striking slower-moving molecules transfer some of their energy to the slower-moving ones. Thus, heat energy is transferred from a warmer substance to a cooler one. In cooking, heat is transferred to food.

In this chapter, the following will be discussed:

- Why cook food?
- Measurement of temperature
- Heat involved in change of state
- Types of heat transfer
- Media for heat transfer
- Induction cooking
- Microwave cooking

WHY COOK FOOD?

There are several important reasons for cooking food. Edible and safe foods are essential outcomes of cooking. Additionally, cooking improves the digestibility and, therefore, the nutritive value of some foods. Cooking also enhances the aesthetic appeal of many foods.

Food Safety and Shelf Life

Proper cooking destroys most **pathogenic microorganisms** that may be present in raw foods (see Chapter 2) or natural toxins (phytohaemagglutinin) as found in raw kidney beans. The risk for a foodborne illness can be significant when consuming some foods without cooking to recommended endpoint temperatures (see Chapter 2). **Pasteurization** is essentially a mild cooking process with carefully controlled times and temperatures. It is used to destroy pathogenic microorganisms in milk as well as in some other food products such as eggs.

The keeping quality, or shelf life, of some foods is extended by cooking. For example, very perishable fresh peaches or other fruits keep longer if cooked. Canned foods (see Chapter 28) may be stored much longer than fresh foods because of the high heat processing and protection from contamination in the sealed can.

Making Foods Edible

Cooking is needed to make some basic staple foods, such as dry legumes and whole grains, edible. These products are not edible as harvested and must be **rehydrated** and softened so that the raw starch is made more palatable and digestible. For baked goods, a remarkable transformation occurs because of cooking. Flour mixtures change in flavor, color, and texture when baked or cooked, thereby resulting in tender cakes, crisp cookies, or chewy brownies.

Digestibility and Nutritive Value

Digestibility and nutritive value may, in some cases, be increased by cooking. Starch in cooked grain products and legumes becomes more readily available to digestive enzymes than that in compact raw **starch granules**. Some anti-digestive factors in dry beans and peas are also destroyed by heating. Of course, cooking may bring about decreases in nutritive value as well. For instance, some loss of vitamins and minerals occurs when vegetables and meats are cooked. Nutrient losses can be reduced by avoiding overcooking and using minimal water when preparing foods high in water-soluble vitamins.

Aesthetic Appeal

Finally, let us not forget that food is to be enjoyed. Cooking foods makes possible the creation of many new delectable dishes, greatly increasing variety and interest in dining. Flavor, **texture**, and color of foods are affected by the cooking process. New flavors are formed by heating, as when meats are browned, breads are baked, and sugars are caramelized. Alternatively, undesirable flavors, textures, or colors may be caused by overcooking of foods.

Texture is often softened by cooking—the fiber of vegetables and connective tissue of meat become more tender. Some foods, however, become crisp on cooking (such as bacon, potato chips, and other fried foods). Eggs, both whites and yolks, become more firm on heating. The entire character of a texture may be changed by cooking. Note the great difference in texture between a cake batter and the finished cake or between bread dough and the baked loaf. A pudding or sauce, containing starch, thickens with sufficient heating.

Color changes occur during cooking as well. Bright green vegetables turn dull and drab when they are overcooked or cooked with acid, whereas a short **blanching** period usually brightens the color of fresh green peas or beans. Rich brown gravy is made from drippings that have browned during the roasting of meat. Light brown crusts on baked goods enhance their eye appeal and improve flavor and texture characteristics. Thus, the effects of cooking on food are truly diverse and, in many cases, highly desirable.

MEASUREMENT OF TEMPERATURE

Thermometers are used to measure *sensible heat*—that which can be felt by the senses. Two thermometer scales commonly may be used to indicate the temperature of a substance. The Fahrenheit scale (F) is used in the United States in connection with the U.S. customary system of weights and measures. The Celsius (or Centigrade) scale (C) is used in most other nations and is used for scientific research in the United States.

Using the Fahrenheit scale, water at sea level freezes at 32° and boils at 212°. On the Celsius scale, water freezes at 0° and boils at 100°. The usual room temperature of 72°F is 22° on the Celsius scale (**Figure 5–1**). This formula

$$1.8(°C) = (°F) -32$$

may be used for conversions from Celsius to Fahrenheit and vice versa [1]. Conversion charts also may be found in Appendix B.

HEAT INVOLVED IN CHANGE OF STATE

A substance may exist as a solid, a liquid, or a gas. When a substance, such as water, changes from a solid to a liquid or from a liquid to a gas, we say that a *change of state* occurs. The physical state of the matter—solid, liquid, or gas—has changed. Energy is involved in this change of state and causes molecules to move more rapidly.

Change of State of Water

Water is being used here as an example of change of state because water is commonly used as a medium for applying heat in food preparation. Water changes from ice to water and then to steam with the addition of heat (**Figure 5–2**).

Solid. The solid form of water is ice. In a chunk of ice, the water molecules have formed an ordered crystalline pattern and are held in a fixed arrangement in relation to each other. In a solid such as ice, the molecules may vibrate in place but do not move around freely.

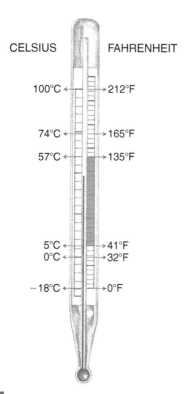

CELSIUS   FAHRENHEIT

100°C → 212°F
74°C → 165°F
57°C → 135°F
5°C → 41°F
0°C → 32°F
−18°C → 0°F

Figure 5–1

Two thermometer scales are used in measuring temperature: the Fahrenheit and the Celsius. At sea level water boils at 212°F (100°C), whereas water freezes at 32°F (0°C). The temperature danger zone supports the rapid growth of bacteria and is shown here to be 41°F (5°C) to 135°F (57°C).

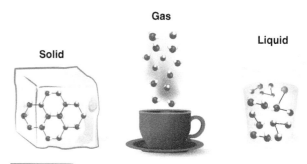

Figure 5–2

Heat changes the state: ice (a solid) to water (a liquid), then to steam (a gas). These diagrams show the structure of the molecules in each, from an ordered crystalline pattern (ice) to the free movement of molecules in a container (water), to widely separated molecules free to move in space (steam).

FOCUS ON SCIENCE

WHY DOES IT TAKE LONGER TO COOK CERTAIN FOODS IN THE ROCKY MOUNTAINS OR OTHER HIGH-ELEVATION LOCATIONS?

Water boils at 212°F (100°C), right? Actually if you are cooking at a high-altitude location such as Denver, Colorado, water will boil *before* 212°F (100°C). Bottom line—water boils at a lower temperature in high-elevation areas.

Because Denver is at a high altitude, the external pressure (atmospheric pressure) on the water is decreased. At high altitudes, less energy is needed to break the water molecules free from the bonded energy. If it takes less energy, less heat is needed. If less heat is required, less temperature is required, and the water will boil at a lower temperature. Therefore, food cooked in boiling water, like pasta or rice, will take longer to cook because it is cooking at a lower temperature than at sea level.

Liquid. Ice melts and becomes liquid water when heat is applied. Heat causes the water molecules to vibrate more rapidly and push against each other. In a liquid, the molecules have broken away from each other and are free to move about; however, they remain together and take the shape of the container in which they are placed.

Gas. Water vapor and steam are both examples of the gaseous form of water. The molecules in a gas are widely separated and move freely in space. When liquid water stands in an open container, some of its molecules vaporize, or become gas, even at room temperature. This phenomenon can be observed when a glass of water, if left uncovered at room temperature, eventually becomes empty. The evaporation of water from a glass is an example of the conversion from liquid water to water vapor at room temperature. The random motion of the water molecules in this example was sufficient to allow escape into the atmosphere.

Boiling of Water. When water is very hot or boiling, steam (the gaseous form of water) comes from the surface. To understand the boiling of water, both atmospheric pressure and vapor pressure need to be defined. **Atmospheric pressure** is the downward pressure from the atmosphere (the gas surrounding the earth). Atmospheric pressure is greater at lower elevations (sea level) as compared to high elevations (mountains) (**Figure 5–3**).

Vapor pressure is the pressure caused by gaseous molecules hovering over the surface of liquid water (**Figure 5–4**). As liquid water is heated, more gaseous molecules form, thus increasing the vapor pressure. When the vapor pressure is equal or slightly greater than atmospheric pressure, bubbles formed in the liquid water will begin to break at the surface. We term this breaking of bubbles as simmering or boiling (**Figure 5–5**) depending on how rapidly the bubbles are breaking the surface. The equalization of the vapor pressure and the atmospheric pressure allows boiling and also the release of steam.

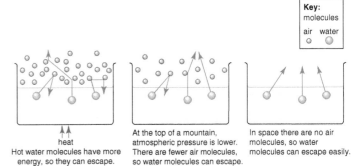

Key:
molecules
air   water
○   ●

heat
Hot water molecules have more energy, so they can escape.

At the top of a mountain, atmospheric pressure is lower. There are fewer air molecules, so water molecules can escape.

In space there are no air molecules, so water molecules can escape easily.

Figure 5–3

Heat adds energy to water molecules to result in boiling. At higher elevations, there is less atmospheric pressure and therefore water molecules can escape easily. Water boils at a lower temperature at high elevations than sea level because of less atmospheric pressure.

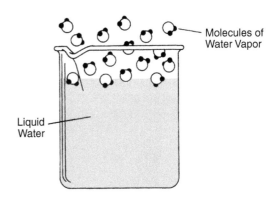

Molecules of Water Vapor

Liquid Water

Figure 5–4

Vapor pressure is the pressure produced over the surface of a liquid, such as water, as a result of escape of some of the liquid molecules into the vapor or gaseous state. This process causes water to gradually disappear or evaporate from an open container even at room temperature.

Figure 5–5

Bubbles in boiling water can be observed in this photo. (Steven Coling/123RF)

Low Atmospheric Pressure versus High Atmospheric Pressure. In the United States, there are a number of cities near or below sea level in areas such as Florida, Louisiana, and the Death Valley in California. In contrast, Denver, Colorado, at 5280 feet (1609 meters) is a mile above sea level. These elevations impact heat transfer and cooking.

At sea level, the temperature at which water boils is 212°F (100°C). At altitudes higher than sea level, the boiling point of water is 1°C (1.8°F) lower for each 900 feet of elevation. Thus, in Denver, Colorado, water will boil at approximately 202°F (94°C). Water boils at lower temperatures at higher elevations because the atmospheric pressure is lower at higher elevations. As a consequence, food must be cooked longer in mountainous regions because it is the temperature, not the boiling action, that influences the cooking time.

Pressure cookers (**Figure 5–6**) cause the buildup of vapor pressure to levels greater than the atmospheric pressure, thereby increasing the boiling point of water to above 212°F (100°C). Thus, foods cook faster in a pressure cooker because higher temperatures are possible than boiling range top. As discussed

Figure 5–6

A pressure canner is necessary to obtain temperatures higher than 212°F (100°C). (Oligo/Shutterstock)

in Chapter 28, pressure cookers are used in canning low-acid foods, because to produce safe-to-eat canned foods, a temperature of 240°F (115°C) is required. At high elevations, longer processing times are also necessary because of the difference in temperatures obtained at high altitudes.

Heat Capacity of Water

Liquid water has a relatively large capacity to absorb heat. In fact, it is used as a standard for measuring the heat capacities of other substances. Water has been assigned a heat capacity of 1.00, called its *specific heat,* which indicates that one **calorie** is required to increase the temperature of 1 gram of water to 1°C. Thus, to take 100 grams of water (about 2/5 cup) from 0°C (32°F) to boiling at 100°C (212°F), 10,000 calories of heat or energy are required. To calculate these calories, the following is used:

1 calorie per gram per degree, therefore 1 calorie × 100 grams × 100 degrees = 10,000 calories.

FOCUS ON SCIENCE
BOILING WATER

To boil water requires energy, and this energy is in the form of heat, which may be introduced by gas flame, electrical, solar, burning wood, and so on. Energy has been introduced into the water to such a point that the bonding energy between the water molecules has exceeded the bond threshold and they have broken away and coalesced into steam.

Water boils at an extremely high temperature for its molecular size because of the extensive network of hydrogen bonds. The hydrogen (H) bonds are cohesive forces—these forces want to hold the water molecules together. Furthermore, there are a number of these bonds. The process of boiling requires that molecules come apart, and this process takes more energy than expected. Additionally, another result of the hydrogen bonding network is that water has a very high specific heat. Once heated, water takes a long time to cool off. Or, in reverse, it takes a good deal of heat to make water hot. These are *small* calories; 1,000 of these equal 1 kilocalorie, which is the unit used in nutrition.

Latent Heat

Up until this point, the focus has been on *sensible heat*, or heat that can be measured with a thermometer. Heat or energy that is required to change the physical state without changing temperature is called *latent heat*. This "hidden" heat or energy cannot be measured by a thermometer. This latent heat is necessary, however, to change ice to water, and then water to steam.

Latent Heat of Fusion and Solidification. The energy or heat required or released to change the state of ice to water or alternatively water to ice are named the latent heat of fusion and solidification (**Figure 5–7**).

Latent Heat of Fusion. For each gram of ice that changes to liquid water, 80 calories of latent heat are needed even though the temperature remains at 32°F (0°C). These 80 calories of energy are absorbed by the melting ice and used to break up the ordered molecules of water in the ice structure. Heat absorbed during a change from solid to liquid state is called *latent heat of fusion*. The latent heat of fusion is utilized when freezing ice cream using an ice-and-salt mixture. As the ice melts, the heat necessary for bringing about this change of state is taken from the ice cream mixture to be frozen, thus making the ice cream colder. Cold is really the absence of heat. The addition of salt to ice causes more rapid melting of the ice and a greater rate of heat absorption from the ice cream mix, which enables the freezing of ice cream in home-style ice cream makers (see Chapter 10). Although too low of a temperature for making ice cream, a mixture of one part salt to three parts ice, by weight, will result in a temperature of −6°F (−21°C).

Latent Heat of Solidification. When energy is released during the change of a liquid to a solid, it is called the *latent heat of solidification*. The same amount of energy as needed to change ice to water—

Figure 5–7

For each gram of ice converted to water, while remaining at 32°F (0°C), 80 calories per gram are necessary. The heat absorbed to cause this change in state is called latent heat of fusion. (Jagcz/123RF)

Figure 5–8

For each gram of water turned into steam, while remaining at 212°F (100°C) at sea level, 540 calories of heat are needed. This is the latent heat of vaporization. (Toa55/123RF)

80 calories per gram—is released from the liquid water as it freezes and forms solid ice crystals.

Latent Heat of Vaporization and Condensation. The energy or heat required or released to change the state of water to steam or alternatively steam to water are named the latent heat of vaporization and condensation (**Figure 5–8**).

Latent Heat of Vaporization. When liquid water changes to a gas in the form of water vapor or steam, the energy absorbed is called *latent heat of vaporization*. For each gram of water vaporized at the boiling point (212°F/100°C), 540 calories are absorbed to produce steam at 212°F (100°C). The energy of latent heat does not change the temperature but is necessary to bring about the wide separation of water molecules from each other as they form a gas.

Latent Heat of Condensation. In the reverse process—the condensation of steam to liquid water—the same amount of energy is released. This release of energy is called the *latent heat of condensation*. We take advantage of this released heat when we steam foods. As steam touches the cooler surface of the food, it condenses to liquid and releases the 540 calories per gram of water condensed. This energy is absorbed by the food, thus actually aiding in the cooking process. It is this same energy absorption that accounts for the severity of steam burns when our skin comes in contact with steam.

TYPES OF HEAT TRANSFER

Conventional cooking methods transfer heat energy from its source to the food by means of conduction, convection currents, and radiation (**Figure 5–9**). In most cooking methods, more than one means of heat transfer is involved. Some cooktops may be specially

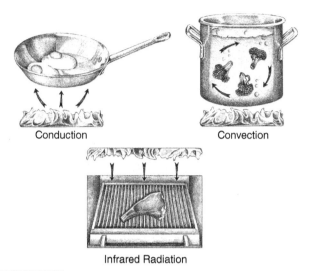

Figure 5–9

Arrows indicate heat patterns during conduction, convection, and infrared radiation.

Figure 5–10

Various styles of cookware allow for a variety of preparation methods.

designed to cook by magnetic induction, whereas microwave ovens utilize electromagnetic waves of radiant energy to heat food. Cooking using induction and microwaves will be discussed later in the chapter.

Conduction

Conduction is the transmission of heat through direct contact from one molecule or particle to the next one. Heat moves from the heated coil of an electric unit, the touching flame of a gas unit, or other heat sources to the saucepan placed on it and from the saucepan to the first layer of food, water, or fat in contact with the bottom and sides of the pan. Heat is then conducted throughout the mass of the food in the pan the same way, particle by particle.

Although the process of conduction is similar for both fat and water, fat can be heated to a much higher temperature than water; thus, it is possible to bring more heat into the pan during the frying process. Water boils at 212°F (100°C) at sea level, but it is common to fry foods at about 375°F (190°C).

Quality of Materials for Conduction. Materials used in the construction of cookware vary in their ability to conduct heat efficiently. Metals, glass, ceramic, and silicone are materials often used for cook- and bakeware. All types of pans conduct heat most effectively when the bottom surface is flat and therefore has complete contact with the source of heat.

Metals. Metals that are good conductors in order starting with the best include copper, aluminum, and iron. Aluminum pans may be either cast aluminum or aluminum formed from sheets. Although copper is an excellent conductor, it reacts with alkaline and acidic foods. Therefore, the food contact surface of a copper

pan is usually another metal, such as stainless steel. Cast-iron does not conduct heat as well as copper and aluminum; however, it holds heat well and is an acceptably good conductor. Iron cookware is heavy and must be seasoned with oil to maintain a nonstick surface (**Figure 5–10**).

Stainless steel is an alloy of iron with a small percentage of carbon and other metals, such as chromium and nickel. Stainless steel does not conduct heat as well as copper, aluminum, and iron. Stainless steel is a very durable, easily cleaned metal, and therefore is often used for cookware. To improve the conductivity of stainless steel pans, it is often combined in various ways with other metals to improve heating efficiency and eliminate "hot spots." For example, the heating base of a stainless steel pan may be clad with copper or aluminum, or a core of iron or other high-conductivity metal may be placed between the sheets of stainless steel used to form the pan.

Glass and Ceramic. Heat-resistant glass (such as Pyrex® or Anchor Hocking®) or ceramic materials (such as CorningWare®) offer some advantages as cookware but are not as effective in conducting heat as other materials. Glass cookware does allow radiant heat to travel through the glass, and for this reason when baking in glass pans, reducing the oven temperature by 25°F (3°C) is recommended. Unlike metal cookware, glass and ceramic cookware without metal trim may be used in a microwave oven.

Silicone. Silicone bakeware comes in a variety of colors, is flexible, and has been described as being nonstick if oiled or sprayed with vegetable oil. Silicone conducts heat less readily than copper and aluminum. Researchers compared silicone cake and muffin pans to aluminum counterparts [2, 3]. The bottom and sides of cakes baked in silicone pans were less brown than those baked in aluminum pans [3]. The researchers attributed this difference in browning to the lower heat transfer rate in the silicone pans. The cakes baked in silicone had an increased volume, also likely a result of the slower heat transfer, and thus slower crust development. Researchers also compared silicone muffin pans and observed similar findings to the cake studies in relation to pale bottom and side crust color, and greater muffin volume. However, excessive sticking of the muffins in the silicone pans was observed as compared to similarly treated aluminum pans [2].

Convection

Convection is the transfer of heat through air or liquid currents caused by the movement of different temperature areas of the gas or liquid (Figure 5–9). When gases and liquids are heated, they become lighter or less dense and tend to rise. The colder portions of these gases and liquids are more dense or heavier and move to the bottom. The lighter air rises and cooler, heavier air moves to the bottom, thus setting up circular convection currents.

Convection currents move the molecules around and tend to distribute the heat uniformly throughout. Examples of the usefulness of these currents is evident in the preparation of foods in water, in fat (deep-fat frying), or hot air (baking in an oven). When foods are simmered or boiled in water or deep-fat fried, convection currents move the heated water or fat molecules up and around the food, thereby transferring heat. The heat is then also transferred into the interior of the food by conduction.

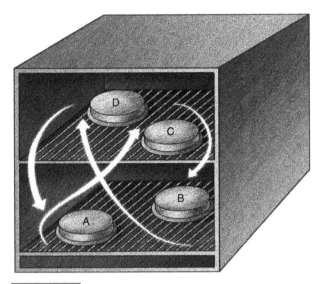

Figure 5–11

Convection currents move heated air around cake surfaces to aid in baking and browning.

Figure 5–12

Muffins are baking in this convection oven. Look carefully to see the large fan on the back of the oven that circulates air to contribute even heat. (Bacho12345/123RF)

In oven baking, without the presence of a convection fan, heated gas molecules of air rise from the energy source in the bottom and move around the surfaces of the baking containers. This movement helps in the browning of the tops of baked products and other foods. Placement of containers in the oven is important to take full advantage of convection currents in cooking and browning. When it is necessary to use two racks, the pans should be staggered so that one is not directly underneath the other (**Figure 5–11**) to allow for air movement.

A convection oven employs a mechanical fan that increases air movement in the oven during baking, thus increasing the efficiency of heat transfer and decreasing cooking time. Convection ovens are common in food services and are becoming popular in homes (**Figure 5–12**). When using a convection oven,

Figure 5–13

Radiant energy travels through air and heats foods without touching, as shown in this toaster oven.

the baking time and temperature should be reduced to avoid overcooking. A temperature reduction of about 25°F (14°C) is suggested.

Radiation

Energy can be transmitted as waves or rays that vibrate at high frequency and travel very rapidly through space. Radiant waves, a form of electromagnetic energy (**Figure 5–13**), go directly from their source to the material they touch without any assistance in the transfer of energy from the air molecules in between. Radiant waves can travel through a vacuum. An example of radiant energy is sunlight, which travels at the rate of 186,000 miles per second. Sunlight includes infrared, visible, and ultraviolet light.

Infrared Radiation. Infrared wavelengths effectively transfer heat [9] and are the type of heat often referred to when radiation heat transfer is discussed. These wavelengths are shorter than those of microwaves but longer than visible electromagnetic spectrum (**Figure 5–14**). This form of thermal radiation

THE ELECTROMAGNETIC SPECTRUM

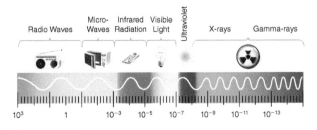

Figure 5–14

The electromagnetic spectrum is shown here with the length of waves provided, ranging from long waves (non-ionizing radiation) to short waves (ionizing radiation). Microwaves are longer than the waves that produce visible light. In cooking, microwaves and infrared radiation, both non-ionizing radiation, are used to heat food. (Designua/Shutterstock)

is usually generated by a hot source, such as burning coals, a hot stove burner, a broiler, or the sides of a hot oven. Broiling, barbecuing, and toasting foods are examples of cooking methods that utilize radiant energy (Figures 5–9, 5–13).

The glowing coals of a fire, the red-hot coils of an electric heating unit, and the burning of a gas flame give off waves of radiant energy that travel from their source in a straight line to the surface of food in close proximity. Energy is absorbed at the surface of the food and produced heat. This heat is then transferred to the interior of the food by conduction. When baking in an oven, convection currents also are a factor in the transfer of radiant heat coming from the hot heating elements in the oven.

Infrared heat may also be produced by high-energy lamps that can be used to keep food warm on a serving line. Infrared radiation has been used to dry fruits and vegetables and for heat blanching.

Cookware. The amount of energy absorbed from the radiant waves is affected by the characteristics of the pans or baking dishes used. Dull, dark, rough surfaces absorb radiant energy readily, whereas bright, shiny, smooth surfaces tend to reflect the waves and absorb less energy, thus slowing the cooking and browning. Sometimes shiny aluminum bakeware is desirable—for example, to protect the edges of a pie crust from browning excessively. Ovenproof glass dishes generally transmit radiant waves, and therefore the oven temperature should be reduced by about 25°F (14°C).

Ultraviolet Radiation. Ultraviolet radiation is part of the electromagnetic spectrum with shorter wavelengths than visible light (Figure 5–14). Ultraviolet radiation can be used to extend the shelf life of products such as milk, baked goods, meats, and fish; disinfect packaging materials; or sterilize surfaces [10]. The ultraviolet light is produced with a mercury-filled UV lamp or for pulsed light a Xenon lamp. As this technology is further tested, it may be used to replace chemicals used to sterilize packaging and other materials [10].

Microwaves. Microwaves are also part of the electromagnetic spectrum. Microwaves have shorter wavelengths than ultraviolet, visible light, and infrared radiation. Microwaves can penetrate food and cause the rapid motion of dipolar molecules (such as water, proteins, and carbohydrates), thereby producing heat. Microwave cooking will be discussed further later in the chapter.

MEDIA FOR HEAT TRANSFER

Media for transferring heat to food include air, water, steam, and fat. Combinations of these media are often used.

Air

Roasting, baking, broiling, and cooking on an outdoor grill are methods that use heated air as the cooking medium. These are generally considered to be *dry-heat* cookery methods because the surface of the food comes into contact with dry air.

Other methods of heat transfer also occur in foods cooked with dry-heat cookery. For example, the transfer of heat in the interior of a moist food will be facilitated by the water in the food by conduction. Conduction heat transfer also occurs when heat is transferred from a hot cookie sheet or baking dish to the food. In convection ovens, a blower circulates the heated air, and the food heats more rapidly.

When cooking in an oven, the surface of a food is dehydrated. The dry surfaces are able to attain temperatures higher than the boiling point of water, thereby aiding in browning. The browning of food contributes to flavor development. The browned crust on breads and seared meats are examples of foods that develop desirable flavors because of browning.

Water

Simmering, boiling, **stewing**, **braising**, and **poaching** are methods that use water as the primary cooking medium. For obvious reasons, these are called *moist-heat* cookery methods (**Table 5–1**). When water is the cooking medium, the highest temperature attainable is that of boiling. At sea level, water boils at 212°F (100°C). Water boils at lower temperatures at higher elevations. Simmering and poaching use temperatures just below boiling (see Table 5–1).

Water is a better conductor of heat than air; therefore, foods cooked in water cook faster. Heat is transferred or conducted directly from the hot water to the food. Convection currents are also set up in hot water and help to distribute heat uniformly throughout the food mass.

Steam

Steaming is also a moist-heat method of cooking. When cooking with steam, heat is transferred from the steam to the surface of the food. The steam condenses on the cooler food, releasing the latent heat absorbed when the steam was formed from boiling water.

Foods are steamed when they are placed on a rack above boiling water in a covered container that holds in the steam. Steaming also occurs when foods that contain water are wrapped in foil or parchment paper or placed in cooking bags. Baked potatoes, meats, and some seafood may be cooked in this way. Cooking a covered casserole in the oven also involves cooking with steam because the steam produced when the liquid boils is contained in the dish.

Table 5–1
DRY, MOIST, AND COMBINATION COOKING METHODS

Type of Method	Media for Heat Transfer	Cooking Method	Description	Primary Method of Heat Transfer
Dry				
	Air	Broiling	Radiant heat from an overhead source is used to cook foods placed on a rack over a pan.	Radiation
	Air	Roasting	Roasting generally applies to meat and poultry. The food is cooked uncovered on a rack or roasting pan in a heated oven.	Radiation Convection Conduction
	Air	Baking	Baking generally applies to portion pieces of meat or poultry and other foods such as bakery products. Foods are baked, uncovered, in a heated oven.	Radiation Convection Conduction
	Air	Grilling	A heat source, such as coals in a barbeque, cooks food placed on hot grates.	Radiation Conduction
	Fat	Sautéing	A shallow pan is heated to a relatively high temperature with a small amount of oil to cook food. Stir-frying is a similar technique.	Conduction
	Fat	Panfrying	A moderate amount of fat is used in a heated pan. The fat should come up to one-half or one-third the height of the food to be cooked. Pan-fried foods are generally breaded. Panfrying uses less heat and more oil than sautéing.	Conduction
	Fat	Deep-fat frying	Foods are submerged in oil heated to as high as 400°F (200°C). Deep-fat frying is a dry-heat cooking method because no water is used.	Conduction Convection
Moist				
	Water	Poaching	Food is placed in a liquid heated to 160°F to 180°F (71°C to 82°C). Water, broth, or other flavored liquids may be used. The food may be poached by submerging or placing in a shallow depth of liquid.	Convection
	Water	Simmering	Food is submerged in a liquid heated to 185°F to 205°F (85°C to 96°C). Often used to tenderize foods through long, slow cooking.	Convection
	Water	Boiling	Boiling liquid is used to cook foods. Water boils at 212°F (100°C) at sea level.	Convection
	Steam	Steaming	The food generally should not touch the liquid but is instead placed in a perforated or wire container above a boiling liquid.	Convection
Combination				
	Fat, water	Braising	Food is browned in a small amount of fat, and then cooked covered in a small amount of sauce or other liquid. Because this method uses both dry and moist heat, it is considered to be a combination method of cooking.	Conduction Convection
	Fat, water	Stewing	Stewing is generally associated with small pieces of food that have been browned in a small amount of fat. The food is immersed in a simmering sauce or liquid for final cooking.	Conduction Convection

Source: References 17, 22.

In a pressure canner, steam is the cooking medium; however, because the close containment of the steam within the canner raises the vapor pressure, the boiling point of the water producing the steam is increased (Figure 5–6). Therefore, the temperature of cooking within the pressure canner is elevated above the boiling point of water at atmospheric pressure, and cooking is much more rapid. In a pressure saucepan, an adjustable gauge on the pan regulates the pressure and thus the temperature by releasing some steam during the cooking process. Canning is discussed further in Chapter 28.

Fat

Fat is the cooking medium in sautéing, panfrying, and deep-fat frying. Cooking in oils and fats does not involve water and therefore is considered a dry-heat cooking method. To *sauté* means to cook quickly in a very small amount of fat at a high temperature. Some sautéed foods may be lightly dusted with flour. Stir-frying is similar to sautéing, but it is commonly done in a wok (Figure 5–10). Panfrying is cooking in a small amount of fat that comes about one-third to one-half of the way up the food to be cooked. Thus, more fat is used in panfrying as compared to sautéing. Panfrying is also at a more moderate temperature, and the foods are frequently coated in breading [17]. Cooking a food immersed in fat at a controlled temperature is deep-fat frying. In all of these cooking methods, heat is transferred by conduction from the energy source through the pan to the fat. Convection currents are set up in the heated fat and aid in distributing the heat. The heated fat then conducts heat to the food it touches.

Fat can be heated to a much higher temperature than the boiling point of water. Because some fat is also absorbed by the food, the flavor and nutritional composition are changed. Frying and nutritional considerations of the use of oils and fats in cooking are discussed in more detail in Chapter 8.

INDUCTION COOKING

Induction cooking utilizes a high-frequency **induction coil** that is placed just beneath the cooktop surface to produce magnetic friction that causes **ferrous** metal cookware to heat. The cooktop is made of a smooth, ceramic material and remains cool (**Figure 5–15**). Only the cooking pan gets hot. The hot pan rapidly transmits heat to the food through conduction.

Flat, not warped, cookware made of cast iron, magnetic stainless steel, or enamel over steel is required for use on induction cooktops; pans made of nonferrous materials cannot be heated. Heating by induction is rapid, and numerous power settings are available. Another advantage of the induction cooktop is the ease of cleaning. Because there is no exposed heating unit and the surface does not get hot, spills do not burn onto the unit.

MICROWAVE COOKING

Microwave heating stemmed from the development of radar during World War II. It recognized that radar antennas generated heat and could be useful in heating

Induction Cooktop

Figure 5–15

Induction cooktops generate a magnetic current to heat cast-iron or magnetic stainless steel cookware. Heat is then transferred to the food through conduction from the hot pan.

FOCUS ON SCIENCE
SOUS VIDE

Sous vide is a cooking method in which the food is vacuum sealed in a plastic pouch and then submerged in a relatively low-temperature water bath (111°F to 140°F/44°C to 60°C) [21]. Sous vide is a French term meaning "under vacuum." This cooking method has been used in restaurants and food services because it can produce precise control over doneness, and the lower temperatures used for longer periods can result in foods more uniformly cooked throughout [21]. Some consumers are now starting to cook using sous vide in the home setting.

Sous vide must be carefully handled to reduce foodborne risks, and should not be used without an understanding of proper procedures. Foods cooked at temperatures below 131°F (55°C) should not be consumed by those at high risk for foodborne illness (see Chapter 2). Some factors that may impact the safety of sous vide–prepared foods can be influenced by the initial pathogenic organism contamination level, the times and temperatures used, and cooling process if the food is not consumed immediately following cooking. *Clostridium botulinum* bacteria grow well in anaerobic environments, such as in vacuum packing; thus, methods to control botulism poisoning are necessary [21].

food. The first microwave oven (called the Radarange) became available for food service establishments in 1947, and the first one for consumer use was introduced in 1955. These early manufactured models were large, heavy, specially wired, and very expensive with price tags around $1,300. Microwave ovens are now used in more than 90 percent of U.S. households [4, 32].

What Are Microwaves?

Microwaves are high-frequency electromagnetic waves of radiant energy. These electromagnetic waves are radio waves of very short wavelength (about 4 inches) [32], falling between television and infrared frequencies on the electromagnetic spectrum (Figure 5–14). In comparing wavelengths, radio waves are measured in kilometers, television frequencies in meters, microwaves in centimeters, and infrared waves in microns [12].

Microwaves are generated in a vacuum tube called a *magnetron,* which converts alternating electric current from a household circuit into electromagnetic energy radiation. Microwaves radiate outward from their original source and can be absorbed, transmitted, or reflected. In most microwave ovens, a stirrer blade in the top of the oven helps to distribute the waves (**Figure 5–16**). Turntables provide another means of distributing energy.

How Do Microwaves Heat Food?

Microwaves heat foods and beverages by causing electrically polarized molecules in the food to produce friction because of rapid rotation. Polarized molecules

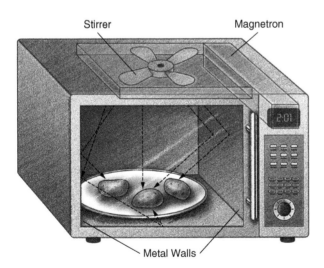

Figure 5–16

Microwaves are produced by a magnetron, from which they enter the oven. A stirrer deflects the microwaves and distributes them to various parts of the oven. They are reflected back from the metal walls of the oven. The food in the oven absorbs the microwave energy, and heat is created in the food as a result of the friction produced between the rapidly moving molecules.

are also called *dipolar molecules* and include water, proteins, and some carbohydrates. These dipolar molecules act like tiny magnets and align themselves in the microwave electromagnetic field. The field alternates millions of times each second, causing the polarized molecules in the food to rotate rapidly because of forces of attraction and repulsion between the oppositely charged regions of the field. Heat is produced in the food by this friction. Positive and negative ions of dissolved salts in the food, including table salt or sodium chloride (NaCl), also migrate toward oppositely charged regions of the electric field and generate additional heat by their movement [11, 20, 31, 32]. Microwaves are not hot and do not heat directly, but instead heat by causing the movement of dipolar molecules.

Microwaves in the oven reach the food both directly from the magnetron unit and indirectly by reflection from the metal walls. Thus, the metal walls of a microwave oven reflect and contain the microwaves within the oven. Microwaves generally penetrate about 1 to 2 inches into the food. The depth of penetration varies with the frequency of the microwaves and the composition of the food. Further distribution of the heat, particularly toward the center of a relatively large mass of food, occurs by conduction, as it does in conventional heating. Microwaves do not, as sometimes suggested, cook from "the inside out" [32, 33]. Microwave cooking is faster, however, because microwaves penetrate farther into food than the infrared radiant waves used in conventional cooking. The depth of penetration is variable depending on the type of food being microwaved [31].

Food-Related Uses of Microwaves

Microwave heating of food is useful in households, commercial and noncommercial food services, and also in the food industry for processing.

Household. Microwave ovens are used most frequently in the home to boil water, heat frozen foods, defrost frozen foods, or make popcorn. Consumers have not embraced cooking entire meals in the microwave [30], even though there are cookbooks that provide recipes and guidance for microwave cooking. Instead, consumers often use the microwave for speed and convenience.

Younger members of the household use microwave ovens. Some parents may be more comfortable allowing their older children to heat a snack in the microwave rather than in an oven. The interiors of microwave ovens, as well as potentially the food container, stay cool when heating a food item, and thus may be perceived as safer even though the food itself can become very hot and result in burns.

Food Service. Heavy-duty commercial microwave units are often installed in food service establishments. These units have high-output capabilities and are designed to withstand frequent use. Hospital food services may use microwaves to reheat individual plates of chilled menu items just prior to service to the patient [15]. Because little or no time savings occur when cooking large quantities of food in a microwave oven, food services rarely use microwaves for food production.

Food Industry. Specialized microwave equipment is used by the food industry. Conveyer belts are often used to move products through a microwave field, resulting in more uniformity in the distribution of energy throughout the food products [20, 23]. Meat **tempering**, bacon precooking, and sausage cooking represent the largest uses of microwave processing by the food industry [20, 23]. Microwave processing equipment is used to temper billions of pounds of food each year. As the foods are tempered, they are brought to a temperature just below the freezing point of water. Microwave tempering can be completed within minutes (instead of hours or days), with less drip loss and reduced microbial growth [20].

The food industry also may use combination of microwave and conventional heating for drying foods such as pasta and snack foods [20]. High-intensity microwaves may be combined with external heat sources, such as hot-air or infrared energy, to cook products quickly while simultaneously producing a browned surface [23]. Yeast-leavened products may be **proofed** in a short time with the use of microwaves. Microwaves may also be used for baking bread, pizza, cake, and pastry products, often in combination with conventional baking methods [14]. The microwave **pasteurization** and **sterilization** of food are becoming more prevalent. Foods pasteurized and sterilized with microwaves can result in high-quality foods subjected to less heat than other preservation processes [6, 20, 31].

Microwave Ovens

Microwave ovens used in homes and in food service operations are available with a variety of features, such as variable power outputs, calculation of cooking times, automatic cooking, sensors, and more. Reduced-power settings in microwave ovens give full power intermittently, with on–off cycling, which reduces localized overheating and helps to protect sensitive foods. Many microwave ovens include sensors to automatically determine doneness of foods such as vegetables, or provide a cook time and power level to thaw, reheat, and cook foods when provided the weight or volume.

Microwave ovens may be purchased with varying power outputs. Microwave ovens for consumer use usually have an output capability of 600 to 700 watts, whereas commercial units often have a higher wattage. The design assumption for the heavy-duty units is that they will be used hundreds of times per day. Microwave ovens with lower power—400 to 500 watts—are also available for home use, but heat food more slowly.

Regulations and Safety

The Federal Communications Commission assigned frequencies of 915 and 2,450 megahertz (million cycles per second) for microwave cooking to avoid interference with communication systems that operate in closely associated frequencies. The 2,450-megahertz frequency is used in today's microwave ovens. The shorter wavelengths (approximately 4.8 inches) produced by a frequency of 2,450 megahertz result in more uniform heating and better results for small items being cooked [12].

Since 1971, the Food and Drug Administration (FDA) has regulated the manufacture of microwave ovens in terms of performance standards and design safety. A radiation safety standard enforced by the FDA limits the amount of microwaves that can leak from an oven throughout its lifetime [34]. The limit is 5 milliwatts of microwave radiation per square centimeter at a distance of 5 centimeters (2 inches) from the oven surfaces. This amount is far below the level known to harm people, and the exposure decreases as one moves away from the oven. For example, the exposure to microwave radiation at 20 inches from the oven is only one-hundredth of the level at 2 inches.

Microwave ovens also are required to have two interlocking systems to prevent the production of microwaves if the latch is opened. The FDA tests microwave ovens in their labs and oversees manufacturers to ensure that radiation control standards are met [34].

Packaging Materials and Cookware

When cooking with a microwave in homes, plastic, ceramic, and glass containers that are labeled as microwave safe must be used [32, 33]. Generally, materials that are transparent to microwaves should be utilized, so that the microwaves pass through these materials to heat food inside the container. Metal containers or glass containers with a metal glaze, rim, or trim are not acceptable for microwave use. Recommendations for microwave cookware by the type of material are given in **Table 5–2**.

If it is uncertain that a ceramic container is microwave-oven safe, it should be tested by placing it in the oven with a heat-resistant glass cup containing one cup of water and running the oven on high power for one minute. If the dish remains cool, it is suitable

FOCUS ON SCIENCE

SOME MICROWAVABLE FOODS HAVE SPECIAL PACKAGING TO USE WHEN COOKING. WHY?

Microwavable popcorn, pizza, sandwiches, and some other products depend on a concentration of heat in a microwave oven to produce a pleasing food. This concentrated heat is produced with a *heat susceptor* [5]. The next time you pop microwave popcorn, look at the part of the package that is to be "this side down" or the pizza tray with the silver surface. These are heat susceptors.

Heat susceptors may consist of metallized paperboard, which strongly absorbs energy and becomes very hot. The metal itself does not absorb the microwave energy, but it readily absorbs the heat produced by the other materials in the packaging. Thus, the use of susceptors allows popcorn to become hot enough to pop. Likewise, susceptors are used for microwavable pizza, sandwiches, and other products where the concentration of heat is useful to promote browning or crispness.

Table 5–2
MICROWAVE COOKWARE

Type of Material	Microwave Safe	Not Recommended
Glass (such as Pyrex® or Anchor Hocking®), ceramic, and CorningWare®	Glass and ceramic containers are recommended if heat resistant and without metal.	Some glazed ceramics are not recommended because these dishes become hot before the contents are heated. The heating may be because of metal in the glazing. Dinnerware with silver or gold trim is not recommended.
Utensils with metal trim or screws in lids or handles		Not recommended because arcing is likely to occur, causing sparks in the microwave oven. Stop cooking immediately if arcing occurs.
Ceramic mugs or cups with glued-on handles		Not recommended because handles may fail.
Paper products	White, microwave-safe paper towels may be used to absorb moisture and splatters during cooking. Paper plates labeled microwave safe are recommended. Parchment paper and wax paper are acceptable.	Dyed paper products are not recommended to avoid migration of dye into the food product. Newspaper and brown paper bags should not be used because of inks and other chemicals that may have been used in manufacture.
Plastics	Microwave plastics designed for use in the microwave oven are recommended. When using microwave-safe plastic, slitting the top is recommended to prevent pressure buildup. Minimal contact between the food and the plastic is recommended to avoid migration of plasticizers into the food. Levels of migration have been found to be highest when direct contact occurs between the film and foods with a high fat content.	Thin storage bags, plastic wrap on meats from the store, foam meat trays, takeout containers, and one-time-use plastic containers such as margarine tubs should not be used in the microwave oven. These plastics have not been produced for microwave use and may melt or distort. Do not use foods cooking in plastic containers that have warped or melted when microwaved.
Metal containers		Not acceptable for use in microwave ovens. Also avoid metal twist ties and Chinese takeout containers with metal handles.
Aluminum foil	Some microwave manufacturers may indicate that very small strips of aluminum may be used to reduce excessive cooking of certain areas.	Do not use large pieces of aluminum. Foil should not be closer than 1 inch from the oven walls or metal shelves. Do not use aluminum unless safe use is specifically described in the owner's manual provided by the manufacturer.

Source: References 12, 32, 33.

for microwaving. If it becomes hot, it has absorbed some microwave energy and should not be used in a microwave [32].

Advantages and Limitations of Microwave Cooking

Microwave cooking offers advantages in the speed of cooking or reheating some foods, reduction of nutrition loss, and energy conversation. However, foods that need to brown for optimum appearance and flavor are not ideally prepared in microwave ovens. Super-heated water has been known to result in significant burns for the food preparer, and food safety can be impacted by uneven heating. Additionally, foods needing to rehydrate as part of the cooking process do not cook effectively in microwaves.

Reheating of Foods.   One of the great advantages of using a microwave oven is the speed with which cooking can be accomplished—2 to 10 times faster than conventional methods. The cooking time in microwave ovens varies with the volume and type of food being cooked. Microwave ovens are not ideal for quantity cookery, because cooking time must be extended as the quantity of food is increased. One potato, for example, cooks in 4 to 6 minutes in a microwave oven, whereas four potatoes require about 16 to 19 minutes to cook.

Microwave cooking offers advantages in reheating precooked foods, both individually packaged and packaged in meals, and in thawing frozen foods.

Not only does the microwave oven reheat precooked foods more rapidly than conventional methods, but it has been shown to reduce reheated or warmed-over flavor in poultry [8].

Reduction in Nutrient Loss.   Vegetables can be cooked in a microwave oven using minimum water, thus conserving water-soluble nutrients. Researchers have found that microwave blanching of vegetables as compared to blanching in water resulted in less nutrient loss [27]. Antioxidants in vegetables are also well retained when cooked in a microwave oven as compared to other cooking methods, especially when compared to conventional cooking methods utilizing water [13, 16].

Energy Conservation.   The microwave oven saves energy when compared with conventional ovens, particularly for cooking up to about six servings at one time. In cooking pork sausage links, the microwave oven had the lowest energy requirement, followed by the convection oven, with a standard oven requiring the most energy [19]. Energy savings from microwave use also come from the lesser amount of dishwashing that is generally required. Containers used for microwave cooking are usually suitable for serving as well. Finally, during warm seasons of the year, a microwave oven, in contrast to a conventional oven, will not contribute heat to the kitchen. In microwave cooking, the oven walls and surrounding air do not become hot.

FOCUS ON SCIENCE
WHY SOME FOODS COOK MORE QUICKLY THAN OTHERS IN A MICROWAVE OVEN

The composition of a food affects the rapidity of heating. Fats and sugars have low *specific heats* compared with water; therefore, foods high in fat or sugar heat more rapidly than foods high in water. Foods with less *density* also heat more rapidly than high-density foods when similar weights of these products are heated. Dense foods limit the depth of penetration of the microwaves.

FOCUS ON SCIENCE
WARMED-OVER FLAVOR AND MICROWAVED FOODS

What is warmed-over flavor?

Warmed-over flavor (WOF) occurs when food is reheated. The culprit is fat. Meats, especially those high in polyunsaturated fatty acids, are prone to oxidation, leading to rancidity development. Fish is also at risk, followed by poultry, pork, beef, and lamb. The oxidized fats produce volatiles; when the food is reheated, off flavors such as "cardboard," "rancid," "icebox," and even "freezer burn" are characterized.

How can microwavable foods avoid WOF?

In order to make some foods more acceptable, the manufacturer might include flavors that mask "warmed-over" tastes. Several flavor manufacturers encapsulate flavor systems so that they release flavor only on microwave heating. Use of various spices that contain natural antioxidants is another method to avoid the problem of WOF. Also, the manufacturer may use technology that releases aromas in the heated food to enhance product appeal.

Surface Browning. Lack of surface browning is a disadvantage of microwave cooking for some foods. When breads, cakes, and meats do not brown, the flavor, appearance, and potentially the texture are negatively affected. A loaf of bread without a crisp, golden-brown crust does not have the same appeal. A meat roast that cooks in a microwave for a relatively long time may develop some browning, but it may be overcooked before significant browning occurs.

The lack of browning of microwave-cooked products is because of the cool air temperature inside the microwave oven and the cooling effects of moisture evaporation at the surface of foods cooked with microwaves. The temperature inside the microwave-cooked food is actually higher than it is at the surface [11]. To overcome some of the problems created by the lack of browning in microwave cooking, a special browning dish can be used to sear chops, meat patties, steaks, and similar products. A special coating on the bottom of the dish absorbs the microwave energy and becomes very hot (450°F to 550°F/232°C to 289°C). Alternatively, sauces and gravies can add color and flavor to meats cooked in a microwave. Similarly, icings will add flavor to cakes or cupcakes while covering the pale surface.

Quality Considerations. Foods that need long cooking periods at simmering temperatures to tenderize or to rehydrate are not as satisfactorily prepared in a microwave oven as in a conventional oven. Dried pasta and rice are examples of foods that do not cook much more quickly in the microwave because rehydration must occur. In other foods, such as sauces and meats, flavors do not have an opportunity to develop in the short cooking periods of microwave ovens.

Stale bread is freshened with heating by conventional methods, but bread reheated in a microwave oven becomes tougher. The addition of emulsifiers and increased water content (by use of fiber) has decreased the toughness of microwave-reheated bread

[24]. Food processors are able to improve the quality of microwavable food products in part by the use of **hydrocolloids**, such as xanthan gum, carrageenan, and microcrystalline cellulose, which have high water-binding capabilities. These ingredients help to stabilize many microwavable products and prevent dry spots due to uneven heating and loss of moisture [7].

Overcooking and Erupted Hot-Water Phenomena. It is relatively easy to overcook foods in the microwave oven because heating is rapid. Caution must be exercised to avoid the dehydrating effects that may result from as little as a few seconds of overheating.

Safety is also a concern when some products such as liquids are overheated. Superheated water has been reported to the FDA [32, 33, 34]. Superheated water is water that has been heated past its boiling temperature without appearing to boil. This is most likely to occur in a very clean cup when a liquid has been heated too long. When superheating has occurred, a slight movement, such as picking up the cup or adding instant coffee, may result in a sudden, violent eruption of boiling water that may cause a severe burn.

Uneven Heating and Food Safety Implications. Uneven heating is a major disadvantage in the use of the microwave oven. This lack of uniformity in heat distribution raises concern about the microbiological safety of certain foods heated with microwaves; sensory characteristics may also be affected. In the heating of meals made of ground meat patties, sauce, mashed potatoes, and carrots, it was reported that cold and hot spots were present near each other. The high–low temperature difference could be greater than 54°F (30°C) at spots within a few centimeters of each other [28]. When individual portions of meat loaf (beef), mashed potatoes, and green beans were heated in a microwave oven during one study that simulated procedures used in cook–chill food service systems, a wide range (up to 83°F/46°C) of endpoint temperatures was observed [11].

FOCUS ON SCIENCE
STARCHES AND HYDROCOLLOIDS IN MICROWAVABLE FOODS

Starch and hydrocolloids are used to build viscosity in food, but they are a challenge to the food scientist to use in microwavable applications because the desired consistency needs to be obtained with shorter heating times. An instant starch or a cold-soluble colloid will aid in obtaining the desired viscosity with shorter cooking times.

What role do starches and hydrocolloids play in the quality of microwavable foods?

Even though a food may taste good, if the texture is dry, crumbly, mushy, or soggy, it may be unacceptable

to the consumer. These texture variations can be associated with rapid heat and vaporization that occurs during microwaving. Texture is also affected by uneven heating that is common when using a microwave oven. Starches or hydrocolloids can benefit microwavable foods by (1) inhibiting the rapid loss of moisture during heating, (2) keeping water bound (as in meats), and (3) preventing syneresis (weeping or loss of moisture).

It has also been reported that the usual procedures followed in cooking chicken by microwaves may not destroy all of the **Salmonella** organisms that may be present [18]. Concern has been expressed in regard to the destruction of *Trichinella spiralis* in pork prepared in the microwave oven. It is important to ensure the safety of these foods by checking the final temperature in several locations within the product with a meat thermometer or the oven's temperature probe. Historically it has been recommended that meats cooked by microwaves be heated 25°F (14°C) higher than those attained with conventional heating. Current recommendations, however, suggest cooking meats in a microwave oven to 165°F (74°C) throughout [26].

General Cooking Recommendations

Steps may be taken when cooking in a microwave oven to prepare high-quality foods. Suggestions to address browning concerns, evenness cooking, avoidance of overcooking, and effective defrosting can be useful.

Browning. Large pieces of food, such as meat roasts, may brown during cooking in a microwave oven because cooking time is relatively long, but smaller quantities of food cooked for short periods need to be browned by some means other than the use of microwave energy. Small cuts of meat may be broiled conventionally after microwave cooking to develop browned color and flavor. Bacon is easily cooked in a microwave oven, however, and does brown. The fat on the surface of the bacon aids in browning.

The optimum time for cooking should not be extended to increase the likelihood of browning. Foods dry out very rapidly with only slight overcooking when using microwaves. Creative use of dark-colored toppings, sauces, melted cheese, gravies, crumbs, and spices can compensate for lack of browning in many dishes.

Stirring and Turning. Power is unevenly distributed in the microwave oven; therefore, foods need to be turned around, turned over, stirred, or relocated in the oven at various times during cooking. Multiple items such as individual potatoes, pieces of fish, and custard cups should be placed in a circle. Most microwave ovens have a turntable whose rotation automatically distributes power more evenly. Although metal is generally not acceptable for use in a microwave oven, small strips of aluminum foil may be used in many brands of microwave ovens to shield thin or sensitive parts of the food. The foil should not be allowed to touch the inside of the oven [1, 32].

Standing Time or Carry-Over Cooking. A food continues to cook for several minutes after it is removed from the microwave oven; this is also called carry-over cooking [32]. During this standing time, heat continues to be conducted from hotter parts of the food mass to cooler ones, and the internal temperature of the food evens out and may also increase. Many convenience microwavable foods specify the holding time needed to allow the product to finish cooking. When preparing foods in the microwave without pre-packaged instructions, the cooking time should be planned to include a holding period to avoid overcooking. A longer standing time is desirable for foods of large volume and density, such as meat roasts.

Defrosting. One benefit of a microwave oven is the ease of defrosting. Most ovens have a defrost setting with a low- to medium-power input. The oven cycles on and off, and during the off periods, the heat produced in the food is distributed or equalized throughout.

As defrosting proceeds, some attention to the product improves the outcome. Ground meat, stew meat, whole poultry, or whole fish should be turned, and as soon as possible, pieces of the frozen food should be broken apart. Meat and poultry should be cooked immediately after defrosting.

Arrangement of Foods When Heating Meals. Factors affecting the heating in microwave ovens include, in addition to the oven itself, the packaging and the food. Because different foods have different dielectric properties (and thermal ones), uneven heating may occur in meals with several different components. Temperatures near the edges of a plate or tray of food tend to be higher than in the center; the edge of the food seems to act as an antenna in the microwave field, absorbing energy. The arrangement of the foods on a plate or tray has a pronounced effect on heating rates and final temperatures. Researchers found that the best heating effect was achieved when mashed potatoes were piled up along the sides of the tray [28].

Microwave ovens are widely used, in both homes and institutions, to reheat fully cooked, plated meals. Individual meal items should be chosen and grouped so that they are as compatible as possible in terms of heating rate and uniformity of heating. Dense meal items, including baked potatoes, mounded mashed potatoes, lasagna more than 1/2 inch thick, stuffed peppers, and thickly sliced meat or fish, heat relatively slowly. Therefore, such foods should be thinly portioned. Examples of meal items that heat more rapidly and easily are mashed potatoes with the center pressed down; thinly sliced meats, centered on the plate with gravy over them; and thinly portioned fish without sauce. Denser items should be placed toward the outside of the plate. Subdivided vegetables or loose rice and pasta may be placed in the center of the plate.

STUDY QUESTIONS

Why Cook Food

1. List and explain five reasons for cooking food.
2. Give examples of changes in flavor, texture, and color of foods that may occur during cooking.

Measurement of Temperature

3. Compare the Fahrenheit and Celsius thermometer scales.
4. Explain why heat measured by thermometers is called sensible heat.

Heat Involved in Change of State

5. Identify the three states of water.
6. Compare and contrast *vapor pressure* and *atmospheric pressure* and their impact on the boiling of water.
7. Explain why water boils at different temperatures depending on the elevation (feet or meters above sea level).
8. Explain the impact of elevation on the speed of cooking in boiling water.
9. Define specific heat and explain in relation to the energy required to heat water.
10. Define and compare *latent heat* and *sensible heat*.
11. How much energy is involved in each of the following?
    (a) The latent heat of fusion for water.
    (b) The latent heat of solidification.
    (c) The latent heat of vaporization at boiling point.
    (d) The latent heat of condensation.

Types of Heat Transfer

12. Describe how heat is transferred in food preparation by (a) conduction, (b) radiation, (c) convection currents.
13. Discuss the types of cookware that are best suited for (a) conduction and (b) radiation.
14. Explain why a 25°F (14°C) reduction in oven temperature is recommended when cooking in a convection oven or when cooking in a standard oven with a glass baking dish.

Media for Heat Transfer

15. (a) Name four different media commonly used for transferring heat to food and explain several cooking methods that use each medium.
    (b) What types of heat transfer are generally used in each method that you cited?
16. Describe each of the following cooking methods: broiling, roasting, baking, grilling, sautéing, panfrying, deep-fat frying, poaching, simmering, broiling, steaming, braising, and stewing.
17. Compare and contrast moist, dry, and combination cooking methods.
18. Identify what media (air, water, steam, or fat) for heat transfer must be used for moist heat cooking methods.

Induction Cooking

19. Explain how an induction cooktop heats food. Include in your description how both the pan and the food are heated.
20. What types of pans will heat on a conduction burner/cooktop, and what types of pans will not heat with an induction cooktop?

Microwave Cooking

21. Describe microwaves in relationship to the electromagnetic spectrum.
22. How do microwaves produce heat when they are absorbed by food?
23. Identify several ways microwaves may be used in the heating of food at (a) home, (b) in food service, or (c) by the food industry.
24. Discuss several advantages and several limitations to the use of microwave equipment in home cooking, institutional food service, and industrial food processing.
25. Discuss the regulations and government oversight of microwave ovens.
26. Identify packaging materials and cookware that are acceptable for use in a microwave oven, and provide a rationale for why some materials should not be used in a microwave oven.
27. Discuss several advantages and disadvantages when cooking or heating food in a microwave oven.
28. Explain superheated water and why it can occur.
29. Provide recommendations for safe endpoint cooking temperatures when using a microwave oven to prepare foods that may cause a foodborne illness.
30. Explain why foods should be stirred or turned at intervals during cooking in a microwave oven. Of what value is standing time after cooking? Explain.
31. Discuss the precautions to be taken when reheating fully cooked, plated meals in a microwave oven.
32. Give several suggestions for using the microwave oven in combination with conventional methods of cooking.
33. Explain why the arrangement of foods in a microwave and the density of the food can influence the evenness of heating.

6

Seasonings, Flavorings, and Food Additives

Our senses determine the pleasure we derive from eating food. We may eat to maintain life, but this becomes a difficult task without enjoyment. Food flavors that tantalize the senses provide a pleasurable eating sensation. *Flavor* is the complex sensory combination of taste, aroma, and mouthfeel derived from eating a particular food. Flavor is defined by ASTM International as:

(1) perception resulting from stimulating a combination of the taste buds, the olfactory organs, and chemesthetic receptors within the oral cavity; (2) the combined effect of taste sensations, aromatics, and chemical feeling factors evoked by a substance in the oral cavity. [1]

Natural flavors of many foods—fresh, ripe strawberries, for example—are enticing in themselves, but the judicious use of seasonings and flavoring products can enhance natural food flavors. Flavorful food is the ultimate goal of the cook and food manufacturer. The proper use of seasonings and flavorings is essential in achieving this goal.

Flavorings, including herbs and spices, represent the largest category of food additives. A broad definition of food additives is anything added to processed foods. Food additives are natural or synthetic; these substances are added to foods for functional purposes. In addition to flavorings, food additives perform a number of desirable functions including nutritional value improvement, spoilage reduction, consistency enhancement, and appearance improvement.

In this chapter, the following topics will be discussed:

• Consumption trends and nutritive value
• Seasonings such as salt and pepper
• Flavor enhancers and masking agents
• Spices and herbs
• Flavor extracts
• Vegetables, fruits, and fresh flowers as flavorings
• Condiments and alcohol flavorings
• Food additives

CONSUMPTION TRENDS AND NUTRITION

Consumption Trends

Global food trade, immigration, and worldwide travels have increased awareness and expanded availability of new food flavors in the American cuisine [69, 68, 71]. Spices have been used for centuries to flavor food. Continued heightened awareness of ethnic cuisines has increased flavor options in the marketplace [70]. Spicy hot, exotic, and floral flavors are some popular trends. Consumer demand for organic foods has precipitated organic flavor and additive production.

Nutritional products and functional foods often need masking agents to cover up undesirable flavors and bitterness caused by added ingredients such as amino acids, herbs, vitamins, and minerals [42]. Biotechnology that alters taste perceptions at the cellular level will continue to play a major role in flavor enhancers and masking agents used in processed foods [42]. Novel flavors are premium flavors sold in fine dining or specialty retail markets [46]. Examples of novel flavors include the sweet and tangy pichuberry, the maplelike flavor from lucuma, tart cloudberry, or the earthy tigernut [46]. Novel flavors are used in items such as premium drinks and ice creams.

The shift from traditional home cooking to packaged foods, processed foods, and restaurant dining has expanded flavor offerings. This shift to processed foods and restaurant dining has also increased salt (sodium chloride) intake. The 2015–2020 *Dietary Guidelines for Americans* states that 75 percent salt is from processed foods, and 5–10 percent salt added to food while cooking or from the salt shaker at meals [77]. Sodium intake in the United States averages around 3,409 mg/day excluding salt added at meal time; this far exceeds the recommended 2,300 mg levels for healthy populations [22, 76, 77, 75] (**Figure 6–1**).

Food processors are constantly exploring flavor options to entice consumers. Flavorings are usually less than 1 percent of a food, but have a big impact. New guidelines lowering food sodium levels challenge food processors to produce food with less sodium and high

Figure 6–1

The survey data shows that people consume the equivalent of more than 1.5 teaspoons of salt—nearly 3,430 milligrams of sodium—each day. Most U.S. adults consume on average more than twice the maximum daily sodium intake recommended. (Peggy Greb/USDA)

consumer appeal [29, 25, 30]. Simple clean labeled foods with fewer ingredients and more natural ingredients are changing food additive use.

No federal standard of identity exists for spices. The FDA Compliance Policy Guide (CPG) provides guidance for spice labeling and safety. Color additives and spices such as turmeric, paprika, and saffron used as colorants must comply with federal regulations [78].

Nutritive Value

Seasonings, flavorings, and other food and color additives are added to food in very small amounts limiting caloric contribution. Food additives such as vitamins and minerals added to food for fortification and enrichment can have a positive impact on nutritional value. Compounds extracted from spices and herbs are being researched for medicinal roles such as anti-inflammatory, obesity and tumor suppression, and other cancer issues [12, 81, 23].

Salt (sodium chloride) is the most widely used seasoning, flavoring, and food additive [18]. Table salt and kosher salt are 60 percent chloride and 40 percent sodium. Salt provides the essential nutrient sodium. Sea salts may have around 2 percent mineral content. Sea salt minerals vary based on region and harvesting methods. Minerals found in sea salt include calcium, potassium, magnesium, iron, copper, fluorine, iodine, molybdenum, manganese, cobalt, and zinc. These different minerals influence salty perception and taste in foods [8, 4]. The essential nutrient iodine is added to some table salt for iodine deficiency prevention [34].

However, pervasive salt use in processed foods has resulted in negative cumulative effects [72].

Sodium is an essential nutrient, but excessive intake has been linked to increase risk for high blood pressure, stroke, cardiovascular disease, and cancer [28, 72, 77]. Potassium chloride is commonly used as a salt substitute, [73]. Other seasonings, including herbs and spices, offer another way to reduce salt consumption [29, 31]. Flavor enhancers and umami-rich ingredients such as mushrooms, vinegar, and soy sauce have been found to increase salt perception, thus offering an additional option for salt reduction in foods [7, 20, 30, 38, 39, 43].

BASIC SEASONINGS

Seasonings are substances that enhance the flavor of food. Basic seasonings—salt and pepper—are added to improve the flavor of foods without being specifically perceived or detected as individual ingredients. Salt and pepper may bring out hidden flavors in foods or, in the case of pepper, add flavor (**Figure 6–2**).

Salt

Salt is the most important and basic seasoning agent [9]. Salt acts to heighten flavors and provide a salty taste. Foods without salt are often described as tasting "flat." Adding salt to food makes it more palatable [25]. Salt accentuates sweet and sour notes while suppressing bitter taste.

Salt is one of the oldest known commodities. It is valued not only as a seasoning, but also as a preservative [60]. Salt was so important in early history that Roman

Figure 6–2

Salt and pepper are basic seasonings. Salt is considered the most important seasoning valued for its taste, flavor-enhancing capabilities, and use as a preservative. (Danny Smythe/Shutterstock)

Figure 6–3

Unprocessed rock salt mined in Hutchison, Kansas. (© Amanda Frye)

Kosher salt

Rock salt

Fleur de sel

Himalayan pink salt

Black salt

Figure 6–4

Kosher salt, rock salt, *Fleur de sel*, Himalayan pink salt, black salt. (Richard Embery/Pearson Education)

soldiers were sometimes paid in salt. Our word *salary* comes from the Latin word *sal,* meaning "salt" [55].

Salt is a **crystalline** substance with the chemical name sodium chloride (NaCl). It is found naturally in some foods, but the salt added to foods is mined from salt beds or harvested via evaporation of saline ocean waters. Salt is purified before being marketed for food use. **Figure 6–3** shows unpurified mined salt. An anticaking agent can be added to prevent clumping. Salt may be **iodized** for nutritional purposes. Federal code requires the statement "This salt supplies iodide, a necessary nutrient" to appear on the label of iodized table salt. Non-iodized table salt must be labeled "This salt does not supply iodide, a necessary nutrient." If anticaking agents are added, the salt is labeled as "free flowing."

Various types of salt available in the marketplace are described in **Table 6–1**. Land and sea salts around the world have different color, flavor, mineral content, and saltiness [8]. **Figure 6–4** shows some different types of salt. In 2015, the FDA issued nonbinding recommendations called the "Guidance for Industry: Colored Sea Salts." Sea salts with charcoal or red clay may not meet current FDA codes for safe color additives [15]. Salts may be sold in many different forms depending on end use. Food manufacturers have access to many different forms of salt and crystalline sizes to fit processing needs.

The optimal amount of salt used in a dish depends on the food product being prepared and personal preference. For most cooked dishes, salt and other seasonings should be added in small increments, with a tasting after each addition, until the most desirable taste is achieved. Many recipes specify the amount of salt as "to taste" or "tt," which means salt is added just until the salt taste is perceptible. In products such as soups and sauces, which are likely to evaporate during cooking, salt should be added at the end of the cooking period to avoid the dish from becoming too salty as it cooks and concentrates. More salt can always be added to food, but too much salt cannot be removed.

Salt interacts with other flavors. Salt will enhance sweet flavors while suppressing sour [50] and bitter flavors [9]. These interactions explain the preference for salting watermelon or cantaloupe to enhance sweetness and the salting of eggplant to reduce bitterness. In soup, the influence of salt on sweetness and bitterness has been demonstrated [18]. Salt also affects the mouthfeel of the soup, giving the impression of increased thickness and fullness, as if the product were less watery and thin. The addition of salt produces an overall flavor balance that is more "rounded out" and "fuller." **Figure 6–5** compares the flavor profile for tomato soup to which salt was added with those for soup to which dill seed or onion powder was added.

Other ingredients also interact with our perception of saltiness. Salt is detected at lower concentrations when vinegar is added [20]. Thus, substituting vinegar for part of the salt in a dish can provide the desired saltiness with the use of less salt. In a study using chicken and beef bouillon, perceived saltiness was found to be enhanced by savory aroma compounds [4]. The use of soy sauce, a source of umami,

Table 6–1
VARIETIES OF SALT FOR USE IN COOKING

Type of Salt	Description
Table salt	Usually produced by pumping water through underground salt deposits. The water is evaporated leaving crystals.
	Table salt may have a magnesium carbonate or another anticaking agent added to promote a free-flowing product.
	Iodized table salt contains the nutrient iodine.
Kosher salt	Large coarse salt flakes. No iodine. Sometimes anticaking agents. Large flakes adhere to food and dissolve more quickly. Used for "koshering" meat. Also, used for brining meats and other applications.
Sea salt	Salt produced by evaporating sea water. Flavor is more complex due to additional minerals such as magnesium, calcium, and potassium. Mineral content varies by the sea source, but may be as much as 2 percent. Color also varies white, grey, black, pink, peach, and brownish red. May contain anticaking agents. Sea salt has about the same amount of sodium as table salt; however, some sources of sea salt may have higher sodium content. Because some sea salts vary in salty taste intensity, it may be possible to use less sea salt than table salt and therefore reduce sodium consumption. Sea salt is available from coarse to fine grades and in sea salt flour depending on end use and food processing.
Rock salt (edible and inedible)	Rock salt has been mined from underground deposits. The unpurified rock salt is used for making homemade ice cream or for deicing a driveway or walk area. Edible rock salt, which has been purified, may be used in a salt mill.
Potassium chloride (salt substitute)	A metal halide salt with a similar crystalline structure to sodium chloride. It may have a bitter or metallic aftertaste depending on the amount used.
Pickling or canning salt	Pure granulated salt. No iodine, anticaking agents, or other additives. Used for brining, pickling, and canning. Dissolves completely in brine. Dissolved solution is clear.
Sel gris	Sea salt from France's Normandy coast. Slightly wet and grey from minerals and clay.
Fleur de sel	Delicate crystals harvested from marsh rocks in Sel gris. Means "flower of salt."
Himalayan pink salt	Pink salt mined in Himalayan mountains. The pink color and unique flavor are from iron and copper.
Black salt (kala namak)	Indian mined black rock salt; minerals and other compounds give color and sulfur flavor. Used in traditional Indian recipes.
Palm Island Bamboo Jade	Olive green sea salt from Hawaii. Green herbal aroma probably from drying sea water on bamboo shoots.

Source: Adapted from References 8, 33, 49, 73.

also enables a reduction of salt in certain dishes while maintaining a desirable flavor profile [30].

Pepper

Pepper was the first Asian spice to arrive in Europe and today remains one of the most widely used spices in the world. The "hot spices," which include mustard seed as well as black, white, and red pepper, represent a large percentage of U.S. spice usage. Pepper is cultivated in the tropics, with most of the black pepper grown in India, Indonesia, Brazil, and Vietnam. The *Tellicherry* peppercorns from the southwest Indian coast are considered some of the best peppercorns in the world [33].

Not all pepper are the same. Black pepper is best used as a seasoning in dark-colored foods to avoid black flecks in light-colored foods. Light peppers,

white and red, are used in both light and dark menu items (**Figure 6–6**). Red pepper is known for its heat and pungency. Ground white pepper is good for all-around seasoning. It blends well, both in appearance and in flavor, in white dishes, and it has the necessary strength to season dark dishes. White pepper is generally perceived as milder than black pepper.

Black and white pepper is produced from the berry of the vine *Piper nigrum L.* [78] (**Figure 6–7**). The pepper berries are referred to as "peppercorns." The peppercorns may be used whole or ground fine to coarse depending on use. *Piperine* is an amide compound (**Figure 6–8**), responsible for the pungency in black and white pepper [78, 35].

Pungency is flavor sensation characterized by the collective hot, sharp, and stinging feelings in the

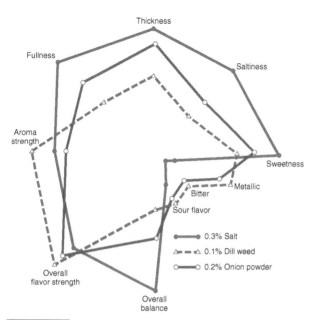

Figure 6–5

Aroma and flavor profiles for tomato soup with (1) 0.3 percent salt, (2) 0.1 percent dill weed, or (3) 0.2 percent onion powder. The farther away a point is placed from the center point, the more pronounced is the attribute. (Based on Gillette, M. (1985). Flavor effects of sodium chloride. *Food Technology*, 39(6), 47. Copyright © Institute of Food Technologists)

Figure 6–6

Black pepper, white pepper, green peppercorns, pink peppercorns, and Szechuan peppers. (Richard Embery/Pearson Education)

Figure 6–7

(left) Unripe berries from *Piper nigrum* L. (right) Ripe berries for white berries. (Fisfra/123RF)

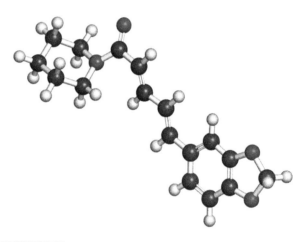

Figure 6–8

Piperine is the molecule responsible for the pungent flavor of the black and white pepper. (Molekuul_be/Shutterstock)

oral cavity [35]. There is a loss of pungency during exposure to light and storage due to isomerization of the double bonds [35]. Other volatile compounds also contribute to pepper's flavor [35]. Pepper quality characteristics are measured by volatile oil, nonvolatile methylene chloride extract, total and acid insoluble ash, crude fiber, and moisture [78].

Black pepper berries are picked while immature and still green, then fermented and sun-dried [33, 78]. The dried peppercorn is deep dark brown-black with deep wrinkles [78]. Ground black pepper is described as having a characteristic penetrating odor [78]. Black pepper has a hot, biting, and warm pungent flavor and aroma [33, 78].

White pepper is from mature berries [69]. The berries are harvested when they are ripe and changing color from green to yellow typically before they turn red [35]. The outer covering is removed to reveal the white interior [32, 49].

Green peppercorns are unripened peppercorns that have been freeze-dried or pickled. Pickled green peppercorns are similar to capers with a fresh, pickled sour flavor often used in sauces and fish [33].

Pink peppercorns are peppercorns from South American shrubs or trees depending on type and source [33]. They are unrelated to black and white peppercorn vines. During the 1980s, the FDA placed a temporary ban on Brazilian pink peppercorns (*Anacardiaceae*) because of allergic reactions similar to poison ivy. However, pink peppercorns (*baies roses*) are popular in France. Pink peppercorns lack the hard outer cover and *piperine* found in black pepper, but provide color and a delicate peppery and juniper flavor.

Szechuan pepper is also known as anise pepper, Chinese pepper, or Sichuan. It is a dried red berry of a prickly ash tree native to China. These peppercorns are extremely hot, spicy with citrus and pepper overtones [33]. They are used in Chinese five spice powder and many Chinese dishes. Japanese cuisine uses a similar green variety called *sancho* to season grilled meats and fish [33].

Red pepper, sometimes called *cayenne* red pepper, comes from plants of the genus *Capsicum*, and although hot and pungent, it is not botanically related to *P. nigrum*, which produces the berries for black and white pepper [5]. Red pepper is typically a fine-ground blend of hot-dried red chili peppers; the color is bright orange to brown red [33, 78]. The compound *capsaicin* is responsible for cayenne pepper's pungency [78]. *Sweet paprika* is from a red pepper that contains low levels of the pungent compounds and is primarily used to color foods [35]. Paprika can also be a coloring spice

and subject to Code of Federal Regulations 101.22(a)(2). Quality characteristics of red pepper pungency are measured by Scoville units pungency ratings, total and acid insoluble ash, and moisture [78].

FLAVOR ENHANCERS AND MASKING AGENTS

Flavor enhancers and masking agents act somewhat differently from seasonings. Flavor enhancers accentuate flavors. Masking agents hide the undesirable flavors or modify taste perception. Both flavor enhancers and masking agents are important in food processing, food development, and reformulations as they enhance food palatability while "hiding" bitterness or other unpleasant qualities.

Bitter taste masking is a major issue with nutritional and functional food products [42]. These products often have added ingredients, such as amino acids, vitamins, minerals, herbs, or artificial sweeteners, which can produce a bitter taste. Bitter masking agents can involve encapsulation so bitter tastes are not perceived. Another masking technique involves stimulating sweet and salty receptors to alter taste perception. Molecular compounds that trigger bitter perception can be identified then altered to prevent the bitter taste perception. Product reformulation to reduce sodium and carbohydrates, or to increase protein often relies on flavor enhancers and masking agents to improve the new product taste and flavor.

Ingredients that enhance flavor and suppress undesirable traits are important in food processing [57]. Product development involves optimizing flavor and suppressing negative traits; the understanding of taste and flavor of molecular and chemical components is essential. Enhancing and masking ingredients are important in sweet and savory foods as well as those foods with heating, cooling, and tingling sensations [57].

FOCUS ON SCIENCE
SALT AND PICKLING

Adding salt to pickling brine is one important way to help lactic acid bacteria win the microbial race. At a certain salt concentration (as low as 5 percent NaCl) and a pH of 4, lactic acid bacteria have a competitive advantage and grow quicker than other microbes. Below this "right" concentration, bad bacteria may survive and spread more easily, possibly outcompeting lactic acid bacteria and spoiling the pickles. If too much salt is added, lactic acid bacteria will not thrive, the vegetables will not be pickled, and salt-tolerant yeasts will be able to thrive. These salt-tolerant yeasts consume the lactic acid, thereby making the pickles less acidic—and more hospitable to spoilage.

Pickles also may be brined in bulk with a controlled fermentation of cucumbers, producing a uniform product in a shorter time period. The controlled fermentation method employs a chlorinated brine of 25° salinometer, acidification with acetic acid, the addition of sodium acetate, and inoculation with *P. cerevisiae* and *L. plantarum* or the latter alone with a 10- to 12-day fermentation required.

Source: J. M. Jay, "Fermented Foods and Related Products of Fermentation," in *Modern Food Microbiology*, 3rd ed. (New York: Van Nostrand Reinhold Co., 1986), p. 382.

A flavor enhancer heightens the perception of flavor. Examples of flavor enhancers include monosodium glutamate (MSG) and some other substances called **5′-ribonucleotides** (adenosine-5′-monophosphate [AMP], inosine-5′-monophosphate [IMP], and guanosine 5′-monophosphate [GMP]) [22]. The distinctive taste that MSG and the 5′-ribonucleotides produce has been called *umami*. This word is derived from the Japanese word meaning "delicious" or "savory." Umami is found naturally in foods such as mushrooms, aged cheese, tomatoes, and meats. Sometimes umami is described as a fifth taste along with sweet, sour, salty, and bitter (see Chapter 1 for more information about taste). Umami interacts with the four basic tastes by enhancing taste sensitivity to salt and sweet while reducing the perception of sour and bitter tastes [7, 37, 39]. Umami also appears to favorably influence our perception of thickness.

Kokumi is another Japanese flavor enhancer word that means a mixture of different taste or mouthfeel characteristics. It describes a food's impact, "mouthfulness," mildness, and taste continuity [57]. The term *kokumi* is often used to describe well-cooked, aged, or fermented products. An example of *kokumi* is the richness and fullness from a soup that is simmered for hours. Japanese scientists have isolated compounds in garlic responsible for the *kokumi* taste response. These *kokumi*-inducing compounds were identified as S-allyl-cysteine sulfoxide (allium) and glutathione. Yeast extracts have been used for *kokumi* attributes in savory snacks such as cheddar cheese popcorn [47].

MSG

MSG has a long history as a flavor enhancer. Many hundreds of years ago, Asian cooks used dried seaweed called *sea tangle* to make a stock that made foods remarkably full and rich flavored. Tokyo professor Kikunae Ikeda discovered in 1908 that glutamate in the seaweed was responsible for flavor enhancement. MSG was formulated in Japan the following year and then introduced into the United States in 1917 [38, 39].

MSG is a crystalline material that looks something like salt. Chemically, it is the sodium salt of an amino acid called *glutamic acid*. It is made in a **fermentation** process that starts with molasses or some other carbohydrates such as starch from tapioca or cereals. MSG is a flavor enhancer or intensifier, bringing out the flavors of other foods. At the levels ordinarily used in cooking, MSG does not have a taste of its own; however, when used in sufficiently large amounts, it may add its own flavor. MSG is typically used in soups, sauces, vegetables, meats, poultry, and fish.

5′-Ribonucleotides

A group of compounds called 5′-ribonucleotides are naturally present in some foods, such as beef, chicken, fish, and mushrooms. They may act as flavor enhancers and masking agents, independently or in combination with MSG, creating the umami taste. Their action with MSG has been called synergistic. Synergism refers to cooperative action among two or more substances so that the total effect of the mixture is greater than the sum of the individual effects. Even a very small amount of the ribonucleotides increases the flavor-enhancing properties of MSG [24].

Ribonucleotides may be prepared from hydrolyzed yeast extracts, **yeast autolysates**, and enzyme hydrolyzed vegetable protein. Hydrolyzed yeast extracts are rich in 5′-ribonucleotides, especially IMP and GMP. Hydrolyzed vegetable proteins are naturally high in glutamic acid and thus contribute umami taste [27]. These ingredients may be used in soups, sauces, marinates, and flavor seasonings.

AMP works by blocking the activation of the molecule *gustducin* in the taste receptor cells and preventing taste nerve stimulation so the brain never perceives the bitter taste [42]. AMP has been shown to decrease bitter taste associated with grapefruit juice, diet soft drinks, and potassium chloride salt substitutes.

Monoammonium Glycyrrhizinate (MAG)

Monoammonium glycyrrhizinate (MAG) is a flavor enhancer and masking agent that sweetens, as it enhances other flavors, and masks chemical and bitter flavors in foods. MAG is a licorice derivative. The glycyrrhizin molecule is an ammonia salt form of

---

FOCUS ON SCIENCE
WHAT MAKES PEPPER HOT?

Although we commonly think of heat in reference to our sensory reaction to peppers, the effect is really not thermal, but rather a chemically induced irritation that stimulates the endings of the trigeminal nerve—quite different from the sense of taste or the sense of touch. The chemical responsible for this stimulation in black pepper is called *piperine*, and the active agent in red pepper is *capsaicin*. The chemical composition of capsaicin ($C_{18}H_{27}O_3N$) is similar to piperine ($C_{17}H_{19}O_3N$) [5]. However, capsaicin is about 100 times more potent than piperine.

glycyrrhizic acid, the active ingredient in licorice, and makes up about 10 percent of pure licorice extract.

Glycyrrhizin is extracted from licorice root. It is a pure white powder that is sweet with no residual licorice taste. Licorice glycyrrhinates are 50 times sweeter than sucrose; it is used to sweeten and potentiate other flavors such as cocoa. Other applications include use in bakery products, frostings, puddings, candy, fruits, coffee, meats, soups, and sauces. MAG is used in carbonated diet colas to enhance mouthfeel and eliminate the metallic artificial taste associated with diet colas. MAG is effective at extremely low levels around 40–60 parts per million [57].

Enhanced Cooling Sensation

Cooling sensations in the oral palate are imparted not from the sense of cold, but also by stimulating the taste buds. This sensation is typically associated with mint-flavored chewing gums or mints. However, biotechnology can use molecules to stimulate the cold perception. Non-mint derivatives can be used to impart the cooling sensation in fruits, dairy products, energy drinks, flavored waters, ice tea, savory products, and many more products. This enhanced cooling sensation is without the traditional mint menthol aroma or burn.

SPICES AND HERBS

Since antiquity, spices have been treasured for their ability to flavor and preserve foods (**Figure 6–9**). Spices have been valued for nonfood purposes too—as ingredients of incense, perfumes, cosmetics, embalming preservatives, and medicines. The desire and quest for tropical spices was instrumental in provoking trade wars and in encouraging exploration. Marco Polo went to the Far East in search of spices and precious stones; Columbus was searching for a new trade route when he discovered America. Spices were so important, costly, and scarce—even being accepted as currency in the late thirteenth century—that wars were fought over them [62].

The United States is now the world's largest importer of spices and herbs. Three-fourths of the spices imported into the United States come from India, Indonesia, China, Brazil, Peru, Madagascar, Mexico, and Vietnam plus several countries in Africa [74]. The spice market in the United States is growing as consumers explore new flavors and cuisines [16, 56, 69, 71]. According to the International Trade Centre, the global market for seasonings, spices, and herbs is over $6.5 billion. There is an upward trend in spice trade volume and value with expansion of global cuisines. **Figure 6–10** shows a steady increase in U.S. spice imports.

Classification

The term *spice* is used broadly to describe a wide variety of dried, **aromatic** vegetable products that are used to flavor prepared foods. The American Spice Trade Association and the FDA define spices as "any aromatic vegetable substance in the whole, broken or ground form except those substances which have been traditionally regarded as foods, such as onion, garlic, and celery; whose significant function in food is seasoning rather than nutritional; that is true to name; and from which no portion of any volatile oil or flavoring has been removed." [42] (**Figure 6–11**).

This definition includes tropical aromatics (pepper, cinnamon, and cloves), leafy herbs (basil and oregano), spice seeds (sesame, poppy, and mustard), and spice blends. The FDA does not consider dehydrated vegetables such as garlic and onions as part of the spice group.

The Federal Code of Regulations provide details regarding spices generally recognized as safe (GRAS) as well as for labeling requirements [80]. There are no standards of identity for spices. FDA's Compliance

Figure 6–9

Since ancient civilizations, spices have been used to flavor food. (Jag_cz/Shutterstock)

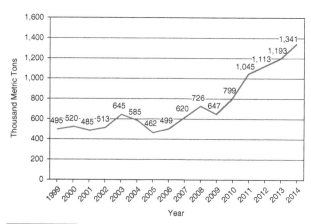

Figure 6–10

U.S. spice imports have been increasing for the last two decades. (Data from USDA/ERS. Graph © Sam Frye and Amanda Frye)

Figure 6–11

Spices are any aromatic vegetable substance in the whole, broken, or ground form whose significant function in food is seasoning. (Kerdkanno/Shutterstock)

Figure 6–12

Herbs, aromatic leaves and stems of plants used for flavoring. (Valentina Razumova/Shutterstock)

Policy Guidelines (CPG) provide definitions, description, and guidance for use in labeling spices and the foods in which they are used, and also requires spices such as paprika, saffron, and turmeric to be labeled as "spice and coloring."

Spice. In common usage, spices are more narrowly defined by only referring to the bark, roots, buds, flowers, fruits, and seeds of aromatic plants grown in the tropics [32, 49]. Using this definition, allspice, anise, cardamom, cayenne pepper, cinnamon, cloves, cumin, ginger, mace, nutmeg, paprika, and turmeric are all spices. Some spices are sweet, some are spicy sweet, and some are "hot."

Spices are available in whole or ground forms. Ground spices allow for more uniform distribution and more rapid release of flavor than whole spices; thus, they are often added near the end of cooking. Whole spices should be added early in the cooking process. Spice extracts are available to food processors. Spice extracts are produced by grinding or crushing the spices, then extracting the spice with steam distillation, solvent extraction, or other processing methods [62].

Herb. The term *herb* usually refers to aromatic leaves and stems of soft-stemmed plants used for flavoring that grow in temperate climates (**Figure 6–12**). However, some woody-stemmed plants, such as sage, also produce culinary herbs. Bay leaves come from an evergreen tree—the laurel [32]. Other herbs include basil, marjoram, mint, oregano, rosemary, savory, tarragon, and thyme (**Figure 6–13**).

Herbs may be fresh or dried. Fresh herbs are preferred by many cooks because drying can alter the flavors and aromas [32]. For the best flavor, fresh herbs are typically added near the end of cooking. Dried herbs are more concentrated; therefore,

when substituting dried herbs for fresh, reduce the quantity by one-third to one-half (e.g., 1 teaspoon fresh equals one-third or one-half teaspoon of dried herbs).

Many herbs can be successfully grown in home gardens, and then gathered fresh for use in cooking. In the fall, fresh herbs may be dried or frozen for use throughout the winter. Alternatively, some fresh herbs may be grown inside during the winter months. Common homegrown herbs include mint, tarragon, basil, rosemary, chives, oregano, parsley, and cilantro. Micro herbs are the first true leaves of any herb [33] (**Figure 6–14**). The tiny leaves are fragile with intense flavor. These micro herbs must be picked by hand, and are often used as garnish, especially on canapés [33].

Spice and Herb Blends. Mixtures of spices, herbs, seeds, or dehydrated vegetables are marketed as spice blends for use in food preparation. *Chili powder,* for example, is a blend of ground chili pepper (usually about 85 percent by weight) and some combination of cumin, garlic powder, and oregano [32].

Bouquet garni is a mixture of fresh herbs and sometimes vegetables tied with a string. Bouquet garni is used to flavor soups, stews, sauces, braised meats, and vegetables. A bouquet garni commonly consists of parsley, thyme, and a bay leaf. Likewise, a sachet, also known as a *sachet d'épices,* is a bundle of herbs and spices tied in cheesecloth (**Figure 6–15**). A sachet consists of peppercorns, bay leaves, parsley, thyme, whole cloves, and possibly garlic, depending on the recipe. Bouquet garni and sachet d'épices are removed from the dish before serving.

The description and use for some herbs and spices are given in **Table 6–2**. As you use herbs and spices, your ability to identify each by its aroma, color,

Basil

Cilantro

Oregano

Rosemary

Curly Parsley

Italian Parsley

Spearmint

Thyme

Dill

Garlic Chives

Figure 6–13

Fresh herbs include basil, cilantro, oregano, rosemary, curly parsley, Italian Parsley, spearmint, thyme, garlic chives, dill. (Richard Embery/Pearson Education)

Figure 6–14

Micro herbs are the fragile first leaves of any herb. The leaves are intense with flavor. (Richard Embery/Pearson Education)

and appearance will increase. Spice and herb blends may be made in the kitchen too. Other spice and herb blends are listed in **Table 6–3**.

Use

Both spices and herbs are generally used as "flavor builders" in the cooking process so that their separate flavors merge indistinguishably to develop an overall flavor. Just as music is composed of many notes that blend together for a pleasing sound, herbs and spices in a dish should create a delicious flavor. To maintain a balance of flavors when increasing a recipe yield, the amount of herb or spice should be increased to a lesser degree, as shown in **Table 6–4**.

The choice of herbs and spices used in a dish often creates an immediate impression about the ethnic cuisine being prepared. Some herbs and spices have distinctive flavors and, when used in quantities large enough to taste, become major flavors rather than blending into the total flavor of the dish.

Food processors may add some flavoring ingredients, such as cinnamon, in **encapsulated** forms [51]. Flavors are encapsulated for a number of reasons: the

process helps to retain flavor in food products during storage, protects the flavor from undesirable interactions and flavors, minimizes oxidation, and allows for controlled flavor release [51].

Storage

The storage life of spices depends not only on the storage conditions, but also on the age, type, and source of the spice. **Table 6–5** provides suggestions for shelf life for dried herbs and spices. Whole spices retain flavor strength longer than ground because the increased surface area results in loss of flavor more quickly. In general, spices and herbs should be stored in a cool, dry, and dark place in airtight containers. Because moisture will decrease the length of storage, it is best to avoid shaking spices from the container over a steaming pot of food.

The quality of spices may be assessed by checking for (1) a vibrant, not faded, color; (2) rich, full, and immediate aroma; and (3) the "best by" freshness date on the container. Because spices and herbs are composed of numerous flavor components, the overall balance of flavors can be altered with aging. Therefore, a spice or herb stored too long may not only lack in flavor, but also provide a different and disappointing flavor profile to the dish.

Quality Issues

Spices come from every part of the world including many poorer underdeveloped countries where spice trade is crucial for the economy. Herb and spice contamination and adulteration has been a historical problem. Quality can be difficult to control. Adulteration may be unintentional or intentional to increase spice value. Many spices and herbs are grown and harvested on many small farms; some are even found growing wild. Metal and metallic contamination from

(a)   (b)

Figure 6–15

(a) This bouquet garni includes parsley, leeks, celery, fresh thyme, and carrots. (b) The sachet includes peppercorns, bay leaves, parsley stems, thyme, cloves, and garlic. (Richard Embery/Pearson Education)

Table 6–2
CHARACTERISTICS AND USES OF SOME SPICES AND HERBS

Spice/Herb	Description	Flavor Characteristics	Applications
Allspice	Dried berry of tree grown in West Indies and Latin America	Resembles mixture of nutmeg, cloves, cinnamon, and pepper	Pickling, meats, fish, cakes, soups, vegetables, chili sauce
Anise seed	Dried greenish-brown seed of annual herb of the parsley family	Strong black licorice-like flavor and odor	Beverages, baked 6-2 goods, confections, lunch meats, soups
Basil	Leaves and tender stems from annual herb of the mint family	Pungently aromatic, sweet, spicy flavor	Tomato paste, tomato sauce, vegetables, pizza, chicken dishes, salad dressing
Bay leaves	Leaves of evergreen member of the laurel family	Aromatic, bitter, spicy, pungent flavor	Bouillons, meats, fish, barbeque sauces, soups, vegetables
Capsicum, red pepper	Dried pod of member of nightshade family	Intensely pungent, biting, hot, sharp taste	Chili powder blends, meat seasonings, condiments, soups, beverages, baked goods
Caraway seed	Fruit of biennial herb of the parsley family; long curved seeds tapered at one end	Warm, biting, acrid but pleasant, slightly minty, medicinal flavor	Rye breads, baked goods, cheese, goulash, vegetables
Cardamom	Seeds from the fruits of a perennial herb of the ginger family	Sweet, pungent, highly aromatic, camphoraceous flavor	Baked goods, Indian curry dishes, lunch meats, pickles
Chervil	Leaves of an annual of the parsley family	Highly aromatic; resembles mixture of anise, parsley, caraway, and tarragon	Instant soups, fish dishes, condiments, baked goods
Chives	Leaves of a perennial of the onion family	Delicate onion flavor	Soups, salad dressings, dips
Cilantro	Leaves of plant that resembles flat parsley and produces coriander seeds	Aromatic and spicy with sage, citrus, and parsley flavors	Used in Mexican, Chinese, Indian, and Thai cuisines
Cinnamon	Dried inner bark of an evergreen tree of the laurel family	Warm, spicy, aromatic, pungent flavor	Confections, ice cream, cakes, pies, cookies, beverages, soup bases, processed meats
Cloves	Dried flower buds from evergreen of the myrtle family	Warm, spicy, astringent, fruity, slightly bitter flavor	Pickling, beverages, baked goods, confections, spiced fruits, processed meats, pudding mixes
Cumin seed	Dried ripe fruits of an annual herb of the parsley family	Aromatic, warm, heavy, spicy, bitter flavor	Chili powder, chili con carne, curry powder, salad dressings
Ginger	Rhizome (underground stem) of perennial tropical plant	Aromatic, biting, fragrant, pungent, warm, camphoraceous flavor	Baked goods, beverages, gingerbread, cookies, sauces, condiments, processed meats
Lemongrass	Stalk of a perennial plant that resembles a woody green onion	Lemony flavor	Thai and Vietnamese dishes
Marjoram	Leaves and floral parts of a perennial of the mint family	Warm, aromatic, sweet-minty, slightly bitter flavor	Gravies, soups, stews, poultry, fish, processed meats

(Continued)

Table 6–2
CHARACTERISTICS AND USES OF SOME SPICES AND HERBS (CONTINUED)

Spice/Herb	Description	Flavor Characteristics	Applications
Nutmeg	Seed of a fruit of the evergreen nutmeg tree	Sweet, warm, pungent; highly spicy flavor	Sauces, custards, puddings, baked goods, dehydrated soup mixes, processed meats
Oregano	Leaves of a perennial of the mint family	Strong, pungent, aromatic, bitter flavor	Tomato dishes, pizza, meats, omelets, soups, vegetables
Parsley	Leaves of a biennial	Grassy, herbaceous, bitter flavor	Chicken and tomato soup bases, lasagna, salad dressings, potato chips
Rosemary	Narrow leaves of small evergreen shrub of mint family	Sweet, fresh, spicy, peppery	Soups, stews, vegetables, beverages, baked goods
Saffron	Dried stigmas of crocus; bright yellow; very expensive	Earthy, bitter, fatty, herbaceous flavor	Baked goods, rice dishes
Sage	Leaves of a perennial semi-shrub of the mint family	Fragrant, warm, astringent, camphoraceous flavor	Sausages, poultry seasonings, fish, meat loaf, condiments
Savory	Leaves of an annual of the mint family	Spicy, peppery taste	Meats, fish sauces, chicken, eggs, dry soup mixes, baked goods
Sesame seed	Seeds of an annual herb	Nutty flavor	Breads, rolls, crackers, cakes, salad dressings, confections
Tarragon	Flowering tops and leaves of a perennial herb	Minty anise-like flavor	Salad dressings, vegetables, meats, fish, soup bases, condiments
Thyme	Leaves and flowering tops of a shrub-like perennial of the mint family	Biting, sharp, spicy, herbaceous, pungent	Fish, meat, poultry, vegetables, fresh tomatoes, poultry stuffing, canned soups
Turmeric	Rhizomes of tropical perennial herb	Mild, peppery, mustardlike, pungent taste	Curry powders, mustards, condiments

Source: Adapted from References 11, 44, 64.

soil or harvesting can pose serious health risks too. Cleanliness, insect and rodent infestation, and microbiological quality are important concerns. Pathogenic bacteria may be introduced via growing conditions, environment, poor hygiene and sanitation practices of harvesters, and lack of proper agriculture and manufacturing practices.

Since most spices are imported, strict standards exist for whole and ground spices being brought into the country or during interstate transport. The FDA governs these imports and compliance laws. Federal law governs the safety of the U.S. food supply. In 2007–2009, spice shipments from 37 of 79 countries to the United States had *Salmonella* contamination with prevalence of 6.6 percent. Furthermore, 12 percent of the spices were adulterated with filth, insects, and animal hair. Since that time, the FDA has been working with the international CODEX Committee on Spices and Culinary Herbs (CCSCH) to develop worldwide standards for spices and culinary herbs in dried, dehydrated, whole, ground, cracked, or crushed form.

Spices imported into the United States must meet American Spice Trade Association (ASTA) specifications and standards established by FDA, the U.S. Department of Agriculture, and CODEX CCSCH [62]. The ASTA, FDA, CPG, and other standards quality specifications control for cleanliness, impurities, adulteration, moisture content, microbial growth, pesticide levels, mycotoxin/aflatoxin levels, and particle size.

No standards of identity exist for spices. However, FDA Compliance Policy Guides (CPG), "Section 525.750 Spices-Definitions," provide spice descriptions for labeling spices and the foods which they are used. For example, black, red, and white pepper are described in these definitions. Pepper and other spice standards are listed as "generally recognized as safe" (GRAS) under federal law. The CPG provides criteria for spice compliance and seizure. For example,

Table 6–3
SOME SPICE AND HERB BLEND INGREDIENTS AND USES

Name	Main Ingredients	Use
Blackening spice (Cajun Dry Rub)	Black peppercorns, salt, fennel seeds, thyme, paprika, mustard, garlic powder, sage, red pepper	Dry rub for chicken, fish, steak, vegetables before broiling, grilling or sautéing
Chinese five spice powder	Szechuan pepper, star anise, cloves, cinnamon, and fennel seeds	Chinese and Vietnamese foods
Curry powder	Black pepper, cinnamon, cloves, coriander, cumin, ginger, mace, and turmeric	European blend to replicate Indian "curry" flavor for sauces
Fine herbs (Fr. *Fines herbes*)	Parsley, tarragon, chervil, and chives	Used primarily in French cooking fresh or dry
Jamaican jerk seasoning	Thyme, allspice, black pepper, salt, basil, mustard, cinnamon, cloves, and ginger plus onion, hot peppers, and garlic	Jerk is typically a paste made with vinegar or lime juice. Traditionally used with pork or chicken
Herbes de provence	Thyme, rosemary, bay leaf, basil, fennel seeds, savory, and lavender	Dried herb blend from Southern France. Used with grilled or roasted meats, chicken, fish, or vegetables
Italian seasoning blend	Basil, oregano, sage, marjoram, rosemary, thyme, savory	Dried blend commercially available. Used for Italian flavoring in dishes
Garam masala	Peppercorns, cardamom, cinnamon, cloves, cumin, mace, coriander, nutmeg, turmeric, bay leaves, fennel seeds. Ingredients may vary	Spices of Northern India and Pakistan. Often used in tandoori cooking
Pickling spice	Black peppercorns, red chilis, allspice, cloves, ginger, mustard seed, coriander seeds, bay leaves, and dill	Used in cucumber or vegetable pickles as well as stews and soups
Pumpkin pie spice	Cinnamon, ginger, nutmeg, and allspice (other ingredients: lemon peel, and cardamom)	Used to make pumpkin pie. Sometimes sprinkled on egg nog.
Lemon pepper	Salt, black pepper, citric acid, lemon peel, optional ingredients, garlic, and minced green onion and salt omitted	Used to season seafood, eggs, meats, and more
Seasoning salt	Salt, garlic, spices, celery seeds, paprika, many variations of spices often with MSG	Used to season meat, eggs, vegetables
Za'atar	Dried thyme, oregano, sumac, and sesame seeds	Middle Eastern. Used on flatbreads or mixed with olive oil as condiment
Quatre-épices	Black peppercorns, nutmeg, cloves, and dried ginger Optional inclusions: allspice and cinnamon	Used in *charcuterie* (form of meat preservation) and stews
Ras elhanout	Typically contains 20 spices such as turmeric, cinnamon, cloves, grains of paradise, coriander, cumin, cardamom, peppercorns, dried chilis, dried flower petals, and more	Moroccan spice blend sold ground or whole used in stews, rice, couscous, and game dishes

Table 6–4
GUIDELINES FOR ADJUSTING RECIPES WITH HERBS AND SPICES

Herb or Spice	Original Recipe	Double Recipe	Triple Recipe
For these spices, increase in the same proportion as the recipe: black pepper, cinnamon, ginger, curry, chili powder, allspice, and cloves.			
For herbs, increase the amount of herbs by one-half of the original amount as illustrated when increasing the recipe by more than double.			
Red hot pepper will build intensity. Increase red pepper by one-quarter of the original amount as illustrated when increasing a recipe by more than double.			

the CPG Sec. 525.625., "Whole and ground pepper – Adulteration with insect & rodent filth; mold a mammalian excreta; foreign matter," states that insect matter, mold, and foreign matter must be less than 1 percent by weight in whole pepper with "mammalian excreta" less than 1 mg per pound in whole or part. Ground pepper criteria for legal action includes insect filth when "The ground pepper in six or more subsamples contains an average of 475 or more insect fragments per 50 grams." Rodent filth in ground pepper is defined as "six or more subsamples containing an average of 2 or more rodent hair fragments per 50 grams" [79].

Other herbs and spices also have similar but different tolerances for contamination depending on the spice in the CPGs. These standards and guidelines are important for protecting public health and safety. In October 2013, FDA issued a draft risk profile report that found pathogen contamination and filth to be problematic in spices.

Processing methods to reduce spice microbial contamination include fumigating with ethylene oxide, propylene oxide, methyl bromide, irradiation, and vacuum-assisted steam [9, 3]. Ethylene oxide has been banned in some European countries but is approved by the U.S. Environmental Protection Agency (EPA). Methyl bromide was phased out by the EPA in 2005 [62]. Treatment with ethylene oxide is effective

Table 6–5
RECOMMENDED STORAGE LIFE FOR SPICES, HERBS, AND EXTRACTS

Ingredient	Shelf Life
Spices, ground	2–3 years
Spices, whole	3–4 years
Seasoning blends	1–2 years
Herbs, dried	1–3 years
Extracts	4 years, except pure vanilla, which will last nearly indefinitely

Note: Storage conditions should be optimum. Light, warm, humid storage conditions will reduce shelf life.

in eliminating and reducing pathogens, but it results in alteration of spice flavor and color due to volatile compounds lost during processing. It was shown that black pepper and allspice lost half their volatile oils when processed by ethylene oxide [10].

Irradiation is the process where foods are exposed to ionizing radiant energy such as gamma rays or x-rays. Irradiation is an approved method for microbial disinfection of spices [3]. Irradiated spices sold directly to the consumer must be identified as irradiated. A food containing an irradiated spice does not need to be identified as irradiated. Irradiation, as with thermal pasteurization or sterilization, results in physical changes of spices. Color pigments of herbs and spices may be altered during processes to kill pathogens. There is alteration of sensory qualities in treated spice and herb compared to untreated spices and herbs [10]. Effective processing methods that preserve spice and herb culinary qualities while ensuring public safety remain a challenge to regulators, processors, and end users [3, 10].

FLAVOR

Flavor is the combination of aroma, taste, and any oral chemical heat or cooling sensation [54]. Foods are characterized by their flavor. Home cooks, traditional restaurants, fast-food restaurants, institutional dining services, and commercial food processors are all concerned about the flavor of foods produced.

Flavor delivery and type of flavorings are essential in home or commercial food production. The wrong type of flavoring, flavoring added at the wrong time, or wrong delivery system will impact the final food product and consumer experience. Liquid flavoring agents are emulsions and extracts. Fruits, beans, pods, spices, and seeds provide essential oils that contain the flavoring compounds. Essential oils are the pure oils extracted from the skins, peels, or other plant parts that give the aroma of the flavoring agent [33, 13].

Alcohol and oil-water emulsions act as a carrier for natural and artificial flavors. The volatile flavor compounds are responsible for the aroma associated with specific flavors such as vanilla. These essential oils are carried in emulsions or alcohol. Flavor emulsions are essential oils mixed into water with emulsifiers.

Extracts use ethyl alcohol as the carrier for natural and artificial volatile flavoring compounds or essential oils. Flavor extracts are typically used in baked goods and puddings. Vanilla, almond, lemon, and anise are common extracts. Only small amounts of these flavorful materials are required, but they add their own distinctive flavors to the final products. The extract solvent is alcohol which is volatile. Consequently, the flavorings should be stored in tightly closed containers and kept in a cool place. In puddings and other products cooked on surface units, the flavorings should be added at the end of the cooking period. In baked products, they should be added to the fat during preparation to reduce volatilization.

Flavored oils as emulsions are more potent than extracts. Flavored oils are used in most hard candy production and commercial food processing.

Flavor encapsulation is the food industry term used to describe delivering liquid flavors in a functional form. Encapsulated flavors are beneficial since they convert the liquid flavor to an easily dispersed

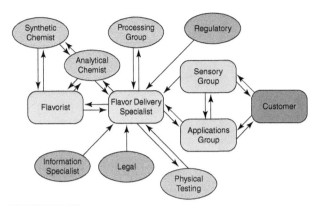

Figure 6–16

Interactive flow diagram of developing a flavor and delivery method for a commercial food producer. (Reprinted from Porzio, M.A. (2007) Flavor Delivery and Product Development. *Food Technology*, 61 (1), 22–29. Copyright © Institute of Food Technologists)

powder, protect key flavor components, deliver more flavor impact in the finished product, provide thermal stability, supply visual flavored particles in food, and sometimes provide controlled reactions in food [52]. Some flavor encapsulations are time released so their volatile compounds are protected.

Liquid flavors can be natural or artificial, extracts, essential oils, a flavor oil, flavor essence, or combination. These liquid volatile flavor compounds undergo numerous processes to coat and put flavor into a form easily used for a specific food product. Flavors and flavor processes are different for each food and application [54].

Flavorists work with suppliers and food processors to develop the right flavors and flavor delivery methods in processed foods [53]. The interactive flow diagram in **Figure 6–16** demonstrates the steps food manufacturers go through to develop flavor for the foods they produce.

VEGETABLES, FRUITS, AND FLOWERS AS FLAVORINGS

We season and flavor foods not only with basic seasonings, herbs, and spices but also by the ingredients we choose to include. Onions, garlic, tomatoes, mushrooms, peppers, and many other vegetables have pronounced flavors that influence the final taste of the product [49] (**Figure 6–17**). Many soup, sauce, and braised meat recipes use a *mirepoix* to flavor the dish. A standard mirepoix is a mixture of diced vegetables including 50 percent onions, 25 percent carrots, and 25 percent celery [32].

Hot Peppers

"Hot" peppers originated in the New World and were taken back to Europe by Christopher Columbus. Hot peppers, commonly called chilies (or chiles), are basic to

Figure 6–17

Vegetables and roots used to build flavor. (Richard Embery/Pearson Education)

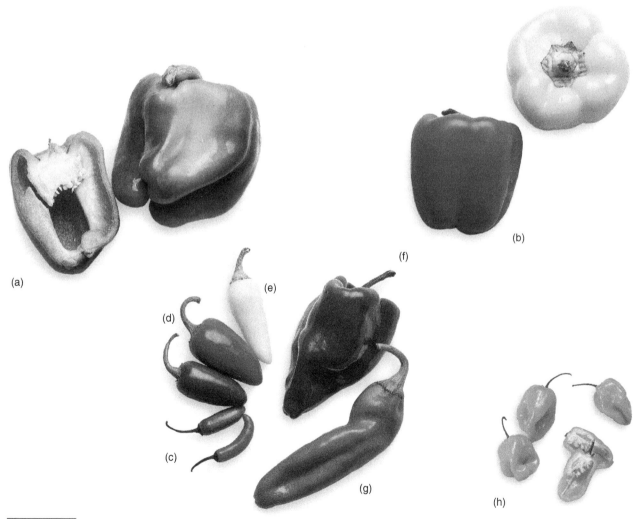

Figure 6–18

Some peppers used as flavoring. (a) Green Bell Pepper (b) Red and Yellow Bell Pepper (c) Red and Green Serrano (d) Green and Red Jalapeño, (e) Yellow Hot Pepper (f) Poblano Chile Pepper, (g) Anaheim Chile Pepper and (h) Habañero Pepper (Richard Embery/Pearson Education)

many **cuisines** of the world and are increasing in popularity in the United States. In the United States, ethnic trends, including an interest in Caribbean, Mexican, and South American dishes, is promoting the consumption of "hotter" dishes. Worldwide, the cuisines of India, Asia, Africa, and many other countries utilize the hot flavors of capsicums in their dishes to convey distinctive flavors.

Chilies are from the *Capsicum* genus, which encompasses over 300 varieties of plants varying in hotness, color, and flavor [5, 56]. Some of the commonly used peppers include the *sweet green pepper, habañero* or *scotch bonnet, jalapeño, chipotle, poblano, ancho, anaheim,* and *paprika.* Sweet green peppers, unlike many other chilies, are not hot but are nevertheless flavorful (**Figure 6–18**). The habañero or scotch bonnet is generally considered to be the hottest chili in the world at 100,000 to 300,000 **Scoville Heat Units**. Jalapeños are hot to medium-hot and are used in many Mexican

---

FOCUS ON SCIENCE
ESSENTIAL OILS AND VANILLA EXTRACT

Essential Oils

Essential oils found in the skin of citrus fruit (orange and lemon) contribute flavor and aroma thought to hold the essence of the plant. The flavor and aroma of spices are made by oil deposits in seeds (cumin), pods or fruits (nutmeg), bark (cinnamon), and even stems (sassafras). Essential plant oils, whether from orange zest or coriander seeds, are highly volatile—that is, they evaporate quickly when exposed to air.

Vanilla Extract

Vanilla is a plant (an orchid), and the beans are its pods (**Figure 6–19**). The mature pod shrivels and turns black after picked. Vanilla can be traced back to indigenous Mexican cultures. Today vanilla is grown in five main areas throughout the world; each region produces vanilla beans with distinctive characteristics.

Figure 6–19

Vanilla orchid with green pods. (Bjul/123RF)

Madagascar is the largest producer of vanilla beans known as Bourbon vanilla, which is known as the highest quality vanilla. Bourbon vanilla applies to vanilla beans grown on Bourbon Islands. Bourbon vanilla is from Madagascar and popular in the United States. Tahitian vanilla is popular in Europe. Indonesia is the second largest producer of vanilla beans which are woody and astringent. Madagascar and Indonesia produce 90 percent of world's

vanilla beans. Southern Indian vanilla crop is expanding, while Mexican production is very small.

The growing location and processing method impact the final flavor. Much like coffee and chocolate, the beans are picked and dried or "cured" to develop flavor and aroma. Vanilla beans are mixed and steeped with ethyl alcohol and water then extracted and bottled. In the United States, real vanilla extract must contain 35 percent ethyl alcohol and 13.35 ounces of vanilla beans per gallon. Double-strength extracts (twofold vanilla) contain the same amount of alcohol but twice the beans.

Artificial vanilla is a combination of chemicals, vanillin, and other ingredients to replace the flavor and aroma of vanilla. Vanilla flavoring has an alcohol content of less than 35 percent. Code of Federal Regulations Title 21 part 169 gives standards of identity for various vanilla and vanillin extracts, powders and flavorings [63].

Whole vanilla beans can be purchased and used to flavor foods (**Figure 6–20**). Vanilla beans should be stored in an airtight container in a cool, dark place. Sometimes vanilla bean will develop a white crystalline coating during storage that is crystalline vanillin, not mold. The beans are still edible with the vanillin crystals [33].

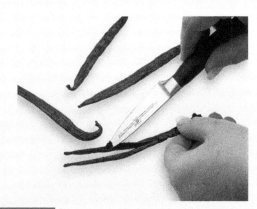

Figure 6–20

Vanilla beans are first split lengthwise. Seeds are scraped and stirred into mixture being flavored. Seeds will not dissolve. Remaining pod can be placed in sugar to create a vanilla sugar. (Richard Embery/Pearson Education)

dishes. The chipotle is a smoke-dried jalapeño with a deep smoky flavor. The ancho chili is a dried poblano chili; both types are mild to medium-hot. Paprika is the powder of a mild sweet chili and is frequently valued in cooking for the rich, red color it adds to a dish [78]. Use of the seeds in chilies, such as jalapeños, adds heat and flavor [65]. If less heat is desired, strip the seeds and discard. When handling chili peppers, "burning" of the hands can occur, and therefore latex gloves are recommended. Likewise, care should be taken to avoid touching the face or eyes when working with chili peppers.

Fruits

Fruits are compatible with savory, salty, hot, and sweet ingredients [61]. Citrus fruits are aromatic and flavorful. Lemons, limes, and oranges contribute to the flavor of many dishes including baked products, entrees, vegetables, or sweet desserts. Fruit salsas made with mangoes or peaches have also become popular.

Edible Flowers

Floral scents and flavors are being recognized as a major flavor trend [61]. Yellow chrysanthemum flower extracts can add floral notes to herbal blends [61]. Flavor pairing such as hibiscus and mango or orange blossom and vanilla result in a new tantalizing flavor [61]. Floral flavored extracts are one way that floral flavors can be added to beverages, candies, and other foods [59]. In addition to flavor, edible flowers add beauty to foods. Nasturtium blossoms have a peppery taste; they are good in salads where the flavor will be complementary (**Figure 6–21**). Roses are sweet and pleasing with desserts.

In selecting flowers, be sure that they have been grown to be eaten and have not been subjected to pesticide sprays. Also, you should be aware that not all flowers are edible. Some flowers, like lily of the valley and daffodils, are poisonous. Rose petals, nasturtiums, Johnny-jump-ups, pansies, calendulas, carnations, snap dragons, and squash blossoms are examples of edible flowers.

CONDIMENTS

Condiments may be described as ingredients used to enhance the flavor, texture, or appearance of food [58]. They can be added after the food is ready to consume or used during preparation. Condiments, however, frequently have a significant impact on the flavor of foods we consume. Some condiments include catsup, mustard, horseradish, hot sauces, salsas, pickle relish, barbeque sauces, soy sauce, wasabi, Hoisin sauce, horseradish, Worchester sauce, sriracha sauce, and fruit chutney (**Figure 6–22**).

ALCOHOL

Wines, liqueurs, and distilled spirits can be used in preparing main dishes, sauces, and desserts, creating new and interesting flavors. The use of bourbon and various ales are being used to flavor foods [61]. Brandy and rum are common bakery and custard flavors. Liqueurs are used to impart flavors such as amaretto which gives almond flavor or Kalhulá for coffee flavor [33].

It has generally been assumed that, because of its low boiling point, the alcohol is evaporated from the foods during cooking. However, a study of six alcohol-containing recipes found that from 4 to 85 percent of the alcohol was retained in the food [2]. A pot roast that was heated over 2 hours, had 4 to 6 percent alcohol retention. Grand Marnier added to a boiling sauce led to alcohol retention of 83 to 85 percent. Flamed

Figure 6–22

Chutney is a pungent spicy relish made from fruit, spices, and herbs. Chutney is used in Indian cuisine. (Richard Embery/Pearson Education)

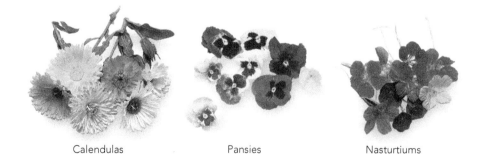

Calendulas   Pansies   Nasturtiums

Figure 6–21

Calendulas, pansies, and nasturtiums are edible flowers that can be used to liven up any salad or dish. (Richard Embery/Pearson Education)

cherries jubilee retained 77 to 78 percent of the alcohol. The presence of alcohol in significant amounts affects the energy value of a food because alcohol contributes approximately 7 kilocalories per gram. Alcohol retention can be problematic for people who are abstaining from alcohol.

FOOD ADDITIVES

A food additive may be broadly described as any substance added to food or beverages either directly or indirectly. The Code of Federal Regulation sets standards for direct, indirect, primary, and secondary food additive sources. Indirect additives are those ingredients that become part of the food in trace amounts from packing, storage, or handling. Direct additives have been added to food.

Numerous additives are used in foods; each has a specific purpose. Many of the additives in foods are very familiar and include salt, vanilla, pepper, baking soda, and spices. Food additives may be used in foods to do the following:

- Maintain or improve safety and freshness
- Improve or maintain nutritional value
- Improve taste, texture, and appearance

Additives cannot be placed in food to conceal damage or spoilage or to deceive the consumer. The FDA regulates the use of additives in foods and maintains a list of additives called "Everything Added to Food in the United States." Some additives, such as salt, are on the GRAS (generally recognized as safe) list and are not subject to the same regulatory process as other ingredients. More information about the regulation of food additives may be found in Chapter 3.

Food additives can be grouped into classes based on similar function. Some of the more important classes or types of additives follow. Examples of each class are given in **Table 6–6**.

Table 6–6
SOME ADDITIVES AND FOOD INGREDIENTS IN USE FOR VARIOUS TYPES OF FOODS

Type or Class	Purpose	Examples	Food in Which Used
Nutrients	Replace vitamins and minerals lost in processing (enrichment) or add nutrients lacking in diet (fortification)	Thiamine, riboflavin, niacin, folate or folic acid, beta carotene, iron or ferrous sulfate, ascorbic acid, vitamin D, alpha tocopherols, potassium iodine	Flour, breads, and cereals in enrichment process. Fruit juices, fruit drinks, dehydrated potatoes, and margarine.
Preservatives (includes antimicrobials and antioxidants)	Prevent food spoilage from bacteria, molds, fungi, or yeast; slow or prevent changes in color, flavor, or texture; delay rancidity; maintain freshness	Ascorbic acid (vitamin C), citric acid, sodium benzoate, calcium propionate, sodium erythorbate, sodium nitrate, calcium sorbate, potassium sorbate, butylated hydroxyanisole, butylated hydroxytoluene, tocopherols (vitamin E)	May be used in a variety of foods. Antioxidants often found in foods containing fats to prevent rancidity. Browning of fruits is prevented by ascorbic and citric acid. Propionates retard molding and development of "rope" in bread. Benzoates provide antimicrobial function in carbonated beverages and fruit drinks.
Coloring agents	Offset color loss, correct natural variations in color, provide color to colorless foods	FD&C Blue #1 and #2, FD&C Green #3, FD&C Red #3 and #40, FD&C #5 (tartrazine), and #6, Orange B, Citrus Red #2, beta-carotene, grape skin extract, paprika oleoresin, cochineal extract or carmine, saffron, caramel color	Found in many processed foods.

(Continued)

Table 6–6
SOME ADDITIVES AND FOOD INGREDIENTS IN USE FOR VARIOUS TYPES OF FOODS (CONTINUED)

Type or Class	Purpose	Examples	Food in Which Used
Flavors and spices	Add a specific flavor, which may be natural or synthetic	Natural flavoring, artificial flavor, spices	Found in a wide variety of foods.
Flavor enhancers	Enhance flavors already in foods without providing a separate flavor	MSG, hydrolyzed soy protein, autolyzed yeast extract, disodium guanylate, or inosinate	Many processed foods.
Emulsifiers	Prevent separation, keep emulsified products stable, allow smooth mixing of ingredients, and control crystallization	Soy lecithin, mono- and diglycerides, egg yolks, polysorbates, sorbitan monostearate	Margarines and shortenings, salad dressings, peanut butter, frozen desserts, chocolate.
Stabilizers and thickeners	Produce uniform texture, improve mouthfeel	Gelatin, pectin, guar gum, carrageenan, xanthan gum, whey	Frozen desserts, dairy products, cakes, pudding, jams, jellies, sauces.
Sequestrants	Bind small amounts of metals which may be undesirable	Ethylenediamine tetraacetic acid	Wine and cider.
Humectants	Retain moisture	Glycerine, sorbitol	Marshmallows, flaked coconut, and cake icings.
Anticaking agents	Prevent moisture absorption; keep powdered foods free-flowing	Calcium silicate, iron ammonium citrate, silicon dioxide	Table salt, powdered sugar, and baking powder.
Bleaching and maturing agents	Improve baking properties of wheat flours	Chlorine, chlorine dioxide, benzoyl peroxide	Cake flour and all-purpose flour.
Leavening agents	Promote rising of baked goods	Baking soda, monocalcium phosphate, calcium carbonate	Breads and other baked goods.
Yeast nutrients	Promote yeast growth	Calcium sulfate, ammonium phosphate	
Dough strengtheners and conditioners	Stabilize dough	Ammonium sulfate, azodicarbonamide, L-cysteine	Breads and other baked goods.
Firming agents	Maintain firmness and crispness	Calcium chloride, calcium lactate	Processed fruits and vegetables.
Enzyme preparations	Modify polysaccharides, fats, and proteins	Enzymes, lactase, papain, rennet, chymosin	Cheese, dairy products, meat.
Acids, alkalis, and buffers	Adjust and control pH	Citric acid and its salts, acetic acid, sodium bicarbonate, sodium hydroxide	Soft drinks, processed cheese, baking powders, Dutch processed cocoa.
Sweeteners	Add sweetness with or without added calories	Sucrose (sugar), glucose, fructose, sorbitol, mannitol, corn syrup, high fructose corn syrup, saccharin, aspartame, sucralose, acesulfame potassium (acesulfame-K), neotame	Beverages, baked goods, sweetener substitutes, many processed foods.

Table 6–6
SOME ADDITIVES AND FOOD INGREDIENTS IN USE FOR VARIOUS TYPES OF FOODS (CONTINUED)

Type or Class	Purpose	Examples	Food in Which Used
Fat replacers	Provide texture and creamy mouthfeel in reduced-fat foods	Olestra (sucrose polyester), cellulose gel, carrageenan, polydextrose, modified food starch, microparticulated protein (as Simplesse®), guar gum, xanthan gum, whey protein concentrate	Baked goods, dressings, frozen desserts, confections, cake and dessert mixes, dairy products.
Bulking agents	Add texture and body	Polydextrose	Baked goods, confections, puddings, and other foods.
Gases	Serve as propellant or create carbonation	Carbon dioxide, nitrous oxide	Oil cooking spray, whipped cream, carbonated beverages.

Nutrient Supplements

Vitamins and minerals are often added to processed foods either to restore or to improve their nutritive value. Examples include the enrichment of bread and cereals, the addition of iodine to salt, and the fortification of milk with vitamin D. Some vitamins, such as vitamins C and E, also play functional roles, such as acting as **antioxidants**.

Preservatives

Antioxidants are a group of preservatives. Fatty foods are particularly susceptible to spoilage known as **rancidity**, which causes unpleasant off-odors and flavors. Some antioxidants retard the development of rancidity. Another type of antioxidant may prevent **enzymatic oxidative browning** in fresh fruits and vegetables. Vitamin C is an effective antioxidant in this regard.

Antimicrobial agents are another group of preservatives. These additives prevent or inhibit spoilage caused by such microorganisms as molds and bacteria. The effectiveness of such preservation methods as refrigeration may be enhanced by the judicious use of certain antimicrobial agents.

Coloring Agents

Color additives are used in foods: 1) to make foods more visually appealing, 2) to correct natural variations, 3) to correct color loss due to exposure to light, air, temperature extremes, moisture, and storage conditions, 4) to enhance natural color, 5) to provide color for colorless foods, and 6) to make "fun" colorful foods. Color additives are defined by the FDA as any dye, pigment, or other substance made or obtained from a vegetable, animal, mineral, or other source capable of coloring a food. The Federal Food Drug and Cosmetic Act declares that any substance that imparts color is a color additive. Color additives are subject to premarket

approval requirements unless used only for a purpose other than coloring. The FDA classifies color additives as either "certified color additives" or "color additives exempt from certification." Synthetic color additive use is decreasing as manufacturers replace them with natural colors to meet consumer demand for simple clean labels and more natural food products [41, 45].

Certified colors are synthetically produced. These certified color additives are used in food because they are less expensive to produce, provide more intense and uniform color, plus they are easily mixed to provide a desired color hue. Certified colors are referred to in the food industry as artificial colors, synthetic colors, or FD&C colors (FD&C-an acronym referring to the Food, Drug, and Cosmetic Act which is codified into the Federal Code known as Title 21). There are nine certified colors approved for use in the United States; they must be certified to meet specifications set by the FDA on a batch-by-batch basis. Ingredient labels must list FDA certified colors by name such as FD&C Blue No. 1. The U.S. federal regulations for colors and listings are found in the Code of Federal Regulations Title 21 parts 70–82. Color regulations may differ between countries.

Certified colors may be classified as *dyes* (water soluble) or *lakes* (water insoluble) [19]. Dyes dissolve in water and are available as liquids, granules, powders, or other special use forms. Food manufacturers use dyes in beverages, dry mixes, baked goods, confections, dairy products, pet foods, and other products. Lake dyes produce more stable colors and are suited for high fat or low moisture products as they do not dissolve in water. Common uses for lake dyes are hard candies, cakes and donuts mixes, coated tablets, and chewing gum.

Color additives exempted from FDA certification are commonly called "natural" or "exempt colors" in the food industry, but legally the FDA does not

---

UP CLOSE

FDA BANS SEVEN FLAVORING SUBSTANCES

In 2018, the FDA banned seven artificial flavors and flavor enhancers. These synthetically derived flavoring additives (benzophenone, ethyl acetate, methyl eugenol, myrcene, pulegone, pyridine, and styrene) were listed as "artificial flavorings" and used in very small amounts. These artificial flavors and flavor enhancers were used in candy, chewing gum, ice cream, and baked goods. Styrene was no longer used by the food industry. Consumer activist groups petitioned the FDA to ban these substances based on animal studies showing that these substances caused cancer. These synthetic flavorings are being banned based on the 1958 Delaney Clause of the Federal Food, Drug and Cosmetic Act that says the FDA cannot approve as safe any food additive that has been found to induce cancer in humans or animals at any dose. The FDA allowed food processors 24 months to find suitable ingredient replacement and to reformulate food products. See Chapter 3 for more information on food regulations. ∎

---

allow the term "natural" to describe the labeling of these color additives. Exempt color additives may be listed on labels as "color added" or "colorings." Natural pigments obtained from fruits and vegetables are available for use in foods and are exempt from certification. Natural sourced coloring in food and beverages is increasing to meet consumer demands. Natural colors are derived from chlorophylls, carotenoids, and anthocyanins that are common in foods [19]. Common natural colorings include annatto, saffron, paprika, beetroots, grape skin extracts, and turmeric [19]. Common natural pigments are generally less stable, paler than artificial colors, and more expensive to produce [19]. Natural colors may not perform the same in all food systems [45]. For example, red beet juice extract may work great in yogurt, but the color compounds brown in baking. New heat stable natural red colorings have recently been developed [45]. Potential risk from natural colorants include pathogen, trace metals, insecticide, and herbicide contamination [19, 41].

All color additives are considered artificial for labeling purposes in the United States. All color additions in a food or beverage must be identified and labeled. "Natural color" is not permitted on the label since color added to food or beverage is considered artificial. Both natural sourced colors and chemically derived colors have the potential to pose risks in foods, hence the need for regulation [41].

Flavorings

Flavorings, which include herbs and spices, make up the largest group of intentional additives. A wide variety of substances are used to improve the flavor of processed foods. These include natural extracts and **essential oils** as well as synthetic or artificial flavorings. Flavor enhancers such as MSG round out flavor profiles. Flavors may be in liquid or powdered forms. Flavored essential oils are more concentrated and potent flavors compared to extracts. Flavor delivery systems such as encapsulation, microencapsulation, and thermal stable flavors are used by food manufacturers [45, 53, 26].

Emulsifiers

Emulsifiers are widely used to mix two immiscible liquids, such as fat and water, uniformly together in the making and stabilizing of **emulsions**. They are also used to stabilize foams and suspensions. Emulsions are discussed further in Chapter 8.

Stabilizers and Thickeners

Texture and body are important characteristics of many foods. A variety of stabilizers and thickeners are used to achieve desired smoothness and consistency, including many vegetable gums, such as carrageenan, and a number of starch products.

Sequestrants

Sequestrants are used to bind (chelate) small amounts of metals, such as iron and copper, that may have undesirable effects on flavor or appearance. These chelating agents help stabilize foods through reactions that alter the effects on food [36].

Humectants and Anticaking Agents

Humectants are used to retain moisture and keep certain foods soft. Some humectants are added to finely powdered or crystalline foods to prevent caking as moisture is absorbed. Anticaking agents are added in small regulated quantities to dry powder or crystalline foods such as salt, sugar, and other dry ingredients to prevent clumping. Calcium silicate, iron ammonium citrate, silicon dioxide, and yellow prussiate of soda are four anticaking agents.

Bleaching and Maturing Agents

The baking properties of wheat flours are improved by the addition of certain oxidizing agents (**maturing agents**). Many of these also have a bleaching effect.

Acids, Alkalis, and Buffers

Acidity or alkalinity is very important in many processed foods. Acids, alkalis, and **buffers** are used to adjust and control the pH. Buffers will resist changes in acidity and alkalinity and thus help to stabilize the pH. The alkaline salt—sodium bicarbonate or baking soda—is also used to produce carbon dioxide gas to leaven baked products.

Alternative Sweeteners

A sweet tooth has apparently always been part of the human anatomy. The harvesting of honey and sugarcane has a long history. However, substitutes for the taste of caloric sweeteners, including sucrose (table sugar), honey, and corn syrups, have been developed only in the past century. A number of alternative sweeteners have been approved by the FDA for use in food and are discussed in Chapter 9.

Fat Replacers

The food industry is motivated to develop substances that can replace fat but leave flavor and texture unchanged or minimally changed. Some of the approved fat replacers are GRAS, whereas others require special approval by the FDA as food additives. Fat replacers may be carbohydrate based, fat based, or protein based. Additional information about fat replacers is discussed in Chapter 10.

Bulking Agents

Bulking agents aid food formulations with reduced fat, carbohydrates, or calories. These ingredients replace the reduced fat or carbohydrate functional properties such as bulk, mouthfeel, and texture attributes. The bulking agents contribute to the desirable bulk provided by omitted fat and carbohydrates [14]. Polydextrose contains only 1 calorie per gram and helps to add texture and body when fat and sugar are reduced in some food products. Polyalcohols and maltodextrins also add body and texture to low-fat or low-sugar products. When used to provide texture and body in reduced-fat or reduced-sugar food products, these substances are called *bulking agents*.

STUDY QUESTIONS

Consumption Trends and Nutritive Value

1. Discuss some seasoning and flavoring trends.
2. How do seasonings impact nutrition?

Seasonings

3. Distinguish among seasonings, flavorings, and flavor enhancers.
4. Describe the basic effects or roles of salt and pepper in cooking.
5. Why is salt used in pickles?

Flavor Enhancers and Masking Agents

6. What is a flavor enhancer? Give examples.
7. What is MSG? How was it discovered? With which types of food is it most effectively used?
8. What is meant by the *umami* taste?
9. What are masking agents? How and why are they used in foods?

Spices and Herbs

10. In a strict classification, what are *spices,* and what are *herbs*?
    (a) Give examples of each.
    (b) Describe their basic roles in cooking.
    (c) Give suggestions for proper storage.
    (d) Suggest uses for fresh herbs.
    (e) How should selected herbs and spices be adjusted when increasing a recipe yield?
11. Discuss quality issues with spices. Describe how these issues are monitored.

Flavorings

12. Flavorings are important in food. Discuss some delivery methods and types of flavorings used in foods.

Food Additives

13. Identify and discuss ingredients other than spices, herbs, and basic seasonings that add flavor in recipes.
14. List at least 10 different types or groups of food additives and give examples of specific additives for each group.

7

Food Composition

Water, protein, carbohydrates, and fats are the four main food components. Each component can be thought of as chemical **molecules** put together and interacting in a variety of ways for different foods. *Chemical composition* is the determination of the food chemical components through laboratory analysis (**Figure 7–1**). Water, carbohydrates, fats, and proteins are the chemical substances found in largest amounts in foods. Enzymes are special types of proteins found in small amounts in unprocessed plant and animal tissues. Minerals, vitamins, acids, pigments, and flavor substances are also present in foods in minute amounts.

Comprehensive food composition tables have been produced by compiling the results of laboratory food sample analyses. The Agricultural Research Service in the U.S. Department of Agriculture (USDA) provides a database that reports nutrients in over 180,000 foods. This database, called the *USDA National Nutrient Database for Standard Reference*, is available from the USDA website (See Appendix C) [19]. The USDA also has food composition database tables for "Branded Food Products." Flavonoids, isoflavones, and proanthocyanidins values were added in 2015. The USDA nutrient databases are maintained by the Nutrient Database laboratory, Beltsville Human Nutrition Research Center, located in Beltsville, Maryland (**Figure 7–2**).

Figure 7–2

USDA Beltsville Nutrition Laboratory. (USDA)

Figure 7–3

USDA Food technologist Steven Shackelford makes computerized images of steak samples to predict beef composition. (Keith Weller/USDA)

In addition to knowing the quantity of each chemical component present in foods, we need some knowledge of the characteristics and properties of the major constituents (**Figure 7–3**). Changes may occur in these components as a food is processed and prepared (**Figure 7–4**). For example, water is removed in large quantities from fruits, vegetables, and meats when they are dehydrated. Fat melts and is found in the drippings when meat is roasted. Oil and water or vinegar separate from each other when the **emulsion** in mayonnaise is broken. The addition of fresh pineapple to a gelatin mixture prevents gel formation. Gelatin, which is a protein, is broken down into **peptides** or **amino acids** by an enzyme in the fresh pineapple.

Figure 7–1

USDA biological laboratory technician Elizabeth Denvir extracts samples for total lipid and fatty acid composition. (Scott Bauer/USDA)

Figure 7–4

USDA technician Brooke Balsam prepares ground beef for fat analysis. (Jack Dykinga/USDA)

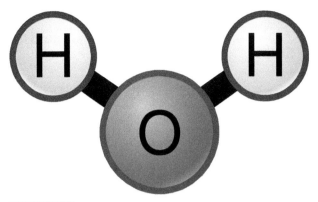

Figure 7–5

Molecular diagram of water molecule with one atom of oxygen and two atoms of hydrogen. (Oxford Designers & Illustrators Ltd/Pearson Education Ltd)

The information presented in this chapter will be helpful in understanding the nature of foods as discussed in other chapters. In this chapter, the following chemical characteristics of the major components of foods will be discussed:

- Water
- Carbohydrates
- Lipids
- Proteins
- Solutions and dispersions

WATER

All foods contain at least some water. Much of the water in plant and animal tissues is held inside the cells. Water in foods may be free water or bound water. Water activity is the ratio of the vapor pressure of water in a food at a specified temperature to the vapor pressure of pure water at the same temperature. Foods with a high water activity level are more perishable than foods with a low water activity level.

Water in Foods

Water is contained in all foods, even in those that appear to be quite dry (**Figure 7–5**). The water content ranges from as low as 1 or 2 percent to as high as 98 percent, although most foods contain intermediate amounts. **Table 7–1** gives the water content of selected foods. Foods high in water are raw vegetables and juicy fruits. Fresh greens contain about 96 percent water, and watermelon has about 93 percent water. Crackers, a low-moisture food, usually contain only 2 to 4 percent water.

Water can exist as a solid (ice), liquid, or gas (steam) depending on the temperature and pressure (**Figure 7–6**). Each water phase is important in food. Water is an essential component in many

Table 7–1
WATER CONTENT OF SELECTED FOODS

Food	Water Content %
Lettuce, iceberg, raw	96
Celery, raw	95
Broccoli, cooked	90
Carrots, raw	88
Milk, whole	88
Orange juice	88
Oatmeal, cooked	85
Apples, raw	84
Creamed cottage cheese	79
Eggs, raw, whole	75
Bananas	74
Chicken breast, cooked	65
Ice cream	61
Beef roast, lean, cooked	57
Pork, ham, cooked	53
Pizza, cheese, baked	46
Potatoes, french-fried	38
Cheddar cheese	37
Bread, whole wheat	38
Bread, white	37
Cake, white layer	24
Butter	16
Raisins	15
Brownies	10
Cookies, chocolate chip	4
Popcorn, popped, plain	4
Cornflakes	3
Peanuts, roasted in oil	2

Source: Reference 14.

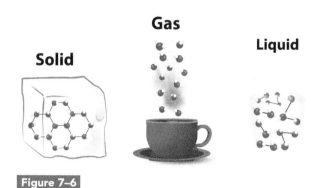

Figure 7–6

Water can exist as a solid (ice), liquid, or gas (steam).
(Designua/Shutterstock)

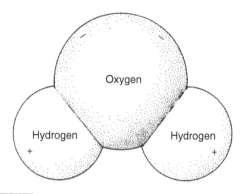

Figure 7–7

The water molecule is called a dipolar molecule because part of it is positively charged and another part is negatively charged.

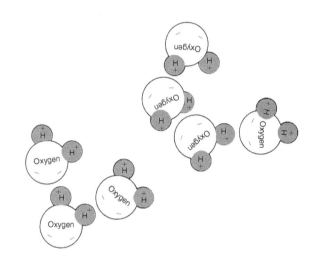

Figure 7–8

Water molecules cluster together because the positive charge on the hydrogen side of the molecule is attracted to the negative charge on the oxygen side of the molecule, forming a weak bond.

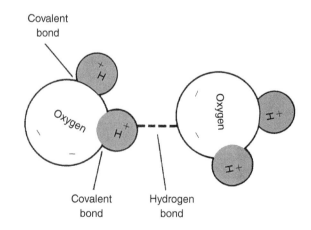

Figure 7–9

A hydrogen bond forms as water molecules are attracted to each other.

foods. It plays a major role in the heating and cooking of foods. Water affects the appearance, flavor, and texture of food. Food storage, food preparation, food systems, and food safety are all dependent on water. Water's importance in food is essential to understand; this ubiquitous substance is so often taken for granted.

The Nature of Water

Water is a small molecule containing two hydrogen atoms and one oxygen atom (H_2O) bonded strongly together by **covalent bonds**. However, water does not behave in the same manner as most other similar size molecules due to water's physical properties and chemical nature. Water is a unique molecule that we all depend on for our existence.

Water is unique because of its **polar** nature [5]. Although the hydrogen and oxygen atoms are joined by strong covalent bonds, the positive and negative charges are not evenly distributed over the whole molecule. **Figure 7–7** is a representation of a water molecule with a negative (−) charge on the oxygen side and positive (+) charge on the hydrogen sides. The water molecule has positive and negative poles and thus is *dipolar*. Because opposite charges attract each other, the negative part of one water molecule is attracted to the positive part of another water molecule, causing these molecules to cluster together, as demonstrated in **Figure 7–8**. The attraction between the negatively charged oxygen and the positively charged hydrogen is a type of bonding that is much weaker than covalent bonding. This special bond is called a *hydrogen bond* (**Figure 7–9**).

Because water molecules have such a special attraction for their fellow molecules, considerable energy is necessary to separate them from each other. This fact is apparent when water is boiled and its state is changed from the liquid to the gaseous molecules of steam or water vapor. The boiling point of water (212°F/100°C at sea level) is quite high, considering the small size of this molecule.

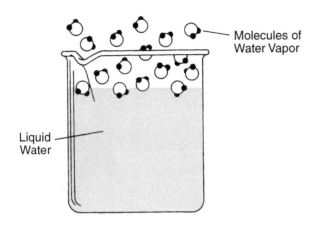

Molecules of
Water Vapor

Liquid
Water

Figure 7–10

Vapor pressure is the pressure produced over the surface of a liquid, such as water, as a result of the escape of some of the liquid molecules into the vapor or gaseous state. This process causes water to gradually disappear or evaporate from an open container even at room temperature.

Water does not readily change to a gaseous state; a considerable amount of heat must be applied to the water to overcome the special attraction of the molecules for each other and raise the vapor pressure before the water will boil. The *vapor pressure* is the pressure produced by those water molecules that have already become vapor. Water molecules are close to the surface of the liquid water even at room temperature (**Figure 7–10**). Water's vapor pressure is comparatively low. The amount of energy or heat (called latent heat of vaporization) required to change water from the liquid state to a gaseous state at its boiling point is 540 calories (0.54 **kilocalorie**) for each gram of water changed to steam. The temperature of the steam itself is the same as the temperature of the boiling water. The boiling point of water is discussed in more detail in connection with boiling sugar solutions in **Chapter 9**.

Free Water.   Much water in plant and animal tissues is held inside the cells (intracellular). In many cases, it is held within the cells as a hydrate, which means that it does not flow from the cells when the tissues are cut or torn. For example, by visual observation, lean broiled beefsteak does not appear to contain about 60 percent water, and a sliced stalk of celery does not appear to be 94 percent water. A food's ability to hold water is referred to as its *water-holding (binding) capacity.*

Although much of the water in plant and animal tissues is held as a hydrate, it is still available. That is, it may be removed by pressure, and it retains the properties of pure water—it can be frozen or act as a **solvent** to dissolve other molecules. This available water that retains properties of pure water is called *free water.*

Bound Water.   Some of the water in foods is held in an extremely tightly bound form and is called **bound water**. Bound water becomes part of the structure of large molecules such as proteins and **complex carbohydrates**. This bound water has reduced mobility, and does not have the same properties as free water—it does not readily freeze or boil and cannot easily be pressed from the tissue. Some water is bound by the interaction with **ions** and small molecules.

Water Activity.   Water activity (a_w) is measured on a scale ranging from 0.0 (no activity) to 1.0 (water). The more water that is bound in a food, the less the activity of the water. Water activity (a_w) is defined as the ratio of the **vapor pressure** of water in a food (p) at a specified temperature to the vapor pressure of pure water (p_o) at the same temperature, as shown here:

$$\text{Water activity } (a_w) = \frac{\text{Vapor pressure of water in food sample } (p)}{\text{Vapor pressure of water of pure water } (p_o)}$$

The presence of **nonvolatile** substances in a food, such as sugars and salts, lowers the vapor pressure of the water present. Therefore, the water activity of foods will be less than 1.0.

The perishability of a food is related to its water content. Food with higher water content is generally more perishable. This relationship occurs because microorganisms require water for their growth. However, an even closer relationship exists between water activity and perishability. Water activity can be reduced by drying a food. In this case, some water is removed by vaporization, thus causing the substances that are dissolved in the water remaining in the food to become more concentrated and the vapor pressure, therefore, to be lowered. Water activity can also be reduced by freezing because water is removed from the system when it forms ice. The addition of sugar or salt lowers the water activity of a food because some water is bound by these substances; that water is then unavailable for use by microorganisms.

Foods with a water activity of 0.85 or higher are susceptible to bacterial growth. Intermediate-moisture foods normally have water activity between 0.7 and 0.9 and are soft enough to eat without rehydration. Fresh meats, fruits, and vegetables have usual water activity values of 0.95 to 0.99 and are susceptible to spoilage.

Uses of Water in Food Preparation

Water plays several important roles in food preparation, affecting both the sensory characteristics of food [13] and the processes by which heat is transferred and foods are cooked. A negative aspect of water when it is used in cooking is that it may leach out and dissolve some important nutrients, such as vitamins and minerals. For this reason, it is suggested that vegetables be cooked in as little of water as possible, or else the cooking water is consumed.

Figure 7–11

Water is sometimes considered the "universal solvent" or dispersion medium. Food dispersion may be simple like a sugar solution or complex as a cake batter. Food dispersion may be gas bubbles, solid matter and crystals (such as salt or sugar). (Coleman Yuen/Pearson Education Asia Ltd)

Figure 7–13

Vinaigrette salad dressing is an example of an oil in water emulsion. (Richard Embery/Pearson Education)

Universal Solvent.   Water has been called a *universal solvent,* indicating that it can dissolve many different substances (**Figure 7–11**). Water acts as a solvent or a dispersing medium for most of the chemical substances in foods. This dispersion may be as simple as sugar in water solution or complex like a cake batter. The dispersion may be in the form of a solution, colloidal dispersion, emulsions (**Figure 7–12**), or suspension. Liquids may be dispersed in solids such as meats and jellies [4].

In a solution, water dissolves substances such as salt, sugar, vitamins, minerals, flavoring agents, and other substances. Solutions may be ionic or molecular in nature. Solutions are an essential part of many foods and food systems. Flavor molecules in beverages such

as coffee and tea are dissolved in water, and sugars are dissolved in fruit juices and in syrups.

Colloidal dispersions are found in foods that are not true solutions and differ in size of molecules involved. Colloidal dispersion molecules are larger. Gelatin is an example of a colloidal dispersion. A solid dispersed in a liquid is called a sol. Gels are a liquid-solid dispersion that are rigid structures. Gels may be carbohydrate or protein based.

Emulsions are liquid and liquid dispersions typically oil in water such as homogenized milk and salad dressings. Emulsions can also be a water in oil dispersion, such as butter (**Figure 7–13**).

Suspensions have large molecules that are neither a solution nor a colloidal dispersion. Starch in

Figure 7–12

Oil in water emulsion is common in foods. Emulsifiers are sometimes used to create a uniform dispersion of oil in the water medium. (Richard Embery/Pearson Education)

water is an example of a suspension. Starch granules may first be dispersed in cold water and then heated, absorbing large amounts of water to produce a thickened mixture, such as a pudding or sauce. More detailed discussions on solutions, emulsions, colloidal dispersions, and suspensions will be presented later.

Heat Transfer. In cooking, water is an important medium for applying heat. It may be used for this purpose both in its liquid form as hot or boiling water and in its vapor form as steam. When water boils, the forces of attraction between water molecules are overcome, and the water molecules become gaseous. They leave the container in bubbles of steam (**Figure 7–14**).

Factors affecting the boiling point of water are altitude, barometric pressure, steam pressure, salt, and sugar. At sea level, the temperature of boiling water is 212°F (100°C). However, in Denver, Colorado, which is at an elevation of approximately 5,000 feet, water boils at 203°F (95°C). Thus, food will cook slower at high elevations. Making water boil rapidly does not increase this boiling temperature at any elevation. Steam that is not under pressure has the same temperature as boiling water.

The boiling point of water may be raised above 100°C under pressure, such as in a pressure canner or saucepan (**Figure 7–15**). As pressure rises, more energy and more heat must be applied to give water molecules enough energy to convert the water to steam. Given water boils at 100°C (212°F), then at 5 pounds steam pressure, water boils at 109°C (228°F), 10 pounds pressure 115°C (240°F), and 15 pounds pressure 121°C (250°F) [7].

Barometric pressure can cause fluctuations in the boiling point of water at the same altitude. If barometric pressure is low, water boils below 100°C (212°F). When barometric pressure is low, the air is less dense, so boiling point of water is lower. Weather changing from clear to cloudy typically causes a lower barometric

Figure 7–15
Steam that is not under pressure has the same temperature as boiling water. The boiling point of water may be raised under pressure such as in a pressure cooker. (Steve Heap/Shutterstock)

pressure and cloudy to clear a higher barometric pressure. The boiling point of water may need to be checked with the thermometer and adjusted to endpoint temperatures prior to making certain foods, such as candy or jelly, that rely on precise temperatures for quality products. To calibrate the boiling point, simply insert a candy thermometer in a rapid boiling pot of water. If the boiling point is above or below 100°C (212°F), then add or subtract this number of degrees to the endpoint cooking temperature.

Salt and sugar both increase boiling point and depress freezing point. The salt and sugar molecules dilute water molecules and lower water vapor pressure. Salt and sugar raise solution boiling points to a higher temperature and lower freezing points to a lower temperature [7]. These facts are important in understanding food systems and the production of foods such as ice cream, which will be discussed in Chapter 10.

A certain amount of energy, called **latent heat** or *heat of vaporization,* is necessary to change the state of water from its liquid form to its vapor form as steam. This heat is absorbed by the steam but does not register on a thermometer. When steam condenses on a cooler surface and returns to its liquid form, the latent heat is released and helps to cook the food. For example, steamed vegetables are cooked both by the heat of the steam itself and by the release of latent energy from the steam as it condenses on the surface of the vegetables and changes back to its liquid water form. The energy released by the changing state from vapor to liquid is stored energy, so this energy becomes available to cook the food [4]. Heat transfer was discussed in Chapter 5.

Steam. When water vaporizes, it becomes steam. Steam is an important leavening agent in many baked

Figure 7–14
Water is important in food preparation. It serves as a medium when applying heat as a boiling liquid or vapor from steam. (Joe Belanger/Shutterstock)

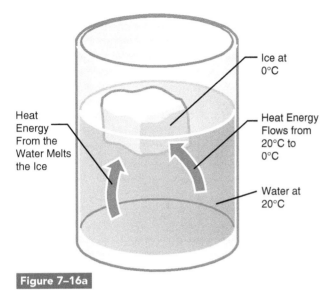

Figure 7–16a

Latent heat of fusion is involved in the melting of ice.

(HL Studios/Pearson Education Ltd)

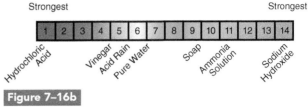

Figure 7–16b

pH affects characteristics and chemical reactions in many foods.

goods. Steam also serves as a cooking method. In pressure cooking, steam pressure is an essential element as steam confined to a small space previously occupied by air causes a rapid pressure buildup. As steam pressure rises, so do boiling points. One teaspoon of water can yield 2 gallons of steam [7].

Freezing. Water is involved in the preparation of **freezing mixtures** that may be used to freeze ice creams and other frozen desserts, particularly those made at home. When crushed ice (water in its solid form) is mixed with salt, the salt dissolving on the surface of the ice increases the melting rate. As ice changes from its solid form to liquid (water), heat is absorbed. This energy is called *latent heat of fusion*. See **Figure 7–16a**. The same amount of heat is given off when water freezes to ice. Water freezes at 32°F (0°C).

Cleansing Agent. Water also performs an important function as a cleansing agent both for food itself and for utensils and equipment used in the preparation and serving of food. It removes soil particles and many microorganisms as well. Cleaning agents, such as soaps and detergents, increase the cleaning capacity of water.

Chemical Changes. Water promotes chemical changes in certain cases. Some mineral salts become ionized in solution—they break apart, and each part develops either a positive (+) or a negative (−) charge. For example, common table salt is known chemically as sodium chloride or NaCl. When this salt is placed in water, it dissolves and ionizes into sodium and chlorine ions as follows:

$$NaCl \rightarrow Na^+Cl^-$$

Ionization of salt in water increases the temperature at which water boils; however, the effect is minimal with the amount of salt typically used.

Ionization causes other chemical reactions to occur. As long as baking powder remains dry, no chemical reactions take place. However, when baking powder dissolves in water, some of the chemicals that it contains ionize and then react with each other to produce new chemical substances. Among these products is carbon dioxide (CO_2) gas, which rises in tiny bubbles and makes a baked product light or leavened.

Water also affects the reactions of acids and bases (also called alkalis). The chemical phenomenon that characterizes an acid substance is the ionization of a hydrogen atom, producing a positively charged hydrogen ion (H^+). This hydrogen ion, among other things, stimulates our taste buds to give us the impression of sourness. The ion that is characteristic of bases or alkalis is a negatively charged hydroxyl ion (OH^-).

Water and pH. The degree of acidity or alkalinity affects the characteristics of many foods and food mixtures during preparation. Acidity affects the color of fruit juices and vegetables during cooking and chocolate in baked products. The pH scale was developed for quantification of the acidity degrees. This scale runs from 1 as the most acidic to 14 as the most alkaline, as shown in **Figure 7–16b**. A pH of 7, in the middle, indicates an essentially neutral solution (neither acidic nor basic).

Pure water that has an equal number of hydrogen (H^+) and hydroxyl (OH^-) ions has a pH of 7. Tap water, however, usually has small amounts of other ions that affect its acidity or alkalinity, thus changing the pH from 7. For example, the harder the tap water, the more calcium and magnesium ions it contains. The presence of these ions increases the alkalinity of hard water, so its pH is above 7. This alkaline or basic pH will affect the color of some vegetables cooked in the water.

The pH of foods also has a connection to food safety. Foods with a pH of 4.6 to 7.5 are most likely to support the growth of pathogenic organisms. The pH values of selected foods are given in **Table 7–2**.

Hydrolysis. Water has an active part in a special type of chemical reaction called *hydrolysis*, which refers to the breaking of a linkage between units of a larger or more complex molecule to yield smaller molecules. If a complex molecule is completely hydrolyzed, all of the linkages between the small building blocks that make up the larger molecule are broken. In this process, a water molecule actually becomes part of the end product.

Table 7–2
pH OF SELECTED FOODS

Food	pH
Limes	2.0
Lemons	2.2
Vinegar	2.9
Strawberries	3.4
Pears	3.9
Tomatoes	4.2
Buttermilk	4.5
Bananas	4.6
Carrots	5.0
Bread	5.4
Meat, ripened	5.8
Tuna	6.0
Potatoes	6.1
Corn	6.3
Egg yolk	6.4
Milk	6.6
Egg white	7.0–9.0

Source: Adapted from Reference 2.

as *scale* in hot-water heaters and kettles used over a long period primarily for boiling water. *Permanently hard water* contains calcium, magnesium, and iron sulfates that do not precipitate on boiling. They form insoluble salts with soap and decrease its cleaning capacity.

Hard Water and Food Preparation. The mineral salts of hard water may affect food preparation in various ways. Calcium retards the rehydration and softening of dried beans and peas during soaking and cooking. Hard water is often fairly alkaline and may thus affect the color of some of the pigments in cooked vegetables. Iced tea may be cloudy because some compounds in the tea (polyphenols) precipitate with the calcium and magnesium salts in hard water. Water that is naturally soft contains very few mineral salts.

Softening Water. Hard water may be softened by several different processes. In one method, water-softening agents, such as washing soda and polyphosphates, may be added to water to precipitate the calcium and magnesium salts. Another method uses an ion-exchange process in which calcium and magnesium ions are exchanged for sodium ions (**Figure 7–18**). A resinous material may be contained in a water-softening tank through which the hard water flows. Sodium ions held by the resin are exchanged for calcium and magnesium in the hard water until the resin has exhausted its sodium supply. At this point, the resin may be recharged with sodium by flushing it with a strong salt solution. Water softened in this manner is, of course, higher in sodium than it was originally.

Starch can serve as an example of hydrolysis. Starch is a complex carbohydrate molecule made up of hundreds of small glucose (a simple sugar) molecules linked together. When starch is hydrolyzed, the chemical linkages between the glucose units are broken. For each linkage that is broken, one molecule enters into the reaction and becomes part of the glucose molecules, as shown in **Figure 7–17**.

Water Hardness

Water is generally classified as being soft or hard to various degrees. What is it that makes water hard? Basically, it is the presence of various mineral salts.

Types of Hard Water. The two general types of hard water are temporary and permanent. *Temporarily hard water* contains calcium, magnesium, and iron bicarbonates that precipitate as insoluble carbonates when the water is boiled. These mineral deposits may accumulate

CARBOHYDRATES

What comes to mind when you hear the word *carbohydrate*? You may think of sugars and starch and perhaps fiber. Sugars are *simple carbohydrates*, consisting of either one basic sugar unit or a few of these small units linked together. Starch and fiber belong to the class of *complex carbohydrates* because they may have thousands of basic sugar units linked together to form very large molecules. Thus, carbohydrates are either sugars or more complex substances, such as starch, that are formed by the combination of many sugars.

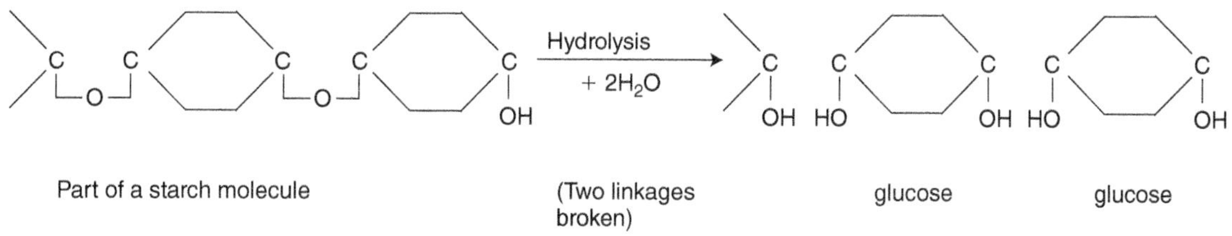

Part of a starch molecule   (Two linkages broken)   glucose   glucose

Figure 7–17

Hydrolysis of a starch molecule is depicted here. The addition of two molecules of water (H_2O) is needed when the linkages are broken in the starch molecule to produce two molecules of glucose after hydrolysis.

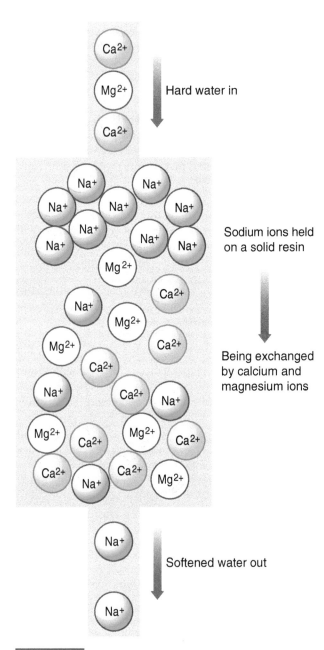

Figure 7–18

Water softeners work by exchanging ions of Ca and Mg for Na ions. This diagram shows how water is softened using ion exchange column: exchanging calcium and magnesium ions by sodium ions. (Oxford Designers & Illustrators Ltd/Pearson Education Ltd)

Ca²⁺ / Mg²⁺ / Ca²⁺ — Hard water in

Sodium ions held on a solid resin

Being exchanged by calcium and magnesium ions

Softened water out

the atmosphere and water (H_2O) from the soil into the simple sugar, glucose ($C_6H_{12}O_6$). Oxygen (O_2) is given off by the plant during this photosynthetic process. Thus, begins the cycle of nature on which animal life depends on plants.

High-carbohydrate foods, including various cereal grains, legumes, and starchy roots or tubers, are staples in the diets of millions of people throughout the world. Foods classified as largely carbohydrate include the following:

Sugars	Jellies and jams
Syrups	Flours
Molasses	Dried fruits
Honey	Legumes
Candies	Cereal products

Chemical Classification

Carbohydrates are classified according to the number of basic sugar units that are linked together. They may thus be grouped in the following way:

Monosaccharides	Simple sugars with one basic unit (glucose, fructose, and galactose)
Disaccharides	Simple sugars with two basic units (sucrose, lactose, and maltose)
Oligosaccharides	Intermediate-size molecules containing approximately 10 or fewer basic units
Polysaccharides	Complex carbohydrates with many basic units (up to thousands)

Monosaccharides. The simplest sugar carbohydrates are monosaccharides. *Saccharide* refers to their sweetness and *mono* to the fact that they are a single unit. Those that we are most concerned in food preparation contain six carbon atoms and are thus called **hexoses**, although some five-carbon sugars, called **pentoses**, are important components of certain fibers and **vegetable gums**.

Three important hexose monosaccharides are glucose, fructose, and galactose. Another name for glucose is *dextrose*; fructose is sometimes called *levulose*. Each sugar has the same number of elements, $C_6H_{12}O_6$, but slight differences in the position of the chemical groups produce differences in properties, including sweetness and solubility. Chemical structures for these sugars are shown in **Figure 7–19**, and some sources are given in **Table 7–3**. Sugars are discussed in more detail in Chapter 9.

Glucose. The most widely distributed monosaccharide in foods is glucose, which is present in at least small amounts in all fruits and vegetables. The sugar that circulates in the bloodstream is glucose. Many complex

Carbon (C), hydrogen (H), and oxygen (O) are the elements that make up carbohydrates. The ratios of these elements to each other form a pattern: One molecule of water (H_2O), containing the hydrogen and oxygen, is present for each atom of carbon. *Hydrated carbon* is suggested by the ratio $[C_x(H_2O)_y]$, and from this the name *carbohydrate* has been derived.

Carbohydrates are formed in green plants through *photosynthesis* where energy from the sun is harnessed to convert carbon dioxide (CO_2) from

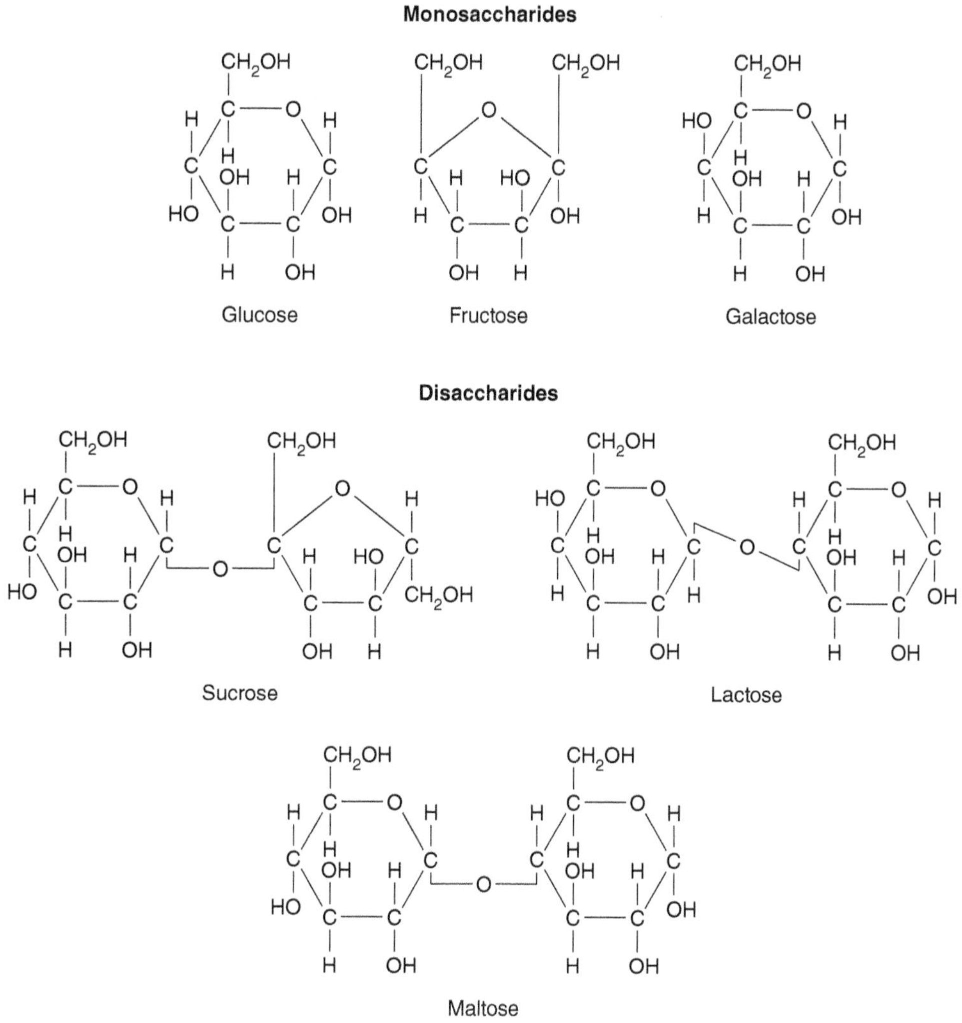

Monosaccharides

Glucose   Fructose   Galactose

Disaccharides

Sucrose   Lactose

Maltose

Figure 7–19

Chemical structures are shown for monosaccharides and disaccharides of importance in food preparation.

carbohydrates, including starch, have glucose as their basic sugar unit. Glucose is a major component of corn syrup, which is produced by the breakdown or hydrolysis of the complex starch molecule. Crystalline glucose and corn syrup are widely used in bakery products and other manufactured foods. Glucose is present in honey with relatively large amounts of fructose.

Fructose. Probably the sweetest of all the common sugars is fructose. It contributes much of the sweetness to honey and is found in many fruits, sometimes being called fruit sugar. Because it is very soluble, fructose is not easily crystallized.

Technology has made possible the production of a high-fructose corn syrup by employing a special enzyme, called *glucose isomerase*, to change glucose to fructose. This syrup is widely used in processed foods, particularly soft drinks.

Galactose. Although galactose is generally not found free in natural foods, it is one of the two

building blocks of milk sugar (lactose). Some galactose is formed from the breakdown or **hydrolysis** of lactose when fermented milk products, such as yogurt, are made. Galactose is also present in some oligosaccharides, such as raffinose. A derivative of galactose (galacturonic acid) is the basic unit of pectic substances. Pectic substances are polysaccharides found in plant cells that are associated with gelling properties in jelly and jam. Additionally, galactose is a basic building block of many vegetable gums, which are complex carbohydrates.

Disaccharides. Monosaccharides are the building blocks of disaccharides, which consist of two monosaccharides linked together. The primary disaccharides in foods are sucrose, lactose, and **maltose**. Their chemical structures are shown in Figure 7–19, and some sources are listed in Table 7–3.

Sucrose. Sucrose is table sugar and is widely used in crystalline form for food preparation. It is usually

Table 7–3
SUGARS, THEIR SOURCES, AND PRODUCTS OF HYDROLYSIS

Sugar	Common Sources	Products of Hydrolysis
Monosaccharides, $C_6H_{12}O_6$		
Glucose or dextrose	Fruit and plant juices. Often present with other sugars. Honey. Can be result of hydrolysis of sucrose, lactose, and maltose.	
Fructose or levulose	Fruit and plant juices. Often present with other sugars. Honey. Can be result of hydrolysis of sucrose.	
Galactose	Does not occur free in nature. Formed by hydrolysis of lactose or galactans.	
Disaccharides, $C_{12}H_{22}O_{11}$		
Sucrose	Present with other sugars in many fruits and vegetables. Sugarcane and sugar beets are rich sources. Maple sugar and syrup. Used in many processed foods.	One molecule each of glucose and fructose. A mixture of equal amounts of glucose and fructose is called *invert sugar*.
Lactose	Milk and whey.	One molecule each of glucose and galactose.
Maltose	Malted or germinated grains. Corn syrup. Can be result of hydrolysis of starch.	One molecule yields two molecules of glucose.
Oligosaccharides		
Raffinose (a trisaccharide)	The seed coats of legumes, nuts, and dried beans.	One molecule each of galactose, glucose, and fructose.
Stachyose (a tetrasaccharide)	Legumes, nuts, seeds, and dried beans.	One molecule of raffinose plus galactose.

extracted from sugarcane or the sugar beet. Sucrose is composed of one molecule of glucose and one of fructose. These two monosaccharides are linked through their most reactive chemical groups, the aldehyde group $(HC{=}O)$ of glucose and the ketone group $(C{=}O)$ of the fructose.

When sucrose is hydrolyzed, the linkage between glucose and fructose is broken, and a molecule of water is added in the reaction. The resulting mixture, containing equal molecular amounts of glucose and fructose, is called *invert sugar* and is important in controlling sugar crystallization during the process of making crystalline candies (see Chapter 9). Sucrose may also be hydrolyzed by an enzyme called *sucrase* or *invertase*, as is used in the making of chocolate-covered cherries with the liquid interior.

Lactose. Lactose, commonly called milk sugar, is found naturally only in milk and milk products. The two monosaccharides that make up lactose are glucose and galactose. Whey, produced during cheesemaking, is a rich source of lactose and is sometimes used in processed foods. Whey also contains whey protein.

Maltose. Two molecules of glucose link to form maltose. Maltose is one of the products of hydrolysis

when the complex carbohydrate starch is broken down. Therefore, it is present in germinating or sprouting grains, where starch hydrolysis provides energy for the grain growth. It is also an important component of corn syrup, which is made by breaking down corn starch.

Oligosaccharides. The term *oligosaccharide* may be used to refer to carbohydrate molecules containing 10 or fewer monosaccharide units. (*Oligo* is a Greek word meaning "few.") This category includes the trisaccharide (three sugar units) raffinose and the tetrasaccharide (four sugar units) stachyose. These carbohydrates are not digested by humans and may be broken down by bacteria in the intestinal tract, resulting in some gas formation. They are present in dried beans.

Oligosaccharides are added to several foods, including soft drinks and cereals, to act as **prebiotics** by stimulating the metabolism of indigenous bifidobacteria in the colon [18]. Growth of bifidobacteria apparently suppresses the activity of putrefactive bacteria.

Polysaccharides. Polysaccharides are complex carbohydrates containing monosaccharide units numbering from about 40 to thousands. These basic units are linked in various ways. Linkages may produce long, straight chains in some cases and branched-type molecules in other instances.

Starch and Dextrins. Starch is the basic storage carbohydrate of plants and is therefore found in abundance in seeds, roots, and tubers. Hundreds or even thousands of glucose molecules join to make a starch molecule. Basically, there are two kinds of starch molecules, sometimes called *fractions of starch*. One is a long chain or linear type of molecule called *amylose*. The other is a highly branched, bushy type of molecule referred to as *amylopectin*. Most natural starches are mixtures of these two fractions, each contributing its own properties in relation to thickening and gelling. Illustrations for the chemical structures of amylose and amylopectin are shown in **Figure 7–20**.

As starch molecules are produced in a growing plant, they are placed in a tightly organized formation called a *granule*. **Starch granules** are large enough to be seen under an ordinary microscope. When starch granules are heated in water, they swell tremendously in a process called *gelatinization*. The swollen starch granules are responsible for the thickening that occurs when starchy puddings and sauces are cooked. Starch and gelatinization are discussed in more detail in future chapters.

Dextrins are produced when starch molecules are partially broken down by enzymes, acid, or dry heat. We might think of dextrins as large chunks of broken starch molecules. They are formed from starch when corn syrup is made, when bread is toasted, and when flour is browned. Dextrins have less thickening power than starch.

Glycogen. Glycogen, a polysaccharide, is sometimes called *animal starch* because it is found in animal tissues. It is similar in structure to the amylopectin or branched fraction of starch. When completely hydrolyzed, it yields only glucose. The liver stores glycogen on a short-term basis until it is hydrolyzed to help maintain a normal blood sugar level. The muscles also temporarily store glycogen.

Plant Fiber Components. The term *dietary fiber* refers to the "edible parts of plants or analogous carbohydrates that are resistant to digestion and absorption in the human small intestine with complete or partial fermentation in the large intestine" [1]. **Fiber** is sometimes called *roughage* or *bulk* and is a complex mixture composed primarily of *cellulose, hemicelluloses, beta-glucans, pectins,* and *gums,* which are all polysaccharides. The fact that oligosaccharides are indigestible by human digestive juices may qualify them to be called low-molecular-weight, water-soluble dietary fibers. A non-carbohydrate molecule called **lignin** also is part of the fiber complex, particularly

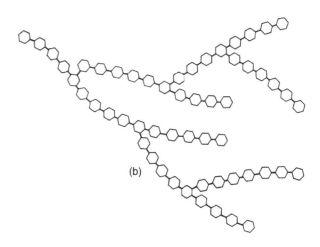

Figure 7–20

Portions of starch molecules, of which there are two types: (a) amylose, a long-chain-like molecule, also called the linear fraction, contributes gelling characteristics to cooking and cooled starch mixtures, and (b) amylopectin, the branched fraction, contributes thickening properties to cooked starch mixtures. Each small unit represents one molecule of glucose.

in woody portions of vegetables. The Food and Nutrition Board at the National Academy of Sciences has proposed new definitions of "dietary fiber" and "added fiber" that distinguishes between intact fiber in plants and fiber that has been isolated and added to foods [3, 10].

The fiber components are found primarily in or around the cell walls of plants. Many of them play important structural roles, whereas some, including various gums, are nonstructural. The importance of fiber in our diets for the prevention or control of several chronic disorders, including colon cancer, cardiovascular disease, and diabetes, has been recognized by the health and scientific communities [3]. The outer bran layers of cereal grains, legumes, nuts, and seeds, as well as fruits and vegetables, contain relatively large amounts of dietary fiber, many of whose components have the capacity to absorb water and swell.

Cellulose. Cellulose has thousands of glucose units linked together. Starch and cellulose are both polymers of glucose, but the difference is in the way the glucose units are linked together based on how the hydroxyl groups are oriented. Starch has an alpha 1–4 linkage where the –OH (hydroxyl group) is oriented in the same direction at both 1 and 4 carbons. Cellulose has a beta 1–4 linkage where the hydroxyl group (–OH) is oriented in opposite directions at the 1 and 4 linkage. Cellulose linkages, which are different than starch, form long, strong fibers. The linkage of glucose molecules in cellulose is not subject to hydrolysis or breakdown by human digestive enzymes (**Figure 7–21**). Therefore, unlike starch, which is digestible, cellulose is indigestible and is known as fiber. The cell walls of plant tissues contain cellulose in tiny fibrils, helping to give structure to these tissues.

Cellulose may be chemically modified to make it more soluble and able to form gels. Examples of modified cellulose include methylcellulose and carboxymethyl cellulose, which are used to thicken, stabilize, gel, and provide bulk in various processed foods [9].

Hemicelluloses. Also found in plant cell walls are hemicelluloses. These are a heterogeneous group of polysaccharides that contain a variety of different monosaccharide building blocks. In many cases, these molecules have branching side chains. Hemicelluloses, along with cellulose, play important structural roles in plants. Xylose and arabinose, which are pentoses (monosaccharides with five carbon atoms), are common components of hemicelluloses.

Beta-glucans. Beta-glucans are polysaccharides made up of glucose building blocks that are linked together differently from the glucose components of cellulose. Beta-glucan molecules are less linear than cellulose molecules and more soluble in water. Oats and barley are rich sources of beta-glucans [3, 15]. Foods high in beta-glucans are authorized by the U.S. Food and Drug Administration (FDA) to be labeled with a health claim stating that the food may reduce the risk of heart disease.

Pectic Substances. Pectic substances are polysaccharides found in the spaces between plant cells and in the cell walls and aid in cementing plant cells together. **Galacturonic acid**, a derivative of the sugar galactose, is the basic building block of pectic substances. The largest of the pectic molecules, sometimes called the parent, is *protopectin*. It is present in largest amounts in unripe fruit and is hydrolyzed by enzymes in the tissues to the less complex *pectinic acid*, also called **pectin**, as the fruit ripens. *Pectic acid* is produced from pectin by additional hydrolysis of special chemical groups on the molecule called **methyl esters**. Pectin is the substance responsible for forming gels in various jams, jellies, and preserves; it also occurs naturally in many fruits.

Vegetable Gums. The term *vegetable gum* or *gum* describes a wide variety of water-soluble polysaccharides that have the ability to act as thickeners or gelling agents in food products [6]. They are a major part of a group of food-processing aids called **hydrocolloids**. Gums are long-chain **polymers** of monosaccharides; various hexose and pentose sugars and their derivatives are the basic building blocks. When they are dissolved or dispersed in water, they have a thickening or texture-building effect, creating *body* and improving mouthfeel in a variety of food products [16, 17]. They also make it more difficult for dispersed materials to separate. In other words, they *stabilize* suspensions (solids dispersed in water). Thus, gums may help to retain water, reduce evaporation rates, modify ice crystal formation, and produce other desired changes in the consistency and flow characteristics of various foods. The preparation of low-calorie and reduced-fat foods often requires the ingenious use of hydrocolloids; for example, gums can thicken and stabilize low-calorie salad dressings made with reduced amounts of oil or no oil. The FDA regulates gums, classifying them as either food

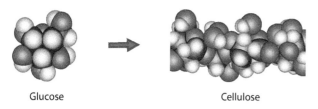

Glucose   Cellulose

Figure 7–21

Cellulose is made up of many glucose units linked together. Humans do not have the enzymes to break the cellulose links, thus cellulose acts as fiber in humans. (Oxford Designers & Illustrators Ltd/Pearson Education Ltd)

additives or GRAS (generally regarded as safe) substances [9]. Vegetable gums include the following:

Source	Examples
Extracts from seaweed	Agar
	Alginates
	Carrageenan
Seed gums	Guar gum
	Locust bean gum
Plant exudates	Gum Arabic
	Gum tragacanth
	Gum karaya
Chemically modified materials	Methyl cellulose
	Sodium carboxymethyl cellulose
Fermentation products	Xanthan gum
	Gellan gum

Browning

Chemical reactions that cause browning of foods often occur during preparation and storage. In some cases, this color is desirable, but in other cases it is not. It is important to be able to control browning so that it can be inhibited or encouraged as needed. Some browning reactions are **catalyzed** by enzymes. Those involved in the browning of fresh fruits and vegetables are discussed in Chapter 20. Other browning of foods results from non-enzymatic reactions, some of which involve carbohydrates.

Caramelization. Caramelization is a nonenzymatic browning that produces caramel pigments from sugars in food. When sugars are heated to temperatures above their melting points, they undergo a series of chemical reactions that begin with dehydration and end with **polymerization**, which produces brown compounds. This process is called **caramelization**, yielding a desirable caramel flavor and a light brown color. If sugar

FOCUS ON SCIENCE
MORE ON CARAMELIZATION

The caramelization reaction can be summarized as follows:

- First, the sugar melts at temperatures above 300°F (149°C), which is followed by foaming.
- Sucrose decomposes into glucose and fructose.
- A condensation reaction occurs in which the individual sugars lose water and react with each other.
- Hundreds of new aromatic compounds are formed having a range of complex flavors.

Some flavors formed during caramelization are as follows:

- *Diacetyl (2,3 butanedione)* is an important flavor compound produced during the first stage of caramelization. Diacetyl is responsible for a buttery or butterscotch flavor.
- *Esters* and *lactones* have a sweet, rum-like flavor.
- *Furans* have a nutty flavor.
- *Maltol* has a toasty flavor.
- Bitter flavors can be formed if caramelization is allowed to proceed too far because the original sugar will be destroyed.

FOCUS ON SCIENCE
HOW IS THE MAILLARD BROWNING DIFFERENT FROM CARAMELIZATION?

Both Maillard browning and caramelization are nonenzymatic browning reactions, but Maillard browning is a chemical reaction between a free amino group or an amino acid (usually lysine) and a reducing sugar (glucose).

In Maillard browning, different types of sugars react more readily than others. In order of reactivity, they are the following:

- Pentose sugars such as ribose. Pentose sugars are five-carbon sugars.
- Hexose sugars such as glucose, fructose, and galactose. Hexose sugars have six carbon atoms.
- Disaccharides such as sucrose, lactose, and maltose.

Likewise, different amino acids produce varying degrees of browning, with lysine being the most reactive. Because, the Maillard reaction produces water, having a high water activity environment inhibits the reaction: therefore, intermediate water activity (a_w) values of 0.5 to 0.8 allow the reaction to proceed rapidly. The effect of pH is not clear-cut, and reactions take place by different pathways with the pH of the system influencing the ratio of products formed. Therefore, a pH < 6 will favor the formation of furfurals, whereas a pH > 6 will produce reductones and fission products.

heating is continued, many bitter compounds are produced, and the color becomes very dark.

Maillard Reaction. *Maillard reaction* is another nonenzymatic browning that is important in foods. Maillard reaction can be desirable or undesirable in foods. The browning of a loaf of bread during baking is due mainly to the Maillard reaction. The flavor and color of golden brown bread are desirable. However, the browning and off-flavors developed during nonfat dry milk solids or canned evaporated milk storage are not desirable.

The Maillard reaction is a sequence of events. The reaction involves a carbohydrate—a sugar—in its initial step. The **carbonyl group** of a sugar combines with the **amino group** of an amino acid or protein with the removal of a molecule of water. After this, a series of chemical reaction occurs, including fragmentation and then polymerization, with the eventual formation of brown pigments. The specific compounds involved and the conditions of temperature, pH, moisture, and so on under which the reaction occurs all affect the final flavor and color, which may be desirable or not desirable.

LIPIDS OR FATS

The term *lipids* describes a broad group of substances with similar properties or characteristics of insolubility in water and a greasy feel. The lipid classification includes at least three major groups with which we are particularly concerned in the study of food and nutrition: (1) neutral fats known as triacylglycerols or triglycerides, (2) phospholipids, and (3) sterols.

Triglycerides (Triacylglycerols)

Approximately 90 to 95 percent of the fatty substances in foods fall into the triglyceride group. Thus, when we talk of fats in food, we are actually talking about triglycerides or triacylglycerols; both terms refer to the same chemical molecule. *Triglyceride* will be the term used in the discussions in this text.

Triglycerides are made up of three *fatty* acids combined with one molecule of an alcohol called *glycerol*. Glycerol has three carbon atoms and three hydroxyl groups (–OH). Fatty acids are commonly composed of linked chains of carbon atoms, with an organic acid group $\overset{O}{\underset{(-C-OH)}{\|}}$ on the end of the chain. The fatty acids are joined to the glycerol molecule by what is called an *ester linkage*, as shown in **Figure 7–22**.

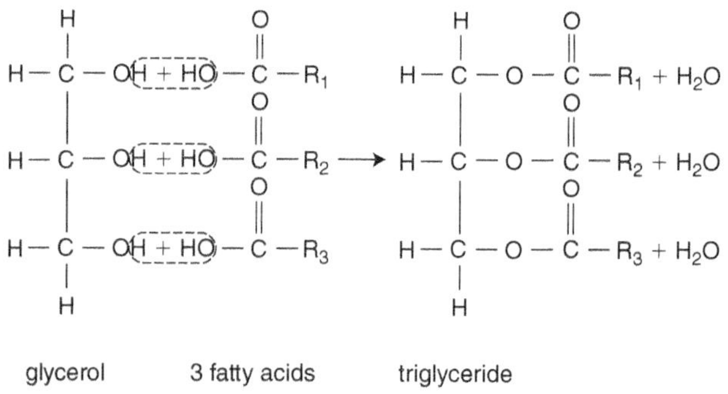

Fatty Acids. Most fatty acids in foods are not free fatty acids, but rather are combined in triglycerides. Different fatty acids may be joined with the glycerol in the same triglyceride molecule. Fatty acids vary in two important ways—they differ in the length of the

Figure 7–22

Glycerol and three fatty acids are joined by an ester linkage to produce triglyceride as shown. Take note how the circled (with a dotted line) H + HO result in the production of H_2O as shown next to the depiction of triglyceride.

chain of carbon atoms and in the number of hydrogen atoms that are attached to the carbons.

The carbon chain in fatty acids may be as short as four carbons or as long as 24 or more carbons. Generally, however, the fatty acids in foods have an even number of carbons. Names of some common fatty acids and the lengths of their carbon chains are listed in **Table 7–4**.

A carbon atom has four bonds with which it joins to other atoms as shown here $-\overset{|}{\underset{|}{C}}-$. Within a carbon chain, two of the bonds join with adjacent carbon atoms. Each of the remaining two bonds on a carbon atom may bond with a hydrogen atom. Some fatty acids have all of the hydrogen atoms with which the carbon atoms can bond (**Figure 7–23**). There are no *double bonds* between carbon atoms, which might be broken to allow bonding with more hydrogens. These types of fatty acids are called *saturated*. Other fatty acids contain double bonds between some carbon atoms and are *unsaturated* in terms of the amount of hydrogen they contain. Examples of saturated fatty acids are butyric, stearic, and palmitic acid. Butyric acid is present in butter, and stearic acid is a major component of beef fat. Palmitic acid, a saturated fatty acid with 16 carbon atoms, is widely distributed in meat fats, vegetable oils, and cocoa butter.

Oleic acid contains one double bond (**Figure 7–24**). It is thus a *monounsaturated* fatty acid. Linoleic, linolenic, and arachidonic acids contain two, three, and four double bonds, respectively. Fatty acids with more than one double bond are often called *polyunsaturated*. Polyunsaturated fatty acids that have a double bond between the third and fourth carbon atoms from the left are called omega-3 (ω-3) polyunsaturated fatty acids. Some ω-3 fatty acids appear to be of importance in body metabolism

Table 7–4
FATTY ACIDS FOUND IN FOODS

Fatty Acid Common Name	Systematic Name	Number of Carbon Atoms
Saturated		
Butyric	Butanoic	4
Caproic	Hexanoic	6
Caprylic	Octanoic	8
Capric	Decanoic	10
Lauric	Dodecanoic	12
Myristic	Tetradecanoic	14
Palmitic	Hexadecanoic	16
Stearic	Octadecanoic	18
Arachidic	Eicosanoic	20
Monounsaturated		
Palmitoleic	Hexadecenoic	16
Oleic	*Cis*-Octadecenoic	18
Polyunsaturated		
Linoleic	Octadecadienoic	18
Linolenic	Octadecatrienoic	18
Arachidonic	Eicosatetraenoic	20

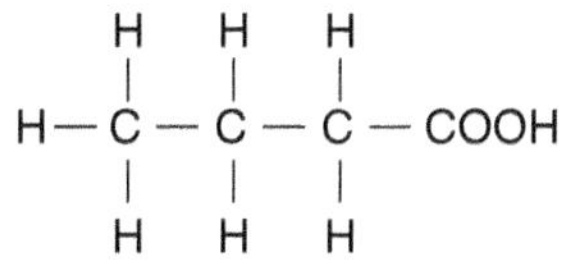

(butyric acid; 4 carbon atoms)

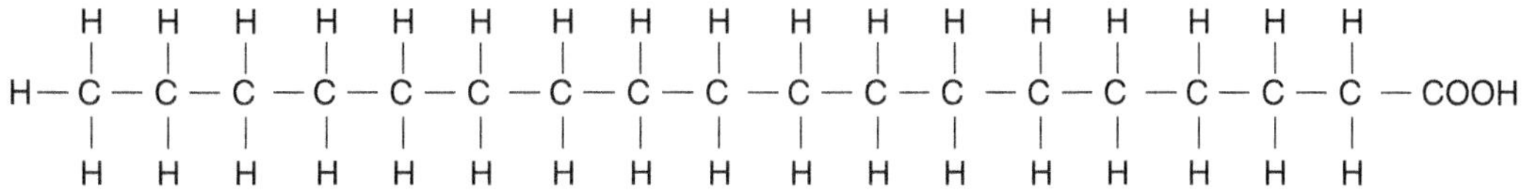

(stearic acid; 18 carbon atoms)

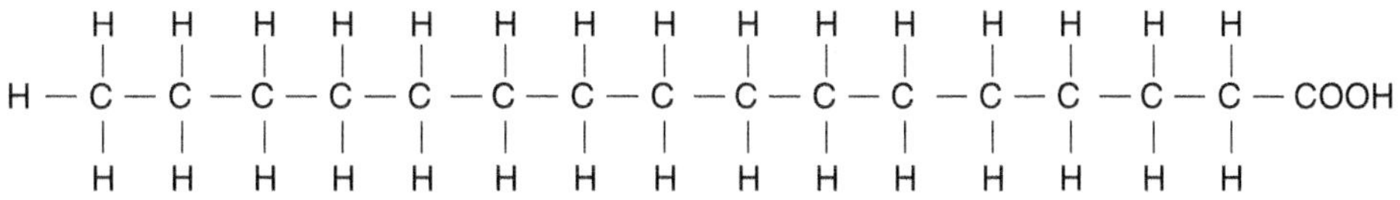

(palmitic acid; 16 carbon atoms)
Saturated Fatty Acids

Figure 7–23

The structures of three saturated fatty acids (butyric, stearic, and palmitic) are shown. Saturated fatty acids have either a carbon (C) or a hydrogen (H) atom attached to each of the four possible carbon bonds. Thus, these fatty acids are saturated with hydrogen, leaving no room for the bonding of additional hydrogen.

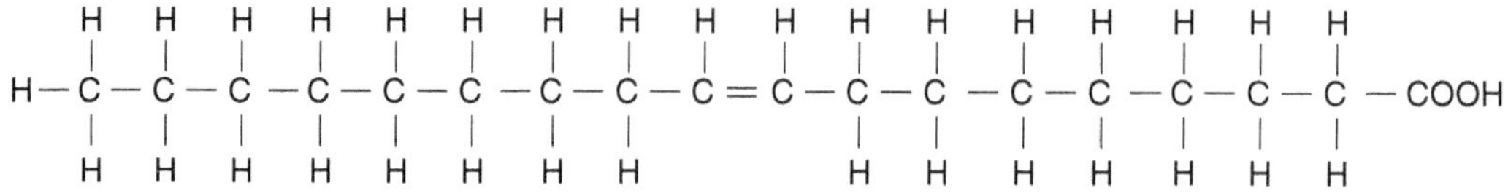

(oleic acid; 18 carbon atoms)

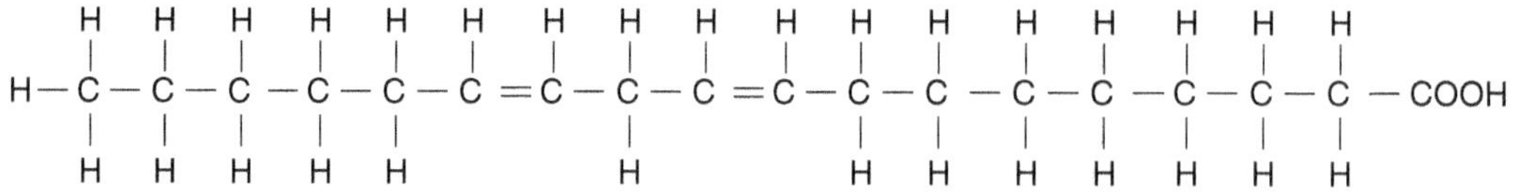

(linoleic acid; 18 carbon atoms)
Unsaturated Fatty Acids

Figure 7–24

Oleic and linoleic unsaturated fatty acids are shown in this figure. Oleic is a monounsaturated fatty acid containing only one double bond between carbons (C). Linoleic acid is a polyunsaturated fatty acid with two double bonds between carbons (C). If the double bonds were broken by adding hydrogen, these fatty acids would become more saturated.

related to the prevention of coronary heart disease. Fish, particularly fatty fish, contains (ω-3) fatty acids.

The body is not able to make linoleic acid (Figure 7–24) with its two double bonds. Linoleic acid is therefore considered to be an essential fatty acid for both infants and adults because it must be obtained in the diet. Skin lesions and poor growth have been reported in infants receiving a diet limited in fat, and these symptoms disappeared after a source of linoleic acid was added to the diet. It has been suggested by the Food and Nutrition Board of the National Research Council of the National Academy of Sciences that a linoleic acid intake equivalent to 2 percent of the total dietary kilocalories for adults and 3 percent for infants is probably satisfactory to avoid any deficiency. The average American diet apparently meets this recommendation.

Good food sources of linoleic acid include seed oils from corn, cottonseeds, and soybeans (50 to 53 percent linoleic acid) and special margarines and peanut oil (20 to 30 percent). Corn oil contains more than six times as much linoleic acid as olive oil, and chicken fat contains up to 10 times as much as the fat of **ruminant animals** such as cattle. The fat from an avocado is about 10 percent linoleate.

Cis-Trans Configuration. The shape of a fatty acid is changed by the presence of a double bond because the double bond limits the rotation of the carbon atom at this point. The particular molecular shape produced by a double bond is dependent on the configuration of the bond. It may be either *cis* or *trans*. A *cis* configuration has the hydrogen atoms on the same side of the double bond, and in the trans

configuration, the hydrogen atoms are on opposite sides of the double bond, as shown in **Figure 7–25**.

Because it is part of a triglyceride molecule, the fatty acid's shape affects the melting point of the triglyceride. An unsaturated fatty acid with a trans configuration has a higher melting point than the same-size molecule with a *cis* configuration. The bending of the chain in the *cis* fatty acid does not allow the triglyceride molecules to pack as closely together when they crystallize in a solid state; thus, less energy is required to separate them when they melt. Therefore, triglyceride molecules in the *cis* configuration melt at a lower temperature than those in the trans configuration.

Types of Triglyceride Molecules. A triglyceride molecule may be formed with three of the same kind of fatty acids, for example, three palmitic acid

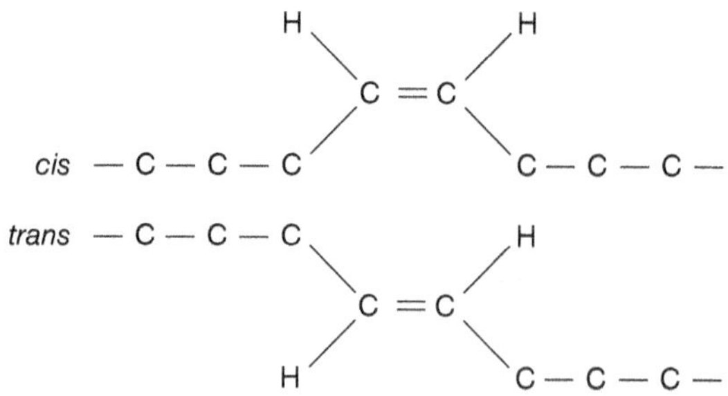

Figure 7–25

The *cis* and *trans* configurations of triglycerides are depicted here. *Cis* hydrogen atoms are on the same side of the double bond between the carbons (C). Trans hydrogen atoms are on the opposite sides of the double bond between the carbons (C).

molecules. In this case, the triglyceride would be called a *simple* triglyceride and could be named tripalmitin. More commonly, however, triglycerides in foods are *mixed*; that is, they contain different fatty acids, either all three different or two alike and one different.

Phospholipids

Phospholipids are present in foods in relatively small amounts but play some important roles, chiefly as **emulsifying agents**. Lecithin is a phospholipid that is used as a food additive in various processed foods, including margarines. Lecithin is found naturally in several foods, including egg yolks.

Structurally, phospholipids are much like triglycerides. They contain glycerol attached through an ester linkage to two fatty acids; however, they differ from triglycerides in that, instead of a third fatty acid, there is a phosphoric acid group joined to the glycerol. A **nitrogen base**, such as choline, is also linked with the phosphoric acid (**Figure 7–26**).

In a mixture, the fatty acid portions of the phospholipid molecules are attracted to other fat substances, whereas the phosphoric acid–nitrogen base portion is attracted to polar molecules such as water or vinegar. Thus, the phospholipid may act as a bridge between fat and water and allow them to be mixed in an emulsion. The phospholipid functions as an emulsifying agent.

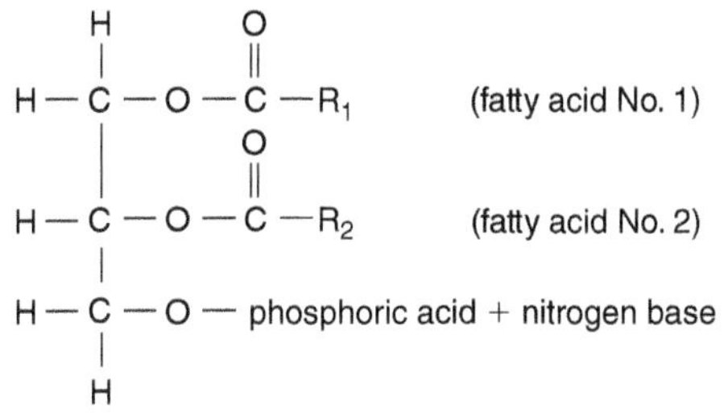

Figure 7–26

The structure of a phospholipid is shown here. Phospholipids differ from triglycerides by the joining of a phosphoric acid and nitrogen base to the glycerol instead of a third fatty acid as found in triglycerides. Compare this figure with Figure 7–22 to see the similarities.

FOCUS ON SCIENCE
TRANS FATTY ACIDS PARTIALLY HYDROGENATED OILS (PHOs) NO LONGER GRAS

In 2015, the FDA finalized a determination that partially hydrogenated oils (PHOs) are not "generally recognized as safe" (GRAS) in human food. PHOs were the primary dietary source of *trans* fats in processed foods [21]. *Trans* fats were found in vegetable shortenings, some margarines, baked goods, crackers, cookies, snack foods, and other foods made with or fried in partially hydrogenated oils (**Figure 7–27**). Unlike other fats, the majority of *trans* fat is formed when the food manufacturers turn liquid oils into solid fats, such as shortening and margarine. Also, oils may be lightly hydrogenated to preserve their quality and prevent rancidity because of their amount of unsaturated fatty acids, which are prone to becoming rancid.

Because of the association between the *trans* fatty acid consumption and heart disease, the FDA started to reexamine the use of PHOs in food. In 2006, manufacturers were required to list *trans* fats on "Nutrition Facts" labels. Between 2003 and 2012, a 78 percent decrease in *trans* fat consumption was contributed to labeling and manufacturer reformulation [8]. A tentative ruling on trans fat and partially hydrogenated oils was made by the FDA in 2013 [20]. In 2015, after examining scientific evidence, manufacturer input and public comments, the FDA ruled to remove partially hydrogenated oils *trans* fats from the GRAS list in hopes of preventing thousands of heart attacks and deaths each year [21]. Small amounts of trans fat do naturally exist in nature. Processed foods were contributing the overwhelming majority of trans fats to the American diet via partially hydrated oils. Manufacturers are using different methods of hydrogenation to produce shortenings and other solid fats that may be labelled as *trans* fat free. Manufacturers were given three years until June 2018 to ensure their products no longer contained partially hydrogenated oils for uses that have not been otherwise authorized by the FDA [21].

Figure 7–27

Trans fat from partially hydrogenated oil was found in many processed foods such as the ones shown in the photograph. Manufacturers were required to remove PHOs from ingredient formulation by June 2018. (US FDA)

Sterols

Cholesterol is probably the most widely known sterol and is found only in animal foods—meat, fish, poultry, egg yolks, and milk fat. Cholesterol is an essential component in the cells of the body, but too high a level of cholesterol in the bloodstream is one factor associated with an increased incidence of coronary heart disease. Vitamin D is also a sterol.

Plants do not manufacture cholesterol, but plant oils do contain some other sterols, generally called *phytosterols*. These sterols, however, are not well absorbed from the human digestive tract and actually interfere with the absorption of cholesterol. In 2000, the FDA authorized a health claim identifying the role of plant sterols or plant sterol esters in lowering the risk of heart disease [11, 12, 15]. The chemical structures of sterols are complex and quite different from those of the triglycerides.

Fats in Food Preparation

Several important roles are filled by fats in food preparation. They act as primary tenderizing agents in baked products, contribute to leavening when air is incorporated into a batter during the creaming of fat and sugar, and promote moistness. For example, contrast the marked tenderness of a croissant, which contains a high proportion of fat, with the chewiness of a bagel, which is made with very little fat.

Oils are major components of salad dressings and mayonnaise. Fats may be heated to high temperatures and act as a medium of heat transfer in the frying of foods. High-fat products such as butter and margarine are used as table spreads. Several flavor compounds are fat soluble and are carried in the fat component of many food products. The properties and processing of fats are discussed in Chapter 8.

Foods high in fat include the following (see also Table 8–2 and 8-3 in Chapter 8):

Butter	Deep-fat fried foods
Cream	Chocolate
Lard	Cheese
Oils	Nuts
Margarine	Fat meats
Hydrogenated shortening	

PROTEINS

Proteins are large, complex molecules found in every living cell. The name *protein* is derived from the Greek word *proteos,* meaning "of prime importance" or "to take the first place." Thus, all foods that were once living animal or plant tissues, including meats, vegetables, and cereal grains, contain some protein. Protein is an essential nutrient for human life and growth. In food preparation, proteins play important functional roles, for example, binding water, forming **gels**, thickening, producing **foams**, and aiding browning. In addition, enzymes, which are special kinds of protein molecules, catalyze many reactions that affect the characteristics of prepared foods.

Structure of Proteins

Proteins are unique because, in addition to the elements carbon, hydrogen, and oxygen, they also contain nitrogen. Often, sulfur is present as well, and some proteins contain phosphorus or iron. Proteins are large molecules made up of hundreds or thousands of small building blocks called *amino acids,* which are joined in a special chemical linkage called a **peptide linkage**. These linkages produce long chains that are said to constitute the *primary structure* of proteins.

The *secondary structure* of proteins results from the springlike coiling of the long peptide chains (**Figure 7–28**). The characteristic coil is called an *alpha helix,* and special bonds called **hydrogen bonds** help to hold the coils in place.

The secondary coils of peptide chains may fold back on themselves, usually in an irregular pattern, to form more compact structures. This folding, which is characteristic for each particular protein, produces what is called the *tertiary structure* of a protein molecule. The long chains of amino acids, when coiled and folded, often produce a globular shape for the protein. A still higher level of organization, called the *quaternary structure,* may result when some globular proteins combine with others, and each forms subunits in a more complex whole. The structure of many protein molecules is indeed intricate, but the final shape of the protein is often of critical importance to its function in a living cell or in food preparation.

Amino Acids. About 22 different amino acids are used as building blocks for proteins. Each of these amino acids has two chemical groups that are the

Figure 7–28

Representation of an alpha helix.

same for all of the amino acids—an amino group (H_2N-) and a carboxyl or acid group as shown here.

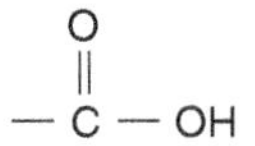

$$
\begin{array}{c}
\quad\ \ O \\
\quad\ \ \| \\
-\,C\,-\,OH
\end{array}
$$

The remainder of the molecule differs specifically for each amino acid. A general formula for amino acids is written as follows, with the R representing a side chain of variable structure.

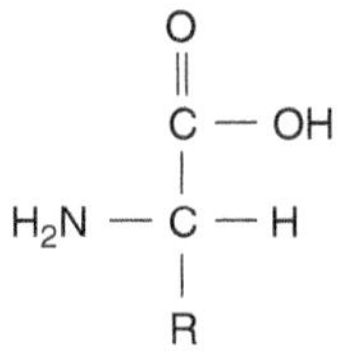

$$
\begin{array}{c}
\qquad O \\
\qquad \| \\
\qquad C\,-\,OH \\
\qquad | \\
H_2N\,-\,C\,-\,H \\
\qquad | \\
\qquad R
\end{array}
$$

The side chains or R groups give a protein its particular characteristics. Some R groups have short carbon chains, some contain sulfur, some have additional amino acid groups, and some have a cyclic structure. The side chain structures are shown in **Table 7–5**.

Protein molecules are formed as hundreds of peptide linkages are made to connect amino acids. The peptide linkage is between the amino group of one amino acid and the acid or carboxyl group of another.

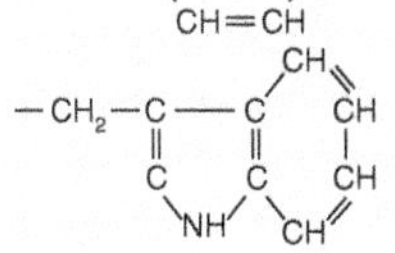

Protein Quality

Nine amino acids are considered nutritionally essential for tissue maintenance in the adult human in the sense that the diet must furnish them in suitable amounts. These essential amino acids are isoleucine, leucine, lysine, methionine, phenylalanine, threonine, tryptophan, valine, and histidine. The other amino acids, considered nonessential, may be synthesized in the body if nitrogen sources are available.

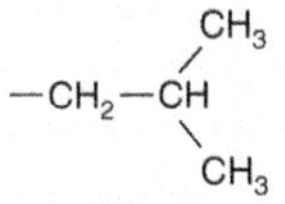

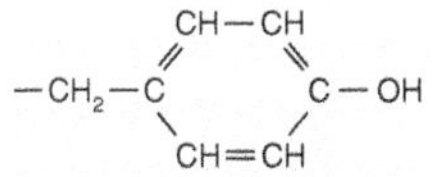

The balance of essential amino acids in a protein determines the biological value of that protein. Proteins of high biological value contain adequate amounts of the essential amino acids to promote the normal growth of animals and are sometimes called *complete proteins,* whereas proteins of low biological value do not. Because the amino acid requirement for growth is more rigid than that for the maintenance of tissues, some proteins that are inadequate for growth may function satisfactorily for maintenance or repair of body tissues. Specific examples of proteins of high biological value are those found in milk, cheese, eggs, meat, poultry, and seafood.

Vegetable sources of protein are often lacking to some degree in one or more of the essential amino acids and have a lower score for biological value. In addition, the total amount of protein in relation to the total calories found in certain vegetable products, such as cereal grains, is low. An exception among plant protein foods is the soybean, which contains a relatively large amount of high-quality protein. Some protein foods of relatively low biological value may be

Table 7–5
SIDE CHAIN (R) GROUPS FOR SELECTED AMINO ACIDS

Amino Acid	Structure for Side Chain (R) Group
Glycine	$-H$
Alanine	$-CH_3$
Valine	$-CH$ with two CH_3
Leucine	$-CH_2-CH$ with two CH_3
Isoleucine	$-CH-CH_2-CH_3$ with CH_3
Serine	$-CH_2-OH$
Threonine	$-CH$ with OH and CH_3

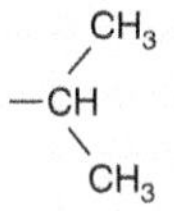

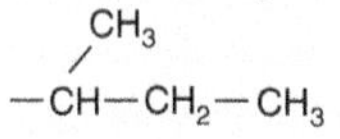

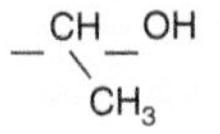

Sulfur-Containing

Cystine	$-CH_2-S-S-CH_2-CH-NH_2$ (with $-C-OH$ carboxyl, O double bond)
Cysteine	$-CH_2-SH$
Methionine	$-CH_2-CH_2-S-CH_3$

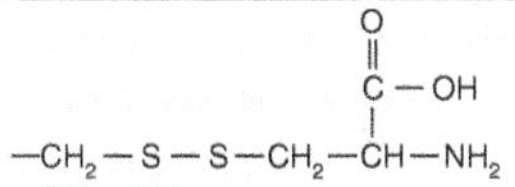

Acidic

Aspartic acid	$-CH_2-\underset{\|\|O}{C}-OH$
Glutamic acid	$-CH_2-CH_2-\underset{\|\|O}{C}-OH$

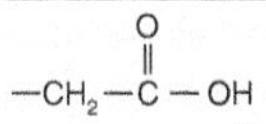

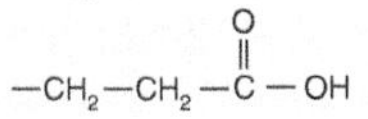

Basic

Lysine	$-CH_2-CH_2-CH_2-CH_2-NH_2$
Arginine	$-CH_2-CH_2-CH_2-NH-\underset{\|\|NH}{C}-NH_2$
Histidine	$-CH_2-C=CH$ (ring with N, NH, CH)

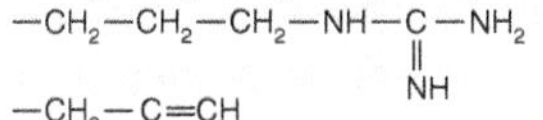

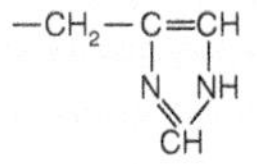

Aromatic

Phenylalanine	$-CH_2-C$ (benzene ring)
Tyrosine	$-CH_2-C$ (benzene ring) $-OH$
Tryptophan	$-CH_2-C$ (indole ring)

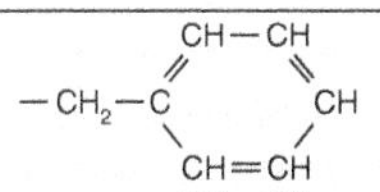

combined with other protein sources that complement them, one supplying more of an essential amino acid(s) than the other is able.

Cereals or legumes are more valuable in the diet if they are combined with even a small amount of protein from an animal source, such as milk, cheese, egg,

Table 7–6
SOURCES AND QUALITATIVE VALUES OF SOME COMMON PROTEINS

Protein	Source	Biological Value
Casein	Milk or cheese	High
Lactalbumin	Milk or cheese	High
Ovovitellin	Egg yolk	High
Ovalbumin	Egg white	High
Myosin	Lean meat	High
Gelatin	Formed by hydrolysis from certain animal tissues	Low
Gliadin	Wheat	Low
Glutenin	Wheat	High
Hordein	Barley	Low
Prolamin	Rye	Low
Glutelin	Corn	High
Zein	Corn	Low
Glycinin	Soybean	High
Legumelin	Soybean	Low
Legumin	Peas and beans	Low
Phaseolin	Navy beans	Low
Excelsin	Brazil nut	High

meat, fish, or poultry, or with soy protein, which furnishes amino acids that cereals and most legumes lack. Cereals and legumes also complement each other to improve protein quality. For example, a peanut butter sandwich contains a better-quality protein mixture than the bread or peanut butter eaten separately. **Table 7–6** lists the common names of several food proteins, their sources, and their general biological value.

Food Sources

Protein is present in many foods, but in varying amounts. Because protein is an essential substance for living cells, one would expect to find it in both plant and animal tissues. Foods that are relatively high in protein (20 to 30 percent) include meats, fish, poultry, eggs, cheese, nuts, and dry legumes. Even after dry legumes are rehydrated and cooked, they make an excellent contribution to dietary protein requirements. Although milk contains only about 4 percent protein, it is an excellent source of good-quality protein because of the amounts usually consumed on a regular basis. Cereal grains contain lesser amounts of protein; however, in the quantities of cereal grains that are often eaten, they make an important contribution to protein needs.

Properties and Reactions

Buffering. Amino groups act as bases or alkalis, whereas carboxyl groups act as acids. As both of these groups are present on the same amino acid or protein

structure, amino acids and proteins may act as either acids or bases and are said to be *amphoteric*. This characteristic is important for many aspects of food preparation when the degree of acidity or alkalinity affects the quality of a food product. Proteins may combine with either the acid or the base within a limited range and resist any change in acidity. Because of this characteristic, they are called **buffers**.

Denaturation and Coagulation. The large complex protein molecules may undergo changes in their structures when they are subjected to the various conditions commonly encountered in food processing and preparation. If the protein molecule unfolds to some degree yet still retains all peptide linkages between the amino acids that make up the molecule, it is said to be *denatured*. The process of **denaturation** is illustrated in **Figure 7–29**.

When protein is denatured, some of the properties change. For example, it usually becomes less soluble. If it is an enzyme, it loses its ability to function. The extent of denaturation may be either limited or extensive. If the conditions causing denaturation persist, additional changes may occur in the protein. The unfolded parts of the molecule recombine in different ways to produce a new molecular shape, and protein molecules may bond together to form a continuous network. The term **coagulation** has been used to describe some of the later stages of protein denaturation in which denatured protein molecules bind together and produce a gel or a solid mass. The coagulation of egg white on being heated is an example of this denaturation process.

Applying heat in the cooking of food produces denaturation and/or coagulation of proteins. An example is the roasting of meat, which denatures the meat proteins. Proteins may also be denatured by mechanical beating. For example, when egg whites are whipped to produce a foam, denaturation and coagulation of the egg white proteins occur. Changing the degree of acidity, changing the concentration of mineral salts, and freezing may also cause denaturation.

Enzymes. Enzymes are protein molecules with a special function. Produced by living cells, they act as *catalysts* to change the rate of a chemical reaction without

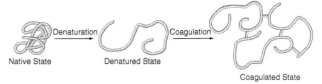

Figure 7–29

Denaturation of a protein involves unfolding of the molecule. The denatured molecules may bond together again to form a coagulated mass.

actually being used up in the reaction itself. Enzymes catalyze a wide range of reactions in living matter, from the digestion of foods in the digestive tract of animals to most of the complex processes occurring in plant and animal metabolism. Enzymes in plant and animal tissues do not stop functioning when the animal is slaughtered or the plant tissue is harvested. Thus, we must deal with enzymatic activity when we handle foods from these sources. Enzymes and enzymatic action in foods are mentioned frequently throughout the text.

Nomenclature. Names of enzymes often include the substrate or substance on which they act, joined with an "*ase*" ending. For example, *lactase* is an enzyme that works on lactose to bring about its hydrolysis, and *maltase* catalyzes the hydrolysis of maltose to yield **glucose**. Sometimes an enzyme is named for the product that results from its action. Sucrase, for example, is sometimes called *invertase* instead because its action to hydrolyze sucrose produces an equimolecular mixture of glucose and fructose, which is commonly called *invert sugar.* In other cases, the name describes the reaction catalyzed; **oxidase**, for example, is the name of an enzyme involved in an **oxidation reaction**. Still other names, such as *papain* and *bromelin,* do not provide any information about the substrate, end products, or reaction.

A systematic nomenclature program that attempts to describe both the substrate and the type of reaction has been established; however, the names are often cumbersome and difficult to use on a practical basis. Numerical codes are sometimes used, but they, too, are difficult to use.

Mechanism of Action. It has been suggested that enzymes function somewhat like a lock and key. They first combine with the substrate on which they will act, forming an intermediate compound sometimes referred to as the *enzyme–substrate (E–S) complex.* This complex formation undoubtedly involves a specific catalytic site on the enzyme. When the reaction is complete, the enzyme separates from the product and is free to react with another molecule of substrate. This process may be depicted as follows:

enzyme (E) + substrate (S) $\rightarrow$ E$-$S $\rightarrow$ E + product (P)

Some Types of Enzymes. Enzymes may be classified into groups according to the type of reaction they catalyze. For example, some enzymes catalyze hydrolysis reactions (*hydrolytic enzymes*), and some catalyze oxidation and **reduction reactions**. Hydrolysis is a chemical reaction that involves the breaking or cleaving of a chemical bond within a molecule. Water plays an essential role in this reaction, and the hydrogen and oxygen atoms of water are added to the two new molecules formed. Within the classification of hydrolytic enzymes, some are designated *proteases*, or *proteinases*, because they hydrolyze or digest proteins; *lipases* hydrolyze fats; and *amylases* act on starch. *Sucrase* breaks down sucrose into two simpler sugars. Some enzymes that catalyze oxidation-reduction reactions are commonly called oxidases or **dehydrogenases**.

Some hydrolytic enzymes occur in plant tissues and have importance in food preparation. For example, the enzyme bromelin, which occurs in pineapple, is a protease and causes gelatin (a protein) to liquefy when fresh or frozen uncooked pineapple is added to gelatin. It is necessary to inactivate (denature) bromelin by heating the pineapple before adding it to a gelatin mixture if the gelatin is to set. Bromelin has been used as a meat tenderizer because of its proteolytic action. Papain, which is obtained from the papaya plant, also acts on proteins to hydrolyze them. It forms the basis of some tenderizing compounds applied to less tender meats. Enzymes used as meat tenderizers do not penetrate very far into the meat and may tenderize only on the surface. Certain oxidases in plant tissues are involved in the darkening of cut or bruised surfaces of many fresh fruits and vegetables. *Chymosin*, or *rennin*, is an enzyme that brings about the clotting of milk and is used in the manufacture of cheese.

Enzyme Activity. Each enzyme acts most effectively under optimal conditions. Temperature, degree of acidity or pH, amount of substrate, and amount of enzyme are all important. In general, the rate or speed of an enzymatic reaction increases as the temperature increases until a critical level is reached, at which point denaturation or coagulation of the enzyme by heat stops the activity. At its optimum temperature, enzymatic activity is greatest, and denaturation does not occur. For example, the optimum temperature for the activity of papain is 140–160°F (60−70°C). When it is used as a meat tenderizer, it does not begin to hydrolyze meat proteins to any significant extent until this temperature range is reached during the cooking process. The enzyme is then inactivated as the temperature rises above 160°F (70°C).

Each enzyme also has an optimal pH. Often, this pH range is quite narrow, outside of which activity does not occur. For example, chymosin (rennin) clots milk most effectively when the pH is about 5.8. Clotting does not occur if the pH is strongly alkaline.

The rate of an enzymatic reaction increases with increasing substrate up to a certain point and then remains constant. The rate of an enzymatic reaction also increases with increasing amounts of enzyme. Enzyme activity in foods may thus be at least partially determined by controlling the conditions under which the food is held or handled.

SOLUTIONS AND DISPERSIONS

Foods are usually mixtures of the various chemical substances that we have discussed—sugars, starch, fiber, fats, proteins, minerals, vitamins, and water—and also air. To complicate things still further, some of these substances may be in different states—solid, liquid, or gas. Substances combined with other substances are often called *dispersion systems.* One (or possibly more) substance called the *dispersed phase* is scattered or subdivided throughout another continuous substance called the *dispersion medium* (**Figure 7–30**). For example, table sugar or sucrose may be dispersed in water; the individual molecules of sucrose are the dispersed phase; and the water surrounding each of the sucrose molecules is the dispersion medium or continuous phase.

Dispersion systems may be classified by state of matter in each phase. Some foods may consist of multiple food systems. According to this classification, a food system may have the following:

* gas dispersed in a liquid (air in whipped egg white—a foam),
* a liquid dispersed in a liquid (oil dispersed in vinegar to make mayonnaise—an emulsion),
* or a solid dispersed in a liquid (proteins such as **casein** dispersed in milk or **ovalbumin** dispersed in egg white).

Another classification of dispersion systems is according to the size of the dispersed particles (see **Table 7–7**). In this classification, the tiniest molecules or particles dispersed in a liquid are said to form true solutions. Particles of intermediate size, although still very small, form colloidal dispersions. Comparatively large particles, such as corn starch granules dispersed in cold water, form suspensions. In line with this classification, small molecules or ions, such as sugars, salts, and vitamins, are usually found in true solutions; larger molecules, such as proteins, pectic substances, cellulose, hemicelluloses, and cooked starch, are usually colloidally dispersed; and clumps of molecules, such as fat globules and

Table 7–7
PARTICLE SIZE IN VARIOUS TYPES OF DISPERSION SYSTEMS

System	Particle Size
True solutions	Less than 1 nm[a] in diameter
Colloidal dispersions	1 nm to 0.1 or 0.2 μm[b] in diameter
Suspensions	Greater than 0.2 μm in diameter

[a] A nanometer (nm) is one thousandth of a micrometer.
[b] A micrometer (μm) is one millionth of a meter.

uncooked starch granules, are usually suspended and readily separate from the dispersion medium on standing. In true **solutions**, the dispersed phase is called the **solute** and the dispersion medium is referred to as the **solvent**. In food systems, water is the most common solvent or dispersion medium; however, in a few cases, such as those of butter and margarine, fat is the dispersion medium, and small droplets of water form the dispersed phase.

Characteristics of Solutions

Solutions are common phenomena with respect to food systems. Sugars are in water solutions in fruits, fruit juices, and vegetables. In fact, in all foods containing sugars or salts and water, a solution is formed.

The solutes in solutions are always tiny molecules or ions. These minute particles are in constant **kinetic motion**, but are evenly distributed throughout the solvent; therefore, the mixture is homogeneous. Because solutions are very stable, they remain unchanged indefinitely unless water evaporates and the solute becomes so concentrated that it **crystallizes** out of solution. The solute is so finely dispersed that it passes through most membranes and filters and cannot be seen under a microscope. True solutions do not usually have the capacity to form gels.

Characteristics of Colloidal Dispersions

The colloidal state is intermediate between a true solution and a coarse suspension, with dispersed particles that are either large molecules, such as proteins or pectin, or smaller molecular clumps such as minute fat globules containing small bunches of triglyceride molecules. Because colloidal particles are larger than those in a true solution, they do not have as much kinetic energy and do not move as rapidly in the dispersion medium. Therefore, they are not as homogeneous and not as stable. However, colloidal particles remain dispersed under usual food preparation and storage conditions.

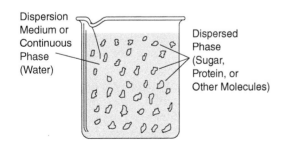

Dispersion Medium or Continuous Phase (Water)

Dispersed Phase (Sugar, Protein, or Other Molecules)

Figure 7–30
A dispersion system.

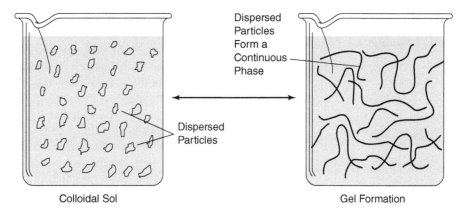

Figure 7–31

A representation of gel formation. This is sometimes called sol-gel transformation and is typical of colloidal dispersions.

Three major factors are responsible for the stabilization of colloidal dispersions. (1) The colloidal particles are moved back and forth by the smaller, faster-moving water molecules of the dispersion medium in what is called *Brownian movement.* (2) There are similar net electric charges on the dispersed particles—either all positive or all negative—and like charges repel each other, keeping the colloidal particles separated. (3) The colloidal particles often bind water closely around them (called *water of hydration*), forming a somewhat protective shell.

Many colloidal systems have the unique ability to form gels. Gels essentially are liquids trapped in a polymer network resulting in a more or less rigid system. A colloidal dispersion in a liquid, pourable condition is called a *sol,* thus distinguishing it from a true solution in which the dispersed particles are smaller. The sol, under proper conditions of temperature, pH, and concentration, may be transformed from a pourable mixture into a gel. It has been suggested that during gel formation, the relatively large colloidal particles loosely join to form a continuous network, sometimes called a *brush-heap structure,* trapping the liquid dispersion medium in its meshes. **Figure 7–31** suggests how this might happen. Gel formation in foods may involve proteins, such as egg and gelatin gels, or carbohydrates, such as pectin jams or jellies and starch-thickened pies or puddings. Future chapters have more discussion on gels.

Foams, characterized as a gas dispersed in a liquid substance, are considered to be colloidal systems. Emulsions are also colloidal dispersions, where one liquid is finely dispersed throughout a second liquid with which the first liquid is generally considered to be immiscible or insoluble (**Figure 7–32**). The formation of a stable emulsion requires a third agent, called an *emulsifying agent* (**Figure 7–33**). Certain proteins and phospholipids often act as emulsifying agents in food products.

Characteristics of Suspensions

Suspensions are generally very unstable. The dispersed particles are composed of large groups of molecules, and the force of gravity tends to cause separation of the particles from the dispersion medium. The particles

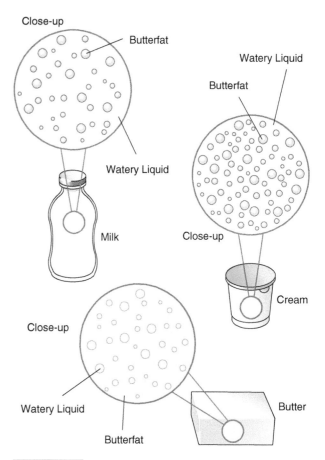

Figure 7–32

Examples of food emulsions. Most emulsions are oil in water but some emulsions are water in oil emulsions.

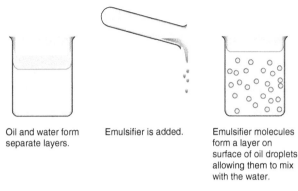

Oil and water form separate layers.   Emulsifier is added.   Emulsifier molecules form a layer on surface of oil droplets allowing them to mix with the water.

Figure 7–33

Oil and water are immiscible liquids. Emulsifiers aid in the formation of a stable emulsion. (Oxford Designers & Illustrators Ltd/ Pearson Education Ltd)

are large enough to be seen under an ordinary microscope. Examples of suspensions in food preparation include French dressings without added emulsifying agents. When the mixture is shaken, the oil becomes dispersed in the vinegar; however, the two phases separate immediately on standing. When corn starch and cold water are mixed together in the preparation of a starch-thickened pudding, the starch granules are suspended in the water; however, on standing only a short time, they settle to the bottom of the container. Tiny crystals of sugar in a crystalline candy such as chocolate fudge also represent an example of a suspension. In this case, the system is more stable; however, larger crystals may form, and the candy may become "sugary" if it stands too long in a dry atmosphere where moisture is evaporated from the product.

STUDY QUESTIONS

Food Composition

1. The chemical composition of food can be determined in the laboratory. List the major components and the minor components that are present in foods.

2. Select a food. Look up this food in the *USDA National Nutrient Database for Standard Reference*. Discuss the composition of the food.

Water

3. Give examples of foods that are high, intermediate, and limited in water content. Explain what is meant by *water activity*.

4. Describe four or five important functions of water in food preparation.

5. What is the pH scale? What does it indicate? Place several common foods on the scale.

6. Describe some unique characteristics of the water molecule.

7. (a) Name two types of hard water and the types of mineral salts contained in each.

   (b) Describe two methods of softening permanently hard water.

Carbohydrates

8. (a) What are carbohydrates? Simple carbohydrates? Complex carbohydrates?

   (b) In the following list of carbohydrates, indicate which are monosaccharides, which are disaccharides, and which are polysaccharides.

Starch	Fructose (levulose)
Glucose (dextrose)	Galactose
Lactose	Dextrins
Cellulose	Glycogen
Maltose	Sucrose

   (c) Identify the monosaccharide building blocks for each disaccharide and polysaccharide listed in question 8b.

   (d) What are oligosaccharides? Give examples.

   (e) Give several examples of vegetable gums and describe some of their uses in food processing.

   (f) Name two fractions of starch and describe the major differences in their chemical structures.

   (g) List at least four chemical components of dietary fiber. Indicate which are carbohydrates.

Lipids

9. (a) Describe in words the chemical structure of a triglyceride.

   (b) Distinguish among saturated, unsaturated, and polyunsaturated fatty acids.

   (c) For each of the following fatty acids, indicate if it is saturated, monounsaturated, or polyunsaturated:

   Palmitic acid

   Linoleic acid

   Butyric acid

   Stearic acid

   Oleic acid

   (d) Distinguish between *cis* and *trans* fatty acids.

   (e) What is a simple triglyceride? A mixed triglyceride?

(f) In the following list of foods, check those that are rich sources of fat:

Whipped cream	Lard	Pork spareribs
Spinach	Walnuts	Potato chips
Pinto beans	Cheddar cheese	Shortening
Corn tortillas	Chocolate	White bread
Margarine	Corn oil	Apples

(g) How do phospholipids differ from triglycerides in chemical structure? What useful role do phospholipids play in food preparation?

(h) List several food sources of cholesterol.

Proteins

10. (a) What chemical groups characterize amino acids?

(b) How are amino acids joined to make proteins?

(c) What is meant by the side chains or R groups of a protein? Explain why proteins may act as buffers in foods.

(d) What is an essential amino acid, and how many amino acids are so designated for adult humans?

(e) From the following list of amino acids, identify those that are nutritionally essential:

Methionine	Threonine	Glutamic acid
Phenylalanine	Isoleucine	Cystine
Tryptophan	Glycine	Leucine
Serine	Alanine	Valine
Lysine	Tyrosine	Histidine

(f) Explain the meaning of *biological value* in relation to proteins. Why do some protein foods, such as eggs and milk, have high biological value while others, such as kidney beans and wheat flour, have lower biological value?

(g) Explain how proteins can supplement each other to improve the net nutritional value.

(h) Name several food sources that are relatively high in protein.

(i) Describe, in general, the primary, secondary, tertiary, and quaternary structure of proteins.

11. (a) Describe what probably happens when a protein is denatured. List at least four treatments, likely to be applied to foods, that can cause protein denaturation.

(b) Explain what probably happens when proteins are coagulated and describe some examples of coagulation in foods.

Enzymes Are Special Type of Proteins

12. (a) What is a catalyst? What are enzymes, and how do they act as catalysts?

(b) Suggest a general mechanism of action for enzymes.

(c) Give examples of hydrolytic enzymes.

(d) Explain why enzymes are important in food processing and preparation.

Dispersions, Solutions, Emulsions, and Suspensions

13. (a) Describe what is meant by the terms *dispersion system, dispersed phase, dispersion medium, solution, solute,* and *solvent.*

(b) Give examples of foods in which types of dispersion systems are classified according to the state of matter in each phase.

(c) Describe three types of dispersion systems classified on the basis of size of dispersed particles.

(d) Describe what probably happens during a sol-gel transformation in a food product. What types of dispersion systems are likely to show this phenomenon?

8

Fats, Frying, and Emulsions

Fat is naturally present in many foods (**Figure 8–1**). The chemical composition of many foods includes fats. **Invisible fat** is the fat naturally present in food. Invisible fat examples include meat, poultry, fish, dairy products, eggs, nuts, seeds, and chocolate. **Visible fats** are products that are essentially 100 percent fat such as shortening, lard, salad and cooking oils, margarine, and butter. These visible fats are often incorporated by home cooks, food processors, and food services into baked products (e.g., cakes and cookies), fried foods (e.g., french-fried potatoes and doughnuts), or other prepared foods. Consumers who are unfamiliar with food composition and food preparation may perceive shortening, oils, and butter as invisible when present in prepared foods.

Triglycerides are the main fat in food preparation and processing. These triglycerides consist of one glycerol unit with three units of fatty acids attached. Triglycerides are the majority of fat naturally found in foods and more purified fats. Usually these triglycerides are just referred to as fats.

Fats are insoluble in water with a lower density than water. Fats may be a liquid or solid at room temperature. When fats are liquid at room temperature they are referred to as *oils* and fats that are solid at room temperature are referred to as *plastic fats, solid fats, or* sometimes just *fats*. *Lipids* is a broader category that encompasses more than fats and oils, including chemical substances beyond **triglycerides** (triacylglycerols). Lipids also include mono- and diglycerides, **fatty acids**, **phospholipids**, **sterols**, and other substances. Chapter 7 provided discussion on lipids and this category is summarized in **Table 8–1**.

In this chapter, the following topics will be discussed:

- Fat consumption and nutrition
- Functions of fat in food
- Properties of fats
- Processing, refining and types of fat
- Oils
- Oil and fat refining
- Shortening and margarine
- Milk fats
- Fat foams
- Butter
- Ice cream
- Deterioration of fat and its control
- Frying
- Buying fats
- Fat replacers
- Emulsions
- Salad dressings

CONSUMPTION TRENDS AND NUTRITION

Fats are essential in the human diet, and current dietary guidelines offer guidance for incorporating a fat in the diet. For years, the American Heart Association, the U.S. Surgeon General, the Dietary Guidelines for Americans,

Figure 8–1

Oils and fats are an integral of part foods. (JPC-PROD/Shutterstock)

TABLE 8–1
TRIGLYCERIDES, FATTY ACIDS, PHOSPHOLIPIDS, AND STEROLS

Type of Lipid	Description	Chemical Structure
Triglycerides	Most fats found in foods are triglycerides. Triglycerides are composed of three fatty acids combined with an alcohol molecule called glycerol.	Triglyceride molecule (the R represents the chain of carbon atoms).
Fatty acids	May be saturated, monounsaturated, or polyunsaturated. A saturated fatty acid is "saturated" with hydrogen. An "unsaturated" fatty acid has double bonds between carbon atoms, which, if broken, would allow the addition of hydrogen. The carbon chain length of fatty acids varies from four carbon atoms to more than 24.	Butyric acid is a saturated fatty acid with a carbon chain length of four.
Phospholipids	Function as emulsifiers. Lecithin, found in egg yolk, is an example of a phospholipid. Structurally have similarities to triglycerides.	Phospholipid (the R represents the carbon chain).
Sterols	Cholesterol, vitamin D, and phytosterols are all sterols. Found in animal and plant oils. Amount varies with source.	
Free Fatty Acids (FFA)	Unattached fatty acids present in a fat. Some unrefined oil 1 percent FFA. Refined oil <0.1 percent	
Tocopherols Tocotrienols	Minor constituent of vegetable oil. Vitamin E source and antioxidants. Palm oil and wheat germ oil tocotrienols.	
Mono- and diglycerides	Mono- and diglycerides are diesters of fatty acid and glycerol with one or two fatty acids attached to glycerol backbone. Used frequently as emulsifiers. Found in animal fat and vegetable oils.	Cholesterol

and various health organizations have called for a reduction in total dietary fat and saturated fats. Recently the Food and Drug Administration (FDA) removed artificially produced trans fats found in partially hydrated oils (PHOs) from the "generally recognized as safe" (GRAS) list. Food manufacturers and food-service operations were forced to find substitute for PHOs in many fried and baked products [115]. More about the FDA, the PHO, and artificial trans fat status was discussed in Chapter 7.

Consumption Trends

The promotion of low-fat diets became prominent in the 1970s and early 1980s [79, 120]. How fat is replaced in the diet is important, as replacing dietary fats with refined sugars remains a concern [81, 137]. The national debate over fat in diets during the 1980s led to the publishing of the first dietary guidelines [120]. Ironically in 1980 approximately 14 percent of the U.S. population was obese, but these numbers have risen by 35–40 percent since that time [120].

TABLE 8–3
APPROXIMATE AMOUNTS OF VARIOUS FAT AND FAT-RICH FOODS REQUIRED TO FURNISH 100 KILOCALORIES

Food	Fat Content (%)	Weight (g)	Approximate Measure (Tablespoons)
Butter	80	13	1
Margarine	80	13	1
Hydrogenated fat	100	11	1
Lard	100	11	1
Salad oil	100	11	1
Bacon fat	100	11	1
Peanut butter	46	16	1
Cream, light	20	50	3
Cream, whipping	35	33	2, or about double the volume if whipped
Cream, sour	25	48	4
Cheese, cheddar	32	24	1-inch cube
Egg, scrambled	11	61	1 egg
Ground beef, regular, broiled	21	35	1 ounce
Doughnut, yeast	21	26	½ doughnut

FUNCTION OF FATS IN FOOD PREPARATION

Fats play a variety of roles in food preparation (see **Table 8–4**). They give flavor and a mouthfeel that is associated with moistness, thus contributing greatly to palatability, eating pleasure, and satiety value [34]. Fats also act as a flavor carrier. Some fats, such as butter, bacon fat, or sesame oil, are used specifically to add flavor. As an ingredient in baked products, fats "shorten" strands of the protein—**gluten**—and thereby tenderize it. Some fats also contribute to the aeration of batters

TABLE 8–4
FUNCTIONS OF FAT IN FOOD

Functions of Fat	Examples
Flavor	Fats such as butter and olive oil add distinctive flavors and may carry and enhance flavors in some foods. Fat also acts as a flavor carrier.
Color	Butter adds a yellow, creamy color to some dishes. Foods fried in fat are browned. Pigments are carried in fat. Carotenoids are yellow to deep orange to red; palm oil is highest in carotenoids. Chlorophyll is green in color; canola oil is highest in chlorophyll. Gossypol is a yellow pigment only found in cottonseed oil; gossypol can be toxic [44]. Most color is reduced during normal processing to give acceptable color, flavor, and stability [114].
Texture	In a properly prepared pastry, shortening or lard provides for a flaky texture. Shortening creamed with sugar when making a cake will contribute to a fine cell structure and moist crumb. Fried foods become crisp. Milk fat and other fats contribute viscosity or creaminess.
Tenderness	In baked goods, fats and oils interfere with the development of gluten and shorten the gluten.
Emulsification	Vegetable oils are one phase of the emulsion in salad dressings.
Heat transfer	Fats can be heated to a high temperature that is well above the boiling temperature of water, resulting in desirable texture, flavor, and color changes for foods cooked in fat.
Control of crystallization	Crystal formation in ice cream is controlled in part by milk fat from cream.
Moistness in meat	Fat contributes to the sensation of moistness.

and doughs. Their capacity to be heated to high temperatures makes them an excellent medium for the transfer of heat to foods in the process of frying. Fats are major components of salad dressings, in which they usually constitute one phase of an **emulsion**. Lecithin, a phospholipid, is an example of a fat that may act as the **emulsifying agent**, or emulsifier. Some emulsions can be made into fat foams. Foams can be defined as an agglomeration of bubbles [113]. Fat foams contain air, a free ingredient for processors, that impart textural characteristics desired by consumers. Fat foams are an integral part of whipped cream, whipped topping, and ice cream. Functions of fats in food preparation are summarized in Table 8–4 and discussed in later chapters.

PROPERTIES OF FATS

Fats exhibit several unique properties that influence their use in food preparation. Solubility, melting point, smoke point, plasticity, and flavor will be discussed. The chemical structure of triglycerides and their component fatty acids was discussed in Chapter 7.

Solubility

Fats or lipids are insoluble in water and therefore do not mix readily with water-based food systems (**Figure 8–2**). They also have a greasy feel. In the laboratory, fats are soluble in a group of organic solvents that include chloroform, ether, and petroleum ether.

Type of Fatty Acids

Fatty acids may be saturated or unsaturated (**Figure 8–3**). Unsaturated fats may be classified as **mono-unsaturated fatty acids** or **polyunsaturated fatty acids**.

Saturated Fats. A saturated fatty acid contains only single carbon to carbon bonds. Saturated fats hold all

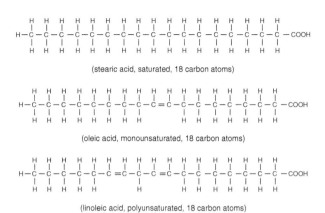

(stearic acid, saturated, 18 carbon atoms)

(oleic acid, monounsaturated, 18 carbon atoms)

(linoleic acid, polyunsaturated, 18 carbon atoms)

Figure 8–3

These fatty acids are saturated, monounsaturated, and polyunsaturated. Stearic acid is fully saturated with hydrogen. Oleic has one double bond and is a monounsaturated fatty acid. Linoleic has two double bonds and is a polyunsaturated fatty acid.

of the hydrogen that may be attached to carbon atoms (see Chapter 7). Therefore, there are no double bonds between the carbon atoms. Palmitic and stearic acids have a high proportion of saturated fatty acids. These fatty acids have relatively high melting points and are usually solid at room temperature.

Unsaturated Fats. Unsaturated fatty acids contain one or more carbon-to-carbon double bonds. Unsaturated fats are capable of binding more hydrogen. Monounsaturated fatty acids have one double bond between carbon atoms. Polyunsaturated fatty acids contain multiple double bonds between carbons. When the ratio of polyunsaturated fatty acids to saturated fatty acids (**P/S ratio**) is high, oils are called *polyunsaturated oils* or *fats*. **Figure 8–4** provides the percentage of polyunsaturated, monounsaturated, and polyunsaturated fatty acids found in several kinds of dietary fat. *Iodine value* (IV) is the analytical chemistry test used to determine the degree of unsaturation in fatty acids, oil, fat, or wax. A saturated fat will take up no iodine, whereas a polyunsaturated fat is very reactive with iodine having a high iodine value.

Main food polyunsaturated fatty acids are essential fatty acids linoleic (2 double bonds), linolenic (3 double bonds), as well as arachidonic (4 double bonds), eicosapentaenoic (EPA) (5 double bonds), and docosahexaenoic acids (DHA) (6 double bonds). Vegetable oils are the main source for essential fatty acids linoleic and linolenic acids. Arachidonic acid is found in small amounts in lard, which also contains about 10 percent linoleic acid [114]. Fish and algae oils contain large quantities of long-chain fatty acids with three or more bonds including EPA and DHA.

Fatty Acid Nomenclature. Fatty acid nomenclature can be confusing. Carbons in fatty acid chains are commonly numbered consecutively from the end

Figure 8–2

Fats are insoluble in water, thus they do not readily mix in water-based food systems. Oil is less dense than water. (PHOTO FUN/Shutterstock)

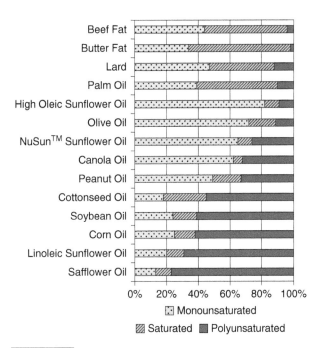

cis hydrogen atoms are on the same side of the double bond

H H
| |
(–C=C–)

trans hydrogen atoms are on opposite sides of the double bond

H
|
(–C=C–)
|
H

Figure 8–5

Cis and *trans* fatty acid configurations are shown. The shape of the fatty acid is influenced by the presence of the double bond between the carbon atoms. This double bond limits the rotation of the carbon atom and therefore the placement of the hydrogen atoms. Some trans fatty acids occur naturally in certain fats; however, trans fatty acids most frequently are found in food as the result of hydrogenation.

Figure 8–4

Dietary fats vary in the percentage of polyunsaturated, monounsaturated, and saturated fats. Saturated fats are associated with an increased risk of heart disease. Polyunsaturated and monounsaturated fats therefore are preferable from a health perspective.

of the chain with the carboxyl group as carbon 1 with the double bonds being identified by the lower number of the two carbons it joins.

Omega or (n-) is another nomenclature for identifying unsaturated fatty acids which identifies sites of enzyme reactivity. Omega or "n minus" refers to the position of the double bond closest to the methyl end. Oleic acid has a double bond 9 carbons from the methyl end so is an omega-9 fatty acids. Eicosapentaenoic acid (EPA) found in fish oils and algae oils is omega-3 (or n-3) fatty acid [114].

Cis and Trans Fatty Acids. Unsaturated fatty acids can exist either in *cis* or *trans* form depending on the configuration of the hydrogen atoms around the carbon atoms with the double bond. *Cis* forms have hydrogen atoms on the same side of the carbon chain. *Trans* forms have hydrogen atoms on opposite side of carbon chain (**Figure 8–5**). Both *cis* and *trans* fatty acids naturally occur. The artificial *trans* fatty acids are typically manufactured as partially hydrated oils (PHOs) that are no longer recognized as GRAS.

Most oils and fats in natural state are *cis* formation. However, naturally occurring *trans* bonds are formed as a result of microbial action in rumen where polyunsaturated fatty acids of feed are partially hydrogenated [114]. Thus, *trans* fats are found naturally in milk fats of ruminant animals such as cows, goats,

and sheep [70]. Butter, milk, beef tallow, and lard naturally contain small amounts (2–5 percent) of *trans* fats [70]. Milk fat has 2–11 percent naturally occurring trans fats with seasonal and laboratory method variance [27]. The amount and type of feed can influence rumen microbial population, which influences hydrogenation and formation of trans fat isomers in milk fat [27]. Seasonal milk fat varies, *trans* fat levels are about 2 percent higher in the spring and summer has when cows graze in the pasture versus winter months [27]. However, the presence of naturally occurring *trans* fat does not mean these products should be eliminated from the diet since these products contain many important nutrients.

Length of Carbon Atoms. Fatty acids usually contain an even number of carbon atoms ranging from 4 to 24 carbon atoms in length (see Chapter 7 for more discussion). Longer chain fatty acids are formed as the number of carbon atoms in the fatty acids increases and the melting point increases too. For example, butyric acid with four carbon atoms melts at a lower temperature than stearic acid with 18 carbon atoms. Both of these fatty acids are saturated. Butter contains a relatively large proportion of short-chain fatty acids, many of them saturated, and melts at a lower temperature than beef fat or hydrogenated shortenings, which contain more long-chain fatty acids.

Fat Crystals and Polymorphism

Most fats can exist in several different crystalline forms exhibiting polymorphism depending on how the fat molecules align in a solid state. Fat crystals form when liquid fat is cooled and heat is removed. As a result, there is a slowdown in the molecular movement, allowing fatty acids to attract via van der Waal forces then bond to form crystals. More symmetrical fat molecules with similar chain length fatty acids align and form crystals more readily [114, 17].

The fat crystal formation affects the fat melting point and how the fat performs in foods. The fat crystal forms can transform from lower melting points to higher melting points depending on the molecular composition, fat configuration, crystallization configurations, temperature, and storage conditions. Mechanical agitation and temperature flux during processing and storage tend to accelerate the rate of crystal formation. Fatty acid chains can form into three different basic arrangements with other subcellular configurations. The three basic fat crystalline forms are known as α (alpha), β (beta), and β' (beta prime) (**Figure 8–6**). The fat crystal transformation is classified and ordered as α (alpha) to β' (beta prime) to β (beta). If fat is chilled, it forms many small transparent alpha crystals that rapidly change to more stable beta prime crystals. Rapid cooling and agitation form small fat crystals that are important in frozen desserts and candies. Slow cooling of melted fat results in the formation of large coarse crystals [27]. Butter in solid form has small unnoticeable crystals, but when butter is melted and cooled large, coarse crystals form that are easy to see. The melted cooled butter is coarse and crystals are visible. The butter's coarse crystal state can be reversed by melting butter again by cooling rapidly and agitating as it cools to form small crystals again [27].

The fatty acids composition of a triglyceride will influence the crystalline form stability. More heterogeneous fatty acid triglycerides with many different fatty acids attached to the glycerol backbones yield more stable fine beta prime crystalline forms such as found in tallow, milk fat, and palm oil. More homogenous fatty acid triglycerides have more beta coarse crystalline forms such as in lard.

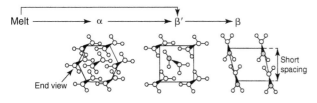

Figure 8–6

Basic fat crystalline forms (a) alpha, (b) beta prime, and (c) beta. Illustration of milk fat crystals melting from alpha crystal form to beta prime crystal to beta crystal. Beta crystals are primarily formed by recrystallization of beta prime crystals. (Based on Rønholt, S., Mortensen, K. and Knudsen, J. C. (2013), The Effective Factors on the Structure of Butter and Other Milk Fat-Based Products. *Comprehensive Reviews in Food Science and Food Safety*, 12: 468–482. oi:10.1111/1541-4337.12022)

Food manufacturers use this understanding of fat's crystalline state to determine processing needs and to use fats that will work best in certain foods. Beta crystals tend to be coarse and are desirable for frying and liquid shortenings or creating pie crusts. Beta prime crystals are fine and create smooth and creamy products such as shortening or margarine. Beta prime crystals will aerate and cream well so are used in baking and frostings [114]. Fats can be processed and structured to develop desirable crystal forms for various food-processing needs [114].

Melting Point

Most natural fats are complex mixtures of triglycerides. Each triglyceride in the natural fat has varying fatty acids making a complex mixture with varying melting points. Most fats tend to melt gradually and in stages as temperature is increased because of this complex triglyceride mixture. As temperature is increased, most unsaturated components melt first and saturated components last. Some fats such as cocoa butter are described as having a sharp melting point since there is little difference in their component fatty acids. Cocoa butter's sharp melting point is not because of the fatty acids but because of the similar simple triglycerides (see discussion on chocolate in this chapter.) Mutton tallow has similar fatty acid composition but more diversity in triglycerides leading to different melting properties [17].

Fat melting point refers to measuring the strength of bonding forces between fatty acids within the crystals. The more attraction between molecules, the easier it is to crystalize, and the higher the melting point since it takes more energy in the form of heat to melt the crystals [17]. Fats that contain more asymmetrical molecules have lower melting points.

In common usage, fats that have a relatively high **melting point** and are solid at room temperature are called *fats,* whereas those that have lower melting points and are liquid at room temperature are called *oils.* The melting point of a fat is influenced by the type, form, and length of the fatty acids. Long-chain fatty acids have higher melting points since the long hydrocarbon chains interact more strongly than shorter ones. Melting point decreases with increased double bonds; increased double bonds result in more bends in the carbon chain and a poorer fit for molecular attraction. The position of the double bond in the chain also affects melting point.

An isomer is two or more substances such as fatty acids that are identical except for molecular structure. Conversion of *cis* fatty acid to corresponding *trans* isomers results in increase melting point [114]. The trans form of a fatty acid has a higher melting point than its cis form, likely due to the shapes of the molecules. The cis form is more bent and thus less able to pack tightly together with other molecules. Tightly packed triglyceride molecules require more heat or energy to move them apart, thus increasing the melting point.

Fats in the trans formation have higher melting points. Thus, the fatty composition of the triglyceride influences the melting point of fats. The melting point of a fat increases with each shift in polymorphic form so beta form melting points are higher than alpha form melting points.

These melting point and fat characteristics play a significant role in food preparation, food processing, and nutrition. The melting points of triglycerides making up a fat determine if the fat will be liquid, solid (plastic), hard, or brittle at room temperature [27]. The fat consistency determines the functional properties in food preparation and processing. Manufacturers use this knowledge to produce and apply various fat products and shortenings suitable for specific food products [35].

Smoke Point

The **smoke point** of a fat is the temperature at which smoke comes from the fat surface when heated, which is measured in a laboratory under controlled conditions. The smoke point measures thermal stability of

fat when heated in contact with air [114]. Fats should not be heated higher than necessary. When fat is overheated, hydrolysis of the fat molecules occurs, creating free glycerol. The fat smoke point is dependent upon ease of hydrolysis to glycerol and percentage of free glycerol in the fat [17]. Monoglycerides have lower smoke points than triglycerides. Fats previously used in frying have a lower smoke point because some fat hydrolysis has previously occurred. (See **Table 8–5** for smoke points of various fats and oils.)

Fats have different smoke points. For example, whole butter has a smoke point of approximately 260°F (127°C) compared to the smoke point of soybean oil, which is 495°F (232°C). Soybean, corn, canola, and peanut oils are types of fats better suited for high-heat applications, such as deep-fat frying or sautéing, because of their high smoke points.

Clarified butter also has a high smoke point. Butter is clarified by melting, followed by skimming off the milk solids and then ladling off the butter fat to leave the water in the bottom of the pan (**Figure 8–7**) [67]. *Ghee* is a clarified butter used in Southern Asian and Middle Eastern cuisines.

Acrolein is a substance produced when fats are heated to excessive temperatures and smoke. This

Table 8–5
REACTION TEMPERATURES OF FATS

FAT	MELT POINT	SMOKE POINT	FLASH POINT
Butter	92–98°F/33–36°C	260°F/127°C	Possible at any temperature above 300°F/150°C
Butter, clarified	92–98°F/33–36°C	335–380°F/168–193°C	Possible at any temperature above 300°F/150°C
Lard	89–98°F/32–36°C	370°F/188°C	n/a
Deep-fryer shortening, heavy-duty, premium	102°F/39°C	440°F/227°C	690°F/365°C
Canola oil	n/a	430–448°F/221–230°C	553–560°F/289–293°C
Corn oil	40–50°F/4–7°C	450°F/232°C	610°F/321°C
Cocoa butter	88–93°F/31–34°C	n/a	n/a
Cottonseed oil	55°F/13°C	450°F/232°C	650°F/343°C
Margarine	94–98°F/34–36°C	410–430°F/210–221°C	Possible at any temperature above 300°F/150°C
Olive oil, extra virgin	32°F/0°C	350–410°F/177–210°C	n/a
Olive oil, pure or pomace	32°F/0°C	410–440°F/210°C–227°C	437°F/225°C
Peanut oil	28°F/−2°C	450°F/232°C	540°F/282°C
Shortening, vegetable, all-purpose	120°F/49°C	410°F/210°C	625°F/329°C
Soybean oil	−5°F/−20°C	495°F/257°C	540°F/282°C
Walnut oil	n/a	350–400°F/177–204°C	620°F/326°C

n/a = not available

This data was compiled from a variety of sources and is meant as a guideline only. Because reaction temperatures depend on the exact type and ratio of fatty acids present, the actual temperatures will vary depending on the brand or manufacturer of the fat in question. Temperatures are for clean, previously unused fats. Heating a fat, even one time, can lower the smoke and flash points dramatically.

(a)   (b)

Figure 8–7

The steps in the clarification of butter are shown here. First, melt the butter, then (a) skim the milk solids from the surface and (b) ladle the butter from the pan, leaving the water. (Richard Embery/Pearson Education)

acrolein gas results from the dehydration of glycerol. During frying, fat's triglyceride molecules can be hydrolyzed to their component parts of free fatty acids and glycerol. When the free glycerol decomposes with continued heat, it produces acrolein and water. The chemical change of glycerol to acrolein and water is shown in **Figure 8–8**. The volatized acrolein is a mucous membrane irritant. It may result in eye and throat irritation when you are near smoking cooking fat.

Flash Point and Fire Point

Fat *flash point* is the temperature at which the volatile products are at the point of being ignited, but not capable of sustaining combustion [114]. *Fire point* is the temperature at which the volatile products will support continued combustion [114]. For canola oil, the smoke point is 457°F (236°C), the flash point is 619°F (326°C), and fire point is 662°F (350°C); however, for canola oil with high oleic acid content, the values are higher [114]. Oils that have been used for an extended period of time will have lower smoke, flash, and fire points [114]. Care is always warranted in frying. If the fat starts to smoke during cooking, the

$$
\begin{array}{ccc}
CH_2OH & & CH_2 \\
| & & \| \\
CHOH & \xrightarrow{\text{heat}} & CH \qquad + 2H_2O \\
| & & | \\
CH_2OH & & C = O \\
& & | \\
& & H \\
\text{glycerol} & & \text{acrolein} \qquad \text{water}
\end{array}
$$

Figure 8–8

Acrolein is produced when fats are heated to the smoking point. As shown, glycerol, when heated, produces acrolein and water.

heat should be reduced. Fat that ignites during cooking should be covered with a lid to smother flames and extinguish fire; turn off heat. Never move a flaming pan. Do not try to extinguish with water.

Plasticity

Plastic can be defined as something that does not undergo permanent change in shape until a stress or force has been applied. A solid fat can be described as a plastic; fat can be described as exhibiting **plasticity**. Shortening is an example of a **plastic fat**.

The plasticity of a fat is related to the fatty acid profile and the arrangement of the fatty acids after they are heated and manipulated. β' crystals are smooth and creamy. The fatty acids, which vary in saturation, isomerism, and length, require time to rearrange into the dense three-dimensional packing crystal. Cottonseed oil contains a fatty acid profile that promotes β' crystals, and for this reason it is used in the manufacture of some plastic fats.

Most fats, such as shortening or margarine, that appear to be solid at room temperature actually contain both solid fat crystals and liquid oil. Butter contains free oil, fat crystals, water, and fat globules [26]. Plastic fats have a range that they are neither too hard nor too soft, which depends on the crystals and the liquid portions. The liquid part is held in a network of small crystals. Because of this unique combination of liquid and solid, the fat can be molded or pressed into various shapes without breaking, as would a brittle substance. Manufacturers of plastic shortenings and margarines use the β' stability of mixed glycerides to produce products with this desired creaminess [10]. The type and size of the crystals in a plastic fat influence the performance of the fat in baked products and pastry. Plastic fats can be creamed with sugar, as is commonly done in the mixing of cookies and some cakes.

Flavor

Some fats that are used for seasoning at the table and in salad dressings possess distinctive and pleasing flavors. These include butter, bacon fat, olive oil, sesame seed oil, and margarines. Fats can be flavored with desirable flavors such as butter flavors. In choosing fats for flavor purposes, the cost may also be considered. For example, olive oil and butter are more expensive selections compared to other oils or margarine.

Fats can act as carrying agents. The ability of fats to carry aromatic flavor substances is frequently used in food preparation. Onions, celery, peppers, and similar flavorful foods are cooked in fat to produce a savory fat that can be incorporated into food mixtures. Aromatic fruit and other flavors are carried by fat.

Cocoa Butter and Chocolate

Cocoa butter is the fat found in the cocoa bean, which can be processed into chocolate (**Figure 8–9**). Cocoa beans growing on trees are shown in **Figure 8–10**. The cocoa beans are processed by undergoing fermentation, roasted, and dried to develop flavor compounds from the sugar and proteins in the bean. The beans are shelled (winnowed) revealing an inner bean called a "nib" that contains about 53 percent cocoa butter [113] (**Figure 8–11**). These nibs can be further processed into a paste called the chocolate liquor or mass that contains the aroma compounds that are associated with the chocolate flavor [133]. The cocoa butter can be extracted from the liquor or blended to distribute cocoa butter [67]. The cocoa butter has little flavor, but it acts as a flavor carrier. Cocoa butter acts to trap the flavor aroma compounds that are only released when the cocoa butter is melted. Cocoa butter has a unique and precise narrow melting point

Figure 8–10

Cocoa pods growing on tree. (Jerome Scholler/Shutterstock)

temperature range (88−93°F or 31−34°C) depending on the type of chocolate and percentage of cocoa butter [67].

Cocoa butter is a unique fat. Many of cocoa butter's triglycerides are identical consisting of palmitic, oleic and stearic fatty acids. The other triglyceride is oleoyldistearin with two stearic and an oleic fatty acid radical. Both triglycerides have oleic acid in the central position on the glycerol backbone. The two triglycerides have a melting point within two degrees of each other.

Chocolate melts over a fairly narrow temperature range that is close to body temperature. In the chocolate, the cocoa butter entraps, carries, and distributes chocolate flavor and aroma compounds. When chocolate melts in the mouth, it releases the volatile flavor compounds and produces a smooth mouthfeel. It is only when the cocoa butter melts that the chocolate aroma and volatile compounds are released [133].

In food processing, the melting of chocolate is called "tempering." Cocoa butter has a unique complex polymorphism since its solid form can take several crystalline forms, which are six forms of α (alpha), β (beta), and β' (beta prime) crystals. Only one of the crystal forms is stable [18]. The fats in cocoa butter can crystallize into six different forms each with a different melting point [113]. Good

Figure 8–9

Cocoa butter. (Diana Taliun/Shutterstock)

Figure 8–11

Halved cocoa bean and fruit. (Digital Genetics/Shutterstock)

Figure 8–12

Chocolate bloom is visible on these improperly stored chocolates. (© Amanda Frye)

chocolate that is glossy, uniform in appearance and has a good texture that "snaps" when broken contains beta (β) "V" type crystals. Dipping chocolate is tempered, cooled, and agitated to develop many beta V type fat crystals [17]. During tempering, all six crystal forms are melted around 113°F (45°C) [74]. Upon cooling, crystals known as IV and V form around 80°F (27°C). The chocolate is agitated to seed other small crystals that serve as the nuclei for other small crystals. The chocolate is heated to 88°F (31°C) to eliminate the IV crystal form and leave only the stable desirable βV crystal [74, 18]. When melting chocolate for dipping or other uses, proper tempering is essential for melting chocolate so the cocoa butter achieves the proper gloss, texture, and stability [133].

Cocoa butter is solid below 88°F (31°C) and melts around 93°F (34°C) [17]. Chocolate should be stored at temperatures between 64 and 70° F/18 and 21°C [133]. Improper tempering or storage at high temperatures above 70°F (21°C) over time will alter the chocolate quality. Chocolates containing cocoa butter must maintain a stable state after cooling and stored within a precise temperature zone [18].

The unstable fat crystals will migrate to the surface and recrystallize resulting in the development of chocolate or fat *bloom* [17, 67]. *Fat bloom* is from small fat crystals on the chocolate surface

that gives a white or grey appearance. See **Figure 8–12** to see chocolate bloom on improperly stored chocolate. The fat bloom has no effect on the taste and can be reversed by tempering the chocolate [67, 18]. See Chapters 9 and 27 for more information on cocoa and chocolate.

PROCESSING, REFINING, AND TYPES OF FAT

Fats and oils commonly used in food preparation originate from plant or animal. Plant-based oils are extracted from seeds, fruits, or nuts. Animal fats are obtained as a by-product from the meat processing industry. The animal fats are obtained from carcasses when animal protein tissue is separated from other material such as the hide and bones. Milk fats are most commonly from milk from the cow, goat, or sheep. Vegetable, fruit, and oilseed oils are extracted or pressed from the seed, vegetable, or fruit source. Cold and hot express methods are used to obtain the oil [114]. The fat and oils obtained directly from the rendering or extractions are called "crude" oils or fats. These oils and fats must undergo further processing to remove impurities. The oils are processed to protect desirable components.

Rendering Animal Fat

The term for extracting animal fat is called *rendering*, which the USDA defines as "to extract fat or oil from livestock or poultry by melting down or reprocessing meat, bone, feathers, or other by-products." Rendering is done either by dry heat or steam method; some rendering plants use highly sophisticated and automated continuous flow equipment. All rendering and meat processing occurs at USDA-inspected plants. This extracted animal fat is either edible or inedible fat. Tallow is the fat rendered from the adipose tissue of cattle and sheep; it is used in candle making, soap manufacture, etc. Grades are based on hardness, moisture, insoluble, titer, clarity, and free fatty acid content.

Animal fat rendering is a type of sustainable recycling; it is healthy for the environment. Rendering is a multi-million ton business and an important subsector of the economy. The meat processing industry produces more than meat to eat; they also efficiently use everything from the animal carcass so nothing is wasted. Secondary markets include hides or skins, bones, and fat. The food-processing industry uses the edible fat and other by-products for fats, gelatin, and blood meal.

Tallow. Animal tissues containing fat are converted to tallow by rendering. U.S. edible tallow is from the highest quality beef and processed for human consumption and inspected by the USDA Food Safety and Inspection Service (FSIS). Edible tallow renderers can only render one type of animal per processing plant. The tallow is either "deodorized" tallow that does not alter taste of food or "undeodorized" tallow that is used to enhance flavors in food [93]. Deodorizing is a process to remove volatile odor compounds using steam [114]. Certified halal and kosher tallows are also available in the United States.

Lard. Is the fat rendered from fresh and clean tissues of pigs in good health at time of slaughter. Lard composition, consistency, and characteristics vary based on feeding regime. Pigs fed high unsaturated fats will yield softer lard [93]. Rendering involves subdividing the fatty tissue into small particles and heating. The melted fat then separates from the connective tissue and other cell residues. Leaf fat, which lines the abdominal cavity, is used to make the better qualities of lard.

Lard is one of the oldest culinary fats; however, the high saturated fat content, lack of uniformity in the production of lard, its flavor, and a potentially grainy texture have resulted in a reduction in the use of lard by Americans. In 1970, the per capita annual availability of lard in the food supply was 4.5 pounds as compared to 1.0 pound in 2008 [127]. Lard is still the preferred fat in Mexican cuisine for such dishes as re-fried beans. It also has excellent shortening power, resulting in tender pie crusts.

A chemical modification, called *interesterification,* can be applied to lard to improve its plasticity and creaming qualities. Interesterification involves treating the fat with a catalyst at a controlled temperature to create a random distribution of fatty acids on the triglyceride molecules. The degree of saturation is not changed, but the properties of the lard are improved.

Lard is susceptible to spoilage by the development of rancidity. **Antioxidants** are added to lard in processing to increase its shelf life. Some lard samples have relatively low smoking temperatures and have not been commonly used for frying; however, lards with high smoke points can be produced.

Choice white grease. This is a specific grade of mostly pork fat defined by hardness, color, fatty acid content, moisture, insoluble, unsaponifiables (materials that will not convert to soap), and free fatty acid. Choice white grease is used in pet foods and animal foods. It provides an excellent source of fatty acids and energy. It is also used to produce shortenings or the oleo chemical industry [93].

Inedible Rendering Fats

Yellow Grease. Restaurants and food processors render or recycle old or "spent" frying oil and grease. Inedible fat renderings are also further processed. This grease is called *yellow grease*; it is a by-product of the restaurant and industrial cooking operations. Sometimes low-quality rendering plants produce low-quality tallow that is classified as yellow grease. Spent grease may be old cooking and frying grease from animal and plant sources. This grease is often used for biofuels.

Other Fat Sources. The renderer may obtain his fat sources from animal processing businesses, restaurants for spent grease, meat boning and trimming businesses, aquaculture productions, and fallen animals [93]. There are over 3,000 industries that rely on the edible and inedible rendered fat. These secondary market products are important in the fashion industry (leather), chemical industry, pet food industry, metallurgy, plastic industry, rubber and fertilizer industries. Inedible tallow provides key ingredients for soaps and personal care products. Tallow is a basic ingredient in toiletries and laundry soaps. Inedible tallow is now the most common with 3.5 billion pounds produced in 2016 versus choice white grease production of 1.37 billion pounds in 2016 [128]. Bio-diesel from animal fats and used cooking oil is a growing industry. Finding high value use for animal by-products is an important part of the economy and sustainable agriculture. Rendering is not only valuable to the economy, but also protects public health by the disposing of animal carcasses and by protecting the environment, too [93, 114].

OILS

Oils come from a variety of plants and fish. Some foods are naturally high in oils, like nuts and olives (**Figure 8–13**). Vegetable oils are obtained from

Figure 8–13

Olive oil. (Margouillat/123RF)

fruits, seeds, and nuts. Soy and palm are the sources of nearly two-thirds of the world's vegetable oil [19]. Oil most often is removed from oil-containing seed fruits or nuts by pressing in batches or a continuous expeller press. The meal leaving the expeller may contain some residual oil that is removed by solvent extraction. Hexane is the most common solvent used and is evaporated from the oil. The meal remaining after the oil has been obtained is used for animal feed, some select human food applications, fuel, or fertilizer [19].

Most oils are high in monounsaturated or polyunsaturated fats and low in saturated fats. Interest in omega-3 oils has driven production in the fish oil market. Single cell algae are also used for oil production. Few plant oils, including coconut oil and palm kernel oil, are high in saturated fats and maybe classified as *solid fats*. Oils are not a food group, but recommended amounts of oils are included in food intake patterns since they are a source of essential fatty acids and vitamin E.

Global oilseed production is over 579 million tons. Common oilseeds include copra (dried coconut kernels), cottonseed, palm, palm kernel, peanut, canola (rapeseed), soybean, corn, safflower, sunflower, flaxseed, pumpkin seed, grape seed, and sesame seed from which oil is extracted. The olive is the most common fruit used for oil. Nut oils such as walnut, almond, hazelnut, and macadamia nut may also provide oil. Soybean oil is the most common oil used in the United States. Some common oils are corn, soybean, canola, cottonseed, olive, safflower, sunflower, walnut, and sesame oil.

The crude oils are further refined to remove free fatty acids, color, and suspended meal particles [19]. An alkaline material is added to remove the free fatty acids not attached to a glycerol molecule. Free fatty acids in excess can detract from the oil's flavor and decrease its effectiveness when used for frying. The unwanted products of this reaction are then removed by centrifuging and washing, with a final drying process, followed by bleaching and deodorizing to remove color pigments and further purify the oil [68]. *RBD* refers to refined, bleached, and deodorized oil. These steps are discussed in more detail later.

Kinds of Oils

Vegetable oils may be used in cooking as oils or hydrogenated to produce shortenings and margarines. A number of different oils may be found in the marketplace. The flavor, cooking characteristics, fatty acid composition, properties, nutrition profile and price influence the choice of oil [122].

Soybean. Soybean oil is the dominant edible oil used and produced in the United States (**Figure 8–14**). Until the early 1940s, it was not used in this country chiefly because of its susceptibility to oxidation and development of off-flavors described as being "grassy" and "painty." These off-flavors, or flavor reversion (discussed later in this chapter), appear to be related to the content of linolenic acid. Partial hydrogenation of soybean oil improves stability but forms trans-fatty acid; however, partially hydrogenated oil is no longer GRAS [77]. High-oleic soybeans are low in linoleic and linolenic acid as compared to traditional soybeans. Some varieties of high-oleic soybeans have been developed through conventional plant-breeding methods [40] and with genetic engineering [77]. Oils produced from high-oleic soybeans are two to three times more stable as compared to regular soybean oil.

Figure 8–14

Soybean, pods of soybeans, and soybean oil. (Spline_x/Shutterstock)

Cottonseed. Cottonseed oil was America's first vegetable oil, developed over a century ago as a by-product of the cotton industry. It has a neutral flavor and has a high level of stability to flavor reversion even when used for frying [98]. Much of the cottonseed oil used in the United States is used by food-service operators and snack food processors.

Olive. One of the most expensive edible oils is olive oil; it is also one of the most ancient oils. Ancient civilizations (ca. 500 B.C.) first extracted olive oil with primitive stone mortar and fallen olives (**Figure 8–15**) [110]. The Romans developed the millstone crusher and the olive press to extract olive oils; a technique modified and used for many years (**Figure 8–16**) [47]. Today three basic olive oil extraction techniques exist—pressure, percolation, and centrifugation; centrifugation is most widely used today [47]. The highest-quality olive oils are those that have not been refined, deodorized, or otherwise processed. The terms *extra virgin, virgin,* and *pure* indicate the acidity level and amount of processing. New grade standards set by the U.S. Department of Agriculture (USDA) for olive oil took effect in 2010, but are voluntary. A description of the various types of olive oils is in **Table 8–6**.

Figure 8–16

People have used olive presses since Greeks first began pressing olives over 5000 years ago. (EZeePics/Shutterstock)

Olive oil has always been prized for its flavor, particularly by those who have lived in the Mediterranean area, where olive oil is the major cooking and salad oil. The popularity of olive oil in the United States has grown as consumers embrace world cuisines and seek to use oils with perceived health benefits. Olive oil

Figure 8–15

An ancient olive tree. (Luri/Shutterstock)

TABLE 8–6
TYPES OF OLIVE OIL

Type	Description
Virgin olive oil	Applies only to oil obtained from the first pressing of the olives without further processing.
Extra virgin olive oil	Top grade of virgin olive oil because of its low acidity level.
Olive oil or pure olive oil	A blend of refined olive oil and extra virgin or virgin olive oil. Is less expensive and less flavorful as compared to extra virgin and virgin olive oils. Has a higher smoke point (468°F/242°C) compared to other types of olive oils and is therefore a better choice for higher-temperature cooking techniques, such as sautéing.
Olive-pomace oil	A blend of olive oil and refined olive-pomace oil. Refined olive-pomace oil is produced by extracting oil from crushed olive material with the use of solvents.

Figure 8-17

Ripening olives in different stages of ripeness. (© Amanda Frye)

Figure 8-18a

Grinding olives for oil extraction. (Dmytro Surkov/123RF)

Figure 8-18b

Oil after extraction. (Vasileios Karafillidis/123RF)

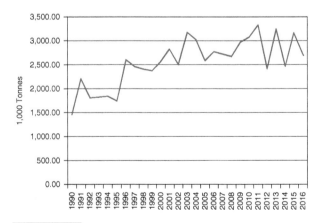

Figure 8-19

World olive oil production. (Source: International Olive Council)

contains a high percentage (55 to 83 percent) of the monounsaturated fatty acid oleic. It is also more stable to oxidation than most oils because of its low content of linoleic acid, a polyunsaturated fatty acid. Olive oil is high in free radical scavenging polyphenols that are thought to be an important health benefit in preventing cardiovascular disease and cancer [130, 49, 57]. Harvest time and olive variety influence the polyphenol compounds [47, 110] (**Figures 8-17, 8-18a,** and **8-18b**). See **Figure 8-19** for worldwide olive oil production.

Canola. Canola oil is a highly stable oil that is high in unsaturated fat (94 percent), 58 percent of which is the monounsaturated fatty acid oleic [37]. This oil has increased in popularity because of its health advantages over other oils [92]. Canola oil is high in omega-3 fatty acid alpha linolenic acid (ALA) and low in saturated fatty acids [83].

Canola oil is relatively new on the market compared to other oils. In the 1970s, Canadian plant breeders developed an edible variety of rapeseed low in erucic acid and glucosinolates and named it Canola (**Figure 8-20**). The FDA has approved canola oil for use in the United States and granted it GRAS status. The name canola comes from "Can" for Canada and "oleo" for oil. Canola oil is used widely in Europe, but it often is called oilseed rape or rape oil. It is used in salad oil, salad dressings, margarines, shortenings, and fats produced for commercial frying operations. Canola oil has a high smoke point between 468° F and 475°F, making it ideal for frying.

Sunflower, Safflower, Peanut, Flaxseed, and Corn.
Sunflower oil has good flavor stability and is growing in popularity (**Figure 8-21**). Safflower oil, with 78 percent linoleic acid, has the highest polyunsaturated fatty acid content. However, it is more expensive than many other oils and lacks flavor stability [68]. Peanut oil, on the other hand, has excellent oxidative stability. It is preferred by some snack food manufacturers because of its flavor [37]. Peanut oil is used for frying due to its high smoke point. Corn oil has a naturally sweet taste and is used primarily in margarines. It is a relatively stable source of polyunsaturated fatty acids because of its low

Figure 8–20

A field of Canola plants. (Alexander Kolomietz/123RF)

Figure 8–21

Sunflower seeds and oil. (Bitt24/Shutterstock)

Figure 8–22

Corn oil. (Dino Osmic/Shutterstock)

Figure 8–23

Flaxseed. (Shapiso/Shutterstock)

linolenic acid content [51] (**Figure 8–22**). Flaxseed oil is produced by cold pressing (**Figure 8–23**). Flaxseed oils are rich in omega-3 fatty acids [92]. A flaxseed oil, high in alpha linoleic acid, has been developed that is about 20 to 30 percent higher in omega-3 fatty acids compared to other flaxseed oils [98].

Tropical Oils. Coconut, palm, and palm kernel oil are known as tropical oils, but unlike other oils, they are high in saturated fats. *Copra* is the dried coconut kernel from which coconut oil is extracted. Coconut oil is solid at room temperature because it contains a high proportion of saturated fatty acids, about 92 percent. Many of these are short-chain fatty acids, particularly lauric acid. Coconut oil has a sharp melting point, similar to the fat found in chocolate, and is therefore useful in confections and cookie fillings.

Palm kernel oil is extracted from the dried palm kernel. Palm kernel oil is much like coconut oil and composed of a high proportion of saturated fatty acids. Palm oil, unlike palm kernel oil, is extracted from the fruit rather than the kernel of the palm tree [9] (**Figure 8–24**). Palm oil is semisolid at room temperature and has a long shelf life. It may be used in margarine and shortening and thus is on the labels of a number of processed foods. Palm oil is being used in conjunction with soybean oils to produce margarines free of trans fatty acids [70].

Marine Oils

Marine oils include fish oils, fish liver oils, krill, squid, and some mammals such as seal, plus algae. Some fish have up to 20 percent oil. The omega-3 fatty acid fish oil market is about 10–12 percent of total marine oil [11] (**Figure 8–25**). Marine oils typically are long-chain polyunsaturated fatty acids with up to six double bonds. These oils are rich in vitamin A and D.

Figure 8–24

Palm oil comes from the fruit itself (reddish orange). (Wasu Watcharadachaphong/Shutterstock)

Figure 8–25

Omega-3 fish oil capsules. (Smal Marina/Shutterstock)

Fish liver oil use can be traced back to the Middle Ages and populations in Norway, Iceland, Greenland, and Scotland have used fish liver oil for thousands of years. Cod liver oil is probably one of the best known oils, although other fish liver oil production is higher. Liver is processed under low steam pressure, which cooks the liver; then as steam condenses the oil floats on top, which is skimmed off to storage tanks. Some oil is from fresh catch but much is from aquaculture-raised fish, incidental catch and fish by-products from fileting, fish cannery wastes, *surimi* such as "imitation crab" processing, and roe fishery waste.

The most common method for extracting marine oil is wet reduction rendering process involving cooking, pressing, separation of the oil and water with recovery of oil, and drying of the residual material. Other methods exist such as dry rendering and solvent extraction enzymatic hydrolysis, silage autolysis, or solvent extraction [11]. The crude oils are further refined to remove free fatty acids, color, and suspended meal particles [19]. An alkaline material is added to remove the free fatty acids not attached to a glycerol molecule. Free fatty acids in excess can detract from the oil's flavor and decrease its effectiveness when used for frying. The unwanted products of this reaction are then removed by centrifuging and washing, with a final drying process, followed by bleaching and deodorizing to remove color pigments and further purify the oil [68].

Some single cell organisms such as modified yeast and algae can yield omega-3 fatty acids EPA and DHA as well as omega-6 fatty acid ARA (arachidonic acid). These can be easily grown in fermenters or outside ponds. Processing the oil requires separating the biomass, drying then using a solvent to extract the oil which is then refined [11]. Marine oils are less stable and subject to oxidation because of their high degree of unsaturation.

OIL AND FAT REFINING

Refining crude oils and fats is the process to remove undesirable components that impart undesirable characteristics to the color and flavor, keeping qualities, and safety. The goal of refining is to keep the desirable qualities such as antioxidants, phytosterols, vitamins, and essential fatty acids, yet remove undesirable substances such as free fatty acids, phospholipids, carbohydrates, proteins and their degraded products, water, pigments and fat oxidation products, volatiles, and contaminants [106, 85]. The basic standard refining processes are physical or alkali chemical processes [106]. Alkali chemical process uses sodium hydroxide (also known as caustic soda or lye) to neutralize the oil after physical processing. Free fatty acids are removed by distillation. Physical refining cannot be used on all oils. Physical refining reduces loss of neutral oils and minimizes chemical pollution in the environment. Alkali refining is required for high acidic or highly pigmented crude oils.

Settling

Settling allows water and oil to separate so the water can be withdrawn. The fat or oil is heated and then allowed to stand until the aqueous phase separates. This rids the oil and fat from water, protein materials, phospholipids, and carbohydrates [85].

Degumming

Degumming is the process to remove gums and phospholipids from the crude oil since they will darken the oil and result in high product loss. Some oils such as soybean, canola, and sunflower oils contain a substantial amount of phospholipids [85]. Degumming is essential in physical refining. The phospholipids may be either hydratable or non-hydratable forms. Non-hydratable phospholipids are typically calcium or magnesium salts of phosphate compounds. Hydratable phospholipids are hydrated with 1–3 percent water, agitated at 122°F (50°C) and then separated by settling or centrifuging [85]. The non-hydratable forms are treated with 0.1–0.3 percent phosphoric acid that chelates with the calcium and magnesium salts that convert the phospholipids to a hydratable form [106]. Other degumming alternative methods exist such as organic refining using citric acid, acid refining, and EDTA and enzymatic degumming [25]. The degumming process used depends on the oil.

Neutralization

Neutralization is used to remove free fatty acids. Sodium hydroxide, commonly referred to as caustic soda or lye, is mixed with heated oil or fat then allowed to settle separating aqueous phase or centrifuged. The resulting aqueous solution called foots or soapstock is separated and used for making soap [85]. The soapstock is removed from the neutral oil by washing it with hot water followed by settling or centrifuging [85]. The neutralization also removes residual phospholipids and improves oil color.

Bleaching

Bleaching is a common step in both physical and alkali refining to remove color, trace metals, and oxidation products. Chlorophyll is only removed from oil by bleaching, and heated with special natural adsorbents like acid-activated clay. However, peroxides that are present in oil can have negative oxidative effects. Temperature, mixing, time, and vacuum are variables that affect the bleaching process and must be carefully controlled.

After a steep and long decline following World War II, U.S. per person butter consumption began rising in 2005

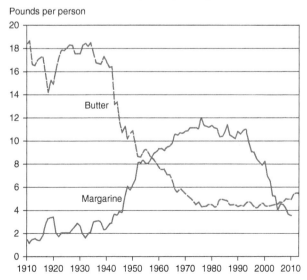

Figure 8–26

Per capita butter and margarine consumption. (Source: USDA Economic Research Service, Food Availability Data. Reprinted from: Bentley, J. & Ash, M. (2016). Butter and Margarine Availability over the last Century. Amber Waves. Washington, DC: United States Department of Agriculture, Economic Research Service.)

Winterization (Dewaxing)

Winterization and dewaxing is a process to improve the clarity of the oil. The cloudiness of these oils occurs because some of the triglyceride molecules in the oil have higher melting points than other molecules in the mixture and crystallize or become solid at the low refrigerator temperature. The cloudy appearance does not affect the functionality of oil. A winterized oil, usually called *salad oil,* has a lower melting point and does not crystallize at refrigerator temperatures [68]. To produce winterized oil, the temperature of the oil is lowered to a point at which the higher-melting triglycerides crystallize. Then the oil is filtered to remove these crystals. The remaining oil remains clear and liquid under refrigeration. Some cooking oils become cloudy when stored in the refrigerator, and thus are undesirable for salads and salad dressings that will be refrigerated.

Deodorization

Deodorization typically uses steam distillation at elevated temperatures 185°F (85°C) under low pressure to remove volatile compounds. Many of these undesirable flavor compounds are from oil oxidation. Other volatile compounds are ketones and aldehydes give an undesirable flavor and odor.

Modification of Fats and Oils

The ideal edible oil characteristics are described as having oxidative stability, functionality, and nutrition. So ideally a fat or oil should have a high oxidative stability at high and ambient temperatures, contain enough solid fat for use as margarines, shortenings, and frying fats, be both low in saturated fatty acid, and high in polyunsaturated acids. However, no single fat or oil fulfills these requirements [35]. Oil and fat processing technology is used to achieve these ideals while reducing *trans* and saturated fatty acids but yielding desirable characteristics.

Hydrogenation

Hydrogenation is the process of adding hydrogen to the points of unsaturation in a fatty acid. If an oil were completely hydrogenated, the carbon-carbon double bonds would be converted to single bonds; the fat would be saturated. The process of hydrogenation changes liquid oils into plastic shortenings or margarines. Hydrogenation also increases an oil's oxidative and thermal stability. Hydrogenation has been used since 1902 [30]. Hydrogenated shortenings are neutral in flavor, have a smoke point high enough to be used for frying, and have good shortening power for baked goods. Hydrogenated fats also resist oxidation, which results in undesirable **rancid** flavors and odors. The plastic quality of hydrogenated shortenings is important in the preparation of baked goods. A plastic fat may be creamed into sugar, as in cookies, or cut into flour when making pie crusts and biscuits. Traditional shortenings, not trans fat reduced, contain 25 to 29 percent trans fatty acids and 25 to 29 percent saturated fats [96].

Hydrogenation can be controlled and stopped giving oils the characteristics desired, thus turning oils into a solid appearance such as shortening or margarine. Partial hydrogenation was used for cooking oils, liquid shortenings and liquid margarines because of the functionality and stability of the fats. However, oils that have been partially hydrogenated contain some trans fatty acids which are no longer generally recognized as safe according to the FDA. Food manufacturers have had to replace trans hydrogenated oils with natural saturated palm oils, shortenings made through interesterification or modified hydrogenation processes producing reduced trans fat shortenings [96].

Traditional Oil Hydrogenation

Traditional oil hydrogenation occurs in a reactor, where hydrogen gas is bubbled through the liquid oil in the presence of a nickel catalyst, which speeds the reaction. In the process of hydrogenation, some of the double bonds between the carbon atoms of the fatty acid portion of the triglyceride molecule are broken, and hydrogen is added. This chemical change makes the fatty acids more saturated and increases the melting point of the fat. With sufficient hydrogenation, it becomes a solid at room temperature. Often, products that have received different degrees of hydrogenation are combined to produce the desired effect [68]. Some oils, such as frying fats used in food-service operations, are partially hydrogenated yielding trans fatty acids. Various approaches are being used by manufacturers to reduce trans fatty acid content of shortenings and margarines [70, 119]. A modification of the hydrogenation process can reduce the development of trans fatty acids.

Structured Lipids

Structured lipids are lipids that are modified from their natural form to alter characteristics for use in a specific food, increase stability or use in foods. The modification involves an alteration of chemical structure of the lipid by fatty acid addition or rearrangement on the glycerol backbone [112]. Fat interesterification involves rearranging the fatty acids on the triglyceride molecule by chemical catalyst or enzymes creating thus a "new" triglyceride [76]. Stability of oil in water emulsion high in polyunsaturated fats can be increased by using interesterification making the lipid more resistant to oxidation [108]. Structural lipid processes used in foods include the production of shortening through interesterification, production of mono- and diglyceride and phospholipid emulsifiers, production of low trans fats shortenings and margarines, as well as cocoa butter alternatives [112, 131]. Structured emulsions can be formulated to have a solid-like structure suitable for many trans PHO applications including shortening [131, 108]. Structured

lipids or interesterified fats provide another non-trans solid fat alternative [76, 109]. These structured lipids have nutraceutical application such as infant formula or medium chain triglyceride (MCT) oils. Interesterified margarine has been produced for many years.

Interesterification

Interesterification by a chemical or enzymatic process is one way to produce hydrogenated fats, such as margarine, with fewer trans fatty acids [16, 119]. This process was used in shortening production and to replace partially hydrogenated oils. Interesterification of fully hydrogenated oil with high-oleic soybean oil closely resemble the functionality of partially hydrogenated oils [84].

Interesterification is a process in which the ester bonds linking fatty acids to the glycerol backbone are split, then the newly liberated fatty acids are randomly shuffled within a fatty acid pool and re-esterified onto a new position, either on the same glycerol (intraesterification) or onto another glycerol (interesterification) [105]. The fatty acids bonded to the glycerol backbone can vary in chain length, number and position of double bonds, and geometrical configuration, which provide the fat's physical, chemical, and nutritional properties [41]. The plasticity, melting point, smoke point, crystalline properties, and the liquid or solid form are physical properties important in food. Interesterification can rearrange fatty acids on the triglyceride molecule so to change the composition, but preserve the fatty acid profile [41]. Interesterification does not change the fatty acids; it just rearranges them on the glycerol backbone to synthesis a new triglyceride with desired properties [31]. A reaction is usually carried out with a high melting point fat (such as a palm oil fraction or fully hydrogenated vegetable oil) and a liquid oil to create a triglyceride molecule with desirable properties such as texture, plasticity, and mouthfeel.

Interesterification has been industrially viable in the food industry since the 1940s to improve the spreadability and baking properties of lard. In the 1970s, there was a renewed interest in this process, particularly as a hydrogenation replacement in the manufacture of zero-trans-fat margarines [105]. Foods with less than 0.5 grams of trans fat may be labeled as "trans fat free," and therefore some have called for stricter labeling guidelines [103].

Interesterification can provide hydrogenation of oils without the trans fat to yield shortenings with desirable function and properties with no trans fats [101, 76, 41]. The use of low temperatures, high pressures, and high catalyst concentrations has been found to reduce the trans fatty acids by 50 percent [35]. Enzymatic interesterification is the desired method to create these new triglyceride fats since it is more stable and controlled. Interesterified lipids can be feasible and economically viable food-processing solution, but question on health impacts are still being researched [76].

Fractionation

Fractionation is a technique used to separate triglyceride in fats and oils by difference in melting points, solubility, or volatility. It can be used to separate fats or liquid oils. Fats are typically a mixture of triglycerides with different melting points. These triglyceride components can be separated by the fractionation process to yield a product with desired characteristics. Fractionalization is another approach used to reduce trans fats and involves the batch cooling of the refined oil followed by batch filtration [19]. Often solvents are used to separate components. Fractionations are often used in processing palm oils and palm kernel oils. The individual triglyceride fractions form products with desired liquid solid characteristics. *Winterization* is a form of fractionation.

Esterification

Esterification is a technique where edible acids, fats, and oils can be reacted with edible alcohols to produce esters such as mono- and diglycerides or emulsifiers [114]. Esters may also be used as fat replacers.

Additives and Processing Aids

Fat and oil manufacturers often add FDA-approved food additives to fats and oils to protect the quality and prolong storage. These additives must meet the Federal Code of Regulations as direct food additive. These additives include antioxidants to retard rancidity such as BHA and BHT. Sometimes coloring agents are added to fats to enhance color with carotenes and annatto as in margarine or butter flavored shortenings. Lecithin is sometimes added as an emulsifier. Citric acid is often added as a metal chelating agent to inhibit oxidative breakdown that induces rancidity. Polyglycerol esters are added to modify and inhibit crystallization. These are just a few examples of additives and processing aids added to fats and oils during processing [114].

Blending

Blending of oil and fats is common for food manufacturers. Oils are modified and blended with fats in many combinations to produce a functional ingredient with desirable properties for baking, frying, salad dressing, and more. Interesterification and fractionation are used for these purposes [114].

SHORTENING AND MARGARINE

Shortening

Shortenings are used in many baked goods, including cakes, pie crusts, biscuits, and cookies as well as many commercially prepared crackers, cookies, and other snack foods. Shortenings were originally produced from animal and vegetable fats or hydrogenated oils which yielded 12–25 percent trans fats. Now that trans fats have been found to have negative health consequence, shortenings [79, 80, 89, 66, 124, 115] are often made through interesterification. Shortenings often have emulsifiers, such as **monoglycerides** and **diglycerides**, added to them. The use of shortening with an emulsifier is desirable in some cake formulas to allow higher proportions of sugar and liquid to fat. The presence of mono- and diglycerides in shortening decreases the smoke point of the fat, thus making it less desirable for frying purposes. In the home, often only one type of general-purpose shortening is used. Commercial food-processing and food-service establishments may use several different shortenings that have been formulated for specific purposes, such as deep-fat frying, cake making, or icings.

Margarine

Oleomargarine was first developed in 1869 by a French chemist, Mège-Mouries, in response to the offer of a prize by Napoleon III for a palatable, nutritious, and economical alternate for butter. Beef tallow and whey were the chief constituents of the original margarine [16]. Since that time, many changes have occurred in the composition and processing of margarine. Code of Federal Regulations Title 21 B 166.110 gives standard of identity for margarine. Margarine (oleomargarine) is defined as a "food in plastic form or liquid emulsion containing not less than 80 percent fat." Margarines can be made from edible vegetable or marine oils or rendered animal fat such as tallow. Margarine is required to have not less than 15,000 International Units of Vitamin A per pound. *Spreads* are typically lower in fat and higher in water and thus are not suitable for substitution for margarine during baking. A variety of margarine products are available and are described in **Table 8–7**. The reduced-fat and whipped margarines, while desirable for use as table spreads, are generally not recommended for baking. Recipes for cookies and other baked items have been formulated for a specified amount of fat, and thus the use of a lower-fat margarine spread is likely to impact quality. The functions of fat in baking are discussed in following chapters.

Ingredients. Margarine is most commonly made with hydrogenated vegetable oils or liquid vegetable oils; milk, buttermilk, or whey products; and additives that provide desirable characteristics. Traditional margarine and margarine spreads contained approximately 15 percent trans fatty acids; thus manufacturers had to change process from traditional hydrogenation methods to meet FDA requirements [70]. U.S. formulations and production of margarine have been forced to change from PHO trans producing hydrogenation to interesterification and fractionation methods [16]. Fat crystalline forms of beta and beta prime structures are important for textural qualities in stick and tub margarines [28].

TABLE 8–7
VARIETIES OF MARGARINE

Type of Margarine	Description and Characteristics
Regular or standard	Contains 80 percent fat. Appropriate for cookies and other baked goods.
Light or reduced fat	Contains a lesser amount of fat, a greater amount of water, and a stronger emulsifying system than regular margarines. Amount of oil between 45 and 75 percent.
	Generally not appropriate for cookies and other baked goods. Also not desirable for sautéing because the added water will result in spattering.
Whipped	May contain an inert gas to increase the volume and decrease the density and thus has six sticks to the pound instead of four.
Margarines made with canola oil, olive oil, or other	May be made with specialized oils to add unique flavor, to meet consumer preferences, or to provide other desirable characteristics.
Trans fat free	Vegetable oils hydrogenated using a process to avoid trans fatty acids.
Margarine and butter blends	Contain both margarine and butter to offer more butter flavor while having less cholesterol than 100 percent butter.
Unsalted	Does not contain added salt.
Plant stanol or sterol ester	Margarine containing plant stanol or sterol esters that have been shown to reduce cholesterol levels.

Margarine is a *water-in-fat emulsion* and must contain not less than 80 percent fat according to the **standard of identity** for margarine established by the FDA. Most regular margarines contain about 80 percent fat. Other ingredients permitted in margarine by the federal standard of identity are listed in **Table 8–8**.

MILK FATS

Most common milk fat is from the cow when cream is separated from the milk, which will be the focus of the following discussion (**Figure 8–27**). Milk fats are important for butter, creams, whipping cream, and cheesemaking. Milk fat and butterfat are the same

TABLE 8–8
INGREDIENTS IN MARGARINE

Purpose	Ingredients
Fat source	Hydrogenated vegetable oils or liquid vegetable oils, rendered animal fats, or marine oils
Nutrient fortification	Vitamins A and D
Flavor	Diacetyl and salt
Emulsifying agents	Lecithin, monoglycerides, and/or diglycerides
Preservatives	Citric acid or certain citrates; sodium benzoate, benzoic acid, or sorbic acid
Color	Various colorings—may be artificial or natural

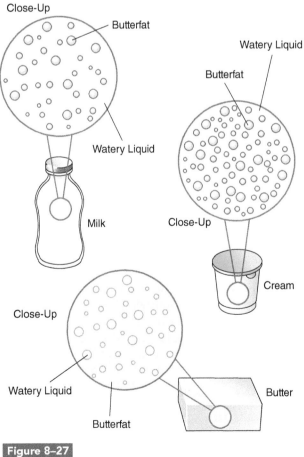

Figure 8–27

Milk fat to cream to butter.

thing. Anhydrous milk fat (AMF), sometimes called butteroil, is a milk fat in an extracted commercial product that may not have all the milk fat components. Milk fat is also discussed in Chapters 7, 10, and 22.

Triglycerides account for 98.3 percent of milk fat with the remaining fat as free fatty acids and mono- and diglycerides from lipolysis or incomplete formation. Long-chain saturated fatty acids C14–myristic (11 percent); C16–palmitic (26 percent); and C18–stearic (10 percent) are two-thirds milk fatty acids and C18:1 oleic (20 percent) fatty acid, the most common unsaturated fatty acid. Short-chain fatty acids C4–butyric; C6–caproic; C8–caprylic; and C10–capric account for 11 percent of the milk fat.

About 5 percent of the fatty acids are naturally trans due to rumen microbial conversion. There are small amounts of essential fatty acids 18:2 linoleic (3–5 percent) and 18:3 linolenic (1–2 percent) including highly bioactive isomers of linoleic acid cis 9 and trans 11 in 18:2 [134, 24]. Butyric acid is specific to milk fat and is subject to lipase lipolysis that is responsible for rancidity. Milk fats nutritional and textural properties can be manipulated by fractionation and interesterification, but the acceptance of these products is low and the cost is high [24]. Other milk fat lipids include 0.8 percent phospholipid in the fat globule membrane and 0.3 percent cholesterol in the fat core.

The overall milk fat melting point is the same temperature as the cow: 101.5°F (38.6°C). Individual triglycerides in the milk fat have a wide distribution of melting points producing a complex melting curve. There are four known milk fat crystal forms—alpha, beta, and beta prime 1 and 2; the alpha crystals are the least stable [53].

Most milk fat is in a small droplet globule surrounded by a protein and phospholipid membrane. The phospholipid is involved in milk fat oxidation. If raw milk is allowed to stand at room temperature, the fat will float to the top of the milk and separate because of density difference. However, if refrigerated, the fat globules will cluster, rising quicker and forming a cream layer within 20–30 minutes in cold milk.

Fat destabilization is important to fat emulsions such as butter or fat foams as found in whipping cream and ice cream [54]. Fat destabilization refers to clumping and clustering of fat globules leading to a fat matrix in a product. With this milk fat destabilization there is an irreversible increase in size of fat globules as they join together losing individual identity in a process known as *coalescence*. The term *flocculation* refers to reversible clustering fat globules with no loss of fat globule identity and the fat globules can be re-dispersed. *Partial coalescence* occurs as fat globules are held together by fat crystals and liquid fat as long as the crystal structure is maintained. These processes are temperature dependent. Once the fat crystals melt, the fat globules

coalesce. When cream is whipped, the fat crystals come together by shear force of the whipping action with the fat crystals coming together as they collide with each other during the agitation. The liquid fat is said to act as the cement to bind these crystals. Partial coalescence is important in dairy emulsions due to fat crystals. These fat crystals surround air pockets as whipping cream turns into a cream foam [54].

Milk fat provides the lubricating mouthfeel in foods such as butter and ice cream. It provides a creamy texture to product as well as flavor. Butter flavor is uniquely derived from short-chain fatty acids. Rancidity is caused by the hydrolysis of the short-chain fatty acids. These butter fats also provide flavor for aged cheese and provide a shortening effect of the cheese protein matrix. Butter is not spreadable at refrigerated structure due to its fatty acid crystalline nature. The spreadable butter fat is 61–75°F, (16–24°C) which is determined by the solid fat content (SFC) [53].

FAT FOAMS

Fat foams are important in food systems such as whipped cream, ice cream, and even layer cakes. Food foams are composed of gas (air), liquid (water), and a surface active agent (fat or protein) [63]. In fat foams, bubbles of air are surrounded by fat globules. The air cells impart body and smoothness giving a light texture and disperse flavors in foods. Soluble milk proteins, which are only about 1–2 percent of milk, are 12 percent of whipping cream composition [86]. These milk proteins initially stabilize the air cells as the adsorption of fat globules encases the air cell [113, 86]. The subsequent encasing of fat globules around the air cell is a secondary process. The individual surrounded fat globule encased air sacs are joined together to form a 3D structure that is probably due to exposed fat crystals and partially coalesced fat globules [86, 113].

After 20 seconds of whipping the cream, the air bubbles are initially surrounded and stabilized by milk protein films [14, 113]. During whipping, the air bubbles decrease in size until maximum foam strength is achieved [107]. As whipping continues, the fat globules become predominant around the air cell. Fat globules penetrate the protein membrane leaving only original protein remnants visible at the fat-encased air bubble surface [14, 107]. Partial coalescence in whipped cream also increases mixture viscosity [113]. Stabilizers can be added to the whipping cream to increase foam stability [39], enhance viscosity, and prevent foam drainage during storage. However, added stabilizers decrease over run or the volume in whipped cream foams [113]. Added emulsifiers to cream can act to promote fat globules on the foam bubble surface, promoting partial coalescence during whipping [113].

Temperature is important in forming a milk fat foam due to the fat crystallization properties. Foam will collapse if temperature is too high (70°F or 21°C) [17, 14]. Chilled whipping cream 45–50°F (7–10°C) and a chilled bowl are desirable to prepare whipped cream [17].

Fat destabilization is essential for fat foams (unlike homogenization used to stabilize fat molecules in milk; see Chapter 22). Fat destabilization is sometimes referred to as fat agglomeration, which includes fat coalescence, flocculation, and partial coalescence. Coalescence is an irreversible state that increases the fat globule size with loss of identity of the coalescing globules. This can be thought of as many individual small fat globules morphing into one big fat globule. Flocculation is when individual fat cells cluster together; they do not lose their individual identity. However, flocculation is not a permanent state. The cluster of fat cells is easily separated into the individual fat globules. Partial coalescence can be thought of as somewhere between flocculation and coalescence. Partial coalescence is irreversible as a force like whipping causes the individual fat globules to join together. The fat crystals maintain the fat globule identity as they link together. The liquid fat binds these individual globules together. The fat crystalline structure and temperature are responsible for the formation of fat foams [53].

Cream is an oil-in-water emulsion with a fat content of 35–40 percent [113]. The conversion of an emulsion to a stable foam requires a structure capable of retaining air bubble integrity [3]. Thus, whipping cream is the process of transforming the liquid emulsion into an aerated viscoelastic solid foam [3]. When heavy cream is agitated by whipping, initially milk protein stabilizes the air bubbles (**Figure 8–28**). The protein thins and the air cell becomes surrounded by fat globules that have partially coalesced in chains and clusters, which spread around the air bubbles [53]. The partial coalescence causes one air cell to be linked to one stabilized air cell than another. The fat's crystalline state is essential and temperature dependent so the fat only partially coalesces around fat globules to form a 3D network around the air cells. Individual fat globules retain their identity, as long as the fat crystal structure is maintained; thus the importance of a cool temperature during whipping [3, 17]. Whipped cream foams are stable and lasting due to the semisolid fat particles in the cream exerting the stabilizing influence by partial coalescence [113] (**Figure 8–29**). Excessive partial coalescence will lead to foam collapse [82]. Fully coalesced fat globules cannot form a stable foam 3D network [53]. The crystalline fat structure is extremely important. A well-whipped cream should be a stiff foam with an overrun of 100–120 percent [3].

Figure 8–28

Metal whisk used to whip cream. (Denis Pogostin/Shutterstock)

Figure 8–29

Whipped cream is a milk fat foam. (Magone/123RF)

Sugar added to the whipped cream mixture can have an effect on the fat foam. If sugar is added to whipped cream before it reaches maximum stiffness it will delay the clumping of fat. If the cream is whipped too much, a loss of air bubbles ensues followed by an irreversible emulsion phase inversion from oil-in-water emulsion to a water-in-oil emulsion. The whipped cream fat will begin to clump (churn) and the mixture turns to butter.

BUTTER

Butter is essentially transformed milk fat (Figure 8–27). Butter contains approximately 80 percent milk fat, 18 percent water, and milk solids. It is made from milk fat

UP CLOSE
FOAM ASSESSMENT

Foam assessment and stability can be assessed through some simple measurements and calculations. Overrun can be used to calculate the amount of air incorporated into the foam.

Foam stability can be measured by the amount of liquid that leaks or drains from the foam when standing, which is typically measured over time.

$$\text{Overrun} = 100 \times (\text{total volume of the foam} - \text{volume of the original fluid})/(\text{volume of the original fluid.})$$

that is separated more or less completely from the other milk constituents. Historically, butter was made from clabbered milk, which is raw milk that was allowed to stand and sour. The milk fat cream would separate and then was skimmed off the top into a wooden tub and churned by hand to make butter (**Figures 8–30a** and **8–30b**). However, natural milk souring is sensitive and prone to microbacterial contamination.

Today, butter is manufactured under carefully controlled processing conditions. Temperature control is essential to obtain the desired texture and functional properties in the final butter product. Butter formation is an example of the breaking of an *oil-in-water emulsion* (the cream) by agitation.

The cream oil in water undergoes a transformation (phase inversion) and the resulting emulsion that forms in butter is a *water-in-oil emulsion*. The butter contains about 18 percent water being dispersed in about 80 percent fat and a small amount of protein acting as the emulsifier (**Figure 8–31**). Buttermilk, a

Figure 8–30a

Stoneware butter churn and wooden dasher. (Warren Price Photography/Shutterstock)

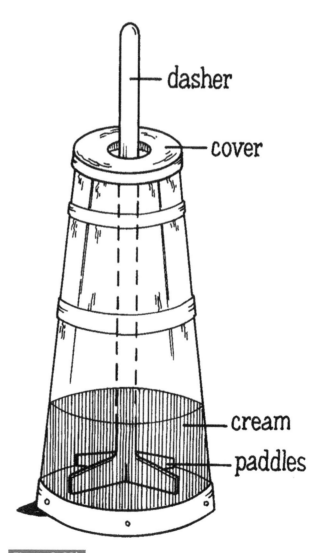

Figure 8–30b

Inside the butter churn.

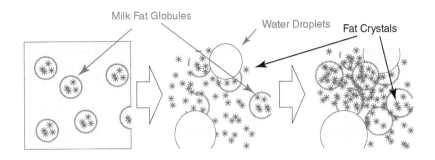

Figure 8–31

The milkfat microstructure within the fat globule (left) Cream is an oil-in-water emulsion (center) fat globule ruptures during cream churning causing a phase inversion to water-in-oil emulsion with fat crystals found in the continuous phase and fat globule. (right) Upon storage the fat crystals form a dense fat network which holds water.   (Reprinted from Rønholt, S., Mortensen, K. and Knudsen, J. C. (2013), The Effective Factors on the Structure of Butter and Other Milk Fat-Based Products. Comprehensive Reviews in Food Science and Food Safety, 12: 468–482. Copyright © Comprehensive Reviews in Food Science and Food Safety)

low-fat milk product, remains after butter is churned from cream. The key steps in butter production are provided in **Table 8–9**.

Butter is typically made with sweet cream and added salt (1.2 percent) for taste and to accentuate flavor [134]. Unsalted butter is also available; it is typically used for baking. Butter has fat soluble vitamins A, D, E, and K as well as calcium, choline, potassium, and other nutrients [120]. Butter can be made from acidulated or bacteriologically produced sour cream as well. *Cultured butter* pasteurized cream is aged with cultures *(S. cremoris, S. lactis diacetyl lactis)* to develop flavor components at pH 5.5 at 21°C and then pH 4.6 at 13°C. Most flavor development takes place in this pH range and colder temperature [53]. Cultured cream is not washed or salted.

Today, only pasteurized cream is used to produce butter. Butter manufacturers may purchase the pasteurized cream or buy milk, pasteurize, and separate the milk fat. Pasteurization causes the fat in the fat globules to liquefy then once cooled some of the fat will crystallize. The rate that the cream is cooled after pasteurization is key to the butter hardness [134]. The pasteurized cream is typically "ripened" or "aged" at a chilling temperature prior to churning. This ripening phase equalizes the temperature and controls fat crystal development that helps assure final product. Processing temperature is extremely important at all phases around 50°F (10°C), so cream is aged [53]. Cream aging takes between 12 and 15 hours to maximize fat crystalline structure.

The appropriate amount of liquid fat during chilling allows for components with higher melting point crystals to encourage fat crystallization later during processing [134]. The cooling rate determines the solid-to-liquid ratio. During cooling many small fat crystals form ultimately leading to a large crystal surface area. The large crystal surface area will allow the liquid fat to absorb onto the crystal surface ultimately reducing the amount of liquid fat during churning.

TABLE 8–9
KEY STEPS IN BUTTER PRODUCTION

Step	Description
Cream	Cream is separated from milk and standardized to a fat percent level for quality control.
Pasteurization	By law, cream is heated to reduce pathogenic bacteria and enzymes.
Aging	Cream is held under refrigeration to ensure proper churning and butter texture.
Ripening (optional)	If cultured butter is desired, a culture of lactic acid bacteria is added to develop flavor and aroma characteristic of cultured butter.
Churning	Cream is agitated by a continuous or batch method.
Draining buttermilk	The liquid remaining after the fat globules coalesce is buttermilk. This low-fat by-product of butter churning is drained from the butter.
Washing (optional)	The butter may be washed.
Working	The butter is worked (mixed) to remove any remaining water or buttermilk and to mix in salt and coloring, if desired.
Packing and storage	Butter is packaged and cooled to storage temperature.

Source: Based on Wisconsin Dairy Association *Key steps in butter production*

Rapid cooling will yield many small crystals, whereas gradual cooling yields fewer but larger crystals. A cooling process that involves lots of agitation causes more fat to crystallize early and form a solid phase with less liquid fat to release during churning and working phases.

Butter Manufacturing

Butter is manufactured by traditional batch processing or in a continuous process that is the most common [134]. The continuous process method produces harder, less spreadable butter that is related to fat crystallization and morphology [134]. Fat crystals of batch produced butter are larger and more irregular [134]. Continuous processing has more rapid cooling, greater fat globular destruction, and more mechanical agitation before crystallization compared to batch [134].

The cream is churned through mechanical agitation. The mechanical rupture of the protein film that surrounds each of the fat globules in cream allows the globules to coalesce. The temperature of the cream is important since if fat is liquid at high temperature then agitation will not break fat globule membrane or the churning (clumping) of the fat globule. Butter churning forces more oil and fat crystals from the damaged fat globule and also disperses the water [134].

The cream is pumped for churning for continuous butter making where the cream is violently agitated to break apart fat globules. As the cream churns, it separates and buttermilk is siphoned off. In traditional churning, the agitation would stop and buttermilk would be siphoned off, versus the continuous churning where the buttermilk is continuously siphoned off.

Gradually with churning, there is an increase in solid fat content leading to an increase in hardness, which is referred to as "setting." This butter setting is a plasticizing step and is crucial in manufacturing [134]. As fat globules clump, they begin to associate with air bubbles so that a network of air bubbles is formed. The air bubble network with fat clumps and globules entrap liquid to produce a stable foam. As the beating continues the fat clumps increase in size until they become too large and too few to enclose the air cells, hence air bubbles coalesce, the foam begins to "leak" and ultimately butter and buttermilk remain. As the buttermilk is drained off, the butter is formed existing as water-in-oil emulsion with remaining water trapped inside the fat network.

Salted butter has 1–3 percent salt added, which provides flavor and extends shelf life. The salt is either worked into the continuous phase with the aqueous cream by adding (10 percent) salt slurry, since some is drained off with the buttermilk, or worked into the butter in batch production. The salt is "worked" into the butter and fat moves from globular form to free fat form. Overworked butter will be brittle and underworked butter will show water droplets. The finished butter is packaged and placed in cold storage.

Spreadability

Butter texture is essential to consumer acceptance. Butter spreadability is the rheological phenomenon determined by hardness, functionality, and melting properties. The crystalline milk fat network affects the spreadability, appearance, and texture [53, 104]. Rheological properties of butter and spreads depend on the ratio of solid fat and liquid fat [15]. Without solid fat the butter would be liquid; without liquid the butter would be hard and brittle [104]. The rheological properties of butter and products are influenced by the fat crystal structure, solidification, and transformation behavior [104, 15] (Figure 8–31).

Butter Milk Fat Crystallization

The structure of butter is complicated involving the fat crystalline structure and a phase inversion of oil-in-water emulsion of cream to the butter water-in-oil emulsion. The milk fat crystals are responsible for the butter texture and structural integrity [134]. A lower temperature fat is in a more solid state due to crystalline fat structure (Figure 8–31).

Crystallization is the change of state from a liquid to a solid that involves crystal nuclei and then growth [134]. Once the fat crystals form the crystals in the liquid oil aggregate into the 3D network due to weak attractive Van der Waals forces, the crystals become interlinked [104]. Crystallization is temperature dependent. Smaller crystals are associated with harder butter [134]. Above 104°F (40°C), the milk fat is liquid and below 40°F (5°C), completely solid and between these temperatures, butter is partly crystalline [134]. Solid fat content (SFC) refers to the proportion of fat that is solidified and determines hardness in the fat crystal network (**Figure 8–32**). Once butter is churned, it undergoes a plasticizing step. Hardening of fat crystals can continue for a month. The butter milk fat remains primarily as beta prime crystalline state even after prolonged storage. Post-crystallization increases solid fat content and strengthens the crystalline fat network [104].

Butter Characteristics

Spreadability is achieved between 20 and 40 percent solid fat. More saturated fatty acids yield harder solid fat content, thus a harder fat such as butter. Plasticity of milk fat-based spreads can be altered by changing proportion of unsaturated and saturated molecules. Altering proportions can be achieved by fractionating, blending, and manipulating milk composition through feed or genetic means. Winter butter is harder than summer butter due to seasonal difference in cow feed influencing fatty acid composition.

Butter is made from either sweet or sour cream. Cultured butter is made from cream *cultured* with bacteria. It has a more pronounced flavor. Clarified butter contains only the butter fat. Either sweet or cultured butter may be clarified by melting the butter and removing the milk solid and water components (Figure 8–7). Ghee, used in Indian cooking, is made by simmering butter until the water is cooked off and milk solids begin to brown [33].

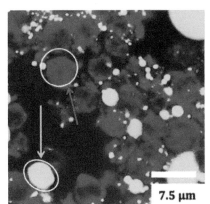
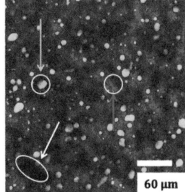

Figure 8–32a

Images of butter structure using confocal laser scanning microscopy. Water is shown in green and continuous phase purple or red. Fat crystals are dark and gray. Phospholipids surround milk fat globules as shown with red arrow (left). The red shows the liquid fat network shown with red arrow and white circle (right). (Reprinted from Rønholt, S., Mortensen, K. and Knudsen, J. C. (2013), The Effective Factors on the Structure of Butter and Other Milk Fat-Based Products. Comprehensive Reviews in Food Science and Food Safety, 12: 468–482. Copyright © Comprehensive Reviews in Food Science and Food Safety)

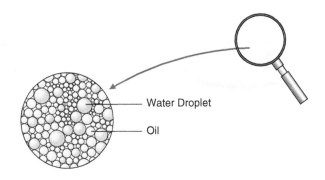

Figure 8–32b

Butter is a water-in-oil emulsion. See fat network surrounding water. (HL Studios. Pearson Education Ltd)

Salted or Unsalted. Some sweet-cream butter is marketed unsalted as sweet butter. Salted butter is preferred by most Americans; unsalted butter is used extensively in Europe and by European-trained chefs. Unsalted butter in cooking offers the advantage of allowing the cook to control more fully the seasoning of the dish. Unsalted butter may be especially desirable when baking [33].

Coloring. Butter produced when cows are on green feed is naturally more pigmented than butter produced when green feed is not consumed. Thus, the season of the year and consumer preferences for butter of different degrees of color determine the use of coloring so that a uniform color may be sold throughout the year. Carotene is the coloring agent commonly used.

Grade Standards. The USDA has set grade standards for butter [1]. Grades for butter include U.S. Grade AA and U.S. Grade A. U.S. Grade AA butter must have a smooth, creamy texture and delicate sweet flavor and be made from high-quality, fresh, sweet cream. U.S. Grade A butter rates close to the top grade but may not

be as smooth and spreadable as Grade AA. Butter must have at least 80 percent milk fat by federal law.

Flavor. Butter flavor is complex, resulting as it does from the combination of many flavor compounds. A substance called *diacetyl*, formed from bacterial action, is an important flavor component of butter. Butter is used in many recipes because of its flavor.

ICE CREAM

Ice cream is a complex mixture. It is a colloidal mix, frozen emulsion, and a milk fat foam. This frozen emulsion is composed of air bubbles, ice crystals, milk fat globules, milk proteins, and stabilizers such as gums in the continuous phase [72] (**Figure 8–33**). The fat globules can be coated with an emulsifying layer; egg yolk traditionally provided emulsifiers for ice cream mixtures [55]. The milk sugar lactose is in a supersaturated state or the undesirable crystallizing form that causes a sandy gritty mouthfeel (see Chapter 10 for more information). Unsaturated fats or liquid fats do not create fat crystalline structure needed for ice creams; the fat crystallization and liquid fat properties are key in determining quality of ice cream [75, 46].

During ice cream processing, the ice cream emulsion fat is composed of partially crystalline fat aggregates that form a large fat network throughout the aerated mixture. During mixing of the ice cream emulsion, air is introduced forming a foam. The ice cream mixture foam is due to partial coalescence of the fat wrapping around the air bubbles giving the foam microstructure in the oil-in-water emulsion. The fat partially coalesces around air cells initially stabilized by protein to form air cells that are interconnected by fat microbridges and supported by solid aggregated fat particles to form a *foam* [75]. The solid-to-liquid fat

---

MAKING BUTTER AT HOME

Butter may be made at home relatively easily with today's appliances. Here's how to do it:

Take 1 to 2 cups of chilled heavy, pasteurized cream (preferably without added stabilizers) and blend in a chilled food processor bowl using the plastic blade, whisk, or normal chopping blade. You will see (1) soft whipped cream, (2) firm whipped cream, (3) coarse whipped cream, (4) seizing of the cream followed by fine bits of butter in

buttermilk, and (5) yellowish butter separated from milky buttermilk. Drain the buttermilk, leaving the butter.

The butter produced at this stage may be eaten, or additional steps may be followed for better storage. To further process the butter, add one-half cup of ice-cold water and blend. Discard the wash water and repeat until the water is clear. Finally, knead the butter with a potato masher and pour out water as it separates. Enjoy!

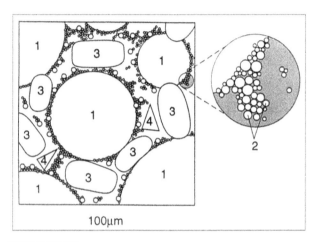

100μm

Figure 8–33

Ice cream internal structure—(1) air cells; (2) fat globules, some agglomerated and supporting the air cell structure; (3) ice crystals; and (4) lactose crystals. Colloidal casein protein and gums are suspended in the continuous phase. (Reprinted with permission Marshall, R. T. & Goff, D. (2003) Formulating and manufacturing ice cream and other frozen desserts. Food Technology. 57 (5), 32–45. © Institute of Food Technologists)

ratio is essential to producing ice cream since the crystalline fat is required for partial coalescence [75]. The solid fats are typically from the saturated milk fat fatty acids. Replacing the saturated solid fats in ice cream with emulsifiers or colloids decreases quality [75]. See Chapter 10 for more information on ice cream.

DETERIORATION OF FAT AND ITS CONTROL

Rancidity is the spoilage of fat. It may develop on storage, particularly if the fats are highly unsaturated and the environmental conditions are appropriate for initiating the reaction. Hydrolysis and oxidation cause rancidity in fats.

Hydrolytic Rancidity

Hydrolysis involves breaking chemical bonds and, in the process, adding the elements of water—hydrogen and oxygen. When triglycerides are hydrolyzed, they

yield free fatty acids and glycerol. Heat acts as a catalyst. When foods are fried, excess water in the fat can cause rancidity of the fat. The enzyme *lipase* also acts as a catalyst for fat hydrolysis. The release of free fatty acids does not produce undesirable odors and flavors in fats unless they are short-chain fatty acids, such as **butyric acid** and **caproic acid**. These fatty acids predominate in butter. They are volatile and largely responsible for the unpleasant odor and flavor in rancid butter. Butter is inedible even when these components are present in low concentrations. Long-chain free fatty acids do not usually produce a disagreeable flavor unless other changes, such as oxidation, also occur. Stearic, palmitic, and oleic acids are examples of long-chain fatty acids.

Oxidative Rancidity

The oxidative rancidity of fats causes a widely recognized but difficult-to-describe unpleasant odor. Oxidative rancidity requires oxygen but is more likely to occur when the fat also is exposed to heat, light, or metals, such as iron and copper. *Autoxidation* is the process of oxidation induced by air at room temperature [114]. Autoxidation is typically a slow process, but light can increase the rate. Factors that affect the rate of oxidation include: amount of oxygen, degree of unsaturation in a lipid, presence of antioxidants, presence of pro-oxidants such as copper, iron, heme containing molecules, and lipoxidases, light exposure, and storage temperature. Rancidity is noticeable by off-flavor and odors. Manufacturers protect fats and oils from oxidation to extend shelf life by blanketing oil and fats with nitrogen to protect against oxygen during processing, storage, and transportation. Chelating agents and antioxidants are also used to deter autoxidation.

Lipoxygenase is an iron-containing enzyme present in some plant and animal foods that may cause oxidative rancidity. Lipoxygenase activity can lead to off-flavors in underblanched vegetables and is found in soybeans. Unsaturated fatty acid molecules are subject to oxidation. The rancid odor of these rancid fats is due to decomposing volatiles from hydroperoxides. Rancidity most often results from a strictly chemical reaction that is self-perpetuating, called a *chain reaction* (**Table 8–10**).

TABLE 8–10
CHAIN REACTION OF OXIDATIVE RANCIDITY

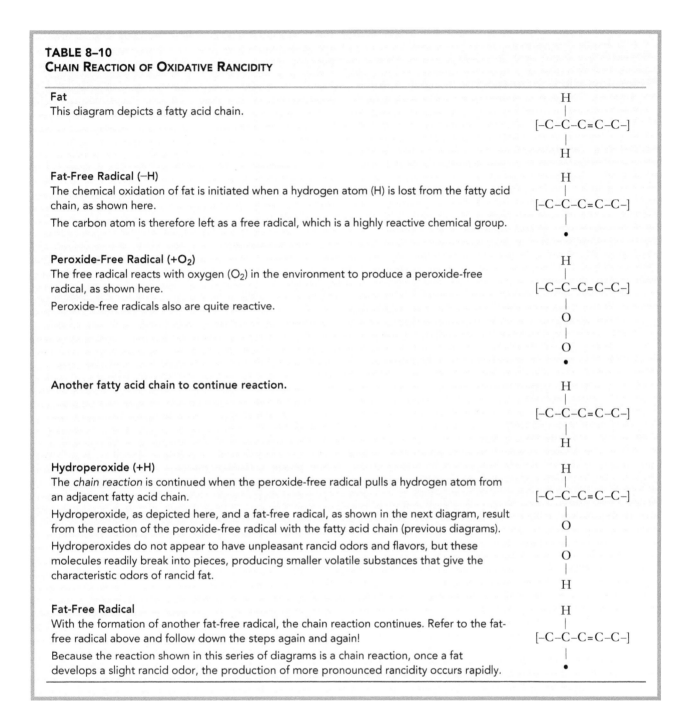

Fat
This diagram depicts a fatty acid chain.

$$\begin{matrix} & & \text{H} & & & & \\ & & | & & & & \\ [-\text{C}-&\text{C}-&\text{C}=&\text{C}-&\text{C}-] \\ & & | & & & & \\ & & \text{H} & & & & \end{matrix}$$

Fat-Free Radical (–H)
The chemical oxidation of fat is initiated when a hydrogen atom (H) is lost from the fatty acid chain, as shown here.

The carbon atom is therefore left as a free radical, which is a highly reactive chemical group.

$$\begin{matrix} & & \text{H} & & & & \\ & & | & & & & \\ [-\text{C}-&\text{C}-&\text{C}=&\text{C}-&\text{C}-] \\ & & | & & & & \\ & & \bullet & & & & \end{matrix}$$

Peroxide-Free Radical (+O₂)
The free radical reacts with oxygen (O_2) in the environment to produce a peroxide-free radical, as shown here.

Peroxide-free radicals also are quite reactive.

$$\begin{matrix} & & \text{H} & & & & \\ & & | & & & & \\ [-\text{C}-&\text{C}-&\text{C}=&\text{C}-&\text{C}-] \\ & & | & & & & \\ & & \text{O} & & & & \\ & & | & & & & \\ & & \text{O} & & & & \\ & & \bullet & & & & \end{matrix}$$

Another fatty acid chain to continue reaction.

$$\begin{matrix} & & \text{H} & & & & \\ & & | & & & & \\ [-\text{C}-&\text{C}-&\text{C}=&\text{C}-&\text{C}-] \\ & & | & & & & \\ & & \text{H} & & & & \end{matrix}$$

Hydroperoxide (+H)
The *chain reaction* is continued when the peroxide-free radical pulls a hydrogen atom from an adjacent fatty acid chain.

Hydroperoxide, as depicted here, and a fat-free radical, as shown in the next diagram, result from the reaction of the peroxide-free radical with the fatty acid chain (previous diagrams).

Hydroperoxides do not appear to have unpleasant rancid odors and flavors, but these molecules readily break into pieces, producing smaller volatile substances that give the characteristic odors of rancid fat.

$$\begin{matrix} & & \text{H} & & & & \\ & & | & & & & \\ [-\text{C}-&\text{C}-&\text{C}=&\text{C}-&\text{C}-] \\ & & | & & & & \\ & & \text{O} & & & & \\ & & | & & & & \\ & & \text{O} & & & & \\ & & | & & & & \\ & & \text{H} & & & & \end{matrix}$$

Fat-Free Radical
With the formation of another fat-free radical, the chain reaction continues. Refer to the fat-free radical above and follow down the steps again and again!

Because the reaction shown in this series of diagrams is a chain reaction, once a fat develops a slight rancid odor, the production of more pronounced rancidity occurs rapidly.

$$\begin{matrix} & & \text{H} & & & & \\ & & | & & & & \\ [-\text{C}-&\text{C}-&\text{C}=&\text{C}-&\text{C}-] \\ & & | & & & & \\ & & \bullet & & & & \end{matrix}$$

Triglyceride unsaturated fatty acid portions are most susceptible to oxidative changes. Therefore, more highly unsaturated fatty acids, such as linoleic acid, are most likely to develop oxidative rancidity. Highly hydrogenated fats and natural fats composed largely of saturated fatty acids are relatively resistant to this type of chemical change, but all natural fats contain some unsaturated fatty acids and therefore may become rancid.

Oxidative rancidity is responsible for most of the spoilage of fats and fatty foods. Lard is susceptible to oxidative rancidity when it is exposed to oxygen. It may also be a problem in dry foods containing only small quantities of fat, such as wheat germ, prepared cereals and whole grains. When rancidity develops in fatty foods, the fat-soluble vitamins A and E that are present also may be oxidized.

Higher temperatures greatly accelerate the oxidation rate at higher temperatures. The difference in fat and oil stability becomes more noticeable during frying and baking. The stability of fats or oils may be predicted by oxidative stability index (OSI). The more unsaturated the fat or oil, the greater the susceptibility to oxidative rancidity. Dimethyl silicone is usually added to frying fats and oils to reduce oxidation and foaming of fat for frying. Partially hydrogenated oils used to be used for frying because of their stability [114].

Flavor Reversion.   A special type of oxidative deterioration is called *flavor reversion*. It involves a change in edible fats, evident by an objectionable flavor prior to the onset of true rancidity. The kinds of off-flavors that develop during reversion vary with the particular fat and with the conditions that cause the change. No fat is entirely free from the tendency to develop flavor reversion, but some oils, such as corn and cottonseed oils, are quite resistant to this type of deterioration. Soybean oils that contain high levels of linoleic acid are highly susceptible to flavor reversion. Reverted soybean oil has been described as "painty," "beany," "haylike," "grassy," and, in the final stages, "fishy."

Reversion may develop during exposure of the fat to ultraviolet or visible light or heat. A small amount of oxygen seems to be necessary for the reaction, which is catalyzed by the presence of small amounts of metals, such as iron and copper. Soybean oil is known to contain traces of iron and copper, which may act as **pro-oxidants**. Thus, the flavor of soybean oil is stabilized by the use of metal inactivators or sequestrants that tie up the trace amounts of iron and copper that are present.

The chief precursors of the reversion flavor in oils are thought to be the triglycerides containing **linolenic acid**, although linoleic acid is probably also involved to some degree [111]. The fats that are most susceptible to reversion contain linolenic acid in larger amounts than the relatively stable fats. Flavor reversion may be prevented by the selective hydrogenation of soybean oil to decrease the amount of linolenic acid. Plant breeding and genetic engineering are developing oils resistant to flavor reversion and oxidation without hydrogenation. These oils are lower in linolenic acid content and higher in oleic acid [77].

Warmed-over flavor (WOF) is the term given to describe the flavor that develops in cooked meats after short-term refrigeration or freezing. The flavor is a result of lipid oxidation and is described as "rancid," "cardboard," or "painty" flavor. The warmed-over flavor is a problem in precooked frozen or refrigerated convenience meats such as turkey or chicken that is to be reheated. Volatiles from oxidized lipids are thought to be the source of warmed-over flavor.

Antioxidants and the Prevention of Rancidity

Natural antioxidants are present in most vegetable fats. The Native Americans used to protect animal fat with oak bark extracts to prevent spoilage. Fats can be protected to some degree against the rapid rancidity development by controlling the storage conditions. Rancidity can be prevented or delayed by storage at refrigerator temperature with the exclusion of light, moisture, and air. Because only certain rays of light catalyze the oxidation of fats, the use of colored glass containers that absorb the active rays protect fats against spoilage. Certain shades of green bottles and yellow transparent cellulose have been found to be effective in retarding rancidity in fats and foods, such as bacon. Vacuum packaging also helps to retard the development of rancidity by excluding oxygen.

Antioxidants have been used in the United States since 1947 to stabilize fats and control the development of rancidity [36]. Several compounds with antioxidant activity, including the nutrients vitamin C and beta-carotene, are naturally present in certain foods. Vitamin E (tocopherols), present in seeds and in the oil extracted from seeds, is an effective antioxidant that protects edible vegetable oils [94, 45]. Four synthetic antioxidants approved as food additives by the FDA are butylated hydroxyanisole (BHA), butylated hydroxytoluene (BHT), tertiary butyl hydroquinone (TBHQ), and propyl gallate. These four substances have found widespread use in food processing [32, 44].

Some substances, such as citric acid, may be used with antioxidants in foods as *synergists*. A synergist increases the effectiveness of an antioxidant. Metals such as iron and copper may be present in trace amounts in foods and will encourage the development of oxidative rancidity. Some synergists are effective because they bind or **chelate** metals and prevent the metals from catalyzing the oxidation process. Chelating agents are sometimes called *sequestering agents*.

Antioxidants generally act as oxygen interceptors in the oxidative process that produces rancidity, providing a hydrogen atom to satisfy the peroxide-free radical (Table 8–10). Thus, the chain reaction that perpetuates the process is broken or terminated, until another hydrogen atom is lost from a fatty acid chain, and the chain reaction begins again. Antioxidants, therefore, greatly increase the shelf life of fats, and foods containing fat, such as processed meats, whole-grain and dry-prepared cereal products, nuts, fat-rich biscuits and crackers, potato chips, and flour mixes.

FRYING

Fats and oils are used when cooking foods by frying. Frying is considered to be a dry-heat cooking method. Frying foods maybe used by home cooks, foodservice operations or large industrial food processors with continuous production of a thousand pounds per hour [21]. Two methods of frying are panfrying, in which a shallow layer of fat is used (**Figure 8–34**), and deep-fat frying, in which the food is submerged in heated fat (**Figure 8–35**). Sautéing uses a very small amount of fat. Liquid hot fat is a good conductor of heat. Food cooked in fat is cooked with surface browning due to caramelization of sugars and Maillard reaction. Frying

(a)   (b)

Figure 8–34

(a) Panfrying breaded veal cutlets produces a tender, juicy cutlet with a golden brown and crisp coating. (b) Stir-frying asparagus and mushrooms in a wok or sauté pan uses only a small amount of oil and results in a flavorful dish. (Richard Embery/Pearson Education)

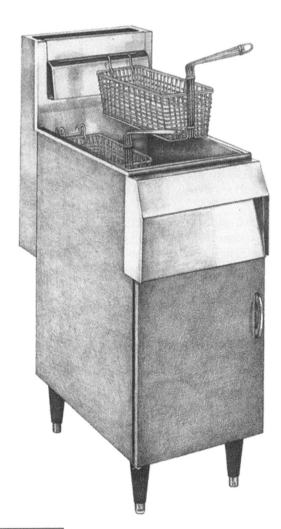

Figure 8–35

Deep-fat frying is common in many food-service establishments. Deep-fat fryers, such as this one, have the capacity to cook several pounds of food at one time.

fat should be odorless and colorless. Frying temperatures vary based on fat properties such as smoke point, flash point, and melting point.

Panfrying

Panfrying is used to cook such foods as meats, potatoes, vegetables such as eggplant, and eggs (Figure 8–34). When frying, the depth of the fat is usually less than ½ inch; therefore, measuring the fat temperature can be difficult. However, if the fat smokes, it is too hot, and decomposition is occurring. Moderate temperatures are generally used. Fry pans should be seasoned before the first use by pouring a small amount of oil into the warm fry pan and rubbing the pan surface with a cloth to produce a mirrorlike finish.

Panfrying is often done using a vegetable oil, shortening, or clarified butter. Both butter and margarine, as purchased, have a low smoke point and contain water, which can cause spattering. Butter and margarine are therefore generally not desirable for frying. As discussed earlier in the chapter, vegetable oils are a healthier fat choice.

Deep-Fat Frying

Deep-fat frying is commonly used to prepare french fries, onion rings, breaded chicken tenders and nuggets, doughnuts, and a variety of other foods (**Figure 8–36**). The food is completely surrounded by hot fat, so food cooks very rapidly. Many foods that are deep-fat fried are battered or breaded prior to frying. Battered foods typically sink to the bottom when placed in the fryer and then rise to the top when cooked. Most deep-fat fried foods should be lightly brown, crisp on the exterior, moist and tender inside, and without the sensation of excessive fat. In the home, foods may be deep-fat fried in a heavy pan with a deep-fat frying thermometer to monitor

Figure 8–36

(left) Basket method of deep-fat frying. (center) The double basket method. (right) The swimming method of deep-fat frying. (Richard Embery/Pearson Education)

temperatures or, more easily, by the use of a small electric deep-fat fryer. Deep-fat fryers come in a variety of sizes for food-service operations (Figure 8–35).

Methods for deep-fat frying are basket or swimming (Figure 8–36). Food can be placed in a frying basket and lowered into hot fat. Sometimes, a second basket is placed on top of food to prevent floating and promote even cooking. This is called a double basket method. Swimming method is used for batter foods that would stick to a basket. Food is carefully placed in deep-fat fryer with hot fat and then turned for even browning and removed using a frying spider or tongs. Doughnuts are fried using swimming method. Excessive fat is drained or absorbed with an absorbent paper. Fried food is best kept hot under a heat lamp or oven until ready to serve.

Frying Temperature. The temperature of the fat used when deep-fat frying will influence the food quality and the fat degradation. The oil or fat must be heated to the desired temperature before food is fried. Once food is submerged in hot fat there is a recovery time before fat returns to the desired cooking temperature. This recovery time can be slow with temperatures difficult to control impacting final outcome of fried product. Food fried at a temperature that is too high will become too dark on the exterior before being cooked fully in the interior. When foods are cooked at a temperature that is too low, excessive fat is absorbed. Smaller foods are generally cooked at higher temperatures, whereas larger foods, such as a breaded chicken breast, should be cooked at a lower temperature. Alternatively, these larger food items may be partially cooked in the fryer until the desired level of browning has been achieved and then immediately finished in the oven. Holding partially cooked foods before final cooking is not recommended for food safety reasons. **Table 8–11** provides a range of temperatures that can be used for deep-fat frying.

Many deep-fat fryers will control the temperature of the fat with a thermostat that will automatically control the heat based on the oil temperature. Some simple home deep-fat fryers have only one factory preset temperature, which is satisfactory for most foods. Food service and more sophisticated home fryers allow for a choice of temperature [13].

Frying Technology

Excess Oil Removal, a patented system, fries the food then spins away excess oil. The food is reported to retain less oil [21]. *Vacuum frying* can fry at a lower temperature and leave foods with a lower oil content. It lowers the frying temperature as the pressure is low. Conventional frying results in fried foods with an oil content of 30–40 percent, but vacuum frying reduces food oil content to 20–25 percent. Less acrylamide results in vacuum frying [56]. Reducing frying temperatures from 356°F to 325°F (180°C to 165°C) reduces potato chip acrylamide levels 63 percent with vacuum frying [56]. Compared to traditional frying, vacuum frying methods can reduce acrylamide formation by 94 percent [56]. Vacuum frying decreases frying fat oxidation, polymerization, and hydrolysis thus extending the use of frying fat. Polyunsaturated frying oils have

TABLE 8–11
TEMPERATURE RANGES FOR DEEP-FAT FRYING

Type of Product	Temperature of Fat
Doughnuts	350–375°F (175–190°C)
Fish	350–375°F (175–190°C)
Fritters	350–375°F (175–190°C)
Oysters, scallops, and soft-shelled crabs	375°F (190°C)
Croquettes	375°F (190°C)
Eggplant	375°F (190°C)
Onions	375°F (190°C)
Cauliflower	375°F (190°C)
French-fried potatoes	385–395°F (195–200°C)

Note: A thermometer- or thermostat-controlled fryer is the preferred method of controlling temperature.

HOT TOPIC
ACRYLAMIDES

The U.S. Environmental Protection Agency classifies acrylamide, a colorless, crystalline solid, as a medium hazard and probable human carcinogen [52]. Acrylamides are formed by a high-temperature reaction of reducing sugar such as glucose and fructose plus the amino acid asparagine. Five international groups have confirmed a major Maillard reaction pathway for acrylamide formation, but other acrylamide forming pathways are thought to exist [23]. Acrylamide is an industrial chemical used in water purification systems and grouts, and is found in cigarette smoke plus heated and fried foods cooked at high temperatures. Acrylamides form when frying or baking above 120°C (248°F) [129].

In 2002, scientists released data of extremely high levels of acrylamides in french fries and potato chips, around 30–2, 300 ppb [23]. French fries and potato chips have been found to have high levels of acrylamide partly because potatoes are high in the amino acid asparagine. Cold storage of potatoes increases reducing sugars and thus acrylamide formation during cooking. Never store potatoes in the refrigerator. Careful handling to avoid bruising of potatoes is important; avoid using sprouted potatoes [129]. Overcooked french fries have extremely high levels of acrylamides indicating that frying temperatures and frying times influence acrylamide formation. French fries deep-fat fried where silicone was used as a frying additive showed higher levels of acrylamide formation than those fried without silicone [48].

Acrylamides are also found in cereals, breads, coffee, and bakery products. Prune juice and canned ripe black olives also have high levels of acrylamide. Frying, baking, and roasting produces acrylamides but not microwaving, boiling, or steaming. Toasting bread to very brown color should be avoided because of the acrylamide levels. High asparagine levels in cereal grains can increase acrylamide during frying, baking, and processing of cereal-based products [129]. Replacing reducing sugars such as glucose and fructose with sucrose can also help lower acrylamide levels in processed grain-based products and baked goods.

Coffee has a significant amount of acrylamide with light roasts having more than dark roast, since acrylamides are formed early in the roasting and destroyed later in the roasting process [129]. Robusta coffee beans produce more acrylamide than Arabica beans. Frying should be done at lowest temperature possible and frying oil not over used [129].

California's Safe Drinking Water and Toxic Enforcement Act of 1986 (Proposition 65) requires cancer or reproductive toxicity warnings, if foods and drinks exceed 0.2 micrograms/day. In 2010, WHO/FAO Joint Expert Committee on Food Additives (JECFA) stated that acrylamides may be a "human health concern" [129]. The FDA issued nonbinding guidelines on acrylamides for industry in 2016; they continue to study the matter. In 2017, the European Union adopted regulation to reduce acrylamides in food.

---

less breakdown in vacuum frying [21]. *Pressure frying* has been used for many years. Pressure frying is batch processing frying method typically used for cooking meats such as fried chicken. Pressure frying is done in an enclosed vessel where steam releases pressure, raising the boiling point of water and the temperature at which food is cooked—347°F to 363°F (175°C to 184°C). Pressure frying results in shorter cooking time and greater moisture retention in foods. Oxidation is reduced since oxygen is expelled from the vessel during cooking [21]. Another frying technology is *air frying* where food is heated in hot air containing fine oil droplets. The process results in longer cooking time, lower fat absorption, less starch gelatinization, and sensory quality differences compared to traditional deep-fat frying.

Fat Absorption. A minimum level of fat absorption is desirable when frying foods. A reduction of fat in the diet is desirable from a nutritional perspective, and excessively greasy foods are of poor sensory quality. Fat absorption is influenced by (1) frying temperature, (2) length of cooking time, (3) food characteristics, and (4) condition of the frying fat.

Foods fried at low temperatures will absorb more fat because the food will be cooked for a longer period. As noted previously, it is necessary to fry larger foods at lower temperatures to allow complete cooking of the interior while avoiding a dark brown exterior. Some foods, however, are inadvertently cooked at a low temperature due to overloading the fryer. Overloading a fryer with an excessive amount of food will cause a significant temperature drop, and the food will be sitting in the fat but not frying. An overloaded fryer will require an extended period of time to recover to an appropriate frying temperature. While the fat temperature is too low, the food will absorb fat, and a greasy product will be the result.

The proportions and types of ingredients in doughnuts and various manipulative procedures affect fat absorption. Doughnuts or fritters will absorb more fat when the recipe or formula contains a higher level of lecithin (a phospholipid), eggs (which contain lecithin), or sugar and fat [73]. Doughnuts made from soft wheat flours and from soft doughs absorb more fat than doughnuts made from strong flours and from stiff doughs. The development of gluten by the extensive manipulation of the dough decreases fat absorption. Lastly, if the surface of the dough is uneven, surface area will increase, and therefore fat absorption will increase.

A pectin coating for french-fried potatoes and some breaded items such as fish and chicken reduces the amount of fat absorbed by these products. Barley flour that is beta-glucan rich used in batters also appears to reduce the amount of oil uptake [69]. A protein substance extracted from muscle tissue is another approach that has been found to reduce food moisture loss and the amount of oil absorbed during frying [97]. The total calorie content of the fried items is therefore reduced when less fat is absorbed.

The type of fat used for frying does not appear to affect significantly the amount of fat absorbed. Under identical conditions of time, temperature, and type of food being fried, various fats commonly used for frying appear to be absorbed in similar amounts.

Fat Selection. The food-service industry has five basic criteria for selecting frying fat. These criteria are (1) flavor, (2) texture, (3) mouthfeel, (4) stability (life of fat), and (5) cost and availability [100]. These factors may be considered in choosing a frying fat. Fats used for frying must produce foods with a desirable flavor and color. Frying fats must also be stable, resistant to foaming and gum formation. Frying fats must be able to tolerate high cooking temperatures and have a relatively high smoking point. Lastly, although consumers enjoy fried foods, the preference for the use of fats with a more favorable nutritional profile is desired. Many restaurants, in the past, used a mixture of animal **tallow** and vegetable fat for frying. While this blend of frying fat had many desirable characteristics, consumers who are vegetarians and those concerned about saturated fat and cholesterol prefer all-vegetable frying fats with no trans fatty acids. Polyunsaturated fats may be nutritionally healthier, but they are prone to oxidation that affects food flavor and quality. Partially hydrogenated oils with 16–26 percent saturated fat improved frying stability but are high in trans fat, so now they are no longer recommended or recognized as safe [100]. Palm oil and structured lipid-derivative palm olein are resistant to oxidation and thus an extended life frying medium [10].

Frying fats are processed to improve their functionality in frying applications. A certain amount of hydrogenation of the frying oil was historically used to provide stability and to increase frying life of the fat before too much degradation occurs. The trans fat (PHO) ban changed frying fat processing and use. Blends of corn oil and cottonseed oil have good stability, are naturally low in linolenic acid and no trans fats [100]. Corn and cottonseed oils can also be blended with canola or soybean oils for linolenic acid levels under 3 percent [100]. New soy-based, low-linolenic oils are being developed that are resistant to oxidation, exhibit strong flavor stability, do not require hydrogenation, and yet function well as frying oils [97, 122]. Antioxidants may also be used to increase shelf life of fried foods (e.g., potato chips) or to help prevent the breakdown of the fat during frying [122]. Peanut oil with a high smoke and 19 percent saturated fats and 33 percent linoleic acid is a top choice for a stable frying fat [100].

Care of Fat. To maintain high quality in fried foods, it is important to monitor the frying fat. A frying fat may be used for a considerable period if the turnover with fresh fat is fairly high and if the fat is cared for properly. Fat is damaged by salt, water, high temperatures, food particles, and oxygen contact. Thus, food should not be salted above the frying fat, and ice crystals on foods should be removed as much as possible before frying. Not only will water damage the oil, but water in hot oil will cause spattering and can result in burns to anyone nearby. Aeration of fat should be minimal to prevent oxidation [100]. A smoking oil is an indication that the temperature is too high, and if the temperature is not reduced, the oil could reach a *flash point* and ignite. Thermostats on fryers should be checked with a fryer thermometer to ensure proper functioning (**Figure 8–37**).

Frying fats need to be filtered regularly at the end of each day or if there is heavy use, more often. Various filtration systems are available for food service, including screens, cartridges, and paper filters with and without filter aids. Filtering machines specifically designed for this purpose are available. Some commercial fryers have built in filters. Fat can also be filtered through a paper filter. Filtering the fat removes charred batter, breading, and other materials that have accumulated in the frying fat. These crumbs, sometimes called *fines,* can ruin the appearance of the fried product, contribute bitter flavor, lower the smoke point, and darken the fat.

In the home, frying fat should be filtered after each use through cheesecloth, paper filter, or a fine metal mesh strainer and stored in a cool place out of contact with light and air.

Frying fats that have darkened considerably, show evidence of a lowered smoke point, have developed off-odors, or are foaming should be discarded.

Figure 8–37

Clean fat/oil should only be used for frying (left). Clear, free of food particles, off odors, and light in color. (right) Fat/oil that has darkened should be discarded. (Richard Embery/Pearson Education)

Foaming of frying fats is distinctive and can be distinguished from the normal bubbling that occurs when frying by the very small bubbles that are present and the tendency of these small bubbles to proliferate much like sudsy water. Foods prepared with degraded fats will be of poor quality and impart undesirable off-flavors in food.

Fat Turnover. *Turnover* indicates the amount of fat in the fryer that is replaced by fresh fat in a given period. Because fat is absorbed by the foods that are fried, the amount of fat continuously decreases, and fresh fat will need to be added to maintain the correct depth of the fat that is sometimes called "topping off." The rate of turnover varies depending on how much food is fried. When turnover is slow, it is necessary to discard periodically all of the fat in the deep-fat fryer and start again with fresh fat.

Changes to Fat Used for Deep-Fat Frying. Frying fats change when used for deep-fat frying. *Acrolein* and surfactants are chemicals that may be produced in frying fat. Food can interact with the fat and cause changes, including a lower smoke point and fat darkening. Smoke, flash, and fire points are lowered with each frying.

Polymerization. Polymerization is a reaction where fats high in polyunsaturated fatty acids form new, larger molecules or *polymers* when heated at a high temperature for a long period of time. Polymerization occurs in fats that are held at frying temperatures (374°F/190°C) for extended periods. These polymers contribute to increased viscosity and darkening of the fat. Polymerization is thought to be caused by carbon linkages.

Change in Smoke Point. A high smoke point is desirable in a fat used for deep-fat frying. The smoke point of a fat will lower over time when used. It is one of the reasons frying fats must be replaced. The smoke point of fats will lower as the result of the following:

- Free fatty acid formation resulting from high heat or the frying of high-moisture foods
- Suspended matter, such as flour or batter particles, in the fat
- Greater surface area of the fat exposed to air

Surfactants. Oxygen from the air may react with the fat in the fryer at the oil–air interface, thus creating many different chemical compounds in the frying fat in addition to the basic triglyceride molecules that originally made up the fat. Some of the chemicals produced are surfactants—molecules that interact at the air–oil or oil–food interfaces. These surfactants lower the surface or interfacial tension. A surfactant theory of frying suggests that the lowered **surface tension** allows oxygen to be drawn in, producing some oxidized compounds that aid in heat transfer. Also, the contact time between the hot oil and the aqueous food surfaces is increased, and more heat is transferred to cook the food. If surfactant levels become too high, however, degradation of the fat is enhanced, **polymers** are formed, increased viscosity results from the gum formation, and foaming is excessive [13].

Darkening of Fats. As frying fat is used, darkening occurs (Figure 8–37). As the fat darkens, the foods fried in it darken more rapidly and may be uneven in color. Color is one of the indicators used commercially to determine when the oil should be replaced. The ingredients in the product being fried influence the color changes of the frying fat. Potatoes form little color in the frying fat, whereas chicken causes considerably more darkening. The composition of the breading mixture also affects darkening. The presence of egg yolk in a batter or dough causes greatly increased darkening of the fat with continued use.

Changes to Food during Frying. In deep-fat frying, there is a direct transfer of heat from the hot fat to the cold food. Water present in the food to be fried plays some important roles in heat transfer and the frying process. Water is lost from the exterior surfaces of the food as it is converted to steam. The steam carries off energy from the surface of the food and prevents charring or burning. While water is being evaporated, the temperature of the food is only about 212°F (100°C). Water then migrates from the central portion of the food outward to the edges to replace that lost by evaporation. Finally, the interior of the food is cooked. Sufficient heat must be transferred to gelatinize starch and coagulate proteins that may be present in the food.

FOCUS ON SCIENCE
WHY DOES MY DEEP-FAT FRYER BASKET DEVELOP A STICKY BUILDUP?

The hydrolysis of triglycerides occurs during frying because of the heat and moisture from the food. As a result of triglyceride hydrolysis, free fatty acids are formed in the frying fat. These free fatty acids join together (polymerize) and form long chains. These long compounds cause an increase in viscosity of the frying fat. This thickening is the reason the side walls of a fryer and the fryer basket will develop a sticky buildup.

BUYING FATS

It is important when purchasing fats to consider their specific uses in food preparation and to select fats in accordance with needs, budget, and health. Fats and oils are often tailored for specific uses in food-service operations, such as deep-fat frying, panfrying or griddling, cake making, or salad dressings.

Most consumers probably do not need to keep more than three or four different household fats on hand. Mono- and polyunsaturated oils are desirable for many cooking applications and are healthier than solid fats and tropical fats, which contain a high proportion of saturated fats. Butter, because of its flavor, is sometimes preferred for table use as well as for use in some baked products and for seasoning certain foods. Margarine serves a similar purpose, usually at a somewhat lower cost. Margarines, when high in polyunsaturated fatty acids, may be chosen over butter for health reasons. Olive oils are considered healthy, and also offer a desirable flavor.

Most households will need shortening for selected baked goods and pastries. In food service, several different shortenings may be purchased that have been formulated for specific purposes. Lard is preferred by some for use in pastry, biscuits, refried beans, or tortillas.

FAT REPLACERS

Food processors can use a wide variety of ingredients to replace or partially replace fat in food products. Fat plays many different roles in food products. It is very difficult, if not impossible, to find a fat substitute that will perform well in all food products [117]. Several different fat replacers are used separately or in combination. Generally, fat replacers can be classified into two groups: (1) fat substitutes and (2) fat imitators. Fat substitutes can replace fats in foods. They are macromolecules that chemically and physically resemble triglycerides and are often referred to as *fat-based fat replacers*. Fat substitutes are usually stable at cooking and frying temperatures [2].

Fat imitators are substances that imitate sensory properties of triglycerides but cannot replace fat on a weight-to-weight basis. Many are modified common ingredients, such as starch and cellulose, and act to bind a substantial amount of water [2]. No one fat replacer mimics all the roles of fat in ice cream [72].

Fat replacements may be carbohydrate, fat, or protein based. Starches, gums, proteins, fiber-based ingredients, emulsifiers, and other fat derivatives have traditionally been used to reduce fat levels [97]. Structured lipids, esters, and microcrystallized fat derivatives are also used to mimic fat properties in foods for low or reduced fat alternatives. Microparticulated-protein fat replacer can be produced by reshaping proteins from milk and egg into tiny round particles. These particles are so small that they are perceived as fluid. Microparticulated protein has a caloric value of 4 kilocalories per gram on a dry basis compared with 9 kilocalories per gram for the fat it replaces.

Emulsifier systems can be designed to function well in many low-fat products, but other ingredients must also be used in conjunction with the emulsifier system to help replace the fat that is lost. Included in the emulsifier group are fatty acid esters of sucrose. Also used are carbohydrate derivatives of cellulose, inulins, maltodextrins, gums, modified starches, pectin, and polydextrose. Several fat replacers come from protein sources, including egg, milk, whey, soy, gelatin, and wheat gluten. Some are microparticulated to form microscopic, coagulated, round, deformable particles that give a mouthfeel and texture similar to fat. Others are treated in ways to modify their functional properties, such as water-holding capacity and emulsifying characteristics. These substances are generally not heat stable but are used in dairy products, salad dressings, frozen desserts, and margarines [2].

As fat replacement technology has changed over the years, fat replacers increasingly are being used in customized applications [97]. Any fat replacer must be approved by the FDA as a food additive unless the fat replacer is GRAS. Wellness trends and replacing trans fats in foods have been the focus of food manufacturers [97].

EMULSIONS

The term *emulsion* is applied to a system consisting of one liquid dispersed in another liquid with which it is **immiscible**. The two general types of emulsions are an *oil-in-water* emulsion and a *water-in-oil* emulsion. Oil-in-water emulsions are most common in foods. Butter and margarine, however, are examples of water-in-oil emulsions. The type of emulsion formed depends to a considerable extent on the nature of the emulsifier. An emulsifying agent or emulsifier is necessary to stabilize the system and keep one liquid dispersed in the other on a permanent basis (**Figures 8–38a** and **8–39**). Emulsifiers play a key role in commercially formulating food products [99].

Emulsions in Foods

Emulsions are found naturally in many foods, such as milk, cream, and egg yolk. In all such foods, the fat is divided into small particles or globules and dispersed throughout the watery portion of the food. Many food products are emulsions that have been formed during processing or preparation. See **Figure 8–38b** for common food emulsions. Work is necessary to divide the fat into tiny globules or droplets. These newly formed

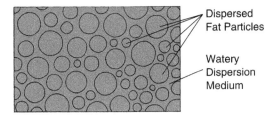

Figure 8–38a

An emulsion consists of one substance dispersed in another substance with which it is immiscible. An emulsifying agent surrounds each dispersed particle. This diagram represents an oil-in-water emulsion; the oil droplets, surrounded by an emulsifying agent, are dispersed in water.

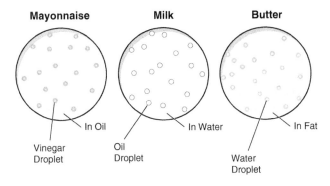

Figure 8–38b

Variety of emulsions—vinegar and oil, mayonnaise and butter. (Oxford Designers & Illustrators Ltd. Pearson Education Ltd)

globules must be rapidly protected against coalescence by the **adsorption** of an emulsifier at their surface. Shaking, beating, stirring, whipping, and high-pressure homogenization are some methods used to form an emulsion of one immiscible liquid dispersed in another. Homogenized milk is a processed emulsion.

From food preparation, examples of emulsions are mayonnaise and other salad dressings, sauces, gravies, puddings, cream soups, shortened cake batters, and other flour mixtures in which the fat is dispersed. Other emulsions are produced in the commercial processing of foods such as butter, peanut butter, and margarine. The *dispersing medium (continuous phase)* may be water, milk, dilute vinegar, lemon or other fruit juice, or some similar liquid. The *dispersed substance* may be any of the commonly used food fats and oils. Water-in-oil emulsions, such as butter or margarine, have fat as the dispersing medium and water as the dispersed substance. A food system is still called an emulsion even when the fat is not liquid at usual storage temperatures.

Temporary and Permanent Emulsions

Temporary Emulsions. If oil and water alone are shaken together, an emulsion is formed, but on standing, the oil particles reunite and separate from the water. Emulsions of this kind are called *temporary emulsions*. They must be used immediately, or if made in quantity and stored, they must be re-shaken or beaten before each use. Simple French and Italian dressings are examples of this type of emulsion.

Permanent Emulsions. Permanent emulsions, which can be held or stored without separation of the two immiscible liquids, require an emulsifying agent or emulsifier to form a protecting or stabilizing film around the dispersed droplets and prevent them from reuniting. The term *stabilizer* is also used to describe the emulsifier or the substance that assists the emulsifier in some food products. An example of a permanent emulsion is mayonnaise. Actually, any food containing fat that is distributed throughout and does not appear on the surface as a separate layer is a permanent emulsion.

Emulsifiers

How does an emulsifier act to form an emulsion? Emulsifiers have a special type of chemical nature: They are **amphiphilic** molecules. Part of the emulsifier molecule is attracted to or soluble in water is ionic and described as hydrophilic. The other part of the same molecule is soluble in fat described as lipophilic and typically has a long-chain carbon region such as a fatty acid. Thus, the emulsifier molecule may be oriented at the interface of the two immiscible liquids with its hydrophilic group in the watery phase and its lipophilic group in the fat or oil phase. One of these amphiphilic groups is a little stronger than the other and causes one phase to form droplets that are dispersed in the other continuous phase, with the emulsifier between them as it surrounds droplets of the dispersed phase. **Figure 8–39** suggests how an emulsifier might orient itself at an oil–water interface to form an emulsion.

If the emulsifier is more attracted to the water, or more water soluble, it promotes the dispersion of oil in water. If the emulsifier is more attracted to the oil, or more oil soluble, it tends to produce a water-in-oil emulsion. Emulsifiers are characterized by their hydrophilic lipophilic balance (HLB), which is represented on a 1–20 scale where HLB values less than 6 favor water-in-oil emulsions and 8 or great values favor oil-in-water emulsions [20]. Breaking of emulsions or separation of the two phases may occur under certain conditions. In some cases, the emulsion can re-form.

There are both natural and synthetic emulsifiers. Lecithin is a natural emulsifier found in egg yolk. Egg yolk is the emulsifier used in mayonnaise, which is discussed below. A variety of substances act as emulsifying agents in manufactured food systems, including esters of fatty acids, mono- and diglycerides, poly hydroxyl substrates such as lactic acid, sucrose, and polysorbates. Sugar beet pectin and soap bark tree *Quillaja saponaria* are used in novel emulsifier systems

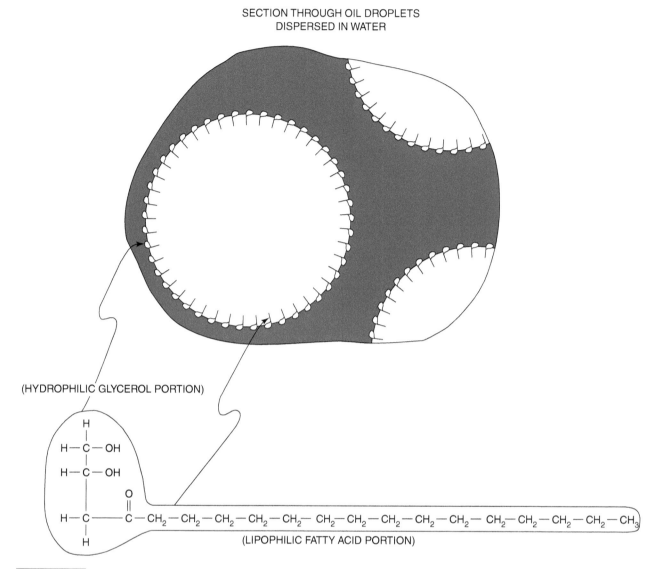

SECTION THROUGH OIL DROPLETS
DISPERSED IN WATER

(HYDROPHILIC GLYCEROL PORTION)

(LIPOPHILIC FATTY ACID PORTION)

Figure 8–39

An emulsifier stabilizes an emulsion by virtue of its chemical structure. In a simplified presentation, this structure includes one part that is attracted to water and another part that is attracted to fat. The attraction of one of the groups is somewhat stronger than the other. For example, a monoglyceride molecule is shown with the fatty acid portion being attracted to the oil and the glycerol portion attracted to the water, forming a filmlike layer around the oil droplets and keeping them dispersed in the continuous watery phase.

[71, 99]. Novel nanoscale emulsifiers show potential in many food systems [29]. Stabilizers can be used to stabilize emulsions by increasing stability of continuous phase by increasing viscosity (thicker is better); affecting droplet size (smaller is better); or lessening the difference in two immiscible liquid phases [20]. Emulsifiers may be used to distribute color in food [99]. Emulsions may be used to offer stability.

Some stabilizers are from the isolated milk protein casein, whey proteins and concentrated whey products, isolated soy proteins, oilseed protein concentrates, gelatin, lecithin, cellulose derivatives, fine dry powders such as ground spices, various vegetable gums, and starch pastes. Several emulsifiers

are present in some batters. For example, shortened cake batter may contain egg lipoproteins and mono- and diglycerides that have been added to the shortening.

Making an emulsion involves making small droplets to increase droplet surface area. This can be done by vigorous beating, shaking as in a bottle of salad dressing, or by whisking by hand or mixer. Food manufacturers may do this in a batch or continuous process using special equipment. The addition of ingredients used in the emulsion is critical. The emulsifier is added to the continuous phase and then the dispersed phase is slowly added with vigorous agitation. The process of mayonnaise discussed below is a good example. Temperature can destabilize emulsions. Emulsions are not typically frozen [20]. Low temperatures can cause fat to harden and high temperature can cause coalescence. Commercial food processors use specialized equipment to process food emulsions. Homogenizers, colloid mills, and immersion mixers are examples of emulsion equipment.

SALAD DRESSINGS

Classification

Definitions and standards of identity for mayonnaise, salad dressing, and French dressing have been published by the FDA. If products are labeled and sold under these names, they must meet the standards of identity as defined in the code of federal regulations. If the product is labeled with a nutrient claim, such as "reduced fat," these modified products must not be nutritionally inferior and must function like the standard product. A summary of

the standard of identities for mayonnaise, French dressing, and salad dressing are provided in **Table 8–12**. Because mayonnaise and salad dressing contain different ingredients and flavors, the names *mayonnaise* and *salad dressing* should not be used interchangeably.

All three dressings contain an acidifying ingredient. Many variations of these three basic dressings are created by using different, optional ingredients. Thus, a wide variety of dressings are available commercially, such as Thousand Island, blue cheese, bacon and tomato, creamy cucumber, Italian, ranch, and taco dressings. Citrus flavors in dressings have gained popularity in recent years [95]. Exciting new flavors in salad dressings may encourage healthful eating, bringing into the daily diet more vegetables, salads, and nutritious sandwich fillings (**Figure 8–40**).

Dressings for salads made in home kitchens are not, of course, governed by standards of identity. Many of these dressings are simple combinations

TABLE 8–12
MAYONNAISE, SALAD DRESSING, AND FRENCH DRESSING STANDARDS OF IDENTITY

Type	Description
Mayonnaise	An emulsified semisolid food prepared from edible vegetable oil, vinegar, and/or lemon juice or citric acid, egg yolk, or whole egg (*Federal Register* 21 CFR 169.140). If there is no FDA-qualified health claim, the edible oil content of mayonnaise must be not less than 65 percent by weight. The oil is dispersed in vinegar or lemon juice. Optional ingredients may include spice (except saffron or turmeric), a nutritive sweetener, monosodium glutamate, sequestrates, or crystallization inhibitors. Lecithin, found in the egg yolk, acts as the emulsifying agent, producing a permanent emulsion.
Salad dressing *Commonly known by the brand name Kraft Miracle Whip*	An emulsified semisolid food prepared from edible vegetable oil, an acidifying ingredient, egg yolk or whole egg, and a cooked or partly cooked starchy paste prepared with a food starch or flour. Water may be added in the preparation of the starchy paste. Must contain not less than 30 percent by weight of edible vegetable oil and not less than 4 percent by weight of liquid egg yolks (*Federal Register* 21 CFR 169.150) or their equivalent unless a legally defined nutrient claim has been made. Optional seasonings and emulsifying agents may also be used.
French dressing *Legal name for a wide variety of dressing types with the specified ingredients*	A separable liquid food or the emulsified viscous fluid food prepared from edible vegetable oil (oil content not less than 35 percent by weight), specified acidifying agents (vinegar, lime, or lemon juice), and optional seasonings (*Federal Register* 21 CFR 169.115). Reduced-fat or reduced-calorie dressings may be called French dressing with an approved FDA nutrient claim. Optional ingredients may include spices, salt, nutritive sweeteners, tomato paste, puree, catsup, sherry wine, eggs, coloring, stabilizers, citric or malic acid, sequestrants, and crystallization inhibitors. Functionally, paprika and other powdered seasonings help to keep the oil and acid emulsified on a temporary basis when shaken or beaten. French dressings may be prepared in the home by using $3/4$ cup salad oil for each $1/3$ cup vinegar or lemon juice and various seasonings, as desired.

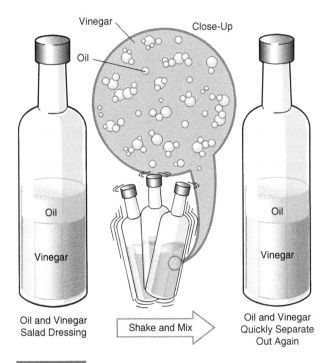

Figure 8–40

A basic vinaigrette dressing made from vinegar and oil that when shaken forms a temporary emulsion. Upon standing the oil particles reunite and separate from the vinegar.

of ingredients and are difficult to classify. In fruit dressings, fruit juices replace vinegar and other liquids. Sour cream, sometimes with added ingredients, such as crumbled cheese, can be added to vegetable or fruit salads. Mixtures of vinegar or lemon juice and seasonings, with or without small amounts of fat-containing ingredients, are sometimes used as low- or reduced-calorie dressings.

Dry salad seasoning mixes can also be purchased or prepared. A mixture of seasonings and emulsifiers or stabilizers are included in dry salad dressing mixes. These mixes are usually added to sour cream or to milk and mayonnaise to make a creamy dressing or to vinegar and oil to make a French-type dressing.

Reduced-Fat Dressings

Reduced-fat salad dressings, French dressings, mayonnaise, and dressing mixes are sold on the retail market and are prominently labeled as such. The caloric content of reduced-calorie dressings depends on how much oil is used.

A mixture of emulsifying agents and stabilizers, including xanthan gum, alginate, cellulose gum, locust bean gum, and modified starch, is used to produce an emulsion and to substitute for the fat that is being eliminated. These stabilizers are hydrophilic and hold relatively large amounts of water, giving body or thickness to the product.

Mayonnaise Preparation

Mayonnaise can be made in the home kitchen (**Figure 8–41**). The factors that affect the formation of mayonnaise, its stability, and the ease of preparation are similar wherever the product is made. However, recipes with raw egg yolks should be modified through the use of a pasteurized egg yolk to reduce the use of foodborne illness. For food-safety reasons, in addition to the time involved in the preparation of mayonnaise, few make this product from scratch.

Factors Affecting Mayonnaise Preparation. Cold oil is more difficult to break up into small globules than warm, less viscous oil. Thus, the start of emulsification is delayed by chilling, but after the emulsion is formed, chilling thickens and stabilizes the product.

Egg yolk is the chief emulsifying ingredient in mayonnaise. Salt, mustard, paprika, and pepper are used mainly for flavor, but both the salt and the powdery seasoning ingredients help to stabilize the emulsion as well. Mayonnaise usually contains about ¾ to 1 cup of oil per egg yolk and 2 tablespoons of acid ingredient (usually vinegar).

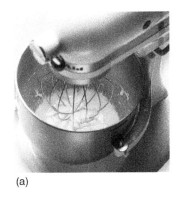
(a)

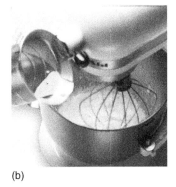
(b)

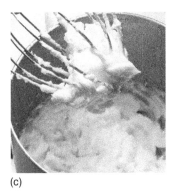
(c)

Figure 8–41

Mayonnaise may be made in the home. The use of pasteurized eggs is recommended. (a) Whip egg yolks until frothy. (b) Drizzle the oil slowly into the yolks while mixing to allow the emulsion to form. (c) The finished mayonnaise. (Richard Embery/Pearson Education)

Stable mayonnaise can be mixed by various methods. The acid may be added (1) to the yolk with the seasonings before any additions of oil, (2) at various intervals during the mixing, (3) alternately with the oil, or (4) after a large percentage of the oil is added to the egg yolk. The first additions of oil must be small to allow a stable emulsion to form. After the first two or three additions of oil, the volume that is added at one time may be increased to a variable extent, depending on the temperature of the ingredients, the rate of beating, and other factors, but in any case it should be less than the volume of emulsion that is already formed.

Breaking and Re-Forming an Emulsion. If oil particles coalesce, the emulsion breaks, and the oil separates from the watery portion of the dressing. When this occurs while the emulsion is forming, the cause is incomplete preliminary emulsification, too rapid an addition of oil, too high a ratio of oil to emulsifier (or another wrong proportion), or an inefficient method of agitation.

Prepared emulsified mayonnaise may separate during storage. Freezing may damage or rupture the film of emulsifying agents and allow the dispersed oil to coalesce, resulting in a broken emulsion. Mayonnaise stored at too high a temperature may separate because of differences in the rate of expansion of warm water and oil. Mayonnaise stored in an open container may lose sufficient moisture from the surface by evaporation to damage the emulsion. Excessive jarring or agitation, particularly during shipping and handling, can cause separation, but this occurrence is uncommon.

A broken mayonnaise emulsion may be re-formed by starting with a new egg yolk or with a tablespoon of water or vinegar and adding the separated mayonnaise to it gradually. Thorough beating after each addition of separated mayonnaise is important. If separation occurs in the preparation of mayonnaise before all the oil is added, the remainder of the original oil may be added only after re-emulsification has been achieved as described.

Variations. Additions can be made to mayonnaise to vary the flavor and consistency. Chopped foods, such as vegetables, olives, pickles, hard-cooked eggs, and nuts, may be added with discretion. Chili sauce, sour cream, and whipped cream can also enhance flavor and consistency for certain uses.

STUDY QUESTIONS

Fat Consumption Trends and Nutritive Values

1. Discuss the role of fat in the diet. How can fats be used to meet dietary guidelines?

2. What are essential fatty acids? Name the essential fatty acids.

3. Discuss removing partially hydrogenated oils from the GRAS (generally recognized as safe). What impacts did this have to food processing and fat supplies?

Fat in Food Composition

4. Compare and contrast visible versus invisible fats. Give examples of each.

5. Discuss triglycerides role in food.

6. Discuss the difference between lipids and triglycerides.

Properties of Fat

7. Discuss the role of fat in food systems.

8. Identify fats classified as solid fats. Explain why limiting the consumption of solid fats is recommended.

9. Explain how saturated, monounsaturated, and polyunsaturated fats are chemically structured. Identify which of these types of fats are considered more healthy.

10. For what general purposes are fats used in food preparation? Name at least four uses.

11. Discuss why understanding of fat crystallization is important. What role does fat crystallization play in food?

12. Explain two chemical reasons why fats vary in their melting points so that some are liquid at room temperature while others are solid.

13. Describe the chemical structure of cis versus trans fatty acids. Explain the significance of cis versus trans from (a) a health perspective and (b) a food preparation perspective.

14. Define and discuss smoke point, fire point, and flash point. Why are these principles important in food preparation and processing?

15. What is a plastic fat? Give examples.

16. Discuss how fat impacts flavor.

17. What makes cocoa butter a unique fat?

18. What is fat bloom?

Fat and Oil Processing

19. Most fats used in food preparation are separated from other tissues and refined or processed. Briefly describe how each of the following fats is produced. Also indicate for which of the general uses listed in question 4 each fat may be appropriate.

(a) Butter

(b) Margarine

(c) Lard

(d) Hydrogenated shortening

(e) Oil

(f) High-oleic, low linolenic–acid oil

(g) Marine oils

20. (a) Explain what happens when oils are hydrogenated? Winterized?

21. What is the purpose of interesterification? How does this process serve in the production of food fats?

22. Discuss the general process of producing vegetable oils.

Shortenings and Margarine

23. Compare and contrast shortenings and margarines.

Milk fats

24. Discuss the qualities of milk fat.

25. Describe a milk fat foam and some examples in food systems.

26. Describe butter from a food science perspective.

27. How is butter processed?

28. Discuss the qualities of butter and impact on food systems.

Deterioration of Fats

29. (a) What is rancidity? How is it controlled?

(b) Distinguish between hydrolytic rancidity and oxidative rancidity.

(c) Explain what probably happens when a fat is oxidized and becomes rancid.

(d) List several factors that may contribute to the development of rancidity. How can these be controlled?

(e) How does an antioxidant retard the development of rancidity?

(f) Name several antioxidants that may be added to or that are present in fatty foods.

Frying

30. Compare and contrast panfrying and deep-fat frying.

(a) What is *panfrying*? What is *deep-fat frying*?

(b) Explain the importance of using a proper temperature in frying foods. What do smoke point and acrolein have to do with the proper temperature for frying?

(c) Discuss factors to consider when choosing a frying fat.

(d) Give suggestions for the appropriate care of used frying fat.

(e) What is meant by fat *turnover*? Why is it important in frying?

(f) Discuss several factors that may influence the amount of fat absorbed during frying.

31. Discuss why fat temperature is important in foods.

32. Discuss several factors to consider in deciding which fats to purchase.

33. What are acrylamides? Where are they found? How can intake be reduced?

Emulsions

34. (a) What is an *emulsion*? What is necessary to produce a permanent emulsion?

(b) Give several examples of emulsions in natural foods and of emulsions in prepared or processed foods.

(c) Describe the difference between an oil-in-water emulsion and a water-in-oil emulsion.

(d) How does an emulsifier act to stabilize an emulsion?

35. (a) Standards of identity have been published for which three types of dressings for salads?

(b) What percentage of oil is specified for each type?

(c) Which governmental agency is responsible for these standards?

36. (a) Describe mayonnaise and list its major ingredients.

(b) Discuss several factors that may affect the formation of a stable emulsion in the making of mayonnaise.

(c) Describe what happens when an emulsion breaks. How can a broken mayonnaise emulsion be re-formed?

(d) Why can no egg mayonnaise be called mayonnaise?

37. Describe French dressing and list its major ingredients.

38. Explain how salad dressing generally differs from mayonnaise.

9
Sweeteners and Sugar Cookery

Sweeteners have been used for food since prehistoric times, probably beginning with the discovery of honey. From drawings in Egyptian tombs we learn that, as early as 2600 B.C., beekeeping was practiced for honey production. It is doubtful, however, that the honey was available to anyone but the rich and powerful. Today, some type of sweetener is found in most people's diets.

Commonly used sweeteners are generally extracted from plant sources and refined. The term *sugar* usually refers to crystallized sucrose (table sugar). In addition, sweeteners include other concentrated sources of sugar such as corn syrups, maple syrup, molasses, and honey. Artificial or alternate sweeteners produce sweetness, but are usually noncaloric substances.

In this chapter, the following topics will be discussed:

• Sweetener consumption and nutritive value
• Sugar properties
• Sugar types including crystalline sugars and syrups
• Alternative sweeteners
• Sugar cookery
• Candy

CONSUMPTION TRENDS AND NUTRITION

Consumption Trends

The United States is the world's largest consumer of sweeteners including high-fructose corn syrup. As a global leader in sugar production, the United States is one of the few countries that is a significant producer of both sugar beet and sugarcane. Sugar is over a $3 billion industry in the United States. Sugar-cane accounts for 45 percent and sugar beets 55 percent of total sugar production. U.S. sugar production is around 7.9 million tons and imports between 3 and 4 million tons. U.S. sugar production has increased since the 1980s due to improved processing equipment, better crop varieties, new technology, and increased production acreage expansion. Global markets of sugar production have been increasing with 2017/2018 hitting over 180 million tons of raw value sugar, but consumption trends remain flat at 172 million tons. In recent years, sugar production in Brazil, China, the European Union, India, and Thailand has increased. Mexico is a major producer and

competitor in sugar trade. Consumption trends remain flat and many factors increase pricing of sugar including trade agreements, quotas, tariffs, and commodity factors.

The United States is also a major importer of sugar. Sugar has been an important economic issue since colonial times where sugar quotas were part of colonial trade. Today, the sugar is an important part of U.S. trade agreements. The U.S. sugar program is built on price supports, domestic marketing allotments, and tariff-rate quotas to influence U.S. sugar markets.

From food availability data published by the U.S. Department of Agriculture (USDA), it is apparent that the consumption of sugar and sweeteners in the United States has increased since 1909 (**Figure 9–1**). According to the USDA, the 2014 U.S. per capita annual availability of cane and beet sugar, edible syrups, honey, high-fructose corn syrup, glucose, and dextrose was 131 pounds compared to 119 pounds in 1970. Cane and beet sugar use has declined since 1970, whereas the use of high-fructose corn syrup has increased considerably (0.55 pound per capita in 1970

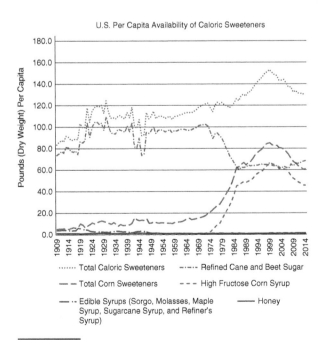

Figure 9–1

The amount of added sugars has increased over the years. (Data USDA/ERS Graph © Sam Frye/Amanda Frye)

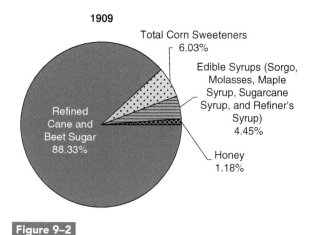

Figure 9–2

1909 Per capita sweeteners percentage. (Data USDA/ERS Graph © Sam Frye/Amanda Frye)

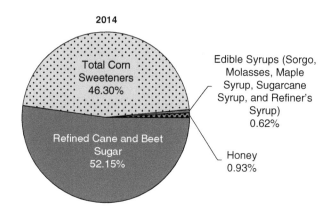

Figure 9–3

2014 Per capita sweetener percentages. (Data USDA/ERS Graph © Sam Frye/Amanda Frye)

to 45 pounds in 2014). Charts compare usage between 1909 and 2014 (**Figure 9–2**). High-fructose corn syrup use has increased in large part to beverage producers shifting from sugar to high-fructose corn syrup in many soft drinks (**Figure 9–3**). Food availability data may overestimate consumption. See Chapter 1 for a discussion about food availability data and consumption surveys as measures of food consumption.

Maple syrup production depends on sap flow, length of season and number of trees tapped. (**Figure 9–4** and **Figure 9–5**). In 2018, over 13.6 million trees were tapped for maple syrup production

with the largest number of taps in Vermont. According to the USDA, Vermont, New York, and Maine produce 75 percent of the U.S. maple syrup (Figure 9–4). Price per gallon has also been on the rise over the past two decades. According to the USDA, total production of U.S. maple syrup in 2016 was 4.2 million gallons, significantly up over 28 percent from past years with further increases in 2017 followed by a decline in 2018 (Figure 9–5).

Sweet sorghum syrup or sorgo production was over 2 million gallons in the 1960s, but has been declining for decades. The exact production numbers

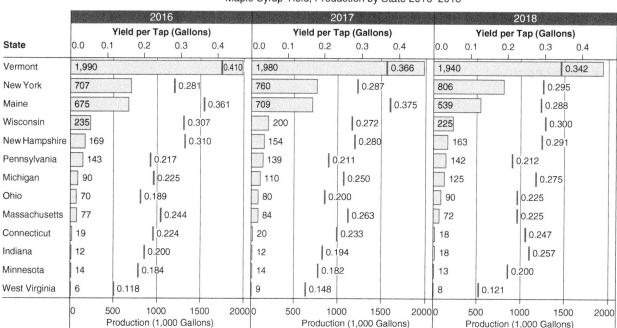

Figure 9–4

Vermont, New York and Maine are the largest of the 13 U.S. maple syrup producing states. (© Sam Frye/Amanda Frye Data: USDA/ARS)

United States Maple Syrup Production, Length of Season 2016–2018

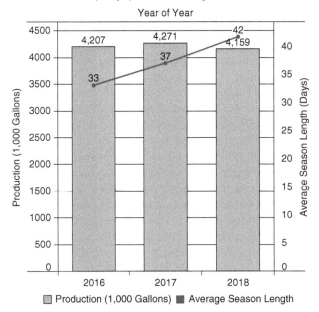

U.S. maple syrup production and price have trended upward since 2000 with further increases in 2017 and slight decline in 2018. The season or period of sap flow for collecting sap increased between 2016 and 2017. (Data USDA/ARS Chart © Sam Frye/Amanda Frye)

are not available, but estimated to be less than 2 million gallons annually. Sweet sorghum is also used for some whiskey and rum production as well as biofuel.

The USDA is conducting a great deal of research on honey bees and the die-off phenomenon that has been occurring at epidemic proportions over the last decade. However, honey production has increased in recent years. Honey production increased in 2016 with over 162 million pounds of honey produced. Small producers (under 5 colonies) had the biggest increase. Large colony producers had yields of 58.3 pounds honey per colony versus small producers' yields of 31.9 pounds per colony. Per capita consumption of honey in the United States has been around 1 pound over the last four decades, with consumption between 0.9 and 1.2 pounds.

Nutritive Value

Sugar provides essentially energy (calories) for the body at 4 kcal/g. Foods containing large amounts of sugar may be low in nutrients. One teaspoon of sugar contains 15 calories. If overconsumed without following healthy eating patterns, sugar-laden foods may lead to an unbalanced diet, resulting in decreased consumption of vitamins, minerals, fiber, and protein. The 2015–2020 Dietary Guidelines for Americans recommend cutting back on the consumption of added sugars to 10 percent, a decreased target from previous dietary guidelines. The American Heart Association

recommends added sugars be no more than 6 teaspoons or 100 kcals/day for women or 9 teaspoons or 150 kcal/day for most men [60]. Beverages account for 47 percent of all added sugars consumed by the U.S. population, including soft drinks (25 percent), fruit drinks (11 percent), sports and energy drinks (3 percent), coffee and tea (7 percent), and alcoholic beverages (1 percent). Recently, corporate food scientists discovered a method to change the shape and restructure sugar from a rectangle to a hollow sphere. These spheres are reported to deliver sweetness to tongue taste receptors by maximizing the surface area relative to volume allowing for food manufacturers to use less sugar in candy products. Now the candy manufacturers can use 40 percent less sugar in their confectionary. The altered sugar crystals are not applicable in all food products since they dissolve too quickly to be used in beverages [2].

Molasses, which contains the natural ash of the plant juices from which it is made, provides a small amount of antioxidants [40], calcium, and iron. Sorgo, honey, and maple syrup also contain some mineral value. However, the less refined sugars and syrups, including honey, provide the macronutrient carbohydrate that provides calories for energy. Although sugar has been used to sweeten foods for many decades, concerns about caloric excess in the diet, tooth decay, or specific dietary concerns, such as diabetes, have sparked a desire for alternatives. The food industry has responded with a variety of "sugar-free" products. Nutritive and nonnutritive sweeteners are acceptable when consumed in moderation and within the context of a diet consistent with the dietary guidelines for Americans and the dietary reference intakes [3].

Some examples of added sugars are provided in **Table 9–1**. Added sugars account for 16 percent of the calories consumed by many Americans (**Figure 9–6**). The major source of added sugars in our diets include

Sugar may be included in several forms as identified on this food label ingredient list. (shakzu. 123rf.com)

Table 9–1
SOURCES OF ADDED SUGAR IN THE DIET

White sugar
Brown sugar
Honey
Pancake syrup
Maple syrup
Molasses
Corn syrup
High-fructose corn syrup (HFCS)
Corn syrup solids
Raw sugar
Malt syrup
Fructose sweetener
Liquid fructose
Anhydrous dextrose
Crystal dextrose
Sorgo
Nectar
Cane juice
Evaporated corn sweetener
Confectioner's powdered sugar
Corn syrup solids
Lactose
Maltose

Source: USDA ChooseMyPlate (2017).

sodas; energy drinks; sport drinks; desserts, such as cookies, cake, pudding, and ice cream; sugar-sweetened fruit drinks; and candy. Global studies, however, indicate that economic facts such as cost and income are the biggest drivers in consuming these sugar-laden beverages [34]. Globally, as price increases and income decreases there is less consumption of sweetened beverages. Price and income are the most important factors of consumption of sweetened beverages [34].

The Academy of the Nutrition and Dietetics 2012 position paper "Use of Nutritive and Non-nutritive Sweeteners" says that consumers can safely enjoy a range of nutritive and nonnutritive sweeteners when consumed within an eating plan that meets Dietary Guidelines for Americans and the Dietary Reference intakes [3]. The Academy recognizes the role of sugar in providing necessary calories and that sweetness is innate and a pleasurable eating experience. It also recognized that an overconsumption of sugar calories may contribute to obesity and other disease states. On average, adults consume 17 percent and children 14 percent of their energy intake from sugars [3, 60]. Sugars can contribute, along with other fermentable carbohydrates, to acid production in the mouth, which promotes dental cavities [3]. Present research evidence shows dietary sugars do not appear to be responsible for behavioral changes such as hyperactivity [3]. Sugars have their place in food preparation, providing variety and satisfying the desire for sweet taste.

HEALTHY EATING
SUGAR CONSUMPTION AND CALORIES

There are reasons to reconsider your sugar consumption. The percentage of Americans who are overweight or obese has increased with approximately 17 percent of youth and one-third of the adult population obese. The following table compares obesity rates present to the past [36].

Percent Who Are Obese in the United States, 1970s to Present		
	1970s	Present
2- to 5-year-olds	5	8.9
6- to 11-year-olds	4	17.5
12- to 19-year-olds	6	20.5
Adults	15	37

Why the Concern?

Obesity is associated with a higher prevalence of type 2 diabetes, heart disease, high blood cholesterol levels, and high blood pressure [60]. To rein in our waistlines, Americans need to eat fewer calories and increase activity levels.

Why Reexamine Our Sugar Consumption?

Clearly, sugar is not the only source of calories in our diets. But sugar, when consumed in excess, contributes calories and little else. Sugar-sweetened carbonated beverages, energy and sports drinks, and fruit drinks are primary sources of added sugars in our diets. An increased risk of overweight and obesity among children, adolescents, and adults has been associated with the consumption of high-sugar beverages [23, 25]. The following are some tips to consider:

- Reduce overall calorie consumption and increase activity level if overweight.
- Look for sugar and syrups on the ingredient label and select lower-sugar products. Look for words ending in "ose," such as sucrose and dextrose, to identify sugars.
- Avoid sugar-sweetened beverages—enjoy water and other beverages.
- Enjoy naturally sweet foods that are packaged with other nutrients, such as fresh fruit or nonfat and low-fat milk [23].

CHEMICAL CLASSIFICATION OF SUGARS

The chemical classification of sugars as **monosaccharides** and **disaccharides** and a description of some of the common sugars were provided in Chapter 7. Monosaccharides and disaccharides are briefly summarized in **Table 9–2**.

Nutritive versus Nonnutritive Sweeteners

Sweeteners can be classified as nutritive, meaning they provide nutritional value as calories, or nonnutritive, basically calorie free. Nonnutritive sweeteners must contain less than 2 percent of the calories as an equivalent amount of sugar (sucrose). Sucrose is the main sweetener used throughout the world. Sugar, sugar alcohols, corn and maple syrup, molasses, honey, fructose syrups, agave syrup all provide energy and so are considered nutritive sweeteners providing some calories.

Nonnutritive sweeteners are used in small amounts and provide little to no nutritional value or calories. These high-intensity sweeteners do not replace the many properties of sucrose. Thus, high-intensity sweeteners are never substitutes for sucrose. The following six high-intensity sweeteners have been approved by the FDA for use as food additives in the United States: saccharin, aspartame, acesulfame potassium (acesulfame-K), sucralose, neotame, and advantame. According to the FDA, aspartame is the only approved nutritive

---

Table 9–2
MONOSACCHARIDES AND DISACCHARIDES

Monosaccharides
The simplest sugars (carbohydrates) are a single unit. Hexoses contain six carbon atoms.

Glucose	Found in many fruits and vegetables naturally. Type of sugar that circulates in our bloodstreams. Basic building block of many starches (**Figure 9–7**).
Fructose	Found in honey and in many fruits naturally (**Figure 9–8**).
Galactose	Found as one of the two building blocks for lactose, a disaccharide (**Figure 9–9**).

Disaccharides
Are composed of two monosaccharide molecules linked together.

Sucrose	Composed of glucose + fructose. Known as table sugar. Usually extracted from sugar cane or sugar beet (**Figure 9–10**).
Lactose	Composed of glucose + galactose. Naturally found only in milk and milk products (**Figure 9–11**).
Maltose	Composed of glucose + glucose. The product of the breakdown of starch (**Figure 9–12**).

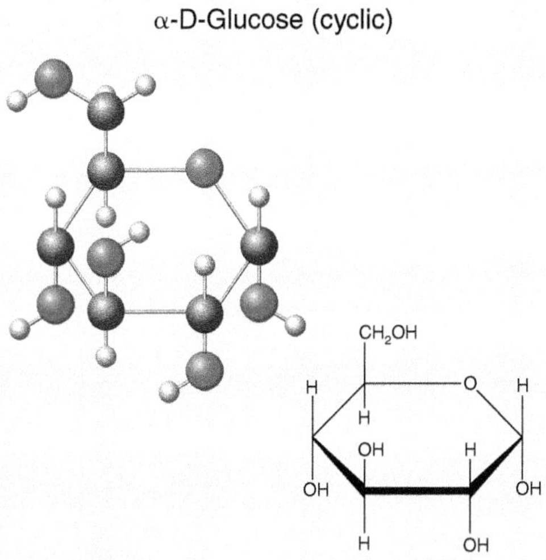

α-D-Glucose (cyclic)

Figure 9–7
Glucose molecules. (Anton Lebedev/123RF)

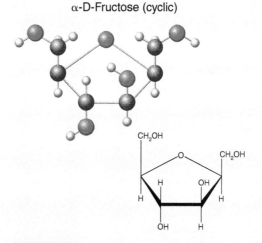

α-D-Fructose (cyclic)

Figure 9–8
D-fructose molecule structural chemical formula and model of fructose (alpha-D-fructose) 2D and 3D illustration vector. (Anton Lebedev/123RF)

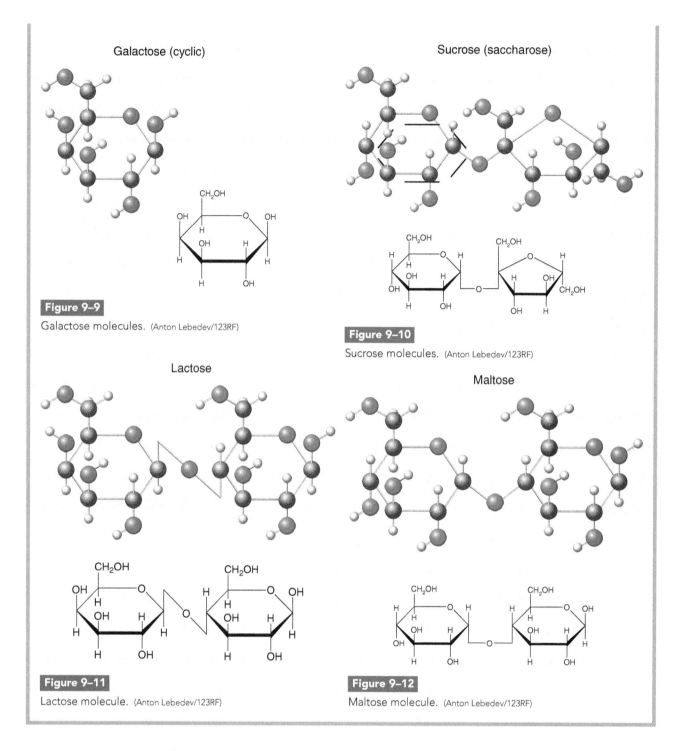

Figure 9–9

Galactose molecules. (Anton Lebedev/123RF)

Figure 9–10

Sucrose molecules. (Anton Lebedev/123RF)

Figure 9–11

Lactose molecule. (Anton Lebedev/123RF)

Figure 9–12

Maltose molecule. (Anton Lebedev/123RF)

high-intensity sweetener that contains more than 2 percent of the calories in an equivalent amount of sugar.

Nutritive Sweeteners
Sugar Beets and Sugarcane

Sucrose is the main sweetener of human consumption and is commonly referred to as "sugar." Plants all produce sucrose through the process of photosynthesis (**Figure 9–13**). However, sugarcane (**Figure 9–14**) and sugar beets (**Figure 9–15**) accumulate large amounts of sucrose in their storage tissues.

Sugarcane and sugar beet supply granulated table sugar supply of 4 kcal/gram or 15 kcal per teaspoon [29]. Sugar is an important worldwide industry; since American colonial time, quotas and trade have made sugar valuable economic indicator and commodity. **Figure 9–16** shows where sugar beets and sugarcane are grown in the United States.

The sugarcane stalk (culms) (**Figure 9–17**) and the sugar beet's (**Figure 9–18**) swollen tap root are highly prized sugar storage organs [39]. Commercial sugarcane and sugar beet plants have been bred for

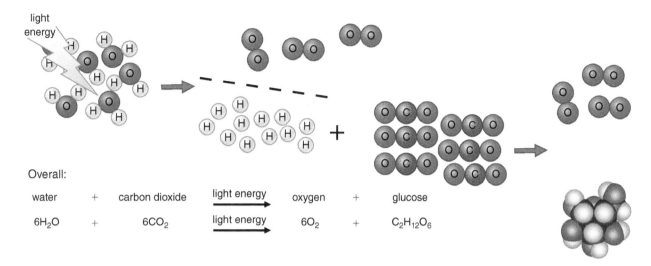

Overall:

| water | + | carbon dioxide | light energy → | oxygen | + | glucose |
| 6H$_2$O | + | 6CO$_2$ | light energy → | 6O$_2$ | + | C$_2$H$_{12}$O$_6$ |

Figure 9–13

How photosynthesis turns sun energy to sugar. (Oxford Designers & Illustrators Ltd/Pearson Education Ltd)

Figure 9–14

Sugarcane plantation. (Hywit Dimyadi/Shutterstock)

Figure 9–15

Sugar beets are a major source of sugar. (Igorstevanovic/Shutterstock)

high sweetness levels and low invertase levels leading to high levels of sucrose that can be extracted and processed into "sugar" [62]. Sugarcane and sugar beets have low levels of starch storage as a result.

The refining processes that extract the sucrose from the sugar beets and sugarcane are different [29] (**Figure 9–19**), but both go through the same basic process. The canes or tubers must be crushed or shredded to start the sucrose juice extraction process. The extracted "juice" containing 10–15 percent sugar is processed and filtered to remove impurities before evaporation under vacuum. Molasses is spun off for white crystalline table sugar. The process of molasses removal, purification, and sugar crystallization is termed "refining." The sugar goes through more purification so crystals are the proper size and moisture levels. Various forms of sugar are discussed below. The waste sugar refining by-products called bagasse are used as a fuel source, often used as energy for the sugar refining factory.

CRYSTALLINE FORMS OF SUGAR

Crystals will form in a supersaturated sugar solution (**Figure 9–20**). In the process of crystallization, molecules that are dispersed in a liquid solution pack closely together in a precise, organized, set pattern to form a solid substance. The tiny crystals, which have a characteristic shape for each substance crystallized, may sometimes be gathered into clusters of crystals.

The size of the crystals formed depends on several factors, including concentration, temperature, agitation, and the presence of other substances that interfere with crystal formation. These factors are carefully controlled both in the crystallization of commercial sugars and in the making of candies.

U.S. Sugar Producing States

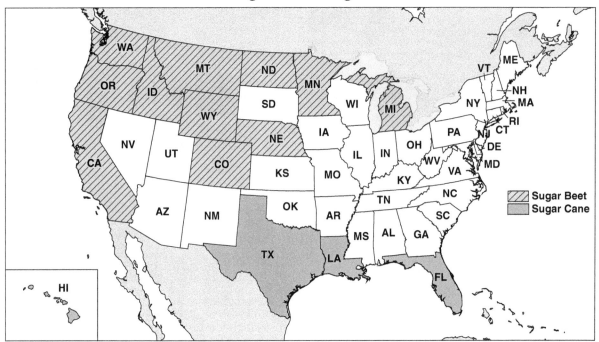

Figure 9–17
Fresh-cut red sugarcane that will be refined into white granulated sugar. (Mohammed Anwarul Kabir Choudhury/123RF)

Figure 9–18
Sugar beet can weigh 2–4 pounds and have 13–22 percent sucrose. (Luis Carlos Jimenez del rio/Shutterstock)

Granulated Sugar

Granulated sugar or crystalline sucrose, called *table sugar*, plays a variety of roles in food systems. To the food scientist, sucrose is much more than a sweetener. For example, it affects the texture of many baked products, improves the body and texture of ice creams, is fermented by yeast to produce carbon dioxide gas that leavens breads, and preserves jams and jellies by retarding the growth of microorganisms.

Table sugar is produced commercially from both sugar beets and sugarcane. The product, refined sucrose, is chemically the same from both sources. In the production of table sugar, the plant materials are crushed or sliced, and the high sugar content is extracted. The juice is filtered, clarified, and evaporated under a vacuum to form a concentrated sugar syrup from which the sugar is crystallized (**Figure 9–21**). In the processing of cane sugar, an intermediate product with 2 to 3 percent impurities is *raw sugar*. Raw sugar is sent to refineries for further treatment through a series of steps involving dissolving, purifying, and recrystallizing to produce granulated sugar. The crude raw sugar is not suitable for human consumption. Beet sugar production is done in one continuous stage, without a raw sugar intermediate.

Many grades and granulations of refined sugar are available. Fine granulated sugar with uniform grain size is the principal granulated sugar for consumer use. Forms of sugar that may be found in the marketplace are described in **Table 9–3**.

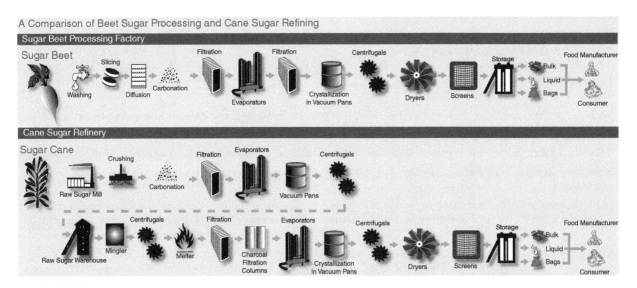

Figure 9–19

Sugarcane and sugar beet refining process. (Courtesy of the Sugar Association Inc.)

Figure 9–20

Sugar crystals. (Kichigin/Shutterstock)

Figure 9–21

The crystalline structure of ordinary table sugar is evident when viewed under a microscope. (Artem Povarov/123RF)

Other Crystalline Sugars

A white crystalline form of glucose, 75 to 80 percent as sweet as sucrose, is produced by the complete hydrolysis of cornstarch (**Figure 9–22**). It can be obtained in various particle sizes, including powdered and pulverized, but is used chiefly in the food industry. Crystalline glucose may also be found when crystals form in honey; the fructose remains in the syrup.

Crystalline fructose, like crystalline glucose, is used mainly by food processors. When used in combination with sucrose, the sweetness is greater than when an equal amount of either sugar is used alone, thus allowing less sugar to be used. Compared with sucrose, fructose produces more rapid development of viscosity and increased gel strength in starch-thickened pies and puddings [51]. Crystalline lactose, which is about one-sixth as sweet as sucrose, and maltose also are available for special uses (**Figure 9–23**).

Maltodextrins, which are derived from cornstarch, are available as dry products and as concentrated solutions. The starch in maltodextrins is less completely hydrolyzed to glucose than corn syrup solids; therefore, they are less sweet and have a bland flavor. They also contribute chewiness, binding properties, and viscosity to candy [16].

Brown Sugars

Brown sugar is obtained from cane sugar during the late stages of refining. It is composed of clumps of sucrose crystals coated with a film of molasses. Molasses is a by-product of the sugar production process; it is the liquid

Table 9–3
FORMS OF GRANULATED SUGAR

Forms of Granulated Sugar	Description
"Regular" white sugar	Sugar usually used in cooking or in sugar bowls. May be "fine" or "extra fine" crystal size.
Fruit sugar	Slightly finer than "regular" sugar. Often used in dry mixes and powdered drinks.
Baker's special sugar	Finer than fruit sugar. Developed for baking industry for cakes and sugaring cookies or doughnuts.
Superfine, ultrafine, or bar sugar	Finest crystal size of all of the crystalline sugars. Dissolves very easily and thus is ideal for meringues, delicate cakes, or iced drinks. In England, is known as caster sugar.
Confectioner's or powdered sugar	Granulated sugar ground to a smooth powder and sifted. Contains about 3 percent cornstarch to prevent caking. May be ground to different degrees of fineness; powdered sugar sold in grocery stores is 10X.
Coarse sugar	Crystal size is larger than regular sugar. Is resistant to color changes and inversion to glucose and fructose (invert sugar). Used for making fondants, confections, and other products where this stability is desirable.
Sanding sugar	A large crystal-size sugar used in the baking industry to sprinkle on baked goods. The large crystals appear to "sparkle" in light.
Liquid sugar	White granulated sugar that has been dissolved in water for use in recipes requiring dissolved sugar.
Invert sugar	Invert sugar is used primarily in food manufacturing to retard crystallization of sugar and retain moisture in packaged foods. Sucrose is split into fructose and glucose via inversion. Since fructose is sweeter than sucrose or glucose, the commercial invert sugar mixtures may vary. Total invert sugar is 50 percent fructose and 50 percent glucose. A 50 percent invert sugar has half sucrose and 25 percent glucose and 25 percent fructose. Invert sugar can be made by boiling sugar solution and lemon juice.

Source: Adapted from the Sugar Association, Inc.

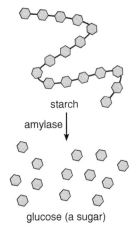

Figure 9–22

Starch can be turned to sugar via hydrolysis. (Oxford Designers & Illustrators Ltd/Pearson Education Ltd)

Figure 9–23

A variety of sugars. (Dream79/Shutterstock)

remaining after most of the sugar crystals have been separated from it. Some invert sugar (fructose and glucose) is present in molasses, and thus in brown sugar. A small amount of ash, an organic acid, and flavoring substances are also present in brown sugar, contributing to the characteristic pleasant caramel flavor and light yellow to dark brown color. The lighter the color, the higher the stage of purification and the less pronounced the flavor. The types of brown sugar are described in **Table 9–4**.

Cocrystallized Sucrose

A process known as *cocrystallization* can be applied to the crystallization of sucrose. Cocrystallization is a process whereby a second ingredient is incorporated in or plated onto a microsized sucrose crystal by spontaneous crystallization [4]; there is no settling out of the second ingredient. The resulting sugar product is homogeneous and readily dispersed in food ingredients. The second ingredient may be flavorings, such as honey, fruit juice,

Table 9–4
FORMS OF BROWN SUGAR

Forms of Brown Sugar	Description
Turbinado sugar	Partially processed raw sugar. Only surface molasses has been removed; thus, it is blond in color and has a mild brown sugar flavor.
Light and dark brown sugar	Dark brown sugar is deeper in color and has more molasses flavor compared to light brown sugar.
Muscovado or Barbados Sugar	British specialty brown sugar that is very dark brown with a strong molasses flavor. Sugar crystals are coarser and stickier in texture compared to "regular" brown sugar.
Free-flowing brown sugar	Produced by cocrystallization, free-flowing brown sugars are fine and powderlike and pour like white sugar.
Demerara sugar	A light brown sugar with large golden crystals that is popular in England.
Evaporated Cane Juice	A food-grade, cane-based sweetener made directly from milled cane. Filtered clarified juice is evaporated into syrup. Syrup is free flowing, golden in color, and has a hint of molasses flavor.

Source: Adapted from the Sugar Association, Inc.

maple, peanut butter, chocolate, and alternate sweetener–sugar combinations. The incorporation of mixtures of ingredients into a crystallized sugar matrix is also used to make instant-type products with improved functions in gelling, aeration, and emulsification, such as mixes for pudding, gelatin dessert, flavored drink, and icing.

In the cocrystallization process, spontaneous crystallization of a purified supersaturated sugar solution is accomplished by rapid agitation, resulting in the production of microsized crystal aggregates as cooling proceeds. The aggregates have a spongelike appearance, with void spaces and an increased surface area. In the presence of a second ingredient, an infinite dispersion of this ingredient occurs over the entire the sucrose aggregate surface area.

SYRUPS, MOLASSES, AND HONEY

Corn Syrups

Regular corn syrups contain about 75 percent carbohydrate and 25 percent water; however, the proportions of the various sugars present in the carbohydrate portion may vary from 20 to 98 percent glucose, depending on the manufacturing process and the proposed use of the product [16]. Corn syrup also may be called glucose syrup on food labels.

Corn syrup has traditionally been produced in the United States by using acid and high temperatures to hydrolyze cornstarch. The carbohydrate of the resulting product is composed of 10 to 36 percent glucose and 9 to 20 percent maltose, the remainder consisting of higher sugars and **dextrins** [26]. With the additional use of selected enzymes, a corn syrup that contains a much higher proportion of glucose and/or maltose may be prepared. The use of **glucoamylase** yields more glucose, whereas the use of

β-amylase yields more maltose. High-glucose syrups have lower viscosity and higher sweetening power.

The extent of conversion of starch to glucose is described by the term *dextrose equivalent* (DE), which is defined as the percent of **reducing sugar** calculated as dextrose (glucose) on a dry-weight basis. Dextrose or glucose thus has a DE of 100. Corn syrups are available with different sugar compositions having DEs of 20 to 95 [16].

Corn Syrup Solids. Dried corn syrups or corn syrup solids are produced by the spray or vacuum drying of refined corn syrup. The dried product is useful in such foods as dry beverage mixes, instant breakfast mixes, cereal bars, and sauce mixes.

High-Fructose Corn Syrup. A high-glucose corn syrup is used as the basis for production of a high-fructose corn syrup by use of the enzyme **glucose isomerase** (**Figure 9–24**). This enzyme catalyzes the chemical reaction that changes about half of the glucose in the mixture to fructose. High-fructose corn syrup containing about 42 percent of the carbohydrate as fructose was produced in the early 1970s. Syrups containing up to 90 percent fructose have since been prepared by a fractionation process that removes much of the glucose from a 42 percent high-fructose corn syrup. To produce a syrup of 55 percent fructose content, a stream of 90 percent fructose syrup is blended into a stream of 42 percent fructose syrup [42]. The primary feature of high-fructose corn syrup is sweetness.

High-fructose corn syrups are widely used in the manufacture of soft drinks. They are also used in a variety of other products, including prepared cereals, chocolate products, icings, canned and frozen fruits, frozen desserts, confections, and sauces [14].

Stage 1: production of glucose syrup

starch from maize grains

The enzyme amylase is added to
the starch to digest it into glucose.

glucose syrup

**Stage 2: conversion of glucose
to fructose**

glucose syrup

isomerase enzyme

fructose syrup

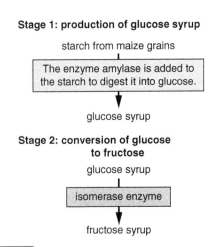

Figure 9–24

Fructose can be produced from corn (maize) starch by using
the enzymes amylase and isomerase.

Figure 9–25

Molasses is produced as a product from sugar refining.
(David Pimborough/123RF)

Molasses (Treacle)

Molasses (treacle) is a by-product of sugar refining
(**Figure 9–25**). Molasses is the residue that remains after
sucrose crystals have been removed from the concentrated juices of sugarcane. It contains about 70 percent
sugar but not more than 25 percent water or 5 percent
mineral ash. The sugar component is a mixture of sucrose, glucose, and fructose, but is primarily sucrose.

Molasses differs in sugar and mineral content, depending on the stage of the crystallization process from
which it is derived. After the first crystallization of sucrose,
the molasses is high in sugar and light in color. After the
final process, a dark and bitter product with a relatively
high mineral content, called *blackstrap molasses,* remains.
Most molasses sold on the market is a blend.

Sweet Sorghum Syrup (Sorgo)

Sorghum syrup called Sorgo is made from the cane
(stem stalk) of sweet sorghum. This sweet sorghum is
closely related to sorghum plants raised for grain, but
the syrup variety is bred for an abundance of sugar in
the cane stalk. However, there is no waste; tops and
leaves of sweet sorghum are used for animal feed.

Sorgo is similar to molasses in appearance. Its total
sugar content is about 65 to 70 percent. Sorghum syrup
is high in iron, calcium, magnesium, and potassium.
According to the National Sweet Sorghum Sweet
Producers and Processors Association, sorghum is de-
headed to increase sugar in the cane. The timing of
the deheading is critical as early deheading leads to
more sugar in the cane at the time of processing and
higher syrup Brix readings. The harvesting of syrup is
best done as seed is hard and ripe.

For syrup production, leaves are stripped and
canes cut to ground. These canes are crushed for juice

extraction and the syrup production is like sugarcane
syrup production.

Molasses and sorgo look and taste very similar;
they can be used interchangeably. Sorgo is sweeter
than molasses so substitution in a recipe requires cutting the amount of sugar by one-third. Sorghum syrup
can also be substituted for honey.

Sorghum syrup does crystallize like honey. This
crystallization can be reversed by sitting jar in warm
water or adding a small amount of invertase to stop
crystallization.

Maple Syrup

Maple sugaring has been an early-spring tradition in some
parts of the United States ever since Native Americans
first discovered that sap from the maple tree cooked
over an open fire produced sweet syrup (**Figure 9–26**).

Figure 9–26

Maple trees that are tapped for sap with buckets collecting
maple sap. (Marc Bruxelle/Shutterstock)

FOCUS ON SCIENCE
MORE ON DEXTROSE EQUIVALENTS AND REDUCING SUGAR

What is meant by dextrose equivalents?

Dextrose equivalents (DE) is a term that is used to indicate the degree of hydrolysis of starch into glucose syrup (or corn syrup). DE is the percent of reducing sugars in the syrup, calculated as the dextrose (glucose) on a dry-weight basis. A simple way to remember this is that DE indicates what percentage of syrup is glucose. If the DE is low, then large numbers of linear chains or long-chain fragments have been retained, and strong gels may be formed.

What is a reducing sugar?

Aldoses (such as glucose) are called *reducing sugars* because of their ability to reduce an agent such as silver or

copper (II) ions. In this reaction, the sugar's aldehyde group is oxidized to a carboxylate group. Fehling's solution, which is an alkaline solution of copper (II) salt, oxidizes an aldose (such as glucose) to an aldonate. In this process, the copper (II) is reduced to copper (I), which precipitates as a brick-red oxide Cu_2O as in the following reaction:

$$2CU(OH)_2 + R - \overset{\overset{\displaystyle H}{|}}{C} = O \rightarrow R - \overset{\overset{\displaystyle O}{\|}}{C} - OH + Cu_2O + H_2O$$

U.S. Maple Sugar Producing States

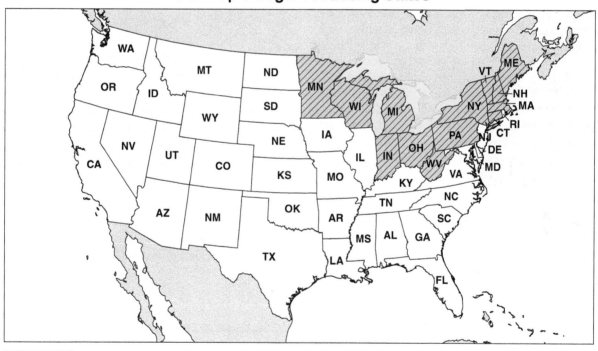

Figure 9–27

Map shows where maple syrup is produced. (Cartographer Charlie Frye and © Amanda Frye)

Vermont is well-known for its pure maple syrup with $15 million in annual direct sales. However, maple syrup production occurs in New Hampshire, Connecticut, New York, Maine, Massachusetts, Pennsylvania, West Virginia, Indiana, Ohio, Michigan, Minnesota, Wisconsin, Minnesota, and Vermont (**Figure 9–27**).

Maple syrup is highly prized of all syrups used for culinary and table purposes. It is made from sugar maple sap that is evaporated to a concentration containing no more than 35 percent water. Maple sap contains between 1 and 7 percent sugar (average 2.5

percent). The greater the sugar sap content, the less sap it takes to make syrup. The sap must be cooked to evaporate water and concentrate sugar and flavorings. Sucrose is the primary sugar in maple syrup sugar with sucrose ranging between 65–68 percent in syrups. Fructose accounts for 0–0.7 percent and glucose 0.4–0.7 percent of maple syrups. Maple syrup pH is around 6.0. Calcium, iron, potassium, magnesium, manganese, sodium, phosphorus, sulfur, and zinc are all natural constituents of maple syrup. Chemical, mineral, and carbohydrate composition has not been found to vary significantly between grades of syrup [59]. One tablespoon of maple syrup contains 50 calories. Maple syrup does not naturally contain sulfites [52].

Maple trees are tapped at the end of winter for about a month to collect sap [30] (Figure 9–26). The special flavor of maple syrup is developed in cooking down the sap into syrup (**Figure 9–28**). Organic acids present in the sap enter into this flavor-developing process. It has been found that evaporating the sap at low temperatures through distillation or freeze-drying results in syrup that is practically flavorless and colorless. Approximately 40 gallons of sap are necessary to yield a single gallon of maple syrup (**Figure 9–29**).

The U.S. Department of Agriculture adopted revised grading standards for maple syrup in 2015. These standards are voluntary, but serve as a basis for producers, suppliers, buyers, and consumers as well as federal inspection and commodity grading. (See **Table 9–5**.) The new standards eliminate "Grade B which allowed for off flavors and odors" and created a new "Grade A Very Dark." Grade A was revised to include four color classes from golden to very dark. Grade A syrups must be a quality maple syrup with solids by weight (Brix) between 66.0 and 69.0. Color uniformity, good flavor, odor, and flavor intensity (maple taste associated with color class) are factors considered in grading. Syrup must be free of off-flavors and odors, cloudiness, turbidity, sediment, and clean with no deviants (**Table 9–6**). Syrup that does not meet Grade A *processing grade* has a "fairly" good maple taste: may contain off-flavors, but is "fairly free'" of damage and turbidity, and is "fairly" clean. Off-flavors are described as "buddy," which is chocolaty to bitter chocolaty. Other off-flavors are "woody" or due to manufacturing burnt, scorched, fermented, or chemical or other odors or flavors developed during handling or storage. The maple syrup color classes are measured by use of a spectrophotometer that measures percent of light transmission. Any syrup containing "off-flavors" regardless of color or grade must not be sold and set aside in 5 gallon minimum for reprocessing [57].

The term *maple flavored* is used for products that are made with chemical substances that imitated

Figure 9–28

Maple sap being boiled down to produce maple syrup. (Kim D. Lyman/Shutterstock)

Figure 9–29

A container of maple syrup. The Grade A color varies. (Louella938/ Shutterstock)

maple syrup flavors and contain no maple syrup. *Pancake syrups* are economical syrups made with sugar or corn syrup and flavoring; maple syrup is not an ingredient. Thus, pancake syrups have a much different flavor profile than maple syrup.

Table 9–5
U.S. STANDARDS FOR MAPLE SYRUP GRADES

Grade A Color Classes	Taste	Light Transmittance (%Tc)
U.S. Grade A Golden	Delicate	≥ 75.0
U.S. Grade A Amber	Rich	50.0–74.9
U.S. Grade A Dark	Robust	25.0–49.9
U.S. Grade A Very Dark	Strong	≤ 25.0
Processing grade	Does not meet Grade A standards. May be any color. Processing grade class, Brix less than 68.9; may contain off-flavors or odors; may have very strong taste.	
Substandard syrup	Fails to meet processing standards and cannot be graded.	

Source: Adapted from Reference 57.

Table 9–6
MAPLE SYRUP TERMINOLOGIES

Brix is the percentage by weight concentration of total soluble solids (mainly sugar).

Turbidity (cloudiness) refers to the suspension of fine particles in the syrup detracting from syrup clearness. These particles are typically malate of lime, niter or sugar sand, or calcium malate.

Malate of lime means fine particles of mineral matter found in maple syrup.

Sugar sand or niter is the harmless gritty matter in maple syrup. Calcium malate results from high calcium and malic acid concentrations; these are least-solubility salts in syrup.

Damaged syrup means defect in appearance, edibility, or quality. Badly scorched syrup, buddy syrup, fermented syrup, or syrup with off-flavor or color is considered damaged.

Buddy flavor or buddiness characteristic of damaged syrup whose sap from trees have come out of dormancy.

Source: Adapted from Reference 57.

Table 9–7
HONEY TERMINOLOGIES

Extracted honey Honey that has been separated from the comb by centrifugal force, gravity, straining, or other means.

Filtered honey Honey that has been filtered to remove all or most of the fine particles, pollen grains, air bubbles, or other materials normally found in suspension.

Strained honey Honey that has been strained to remove most of the particles including the comb, propolis, or other defects found in honey. Grains of pollen, small air bubbles, and very fine particles would not normally be removed.

Propolis The gum gathered by bees from various plants. It varies in color from light yellow to dark brown and causes staining of comb or frame and may be found in extracted honey.

Source: Reference 58.

Honey

Honey is flower nectar that is collected, modified, and concentrated by the domesticated European honeybee. Honey is a supersaturated solution, and, with storage, glucose tends to crystallize out of the solution. Heating will dissolve the crystals, restoring the honey to a liquid form.

Honey contains about 17 percent water and 82.5 percent carbohydrate, with small amounts of minerals, vitamins, and enzymes. The average carbohydrate portion of honey fructose is 38 percent, glucose 31 percent, maltose 7 percent, and sucrose 2 percent. As specified by the U.S. Food and Drug Administration (FDA), honey may not contain more than 8 percent sucrose; a higher percentage is taken as an indication of adulteration. The addition of any other sugar substances—such as high-fructose corn syrup—to honey is also considered to be adulteration. The ratio of glucose to fructose in honey is important to prevent crystallization. A moisture content of 17 percent and a 2:1 glucose to fructose content reduces crystallization. Heat treatment can inactivate enzymes in raw honey. Untreated honey can affect volume and texture of baked goods.

The USDA has set standards for grades of honey, including comb honey and extracted honey (filtered and strained or liquid and crystallized). The grades are based on moisture content, minimum total solids, flavor, aroma, clarity, and absence of defects. (See **Table 9–7** for terminology.) The color of honey may vary from white to dark amber, based on its mineral content and floral source. Grades of honey are independent of color, but darker-colored honey generally has a stronger flavor than the white or light-colored product.

The flavor of honeys varies according to the flavoring compounds in the nectar of different flowers. Different regions of the country produce different flowers and honey. Over half of the honey produced in the United States is mild-flavored sweet clover, clover, or alfalfa honey (**Figure 9–30**). Honeys also come from orange and other citrus blossoms, wild sage, cultivated buckwheat, and the tulip tree. Much of the honey on the market is a blend of different floral types.

Honey is stored in the comb by bees and in that form is marketed as comb honey (**Figure 9–31**). If the comb is uncapped and centrifuged, the honey is

Figure 9–30

Honey can be added to many foods for flavor. (Strelok/123RF)

Figure 9–31

Honey bees making honey. (Irochka/123RF)

Figure 9–32

Agave field for production, Jalisco, Mexico. (T photography/ Shutterstock)

extracted. Extracted honey may optionally be pasteurized by a mild heat treatment to destroy yeasts and to delay crystallization. Honey may be strained to remove wax particles and foreign matter, and filtered to remove pollen, air bubbles, and other fine particles.

Other types of honey products include crystallized, dried, and whipped. Dried honey has a color and flavor similar to original honey. The granular form, is free flowing, and has a long shelf life. Whipped honey may have a higher proportion of glucose. It crystallizes to some degree, resulting in a thickened mixture.

The *United States Standards for Grades of Extracted Honey May 23 1985* provides detail requirements for honey grade assignment based on percent soluble solids, clarity, color, aroma, and flavor. U.S. Grades of Extracted Honey are U.S. Grade A, B, C, and Substandard. The grading requirements vary between filtered or strained honey. Extracted honey may be liquid, crystallized, or partially crystallized [58].

Agave Syrup (Nectar)

Agave syrup (nectar) is typically processed from the succulent blue agave. This species is native to Mexico and is the same plant used for Tequila production (**Figure 9–32**). The agave leaves are cut and removed around the pina base, which is half above and half below the ground. The agave base is removed and taken to a processing facility. The agave base is heated under pressure to no more than 118°F (60°C), which starts the juice flow. If heated above 118°F, carbohydrates will break down and flavor will be lost. The base is then chopped to release the milky agave juice, which is filtered and centrifuged and then bottled. The

Figure 9–33

Agave syrup. (© Amanda Frye)

agave syrup is sweeter than sugar and thinner than honey with a 76 Brix. Agave is 95 percent oligosaccharide (inulin fructose) and 5 percent sucrose/glucose. One tablespoon equals 60 calories (**Figure 9–33**).

The main carbohydrate in agave syrup is fructose stored as polysaccharide called inulins, which is a fructosan. Inulins are made up of about 35 fructose units hooked together with a glucose terminal. Inulins are not digested by the small intestine, but in the large intestine it is a source for bacterial digestion yielding small-chain fatty acids and lactic acid. Plants that store energy as inulin do not typically store energy as starch. Inulins are typically stored in roots or rhizomes. Inulins have one-third to one-fourth the calories of carbohydrates.

Table 9–8 lists some sugar and syrup substitutions that can be made in food preparation. Adjustment must be made for the liquid present in syrups.

Table 9–8
SUBSTITUTION AMONG SUGAR AND SYRUP PRODUCTS

1 cup brown sugar = 1/2 cup liquid brown sugar

1 cup honey = 1¼ cup sugar + 1/4 cup liquid

1 cup corn syrup = 1 cup sugar + 1/4 cup liquid

1 cup sorghum syrup = 2/3 cup sugar + 1/3 cup liquid

1 cup agave syrup = 3/4 cup sugar + 1/4 cup liquid

SUGAR ALCOHOLS (POLYOLS) AND NOVEL SWEETENERS

Low-calorie sweeteners lack the bulk needed for many food products. Sugar alcohols are therefore used with low-calorie sweeteners to improve bulk, mouthfeel, and texture [35]. Eight **polyols** (erythritol, mannitol, isomalt, lactitol, maltitol, xylitol, sorbitol, and hydrogenated starch hydrolysates) are approved for use in the United States. GRAS and Code of Federal Regulations Title 21 sections 184.1835, 180.25, 172.395, and 101.9 regulate sugar alcohols. Foods sweetened with polyols may be labeled with "sugar free" or "does not promote tooth decay" claims; however, these foods may not meet the requirements of a "reduced-calorie food." Reduced-calorie foods must contain 25 percent less calories than the full-calorie product. Those who are following a diabetic or weight reduction diet should be aware of the caloric value of sugar alcohols [31].

Sugar alcohols are only partially digested and absorbed by the body thus decreasing blood glucose response and caloric density. The caloric values permitted by the FDA in the labelling of polyols are provided in **Table 9–9**. However, overconsumption of sugar alcohols can lead to intestinal disturbance.

Sugar alcohols have been used by the food industry for decades in various foods and confectionary products worldwide [22]. Polyols have been used in sugar free gums, mints, baked goods, jams, dairy products, and more [1]. They are touted by food manufacturers for their diverse functionality, sugar-free status, as

"no-sugar added," and ability to create good products [22]. Sugar alcohols are derived from sugars derived from agriculture products. These sugars—sucrose, glucose, fructose, lactose, xylose, or maltose—are then modified by reducing their reactive sites (aldehyde and ketones) thus changing only the reactive group while leaving the underlying sugar structure intact. They leave the bulking properties and functionality of the sugar structure and allow for a 1:1 substitution [22, 1]. However, polyols are not all the same possessing different properties such as cooling effects, sweetness, and solubility. Applications of individual sugar alcohol to food systems vary. The following provides a brief discussion of the different polyols and their properties.

Erythritol

Erythritol is a monosaccharide polyol that is naturally present in some fruits and vegetables, including pears, melons, and mushrooms [3, 27]. It is produced by the hydrolysis and fermentation of starch and purified by crystallization. Like other sugar alcohols, erythritol does not promote tooth decay or sudden increases in blood glucose. Unlike other sugar alcohols, however, it does not cause undesirable laxative side effects. It is about 70 percent as sweet as sucrose, has only 0.2 kilocalorie per gram, and, when used with other

Table 9–9
CALORIC VALUES FOR POLYOLS

Sugar Alcohol (Polyol)	Kilocalories per Gram
Hydrogenated starch hydrolysates	3.0
Sorbitol	2.6
Xylitol	2.4
Maltitol	2.1
Lactitol	2.0
Isomalt	2.0
Mannitol	1.6
Erythritol	0.2

Source: References 27, 35.

ACCEPTABLE DAILY INTAKE OF LOW-CALORIE SWEETENERS

Acceptable daily intake (ADI) is the estimated amount of a substance, such as a low-calorie sweetener, that may be consumed over a lifetime without risk. The ADI is usually set at 1/100th of the maximum level found to cause no adverse effects in animal experiments [1, 27].

The FDA establishes the ADI of low-calorie sweeteners in the United States. International and other

government authorities establish ADI standards for food ingredients in other countries that may vary slightly from U.S.-established levels. The ADI is one of the considerations influencing the approval of sweeteners for use in the food supply.

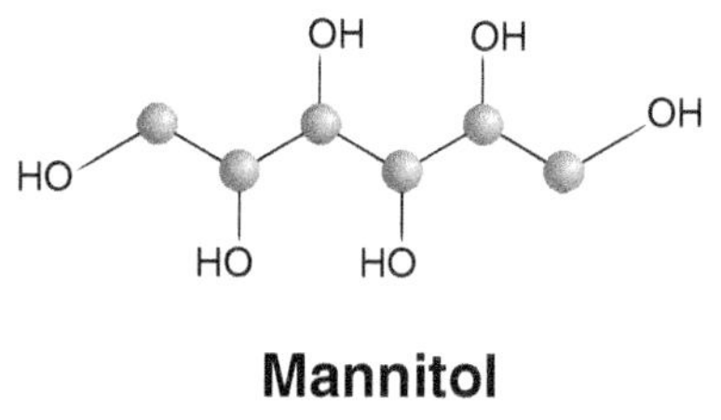

Mannitol

Figure 9–34

Mannitol. (Lyricsaima/Shutterstock)

high-intensity sweeteners, may round off the flavor. The FDA, in 1997, accepted for filing a GRAS affirmation petition [19, 44]. Acceptance of this petition by the FDA allows manufacturers to produce and sell erythritol-containing foods in the United States. Erythritol is suitable for a variety of food products, including chewing gum, candies, bakery products, and beverages.

Mannitol

Mannitol is used in food and pharmaceutical products. Mannitol is about 65 percent as sweet as sucrose [1, 22] (**Figure 9–34**). It is often used as a dusting powder for chewing gum to prevent the gum from sticking with the wrapper. In medications, it effectively masks the bitter tastes of vitamins, minerals, and other ingredients. If the daily consumption of a particular food may exceed 20 grams of mannitol, the FDA requires the statement "excess consumption may have a laxative effect" on the label [27, 35].

Isomalt, Lactitol, and Maltitol

Isomalt is 0.45–0.6 times as sweet as sugar and can replace sugar in many products, often with minimal modifications in the formula [35, 45]. Unlike most polyols, it does not produce a cooling effect.

Lactitol is 0.3–0.4 times as sweet as sucrose [45]. It is produced by hydrogenation of the milk sugar lactose [9]. A low-calorie sweetener may need to be used in combination with lactitol to achieve the desired level of sweetness in some products [35].

Maltitol is made by hydrogenation of maltose [51]. It has a sweetness level that is 0.8 times that of sucrose. Like isomalt, maltitol does not produce a cooling effect. Maltitol can be used as a fat replacer in some products in addition to its use as a sweetener.

Xylitol

Xylitol is used primarily in confections such as chewing gums, candies, chocolates, and gum drops. Xylitol is as sweet as sugar and has a significant cooling effect that enhances mint flavors. It has the advantage of being associated with the significantly reduced formation of new caries [35]. Sugar alcohols, such as xylitol, are **noncariogenic** because they are not fermented by bacteria [16]. Xylitol appears to be the best nutritive sweetener with respect to caries prevention.

Sorbitol

Sorbitol has been used for half a century in processed foods [35]. Small quantities of sorbitol are found naturally in some plant species [39]. Sorbitol is 0.6 times as sweet as sucrose and exhibits a cool, pleasant taste. Sorbitol is used in many food products for its sweetening, moisture stabilizing, and texture properties. The FDA requires that if the consumption of a food might exceed 50 grams of sorbitol, the product must be labelled to inform consumers of the potential laxative effect [27].

Hydrogenated Starch Hydrolysates

Hydrogenated starch hydrolysates describe the broad group of polyols that contain hydrogenated oligo- and polysaccharides in addition to polyols such as sorbitol, mannitol, or maltitol. However, if the polyol mixture contains more than 50 percent sorbitol, for example, it would be called sorbitol syrup [35]. Hydrogenated starch hydrolysates are 40 to 50 percent as sweet as sugar, and like the other polyols discussed, they are used as bulk sweeteners, bulking agents, and humectants, along with other functional roles.

Novel Sugar Sweeteners

Two novel sugar sweeteners, trehalose and tagatose, are relatively new to the marketplace [27]. Trehalose is a naturally occurring disaccharide that provides 4 kilocalories per gram like sugar, but is less sweet and results in a lower **glycemic response** [27, 45]. This sweetener is valued for the ability to stabilize foods during freezing or hydration [27]. It was approved for GRAS status in the United States in 2000 and occurs naturally in mushrooms, yeast, seaweed, and lobster [45].

Tagatose occurs naturally in some dairy products. It is an **isomer** of fructose that is manufactured using lactose as the raw material. It is almost as sweet as sugar and is similar in bulk. Tagatose, however, provides fewer calories (1.5 kilocalories per gram) and a lower glycemic response due to differences in how it is metabolized [27, 46]. Tagatose has been approved for GRAS status and may be labeled with the claims "does not promote tooth decay" or "may reduce the risk of tooth decay" [45].

Aspartame

Aspartame was discovered in 1965 and initially was approved for use in several foods by the FDA in 1981 [27]. In 1996, the FDA approved the use of aspartame as a general-purpose sweetener, meaning that it may be used in all categories of foods and beverages. It is regulated under 21 CFR 172.804. Aspartame is the only nutritive high-intensity sweetener.

Aspartame is made by joining two amino acids—aspartic acid and phenylalanine—and adding methyl alcohol to form a methyl **ester** (**Figure 9–35**). Aspartame is a white, odorless, crystalline powder that has a clean, sugar-like taste and a sweetness potency

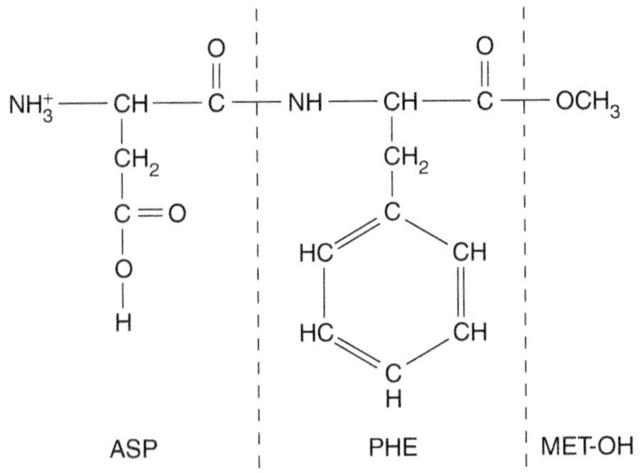

Figure 9–35

Chemical structure of aspartame. ASP, aspartic acid; PHE, phenylalanine; MET-OH, methyl alcohol.

180–200 times that of sucrose [21]. No bitter aftertaste is associated with aspartame. The registered trade name for aspartame as a food ingredient is NutraSweet®. Equal® is a tabletop low-calorie sweetener containing NutraSweet®. Another tabletop sweetener is Spoonful®, which consists of aspartame and maltodextrin. It is designed to measure like sugar. Aspartame can be utilized as an energy source in the body; however, it is used in such small amounts that its caloric value is insignificant.

Because aspartame is not stable to heat but changes chemically and loses sweetness, it has not been useful in such foods as baked layer cakes [18]. Its heat instability can be corrected, however, by encapsulating a core of granulated aspartame with a water-resistant coating of polymer and/or a layer of fat. After the outer layer melts, the core layer slowly hydrates, releasing the aspartame in the final stages of baking. The use of low-calorie bulking agents with aspartame is also necessary to produce the effects on volume and texture that sugar provides in many baked products.

Rigorous testing has been done to ensure the safety of aspartame [20, 27, 26]. Although some have questioned the wisdom of its use, particularly in soft drinks kept at high temperatures, research from several sources has documented the safety of aspartame use by healthy adults and children and by individuals with diabetes. Aspartame-containing foods should not, however, be used by individuals with **phenylketonuria (PKU)** because phenylalanine is released during its metabolism.

NONNUTRITIVE HIGH-INTENSITY SWEETENERS

Nonnutritive sweeteners are often referred to as high-intensity or high-potency sweeteners since they can be in small quantities to sweeten food and drink [1]. These high-intensity sweeteners are many times sweeter than sucrose so they contribute few to no calories and typically do not raise blood sugars. No sweetener is best for every food product [35, 46]. High-intensity sweeteners are never substitutes for sucrose since they only provide sweetness. The future chapters discuss the many roles of sucrose in food systems such as a bulking agent, browning, and temperature depression. Therefore, sugar replacers are chosen for the applications for which they will be best suited. Combinations of different non-sucrose sweeteners, called sweetener blends or combinations with nutritive non-sweet carbohydrates such as maltodextrins, offer promise for improved taste and stability and can overcome the limitations of the individual sweeteners [35, 45]. Terminologies often used in relation to non-sucrose sweeteners and substitutes are provided in **Table 9–10**.

High-intensity sweeteners may be derived from natural or artificial chemicals. High-intensity sweeteners are regulated as food additives or GRAS by FDA through the code of federal regulations title 21. Aspartame is a nutritive high-intensity sweetener as discussed above. The FDA received GRAS request notices for certain steviol glycosides–derived sweeteners from the stevia plant (*Stevia rebaudiana* (bertoni) bertoni) and extracts from the swingle fruit (*luo han guo* or monk fruit). Rebaudioside A, produced from the stevia plant, was declared generally recognized as safe (GRAS) by the FDA in 2008 [32]. However, cyclamates and cyclamate salts from sodium, calcium, potassium, and magnesium cyclamates are prohibited from use in the United States. Import alerts are placed on whole leaf and "crude" stevia that are different than the GRAS approved highly purified stevia "steviol glycosides" low-calorie sweeteners and other sugar substitutes.

Saccharin

Saccharin was first synthesized in 1879, when it was accidentally discovered that it has a sweet taste. It has been used in the United States since 1901 for both food and nonfood purposes. It is intensely sweet, 300–500 times as sweet as sucrose, and comes in a wide variety of products under extreme processing conditions [20] (**Figure 9–36**). It can be synthesized with relatively few impurities and is inexpensive. One major disadvantage of saccharin is its perceived bitter aftertaste, particularly at higher concentrations. When used in combination with other nonnutritive sweeteners, sweetness is enhanced and bitterness decreased somewhat (**Figure 9–37**).

Saccharin (sold under the trade name Sweet'N Low®) has been the only approved nonnutritive sweetener used in the United States during certain periods. In 1977, the FDA proposed banning this GRAS substance because an increase in bladder tumors in laboratory rats was found to be associated with the ingestion of

Table 9–10
TERMINOLOGIES OF HIGH-INTENSITY SWEETENERS AND SUGAR SUBSTITUTES

Definition	Terms Used	Examples

Sweeteners with very intense sweet taste used in small amounts.
 	
Contributes very few or no calories to the food in which the sweetener is used.
	Low-calorie sweetener
	
	   Indicates the purpose for the sweetener and is term preferred by some authors.
	
	Alternative sweetener or sugar substitute
	
	   These terms are used but also may be used for other types of sweeteners, thus resulting in confusion.
	
	High-potency sweetener
	
	   May confuse some consumers who may perceive the foods using these ingredients are extremely sweet.
	
	Nonnutritive sweetener
	
	   This term is used by some authors, but other authors suggest this description is not entirely accurate, especially with regard to aspartame.
	
	Artificial sweetener
	
	   Another term used by some authors. Not accurate.
		Acesulfame-K
		Aspartame
		Neotame
		Saccharine
		Sucralose
		Rebaudioside A (stevia)

Sweeteners used in place of sugar to reduce calories while still providing the same "bulk" as sugar. Unlike the low-calorie or nonnutritive sweeteners that provide essentially no calories, polyols provide 0.2 to 3.0 kilocalories per gram. May be used in combination with a low-calorie sweetener.	Polyols Sugar alcohols Bulk sweeteners	Sorbitol Mannitol Xylitol Erythritol Isomalt Lactitol Maltitol Hydrogenated starch Hydrolysates

Source: References 1, 27, 55.

Figure 9–36

Saccharin is a sweetener typically identified in the pink packet. Saccharin is 200–700× as sweet as sucrose. (Karin HildebrPDF Lau/Shutterstock)

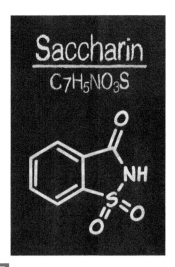

Figure 9–37

Chemical formula and structure of saccharin. (Zerbor/123RF)

high levels of dietary saccharin. Strong public protest influenced the U.S. Congress to impose a moratorium against any action to ban saccharin, in part due to the highly controversial methodology of the laboratory rat study. The moratorium was extended periodically to allow continued use of saccharin as further research clarified saccharin's role in the **carcinogenic** process [13]. Congress ruled, as a compromise measure, that a warning statement be placed on labels of foods containing saccharin. Saccharin has since been found to be a carcinogen only in rats and only if administered over two generations. **Epidemiological** studies in humans have not shown the risk of developing bladder cancer to be increased with exposure to saccharin.

In December 1991, the FDA officially withdrew the proposed federal ban on saccharin, indicating that "the safety of saccharin is no longer of concern and that these 1977 proposals have become outdated" [8]. A National Toxicology Program panel, which reports to the National Institute of Environmental Health Sciences, removed saccharin from the list of substances known or anticipated to be human carcinogens in 2000 [27]. The warning label requirement was rescinded in 2001 [27, 55]. Saccharin is regulated under the Code of Federal Regulation Title 21 180.37.

Acesulfame-K (Acesulfame Potassium)

Acesulfame is a synthetic derivative of acetoacetic acid. It is apparently not metabolized in the body and is excreted unchanged. This sweetener is characterized by a rapid onset of sweetness. It has little undesirable aftertaste, although at high concentrations it does exhibit lingering bitter and metallic flavor attributes [20]. Acesulfame-K, the potassium salt of acesulfame, is up to 200 times sweeter than sucrose [1, 27] (**Figure 9–38**).

Acesulfame-K was inadvertently discovered by a German chemist in 1967. The FDA approved this compound as a food additive in 1988. In 2003, acesulfame-K was approved as a nonnutritive sweetener and flavor enhancer for general use in foods except for meat and poultry in 2003 [55]. It is used in a variety of products and is marketed under the brand name Sunette® [20, 27]. Acesulfame-potassium is regulated under 21 CFR 172.800.

Acesulfame-K is heat stable. It does not decompose under simulated pasteurization or baking

conditions [35]. It thus has potential for use in cooked and baked products. In mixtures of acesulfame-K and aspartame (1:1 by weight), there is a strong **synergistic** enhancement of sweetness.

Sucralose

Sucralose is a white, crystalline solid produced by the selective addition of chlorine atoms to sucrose (**Figure 9–39**). It is 600 times sweeter than sugar, tastes very much like sucrose, and has no bitter aftertaste [20]. It is highly soluble in water and is stable under extreme pH conditions and at high temperatures; therefore, it can be used in **retort** applications (a sterilization procedure), hot-filled and carbonated beverages, and baked goods. Sucralose does not interact with any other food components. Because absorption of sucralose is limited and the small amount that is absorbed is not metabolized, it imparts no caloric value to foods [1, 27, 44, 55].

Sucralose was approved by the FDA for use in several food and beverage categories in 1998 and then as a general-purpose sweetener in all foods the following year [55]. This sweetener was developed by a British firm and licensed for U.S. distribution. As a tabletop sweetener, it is marketed in packets, tablets, and granular form under the Splenda® brand. Regulated as a food additive 21 CFR 172.831.

Neotame

In July 2002, the FDA approved neotame for use as a general nonnutritive sweetener and flavor enhancer in foods except for meat and poultry (**Figure 9–40**).

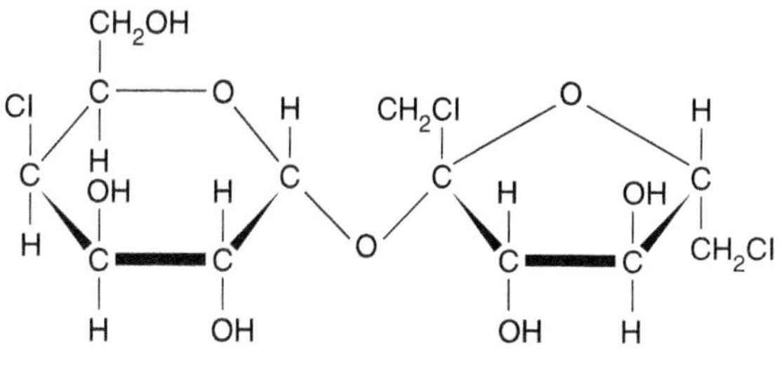

Structure of sucralose

Figure 9–39

Chemical structure of sucralose.

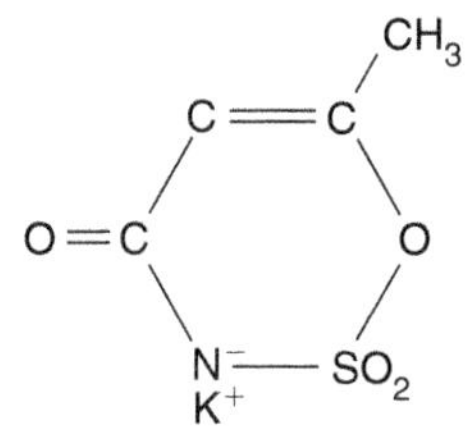

Figure 9–38

Chemical structure of acesulfame-K.

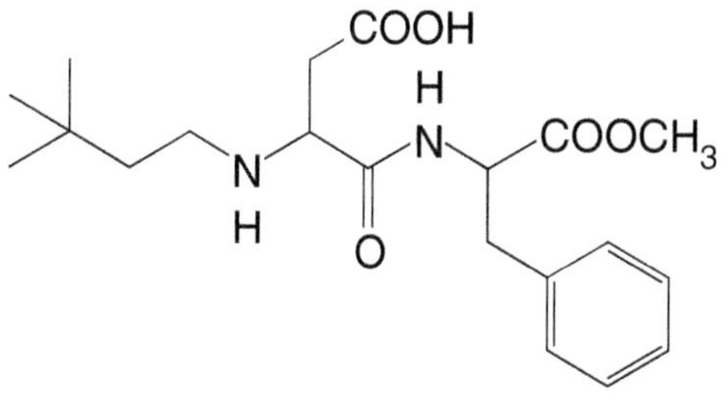

Figure 9–40

Structure of neotame. (*Source:* Adapted from Reference 28.)

Neotame is 7,000–13,000 times sweeter than sucrose [32]. It functions as a low-calorie sweetener and a flavor enhancer. Neotame has a clean sweet taste that is "sugar-like" without undesirable taste characteristics. It has been shown to enhance some flavors, such as mint, and to suppress other flavors, such as bitterness and the "beany" flavors in some soy products.

The stability of neotame has some similarities to aspartame, although neotame is more stable in neutral pH conditions and can be used successfully in dairy foods and baked products. Neotame is heat stable and can be used in cooking and baking [27].

French scientists Claude Nofre and Jean-Marie Tinti, in work with the NutraSweet Company, developed this alternative sweetener [41]. Neotame can be made by the reaction of aspartame with 3,3-dimethylbutyraldehyde. However, unlike aspartame, neotame does not metabolize to phenylalanine, and thus no special labelling is needed for those with PKU. Neotame has been found safe for the general population, including children, pregnant women, and people with diabetes [1, 27, 41]. Neotame is sold under the brand name Newtame® and regulated under 21 CFR 172.829.

Advantame

In 2014, FDA approved advantame as a nonnutritive sweetener and flavor enhancer for general-purpose use except in meat and poultry. Advantame is 20,000 times sweeter than sucrose. Advantame is heat stable and stays sweet during baking. Advantame is regulated under 21 CFR 172.803. Advantame is synthesized from aspartame and propylaldehyde and has 70–120 times the sweetness of aspartame [38]. It is stable in dry form, but in liquid systems degradation does occur over time. Manufacturer suggested use is as a sole sweetener or blended with other sweeteners.

GRAS Approved

Rebaudioside A (Stevia High-Purity Steviol Glycosides) *Stevia, steviol glycosides, stevioside,* and *rebaudioside A* are all terms used to describe the sweetening substance extracted from a South American shrub of the chrysanthemum family [27, 47]. Leaves from the stevia plant are harvested, dried, and then steeped in water, followed by purification. Because of how this sweetener is derived, many consider it to be a natural calorie-free sweetener. (**Figure 9–41**).

Stevia glycosides are 200–300 times sweeter than sugar [27, 48, 50]. Stevia is shelf and heat stable [49]. The FDA declared this sweetener GRAS in 2008 for use as a general-purpose sweetener. It is being marketed as Truvia™, although other stevia-based sweeteners are available or under development.

Swingle Fruit Extracts (SGFE)—Luo Han Guo Swingle fruit (*Siraitia grosvenorii*), also called luo han

Figure 9–41

Stevia leaves are the source of the GRAS—95 percent purified steviol glycosides sweetener. It is 200–400× more sweet than sucrose. (Dinko Bence/Shutterstock)

guo or monk fruit, is a plant native to Southern China and Thailand. In 2016, FDA placed SGFE on the GRAS list with notices for specific use. The small round fruits grow on vines. The edible pulp contains approximately 1 percent mogrosides that are responsible for the sweet taste. The sweetener fruit extracts are considered nonnutritive and reported to be 100–250 times sweeter than sugar. Swingle fruit has been used in Chinese medicine.

Other Alternative Sweeteners Not Yet Approved in the United States

Cyclamates. Cyclamates are 30 times sweeter than sucrose, taste much like sugar, and are heat stable. The sweetness has a slow onset and then persists for a period of time. Although cyclamates were considered GRAS by the FDA at one time and are currently approved for use in 50 countries, they are now banned from use in the United States [35]. A chronic toxicity study implicated sodium cyclamate as a possible bladder carcinogen in rats and resulted in the removal of cyclamates from the GRAS list in 1970. Since 1970, several additional safety studies have been done that have not been able to confirm the original findings of bladder cancer. A petition for approval of cyclamates as a food additive was again filed with the FDA; however, it has not been reapproved for use in the United States [27].

Alitame. Alitame is a **peptide** that is 2,000 times sweeter than a 10 percent solution of sucrose. It may be metabolized in the body but would give minimal caloric value, because only a small amount of sweetener would be required to match the sweetness of sucrose. Alitame is highly soluble and has good stability under a variety of manufacturing conditions, although an off-taste may occur in warm acidic solutions. It may be used in combination with other low-calorie sweeteners. Alitame is already in use in several other countries, including Mexico [19]. A petition for the approval of alitame is being held in abeyance until additional data documenting safety are provided to the FDA [27].

Thaumatin. Thaumatin is a small protein extracted by physical methods from the berry of a West African plant—sometimes called the miraculous fruit. It is listed in the *Guinness Book of World Records* as the sweetest substance known—2,000–2,500 times sweeter than an 8–10 percent solution of sucrose. Although it is metabolized in the body and yields 4 kilocalories per gram, its low usage levels make it basically noncaloric. It is listed as GRAS in the United States as a flavor modifier but not as a sweetener [27]. This protein interacts with taste receptors on the tongue to mask unpleasant tastes, such as metallic and bitter flavors. As a flavor enhancer, it acts in a similar fashion to monosodium glutamate and the 5'-nucleotides. It functions synergistically with other high-intensity sweeteners, allowing reduced levels of these substances [54]. A British company produces and markets thaumatin under the trade name Talin®.

Neohesperidin Dihydrochalcone. Neohesperidin dihydrochalcone is 1,500 times sweeter than sucrose, but it has a flavor profile that is different from sucrose [1, 27]. It is derived from grapefruit rinds and is approved in the United States as a flavor modifier but not for use as a sweetener.

Glycyrrhizin. Glycyrrhizin is 30 times sweeter than sugar but has a different flavor profile. It is derived from licorice extract and is considered GRAS in the United States as a flavoring agent, flavor enhancer, or surfactant. Glycyrrhizin, however, is not approved as a sweetener [27].

BULKING AGENTS

Although many consumers today are looking for foods that are low in calories or "light," they still want an appealing flavor. Often, good-tasting food is synonymous with sweet food. Although it is relatively easy, with the approved nonnutritive sweeteners, to make a low-calorie product sweet, it is more challenging to match the other functions provided by sugar in the formulation [15]. One method is to use a bulking and bodying agent—something that is low in calories but provides volume, texture, and a thickened consistency. Bulking agents are also called *macronutrient substitutes*.

Polydextrose is a bulking agent that has been shown to be safe through extensive testing. It is an approved food additive used—often with an artificial sweetener—in such products as frozen desserts, puddings, baked goods, frostings, and candies. Polydextrose contributes 1 kilocalorie per gram, only one-fourth of the calories that sucrose or other sugars provide. Therefore, when used with aspartame or saccharin, it can reduce the caloric content of an item by 50 percent or more [15]. The materials used in the production of polydextrose are an 89:10:1 mixture of dextrose, sorbitol, and citric acid. One polydextrose product is marketed under the brand name Litesse™.

Other bulking agents include cellulose and maltodextrins. Maltodextrins consist of glucose units with a DE of less than 20 and contribute 4 kilocalories per gram. Maltodextrins are not sweet. Some fat-free products in which bulking agents may be used, such as fat-free cookies and granola bars, contain concentrated fruit juices and dried fruits as substitutes for added sugar. See Chapter 7 for a discussion on cellulose.

PROPERTIES OF SUGARS

Properties of sugar, including solubility, melting point, moisture absorption, fermentation, acid and enzyme hydrolysis, decomposition, and sweetness, are discussed in the following section.

Solubility

In the natural state of foods, sugars are in a **solution**. **Crystallization** of sugar occurs from a sufficiently concentrated sugar solution, a fact that is used in the commercial production of sugar from sugarcane and beets.

The common sugars vary in solubility. Fructose, a monosaccharide, is the most soluble; lactose, a disaccharide, is the least soluble. The relative solubility of sugars is provided in **Table 9–11**. The solubility of all sugars in water is increased by heating. As shown in **Table 9–12**, the amount of sucrose that may be dissolved in 100 grams of water more than doubles when the temperature increases from 68°F (20°C) to 212°F (100°C).

Table 9–11
RELATIVE SOLUBILITY OF SUGAR AT ROOM TEMPERATURE LISTED FROM MOST TO LEAST SOLUBLE

Most soluble	Fructose
	Sucrose
	Glucose
	Maltose
Least soluble	Lactose

Table 9–12
THE SOLUBILITY OF SUCROSE IN WATER INCREASES WHEN THE TEMPERATURE OF THE WATER INCREASES

Grams of Sugar Dissolved in 100 Grams of Water	Temperature
203.9	68°F/20°C
320.5	158°F/70°C
487.2	212°F/100°C

Saturated and Unsaturated Sugar Solutions.
When small amounts of sugar are added to water and the mixture is stirred, the sugar dissolves, and the solution appears to be transparent. We call this solution *unsaturated* because it will dissolve more sugar if it is added. The solution becomes *saturated* when it has dissolved all of the sugar that it can at that particular temperature. A solution is truly saturated when sufficient solute (sugar in this case) has been added so that some remains undissolved at the bottom of the container.

Supersaturated Solutions.   A solution is *supersaturated* when it holds more solute than is usually soluble at a particular temperature. To produce a supersaturated sugar solution, more sugar than can be dissolved at room temperature is added to water, and the mixture is heated to the boiling temperature, at which point all of the sugar dissolves. As this solution is carefully cooled to room temperature without being disturbed, the solution gradually becomes saturated and then supersaturated.

Only by careful cooling and avoiding factors that promote crystallization can a solution be held in the supersaturated state. Because supersaturation is such an unstable state, crystallization eventually occurs, and all excess solute beyond saturation is precipitated or crystallized. Some substances require more time to crystallize from a supersaturated solution than others, unless agitation or seeding (adding a few already formed crystals) starts the process of crystallization. The sugars that are the most soluble, such as fructose, are the most difficult to crystallize; those that are the least soluble, such as lactose, crystallize readily. In making candies, close attention is given to the solubility and ease of crystallization of sugars. (**Figure 9–42**.)

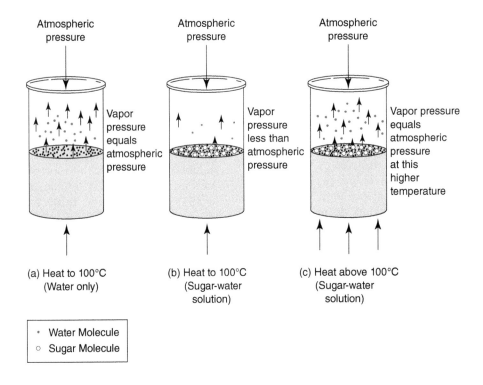

(a) Heat to 100°C (Water only)

(b) Heat to 100°C (Sugar-water solution)

(c) Heat above 100°C (Sugar-water solution)

· Water Molecule
○ Sugar Molecule

Figure 9–42

Pure water boils at 212°F (100°C) at sea level, because its vapor pressure is equal to atmospheric pressure at this point: An equilibrium is established. When sugar or other nonvolatile solute is dissolved in water, some of the nonvolatile sugar molecules displace water molecules on the surface. The vapor pressure of the solution is therefore decreased. Heating to 212°F (100°C) does not increase the water vapor pressure enough to be equal to the atmospheric pressure at this point. More heat must be put into the solution to vaporize more water and increase the vapor pressure enough to equal the atmospheric pressure. Therefore, a sugar solution boils at a higher temperature than pure water. The higher the concentration of sugar or other nonvolatile solute, the higher the boiling point of the solution.

Melting Point and Decomposition by Heat

Granulated sugar, when heated dry in a heavy pan, caramelizes. This process starts with the melting of sucrose (table sugar) at about 320°F (160°C). This clear liquid sugar will undergo several decomposition changes as heating continues. At about 338°F (170°C), the sugar browns and is said to be caramelized. Caramelized sugar has a characteristic caramel flavor along with the brown color. If hot liquid (such as water) is added, the caramelized sugar dissolves and can be used to flavor puddings, ice creams, frostings, and sauces. Sugar is caramelized during the cooking of such foods as peanut brittle and caramel candy.

Caramelization is one type of browning, called *nonenzymatic browning*, because it does not involve enzymes. It is a complex chemical reaction, involving the removal of water, **polymerization**, and the formation of organic acids. Caramel is noncrystalline, soluble in water, and much less sweet than the original sugar from which it was made. Both the extent and the rate of the caramelization reaction are influenced by the type of sugar being heated. Galactose and glucose caramelize at about the same temperature as sucrose (338°F/170°C), but fructose caramelizes at 230°F (110°C) and maltose at about 356°F (180°C).

Absorption of Moisture

Sugars absorb moisture from the atmosphere and are therefore said to be *hygroscopic*. For example, crystalline sugars become caked and lumpy unless stored in dry places. Baked flour mixtures that are rich in sugar take up moisture when surrounded by a moist atmosphere in tightly closed containers.

Fructose is more hygroscopic than the other sugars commonly found in food. Therefore, higher moisture absorption occurs in products containing fructose, such as cakes or cookies made with honey, molasses, or crystalline fructose. These baked products remain moist noticeably longer than similar products made with sucrose.

Fermentation

Most sugars, except lactose, may be fermented by yeasts to produce carbon dioxide gas and alcohol. **Fermentation** is an important reaction in the making of bread and other baked products; the carbon dioxide leavens the product, and the alcohol is volatilized during baking. Fermentation is also important to beer and wine making. The spoilage of canned or cooked products containing sugar may occur by fermentation.

Acid Hydrolysis

Disaccharides are hydrolyzed by weak acids to produce their component monosaccharides. Sucrose is easily hydrolyzed by acid, but maltose and lactose are slowly acted on. The end products of sucrose hydrolysis are a mixture of glucose and fructose. This mixture is commonly called **invert sugar** and is important in candy making. Acids have little effect on monosaccharides.

UP CLOSE
ROCK CANDY

Have you ever enjoyed a sweet treat called rock candy? Rock candy is crystallized sugar made from a supersaturated sugar solution (**Figure 9–43**). Here's how it is made:

- Collect a clean cotton string, popsicle stick, and clean pint-sized canning jar.
- Tie the string to the stick and place the stick across the top of the jar with the string hanging into the jar without touching the bottom.
- Using a heavy pan on a range, heat 2 cups of sugar in 1 cup of water until the sugar dissolves or the temperature on a candy thermometer reads 240°F (116°C).
- Remove the sugar mixture from the heat and add flavoring or coloring if desired.
- Carefully pour the hot sugar mixture into the pint-sized jar, being careful not to spill.
- Let the sugar mixture sit undisturbed for 3 to 10 days with the string hanging into the jar.
- Watch the sugar crystals grow.
- When ready to eat, remove from the jar and break the rock candy into pieces and enjoy!

The science behind rock candy is that a *supersaturated* sugar solution was made by heating more sugar in water than would dissolve without heat. Supersaturated sugar solutions are unstable, and the sugar will begin to crystallize. The string serves as a place for sugar crystals to collect, thereby making rock candy.

Figure 9–43

Rock candy on sticks. (Leonid Nyshko/123RF)

IN DEPTH
THE ROLE OF SUGAR AND BROWNING OF FOODS

Sugar in foods is associated with three types of nonenzymatic browning: (1) caramelization, (2) Maillard reaction, and (3) decomposition by alkalis.

Caramelization

Sugars are caramelized when subjected to dry heat. Sucrose decomposes into glucose and fructose, resulting in buttery, rum-like, nutty, and toasty flavors. If sugar is browned too extensively, bitter off-flavors will result.

Maillard Reaction

Maillard browning can be desirable (browning of baked bread) or undesirable (browning of nonfat dry milk solids after extensive storage). The Maillard reaction is the result of a carbonyl group of a reducing sugar combining with the amino group of a protein with the removal of a molecule of water. Glucose, fructose, galactose, lactose, and maltose are reducing sugars [33]. Sucrose must be broken into glucose and fructose to be involved in a Maillard browning. Maillard browning may occur at room temperature but is accelerated at higher temperatures.

Decomposition by Alkalis

Monosaccharides (glucose and fructose) will brown in the presence of an alkaline solution. In some cases, this type of browning is undesirable (fondant), but in other cases, it can be acceptable or preferred (baked beans and some baked goods).

The extent of acid hydrolysis in a sugar solution is variable, depending on whether the solution is heated, the rate and length of heating, and the kind and concentration of acid used. Application of heat accelerates the reaction. Long, slow heating tends to bring about more hydrolysis than rapid heating for a shorter period. A high acidity level encourages a greater rate and extent of sugar decomposition. Hydrolysis may occur incidentally, as in the cooking of acid fruits and sugar, or it may be brought about purposely as a means of improving the texture or consistency of certain sugar products. In fondant, hydrolysis is often produced by the addition of **cream of tartar**.

Enzyme Hydrolysis

Enzymes also hydrolyze disaccharides. The enzyme *sucrase*, also called *invertase*, is used in the candy industry to hydrolyze some of the sucrose in cream fondant to produce invert sugar composed of fructose and glucose. This process produces soft, semifluid centers in chocolates such as in chocolate-coated cherries.

Invertase is added to fondant during beating or molding. Heat will inactivate the enzyme, and therefore it should not be added before boiling of the sugar solution. Invertase acts best in an acid medium, such as fondant acidified with cream of tartar.

Decomposition by Alkalis

The decomposition of sugars by alkalis also has significance in sugar cookery. Alkaline waters used in boiling sugar solutions may bring about some decomposition of sugars. The monosaccharides, which are only slightly affected by weak acids, are markedly affected by alkalis. Both glucose and fructose are changed into many decomposition products by both standing in and being heated in alkaline solutions. The stronger the alkali solution, the more pronounced are the effects on sugars. The decomposition products of glucose and fructose are brownish, and when the process is extensive, the flavor may be strong and bitter. Examples of the decomposition of sugars by alkalis in food products are provided in **Table 9–13**.

Table 9–13
FOOD EXAMPLES OF THE DECOMPOSITION OF SUGARS BY ALKALIS

Food Product	Characteristics as a Result of Decomposition of Sugars by Alkalis
Fondant	Cream of tartar is often added to a fondant mixture to make it more acidic to prevent the alkali decomposition.
	Fondant is less white when made with glucose or corn syrup *without* the addition of cream of tartar. Hard water is alkaline, and when used for making fondant, an off-white color may be pronounced.
Baked beans	Baked beans are browner in color and have a greater caramelized flavor when made with glucose- or fructose-containing sweeteners, such as corn syrup, rather than table sugar.
Cakes and cookies	Cakes and cookies are browner in color and have a stronger flavor when made with honey and baking soda. Baking soda is alkaline and contributes to the decomposition of sugars.

Sweetness

The flavor of purified sugars is described as being sweet. We humans love sweetness, as do virtually all mammals since history began, with honey, dates, and figs providing early sources of sweetness [7]. The degree of sweetness that we perceive is affected by several factors, including genetic variation among individuals as well as concentration of the sweetener, temperature, viscosity, pH, and the presence of other substances with the sweetener. It is therefore sometimes difficult to make consistent and reproducible comparisons of sweetness among the various sweeteners, including the common sugars.

Lactose is the least sweet of the sugars, followed by maltose, galactose, glucose, and sucrose, with fructose being the sweetest. However, these orders of sweetness do not hold at all temperatures or in all products. For example, fructose was reported to give sweeter lemonade than sucrose when added in equal weights, but sugar cookies, white cake, and vanilla pudding were sweeter when made with sucrose compared with fructose [17]. A maximum sweetness from fructose is most likely to be achieved when it is used with slightly acid, cold foods and beverages.

FUNCTIONS OF SUGAR IN FOOD AND SUGAR COOKERY

Sugar performs a variety of roles in food preparation. Sugar impacts flavor, texture, viscosity, browning, and preservation of foods. Functions of sugar in food are summarized in **Table 9–14**. The importance of sugar in desserts and baked goods will be discussed in Chapters 10 through 17. Sugar in candies and confections will be discussed here.

Sucrose, or table sugar, is a key ingredient in fudge, fondant, brittles, and other candies. In the preparation of concentrated sugar products, such as candies and icings, many of the chemical and physical properties of sugar are of particular importance.

The foundation for candies and cooked frosting is a boiled sugar solution. A boiled sugar solution acts differently than boiled water. Thus, in our discussion of candies, we will start by overviewing properties of solutions.

Boiling Points and Solutions

Boiling Pure Liquids.   Water boils when the **vapor pressure** of water is equal to the atmospheric pressure resting on its surface. Vapor pressure is the pressure caused by gaseous molecules hovering over the surface of liquid water. At the boiling point, the vapor pressure of the liquid pushes against the atmospheric pressure, allowing bubbles in the liquid to break the surface. Once boiling occurs, the temperature of the boiling liquid does not increase; an equilibrium is established. Thus, at sea level, water boils at 212°F (100°C) and no higher, regardless of whether additional heat is applied.

The boiling point of a liquid varies with altitude. At sea level, the atmospheric pressure is about 15 pounds per square inch. However, at higher elevations, the atmospheric pressure is lower. Consequently, the boiling point at higher elevations is lower than that at sea level. For each 960 feet above sea level, the boiling point of water drops 1°C (1.8°F). Thus, in Denver, Colorado, water will boil at about 203°F (95°C). In mountainous areas, the low boiling point of water can significantly interfere with many cooking operations, and thus methods and formulas are modified. A more extensive discussion of vapor pressure, atmospheric pressure, and pressure cookers in relation to the boiling point of water is provided in Chapter 5.

Table 9–14
FUNCTIONS OF SUGAR IN FOOD

Functions of Sugar	Examples
Flavor	Icings, ice cream, cookies, cakes, beverages, and other foods are sweetened with sugar. Acidity is balanced with sugar in foods such as salad dressings, sauces, and condiments.
Color and flavor	Sugar caramelizes, thereby resulting in browning as well as desirable flavors in a wide variety of foods, including meats, vegetables, and baked desserts.
Texture	Sugar can help to control crystal formation in frozen desserts such as ice creams and in candies.
Bulk, volume, or body	Sugar provides "bulk" in foods such as ice cream, preserves, jams, baked goods, and beverages. Beverages that are usually sweetened with sugar may seem thin and watery without the sugar.
Food source	Sugar provides nourishment for the growth of yeast used in yeast breads.
Preservation	Spoilage is prevented in jellies, jams, and preserves by a high sugar level. The sugar binds with the water, thus reducing the moisture available for microbial growth. The natural flavor, texture, and color of frozen or canned fruits are preserved in part with sugar.

Table 9–15
BOILING POINTS OF SUCROSE SOLUTIONS OF VARIOUS CONCENTRATIONS AT SEA LEVEL

Percent Sucrose	10	20	30	40	50	60	70	80	90.8
Boiling point									
°F	212.7	213.1	213.8	214.7	215.6	217.4	223.7	233.6	266.0
°C	100.4	110.6	101.0	101.5	102.0	103.0	106.5	112.0	130.0

Source: Browne's *Handbook of Sugar Analysis.* Reprinted by permission of John Wiley & Sons, Inc.

Boiling Solutions. Anything that *decreases* the vapor pressure of a liquid *increases* its boiling point. Sugar and salt, in solution, decrease vapor pressure and therefore increase the boiling point. Substances in a true solution (e.g., sugar and salt) that do not become volatile or gaseous at the boiling point of water displace water molecules on the surface of the liquid, thereby lowering vapor pressure. More heat is needed to raise the lowered vapor pressure to the point where it is equal to atmospheric pressure (Figure 9–42), and consequently the boiling point is increased.

When dissolved substances ionize in solution, as does salt, the vapor pressure is decreased, and the boiling point of the water is raised to an even greater degree. The larger the number of particles of solute in the solution, the more the vapor pressure is lowered and the higher the temperature of boiling.

Boiling sugar solutions do not reach a constant boiling point the same as plain water. As water evaporates from a sugar solution, the sugar becomes more concentrated, and the boiling temperature further increases. This process continues until all of the water is evaporated or the solubility of the sugar is exceeded. The boiling points of some pure sucrose solutions of various concentrations are given in **Table 9–15**. These boiling points are for sucrose solutions alone and do not apply to mixed sugar solutions, such as sucrose solutions containing corn syrup, glucose, or molasses.

Calibrating and Reading the Thermometer. The first step in candy making is to calibrate the thermometer by taking the temperature of boiling water. If the thermometer does not show the proper temperature for the altitude, an adjustment is made by adding or subtracting, as appropriate, the difference in degrees between the expected and observed temperatures.

In taking the temperature of boiling sugar solutions, the bulb of the thermometer should be completely immersed in the solution but should not touch the bottom of the pan. In reading the scale, the eye should be on a level with the top of the mercury column.

Inversion of Sucrose

Equal amounts of glucose and fructose are called *invert sugar.* Invert sugar is made through the hydrolysis of sucrose. It is important in candy making because invert sugar helps control sugar crystallization in candy making.

Invert sugar helps to control the process of sugar crystallization because a mixture of invert sugar and sucrose is more soluble than a sucrose solution alone and is less easily crystallized. Invert sugar therefore helps to produce desirably small sugar crystals in crystalline candies, such as fondant and fudge.

A small amount of invert sugar is formed by the long, slow heating of a plain sucrose solution; however, the reaction is accelerated by the presence of a weak acid. Cream of tartar, an acid salt, is probably the preferable acid to use in most candy making, because its composition is fairly uniform and measurements are usually quite accurate. In addition, fondant made with cream of tartar is snowy white.

The rate of heating, the duration of heating, and the quantity of cream of tartar used affect the amount of invert sugar formed. If too much acid is used or if the period of heating is too long, too much inversion occurs, with the result that the fondant is extremely

FOCUS ON SCIENCE
THE CHEMICAL REACTION FOR INVERSION OF SUCROSE

The chemical reaction for the inversion of sucrose is provided below. The acid or enzyme enables the reaction but is not consumed in the reaction:

$$C_{12}H_{22}O_{11} + H_2O \xrightarrow[\text{invertase}]{\text{Acid + Heat}} C_6H_{12}O_6 \text{ (glucose)} + C_6H_{12}O_6 \text{ (fructose)}$$

soft or fails to crystallize at all. It has been found that the presence of 43 percent invert sugar prevents crystallization completely. In a fondant cooked to 239°F (115°C) in 20 minutes, 11 percent invert sugar was produced with 1/8 teaspoon cream of tartar and 1 cup (200 grams) of sugar [61]. Glucose, fructose, or invert sugar may be added directly to sucrose solutions in candy making rather than producing invert sugar during cooking by the addition of cream of tartar. Direct addition of these substances makes control of their quantity easier than trying to regulate the amount of invert sugar produced by sucrose hydrolysis. Corn syrup, which contains a high proportion of glucose, is sometimes used instead of cream of tartar in fondant mixtures. The glucose in the sucrose solution has an effect similar to that of invert sugar in increasing the solubility of the sucrose and allowing better control of the crystallization process so that small sugar crystals are produced in the final product.

CLASSIFICATION OF CANDIES

Either *crystalline* or *noncrystalline* candies may be produced from boiled sugar solutions. Crystalline candies are generally soft. If properly made, they are so smooth and creamy that the tiny sugar crystals that make up their microscopic structure cannot be felt on the tongue. The principal crystalline candies are fondant, fudge, and penuche. Divinity, with added egg white, also is a crystalline candy.

Noncrystalline candies are sometimes called *amorphous,* which means "without form." In their preparation, by use of various ingredients and techniques, crystallization of sugar is prevented. Noncrystalline candies may be chewy, such as caramels, or hard, such as butterscotch, toffees, and brittles.

Crystalline Candies

Essential steps in the making of most crystalline candies include: (1) development of a complete solution of the crystalline sugar; (2) boiling of the sugar solution to concentrate the sugar; (3) control of crystallization to form small, fine crystals; and (4) ripening.

Boiling of Sugar Solution. Sugar is boiled in liquid (e.g., water or milk) to dissolve the sugar and evaporate part of the water to create the desired concentration of sugar. Undissolved sugar crystals in the sugar solution need to be prevented because these sugar crystals will seed the mixture, causing premature crystallization and a grainy candy.

During the cooking of the sugar solution, one of two methods may be used to remove all undissolved sugar crystals from the side of the pan. A lid may be used to cover the pan during initial cooking. As steam is produced, all crystals on the sides of the

pan will be dissolved. Because evaporation of water is necessary to concentrate the sugar, the lid is removed for the majority of the cooking period. A second method of dissolving sugar crystals is to wash the crystals from the pan with a small piece of moistened paper towel or cheesecloth wrapped around a fork (**Figure 9–44**). Both methods (initial covering of the pan or washing pan sides) are designed to ensure that no sugar crystals remain. An alternative method is brushing down side of pan with cold water using a pastry brush (**Figure 9–45**).

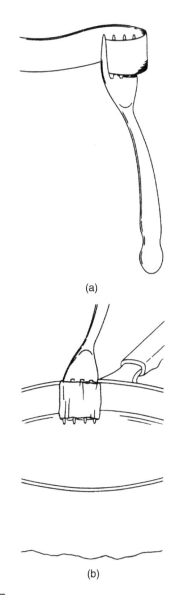

(a)

(b)

Figure 9–44

Complete solution of sugar. Wipe all sugar crystals from the sides of the pan as the candy mixture begins to boil. (a) Roll a small strip of moistened paper towel or cheesecloth around the tines of the fork. (b) Dip the covered fork in and out of a cup of clean water as the sides of the pan are wiped free of sugar crystals. The extra water on the wrapped fork goes into the boiling sugar solution.

Figure 9–45

Cold water can be brushed on side of the pan with a pastry brush to remove sugar crystals. (Richard Embery/Pearson Education)

Figure 9–46

A special candy thermometer that measures very high temperatures is used to determine end point temperatures when cooking points of candy. Temperatures may need to be adjusted for every 500 ft above sea level. (Richard Embery/Pearson Education)

Later contamination of the sugar solution with crystals also must be avoided. Sugar crystals may contaminate the solution if stirring and vigorous boiling splash syrup on the sides of the pan above the liquid. This splashed syrup can dry, crystallize, and drop into the sugar syrup when cooling. The stirring spoon can be another source of sugar crystals. Therefore, the stirring spoon should be well rinsed before each use to avoid the introduction of dried crystals.

Boiling to Concentrate Sugar Solution. As a sugar solution is boiled, water evaporates and the temperature of the mixture rises. Each candy has a recommended final cooking temperature (**Figure 9–46**). Crystalline candies are generally cooked to the soft ball stage, or about 234°F (112°C). If a candy is undercooked, the sugar concentration will be too low, and the candy may be soft or runny. Testing the doneness of candy mixtures may be accomplished by the use of a thermometer or by evaluating consistency after dropping the hot candy mixture into very cold water.

At altitudes above sea level, the final boiling temperatures should be lowered to the extent that the boiling point of water is decreased below 212°F (100°C). The results of the cold-water tests of doneness are compared with the temperatures of cooking in **Table 9–16** and are shown in **Figure 9–47**. The traditional cold water test is useful if a candy thermometer is not available. The cold water test involves dropping a few drops of cooked sugar mixture into a small bowl of very cold water. Hardness of sugar mixture is then checked with fingers—soft ball, hard ball, hard crack, etc. [28].

Humidity, ingredients, and rate of cooking may all have an impact on the cooking of sugar solutions. Candies are best prepared on a day with low humidity. When the humidity is high, higher temperatures are needed to evaporate the additional liquid absorbed in damp weather. When corn syrup is used in

(a)

(b)

(c)

Figure 9–47

The concentration of sugar syrups is best measured with a candy thermometer. Spooning a few drops of the syrup into very cold water will provide another measure of concentration as shown by the soft, hard, and hard crack stages in these pictures. (a) Soft ball stage. (b) Hard ball stage. (c) Hard crack stage. (Richard Embery/Pearson Education)

Table 9–16
TEMPERATURES AND TESTS FOR SYRUP AND CANDIES

Test of Doneness	Temperature of Syrup at Sea Level*	Description of Test	Kinds of Products
Thread	230–233°F (110–112°C)	Syrup spins a 2-inch thread when dropped from fork or spoon.	Syrup
Soft ball	234–240°F (112–115°C)	Syrup, when dropped into very cold water, forms a soft ball that flattens on removal from water.	Fudge, fondant, penuche, and pralines
Firm ball	244–248°F (118–120°C)	Syrup, when dropped into very cold water, forms a firm ball that does not flatten on removal from water.	Caramels and marshmallows
Hard ball	250–266°F (121–130°C)	Syrup, when dropped into very cold water, forms a ball that is hard enough to hold its shape yet is plastic.	Divinity, butterscotch, saltwater taffy, and syrup for popcorn balls
Soft crack	270–290°F (132–143°C)	Syrup, when dropped into very cold water, separates into threads that are hard but not brittle.	Toffee and taffies
Hard crack	295–310°F (146–154°C)	Syrup, when dropped into very cold water, separates into threads that are hard and brittle.	Brittle (peanut brittle), hard candy, and lollipops
Clear liquid followed by browning	310–338°F (154–170°C)	Sugar liquefies, followed by browning. Continued browning will result in blackening and burning.	Sugar caramelization

* For each increase of 500 feet in elevation, cook the syrup to a temperature 1°F lower than the temperature called for at sea level. If readings are taken in Celsius, for each 960 feet of elevation, cook the syrup to a temperature 1°C lower than that called for at sea level.

candy, a slightly lower temperature will result in the desired stage of firmness. The desired rate of cooking depends partly on the proportions of ingredients used. Faster boiling is necessary if a high proportion of water is used to avoid too long a cooking period and consequently the production of too much invert sugar. Violent boiling is also best avoided because of the larger amount of syrup that is splashed on the sides of the pan.

Control of Crystallization. The control of crystallization is important to produce a smooth and creamy crystalline candy. Crystallization is in part controlled by ingredients in the recipe. The presence of glucose, corn syrup, invert sugar, fats, and proteins interfere with crystallization in fondant, fudge, and other candies. Glucose, corn syrup, or invert sugar affect crystallization because they make the sugar solution more soluble and therefore decrease the ease of crystal formation. Other substances, including fats from milk, cream, butter, margarine, and chocolate and proteins from milk and egg white do not themselves crystallize. They do, however, physically interfere with the process of sugar crystallization, retarding the growth of crystals.

Crystallization is also controlled by the candy-making procedures followed. As discussed previously, a complete solution must be obtained by ensuring that undissolved sugar crystals do not seed the sugar solution. The cooling process is also important. Most crystalline candies should be cooled to about 104°F (40°C) either in the pan or on a marble-top counter. Cooling of the sugar syrup will be more rapid on a cool marble-top surface. If poured onto a marble-top surface, the sugar syrup should be poured quickly from the pan. Scraping, prolonged dripping from the pan, or jostling of the poured syrup will usually start crystallization and should therefore be avoided. If a thermometer is placed in the syrup to determine when the syrup is ready for beating, it should be read without moving it in the syrup.

As the hot syrup cools, it becomes saturated and then supersaturated because it is holding in solution more solute (sugar) than is normally soluble at the lower temperatures. To produce a smooth, creamy texture, many fine crystals—not large crystals—must be formed. Thus, conditions must be conducive to the formation of many nuclei or small clumps of molecules within the supersaturated solution. These nuclei act as centers around which crystal formation may begin. Sugar solutions usually require a high degree of supersaturation before formation of nuclei and crystallization start.

Cooling the candy mixture to about 104°F (40°C) before starting to beat or otherwise agitate favors the formation of more nuclei and finer crystals. Agitation also promotes the formation of finer crystals. Therefore, it is important to stir a crystalline candy not only until crystallization starts but also until it is complete. As crystallization proceeds, the candy stiffens and becomes dulled. It may soften temporarily as the result of the heat of crystallization being given off as the crystals form.

The temperature of the candy before beating is started is important, because the temperature at which crystallization occurs affects the size of crystals. In general, the higher the temperature at which crystallization occurs, the faster the rate of crystallization and the more difficult it is to keep the crystals separated, resulting in larger crystals. The viscosity of the solution is also greater at lower temperatures. High viscosity is a further aid in the production of fine crystals because it retards crystallization. **Figure 9–48** shows the sizes of crystals formed in fondant beaten at different temperatures. The syrup could be cooled to so low a temperature that beating is impossible. Too low a temperature also may hinder the formation of many nuclei.

Ripening. As crystalline candy stands after crystallization is complete, it becomes somewhat more moist and smooth and kneads more easily because some of the very small crystals dissolve in the syrup. Changes that occur during the initial period of storage are called *ripening*. Adsorbed substances that interfere with crystallization aid in retarding the growth of crystals during storage.

Fudge. Fudge is a crystalline candy and therefore follows the basic principles of crystalline candy preparation. Like other crystalline candies, a sugar solution is first boiled and then cooled, followed by beating. Fudge is usually beaten in the pan. When crystallization is almost complete, the initially glossy fudge becomes dull, and the whole mass softens slightly (**Figure 9–49**). Fudge should be poured from the pan before it hardens.

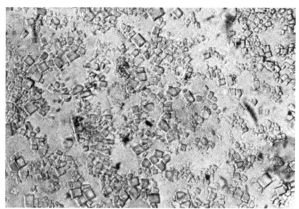

Crystals from fondant made with sugar, water, and cream of tartar, boiled to 239°F (115°C) and cooled to 104°F (40°C) before beating.

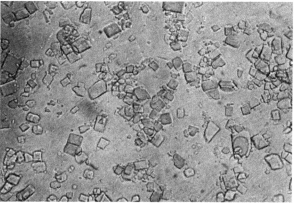

Crystals from fondant made with sugar and water with 7 percent glucose added, boiled to 239°F (115°C) and cooled to 104°F (40°C) before beating.

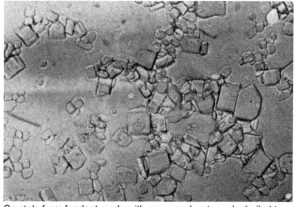

Crystals from fondant made with sugar and water only, boiled to 239°F (115°C) and cooled to 104°F (40°C) before beating.

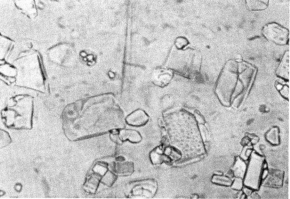

Crystals from fondant made with sugar and water only, boiled to 239°F (115°C) and beaten immediately.

Figure 9–48

Comparison of sugar crystal size with various methods of making fondant. (Courtesy of Dr. Sybil Woodruff and the Journal of Physical Chemistry)

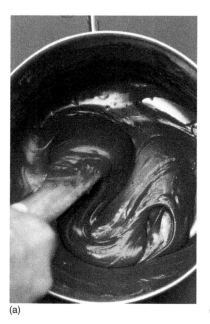
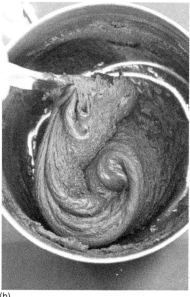

(a)   (b)

Figure 9–49

(a) Traditionally, fudge is heated to 234°F (112°C), then cooled to 120°F (49°C) when it should be vigorously beaten as it begins to thicken. During beating, the fudge becomes thicker and less glossy, but it remains smooth. When properly beaten, the fudge is thick, not runny, and it can be poured into a pan for final cooling. (b) When fudge is beaten too long, it becomes very dull, grainy in texture, and it may be too stiff to pour into a pan. (© Douglas and Barbara Scheule)

In fudge, usually the butter or margarine, the fat of chocolate, and the milk proteins and fat furnish the substances that interfere with crystallization. Acid is sometimes used, and corn syrup may be used. If brown sugar replaces part or all of the white sugar, as in penuche, some invert sugar is introduced into the mixture. Also, a small amount of acid in the brown sugar helps invert sucrose. Therefore, brown sugar fudge (penuche) crystallizes less rapidly than white sugar fudge.

Fondant.   Fondant is a soft, smooth candy made from sugar, water, and cream of tartar or corn syrup (**Figure 9–50**). Fondant has many possible uses. It may be made into bonbons, which are fondant centers dipped in melted fondant, or into fondant loaves, which have fruit and nut mixtures added. Chocolate candies often have centers made of fondant, including chocolate-covered cherries. Fondant patties are made from melted fondant that is flavored and colored as desired. Rolled fondant is used to create a smooth surface on

decorated cakes. Candy cookbooks suggest many specific combinations of fondant with other ingredients.

In fondant, invert sugar is encouraged with the addition of a cream of tartar (an acid) or corn syrup to promote the development of small crystals. Some recipes may use milk or cream (as the liquid), which will increase the creamy character of fondant. Standard proportions for fondant are provided in **Table 9–17**.

Fondant is usually poured out onto a flat surface such as a cool marble top. After initial cooling, the outer edges are scraped and folded into the center with a spatula until it becomes opaque. Once it can be handled by hands dusted with confectioner's sugar, it should be kneaded until thick and smooth. Fondant is usually stored for 24 hours to ripen. Various color and flavor combinations can be added to fondant, as suggested in **Table 9–18**.

Table 9–17
PROPORTIONS FOR FONDANT

With Cream of Tartar	With Corn Syrup
2 cups (400 g) granulated sugar	2 cups (400 g) granulated sugar
¼ tsp cream of tartar	1 to 1½ Tbsp (21–39 g) syrup
1 cup (237 mL) water	1 cup (237 mL) water

Table 9–18
COLOR AND FLAVOR COMBINATIONS USED FOR CANDY

Color	Flavor
Red	Oil of cinnamon or cloves
Green	Oil of lime
White	Oil of peppermint
Pink	Oil of wintergreen
Yellow	Oil of lemon
Orange	Oil of orange

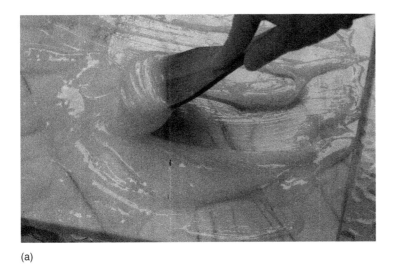
(a)

(b)

Figure 9–50

(a) Fondant is heated until it reaches the soft ball stage at 240°F (115°C) and then poured out on a flat surface to cool to 104°F (40°C). It is then manipulated until it begins to thicken and whiten in color. (b) The still warm fondant is gathered into a ball and kneaded until smooth. (© Douglas and Barbara Scheule)

Noncrystalline Candies

Sugar does not crystallize in noncrystalline candies. The crystallization is prevented by (1) cooking to very high temperatures so that the finished product hardens quickly or solidifies before the crystals have a chance to form, (2) adding such large amounts of interfering substances that the crystals cannot form, or (3) combining these methods.

Brittles. Brittles are cooked to temperatures that are high enough to produce a hard, brittle candy that solidifies before it has a chance to crystallize. The brown color and characteristic flavor of brittles result from nonenzymatic browning reactions, probably both the **Maillard** type and the caramelization of sugar. The development of caramel also helps to prevent crystallization of sugar in the brittles because it is noncrystalline.

Some brittles are made merely by melting and caramelizing sucrose. Soda is sometimes a constituent of brittles and is added after cooking is completed. It neutralizes acid decomposition products and forms carbon dioxide gas, which gives the candy a porous texture. The flavor is also made milder and less bitter by the use of soda. The degree of bitterness in a brittle depends on the extent of decomposition of the sugar. Brittles include butterscotch, nut brittles, sesame seed, and toffee.

Caramels. Caramels are firm, noncrystalline candies containing large amounts of interfering substances. They are cooked to temperatures between those for crystalline candies and hard brittle candies.

The added substances that interfere with crystallization are usually butter or margarine and viscous corn syrup or molasses, which contain glucose, fructose, or invert sugar. Corn syrup also contains dextrins, which do not crystallize. Acid hydrolysis may be used to produce invert sugar, but more inversion is necessary for caramels than for fondant. Fats and proteins in milk or cream also aid in preventing crystallization. The final cooking temperature varies with the kind and proportion of ingredients. The brown color of caramels results chiefly from the Maillard reaction. The color and flavor of caramels develop better with long, slow heating than with rapid cooking. The characteristic flavor of plain caramels may be modified somewhat by the addition of chocolate or molasses.

Taffy. Taffy can be made from a simple sucrose syrup with the addition of cream of tartar, vinegar, or lemon juice to invert part of the sucrose and prevent crystallization. Flavoring extracts may be added when the solution has cooled sufficiently for pulling. Glucose, corn syrup, or molasses can be used instead of acid. Taffies are harder than caramels and therefore require higher cooking temperatures.

Spun Sugar

Spun sugar looks like long hairlike threads of sugar (**Figure 9–51**). A two-to-one sugar-to-water solution with inverted sugar cooked to hard crack stage can be used to make long hairlike threads of sugar by whisking hot syrup across dowels. The syrup hardens immediately and retains the threads-of-sugar shape.

FOCUS ON SCIENCE
WHAT IS HAPPENING WHEN FUDGE IS COOLING?

After boiling the solution and reaching the end-point temperature, the syrup reaches saturation very soon after it starts to cool. If everything was done precisely, the sugar does not come back out of the solution. Instead, the syrup continues to cool as a supersaturated solution. The solid phase—in this case, sugar—cannot start to crystallize without something to serve as a nucleus. If a single sugar crystal is present, however, the syrup will start to crystallize, and the crystals will grow steadily as the syrup continues to cool, resulting in grainy fudge.

That is why the inversion of sugar is important in the syrup. Large crystals of sucrose have a harder time forming when molecules of fructose and glucose are present. Crystals interlock together and form large molecules. If some of the molecules are a different size and shape, they will not fit together, and a crystal does not form.

CHOCOLATE DIPPING

The chocolate used for ordinary culinary purposes is not ideal for dipping candies. Dipping chocolate should be of fine quality and contain sufficient cocoa butter to promote hardening with a smooth, glossy finish. Confectionary chocolate or other chocolates specifically intended for dipping may be purchased. If using chocolate chips or other culinary chocolate, use 12 ounces of chocolate with 2 tablespoons of shortening and temper it over hot water.

Candy centers to be coated with chocolate should be prepared several hours before dipping so that they are firm enough to handle easily. An exception is fondant centers to which invertase enzyme has been added; this type of fondant becomes softer the longer it stands (**Figure 9–52**).

Successful chocolate dipping depends largely on the use of a suitable chocolate, the control of temperatures and avoidance of a humid atmosphere, and thorough stirring or hand manipulation of the chocolate while it is melting and cooling and, as much as possible, while dipping. Manipulation of the chocolate ensures uniform blending of the cocoa butter with the other chocolate constituents and produces a more even coating (**Figure 9–53**).

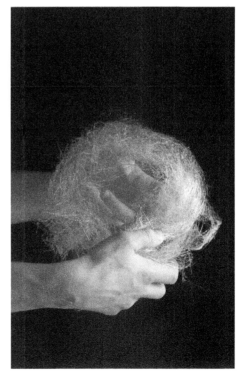

Figure 9–51

Spinning sugar solution to hard crack stage and sugar threads of boiled mixture will harden immediately and retain their form. (Richard Embery/Pearson Education)

Figure 9–52

A dipping fork with two or more long prongs can be used to dip chocolates. (© Amanda Frye)

Figure 9–53

Dipping chocolate truffle centers into tempered chocolate coating. (Richard Embery/Pearson Education)

Temperatures and Techniques

Room temperature and humidity are well controlled in commercial chocolate dipping rooms. The temperature should be 60−70°F (15−20°C). A clear, cool day of low relative humidity is desirable. Drafts should be avoided, as uneven cooling affects the gloss and color of chocolates.

Even melting of the chocolate is facilitated by grating, shaving, or fine chopping. The chocolate should be melted over hot (not boiling) water; higher temperatures may allow the cocoa butter to separate out. While the chocolate is melting, it should be stirred continuously. Stirring prevents uneven heating and overheating and maintains a uniform blend. Water should not be allowed to get into the melting chocolate, as it can cause the chocolate to *seize* and become lumpy.

After the chocolate has melted, it should be taken to a temperature of about 120°F (49°C) for tempering. It should then be continuously stirred while being cooled to about 85°F (29°C). At this point, the chocolate is ready for dipping. The range of temperatures at which chocolates can be satisfactorily dipped is narrow; hence, rapid dipping is necessary. Fondant centers may be dropped into the chocolate, coated, and lifted out with a wire chocolate dipper or a two-tined fork. The coated chocolate is inverted on waxed paper. Another method of dipping chocolates is to pour the melted chocolate onto a marble-top surface and stir it by hand. Fondant centers may be rolled in the melted chocolate; the surplus chocolate is removed by tapping the fingers lightly on the marble surface, and then the coated chocolate is dropped quickly onto waxed paper.

Defects of Dipped Chocolates

The chief defects of dipped chocolates are gray or streaked surfaces, a broad base on the dipped chocolate, or sticky spots on the surface. Gray surfaces are caused by unfavorable room temperatures, incorrect temperatures during melting and handling the chocolate, direct drafts, excessive humidity, insufficient stirring of the chocolate, and not rapid enough cooling of the chocolate. The surface of a defective chocolate appears dull and gray because the fat of the chocolate has not crystallized in a stable form.

A broad base on the dipped chocolate results from dipping at too high temperatures or from failure to remove excess chocolate after dipping. Sticky spots result from leakage of the centers because of incomplete coating with chocolate. These spots are particularly likely to occur in chocolates made from fondants that liquefy on standing.

THE CONFECTIONERY INDUSTRY

A variety of ingredients are available to the commercial confectioner to help improve texture, prevent defects, add gloss, enhance flavor release, and aid processing in the manufacture of candies. New candy, flavor and texture combinations are being introduced in the marketplace. Quick-setting starch to reduce drying time for jelly gum candies, encapsulated flavors and colors for customized products, blends of acidulants to improve taste properties of hard candies, lecithin products to act as emulsifiers in caramels and toffees, and polishing and sealing systems for chocolate-based products have been used in the confectionary business. Sugar-free and low-fat confections are being developed in increasing quantities. Various hydrocolloids, such as pectins, starches, gelatin, and gums, are playing important roles as textural or stabilizing agents in the manufacture of many confectionery products, including lower-fat and calorie-reduced

Figure 9-54
Candy being chocolate coated. (Photowind/Shutterstock)

items [11, 43]. Automated and specialized equipment are also used in the confection industry (**Figure 9–54**), but food science principles are the same.

SUGAR SYRUPS (SIRUPS)

Sugar syrups are important in food preparation. These sugar syrups are also important in some beverages, canning, candy production, frosting, meringues, cake moisteners, and so on. These syrups may be simple syrups or cooked syrups (discussed earlier).

Simple syrups are referred to as "stock" syrups. Simple syrup serves the basis for cocktails and sweetened beverages such as lemonade and sweetened ice teas. Sometimes simple syrup is called moistening or dessert syrup when it is used to moisten cake, sauces, or beverages.

Simple syrups are a solution of granulated sugar and water. The simple syrup's concentration is based on sugar to water ratio. Syrups are typically classified as light, medium, or heavy depending on the ratio of sugar to water. The syrup concentration depends on the end use purpose. Syrup concentrations are important in canning. Cold water can dissolve double its weight of sugar. Concentrated syrups must be heated to form a solution [28].

Hydrometers measure specific gravity and show sugar concentration of syrup or Brix (**Figure 9–55**). Brix is the measurement in percentage by weight of sucrose in pure water solution. Brix degrees (°Brix) is only valid for pure sucrose solutions; pure sucrose is only that extracted from sugarcane or sugar beet. Density meters and refractometers are used to measure density of other sweetened solutions such as high-fructose corn syrups (HFCS); pure sucrose solutions can also be measured. Baumé scale shows degrees of concentration 0°–50°. The density (D) is the relationship between the mass (m) and volume (v) of a substance (D = m/v). The more sugar dissolved in a liquid, the denser the solution, which will be measured on the hydrometer Baumé scale. The higher the number, the more concentrated the solution. Hydrometer should register 0° at 58°F (15°C) in water.

The exact sugar content is a crucial parameter of end food products. Brix hydrometers, density meters, and refractory are used to measure sugar concentrations in the food and beverage processing industry; but digital density meters and digital refractometers are the newer technology.

Procedures for preparing simple syrups involve combing water and sugar in heavy saucepan. Bring mixture to boil without stirring to prevent crystallization. Boil syrup for 1 minute or until proper density is reached. Remove syrup from heat. Flavorings can be added after cooking for a flavored syrup. Cool and refrigerate [28]. **Table 9–19** shows proportions, Baumé readings, and some standard uses for light, medium, and heavy syrups.

Table 9–19
SIMPLE SYRUP PROPORTIONS

Type of Syrup	Sugar	Water	Baumé Scale	Use
Light	1 parts	2 part	17°–20°	Canning, sorbets, spongecake moisteners
Medium	1 parts	1½ part	21°–24°	Canning, candied citrus peels
Heavy	1 part	1 part	28°–30°	All-purpose syrup, canning

Source: Reference 28.

STUDY QUESTIONS

Consumption Trends and Nutrition

1. Discuss the sweetener production and consumption trends. How have these trends impacted Americans' health?

2. Discuss the nutritive value of sweeteners. What healthy and unhealthy roles might be associated with sweeteners?

3. Discuss trends in sweetener consumption in the United States in recent years.

Crystalline Forms of Sugars and Syrups, Molasses and Honey

4. Various types of sugars and syrups are available on the market. Describe the major characteristics of each of the following:
   (a) Granulated sugar (sucrose)
   (b) Powdered sugar
   (c) Brown sugar
   (d) Corn syrup
   (e) High-fructose corn syrup
   (f) Molasses
   (g) Honey
   (h) Maple syrup

5. Describe the similarities and differences between nutritive and nonnutritive sweeteners.

Nutritive versus Nonnutritive Sweeteners

6. (a) Give several examples of nonnutritive, high-intensity, or alternative sweeteners.
   (b) Discuss some advantages and limitations to the use of alternative sweeteners in manufactured foods.
   (c) Give examples of bulking agents and describe their role in the production of reduced-sugar foods.

7. Discuss the sweeteners produced in the United States.

8. List some sugar alcohols and describe their possible uses in foods.

Properties of Sugars

9. Sugars have many properties that are important in the preparation of candies and other sugar-containing foods.
   (a) List the common sugars in order of their solubilities in water at room temperature. Describe how the solubility of sugars is affected by temperature.

   (b) Describe a saturated and a supersaturated solution. Explain the significance of a supersaturated solution in making crystalline candies.

   (c) What happens when sugar is heated in a dry state above its melting point? Why is this reaction important in food preparation?

   (d) What is meant by *hygroscopic*? Which is the most hygroscopic sugar?

   (e) Name the two monosaccharides that result from the hydrolysis of sucrose. What catalysts may cause sucrose hydrolysis? Describe examples of the importance of this reaction in food preparation, particularly in candy making.

   (f) Describe examples from food preparation of the effect of sugar decomposition by alkali.

   (g) Compare the common sugars for relative sweetness. Discuss several factors that affect these comparisons. Under what conditions is fructose likely to taste most sweet?

Functions of Sugar in Food and Sugar Cookery

10. (a) What is the effect of sugar on the boiling point of water? Explain.
    (b) Describe what happens as you continue to boil a sugar solution.

Classification of Candies

11. (a) Name two major classifications for candies. Describe the general characteristics of each type.
    (b) Classify caramels, toffee, fondant, taffy, butterscotch, fudge, brittles, and penuche into the appropriate groups described in question 11a.

12. Describe the basic steps involved in the preparation of crystalline candies such as fondant and fudge. Explain what is happening in each step and how crystallization is controlled.

13. Describe the basic steps involved in the preparation of brittles and caramels. Explain how crystallization is prevented in each case.

14. Suggest several uses for basic fondant.

Chocolate Dipping

15. Describe and explain several precautions that must be observed for successful dipping of chocolates.

10
Frozen Desserts

Frozen desserts have been enjoyed in one form or another since as early as the second century B.C. (**Figure 10–1**). Frozen ices and flavored snow evolved into ice cream and the wide variety of other frozen desserts we enjoy today. The first advertisement for ice cream in the United States appeared in 1777. President Thomas Jefferson's handwritten vanilla ice cream recipe is housed in the Library of Congress archives (**Figure 10–2**) [21]. Until 1800, ice cream was rare and enjoyed primarily by the affluent. Around 1800, the insulated ice house was invented, allowing ice to be stored and used year round. Ice cream production became a commercial enterprise as technologies continued to change. By the mid-1800s, however, ice cream became more widely available in soda fountain shops [15]. The improvement of freezer technology and affordable freezers for consumers also boosted the ice cream manufacturing since consumers could store frozen ice creams and novelties in their home freezers. The first home freezers were produced in 1940. Before that time, Americans had to make their own ice cream at home or eat at a location that could store frozen goods. Today, many consumers enjoy ice cream and other frozen desserts purchased from their local grocery stores, although ice cream parlors and custard stands remain a treat.

The ingredients, method of freezing, and storage all have an impact on the quality of frozen desserts. In this chapter, the following topics will be discussed:

- Consumption trends and nutritive values
- Types of frozen desserts

Figure 10–2

Thomas Jefferson's handwritten ice cream recipe is housed in the Library of Congress, Manuscript Division. Thomas Jefferson was an American Founding Father, statesman, diplomat, principal author of the Declaration of Independence, and third President of the United States (1801–1809). He was the first to serve ice cream at the White House. (Library of Congress, Manuscript Division)

- Characteristics of frozen desserts
- Ingredients in frozen desserts and light frozen desserts
- Commercial ice cream processing
- Ice cream preparation at home
- Storage

CONSUMPTION TRENDS AND NUTRITION

Consumption Trends

The average American consumes almost 22 pounds of ice cream and frozen dairy products per year. The United States, New Zealand, and Australia are the top ice cream consumers in the world. The United States Department of Agriculture publishes market data on ice cream production. Overall, there has been a general decrease in frozen dairy products since 1975 (**Figure 10–3**). However, a slight pick-up in the category was

Figure 10–1

Frozen desserts such as ice cream are often served in a waffle cone. Waffle and wafer cones are discussed in Chapter 16. (Phovoir/Shutterstock)

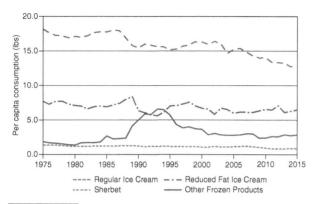

Figure 10–3

U.S. frozen dairy product consumption 1975–2015. (USDA/ERS/ Graph Credit © Amanda Frye and Sam Frye)

Figure 10–4a

Frozen novelty item such as this are typically called drum sticks. (Anette Linnea Rasmussen/Shutterstock)

Figure 10–4b

Frozen novelty ice pop, sometimes called a popsicle, is a frozen colored, flavored ice on a stick. It was first introduced in the United States in 1905. (Svetlana Foote/Shutterstock)

seen in 2015. The frozen novelties represent an annual $4.9 billion business with increasing sales up to 4 percent in 2017 [26] (**Figure 10–4**). Growth trends focusing on premium, super premium, and snack novelty products are predicted through 2022.

Ice cream represents 87 percent of the total sales, with frozen yogurt, water ices, sherbets, and other products representing the remainder of the market.

Figure 10–4c

Ice cream sandwich is another novelty with cookie sandwiched with ice cream filling. (Viennetta/Shutterstock)

Figure 10–4d

Ice cream bars are molded novelty ice cream products. Continuous ice cream freezers can allow for ice crystal ice cream to be extruded into individual molds that are quick frozen. Ice cream is unmolded and enrobed or coated. A stick used to hold the coated ice cream is inserted; the product is hardened, packaged, and stored (−28 degrees C). (Johan Swanepoel/Shutterstock)

Vanilla is the most popular ice cream flavor followed by chocolate. Of the total soft and hard ice cream market, 26 percent is low fat and nonfat. Gelato sales have picked up in the United States. The U.S. Department of Agriculture food availability data figures are reported in pounds. In 2015, this data set reported the following annual per capita figures: 13.1 pounds ice cream, 6.5 pounds of low-fat ice cream, 0.9 pound of sherbet, and 2.9 pounds of frozen yogurt and other miscellaneous frozen desserts, including frozen ices [21].

The new 2018 nutrition labeling regulations are expected to impact ice cream with declaration of added sugars and increased serving size of ice cream from ½ cup to ⅔ cup as manufactures seek ways to minimize added sugars [19] (**Figure 10–5**). New trends in fewer ingredients and clean labels may be boosting smaller

Figure 10–5

Ice cream can be scooped into individual servings. (Subbotina Anna/Shutterstock)

ice cream novelty manufacturers [7]. Artificial flavors are being replaced with natural flavors. New flavors including tea-flavored ice cream are being introduced [6]. Inclusions, an item added to an item or "included," are popular in frozen dairy products [1]. Frozen desserts made from nondairy almond milk and frozen cake batter with coating are other frozen dessert items. Trends are moving away from bioengineered ingredients to "clean labels" with few ingredients.

Nutritive Value

Ice cream, frozen yogurt, and other frozen desserts contribute protein, calcium, vitamin A, riboflavin, and other nutrients to the diet. Those desserts containing higher percentages of milk will result in a greater contribution of nutrients. Fat and sugar are also found in frozen desserts, thereby resulting in a generally high caloric value. Frozen desserts must have a higher sugar content to taste desirably sweet compared to most other types of desserts because of the dulling effect of cold temperatures on taste sensations. Fruit ices, sherbets, and

Figure 10–6

Lemon sorbet is one of the several types of frozen desserts that may be prepared and served. (Richard Embery/Pearson Education)

Figure 10–7

Gelato is an Italian-style ice cream rich in egg yolks with little air incorporation. There is no standard of identity for gelato in the United States. Products sold as gelato may not meet ice cream standards or may contain oil instead of milk fat. (CoolR/Shutterstock)

sorbets, although generally lower in fat than ice cream, have a higher sugar content (**Figure 10–6**).

Reduced-fat and reduced-sugar frozen desserts are available in the marketplace. Prior to the passage of the 1990 Nutrition Labeling and Education Act, reduced-fat ice creams were labeled "ice milk." Starting in 1994, reduced-fat, low-fat, light, and fat-free ice creams were sold in place of ice milk [15]. The regulatory limitations for these various types of desserts may be found in **Table 10–1**. (See Chapter 3 for more information about the Nutrition Labeling and Education Act.)

TYPES OF FROZEN DESSERTS

The three main types of frozen desserts are ice creams, sherbets, and water ices [3]. Some ice creams contain enough egg yolk solids to be considered a custard-type ice cream. Several ice creams also

Figure 10–8

Soft-serve ice cream served in plain wafer cone. (Shutterstock)

TABLE 10–1
CLASSIFICATION OF COMMERCIALLY FROZEN DESSERTS

Frozen Dessert	Description
Ice cream	Ice cream is produced by freezing (while stirring) a pasteurized mix containing at least 10 percent milk fat, 20 percent total milk solids, sweeteners, and other optional ingredients that stabilize or flavor the mix. The finished ice cream must weigh at least 4.5 pounds per gallon and contain at least 1.6 pounds of food solids per gallon.
Frozen custard, French ice cream, French custard ice cream	Eggs are added to the ingredients found in ice cream. The total weight of egg yolk solids is not less than 1.4 percent of the finished weight. If it is a bulky ice cream, the egg solids must be not less than 1.12 percent of the finished weight.
Reduced-fat ice cream	Ice cream made with 25 percent less fat than in the standard reference ice cream.
"Light" ice cream	Contains at least 50 percent or less total fat or 33 percent less calories compared to the standard reference ice cream.
Low-fat ice cream	Not more than 3 grams of milk fat in a 4-fluid-ounce serving.
Nonfat ice cream	Less than 0.5 gram of milk fat per serving.
Gelato	An Italian-style ice cream that is rich in egg yolk solids and total solids. Contains little air and no stabilizers or emulsifiers. Denser than ice cream with 3–8 percent fat (**Figure 10–7**).
Bulky flavored ice cream (Inclusions)	Contains a significant amount of ingredients such as nuts, fruit, confections, cookies, and cocoa. The minimum level of fat may be reduced in these ice creams.
Soft-serve	Ice cream that is served after being drawn from the freezer without hardening (**Figure 10–8**).
Mellorine	Milk fat is replaced in whole or part by vegetable or animal fat. Must contain not less than 6 percent fat and 2.7 percent protein.
Parevine	A frozen dessert similar to ice cream; however, it contains no dairy ingredients.
Tofutti	Brand name of a frozen dessert that resembles ice cream but contains no dairy ingredients. Contains tofu or soybean curd with sweeteners, stabilizers, and a nondairy fat.
Frozen yogurt	Frozen yogurt is similar to ice cream; however, it is generally lower in fat, and it must contain bacteria cultures, which are typical for yogurt.
Fruit sherbet	A pasteurized frozen product containing fruit juices, sweeteners, stabilizers, 2 to 5 percent total milk solids, 1 to 2 percent milk fat, and a minimal acidity of 0.35 percent. Sherbet must be a minimum of 6 pounds per gallon, which is equivalent to a 50 percent overrun. Sherbet is generally higher in sugar than ice cream. Often has gelatin as a stabilizer.
Sorbet	Contains frozen fruit and/or fruit juice, sugar, and stabilizers. The volume of air whipped into the product may be up to 20 percent. Sorbet is generally high in sugar (**Figure 10–9**).
Italian ice (Granita)	Composed of sugar, water, and flavoring. Large ice crystals are generally present.
Frappé	An ice frozen to a slushy consistency and served as a drink. Often contains fruit juices (**Figure 10–10**).
Novelties	Examples of novelties include ice cream sandwiches, ice cream bars, cones, cake rolls, and molded items.
Milkshakes and Malts	Thin drinkable ice cream mixtures that are served as a beverage (**Figure 10–21**).

Source: Reference 15.

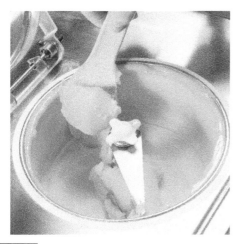

Figure 10–9

Mango sorbet being scooped. (Richard Embery/Pearson Education)

Figure 10–10

A coffee-flavored frappé. (Palo_ok/Shutterstock)

UP CLOSE

LIQUID NITROGEN AND ICE CREAM PRODUCTION

In 1992, a patent was issued for the manufacture of a "free-flowing alimentary dairy product." Today this product is known as Dippin' Dots®. It is produced by releasing droplets of the flavored ice cream mix into liquid nitrogen. On removal from the nitrogen, the product is stored at −22°F (−30°C). For consumption, it is warmed above this temperature. Chefs and ice cream shops now manufacturer ice cream using liquid nitrogen too (**Figure 10–11**). ■

Source: Reference 15.

Figure 10–11

This chef is using liquid nitrogen to quickly freeze a specialty ice cream. (Fedorkondratenko/123RF)

contain inclusions or bulky flavoring ingredients, such as fruits, nuts, chocolate syrup, cookie pieces, and peanut butter mixtures. Table 10–1 summarizes the distinguishing characteristics of commercial frozen desserts.

Ice cream may be further classified as *superpremium*, *premium*, *standard*, or *economy*. Superpremium ice cream contains a high fat content (12 percent or higher milk fat); a very low overrun, which indicates that little air has been mixed into the product during freezing; and very high-quality ingredients. Likewise, premium is high in fat and has little overrun. These premium ice creams are rich and creamy, but will have a high calorie and high fat content compared to standard ice cream. Standard ice cream is defined as containing the minimum requirements of the U.S. Food and Drug Administration (FDA) standard of identity, which is 10 percent milk fat, 20 percent total milk solids, and 4.5 pounds per gallon. Economy ice cream meets the standard identity for ice cream; however, it is generally sold for a lower price. Refer to Chapter 3 for a discussion of FDA standards of identity.

CHARACTERISTICS OF FROZEN DESSERTS

Frozen desserts are complex food systems-solutions, suspensions, and foams. Ice cream and other products that contain fat are also an emulsion. These frozen systems are foams with air cells dispersed in a continuous liquid phase that contains ice crystals, emulsified fat globules, proteins, sugars, salts, and stabilizers. Ice cream in particular has a

colloidal structure [10]. (Refer to Chapter 7 for more about colloidal dispersions.) Small air bubbles and ice crystals are dispersed among liquid water and destabilized, clustered fat globules, thus contributing to the characteristic taste and mouthfeel of ice cream (**Figure 10–12**) [11, 16].

High-quality ice cream products are characterized by a smooth, creamy, somewhat dry and stiff texture with tiny ice crystals. The ice cream should have enough body so the product melts slowly and uniformly. The taste should be sweet with a fresh characteristic flavor. In addition, the color should be pleasing. **Table 10–2** provides an overview of some quality attributes and potential defects that may be present in ice cream.

Crystal Formation

All types of frozen desserts are crystalline products in which water is crystallized as ice. The aim in preparation is generally to obtain fine crystals and produce a smooth mouthfeel. Differences in crystal size and creamy texture are apparent among products, depending on the fat content and the use of stabilizers. For example, fruit ices containing no fat usually have a more crystalline texture than high-fat, creamy ice creams. Many of the same general factors that tend to produce fine crystals in crystalline candies, in which the crystals are sugar, also produce fine ice crystals in frozen desserts. Both fat and nonfat solids, such as proteins, interfere mechanically with crystal formation and growth. Many stabilizers, including vegetable gums, are hydrocolloids that bind large amounts of water, increase viscosity, and interfere with crystallization. Agitation of the mix during freezing also promotes the development of small ice crystals.

Overrun

Overrun is the volume of ice cream obtained above the volume of mix frozen. Overrun results from whipping air into the mix during freezing and expansion because of freezing. Ice cream is a partly frozen foam and typically contains 40 to 50 percent air by volume [2]. Thus, during freezing, the volume of the ice cream mix increases by 70 to 100 percent. Homemade ice creams usually have no more than 30 to 40 percent

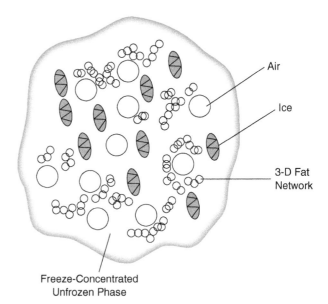

Air

Ice

3-D Fat Network

Freeze-Concentrated Unfrozen Phase

Figure 10–12

Ice cream has a three-dimensional structure of fat, air, and ice. The structure of ice cream can be described as a partially frozen foam with the majority of the space taken by ice crystals and air bubbles. Tiny fat globules surround the air bubbles with proteins and emulsifiers surrounding the fat globules. Finally, a very concentrated, unfrozen solution of sugars forms a continuous phase.

overrun. The higher percentage of overrun in commercial ice creams in comparison with homemade products results from a better control of freezing conditions, such as the rate of freezing and the stage of hardness at which the freezing is discontinued. **Homogenization** increases the viscosity of the mix, and also favors air retention.

Too little overrun produces a heavy, compact, coarse-textured frozen dessert, which is more expensive per serving, whereas too great an overrun results in a frothy, foamy product. Better ice creams are often sold by weight. Federal standards require weight of 4.5 pounds per gallon, thereby controlling the amount of overrun. Sherbet must weigh not less than 6 pounds per gallon [4].

Overrun may be calculated by volume or by weight using one of the following formulas:

$$\text{Percent overrun} = \left(\frac{\text{volume of frozen ice cream} - \text{volume ice cream mix}}{\text{volume of ice cream mix}} \right) \times 100$$

$$\text{Percent overrun} = \left(\frac{\text{weight of mix} - \text{weight of ice cream}}{\text{weight of ice cream}} \right) \times 100$$

Body

The term *body* as used in connection with frozen desserts implies firmness or resistance to rapid melting. Homemade ice creams usually have less body than commercial ice creams because stabilizers used in the commercial products often add body. Homemade ice creams generally melt faster in the mouth and give the impression of being lighter desserts, although they may

TABLE 10–2
SELECTED QUALITY ATTRIBUTES AND POTENTIAL DEFECTS IN ICE CREAM

Quality Attribute	Potential Defects and Causes
Flavor	Sweetness and flavorings—too much or too little
	• Amount or type of sweeteners and flavors may result in poor flavor.
	Off-flavors—cooked flavor or "lacks freshness"
	• Milk products were cooked to too high of a temperature, or ice cream was stored where the storage atmosphere allowed the absorption of undesirable volatile flavors.
Body	Crumbly—flaky or snowy
	• Overrun too high, low stabilizer or emulsifier, low total solids, or coarse air cells.
	Gummy—pasty or puttylike body
	• Overrun too low, too much stabilizer, or poor stabilizer.
	Weak body—melts quickly into watery liquid
	• Overrun too high, low total solids, insufficient stabilizer.
Texture	Coarse or icy—ice crystals are large
	• Most likely cause of large ice crystals is fluctuating temperatures during storage or distribution.
	• Other causes include insufficient total solids, protein, stabilizers in the mix; insufficient aging of the mix following pasteurization; slow freezing; slow hardening; incorporation of large air cells due to type of freezer; or rehardening of soft ice cream.
	Sandy—a rough, gritty mouthfeel that does not melt and disappear
	• Caused due to formation of lactose crystals.
	• Prevented by hardening ice cream quickly, maintaining low hardening temperatures, and preventing temperature fluctuations.
Volume	Shrinkage—ice cream pulls away from side of container; thus, it "shrinks"
	• Is the result of a loss of air bubbles.
	• Potential causes include too low of temperatures during hardening, too high or too low storage temperatures, excessive overrun, or pressure changes as might occur when transporting ice cream from high to a low altitude.
Melting	Ice cream should melt not too slow or too fast. Once melted, the product should form a homogeneous fluid base.
	Curdy—irregularly shaped curd particles are visible in melted product
	• Caused by protein destabilization or overstabilization by gums.
	Does not melt—ice cream retains shape after 15 to 20 minutes at room temperature
	• Excess fat destabilization.
	• Too much stabilizer.
	Foamy—large air bubbles retain shape in melted product
	• Too high a level of emulsifiers and egg yolks.
	Wheying off—watery fluid appears that may have curd particles in the fluid
	• Caused by protein destabilization or separation between proteins and polysaccharides.
	Low viscosity—melted product is thin like milk
	• Caused by low solids in mix.

Source: Reference 15.

actually be richer mixtures than many commercial ice creams.

Texture

Texture refers to the fineness of particles, smoothness, and lightness or porosity. The size and distribution of ice crystals is a major factor influencing the texture of frozen desserts. Substances that interfere with large-crystal formation, such as fat and certain stabilizers, help produce a fine, smooth texture in frozen desserts. Consumers generally prefer smooth, fine-grained ice cream.

INGREDIENTS IN FROZEN DESSERTS

Ice cream ingredients include milk, milk fat, sweeteners, and flavorings (**Figure 10–13**). Additionally, ice cream may include eggs, emulsifiers, and stabilizers. Cream is typically the ingredient that supplies milk fat. Nonfat dried milk or whey may make up part of the nonfat milk solids in ice cream. **Table 10–3** provides a listing of several different types of ingredients that may be used in making ice cream.

Milk fat

An optimum amount of cream, supplying milk fat, gives desirable flavor to ice cream, and also improves body and texture, resulting in a firm, smooth product. The amount of milk fat influences the viscosity of the mix,

Figure 10–13

Base ingredients for ice cream are milk, cream, sugar, vanilla, and eggs (optional). (Richard Embery/ Pearson Education)

TABLE 10–3
ICE CREAM INGREDIENTS

Ingredient Category	Potential Ingredients Used
Dairy	Cream, milk, evaporated milk, condensed milk, dried milk, nonfat milk, whey, hydrolyzed milk protein, and others
Sweeteners	Sugar, dextrose, invert sugar, corn syrup, maple syrup, honey, brown sugar, malt syrup, lactose, fructose, aspartame, acesulfame-K, sucralose, high-fructose corn syrup, and others
Egg products	Whole eggs or egg yolks, which may be liquid, dried, or frozen
Stabilizers and thickeners	Guar gum, locust bean gum, sodium carboxymethyl cellulose, sodium alginate, propylene glycol alginate, xanthan, gelatin, calcium sulfate, carrageenan, gum acacia, gum karaya, oat gum, gum tragacanth, furcellaran, and others
Emulsifiers	Mono- and diglycerides, polyoxyethlene sorbitan monostearate (60) or monoloeate (80), microcrystalline cellulose, diocytyl sodium sulfosuccinate, and others
Caseinates	Ammonium caseinate, calcium caseinate, potassium caseinate, sodium caseinate
Coloring	Natural or artificial colors
Mineral salts	Sodium salts of citric acid

Source: References 15, 5.

thereby affecting the incorporation of air. A moderate viscosity is desirable, as both a highly viscous mixture and a thin, nonviscous mixture resist the incorporation of air. The air cells are desirably small, and the texture is smooth in a mixture with optimum viscosity.

Homemade ice creams with a high milk fat content may have a tendency to churn, producing agglomerated particles of butter. The homogenization of commercial ice cream mixes helps avoid this problem. Commercial ice creams usually contain 10 to 14 percent milk fat.

Nonfat Milk Solids

Nonfat milk solids often are added to improve the flavor and texture of the ice cream. A relatively high percentage of milk solids reduces the free water content of ice cream, and improves its texture by encouraging finer ice crystal formation. The added lactose found in the nonfat milk solids enhances sweetness [16]. Nonfat milk solids also promote the development of overrun.

Commercial ice creams can be reinforced with milk solids by the use of evaporated skim milk, nonfat dry milk, or dry whey solids. Whey solids, however, may substitute no more than 25 percent of the nonfat milk solids according to U.S. regulatory standards. Homemade ice creams usually are not reinforced with milk solids, although nonfat dry milk may be found in some recipes. Unless reinforced with nonfat dry milk, homemade ice creams probably contain no more than 6 percent milk serum solids compared with an average of about 9 or 10 percent in commercial ice creams.

Too high a percentage of nonfat milk solids gives a sandy ice cream as a result of the lactose crystallization at the low holding temperature. About 11 percent nonfat milk solids is close to the upper limit for prevention of a "sandy" product, unless the enzyme *lactase* is added to hydrolyze the lactose. In this case, a higher level of nonfat milk solids can be used without the development of sandiness. Too low a percentage of nonfat milk solids encourages high overrun, creating fluffiness and poor body.

Sweeteners

Sweeteners, of course, affect flavor. Consumers generally seem to prefer a fairly sweet ice cream (one containing about 14 or 15 percent sugar). Sugar also lowers the freezing point and affects the amount of water frozen at the usual holding and serving temperatures for ice cream, thus improving texture. If too much sugar is added, the freezing point is lowered excessively, and freezing is retarded. If too little sugar is used, the freezing point is high enough that much of the water is frozen, adversely affecting the texture of the ice cream [18].

Although table sugar is the usual sweetener in homemade frozen desserts, various sweeteners are used in commercial products. These include corn syrups and high-fructose corn syrups (HFCSs) as well as sugar. The use of corn sweeteners is increasing. A comparatively large amount of high-fructose corn syrup, which produces a lower freezing point, has been reported to contribute to the development of iciness on storage of ice cream [23].

Eggs

Custards thickened with egg yolk or whole eggs are sometimes used in ice creams. Eggs or egg yolks have been a traditional emulsifier in ice cream mixes and are one of the reasons for the traditional smoothness found in French vanilla or custard ice creams [16]. Eggs also improve the whipping ability of the mix. Frozen custard must have 1.4 percent egg yolk solids as percent of finished product [4].

Commercially, eggs are added to the mix prior to pasteurization. In home preparation, the eggs should be cooked with the sugar, milk, and cream until a minimum temperature of 165°F (74°C) has been reached. Raw eggs should not be used in frozen desserts because of the possible salmonella presence even in unbroken eggs. This cooked custard should then be cooled under refrigeration for several hours prior to freezing.

Stabilizers and Emulsifiers

Emulsifiers affect the fat-globule structure and the agglomeration of these globules during freezing, which contributes to improved whipping quality and texture. Stabilizers interfere somewhat with ice crystal formation, helping keep the crystals small; they also give body to the mixture [20]. Some of the water in frozen desserts is bound by the stabilizers, thus inhibiting ice crystal growth, particularly during distribution and storage [23, 5].

Several different **stabilizers** and **emulsifiers** are used in commercial frozen desserts in amounts up to 0.5 percent. Gelatin is one example of a stabilizer that may be used in home recipes. Although once commonly used in commercial ice cream, gelatin has been largely replaced by other polysaccharides of plant origin [16].

Acids

Citric acid is an acid commonly used in sherbets and ices. The addition of citric acid provides a tart flavor and reduces the perception of sweetness. Sherbets and ices generally have about twice the sugar content of ice cream to produce the desirable flavor, body, and texture [16]; thus, the reduction in sweetness perception is desirable in these frozen desserts.

Fruit and Flavorings

A variety of fruits and flavorings may be used in ice cream and other frozen desserts. Vanilla is a traditional flavoring for ice cream and may be added as pure vanilla extract or as imitation or artificial vanilla flavoring. Vanilla extract provides a more desirable flavor profile. Chocolate and cocoa also are popular flavorings for frozen desserts.

Fruit ice creams follow vanilla and chocolate in popularity. Strawberries, raspberries, and peaches are examples of fruits that may be used in ice cream, frozen yogurt, and other frozen desserts. Strawberry is a popular fruit ice cream and frozen dairy dessert flavor. Additional sugar is often used with fruit to form a fruit and sugar syrup and to counteract the tartness of the fruit. Studies show that strawberry frozen yogurt with higher sugar levels is preferred over lower sugar levels [9].

Many different inclusions such as candies, cookies, and nuts may be used in frozen desserts. Cobranding is becoming increasingly popular in the marketplace as well-known candies, cookies, and other ingredients are used and advertised prominently with the ice cream. Oreo® cookie ice cream and Snickers® candy ice cream are examples of this trend [1].

INGREDIENT MODIFICATIONS FOR "LIGHT" FROZEN DESSERTS

Major changes in the composition of frozen desserts are necessary to achieve reduced calories and/or fat and to attain "light" status. It is a complex process to produce acceptable frozen desserts with useful reductions in sugar and fat. Understanding the role of ingredients for the production of acceptable light frozen desserts is essential if high-quality products satisfying customers' appetite for low-fat and low-calorie desserts are to be achieved.

Fat Modifications

Fat contributes greatly to the flavor and richness that consumers have come to expect in frozen desserts that are similar to ice cream. The smooth mouthfeel of fat may be only partially replaced by the addition of low-calorie texturizers, such as vegetable gums and cellulose derivatives. However, a variety of fat substitutes and fat-replacement technologies is available to produce a product of desirable texture. Maintaining flavor quality may be even more difficult. Fat serves as a reservoir of flavor, as it interacts with many flavor components. Thus, flavor is slowly released in the mouth, resulting in a pleasant aftertaste. Flavor challenges are increased as fat is decreased in a creamy frozen dessert [12].

Fat replacers used in ice cream are usually carbohydrate, protein, or lipid based [16]. Microparticulated proteins, such as Simplesse®, are relatively successful fat replacers in frozen desserts. Fantesk™, another fat replacer that is composed of a starch–lipid composite, was tested in soft-serve ice cream and found to produce a product similar to standard commercial products [3]. More information about fat replacers are found in Chapter 8.

Sugar Modifications

In frozen desserts, sugar has important functions beyond its sweetening power. For example, the freezing point of the mixture is markedly increased when sugar is replaced by a high-intensity sweetener such as aspartame. This exchange increases the amount of water frozen at any given temperature below the freezing point of the mixture and thus affects the texture and body of the frozen dessert [16]. It also affects the overrun of the finished product, modifying its usual characteristics.

So-called **bulking agents** have been used to replace some of the non-sweetening functions of sugar in frozen desserts, including **polydextrose**, **maltodextrins**, and **sorbitol**. However, some disadvantages of these ingredients include the development of off-flavors and the possible gastrointestinal distress. In addition, some bulking agents have the same caloric value as sucrose [13]. Bulking agents and polyols were discussed extensively in Chapter 9.

Nonfat Milk Solids

Another adjustment sometimes made in light frozen desserts is an increase in the nonfat milk solids. A defect of frozen desserts with high levels of nonfat milk solids is sandiness. As nonfat milk solid levels increase, the amount of lactose in the mix also increases. Crystals of lactose may form at these higher levels and will create a sandy mouthfeel. If the enzyme lactase is added to the mix before processing, lactose is hydrolyzed to glucose and galactose. These sugars are more soluble and sweeter than lactose and allow an acceptable light product to be made with increased milk solids [14].

PREPARATION OF FROZEN DESSERTS

Most ice cream used in this country is commercially manufactured, although some ice cream is still prepared at home. The preparation of frozen desserts, whether made commercially or in the home, starts with the preparation of the mix. Ingredients are mixed together, heated, allowed to cool, frozen, and then hardened in a container in frozen storage. Even though commercial and homemade ice creams differ, the basic principles involved in their preparation are similar.

Commercial Ice Cream Processing

Pasteurization, Homogenization, and Aging. The steps in the manufacture of ice cream include blending of ingredients, pasteurization, homogenization, aging the mix, freezing, packaging, and hardening. The mix is **pasteurized** to destroy pathogenic organisms. Pasteurization also aids in the blending of ingredients, makes a more uniform product, and improves flavor and keeping quality. Next, the hot mix is homogenized by forcing the liquid through a small orifice under conditions of temperature and pressure suitable to divide the fat globules finely, which are reduced to about one-tenth of their usual size. The texture and palatability of ice cream are improved by homogenization. The homogenized mix is cooled and aged for a minimum of 4 hours, but overnight is usually preferred. During this time, the fat globules solidify, and the viscosity increases, thereby improving the body and texture of the ice cream [16].

Freezing and Hardening of the Mix. The ice cream mix is frozen in continuous or batch freezers. The continuous method allows the continuous freezing and withdrawal of ice cream. Both methods utilize a liquid refrigerant, usually ammonia, which enters a chamber surrounding a cylinder containing the mix. The liquid refrigerant absorbs heat and results in the freezing of the mix. Some self-contained models operate with another type of refrigerant such as Freon® [16]. Within the cylinder, holding the ice cream mix, dashers scrape freezing ice cream from the walls of the chamber while whipping air into the mix. This agitation of the ice cream mix causes some of the fat globules to **agglomerate** into a form similar to a bunch of grapes. Although this agglomeration process is desirable, if too extensive, actual churning may take place, resulting in clumps of butter. Emulsifiers and stabilizers in commercial ice cream mixes help to control the degree of agglomeration and thus decrease freezing time, improve whipping quality, and produce an ice cream with a fine, stiff texture that melts slowly and uniformly [2].

Ice cream produced in the continuous or batch freezers is essentially "soft-serve" ice cream at the end of this freezing process. To produce the ice cream purchased in grocery stores and in ice cream stores featuring "hand-dipped" ice cream, the soft ice cream is drawn from the freezer into packages and quickly transferred to cold storage rooms. Here the freezing and hardening process is completed without agitation [16].

Soft-Serve. Soft-serve ice cream and frozen yogurt are popular items in many fast-food and buffet-type food service establishments. These products are similar in composition to their harder frozen counterparts, but they are served directly from the ice cream maker and therefore do not undergo the hardening process. Additional stabilizers or emulsifiers may be used in soft-serve ice cream, yogurt, and reduced-fat ice cream products. State regulations vary regarding the sale of soft-serve products.

Ice Cream Preparation at Home

When homemade ice cream is prepared from pasteurized milk, cream, and eggs, the ice cream mixture does not require heating before the freezing process. Heating in a double boiler for 15 to 20 minutes at 145°F (63°C) can be advantageous, however, because

it will blend the ingredients thoroughly. If raw eggs are added to the mix, the ice cream must be heated to a minimum of 165°F (74°C) to destroy pathogenic bacteria that may be present in the raw eggs. After it is heated, the mixture should be cooled quickly. A smoother ice cream and improved flavor will result from aging or holding the mix for 3 or 4 hours at refrigerator temperature before freezing. Replacing part of the granulated sugar with corn syrup may also help to make a creamier homemade ice cream [17].

Home Ice Cream Freezers. **Figure 10–14** illustrates the structure of an ice cream freezer. Ice cream freezers may be electric or hand cranked. The outer container or bucket of the freezer is usually made of a material that conducts heat poorly, such as wood or plastic foam, which minimizes the absorption of heat from the air. The container that holds the ice cream mix inside the outer container is metal, which conducts heat readily and permits the rapid absorption of heat from the ice cream mix. A paddle or dasher inside the metal can agitates the ice cream mixture and scrapes mixture from the side walls as it is turned (Figure 10–14).

The ice cream mix should occupy two-thirds or less of the capacity of the inner metal can to allow for overrun or swell during freezing (**Figure 10–15**). If the container is filled to the top before freezing, the ice cream will overflow as air is incorporated, and the mix freezes.

Packing the Freezer with Ice and Salt. Although refrigerants are used to remove heat from the mix commercially, in the home setting, a mixture of ice and salt packed in the space between the metal can holding

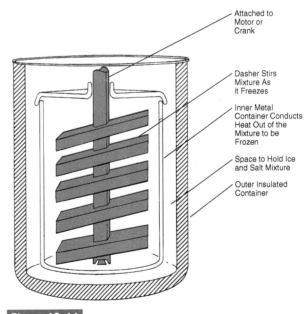

Attached to Motor or Crank

Dasher Stirs Mixture As it Freezes

Inner Metal Container Conducts Heat Out of the Mixture to be Frozen

Space to Hold Ice and Salt Mixture

Outer Insulated Container

Figure 10–14

Structure of an ice cream freezer.

(a) The ice cream mixture is placed in the freezing canister and the dasher is in place.

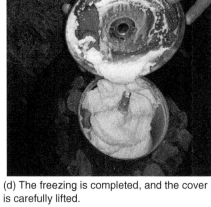

(d) The freezing is completed, and the cover is carefully lifted.

(b) The freezer is closed; crushed ice and rock salt are added.

(e) The dasher is removed from the freezing canister.

(c) Brothers can help each other in turning the freezer as they eagerly await the final result.

(f) Anticipation is finally at an end, and the boys can spoon out the delicious frozen ice cream.

Figure 10–15

Freezing ice cream at home can be a family activity. (© Barbara Scheule)

Figure 10–16

Rock salt is a coarse crystal salt used in ice cream making. The salt is not refined for human consumption. (© Amanda Frye)

the mix and the outer container performs the same function. The container should be filled about half full with ice before beginning to alternate the addition of ice with salt. According to home ice cream maker White Mountain® brand, the goal is to keep the ice salt brine between 8°F and 12°F. *Rock salt* a coarse sodium chloride (NaCl) is used for ice cream freezing and is unrefined and not intended for human consumption (**Figure 10–16**). Regular table salt is undesirable because of the crystal size, expense, and it tends to lump and collect in the bottom of the freezer [5].

One part rock salt to six parts crushed ice by weight is an efficient proportion of salt to ice for home freezing. This amount is equivalent to about 1 to 12 by measure. For faster freezing, a proportion of about one part salt to eight parts ice, (¼ cup rock salt per quart of chipped ice) by measure, also is satisfactory

[5]. The higher the percentage of salt, the shorter the time required for freezing. If freezing is too rapid, however, there is not enough time to keep the ice crystals separated and small while stirring; the crystals of ice formed may be large enough to produce a granular texture. The mixture will then harden before enough air is incorporated.

As the ice is melted by the salt, a water brine will be produced. This brine should not be drained off except through the small overflow drain hole found near the top of the outer ice cream container. This brine effectively draws heat from the mix and thus promotes rapid freezing.

Rate of Cranking the Mix. When cranking ice cream by hand, slow agitation of the ice cream mixture is desirable at the beginning of the freezing period until the temperature of the freezing mixture is lowered below the critical churning temperature. This slow initial crank phase should take about 3 minutes until the mixture is lowered to a temperature that it begins to freeze [5]. At 40°F (4°C) or above, agitation tends to cause the formation of clumps of butterfat, resulting in a buttery ice cream or in actual butter. Rapid agitation after the mixture is chilled incorporates much air and also favors the formation of many nuclei and fine ice crystals. The rapid cranking should be about 160 revolutions per minute for about 6 minutes [5]. After that cranking continues until the mixture is too stiff to turn. At this point about 60 percent of the mixture will be frozen. The metal container with the frozen churned mix should be left in the brine to harden for a half hour [5]. Electric freezers will crank the ice cream at a rate pre-set at the factory.

Freezing of the Mix. As the salt melts the ice, heat is absorbed from the mix as well as the surrounding area. The rapid melting of ice that occurs when salt is added to it increases the rate of heat absorption. When the mixture to be frozen reaches its freezing point, ice crystals begin to form and precipitate out. The dasher turned by hand or with an electrical motor scrapes the mixture from the side walls, permitting a new layer of mixture to

---

IN DEPTH
THE SCIENCE BEHIND THE FREEZING OF LIQUIDS

Pure liquids have characteristic freezing points at constant pressure. For pure water, freezing occurs when the liquid water is in equilibrium with the solid state, which is ice. Thus, water freezes at 32°F (0°C) at a pressure of 760 millimeters of mercury. Unlike many substances, water expands during freezing to occupy more space than it did in the liquid form due to an expanded lattice-like structure when frozen. Although water freezes at 32°F (0°C), after freezing, the temperature of ice may be lowered below 32°F (0°C) if in colder surroundings.

Substances dissolved in a liquid to form a true **solution** cause the freezing point of the solution to be lower than the freezing point of the pure liquid. A sugar solution, which is the basis for frozen desserts, has a lower freezing point than pure water. Ices and sherbets that contain acid fruit juices have a higher percentage of sugar than ice creams and therefore freeze at a lower temperature. ■

come in contact with the can. This agitation also tends to form many nuclei on which ice crystals may form, favoring small-crystal formation. As this mixture freezes, water is removed from the mix by becoming ice, thereby causing the mix to become more concentrated. This sweeter, more concentrated unfrozen mix will have a lower freezing temperature than the original mix. Thus, as freezing proceeds, the freezing temperature is gradually lowered, just as the evaporation of water that occurs in the boiling of a sugar solution produces a gradual increase in the boiling temperature of the mixture.

The initial freezing of the mix is complete when the crank is too difficult to turn by hand or the electric motor is laboring, as will become apparent by the sound of the motor. The ice cream, if served at this point, will be similar in consistency to soft-serve. To harden the ice cream, drain off excess brine and re-pack with a freezing mixture of ice and salt containing a higher percentage of salt than used for the original freezing. The hardening of the dessert to a consistency desirable for serving is thus accomplished more rapidly.

Still-Frozen Desserts

Still-frozen desserts are prepared without the agitation of a dasher as is used in commercial or home ice cream freezers (**Figure 10–17**). It is difficult to produce fine crystals in ice creams that are frozen without stirring because relatively few nuclei for ice crystal formation are present, and thus large crystal growth can occur (**Figure 10–18**). Mixtures that can be frozen most successfully without stirring are those rich in fat, such as whipped cream products, or mixtures containing gelatin, cooked egg custard, evaporated milk, or a cooked starch base. These substances interfere with the formation of large ice crystals. Because these mixtures are not stirred to incorporate air, air must be beaten into cream or evaporated milk prior to freezing (**Figure 10–19**). Partially frozen mixtures may be removed from the freezing trays and beaten once or twice during the freezing period. Air cells tend to interfere with coarse-crystal formation.

Still-frozen desserts may be frozen in a home freezer compartment or by packing in a freezing mixture. The time required for freezing refrigerator desserts depends on the quantity being frozen, the composition of the mixture, and the temperature. About 4 to 6 hours may be needed, and the cold control is best set on the lowest temperature (**Figure 10–20**). When the mixture is frozen without stirring, freezing quickly promotes the production of many small ice crystals. Faster freezing occurs if the mixture is stirred occasionally in the tray to permit unfrozen portions to come in contact with the tray.

If a still-frozen dessert is frozen in a mixture of ice and salt, two parts ice and one part rock salt should be used. Mixtures frozen without stirring require a longer time and a colder temperature to freeze than stirred mixtures. Removing heat from the center of the mass

Figure 10–17

Frozen mousse, a still frozen product. (Liv friis-larsen/Shutterstock)

Figure 10–18

Lemon Italian ice placed in a hollowed-out lemon shell. *(Olexiy Bayev/123RF)*

Figure 10–19

The whipped cream is gently folded into gelatin-thickened pureed raspberry mixture prior to freezing. (Richard Embery/ Pearson Education)

may be difficult in unstirred frozen desserts because these desserts are usually high in fat and have air beaten into the heavy cream base. Both cold fat and air are poor conductors of heat. The fineness of the division of salt and ice is also a factor influencing the rate of freezing in the preparation of frozen desserts. Finely crushed ice has more surfaces exposed to the action of salt than coarsely chopped ice; hence, the finer ice melts faster.

(a)

(b)

Figure 10–20

Granita is an Italian ice. The mixture is not churned but still frozen and scraped to or frequently stirred to yield flaky ice pieces. These photographs show a coffee-flavored granita being made. (a) Mixture is being stirred once it has begun to freeze, and then the mixture is refrozen and the partial frozen mixture is stirred again. (b) Final coffee granita is being scraped and served. (Richard Embery/ Pearson Education)

STORAGE OF FROZEN DESSERTS

Frozen desserts must be kept cold. Ice cream exposed to temperatures above 10°F (−12°C) will develop adverse changes in body, texture, and flavor. Temperature fluctuations are especially of concern and will cause the small ice crystals to turn into large crystals, resulting in an icy, crystalline texture. When purchasing ice cream, it should be −20°F (−28°C) and quickly returned to freezer storage in the home or food service. When storing ice cream, keep it between −5°F and 0°F (−21°C and −18°C) in an area of the freezer where temperature fluctuations will be minimized. Thus, storage in the door compartment is not recommended. Although many home freezers are self-defrosting, storage in a non-defrosting freezer, such as in deep freeze, is preferable so that the temperature fluctuations necessary for the defrosting feature can be avoided. Finally, because ice cream will absorb odors, store with the container lid tightly closed away from foods with strong odors.

Figure 10–21

Milk shakes and malts are ice cream beverages. (29September/ Shutterstock)

STUDY QUESTIONS

Consumption Trends and Nutrition

1. Discuss what new frozen ice cream, dessert, or novelty items you have seen available to consumers in the retail and commercial foodservice market? Did the item have inclusions? Was it a novelty item or premium product?

2. Discuss some nutritional similarities and differences among different frozen dairy products?

Types of Frozen Desserts

3. Discuss why standards of identity are important.

4. Describe identifying characteristics of each of the following:

   (a) Sherbet

   (b) Water ice

   (c) Ice cream

   (d) Mousse

   (e) Sorbet

   (f) Frozen yogurt

   (g) Mellorine

   (h) Parevine

   (i) Reduced-fat ice cream

Characteristics of Frozen Desserts

5. Discuss these various food systems in ice cream. Give ingredients involved in each of these systems.

Ingredients in Frozen Desserts

6. What is the effect of each of the following on the flavor, texture, and/or body of a frozen ice cream?

   (a) Milk fat

   (b) Nonfat milk solids

   (c) Sweeteners

   (d) Stabilizers

   (e) Overrun

Preparation of Frozen Desserts

7. Describe how overrun affects the quality of the product. Discuss the difference in overrun between premium- and economy-style ice creams.

8. How does sugar affect the freezing point of the ice cream mix?

9. Discuss some of the problems often involved in the formulation of acceptable "light" frozen desserts. What are some possible solutions to these problems?

10. Discuss the steps in ice cream production

11. Explain how a mixture of ice and salt is able to act as a freezing mixture to freeze frozen desserts.

12. Describe an appropriate procedure for preparing homemade ice cream in an ice cream freezer. Explain what happens at each step.

13. What procedures should be used when freezing a frozen dessert without stirring? Why?

Storage of Ice Cream and Frozen Dessert Products

14. Discuss proper storage for ice cream and other frozen dessert products. What happens if not stored properly?

15. What is the "sandiness" in ice cream caused from? How can it be prevented?

11
Starch

Starch, one of the most abundant substances found in nature, is a carbohydrate. Starch is a **polysaccharide** molecule made up of hundreds or thousands of glucose molecules (refer to Chapter 9 for more about carbohydrates). Plants store energy in the form of starch (**Figure 11–1**). Glucose is formed in plants from carbon dioxide absorbed from the air using the sunlight as energy. The glucose is made into long chains (polymerization), which are stored as starch in granules. The starch serves as a plant energy reserve. These energy starch stores are in roots, seeds, fruits, and stems. In plants, as in humans, starch provides energy. The starch is broken down to provide energy for growth. For example, during **germination** of a seed, this stored polysaccharide molecule (the starch) undergoes enzymatic **hydrolysis** to yield **glucose**, which then supplies energy for the germination and early stages of plant growth. Factories can emulate this conversion of starch to glucose by using enzymes to produce sugars such as high-fructose corn syrup (HFCS). Starches fall into two categories: (1) native starch and (2) modified starch.

Human starch use dates back to 1000 B.C. when Egyptians used starch from various grains in cosmetics

Figure 11–2

A new starch-based coating makes paper water resistant. Developed by the United States Department of Agriculture, Agriculture Research Station. (USDA/Photo by Peggy Greb)

and as papyrus page adhesive. Around 500 B.C., upper-class Romans starched their togas for a crisp neat look. In 1841, Orlando Jones, was awarded U.S. patent number 2000 for a process using alkali that sped up and improved starch production. A year later cornstarch was isolated, leading to the discovery of corn laundry starch and other industrial uses including a food thickener.

Starch is renewable and biodegradable. Scientists are still exploring new applications of starch, such as using food-grade starch as a plastic film coating (See Chapter 28). In 2017, USDA research scientists developed a paper coating made from starch (**Figure 11–2**).

Starch is available as a purified material to the food industry. In this form, it belongs to a group of substances called **hydrocolloids**, a group that also includes **pectin** and gums, sometimes called **vegetable gums**. Hydrocolloids are water loving and absorb relatively large amounts of water.

Starch gives foods texture and desirable consistency. In food systems, starch serves as a thickener, binder, stabilizer, and gelling agent. Starch is used to thicken sauces, soups, puddings, and other foods; it also serves as a gelling agent, as in cream pies. It also plays an essential role in cooked products like potatoes, rice, and pasta, which are discussed in later chapters. Starch is a primary component of flour mixtures

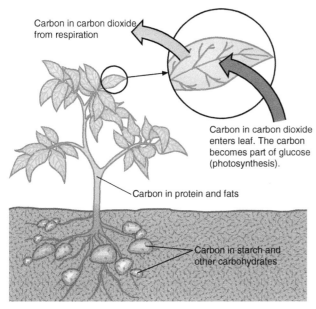

Carbon in carbon dioxide from respiration

Carbon in carbon dioxide enters leaf. The carbon becomes part of glucose (photosynthesis).

Carbon in protein and fats

Carbon in starch and other carbohydrates

Figure 11–1

How a plant stores energy as starch. (Oxford Designers & Illustrators Ltd. Pearson Education Ltd.)

and baked goods, which will be addressed in future chapters. Starch cookery and its role as a thickener and gelling agent are also discussed.

In this chapter, the following topics will be examined.

- Consumption trends and nutritive value of starch
- Sources of starch
- Starch structure
- Kinds of starch
- Gelatinization, gel formation, and retrogradation
- Factors affecting starch pastes
- Starch cookery
- Starch to sugar and more

CONSUMPTION TRENDS AND NUTRITION

Consumption Trends

Cornstarch is the most widely used starch in the United States (**Figure 11–3**). One corn kernel is about 70–72 percent starch. According to the USDA Economic Research Service (ERS), corn food, seed, and industrial uses including starch account for about one-third of domestic corn use (**Figure 11–4**). Corn use has steadily grown and is expected to keep on this trajectory in the future. Total Food, Seed, and Industrial (FSI) domestic starch usage has fluctuated from 214 million bushels to 277 million bushels since 1986 (**Figure 11–5**). See **Figure 11–6** to understand more about measurements used in the discussion of starch production and usage.

In the United States, a minor amount of starch is obtained from wheat, potatoes, and other plants. The USDA does not collect separate end-use starch data, but it has been noted that total wheat flour and potato use has been in the decline for the past two decades (**Figure 11–7**). USDA's Economic Research Service claims that the downward carbohydrate consumption trends and changing taste preferences have created "downward pressure" for use of other plant-based starch such as potatoes.

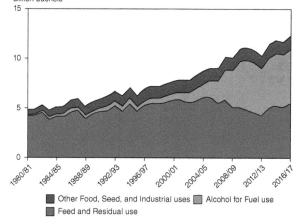

Figure 11–4

Corn use for starch products has increased since 1980. (USDA/ERS)

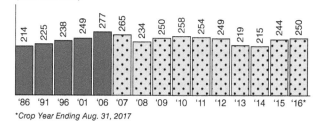

Figure 11–5

Starch usage 1986–2016. (USDA/ERS)

Denmark is the home of the International Starch Institute and a major producer of potato starch, leading the world in per capita starch production. The European Union (EU) has been increasing starch production over the last decade, producing 10.7 million metric tons (tonnes) in 2015. Annually, the EU uses around 9.3 tonnes of starch: 61 percent being food, 1 percent feed, and 38 percent nonfood, primarily paper making. Of this, 26 percent is native starch, 19 percent modified starch, and 55 percent is made into sweeteners. In 2015, the EU processed corn (maize) (8 million tonnes), wheat (8 million tonnes), and potato (7 million tonnes) into 11 million tonnes starch and 5 million tonnes co-products such as oil, protein, and fiber. Thailand is a large producer and exporter of cassava (tapioca) starch. Over the last decade, Thailand has increased production of tapioca from 26 to near 32 million tons. Worldwide starch production has increased over the last decade. Starch sales have been increasing by 2–7 percent, reaching over $77.4 billion in 2018. Global market for starch is projected to reach 182 million metric tons by 2022, driven by use in food processing and industrial use as adhesive, biodegradable, and renewable polymers. Consumer demand has led to non-GMO and organic starches being introduced in the marketplace.

Understanding Agriculture Commodity Math

Standard weights, measures, equivalents, and conversion factors for agriculture commodities

Bushel (BU) is a dry unit of measure. A level bushel is called a "struck bushel"
    1 Bushel (U.S.) = 2,150.42 cubic inches (35,245.38 cubic cm)
    1 Bushel = 32 quarts or 4 pecks (1 peck = 8 quarts)
    1 barrel (bbl) of liquid = 42 gallons
    1 barrel (bbl) (dry, standard) = 2.709 bushels, struck
A Bushel of grain has a different weight depending on the grain, vegetable, or fruit and grade
    1 bushel = 56 pounds (25.4 kg) for shelled corn, rye, sorghum grain, and flaxseed
    1 bushel = 60 pounds (27.2 kg) for wheat, white potatoes, soybeans
    1 bushel = 48 pounds (21.8 kg) for barley
Countries using the Metric System use the Metric Ton (Tonne)
    1 Tonne (Metric Ton) = 1000 kg
    1 Tonne = 2,204.62 pound (U.S.)
The U.S. uses short tons and the U.K. uses long tons
    1 Short Ton (U.S.) = 2000 pounds   1 Short Ton (U.S.) = 0.907185 metric ton (Tonne)
    1 Long Ton (U.K.) = 1.016047 metric ton (Tonne)   1 Long Ton (U.K.) = 1.12 short ton (US)
    1 Short Ton (U.S.) = 0.89 long ton (U.K.)   1 million pounds = 500 short tons
Reference: United States Department of Agriculture, Economic Research Service, Agricultural Handbook Number 697, (1992), *Weights, Measures, and Conversion Factors for Agricultural Commodities and Their Products.*

Figure 11–6

Agriculture commodities such as corn, potatoes, wheat, and starch are measured in different ways using special terms.

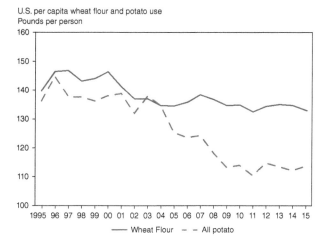

Figure 11–7

There has been a steady decrease in demand for wheat and potatoes including starch production over the last two decades. (USDA/ERS)

Nutritive Value

Both starch and sugar are carbohydrates providing 4 kcal/gram. A diet with a 45 to 65 percent carbohydrate intake is recommended with products such as refined starch limited to 13–15 percent of calorie intake [40, 43]. Refined starch can be defined as the starch component of grains, tubers, seeds, and other foods used as an ingredient in another food. These starches have been refined to remove other components of the food such as fat, protein, vitamins, and minerals. Refined starches are added to other foods and act as

thickeners, stabilizers, bulking agents, and anticaking agents, but only contribute calories and little other nutritional value [40]. Starch, as a component of breads, cereals, grains, potatoes, and other foods, is associated with needed nutrients. Starch in its refined purified form, such as found in cornstarch, offers few nutrients outside of calories; it will be the focus of this chapter.

Starch is a polysaccharide that through human digestion is converted to glucose. The human digestive system produces enzymes, called **amylases**, that break down or hydrolyze starch, yielding the disaccharide **maltose**. Maltose is then hydrolyzed to glucose, which is absorbed and metabolized by body cells, providing energy.

SOURCES OF STARCH

Plants store energy in the form of starch granules. Seeds, roots, and **tubers** serve as starch storage (**Figure 11–8**). Thus, the most common sources of food starch are cereal grains, including corn, wheat, rice, grain sorghum, and oats; legumes; and roots or tubers, including potato, sweet potato, arrowroot, and the tropical cassava plant (marketed as tapioca). Sago comes from the pith or core of the tropical sago palm. See **Table 11–1**.

Purified native starch may be separated from grains and tubers by a process called *wet milling*. The wet milling of corn results in starch, germ, fiber, and protein. Approximately 32 pounds of starch can be produced from 1 bushel of corn. The steps involved in

Figure 11–8

Cassava (tapioca) plants with tuber where starch is stored. The tubers are grated and starch extracted and processed into starch (tapioca). (My Life Graphic/Shutterstock)

the wet milling of corn are explained in **Table 11–2**. Manufacturing of starch is plant specific, but the steps are basically the same: (1) cleaning, (2) grinding or grating, (3) slurry, (4) separation/refining, and (5) drying.

The slurry can be dried into white odorless native starch powder or modified and dried into a modified starch. Native starch is the pure starch isolated from the original plant material. Modified starch is a native starch that has undergone physical or chemical processes to change starch properties for specialty food use or industrial applications. Modified starches are discussed in more detail later. All by-products such as fiber, protein, gluten, etc., are used for other products such as animal feed. Wheat starch production yields a valuable by-product called gluten, which is more valuable than the starch itself.

COMPOSITION AND STRUCTURE

The Starch Molecule

Starch is a polysaccharide made up of hundreds or even thousands of glucose molecules joined together. The molecules of starch are of two general types, called *fractions*: amylose and amylopectin. Most starches found in nature are mixtures of the two fractions: amylose and amylopectin. Corn, wheat, rice, potato, and tapioca starches contain 16 to 24 percent amylose, with the remainder being amylopectin. The root starches of tapioca and potato are lower in amylose content than the cereal starches of corn, wheat, and rice.

Amylose. Amylose is a long chain-like molecule, sometimes called the *linear fraction*, and is produced by linking together 500 to 2,000 glucose molecules. The glucose units in amylose molecules can be thought of as beads on a string. A representation of the amylose molecule is shown in **Figure 11–9**. The amylose fraction of starch contributes gelling characteristics to cooked and cooled starch mixtures. A **gel** is rigid to a certain degree and holds a shape when molded (**Figure 11–10**). The starch gel network holds free water between the spaces in the rigid

Table 11–1
STARCH PLANTS

Major Industrial Starch	Local Confined Use	Limited and Potential Use	
Corn	Arrowroot	Amaranth	Pea
Cassava (Tapioca, Manioc)	Barley	Banana	Cocoa Bean
Potato	Millet	Rye	Coleus Tuber
Wheat	Oat	Yam	Cow Cockle
	Rice	Black Pepper	Field Bean
	Sorghum	Breadfruit	Ginger Root
	Sago	Buckwheat	Horse Gram
	Sweet Potato	Quinoa	Buffalo Gourd
	Mung Bean	Kuzu (Kudzu)	Wild Rice
	Taro Root	Lily	Winged Bean

Source: International Starch Institute, Starch Europe, and [45].

Table 11–2
STEPS IN THE WET MILLING OF CORN TO PRODUCE STARCH

Steps in the Wet Milling Process	Description
Inspection and cleaning	Dust, chaff, and other foreign materials are removed from shipments of corn.
Steeping	Corn is soaked in mildly acidic 50°F (10°C) water for 30 to 40 hours. Gluten bonds are loosened and begin to release starch. Coarse grinding, following the steeping period, breaks the germ loose from other components.
Germ separation	The low-density corn germs are spun out of the water slurry containing the coarsely ground corn. Corn oil is produced from the germ.
Fine grinding and screening	The corn and water slurry is ground more thoroughly to release the starch and gluten from the fiber. The starch–gluten suspension resulting from this step is called *mill starch*.
Starch separation	The mill starch is passed through a centrifuge to separate out gluten still present. The remaining starch is washed several times to remove any remaining protein. The starch, once dried, is 99.5 percent pure.

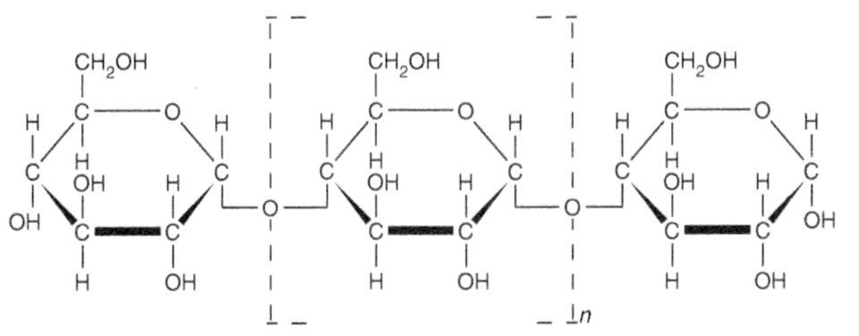

Figure 11–9

Amylose is a linear molecule with hundreds of glucose units linked together. A portion of the molecule is represented here. The glucose units are joined between the no. 1 carbon atom of one glucose molecule and the no. 4 carbon atom of the next one. The *n* may represent hundreds of similarly linked glucose molecules. See also Chapter 9.

Figure 11–10

A cornstarch gel which is rigid and holds its shape when unmolded. Carbohydrate gels are unique with starch fraction amylose primarily responsible for gelling properties. (© Amanda Frye)

structure. For example, a pie pudding thickened with starch will hold its shape so that it can be cut and placed on a plate.

Through genetic manipulation, high-amylose starches have been produced. For example, a high-amylose corn, called *amylomaize*, has starch that contains approximately 70 percent amylose. High-amylose starches have a unique ability to form films and to bind other ingredients. High-amylose cornstarch films are used for transparent edible packing films.

Amylopectin. Amylopectin has a highly branched, bushy type of structure, very different from the long, string-like glucose molecules in amylose. In amylopectin, the glucose units are joined together to form something that more resembles a branching bush or tree.

Glucose is the basic building unit for both amylose and amylopectin, but how these glucose units are joined together is different. **Figure 11–11** represents the chemical nature of amylopectin, with many short chains of glucose units branching from each other, much like the trunk and branches of a tree. Cohesion or thickening properties are contributed by amylopectin when a starch mixture is cooked in the presence of water, but this fraction does not produce a gel.

Certain strains of corn, rice, grain sorghum, and barley have been developed that contain only the amylopectin fraction of the starch. These are called *waxy* varieties because of the waxy appearance of the kernel when it is cut [3]. Waxy starches are non-gelling because of the lack of amylose and may be used successfully in products that will be canned, frozen, and thawed. High glutinous rice is predominantly amylopectin.

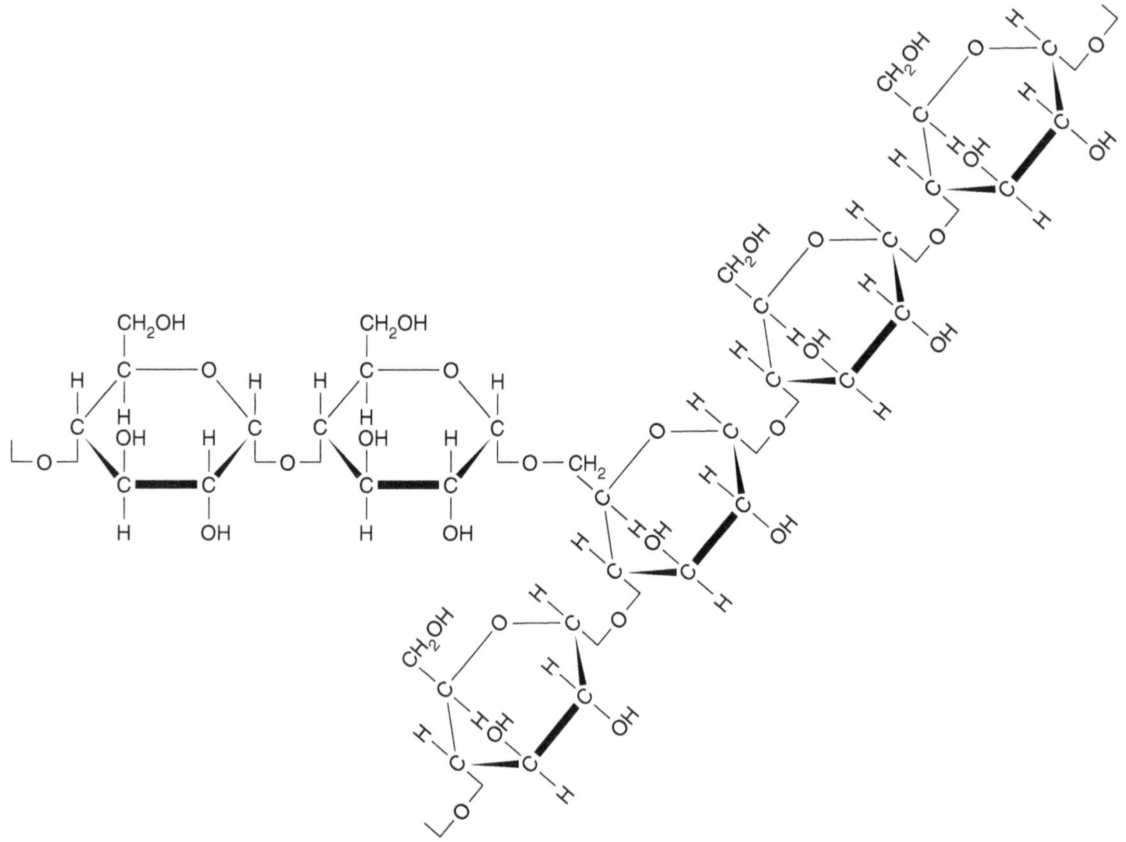

Figure 11–11

Amylopectin is a busy, treelike molecule with many sort branches of glucose units linked together. A portion of the molecule is represented here. The glucose units in the chains are joined between the no. 1 and the no. 4 carbon atoms. However, at the points of branching, the linkage is between the no. 1 carbon atom of one glucose unit and the no. 6 carbon atom of the other. See also Chapter 9.

The Starch Granule

In the storage areas of plants, notably the seeds and roots, molecules of starch are deposited in tiny, organized units called *granules*. The shape and size of the granules depend on the botanical origin ranging from 2 to 100 micrometers [41]. Shapes can vary from round, perfect spheres, elongated filaments, discs, polyhedral and rounded, oval, large oval, and compound [7].

Inside the starch granule, the amylose and amylopectin molecules are placed together in tightly packed stratified layers formed around a central spot in the granule called the *hilum*. The starch molecules are systematically structured in the granule to form crystalline-like patterns. Each different plant starch has granules with distinct sizes and shapes. The surface of the granules has small pores, which are thought to be the entry point of amylases that would break down the starch energy reserves into units needed for germination [10].

If the starch granules, in a water suspension, are observed microscopically under **polarized light**, the highly oriented structure causes the light to be rotated so that a Maltese cross-pattern on each granule is observed (**Figure 11–12**). This phenomenon is called **birefringence**. The pattern disappears when the starch mixture is heated and the structure disrupted. The sizes and shapes of granules differ among starches from various sources, but all starch granules are microscopic in size. **Figure 11–13** shows a photomicrograph of different types of starch granules.

Iodine Test for Starch. The presence of starch can be tested with a simple test using a dilute iodine solution. The brown iodine solution will

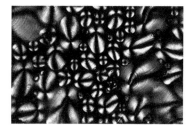

Figure 11–12

Potato starch seen under polarized light shows birefringent crosses resulting from the highly organized nature of the granules (magnified 700×). (Zoonar GmbH/Christian Wei/Alamy Stock Photo)

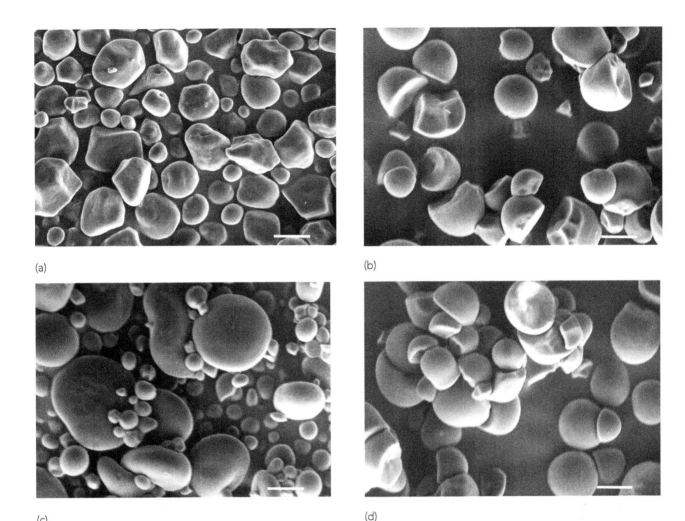

(a)

(b)

(c)

(d)

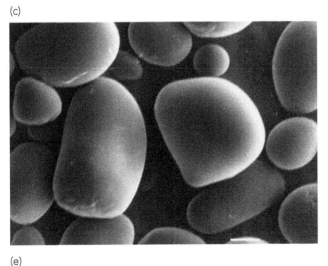

(e)

Figure 11–13

Starch granules from various plant sources have unique size and shape. (a) Cornstarch (b) Arrowroot starch (c) Wheat starch (d) Tapioca starch (e) Potato starch. Starch granules from other plant sources will have some similar characteristics to cornstarch granules but will vary in size. The bar at the bottom of the photographs represents 10 micrometers. (Dr. James BeMiller)

turn blue-purple if starch is present. Molecules of starch, especially amylose, exist in water as random coils. When iodine is present, or certain fatty substances, the starch forms a helix with at least six to seven glucose units in each coil [8] (**Figure 11–14**). When iodine is added to a starch mixture, it changes color. The blue color is due to the formation of a single amylose helix surrounding the iodine molecule

[6]. The color of the starch–iodine complex depends on helix length and the number of iodine molecules involved. A long starch–iodine helical complex will yield a blue color; a short starch–iodine complex will turn red. Due to amylose's linear nature, a blue color will occur with iodine; amylopectin's short branched structure will yield a red-purple color [8, 6]. Note along this same principle that amylose also has the

FOCUS ON SCIENCE
THE CHEMICAL STRUCTURES OF AMYLOSE AND AMYLOPECTIN

Amylose

Amylose is a linear polymer of glucopyranose units with carbon atom number 1 of one glucose connected to the hydroxyl of carbon atom number 4 of the adjacent glucose unit forming an α (alpha) (1 → 4) linkage. In the α (alpha) form, the hydroxyl (−OH) unit on the 1 carbon is oriented on the same side as the hydroxyl unit on the 4 carbon. When two units of glucose are joined with α (1 → 4) linkage, maltose is formed. Note: If glucose was a beta (1 → 4) linkage where the −OH (hydroxyl) of 1 carbon is oriented the opposite direction of 4, then this would produce a cellulose.

Amylose is a very flexible and mobile molecule and can easily assume random shapes. It has many hydroxyl groups that allow hydrogen bonding with other starch molecules. It is responsible for the three-dimensional gel structure in starch-containing food products.

Amylopectin

Amylopectin is composed of amylose subunits, which are joined by α (1 → 4) and α (1 → 6) linkages. The α (1 → 6) linkages about every 20 glucose molecules create branched points within the molecule which give it profoundly different characteristics from the amylose molecule. Amylopectin shows the primary structure within one growth ring. It shows clusters of short chains of different lengths. Each cluster has branch points in a narrowly defined region that allows close spacing (packing) of the linear short chains. The terminal end group of each chain is nonreducing, encouraging some double helix and crystal formation of parallel chains. The interior of the helix is mainly hydrogen atoms attached to carbon atoms giving a hydrophobic surface [45]. See **Table 11–3**.

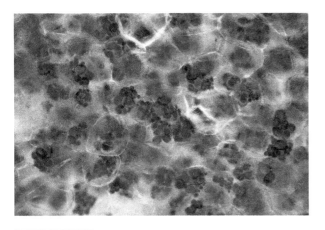

Figure 11–14

Iodine stained waxy potato starch. Starch high in amylose will stain blue and those high in amylopectin will stain reddish purple. (Paweł Burgiel/Fotolia)

ability to bind with fatty acid chains, forming stable amylose–lipid complexes [6].

KINDS OF STARCH

The starch may be classified from more than one perspective. Starch may be classified based on the kind of plant from which it was derived, for example, corn, potato, and so forth. These are native starches. Another classification of starch is based on whether the starch has been produced from a plant found in nature or from a plant developed through the use of biotechnology and genetic crossbreeding.

Starches can also be classified based on their "pasting" properties. The pasting or gelatinization properties

Table 11–3
GENERAL PROPERTIES OF AMYLOSE AND AMYLOPECTIN

	Amylose	Amylopectin
Molecular structure	Linear	Branched
Degree of polymerization (glucose units)	α-(1 → 4) 350–1000	α-(1 → 4) α-(1 → 6) Several thousands
Iodine test	Blue	Red-purple
Gel	Gel structure, stiff, strong, irreversible Opaque Subject to retrogradation	Soft and reversible Solution at low concentrations Translucent No retrogradation
Film formation	Flexible transparent coherent films	Brittle

depend on the gelatinization temperature of each starch and the type of gel or paste it forms.

When starch is put in cold water and heated slowly, the starch granules start to swell absorbing water. The initial starch water mixture has a milky appearance and gradually loses its opaqueness. The mixture becomes more translucent as the granules lose their birefringence. The granules increase in size losing their structural integrity. The mixture begins to thicken and becomes more viscous until a paste or gel is formed. This is called pasting or gelatinization. The temperature at which gelatinization takes place that can differentiate starches relies on the control of variables. Variables such as starch concentration, pH, rate of heating, and the presence of certain salts can affect gelatinization. Food ingredients such as salts, acids, and sugar impact gelatinization and the type of gel formed.

Some starches, called *modified starches*, may be modified through chemical or physical means to produce starches with specific useful characteristics. Starches may be called *resistant* because they cannot be digested by the human digestive tract. All of these starch will be discussed in the following sections.

Native Starches

Native starch is starch that is derived from plants without chemical or physical modification. Cornstarch is commonly used in cooking and is an example of a native starch. Tapioca, potato, arrowroot, and other kinds of native starches are described in **Table 11–4**. Each type of native starch has unique properties and characteristics. These unique starch traits are applied to food preparation and processing.

Table 11–4
KINDS OF NATIVE STARCHES

Native Starch	Description	Characteristics in Food Preparation
Cornstarch	Derived from the wet milling of dent corn. May be called maize. Common cornstarch contains about 25 percent amylase. Waxy maize starch is almost entirely amylopectin. High-amylose cornstarch contains 55 to 75 percent amylose.	Used to thicken sauces, gravies, and puddings. Compared to wheat starch (flour), results in a clearer, glossy sauce. Thickening is reduced when mixed with an acid. Common cornstarch should not be used in foods to be frozen and thawed.
Tapioca	Produced from the root of the cassava plant. Contains 15 to 18 percent amylose.	May be used to thicken pudding or pie fillings. Thickens quickly at a lower temperature than other starches. Is more tolerant of freezing and thawing than some other starches. Pearl tapioca (small or large) is characterized by the "pearls" of starch in the cooked product.
Wheat	Produced from the milling of wheat. Wheat starch has an amylose content of 25 percent.	Products thickened with wheat flour are not glossy like those thickened with other starches, such as cornstarch or arrowroot.
Potato	Derived from potatoes. Contains 20 percent amylose.	Is gluten free. May be used to thicken soups and gravies. Avoid boiling liquids thickened with potato starch.
Rice	Sweet rice flour or starch is produced from sweet rice. Sweet rice has a higher starch content compared to other kinds of rice. Contains 20 percent amylose and 80 percent amylopectin.	Used in Asian desserts. Tolerates freezing.
Arrowroot	Extracted from the roots of plant growing in tropical countries. Bermuda arrowroot is grown in Central America. Arrowroot is similar to tapioca starch. Some commercial "arrowroot" starch is produced from the cassava plant and therefore would not be considered true arrowroot although it is often called Brazilian arrowroot.	Imparts a shiny gloss to foods. Is neutral in flavor. Thickens at a relatively low temperature and will tolerate acidic ingredients and prolonged heating better than some starches. May be frozen and thawed more successfully than other kinds of native starches. Is not recommended for dairy-based sauces because a slimy texture may result.
Sago	Prepared from the pith of palms native to the East Indies.	Used to thicken pudding or a variety of other dishes.

Source: References 14, 18, 19.

Improved Native Starches

Improved native starches provide some of the functional benefits found in modified starches without chemical or physical starch modification. These improved native starches may be developed through traditional plant breeding methods or genetic engineering. Corn modified to contain only amylopectin (no amylose) is called waxy maize. Other corn with high amylose (70 percent) levels is called high-amylose corn. High-amylose cornstarch will not gelatinize even at boiling temperatures and must be pressure cooked. Genetic engineering was discussed further in Chapter 1.

Improved native starches are modified starches without the use of chemicals. Public interest and government constraints on the amount and type of chemicals used to modify starches encourage starch producers to seek hybrid plants offering desired functional properties [15, 44]. Improved native starches may provide better texture with enhanced taste qualities when compared with traditional modified starches [29, 33]. Soft white wheat with 100 percent amylopectin has been developed through conventional plant breeding [34].

Modified Starches

Starches may be modified using chemical or physical methods to tailor the functional characteristics of the starch for desired applications. Native starches from different sources (wheat, corn, potato, and tapioca) behave differently in food preparation because of varying compositions and ratios of amylose to amylopectin fractions. These differences should be considered when choosing a starch for a particular use.

Traditional natural or native starches may have limitations when used in food processing and manufacturing or in homes when freezing and thawing are desired. Consequently, chemical modification of natural starches is used in the food processing industry to achieve a desired texture and flavor in a finished product that must undergo high temperatures, high shear, low pH, or freeze–thaw cycles during its production [26]. Clear gel is an example of a modified cornstarch that is used in foods to be frozen and thawed or in canned pie fillings because of its stability in these applications.

The U.S. Food and Drug Administration (FDA) Title 21 Code of Federal Regulations has regulations governing the modification of natural food starches, providing guidelines concerning the types and amounts of modifiers allowed, the residuals permitted (if any), and the combinations that are acceptable. Within these guidelines, starch manufacturers work to develop new and innovative starch derivatives. The most common chemical modifications of starch utilized by the food industry involve *hydrolysis*, *cross-linking*, and *substitution*. However, over the last decade starch-converting enzymes, the alpha amylases, have been favored for hydrolysis [41]. Chemically modified starches are listed as modified starch on food labels.

Hydrolysis or Acid-Converted Starch. Hydrolysis of starch may be accomplished by mixing starch with water and an acid to produce a random breaking of linkage points along the molecular chain. Most of the starch still remains in the form of granules and is dried after the acid treatment. This modified starch is known as *thin-boiling* or *acid-thinned starch*. It produces a paste with low viscosity when boiled, and it hydrates at a lower temperature than the unmodified starch, but then produces a stiff gel. Acid-thinned starch often is used in the confectionery industry.

Cross-Linked or Cross-Bonded. Cross-linked starches are modified to improve viscosity and textural properties. The crosslinking reinforces hydrogen bonds with chemical bonds that act like bridges between starch molecules. The temperature for hydration is increased. The crosslinking improves resistance to high temperatures, low pH, and high shear. Thus, the cross-linked starches have improved stability in acid conditions, increased resistance to **shear** or stirring, and are more tolerant to heat. Food processors, therefore, have greater flexibility and control when they use cross-linked modified starches in manufactured foods. Starches modified

---

IN DEPTH
HYDROLYSIS OF STARCH

Hydrolysis is the breaking of a chemical linkage between basic units in a more complex molecule to produce smaller molecules. Water is involved in this reaction. Starch hydrolysis may be brought about or catalyzed by the action of enzymes called *amylases*. Starch hydrolysis replicates what happens in a plant as it needs to break down starch stores for energy (glucose) during germination. Acid may also act as a **catalyst** in the breakdown.

The complete hydrolysis of starch produces glucose because glucose is the basic building block for starch molecules. Intermediate steps in the hydrolysis of starch include the following:

- **Dextrins**—large chunks of starch molecules that are still large enough to be classified as polysaccharides

- **Oligosaccharides**—sugars that contain several glucose units

- Maltose—a **disaccharide** with two **monosaccharide** units, yielding only glucose ∎

by cross-linking are valuable for foods that are heated for extended periods of time or are subjected to exceptionally high shear (e.g., canned soup, spaghetti sauces, and certain pie fillings).

Cross-linking is produced by the use of reagents that have two or more reactive groups. These groups react with starch molecules at selected points and create a cross-bond between two chains of the starch molecule. Reagents include phosphorus oxychloride and adipic acid. Cross-linking may be thought of as welding molecular starch chains together at various spots or locations, thus limiting the swelling of the granules.

Improved properties that result from modification of starches is demonstrated in cross-linked **waxy maize** starch. The natural starch is non-gelling because it contains no amylose fraction, only amylopectin. In this regard, it should make a good thickening agent for fruit pies, providing a soft, thickened, but not rigid mixture; however, it is quite stringy in texture, which is an undesirable characteristic for fruit pies. When it is chemically treated to produce cross-linking, the resulting starch retains its non-gelling properties, but loses the stringy characteristic. It also is much more stable to heating and freezing making it an ideal thickening agent for frozen fruit pies.

Substitution or Stabilization. Substitution is used to prevent **retrogradation** of cooked starch, which may be likely to occur in frozen and refrigerated products. Retrogradation can lead to *syneresis*, or weeping, of liquid from the cooked starch mixture upon on standing. Syneresis can be seen as water beads on top of starch-based cream pies, puddings, or gels. The free water held in the spaces of the gel network has been forced out as the starch fractions realign squeezing the water out of the gel. Starches with a high percentage of amylose are most likely to experience retrogradation due to the linear amylose molecules that may re-associate. Substitution keeps the linear molecules from becoming realigned by repulsing the fragment reassociation (re-crystallization), thus improving clarity and reducing syneresis.

Starches are modified by substituting or adding a bulky blocking group on the starch backbone, preventing the original starch molecule from reassociating or recrystallizing. This can be achieved by adding certain mono-functional chemicals (those having only one reactive group, such as acetate) on the hydroxyl groups (–OH) of the starch molecule at random points, which decreases the tendency of bonding between molecular chains of the starch and increases the stability of the starch-thickened product as it is frozen and then thawed. Starches can also be made with emulsifying properties by adding a hydrophobic fraction. Substitution also lowers pasting and gelatinization temperature.

Physically Modified Starch. Physically modified starches may be modified by drum-drying, extrusion, spray drying, heat, or moisture treatment. Through one or more of these physical modifications, starches that hydrate or absorb water in cold liquid systems may be produced. The three major types of physically modified starches are instant, cold-water swelling, and heat-treated starches.

Instant or Pregelatinized Starches. Instant starches are made by cooking a starch in water, and then cooking it on a drum dryer or extruder. This cooked starch is then ground and may be used in products that do not include further heat treatment. The integrity of the starch granules is lost; however, the finished product has a smoother texture provided that the starch is adequately dispersed to prevent lumps [18]. Instant starches are utilized in instant dry-mix puddings, gravies, and sauces.

Cold-Water Swelling Starches. Cold-water swelling starches also are pregelatinized but retain their granular integrity [18]. These starches swell in room-temperature water and have a smooth texture. Cold-water swelling starches are produced by heating the starch in an ethanol–water solution or by a spray-drying cooking process.

Heat-Treated Starches. Starches may be treated by specialized heat processes to produce starches with desirable characteristics that may be labeled as "starch" and not "modified starch" because no chemicals are involved. Heat-treated starches have greater viscosity and stability [13]. The starch may be heated beyond its gelatinization point in insufficient water or heated with water below its gelatinization point for an extended period to result in the increased functionality.

Resistant Starches

Resistant starch is not digestible by the human body. A part of the ingested starch is not digested in the small intestine [31]. There are four main types of resistant starch called RS1, RS2, RS3, and RS4 (see **Table 11–5**). Of these, only RS4 is a chemically modified starch; the other types are found in nature. Although each of these kinds of resistant starch has different characteristics, all are useful in foods to increase total dietary fiber in food products without significantly impacting product quality as can occur with other sources of fiber [23, 35].

EFFECT OF HEAT AND COOLING ON STARCH

When starch is used in food preparation, several steps occur. First, when starch is placed in water, but not cooked, it will absorb water (**Figure 11–15**). Without heat, this water absorption is reversible. When starch granules are heated in water, however, an irreversible change called *gelatinization* occurs. Gelatinization is observed when a starch-based sauce, gravy, or

Table 11–5
RESISTANT STARCH: TYPES AND SOURCES

Type	Description	Food Sources
RS1	Physically inaccessible or digestion resistant	Whole grains, partly milled grains, seeds, and legumes
RS2	Ungelatinized resistant granules with a type B crystallinity; resists digestion because of dehydration level and compact structure	Raw potatoes, green bananas, some legumes, and high-amylose corn
RS3	Retrograded starch	Cooked and cooled potatoes, bread, cornflakes, and food products with repeated moist heat treatment
RS4	Chemically modified food starches producing cross-linking	Foods containing modified starches

Source: Reference 35.

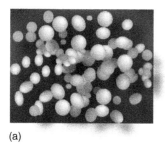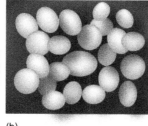

(a)   (b)   (c)

Figure 11–15

Starch gelatinization (a) Uncooked starch granules floating in liquid. (b) Starch begins to swell when heated. (c) Fully gelatinized swollen starch granules.

Figure 11–16

A white sauce, also called béchamel, is thickened with a roux composed of flour and butter. The flour provides starch that when heated will gelatinize and thicken the sauce. (Richard Embery/Pearson Education)

pudding thickens as it is cooked (**Figure 11–16**). With continued heating, a cooked *starch paste* is produced. A starch paste is a viscous mass of swollen starch granules and potentially also granule fragments [3].

Gel formation may occur as the starch paste cools if the starch used contains a high proportion of amylose. Cooling also may result in the reassociation of some of the starch molecules, thereby forming a tight gel matrix. This state is known as *retrogradation* and can cause syneresis, or weeping. In the following section, the impact of dry heat, moist heat, and the influence of ingredients when cooking starch in a liquid will be explored as related to gelatinization, gel formation, and retrogradation.

Dry Heat

When dry heat is applied to starch or starchy foods, the starch becomes more soluble in comparison with unheated starch and has reduced thickening power when it is made into a cooked paste. As starch is heated with dry heat, nonenzymatic browning occurs and a toasted flavor develops. If the heat is excessive, a burned flavor will result. During the dry heating of starch, some of the starch molecules are broken down to dextrins in a process called *dextrinization*. Dry-heat dextrins, known as *pyrodextrins*, are formed in the crust of baked flour mixtures, on toast, on fried starchy or starch-coated foods, and on various ready-to-eat cereals.

Figure 11–17

Espagnole (brown sauce) is made from a dark roux.   (Richard Embery/Pearson Education)

Dry heat is used to brown flour in the preparation of a brown roux used in an **espagnole sauce**, gumbo, or brown gravy (**Figure 11–17**). The dry flour is browned either in a dry pan or with butter to produce a **brown roux**. The browning of the flour is desirable when making espagnole sauce because of the change in color and development of a toasted, peanut, or nutty flavor. However, because the flour was browned and has less thickening ability, a larger proportion of browned flour to liquid or brown roux is needed to achieve the desired thickness.

Moist Heat

The starch granule is generally insoluble in cold water. A nonviscous suspension of starch is formed when raw starch is mixed with cold water and, on standing, the granules gradually settle to the bottom of the container. After this starch–water suspension is heated, gelatinization occurs, producing a colloidal dispersion of starch in water. The resulting thickened mixture is called a *starch paste*.

Gelatinization. As starch is heated in water, water is absorbed, the starch granules swell, small crystallite areas within the granule melt, and the structure of the starch is changed, resulting in the loss of the cross-pattern called birefringence (Figure 11–12) [1, 3]. The point at which the birefringence disappears is called the *gelatinization point*. The process is called **gelatinization**. Gelatinization results in an increase in **viscosity** or thickness until a peak viscosity is reached. The changes that occur during gelatinization are irreversible. Without sufficient water, starch granules cannot gelatinize.

The starch dispersion also increases in **translucency** to a maximum as heating continues [17]. The degree of translucency varies with the type of starch. Starches made with root starches, such as potato and tapioca, generally are clearer. Cornstarch produces a more opaque gel (Figure 11–10).

Gelatinization occurs over a temperature range that is characteristic for a particular starch and in part is related to the size of the starch granules. There are various stages in the heating of starch in water. Large granules swell first. Potato starch granules, generally larger than those of other starches, begin to swell at a lower temperature than cornstarch or tapioca. In any case, swelling is usually complete at a temperature of 190 to 194°F (88 to 92°C). Starch gelatinization temperatures for various starches are provided in **Table 11–6**.

Pasting. When the heating of the starch–water mixture continues after gelatinization, further granular swelling, leaching of soluble components (often amylose), and disruption of the granules occur [3]. This process is called *pasting*. Gelatinization and the development of a viscous starch paste are generally described as sequential processes [1].

Gel Formation (Gelation). Carbohydrate gel formation or *gelation* is different from *gelatinization*. Also carbohydrate gels are different than protein gels such as gelatin or custard, which will be discussed in other chapters. The ability of starch grains to gelatinize is different than forming a 3-D network called a gel.

Table 11–6
STARCH GELATINIZATION TEMPERATURES FOR SELECTED TYPES OF STARCH

Type of Starch	Approximate Gelatinization Temperature
Corn (common)	149–163°F (65–73°C)
Corn (waxy)	149–156°F (65–69°C)
Corn (55 percent high amylose)	183°F (84°C)
Corn (70 percent high amylose)	199°F (93°C)
Wheat	136–147°F (58–64°C)
Tapioca	138–149°F (59–65°C)
Potato	135–149°F (57–65°C)

Gelatinization describes the process involving water that causes the swelling of starch granules that are heated. In the presence of excess water, these swollen starch granules will rupture when heated and form a gel structure [27]. Starch can gelatinize into a wide variety of viscous pastes depending on the starch used, concentration, and other ingredients, but amylose at an essential concentration is essential for gel formation [9]. The 3-D gel structure is due primarily to the amylose fraction in the starch that was freed from the starch granule. Although the free amylopectin fraction may interact in the gel structure, it is the amylose fraction that is essential for a gel structure [27]. Non-covalent hydrogen bonding between the amylose fractions is thought to be essential to build the 3-D gel structure via intermolecular and intramolecular hydrogen bonding [27]. The water hydrogen bonds are thought to act as cross-linking bridges between the amylose fractions for the gel structure [27]. As the gel cools, the gel structure becomes rigid. There is a proposed phase separation (water) and crystallization aggregation (amylose) for the gel structure [27]. Water becomes entrapped in this crystalline gel network. If amylopectin fractions are present, they fill in the amylose gel network [22]. This starch gel phenomenon can be witness in such items as a gel holds its cream pie that when cut holds its shape.

The strength of the gel is dependent on the junction points of the starch network. Branched chains form weak junction zones. Short starch chains that are weakly held together will separate at the slightest increase of temperature movement causing a weak gel. Long chains with strong junction zones form strong sturdy gels [6]. Gel formation in cooked starch pastes is a gradual process that continues over several hours as the paste cools. Starches containing relatively large amounts of amylose, such as cornstarch, form firmer gels than starches with a somewhat lower concentration of amylose, such as tapioca. Waxy varieties of starch without amylose do not form gels. Thus, non-gelling modified waxy starches are effectively used for products that are frozen or items such as a stir-fry sauce or gravy that is to be cooled and reheated for later use. A wheat flour or cornstarch sauce or gravy is difficult to reheat into a smooth sauce after cooling due to gel formation. More about the science of gel formation is provided in the "In Depth: Gel Formation" feature.

Retrogradation or Setback. Retrogradation describes what happens to a gelatinized starch as it cools and ages. As starch-thickened mixtures cool, some starch molecules begin to reassociate, resulting in increased opacity and then a precipitate or gel [3]. This process, called retrogradation or setback, is responsible for defects in starchy foods such as the loss of viscosity in soups and the staling of bread.

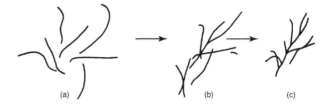

Figure 11–18

Diagram representing gel formation and further retrogradation of a starch dispersion: (a) solution, (b) gel, (c) retrograded. (From Elizabeth Osman, Starch and other polysaccharides. In *Food theory and applications*, edited by Pauline C. Paul and Helen H. Palmer. Copyright © 1972, John Wiley & Sons, Inc. Reprinted by permission of John Wiley.)

The term *retrogradation* is used for this process because it refers to the starch molecules associating more closely together and ultimately again forming an organized, crystalline pattern [1, 3]. The starch molecules form a network that traps free water. During retrogradation, the free water is squeezed out of the gel network. Amylose molecules are subject to this reassociation or recrystallization. As retrogradation proceeds and the starch molecules pull together more tightly, the gel network shrinks and water is pushed out of the gel. Starches that are high in amylose (such as cornstarch) undergo retrogradation more rapidly than those higher in amylopectin [3]. However, amylopectin molecules recrystallize with long-term storage causing even more gel rigidity [22]. Freezing and thawing increases retrogradation [9]. Syneresis, or weeping, results from the increased molecular association as the starch mixture ages [1]. This can be seen in foods such as cream-based pies which may have tiny beads of water on the surface. Bread staling is due to starch retrogradation as the starch units realign over time causing crumb hardening, known as staling. Retrogradation of starch occurs faster at refrigerator temperatures. Freezing prevents staling. More on this issue is discussed in later chapters.

Freezing a cooked starch gel has a similar effect. The starchy framework remains intact but the water turns to ice crystals. Upon thawing, the water is not able to reassociate with the starch network, and water can be squeezed from the spongy amylose gel structure. Modified starch must be used when freezing. Gel formation and retrogradation are illustrated in **Figure 11–18**.

FACTORS AFFECTING STARCH PASTES

Certain conditions must be standardized and controlled to obtain uniformity in the cooking of starch pastes. These include temperature of heating, time of heating, intensity of agitation or stirring (shear), acidity (**pH**) of the mixture, and addition of other ingredients.

Temperature and Time of Heating

Starch pastes may be prepared most quickly by bringing to a boiling temperature over direct heat, constantly stirring during thickening, and simmering for approximately 1 minute. Longer cooking to improve the flavor is not necessary; however, if a starch mixture is not fully cooked, then a **raw starch flavor** and a less smooth or silky mouthfeel will be evident. Continued heating after gelatinization is complete can result in decreased thickness. However, in home cooking situations, boiling or cooking starchy sauces and pudding for longer periods usually does not produce thinner mixtures, because the loss of moisture by evaporation is not controlled. The loss of moisture results in an increase in starch concentration and therefore an increased thickness that then offsets the thinning from excessive heat.

Under carefully controlled conditions, starch pastes that are heated rapidly are somewhat thicker than similar pastes heated slowly [16]. More concentrated dispersions of starch show higher viscosity at lower temperatures than less concentrated mixtures because of the larger number of granules that can swell in the early stages of gelatinization.

Agitation or Stirring

Stirring, while cooking starch mixtures, is desirable in the early stages to obtain a smooth product of uniform consistency. However, if agitation is too intense or is continued too long, it accelerates the rupturing of the starch granules, decreases viscosity, and may give a slick, pasty mouthfeel. Stirring should therefore be minimized.

Acidity (pH)

A high degree of acidity appears to cause some fragmentation of starch granules and hydrolysis of the starch molecules, thus decreasing the thickening power of the starch [13]. In cooked starch mixtures containing fruit juices or vinegar, such as fruit pie fillings and salad dressings, the acidity may be high enough (pH below 4) to cause some thinning.

Specially prepared modified starches resistant to acid breakdown are used in commercial food processing when this may be a problem. When a high concentration of sugar is also present in a starch paste, the sugar may help to decrease the effect of acid because sugar limits the swelling of starch granules, and the starch molecules are therefore not as available for hydrolysis by acid. Proportions of ingredients in recipes for acid–starch products, such as lemon pie filling, have been adjusted to compensate for the usual effects of acid and sugar so that a desirable consistency results. Acid juices, such as lemon juice, should also be added after the starchy paste has been cooked, thus limiting the acid's contact with starch molecules.

Water Availability

Water is essential for gelatinization. If adequate water is not available or is "bound" by another ingredient, then starch cannot undergo gelatinization. Water-to-starch ratio should be above two to three parts of water to starch based on weight. Later chapters will demonstrate the importance of water and gelatinization in food systems.

Sugar

Sugar raises the temperature at which a starch mixture gelatinizes [2, 38]. The use of a relatively large amount of sugar delays the swelling of the starch granules and thus decreases the thickness of the paste, at least partially, by competing with the starch for water. If not enough water is available for the starch granules, they cannot swell sufficiently. In a recipe calling for a large amount of sugar, only part of the sugar needs to be added before cooking. After the starch mixture has been cooked, the remainder of the sugar can be added with much less effect on viscosity.

High concentrations of sucrose (table sugar) are more effective in delaying swelling or gelatinization than are equal concentrations of monosaccharides such as glucose and fructose. At a concentration of 20 percent or more, all sugars and syrups cause a decided decrease in the gel strength of starch pastes.

IN DEPTH

GEL FORMATION

Many starch molecules are disrupted during the process of gelatinization as the starch granules swell. Some of the molecules of amylose, the linear starch fraction, leach out from the granule. Two or more of these chains may form a juncture point, creating a new bond and gradually leading to more bonds and more extensively ordered regions. Bonding with the amylose molecules begins immediately after cooking.

Amylopectin, the branched fraction, usually remains inside the swollen granule, where it more slowly forms new bonds between branches in a process of recrystallization [42]. Bonds formed between the branches of the bushy amylopectin molecules are weak and have little practical effect on the rigidity of the starch paste; however, bonds between the long-chain amylose molecules are relatively strong and form readily. This bonding produces a three-dimensional structure that results in the development of a gel, with the amylose molecules forming a network that holds water in its meshes. The rigidity of the starch mixture is increased. ∎

The presence of fats and proteins, which tend to coat starch granules and thereby delay hydration, also lowers the rate of viscosity development.

Other Ingredients

Various ingredients are used with starch in the preparation of food. Some of these ingredients have a pronounced effect on gelatinization and on the gel strength of the cooled starch mixture. Salt (sodium chloride) is commonly used in starch-thickened sauces. Salt effects on gelatinization vary but are typically not an issue in most food systems. Salt is typically about 1–2 percent, so it plays a minor role in starch cookery. Surfactants such as emulsifiers are sometimes used in starch cookery. Surfactant roles may have some minor effect on starch cookery.

STARCH COOKERY

Understanding techniques and principles behind starch cookery is necessary to produce lump-free smooth gels and pastes since a uniform thickened or gelled product is desired with starch cookery. Starch granules must be separated before heating in the liquid. There are several techniques that are used to achieve this separation depending on if cold or hot liquids will be used. The first step in starch cookery involves separating starch granules before heating in the liquid. The second step requires the even and uniform distribution of the separated starch granules in the liquid before heating. Starch granules should swell uniformly so that some granules do not take up more water than others leaving some ungelatinized starch in a cooked mixture. Water (liquid) is essential to gelatinize starch. The following discussion reviews several options of starch cookery.

Combining Starch with Cold Liquids

Starch separation can be achieved by suspending starch in cold liquid prior to heating. Disperse the starch evenly in the cold liquid by whisking, stirring, or even shaking in a sealed container to mix the starch and liquid. Although not impossible, wheat flour is a bit more difficult to disperse with cold water method. Flour with cold water can be placed in a sealed jar or container and shaken to form a uniform thin slurry. The slurry can be strained prior to heating to rid any remaining lumps. Using instantized flour (modified flour discussed in upcoming chapters) does make cold water flour dispersion easier. Starch can also be separated by combining with sugar and then adding the cold liquid prior to heating. This method is often used for cooked thickened pie fillings or puddings.

Once starch is uniformly distributed in the cold liquid, the liquid can be slowly heated. Stirring to keep starch particles separated and distributed while preventing starch to settle to the bottom of the pan is important. Stirring also helps to uniformly distribute the heat. Once starch begins to thicken, the stirring is gentle and limited so not to thin and damage the paste or gel. The starch paste can be cooked over direct heat or in a double boiler (pan, bowl set in a pan of boiling water). The double boiler method takes longer to reach gelatinization temperature. Sometimes the double boiler requires covering the mixture to prevent a skin forming over the top of the mixture.

Combining Starch with Hot Liquids

A potential problem in starch cookery results from the tendency of dry starch particles to clump or form lumps. Before hot liquids are combined with starch, the particles of starch must be separated to bring about a uniform dispersion of well-hydrated starch granules. This process can be accomplished by (1) dispersing the dry starch with melted fat to make a **roux**, (2) mixing the starch with cold water to form a **slurry**, or (3) blending the starch with sugar.

Roux. A roux is prepared by blending melted fat, such as clarified butter, with flour to form a paste the consistency of wet sand (**Figure 11–19**). A roux may be white, blond, or brown (**Figure 11–20**). A white roux is cooked only briefly, whereas a blond roux is cooked until a light brown color. Brown roux is cooked until a darker color has been achieved [24]. A brown roux will have less thickening power due to dextrinization, as described earlier in this chapter. The roux is then incorporated into a liquid to thicken it. To avoid lumps, a cold liquid should be added to a hot roux, or, alternatively, a cold roux should be added to a hot liquid with vigorous stirring until blended (**Figure 11–21**). Further cooking will result in the gelatinization of the starch.

Figure 11–19

Steps for cooking roux. (1) In a heavy saucepan melt fat (2) Add all flour and stir to form a paste. (3) Stir and cook to form desired roux color. (Richard Embery/Pearson Education)

Figure 11–20

Roux (roo) is principal thickener for sauces. Fat is combined with flour to form a cooked paste prior to adding liquid. Fat coats flour particles so they are separated and will not lump when liquid is added and cooked. (a) A white roux is cooked only briefly to coat flour particles. Serves as the base for white sauce (bèchamel). (b) Ivory roux cooked longer to develop some caramelized color and richer flavors. Used as the base for velouté. (c) Brown Roux is cooked to develop darker color, nutty aroma, and flavor. Used for dark sauces. (Richard Embery/Pearson Education)

Figure 11–21

When thickening a liquid with a roux, (a) add cold liquid or stock to a hot roux or (b) add cold roux to a hot liquid or stock. Blending a hot roux into a hot liquid is not recommended because it is very difficult to smoothly blend the roux into the liquid before lumps are formed due to the rapid gelatinization of the starch. (Richard Embery/Pearson Education)

Figure 11–22

A cold cornstarch slurry is whisked into a hot liquid and cooked until the sauce is thick and the raw starch flavor is cooked out. (Richard Embery/Pearson Education)

Slurry. A slurry is prepared by mixing flour or starch with some of the cold liquid to form a "slurry" with the consistency of thick cream. The slurry is added to a hot liquid while stirring and then cooked over direct heat until the mixture boils (**Figure 11–22**). The slurry method is often useful in making gravy from meat drippings. Although the slurry method is useful for many products, it may not provide as rich a flavor and generally will be less stable in a soup or sauce than when these products are prepared with a roux. A sauce or gravy, however, will be more clear and glossy when cornstarch is used instead of flour; therefore, some dishes, such as stir-fry vegetables, are best prepared with cornstarch slurry.

Sauces

A variety of sauces may be made with starch used as a thickening agent. A white sauce is a starch-thickened sauce made from fat, flour, liquid, and seasonings. When the liquid is milk, the basic sauce is called a white sauce or *béchamel* (bay´-sha-mel *or* besh´-a-mel). When the liquid is a light stock of veal, chicken, or fish, the sauce is called a *velouté* (vayl´-oo-tay´). The five basic mother sauces are described in **Table 11–7**. All of the five mother sauces, except hollandaise, are thickened with a roux that has starch in the form of flour.

White sauces are used in the preparation of a variety of dishes, including cheese sauce, cream soup, soufflés, and various casseroles. The finished sauce should be smooth, satiny, and free of lumps. The consistency depends on the amount of starchy agent used. **Table 11–8** gives proportions for standard white sauces of various consistencies along with suggested uses. If cornstarch is substituted for flour in making a white sauce, only half as much cornstarch should be used compared to the original amount of flour. Cornstarch is composed of nearly all starch, as compared to flour, which also contains protein.

Table 11–7
THE FIVE BASIC MOTHER SAUCES. These basic sauces can be used as a base to make additional sauces.

Sauce Name	Description
Béchamel	Milk thickened with roux and flavored with onion, nutmeg, salt, and pepper. Cheese sauce, mornay, and other sauces may be made using béchamel.
Velouté	Fish stock, chicken stock, or veal stock is thickened with roux and seasoned with salt and pepper. A suprême sauce is made by adding cream to a chicken velouté sauce.
Espagnole	Brown stock, such as a beef stock, is thickened with a brown roux and seasoned with tomato purée, diced carrots, onions, and celery and additional herbs and spices. This sauce is used to make demi-glace by adding equal parts espagnole to a brown stock and simmering until the mixture is reduced by half due to evaporation.
Tomato sauce	Tomatoes, diced carrots, onions, and celery with additional herbs and spices are cooked together and may or may not be thickened with a roux, depending on the desired use of this sauce. A vegetable or white stock also may be included.
Hollandaise	Composed of egg yolks, white wine vinegar, water, lemon juice, clarified butter, and seasonings, this sauce is thickened as a result of the egg yolks and the emulsion formed when making this sauce. A béarnaise sauce is made using hollandaise as a base.

Source: Reference 24.

Table 11–8
PROPORTIONS OF INGREDIENTS AND USES FOR WHITE SAUCE

Sauce	Fat*	Flour*	Liquid	Salt	Pepper	Uses
Thin	1½ tsp (7 g)	1 Tbsp (7 g)	1 c (237 mL)	1/4 tsp (1.5 g)	**	Cream soups
Medium	1 Tbsp (14 g)	2 Tbsp (14 g)	1 c	1/4 tsp	**	Creamed vegetables and meats; casseroles
Thick	1½ Tbsp (21 g)	3 Tbsp (21 g)	1 c	1/4 tsp	**	Soufflés
Very thick	2 Tbsp (28 g)	4 Tbsp (28 g)	1 c	1/4 tsp	**	Croquettes

*Amounts may be adjusted, if desired. A roux (mixture of flour and fat) should be the consistency of wet sand. If too dry, then add fat, or if too wet, add more flour.

**Add pepper to taste.

**fg = few grains.

Cream Soups

Cream soups may vary in consistency, but their usual thickness corresponds to that of thin white sauce. One tablespoon of flour is used for each cup of liquid, which may be part milk and part vegetable cooking water or meat broth and finely diced vegetables. Combined vegetable waters sometimes produce a soup of better flavor than the water from a single vegetable. A **mirepoix**, composed of diced onions, carrots, and celery, is used in many soups because of the flavor provided. If starchy vegetables are used for pulp, such as is done in some purée or cream soups, the flour should be reduced to about one-half the usual amount. The fat must also be reduced, or, lacking enough flour to hold it in suspension, the fat will float on top of the soup. Some flour is desirable for starchy soups, such as potato or dried bean soup, to hold the pulp in suspension. In preparing a cream soup, a medium white sauce can be made from milk, fat, flour, and seasonings (Table 11–8). An amount of vegetable juice and pulp equal to the milk used is then heated and added to the sauce, thus diluting the mixture to the consistency of a thin white sauce.

If acid juices, such as tomato, are used, the acid is added gradually to the white sauce at serving time to minimize the tendency to curdle. Fresh, recently opened milk will be more stable in resisting curdling, and whole or reduced-fat milk generally is less likely to curdle than nonfat (skim) milk. Although a curdled cream soup is edible, it is aesthetically undesirable. As shown in **Figure 11–23**, a cream soup should be smooth and creamy without evidence of curdling. Making a tomato sauce from the tomato juice, fat, and flour (roux) instead of making a white sauce is preferred by some cooks and is a common practice in the production of canned tomato soup.

Figure 11–23

This New England clam chowder has an attractive appearance and has been properly prepared so that the sauce is smooth and creamy. (Richard Embery/Pearson Education)

Figure 11–24

Meringue is placed on this chocolate cream pie. This pudding, thickened with starch and eggs, will hold its shape when cut and served on a plate. (Richard Embery/Pearson Education)

Baking soda may be used by some in cream of tomato soup because the soda will offset the acid in the tomato and therefore reduce the tendency toward curdling. Baking soda, however, is not recommended because it may increase the alkalinity of the soup so much that vitamin C and some of the B vitamins are essentially destroyed by **oxidation**. The use of excess baking soda may also seriously mar flavor.

Starch-Thickened Desserts

Cornstarch pudding is probably the most common starch-thickened dessert. Although similar desserts are made from other cereal sources, including wheat flour alone or combined with tapioca or sago, puddings made with cornstarch are often considered to have a smoother mouthfeel and less "pasty" texture than those made with flour. The consistency of starchy puddings varies according to personal preference. If a pudding stiff enough to form a mold is desired, it will have better flavor and texture if it is made as soft as possible while still holding its form when unmolded. Many prefer pudding to have a relatively soft consistency, in which case it must be spooned into

individual dishes. Tapioca and sago puddings are usually more acceptable when they are relatively soft.

The preparation of puddings and pie fillings often combines starch and egg cookery to produce a creamy mixture (**Figure 11–24**). The product is thickened with starch before the egg is added because starch tolerates higher temperatures than egg. The pudding is first prepared in the same manner as a cornstarch pudding containing no egg. After starch gelatinization is complete, a small amount of the hot starchy mixture may be added to the egg. This dilutes, or **tempers**, the egg so that it does not coagulate in lumps when it is added to the bulk of the hot mixture (**Figure 11–25**). Alternatively, a small amount of cold milk may be withheld in the beginning of the preparation and mixed with the egg to dilute it. This milk–egg mixture is then added all at once, with stirring, to the hot starchy pudding mixture, producing a smooth, creamy product.

Starchy puddings containing egg should be cooked sufficiently after the addition of the egg to coagulate the egg proteins. If this is not done, the pudding may become thin on standing. If a fairly large amount of egg is used, the temperature of the pudding after the egg is added should not reach boiling

(a)

(b)

Figure 11–25

(a) Hot liquid is slowly poured into eggs while beating to warm the eggs gradually. (b) The egg and hot liquid are returned to the range to finish cooking. (Richard Embery/Pearson Education)

because this may result in curdling of the egg with a consequent grainy texture of the pudding.

Numerous additions or substitutions may be made to the basic formula for cornstarch pudding to vary the flavor. These additions include chocolate or cocoa, caramelized sugar, shredded coconut, nuts, maple syrup, or diced fruits. Recipe books should be consulted for specific directions in preparing the variations. A basic recipe for pudding is provided in the accompanying "Up Close" feature.

Microwave Cooking of Starch Mixtures

The microwave oven is a quick and convenient tool in the preparation of relatively small quantities of starch-thickened sauces and puddings. If preparing larger quantities, the use of the microwave oven will not necessarily be a timesaver.

A smooth, creamy chocolate pudding to serve only one or two persons may be prepared in just a few minutes. First, semisweet baking chocolate is heated in milk in a two-cup measure with the microwave oven on high for 1 to 2 minutes until the mixture is hot. A blend of dry cornstarch and sugar is then added to the hot chocolate milk, and the mixture is heated on high for 30 seconds to 1 minute, stirring after each 30 seconds. Vanilla, butterscotch, and other types of starch-thickened puddings are prepared in a similar manner. Microwaved

sauces and puddings need less stirring than conventionally cooked sauces and puddings because there is no tendency for the material on the bottom of the container to scorch, as in range-top cooking.

It is just as easy to prepare small amounts of a basic white sauce in the microwave oven. First, butter or margarine is melted by heating on high for 30 seconds to 1 minute to make approximately 1 cup of sauce. The flour and seasonings are then added, and milk is blended into the fat–flour mixture. Microwaving 6 to 8 minutes then produces a smooth, creamy white sauce. The mixture is stirred at approximately 1-minute intervals during the cooking. Using a similar technique, gravies may be prepared in the microwave oven using meat stock and meat drippings.

STARCH TO SUGAR AND MORE

Sweetener production is a major use of starch in food processing. The United States is a leader in the conversion of cornstarch to high-fructose corn syrup (HFCS). HFCS has replaced traditional cane sugar in many foods.

The starch industry can emulate the plant breakdown starch to sugar by hydrolyzing starch into sugar by adding acids or enzyme (**Figure 11–26**). Any starch can be transformed into classic sweet syrup, high-maltose syrup for beer, and high-fructose syrup for soft

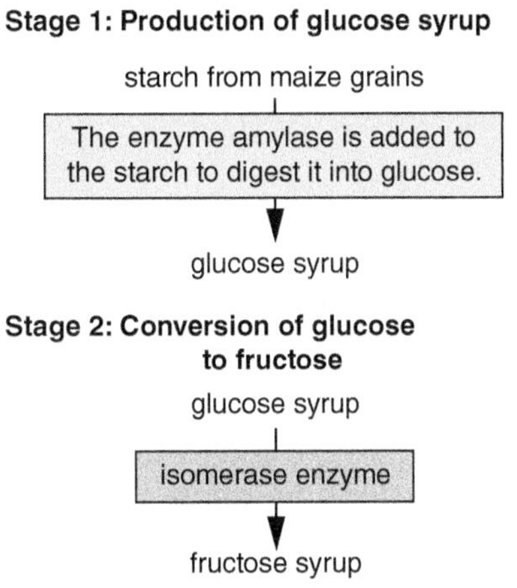

Stage 1: Production of glucose syrup

starch from maize grains

The enzyme amylase is added to the starch to digest it into glucose.

glucose syrup

Stage 2: Conversion of glucose to fructose

glucose syrup

isomerase enzyme

fructose syrup

Figure 11–26

Production of fructose syrup from corn (maize) starch.

Figure 11–27

USDA microbiologist and biochemical engineer add yeast to starch in a bioreactor to begin ethanol fermentation. (USDA/ Scott Bauer)

drinks or sugar substitute. Starch hydrolysis to sugar is characterized and measured as dextrose equivalent (DE), where DE 100 is equal to pure glucose (dextrose) and DE 0 is pure starch. High DE crystallizes easily and yields a powder of granular form used in medicine and chewed tablets. High-fructose syrups from starch are produced from refined high-DE glucose syrups. Isomerase enzymes convert the glucose to fructose and contain about 42 percent fructose in equilibrium with glucose or DE 42. In sucrose-based liquid sugar from sugarcane and sugar beets, the fructose content is about 55 percent. Enrichment of the DE 42 can be done to bring levels in line with natural sugar syrups for DE 55. So HFCS either have 42 percent fructose and 58 percent glucose or 55 percent fructose and 45 percent glucose. Table sugar is equal 50 percent fructose and 50 percent glucose and honey is 48 percent fructose and 52 percent glucose. So the molecules found in starch-converted syrups are the same glucose molecules naturally found in honey and table sugar.

Starch can also be converted to sugar alcohols such as sorbitol. This process involves enzymatic hydrolysis and then catalytic hydrogenation. The starch is hydrolyzed to a dextrose syrup and then hydrogenated with a catalyst in a reactor where it is vigorously stirred under pressure and a controlled temperature. The hydrogenated solution undergoes further refinement to produce the sugar alcohol such as sorbitol. Sugar and HFCS are further discussed in Chapter 9.

Maltodextrins are derived from starch and are used as food additives and bulking agents. They are made from acid or enzymatic starch hydrolysis. Maltodextrins are a non-sweet, nutritive polymer of glucose units linked by alpha 1–4 bonds with DE less than 20. Maltodextrins are odorless, flavorless powders with a DE less than 20. They are sometimes referred to as dextrins. Maltodextrins and HFCS are on the generally recognized as safe (GRAS) and defined in the Code of Federal Regulations Title 21. Much caramel coloring and flavoring start before starch is hydrolyzed to sugar and caramelized. Although bioethanol is used for automobile fuel and not food, starch plays an important role in its production, as starch is converted to glucose and yeast ferments the sugar to alcohol (bioethanol), which is used as fuel for automobiles (**Figure 11–27**).

STUDY QUESTIONS

Consumption Trends and Nutrition

1. Discuss the consumption trends with starch. Why? What is the major starch source in the United States? How is that starch source used?

2. What is the nutritive value of starch? How does starch fit into the U.S. Dietary Recommendations?

Composition and Structure

3. **(a)** Describe the appearance of starch granules when viewed under a microscope. How do their size and shape differ from one plant source to another?

(b) Name the two fractions of starch. Explain how they differ in structure.

(c) Explain why some natural starches are chemically modified. Give examples of the types of chemical modification most commonly used.

(d) How can native starches be improved for desirable uses in food processing, lessening the need for chemically modified starches?

(e) What products are produced as starch is hydrolyzed? What may catalyze this process?

(f) What are resistant starches?

Starch Processing

4. What is wet milling? Why does this vary between raw materials? How are the methods similar or different?

Kinds of Starch

5. Compare and contrast the use of each of these sources of starch.

(a) Cornstarch

(b) Tapioca

(c) Wheat

(d) Potato

(e) Rice

(f) Arrowroot

(g) Sago

Effects of Heat and Cooling on Starch

6. (a) Describe what happens when dry starches are heated. What is this process called?

(b) Why is gravy made from browned flour usually thinner than gravy made from the same amount of unbrowned flour? Explain.

(c) Describe what happens when starch granules are heated in water. What is this process called?

(d) What is birefringence? What does its presence or absence tell you about the starch?

(e) Distinguish between the process described in question 6c and *pasting* of starch.

(f) Describe the general effect of each of the following on the thickness of a cooked starch mixture: (1) rate of heating, (2) excessive stirring, and (3) addition of sugar.

7. How does a thickened starch mixture become a gel?

(a) What is this process called? What happens in the starch mixture to bring it about?

(b) How does the amount of amylose in the starch affect the rigidity? Why?

(c) What is meant by *retrogradation* of a starch paste?

(d) What is *syneresis*? Why may it occur in cooked starch mixtures?

(e) Which of the common starches forms the stiffest and which the softest pudding when used in equal amounts? Explain.

8. Distinguish between *gelatinization* and *gelation* of starch mixtures.

Starch Cookery

9. Describe three ways to keep powdery starches from lumping when they are added to hot liquid. Explain what is happening in each case.

10. Describe appropriate methods for preparing each of the following items. Explain why these methods should be successful.

(a) White sauce

(b) Cream of vegetable soup

(c) Cream of tomato soup

(d) Cornstarch pudding

(e) Cornstarch pudding with egg

(f) Roux

(g) Slurry

11. What two types of instant starch are available to the food processor? How do these differ from each other? Give examples of products in which the consumer may expect to find instant starches used.

Microwave Starch Cookery

12. Suggest appropriate procedures for preparing puddings and white sauces in the microwave oven.

Starch to Sugar and More

13. Discuss how starch is used beyond a thickening agent.

12

Cereal Grains, Noodles, and Pasta

Cereal grains are members of the grass family which produce a dry, edible one-seeded fruit "caryopsis," commonly called a kernel, grain, or berry (**Figure 12–1**). **Table 12–1** lists cereal grains recognized by American Association of Cereal Chemists International. The word *cereal* is derived from *Ceres*, the Roman goddess of grain.

Table 12–1
CEREAL GRAINS

Wheat[1]	Millet
Rice	Fonio[4]
Corn[2]	Triticale
Oats	Sorghum[3]
Barley	Teff
Rye	Job's tear[4]
Canary seed	

Source: AACCI and Wheat Foods Council.

[1] Includes spelt, emmer, faro, einkorn, Kamut®, durum
[2] Includes maize and popcorn
[3] Commonly referred to as milo
[4] Coix seed or Chinese pearl barley

Wheat, corn (maize), rice, oats, rye, barley, millet, and sorghum are the most important cereals used for human food. Sorghum is used chiefly for animal feed in the United States, but it is an important food source in other parts of the world. Triticale is a grain produced by crossbreeding wheat and rye. Pseudo-cereal or false grains are similar to cereal grains, but have different botanical origins. Quinoa, amaranth, and buckwheat are popular pseudo-cereal grains. Buckwheat is not a seed of the grass family, but is often classified with the cereal grains because buckwheat flour has properties and uses similar to cereal flours. A rediscovered cereal-like plant is amaranth, which produces an abundance of tiny seeds. About 1,000 of these seeds weigh approximately 1 gram. Amaranth is one of those rare plants whose leaves are eaten as a vegetable and the seeds are used as cereals [86].

Cereal is not limited to breakfast foods—it applies to a large group of foods made from grains, including flours, meals, breads, and alimentary pastes or pasta. The ease with which grains can be produced and stored, together with the relatively low cost and nutritional contribution of many cereal foods, particularly whole-grain products, has resulted in the widespread use of grain commodities throughout the world. Cereal grains are the principal crops that have

CORN — Cornmeal

RICE — Brown Rice

WHEAT — Bulgur

OATS — Rolled Oats

BARLEY — Pearled Barley

Figure 12–1

Milled grains commonly consumed in the United States. (Richard Embery/Pearson Education)

made the continuation of humankind possible. They are the staple in the diets of most population groups.

In this chapter, the following topics will be discussed:

• Consumption trends
• Nutritive value
• Structure and composition of grains
• Cereal grains and pseudo-cereal grains
• Breakfast cereals
• Cooking of rice
• Noodles
• Pasta

CONSUMPTION TRENDS AND NUTRITION

Consumption Trends

From a dietary perspective, Americans eat enough *total* grains; however, no age group consumed recommended amount of *whole* grains [96, 87] (**Figure 12–2**). According to the USDA Economic Research Service, the average daily intake of grains for the population is 6.46 ounces. However, rice data is not factored into this number or per capita total U.S. grain consumption since 2010.

Figure 12–2

Americans' total grain consumption meets recommendations but no age group eats enough whole grains. (Elena Schweitzer/ Shutterstock)

Wheat is the major grain eaten in the United States, but rice, corn, and oat products are gaining popularity and have increased their share of total grain consumption since 1970 [93]. Interest in ancient grains and alternative pseudo-cereals has increased too. Future projection of grain production is shown in **Figure 12–3**.

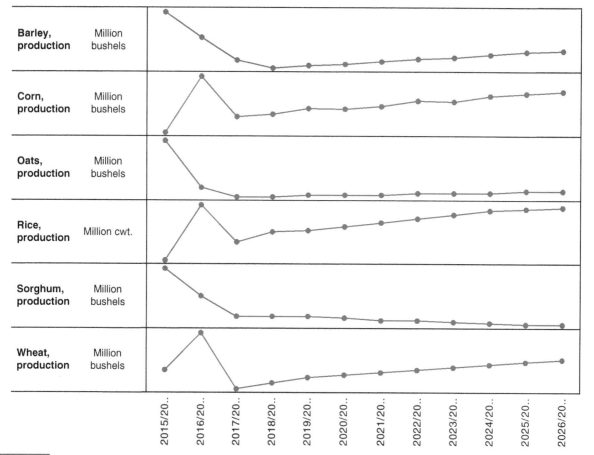

Figure 12–3

The USDA uses complex modeling to predict future cereal crop productions. This chart shows crop production prediction through 2026. (USDA Economic Research Service)

Figure 12–4

Eating whole grain breads is a way to increase whole grain consumption. (Smileus/Shutterstock)

There have been many efforts to increase Americans' whole-grain consumption through education programs, labelling, dietary guidelines, and government programs [25, 39] (**Figure 12–4**). The International Food Information Council Foundation cites that *2016 Food and Health Survey* reported 59 percent of Americans were trying to consume more whole grains in their diets, which was up from 53 percent in 2014 to 56 percent in 2015. Whole-grain consumption increased with consumer awareness [39] (**Figure 12–5**). Ready-to-eat cereal has been demonstrated to increase nutritional intake and cereal grain consumption in children [8]. However, a reversal in this whole-grain trend was posted by the USDA in 2017. Rye flour production experienced a double digit decline [5]. Whole wheat flour production decreased by 8 percent with whole wheat flour only 5.2 percent of flour produced [6]. In 2017, the USDA introduced flexibility for federal whole grain requirements in child nutrition programs [7].

However, total flour production increased starting in 2017 [5]. Pasta consumption may be on an upward swing with Google citing pasta as one of the top five food trends in 2016 based on individual search terms according to *Think with Google Food Trends 2016 U.S. Report*. Increase in durum semolina production confirms this trend up 9.8 percent in 2017 over the previous year [5]. Instant noodles are quick for busy, fast-paced lives and available in single serving packages. Worldwide and in the United States, instant noodles are a growing market [80].

Nutritive Value

Cereal grains are important dietary components for several nutritional reasons. Grains provide the world population with a majority of its food calories and about half their protein. Cereal grains are a "made to order" food with the emphasis on dietary fat reduction and increased complex carbohydrate intake—starch and fiber. Grains are excellent sources of starch, the nutritive polysaccharide, and indigestible fiber. Cereal grains are low in fat and supply a number of valuable vitamins and minerals. The nutritive value for various cereals may be obtained from the USDA nutrient database (see Appendix C).

Protein. Cereal grain proteins are generally of relatively low biological value. Various cereals and legumes, however, supplement each other with respect to essential amino acid content so that the quality of the protein actually eaten is considerably increased. In a vegetarian diet, the lack of the essential amino acid lysine in cereal grains is complemented by lysine in legumes, including soybeans. Likewise, the amino acid methionine is lacking in legumes, but found in cereal grains.

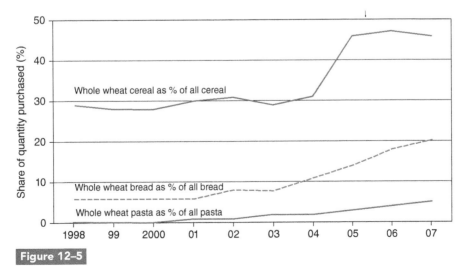

Figure 12–5

Whole grain consumption increased following advice and education to eat more whole grains. (Reprinted from Ho, E., Marquart, L.F., and Camire, M.E. Whole Grains and Health: Empowering Dietary Change. Food Technology, 46-51(4), 2016. Copyright © Institute of Food Technologists)

Refined and Enriched Grains. The nutritive value of cereal products varies with the part of the grain that is used and the method of processing. Refined flours and cereals are made from the endosperm, which contains chiefly starch and protein. Therefore, refined cereals and flours furnish little more than starch or protein unless they are enriched with some of the vitamins and minerals lost in milling.

Enriched and **fortified** flour, according to a legal definition, is white flour to which specified B vitamins (thiamin, riboflavin, and niacin) and iron have been added. In 1996, the U.S. Food and Drug Administration (FDA) mandated the addition of folic acid to help prevent birth defects due to a deficiency of this vitamin [49]. Optional enrichment ingredients include calcium and vitamin D. Whole-grain breads fortified with vitamin D, folic acid, and fiber have been marketed to meet consumer dietary needs [66]. The standards for enriched white flour published by the FDA are listed in **Table 12–2**. Enrichment is required for refined cereal products that enter interstate commerce. Many states also have passed laws requiring enrichment of refined cereal products and flours sold within their boundaries.

Enrichment of white flour increases nutritional quality, but it does not make it nutritionally equivalent to whole-grain flour because only a few of the nutrients lost in milling are replaced by the enrichment process. Many breakfast cereals are highly fortified with vitamins and minerals, well beyond the usual enrichment standards. One study found that ready-to-eat cereals consumed by 10-year-old children made an important contribution to their diets in terms of vitamins and minerals [61]. Enrichment of flour is discussed further in Chapter 13.

Whole Grains. Whole grains are cereal grains with the endosperm, germ, and bran present in the same relative proportions as in the intact grain [88, 94]. Whole grains may be intact, ground, cracked, or flaked. Whole grains are a source of nutrients, such as dietary fiber, iron, zinc, manganese, folate, magnesium, copper, thiamin, niacin, vitamin B_6, phosphorus, selenium, riboflavin, and vitamin A. Whole grains vary in their dietary fiber content.

The *2015–2020 Dietary Guidelines for Americans* recommends that on a daily basis Americans should consume half of their grains as whole-grain products [88]. However, there has been a great deal of debate about defining a whole-grain product. Defining "whole grain" has been controversial over including pseudo-cereal grains, seeds, and oil seeds even though they are not technically "grains." Seeds such as chia, hemp, flaxseed, and sunflower seeds would not qualify for whole-grain status [20]. In 2013, American Association of Cereal Chemists (AACC) approved the following definition: "A whole grain food must contain 8 grams or more of whole grain per 30 grams of product."

The 2007–2010 National Health and Nutrition Examination Survey (NHANES) study found that recommended daily intake of whole grains for all age groups was below recommended range and refined intake above recommended range [96]. Recommendations to increase whole grains in the diet include shifting to whole-grain bread and pasta, and brown rice instead of white, making sure whole grains are listed first on the labels of foods eaten. The number of new product launches featuring whole grains has increased considerably in recent years, making whole-grain foods more widely available in the

Table 12–2
ENRICHMENT STANDARDS COMPARED WITH WHOLE-WHEAT FLOUR (MILLIGRAMS PER POUND)*

	Thiamin	Riboflavin	Niacin	Iron	Folic Acid
Whole-wheat flour	2.49	0.54	19.7	15.0	
Enriched white flour	2.0–2.5	1.2–1.5	16–20	13.0–16.5	0.43–1.4
Enriched bread, rolls, or buns	1.1–1.8	0.7–1.6	10–15	8.0–12.5	0.43–1.4

*One pound of flour is usually equivalent to 1½ pounds of bread.

HEALTHY EATING
CAN YOU IDENTIFY YOUR WHOLE GRAINS?

Whole grains include cereal grains consisting of the intact, ground, cracked, or flaked grains that contain all of the bran, germ, and endosperm in the same relative proportions as found in nature [94].

Keep in mind that color is not a good indicator of whole grains because a brown color can be obtained through the addition of molasses or other ingredients.

Furthermore, products made with whole, white wheat will not be brown but are whole grain. Finally, label terms *wheat bread*, *stone-ground*, and *seven-grain bread* should not be assumed to imply the product is whole grain. Instead, look for *whole* wheat as well as the other whole grains listed above on the ingredient label to identify whole grains [25]. ■

marketplace [63, 70]. Whole-grain and whole-wheat pastas, brown rice, whole-grain breakfast cereals and granola bars, and whole-grain breads are some of the featured products (Figure 12–4). Consumers may look for the Whole Grains Council's "Whole Grain Stamp" to guide their selection of foods that contain whole grains.

Whole-grain products provide vitamins, minerals, dietary fiber, lignans, beta-glucans, inulins, phytochemicals, phytosterols, phytins, and sphingolipids [46, 77]. Diets high in whole grains are associated with a reduced risk of cancer, cardiovascular heart disease, diabetes, and obesity [18, 46, 76, 75, 81, 98, 38]. Whole grains provide fiber for the diet. Adequate amounts of dietary fiber should be consumed from a variety of plant foods [12].

Sprouted grains are now popular adding whole-grain nutrition and texture to baked products. According to AACC definitions, "Malted or sprouted grains containing all of the original bran, germ, and endosperm shall be considered whole grains as long as sprout growth does not exceed kernel length and nutrient values have not diminished. These grains should be labeled as malted or sprouted whole grain."

STRUCTURE AND COMPOSITION

All whole grains have a similar structure: outer bran coats, a germ, and a starchy endosperm portion (**Figure 12–6**). Cereal products such as flours,

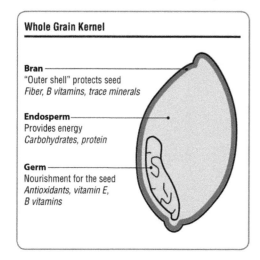

Whole Grain Kernel

Bran
"Outer shell" protects seed
Fiber, B vitamins, trace minerals

Endosperm
Provides energy
Carbohydrates, protein

Germ
Nourishment for the seed
Antioxidants, vitamin E, B vitamins

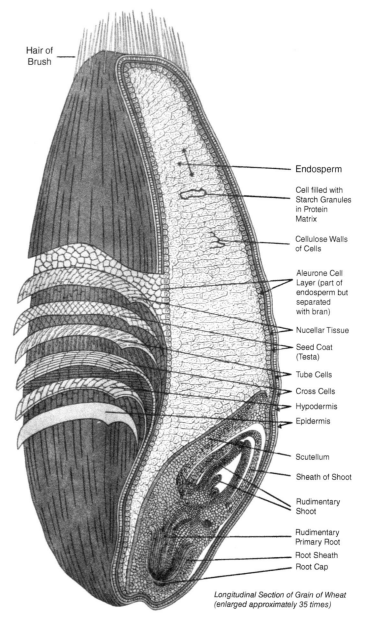

A Kernel of Wheat

Hair of Brush

Endosperm

Cell filled with Starch Granules in Protein Matrix

Cellulose Walls of Cells

Aleurone Cell Layer (part of endosperm but separated with bran)

Nucellar Tissue

Seed Coat (Testa)

Tube Cells

Cross Cells

Hypodermis

Epidermis

Scutellum

Sheath of Shoot

Rudimentary Shoot

Rudimentary Primary Root

Root Sheath

Root Cap

Longitudinal Section of Grain of Wheat (enlarged approximately 35 times)

Figure 12–6

Left: Whole grain kernel: the three basic parts: (1) bran, (2) endosperm, and (3) Right: In-depth view of a wheat kernel. (Wheat Foods Council). (United States Department of Agriculture (USDA))

pasta, and various cereals vary in composition, depending on which part or parts of the grain are used.

Bran

The chaffy coat that covers the kernel during growth is eliminated when grains are harvested. The outer layers of the kernel proper, which are called the *bran*, constitute about 5 percent of the kernel. The bran has a high content of fiber and mineral ash. Milled bran also may contain some germ. The *aleurone* layer comprises the square cells located just under the bran layers of the kernel. These cells are rich in protein, phosphorus, and thiamine and also contain some fat. The aleurone layer comprises approximately 8 percent of the whole kernel. In the milling of white flour, the aleurone layer is removed with the bran.

Endosperm

The *endosperm* is the large central portion of the kernel and constitutes about 83 percent of the grain. It contains most of the starch (**Figure 12–7**) and most of the protein of the kernel. The vitamin, mineral, and fat content of the endosperm is generally low. Milled white flour comes entirely from the endosperm.

Germ or Embryo

The *germ* is a small structure at the lower end of the kernel from which sprouting begins and the new plant grows. It usually comprises only 2 to 3 percent of the whole kernel. It is rich in fat, protein, ash, and vitamins. When the kernel is broken, as it is in certain processing procedures, the fat is exposed to oxygen in the air. This greatly reduces the storage life of the grain because the fat may become rancid. The broken or milled grain also is more susceptible to infestation by insects.

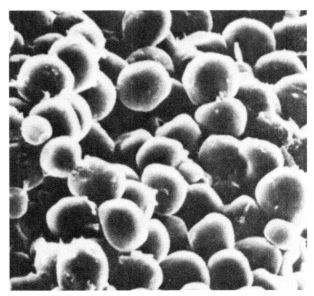

Figure 12–7

A scanning electron micrograph of the fractured surface of corn endosperm showing the cornstarch granules. (Northern Regional Research Center, U.S. Department of Agriculture)

CEREAL GRAINS

Wheat

Wheat has been cultivated since early times and is one of the most widely cultivated plants on earth (**Figure 12–8**). Wheat is commonly milled into flour and is used for the production of wheat starch and, in large quantity, for the making of various types of breakfast cereals. Wheat flour is uniquely suited for bread making because it contains proteins that develop gluten and result in strong, elastic properties in dough. No other common cereal grain equals wheat in bread-making qualities.

Classes of Wheat. Thousands of varieties of wheat may be grouped into six classes, including hard red

---

HEALTHY EATING

WHOLE-GRAIN FOODS—HOW MANY SERVINGS TODAY?

How many servings of whole-grain foods have you eaten today? If you are an average consumer in the United States, the answer to this question is "less than one." According to the *2015–2020 Dietary Guidelines for Americans*, three or more ounce-equivalents of whole grains are recommended on a daily basis [88].

Whole-grain consumption reduces the risk of certain cancers, stroke, diabetes, and cardiovascular disease [78, 79]. The total protectiveness of whole-grain intake against heart disease appears to be greater than the sum of the protection seen with the parts—vitamins, minerals, soluble fiber, and so on—that are

found in whole grains [79]. Whole grains also provide phytochemicals that function as nutrients, antioxidants, and phytoestrogens.

The FDA has approved a health claim for whole grains: "Diets rich in whole grains and other plant foods that are low in total fat, saturated fat, and cholesterol may reduce the risk of heart disease and some cancer." For foods to be labeled with this claim, the food must contain at least 51 percent whole-grain ingredients.

Food manufacturers are offering more healthful whole-grain products. So, how many servings of whole grains will you eat tomorrow? ■

Figure 12–8

Wheat is the most widely cultivated plant on earth. (Repina Valeriya/Shutterstock)

winter, hard red spring, soft red winter, durum, hard white, and soft white [42]. These classifications are based on three factors: (1) winter or spring, (2) hard or soft, and (3) color. Winter wheats are planted in the fall, lie dormant over the winter, and then grow in the spring for harvesting later in the summer. Spring wheats are planted in the spring and harvested during the same growing season. Hard wheats are higher in protein content than soft wheats and usually have greater baking strength in that they result in a bread loaf of large volume and fine texture. Soft wheats are therefore commonly used to make pastries, cookies, crackers, and other products where a high protein content is undesirable [29].

White wheat is gaining favor for bread making because flour made from whole white wheat is whole grain, yet unlike whole red wheats, offers a white color. Whole white wheat flour has a fine, uniform particle size similar to that of refined flour due to a specialized milling process [56, 68]. Whole-wheat flours made from red wheats will have a characteristic light brown color. The following chapters discuss wheat, wheat classes, and enrichment in more detail.

Durum wheat is a very hard wheat of high protein content which requires special milling. It is grown chiefly for use in making macaroni and other pasta. The majority of durum wheat produced in the United States is grown in North Dakota. Classes of wheat, milling, and flour are discussed in more detail in Chapter 13 and later in this chapter.

Processing. Wheat is often ground into flour; however, a variety of forms of wheat may be found in the marketplace, including wheat berries, bulgur, cracked wheat, and wheat germ. Wheat is also used to make a variety of breakfast cereals, which may be shredded, puffed, flaked, or rolled. Various types of wheat products are described in **Table 12–3**.

Table 12–3
TYPES OF WHEAT PRODUCTS

Types	Description
Wheat berry	Wheat berry is another name for the wheat kernel with only the inedible outer hull removed. When used for cooking, it will need to be cooked for an extended period of time to soften.
Bulgur	Bulgur is made from white or red, hard or soft whole-wheat kernels that are parboiled and then dried. A small amount of the outer bran layers is removed, and the wheat is then usually cracked. Bulgur is also cracked. Bulgur is also called *tabouli wheat*. Armenian restaurants serve cooked bulgur pilaf. Bulgur may also be found in vegetarian dishes. Additionally, bulgur may be present in recipes originating in Turkey, Greece, Cyprus, the Middle East, North Africa, and Eastern Europe.
Cracked wheat	Made from the whole kernel which is broken into small pieces. Similar to bulgur but unlike bulgur is not cooked and dried. Provides a nutty flavor and crunchy texture to baked goods. Presoaking or cooking before use is recommended.
Wheat germ	Germ of wheat kernel may be added to foods to provide a nutty, crunchy texture. It is high in protein, fat, B vitamins, and vitamin E. Wheat germ can become rancid because of fat content.
Wheat bran	Bran is the outer layer of the wheat kernel. It is a good source of fiber, B vitamins, protein, and iron. Bran may be added to baked goods.
Farina	Farina is the coarsely ground endosperm of hard wheat. It may be used as a breakfast cereal which is commonly known as cream of wheat.
Semolina	Semolina is the coarsely ground endosperm of **durum** wheat that is primarily used for pasta. It may also be used for couscous and some bread.

Source: References 40, 11.

Corn (Maize)

Maize, commonly called corn in the United States, is a plant that is native to America. Early settlers in the New World were introduced to the uses of corn by Native Americans. Corn is grown in most of the states. Major corn production is in the heartland; Iowa, Illinois, and Minnesota are top corn producing states. The United States is the leading exporter of corn. Corn production has increased dramatically over the last 75 years (**Figure 12–9a** and **b**).

Corn used as a grain is called *dent* or *field* corn and is different from sweet corn that is consumed as a vegetable (**Figure 12–10**). Field corn is harvested

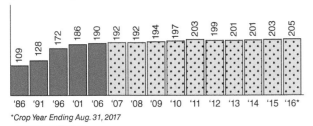

Cereal and Food 1986–2016
(million bushels)

*Crop Year Ending Aug. 31, 2017

Figure 12–9a

Corn for cereal and food use has increased since 1986. This trend has continued for the past 75 years. (National Corn Growers Association)

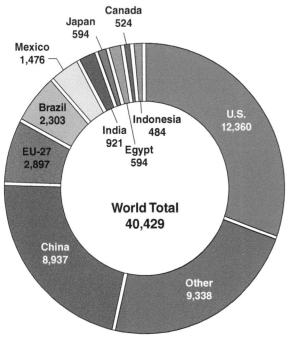

World Corn Consumption
2016–2017*
(million bushels)

Canada 524
Japan 594
Mexico 1,476
Brazil 2,303
Indonesia 484
India 921
Egypt 594
U.S. 12,360
EU-27 2,897
World Total 40,429
China 8,937
Other 9,338

*Marketing Year Oct. 1, 2016—Sept. 30, 2017

Figure 12–9b

World corn consumption. (National Corn Growers Association)

Figure 12–10

Field or dent corn. (Fotokostic/Shutterstock)

in the fall when it is dry and the kernel has formed a dent. Flint is yet another variety of corn. Indian corn, with its colorful kernels and hard pericarp (bran coat) (**Figure 12–11a** and **b**), is an example of flint corn. Blue tortilla chips are produced from blue maize, which has anthocyanins (a blue pigment) in the aleurone layer on the kernel [75]. **Figure 12–12** describes uses of corn.

Processing. Corn is processed for use in a wide variety of foods and other products. Corn is processed by one of the following ways: (1) stone ground or non-degerming, (2) tempering and degerming, or (3) alkaline cooked.

Figure 12–11a

Flint corn is a colorful corn variation. (USDA)

Figure 12–11b

To increase the genetic diversity of U.S. corn, the Germplasm Enhancement for Maize (GEM) project seeks to combine exotic germplasm, such as this unusually colored and shaped maize from Latin America, with domestic corn lines. (Keith Weller. USDA)

Mills using the stone-ground process produce coarse whole-grain corn meal. Whole-grain meals have a shorter shelf life because the oil and germ content makes the meal prone to rancidity [75]. In the degerming process, the majority of the outer bran and germ are removed. Various particle sizes may be produced using rollers, sifters, and grinders ranging from flaking, coarse, medium, and fine grits to corn meals and corn flours [75]. Grits are the most important ground portion. Flaking grits are used for breakfast cereals such as corn flakes, whereas meals and flours are used for cornbread and other baking items. Snack foods use corn grits, meal, and corn flour for a variety of baked goods. Corn uses are discussed in more detail in other chapters.

The alkaline-cooked process involves the cooking of the corn in a boiling lime solution followed by steeping. Excess alkali and the loose pericarp tissue are washed away, and the remaining corn product is ground to form masa harina flour [75]. Masa harina flour is used for tortillas, corn chips, taco shells, and other similar products. Hominy and hominy grits are also produced with the alkaline-cooked process (**Figure 12–13**).

Milling is either wet or dry. Dry milling is used for most food cereal products, such as grinding corn into grits, corn meal, or corn flour. Wet milling involves steeping the corn in water to soften the kernel. Wet milling is used for corn oil, starch, alcoholic beverages and numerous industrial applications including ethanol and bioplastics. The starch can be broken down into sweeteners such as corn syrup or high-fructose corn syrup.

Uses for Corn. Corn is used in breakfast cereals such as corn flakes, corn breads, grits, corn tortillas, and tamales (**Figure 12–14**). Corn meal mush is cooked then refrigerated to set, sliced and fried. Polenta, an

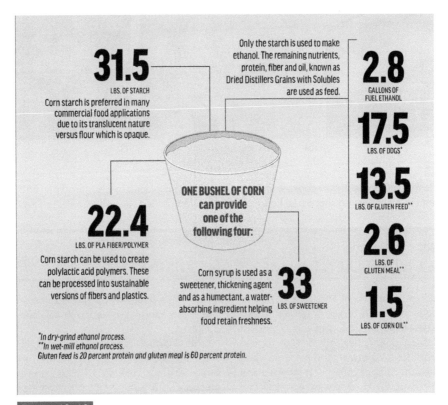

31.5 LBS. OF STARCH
Corn starch is preferred in many commercial food applications due to its translucent nature versus flour which is opaque.

22.4 LBS. OF PLA FIBER/POLYMER
Corn starch can be used to create polylactic acid polymers. These can be processed into sustainable versions of fibers and plastics.

ONE BUSHEL OF CORN can provide one of the following four:

Corn syrup is used as a sweetener, thickening agent and as a humectant, a water-absorbing ingredient helping food retain freshness.
33 LBS. OF SWEETENER

Only the starch is used to make ethanol. The remaining nutrients, protein, fiber and oil, known as Dried Distillers Grains with Solubles are used as feed.

2.8 GALLONS OF FUEL ETHANOL

17.5 LBS. OF DDGS*

13.5 LBS. OF GLUTEN FEED**

2.6 LBS. OF GLUTEN MEAL**

1.5 LBS. OF CORN OIL**

*In dry-grind ethanol process.
**In wet-mill ethanol process.
Gluten feed is 20 percent protein and gluten meal is 60 percent protein.

Figure 12–12

One bushel of corn provides many food and industrial products. (National Corn Growers Association)

Figure 12–13

Hominy is corn processed in an alkaline solution. (Yai/Shutterstock)

Italian dish, is a variation of mush (**Figure 12–15**). In South Africa, *mieliepap* is the staple corn porridge; other corn mush variations can be found throughout the world.

Corn oil, which contains a high proportion of polyunsaturated fatty acids, is extracted from the germ of the corn kernel. (See Focus on Science Corn Oil

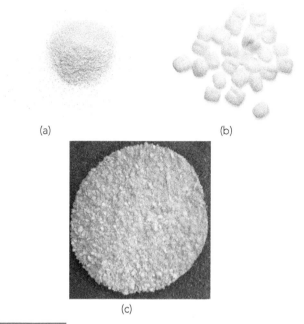

Figure 12–14

(a) Cornmeal, (b) Hominy, (c) Grits. These products may be yellow or white depending on the color of corn used to make them. ((a), (b) Richard Embery/Pearson Education Grits and (c) © Amanda Frye)

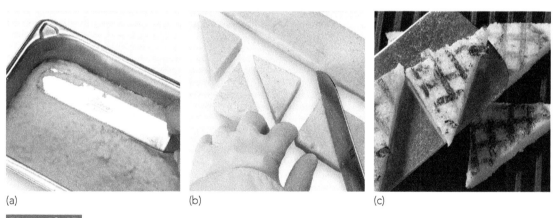

Figure 12–15

Polenta is made from cornmeal that is cooked. (a) The cooked mush is placed in a buttered pan and refrigerated to set. (b) Polenta is cut in desired shapes. (c) Polenta is then grilled or fried. (Richard Embery/Pearson Education)

MULTICULTURAL CUISINE
CORN—A KEY INGREDIENT IN MEXICAN CUISINE

Corn is a major food for people from Mexico and Central America; it is a staple ingredient in one of America's fastest-growing ethnic cuisine—Mexican. The corn tortilla plays a central role in Mexican cuisine. Either corn or flour tortillas make excellent "wraps" for a variety of food mixtures. Corn tortillas are traditionally made from corn that is **steeped** and cooked in alkali solution, washed to remove excess alkali, and ground on a stone mill to produce fresh *masa preparada*.

Dough can also be made from *masa harina* flour, which is the dried mixture of the ground alkaline treated corn.

Masa harina flour can be ground fine, medium, or coarse. The masa harina is mixed with salt and water to make a dough.

Masa dough is pressed into flat, circular shapes that are then cooked on a hot griddle [48]. This traditional procedure for making tortillas, however, is being replaced by large-scale commercial operations in which corn is cooked and ground immediately with little or no steeping, and the tortillas are cooked in large, automated cookers. ■

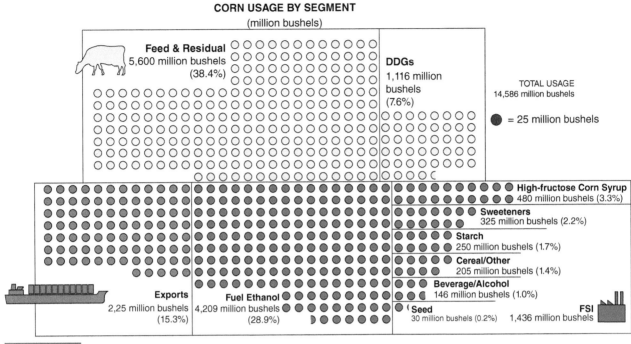

CORN USAGE BY SEGMENT
(million bushels)

TOTAL USAGE 14,586 million bushels

● = 25 million bushels

Feed & Residual 5,600 million bushels (38.4%)

DDGs 1,116 million bushels (7.6%)

High-fructose Corn Syrup 480 million bushels (3.3%)
Sweeteners 325 million bushels (2.2%)
Starch 250 million bushels (1.7%)
Cereal/Other 205 million bushels (1.4%)
Beverage/Alcohol 146 million bushels (1.0%)
Seed 30 million bushels (0.2%)

Exports 2,25 million bushels (15.3%)
Fuel Ethanol 4,209 million bushels (28.9%)
FSI 1,436 million bushels

Figure 12–16

USDA (2016) data reflecting corn use by segment. Distiller's dried grain with solubles (DDGs) are a co-product leftover from converting corn to ethanol. The distiller's grain is high in fat energy, easily digested protein, vitamins, and minerals. These DDGs are used in animal feed. (National Corn Growers Association/USDA)

Figure 12–16 and **Figure 12–17**). Cornstarch is the primary starched in the United States for culinary purposes (see Chapter 11). Corn syrups and glucose are produced by the hydrolysis of cornstarch (see Chapter 9). Cornstarch is the primary starch used in the United States for culinary purposes (see Chapter 11).

Not only is corn used for food, but it is also used in all kinds of consumer and industrial products. Zein is the major protein in corn which behaves as a polymer for industrial use applications [51]. However, zein is affected by water and humidity which limits the use in many applications. Corn is the source of the ethanol that is blended with gasoline for cleaner-burning fuel, and cornstarch is used as a clay binder in ceramics, an adhesive in glues, and a bodying agent in dyes (**Figure 12–16**).

Rice

Rice is one of the most used cereal grain throughout the world, a staple for more than half the world's population. Asia, South America, and Sub-Saharan Africa consume the most rice. Rice is the world's second or third staple crop. In America, rice consumption has increased considerably in the last 20 years. According to the USDA, rice supplies increased 11 percent in 2016/2017 (**Figure 12–19**). About 80 percent of the rice consumed in America is grown in the United States. Six states (Arkansas, California, Louisiana, Mississippi, Missouri, and Texas) produce more than 99 percent of the rice grown in America (**Figure 12–20**).

FOCUS ON SCIENCE
CORN OIL

Corn oil is a by-product of corn wet-milling industries and is recovered from the germ of dent corn. Dent corn has a very thick outer skin and has been shown to have a constant fatty acid composition. Studies have shown that oil content and composition of some corn lines are affected by the geographic locations in which corn is grown (**Figure 12–17**).

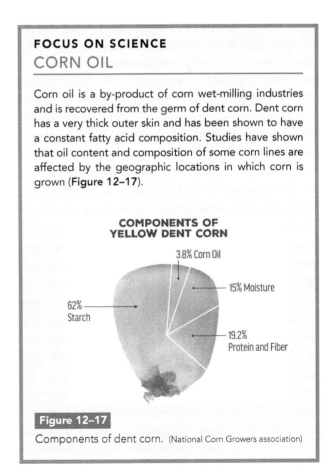

COMPONENTS OF YELLOW DENT CORN

3.8% Corn Oil
15% Moisture
62% Starch
19.2% Protein and Fiber

Figure 12–17

Components of dent corn. (National Corn Growers association)

POP, POP, POPCORN!

Popcorn is a corn variety that is uniquely designed to pop. Moisture inside the kernel surrounded by a hard outer surface will pop open and provide a tasty treat when heated due to a buildup of pressure from the expanding moisture (**Figure 12–18**).

Popcorn that fails to pop may be the result of popcorn that has dehydrated over time during extended storage. Recently, however, scientists have found the chemical structure of the pericarp (outer hull) may play a major role in which popcorns pop the best [69]. The pericarp not only needs to function like a pressure cooker, holding in the moisture until a high level of pressure is produced during heating, but also needs to hold the moisture in during storage. Those kernels that fail to pop had essentially leaky outer hulls which allowed the moisture to escape before cooking. ■

Figure 12–18

Kernels of popped and unpopped popcorn. (Gordine N/ Shutterstock)

Rice was domesticated as early as the 5000 B.C.E. Rice requires high average temperature and a plentiful water supply for growing. Four major types of rice are (1) Indica, (2) Japonica, (3) Aromatic rice, and (4) Glutinous (sweet) rice.

Indica rice grows in tropical and subtropical regions. This rice accounts for 75 percent of global rice trade. Indica rice cooks to a dry state and grains separate. *Japonica* rice grows in cooler climates accounting for about 8 percent of global rice. Japonica rice is short grain rice used by Japanese for sushi and sake [60]. *Aromatic* rice accounts for 15 percent of the global rice trade and draw a premium price. Aromatic rice are primarily jasmine

from Thailand and basmati from India and Pakistan. *Glutinous* rice or sweet rice is grown in Southwest Asia and used in dessert and ceremonial dishes.

Varieties of Rice. More than 40,000 different varieties of rice are grown worldwide [67], although only about 100 are grown commercially in the United States [89]. Rice is classified as long-, medium-, and short-grain varieties (**Figure 12–21**). The food industry also recognizes a fourth category called *specialty rices*. These are distinguished by characteristics other than shape and size and include varieties such as jasmine, basmati, arborio, and sweet glutinous or waxy rice (**Figure 12–22**).

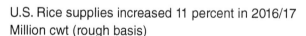
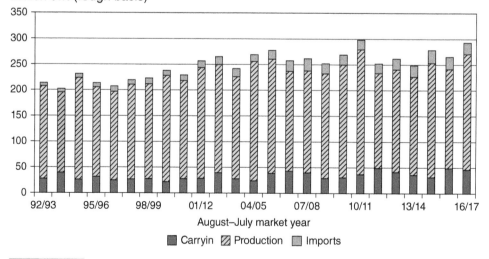

Figure 12–19

U.S. rice supply is composed of rice grown in the United States and imported from other countries. Rice supply has been increasing since 1992. (USDA World Agricultural Outlook Board)

FOCUS ON SCIENCE
WHAT IS LIPASE, AND HOW DOES IT AFFECT QUALITY OF RICE PRODUCTS?

Rice bran contains unsaturated fatty acids: linoleic acid and linolenic acid. Lipase, a hydrolytic enzyme specific to fatty acids, is also present in the bran. Lipase will cause the removal of the fatty acid from the glycerol. Once the fatty acid is free, and if it is an unsaturated fatty acid, rancidity will occur. Unsaturated fatty acids break down to volatile compounds that will produce off-aromas and flavors.

U.S. Rice Producing States

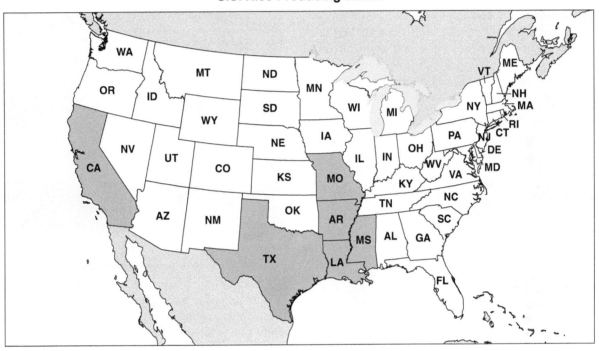

Figure 12–20

Rice is grown in six states in the United States. (© Amanda Frye/Cartographer Charlie Frye)

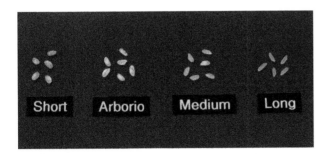

Figure 12–21

Different varieties of rice have different shapes of kernels which then influence the texture of the cooked rice. Shown here are short, arborio, medium, and long grain rice. Arborio rice is often used to make risotto. (Douglas and Barbara Scheule)

Figure 12–22

Rice comes in different colors, shapes and sizes. (Marekuliasz/Shutterstock)

Some of these have fragrant aromas. Other specialty rices are red or black.

Long-, Medium-, and Short-Grain Rice. *Long-grain* rice kernels are three to four times length than width. Long grain varieties of rice have comparatively high **amylose** content and are light and fluffy when cooked (**Figure 12–23**). The cooked kernels tend to separate. They are typically used in dishes such as pilaf, jambalaya, and gumbo.

Medium- and short-grain varieties contain less amylose, absorb less water in cooking, and the kernels are clingy or sticky when cooked (**Figure 12–24**). The medium-grain rice has short kernel two to three times the width. Cooked grains are moist and tender clinging together. They are often used in sushi and rice puddings. Short-grain rice is short and plumb almost a round kernel. The preference for fluffy versus sticky rice depends on the culture of the consumer and the desired characteristics of the dish being prepared.

Specialty Rices. Specialty rices have become more popular in the United States as the interest in ethnic cuisines and new flavors has increased. Aromatic rices such as della, jasmine, and basmati have a flavor and aroma similar to roasted nuts or popcorn. Della is an aromatic rice developed in the United States for improved yield and milling qualities. Della and basmati

Figure 12–23

This long grain rice is grown in the United States. (USNDA)

(a)   (b)

(c)

Figure 12–24

(a) Converted rice, (b) Arborio rice, (c) Basmati rice. (Richard Embery/Pearson Education)

are dry, separate, and fluffy when cooked, whereas jasmine tends to cling together [67]. Arborio is a medium-grain rice with a characteristic white dot in the center of the grain. Arborio is typically used in risotto, a classic Italian dish, because it will absorb flavors and produce a creamy texture.

Processing of Rice. Rice may be processed in several ways to produce brown rice, polished white rice, enriched rice, parboiled or converted rice, precooked or instant rice, and rice flour. These rice products are described in **Table 12–4**. Brown rice has most of its bran, germ, and endosperm and is therefore considered to be a whole grain [23] (**Figure 12–25**).

Rice Flour. Rice flour is primarily used to make rice paper for spring rolls. Vietnam and Thailand are major rice flour consumers. Rice based batter was developed by a team of USDA Agricultural Research Service scientists [13]. This rice batter absorbs 50 percent less oil during frying than wheat batters [13] (**Figure 12–26**). Rice flour used in noodles is discussed later.

Rice and Arsenic. Rice has been a identified as a food with key exposure to arsenic [102]. Foods and drinking water exposed to water or soil containing arsenic are

Table 12–4
KINDS OF RICE PRODUCTS

Kinds	Description
Brown rice	Least processed form of rice. Only the outer husk or chaffy coat is removed from the kernel. The germ and most of the bran is retained. Rich in vitamins, minerals, and fiber. Takes longer to cook than more highly processed forms of rice.
White polished rice	Bran coats and germ are rubbed from the rice grain by an abrasive process, thus leaving the starchy endosperm. The polishing procedure also removes more than half of the minerals and most of the vitamins from the kernel.
Enriched rice	White polished rice may be enriched with vitamins and minerals lost in processing. Often, a powdery material is applied to the surface of the grain. Enriched rice should not be washed before cooking or rinsed after cooking to avoid loss of the enrichment nutrients.
Converted or parboiled rice	Is soaked in water, drained, and then heated, typically by steaming, before it is dried and milled. This heat process retains nutrients normally lost during milling in the rice kernel by causing nutrients in the outer coats to migrate to the interior. Benefits of parboiled rice include improved nutritive value, improved keeping quality, less disintegration during cooking, and better retention of shape and texture during cooking and hot holding. Parboiled rice takes somewhat longer to cook than regular milled white rice.
Instant or precooked rice	A long-grain rice that has been cooked, rinsed, and dried by a special process. It may be cooked quickly and therefore is convenient to prepare.
Rice flour	Made from grinding the grains that are broken during milling. Rice flour is relatively resistant to syneresis in frozen/thawed foods and may replace modified starch in some applications. Shown to reduce the absorption of oil by as much as 70 percent in donuts and 60 percent when used in a batter for fried chicken [32]. Is a nonallergenic alternative to wheat flour products [64].
Rice bran	Is the outer brown layer removed during the milling of white rice. It deteriorates rapidly once it is separated from the rice kernel because a **lipase** enzyme is exposed to the oil in the bran. The fat breaks down, and an unacceptable musty taste rapidly develops. May be heat treated so that the enzyme is deactivated and the bran is stabilized [26].

Figure 12–25

Brown rice has most of its bran, germ, and endosperm and is therefore considered to be a whole grain. (Richard Embery/ Pearson Education)

Figure 12–26

These lemon poppyseed muffins and chocolate chip cookies are made with a U.S. Department of Agriculture ARS-patented special blend rice flours. (Peggy Greb/ USDA/ARS)

at risk for contamination. Arsenic is found naturally in the environment in soil and water from erosion of arsenic containing rocks, volcano eruptions, mining and smelting ore, and arsenic containing pesticides [43]. Arsenic is a known human carcinogen, especially the inorganic form [28]. Rice grows in flooded fields of about 5 inches of water for about 5 months until harvest so it is vulnerable to water contaminated with arsenic (**Figure 12–27**). In 2012, rice from Taiwan and Chile tested high for arsenic [45]. These findings led to concerns about arsenic levels in all rice and other foods. Rice grown in the United States has the lowest levels of arsenic in the world. Some rice from China, the EU, and Japan have tested above international standards of 200 parts per billion (ppb). FDA standard recommendations are under 100 ppb. FDA studies found arsenic in rice and rice products, but the levels in the United States are below recommended standards [102] (**Figure 12–28**). America's rice farmers are committed to producing safe rice that meets FDA standards. Scientists have confirmed that rice grown in America presents no public health risk [102] (**Figure 12–29**).

Figure 12–29

Scientists examine many aspects of rice. The USDA geneticist compares two kinds of low-phytate rice.
(U.S. Department of Agriculture)

Figure 12–27

A rice paddy. (Patpitchaya/Shutterstock)

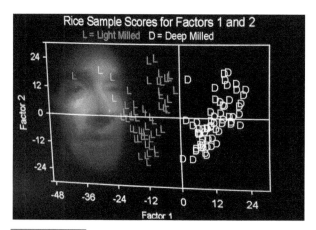

Figure 12–28

Scientists examine many aspects of rice making sure it is high quality and safe to eat. USDA food scientist William Windham analyzes texture data for rice samples separated into groups for light (L) or deep milling (D). (Keith Weller/USDA)

Oats

Only about 10 percent of oats grown in the United States are used for human consumption, the rest are for animal feed (**Figure 12–30**). Many prepared breakfast cereals contain oats. In addition, oats are used in the making of cookies, granola bars, baby foods, variety breads, candy, and snack items. Oats are utilized in a rolled form as both old-fashioned, quick-cooking, and instant oat products (**Figure 12–31**).

Processing. Oats are harvested with the hulls. When oats are processed, the outer hull is removed, but most of the germ and bran remain with the endosperm. Thus, oats are a whole grain. Oat kernels with the outer hulls removed are called *groats*. Once oats are milled the shelf life is short due to lipases. Oats

Figure 12–30

Oat (*Avena sativa*) panicles on the left and oat seeds on the right. (USDA)

FOCUS ON SCIENCE
BETA-GLUCANS

Beta-glucans are nondigestible dietary polysaccharides that have gained prominence for lowering blood cholesterol. They are found in the bran of cereal and occur in especially high concentrations in oat and barley brans.

Chemically, beta-glucan is a linear chain of beta-D-glucopyranosyl units; about 70 percent are linked $(1 \rightarrow 4)$ and about 30 percent $(1 \rightarrow 3)$. The $(1 \rightarrow 3)$ linkages occur singly and are separated by sequences of generally two or three $(1 \rightarrow 4)$ linkages. Thus, the molecule is composed of $(1 \rightarrow 3)$-linked beta-cellotriosyl and cellotetraosyl units. A representative structure of a segment of oat and barley beta-glucans is shown below, where n usually is 1 or 2 but could be larger:

$$- \rightarrow 3)-\beta Glcp-(1-[-\rightarrow 4)-\beta Glcp-(1-\rightarrow]_n$$

Source: R. L. Whistler and J. N. BeMiller, "Cellulosics," in *Carbohydrate Chemistry for Food Scientists* (St. Paul, MN: American Association of Cereal Chemists, 1997), pp. 166–67.

Figure 12–31

Old-fashioned rolled oats are rolled without cutting. Oats are high in beta-glucans. (Penny Hillcrest/Shutterstock)

are cleaned and sorted. Rolled oats are made by passing groats through rollers to form flakes. For quick-cooking rolled oats, the groats are cut into smaller particles, steamed and then rolled into thin, small flakes. Regular or old-fashioned rolled oats are rolled without cutting. Steel-cut oats are whole groats cut into pieces, but not rolled. Because of the retention of most of the germ, rolled and steel-cut oats are higher in fat than most other cereals. Oats are stored in packaging that "breathes" such as the standard cardboard cylinder containers. This is essential to allow air to circulate and remove rancid odors. Oats are also a good source of thiamine and other B vitamins and iron.

Beta-Glucan. Oatmeal has been a common breakfast cereal for many years, but it has become even more popular with the publication of research

indicating that oat bran is particularly effective in diets designed to lower elevated blood cholesterol levels. The use of oat fiber by the food industry thereafter increased greatly, as evidenced by a dramatic rise in the sale of oat bran by the Quaker Oats Company from 1 million pounds per year in 1986 to 2 million pounds per month by 1989 [72]. The benefit appears to come from oat bran's content of beta-glucan, a glucose polymer. Still, there are other cereal sources of beta-glucan, including barley, which is the subject of continuing nutrition research.

At the USDA Northern Regional Research Center, a process was developed for producing a granular or powdered material that contains an appreciable amount of beta-glucan from enzyme-treated oat bran or oat flour. This product is called *oatrim* and is being marketed commercially as a fat replacer (**Figure 12–32**). Scientist at the USDA also developed a product called *Nutrim* made from oats, oat bran and flour. Recent USDA studies combined oats and chia seeds (**Figure 12–33**) to provide a "healthy" cookie high in fiber, Beta-glucans and omega-3 fatty acids [15].

Rye

Rye is grown and used in the United States chiefly as a flour, but it is also available as rye flakes and as a **pearled** grain. Although rye is a dark cereal grain, it actually has a mellow taste that may enhance the flavor of breads and cereals without overpowering them. Rye is used in the United States much less than wheat, but its use more nearly approaches wheat in baking quality than other grains. In parts of Europe, rye is an important bread flour. Rye flour is available in three grades: light, medium, and dark (see Chapter 13 for more about rye).

Barley

Barley ranks fourth in world cereal grain production. In the United States, barley growers raise about 200 million bushels of barely every year. The Pacific Northwest and

Figure 12–32

Oatrim is a tasteless fat substitute powder that can be incorporated into baked goods. It can also be used to prepare a frozen dessert that resembles soft ice cream. Oatrim was developed by an USDA Agriculture Research Service (ARS) scientist. The product went from lab to supermarket shelves in five years. (Scott Bauer/USDA)

Figure 12–33

USDA scientists used whole ground chia seeds as an ingredient in their nutritious cookies. (Al Probyn/USDA)

Northern plains including Colorado, Idaho, Minnesota, Montana, North Dakota, Oregon, Washington, and Wyoming. According to the National Barley Growers Association, three-fourths or more the barley is used for malting. USDA grain standards provide standards for barley including malting barley (**Figure 12–34**).

Figure 12–34

Plant physiologist Allen Budde examines barley partway through the malt kilning process. (David Peterson./USDA)

Malting is the controlled process of germinating and then drying the grain. Sprouted barley is a source of malt, which is rich in the enzyme **amylase**. Malted barley is used in the baking industry for as an enzyme source, flavor, and color source. Malted barley is sometimes used to increase the alpha-amylase levels in flour. The breakfast food industry uses malt primarily as a flavoring agent [40]. Malted milkshakes (malts) are milk shakes with the addition of malt.

The most important use of malt is in the brewing and distilled malted liquor products. Malted barley is an important ingredient for beer production with U.S. barley crops producing over 190 million barrels of beer every year (**Figure 12–35**). Craft beer has increased barley demand and also, demand for imported barley [24] (**Figure 12–36**). Craft beer brewers used four times the amount

Figure 12–35

Beer is a fermented grain product. (Valentyn Volkov/Shutterstock)

Craft vs. Non-Craft
Billion Pounds

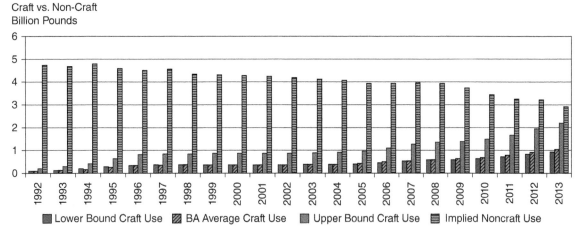

Implied Craft use is determined as the residual of total malt and malt products usage less craft
use based on Brewers Association average per barrel usage estimates.

Figure 12–36

Malt use in craft beer versus non-craft beer. (USDA)

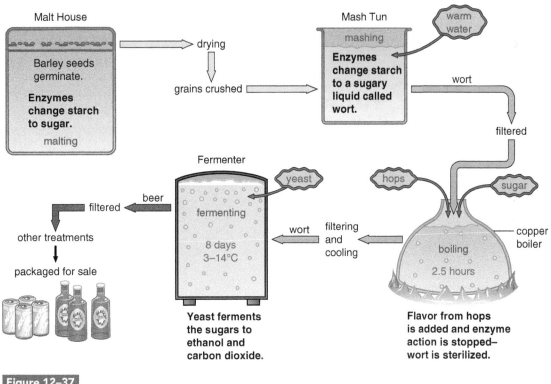

Figure 12–37

Beer brewing steps. (Oxford Designers & Illustrators Ltd. Pearson Education Ltd.)

of barley per barrel compared to non-craft brewers. Craft India Pale Ales (IPAs) require more malt than other craft beers. Malt provides enzymes, fermentable carbohydrates, color, and flavor in beer. Beer brewing steps are shown in **Figure 12–37**. Dark beers require a dark malt. Malt provides the enzymes (amylases) that convert starch into simple sugars to feed the brewer's yeast, which is necessary to produce CO_2 and alcohol (**Figure 12–38**).

Yeast is discussed in greater detail in later chapters. Malted liquors also use malted barley for their production [40].

In the United States, a small proportion of barley is **pearled** (**Figure 12–39**). Pearling is a process that removes the outer hull of barley, leaving a small, round, white pearl of grain, the kind seen in some soups or cooked and served as a starchy side dish. Barley has become a valuable source of beta-glucan

Figure 12–38

USDA chemist Mark Schmitt and biologist Leslie Zalapa prepare a 96-well microplate for use in high-throughput assays of barleys being evaluated for their malting potential. (Stephen Ausmus/USDA)

Figure 12–39

Pearled barley. (ifong/Shutterstock)

for the food industry. Barley flour, whole-grain barley, barley flakes, and barley bran are available and may be used in breakfast cereals, baby foods, and other products [63]. Barley is high in beta-glucans [54].

Triticale

Triticale is a "man-made" hybrid cereal plant produced by crossing durum wheat and rye. Triticale was first grown in 1875, but development didn't begin until the 1930s and production in 1969. Most triticale is grown in Europe and about 7 percent in North America. Triticale combines desirable characteristics of each parent species. Triticale combines the high yield qualities of wheat with the disease resistance and rye's ability to grow well on poor ground, dry conditions, and cold climates. Generally, triticale has a higher protein content and better amino acid balance with more lysine than wheat [73]. Triticale could be a valuable

source of nutrients for many peoples of the world. Triticale has weaker gluten; thus yeast bread production is difficult. Certain varieties of triticale have been shown to produce acceptable non-yeast breads, snack crackers, and noodles [47, 73]. However, yeast bread making quality of triticale is not on par with wheat unless there is genetic modification to increase glutenin [44]. Although triticale is now used primarily for animal feed, it may find increasing use in the human diet as research on this grain continues [65].

Millet

Millet is a small round relatively soft seed with a mild flavor. It tolerates adverse growing conditions and is an important food source throughout the world. Pearl millet (**Figure 12–40**), sometimes referred to as "Bulrush millet," is indigenous to the dry African savanna from Sudan to Senegal [55, 103]. Millet is thought to be one of the first grains cultivated by man. Foxtail millet was first cultivated in China then spread to India, Africa, and the United States; it is still an important Chinese grain source [53] (**Figure 12–41**). Millet is sold for human consumption in North America, and some varieties are sold as animal feed. Millet has a relatively high oil content, no gluten, and considered a good protein source, but limited

Figure 12–40

Pearl millet. (Kirat Grewal/123RF)

Figure 12-41

An 1864 illustration of indigenous Africans drinking millet beer. Created by Bayard and Huyot, published on Le Tour du Monde, Paris, 1864. (Antonio Abrignani/Shutterstock)

Figure 12-42

Farro was ancient grain related to wheat. Farro was a staple of the Roman army. (Richard Embery/Pearson Education)

Figure 12-43

Sorghum. (Robert Klein./USDA)

in lysine. Storability of millet is good and long term. Millet is a staple grain in Africa and can be made into porridge, eaten like rice or ground into flour. Millet has also been made into wine [53]. In Africa and India, *eleusine (eleusine coracana)*, otherwise known as finger millet or goose grass, is another cultivated cereal grain [59, 103].

Khorasan (Kamut®)

"Kamut" is an ancient word meaning wheat. However, Kamut® is a modern brand name for the ancient Khorasan wheat. It is a high-protein large wheat like kernels. Kamut is nicknamed King Tut's wheat since it was originally cultivated in the Fertile Crescent area that runs through Egypt to the Tigris-Euphrates valley. Kamut® may be substituted for wheat berries, or the flour may be used similarly to wheat flour. It is a relative of the durum wheat, but with a sweeter taste.

Spelt (Dinkel or Farro)

Spelt is a grain that is a predecessor of wheat believed to be around since 7000 B.C. (**Figure 12-42**). Spelt has a higher protein, but weaker gluten content than wheat. It is used primarily as flour. Spelt is also higher in selenium, phosphorus, and magnesium.

Sorghum (Milo)

Sorghum is the fifth largest crop produced in world, but in the United States it is mainly used for animal feed [62] (**Figure 12-43**). U.S. manufacturers have largely ignored sorghum use for human food [57]. However, the starch is extracted for commercial food use. Specialty sorghum breakfast cereal flakes are on the market [62].

Grain sorghum is primarily grown from South Dakota to Texas including Nebraska, Kansas,

Oklahoma and Colorado. Sweet sorghum is grown most extensively as a source of syrup. Sorghum syrup can be substituted for molasses in any recipe. Sweet sorghum is grown primarily in the South East part of the United States. Kentucky and Tennessee produce the most syrup. See Chapter 9 for more on sweet sorghum.

In Africa and Asia, sorghum is used for human food. It is often consumed as porridge, although it may be also used to make flat breads, couscous, cakes, noodles, and cookies [85]. Gluten free Chinese noodles can be made from sorghum with careful flour quality control including starch damage and flour particle size [52]. Sorghum is high is several vitamins, minerals, and antioxidants and does not contain gluten. Sorghum is high in iron, calcium, and potassium.

Teff

Teff is used widely in Ethiopia, where it is made into a flat bread. Compared to other grains it is high in iron and calcium. Teff has a sweet flavor [63, 71]. More discussion on Teff is in the following chapters.

Job's Tears

Job's tear is also known as adklay, amyuen, Chinese pearl barley, croix see, and hatomugi. It is produced primarily in East and South-East Asia (China, Japan, the Philippines, Burma, and Thailand). Dehulling reveals a seed, an approximate 5 mm oval-shaped seed that is milky white to black on the surface; husks can be black or white (**Figure 12–44**). Typically Job's tear is used as a polished grain. Job's tear has been used as a cereal, in soups, steeped as a tea and degermed it can be ground into flour. A nondairy drink from Job's tear is sold in Japan and Thailand. It has long been used in Chinese medicine.

The germ is large, about a third of the grain enfolded inside the kernel. Job's tear has a high protein content even after being degermed around 13–16 percent. The starch is thought to contain a higher portion of amylopectin compared to amylose [27].

Fonio

Fonio or Acha is a millet-like grass found in Africa that is thought to be the oldest cultivated cereal grain in Africa dating back over 5000 B.C. Although fonio has been mostly replaced by sorghum, it still is a staple in certain isolated areas [59].

Canary Seed

Canary seed is a true cereal grain grown primarily in Canada, Turkey, and Argentina; it is used primarily for animal feed. However, the use of canary seed for human consumption is being explored. The small elliptical grains covered with hairy hulls on the seed have limited its use for human consumption, but hairless canary seed has been developed eliminating this constraint.

Canary seed is about 60–67 percent starch with canary seed flour comparable to that of wheat [1, 2]. The

Figure 12–44

Job's tears. (ZCW/Shutterstock)

starch is found to be higher in amylose than wheat or corn so it forms gels stable to freezing [3]. The protein value of canary seed is approximately 20 percent, about 2 percent higher than that of wheat [1, 2]. The composition of amino acids includes high levels of cysteine, tryptophan, phenylalanine, and arginine with low levels of lysine and proline [4]. The fat of canary seed is about

GENETICALLY ENGINEERED GRAINS

Genetic engineering is a precise way of introducing new traits into plants by moving genes from one plant to another and eliminating or rearranging genes using recombinant DNA techniques [89, 90]. More precise and selective than traditional crossbreeding, genetic engineering allows plant developers to control carefully changes in plant characteristics. Biotechnology, which includes genetic engineering techniques, is regulated in the United States collaboratively by the USDA, the FDA, and the Environmental Protection Agency [91, 92].

The prevalence of genetically engineered crops has increased considerably since the mid-1990s, when only 5 percent of U.S. soybeans was genetically engineered. In 2011, the USDA estimated that 88 percent of corn and 94 percent of soybeans were biotechnological varieties [92]. These genetically engineered crops are herbicide-tolerant or pest-resistant.

A second generation of genetically engineered crops is under development. Golden rice with enhanced levels of vitamin A is one such crop [9]. In areas of the world where vitamin A deficiency is common and rice is a staple in the diet, this rice could have a positive impact on health [76] and has been shown to be an effective vitamin A source [85]. As of 2017, golden rice has not been approved for use, but release may occur soon in The Philippines [83]. Golden rice will probably be released by 2022.

Other researchers are working on rice with lower levels of phytic acid (Figure 12–29). Phytic acid binds several minerals, including iron, calcium, magnesium, and zinc. Because phytic acid is poorly digested, these minerals also become less available for use by our bodies when bound by phytic acid [30]. ∎

9 percent, but contains 55 percent linoleic acid. However, the high unsaturated fatty acids composition makes it subject to rancidity. It is also high in antioxidants. Beta-glucan levels were found to be moderate 1.1–2.3 percent less than oats and barley but higher than other cereal grains [31]. Canary seed contains B vitamins—thiamine, riboflavin, and niacin. However, canary seed contains 15 percent less niacin than wheat. Potential canary seed food applications have been demonstrated by mixing with wheat flour for yeast bread [1].

Pseudo-Cereal Grains

Pseudo-cereal grains are eaten the same way cereal grains are eaten, but they do not meet the technical definition of a grain. Pseudo-cereal grains have different botanical origins, but similar composition and use.

Wild Rice. Wild rice is unrelated to the rice family, but is the hulled and unmilled grain of a reed aquatic natural grass (**Figure 12–45**). Wild rice is indigenous to North America growing naturally in Minnesota, Wisconsin, and Canada. Native American Indians, in what is now Minnesota, relied on harvesting the wild rice staple from aquatic lakes and river beds; the wild rice kernels sustained them through the long winters. The plants grow 8–12 feet tall and serve as a wildlife habitat especially water fowl. The harvest grain must be (1) parched (dried), (2) thrashed (removing hull from grain), and (3) winnowed (separating wild rice kernel from the hull).

There are three grades of wild rice: (1) Giant (the best long grains), (2) Fancy (medium and lesser quality, and (3) Select (the short grains). The wild rice grain is long, slender, and black which opens up into a butterfly shape when cooked. The cooked wild rice has a nutty and earthy flavor. Wild rice is served as a starchy side dish, incorporated into breads or served in a creamy wild rice soup—a Minnesota specialty. Wild rice is grown in lakes or flooded fields. In 1976, methods were developed for

Figure 12–45

Wild rice is actually not a rice but an indigenous grass seed. (Jiri Hera/Shutterstock)

Figure 12–46

Buckwheat plant. (Pamela Pavek. Natural Resources Conservation Service USDA)

cultivating wild rice. It is now grown in California [33]. Ninety-nine percent of wild rice is grown in Minnesota and California with minor production in Wisconsin, Oregon, and Idaho. Wild rice is adapted to colder climates. Like many whole-grain cereals, it has relatively poor keeping quality, especially at warm temperatures.

Buckwheat. Buckwheat is a pseudo-cereal, not a seed of the grass family; it is the seed of an herbaceous plant (**Figure 12–46**). Buckwheat is thought to have originated in China. Today most of the world's buckwheat is grown in China and Russia. Buckwheat has been grown in America since colonial days, but is a minor crop in the United States primarily grown in North Dakota, New York, Montana, and Pennsylvania with smaller production in Illinois, Maryland, Michigan, Minnesota, North Carolina, Ohio, Oregon, South Dakota, West Virginia, and Wisconsin.

Buckwheat has a distinctive three-sided teardrop shape with a hull (**Figure 12–47**). The hull is removed during milling. Buckwheat contains the amino acid lysine and is a good source of zinc, copper, and manganese and is gluten free. The shelf life of buckwheat is limited due to volatile fatty acids which aren't protected when dehulled so rancidity is an issue after milling.

Figure 12–47

Buckwheat has unique teardrop three-sided shape. (Richard Embery/Pearson Education)

Figure 12–49

Quinoa seeds may be yellow, red, and black. (Oliver Hoffmann/ Shutterstock)

Figure 12–48

Japanese Soba noodles are made from buckwheat. (SPE/Shutterstock)

Figure 12–50

Amaranth seeds (left), amaranth flour (right), above the final product, amaranth cookies. (Diejun Chen/USDA)

Buckwheat can be processed into flour, thus it is commonly considered a grain product. The flour is generally dark colored due to presence of hull fragments remaining after milling. Buckwheat is rich in lysine and linoleic acid. It is prized for its distinctive flavor. Buckwheat is commonly used in pancakes, hot cereals, and soups. Buckwheat can be boiled eaten like rice. Buckwheat groats (what remains after the hull is removed) are sometimes used for breakfast food, porridge, and thickener for soups, gravies, and dressings. Buckwheat is used to produce Japanese soba noodles (**Figure 12–48**). (See Noodle section for more discussion.) Gluten-free Turkish eriste noodles can be successfully made with buckwheat [22]. (See Chapter 13 for more discussion.)

Quinoa. Quinoa (pronounced *keenwah*) is a pseudo-cereal grain that is a small seed (**Figure 12–49**). For over 5,000 years, quinoa has been raised in the Andes, but only recently the crop has been rediscovered and marketed as a "super food" due to its unique nutritional

profile being relatively high in protein (12.5–16.9 percent) and linoleic acid (omega-3). Quinoa contains all essential amino acid including lysine; the amino acid profile is similar to that of dried milk. The seed is 58–64 percent starch and about 10 percent fiber [37].

Quinoa is available in a variety of colors yellow, red, and black. Natural food dyes can be derived from quinoa seeds. The quinoa seed coat contains bitter saponins which must be removed prior to consumption. It may be cooked like rice or ground into flour. Quinoa seeds are sometimes fermented to make beer or a traditional South American alcoholic beverage called "chicha" [37]. Quinoa is gluten free and a very stress tolerant crop able to adapt in changing climates [17].

Amaranth. Amaranth is pseudo-cereal (**Figure 12–50**). It is native to the Americas and consumed was consumed by the Inca, Maya, and Aztec civilizations [82]. There are

Figure 12–51

Figure technician Diejun Chen (left) and chemist George Inglett inspect sugar cookies they made with amaranth and oat products. (Z. Lewis Liu./USDA)

over 60 different Amaranth species and not all are safe for human or animal consumption. The small, light-colored kernels have a peppery flavor [71]. The protein content is between a cereal and bean with high lysine and methionine amino acid concentrations. It is high in vitamins and minerals such as riboflavin, niacin, ascorbic acid, calcium, and magnesium. The grain is processed and consumed in different ways throughout the world. The grain can be expanded as a form of popcorn, ground into flour or cooked, extruded, and toasted to form flakes.

As a gluten-free grain, it is used with a blend of grains in baked goods and breakfast cereals [63, 71]. USDA scientists produced gluten free cookies made with amaranth flour and oats [15] (**Figure 12–51**). See Chapter 13 for more discussion of amaranth.

More on cereal and pseudo-cereal grains, their flours, and uses are discussed in the following chapters.

BREAKFAST CEREALS

Breakfast foods made from cereal grains vary widely in composition, depending on the kind of grain, the part of the grain used, the method of milling, and the method of processing [34]. The two major types of cereal are hot and ready-to-eat [75]. The simplest processed food is a porridge made from cooked grain and water [74]. Oatmeal and Cream of Wheat are examples of hot porridge.

Ready-to-eat breakfast cereals are often enriched and fortified and therefore can provide a significant proportion of key nutrients in the diet. Researchers found the consumption of ready-to-eat breakfast cereals by children and adolescence to be associated with higher nutrient intake and a lower prevalence of obesity [8, 32]. Whole-grain cereals and cereals with a limited amount

of added sugar are available in the marketplace. Reading the food ingredients (listed in predominance in the product) and the nutrition facts panel on the label can assist consumers in making selections. (See Chapter 3 for more about food labeling regulation.)

Ready-to-Eat Cereals

Ready-to-eat cereals (RTE) have been described as processed grain formulations that need no further cooking and are shelf-stable [34]. Ready-to-eat cereals were developed at the end of the nineteenth century. The first documented ready-to-eat cereal was "Granula," a health food promoted in New York by Dr. James C. Jackson in the 1860s [74]. Other ready-to-eat cereals followed with shredded wheat presented by Henry Perky in 1894 at the Boston held World's Fair. Mr. Perky sold his shredded wheat invention to the National Biscuit Company (Nabisco) 30 some years later. The Kellogg brothers developed flaked cereal in 1898 for the health sanitarium which led the establishment in 1906 of the Battle Creek Toasted Corn Flakes Company, now known as the Kellogg Company. C. W. Post was a patient at Kellogg's sanitarium [74]. Post developed the cereal-based coffee-like beverage called "Postum" in 1895 then introduced Grape-Nuts in 1897. Quaker Oats was the leader of the hot cereal porridge market in 1905, but branched out to acquire patents and produce puffed wheat and puffed rice. In 1941, General Mills introduced the first extruded product— Cheerios. Originally called "Cheerioasts," Lester Borchardt, is credited with their invention. Nutrient fortification and pre-sweetened RTE cereals entered the market in the 1940s and 1950s. Over the years, many different kinds of cereals have been developed by a number of companies. Ready-to-eat cereal overtook the hot cereal market in America. Infant cereals are another part of the breakfast cereal industry.

Basic processes used in the production of prepared cereals include flakes, puffing, shredding, baking, and extruded. **Table 12–5** provides a brief description of the commonly used methods of manufacture for ready-to-eat cereals, and **Figure 12–52** shows various types.

Cooking of Breakfast Cereals

The main purposes of cereal cookery are to improve palatability and digestibility. Cereal cookery is fundamentally starch cookery because starch is the predominant component of cereals. Other factors involved are fiber, which is found chiefly in the exterior bran layers, and protein, which is a prominent constituent of the cereal endosperm. Until softened, or unless disintegrated mechanically, bran may interfere with the passage of water into the interior of the kernel and presumably retarding starch swelling. If cellulose is finely divided, its affinity for water is greatly increased. The temperatures

Table 12–5
METHODS FOR THE MANUFACTURE OF READY-TO-EAT CEREALS

Name	Description
Flakes, traditional	Corn flakes are produced from yellow dent (field) corn with germ and bran removed. The endosperm which is split into large pieces (half of kernel) called grits. Each large grit will be a flake. The grits are pressure cooked with water and other ingredients, such as sugar and malt, followed by partial drying to 20 percent moisture. These cooked grits are rolled under pressure to produce flakes followed by toasting 50 seconds at 300°C. Nutrients that enrich the flakes and other flavors may be sprayed on the flakes, depending on the product. Wheat and rice flakes are made using a similar process. One wheat kernel equals one flake.
Oven and gun puffed	Cereals may be expanded by oven puffing or gun puffing. The puffing methods depend on water vaporization due to the sudden change in temperature or pressure. To oven puff rice, the rice is first cooked under pressure and then dried in a several-stage process. Once the desired moisture level is achieved, the rice is baked in ovens where it expands or puffs. Gun puffing may be used with rice, wheat, or corn to achieve greater expansion than oven puffing. The grains are cooked, then heated in a sealed pressure container. On the sudden release of pressure, the water vapor exits the grain and causes expansion. The puffed cereal is dried and flavored as final steps before packaging.
Shredded wheat, traditional	The traditional process for shredding wheat starts with cooking followed by holding to allow moisture equilibration and starch retrogradation. The cooked grains are next passed through a pair of rollers, one smooth and the other having circular grooves. The cereal emerges between the grooves as long parallel shreds. The shreds are separated with a comb and cut with knives to produce biscuits. The biscuits are baked to develop flavor and crispiness.
Baked cereals	Grapenuts® was the first baked cereal. Whole wheat is mixed with malt, sugar, water, and other ingredients to form dough. The dough ferments followed by proofing and baking. The resulting bread is then ground into pieces and retoasted.
Extruded	Cereals, as well as other foods such as pasta and snacks, are made using the extrusion process. Extruded cereals start with a flour mixture, not a whole grain. Cereals are usually prepared using a thermal extrusion process that heats the product as it moves through a barrel by the movement of a screw mechanism. The cooked cereal exits the extruder through a die plate that creates the desired shape. Two different extrusion processes, direct expansion or pellets, are commonly used. Products such as Corn Pops®, and Chex® are produced using direct expansion. As part of the extrusion process, these cereals are also expanded. Once extruded, the cereal is dried, toasted, flavored, and packaged. Co-extrusion can be used for filled cereals. Products such as Cheerios ®, Kix®, and Alpha Bits® are produced from extruded pellets. Extruded pellets are further processed by puffing, flaking, or other process to create the desired cereal. Some shredded cereals may also be manufactured using extrusion.
Granolas	Granolas are composed of various ingredients, including rolled oats, puffed cereal, nuts, coconut, sugar, honey, milk, and spices. The water, oil, and syrup are blended with the dried ingredients and then baked. The baked, toasted cereal is then broken into pieces.
Muesli products	Muesli products, like granolas, are made from mixtures of ingredients, including rolled oats and cereal flakes. Muesli products are generally intended to be consumed with milk, whereas granola may often be enjoyed dry.

Source: References 75, 40, 34.

 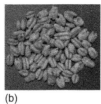 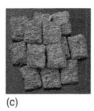 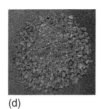 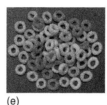 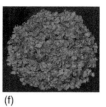

(a)   (b)   (c)   (d)   (e)   (f)

Figure 12–52

Major types of ready-to-eat breakfast cereals: (a) flaked, (b) puffed, (c) shredded wheat, (d) baked, (e) extruded, and (f) rolled oats, which are usually cooked. (Douglas and Barbara Scheule)

necessary to cook starch are more than adequate for cooking the protein in the cereal. (**Figure 12–53a** and **b**)

Combining Cereal and Water. When preparing a cereal with finely divided grains, care should be taken to avoid lumps, such as with cream of rice, farina, malted cereal, or corn meal. The cereal may be (1) added to

Figure 12–53a

Steel Cut Oatmeal with fruit is a an example of a cooked breakfast cereal. (© Barbara Scheule)

Figure 12–53b

Cooked cereal such as this creamy polenta with wild mushrooms can be a savory lunch or dinner option. (Richard Embery/PH College)

cold water and mixed briefly to blend before heating or (2) poured into boiling water and stirred only enough to separate the grains. Cereal can also be made with milk instead of water for a richer taste. Cereal should be added before milk reaches the boiling point and boiling of mixture should be avoided. Excessive stirring should be avoided to prevent breaking up the cereal particles and producing a gummy mass.

Temperature and Time Periods. Factors that affect the cereal cooking time are the size of the particle, the amount of water used, the presence or absence of the bran, the temperature, and the method used. Finely granulated endosperm cereals, such as farina, cook in less time than whole or cracked cereals. Quick-cooking and precooked cereals, of course, can be prepared much faster than completely raw and untreated cereals. For example, whole-wheat cereal may require 1 to 2 hours of cooking to soften the bran and completely gelatinize the starch granules.

Proportions of Water to Cereal. Proportions of water to cereal vary according to the type of cereal, the quantity cooked, the method of cooking, the length of cooking, and the consistency desired in the finished cereal. The majority of people appear to prefer a consistency that is fairly thick, but not too thick to pour. The amount of water must be adequate to permit swelling of the starch granules. If the consistency is too thin, further cooking may be necessary to evaporate the excess water. Most cereal packages provide directions on the recommended ratio of water to cereal.

COOKING OF RICE

White Rice

The challenge of rice cookery is to retain the form of the kernel while at the same time cooking the kernel until it is completely tender. Rice is generally cooked with amounts of water that will be fully absorbed during cooking. Rice can be cooked in about twice its volume of water, although the exact amount will vary with the variety of rice and the cooking method. Regular rice increases to about three times its volume in cooking. One-half teaspoon of salt per

Table 12–6
COOKING METHODS FOR RICE

Cooking Method	Descriptions
Simmering range top	Cook in a kettle with water equal to approximately 2.25 the volume of the rice. Bring to a boil, add rice, and lower temperature to maintain a simmer. Cover with a lid. Rice should be cooked in 15 to 20 minutes depending on the type of rice. Due to evaporation, this cooking method requires more water in proportion to rice.
Double boiler	Place rice and water equaling 1¾ the volume of the rice in the top of a double boiler over boiling water and cover. Due to reduced evaporation, less water is necessary as compared to other methods. Rice should be done in about 45 minutes.
Oven	Place rice in a covered baking dish with an equivalent amount of water as used when cooking by simmering range top. Place in a 350°F oven for about 25 to 35 minutes for white or parboiled rice.
Microwave	Place rice and water in a microwave-safe dish and cook on high until boiling. Cooking should be completed on 50 percent power for 15 to 20 minutes, depending on the type of rice. Only a minimal amount of time is saved when preparing rice in the microwave because the rice kernel still must absorb water and soften during the cooking process.
Rice cookers	Follow instructions for the rice cooker. In general, less water is needed when using a rice cooker compared to other methods.

cup of uncooked rice may be used for seasoning. Enriched rice should not be rinsed before cooking because the enrichment mixture will be washed off. Guidelines for several rice cooking methods are provided in **Table 12–6**.

A number of different ingredients may be used when preparing rice dishes. Rice can be cooked in milk with the use of the double-boiler method. Cooking rice in chicken or beef broth can also give it a desirable flavor. Many ingredients, such as herbs, spices, garlic, sautéed onions, or lemon zest, can result in a delicious rice dish. A variety of hot and cold dishes may be made with rice as a basic ingredient.

In some parts of the country where the water is hard, the minerals in the water can produce a grayish green or yellowish tint to the cooked rice. The addition of ¼ teaspoon of cream of tartar or 1 teaspoon of lemon juice to 2 quarts of water will maintain the white color.

Brown Rice

Brown rice can be cooked by the same methods used to cook white rice, but it must be cooked about twice as long. Because of the longer cooking time, somewhat more water is needed to allow for evaporation—up to 2.5 times the volume of the rice. Brown rice can be soaked for an hour in water to soften the bran and to shorten the cooking period. It does not tend to become sticky with cooking.

Researchers are developing methods of processing brown rice to reduce the cooking time from 45 to 15 minutes to encourage consumers to use brown rice.

Brown rice is highly nutritious and higher in fiber than white rice; however, the longer cooking time discourages some from preparing it. Researchers have found that by "sandblasting" the rice grains with rice flour under 60 to 70 pounds of air pressure per inch, the rice bran develops water-absorbing holes that result in a faster preparation time [84]. Also available is precooked brown rice, which has a slightly different flavor profile than regular brown rice but cooks quickly.

Precooked or Instant Rice

Precooked rice can be prepared very quickly. Boiling water is added to the rice. The mixture is then brought back to a boil, removed from the source of heat, and allowed to stand closely covered until the rice swells.

Rice Pilaf

Browning rice in a small amount of hot fat before cooking it in water converts part of the starch to dextrins. Swelling will also be somewhat decreased. The rice develops an interesting color and flavor that make the method desirable to use as a basis for Spanish rice, as rice pilaf, or as a side dish. Chicken or beef broth rather than water is used as the cooking liquid for pilaf (**Figure 12–54**).

NOODLES

Noodles are made from primarily three ingredients: (1) flour, (2) water, and (3) salt. Wheat flour is the primary flour used for noodles, but other flours can

Figure 12–55

Wheat has an enzyme that can cause gray discoloration in fresh noodles, an undesirable trait in Asian markets. (Peggy Greb/USDA)

Figure 12–54

Rice pilaf is made by first sautéing rice in butter and/or oil, followed by cooking in a vegetable or chicken stock. The finished rice pilaf is shown here. (Richard Embery/PH College)

Figure 12–56

Yellow noodle balls. (Cheuk-king Lo. Pearson Education Asia Ltd.)

be used. Other ingredients may be added to improve dough processing [99]. Noodle dough is made by mixing the flour with water and kneading, rolling, pulling, stretching, dividing into shapes, and then cooking. The main difference between a noodle and pasta is that noodles are typically made from flour rather than durum semolina as pasta.

Oriental Noodles

The noodle is thought to have originated in China. Noodles have been a staple food in many Asian cultures for thousands of years [100, 55, 41, 35]. Grinding sticks and stones dating back over 10,000 years have been unearthed in China [100]. In 2002, during an archaeological excavation in Northwestern China, 4,000-year-old millet noodles were discovered under an inverted blue striped earthenware bowl. The noodles resembled modern noodles; they were yellow in color, and between 3 mm and 500 mm long [100, 55].

Ingredients. There are many different types of Asian noodles depending on culture, climate, region, and many other factors. Oriental noodles can be classified based on raw material they are made from, salt used, color, size, and process used in production [35, 41].

Flour. Wheat flour will be the focus of the noodle discussion, but various other flours are used. Noodle flour consumption in many countries is around 20–50 percent [41]. Non-wheat flours include buckwheat (Soba), mung bean (a round green bean), sweet

potato starch, rice, bean thread, tapioca, sago (starch extracted from palm pith), and corn.

Flour color is very important in Oriental noodles. Chinese noodles are generally made from hard wheats and Japanese udon noodles from soft wheat with medium protein. White noodles are made from white winter wheat (**Figure 12–55**), which has been the subject of much research. Whiteness or brightness decreases with increasing protein levels. Color and texture change during boiling. Gray discoloration of noodles sometimes occurs [16, 14]. White wheat has lower polyphenol oxidase (PPO) which is thought to be responsible for noodle darkening [41].

Salts. Noodles are classified as "salted" or "alkaline." Salted noodles are made with regular salt (NaCl). Alkaline noodles are made with mainly sodium carbonate (Na_2CO_3) or potassium carbonate (K_2CO_3). The alkaline salts affect the color and texture of the noodles. Alkaline salts make yellow noodles (**Figure 12–56**).

Regular salted noodles contain about 1–8 percent salt [35]. Salted noodles can be fresh, dried, boiled, and sometimes parboiled and "long life noodle." The size can vary from very thin to flat. Salted noodles should be a "clean" color ranging from white to creamy with a glossy sheen after boiling. Koreans and Japanese prefer soft, elastic, and smooth salted noodle, whereas Chinese prefer firm, chewy, and elastic noodle [35].

Alkaline salted noodles have a pH 7–11 depending on salts used. They noodles are yellow, firm, and elastic with a distinct aroma and flavor.

Additional Noodles. *Buckwheat* flour (10–40 percent) may be added to wheat to make buckwheat noodles (Soba) found primarily in Japan, sometimes Korea and northeast China. Since buckwheat lacks gluten, a high protein flour must be used. Fresh harvested buckwheat makes the best noodles. These noodles are dark, elastic, and firm [41, 35]. (Soba noodles featured in Figure 12–48).

Rice flour lacks gluten so its ability to form a cohesive dough is limited. However, rice flour is high in embedded starch granules. The starch is high in amylose (see Chapter 11 for more on amylose). It is common to pregelatinize some of this rice flour starch so it can bind better with the remaining flour component [21]. The pregelatinized rice flour is added for binding power. Amylose content has a major effect on textural qualities of rice noodles. They are traditionally made from long to medium grain rice. High amylose rice produces the best bright colored noodles [35].

Noodle Processing. Noodle dough is mixed, and allowed to rest to relax gluten compounds prior to sheeting (rolling). The dough rolled to desired thickness then cut in to desired shapes. Fresh noodles like Chinese raw noodle or Udon noodle (**Figure 12–57**) are ready after cutting. A secondary process occurs depending on the type of noodle being made.

Drying noodles is important for extended shelf life. Moisture may be removed by air drying, vacuum drying or deep fat frying. Steaming noodles is key in instant noodles since it gelatinizes starch in the noodle.

Most *instant* noodles such as shelf stable instant ramen noodles, noodle cups, or noodle bowls are deep-fat fried (**Figure 12–58a**). First the noodle is cut, steamed, and waved against a metal block or glass plates. The waved noodles are then molded into a block of noodles which are deep fat fried for 60–100 seconds at 284–320°F (140–160°C) [35]. Deep fat frying is important (1) to dry noodles, (2) for oil uptake, (3) to gelatinize starch before free water evaporates, and (4) to create internal and external pores in noodle as a result of steam evaporation. Moisture content of instant noodles is 3–6 percent and oil content 15–22 percent [35]. These instant noodles are best prepared for serving by steeping in boiling hot water for 3–4

Figure 12–57

Package of Japanese Udon noodle. (Joey Chan. Pearson Education Asia Ltd.)

minutes [41]. The instant noodle can be boiled but loss of texture occurs. Flavoring ingredients are often stirred into steeped noodle prior to serving. In India, the popular Maggi noodles are flavored with a strong hydrolyzed vegetable seasoning sauce.

Egg Noodles

Egg noodles are made from wheat flour rather than semolina. Egg noodles consist of flour, salt, and eggs. A Standard of Identity exist for egg noodles. Egg noodles, for example, must contain 5.5 percent egg solids to be

Figure 12–58a

Instant ramen noodle. (Kzww/Shutterstock)

Flour Stick Wheat Noodles (without egg)

Fresh Wheat and Egg Noodles

Rice Vermicelli

Cellophane Noodles

Japanese Wheat Somen

Figure 12–58b

Flour stick wheat noodles without egg, rice vermicelli, cellophane noodles, Japanese Wheat Somen. (Richard Embery/Pearson Education)

called a noodle according to U.S. government regulation [92]. Egg noodles are simple to make at home using a food processor [50]. The noodle dough is rolled and cut into long ribbon strips. Commercial noodle production is simple with rolling and cutting processes producing egg noodles that are either frozen or dried [40].

Fresh egg noodles are boiled and served or cooked by adding to soup such as Chicken Noodle soup (**Figure 12–59**). Egg noodles can be boiled and baked in casserole style dishes such as tuna noodle casserole. Traditional Jewish kugel is a baked egg noodle dish. Turkish eriste noodles are a variation of the egg noodle often made at home using semolina flour. Central Asia kesme are egg noodles; the dough sometimes contains milk and may be made without egg. Turkish eriste have been made using chickpea flour for enrichment [19]. Gluten free noodles can be made using buckwheat flour [22].

Egg noodle dough also serves as wrap for Central and Eastern Europe filled dumpling known as pierogi, pirohy, and varenyky (**Figure 12–60**).

Figure 12–59

Chicken noodle soup with egg noodles. (Hannamariah/ Shutterstock)

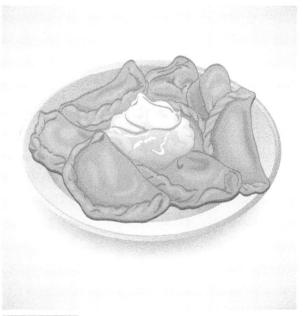

Figure 12–60

Dumpling pierogi, pirohy, varenyky served with sour cream. (Olga Dar/Shutterstock)

Typical fillings are potato and cheese, meat and sauerkraut, and cheese or fruit. Noodle dough is rolled and cut into circles with filling placed in center as dough is folded over and sealed. Dumplings are allowed to dry slightly then boiled and served with melted butter, caramelized onions, or sour cream. Asian dumplings are made with Asian noodle dough and steamed (**Figure 12–61 a**, **b** and **c**).

Instant egg noodle convenience products usually contain noodles which have been steamed and dried to gelatinize the starch allowing the noodles to cook within minutes [40]. Often these convenience side dishes come with a flavorful seasoning stirred into the cooked instant noodles.

PASTA

The terms *pasta* and *alimentary paste* are applied to macaroni products, which include spaghetti, vermicelli, noodles, shells, linguine, rotini, ziti, couscous, and many

Figure 12–61c
Bowl of Chinese wonton dumpling. (Coleman Yuen/Pearson Education Asia Ltd.)

other shapes. There are more than 600 pasta shapes available worldwide, with more being developed [66]. Several different shapes of pasta are shown in **Figure 12–62**. In general, delicate pasta shapes like angel hair should be paired with a delicate sauce, and sturdy pastas should be complemented with a robust, hearty sauce. Pasta with ridges or holes such as Cavatappi, are perfect for chunkier sauces. Some small pastas are added to soups. Some pasta shells are stuffed and baked. Other pasta dough is filled and boiled such as ravioli or tortellini.

The principal ingredient in the making of pasta is a semolina coarsely ground from durum wheat. Durum wheat is the hardest wheat with high-protein levels. Its large kernels contain carotenoid pigments in higher

Figure 12–61a
Steamed Chinese Dumpling. (Leungchopan/Shutterstock)

Figure 12–61b
Traditional Asian sticky rice dumpling steamed in banana leaves. (Kelvin Wong/Shutterstock)

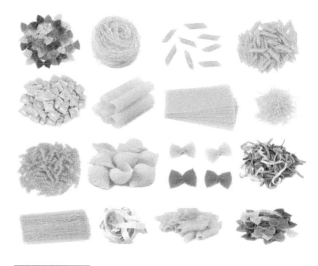

Figure 12–62
Pasta is available in in various shapes and sizes which are used in various pasta dishes. (Photka/Shutterstock)

concentration than is found in bread wheats, giving pasta its characteristic yellow or amber color. When durum wheat is milled the endosperm is ground into a granular product called semolina. Durum is so hard it is difficult to reduce to a fine flour that is high quality.

Fifty-five to sixty-eight percent of durum wheat is grown in North Dakota with 20 percent in Montana and the rest grown in California and Arizona. The United States uses two-thirds of durum wheat and exports the remaining third of supply to Italy, Africa, and Central and South America. Durum is primarily used for pasta in the U.S. market; international markets also use it for couscous and some bread.

Although pasta may be prepared from little more than semolina and water, pasta products may include additional ingredients. Code of Federal Regulations Title 21 has rules on standards of identity for macaroni and other pasta products [95]. Gaining in popularity are whole-grain pastas and pasta made with green pea, chickpea, and lentil flours combined with semolina. These products provide more fiber and, if made with lentils, a higher protein content as well. These additional ingredients do have an impact on flavor, texture, and color of pasta compared to traditional formulations [104]. Spinach and tomato powders may also be used in some pasta products to produce distinctive colors and flavors.

Commercially Manufactured Pasta

In the commercial manufacture of pasta, the flour is mixed with water in large mixers under vacuum. If additional ingredients are used to produce a specialty pasta, it is added during the mixing phase. The tough dough produced during mixing is then shaped into the characteristic shapes by being (1) forced or "extruded" through dies or (2) cut out of flat sheets of dough. Macaroni, for example, is forced through a die with a steel pin in the center to produce a hollow rod. A notch on one side of the rod causes the dough to curve as it passes through. Dough forced through dies is cut into the desired length by a revolving knife.

Next, the pasta is dried in dryers that may be as long as 320 feet. The temperature and humidity are carefully controlled during drying to produce high-quality pasta. Drying that is too rapid may result in pasta that breaks easily. The conventional drying process takes place at approximate temperatures of 140°F (60°C), but the high-temperature process uses temperatures above 212°F (100°C) [36]. Prior to the development of machines that can carefully control the drying of pasta, it was hung on racks to dry in the sun.

Fast Cook or Instant Pasta. Pasta manufacturers are producing pasta to keep up consumer demand for convenience. These pastas may be marketed as instant, faster cooking or one pan no boil products which are mixed with sauce and cooked. These pastas have undergone pre-steaming or cooking to gelatinize starch. The products are dried and marketed as fast cooking, no rinse, instant pastas. Lasagna noodles in this category do not need to be cooked and rinsed prior to lasagna assembly thus saving an extra step in production. Pasta products in this category may retain their structure better if methylcellulose is added to the pasta dough formulation [101].

Traditional pasta preparation relies on temperature and water to gelatinize pasta starch and rehydrate the pasta. Instant pastas are only concerned with the rehydration step. Preparation of instant pasta can be classified into four basic methods: (1) warm water rehydration, which uses boiling water for 2–5 minutes, (2) cold water rehydration using room temperature water for 20–245 minutes, (3) traditional method for shorter time, and (4) microwaving, which uses the principles of the first three methods [97].

Homemade Pasta

Pasta can be made at home. A pasta machine, which is a small kitchen device with a set of rollers and cutters, gives the fastest and best result. The pasta machine is a set of rollers that can be adjusted to make a sheet of pasta dough of desirable thickness. Dough is passed through the rollers several times adjusting the rollers to make a thinner sheet with each pass. Dough can be rolled by hand if no pasta machine. Dough is ready to cut into

FOCUS ON SCIENCE
WHY DOES PASTA MAINTAIN ITS SHAPE WHEN COOKED?

Protein and starch in semolina play an important part in allowing pasta to maintain its shape when cooked. During cooking, the starch granules swell rapidly and tend to disperse and in part become soluble. The proteins, on the contrary, become completely insoluble and coagulate, creating a netlike structure around the starch. Because these mechanisms occur approximately at the same temperatures, the more rapidly the proteins form the netlike structure, the more limited will be the swelling of the starch. The starch components will remain trapped inside the protein network, ensuring a firm consistency and absence of stickiness. If the protein is of poor quality, the starch granules will not be confined, and the soluble material will pass into the cooking liquid, producing a product that will be sticky and of poor consistency.

Source: M. A. Pagani, M. Lucisano, and M. Mariotti, "Traditional Italian Products from Wheat and Other Starchy Products," in Handbook of Food Products Manufacturing, ed. Y. H. Hui (Hoboken, NJ: John Wiley & Sons, 2007), p. 327.

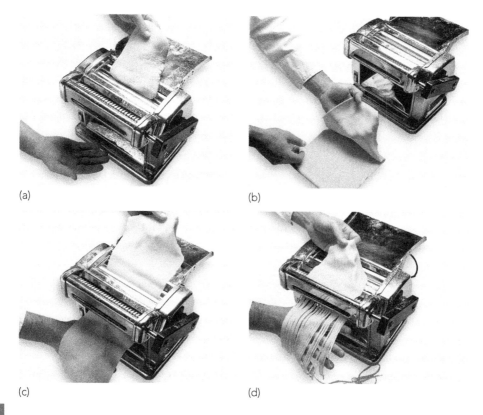

Figure 12–63

(a) Pass pasta dough through pasta machine. (b) Fold dough in thirds. (c) Pass dough through machine until desired thickness. (d) Using the pasta machine cut dough into desired widths. (Richard Embery/Pearson Education)

ribbons when dough is thin enough to see the hand through it, but not so thin it tears. This sheet of dough is referred to as *sfoglia* [50]. The thickness of the final pasta sheet *(sfoglia)* will depend on the type of pasta being made. When dough is at the desired thickness, the dough is cut or filled. Lasagna noodles are pasta ribbons about two inches wide. Spaghetti and fettuccine thin ribbons and many other shapes can be achieved.

Homemade pasta and noodle dough are easy to make with a few simple ingredients. On a work board or bench flour is mounded and well is made in the center. If using eggs, they are beaten with a fork in the well. If any liquid ingredients are used they are added in the flour

well. Liquid ingredients are worked into the flour mixture until the dough is formed. Dough is kneaded until satiny for about 10 minutes. See **Figure 12–64** for the steps. Dough can be made in a food processor, but care must be taken not to over work the dough.

Filled pasta such as ravioli or tortellini are easily made by rolling two sheets of pasta. The pasta sheets are filled with a variety of cheese or meat or vegetable fillings. Pasta dough must be worked with and sealed while still moist.

To make ravioli, place approximately ½ teaspoon of filling mounded onto bottom sheet of pasta about 1 inch apart. Water is then brushed or dabbed around

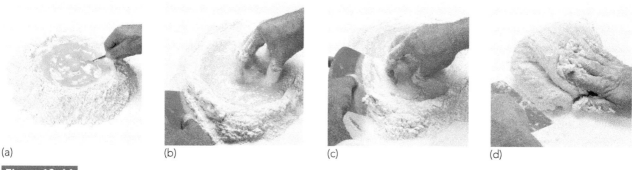

Figure 12–64

Procedure for mixing noodle or pasta dough by hand: (a) Mound the flour with deep well in center. Add eggs into well and whip with fork. (b) Using fingers, stir the eggs gradually bringing more flour into the center. (c) Using a dough scraper, add more flour to the egg mixture, mixing constantly until a firm dough is formed. (d) Knead the stiff dough until smooth. (Richard Embery/Pearson Education)

each mound of filling. Second pasta sheet is placed on top of filled pasta sheet. Top and bottom pasta layers are pressed together around each mound. A sharp chef's knife, ravioli cutter, or pizza cutter is used to cut the ravioli into squares between each sealed mound of pasta. Ravioli is then carefully transferred to floured clean kitchen towels or baking sheets to dry for an hour before boiling.

Tortellini is made in a similar way to ravioli except a round biscuit or cookie cutter is used to cut around filling mounds. The dough is folded over to form a semicircle and sealed. Tail ends are brought together, overlapped, and pinched together to form ring shape or what is described as a brimmed hat. The tortellini is then dried and cooked the same as ravioli (**Figure 12–65**).

Pasta is cooked in salted boiling water until al a dente or filled pieces are cooked. The salt flavor transfers to the pasta which is usually desirable. However, sodium content is also increased in pasta cooked in salted water. About 30 percent of the sodium can be removed by pasta cooked in salted water by rinsing before serving [10]. Pasta is drained and served hot with favorite sauces or chilled and used in salads.

Couscous

Couscous is made from semolina which is steamed and formed into small pieces about 2 mm in diameter. This product can be dried and rehydrated/resteamed

Figure 12–66

Coucous.

before eating. Couscous originated in Northern Africa regions. Couscous is quick to prepare as it is added to boiling water and allowed to set and resteam around 5 minutes. Pearl Couscous (Israeli couscous) is larger pearl size pieces that takes slightly longer with resteaming about 10 minutes. Couscous can be served as a side dish or with stews [40] (**Figure 12–66**).

Preparation of Pasta

Macaroni, spaghetti, and other pastas are cooked by adding the pasta to boiling water, which is usually salted (**Figure 12–67**). Approximately 2 to 3 quarts of boiling water are used for 8 ounces of pasta

Figure 12–65

Filled pasta can be made from sheets of dough, filling then second piece of dough. Filled dough is cut and sealed. (Richard Embery/Pearson Education)

Figure 12–67

Cooking spaghetti in a boiling pot of salted water. (Lestertair/ Shutterstock)

product. The more water used, the less likely it is that the pasta will stick together; thus, it is important to use an adequate amount of water. A small amount of oil added to the cooking water may help keep the pasta pieces separate. The pasta should be added gradually so that the water continues to boil rapidly. Cooking continues in an uncovered pan with occasional stirring until the pasta is tender yet firm to the bite. The standard for final cooking is called *al dente* (to the tooth). If the pasta is to be further baked or simmered with other ingredients, it should be cooked until almost tender. Cooking then is completed after the pasta is combined with the other ingredients.

Pasta generally increases two to two and a half times its original volume on cooking, although the amount varies with the type of shape of the pasta being prepared. Form is almost always retained on cooking in good quality pasta made from high protein semolina. If cooking time is excessive, however,

the pasta will become soft and sticky and may break up. When the boiling process is complete, the pasta should be drained thoroughly in a colander or strainer. Enriched pasta should not be rinsed in water after cooking to avoid the loss of vitamins and minerals. If cooked pasta must be held a while before serving, it may be placed over hot water in a strainer. Steam will keep the product hot and moist without further cooking. Stickiness is reduced by this procedure, compared with overcooking.

Pasta can be designed especially for use in microwave ovens. Most conventional pastas are too thick to be cooked properly and uniformly by microwaves and will not achieve the desired firm texture. Microwavable pasta has thinner walls and has additional ingredients, such as egg albumen [58]. The additional protein helps to form an insoluble network that traps starch granules and controls gelatinization more effectively [36].

Fresh or high-moisture pasta packaged in barrier trays under a modified atmosphere is being marketed successfully as a convenience food, along with companion sauces [36]. Because microbial safety is not ensured by the modified atmosphere packaging alone, care must be taken to keep the product refrigerated after it has been processed and packaged under carefully controlled conditions.

The variety of dishes that can be prepared with macaroni products is almost endless: soups, salads, main dishes, meat accompaniments, and even desserts can be prepared with pasta. For example, pasta may be combined with flavorful roasted vegetables or with fruits in dishes such as pasta salad with pineapple-mint salsa [66]. Pasta may also be used in dishes with hot and spicy ingredients including peppers and cayenne. Fish and seafood pair nicely with pasta. Traditional Italian sauces are not the only way to serve pasta as a main course.

STUDY QUESTIONS

Cereal Grains

1. Name the most important cereal grains used for food.

2. Describe a pseudo-cereal grain. List and discuss pseudo-cereal grains and role they play in the diet.

Whole Grains

3. Name three major parts of a grain. Describe the general chemical composition of each part.

4. Describe general composition and milling of grain.

5. Describe whole grains. Discuss challenges in defining "whole grain."

The Nutritive Value of Cereal Products

6. What is meant by *enrichment* of cereals and flours? What nutrients must be added to meet the standards of the federal government?

7. Compare the general nutritional value of refined unenriched, enriched, and whole-grain cereal products.

Barley

8. What is malt? How is malt used? What is the primary grain that is malted?

Corn

9. The corn kernel is versatile and can take a great variety of forms. Discuss some of these forms and their role in the diet.

Oats

10. Discuss why oats are packaged in breathable containers.

Rice

11. Discuss rice classes, types, and uses.

12. Discussed the difference between brown and white rice.

13. What is arsenic? Where is it found? Why is it concerned with rice?

14. Define and discuss whole grains. Discuss how whole grains fit into a healthy diet.

Processed Cereal Grains and Preparation

15. Briefly describe the processes involved in preparing the grain.

(a) Uncooked breakfast cereals

(b) Prepared breakfast cereals

(c) Flour

(d) Meal

(e) Hominy

(f) Grits

(g) Pasta

16. What are the main purposes for cooking cereals?

17. Suggest appropriate methods for cooking each of the following cereal products. Explain why these methods are appropriate.

(a) Granular cereals such as farina and corn meal

(b) Rolled oats

(c) Rice

(d) Macaroni or spaghetti

Breakfast Cereal

18. Describe the general processes involved in the production of each of the following types of ready-to-eat cereal.

(a) Puffed

(b) Flaked

(c) Granulated

(d) Shredded

(e) Extruded

19. Discuss several factors to consider when purchasing cereals and other grain products?

Noodles and Pasta

20. Discuss the similarities and differences between noodles and pasta.

21. Describe the similarities and differences between semolina and farina.

22. Discuss the standard cooking methods of pasta.

13
Flour Mixtures
Batters and Doughs

Batters and doughs refer to the *flour mixtures* used in producing bakery products, such as muffins, biscuits and other quick breads, pastry, shortened and unshortened cakes, cookies, and yeast breads. The liquid-to-flour ratio will determine if the flour mixture is classified as a dough or batter. Generally, doughs contain a lower liquid-to-flour ratio versus batters that contain higher liquid content. Doughs are generally stiff, so they can be manipulated by hand versus batters, which are thin enough to pour (**Figures 13–1** and **13–2**).

Flour is the main ingredient of batters and doughs (**Figure 13–3**). Liquid is combined with flour to produce either a batter or dough. Other ingredients are added to produce various bakery products. Common foundation formulas include flour, liquid, and additional ingredients, including fat, egg, sugar, leavening agent, and salt (**Figure 13–4**). These basic ingredients are balanced and manipulated to produce different flour-based bakery products. Flavoring agents are added to some mixtures. Fat and sugar replacers can be important ingredients in reduced-fat or reduced-calorie items. Flour substitution and additives such as gums and starch can be used to produce gluten-free baked goods, but the quality rarely equals those made from flour [3].

Figure 13–1

Dough is generally stiff and manipulated by hand. (Oleksandr Kostiuchenko/Shutterstock)

Figure 13–2

Batters are pourable. (YKTR/Shutterstock)

Producing a high-quality-flour-based bakery product depends on many factors. Understanding bakery ingredients and their function, role, proportion, and interactions are essential to balance product formulas that yield high-quality bakery products. The accuracy in ingredient weighing or measuring will affect final product. Mastering the skills and techniques used in ingredient manipulation is essential for producing high-quality bakery products. Terms used to manipulate batters and doughs have precise meanings. Understanding and applying these terms and techniques is essential to produce a quality product. Appropriate bowl size and equipment are necessary to produce bakery goods of high standards. Oven temperature and heating control are crucial for bakery products.

Understanding the characteristics of a good standard baked product is important to maintain quality control. Correct formulations, techniques, production, and ingredient issues also impact the quality of the baked product. It is important to learn (1) quality characteristics and standards for baked products, (2) proportions of ingredients, and (3) techniques used to achieve the standardized characteristics. Understanding ingredients and mixing methods for bakery products will allow the production of consistent high-quality bakery products.

Figure 13–3

Flour is the main ingredient in batters and doughs. (M. Unal Ozmen/Shutterstock)

Figure 13–4

Flour and liquid are the common ingredients found in batters and doughs. Other ingredients may include sugar, fat, eggs, salt, and leavening agents. (AKZ/123RF)

In this chapter, the following topics will be discussed:

- Classification of batters and doughs
- Structure of batters and doughs
- Basic ingredients, including flour, leavening agents, fat, liquids, eggs, sugar, and other sweeteners
- Mixing methods and terminology
- Dry flour mixes
- Baking at high altitudes
- Kosher and Halal laws related to batters and doughs

CONSUMPTION TRENDS AND NUTRITION

Consumption Trends

Wheat is the world's most important food grain (**Figure 13–5**). It provides 20 percent of the calories and proteins for humans across the globe. Wheat is the staple food in more than 40 countries for over 35 percent of the world population. It is the most widely cultivated food crop and can be grown over a wide range of elevations, varying climates, and soils; plus, it is easily processed and transported (**Figure 13–6**). Wheat is actually a member of the grass family whose seed forms a kernel (**Figure 13–7**). The kernel of wheat is milled (ground) into flour, which is the foundation ingredient for batters and doughs.

Wheat most likely originated as a wild grass. It is thought to have first grown wild in Mesopotamia or the Tigris and Euphrates River Valley where people gathered wheat seeds over 17,000 years ago. The word cereal is derived from the Roman Goddess *Ceres*, who was deemed the protector of grains (**Figure 13–8**). Today, more food is produced from wheat than any other grain.

Wheat was first grown in the United States as a hobby crop in 1777. Now wheat is produced in 42 states (**Figure 13–9**). In 2016, U.S. farmers grew 2.31 billion bushels of wheat. One bushel of wheat contains about a million wheat kernels, weighs about 60 pounds, and produces 42 pounds of white flour or 60 pounds (77.2 kg) of whole-wheat flour. One acre (0.4047 hectares) of land yields about 40 bushels of wheat. One bushel of wheat makes 42 commercial loaves of white pan loaf bread (1½ pound loaf). Sixteen ounces of flour make a 1½ pound pan loaf commercial bread that is sliced into 24 slices (**Figure 13–10**).

Kansas is the largest wheat producer in the United States. North Dakota and Montana produce large amounts of durum wheat used in Mediterranean breads and pastas. Wheat is a valuable export crop for the United States. In the United States, domestic food use of wheat is estimated indirectly because no data are collected on actual wheat consumption.

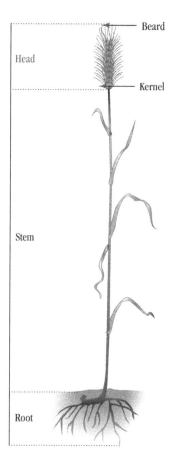

A wheat plant.

Figure 13-5

The wheat head contains kernels. A wheat kernel, like other grains, includes endosperm, germ, and bran. Whole-wheat flour includes the endosperm, germ, and bran in the same proportions as found in nature.

Figure 13-6

Kernels of ripened wheat. (Russal/Shutterstock)

Figure 13-7

Wheat is a grass. (Anest/Shutterstock)

Figure 13-8

Roman Goddess Ceres was the protector of the grain. (Hein Nouwens/Shutterstock)

Across the United States, there are around 190 mills that turn the regional wheat into flour. Monthly estimates of wheat milled are produced by the U.S. Department of Commerce. According to the USDA's Economic Research Service (ERS), consumption of wheat-based products has sharply declined since 2000. This decline reversed a previous 30-year growth trend. The decline was attributed to the public interest in lowering carbohydrate consumption. Recent concerns over gluten may also contribute to declining consumption trends.

Trends in all-day breakfast are boosting consumption of more traditional batter and dough

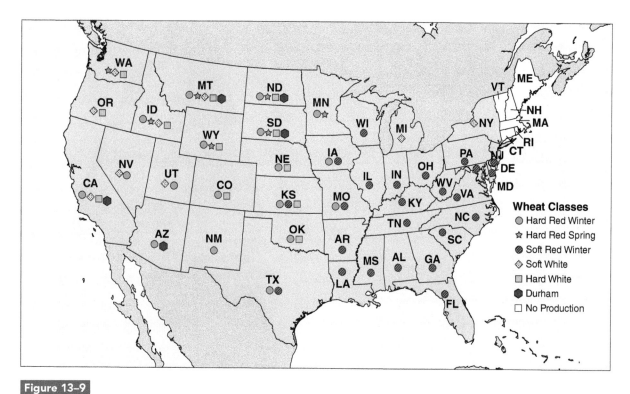

Figure 13–9

Wheat is produced in 42 U.S. states. (Cartographer Charlie Frye/© Amanda Frye)

products. About 20 percent of refined grain consumption is attributed to bakery products such as cakes, cookies, and other sweetened grain bakery products. Sweetened bakery products such as cookies, cakes, sweet rolls, and pies contribute around 30 percent of added sugars in American diets. However, wheat dough is used to make the crust for over 3 billion pizzas sold in the United States each year.

Ancient and sprouted grains are being used in batter and dough products for their texture, flavor, and health benefits [49]. Sprouted grains can add a concentrated source of vitamins, minerals, and antioxidants. They are often added as topping on baked products. Ancient grains gaining in popularity include millet, sorghum, and teff, as well as pseudo cereal grains amaranth, buckwheat, and quinoa [31]. These grains are often added in combinations to make multigrain baked products.

Bite-size baked goods, single-serve packaging, and "take-and-go" products to eat throughout the day are meeting consumer demands for bakery and dough products. Experimental flavors are popular in batter- and dough-finished products. More experimentation with baked items using alternative grains and dairy proteins, hydrocolloids, and gums in baked goods avoiding gluten-bearing grains is being carried out. Replacement of partially hydrogenated shortenings is causing manufacturers to experiment with

alternatives in many batter and dough products [32]. Clean labels with fewer ingredients influence many baked products.

Nutritive Value

Wheat is the main grain used in bakery products, although other grains such as corn and oats may also be used in some bakery products (**Figure 13–11**). Grains are important sources of nutrients, especially the B vitamins (thiamine, riboflavin, niacin, and folate) and minerals (iron, zinc, magnesium, and selenium). Whole grains are also rich in fiber. Most refined grains are enriched, which means the nutrients (B vitamins and iron) taken away during processing are added back (**Figure 13–12**). U.S. Federal code Title 21 defines the standard of identity of cereal grains and products, including nutrient enrichment of flour. Each pound of enriched flour must contain 2.9 milligrams of thiamine, 1.9 milligrams of riboflavin, 24 milligrams of niacin, 0.7 milligrams of folic acid, and 20 milligrams of iron.

Some baked products are naturally low in fat, such as many standard yeast breads and angel food cakes; yet other products such as shortened cakes, cookies, biscuits, pastry, and muffins contain moderate to high amounts of fat. Bakery products such as cakes and cookies may contain high amounts of added sugars. Dietary Guidelines for Americans recommend

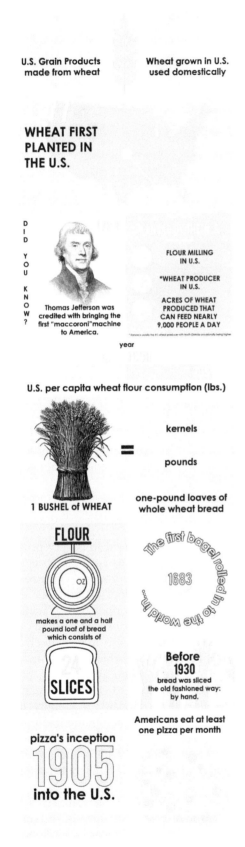

Figure 13–10

Wheat facts. (© Wheat Foods Council)

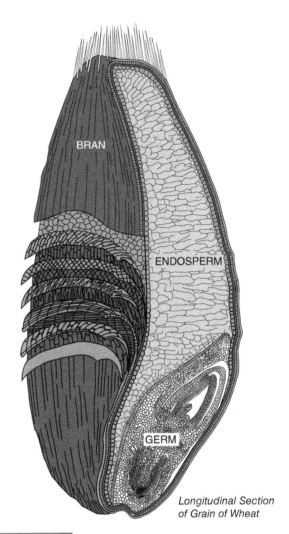

BRAN

ENDOSPERM

GERM

*Longitudinal Section
of Grain of Wheat*

Figure 13–11

Wheat is nutrient-rich and can be incorporated into a healthy meal plan. (© Wheat Foods Council)

healthy eating patterns that include whole grains and limited refined grain products high in saturated fats and added sugar. The FDA ruled in 2015 that *trans fats* from partially hydrogenated oils would be removed from the generally recognized as safe (GRAS) list found in Code of Federal Regulations Title 21 182, 184, 186. Many commercial bakery products that contained trans fats have been reformulated to meet new guidelines.

CLASSIFICATION OF BATTERS AND DOUGHS

Flour mixtures vary in thickness depending largely on the proportion of flour to liquid. Depending on thickness, flour mixtures are classified as batters or doughs. The amount of liquid per cup of flour for batters and

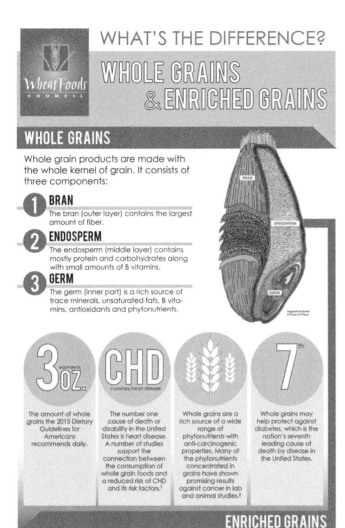

WHAT'S THE DIFFERENCE?

WHOLE GRAINS & ENRICHED GRAINS

WHOLE GRAINS

Whole grain products are made with the whole kernel of grain. It consists of three components:

1 BRAN
The bran (outer layer) contains the largest amount of fiber.

2 ENDOSPERM
The endosperm (middle layer) contains mostly protein and carbohydrates along with small amounts of B vitamins.

3 GERM
The germ (inner part) is a rich source of trace minerals, unsaturated fats, B vitamins, antioxidants and phytonutrients.

3 OZ. equivalents
The amount of whole grains the 2015 Dietary Guidelines for Americans recommends daily.

CHD coronary heart disease
The number one cause of death or disability in the United States is heart disease. A number of studies support the connection between the consumption of whole grain foods and a reduced risk of CHD and its risk factors.[1]

Whole grains are a rich source of a wide range of phytonutrients with anti-carcinogenic properties. Many of the phytonutrients concentrated in grains have shown promising results against cancer in lab and animal studies.[2]

7th
Whole grains may help protect against diabetes, which is the nation's seventh leading cause of death by disease in the United States.

ENRICHED GRAINS

Enriched white flour is the finely ground endosperm of the kernel. The assumption that everything good has been "stripped" away is a fallacy. Many of the nutrients that have been milled out are replaced through enrichment or fortification.

ENRICHED WHITE BREAD IS A GREAT SOURCE OF:

IRON   B VITAMINS   FOLIC ACID   COMPLEX CARBS

1941 When refined grains first became enriched with iron and three B vitamins; riboflavin, niacin and thiamin.

1998 When a 4th B vitamin, folic acid, was added to the enrichment formula. Since then, neural tube birth defects have decreased by 1/3.[3]

1999 A study found that 77 percent of low-income women could consume adequate amounts of folic acid through enriched grain products. The cost of supplements can be expensive, and therefore often not taken by low-income women. Even those who can afford a folic acid supplement often forget to take them.[4]

Figure 13–12

Wheat nutrition and enrichment facts. (© Wheat Foods Council)

Table 13–1
BATTERS AND DOUGHS: AMOUNT OF LIQUID USED FOR 1 CUP OF FLOUR

Type of Batter or Dough	Amount of Liquid for 1 Cup of Flour
Pour batter	$2/3$ to 1 cup liquid
Drop batter	$1/2$ to $3/4$ cup of liquid
Soft dough	$1/3$ cup of liquid
Stiff dough	$1/8$ cup of liquid

doughs is provided in **Table 13–1**. The grain and texture of baked products are a result of gas cells in the protein and starch matrix; thus, flour mixtures are typically classified as a foam system. Ingredients, manipulation, and baking techniques will determine how the gas cells are formed and distributed throughout the baked product.

Batters

Batters are classified as pour batters or drop batters, but considerable variation exists within each group. Pour batters may be very thin, or they may be barely pourable. Pour batters typically have a 1:1 liquid-to-flour ratio. Popovers and thin griddle-cake and shortened-cake batters are examples of pour batters (**Figure 13–13**).

Drop batters are used for muffins, many quick breads, and various kinds of cookies. In drop batters containing approximately one part liquid to two parts flour, gluten development readily occurs on mixing, and therefore the avoidance of over mixing

Figure 13–13

Griddle cakes are an example of a pour batter. (V. J. Matthew/Shutterstock)

Figure 13–14

Muffins are made from drop batters. (Richard Embery/Pearson Education)

Figure 13–15

A sponge is a batter containing yeast. This poolish has a 1:1 flour-to-liquid ratio. (Richard Embery/Pearson Education)

is important. Some drop batters, such as cookies, are stiff enough to require scraping from the spoon (**Figure 13–14**).

A batter containing yeast is called a *sponge*. Sponges such as a *poolish* are thin and have a one-to-one flour-to-liquid ratio (**Figure 13–15**). Other sponges may have higher flour-to-liquid ratio with a consistency of a drop batter.

Doughs

Doughs are thick enough to be handled or kneaded on a flat surface (**Figure 13–16**). Most doughs are rolled in the final stages of preparation, although yeast dough is not usually rolled, except for the shaping of certain types of rolls. Doughs may be soft (just stiff enough to handle) or stiff. Examples of soft-dough

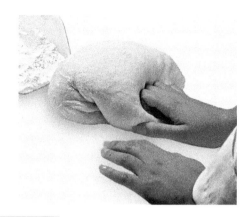

Figure 13–16

Yeast bread dough is thick enough to be kneaded by hand. (Richard Embery/Pearson Education)

products include baking powder biscuits, rolled cookies, yeast bread, and rolls. Pie crust is an example of a stiff dough.

STRUCTURE OF BATTERS AND DOUGHS

The structure that develops in batters and doughs varies according to ingredient type and formula proportions. In all mixtures, except those of high liquid content, hydrated gluten particles adhere and form a continuous mass that spreads out into a network. Some components of the mixture, such as salts and sugar, are partially or completely dissolved in the liquid. The starch granules from the flour tend to be embedded in the gluten network and gelatinize during heating (**Figure 13–17**).

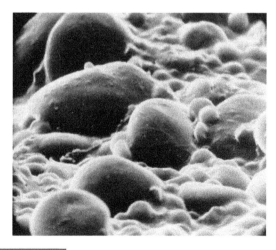

Figure 13–17

Scanning electron photomicrograph of a dough sample showing a developed gluten film covering starch granules of variable sizes. (Reprinted from Varriano-Marston, E. A comparison of dough preparation procedures for scanning electron microscopy. Food Technology, 31:34(10), 1977. © Institute of Food Technologists)

Other components act as emulsifying agents by separating or dividing the fat in the mixture into particles of varying fineness. Ingredient temperature, physical state, and chemical states partially determine the degree of emulsion dispersions. Melted fats or oils may behave differently from solid fats in certain doughs and batters [48].

The texture of the finished product depends largely on the structure obtained in the mixing of the dough or batter. Texture is a combination of such characteristics as the distribution of air cells, the thickness of cell walls, the character of the crumb (elastic, crumbly, velvety, or harsh), and the grain (the size of the cells). Optimum texture of baked goods is product and ingredient dependent. Individual baked good product standards are discussed in later chapters. Variations from typical textures and possible causes for variation are also discussed.

When all of the factors that affect texture are considered, it is not surprising that products made from the same formula may differ from one another. Although a certain degree of control of materials, manipulation, and temperatures is possible, it can be difficult to always control all factors that play a part in determining the quality of the end products obtained. In industrial operations and in many food service establishments, controls are sufficiently precise and reproducible that the same quality product is guaranteed each time.

BATTER AND DOUGH INGREDIENTS AND FUNCTIONS

Understanding batter and dough ingredients and their functions is essential for the production of high quality products. Basic ingredients found in batters and doughs include flour, leavening agents, liquid, fat, eggs, and sweeteners. Leavening gases are important for batter and dough products' grain and texture.

Flour

Flour provides structure and body in baked flour products because of its protein and starch content. Wheat is the grain used for flour in the United States, as codified in the U.S. Code of Federal Regulations. Grain standards for wheat and other grains are listed in the U.S. Code of Federal Regulations Title 7B VIII part 810 (www.eCFR.gov).

Whole-wheat flour includes the endosperm, bran, and germ. In the milling of wheat flour, the endosperm is freed from the bran and germ of the wheat kernel so that specifications for moisture, ash or minerals, and protein content are met. Wheat and flour are tested to meet quality standards, which have a direct relationship with finished product quality [34]. These basic tests, physical tests, milling performance assessment, and product tests are performed on wheat and

flour. Gluten strength and starch properties of flour are important. Millers, manufacturers, and bakers need to know the qualities of the wheat and flour. Starch content and properties are also important. Different characteristics are desired for different end products. Sprouting tests are important to analyze alpha amylase enzyme content. Too much sprouted wheat will yield too much alpha amylase and yield a product that is unusable. Starch damaged during milling affects flour quality and finished baked products. Hard wheat yields more damaged starch during milling, causing increased water absorption capacity and higher availability of oligosaccharides for amylases for yeast bread, but there can be negative effects on dough rheology and baked loaf volume. Increased damage starch in soft wheat causes detrimental effects in cookies and cakes [4].

Controlled laboratory testing provides scientific information on wheat and flour properties, characteristics, and performance in baked products. The American Association of Cereal Chemists (AACC) was formed over a hundred years ago to standardize grain analysis methods. **Table 13–2** summarizes some laboratory tests scientists use to analyze wheat and flours for the worldwide market. Baking tests are time-consuming and laborious; often baking tests are omitted and flour baking performance is predicted from quality parameters (**Figure 13–18**). Crude protein numbers can be a good descriptor of wheat quality and bread volume. Many quality parameters do not adequately replace baking tests [44] (**Figure 13–19**).

Classes of Wheat

There are six major classifications of wheat. Wheat may be classified based on the (1) color of the kernel, (2) hardness or softness of the kernel, and (3) spring or winter planting. Some wheat kernels have a reddish appearance and are called *red wheat*. Wheat with comparatively white kernels is called *white wheat*. *Hard wheat* has a hard, vitreous kernel, whereas *soft wheat* appears to be more powdery (**Figure 13–20**).

Wheat is a versatile crop grown on six continents. In the United States, 42 states grow wheat (Figure 13–9). Kansas is the largest wheat producing state. Geographic location, climate, soil, growing seasons, and moisture levels determine what wheats are grown in the various locations. Because climatic and soil conditions affect the composition of wheat, wide variations can be expected within these classes.

Hard winter wheats are grown mainly in the middle-central states. Hard winter wheat is planted and sprouted in the fall, then goes dormant in the winter, grows again in the spring, and is harvested in the summer. Hard red winter wheat has a high protein content and produces a strong gluten flour. Hard white wheat is the newest class of wheat to be grown and marketed in

Table 13–2
COMMON WHEAT AND FLOUR TESTS

Basic Tests

Moisture Content (percent) Wheat Flour	Low temperature heating Measures moisture content	Flour moisture 12–15 percent Basis for other tests Determines storability Higher moisture leads to decreased storability.
Ash (Mineral) Content Wheat Flour	High temperature incineration Measures ash (mineral) content	Ash concentrated in bran so indirectly determines flour yield during milling. Ash levels specs for flour Ash impacts flour color (low ash–white/high ash-whole wheat).
Protein Content Wheat Flour	High temperature combustion Nitrogen analyses Measures protein content	Protein content relates to water absorption and gluten capacity. Protein varies depending on variety, class, and environmental conditions. Rainfall during kernel development low protein and dry kernel development conditions leads to high protein.
Falling Number Flour	Measures alpha amylase activity Measures the effects of sprout damage Viscosity measured	High alpha amylase enzyme activity means more starch degradation Low falling number too many enzymes, sprout damage and flour is unusable since too much sugar and too little starch.

Physical Tests

Flour Color Analysis	Color analysis Measures flour color	Flour color effects finished product. Often part of end-user specification White is usually most desirable.
Kernel Characterization	Characteristics of kernels Test weight pounds/bushel Wheat hardness Kernel weight	Important for milling and flour yield
Milling Test	Laboratory scale flour mill (Buhler Lab Flour Mill) Determines flour yield and makes flour available for other tests Flour Yield %	Mills small samples of flour Easy to evaluate flour properties for ash, protein content and gluten strength.
Wet Gluten Test	Gluten washing Measures wet gluten content	Provides information on quantity and quality of gluten in wheat or flour samples
Farinograph	Recording Dough Mixer Measures flour water absorption and dough strength	Determines dough and gluten properties of flour Determines if weak or strong gluten flour Weak gluten has lower water absorption. Used to determine water in formulations and mixing tolerance properties
Extensigraph	Visco-elastic recorder Measures dough extensibility and resistance to extension	Determines gluten strength and bread making characteristics of flour Weak gluten flour has lower resistance to extension.
Alveograph	Visco-elastic recorder Measures dough strength	Determines the gluten strength of a dough with the force to blow and break a bubble of dough
Mixograph	Recording dough mixer Measures flour water absorption dough mixing characteristics	Analyzes small amounts of flour for dough and gluten properties

Table 13–2
COMMON WHEAT AND FLOUR TESTS (CONTINUED)

Basic Tests

Flour Starch Viscosity Test

Amylograph Rapid Visco Analyzer	Viscosity analysis Measures flour starch properties	Measures starch properties and alpha amylase enzyme from sprout damage. Sprouting wheat leads to high alpha amylase and problems during processing and products with poor color and weak texture. Sprouted wheat yields less viscous slurries.

Product Baking Tests

Tests flour in finished product Pan Bread Hearth Bread Flat Bread	Controlled protocol for bread type Evaluate flour for bread type application. Evaluates dough qualities and finished baked products. Bread scored for dough qualities, gluten strength, extensibility and stickiness Baked product scored for exterior appearance and internal crumb, grain and texture	Provides bakers with flour quality information Bakers need a flour to give a consistent product with expected volume, color, texture and flavor. Helps optimize production prior to commercial large scale production
Asian Steamed Bread	Asian steam bread steamed not baked	Evaluates dough performance and final product characteristics. Desirable smooth skin, firm and chewy texture and white fine skin and crumb.
Sugar Snap Cookie	Used to evaluate flour in cookie production	Tests spread, low protein and weak gluten produce cookies with high spread and numerous cracks on surface.
Sponge Cake	Tests suitability of flour for sponge cake products	Flour with low protein, low ash and weak gluten are desirable in this test.

*Most common used flour quality test worldwide.
Resources: California Wheat Commission, North Dakota Wheat Commission, and AACC.

Figure 13–18

Food scientist testing flour quality via baking test. (© California Wheat Commission)

Figure 13–19

Wheat baking tests involve evaluating qualities using bench top lab methods carefully controlling, proportioning and evaluating bread dough qualities. (© California Wheat Council)

the United States. The hard white wheat has a hard endosperm, white bran, less bitter taste, and whiter color.

Soft red winter wheat is grown east of the Mississippi River and in the Pacific Northwest. Soft red winter wheats have lower protein and yield flours with lower gluten strength. Soft red winter wheat is used for cookies, crackers, pastries, flat breads, and pretzels. Most wheat grown in the Pacific Northwest is soft red white wheat, both winter and spring varieties. Weaker in gluten, soft red winter wheat is used in Asian-style bakery products, cakes, and pastries.

Hard Red Winter

Versatile, with excellent milling and baking characteristics for pan bread, Hard Red Winter is also a choice wheat for Asian noodles, hard rolls, flat breads, general purpose flour and cereal.

Hard Red Spring

The aristocrat of wheat when it comes to "designer" wheat foods like hearth breads, rolls, croissants, bagels and pizza crust, Hard Red Spring is also a valued improver in flour blends.

Soft Red Winter

A versatile weak-gluten wheat with excellent milling and baking characteristics, Soft Red Winter is suited for cookies, crackers, pretzels, pastries and flat breads.

Soft White

A low moisture wheat with high extraction rates, providing a whiter product for exquisite cakes, pastries and Asian-style noodles, Soft White is also ideally suited to Middle Eastern flat breads.

Hard White

The newest class of U.S. wheat, Hard White receives enthusiastic reviews when used for Asian noodles, whole wheat or high extraction applications, pan breads and flat breads.

Durum

The hardest of all wheats, Durum has a rich amber color and high gluten content, ideal for pasta, couscous and some Mediterranean breads.

Figure 13–20

Six classes of wheat. (© Wheat Foods Council)

The geographical areas in which most of the hard spring wheats are produced are the north-central part of the United States and western Canada. Spring wheat is planted in the early spring, does not go dormant, and has a shorter growing season. Hard spring wheat has a high protein content and strong gluten potential. Durum wheat has a high protein content. Semolina flour produced from durum wheat is used in Mediterranean breads, phyllo dough, and pastries. Milling durum wheat involves specialized techniques [15]. Wheat has also been discussed in Chapter 12.

The class of wheat determines how it is used in food products. Hard winter wheats have a fairly higher water absorption capacity and higher gluten forming protein content; they are suitable for bread-making purposes. These hard wheats are said to have good baking strength and produce a strong flour. Soft wheats have a low protein content, weak gluten properties, and a soft endosperm [27]. Cakes, pastries, muffins, flat breads, and cookies may be made with flour milled from soft wheat. Durum wheat is used in Southern Italy, the Middle East, and Northern African countries to produce batters and doughs for flat breads, leavened breads, and phyllo dough [7, 15].

Milling. Milling of grain is an ancient process that makes the grain more palatable. Grain milling traces back to 6700 B.C. when grain was crushed using handheld stones. Cereal Grain Science is the area of food science that studies composition, structure, and properties of cereals and their reactions or transformations. Wheat milling is a science. The miller analyzes the wheat and then blends it to meet the requirements of the end use. Wheat milling involves analyzing, blending, grinding, sifting, and blending again to produce a desirable flour.

Milling wheat into white flour involves separating the endosperm from the bran and germ and then subdividing the endosperm into a fine flour (**Figure 13–21**). The endosperm contains starch and protein components. The germ contains oils that cause the flour to go rancid faster, so removing the germ allows for longer flour storage. The bran and germ are rich in B vitamins, proteins, fat, and minerals, so milling white flour decreases the quantity of these components compared to the whole-wheat kernel; therefore, white flour is enriched to replace lost vitamin and mineral content.

Many years ago, white flour was made by sifting wheat that had been ground in a stone mill. This method of separation yielded flour that was generally less white and of poorer baking quality than the flour produced in today's mills, where the wheat passes through a series of rollers. The basic steps of milling include the following:

- Cleaning—Dirt, stones, weed seeds, and other debris are removed.
- Tempering—Moisture levels are adjusted to facilitate the separation of the bran, endosperm, and germ.
- Break—Kernels are crushed between rollers to loosen the endosperm. Large chunks of endosperm are called *middlings*.
- Separation and sifting—Sieves and air currents are used to separate the finely ground endosperm from coarse particles as well as the bran and germ.
- Grinding—The coarse endosperm (**middlings**) is ground into flour by reduction rollers [10].

The break, separation, and grinding steps are repeated to produce various streams of flour from the sifters. Flour produced later in the process will contain

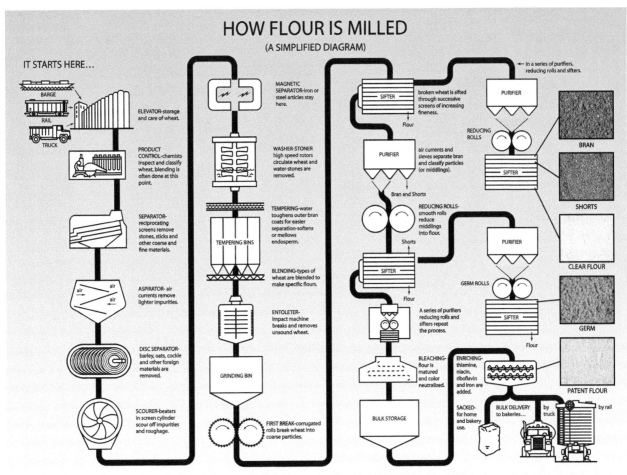

Figure 13–21

Steps involved in the milling of flour. Flour is sifted at various times during milling, and after each sifting, some of the flour stream may be removed. (© Wheat Foods Council)

less endosperm and more bran and germ than previous streams. Flour grades are determined by which **streams** are included in the final flour. The major steps in milling are shown in **Figure 13–21**.

The wheat kernel is divided into three main parts approximately as follows: 83 percent endosperm, 14.5 percent bran layers (including the aleurone layer), and 2.5 percent germ [34]. The endosperm contains many starch granules embedded in a cell matrix that includes protein (**Figure 13–22**). There are other non-starch polysaccharides found in the wheat kernel, such as cellulose and pentosans (hemicellulose). These components are non-digestible or fiber. Pentosans are the non-cellulose polysaccharides that basically act as the glue in the cell. The pentosans can be water soluble or water insoluble. The water-insoluble pentosans make up about 2.4 percent of the endosperm. Water-soluble pentosans can bind large amounts of water and produce viscous solutions; they vary between wheat varieties. The water-soluble pentosans are thought to help stabilize gas cells and decrease gas diffusion from the

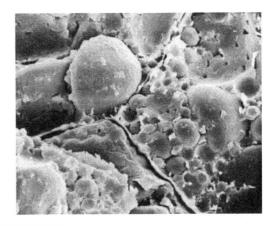

Figure 13–22

A scanning electron micrograph (2,100×) of fractured wheat endosperm cells showing small and large starch granules embedded in the cell matrix. (Reprinted from Freeman, T. P., and Shelton, D. R. Microstructure of wheat starch: From kernel to bread. Food Technology, 45:165(3), 1991. Copyright © by Institute of Food Technologists. Photograph supplied by Thomas P. Freeman.)

cell acting as a stabilizer in batter and dough foams helping to increase final product volume [14]. The water-soluble pentosan *arabinoxylans* were found to have a positive effect on volume of batter-based products such as pancakes [18].

When the parts of the wheat kernel are not separated and the whole kernel is ground, the flour resulting from this process is called *whole-wheat, whole-wheat white, entire-wheat,* or *graham* flour. The endosperm represents approximately 83 percent of the total kernel, therefore, about that same amount of white flour should theoretically be obtained by milling. In actual practice, however, only 72 to 75 percent is separated as white flour [20, 47]. The separation of endosperm from bran and germ is not a simple or an extremely efficient process. The inner bran layers and the germ are tightly bound to the endosperm, and it is impossible to make a complete separation. Non-starch polysaccharides also exist in small quantities. The usual 72 to 75 percent extraction produces white flour containing essentially no bran and germ and exhibiting good baking properties. In times of national emergency, the usual percentage of extraction has been increased as a conservation measure. It has been suggested that the regular extraction rate of white flour could be increased up to 80 percent without sacrificing baking quality [47].

Grades of Flour. The miller grades white flour on the basis of which streams of flour are combined. The grade may be confirmed by measuring ash content because bran is high in minerals [10]. *Patent* flours are the highest quality of commercial flours, coming from the more refined portion of the endosperm from the first streams of flour produced during milling [12, 20]. Patent flours are essentially free of bran and germ and thus are whitest in color. Different grades of patent flour are available, with the highest quality called *extra short* or *fancy patent*. Patent flour can be made from any variety or class of wheat [6].

Straight grade theoretically should contain all of the flour streams resulting from the milling process, but actually 2 to 3 percent of the poorest streams is withheld. Very little flour on the market is straight grade. *Clear grade* is made from streams withheld in the making of patent flours and is high in ash compared to patent flours. Clear-grade flours may be first clear or second clear, with the second clear grade having the highest ash content [6, 25].

Maturing and Bleaching of Flour. Freshly milled flour is yellowish in color and is undesirable for the baking of bread because it will form weak gluten [20]. Therefore, flour may be aged to allow it to whiten and mature. Alternately, the flour may be bleached or treated with additives to mature. These processes favorably affect the baking properties of flours.

Maturing. When freshly milled flour is used to bake bread, the result is a loaf of relatively low volume and coarse texture. A loaf with higher volume and finer texture can be made from the same flour after it has had an opportunity to mature or age. Aging involves simply holding or storing the flour for several weeks or months. During this time, the baking quality improves and the color lightens. The oxidation of portions of the glutenin and gliadin protein molecules that occurs during aging allows more bonds to form when gluten forms and thus results in higher-quality breads [10]. Although the aging of white flour brings about both bleaching and maturing, these two processes are separate and distinct.

Bleaching. Freshly milled flour is yellowish in color, primarily because of naturally present **carotenoid** pigments. With storage, the carotenoid pigments are **oxidized**, and the color of the flour lightens. Natural oxidation occurs when flour is stored and is considered to be "unbleached." The natural bleaching and aging process can be duplicated with chemical agents that speed up bleaching time. If bleaching agents are added to the flour, it is labeled as "bleached." Both bleached and unbleached flours are available on the retail market and have no difference in nutritional quality.

Maturing and Bleaching Agents. Maturing agents are added to freshly milled flour to produce effects similar to aging but in a much shorter period. This process saves the cost of storing the flour. The U.S. Food and Drug Administration (FDA) permits the use of specified chemical substances to mature and bleach flour. Only small amounts of maturing agents are needed to increase flour performance. Maturing agents strengthen gluten as they oxidize gluten subunit proteins, glutenin and gliadin, so they produce more bonds during gluten production. More bonds produce a dough that is stronger, drier, and more cohesive, yielding a more elastic gluten network to trap expanding gases during bread proofing. The baked bread loaf will have a bigger volume and finer crumb. Many maturing agents are more effective than natural methods in strengthening gluten.

Benzoyl peroxide and chlorine are commonly used to bleach flour. Benzoyl peroxide has only a whitening effect and is primarily used for all-purpose and bread flours [20]. Chlorine whitens flour and has an impact on the baking qualities of the flour [6, 12]. It is used mainly in cake flours because it will weaken gluten and allow the starch to absorb water more easily, something that is desirable in cakes [10, 20].

Chlorine dioxide, chlorine, and acetone peroxides have both a bleaching and a maturing effect. Azodicarbonamide may be added to flour as a maturing agent, but it does not react until the flour is made into a dough. Flour that has been treated with any of these chemicals must be labeled "bleached."

Potassium bromide at one time was commonly used as a maturing agent. It strengthens the flour, resulting in higher quality breads. Ascorbic acid (vitamin C) is used as a dough conditioner. Ascorbic acid has gained favor over potassium bromide. Ascorbic acid increases loaf volume. When ascorbic acid is added, the label shall bear the statement "Ascorbic acid added as a dough conditioner" as promulgated by federal law.

Enrichment of Flour.
Enriched flour is white flour with the addition of specified amounts of B vitamins (thiamin, riboflavin, niacin, and folic acid) and iron (Figure 13–12). Flour may also be fortified with vitamin D and calcium. In the United States, flour and cereal products that enter interstate commerce must, by law, be enriched. Many states also have laws requiring enrichment of flour and cereals. Enrichment has been discussed in Chapter 12. Flour enrichment standards can be found in the Federal Code of Regulations.

Flour Storage.
White flour has a shelf life of 18 months if stored in a cool place in an airtight container. Shelf life is decreased once the flour is opened. Refrigerating flour in an airtight container will extend the shelf life. According to the Wheat Foods Council, all-purpose and bread flour will keep for two years when stored in the refrigerator at 40°F. Whole-wheat flour can become rancid; it should be stored in the freezer or refrigerator for long-term use. Whole-wheat flour will keep in the freezer for two to six months.

Protein in Flour and Gluten Formation.
Wheat flour is preferred for bread baking because of proteins in wheat that form gluten when mixed with water. Gluten is the rubbery mass that remains when wheat dough is washed under running water to remove starch granules and water-soluble constituents. It retains cohesiveness on stretching [42, 50] (**Figure 13–23**).

Gluten consists of the flour proteins that determine the viscoelastic properties of dough. Viscoelasticity properties can be described as the extensibility and elasticity. These properties are important to determine their use in batter and dough products. "Strong" flour doughs that are highly elastic are needed for bread making versus "weak" extensible flour doughs that are required for products such as cakes and cookies [42]. Gluten proteins play a key role in determining the baking qualities of wheat and make up about 75 percent of the dry weight mass of flour [42].

Gluten provides essential bread structure, but is less desirable in other baked products. In order for gluten to be formed, the two wheat flour protein components gliadin and glutenin must be hydrated

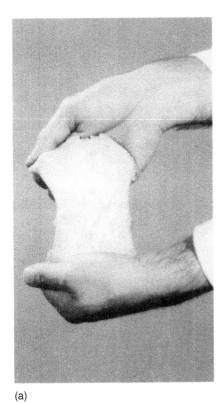  

(a)   (b)   (c)

Figure 13–23

The properties of gluten: (a) the glutenin fraction is tough, rubbery, and gives resistance to extension; (b) the gliadin fraction provides fluidity, stickiness, and cohesiveness; (c) gluten has the properties of both protein fractions. (Baker's Digest/© Sosland Publishing Co. and R. J. Dimler)

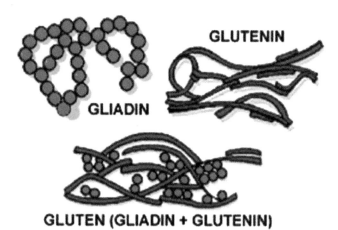

Figure 13–24

Gluten components. (© Wheat Foods Council)

(combined with water) and undergo manipulation so that gluten structural compounds are formed. The type of flour, other ingredients, and the mixing procedure for various baked goods are chosen in large part either to develop gluten, as in yeast breads, or to limit gluten development, as in delicate cakes and pastries.

Proteins in Flour. Wheat contains various proteins whose contents vary depending on wheat variety and growing conditions. The gluten proteins glutenin and gliadin are the storage proteins of wheat, meaning that in a biological seed role they store the carbon, nitrogen, and sulfur to support seed germination and growth [42] (**Figure 13–24**).

Gluten proteins are easy to isolate since they are insoluble in water. Gliadin is responsible for dough cohesiveness, and glutenin provides the resistance to extension. The water-soluble wheat proteins include **albumins** and **globulins**. Albumins and globulins do not appear to play major roles in baking. Gluten proteins are high in amino acids proline and glutamine, but the minor fraction of cysteine is important in structure and function [40]. Cysteine fractions are important in the gluten's crosslinking disulfide bond formation [28, 45].

Eighty percent of flour proteins are gliadin and glutenin, the subunits of gluten. When the subunits are moistened with water and thoroughly mixed or kneaded, gluten is formed. Gluten is primarily responsible for the viscous and elastic characteristics as well as high loaf volume of wheat-flour doughs [8, 12, 17, 27]. The amino acids proline, tyrosine, and glutamine, found in gluten, also appear to have an impact on dough development [9, 46].

The ratio of glutenins and gliadins corresponds to the elastic and viscous properties. When the gliadin and glutenin fractions are separated from each other, the gliadin fraction is found to be a syrupy substance that can bind the mass together. Hydrated gliadins have little elasticity and are less cohesive than glutenin. Gliadins contribute to viscosity and increase extensibility of the dough system [50]. Gliadin fractions reduce stiffness of doughs and make them more extensible [22, 50].

In contrast, the hydrated glutenins are both cohesive and elastic. They are responsible for dough strength and elasticity. The glutenin fractions contribute to dough cohesiveness. The glutenin fraction exhibit toughness and rubberiness or strength and elasticity [26]. Glutenins resist the extension of the dough and contribute to elasticity [12, 26, 50].

Gluten Formation. Gluten is a complex protein network formed when the flour proteins—gliadin and glutenin—are hydrated with water and mixed (Figure 13–24). The dough is a complex viscoelastic system of long protein chains held together by various bonds and links.

Disulfide bonds play a key role in gluten formation. The disulfide bonds give the strength and rigidity to the gluten structure much like the crossbars on a ladder. Gluten is a tightly coiled protein [45]. Long chains of disulfide-linked glutenin chains provide the elastic backbone of gluten. Covalent disulfide bonds (-SS-) are the most significant bonds that react with thiol or sulfhydryl (SH) groups during the mixing process. There are ten times more disulfide groups compared to sulfhydryl groups in wheat flour.

FOCUS ON SCIENCE
GLUTEN PROTEINS

Gliadin and glutenin are the two proteins that make up gluten. Gliadin has a molecular weight of 30,000 to 50,000, whereas glutenin has a molecular weight ranging from approximately 30,000 to 80,000 up to the millions [50].

The glutenin protein is a "heavy-duty worker" in the dough. A variety of glutenin subunits are crosslinked by disulfide bonds, enhancing the strength exhibited during mixing and the formation of the gluten structure [13]. Because of its large size, the glutenin protein forms a network that is mainly responsible for the elasticity and cohesive strength of the dough. The gliadin protein acts as a plasticizer and contributes mainly to viscosity, plasticity, and extensibility of the dough. The quality of these proteins in the wheat flour determines the bread-making performance because gluten quality depends on the gliadin: glutenin ratio of the proteins [42].

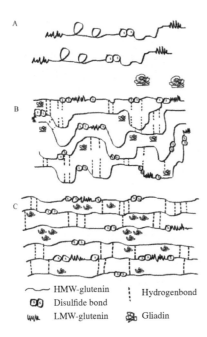

Figure 13–25

(a) Unfolded gluten, (b) gluten without salt, (c) gluten with salt. (Reprinted from HCD Tuhumury, D.M. Small, & Day L. The effect of sodium chloride on gluten network formation and rheology (2014) © Journal of Cereal Science 60(1))

Non-covalent bonds (hydrogen bonds, hydrophobic bonds, ionic bonds) all play a minor but an important role in dough aggregation and dough formation [27] (**Figure 13–25**).

During the mixing of a dough, the long strands of glutenin are aligned in the direction of mixing and interact with gliadin molecules to form a strong, elastic, uniform film that envelops the starch granules in the mixture (Figure 13–17). As gluten develops, it becomes more difficult to stretch, yet it is more elastic and strong with the ability to "spring back" [10]. Dough conditioners sometimes are used to relax the gluten. Dough conditioners such as calcium peroxide work by breaking some of the disulfide bonds, allowing the dough to expand in volume more easily [45]. If a bread dough is over mixed, the gluten strands may tear and the gluten network will break down, resulting in a soft and sticky dough unable to retain leavening gases [10]. Over mixing is most likely to occur when mixing mechanically with a mixer than when kneading by hand.

The development of gluten requires an appropriate amount of water to form a dough. Adequate water is necessary to hydrate gliadin and glutenin. Large amounts of water will dilute these proteins, however, and prevent or reduce gluten development. As air and carbon dioxide gas bubbles are incorporated in the dough, a foam is produced. Interactions probably also occur in the dough between gluten proteins and lipids and other dough components as well [28, 50]. Wheat-flour dough is a complex, but interesting phenomenon.

Gluten Extraction. Gluten can be extracted from a flour-and-water dough that has been vigorously kneaded and then washed to remove the starch. The gluten dough ball should have a satiny surface when gluten is fully developed (**Figure 13–26**). Once the gluten is fully developed in a dough, the gluten can be separated from the remaining flour components such as starch by washing the dough under cold water. Starch is water soluble, so it will be washed away. When most of the starch has been removed from the dough, the water will be clear. The moist gluten thus extracted has elastic and cohesive properties similar to those of chewing gum. Fully developed gluten should be elastic, springy yet extensible. Harder wheat flours require more manipulation and yield doughs that are more elastic and extensible compared to softer flours such as cake flour. Dough from rye flour lacks the elastic characteristics of wheat dough. The ability of dough to retain gases and expand is due to gluten. When gluten dough balls are baked at high heat, the volume increases several times; oven temperature can

(a)

(b)

Figure 13–26

Gluten balls may be made by mixing flour with water to form a dough ball. Then, the dough is washed in cold water to remove the starch, while leaving the gluten. The amounts and characteristics of gluten from flours can thus be compared. Pictured are samples of unbaked and baked gluten balls. The size of the gluten balls corresponds with the level of protein in the flour. Note that it can be difficult to fully wash the starch out of cake flour gluten balls while keeping the protein component together; this may contribute to the very small size of the cake flour gluten balls. All of these gluten balls were made by starting with one cup of flour. (a) Gluten balls before baking; (b) gluten balls after baking. (© Douglas and Barbara Scheule)

be reduced once gluten is set so that the gluten ball is browned and not burnt. Once gluten is inflated, steam pressure maintains the volume until the proteins are set. Bread flour will produce a much larger and stronger gluten ball compared to cake flour.

Types of Wheat Flour. "Flour" in the United States always means that derived from wheat, as defined by the standards of identity in the Code of Federal Regulations Title 21 (see eCFR.gov for current Code of Federal Regulations). Discussions on flour in this book will refer to wheat flour unless otherwise noted. Corn flour, rye flour, and other non-wheat flours do exist but are never referred to as simply flour, which is a term reserved for wheat flour in the United States.

Understanding the differences in the composition and characteristics of wheat flours allows for their appropriate and effective use. Various flour types may be interchanged in different recipes by altering the proportions of the non-flour constituents of the mixture. One of the factors that varies with different types of flours is the protein level. The percentage of protein for several types of wheat flour is provided in **Table 13–3**. The nutritive value of flours may be found in the USDA Nutrient Database (see Appendix C).

Flours milled in the United States are often deficient in essential natural enzymes, primarily alpha amylase. Amylase enzymes help to naturally break down starch and play an essential role in bread making. Federal laws allow correction of enzyme deficiencies by addition of malted barley or malted wheat flour to the final flour.

Protein level is a factor that varies with different types of flours. The harder the wheat, the higher the protein content and vice versa. Low-protein soft wheats or "weak" flours are used for cakes, pastries, cookies, and crackers. High-protein hard wheats or "strong" flours are used for yeast bread production. Durum wheats are used for some Mediterranean and Middle Eastern pastries and breads [15]. The percentages of protein for various wheat flours are provided in Table 13–3. The nutritive value of flours may be found in the USDA Nutrient Database (see Appendix C).

Whole-Wheat Flour. Whole-wheat flour contains essentially the entire wheat kernel—endosperm, bran, and germ (**Figure 13–27**). Whole-wheat flour is also called graham flour. It may be ground to different degrees of fineness and is sometimes referred to as stone ground, which is coarsely ground between mill stones. Whole-wheat flour may be made from red or white wheat and hard or soft wheat. The keeping quality of whole-wheat flour is lower than that of white flour because it contains fat from the germ that may be oxidized during storage, resulting in rancid, off-flavors. Flour ground from freshly harvested wheat in home grinders may be stored at room temperature up to a month before rancidity develops and sensory quality decreases [11]. In fact, fresh-ground wheat should be stored to some extent before use to allow the flour to age so that it has better bread-baking qualities.

Whole-wheat flour is higher in fiber than white flour because it contains bran. Although whole-wheat flour has a fairly high protein level, less gluten is formed; thus, whole-wheat doughs typically are denser and coarser than breads made with refined white flour. Gluten formation is negatively affected by the sharp bran particles that cut gluten strands and components in the germ that interfere with gluten development [10]. Often, whole-wheat flour is mixed with refined bread flour or gluten flour to yield bread products with better volume and texture.

Whole white wheat flour, produced from hard white winter wheat, was recently introduced in the United States and is gaining popularity. With the application of a special milling technology, whole white wheat flour has a softer, smoother texture as compared to traditional whole-wheat flours produced from red wheat [35].

Table 13–3
PERCENT OF PROTEIN OF VARIOUS TYPES OF WHEAT FLOUR

Flour Type	Percent of Protein
Gluten flour	14.0
Durum flour	12.0–15.0
Bread flour	11.5–13.5
Whole wheat	11.0–14.0
All-purpose flour	8.0–11.5
Pastry flour	7.0–9.5
Cake flour	6.0–8.0
Vital wheat gluten	"Vital wheat gluten" is not considered flour but instead an ingredient that may be added to "strengthen" doughs. It contains about 75 percent protein, which can form gluten. It should not be confused with gluten flour.

Source: References 10, 12.

Figure 13–27

Whole-wheat flour. (Richard Embery/Pearson Education)

HOT TOPICS
GLUTEN-FREE DIETS

People who have *celiac disease* (sometimes called gluten-sensitive enteropathy) must avoid foods containing gluten. For these individuals, an autoimmune response results in the production of antibodies that attack and damage the intestinal tract. It is estimated that about 1 percent of Europeans and North Americans are affected [29]. Celiac disease tends to "run in families," although research into the causes and treatment is ongoing.

Gluten is a major component of wheat flour, so replicating its structure-building and water-binding roles is a technological challenge in gluten-free bakery products. In recent years, many new gluten-free products have been introduced into the marketplace; these are engineered from starches, gums, hydrocolloids, non-traditional flours, dietary fiber, and alternative proteins to replicate the standard baked products. Pseudocereals quinoa and buckwheat flours have been shown to produce high-volume bread-like products with good sensory scores [2].

A number of new gluten-free products have been introduced into the marketplace in recent years. The FDA has proposed rules for the labeling of gluten-free products and suggests that no more than 20 parts per million of gluten can be allowed in these products. Various methods for testing of gluten in foods are available [29]. Biochemists are working to develop breeds of "celiac-safe" wheat by identifying the exact DNA that causes the celiac reactivity and eliminating that from the wheat.

Given the important role of gluten in baking, what are the implications of a gluten-free diet? First of all, foods containing gluten must be avoided. Thus, wheat, durum, rye, barley, spelt, kamut or khorasan, einkorn, emmer, club wheat, faro, and triticale grains, which form gluten, should not be used [29]. In place of these grains, rice flour, potato starch, tapioca flour, corn flour, corn starch, and sorghum may be used. Although baked foods made with these alternative flours may have some different characteristics than those made with wheat flour, a variety of resources and recipes is available to help those following a gluten-free diet enjoy a wide variety of foods—including baked goods. ■

FOCUS ON SCIENCE
WHY MAY WHOLE-WHEAT FLOUR BECOME RANCID?

Whole flour contains the bran, germ, and endosperm. Lipoygenase and unsaturated fatty acids are present in the germ. Lipoygenase causes free fatty acids to occur and, at the same time, supplies oxygen to the unsaturated fatty acid. Consequently, rancidity, off-flavors, and aromas may develop in whole-wheat flour [12].

Bread Flour. Bread flour is a white flour made chiefly from hard wheat. It contains a relatively high percentage of protein that develops into gluten. Gluten contributes very strong, elastic properties when the flour is made into dough. Bread flour has a slightly granular feel when touched and does not form a firm mass when pressed in the hand (**Figure 13–28**). It may be bleached or unbleached. Bread flour is used by commercial and food service bakers for yeast breads and also is available for use in the home kitchen. It produces breads of relatively high volume and fine texture with an elastic crumb.

All-Purpose Flour. All-purpose flour is a white refined flour that is sold primarily for home use. All-purpose flour sometimes used in small foodservice operations is labeled *Hotel and Restaurant* flour, but it is not used in commercial bakery operations [19]. All-purpose flour is usually made from a blend of hard and soft wheats to yield a protein content lower than that of bread flour. All-purpose flour is usually enriched and may be bleached or unbleached. Different brands of

Figure 13–28

Squeezing flour in palm of hand: (left) low-protein flour clumps, (right) high-protein bread flour remains free flowing. (Richard Embery/Pearson Education)

all-purpose flour may vary in performance and have protein content ranging from 8 to 11 percent. It may be used for a variety of home-baked products, including yeast breads, quick breads, cakes, pastry, egg noodles, and cookies.

The protein content in all-purpose flour is lower than ideal for some yeast breads and too high for some delicate cakes. The gluten that develops in doughs made from all-purpose flour is less strong and elastic than that produced in bread-flour doughs. Therefore, although all-purpose flour may be used for making yeast bread and rolls under household conditions, food service operations generally use bread flour. Similarly, all-purpose flour may be used for many cakes; however, it has too high a protein content to make a delicate, fine-textured cake.

Pastry Flour.   Used primarily in commercial baking, white pastry flour is usually made from soft wheat. Pastry flour properties are intermediate between all-purpose and cake flours. Pastry flour contains a lower percentage of protein than all-purpose flour. It has a finer texture and lighter consistency than hard wheat flour with a protein content around 8–9 percent. It is well suited for pastry, cookies, and crackers.

Cake Flour.   Prepared from soft wheat, cake flour usually contains only the most highly refined streams of flour from the milling process and is a short patent grade of flour (**Figure 13–29**). The protein content of cake flour is very low compared to other types of flour. Cake flour has a fine silky texture, a high percentage of starch, and low protein content between 7 and 9 percent. Cake flour is bleached with chlorine not only to whiten the flour but also to produce cakes with increased volume [10, 33]. Cake flour is so finely milled that it feels soft and satiny, rather than granular; it forms a firm mass when pressed in the hand. The high starch content and weak quality of gluten produced from cake flour make it desirable for the preparation of delicate and fine-textured cakes.

Instantized Flour.   Instantized flour is a special-purpose flour that is processed so that it instantly disperses in cold water and does not pack down in the packaging. Also called *instant*, *instant-blending*, or *quick-mixing* flour, instantized flour is a granular all-purpose flour that has been processed by moistening and then redrying to aggregate small particles into larger particles or agglomerates. The agglomerated particles are of relatively uniform size and do not pack; therefore, this flour does not require sifting before measuring. It flows freely without dust, is easily measured, and blends more readily with liquid than regular flour. Instantized flour is often used to produce lump-free gravies and sauces. It is most useful when blended dry with a liquid, such as in the thickening of gravies and certain sauces. Some changes should be made in formulas and preparation procedures if this flour is substituted for regular flour in baked products.

Self-Rising Flour.   Self-rising flour is a convenience product made by adding salt and leavening to all-purpose flour (**Figure 13–30**). It is commonly used in biscuits and quick breads but is not recommended for yeast breads. Leavening agents and salt are added to self-rising flour in proportions desirable for baking. Typically, 1 cup of self-rising flour contains 1½ teaspoons of baking powder and ½ teaspoon of salt. Monocalcium phosphate is the acid salt most commonly added in combination with sodium bicarbonate (baking soda) as leavening ingredient. Self-rising flours are popular for preparing quick breads, such as baking powder biscuits.

Gluten Flour.   Gluten flour is usually milled from hard spring wheat, which has a high protein and low starch composition. It is made by mixing wheat flour with dried extracted gluten. This flour has a protein content of 14 percent. The gluten is extracted by the gentle washing of a flour-and-water dough and is dried under mild conditions to minimize any effects on its viscoelastic properties. Gluten flour is used by the

Figure 13–29
Cake flour. (Richard Embery/Pearson Education)

Figure 13–30
Self-rising flour is all-purpose flour containing salt and chemical leavening agent. (Anita Patterson Peppers/Shutterstock)

Figure 13–31

Wheat germ. (Richard Embery/Pearson Education)

baking industry to adjust the protein level in various doughs. Gluten may also be used in breakfast foods.

Other Wheat Products. *Cracked wheat*, although not a flour, is used extensively in baking breads and quick breads. It is prepared by cracking or cutting cleaned wheat into angular fragments. It should be soaked in double its volume of water for 24 hours before use. Cracked wheat may be combined in varying proportions with whole-wheat or white flour. Rolled wheat is also used to make cookies and quick breads.

Crushed wheat or coarse ground wheat is prepared by crushing cleaned wheat. Crushed wheat is sometimes used in yeast bread.

Wheat germ, which represents approximately 2.5 percent of the weight of kernel, is a by-product of wheat milling (**Figure 13–31**). It contains essentially all the fat from the wheat kernel and is available as yellowish tan flakes that may have been toasted. Wheat germ is a rich source of proteins, vitamins, and minerals, including tocopherols (vitamin E compounds), thiamine, riboflavin, iron, calcium, potassium, phosphorous, folic acid, manganese, magnesium, and zinc. It may be added to both yeast and quick breads.

Raw wheat germ, containing up to 10 percent oil, begins to develop rancidity as soon as it is milled.

Specialized milling techniques and vacuum packaging help control the oxidative changes that produce rancidity. Wheat germ may also be purchased as defatted or stabilized. A defatted wheat germ has been treated to remove the fat [5].

A stabilized wheat germ with a six-month shelf life can be made through a careful, controlled heating process to inactivate the enzymes *lipase* and *peroxidase*. These enzymes catalyze the oxidation of fat, and thus, when inactivated, the wheat germ is less prone to spoilage. Stabilized wheat germ retains its vitamin and mineral content, including the antioxidant vitamin E.

Commercial applications for the use of wheat germ include crackers, breakfast cereals, variety breads, and snacks. The vitamin potency of wheat germ is not appreciably decreased when baked in bread; however, the germ has been found to decrease the baking quality of flour. For this reason, a relatively strong flour high in gluten is best used with the wheat germ. Wheat germ may be substituted for one-fifth to one-third of the flour.

Flours and Meals Other Than Wheat Flour. Flours other than wheat are used in quick breads and yeast breads.

Rye Flour. Rye flour is milled from rye kernels (**Figure 13–32**). The milling is similar to wheat except that rye must have less than 8 percent thin kernels and ergot kernels removed during cleaning. Rye is more prone to deadly ergot compared to wheat or other cereal grains (see Focus on Science). The United States produces two basic rye flours, with total flour produced 80 percent light and 20 percent dark. White

Figure 13–32

Rye flour. (Richard Embery/Pearson Education)

FOCUS ON SCIENCE
MORE ON ALL-PURPOSE FLOUR

All-purpose flour is made up of a blend of hard and soft wheat that can be used for all purposes—cakes, cookies, biscuits, pie crusts, and breads. The protein content of all-purpose flour averages about 11 percent. The actual protein content of all-purpose flour may differ from region to region and from brand to brand. Regional differences have influenced manufacturers to place more protein in flour sold in the Northern United States, where yeast breads are more popular, than in flour sold in the South, where biscuits requiring softer flour are more routinely consumed.

FOCUS ON SCIENCE
WHAT DO RYE, WITCHES, AND LSD HAVE IN COMMON?

The answer is ergot.

Ergot is a parasitic fungus (*Claviceps purpurea*) that grows on rye and to a lesser extent on wheat and other cereal grasses (**Figure 13–33**). Ergot infects rye causing the flowering grain head to spew out a fungal-filled yellow mucus that invades developing kernels of grain. The ergot replaces the rye grains with a purplish black "sclerotium," which is sometimes mistaken for dark grains of rye.

Ergot alkaloids can be toxic when consumed; it is important to remove ergot prior to milling, which is dictated by federal law. Ergot poisoning is called ergotism. *Convulsive ergotism* can result in nervous dysfunction, body contortions, convulsions, delusions, hallucinations, and muscle spasms. *Gangrenous ergotism* leads to loss of blood flow, infection, burning sensation, and gangrene in extremities, sometimes leading to extremity loss. Although not common in humans, gangrenous ergotism is common in grazing farm animals.

Outbreaks of ergotism were documented in Europe since 859 A.D. typically among the poor and children who consumed rye and lived in damp areas. During the Middle Ages "St. Anthony's Fire" outbreaks were thought to be gangrenous ergotism. In 1926–1927, an ergotism outbreak affecting over 10,000 people occurred in Southern Russia. The last known ergotism outbreak occurred in 1951 in France among Central European Jewish immigrants who ate bread made from flour contaminated with ergot rye.

Ergotism has been associated with witchcraft and witches since the dark ages. Colonists primarily ate rye bread, and the damp years, 1691–1692, could have promoted ergot growth. Some researchers studying events surrounding the 1692 Salem witch trials believe ergotism may been the cause of the bizarre behavior responsible for the witchcraft hysteria (**Figure 13–34**).

Medicinal uses of ergot extractions were first noted in 1582. In the past, ergot derivatives were prescribed for headaches, to induce childbirth, and for uterine contraction

Figure 13–34

A scene from a Salem Witch Trial. Martha Cory is shown in jail for witchcraft with her prosecutors. She was convicted and executed by hanging on September 22, 1692. (Everett Historical/Shutterstock)

to cure postpartum hemorrhage. New ergot research started in the 1930s to isolate chemical properties of the toxic ergot alkaloids which led to the discovery of lysergic acid.

In 1935, a Swiss scientist, Dr. Albert Hoffman, working in the pharmacological, experimented with the ergot lysergic acid derivatives and developed lysergic acid diethylamide (LSD) (**Figure 13–35**). Self-experimentation notes documented hallucinogenic effects from the product. The military ran experimental drug trials with LSD. The 1960s "Hippy culture" widely used LSD for the hallucinogenic effects to achieve "enlightenment." Research on the medicinal applications of LSD were abandoned in the 1970s and its use outlawed due to the fatal and bad side effects of the drug [51].

Figure 13–33

Rye with Ergot. (PHOTO FUN/Shutterstock)

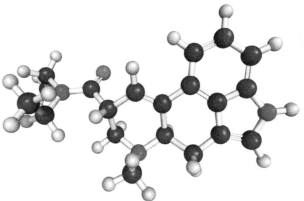

Figure 13–35

LSD (Lysergic Acid Diethylamide). (lculig/123RF)

or patent rye flours are almost entirely obtained from the endosperm. Medium or straight rye flour is obtained by grinding everything except the germ or bran. Rye meal is obtained by grinding the entire rye kernel, yielding dark rye flour sometimes referred to as pumpernickel flour. Protein ranges from 9 to 16 percent [6]. Rye has some gluten-forming properties, but it contains chiefly gliadin with only small amounts of glutenin. Therefore, 100 percent rye flour bread doughs are less elastic and do not hold gases well, yielding a heavy, compact loaf. Rye flour is typically limited to 20–40 percent of total flour content. White flour is often combined with rye flour in making bread to yield a lighter, more porous product than is possible with rye flour alone.

Corn Meal and Corn Flour. Corn meal is a granular product made from either white or yellow corn (**Figure 13–36**). Corn flour has the same properties as corn meal except that it is finer. Corn meal and corn flours are used in several types of quick breads. *Zein* is corn's chief protein, which does not have gluten properties. If a crumbly product is to be avoided, corn meal must be combined with some white flour, preferably all-purpose flour. It is used chiefly in commercial pancake mixes and prepared cereals. Federal standards for corn meal and corn flour include enriched, degerminated, bolted, and self-rising versions of yellow and white corn.

Corn Masa Harina. Corn masa harina flour is produced by cooking corn in alkali and grinding it into flour. Corn masa flour is a staple food for the Latin American culture, including Mexicans and Central Americans living in the United States. It is used to produce corn tortillas. Corn tortillas are made from a dough mixture that is baked on a griddle surface. Corn masa is also used to produce tamales as well as corn tortilla chips, taco shells, and corn chips. In 2016, the U.S. Food and Drug Administration approved the folic acid fortification for corn masa harina. The approval allows manufacturers to voluntarily add up to 0.7 milligrams of folic acid per pound of corn masa harina. Pregnant women with folic acid deficiency are at increased risk of giving birth to a baby with a neural tube defect that affects the brain, spine, and spinal cord.

Soy Flour. Soy flour is made from soybeans, which are legumes. Although soy flour is high in protein, it does not contain the proteins that form gluten. Thus, soy flour must be used with a strong or moderately strong wheat flour for better results in the baking of breads. Soy flour increases protein amount and quality of baked products. In baked items, soy flour also promotes moisture retention, improves crust color, and extends shelf life. Federal standards for commercial white breads permit the use of 3 percent soy flour as an optional ingredient.

Miscellaneous Flours. Many other alternative non-wheat flours from other specialty grains, pseudo-cereals, legumes, nuts, even fruits and vegetables, are ground into flour and used in batter and dough mixtures. *Buckwheat flour* is primarily used in pancakes and waffles. French Brittany crepes use buckwheat flour. Kasha (roasted buckwheat groats) and Japanese Soba noodles are also made from buckwheat. Buckwheat is a pseudo-cereal that yields a grain that is ground into flour. The flour is usually dark due to the presence of hull fragments not removed during milling. It does not have the same baking properties as wheat flour and therefore is often used with wheat flour in recipes. Some of the pancake batters are fermented to increase the flavor. Buckwheat is high in protein, zinc, copper, manganese, potassium, and soluble fiber (**Figure 13–37**).

Teff flour is produced from a tiny seed that is ground into flour (**Figure 13–38**). One gram of Teff contains approximately 3,000 teff seeds. Teff has a sweet, molasses-like flavor and grows in three colors red, brown, and white. It is rich in iron, magnesium, and phosphorus with lesser amounts of calcium, potassium, zinc, niacin, and folate. Teff is used primarily in Ethiopia but is being exported to and grown in the United States. The flour is gluten free and high in calcium. Teff flour is used to produce the spongy

Figure 13–37

The whole raw buckwheat kernel (groat) can be ground into a sandy texture flour. Kasha is a roasted buckwheat groat.

(Richard Embery/Pearson Education)

Figure 13–36

Cornmeal. (Richard Embery/Pearson Education)

HEALTHY EATING
MAKING HEALTHY CHOICES WHEN CHOOSING BAKED GOODS

Batters and doughs can vary widely in their nutritional contribution to the diet. They can be a source of added sugar, added fat, and whole grains. The Dietary Guidelines recommend that Americans *reduce* their consumption of added fat and sugars but *increase* their consumption of whole grains.

When preparing batters and doughs, the amount of sugar and fat per cup of flour in the recipe will provide a rough benchmark to allow comparisons between recipes that are higher or lower in fat and sugar. Yeast breads, for example, may be prepared with little to no added sugar or fat. Alternately, a biscuit is flaky and tender because of its relatively high fat content. Consider not only the recipe ingredients but also the portion size and the frequency at which certain baked goods are consumed.

Batters and doughs contribute B vitamins (including folic acid) and iron to the diet through the use of enriched flours, and many can be prepared with whole grains. The Wheat Foods Council recommends the following when substituting whole-wheat for all-purpose flour:

- Use one-half whole-wheat flour and one-half enriched white flour in the recipe.

- Use 1 cup of whole-wheat flour minus 1 tablespoon for each cup of enriched white flour in the original recipe if seeking all whole wheat.

- For a lighter loaf of whole-wheat yeast bread, add 1 tablespoon of water and 1 tablespoon of gluten flour per each cup of whole-wheat flour. ■

Figure 13–38

Teff flour. (Cokemomo/123RF)

fermented large round Ethiopian flat bread staple called "injera" [49].

Triticale flour, made from the cereal that is a cross between wheat and rye, may be used to make yeast bread of satisfactory quality. Its flavor has been reported to be like that of a very mild rye bread [23].

Rice flour is fundamentally rice starch. It is a low-protein flour that does not produce gluten. *Potato flour* is used in some countries and, like rice flour, is chiefly starch.

Amaranth flour, made by grinding the tiny amaranth seed, is used in some areas of Latin America, Africa, and Asia (**Figure 13–39**). Amaranth seed was the mainstay of the Aztec culture and is now being cultivated in limited amounts in the United States. Amaranth flour has a 13–14 percent protein content and is high in the amino acid lysine, which is limited in wheat flour. It may make a valuable nutritional contribution when combined in wheat breads, cookies, and other baked products [41].

Barley flour is made by hammer milling pearled barley (**Figure 13–40**). Pearl barley is produced

Figure 13–39

Ripened Amaranth seeds can be ground into flour. Leaves are consumed as a vegetable. (Matjoe/Shutterstock)

Figure 13–40

Barley grains can be ground into flour. (Richard Embery/Pearson Education)

Figure 13-41

Sorghum (milo) growing in the field. (Songsak P/Shutterstock)

Figure 13-42

Millet is a high protein cereal grain that can be ground into flour. (Richard Embery/Pearson Education)

Figure 13-43

Tapioca can be ground into flour. (Richard Embery/Pearson Education)

Figure 13-44

Blanched almond flour. (Richard Embery/Pearson Education)

Figure 13-45

Pulses can be ground into flour and used in baked goods. (WitthayaP/Shutterstock)

when the barley is decorticated—that is, removal of the "bark" or outer layers of the grain.

Millet and *sorghum* are also grains that are decorticated and ground into flour; these are more popular in Africa, China, and India [6] (**Figures 13-41** and **13-42**).

Tapioca and *arrowroot* are high tubers that are used to produce starch no gluten flours sometimes used in baked products (**Figure 13-43**).

Nuts such as *almond* and *hazelnuts* are sometimes ground into flours and used to impart distinctive flavors and textures to baked products (**Figure 13-44**).

Pulses, the dried seeds of legume plants, are sometimes ground into flour and used to make gluten-free baked products (**Figure 13-45**). Pea flour, white bean flour, black bean flour, garbanzo bean flour, and fava bean flour are some examples of pulse flours that are occasionally used in dough and batter products. Pulse flour products include yeast and quick breads, pizza doughs, tortillas, pita bread, muffins, cakes, crackers, and cookies.

Major Leavening Gases

To *leaven* means to "make light and porous." Most baked flour products are leavened. This process is accomplished by incorporating or forming in the product a gas that expands during preparation and subsequent heating. Three major leavening gases are air, steam or water vapor, and carbon dioxide. In some flour mixtures, one of these leavening gases predominates, whereas in other products, two or three of the gases play important roles.

Air.   Air is incorporated into flour mixtures by folding and rolling dough, by creaming fat and sugar together, or by beating batters. Beating whole eggs adds some air, but the beating of egg whites adds a significant amount of air. In common practice, some air is incorporated into all flour mixtures.

Steam.   Steam leavening is important in flour mixtures. All flour mixtures contain some water and are usually heated, thus producing water vapor or steam. Steam leavens all flour mixtures to a certain degree. Some products leavened almost entirely by steam are popovers, cream puffs, and éclairs. These mixtures have a high percentage of liquid, and baking is started at a high oven temperature, which rapidly causes steam to form. Because one volume of water increases more than 1,600 times when converted into steam, it has tremendous leavening power. The water available for conversion to steam may be added as liquid or as a component of other ingredients, such as eggs. Egg whites contain enough water to furnish two to three times more expansion in baking angel food cakes than the air that was added by beating. Even stiff doughs, such as pie crust, are partially leavened by steam.

Carbon Dioxide.   Carbon dioxide may be produced in a flour mixture either by a biological process or by a purely chemical reaction. The biological production of carbon dioxide usually results with the action of

yeast. Bacteria may be another biological source for carbon dioxide in some products such as soda crackers. Baking powder and baking soda are chemical leavening agents that are commonly used to produce carbon dioxide in baked goods. Leaveners are not equal in gassing power. Chemical leaveners release gas quickly but have no further leavening action as with yeast. However, yeast may not be desirable in all baked foods [37]. See **Table 13–4** for comparative gassing power of yeast versus baking powder.

Leavening Agents

Yeast and Bacteria.   Carbon dioxide is produced by the action of yeast and certain bacteria on sugar in a process called **fermentation**. Yeast ferments sugar to form ethyl alcohol and carbon dioxide. The alcohol is volatilized by the heat of baking. The fermentation is catalyzed by a mixture of many enzymes produced by the yeast cells. Sugar is usually added to yeast–flour mixtures to speed fermentation and the production of carbon dioxide gas. If no sugar is used, yeast can form gas slowly from the small amount of sugar that is present in flour. **Maltose** also is produced in flour from the action of **amylase** as it hydrolyzes starch. **Maltase**, an enzyme produced by yeast, then hydrolyzes the maltose to yield glucose, which is available

Table 13–4
YEAST VERSUS BAKING POWDER CARBON DIOXIDE PRODUCTION

	Yeast	Baking Powder (Double Acting 30% NaHCO)
Leavener based on dough wt	1.47%	3.42%
CO_2 Evolved per 100 g dough	350 ml CO_2 evolution/hour	214 ml Total CO_2 evolution

Source: Reference 37.

FOCUS ON SCIENCE
WHAT IS SALT-RISING BREAD?

Salt-rising bread dates back to the early 1800s when commercial yeast wasn't available to Americans. Cooks found that they could make a bread "starter" from a mash of cornmeal and potatoes or milk, which produced wild yeasts and bacteria for fermentation. The microorganisms in salt-rising starters are different than sourdough starters [6]. Salt-rising bread is leavened by the fermentation of a salt-tolerant bacterium in corn meal. The corn meal must be stone ground. A mixture of corn meal, milk, and sugar is allowed to stand overnight to ferment in a warm place, preferably between 90 to 100°F (32 to 38°C). This is the leavening agent that will be required for the bread; therefore, yeast in the conventional way is not used in salt-rising bread. Salt-rising bread is traditionally from southern and western portions of the Appalachians, western New York through western Pennsylvania. The bread is a regional specialty and often sold in regional bakeries.

for fermentation by the yeast. Most commercial yeast is contaminated with bacteria, mainly lactobacilli, which add in yeast bread production. The use of yeast in leavening is discussed further in Chapter 15.

Certain bacteria also may produce leavening gas in flour mixtures. One type produces hydrogen and carbon dioxide gases in salt-rising bread. Although the organisms occur normally in the corn meal used to make the sponge for salt-rising bread, they have, in addition, been isolated and put on the market as a starter for this type of bread. Sourdough bread also uses bacteria in producing leavening gas. Soda crackers use bacteria more than yeast for leavening.

Baking Soda. Sodium bicarbonate (baking soda) in a flour mixture gives off carbon dioxide (CO_2) gas when heated in accordance with the following reaction:

$$2NaHCO_3 + heat \rightarrow Na_2CO_3 + CO_2 + H_2O$$

sodium   sodium   carbon water
bicarbonate   carbonate dioxide

However, the sodium carbonate (Na_2CO_3) residue from this reaction has a disagreeable flavor and produces a yellow color in light-colored baked products. Brown spots also may occur in the cooked product if the soda is not finely powdered or is not uniformly distributed throughout the flour.

To avoid the problem of a bitter, soapy-flavored residue in the baked product, sodium bicarbonate is combined with various acids to release CO_2 gas. The flavor of the residue remaining after the release of gas depends on the particular acid involved in the reaction. The salts formed with many acids are not objectionable in flavor. The optimum amount of soda used depends on the acid used. There should be only enough baking soda to neutralize the acid. The baking soda is typically mixed with dry ingredients instead of liquids.

The following food ingredients contain acids and may be combined with soda in flour mixtures to release CO_2 gas:

Buttermilk or sour milk (containing lactic acid)

Molasses (containing a mixture of organic acids)

Brown sugar (which has a small amount of molasses coating the sugar crystals)

Honey

Citrus fruit juices (containing citric and other organic acids)

Applesauce and other fruits

Vinegar (containing acetic acid)

Cream of tartar (potassium acid tartrate)

The acid-containing foods listed vary in acidity and yield variable results when combined with soda; however, the usual amount of soda to combine with 1

Chemical leavening agents such as baking powder are used in many batters and doughs. (Mohammed Anwarul Kabir Choudhury/123RF)

cup of buttermilk or fully soured milk is ½ teaspoon. Less soda is required for milk that is less sour.

Because the pronounced flavor of molasses may mask any undesirable flavor resulting from an excess of soda, up to 1 teaspoon of soda is often recommended for use with 1 cup of molasses, but less may be used. The acidity of honey and brown sugar is too low to allow their use in flour mixtures as the only source of acid to combine with soda.

Cream of tartar is an acid salt (potassium acid tartrate) and may be combined with soda to produce CO_2 gas when the mixture is moistened. The salt that is left as a residue in this reaction (sodium potassium tartrate) is not objectionable in flavor. The chemical reaction between cream of tartar and soda is as follows:

$$HKC_4H_4O_6 + NaHCO_3 \rightarrow NaKC_4H_4O_6 + CO_2 + H_2O$$

cream of   sodium   sodium   carbon water
tartar bicarbonate potassium dioxide
               tartar

Ammonium Bicarbonate. Ammonium bicarbonate is a chemical leavening agent with limited applications. However, it is used commercially only in baked products with low moisture level and large surface areas that are baked at high temperatures, for example, some cookie types and snack crackers. If the product retains water, it retains ammonia, which yields an unpleasant flavor [12]. When ammonium bicarbonate is heated, it releases ammonia, carbon dioxide, and water; this is efficient because two gases are formed.

$$NH_4HCO_3 \rightarrow NH_3 + CO_2 + H_2O$$

ammonium ammonia carbon water
bicarbonate   dioxide

Baking Powder. Baking powders, like baking soda, produce carbon dioxide to leaven baked goods (**Figure 13–46**). Baking powders were developed as one of the first convenience foods containing mixtures of dry acid or acid salts and baking soda. Importantly, *all baking powders are composed of soda and an acid ingredient*. The carbon dioxide gas comes from the soda. Starch is added to standardize the mixture and to help stabilize the components so that premature reactions are avoided. Baking powders have been classified into different groups or types, depending on the acid constituent used; however, not all types are available to consumers.

According to federal law, all types of baking powders must contain at least 12 percent available carbon dioxide gas. Those powders manufactured for home use generally contain 14 percent, and some powders for commercial use have 17 percent available gas. Baking powder containers should always be kept tightly covered to avoid the absorption of moisture that causes the acid and alkali constituents to react prematurely resulting in the loss of some carbon dioxide.

Double-Acting Baking Powder.   The type of baking powder that is generally available for home use is called *sodium aluminum sulfate (SAS)-phosphate* baking powder. It is a double-acting baking powder, which means that it reacts to release carbon dioxide gas at room temperature when (1) the dry ingredients are moistened and (2) heat is applied in the process of baking. Thus, double-acting baking powder releases carbon dioxide twice.

SAS-phosphate baking powder contains two acid substances. Each reacts with soda to release carbon dioxide gas at different times in the baking process. One acid is a phosphate, usually *calcium acid phosphate* (also called *monocalcium phosphate*). This acid salt reacts with soda at room temperature as soon as liquid is added to the dry ingredients. Thus, the batter or dough becomes somewhat light and porous during the mixing process. The other acid substance is *sodium aluminum sulfate*. It requires heat and moisture to complete its reaction with soda. Therefore, additional carbon dioxide gas is produced during baking.

The reactions of calcium acid phosphate and baking soda are complex and difficult to write. Many different salts are probably produced in this reaction, and they may interact with each other:

$$CaH_4(PO_4)_2 + NaHCO_3 \rightarrow \text{insoluble} + \text{soluble}$$

calcium acid phosphate   sodium bicarbonate   calcium phosphate   sodium phosphate

$$+ CO_2 + H_2O$$

carbon dioxide   water

Sodium aluminum sulfate apparently reacts in two stages. The first reaction is with water and results in the production of sulfuric acid as heat is applied, after which the sulfuric acid reacts with soda to produce carbon dioxide gas, according to the following equations:

$$Na_2SO_4Al_2(SO_4)_3 + 6H_2O \xrightarrow{heat} Na_2SO_4$$

sodium aluminum sulfate   water   sodium sulfate

$$+ 2Al(OH)_3 + H_2SO_4$$

aluminum hydroxide   sulfuric acid

$$3H_2SO_4 + 6NaHCO_3 \rightarrow 6CO_2 + 6H_2O + 3Na_2SO_4$$

sulfuric acid   sodium bicarbonate   carbon dioxide   water   sodium sulfate

All baking powders leave residues in the mixture in which they are used. The sodium sulfate (Na_2SO_4) residue from the SAS-phosphate baking powder has a somewhat bitter taste that may be objectionable to certain individuals. Some people are more sensitive than others to this bitter taste.

Amount of Baking Powder to Use.   An optimum amount of baking powder is desirable for any baked product. If too much baking powder is used, the cell walls of the flour mixture are stretched beyond their limit, and they may break and collapse. If too little baking powder is present, insufficient expansion occurs, resulting in a compact product. Use of the minimum amount of SAS-phosphate baking powder that leavens satisfactorily is particularly desirable because of the bitter residue formed with this baking powder. Between 1 and 1½ teaspoons of SAS-phosphate baking powder per cup of flour should be adequate for the leavening of most flour mixtures.

Methods of Adding Baking Powder and Soda.

Dry chemical leavening agents, including baking powders, are usually sifted or mixed with the flour. They are not allowed to become wet and thus do not begin to release their carbon dioxide gas until the later stages of the mixing process, when the liquid ingredients are combined with the dry ingredients.

Some recipe directions suggest that soda be mixed with sour milk or molasses. When soda and molasses are mixed, gas tends to be lost slowly due to high viscosity of the molasses. Carbon dioxide gas, however, is likely to be more rapidly lost from a mixture of buttermilk and soda compared to a batter made by mixing the soda with dry ingredients and then adding the buttermilk. Students in laboratory classes have compared the volumes of chocolate cakes containing soda and buttermilk when the soda was either sifted with the dry ingredients or added directly to the buttermilk. They found that when the soda–buttermilk mixture is added immediately to the batter, the volumes of the finished cakes are quite similar. Allowing the soda–buttermilk mixture to stand before adding it to the batter results in a lower cake volume.

Substitutions of Chemical Leavening Agents.
Buttermilk and soda may be substituted for sweet milk and baking powder and vice versa in many recipes for baked products. One-half teaspoon of soda and 1 cup of buttermilk or fully soured milk produce an amount of leavening gas almost equivalent to that produced by 2 teaspoons of SAS-phosphate baking powder. Other approximately equivalent substitutes include ½ teaspoon of baking powder plus 1¼ teaspoons cream of tartar or ½ teaspoon baking soda plus 1 cup molasses.

Sweet milk can be made sour by taking 1 tablespoon of vinegar or lemon juice and adding enough sweet milk to make 1 cup, or by adding 1¾ teaspoons of cream of tartar to 1 cup of sweet milk. Sweet milk can be substituted for buttermilk with the addition of 1 tablespoon vinegar or lemon for acidity. Or use sweet milk, omit soda, and allow for 1 to 2 teaspoons baking powder to 1 cup flour. An example of making a substitution in a recipe is as follows:

Original Recipe	Recipe with Substitution of Soda and Sour Milk
2 cups (230 g) flour	2 cups (230 g) flour
1 cup (237 mL) sweet milk	1 cup (237 mL) buttermilk
3 tsp (9.6 g) SAS-phosphate powder	½ tsp (2 g) soda and 1 tsp (3.2 g) SAS-phosphate powder

Fat

The major role of fat in flour mixtures is to tenderize, or "shorten," the strands of gluten. This tenderizing effect is produced through formation of layers or masses that physically separate different strands of gluten and prevent them from coming together. To shorten effectively, fat must have the capacity to coat or spread widely and to adhere well to flour particles. The type and amount of fat as well as the way it is incorporated in batters and doughs influence the volume, grain, and textural characteristics of finished products. Fats also impart desirable flavors and increase product mouthfeel [6].

Comparative Shortening Power of Fats. It is difficult to make definite statements concerning the comparative shortening power of various fats because many factors have been shown to modify their effects. For example, the manner in which fat is distributed in a mixture, the extent of distribution, the temperature of the fat and of the mixture, the presence or absence of **emulsifiers** in the mixture, the type of mixture, and the method and extent of mixing, as well as the method by which the fat itself has been processed, may have an effect on the shortening power of the fat.

Emulsification of fat in the batter can influence the smoothness of the batter and desirable texture in some baked products such as shortened cakes. The presence of some **monoglycerides** and **diglycerides** in the fat increases the degree of emulsification of the fat, allowing it to be dispersed in small particles throughout the batter. The addition of emulsifiers to shortened cake batters has been shown to increase volume and produce a finer texture. The *plasticity* of fat is related to its shortening power. In **plastic fat**, some of the **triglyceride** molecules are present in liquid form, and some are crystallized in solid form. The presence of both solid and liquid phases in the fat means that the fat can be molded or shaped rather than fractured or broken when force is applied to it. More plastic fats are more spreadable and, presumably, can spread over a greater surface area of flour particles than less plastic fats. The temperature of fat affects plasticity. At 64°F (18°C), butter is less plastic than at 72 to 83°F (22 to 28°C). At higher temperatures, butter tends to become very soft or to melt completely.

A shortometer was a machine traditionally used to assess the shortening value of fats by measuring the weight required to break a pie crust or a baked wafer. Lards have been shown to have more shortening power than most hydrogenated fats, butter, and margarine. Oils that are high in **polyunsaturated fats** usually produce more tender pastries than lards. One explanation that has been offered is that these oils cover a larger surface area of flour particles per molecule of fat than fats containing a relatively high proportion of **saturated fatty acids**. The relationship between the degree of unsaturation and shortening power of fats, however, needs further clarification.

With other proportions and other conditions standardized, the higher the concentration of fat in a mixture, the greater the shortening power. This point deserves consideration in the substitution of one fat for another. Butter and margarines contain approximately 82 percent fat and about 16 percent water. Reduced-calorie spreads that are marketed as substitutes for margarine or butter contain even lesser fat. Lard, hydrogenated fats, and oils contain essentially 100 percent fat. Disregarding other factors that appear to affect the shortening power of fats, the mere substitution of an equal weight of a fat with a higher fat concentration for one with a lower concentration affects the tenderness of baked flour mixtures. Fats were also discussed in previous chapters.

Role of Fat in Leavening. Plastic fats appear to play important roles in some flour mixtures in the trapping of air bubbles that later contribute to the texture of the finished product. This role of fat may be particularly important in preparation of shortened cakes. Plastic fat is soft and moldable at room temperature. There is a certain ratio of liquid to solid fat present

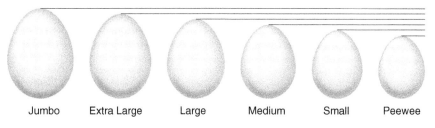

Jumbo   Extra Large   Large   Medium   Small   Peewee

Figure 13–47

Fresh egg sizes can vary which affects the amount of liquid in the recipe.

in the particular fat that makes it plastic. When fat is beaten, it traps air cells, and these cells are dispersed in the batter. When the batter is baked, the air cells produce gas, and the product rises. Creaming fat and sugar crystals together and also vigorously beating fat-containing batters cause air cells to be entrapped in the mixture. Fats that incorporate air readily and allow it to be dispersed in small cells are said to have good creaming properties.

Fat Replacers and Reduced-Fat Formulas. Substances used to replace fat in a flour mixture must mimic the effects of fat on the eating quality of the finished product [3]. This challenges the ingenuity of the food industry as new products are formulated. Cellulose, gums, maltodextrins, modified starches, and polydextrose are carbohydrate-based substances that are used as fat replacers. Dehydrated fruit products, such as banana flakes and prune paste, may be used in low-fat or no-fat bakery products to maintain a desirable texture. Applesauce has also been successfully used to replace fat in some baked goods.

Without jeopardizing the quality of the finished item, the fat in many baked product formulas can simply be reduced. Care should be taken to avoid overmixing lower-fat formulas because gluten can form more readily with less fat. A number of low-fat recipes are available through cookbooks and other sources.

Liquids

Liquids have various uses in flour mixtures. They hydrate the starch and gluten and dissolve ingredients, such as sugar, salts, and baking powder. It is only when baking powders come in contact with liquid that the carbon dioxide starts to release. The typical structure or framework of doughs and batters is not formed until the protein particles are hydrated. **Starch gelatinization** during baking requires moisture. Various liquids may be used in flour mixtures, including water, potato water, milk, fruit juices, and coffee. The water content of eggs is also a part of the total liquid.

Eggs

Eggs may be used as a means of incorporating air into batter because egg proteins coagulate on beating and give some structure or rigidity to the cell walls surrounding the air bubbles (**Figure 13–47**). Egg whites can form a particularly stable foam. As they are beaten, the cell walls become increasingly thinner and more tender to an optimum point. Beaten egg whites can be carefully folded into a batter, retaining much of the air in the foam.

Egg yolks add flavor and color to flour mixtures. They also aid in forming emulsions of fat and water because they contain **lipoproteins**, which are effective emulsifying agents. Because egg proteins coagulate on heating, the addition of eggs to flour mixtures increases the rigidity of the baked product.

Sugar and Other Sweeteners

Sugar is an important ingredient in baked goods to sweeten, tenderize, retain moisture, contribute a brown color, aid in leavening, stabilize egg white foams, and provide foods for yeast. Granulated sugar is used in many flour mixtures for sweetening purposes (**Figure 13–48**). Brown sugar, honey, molasses, and syrups also may be used for the unique flavors and characteristics of these sweeteners (see Chapter 9). Brown sugar produces baked goods that retain moisture longer than those made with granulated sugar. It must be firmly packed into a cup when measured unless substituted by weight.

FOCUS ON SCIENCE

MOISTURE RETENTION IN LOW-FAT BAKED GOODS

A main functions of fat in a baked good is that it contributes moistness. Banana flakes and prune paste are able to trap water or moisture in the baked good. Pectin is present in fruit, and a function of pectin is to trap water or, in this instance, moistness. Therefore, these fruit-based products are able to function relatively well as fat replacers by promoting moistness in baked goods.

Figure 13–48

Sugar is an ingredient in many batters and doughs. Sugar comes in many forms. (Richard Embery/Pearson Education)

Sugar has a tenderizing effect because it interferes with gluten formation, protein coagulation, and starch gelatinization [6, 10]. Gluten development is affected because sugar ties up water, making less water available for the gluten formation. Therefore, more manipulation is necessary to develop the gluten structure when sugar is present. Similarly, the holding of water by sugar interferes with starch and protein and thus delays the formation of structure in baked goods. The **coagulation** temperature of egg proteins is elevated by sugar. For example, sponge-type cakes contain relatively large amounts of egg as well as sugar. Sugar also increases the temperature at which starch gelatinizes, which is of particular importance in high-sugar products, such as cakes of several types. The tenderizing effect of sugar also may result in baked flour mixtures with a greater volume because the tenderized gluten mass expands more easily under the pressure of leavening gases. Additionally, sugar helps to achieve a fine even texture in many baked products [30].

The *hygroscopic* nature, or water absorption tendency, of sugar helps to retain moisture and improve the shelf life of baked goods [10]. Sugar increases softness and moistness and helps to reduce drying and staling. Sugar also contributes to the browning of outer surfaces of baked products and produces desirable flavors. The **caramelization** of sugar occurs at high oven temperatures, producing desirable flavors and a pleasant brown surface.

Sugar contributes to leavening. Creaming of shortening and crystalline sugar adds air to the mixture. In yeast mixtures, sugar is a readily available food for the yeast plant. Sugar also stabilizes egg white foams, whipped whole eggs, and whipped yolks. As a result, whipped eggs are better able to hold air and are less likely to collapse or weep. Angel food, genoise, and chiffon cakes are examples of products made with whipped eggs.

High-intensity or alternate sweeteners, including saccharin, encapsulated aspartame, acesulfame-K, and sucralose, are stable under high temperatures and retain sweetness in baked products. A bulking or bodying agent such as polydextrose must be added with high-intensity sweeteners to substitute for some of sugar's effects on texture. Compensation also must be made for the effect of sugar on the tenderness of the finished product. Again, the food industry faces challenges in formulating no-sugar baked products. Alternate sweeteners have been discussed in Chapter 9.

GENERAL METHODS FOR MIXING BATTERS AND DOUGHS

General objectives in the mixing of doughs and batters are uniform distribution of ingredients and leavening gases, minimum loss of the leavening gases, optimum blending to produce characteristic textures in various products, and optimum development of gluten for the desired individual properties. Sifting flour with a leavening agent helps to evenly distribute the leavening agent. Fat must be evenly distributed throughout the flour mixture. Fat may be cut in with flour, creamed with sugar, or used in a liquid form as oil or melted fat. Liquid fat distribution is least uniform but the fastest method. Distribution of liquid involves distributing water and moistening dry ingredients. The distribution of water dissolves sugars, salts, and acids and sodas in leavening agents. Distribution of liquid is essential to provide a cohesive mixture that forms a batter or dough. Water distribution is also essential to activate leavening agents, starch gelatinization, and gluten formation. The distribution of liquid must be done to maximize leavening gas retention.

Although many different methods are employed for the mixing of batters and doughs, three basic methods—muffin, biscuit or pastry, and conventional—may be adapted for use with a variety of products. Yeast bread, cream puffs, and sponge-type cake are mixed by special methods applicable only to these products. Whatever the mixing method, the optimum amount of manipulation varies with the type of product, with the character and proportion of the ingredients used, and with the temperature of the ingredients. Mixers and other equipment are used to duplicate the mixing methods.

Terminology

Beat—To combine with a vigorous regular over-and-over or circular motion, either to make smooth or to incorporate air. Equipment used are spoon or electric mixer with paddle attachment. (Example: Popover batter is beaten until smooth.)

Blend—To combine two or more ingredients thoroughly. Equipment used are spoon, rubber spatula, whisk, or electric mixer with paddle attachment. (Example: Blending melted chocolate into a batter.)

Cream—Applies to sugar and fat as a method to incorporate air producing a foam system. The sugar crystals are vigorously worked into fat and air is incorporated. The mixture becomes light and fluffy. Equipment used are spoon or electric mixer with paddle attachment on medium speed. (Example: Creaming fat and sugar for shortened cakes.)

Cut—Applies to fat and flour as a method to progressively subdivide fat and coat flour particles and lumps of desired size remain. Equipment used are two knives, pastry cutter, or fingers. Food processor can also be used. (Example: Cut fat into flour as with conventional pie dough.)

Fold—Gently incorporate one ingredient within another. Equipment such as a knife, spatula, rubber scrapper, and sometimes a balloon whisk are used to fold-in ingredients. Method requires minimal, gentle motion, where the edge of the implement leads down to the bottom of the bowl, across the bottom of the bowl, and back up the side of the bowl. For a second pass, move the implement a quarter turn away and repeat the motions in the same down, up, and across motion. Never a beating motion. (Example: Folding in beaten egg whites for angel food cake or soufflé.)

Knead—Stretch, fold, and press dough gently to form and arrange gluten strands. Equipment used hands or electric mixer with dough hook. (Example: Kneading of bread dough or biscuit dough.)

Mix—Distribute and combine ingredients using any technique suitable for the ingredients involved. Equipment used spoon, electric mixer, or other implement.

Stir—Gently combining ingredients until blended, usually with a spoon, in a circular motion. Equipment used spoon, rubber spatula, or whisk. (Example: Liquid and dry ingredients are combined by stirring.)

Whip—Beat rapidly, usually with a whisk, to incorporate air. Equipment used are whisk or electric mixer with whisk attachment. (Example: Whipping egg whites.)

Muffin Method

In the muffin method, dry ingredients are sifted together into the bowl used for mixing. The eggs are lightly beaten, and the liquid and melted fat (or oil) are added to the eggs. The liquid ingredients are then blended with the dry ingredients. The amount of stirring that is desirable will vary with the product.

For thin mixtures, such as popovers, thin griddle cakes, and thin waffle mixtures, lumping can be prevented by adding the liquid ingredients gradually to the dry ingredients. Conversely, the over stirring of thicker batters, such as thick waffle mixtures and muffins, can be prevented by adding liquid ingredients all at once to the dry ingredients. Thicker batters are stirred only until the dry ingredients are dampened to avoid an undesirable development of gluten and a resulting decrease in tenderness (**Figure 13–49**).

Pastry or Biscuit Method

In the pastry or biscuit method, the dry ingredients are sifted together. Fat is cut into the dry ingredients, and liquid is then added to the fat–flour mixture. The "cutting in" of the fat, which results in small fat particles being coated with the flour mixture, results in desirably flaky pie crusts and biscuits. The fat may be cut in by hand (**Figure 13–50**), with a pastry blender, or by lightly mixing in a stand mixer using a paddle or dough cutter attachment.

Figure 13–49

The muffin method of mixing is used to prepare waffles such as this one. (Richard Embery/Pearson Education)

Figure 13–50

A plastic fat, such as shortening or butter, may be cut in by using a pastry cutter, light mixing with a stand mixer paddle or cutter attachment, or by hand, as shown here. (Richard Embery/Pearson Education)

Although the basic method of mixing is the same for biscuits and pie crusts, biscuits are lightly kneaded before they are rolled out and cut into the desired shapes. Thus, biscuit dough is manipulated more than pie dough.

Conventional Method

Although cakes are mixed by more than one method, the conventional method includes (1) creaming together of the fat and sugar, (2) mixing in of beaten eggs, and (3) adding the dry and liquid ingredients alternately until both are fully incorporated into the fat–sugar–egg mixture. This method may also be used for making cookies, various quick breads, and other flour products.

DRY FLOUR MIXES

A wide variety of flour-based mixes for products such as cakes, muffins, biscuits, pie doughs, cookies, and so forth, are marketed. Appropriate directions to the consumer in the use of these prepared mixes result in ensuring uniform, good-quality finished products. In addition to flour, mixes may contain leavening agents, salt, fat (sometimes powdered shortening), nonfat dry milk, dried eggs, sugar, and flavoring ingredients, such as dried extracts, cocoa, ginger, and dried molasses, depending on the type of mixture.

Numerous additives are used and have contributed to the success of commercial flour mixes. These include various emulsifiers, modified starches, caseinate, gums, cellulose, and whipping aids. A combination of added substances is often necessary in the production of reduced-fat or reduced-calorie mixes.

Mixes are convenient time-savers and may cost no more (and sometimes even less) than a similar product prepared in the kitchen. Costs must be determined on an individual basis and are sometimes difficult to compare because of differences in ingredients and yields.

Various flour mixes can also be made in the home kitchen, saving time by measuring and mixing at least some of the ingredients at one time. However, because the techniques used in the production of commercial mixes are not available for home use, homemade mixes do not have as long a shelf life. They should be adequately packaged and stored at cool temperatures. Commercial mixes usually contain a leavening acid that dissolves slowly, such as anhydrous monocalcium phosphate or sodium acid pyrophosphate, to prevent the premature reaction of the baking powder during storage. Also, off-flavors do not readily develop in the mixes with these acids.

BAKING AT HIGH ALTITUDES

Some balancing of ingredients, formulations, and variation of baking temperature may be necessary when baking at high altitudes or geographical elevations above 2,000 feet; the higher the elevation, the more pronounced the effects. Elevations are measured as a geographical point above or below sea levels such as cities. Altitude refers to an object above a certain point, usually sea level. At high altitudes, as compared to sea level, the atmospheric pressure is less. The decreased pressure at higher altitudes results in three key changes that affect cooking: (1) leavening gases meet less resistance and expand more quickly, (2) moisture evaporates more quickly, and (3) water and other liquids boil at lower temperatures.

Air, steam, and carbon dioxide are the three gases found in batters and doughs. The formation rate and greater expansion of leavening gases at high altitudes is of utmost importance in bakery goods. The volume of steam and carbon dioxide produced from their given sources are dependent on pressure and temperature. Basic chemistry laws, Charles' and Boyle's laws, apply to high-altitude baking. These laws state that volume of gas is directly proportional to the absolute temperature and inversely proportion to the pressure [36].

A cubic centimeter of water added to batter at 20°C (68°F) at sea level with atmospheric pressure 760 mm Hg will produce 2,1789 cm^3 of steam at 205°C (400°F). If atmospheric pressure is lowered to 633 mm Hg and all other variables remain constant, there will

Table 13–5
BOILING TEMPERATURE OF WATER AND ATMOSPHERIC PRESSURE AT VARIOUS ELEVATIONS

Elevation (ft)	Atmospheric Pressure (mm Hg)	Boiling Point of Water (°C)	(°F)
Sea Level	760.0	100.0	212.0
1,018	734.0	99.0	210.3
1,977	700.6	98.1	208.5
3,000	683.2	97.0	206.7
4,004	657.8	96.0	204.9
5,000	632.4	95.0	202.0
8,500	556.2	91.5	196.7
10,000	529.0	90.0	194.0
12,500	480.0	87.8	189.8
15,500	429.2	84.0	184.6

Source: References 24, 36.

Table 13–6
ELEVATIONS OF SOME HIGHER ELEVATION CITIES

Location		Elevation (ft)
Arizona	Flagstaff	6,900
California	Big Bear	6,752
Colorado	Colorado Springs	5,985
Colorado	Denver	5,470
Idaho	Idaho Falls	4,742
Montana	Bozeman	4,754
Nebraska	Scotts Bluff	4,662
New Mexico	Santa Fe	7,100
Utah	Salt Lake City	4,345
Wyoming	Laramie	7,159
Bolivia	La Paz	12,795
Colombia	Bogota	8,659
Peru	Cusco	11,440

Source: Reference 24, USGS.

be a 20 percent increase of steam volume. Changes in temperature and atmospheric pressure have the same effect on carbon dioxide production. Therefore, science dictates that less leavening agent is needed to produce the same amount of carbon dioxide with decreasing atmospheric pressure or higher elevations. Liquids boil when the vapor pressure is equal to atmospheric pressure. Higher elevations result in lower boiling points (**Table 13–5**). Evaporation takes place faster at reduced atmospheric pressure. Liquid levels should not be decreased in formulas at high altitudes because the primary role of liquids is to disperse other ingredients not leavening [24].

From a quality perspective, the overexpansion of a baked product may stretch the cells to the extent that they break and collapse, producing a coarse texture and decreased volume. Some of these effects can be seen in bakery products produced above 2,500 feet as cakes may overflow pans or fall, cookies may spread excessively, and breads appear excessively fluffy or over risen. So bakery formulations and methods will differ between Denver, Colorado, located at 5,470 feet versus New York, New York, located approximately at sea level. The United States Geological Survey (USGS) publishes the elevations for cities in the United States (**Table 13–6**). Cookbooks with recipes designed for high altitudes may be used [16], or recipes may be adjusted using general guidelines.

Leavening agents are usually decreased to reduce overexpansion (**Table 13–7**). The strengthening of the cell walls of the product by decreasing the sugar or adding more flour will also counteract excessive leavening. Additional eggs may be added

as another way to strengthen cakes and prevent falling. Oven temperatures may be increased 15 to 25°F (8 to 14°C) to "set" the structure before the leavening gases expand too much. Increased liquid may also be added because of greater loss by evaporation. Suggestions for several types of baked products are provided in **Table 13–8**, and specific ingredient adjustments for shortened cakes are given in **Table 13–9**.

Deep fat frying of batter and dough products is challenging at higher elevations. Doughnuts may have cracked surfaces, increased browning, and high fat absorption at higher elevations. Leavening agents expand dough faster, creating a porous surface before the crust seals. Remedies for high-altitude problems include decreasing formula leavening agents, fat and sugar, adding small portion of hard wheat flour, and decreasing frying temperatures [24, 37].

Table 13–7
ATMOSPHERIC PRESSURE AT VARIOUS ALTITUDES

Altitude	Atmospheric Pressure (Pounds of Pressure per Square Inch of Surface)
Sea level	14.7
5,000	12.3
10,000	10.2

Source: Reference 16.

Table 13–8
HIGH-ALTITUDE SUGGESTIONS FOR BAKED PRODUCTS

Baked Product	General Suggestions for High-Altitude Preparation
Yeast breads	Dough will double in size in much less time at high altitudes. Do not allow to rise more than double in size. To develop good flavor, punch down dough twice to lengthen rising period without overexpansion of structure. Will likely need less flour at high elevations due to drier conditions.
Cakes	Decrease amount of leavening and/or increase the oven baking temperature. Flour levels may need to be increased. Reduce sugar and increase liquid to compensate for excessive evaporation of water at high altitudes. Rich cakes may need less shortening, oil, butter, or margarine. Addition of eggs will strengthen cell structure of rich cakes.
Angel food and sponge cakes	Avoid beating too much air into the eggs. At high altitudes, beat egg whites to the "soft" peak stage. Use less sugar and more flour and increase baking temperature to strengthen cell structure.
Cookies	Many cookie recipes may produce good results at high altitude without modification. Cookies spread increases at higher elevations. Improvement may be observed by a slight increase in oven temperature, liquid ingredients, or flour. Slight decreases in baking powder, baking soda, fat, or sugar may improve quality. Make small changes and test the product to avoid overcompensation for the altitude.
Biscuits	Biscuits often do not need adjustments to compensate for structural issues. A bitter or alkaline flavor can occur at high altitudes due to inadequate neutralization of the baking soda or powder. If flavor is a concern, reduce the amount of leavening agent.
Pie crusts	Some recipes may be improved by the addition of slightly more liquid.

Source: Reference 16, 24.

Table 13–9
ADJUSTMENTS FOR SHORTENED CAKES

Adjustment	3,500–6,500 Feet	6,500–8,500 Feet	8,500–10,000 Feet
Reduce baking powder			
For each teaspoon, decrease:	$1/8$ tsp	$1/8 - 1/4$ tsp	$1/4$ tsp
Reduce sugar			
For each cup, decrease:	0–1 Tbsp	0–2 Tbsp	2½ Tbsp
Increase liquid			
For each cup, add:	1–2 Tbsp	2–4 Tbsp	3–4 Tbsp

Source: Reference 16.

JEWISH AND ISLAMIC DIETARY LAWS ASSOCIATED WITH BATTERS AND DOUGHS

Jewish and Islamic dietary laws impact wheat milling as well as products made from batters and doughs. Jewish dietary laws are derived from the Torah and Talmud. Muslim's dietary Islamic food code is derived from the Quran and the Hadith. Some restrictions and rules govern main ingredients, equipment, storage, and processing; other issues revolve around batter and dough ingredients or undeclared processing aids [1]. These issues are important for worldwide grain trade, millers, bakers, the food industry, food service, and nutritionists [39, 43].

Grain milling for kosher foods goes beyond the basic Jewish dietary laws or *kashrut*. Stringent requirements for milling and grain exist beyond inspecting mills for any non-kosher food practices [40]. Rules regulate what and when wheat may be consumed. Timing of when wheat is planted and harvested is essential [38, 43].

The calendar year for grain resets with Passover, the week-long spring holiday when leavened bread and other products are prohibited. Passover preparation involves cleaning the flour mills, bins, and transport equipment for the holiday. Strict standards and rabbinical supervision exist for products produced for Passover, which includes inspection of the fields where grain is grown. Kosher grain laws are dependent on Passover [21, 38, 43].

These grain laws derive from the Torah passage, which prohibits consumption of new grain until after a barley offering was brought to the Temple on the second day of Passover. Ancient Jews brought an offering of grain to the Temple in Jerusalem on the second day of Passover. The offering served to bless all the flour that was growing or had already been harvested by that day [21, 38, 43].

The blessed wheat that was growing was called "*Chodesh*" *Chodosh* or "new," which could not be consumed until the next Passover. "*Yashon*" (*Yoshon*) is the term for "old" or the already harvested wheat and flour that could be consumed. For wheat to be *chodesh*, it had to be planted and rooted before Passover. Therefore, the new grain *chodesh* would have been planted more than 14 days before the second day of Passover, which is the minimum time required for the wheat seeds to germinate [21, 38, 43].

All winter wheat planted in the fall of the Northern Hemisphere is automatically considered *yashon*. However, spring wheat planted around Passover and harvested in August is more difficult to assure *yashon* status. Typically, spring wheat does not qualify for *yashon* status the year it was harvested; this wheat is permissible for consumption and milling the following year after Passover. Spring wheat is not automatically considered kosher until the following Passover [38]. Worldwide grain imports for kosher grains are affected by these rules [43].

Spring wheat crops such as high gluten flours and durum wheat products are typically *chodesh* not *yashon* unless they are stored and milled the following Passover. *Yashon* and *chodesh* rules govern five grains (wheat, barley, oats, rye, and spelt). Other products like buckwheat, rice, corn, millet, and soybeans are not included in *yashon* and *chodesh* rules [21].

Rye is always a winter grain so it is always *yashon*, but if a bread contains wheat then there may be issues [21]. Spelt is also a winter crop in America but can be a spring crop in other locations. Malt is produced from sprouted barley and occasionally sprouted flour is added to bakery products. The grains used to produce would need to meet yashon and chodesh rules.

Processing aids or undeclared foods added or used in processing batter- and dough-based products and processing may present problems and challenges in Kosher and Halal foods [1]. Processing aids are not required to appear on the product ingredient label. Alpha amylase is derived from sprouted barley or wheat and may be added to flours to increase alpha-amylase levels during milling, but it would not be declared based on federal code.

Halal foods or permissible foods do not have strict rules on cereal grains as Jewish laws. Halal bakery products may be affected by other ingredients that are *haram* (forbidden foods) [40]. Likewise, kosher grains may be impacted by non-kosher food processing aids, non-kosher contamination, or ingredient additives. Kosher laws regarding meat and milk products may impact baked goods too. Insects are generally not kosher, so grain and flour must be free of insects. Additives used in bakery products such as L-cysteine are often made from feathers or parts of non-kosher animals; non-kosher flavor components and some emulsifiers derived from animal sources used in baked goods may not be kosher or halal. Gelatin sources used in baked products in conjunction with gums may not meet halal or kosher standards [1].

Halal additives should be free of contamination and not in contact with haram during processing or storage. Haram ingredients may include some gelatin types, emulsifiers, animal-based enzymes, liquor, pan grease, and release agents that may be used in baked goods but may not be typically halal. L-cysteine, enzymes, mono- and diglycerides, glycerin, lecithin, glycerol ester gums, sodium stearyl lactylates (SSC), polysorbate flavors, and pan release products containing alcohol or animal products would have to be labelled halal or kosher to be used in halal or kosher products.

Food processors should work to find allowed halal and kosher substitutes in these forbidden products if they want to sell their food as halal or kosher. Vegetable oils instead of animal-derived fats are approved and are used for halal and kosher fried foods. GMOs are typically approved for kosher and halal, but there is continued discussion on this matter [11, 38–40]. Kosher and halal supervising agencies work with the food industry to assure compliance and approval status.

STUDY QUESTIONS

Consumption Trends and Nutrition

1. Discuss trends that you have observed in batter and dough products.

2. Describe how batter and dough products can be part of a healthy diet.

Classification of Batters and Doughs

3. What are batters and doughs? Give examples of each.

Mixing Methods and Terminology

4. Describe each of the following general methods of mixing batters and doughs. Give examples of baked products commonly prepared by each method. Discuss the terminology used to describe the mixing methods.

   (a) Muffin method

   (b) Pastry or biscuit method

   (c) Conventional method

Basic Ingredients, Including Flour, Leavening Agents, Fat, Liquids, Eggs, Sugar, and Other Sweeteners

5. (a) What is meant by the *milling* of flour?

   (b) How is white flour produced?

   (c) How is whole-wheat or graham flour produced?

   (d) How do hard and soft wheat flours generally differ in characteristics and composition?

   (e) Name three grades of white flour and indicate which is usually found on the retail market.

6. For each of the following types of flour, describe the general characteristics and uses in food preparation:

   (a) Bread flour

   (b) All-purpose flour

   (c) Pastry flour

   (d) Cake flour

   (e) Instantized flour

   (f) Self-rising flour

   (g) Whole-wheat flour

   (h) Whole-wheat white flour

7. Describe the characteristics and uses of flours made from some other grains, such as corn, soy, buckwheat, rye, potato, rice, triticale, and amaranth. Of these grains, identify the grains that do not contain gluten.

8. About 85 percent of the proteins in white wheat flour are relatively insoluble and play an important role in developing the structure of baked products.

   (a) Name the two wheat-flour protein fractions that develop into gluten with moistening and mixing or kneading.

   (b) Describe the characteristics of wheat gluten. Discuss its role in the preparation of baked flour mixtures.

Leavening Agent

9. (a) What is meant by the term *leaven*?

   (b) Name three leavening gases that are commonly present in baked products.

   (c) Describe several ways in which air may be incorporated into a batter or dough during preparation.

   (d) Explain why steam is such an effective leavening gas. Name two products that are leavened primarily by steam.

10. Carbon dioxide (CO_2) gas may be produced by biological and by chemical means.

    (a) Describe how CO_2 may be produced biologically in baked products.

    (b) Describe examples of the chemical production of CO_2 in flour mixtures.

11. Although CO_2 will be released when soda is heated in a moist environment, explain why it cannot be used satisfactorily for leavening in baked products without an accompanying acid.

12. Baking powders always contain at least two active ingredients. Name them. Which one is responsible for the production of CO_2?

13. Name several acid foods that are commonly used with soda in baked products.

14. Generally, the only type of baking powder available to the consumer is SAS-phosphate baking powder.

    (a) Explain why this baking powder is called "double-acting."

    (b) Name the active ingredients in this baking powder.

    (c) Explain how the active ingredients participate in the production of CO_2 gas.

15. (a) How much soda is normally used with 1 cup of buttermilk in a baked product?

    (b) How much SAS-phosphate baking powder is normally used per 1 cup of flour to leaven a baked product?

Structure of Batters and Doughs

16. Briefly describe the general role of each of the following ingredients in baked flour mixtures:

    (a) Fat

    (b) Flour

    (c) Liquids

    (d) Eggs

    (e) Sugar

17. Why is it a challenge to produce acceptable baked products that are reduced in fat, sugar, and/or calories? Explain.

Dry Flour Mixes

18. Discuss the advantages and disadvantages of using dry flour mixes. Give some examples of dry flour mixes and their use.

Baking at High Altitudes

19. (a) Why do some adjustments need to be made in baked products when they are prepared at high altitudes? Briefly discuss this.

    (b) Suggest appropriate adjustments for shortened cakes that are baked at high altitudes when using recipes standardized at sea level.

Kosher and Halal Laws Related to Batters and Doughs

20. Describe the importance of Kosher and Halal laws related to different aspects of the food industry.

21. Discuss the impact of undisclosed ingredients and processing aids in Kosher and Halal foods.

14
Quick Breads

Quick breads are batter- or dough-based products prepared without the rising or proofing time required by yeast breads (**Figure 14–1**). They are often served warm. Quick breads are made from batters and doughs leavened by steam and chemical leavening agents such as baking powder or baking soda plus an acidifier. Flour, liquid, and salt are the three ingredients found in all quick breads. Examples of quick breads are popovers, pancakes, tortillas, waffles, muffins, biscuits, scones, coffee cakes, nut breads, and fried hush puppies and cake donuts. Cream puffs and éclairs made from steam leavened puff dough are also known as *pâte à choux* (**Figure 14–2**).

In this chapter, the preparation and quality characteristics will be discussed. Individual quick bread ingredients, formulations, manipulation techniques, cooking methods, characteristics, and quality standards will be discussed further.

In this chapter, the following topics will be discussed.

- Consumption trends and nutritional value
- Ingredients, functionality, and proportions
- Cooking methods
- Popovers
- Cream puffs and éclairs
- Pancakes and waffles

Figure 14–1

Cranberry bread. (Andrea Skjold/Shutterstock)

Figure 14–2

Cream puffs. (Ali Safarov/Fotolia)

- Muffins, nut breads, brown breads, cornbreads, and coffee cakes
- Fried quick breads
- Biscuits, dumplings, shortcakes, scones
- Other ethnic and varieties of quick breads

CONSUMPTION TRENDS AND NUTRITION

Consumption Trends

Quick breads have evolved from their origins centuries ago. Pancake predecessors were "hearth cakes" cooked on a griddle over an open hearth. Records from the time of the European Crusades mention soldiers eating bread called *bequis*. In French, the term *biscuit* is used to describe a dry, sweet, or savory flat cake meaning twice baked. Hardtack was an early staple used as bread on long ship voyages eaten by soldiers and early pioneers; hardtack did not mold or spoil like fresh bread (**Figure 14–3**). Hardtack was made from flour, salt, and water docked and baked with an appearance between a biscuit and cracker. Hardtack needed to be boiled, dunked, or fried to make it palatable.

The term *biscuit* in American refers to a unique invention of this country (**Figure 14–4**). The American biscuit are made of flour, fat, salt, leavening agent (baking powder or baking soda), and milk or buttermilk. Variations on basic quick breads presented in this chapter are found among nations and ethnic groups.

Figure 14–3

This hardtack was from the Civil War. Hardtack is a shelf-stable bread made of flour, water, and salt. It was used as ration for Roman soldiers, ship voyages, and extensively during the civil war. This bread had to be dunked in coffee, fried in fat, or crumbled and rehydrated to make it palatable. (The Lincoln Memorial Shrine/© Amanda Frye)

Figure 14–4

Biscuits are an American invention. (© Amanda Frye)

Quick breads continue to evolve. Trends toward fresh bakery items made with few ingredients and "clean label" with simple and limited ingredients are driving the consumer bakery items such as quick breads as consumers move away from processed foods. Fresh in-store bakery sales rose 34 percent to a $11.4 billion business in 2016 [19]. Doughnuts continue to be among best-selling bakery items. All-day breakfast trends have increased traditional breakfast quick bread item consumption [15]. Muffins continue to gain popularity with 30 percent of people said to have a bakery muffin to start their day [19]. Savory and expanded flavor trends carry over to quick bread items such as muffins [7]. All natural and whole grain

single serve packaged items are trends among many quick bread items [7, 19]. Éclairs have risen in popularity with expanded flavored fillings. Ethnic flavor items continue to expand as consumers explore more exotic flavors and products [16]. Hispanic foods such as tortillas continue to increase in popularity [15].

Nutritive Value

Quick bread's nutrition attributes vary depending on the bread type, ingredients, and cooking method. Products with a high fat formulation or fried have a higher caloric and fat content than their baked counterparts. Quick breads are grain-based and meet recommended daily allowance for grains; breads made with whole grain and fruits have additional nutritional value and fiber.

INGREDIENTS AND FUNCTIONALITY

Quick breads are flour-based doughs and batters. They can be made with a variety of ingredients for limitless variations. Some ingredients may contribute different functional properties depending on the type of quick bread produced.

Flour

Flour is the main ingredient found in all quick breads. All-purpose flour is typically used for quick bread products. Flour provides the structural components of quick breads due to gluten formation and starch gelatinization, which give the rigid structural framework. Self-rising flour is used for some quick breads. Self-rising flour has salt and leavening agents added in the correct proportions needed for batters and doughs such as biscuits, pancakes, and waffles. Leavening agents and salt are omitted when using self-rising flours. Sometimes other flours such as cornmeal or corn flour are used instead of wheat flour.

Liquid

Liquid ingredients are essential to dissolve sugar, salt, and chemical leavening agents. Milk, buttermilk, or water are the common liquids used in quick breads. Liquid ingredients provide the water necessary for steam production in quick breads. Water is needed to activate chemical leavening agents. Hydration of flour is required for starch gelatinization and gluten development.

Salt

Salt is a flavor agent that improves the taste of quick breads. Products made without salt taste flat. The typical salt proportion used in quick breads is ½ teaspoon per one cup flour. If salted butter is used, the salt level may be decreased as in cream puffs.

Leavening

Leavening gas sources are varied depending on the type of quick bread. Air incorporation, steam, and chemical leavening methods all play important roles in quick bread leavening, which causes products to rise, increase in volume, and become lighter. Leavening is essential for quick bread grain and texture, as well as the hollow interiors of popover and puff dough products such as cream puffs and éclairs. Air incorporated via foam formation is important in quick breads.

Air may be beaten directly into batter or during the beating of eggs or egg whites. Creaming of fat and sugar incorporates air in some quick breads. *Steam* contributes some leavening in all baked products from water vaporization during baking. Steam is essential for leavening popovers, cream puffs, and éclairs.

Chemical leavening agents such as baking powder or baking soda plus an acid are essential components in many quick breads. Buttermilk is used as the liquid and acid source in many quick bread formulas. Chemical leavening activation distributes gas throughout quick bread batters and doughs. These gases transform the batter and doughs to a foam. The amount and distribution of the leavening gases and the structure surrounding the gases affect the crumb. The ability of dough to stretch, expand, and retain these gas cells is important. The distribution of gases appears as the grain and holes in the baked quick bread.

Fat

Fat acts as a tenderizing agent in quick breads. Fat interferes with gluten production and starch gelatinization. Fat improves flavor and mouthfeel. The fats used in quick breads can vary: no fat, solid fats, and oils are all used in quick bread variations. Butter as a fat adds flavor.

Sugar

Sugar contributes sweetness, which is characteristic of many quick breads. Some quick breads contain no sugar, for example, biscuits, popovers, cream puffs, and éclairs. Other quick breads contain higher amounts of sugar levels, for example, muffins or coffee cakes. Fruit can contribute to sweetness in some quick bread variations. Sugar also serves as a bulking agent. Sugar acts as a tenderizer in quick breads as it takes water away from flour, thus indirectly interfering with gluten production and starch gelatinization. Sometimes the sugar may be creamed into fat to help incorporate air such as in some variations of coffee cakes, muffins, and loaf quick breads. Sugar also contributes to browning in quick breads.

Eggs

Eggs serve various roles in quick breads. Some quick breads such as biscuits contain no eggs, but cream puffs and éclairs contain a high proportion of eggs. Eggs contribute to dough elasticity and the egg proteins coagulate to provide structural components when baked. Beating eggs produces a foam that incorporates air into the quick bread. Eggs also contribute liquid to quick breads. Egg yolks contain emulsifying agents that help to blend the fat and liquid components. This emulsifying property is essential in cream puff and éclair doughs that contain a high percentage of butter. Also, eggs contribute to quick bread's flavor, color, and nutritional value.

Ingredient Proportions

The proportion of flour to liquid varies vastly depending on the type of quick bread. Quick breads are derived from both batters and doughs. Pour batters with flour-to-water ratio of 1:1 are used in quick breads such as popovers. Drop doughs with a flour-to-water ratio of 2:1 are found in muffins. Soft doughs with flour-to-water ratio of 3:1 are found in biscuits (refer to batters and dough in Chapter 13).

The fat level and type of fat used in quick breads also vary. Popovers contain no fat versus cream puffs, which contain a large amount of fat. The fat type may vary from oil to solid. Cream puffs, éclairs, and scones traditionally use butter in their formulations. American style biscuits typically are shortening-based. Muffin, loaf quick breads, cornbread, pancakes, and waffles can be made with solid fat, but typically these products are made using oil. High levels of fat require higher levels of eggs for emulsifying purposes.

Methods of cooking quick breads vary from baking as with muffins, coffee cakes, popovers, cream puffs, éclairs, quick loaf breads, scones, and biscuits. Some quick breads are made on a griddle such as pancakes and tortillas. Other quick breads require special cooking devices such as waffle irons or ebelskiver pans. Other quick breads such as *brown bread* and dumplings are steamed. Products such as hush puppies, fritters, and cake donuts are cooked by frying.

Quick breads can be leavened only by steam, such as popovers, cream puffs, and éclairs. Chemical leavening such as baking powders and baking soda provide the leavening for most quick breads. Baking soda used with various acidifying agents is distinct to certain quick breads such as buttermilk pancakes, buttermilk biscuits, or Irish soda bread. Steamed brown bread and gingerbread use molasses and baking soda for a distinct color and flavor. Buttermilk is a common acidifying agent in many quick breads.

Table 14–1 provides proportions of ingredients for some basic quick breads. Ingredients are balanced to produce the type of product desired. Structural ingredients, such as flour and egg, are balanced against tenderizing ingredients, primarily sugar and fat, so that the product will have form or structure yet be appropriately tender. The consistency of the batter or dough is generally determined by the ratio of flour to liquid ingredients. Higher altitudes may require ingredient proportions to be altered, as discussed in Chapter 13.

Accurate measuring and weighing ingredients is essential in quick breads. Proportion of ingredients

TABLE 14-1
PROPORTIONS OF INGREDIENTS FOR QUICK BREADS

Product	Flour	Liquid	Eggs	Fat	Sugar	Salt	Baking Powder	Soda
Popovers	1 c	1 c	2–3	0–1 Tbsp	–	¼–½ tsp	–	–
Cream puffs	1 c	1 c	4	½ c	–	¼ tsp	–	–
Muffins	1 c	½ c	½–1	1–2 Tbsp	1–2 Tbsp	½ tsp	1½–2 tsp	–
Waffles	1 c	⅔ c	1–2	3 Tbsp	1 tsp	½ tsp	1–2 tsp	–
Pancakes								
Sweet milk	1 c	⅔ c	1	1 Tbsp	1 tsp	¼–½ tsp	1–2 tsp	–
Buttermilk *	1 c	1 c	1	1–2 Tbsp	–	¼–½ tsp	¼–½ tsp (optional)	½ tsp
Sour Cream*	1 c	1 c	1	–	–	¼–½ tsp	¼–½ tsp (optional)	½ tsp
Biscuits								
Rolled	1 c	⅓ c	–	2–3 Tbsp	–	½ tsp	1½–2 tsp	–
Dropped	–	⅓ – ⅜ c	–	–	–	–	–	–
Scones	1 c	⅓ c cream	1	2–3 Tbsp	1 Tbsp	1/8 tsp	2 tsp	–

*Thick

are important in quick breads for satisfactory results (**Figure 14–5**). Leavening agents must be measured with precision. Erroneous substitutions of baking soda for baking powder or omitting acidifying ingredients will have ruinous effects on baked products. Imbalance of liquid and flour will have negative effects on product texture and appearance.

Mixing Bowl

Techniques required to produce different quick breads vary. Bowls and utensils need to be the appropriate size and shape to achieve proper distribution and manipulation of ingredients that affect chemical and physical interactions of batter and doughs [2]. Techniques used to manipulate quick bread need to be appropriate for the ingredients, formulation, and product to achieve a good quality standard product.

Bowl size and shape as well as utensils used are important to properly mix ingredients. The quick bread ingredients are mixed in a bowl with curve and narrowing base, but the base should be sturdy so not to tip when mixing. The bowl should be big enough so ingredients can be properly manipulated. If the bowl is too big, it is difficult to properly manipulate ingredients. Physical and chemical interactions are important to transform ingredients into batters and doughs then to final quality quick bread products. Terms and techniques are discussed in Chapter 13.

Cooking Transformation

During early phases of quick bread baking or cooking the fat melts, if not already liquid. The batter or dough becomes more fluid. Substances dissolve in the hot liquid batter. Baking powder continues releasing carbon dioxide as expansion of air cells takes place in the heat. Protein from flour and egg begin to coagulate; the structure becomes more rigid. Starch gelatinization occurs with the heat. Water is converted to steam, which provides leavening, increasing the product volume. As heat penetrates batter and dough, the structure of the baked product is set with coagulation of proteins and gelatinization of starch. As water evaporation from the surface occurs, the product browns.

Effect of different amounts of leavening (left) 150 percent, (center) 100 percent, correct amount (right) 50 percent—half. (Richard Embery/Pearson Education)

STEAM LEAVENED QUICK BREADS

Popovers, cream puffs, and éclairs are steamed leavened quick breads. These breads contain no chemical leavening agents. Steam from water vaporization causes the rise in these breads giving hollow interiors under a crusty shell. Formulations and manipulation techniques are unique for these quick breads. Popovers and cream puffs have similarities and differences.

Popovers and cream puffs are both made from unsweetened flour mixtures and have the same flour-to-liquid ratio. However, the popover mixture is a batter with low viscosity versus the viscous cream puff mixture which is a soft dough. The high proportion of liquid provides the steam for expansion in both popovers and cream puffs. Both products are baked at an initial high temperature for steam production and early crust formation. Both products have large interior cavity due to rapid steam production and large increase in product volume.

Gluten formation is not a factor in either popovers or cream puffs. Gluten particles are too widely dispersed to adhere to each other to be an issue in the popover batter. Cream puff dough's high fat content plus the starch gelatinization during dough production interfere with gluten formation. Starch gelatinization in the popover occurs during baking, whereas the cream puff starch gelatinization occurs in the stove top heating step of production. Popover and cream puff mixtures both have high concentration of egg that provides structure. However, the egg in cream puff plays an important emulsification role due to the high fat mixture [1]. Each product is discussed in detail below.

Popovers

Popovers are individual unsweetened egg rich batter that balloon several inches when baked to yield a domed light crisp shell with a hollow interior (**Figure 14–6**). The name popover reflects the "pop" effect that occurs during baking. Popovers are made from a simple formulation containing only flour, milk, egg, and salt. They are baked in a hot oven that vaporizes water for a steam leavened crisp hollow quick bread. Popover batter can be the base for timbale (individually baked encased vegetable and meat dishes), Yorkshire pudding, or batter for apple fritters or french fried onion rings. Crêpes are made from a similar batter, but higher proportion of egg and cooked in an oiled skillet.

Ingredients. Popovers are equal part flour and liquid that produce a thin or pourable batter with the addition of egg and salt. They contain a relatively high proportion of liquid, usually milk, and are leavened chiefly by the steam produced in a hot oven in the early baking stages. Popovers are usually mixed by the muffin method, as described in Chapter 13. Proportion of ingredients is more critical than how the ingredients

Figure 14–6

Popover made in muffin tin. (Richard Embrey/Pearson Education)

are combined. A spoon, whip, or rotary beater can be used to combine ingredients into a smooth batter.

Although either pastry or all-purpose flour may be used for making popovers, the crusts are usually more rigid when all-purpose flour is used. The batter should be stirred or beaten to form a smooth and lump-free batter. Excess gluten formation from mixing is unlikely to occur because the high liquid content in popovers prevents the gluten proteins (gliadin and glutenin) from adhering and forming the gluten structure. The liquid is best added gradually at first until the lumps are stirred out due to the high liquid to flour ratio. Proportion of liquid to flour is important as too much liquid produces a batter with a protein structure too weak to hold the steam being produced. Too little liquid will produce a batter with insufficient steam to inflate it.

Popover structure is from starch gelatinization and egg protein coagulation during baking. Gluten structure is not important since as high liquid content keeps gluten proteins widely dispersed so they tend to float in the liquid yielding little gluten development. High concentration of egg is essential for popover structure. Thus, an inadequate amount of eggs in popover batter will result in a heavy product with a very small volume. Two eggs per cup of flour will result in enough extensible and coagulable material to form rigid walls. If the eggs are small or if pastry flour is used, three eggs per cup of flour will provide more desirable results than two eggs.

Too much fat will interfere with weakened batter and cause loss of steam and low volume. Fat tends to float on top of the thin batter and thus affects chiefly the top crust. If as much as 1 tablespoon of fat is used, the top crust may have a flaky appearance. The popover pan wells should be well greased but not so much that excessive fat weakens batter.

Baking.   Special deep-well popover pans (**Figure 14–7**), muffin pans (preferably deep ones), or heat-resistant glass custard cups can be used for baking popovers. The pan wells are greased to keep the popovers from sticking. Popovers made in shallow pans or wells do not "pop" or rise well. When iron pans are used, baking may be speeded up if the pans are prewarmed because iron requires more time to become hot than tin or aluminum. Because steam is the chief leavening agent in popovers, a hot oven temperature (450°F/232°C) is required to vaporize the batter water to form steam quickly and inflate the batter. After 15 minutes at 450°F (232°C), the oven is reduced to 375°F (191°C) for the remainder of the baking time, about 45 minutes. The reduced heat allows proteins coagulation and starch gelatinization to set batter without excessive browning. If popovers are baked for the whole time at a hot temperature, the crusts may become too brown in the time required to set rigid walls. Popovers will collapse if oven door is opened and steam condenses prior to batter being hot enough to set. If the oven is too cold the popovers will start to rise and then collapse. Popovers should be pricked with a fork to allow steam to escape on removal from the oven to avoid a soggy interior. If a crisper popover is desired, turn off the oven and return the pricked popovers to the oven for several minutes.

Browning in popovers is produced primarily by the Maillard reaction. The amount of milk sugar or lactose in the mixture is sufficient for this reaction to occur. **Dextrinization** of starch in the flour may also contribute to browning.

Standard Characteristics.   A good popover should be golden brown that are high rising volume with irregular shaped tops. They should have a crisp hollow tender shell with thick crusty walls. The interior should be divided by thin moist but thoroughly cooked stringy dough partitions. Crusts should not be so brown that their flavor is impaired.

Causes of Failure.   Popovers most likely fail because of insufficient or improper baking. Popovers are not necessarily done when they are brown and may collapse on removal from the oven if the egg proteins are not adequately coagulated. Popovers will not rise to a sufficient volume unless they are baked in a hot oven for the first part of baking so that steam can quickly be generated. An inadequate amount of egg in the formula also may result in decreased volume.

Cream Puffs and Éclairs
(PÂTE À CHOUX)

Cream puffs and éclairs are made from a thick rich unsweetened puff dough (sometimes called a puff paste or éclair paste) known as *pâte à choux* (pronounced "pot a shoo") (**Figure 14–8**). *Choux* means cabbages in French referring to how the cream puffs resemble cabbages. *Pâte à choux* or puff dough takes around 10 minutes to prepare and has multiple uses. The famous chef Julia Childs points out that cream puff paste (dough) is really a "very, very thick white sauce (water instead of milk) … into which eggs are beaten" [3]. The puff dough is the basis for cream puffs, éclairs, *profiteroles*, and many other items (**Figure 14–9**). *Croquembouche* is a

Figure 14–7

Popovers made in deep-well popover pan. Well-made popovers have a large volume and a moist, hollow interior.

(Dejan Stanisavljevic/Shutterstock)

Figure 14–8

A pastry bag is being used to pipe the éclair batter into oblong shapes on a cookie tray prior to baking. (Richard Embery/ Pearson Education)

Figure 14–9

Profiteroles filled with ice cream and drizzles with chocolate sauce. (Richard Embrey/Pearson Education)

Figure 14–10

Croquembouche decorated with caramelized spun sugar. (© Ann Dudko/123RF)

Figure 14–11

Paris-Brest baked rings of puff dough filled with hazelnut pastry cream. Note the open structure of the product. (Richard Embery/Pearson Education)

traditional French Christmas and wedding treat, which is a pyramid of small cream filled puffs held together by caramelized sugar (**Figure 14–10**). *Paris-Brest* are baked piped rings of *pâte à choux*, which are cut and fill traditional hazelnut cream. The interior structure is very open and porous (**Figure 14–11**). *Paris-Brest* resembles a puffed bike tire and takes its name from the famous 19th-century bicycle race between Paris and Brest. Deep-fat-fried *pâte à choux* is called *beignets*. These beignets morsels are typically dusted with powdered sugar before serving (**Figure 14–12**). The dough can be fried to produce Dutch pastry crullers or Spanish/ Mexican cinnamon flavored churros, which are discussed below in fried quick breads. Sometimes choux paste products are referred to as pastries but are discussed here as quick bread because food science principles are similar to popovers.

It is important to note that puff dough has application beyond baked and fried goods. Julia Childs'

Mastering the Art of French Cooking discusses how *pâte à choux* is the foundation for other savory foods. *Gnocchi* and *quenelles* are types of dumplings made from *pâte à choux*, which are shaped in ovals or cylinders and poached in salted water or boullion where they double in size. Gnocchi is made by adding

Figure 14–12

Fried Beignets can be made from choux paste or yeast dough as in New Orleans style. (Richard Embrey/Pearson Education)

mashed potatoes or cooked semolina. If ground fish, veal, or chicken is added to the puff dough, it becomes quenelle paste or is used to make a savory mousse. Childs suggests that quenelle paste that is too soft to poach can be baked as a savory mousse [3].

Éclairs and cream puffs or simply puffs are made from baked puff dough (choux paste). These puffs can be filled with sweet or savory fillings and are sometimes considered pastries. The basic difference between a cream puff and éclair is the shape that the puff dough is placed on the baking sheet. The rich ingredients, ingredient proportions, proper cooking, baking, and dough manipulation techniques are important to produce a product that has a hollow steam risen interior and soft exterior shell [1] (**Figure 14–13**).

Ingredients and Mixing. Cream puffs contain the same ratio of flour to liquid as popovers but contain eight times the fat and a higher quantity of eggs. The

high proportion of fat makes cream puffs more tender and richer than popovers. Like popovers, cream puffs are leavened by steam and baked at a high temperature for early crust formation. Gluten is not an issue as high fat levels interfere with gluten formation. Like in popovers, egg proteins are essential for structure. However, the cream puff mixture requires more egg for the emulsification of the increased fat. Fat levels are so high in cream puff dough, that excessive water loss can result in a broken emulsion that leads to oozing of fat during baking. A broken emulsion can result when there is excessive water is loss during the dough cooking phase (discussed below) prior to baking. The excessive water loss and a broken emulsion might not be apparent until baking.

Even though cream puffs and éclairs contain the same liquid to flour proportions as popovers, prior to baking, the cream puff mixture is a soft dough versus the thinner popover batter. Less salt is added to the cream puff dough if salted butter is used.

The mixing method for cream puff dough is unique (**Figure 14–14**). The fat, usually butter, is melted in hot water. The water should be rapidly boiling to disperse fat in liquid and not just a floating layer on top of the water. Failure to disperse fat evenly in dough will result in a poor emulsion formation and fat oozing during baking. As soon as water–fat boils, flour is added without delay to avoid excessive water evaporation.

Flour is added all at once with vigorous stirring. The fat coats the flour as it is stirred forming a smooth hot ball of paste. Heating is continued until the batter is smooth and forms a ball that pulls away from pan sides. Starch gelatinization during this cooking process causes the mixture to become thick. Although the flour does not have a tendency to lump like popover batter, the dough may have a curdled appearance at this stage as fat and water are not emulsified without the eggs.

The cooked mixture is then cooled slightly to about 140°F (60°C). If paste is not cooled, the eggs will be partially cooked when added. The unbeaten eggs are added one egg at a time to the cooled mixture. Thorough beating is necessary after each egg addition for emulsion formation and a smooth mixture. The egg yolks contain lipoproteins that act as emulsifying agents with their affinity for both water (hydrophilic) and fat (hydrophobic) properties. During cooking, gelatinized starch and melted fat pockets are interspersed throughout the paste. Egg proteins combine these two phases for a smooth paste that will stretch with steam expansion during baking. At this stage, the dough is a smooth, firm, and glossy and not runny or too stiff.

If too much water evaporates during paste cooking, the emulsion will break with no water to form steam leavening during baking; therefore, the puff paste will not rise during baking resulting in an inferior product. Flour also absorbs water during mixing and cooking phases. Curdled paste appearance after the egg addition

Figure 14–13

Cream puffs with crisp exterior and hollow interiors. (Richard Embrey/Pearson Education)

(a)   (b)   (c)

(d)   (e)

Figure 14–14

Steps in making *pâte à choux* (puff dough/paste or éclair paste) (a) Heat butter and milk and/or water. (b) Add flour to hot liquid. (c) Stir dough until "dry" and pulls away from pan. (d) Add eggs one at a time until mixture is shiny, firm, and pulls away from side of pan. (e) Fill pastry bag with large plain tip and pipe mounds for cream puffs or finger strips for éclairs. (Richard Embery/Pearson Education)

indicates excessive water evaporation. Water loss can be remedied by adding hot water gradually back into the paste. Small amounts of hot water are added to paste while stirring until there is a glossy appearance. Too much water in the paste keeps it from rising as the paste consistency is too fluid to trap steam during baking. After eggs are added to the cooked paste, the paste should be stiff enough to be transferred with a spoon or piped through large nozzle pastry bag to a parchment sheet lined or greased baking sheet. The puffs should hold a mounded shape and not be flattened.

Egg also plays a role in obtaining a large volume. Egg proteins aid in the stretching process during the first stages of baking. Later the egg proteins are coagulated by heat to contribute to the rigid structure of the final product. Even though the cream puff batter is stiff, it can be beaten without danger of toughening the puffs. The high percentage of fat and water

in relation to flour interferes with the development of gluten and prevents it from forming a tenacious mass.

Fat also lubricates the paste allowing the paste to expand with steam pressure. Too little fat and the paste cannot expand; too much fat the steam escapes. The ratio of ingredients and paste consistency are essential for a good puffed product.

Baking. Proper baking temperatures are important. Cream puffs like popovers are initially baked in a very hot oven, 450°F (232°C), to create steam for leavening. Baking continues at a lower temperature to finish baking. During this time, protein structures set and starch gelatinizes to hold the steam expanded product. In cream puffs, starch gelatinization starts during the paste cooking process unlike popovers whose starch gelatinizes only occurs during baking. Like popovers, cream puffs will collapse if the steam inflated product's

(a)

(b)

Figure 14–15

(a) Choux puffs should expand evenly with a crisp outside and hollow inside. Puffs on the left made with too many eggs show too much spread and poor expansion. Center puffs are made with too few eggs, which expand unevenly and may ooze butter during baking. Puffs on the right are underbaked and collapse while cooling. (Richard Embrey/Pearson Education) (b) Choux puffs can have many variations. Grated cheese can be stirred into warm choux paste and baked in small mounds for cheese puff hors d'oeuvres. Savory fillings such as tuna salad can be used for puff entrees. Puffs can be filled with fruit, whipped cream or pudding for a sweet dessert. (© Sophia Frye)

structure has not properly set. Products must be firm and dry before removing from the oven. Removing products too soon from the oven will cause collapse. The final product should be raised in volume and hollow cavity with thin dough partitions in the interior (**Figure 14–15**).

The cream puff batter is dropped in mounds or piped onto parchment lined or greased baking sheets, allowing some room between each piece for expansion during baking. Éclairs are piped with a pastry bag into an oblong shape. Oven should be preheated. A high oven temperature of 400–450°F (200–232°C) is necessary to form steam quickly and bring about the puffing or expansion of the batter. The high temperature may be maintained throughout the baking period, if overbrowning does not occur. The baking time is decreased to about 30 to 35 minutes if a high temperature is used continuously. If 450°F (232°C) is used for 15 minutes, followed by about 375°F (191°C) for the

remainder of the baking time, about 45 minutes of total baking time will be required to obtain a rigid structure.

The hollow centers are usually filled when cooled (**Figure 14–16**). A wide variety of sweet and savory fillings may be used, including chicken, tuna, and other types of salads; custards and starch-thickened puddings; flavored and sweetened whipped cream mixtures; and ice cream and other frozen desserts. Smaller puffs are generally used for hors d'oeuvres and larger ones for desserts.

Standard Characteristics. High-quality puffs are hollow shells. The crust is tender and firm to the touch. The mouthfeel should be tender and dry. The top surface may appear irregular, although the surface may vary depending on the dough consistency before baking. The walls are rigid, but tender. The puff interior cavity is hollow and moist with thin and tender dough partitions. If preferred, some of the moist interior dough

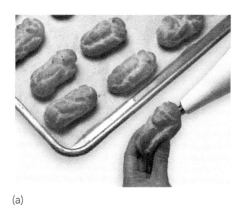

(a)

(b)

Figure 14–16

(a) Filling the éclair with pastry cream with a piping bag. (b) Dipping éclair in chocolate glaze. (Richard Embrey/Pearson Education)

strands may be removed followed by drying in the oven. The crust should have a light golden-brown color.

Causes of Failure. The failure to produce a quality cream puff may be caused by insufficient baking, excessive evaporation of moisture during cooking of the paste, inaccurate ingredient measurements, and inadequate beating of the mixture. Improper baking methods or temperatures not hot enough for steam production will lead to an inferior product. Using too small of eggs will alter ingredient proportions and lead to a poor product.

QUICK BREADS WITH LEAVENING AGENTS

Chemically leavened quick breads are those leavened with baking powder or baking soda and an acid such as buttermilk or cream of tartar. The proportions and cooking methods vary from batters to doughs cooked on a griddle, baked or steamed. Some items require special cooking equipment. At high altitudes, baking soda and baking powder levels will need to be reduced as more carbon dioxide is released from the leavening agents (refer to Chapter 13 for more information on high altitude adjustments).

Pancakes

Pancakes, sometimes called *griddle cakes* or *flap jacks,* are quick breads cooked on a hot griddle. Pancakes are a common griddle bread in American cuisine typically served for breakfast with syrup or fruit compote (**Figure 14–17**). They are usually leavened with baking powder or baking soda and buttermilk. There is more variation in both the proportion of flour to liquid and in the characteristics of the finished product than most flour mixtures. The cooked cakes may be thin and moist or thick and porous according to the proportions of ingredients used (**Figure 14–18**). Many variations of pancakes exist using different grains such as oatmeal, cornmeal and buckwheat. Griddle bread variations are found throughout the world; they are briefly discussed at the end of this chapter.

Figure 14–17

Buttermilk pancakes served with butter and maple syrup.
(Richard Embrey/Pearson Education)

Figure 14–18

Pancakes or griddle cakes may be made thin or thick by adjusting either the amount of liquid (milk) in the recipe or the amount of flour. The thinner pancakes have higher proportion of liquid. (© Douglas and Barbara Scheule)

Ingredients and Mixing. Pancake mixtures are chemically leavened pour batters containing flour, liquid, a leavening agent, egg, and salt. The liquid is usually milk or buttermilk. The batter can be made with a variety of ingredients including fruits, nuts, buckwheat

---

FOCUS ON SCIENCE
LIPOPROTEINS AND CREAM PUFF QUALITY

Emulsifiers allow immiscible substances such as water and oil to mix. Lipoproteins, found in eggs, are emulsifiers that hold cream puff dough together. In cream puffs, an emulsifier is needed because there are high amounts of fat and water but not enough flour to hold everything together. When the dough is beaten vigorously, the lipoproteins in the eggs stabilize the fat by dispersing it throughout the dough. At the end of beating, the dough should feel "sticky." If it has a "greasy" feel, this is an indication that the fat is not completely emulsified. The stabilization of "greasy" dough can be accomplished by beating in a small amount of another egg into the dough to form an emulsion properly and enable the dough to puff when baked.

FOCUS ON SCIENCE
PANCAKES VERSUS CREPES

A true crepe does not contain a leavening agent whereas pancakes do contain baking powder or baking soda and an acid so are leavened by carbon dioxide. The pancake is thicker in structure compared to the crepe. Crepes traditionally have a high ratio of eggs and water to flour, and thus the coagulation of the egg is essential to their structure. Crepes have some similarity to pancakes, but are thin and tender; they contain no leavening agent. Crepes may be filled with sweet or savory fillings. Crepes are discussed in egg cookery. Blintzes are a type of Jewish pancake cooked only on one side and filled with sweetened cheese (**Figure 14–19**). Blintzes should not be confused with *blini*, which are yeasted pancakes typically served with caviar or smoked fish.

Figure 14–19a

A crepe being turned during cooking. (Richard Embrey/Pearson Education)

Figure 14–19b

Blintzes are not turned during cooking and browned only on one side. Blintzes are typically served filled with sweetened cheese mixture. (Richard Embrey/Pearson Education)

or whole grains. Eggs may be separated then egg whites beaten then folded into batter for a fluffier mixture. Sugar caramelizes and therefore may be used to promote browning as well as flavor.

In sweet-milk pancakes, 1⅓ to 1¾ cups of flour may be used per cup of liquid, depending on the type of flour and on the desired thickness of the cake. If thick buttermilk or sour cream is used in the cakes, the proportion of flour to liquid may be about one to one. Because sour cream contains fat, the fat can be omitted.

Pancakes are leavened by carbon dioxide gas produced either from baking powder or from a sour milk and baking soda combination. It is important to avoid overmixing pancake batter. Overstirred pancakes may be soggy because of a loss of carbon dioxide during stirring and may show some tunnel formation. Thin batters tend to lose more carbon dioxide gas on standing than thicker batters. More baking powder may be required if batters are to stand for some time than if they are baked immediately.

Pancakes are usually mixed by the muffin method described in Chapter 13. The stiffer the batter, the less the batter should be stirred to avoid toughening the cakes by developing the gluten. Pancake batters when mixed properly are slightly lumpy rather than completely smooth.

Cooking. Seasoned griddles can be used without being greased, particularly if the batter contains 2 or more tablespoons of fat per cup of liquid used. Specially coated, nonstick cooking surfaces may be used without being greased, although a very small amount of oil may be helpful.

Much of the success in making pancakes depends on the griddle temperature, which needs to be hot prior to pouring pancake batter. Testing the griddle temperature by cooking a few drops of batter may be helpful. If the griddle is too cool, the pancakes cook so slowly that leavening gas is lost and expansion is insufficient producing pale and heavy cakes. Too hot a griddle may burn the cakes before they are sufficiently done. Even if the griddle is not hot enough to cause burning, it may produce uneven browning and a compact texture from too rapid cooking; the pancakes may stick to griddle making flipping difficult. A uniformly heated griddle is also important. A large griddle used on too small of a burner or flame may be too cold on the edges. As pancakes cook on a griddle of a desirable temperature, bubbles of gas expand and some break at the surface. Pancakes should be turned when gas cells break at the surface and edges of the pancakes appear slightly dry. If the entire surface becomes dry, the pancakes will not brown evenly on the second side after turning. Generally, pancakes should be flipped only once in the cooking process. After being turned, the pancakes rise noticeably and become slightly higher in the center. Peaks will not form unless the pancake mixture is very stiff or was greatly overstirred. Pancakes are done when brown on the second side. Browning in pancakes is the result primarily of the Maillard reaction. Cooking pancakes at high altitudes may require the decrease of baking soda or powder by a quarter.

Standard Characteristics. Pancakes should be uniformly round, flat with evenly golden brown tender exterior crust with no pits on surfaces. The pancake should be fork tender. Pancake should be flat and free of peaks. Pancake interiors should have light, tender, with a moist fine, even grained crumb and no tunnels. The flavor should be rich and pleasant.

Waffles

Waffles are a type of griddle cake containing more fat and eggs than pancake and are cooked on a special two-sided plated iron gridded small pockets griddle known as a waffle iron (**Figure 14–20**). The original waffle irons were long-handled pocketed gridded irons used to cook waffles from the hearth.

The pourable waffle batter is cooked on a preheated round or square gridded waffle iron that cooks batter on sides yielding a pocketed type of griddle cake. Sticking of waffles to iron baking plates is influenced by iron plate material, baking time and temperature, and release agent applied to iron baking plates. Iron baking plates with increased hardness, good heat storage capacity, and a smooth stable surface provide better release and less sticking of the waffle. Baking temperature of waffle iron should be high enough to allow rapid crust formation but not so high that burning of exterior occurs, which increases waffle residue left on the iron [11]. The iron must be preconditioned with fat prior to use and may frequently need to be reconditioned by heating fat for 10 minutes on the iron so that iron pores are filled. This keeps the batter from sticking.

Ingredients and Mixing. Waffle batters are similar to pancakes except that waffles contain more egg and more fat (**Figure 14–21**). Frequently, egg whites are separated then whipped and *folded* into batter for a lighter fluffier product. Waffles are leavened by carbon dioxide gas, usually from baking powder, although yeast may sometimes be used in some types of waffles. Tenderness and crispness are desirable characteristics in waffles so a flour of relatively low gluten protein content and weak gluten quality is a good choice (see Chapter 13 for a discussion on types of flours). A stronger flour can be used with higher fat proportions and avoidance of overstirring. In general, a stronger flour tends to yield a less tender, more breadlike waffle.

The proportion of flour in waffles may vary from 1⅓ to 1¾ cups per cup of liquid. With appropriate mixing and cooking techniques, good waffles will be produced. Thinner batters lose their leavening gas more quickly, and it is more difficult to blend beaten egg whites with batters of thin consistency without losing air in the egg whites. Some waffle mixtures that are to be used as dessert or as shortcake are richer in fat than the proportions suggested in Table 16-1. These

Figure 14–20
Waffle iron with graded plates. (© Amanda Frye)

Figure 14–21
Waffle. (Richard Embery/Pearson Education)

specialty waffles often contain sugar and may contain cocoa or molasses. Such mixtures require longer, slower baking than batters with no sugar to produce crisp yet unscorched waffles. Caramelization of the sugar and Maillard reaction contribute to browning.

Waffles of excellent quality usually result when the batter is mixed by a modified muffin method that involves separating the eggs and folding in the beaten egg whites last. However, the whole beaten egg may be used successfully in the muffin method for mixing waffles. Refer to Chapter 13 for further discussion on the muffin method of mixing.

Baking. A waffle iron is preheated before the batter is poured on the grids. An automatic heat control with a light indicator usually shows when the appliance is ready. The batter may stick to the grids if the waffle iron is too hot or insufficiently heated or if there is not enough fat in the batter. Waffle grids should be greased, at least for the first waffle, even if they have a nonstick finish. Manufacturer's directions should be followed in preconditioning and using new waffle irons.

Batters made with 1 cup of flour per cup of liquid are too thin to fill the waffle iron sufficiently to bake the waffle crisp and brown on both sides. Crispness depends on fat and on the depth of batter that the waffle baker holds. A thicker waffle has a tendency to be less crisp than a thin waffle. At high altitudes, a decrease in baking powder or soda may be necessary; see Chapter 13 for more detail.

Standard Characteristics. Waffle exterior should be an even golden brown, which is crisp yet fork tender. Interiors should be moist with a fine even grain. Crust should be golden brown, crisp yet tender. The taste and aroma should be pleasant.

Muffins

Muffins are small individual cake-like quick breads baked in a special pan called a muffin tin. Drop batters are used for muffins. Recipes for muffins and loaf quick breads are typically interchangeable. Many muffin variations can be produced with an array of ingredients (**Figure 14–22**).

Ingredients. Muffin drop batters contain two parts flour (usually all-purpose flour) to one part liquid (usually milk). Muffins typically contain flour, leavening, salt, sugar, fat, egg, and liquid. One egg to 2 cups of flour is standard in a basic muffin recipe with fat and sugar levels increased for richer sweet muffins. Fat may be reduced to 1 tablespoon per cup of flour and still make reasonably acceptable muffins if sugar is present at a moderate level [5].

High levels of sugar will yield a cake-like muffin with a fine grain more like a commercial muffin. Low sugar levels yield a muffin with a more open coarse texture. A waxy crumb may develop when milk and

Figure 14–22

Morning glory muffins made with carrots, pecans, apples, and coconut. (Richard Embery/Pearson Education)

egg are not thoroughly blended prior to addition of liquids to the dry ingredients [1].

Muffins are leavened by carbon dioxide gas, usually produced from baking powder. Typically, 1½ to 2 teaspoons of baking powder per cup of flour are standard. Muffins that contain an acidic ingredient, such as buttermilk or mashed bananas, typically use baking soda or a combination of baking soda and baking powder. Muffins made from cake or pastry flour typically need an increase in flour or reduction in liquids. Structure is provided by the flour components with starch gelatinization, and some gluten formation. Egg protein coagulation during baking also contributes to the structure.

In commercial baking, modified waxy starch, substituted for flour at a 2 percent level, have been reported to enhance the eating quality of low-fat fresh-baked muffins. These starches also could be used in muffin mixes [8]. Composite flour blends may be used to extend wheat flour supplies or to enhance nutritional qualities. For example, wheat-flour formulations containing peanut, sorghum, cassava, or cowpea flours at levels of 12 to 33 percent have been reported to produce acceptable muffins [9]. There were no significant differences observed between the formulations tested and the control muffins made with 100 percent wheat flour for 22 of 31 sensory, physical, and compositional characteristics.

Mixing. Muffins are easily overmixed; the flour-to-liquid ratios in the muffin batter are ideal conditions for gluten development especially if using all-purpose flour. Muffins made from cake flour and pastry flour can tolerate more mixing. Muffins containing relatively large amounts of fat may be mixed by the conventional method. Such muffins are more cakelike in texture. They are sweeter and more tender than plain muffins. Because sugar and fat interfere with the development of gluten in the batter, the effects of increased mixing

IN DEPTH
WHAT HAPPENS DURING BAKING?

Several key changes occur during baking and cooking that allow a batter or dough to come out of the oven or off the griddle with very different characteristics. These changes are described below.

Solid Fats Melt

Flaky biscuits and pie crusts occur when pockets of fat melt. Leavening in other products is enhanced when air and water trapped in solid fat escape. Melting fat also coats gluten strands and thereby contributes to tenderness.

Gases Form and Expand

As gases expand—air, steam, and carbon dioxide—cell walls stretch, become thinner, and therefore become tender. Product size and volume also increase.

Microorganisms Die

Yeast, mold, bacteria, and viruses die. Salmonella, which may be present in raw eggs, is an example of an organism destroyed during baking. Yeast, used for leavening in some products, stops producing carbon dioxide once it dies.

Egg and Gluten Proteins Stretch and Coagulate

Initially, the proteins will stretch as the mixture rises in the oven. Then, as the protein molecules are heated, unfolding and bonding of the molecules occur. The protein becomes rigid and is no longer able to stretch, thus "setting" the structure of the baked product.

Starches Gelatinize

Wheat flour contains about 70 percent starch. When starch is heated in the presence of moisture, gelatinization occurs. The starch granules absorb moisture and swell, thereby providing structure. Starch gelatinization is of minimal significance as a structure builder in low-moisture products, such as pie crust.

Gases Evaporate

As gases escape, a dry or crisp crust develops. The product also will lose weight as moisture is lost.

Caramelization and Maillard Browning Occur

Baked products develop a brown crust and a desirable "baked flavor" due to caramelization and Maillard browning. The absence of this browning can be observed if a product is prepared in a microwave oven where the interior temperature remains cool and browning does not occur. ∎

Source: Reference 4.

---

are less pronounced than in a plain muffin, and tunnel formation is less likely [14]. Rich muffins tolerate and often require more manipulation as fat and sugar interfere with gluten production. Muffins need some gluten production for gas retention and volume, but knowing when to stop stirring is key in muffin mixing.

Muffins are generally mixed by the muffin method. The batter should be stirred just enough to moisten the dry ingredients. The mixture will be slightly lumpy. The fat, if it is solid, is melted and combined with the liquid ingredients, including egg, which are then added, all at once, to the dry ingredients (**Figure 14–23**).

The amount of stirring is more important for muffins than for most mixtures blended by the muffin method. When a muffin batter is stirred only enough to blend the liquid and dry ingredients, dampening dry flour lumps carefully, the batter appears lumpy and drops sharply from the spoon.

Continued stirring of batter causes an elastic gluten mass to form; the batter becomes smooth and tends to string from the spoon (**Figure 14–24**). Overstirring will cause excess gluten formation and the batter will be too elastic. Batter that is too elastic will allow large carbon dioxide bubbles to be retained. The large elongated gas bubbles are referred to as "tunnels." The muffin tin walls confine the large bubble tunnels that start near the bottom and rise toward the top creating large tunnels in the crumb and peaked muffin tops. A crust then forms on the overmixed muffin during baking, before additional carbon dioxide gas is produced by the heat of the oven. As the carbon dioxide gas is produced, it is forced through the softer muffin center and contributes to tunnel formation. Sometimes unbaked batter will push through the top crust that has begun to set causing peaked muffin tops. Overstirred muffins are easily identified due to the peaks and tunnels; they often have pale slick crusts.

The effects of overmixing a muffin batter can be clearly seen in **Figure 14–25**. A more compact texture, rather than an open grain, is associated with peaks or knobs and tunnels in the overmanipulated muffin. With extreme overmixing, sogginess may occur and, owing to the loss of much carbon dioxide gas, tunnels may form. Under stirred muffins are flat with low in volume and coarse crumb. Speckled crust from undissolved baking soda are also symptoms of undissolved baking soda.

Baking. Pans should be prepared by greasing individual muffin tins or using parchment muffin cup liners or pieces of parchment paper before the muffins are mixed. The bottoms of the pans should be greased, but the greasing of the side walls is optional. The muffin

(a)　　　　(b)　　　　(c)

Figure 14–23

Steps in muffin making (a) Combining liquid ingredients. (b) Folding in blueberries with spatula. (c) Portioning muffin batter into greased muffin tins. (Richard Embery/Pearson Education)

(a)　　　　(b)

Figure 14–24

Characteristics of muffin batter. (a) A properly mixed muffin batter results when dry ingredients are just moistened. The batter appears pebbly, not smooth. (b) In an overmixed muffin batter, the gluten has partially developed, and the batter appears to be smooth and cohesive. (© Barbara and Nathan Scheule)

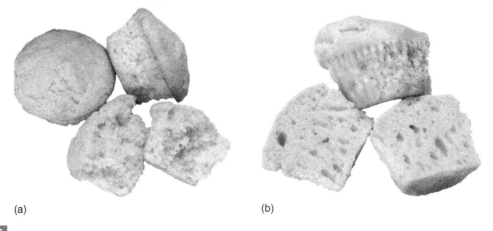

(a)　　　　(b)

Figure 14–25

The corn muffins (a) were properly mixed until the dry ingredients are moistened and the batter is still lumpy. The overmixed muffins (b) have tunnels or large irregular holes after baking. In addition, overmixed muffins often have peaked tops instead of rounded tops. (Richard Embery/Pearson Education)

structure may receive some support from clinging to ungreased sides of the muffin pan as the batter rises in baking; however, muffins may be removed from the pans more easily when the sides are greased.

If pans are not prepared ahead and batter allowed to stand in mixing bowl, gas bubbles form and rise perceptibly in standing batter, which allows leavening gas to escape when cutting into dish batter while portioning batter into muffin cups. The escaped leavening gases decrease the baked muffin volume.

An oven temperature of 400°F (204°C) is satisfactory for baking muffins in about 20 to 25 minutes. A product leavened by carbon dioxide gas must be allowed to rise before crust formation occurs. For that reason, a very hot oven must be avoided. A temperature slightly under 400°F (204°C) is satisfactory if sufficient time is allowed for baking. Browning appears to be the result chiefly of the Maillard reaction, but the caramelization of sugar also may contribute to browning. Muffins baked at too low of a temperature may not develop a pleasing brown crust without being overbaked.

Variations. A wide variety of muffins can be made by modifying the ingredients. For example, corn meal, bran, or whole-wheat flour can be substituted for part of the white flour. Nuts, dates, blueberries, apples, and other fruits may be added to the batter while it is being mixed. Maple syrup muffins are made by substituting maple syrup for half of the milk in the recipe. Chocolate chips or savory add-ins such as cheese, jalapeño peppers or numerous other additions make for endless muffin variations. Another version is to place 1 teaspoon of jelly in a half-filled muffin cup and then add the remainder of the batter, resulting in a "surprise" muffin.

Bran and cornmeal muffins can tolerate more manipulation without undesirable results than muffins made entirely of all-purpose wheat flour. Bran interferes with the development of gluten, and corn meal does not contain gluten proteins. In the making of bran muffins, flavor may be improved by first soaking or hydrating the bran in the liquid before combining it with the other ingredients. The substitution of wheat or corn bran for up to 25 percent of the weight of the flour still allows for an acceptable muffin while increasing the fiber content to a considerable degree [17].

Standard Characteristics. A well-made muffin has a lightly browned surface with a somewhat pebbly appearance, and is rounded, but not peaked. The muffin will be uniform in texture, but the grain is usually not very fine, and the cell walls are of medium thickness. The muffin crumb is slightly moist, light, and tender. The muffin breaks easily without crumbling. The flavor is characteristic of ingredients used but is usually slightly sweet and pleasant tasting. **Figure 14–26** shows well-made muffins.

Figure 14–26
These berry muffins have a rounded, pebbly crust and tender crumb. (Richard Embery/Pearson Education)

Nut Breads and Coffee Cakes

Nut breads and coffee cakes, like muffins, contain flour, leavening, salt, sugar, fat, egg, and liquid. Nut breads are often characterized by the inclusion of ingredients such as bananas, pumpkin, apples, carrots, zucchini, and nuts that provide flavor and moistness (**Figure 14–27**). Nut breads may be baked in small or standard-sized loaf pans. A small crack down the center of the loaf is common and is not considered to be defect (**Figure 14–28**). Because of their larger size, nut breads are typically baked at a lower temperature (350°F/177°C) compared to muffins to prevent too dark of a crust when fully baked.

Coffee cakes are similar to muffins but are made in cake or pie pans (**Figure 14–29**). Many coffee cakes are distinguished by fruit, nut, streusel or crumb toppings that provide flavor, texture, and a decorative

Figure 14–27
Zucchini and other nut breads are usually baked in loaf pans and then sliced to be served, as shown here. (Richard Embery/ Pearson Education)

Banana nut bread with walnuts. (Richard Embrey/Pearson Education)

Skillet cornbread. (© Amanda Frye)

Sour cream coffee cake with Streusel. (Richard Embrey/Pearson Education)

appearance. Although many coffee cakes are classified as quick breads because baking powder is the leavening agent, some coffee cakes are made from yeast bread dough.

Cornbread

Cornbread is a quick bread made from ground corn meal (**Figure 14–30**). There are many variations of cornbread in America; many variations are regional. Cornbread may be made from yellow or white cornmeal. White cornmeal is more popular among Southerners. Opinions vary about standard characteristics for cornbread. Proportions vary depending on style of cornbread. Most recipes use 1 to 1¾ cup ground cornmeal and zero to ¾ cup of flour. Most cornbread is leavened with baking soda and buttermilk and/or baking powder. Milk or buttermilk is typically used

for most modern cornbread recipes. Most but not all cornbread variation contain eggs. Some, but not all recipes contain flour. Salt is added for flavor.

Cornbread's history in America dates back to the Native American Indians that ground parched corn and mixed with boiling water then baked these corn cakes in hot ashes. The Native Americans taught colonist to prepare the unleavened corn cakes or pones. These early cornbreads were soon adapted by trades and trappers who took these corncakes on long journeys, thus the name "journey cakes" or "johnny cakes."

Hoe cakes were simple cornbread in the South. Cornmeal was mixed with water, salted and baked. The hoe cakes were baked on planks or cotton hoes in hot embers. *Spoon bread* is a soft leavened cornmeal mush bread that is baked. Spoon bread is a cornbread derivation; it is soft and eaten with a spoon. Spoon bread can be served as a hot bread for breakfast with butter and maple syrup or for dinner in place of bread or potatoes. Similarly, *batter bread* is a baked custardy cornbread served hot with butter or gravy.

Southern cornbread is typically made with white cornmeal, buttermilk, eggs, baking soda (and sometimes baking powder), and salt with no sugar or flour. This is a moist and crusty cornbread often prepared in a cast iron skillet. Cornbread can be also baked as muffins, in a square pan or in cast iron, cornstick molds (**Figure 14–31**). If using cast iron skillet or cornstick pan, the cast iron skillet and cornstick molds must be seasoned. A well-greased pan helps assure easy removal of baked cornbread product (**Figure 14–32**).

Cornbread is baked in a hot oven 425°F. Cornbread is typically served hot. Many savory additions to cornbread include jalapeño or other spicy peppers, cheese, onions, bacon, and cracklings

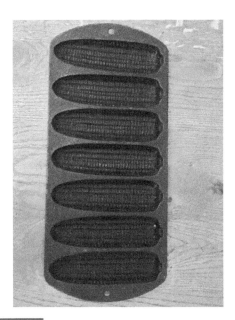

Seasoned cornstick pan for cornbread. (© Amanda Frye)

Cornbread muffins. (Richard Embery/Pearson Education)

(**Figure 14–33**). Hush puppies are deep-fat-fried cornbread pieces and discussed in fried quick breads.

Steamed Bread

Steamed bread is cooked without an oven; this bread is cooked on the stove top in molds in a steamer rather than baked. These steamed breads are quick to mix, but the steaming process takes an hour to several hours. A pressure cooker can be used to make steam bread in much less time, but checking if the bread is done is more difficult.

Bread or pudding molds are used to make steamed bread (**Figure 14–34**). Metal coffee cans or heat-resistant glass bowls or jars can also be used for steamed bread molds. Lids can be improvised with double thick layered aluminum foil secured with kitchen string. Molds and lids must be well greased. Batter is poured to fill mold ⅔ full. Greased lid or aluminum foil is placed greased sides down. Lids are secured to molds

(Left) Jalapeño cheddar corn muffin. (Right) Bacon cheddar corn muffin. (Richard Embrey/Pearson Education)

with clips or aluminum foil secured with kitchen string. Filled and covered molds are placed in a steamer with hot boiling water covering half way up molds or cans. A steaming pot can be improvised by using a large kettle or stock pot with a lid. A trivet or steaming rack must be placed on the kettle bottom to avoid direct contact with bread molds and the bottom of the pot. The kettle is covered and water is kept simmering so the breads cook. Steamer lid should be kept on tightly for steam production during cooking process. Occasionally more boiling water may need to be added during the steaming process. When bread steaming is complete, the bread is unmolded and set on a rack to cool.

Boston brown bread is the most common steamed bread. The bread is moist and slightly sweet. Boston brown bread contains equal parts yellow corn meal, rye flour and whole wheat. The bread is leavened by baking soda and buttermilk. Molasses contributes acid, sweetness, flavor, and color. Salt is used for flavor. Chopped raisins are usually included in this bread. This bread contains no egg, fat, or white flour. The bread is moist, slightly sweet with a medium even grain. Boston brown bread was traditionally served with Boston baked beans but is delicious for breakfast or at any

Brown bread that was steamed not baked. (© Amanda Frye)

(a)

(b)

(c)

(d)

Figure 14–35

Steps in the preparation of biscuits: (a) Sifting the dry ingredients together. (b) Cutting in the fat can be done by hand, as shown here, or with the use of a pastry cutter. (c) Kneading the dough. (d) Cutting the biscuits. (Richard Embery/Pearson Education)

Figure 14–36

The proper amount of kneading improves the volume and quality of baking powder biscuits. The biscuit on the left was prepared from unkneaded dough; the one on the right was made from dough kneaded 15 times before rolling and cutting. (© Barbara Scheule)

Figure 14–37

Dropped biscuits with mounded rough pebbly appearance. (© Amanda Frye)

meal. Commercial canned brown bread is available for retail sale. Dumplings are a steamed bread cooked in minutes on simmering stock and discussed below.

Biscuits

Biscuits are a chemically leavened quick bread that are unique to the United States. A British biscuit is what Americans call cookies. Biscuits are a soft dough that are typically rolled and cut into shapes but can be dropped from a spoon for dropped biscuits. Biscuits contain a larger proportion of fat than other quick breads but are made in a similar manner as standard pastry.

Ingredients. Biscuits are a soft dough made from flour, fat, milk, a chemical leavening agent (typically baking powder), and salt. Biscuits contain between $2\frac{1}{3}$ and 3 tablespoons of fat to one cup flour. A plastic fat is better than liquid fat in biscuits. Soda and buttermilk may be used instead of sweet milk and baking powder for the leavening of biscuits. Buttermilk may be cultured buttermilk or dried churned buttermilk. Dried churned buttermilk contains phospholipids that act as emulsifiers and aid in the fine distribution of fat in baked products. Cultured buttermilk is usually made from fluid skim or low-fat milk, so it does not have the same composition as churned buttermilk. For variation in the preparation of biscuits, grated cheese, chopped chives, or other herbs may be added to the flour mixture before the liquid. The ratio of liquid to flour is critical. The softer the dough the better, provided it is kneaded. Flour absorption capacity variations and the type of milk used causes a difference in the amount of liquid needed. In general, ⅓ cup to ⅜ cup of milk are needed per one cup of all-purpose flour. Self-rising flours that contain chemical leavening and salt are often used.

Mixing. Biscuits are mixed by the biscuit or pastry method, which involves cutting a solid fat into the flour, baking powder, and salt mixture before adding milk and stirring. Milk is added to dry ingredients all at once then mixture is stirred with a fork to moisten dry ingredients. Typically, 20–30 strokes are needed to mix a biscuit mixture containing 2 cups of flour; the size and shape of the bowl, type of milk used, and stroke production will influence the number of strokes needed to make the dough. The stirring also helps to dissolve salt and baking powder or soda. If dough is not stirred and kneaded enough, the soda and acid will not dissolve so "washing soda" is formed from unneutralized acid yielding brown spots on the crust. The dough for rolled biscuits should be a soft rather than a stiff, dry dough (**Figure 14–35**). Biscuit dough that is patted or rolled with no preliminary kneading yields biscuits that are very tender and have crisp crusts; however, they are coarse in texture, are small in volume, and have slightly rough surfaces. Kneading is done lightly with folding strokes where dough is gently folded over itself and turned. Amount of kneading depends on the amount of stirring in mixing phase. The kneading produces a biscuit with a fine texture that displays evidence of layering when broken open. It also rises to a larger volume than an unkneaded biscuit (**Figure 14–36**). The top crust is smoother, and the general external appearance is better in slightly kneaded biscuits than in unkneaded ones. Kneading past the optimum amount produces a compact, toughened biscuit.

Baking. The baking sheet requires greasing for dropped biscuits but not for rolled ones. Rolled biscuits can be placed on the baking sheet about 1 or 1½ inches apart if crusty biscuits are desired. Otherwise, no space is needed between biscuits. A hot oven of 425–450°F (218–232°C) for 8–10 minutes is satisfactory for baking biscuits. The hot oven produces steam that aids in separating sheets of dough as the fat melts. Biscuits may stand for at least an hour before baking without loss of quality.

Standard Characteristics.
Rolled Biscuits. A well-made biscuit usually has a uniform symmetrical shape with smooth level top and straight sides and high volume. The crust should be evenly browned, crisp yet tender without brown specks. The crumb should be a creamy white color, fine grained, moist, and fluffy that peels into layers. Biscuits made with sour milk or cream of tartar and baking powder will have a snowy white crumb due to the lowered pH.

An excess of soda will cause a yellow biscuit crumb and soapy taste with a coarse crumb. A low volume biscuit with a rounded rough top are indication of under manipulated dough. A biscuit with low volume and smooth top is indication of overmanipulated dough, especially if excess liquid was used.

A crumbly crumb is the result of too little liquid or too little manipulation. Flakiness is a desirable characteristic of biscuits that have been rolled. Easily separated sheets of dough can be seen when a flaky biscuit is broken open. The flakiness of a biscuit results from the distribution of fat particles coated with dough. The fat melts on baking and leaves spaces between the sheets of dough. Biscuits high fat levels yield a crisp, more tender crust than muffins. Rolled baking powder biscuits may be compact and flaky or light and fluffy, depending on how much they are kneaded and how thin the dough is rolled before baking.

Dropped Biscuits. Dropped biscuits have slightly more liquid in the recipe and are therefore not kneaded. They are dropped by spoonfuls onto a cookie sheet for baking. The resulting biscuit is usually irregular in shape and rough exterior, lightly coarse in texture but tender with a crisp crust (**Figure 14–37**).

Biscuit Variations
Dumplings. Dumplings are a soft drop biscuit dough that is cooked by steam. Dumplings are steamed on top of a simmering broth typically supported by stewed meat or vegetables. Chicken and dumplings are a chicken fricassee with dumplings steamed on top (**Figure 14–38**). Some dumpling formulations contain a chemical leavening and others do not. Dumpling dough sometimes contains egg; some formulations use cake flour instead of all-purpose flour. Some dumpling variations use cornmeal or potatoes. Dumpling dough can be rolled and cut into squares or dropped by spoonfuls onto the simmering stock or chicken, meat, or vegetable mixtures. There should be enough space so dumplings can expand as they cook. Dumplings floating on top of mixture, not dropped directly into simmering stock, are the fluffiest. Dumplings are cooked and steamed in a covered pot for approximately 10–20 minutes. A tight fitting lid for steaming is important for fluffy dumplings; uncovered pots will produce heavy dumplings. The lid should not be lifted until the dumplings are completely cooked. Dumplings should be light and fluffy. Doneness is checked by inserting a toothpick into the dumpling, which should come out clean when the dumpling is cooked. Dumplings are served hot.

Figure 14-38

Chicken and dumplings. Steamed fluffy dumpling on top of Chicken Fricassee with chicken, and carrots, mushrooms, celery, and onion in a rich creamy stock. (© Amanda Frye)

Figure 14-39

Shortcakes. (Richard Embery/Pearson Education)

Shortcakes. Shortcakes sometimes are made from a rich and sweetened biscuit dough. These shortcakes have a higher fat level, the liquid is often cream, and sugar is added for a richer dough. Shortcakes may be rolled and cut or dropped onto pan for baking. Shortcakes are typically split and served with fresh fruit such as strawberries (**Figure 14-39**).

Scones. Scones, although similar to biscuits, are much richer (**Figure 14-40**). Scones contain flour, eggs, butter, half-and-half, or cream and often sweetened with sugar [13]. Sundry ingredients such as dried fruits such as currants, raisins, or cranberries are common in scones. The biscuit method of mixing is used when making many scones; like biscuits, scones are rolled out and baked on an ungreased cookie sheet. Scones are often patted or rolled in a circle then cut in wedges prior to baking.

Refrigerated Canned Biscuits. Ready-to-bake biscuits in pressurized cardboard tubes are found in the grocery store refrigerated sections. These biscuits are chemically leavened and ready-to-bake. Cardboard tubes "pop" when opened as these are pressurized containers.

At the factory, biscuits are mixed, sheeted, cut, and quickly placed in tubes under controlled conditions. The biscuits are packed in cardboard foil lined cylindrical tubes or cans. The tubes are sealed then placed in a proof box at a temperature to activate leavening system. The activated dough expands to fill tube. Excess air seeps through cardboard foil lined tubes while the dough is contained within the tube. The dough builds pressure inside the tube to about 15 psi (pounds per square inch); this creates a stable condition for 60–90 days in a refrigerated state. Since the dough is not sterile, eventually microorganisms will destroy the quality of biscuits. Leavening agents for refrigerated biscuits is SAPP as it must react on during proofing period, not during mixing or sheeting steps (see Chapter 13 for more about leavening agents.). Shelf life of the biscuits is limited if pH drops or there is improper storage [10].

FOCUS ON SCIENCE
WHY DO THE PROPER MIXING PROCEDURES FOR BISCUITS INFLUENCE QUALITY?

Biscuits should have more structure (gluten development) compared to muffins. For a high, flaky, and tender biscuit, the following key steps should be followed:

1. Cutting fat into the flour—develops tenderness and flakiness
2. Stirring in milk—begins gluten development
3. Kneading of dough to a limited extent—causes more gluten development
4. Rolling dough out to ½- to ¾-inch thickness—is essential to a high flaky biscuit
5. Cutting out biscuits with a straight down motion with no twisting—prevents toughness and uneven biscuits

Figure 14–40

(a) Dough rolled/patted in circle and cut into wedges prior to baking. (b) Baked scone.   (Richard Embrey/Pearson Education)

Figure 14–41

French crullers made from fried *pâte à choux*. Note twisted shaped and large air pockets inside. (Bert Folsom/123RF)

Figure 14–42

Churros. (Fotointeractiva/123RF)

Fried Quick Breads

Cake doughnuts, hush puppies, and fritters are similar to other quick breads. However, these quick breads are deep-fat fried rather than baked. Refer to Chapter 8 for fat and frying information. Doughnuts may be yeast raised too; yeast breads are discussed in Chapter 15. Fritter batter is a popover batter. Cake doughnut batter or dough is a modified muffin formula. Hush puppies are a savory cornmeal batter. Crullers (**Figure 14–41**) and churros are made from fried *pâte à choux* that is piped and fried. Crullers have distinctive twisted shape and large air pocket is in the interior. Churros are rolled in sugar and cinnamon after frying (**Figure 14–42**).

Both hush puppies and fritters are batters that can be dropped by spoonfuls or with small dishers or scoops into the hot fat (**Figure 14–43**). Hush puppies are deep-fat-fried seasoned cornbread mixtures. Fritter applies to a wide variety of sweet and savory fried items. The French term for fritter is *beignet*. Simple *beignets* are *pâte à choux* (puff dough) that is

fried (Figure 14–12) [6]. Fritters fruit or vegetables are dipped in batter then fried (**Figure 14–44**). Fritters may contain small pieces of fruit, such as apple or banana, vegetables, or a spicy ingredient, such as jalapeños. Calas are rice fritters.

Size and shape of product is essential in frying so that batter is allowed to float freely in the fat. To avoid transfer of residual flavor compounds, fat for quick breads should not be the same fat as used for other products such as fish or onion rings. Doughs from high proportions of fat brown too quickly in hot oil. Dough temperatures should be 70°–75°F (21–24°C) [5]. Doughnuts from leaner dough absorb less fat than those from more tender rich dough mixtures. Oil for doughnuts and quick bread products must be fried in oil or fat to a temperature between 375°F and 385°F (190°C and 196°C). The fat needs to be hot enough to cook and seal surface dough quickly so excessive oil is not absorbed to produce a greasy product. If oil is too hot, the exterior will burn before the interior is cooked. Select highest appropriate temperature to minimize oil

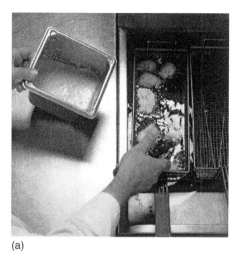

(a)   (b)

Figure 14–43

(a) Hush puppy batter is scooped into hot oil. (b) Once brown, the cooked hush puppies are removed from the oil, drained, and typically consumed hot. (Richard Embery/Pearson Education)

(a)   (b)

Figure 14–44

(a) Dropping the fritters into the deep fat. (b) Dusting fried apple fritters with powder sugar. (Richard Embrey/Pearson Education)

absorption. Doughs with higher percentage of eggs, fats, and sugar will require lower temperatures.

Cake doughnut batter is placed in hot oil directly via equipment called a depositer (**Figure 14–45**). The depositer releases shaped batter in fat about 1½ inches (4 cm) above hot oil. Releasing further away causes misshaped products. Hand production of cake doughnuts uses a soft dough, instead of a batter, that is rolled out and cut with doughnut cutter. Less liquid is used to make a soft dough instead of a batter. Do not overcrowd doughnuts so there is adequate room for expansion. Most dough products will sink to the bottom when placed in hot fat then rise to the top as they cook. When product is properly browned on surface in contact with hot oil the product is turned with a "spider," wooden donut stick, or tongs so it cooks evenly on both sides. Total frying time is approximately 1½–2 minutes. When done, product is removed and drained of excessive oil. Oil should be kept clean. Old oil loses frying ability, browns excessively and

imparts bad flavors. Once cooled, fried donuts can be rolled in sugar mixtures, powdered sugar, frosted or glazed.

Figure 14–45

Cake doughnut batter in depositer releasing donut into hot fat. (Lorna Roberts/Shutterstock)

Other Quick Breads

Variations of quick breads previously discussed are numerous. Quick bread variations are found in cuisines throughout the world. Flat non-yeast griddle bread quick bread variations are found among most ethnic groups. No matter the differences the scientific principles remain behind these breads are the same.

Tortillas are flat thin corn or flour quick bread cooked on a griddle associated with Mexican and Central American cuisine. Flour tortillas' dough is more cohesive and can be made into larger tortillas compared to corn tortillas (**Figure 14–46**). Corn tortillas are made from lime treated corn ground into flour called *masa harina*. The masa is mixed with salt and water to yield a thick dough that is flattened into thin discs and cooked just on a griddle (**Figure 14–47**). Flour tortillas are made from white wheat flour and a small amount of baking powder mixed water and a small amount of fat kneaded into a stiff dough, flattened into disc and baked on a griddle. *Arepas* are a fried simple corn cake from South America primarily in Venezuela and Columbia (**Figure 14–48**). The arepas made from corn meal, water, flour, and salt then fried; often cut in half for sandwich fillings. Salvadoran *pupusa* are another corncake variation.

Native Americans have similar quick breads. Navajo fry bread is stiff flour leavened dough dropped onto a hot greased griddle (**Figure 14–49**). Similar Native American "Indian Fried Bread" is a leavened stiff dough that is flattened then pulled with fingers into a disc that is then fried in oil. Norwegian *lefse* is a large flat griddle bread made from flour and potatoes; often served at the Christmas holiday (**Figure 14–50**). Chapati, also known as *phulka* or roti, is a flat bread made from durum wheat flour called "atta"

Figure 14–47

Cooking tortillas. (Karamysh/Shutterstock)

Figure 14–48

Plate of traditional Colombian arepas made of yellow corn meal with Colombian hogao sauce (tomato and onion cooked). (Ildi Papp/Shutterstock)

Figure 14–46

(Top) Flour tortilla. (Bottom) Yellow Corn Tortilla. (© Amanda Frye)

Figure 14–49

Navajo fry bread. (Gabriela Tsulin/Shutterstock)

Figure 14–50

Lefse is a traditional Norwegian flatbread made with potato. (Amy Kerkemeyer/Shutterstock)

Figure 14–51

Chapati. (Anna Vesna/Shutterstock)

Figure 14–52

Inerja a traditional Ethiopian flat bread. (Otokimus/Shutterstock)

Figure 14–53

Ebelskiver pan. (© Amanda Frye)

(**Figure 14–51**). Chapati is ubiquitous to the Indian subcontinent and parts of Eastern Africa. Chapati is steam leavened. Chapati rolled into disc shapes and baked on a seasoned iron griddle or skillet. Ethiopians make a very large round spongy griddle cake called "injera" from fermented teff flour but featured in this section as an ethnic griddle bread. Injera serves as a sort of plate for traditional Ethiopian stews and sauces (**Figure 14–52**). Teff flour is discussed in Chapter 12.

Chinese Cong Yu Bing is a pan-fried scallion flatbread made from flour and boiling water served with dishes such as moo shu pork and Peking Duck. Vietnamese *Bánh Xao* is a thin lacey crepe pancake made from rice flour and coconut milk are served filled with vegetables and often seafood. Korean Kimchijeon is a large flour pancake made with kimchi (fermented cabbage) [12].

Ebelskivers are sphere-shaped Danish pancakes that are baked on top of the stove in a special seven-welled pan that forms the unique shape (**Figure 14–53**). These sphere-shaped quick breads are akin to pancakes. Ebelskivers may be sweet or savory and filled or unfilled (**Figure 14–54**). These are a traditional fare at Danish Christmas gatherings. Matzo balls are a type of Jewish dumpling made from matzo meal, oil, egg, and typically baking powder (**Figure 14–55**).

Swedish pancakes and German potato pancakes are more variations on pancakes. Baked pancakes, sometimes called Dutch pancakes, puff pancakes, or the German baked pancake (*Pfannkuchen*), Finnish kropser oven pancakes are all versions of filled baked

Figure 14–54

Ebelskivers dusted with powder sugar. (© Amanda Frye)

Figure 14–55

Matzo ball soup. (Brent Hofacker/123RF)

Figure 14–56

Baked Dutch pancake. (Ricky Grant/123RF)

Figure 14–57

Irish soda bread. (Richard Embery/Pearson Education)

quick breads that are fruit filled. These baked pancakes are puffy like giant deflated popovers (**Figure 14–56**). Austrian pancake *Nöckerlen* are mounded dough cooked on a griddle or skillet then transferred to the oven to finish cooking. Irish soda bread is a soft dough quick bread base with raisins leavened with baking soda and buttermilk (**Figure 14–57**). The dough is mounded onto baking sheet [18].

Yorkshire pudding is a popover variation and popular accompaniment for beef rib roast or "Prime Rib." Yorkshire pudding is popover batter baked in a shallow pan of roasted rib roast or prime rib drippings then cut and served.

Gingerbread is a soft cake-like quick bread that was popular in Medieval Europe; Crusaders were thought to spread the slightly sweet spicy treat throughout Europe (**Figure 14–58**). Gingerbread contains baking soda that is acidified for leavening

power by molasses in the formulation. Sometimes rye was used as the flour in gingerbread. Gingerbread was popular ancient European fair food and served by the slice in colonist fairs too. In America, gingerbread was popular with colonist; Martha Washington was noted as serving gingerbread during the Revolutionary War. Gingerbread has been enjoyed for centuries; variations span into cookie form.

The variety of quick breads with ethnic origins is almost limitless. Many other quick breads exist in different ethnic groups and locations produced from products typically available to the area using traditional cooking methods.

Figure 14–58

Gingerbread and garnished with kumquat slices. (Richard Embery/Pearson Education)

STUDY QUESTIONS

Consumption Trends and Nutrition

1. Discuss quick bread's role and nutritional contributions in meal patterns.

2. Discuss the role of quick breads in your dietary intake over the last week.

Ingredients, Functionality, and Proportions

3. For each of the following products, describe (1) the usual ingredients, (2) the usual method of mixing, and (3) any special precautions to be observed in their preparation or potential problems to be avoided.

   (a) Popovers

   (b) Cream puffs

   (c) Pancakes

   (d) Waffles

   (e) Muffins

   (f) Biscuits

4. What characterizes a quick bread?

5. Compare and contrast the following:

   (a) Cream puffs, éclairs, and popovers

   (b) Pancakes and waffles

   (c) Muffins, coffee cake, and nut breads

   (d) Cake doughnuts, hush puppies, and fritters

   (e) Biscuits and scones

6. Compare and contrast products and cooking methods on

   (a) puff dough

   (b) biscuit dough

Other Quick Bread Variations and Ethnic Breads

7. Describe a quick bread you recently purchased or made. What characteristics make this a quick bread. How did this quick bread meet quality standards? Describe how ingredient interactions, manipulations, or techniques impacted the product. How could the product have been improved?

15
Yeast Breads

Yeast breads are baked dough products leavened with yeast. Flour, liquid, yeast, and salt are essential ingredients in yeast breads. Optional ingredients such as sugar, eggs, and fat may be added depending on the type of bread. Wheat flour is the foundation for yeast breads. Wheat flour possesses the unique properties to make a dough when mixed with water; develops a structural network of the flour dough; and retains gases from yeast fermentation. Yeast fermentation produces carbon dioxide, which leavens the bread dough.

Yeast-leavened breads include a wide variety of products, shapes, sizes, and color, including sandwich breads, buns, rolls, bagels, pita bread, focaccia, and many more. Other grain flours and grains may be included in formulations. Grains have different composition and properties that will affect bread-making abilities.

Crusts of standard white yeast bread loaves are golden brown (**Figure 15–1**). However, crust color can vary from white as in Chinese steamed bread to the blackish brown crust of pumpernickel rye bread.

Yeast breads can be divided into two broad categories: (1) lean doughs or (2) rich doughs. Lean doughs are low in fat and sugar (e.g., French bread,

Italian bread, and hard-crust rolls). Rich doughs often include eggs and a higher proportion of fat and sugar (e.g., Brioche and dinner rolls). Rich sweet dough includes products such as cinnamon rolls and coffee cakes. Croissants and Danish pastry are made from laminated or rolled-in yeast doughs that are layered with butter (**Figure 15–2**). The butter is layered into dough by placing butter slices on dough, which is then folded and rolled to produce a flaky texture when baked. Kneading is minimal with laminated doughs as gluten continues to develop during dough rolling and folding of fat. Yeast-raised doughnuts, jelly-filled doughnuts, and bismarks are examples of fried yeast doughs. Yeasted doughnuts are rich doughs cut and proofed to 75 percent volume prior to frying.

Bread baking is a large commercial industry. Most Americans purchase bread rather than make it at home. Commercial bread packaged for the retail market in the United States typically has an extended shelf life for a week or more versus traditional breads throughout the world, which are typically consumed within hours of baking. Artisan breads are a broad category of handcrafted bread products typically made in independent bakeries from high-quality ingredients without additives or preservatives. Artisan breads have become a popular niche market in American bakeshops. Pizza crust is a yeast bread product. Ethnic bakeries sell a variety of specialty yeast bread products.

Figure 15–1

A good-quality white bread with a fine texture, thin cell walls, and a uniform grain. (© Eddy Van Damme/Pearson Education)

Figure 15–2

A croissant is a laminated yeast dough. (Richard Embery/Pearson Education)

In this chapter, the following topics will be discussed:

- Consumption trends and nutritive value
- Ingredients and their functions
- Mixing and handling
- Fermentation and proofing
- Baking bread
- Characteristics of yeast breads
- Rolls
- Whole-grain and variety breads
- Bread staling

CONSUMPTION TRENDS AND NUTRITION

Consumption trends

Bread is a staple food in the diet of many Americans. Retail bread sales in the United States are greater than an annual 20-billion-dollar industry. However, yeast bread consumption in the United States has remained flat with slight decline during the last decade. According to the United States Department of Agriculture (USDA), American consumption of wheat products such as bread has declined since 2000, reversing a 30-year per capita consumption growth trend [54]. Bread sales declined 0.98 percent from 2014 to 2015 [46] with lowered prices in early 2019. Despite decreased consumption trends, bread remains an important part of the American diet.

The Code of Federal Regulations (CFR) Title 21 Part 136 provides legal requirements for the standardization of bread, rolls, buns, and whole-wheat products [55]. Bread sold in the United States must conform to standards as defined in the CFR as well as any additional federal, state, and local laws. It must legally be made from wheat flour. The dough must be leavened with yeast and contain a liquid and salt.

Nutritive Value

Yeast breads are an energy source primarily derived from carbohydrate and protein. Fat content varies with formulations. The 2015–2020 Dietary Guidelines for Americans focuses on making grains consumption half whole grain [53]. Yeast breads can be a healthy component to meet dietary guidelines for the grain group. Whole grain and enriched white bread provides an important source of iron and B vitamins (thiamine, riboflavin, niacin, folic acid). Whole grains provide an important source of fiber too.

CHARACTERISTICS OF YEAST BREADS

Yeast breads come in a wide array of sizes, shapes, textures, tastes, and flavors. High-quality yeast bread standards vary by bread type. Quality attributes to be considered include (1) the texture of the crust and crumb, (2) the appearance of the loaf or roll, (3) flavor, and (4) aroma. Most yeast breads will be light with a large volume in relation to the loaf weight.

Texture

The texture of a good-quality basic white bread is fine, the cell walls are thin, and the grain is uniform (Figure 15–1). Cells tend to be slightly elongated rather than round, although the shape of the cell varies. The crumb is elastic and thoroughly baked so that when cooled it does not form a gummy ball when pressed between the fingers. The fresh crumb should spring back quickly when touched with the finger.

The texture of whole-grain breads is more dense and compact compared to standard white bread. Breads made with a high percent (50 percent or more) of whole-wheat flour tend to be denser than those with less whole wheat [21]. The type of whole-wheat flour also has an impact on the expected texture. Whole white wheat flour is milled more finely and therefore results in a whole-wheat bread with a texture more similar to breads made from refined white flour.

Various traditional or artisan breads, such as sourdough (**Figure 15–3**), ciabatta (**Figure 15–4**), rustic

Figure 15–3

French country sourdough bread has an uneven open texture with relatively large air pockets. (Richard Embery/Pearson Education)

Figure 15–4

A high-quality ciabatta bread has an uneven open texture with relatively large air pockets. (Richard Embery/Pearson Education)

dinner rolls, focaccia, or baguettes, also have a unique texture as compared to other breads [10, 20, 22]. These breads are chewier and have a more open, airy, and uneven crumb.

Ingredients, dough handling, and proofing can all impact bread quality, especially the texture. Allowing the bread dough to proof or rise too long will result in a coarse texture, with an open grain and crumbly character. Bread-making techniques will be discussed in this chapter in greater detail.

Appearance

Standard white loaf breads should have a golden brown crust. Most types of breads should not have a streaked crust, but for some of the artisan breads, this can be expected. The shaping of breads and rolls is another important aspect of appearance to be considered.

A well-shaped bread loaf has a rounded top and is free from rough, ragged cracks on the sides. The **shred** on the sides of the loaf where the dough rises is smooth and even. Careful uniform shaping of the loaf and placing the shaped dough in the center of the baking pan contribute to a well-shaped baked bread loaf. Abnormalities in shape have numerous other causes in addition to problems created by the dough shaping. The stiffness of the dough, strength of the gluten, extent of **fermentation** and **proofing**, baking temperature, and position in the oven may all affect the shape of the loaf as well as its volume and texture.

If a loaf has been over-proofed prior to being placed in the oven, the cells over expand and collapse. The result is a loaf of bread that is flat or sunken on top and has overhanging eaves on the sides, somewhat like a mushroom shape. If a loaf has not proofed long enough before being placed in the oven, it may have wide cracks on the sides after baking because the crust structure will have set before sufficient expansion of the loaf has occurred. Conversely, if the dough is proofed too little, the texture may be somewhat compact and coarse (**Figure 15–5**).

Flavor

The taste and aroma of the bread should be yeasty and characteristic to the type of bread. Yeasty aroma arises from molecules involved in yeast metabolism. Sourdough breads will have a tangy slightly acidic taste and slightly sour aroma [48]. Whole-wheat breads may taste nutty and will have a stronger wheat flavor. Sweet rolls will have a sweeter flavor that complements other ingredients, such as cinnamon or fruits.

INGREDIENTS

Flour, liquid, yeast, and salt are the four essential ingredients in yeast-leavened doughs. Sugar, fat, and eggs are not required to make yeast breads but may be added for texture and flavor attributes desirable

Figure 15–5

(Left) Over-proofed bread loaf with deflated top and coarse crumb. (Right) Under-proofed loaf with a ragged crack on the end and side where the dough rose unevenly during the process of baking and dense crumb. (Richard Embery/Pearson Education)

in certain breads. Liquid ingredients include water, milk, and eggs. Additives also are used commercially in the baking of bread and rolls. These include oxidants (such as ascorbic acid) and vital wheat gluten, which strengthen the dough and assist in the retention of leavening gas. Yeast dough can be classified as a foam food system as gases are dispersed in the dough mixture.

Yeast

Yeast is a living unicellular organism classified in the kingdom of Fungi. Yeasts are ubiquitous in our environment. Yeast serves as a catalyst for the fermentation process, which is essential in yeast breads. The yeast fermentation produces carbon dioxide gas, which leavens the bread [14].

There are many strains of yeast found all around us. Natural wild yeast can be used to make bread. Before commercial yeast development, all bread was made by using a preferment starter from wild yeast. Natural wild yeast starters were essential for ancient and pioneer bread bakers; many artisan bakers use natural yeast starters.

Natural yeast starters are made from a mixture of equal weights of flour and water, which collect yeast and bacteria from the air. Wild yeasts found on grape skins, apple peels, or orange rinds can be added to starters by placing small amounts of these items in the flour–water mixture. The starter is allowed to set at room temperature to grow.

Yeast presence will be noticeable when mixtures start to bubble. Starter mixtures double to triple in volume within 12–24 hours. The natural wild yeast starter is combined with flour, salt, and liquid to make a dough mixture. A portion of the starter is typically saved and "fed" with more flour and water for future use. Wild yeast collection for the starter is time-consuming and leads to variable results. Sourdough bread is an example of a bread made from a natural wild yeast starter.

Ancient Egyptians are credited with being the first bread producers. Archaeologists have found evidence of baking chambers and grinding stones dating back over 4,000 years. The science of bread making didn't develop until after the first microscope was developed in 1676 by Anton Van Leeuwenhoek. In 1859, Louis Pasteur's pioneering scientific work led to the understanding that yeast was a live organism responsible for alcohol fermentation and carbon dioxide for bread leavening. Commercial yeasts were soon developed for making bread. In 1868, Fleischmann's® yeast was commercially produced, changing the baking industry.

The yeast used in breads is known as baker's yeast. Baker's yeast is made from the yeast strain *Saccharomyces cerevisiae* (**Figure 15–6**). Strains of this yeast are carefully selected, grown, and sometimes crossbred to produce a final product with desirable characteristics for baking.

Yeasts can grow with or without oxygen. The production of yeast and early stages of yeast growing are aerobic processes. Many food systems rely on food-grade yeasts for production. Food-grade yeast strains differ based on the unique properties of each yeast strain and their application.

The production of commercial baking yeast is a scientific process. Yeasts are propagated under carefully controlled conditions. A microscope is used to select healthy yeast cell from the desired strain. The yeast cell is placed in a sterile test tube with nutrients so that it can multiply. Yeasts multiply through the process of budding. Next, the mass of budded yeast cells

is transferred to an aseptic flask containing wort. The wort is a nutrient-rich growing medium containing a carbohydrate substrate such as molasses plus vitamins, minerals, and other components. After the yeast cells have multiplied many times, they are ready for the fermentation phase. The flasks are emptied into sterilized fermentation tanks or bioreactors containing more wort. Yeast cells continue to multiply and are transferred to larger tanks so they continue to grow. The final tank may be up to 60,000 gallons as "high as a multi-story building." The yeast would have multiplied 5–8 times over 3 generations by the time it is ready for harvest. When fermentation is complete, the yeast is washed and centrifuged separating the yeast from the wort, yielding a pure active yeast suspension [5].

The yeast cells are living organisms that can be made dormant after the growth process. Dormancy can be accomplished by drying for "active dry yeast" or by low-temperature storage for compressed (cake) or crumbled yeast. Commercial bread yeasts also contain bacteria (typically lactobacilli), which are important in bread production. If compressed yeast is held at room temperature, it will soon die, so proper temperature and storage conditions are important for a viable yeast. Commercial baker's yeast always has an expiration date and directions for storage conditions for successful bread making.

The dormant yeast becomes active again when it is mixed into dough, and the conditions are right for it to come out of dormancy. The yeast cells in the bread dough metabolize fermentable sugars (glucose, fructose, sucrose, and maltose) under anaerobic processes causing carbon dioxide and ethanol to be given off. This series of chemical reactions is collectively called *fermentation*. The alpha and beta amylases in flour provide fermentable sugars for yeast by hydrolyzing damaged starch into maltose unit. Sometimes, alpha amylase, obtained from malted flour or barley, is added to bread flour if alpha amylase levels are insufficient.

Yeast cells contain enzymes (invertases) maltase and sucrase, which can hydrolyze flour starch into maltose and sucrose. Bread formulations often call for the addition of sucrose. Yeast needs fermentable sugar to produce carbon dioxide, but too much added sugar above 10 percent of flour weight will actually retard fermentation and have a negative effect on bread quality. Yeast strains are being isolated and developed to tolerate high sugar formulations [30, 14].

The yeast fermentation is a **metabolic** process that gives off the by-products of carbon dioxide and ethanol. These two by-products affect the dough's functional properties and bread quality. Other metabolites include acetic and succinic acids, which are thought to have an effect on gas-holding capacity and onset of carbon dioxide loss in the dough [40].

Yeast feeds on fermentable sugars (glucose, sucrose, fructose, and maltose) that are the result of flour

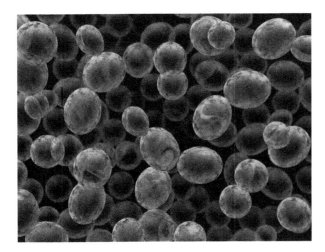

Figure 15–6

Scanning electron micrograph of budding baker's yeast *Saccharomyces cerevisiae*. (Knorre/Shutterstock)

starch hydrolyzed by flour enzymes or added to the bread dough. The yeast fermentation process yields carbon dioxide gases and ethanol. The carbon dioxide gases become trapped in the flour–dough–gluten network, causing the dough to expand in volume. The dough becomes light or is said to be leavened by the production of carbon dioxide gas. Flour gluten provides the dough's viscoelastic structure that traps the carbon dioxide, allowing dough to expand or rise. As the yeast ferments it gives off the carbon dioxide gas, that is trapped in the dough, increasing dough volume and making the dough light. The ethanol evaporates during baking phase, thus making some contribution to product volume. Yeast fermentation rate and yeast metabolites also impact the gas-holding capacity of dough [40].

Since yeast is a living organism, providing favorable temperatures is essential for yeast fermentation and leavening. Yeast fermentation increases up to the optimal temperature around 100°F (38°C). Yeast dough pH between 4.8 and 5.5 allows for maximum yeast activity. Water that is too hot will kill yeast, whereas temperatures that are too cold will result in very slow-rising bread. When yeast is dissolved directly in water, a temperature of 100 to 115°F (38 to 46°C) is suggested. A slightly warmer water temperature is acceptable (120 to 130°F/48 to 54°C) when the water is added to yeast mixed with dry ingredients. If scalded milk is used, it must be cooled to around 27°C (80°F). Yeast cells die at temperatures around 137°F (54.4°C), which is known as the "thermal death point" of yeast.

Baker's yeast is marketed usually as *active dry yeast, instant active dry yeast,* or *compressed fresh yeast* (**Figure 15–7**). Another yeast product used in bread production is *inactive dry yeast.* Inactive dry yeast does not have dough leavening properties, but is used for dough conditioning and flavor development.

Active Dry Yeast. Special strains of *S. cerevisiae* are used for the production of Baker's yeast products such as active dry yeast or instant dry yeast. Active dry yeast are dried dormant live yeast cells that look like grains or beads; and have leavening power upon hydration, food and the proper temperature. Instant dry yeast does not require rehydration prior to use; the yeast can be mixed directly with dry ingredients. Active dry yeast is relatively shelf stable. It may be stored for 1 to 2 years at room temperature if left unopened. Packages of dry yeast are usually dated, after which time optimal activity is not guaranteed. The conditions that contribute to loss of viability in the yeast are mainly air, moisture, and warm temperatures. Therefore, open packages of dry yeast should be stored in the refrigerator.

Active dry yeast must be rehydrated in water before use and is favored for home baking over commercial use. Compared to instant quick-rising yeast,

Figure 15–7

Yeast may be used in breads as dry yeast, fresh yeast, or a starter. Dry yeast has a shelf life at room temperature of about a year if unopened. Fresh yeast must be kept refrigerated and used within about 2 weeks. A starter may be prepared using dry yeast, water and flour, or simply flour and water with wild yeast from the air. (Top) Fresh compressed yeast. (Middle) Dry yeast. (Bottom) Natural yeast starter. (Richard Embery/Pearson Education)

active dry yeast has larger granules, which is the reason it does not rehydrate rapidly. To rehydrate active dry yeast, it should be added to 110 to 115°F (43 to 46°C) water for about 5 to 10 minutes. Water above 130°F (54°C) begins to kill the yeast. Cool water can shock the yeast, causing some of the cell contents to be leached out and resulting in "slackened" dough that flows in the pan when proofed [11]. Active dry yeast should not be added directly to the dry ingredients, as is done with instant quick-rising yeast.

Instant Quick-Rising Active Yeast. Instant quick-rising active yeast hydrates rapidly and may be mixed directly with the dry ingredients. Additionally, it rises quickly compared to active dry yeast. Instant quick-rising yeast can reduce the time for the dough to rise by as much as 50 percent. The same properties of instant quick-rising yeast that allow rapid hydration, however, also contribute to its high instability in air. Therefore, it is packaged in a vacuum or in the presence of inert nitrogen gas with oxygen excluded to preserve its activity [51].

Instant quick-rising active yeast is commonly used by bakers, but is also available for home use. A specially selected strain of *S. cerevisiae* is used, and drying is done in equipment that allows very rapid dehydration. The instant dry yeast consists of cylindrical and porous rod-shaped particles that are very fine and light, with a large surface area.

Bread Machine Yeast. With the popularity of automatic bread machines in homes, an instant quick-rising yeast specially developed for use in automatic bread machines was developed. Although quick-rising active dry yeast also works well in automatic bread-making machines, bread machine yeast has added ascorbic acid (vitamin C), which functions as a dough conditioner. The ascorbic acid promotes dough extensibility (or stretching) during rising. Whether bread machine yeast or instant quick-rising active dry yeast, the yeast should be placed in or near the flour and should not come into contact with liquid or salt, especially when the timer is being used to delay the mixing and baking of the bread.

Inactive Dry Yeast. Inactive dry yeast is used as a dough conditioner and not as a leavening agent. It is produced from Baker's yeast grown by nonalcoholic fermentation with a molasses substrate. The yeast is inactivated by pasteurization during the drying on steam-heated roller dryers. The inactive dry yeast powder is yellow to brown, a source of protein, and rich with B vitamins. Inactive dry yeast is mixed with bread dough and acts as a reducing agent on gluten network. It breaks gluten sulfide bonds, resulting in a more extensible dough which optimizes carbon dioxide retention produced from the active yeast. Inactive dry yeast is typically 0.1–2 percent of flour weight depending on flour strength and product. It has a shelf life of 1 to 2 years [5].

Compressed (Cake) Yeast. Compressed yeast, also called fresh or cake yeast, is highly perishable. It has a shelf life of about 10 days when refrigerated. When used, compressed yeast must be softened in lukewarm liquid at approximately 85°F (29°C) so that it will blend with other dough ingredients. It may be softened either in a small amount of water or in the total amount of liquid used in the dough. Because compressed yeast contains added moisture and conditioners not found in active dry yeast, the dry yeast cannot be substituted interchangeably on a weight basis. The weight of active dry yeast used should be approximately 60 percent of the weight of compressed yeast.

Compressed yeast is produced from a blend of wet yeast cells, water, emulsifiers, and oil that is extruded and then cut into a block form in a variety of sizes. The compressed baker's yeast is packaged and shipped as fresh baker's yeast. It contains about 70 percent moisture, which explains its perishability. If held at room temperature for more than several hours, this yeast loses leavening activity. A fresh sample of compressed yeast is creamy white in color; it is moist but not slimy, crumbles easily, and has a distinctive odor. When stale, the yeast becomes brownish and may develop a strong unpleasant odor. Because compressed yeast undergoes minimal processing, it is the most consistent in quality of all the baker's yeasts [11]. Commercial bakers prefer fresh yeast [14].

Amount of Yeast to Use. Two and one-fourth teaspoons (7 grams) of active dry yeast (equivalent to one package of active dry yeast or one-third of a two-ounce cake of fresh yeast) will leaven bread dough made with up to 4 cups of flour. The amount of yeast used may be altered within limits according to the amount of time to be used for the bread-making process. Bread machine recipes may indicate a greater amount of yeast if selecting a faster bread cycle. Excess yeast causes an undesirable odor, flavor, and texture in bread. Excess yeast and rapid fermentation yield bread with a coarse texture with a gray color crust and crumb. Loaves with excessive yeast have distorted shapes. In general, the smallest amount of yeast that will serve the purpose is desirable. The amount of yeast should be reduced slightly at high altitudes.

Preferments. Yeast may be introduced to bread dough by use of a preferment sometimes referred to as a starter. A preferment is made from a portion of bread dough ingredients prior to final dough mixing. The preferment may be generated with commercial yeast or wild yeasts. The preferment texture varies from stiff starter, sometimes called levain, to loose thin starter, sometimes called barms. A preferment can be a piece of old bread dough. Salt may or may not be included in a preferment. Preferment terminology can be confusing, especially with many foreign terms. It is not always interchangeable as some terms are broad and others specific.

Wild yeast preferment. Wild yeast preferments sometimes called natural sours or natural starters were the only way to make bread before commercial baker's yeast was available. These wild yeast preferments contain wild yeast strains and bacteria collected from the air. The wild yeast produces the carbon dioxide for bread leavening; the bacteria and acid add flavor.

Free amino acids from flour proteolysis are important for bread flavor. Lactic bacteria in sourdough preferment increases amino acid flavor components [48]. The proper balance between yeasts and lactic acid bacteria is important for flavor and leavening (**Figure 15–8**). Sourdough bread is an example of bread often made from a wild yeast preferment. Natural yeasts vary by geographical location. San Francisco sourdough breads are famous for their unique flavor because of the unique yeast in the area. The famous San Francisco Boudin brand of sourdough bread has been made from the same wild yeast starter since 1849.

Flour

Wheat flour is the major and essential component of yeast bread [55, 17]. Only flour from wheat possess unique characteristics that will produce a **viscoelastic** dough that retains gas [17, 23]. Bread flour with the highest quality of gluten proteins are used to yield breads with high volume and fine texture with a cohesive, elastic crumb. Gluten, which is developed when the glutenin and gliadin proteins in wheat flour are hydrated and manipulated, is responsible for extensibility and elasticity in the dough. The glutenin proteins give dough elasticity; gliadin proteins give the fluid or viscous properties.

After the gluten structure has been expanded by gas cells, heat coagulates the gluten proteins and sets the structure. Because of the weakening effect of fermentation on gluten, bread flour is often recommended because of its high protein content and ability to produce gluten. If a low-protein flour is used, the gluten will be weak, and a bread of poor volume and poor quality is likely to result. All-purpose flour used for bread can also be used for yeast bread production [10]. See Chapter 13 for more information about gluten and types of flours.

The starch component gelatinizes during baking giving cell rigidity. Starch also provides essential nutrients needed during fermentation. Yeast obtains fermentable sugars from the starch maltose. Pentosans are the gums found in flour that allow for increased water absorption. These are essential for good loaf volume [17].

The baking performance of flour is measured in the laboratory by food scientists. The variety of wheat and the milling process can have an impact on the performance of the flour. The level of protein, however, appears to be the most important factor influencing loaf volume [17]. (See Chapters 12 and 13 for more on wheat and milling.)

A pound loaf of bread can be made with approximately ¾ pound or 3 cups of flour and 1 cup of liquid. When using a bread flour, about 60 to 65 percent of the weight of the flour as liquid gives a dough the best consistency. The amount of flour required in bread making will vary, however, based on (1) type of flour, (2) type of liquid, (3) humidity, and (4) variety of bread.

Strong, high-protein flours have a higher **hydration capacity** than flours of lower protein content. Thus, the amount of liquid used in making bread varies with the hydration capacity of the gluten-forming proteins in the flour. Weak flours have a low imbibition capacity (ability to absorb liquid) and therefore require a lower percentage of moisture. When milk instead of water is the liquid, a slightly higher proportion of liquid is needed. Milk is composed of 12 to 14 percent of milk solids, which explains the need for additional milk to hydrate the flour.

The amount of flour required in bread making also may vary with the level of humidity in the environment

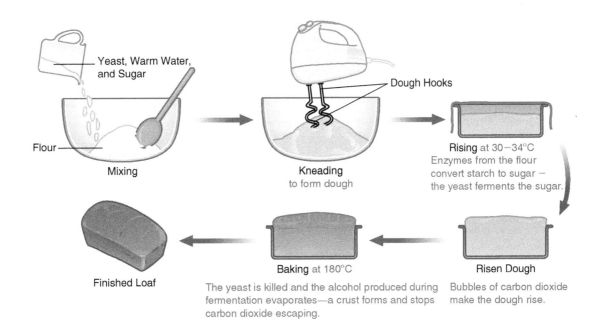

Flour — Yeast, Warm Water, and Sugar

Mixing

Dough Hooks

Kneading
to form dough

Rising at 30−34°C
Enzymes from the flour convert starch to sugar — the yeast ferments the sugar.

Finished Loaf

Baking at 180°C
The yeast is killed and the alcohol produced during fermentation evaporates—a crust forms and stops carbon dioxide escaping.

Risen Dough
Bubbles of carbon dioxide make the dough rise.

Figure 15–8

This diagram shows the bread-making process. (Oxford Designers & Illustrators Ltd./Pearson Education Ltd)

FOCUS ON SCIENCE
VITAL WHEAT GLUTEN

Vital wheat gluten is concentrated dried gluten protein that has been derived from wheat flour by removing starch and the bran. Vital wheat gluten contains 75 to 80 percent protein. Although sometimes called *gluten flour*, vital wheat gluten and gluten flour are not the same. Gluten flour typically has a protein level 40 to 45 percent. Contrast either of these, however, to the protein levels found in all-purpose (9.5 to 11.5 percent) or bread flour (11.5 to 13.5 percent).

Because gluten retains the gas and steam formed during baking, vital wheat gluten is an essential ingredient when baking with soy flour or soy powder. Soy does not contain the proteins needed to form gluten; therefore, the soy-based doughs will not rise or hold shape like doughs made from wheat flour. Either vital wheat gluten or gluten flour may be used in a variety of yeast bread recipes as a means to raise the protein content and therefore result in greater gluten development. Vital wheat gluten is also used to make some meat protein alternatives.

or the type of bread being prepared. When preparing bread on a humid day, more flour may be needed to achieve a soft but not sticky dough. Breads such as ciabatta or European-style dinner rolls may be prepared with water content as high as 70 to 80 percent to create the open texture characteristics of these breads [10, 22]. These bread doughs with very high water percentages will be softer and may require special handling.

Liquid

Yeast breads typically use 3:1 flour:liquid ratio. Bread dough is about 40 percent water depending on formulation. The liquid used in making bread may include water, milk, potato water, whey, or eggs. The yeast needs water for activation, but the temperature is critical. The type of yeast used influences the temperature of liquid as well as how the liquid is added. Active dry yeast must be rehydrated by dissolving yeast in a small amount of warm water ($100-110^{\circ}$F). Yeast cell permeability returns to normal with water between 105 and 115°F ($40-46^{\circ}$C). Hotter water will harm yeast, and over $135-137^{\circ}$F the yeast dies. Cooler temperatures cause low yeast activity resulting in decreased dough quality. Instant dry yeast is added directly to dry ingredients. Liquids are heated to $120-130^{\circ}$F before adding to dry ingredients. Always use a thermometer to check liquid temperature before combining with yeast.

Water is essential in bread dough to hydrate flour starch and proteins contributing to gluten development. Adequate water absorption and mixing are essential for good yeast bread. Flour hydration is a rapid process. If water levels are too low, bread dough is stiff and lacks cohesiveness. If water levels are too high, a batter exists and proper dough development cannot occur. Too much water produces a sticky dough that cannot be properly manipulated. Dough consistency influences how the gluten network can form and flex to capture and maintain the pressure from carbon dioxide gas produced by yeast. Carbon dioxide produces large amounts of pressure inside the

gluten network, so a weak gluten network will collapse under pressure yielding a bread of low volume.

In bread dough, 40 percent of the water is associated with the starch, 31 percent with protein, and 23 percent with flour pentosan gums, which have high water-binding capacity. Water absorption capacity of flour depends on flour protein content and quality, as well as the amount of mechanically damaged starch granules (more damaged starch granules lead to higher water absorption). Water is essential for the partial gelatinization of starch, which contributes to bread structure [18]. Other components, such as sugar or salt, are dissolved or dispersed in the liquid. Salt and sugar also bind water, affecting flour hydration.

The type of liquid used will affect the characteristics of the dough and bread flavor. Water is used in lean doughs when a crisp crust is desirable. Milk is about 87 percent water, so it is often used in bread production. The addition of milk and egg results in a tender bread, improved texture, better dough handling, crust color, flavor, nutritional value, and keeping quality. Milk contributes nutritive value complementing wheat flour's limiting amino acids lysine, methionine, and tryptophan.

A small quantity of mashed potato may be added to bread dough. Cooked potato starch is readily used by amylase, so potato or potato water is often used in bread production. Cooked potato introduces gelatinized starch into the mixture, favoring fermentation and also enhancing the keeping quality and flavor of the baked bread. If the liquid is milk, it should be scalded (heated just below boiling point) to denature serum proteins. Serum milk proteins have a softening effect on gluten and cause a decreased loaf volume. Pasteurization alone does not negate the negative effects of serum proteins. The scalded milk is cooled to $104-113^{\circ}$F ($40-45^{\circ}$C). Dried milk solids and dried whey powders are used by commercial bakers as the proteins are denatured by drying. The dried milk is added with the dried ingredients.

An excessive amount of liquid in a recipe will dilute gluten and result in decreased loaf volume. Too little liquid will make a dry, stiff, inelastic dough that is slow to rise. Too small a proportion of moisture may not provide enough water for optimal gluten development and may result in decreased loaf volume of the finished bread.

Salt

Salt (sodium chloride, NaCl) is an essential ingredient in bread [17, 55]. It is added to bread as a flavor enhancer and has an important role in dough rheology. Salt contributes flavor to the baked product. Bread without salt is rather flat and tasteless.

Salt makes dough stronger [17]. Yeast doughs without salt are slack and sticky with less developed gluten [4, 17]. Salt has a firming effect on gluten structure [45]. It retards yeast fermentation; therefore, salt increases the time required for bread dough to rise. A reduction in salt levels can produce minimal differences in dough rheology and sensory qualities [27]. Bread made without salt has an inferior texture and grain; it is crumbly in texture and may easily become overly light [17, 27].

The amount of salt to produce good flavor in bread is approximately 1 teaspoon per 1 pound loaf or 1–2 percent salt based on flour weight. Excessive salt greater than 3 percent flour weight yields dough that is stiff and difficult to work [4]. An excess of salt should be avoided from the standpoint of both texture and flavor.

Sugar

Although sugar is not a necessary ingredient in a yeast bread formula, it is often added to bread dough formulations. Sugar impacts fermentation, adds sweetness, contributes to a texture, and promotes browning. The sugar in bread dough comes from three sources: (1) present in the flour, (2) produced by the action of enzymes hydrolyzing starch, and (3) added as an ingredient [34].

The rate of fermentation is increased by the addition of sugar. Sucrose is a readily available food for yeast; the yeast will metabolize sucrose as a food source before maltose. Bread with a small amount of sugar rises in a shorter period. If larger amounts of sugar are used, however, as in sweet rolls, the action of the yeast is somewhat repressed. Therefore, a higher proportion of yeast should be used or the fermentation and proofing periods should be extended if the dough is very sweet. Sugar also contributes to the flavor, sweetness, texture, and browning in yeast breads. Although the browning of bread is the result primarily of the **Maillard reaction**, sugar also contributes to browning.

For loaf breads, 2 teaspoons to 1½ tablespoons of sugar per 1 pound loaf are common amounts used. Yeast dough for rich rolls typically contains slightly more sugar—about 2 to 4 tablespoons per cup of liquid. Honey, corn syrup, brown sugar, or molasses may be substituted for granulated sugar for added flavor and color components.

Fat

Fat is not an essential ingredient in yeast bread production. Butter or shortening is typically used when fat is added to yeast bread formulas. Breads with added fat are typically softer and more palatable for longer periods of time than breads without added fat. Thus, fat increases bread shelf life. Fat increases bread crumb tenderness. Improved dough handling is facilitated by fat.

Added fat increases the extensibility of gluten, leading to increased loaf volume and improved texture. Fat can increase bread loaf volume by 10 percent [17, 33, 45, 58]. For loaf breads, 1 to 1½ tablespoons of fat per 1 pound loaf are sufficient to improve tenderness, flavor, and keeping quality. Two to four tablespoons or more per cup of liquid may be used in roll dough for increased tenderness.

Dough Conditioners and Other Ingredients

Dough conditioning formulations are commonly added to commercially prepared yeast doughs. These dough conditioners may be added in countless combinations to strengthen the desirable characteristics of the dough.

Dough conditioners contain functional ingredients to improve processing and product quality. *Vital gluten* is used to increase dough strength, water absorption, and dough tolerance while increasing loaf volume and crumb texture. *Yeast nutrients*, such as monocalcium phosphate and calcium sulfate, are inorganic salts that supply nitrogen or phosphorous needed for yeast growth.

Adjustments to raise or lower pH are accomplished by adding calcium salts (calcium carbonate and calcium sulfate raise pH, monocalcium phosphate lowers pH), which act as *pH regulators*. *Oxidizing agents* act on the gluten structure to produce a better-handling dough and a bread with finer texture, better volume, and a softer crumb. **Potassium bromate** is a slow-acting oxidizer that yields oven spring. Ascorbic acid is now the most commonly used oxidative flour improver [45]. The U.S. Food and Drug Administration has approved several oxidizing substances for use as dough conditioners, including ascorbic acid, calcium iodate, azodicarbonamide, and calcium peroxide [55]. *Reducing agents* such as L-cysteine and non-leavening yeast act on the gluten to increase extensibility and decrease elasticity. They also shorten mixing time [1]. Reducing agents are sometimes combined with oxidizing agents to optimally develop gluten. Ascorbic acid and L-cysteine used together led to increased loaf volume and crumb porosity compared to using each component alone [47].

Emulsifiers enhance dough stability, soften dough to produce a more flexible dough, and result in a finer and softer crumb [45]. Dough conditioning emulsifiers include lecithin, mono- and diglycerides, diacetyl tartaric esters of mono- and diglycerides, polysorbate 60, and sodium stearoyl lactylates.

Enzymes added to flours or doughs can initiate improvements such as retardation of staling, enhancement of bread crust color, oven spring, and softer crumb. Common enzymes used in bread production include **amylases**, disatatic malt syrup, malt flour, **oxidase**, carbohydrase, and **proteases** [1]. Most of the enzymes that are commercially available for use in bakery processing come from fungi and bacteria [12].

New bakery ingredients continue to be developed. Certified organic yeast grown in organic wort is now available. Now baker's yeast gene pool has been tapped to develop yeasts that tolerate high sugar levels and freezing temperatures, combat mold, and increase nutrients such as vitamin D. Isolated strains are being developed to combat the formation of carcinogenic acrylamides that form during bread baking and toasting [14].

Whey protein ingredients have been found to improve the mixing of bread dough while producing high-quality breads with desirable characteristics [36]. Rice bran extracts offer functionality as both a dough conditioner and an emulsifier. Encapsulated flavorings offer advantages in flavor and bread quality. Encapsulated cinnamon is useful because raw cinnamon added to bread dough will inhibit rising [36]. The addition of garlic to wheat flour doughs has been shown to weaken the dough and result in an undesirable crumb and low volume; however, these negative effects are not present when encapsulated garlic is used [31].

MIXING AND HANDLING

The mixing and kneading of bread greatly influence the final quality of the bread. During mixing, ingredients are blended into a mostly homogeneous mass, air is incorporated into the dough creating many small gas nuclei, and gluten is developed. Flour particles rapidly absorb water in the early stages of mixing. With continued mixing, moisture is distributed throughout the dough. The creation of many small gas nuclei during mixing is significant, because during

fermentation, yeast increases the size of existing gas cells but does not create new gas cells. Thus, for a fine crumb, air must be incorporated into the dough during mixing [45].

The characteristics of dough change during mixing and kneading (**Figure 15–9**). Initially on homogenization of the ingredients, the dough tears easily and sticks to the hands. With increased mixing, the dough becomes smoother, is less sticky, and has more coherence. At this stage, the dough will pull away from the sides of a mixer. In the last stage, the dough is well developed. The dough displays strong coherence, and a small ball of dough may be stretched into a thin film without tearing or breaking, sometimes referred to as "the windowpane test" (**Figure 15–10**).

Figure 15–9

Yeast dough (barely mixed, sticky mix, fully kneaded). (© Douglas and Barbara Scheule)

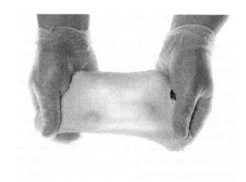

Figure 15–10

The windowpane test. (Knorre/Shutterstock)

FOCUS ON SCIENCE

HOW DO DOUGH CONDITIONERS STRENGTHEN THE YEAST DOUGH?

Oxidizing substances are used as dough conditioners to produce a bread with finer texture, a softer crumb, and better volume. So how does this dough strengthening and conditioning effect occur? Disulfide bonding strengthens gluten. Sulfur atoms on the protein molecules, however, can bind with hydrogen atoms. Sulfur bound to hydrogen cannot form a disulfide linkage. Oxidizers work to improve doughs by "stripping" hydrogen atoms from the sulfur–hydrogen (sulfhydryl) linkages, and therefore more sulfur is available for the formation of the gluten-strengthening disulfide bond.

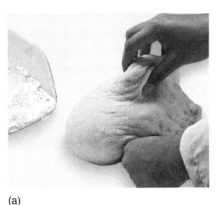 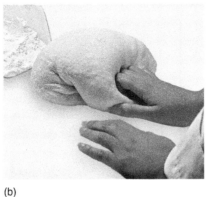 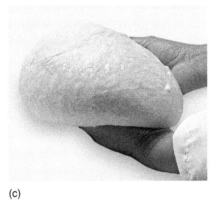

(a)   (b)   (c)

Figure 15–11

To knead bread, (a) bring the edge of the dough toward you, (b) push the dough away from you with your fist or the heel of your hand, and (c) turn the dough one-quarter of a turn and repeat the process until the dough is elastic and smooth. (Richard Embery/ Pearson Education)

The dough cannot be similarly stretched in the earlier stages. If the dough is overmixed, the dough will become sticky, extensible, and excessively soft [45]. Overmixing is most likely to occur when using a mechanical mixer.

Two basic methods of mixing yeast bread are the straight-dough method and the sponge method. The batter method also may be used for some breads. Kneading is an important part of the bread-making process (**Figure 15–11**).

Straight-Dough Method

In the mixing of yeast bread by the straight-dough method, the liquid is generally warmed with the sugar, salt, and softened fat. If milk is used, it must be scalded to denature serum proteins that will interfere with dough quality. Then the scalded milk is cooled so that it will not be so hot that it kills the yeast. Depending on the type of yeast being used, the yeast will be mixed with the dry ingredients or rehydrated in warm water. Instant quick-rising active dry yeast hydrates quickly and is mixed directly with the dry ingredients.

About one-third of the flour is blended with the liquid ingredients and vigorously mixed. Beating the batter blends ingredients uniformly, starts the development of gluten (**Figure 15–12**), and incorporates air cells. The remainder of the flour is added gradually to form a dough that is "kneaded" in the mixer or transferred to a floured board for kneading by hand. The dough is kneaded (see "Kneading" later in the chapter) until it has a smooth, satiny outside surface.

Sponge Method

The sponge method is a two-part fermentation method where 50 to 70 percent of the flour is mixed with the liquid, yeast, and water to form thick batter called the sponge. The sponge is sometimes called a *poolish*. Salt and sugar may also be added at this phase. The sponge is allowed to ferment or ripen until it becomes bubbly and doubled in size. After the sponge is light and full of gas bubbles, it is then made into dough by the addition of the remaining flour, salt (if not added earlier), and other recipe ingredients. The dough is then ready to be kneaded. The sponge may be kept refrigerated for up to 24 hours before using [25]. Much of the bread made commercially in the United States is made using the sponge method [17].

Batter Method

Breads may be made from batters that contain less flour than doughs. The batter method modifies the straight-dough method by eliminating the kneading and shaping steps. The batters are allowed to rise at least once in the bowl and/or in the baking pan. These unkneaded breads usually have a more open grain and uneven surface than kneaded breads and lack the elasticity of the crumb; however, less preparation time is required.

Automatic Bread Machines

Automatic bread machines have gained popularity in the home. With the convenience of these machines, you may, if you desire, plan to return home and find fragrant odors of baking bread permeating your kitchen. In using bread machines, the ingredients are placed in the pan, and the timing cycle is set according to the manufacturer's instructions. At the scheduled time, the loaf of bread will be mixed, proofed, and baked. To make specialty breads, the dough cycle may be used, signaling when the dough may be removed for shaping, final proofing, and baking in a conventional oven. Bread machine or instant quick-rising active dry yeast is well suited for use in bread machines (**Figure 15–13**).

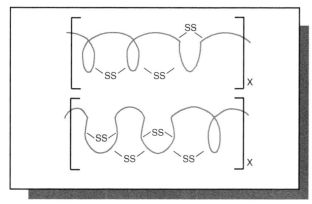

Proposed structure of gluten molecules.

(a)

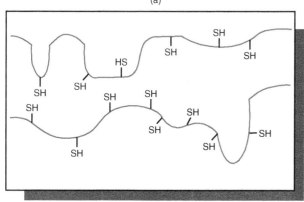

Expanded and relaxed gluten
molecules after mechanical mixing.

(b)

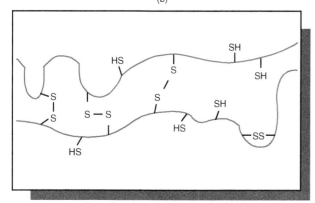

Formation of new linkages by chemical
oxidation to strengthen the expanded
gluten structure.

(c)

Figure 15–12

Gluten molecules. (Reprinted from Tieckelmann, R. E. and Steele, R.E.Higher assay grade of calcium peroxide improves properties of dough. *Food Technology*, 45 Issue (1), 108, 1991. © Institute of Food Technologists)

Figure 15–13

Bread dough containing quick-rising yeast (left) rises substantially faster than dough containing the same amount of regular active dry yeast (right). Both doughs proofed 15 minutes at 100°F (38°C). (Reprinted from N. B. Trivedi, E. J. Cooper, and B. L. Bruinsma. Development and applications of quick-rising yeast. *Food Technology*, 38(6), 51, 1984. Copyright © by Institute of Food Technologists)

swollen particles of the protein fractions, gliadin and glutenin, adhere to each other and become aligned in the long elastic strands of gluten. The development of gluten during kneading is important to provide structure and strength for the dough and the finished loaf of bread. Starch granules from the flour, entrapped in the developing gluten, also play an important role in bread structure.

Kneading by Hand. Skillful handling of the dough ball is necessary at the beginning of kneading. The mass may be collected into a ball of dough that, with proper handling, tends to remain smooth on the outer surface in contact with the board. All wrinkles and cracks are best kept on the side in contact with the hands to minimize the tendency for the dough to stick to the board. Wet spots on the outside surface may require frequent coating with flour until the dough becomes elastic enough to knead easily (Figure 15–11).

The kneading movement is a rhythmical one in which the fingers are used to pull the mass over into position for kneading and the palm or heel of the hand is used for applying pressure to the dough. Forcing the fingers into the dough or using too heavy a pressure tends to keep the mass of dough sticky and difficult to handle.

Kneading by Machine. Various mixers are available with motors powerful enough to mix bread dough completely, thus eliminating the necessity of kneading by hand. The manufacturer's directions should be followed in the use of these mixers. Special attachments called *dough hooks* are commonly used in both commercial and commercial-style home mixers. The dough should cling to the dough hook in one ball as mixing progresses. If the dough is too soft to form a ball, additional flour should be added.

Kneading

Kneading of bread dough is essential for the development of strong elastic gluten strands from relatively high-protein flour. During the kneading process, the

When kneading bread by machine, the dough can overheat due to friction during the mixing and kneading process. This effect can be observed when making large quantities of bread in food service or when using a food processor in the home setting. This undesirable rise in dough temperature can be controlled by a formula that calculates the desired temperature of liquid by taking into account the friction heat generated by the equipment, flour temperature, and room temperature [32]. Recipes provided by home food processors generally recommend a specific water temperature, which is cooler than used in traditional hand-mixed recipes, to control the dough temperature.

Quality Considerations. Whether kneading by hand or by machine, care must be used during kneading to avoid the incorporation of excess flour into the mixture, which results in too stiff a dough. With the development of a good hand-kneading technique, it is surprising how little flour need be used on a board for the handling of any kind of dough. Later handling can be done with practically no flour because of the increased extensibility of the dough after fermentation. Although overmixing by hand is unlikely, dough may be kneaded too much by machine. As discussed earlier, overmixed dough will become sticky and excessively soft.

Properly kneaded dough should be smooth and elastic; there should be evidence of small air pockets or blisters under the surface of the dough. The "window pane" test is a procedure to see if dough has been sufficiently kneaded and gluten formation has occurred. The test involves taking a small piece of kneaded dough and using both hands to gently pull and stretch the dough. A well-kneaded dough will stretch without tearing into a thin translucent sheet resembling bubble gum bubble (Figure 15–10).

FERMENTATION, SHAPING, AND PROOFING

Fermentation may be described as the time between the start of mixing and shaping of the dough. Functionally, the fermentation period continues during dough development while the dough rises or increases in volume and is allowed to rise until it is at least double its original volume, after which it is portioned, shaped, and placed in baking pans. Proofing (the second rising) increases the volume of the shaped dough to result in desirable properties during baking. Decorative finishes may be added to the dough following shaping but prior to proofing and baking.

Fermentation

Fermentation is the stage where the dough is ripened; this is sometimes called the first rising. Time, temperature, environment, gluten strength, and yeast action are important control points for the fermentation process. Fermentation initially is an aerobic reaction before changing to anaerobic reaction. The respiration of the yeast consumes the oxygen trapped in the dough during the first few minutes, and thus the fermentation reaction in bread is mainly an anaerobic reaction [17, 45]. The fermentation reaction may be shown by the following equation [17]:

$$C_6H_{12}O_6 + \text{Yeast} \rightarrow 2C_2H_5OH + 2CO_2$$

glucose   ethanol   carbon dioxide

The carbon dioxide gas produced during yeast fermentation causes the bread dough to expand and volume rises. Ethyl alcohol is volatilized during baking. By-products of the fermentation reaction also include many flavor substances. Organic acids,

---

UP CLOSE
GLUTEN DEVELOPMENT

Protein particles in the flour are moistened and start to swell as the dough is mixed. With mixing, interactions occur and include hydrogen bonding. The hydrogen atoms of –OH or –SH group in the protein molecules interchange and establish weak bonds [17]. Increased interaction leads to the development of the gluten complex. The gluten complex is composed of glutenin and gliadin.

Gluten may be envisioned as a coiled protein that contains a number of disulfide bonds (–S–S–) linking parts of the molecule together to provide more strength and rigidity [50] (see Figure 15–12). During mixing, many of these bonds are broken, and the gluten becomes more expanded and relaxed so that it may be stretched by the leavening gases. The gluten is "developed" and becomes more extensible and elastic.

At one time, gluten development theory suggested that glutenin and gliadin molecules merged to form a network of giant gluten molecules. Recent research, however, suggests that the breakdown of glutenins occurs into smaller subunits that then aggregate into larger proteins after mixing [45]. ∎

amino acids, and other substances produced during fermentation participate in complex reactions that result in characteristic bread flavor.

Favorable Conditions for Fermentation. During fermentation, the dough should be in a warm, moist environment. Fermentation can take place over a wide range of temperatures, but the best flavor is probably developed at 79 to 90°F (26 to 32°C). Cold inhibits yeast activity, and a temperature of about 130°F (55°C) destroys yeast cells.

Dough fermentation can be slowed by chilling or retarding the dough. Retardation may be done for 2–36 hours at temperatures 38–50°F (3–10°C). Commercial bakeries use a special refrigerator called a "retarder." Sometimes commercial bakeries retard formed loaves prior to proofing for production and baking scheduling needs.

Dough undergoing retardation may need to be punched periodically during this process to redistribute yeast cells. Yeast cells will die if they exhaust their nutrient source. Dough containing dead yeast cells result in dough yielding lower volume and deteriorated crumb qualities. Excessively warm temperatures may favor the growth of organisms that produce undesirable flavors in bread. Yeast dough at 98°F (37°C) will rise rapidly, but will often be too sticky and hard to handle.

Dough that is exposed to air develops a crust or film that must later be discarded to avoid the formation of heavy streaks throughout the dough. To avoid crust formation, the dough is covered or placed in a proofing cabinet. Proofing cabinets control the temperature and the humidity, providing ideal conditions for the fermentation and proofing of the dough. If one is not available, the bowl containing the dough may be placed in a pan of warm water and then covered with another pan of the same size. The vaporization of moisture from the surface of the water maintains a humidity that keeps the bread surface from drying out. Alternatively, the surface of the dough may be lightly greased and the bowl covered with a plastic wrap or damp cloth.

Optimal Fermentation. The number of times the dough should be allowed to rise in the fermentation period depends on the flour strength. The strength of the gluten network depends on flour strength determined by flour protein content, which is the strong gluten network foundation. A strong expandable gluten network allows for carbon dioxide gases to be trapped and expand in the gluten network. A weak gluten network will not hold increased pressure from expanding gases. Thus, the weakened gluten network allows gases to escape, yielding a low-volume bread loaf.

Dough made from strong gluten flours may be allowed to rise more times than dough from flours with lower protein content. Weak gluten structures become too highly dispersed with too long a fermentation period. Bread must be baked before gluten strands become so thin and weak that they break, thus allowing carbon dioxide gas to escape.

Optimal fermentation occurs when the dough is light and approximately doubled in size. Fermentation time typically is around an hour or more. However, time required for yeast dough to rise depends on the proportion of yeast in the dough, fermentation temperature, as well as proportion of salt, sugar, and dough stiffness. Sometimes optimal fermentation is tested by quickly pressing two finger tips about ½ inch into dough; if indentation remains, the dough has doubled in size. Dough should barely spring back as an indentation from fingers is left in the dough. In dough made from all-purpose flour, optimal fermentation bulk may be less than in dough made from stronger flours such as bread flour. Fermentation can be slowed by refrigeration.

Overfermentation results in poor oven spring and is likely to produce a loaf that is flat or sunken on top. The bread will have a coarse grain and thick cell walls. It also may have an unpleasant sour odor and flavor and a crust that does not brown well. The volume is small, and the loaf is heavy and compact. In contrast, underfermentation produces bread that has thick cell walls and is heavy, small in volume, and less tender than bread that has fermented sufficiently to bring about a desirable dispersion of the gluten. Dough typically doubles in volume when fermentation is complete.

Punching Down

Once the dough has doubled in size, the dough is punched down or is lightly mixed in the mixer (**Figure 15–14**). The punching should be a gentle handling of dough so not to tear or matt gluten strands as the object is to keep the gluten network around gas cells. The key purpose of punching down the dough is to subdivide the gas cells to produce more smaller cells, redistribute yeast cells, redistribute food substrate, and equalize temperature created in dough by the fermentation process [17, 45]. Yeast cells are immobile in dough and rely on food substrates diffusing to them. As dough expands during fermentation, the food substrates and yeast become farther apart, so punching the dough brings yeast and the food substrates closer together for more carbon dioxide to be produced.

Shaping (Molding) and Panning

After the fermentation stage, the dough is divided into portions (sometimes referred to as scaling the dough) and shaped or molded (**Figure 15–15**). Dough is easier to handle if it is allowed to "relax" or sit covered for a few minutes after being punched down.

(a)

(b)

Figure 15–14

(a) The dough before rising. (b) Punching down the risen dough. (Richard Embery/Pearson Education)

Figure 15–15

Dough being portioned or scaled prior to shaping. A bench knife is used to divide the dough into portions. (Richard Embery/ Pearson Education)

Figure 15–16

Placing three small dough balls into a muffin tin to make cloverleaf rolls. This is a simple yet attractive way to shape rolls before proofing. (Richard Embery/Pearson Education)

Figure 15–17

Lidded Pullman loaf after proofing. The lidded pan makes a bread loaf that can be sliced into perfectly square slices.
(Richard Embery/Pearson Education)

Shaping should be gentle to avoid tearing or matting gluten strands. Large gas bubbles should be expelled during shaping or molding to avoid large air holes in the bread. Dough portions are shaped and placed in pans or on baking sheets. Dough is shaped into a variety of shapes for loafs or individual rolls or buns depending on the product (**Figure 15–16**). Pan loaves are typically rolled into a cylinder. Pullman loaves such as sandwich breads are baked in loaf pans with sliding lids to make bread square, which is ideal for sandwiches (**Figure 15–17**). French bread is long cylinder roll called a bâtards for a French baguette (**Figure 15–18**). Hearth breads are typically round and baked in hearth ovens by placing on a peel. Some breads are molded in cloth-lined baskets called *bannetons* or coiled willow baskets called *brotforms*

Figure 15–18

Shaping bâtards for French baguettes. (Richard Embery/Pearson Education)

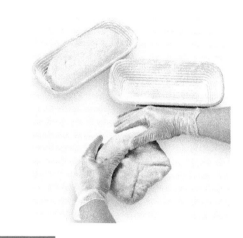

Figure 15–19

Dough proofed in brotform. (Richard Embery/Pearson Education)

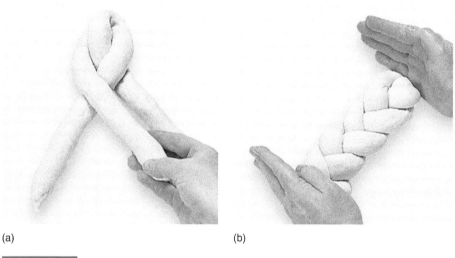

(a)   (b)

Figure 15–20

Bread dough may be braided by rolling three balls of dough into long ropes. The ropes are pressed together at the top and then braided. (a) Ropes of dough are crossed over to begin braiding. (b) Finished braid ready to be proofed and then baked. (Richard Embery/Pearson Education)

(**Figure 15–19**). Free-form loaves can be placed between folds or floured linen or canvas clothes to hold shape during proofing. Dough may be braided for a variety of breads (**Figure 15–20**).

Greasing the inside bottom of the loaf pan prior to shaped dough placement aids in removing the baked bread from the pan. The greasing of side walls is optional, but a somewhat larger volume of loaf may result from allowing the dough to cling to the side walls while rising. The shape of the pan used to bake the bread will influence the product. Shallow pans appear to put less strain on the dough.

In commercial bakeries, in the process called scaling, the dough is divided into equal portions and then rounded into smooth lumps. The rounded portions are benched, which means the portions are allowed to rest a short time to relax gluten strands and make shaping easier. Some bakeries place the round portions in proofers during this period. In many commercial bakeries, the shaping or molding steps are automated. Dough undergoes a process called sheeting as it is passed through rollers. Then the dough is curled and rolled into a cylinder. The seam is placed down in pan or hearth breads to avoid splitting during baking.

Next, the shaped and panned dough is ready for the second fermentation phase. The fermentation of panned dough is called **proofing**, which is discussed below. The proofing fermentation is the second dough rising and proceeds at a faster rate in about half the time.

Decorative Finishes

Before proofing, breads may be shaped into rolls or braided to create rolls and breads (Figure 15–20). Additional decorative touches may be added

Figure 15–21

Decorative slashes on San Francisco Sourdough bread.

(Richard Embery/Pearson Education)

immediately before baking that change the appearance of the bread. A glaze or a wash may be brushed onto the dough to attach seeds, oats, and other toppings to the crust. A wash also may be used to create a shiny, crisp, or soft crust. A whole egg and water wash will promote a shiny crust, whereas a whole egg and milk wash will create a shiny, soft crust. Egg white and water are used when a shiny, firm crust is desired. Milk or cream will make the crust soft, and a water wash will create a crisp crust [24]. Water is sometimes used on hard-crusted products such as French breads.

Many breads are slashed to create an attractive design on the crust (**Figure 15–21**). Doughs are scored or slashed by cutting lightly into the surface-proofed dough with a sharp knife, razor, or baker's "lame" just before baking. Professional bakers use a tool called a lame (pronounced "LAHM"), which is French for "blade." A lame has straight or curved blades attached to a long wooden handle.

In addition to the decorative effect, scoring allows for the escape of gases and additional rising during baking [24]. Scoring loaves prior to baking also ensures the bread loaves expand in the right direction during baking.

Proofing

After the dough has undergone fermentation and is molded into a loaf and placed in a baking pan, it is allowed to rise again. This final rising in the pan is called *proofing*. Proofing is done at 80°F (27°C) or above, typically 86−95°F (30−35°C), and 85 percent relative humidity [17]. During the proofing period, the dough expands and fills pan. Proofing should be terminated when the loaf has approximately doubled in size and the dough does not spring back when it is lightly touched. Proofing time is typically 30–60 minutes. Like the initial fermentation process, the surface of the dough should remain moist by using a proofing cabinet or covering the dough. After proofing, the dough is ready for baking.

Proper proofing will have an impact on the volume of the baked bread. Under-proofed bread will be small and dense after baking. Over-proofed breads will likely collapse in the oven.

Modifications of the above bread-making procedures exist. Bread can be made at home with only one rising period prior to shaping of the loaf or

---

UP CLOSE
WHAT HAPPENS DURING FERMENTATION?

Growth of Gas Nuclei

The gas nuclei in the dough initially contain about 20 percent oxygen and 80 percent nitrogen. As the yeast consumes the oxygen, only nitrogen remains, and the fermentation process becomes an anaerobic reaction. Carbon dioxide, produced by the yeast, is diffused and retained in the dough as (1) gas within the gas cells and (2) dissolved in the aqueous phase of the dough [17]. Cell membranes stretch and the dough rises.

Action of Enzymes

Fermentation is catalyzed by a variety of enzymes produced in the yeast cells. A starch-splitting enzyme called *amylase* is present in flour. In commercial bread baking, additional amylase may be added. This enzyme catalyzes the hydrolysis of starch to dextrins and maltose. Dextrins help to maintain freshness of breads, and maltose may be fermented by the yeast or can contribute to the color of the crust [45].

Proteases are found at low levels in wheat flour, but soften gluten. Thus, proteases at low levels can improve the dough handling during mixing [45]. Proteases hydrolyze proteins to peptides and amino acids. If the proteases are too active, they may hydrolyze too much of the protein and produce harmful effects, such as poor texture and decreased volume.

Increase in Acidity

Acidity increases in bread dough from a pH of about 6.0 when first mixed to a pH of 5.0 during fermentation [17]. The increase in acidity is attributed largely to the carbon dioxide, but also organic acids, mainly acetic and lactic. Increased acidity promotes fermentation and amylase activity, holding some unwanted organisms in check. Greater dispersion of the gluten with loss of elasticity and tenacity also occurs as acidity increases. ∎

rolls. A dough that has been punched down during fermentation and allowed to rise a second time before shaping will have a better crumb texture and larger **oven spring** [45]. Commercial bakeries have experimented with various modifications of standard bread-making procedures with mixed results and limited success. The *continuous bread-making procedure* uses a preferment, and dough is extruded into the pan prior to proofing and baking. Short-time baking systems mixing dough in a partial vacuum have been used in an attempt to save labor costs and time [17]. New equipment, methods, and ingredients are continually being researched, developed, and used by the baking industry.

BAKING BREAD

Conventional Baking

Heat causes changes in bread dough during baking. The gas production and dough expansion are greatly accelerated causing a sharp rising of the dough; this is referred to as *oven spring*. Oven spring is the phenomenon involving the rapid bread volume rise that occurs during the first few minutes of baking. Oven spring can be observed through an oven window. The oven spring period lasts only about ten minutes. Rapid oven spring occurs when loaf interior reaches $131^{\circ}F$ ($60^{\circ}C$); after this point, expansion is reduced. As heat increases, the yeast becomes more active (prior to the point of too hot). Gases increase in volume, water and ethanol vaporize, and carbon dioxide becomes less soluble. Water starts to move from the protein to the starch as gelatinization starts. Baking starts as the elastic dough starts to become a rigid crumb.

Baking temperatures and times vary according to the type of dough and size of mass to be baked. Most recipes recommend oven temperatures of 375 to $425^{\circ}F$ (191 to $218^{\circ}C$) for bread baking. Yeast dough is put into a hot oven. Lean yeast doughs are baked at higher temperature than rich doughs which brown more readily. Whether a hot or a moderate oven is used at the beginning depends on the extent of rising before the bread is placed in the oven. Too hot an oven, however, sets the bread before optimum oven spring occurs, thus reducing the final volume and affecting the texture. Hearth-type breads, such as ciabatta, sourdough, and pizza, are baked in a hearth oven where the proofed shaped dough is placed in oven via a long-handled peel.

Doneness. The interior loaf temperature gradually rises until a temperature is reached that destroys yeast, inactivates enzymes, and stops fermentation. Alcohol produced during fermentation is volatilized and driven off during the bread baking. The remaining baking time is needed to ensure the center loaf reaches around $100^{\circ}C$ ($195-205^{\circ}F$) and moisture is reduced to the desired level. The maximum temperature of the interior of the loaf is approximately the boiling point of water, but as moisture evaporates from the exterior surface and crust formation occurs, the temperature of the crust becomes higher than that of the crumb. Interior temperatures over $100^{\circ}C$ may cause a dry product. Bread interior should be moist with only the crust browning later in the baking cycle.

Gluten undergoes a gradual change in properties over a rather wide range of temperatures (122 to $175^{\circ}F/50$ to $80^{\circ}C$) and finally becomes firm as it coagulates. Partial gelatinization of starch occurs during baking. Starch absorbs only about one-third of its weight of water at room temperature, but because it constitutes about four-fifths of flour, it is responsible for about half the total water absorption of flours made into dough. As the gluten loses water during baking and the starch swells with the imbibition of additional water during heating, at least partial gelatinization of the starch is made possible [28]. In fresh bread, the gluten holds less water, and the starch holds more water than in the uncooked dough. The partially gelatinized starch contributes to bread structure as it is embedded within strands of coagulated gluten proteins.

The Maillard reaction appears to be chiefly responsible for the brown crust color in baked bread. The browning reaction also contributes to bread flavor. Some browning may occur due to caramelization. Malt derivatives are used commercially to enhance crust color. Browning of bread, as with other baked products, is influenced by the type of pan used. Pans with dark or dull finishes absorb heat more readily than bright shiny ones, which reflect heat. Therefore, the surfaces of bread in contact with dull or dark pans brown more readily and uniformly.

Bread is generally considered to be done when the crust is golden brown and the sound of a loaf of bread is hollow. These indicators, however, are subjective. Alternatively, the internal temperature of the bread may be taken with an instant-read thermometer. A temperature reading of 195 to $200^{\circ}F$ (91 to $93^{\circ}C$) is suggested [41].

Hard-crusted breads such as French baguettes are baked with steam injected into the oven. Steam is injected to the oven during the early part of baking. The steam allows the crust to remain soft during the early baking stages so the bread can expand prior to crust formation. The steam delays the crust formation. If no steam is used, the crust forms early, yielding a thick and heavy crust.

UP CLOSE
COMMERCIAL BREAD BAKING

Numerous technological advances have been applied in the baking industry. Basic bread-making principles remain the same, but the equipment, processes, and ingredient variation used differ in commercial bread compared to the home baker.

Pure yeast cultures and standardized ingredients, including dough additives, are available to commercial bakers. Powerful mixers, fermentation rooms, dough dividers, and automatic proofing, baking, and wrapping systems are used. Through the 1940s, the predominant bread-making system in the United States was a sponge-and-dough system. Since then, several alternative methods have been developed, including a conventional straight-dough method, a continuous-dough process, and a short-time bread-making system. Short-time doughs involve a single mixing step and little or no bulk fermentation of the dough before panning. Short-time breads are generally made with warmer doughs, more yeast, and higher levels of oxidants than are used in the preparation of conventional doughs [57]. High-speed mixing of doughs substitutes to some degree for the fermentation period. Addition of oxidizing and/or reducing agents also helps to develop the dough with less fermentation required. Shortening the fermentation period and automation in commercial bread production saves time and labor expense. ■

Microwave Baking

White bread is generally not acceptably cooked by microwaves because of the lack of crust formation; however, relatively dark breads, such as rye and whole-wheat or oatmeal wheat, have been satisfactorily prepared in the microwave oven with little additional heating in a hot conventional oven. Medium (50 percent) power is generally used. Brown-and-serve rolls are successfully prepared in the microwave. They are browned in a hot conventional oven before being served.

Frozen Yeast Doughs

Frozen bread dough that is already shaped into a loaf is marketed at the retail level. Bread dough may also be frozen at home for later use. The dough is thawed at room temperature and allowed to rise before baking. This convenience food allows one to have the aroma of freshly baked bread in the kitchen without the mixing and kneading processes. The most significant problem associated with the freezing of dough is how to maintain the viability and gassing power of frozen yeasts. If the active fermentation time of the yeast is lengthy before freezing, the yeast is less stable to freezing [3]. Commercial frozen doughs use special yeast strains that remain viable for up to 2 years under frozen conditions. When preparing bread dough for the freezer at home, it has been suggested that the best approach is to freeze the bread dough after fermentation but before proofing. The bread proofs during thawing once removed from the freezer [16].

ROLLS

Rolls are individual bread servings that can be formed into a variety of shapes (**Figure 15–22**). Roll dough usually contains larger amounts of fat and sugar than are generally found in bread. Eggs may also be added, although satisfactory roll dough can be made without eggs. The eggs may be beaten lightly and added in the early stages of dough making. An egg adds about 3 tablespoons of liquid.

Rolls require 15 to 25 minutes of baking at 425°F (218°C). Pan rolls require a longer baking time than single rolls separated on a baking sheet or in muffin pans. A pan of rolls may require almost as much baking time as a pound loaf of bread.

Although any roll dough can be held in the refrigerator for 1 or 2 days before baking, refrigerator rolls are probably best made from a dough of slightly different proportions from plain rolls. For refrigerator rolls, only a moderate amount of yeast is used to avoid overfermentation, and slightly more than the usual amount of sugar is added to serve as food for the yeast during the approximately one-week period that

Figure 15–22

White, whole-wheat, and rye rolls in a variety of shapes.
(© Amanda Frye and Sophia Frye)

the dough may be held before baking. When the rolls are first mixed, they are kneaded and allowed to undergo one fermentation, after which they are punched to release gas and stored closely covered at refrigerator temperature to be used as needed. If the dough rises appreciably during holding, it is punched from time to time to release gas. When it is needed, part of the dough is removed from the refrigerator, shaped into rolls, and allowed to rise in a warm room until the rolls double in bulk. This process may require 2 to 3 hours, depending on the temperature of the dough and the room. Rolls can be formed into a variety of shapes and sizes (**Figure 15–23**).

WHOLE-GRAIN AND VARIETY BREADS

Artisan breads, flat breads, hearth breads, and other specialty breads have gained in popularity among American consumers [43, 56]. Restaurants and bakeries are featuring more of these products to satisfy the changing tastes of customers. Contrast in the flavor and texture of breads is made possible by the use of a variety of grains in various forms. Flours, meals, and flakes can all be used. Sometimes whole grains are soaked to hydrate grains prior to incorporation into bread dough. The soaking allows grains to hydrate so dry kernels don't absorb liquid needed for dough formation.

Whole-grain flours contain essentially all the vitamins and minerals, as well as fiber, present in unmilled grain and thus offer nutritional advantages over highly milled flours. USDA dietary guidelines recommend half of grains to be whole-grain products [8, 44, 53].

Whole-Wheat Bread

Whole-wheat bread is prepared with 100 percent whole-wheat flour, as defined in the Title 21 CFR 136 [55]. If some white flour is used with the whole-wheat flour in commercial bread making, the bread is labeled simply "wheat bread." Commercial "wheat" bread describes a bread made from about 75 percent white flour and 25 percent whole-wheat flour; caramel coloring is sometimes added to enhance color. "Wheat" bread should not be confused with whole-wheat bread, which is made from 100 percent whole-wheat flour as defined by Title 21 CFR 136 and 137 [55].

The procedure for mixing, fermenting, and baking whole-wheat dough is similar to that described for white bread dough, although the kneading does not have to be as extensive. The small particles of bran in whole-wheat flour interfere with the development of gluten. Even extensive kneading does not overcome this effect. Whole-wheat loaf volume is typically less white bread.

The volume and texture of whole-wheat flour breads vary by flour type or the preparation technique. If the whole-wheat flour is very finely ground, the volume of the bread made from

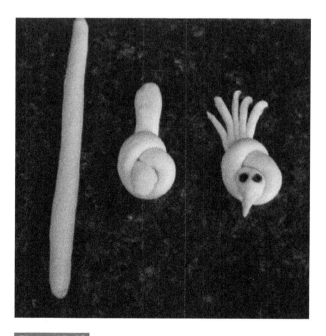

this flour may approach that of white bread. A lighter-textured whole-wheat bread made with as much as 60 percent whole-wheat flour may also be prepared by soaking the whole-wheat flour in water overnight. This soaking period softens the sharp bran edges that tend to interfere with gluten development [21].

Whole white wheat bread is relatively new in the marketplace. It is made from hard white wheat instead of hard red wheat, and thus it is fairly white in color. Because of a specialized milling process, the whole-wheat is finely milled and thus produces a soft bread without the usual hearty texture associated with whole-wheat bread made from hard red wheat. See Chapter 13 for more discussion about types of wheat and whole grains.

High-Fiber Breads

With an emphasis on the need for increased fiber in the diets of most Americans, the baking industry has developed ways of adding extra bran to breads without sacrificing quality [42]. Wheat bran decreases loaf volume. Wheat bran and water interactions appear to be responsible for the detrimental effects. However, pre-soaking and finely grinding wheat bran and the adding of shortening appear to help overcome detrimental effects of wheat bran in bread [26]. Vital wheat gluten and certain conditioners can be used to counteract the deleterious effects of up to 15 parts of bran per 85 parts of flour. Bran flakes or prepared bran cereals may be used at home as added ingredients in wheat bread or rolls to provide additional fiber.

Use of Flours Other Than Wheat

Wheat flour is an essential component of bread according to the Federal Code [55]. Some wheat flour is needed in all yeast breads to provide gluten for bread structure and lightness. Flours milled from grains other than wheat may be combined with wheat flour to give varied and flavorful baked products. Of all the grains, rye flour comes closest to wheat in terms of gluten-forming properties, but rye flour alone does not make a light loaf of bread. Rye yeast bread generally contains some wheat flour for gluten components. Approximately equal portions of rye and wheat flour yield good results. Pumpernickel bread is composed of dark rye flour and molasses.

Wheat germ or other grains are a good source of protein, vitamins, and minerals, but it also contains a **reducing substance** that has a detrimental effect on bread volume. Heat treatment inactivates this substance. A gentle heat treatment may also be used to inactivate enzymes (lipase and peroxidase) that cause rancidity in raw wheat germ, thus producing stabilized wheat germ. Heat-treated wheat germ may be added to bread in amounts of up to 15 percent of the weight of the flour with no deleterious effect on bread volume.

Soy flour increases the protein content of breads and has been used commercially to make high-protein breads. Additives are commonly used by commercial bakers to overcome the adverse effects of soy flour on the absorption, mixing, and fermentation of dough. Bread containing about ⅓ cup of soy flour to 5 cups of all-purpose flour can be satisfactorily made at home. This bread can be made higher in protein by the use of extra nonfat dry milk solids.

Other grains that may be used in bread making, in combination with wheat flour, include oatmeal, cornmeal, barley flakes, and buckwheat flour. Molasses and honey are often used as the source of sugar in whole-grain breads to contribute flavors that blend well with whole-grain products. The relatively coarse textures and dark colors of some specialty breads lend variety to meals.

Other Specialty Breads

Artisan Breads. Artisan breads are old-world-style breads generally prepared with a starter and shaped by hand. French baguettes are prepared from lean dough, which is a dough that contains only water, yeast, bread

---

EVOLUTION OF THE SANDWICH

It was an Englishman, John Montague, the fourth Earl of Sandwich, who in 1762 satisfied his hunger in a hurry by ordering two slices of meat between two pieces of bread. Thus, the sandwich was born. Over 45 billion sandwiches are now being consumed each year in America. Lord Sandwich truly started something.

Bread is the basis of all sandwiches. Around the world, bread is an important component of almost every cuisine. Bread is a great foundation for a vast variety of fillings—meats, fish, eggs, cheeses, peanut and other nut butters, tofu, vegetables, savory herbs, sauces, jelly, and condiments. Sandwiches are a great way to deliver nutritional benefits—healthy vegetables and protein foods along with whole grains [43].

Has the sandwich evolved since 1762? Certainly it has, and it promises to continue to do so in the foreseeable future. Viva la sandwich! ■

French baguettes with thin golden, crisp crust. Pattern on baguette is from scoring proofed loaves with knife to allow steam to escape during baking. (Richard Embery/Pearson Education)

Braided Challah. (Richard Embery/Pearson Education)

Brioche with top knot (Brioche á tête). (© Eddy Van Damme/Pearson Education)

Concha, a Mexican sweet roll that resembles a seashell. (© Eddy Van Damme/Pearson Education)

flour, and salt. A crisp, chewy crust with a tender interior is produced when steam is produced in the oven from a pan of hot water or a specially designed oven capable of injecting steam (**Figure 15–24**).

Brioche. Brioche is a tender bread made from a very rich dough containing butter and eggs. Brioche is often baked in a high-walled fluted pan and has a small piece of dough on top for the top knot or cap (**Figure 15–25**). Brioche has a buttery smell with a fluffy delicate crumb and evenly thin brown crust. Another egg-rich bread is challah (**Figure 15–26**). Challah is a braided loaf traditional for Jewish Sabbath. Challah has a golden brown crust and yellowish, fine, tender, and even cell crumb. A favorite Mexican sweet bread is conchas (shells), which is made to resemble sea shells. The rich sweet rolls are

coated with a colored sugar paste cut out on top to resemble a shell when baked. Conchas are traditionally vanilla and chocolate, but come in every color of the rainbow (**Figure 15–27**). Grissini are long skinny dry Italian bread sticks that are sometimes brushed with olive oil and sprinkled with salt, sesame seeds or herbs.

Flat Breads. Flat breads are traditional in many parts of the world. *Naan* is an Indian flatbread (**Figure 15–28**). Middle Eastern *pita* bread is a flat bread with a large pocket produced by steam. Stuffing the pocket with sandwich fillings can make delicious sandwiches. Other flat breads that do not contain a pocket but may be called pita bread are used for Greek gyros. *Focaccia* is an Italian flat bread that is distinguished by the use of olive oil and savory

Figure 15–28

Naan (Indian flatbread). (Richard Embery/Pearson Education)

Figure 15–29a

Dimpling proofed focaccia prior to brushing with olive oil, seasonings and baking. Proofed dough doubles in bulk and maintains slight depression when finger gently pressed into the dough. (Richard Embery/Pearson Education)

toppings such as fresh rosemary, Parmesan cheese, and cracked black pepper (**Figure 15–29a** and **b**). Lavash is another very thin, rolled, yeasted flat bread from Armenia. Lavash is traditionally cooked in a deep round *tonir* (clay oven).

Bagels. Bagels are doughnut-shaped yeast breads that have been prepared from a yeast dough that is proofed and then shaped and boiled (**Figure 15–30**). The term "bagel" comes from the Yiddish word "beigen," which means to "bend" [6]. Traditional bagels are dense and chewy. Bagels are made from lean formulas with high-protein flours and per flour weight basis, a low proportion of yeast 0.8 percent, 2 percent salt, and 3.0 percent sugar plus water level sufficient for stiff dough. Higher yeast levels (1.2–1.6 percent yeast) produce large bubbles during boiling and often collapse [4].

Retardation of shaped bagels prior to boiling is necessary to develop a chewy tough characteristic and deep coloration [4]. Bagels are boiled for 2–4 minutes per side. Bagels expand and increase in size during boiling due to increased gas production in the dough. Bagels float shortly after being placed in boiling water [4]. Boiling also causes the outer crust to set due to partial gelatinization of starch [52]. Bagels boiled too long are more susceptible to collapse [4]. After boiling, the bagel is drained, quickly transferred to baking racks, and baked in a hot oven approximately 10–15 minutes until brown.

English Muffins and Crumpets. English muffins and crumpets are yeast bread products cooked in ring molds on a griddle. Crumpets are produced from a yeast batter, and English muffins are made from yeast doughs (refer to Chapter 13). Crumpet batter is fermented and

Figure 15–29b

Focaccia (Roman Flatbread) sliced into serving pieces. (Richard Embery/Pearson Education)

Figure 15–30

Bagel formation by wrapping dough around one hand. (Richard Embery/Pearson Education)

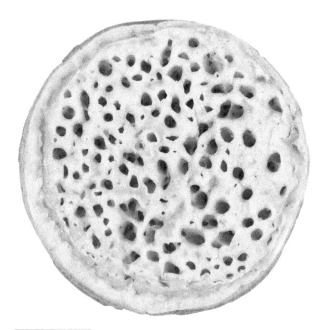

Figure 15–31

Crumpet. (gmstockstudio/Shutterstock)

Figure 15–32

English muffins are griddle-cooked yeast breads. Both sides are cooked and the muffin is split between top and bottom to reveal coarse grain interior. (© Eddy Van Damme/Pearson Education)

then poured into rings and baked on the griddle (**Figure 15–31**). Crumpets are traditionally baked on one side. English muffins originally from London differ from what Americans call muffins. English muffins are yeast-based and American muffins are a quick bread leavened with baking powder [19] (refer Chapter 14).

Traditional English muffin dough contains flour, water, yeast, and salt, with water 75–80 percent flour weight. Dough is mixed and allowed to ferment for several hours and then cut into pieces that are dropped into 3½ to 4 inch iron rings on canvas-covered support, dusted with cornmeal, and proofed until dough level rises to the ring top. Proofed dough pieces are transferred with a metal spatula to 350−450°F heated griddle and cooked approximately 5 minutes per side. The English muffin has the appearance of a heavy bun which is flat on the bottom side and slightly convex on the top side. Top and bottom surfaces are golden brown from cooking and edges white. English muffins split between top and bottom and have an interior characterized by a coarse grain of medium to large holes resembling peaks and valleys on the surface [49] (**Figure 15–32**).

Pizza Dough. Pizza dough is a stiff, lean yeast dough that rises for about 30 minutes before rolling. Rolled pizza dough (or crust) is topped with variations of tomato-based or other sauces, mozzarella and/or other cheeses, meat and/or vegetables, and then baked in a very hot oven. Pizza dough may be used for the Italian American *Calzones*. Calzones are a turnover made from pizza dough folded over a variety of savory fillings (**Figure 15–33**).

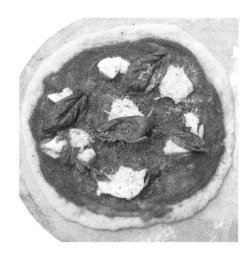

Figure 15–33

(Top) Pizza dough rolled and topped ready to be baked. (Bottom) Calzone. (Richard Embery/Pearson Education)

Figure 15–34

Mantou (Chinese steam buns) in bamboo steaming basket.
(nui7711/123RF)

Steamed Bread. Steamed breads, such as Chinese mantou, such as Chinese *mantou*, are yeast breads that are cooked by steaming under 100°C. These yeast breads are white in color, soft, and tender; have no crust formation. Steaming the yeast dough causes no caramelization and no Maillard reaction resulting in the white coloration (**Figure 15–34**).

Laminated (Rolled-In) Yeast Doughs

Danish pastry and croissants are produced from laminated yeast doughs. Laminated or rolled-in yeast doughs are a rich yeast dough that is layered with fat (typically butter). The fat is incorporated during the laminating process. Typically, laminated doughs are 50 percent fat. The dough is leavened by yeast, but eggs and butter contribute moisture for steam leavening as well. Laminated doughs yield flaky, tender, soft crust products. Kneading is minimal with laminated doughs as gluten continues to develop during dough rolling and folding of fat [24, 25].

Dough can be made using the straight or sponge method. After dough has risen, it is ready to be laminated or layered with fat, folded, and rolled. The fat should be rolled or kneaded so to be the same consistency as the dough. Butter is typically used as the fat, but cheaper shortening substitutes are sometimes used. Rolling, folding, and shaping procedures are described in **Figure 15–35** [25].

STALING OF BREAD

Staling refers to the undesirable changes in bread after baking. Characteristics of bread staling include crust toughening, crumb firming, decreasing crumb capacity to hold moisture, flavor loss, and increasing crumb opaqueness [17]. Bread staling is a complex phenomenon and involves multiple mechanisms [15]. Crust toughening is contributed to water migration from crumb to crust. A freshly baked loaf has a dry crust 2–5 percent moisture and the crust is *friable* (easily crumbled) and desirable. As water migrates from crumb to crust, the crust toughens, losing friability [17].

Crumb staling is not a drying phenomenon as firming occurs and no moisture is lost. Changes in crystallinity that can be detected in the laboratory in the starchy portion of bread have led to the conclusion that starch is mainly responsible for staling. The **amylopectin** fraction of starch is most involved in staling, as it undergoes retrogradation. Retrogradation involves a slow recrystallization or the realignment of the starch-branched fraction (amylopectin). This realignment leads to firming of crumb and makes it

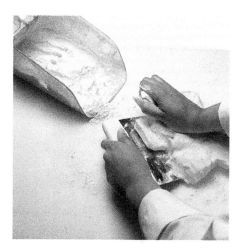

Figure 15–35a

Steps to make laminated yeast bread dough. Knead butter. (Richard Embery/Pearson Education)

Figure 15–35b

Base dough is mixed, kneaded, and fermented. Rolled-out dough. (Richard Embery/Pearson Education)

Figure 15–35c

Spread Butter on two-thirds of rolled-out dough. (Richard Embery/Pearson Education)

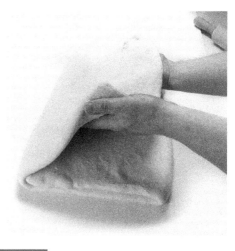

Figure 15–35e

Fold remaining dough. (Richard Embery/Pearson Education)

Figure 15–35d

Fold dough in thirds to cover butter. (Richard Embery/Pearson Education)

Figure 15–35f

Roll out folded dough. (Richard Embery/Pearson Education)

Figure 15–35g

Fold dough in thirds to complete a "turn." Repeat rolling and folding two times for croissant or six times for Danish pastry. Dough can be chilled between turns if necessary. After final turn dough is wrapped, chilled overnight or at least four hours to retard dough and relax gluten. (Richard Embery/Pearson Education)

Shape for croissants. Roll out finished dough, cut into triangles then roll starting from large end to shape into croissant. (Richard Embery/Pearson Education)

Shape for Danish by cutting pinwheel and fill. (Richard Embery/ Pearson Education)

more opaque. Retrogradation of **amylose** (linear star fraction) also occurs, but primarily during baking and initial cooling. However, the firming of bread, associated with staling, can be slowed if moisture loss is controlled, such as is done through the formulation and packaging of ready-to-eat breads [16]. Thus, bread has been shown to firm due to factors in addition to amylopectin recrystallization.

Monoglycerides seem to form a complex with amylose molecules, to decrease retrogradation and to exert a softening effect on the crumb. Some interaction between starch and gluten has also been suggested in explaining staling [29]. Fat in the bread formula helps to retard staling, while emulsifiers added by commercial bakers have a similar effect, as do certain amylase enzymes.

Staling can be reversed by heating. Toasting bread is a method used to reverse staling. If stale bread is reheated to 122–140°F (50–60°C) or above, the staling is reversed, and the bread regains many of the characteristics of fresh bread. The soluble fraction of the starch that decreased during staling is increased. The process can be reversed several times until the bread has lost too much moisture.

Temperature of bread storage is important. Bread stales more rapidly when it is held at refrigerator temperatures than when it is stored at room temperature. Refrigerated temperatures increase rate of firming. Freezing seems to reverse the staling process. Freezing, combined with heating to thaw the frozen product, brings about considerable freshening of stale bread products. This process can be quickly accomplished in a microwave oven; however, microwave energy produces some toughening in bread, and caution must be exercised to avoid the dehydrating effect of microwaving too long. Bread staling is a complicated issue and still an unsolved problem.

SPOILAGE OF BREAD

Bread spoils most commonly by mold spores. Any mold spores in the dough are destroyed in baking, so mold growth on baked bread comes from contamination of the loaf after baking. Conditions favorable to mold growth are moisture and warm temperatures. Commercially, sodium or calcium propionate is added to the bread dough as an anti-molding additive and is quite effective. In warm, humid weather, however, even bread containing this additive is likely to mold if it is held for more than a few days at room temperature. Refrigeration retards mold growth, but also speeds the staling process via starch retrogradation. Bread should be frozen if it is not to be used within a few days.

Rope is a bacterial contamination that can originate in the flour bin or in the various constituents used to make the bread. The spores of this bacterium are not destroyed in baking, and within a few days the interior of the loaf becomes sticky and may be pulled into "ropes" of a syrupy material. The foul "rope" odor resembles overripe melons. Bread is inedible when rope has developed. The cure consists in eliminating the source of the bacteria. Acidifying dough to a pH of 4.5 or lower will prevent rope development. Sour milk or buttermilk may be substituted for one-fourth to one-half of the total liquid, or approximately 1 tablespoon of distilled vinegar per quart of liquid may be added. This addition does not change the flavor of the bread. Calcium or sodium propionate that is added to retard mold production is also effective in preventing rope.

Bread may be packaged in a plastic film under a modified atmosphere, which in most cases is carbon dioxide alone or in combination with nitrogen gas. This method limits the loss of moisture and microbial growth to extend the shelf life of the bread. Carbon dioxide also has an anti-staling effect, possibly due to a change in the ability of amylopectin to bind water in the bread [2]. Ready-to-eat bread is preserved by controlling water activity, pH, oxygen content, and initial microbial load [35].

STUDY QUESTIONS

Consumption Trends and Nutrition

1. Describe the factors that might influence consumption of yeast bread products.

2. Discuss how yeast breads can be incorporated into a healthy meal plan.

Ingredients and Their Functions

3. Explain the role played by each of the following ingredients in the making of yeast bread:
   (a) Yeast
   (b) Flour
   (c) Liquid
   (d) Sugar
   (e) Fat
   (f) Salt
   (g) Dough conditioners

4. Compare the similarities and differences among compressed yeast, active dry yeast, instant quick-rising dry active yeast, and starters as they are used for the preparation of yeast.

5. Based on the Federal Code of Regulations, can "bread" ever be gluten free? Describe why or why not.

Dough Mixing and Handling

6. Compare bread flour and all-purpose flour in terms of mixing, handling, and expected outcome in the making of yeast bread.

7. What steps are involved in mixing yeast bread by the straight-dough method? The sponge method? The batter method?

8. Explain why kneading is such an important step in the preparation of yeast bread at home.

Fermentation and Proofing

9. What is meant by *fermentation* and *proofing* of yeast dough? What occurs during these processes?

10. What are the purposes of *slashing* bread prior to baking?

11. Discuss the role of time, temperature, and humidity during the fermentation and proofing phases.

Baking Bread

12. (a) Describe changes that occur during the baking of yeast bread.
    (b) What is meant by *oven spring*?
    (c) Why is it important to bake bread at precisely the right time after proofing in the pan?

Characteristics of Yeast Breads

13. Describe desirable characteristics of yeast bread.

14. Discuss factors that influence yeast bread characteristics.

Rolls

15. How do ingredients and their proportions generally differ between rolls and bread?

Whole-Grain and Variety Breads

16. What is the difference between wheat and whole-wheat bread? How do whole grain components affect the bread-making process?

17. Identify characteristics of some of the specialty breads available.

Bread Staling and Spoilage

18. (a) What changes occur as bread stales?
    (b) Which component of bread appears to be responsible for staling?
    (c) How can stale bread be refreshened?

19. (a) Give suggestions on how to store bread appropriately.
    (b) What is *rope* in bread, and how can it be controlled?

16
Cakes, Cookies, and Crackers

Cakes are sweet baked products that can be classi-fied into two major groups: shortened cakes and foam cakes. Cakes and cookies are characterized by high sugar levels in the formulations. The word "cookie" means small cake. Most cookie formulas contain less liquid than cake formulas. Some cookies can be made from cake formulas or boxed cake mixes by altering fat and liquid levels. Differences in formulations, in-gredients, and variety exist in each group. High-quality ingredients, correct formulations, and proper proce-dures are essential to yield high-quality products.

Traditional wedding cakes, birthday cakes, and cupcakes are examples of shortened cakes (**Figure 16–1**). Shortened cakes contain fat. The term *short-ened* is derived from fat's role in hindering or short-ening the gluten formation making a tender crumb. Shortened cakes may contain a leavening agent such as baking powder and/or baking soda plus an acid.

Foam cakes are egg foam based. Foam cakes are formed by beating egg whites and adding sugar after which flour is added as a binder and for foam stability. Foam cake's leavening is primarily from air incorporated in whipped egg white or egg foam. Angel food, sponge, and chiffon cakes are examples of foam cakes. Foam cakes may contain oil or a leavening agent. Angel food cake contains no oil, whereas chiffon cake contains oil.

Cookie formulas typically contain less liquid than cakes. Most cookies are made from soft to stiff doughs versus thinner cake batters. Variations in cookie for-mulation and moisture levels result in mixing and shaping differences. Products such as brownies can be difficult to classify as a cake or a cookie since formula-tion variations yield products that are like cake with a light tender crumb to fudgy with a dense crumb.

Cookies differ in several ways from cakes. Cookies are typically individual pieces often shaped by hand or commercially made with specialized equip-ment. Cakes have a finer texture and velvety crumb characteristics compared to cookies. Certain types of cookies, such as rolled cookies or meringue-type cookies, require specialized techniques.

Crackers are individual piece baked cereal prod-ucts that are typically made from soft wheat that is higher in protein. There is some overlap of cookies and crackers; graham crackers are often considered a

Figure 16–1

Chocolate is a favorite shortened cake flavor.
(Cokemomo/123RF)

cookie. The definition of crackers is broad with var-ious formulations but most have a moisture content of less than 5 percent. Most crackers are less than 3 inches in size, but there are a few exceptions.

An adjustment in ingredients, as well as in mix-ing and handling, is needed when baking at high al-titudes. At high altitudes, the atmospheric pressure is less than that at lower elevations. Refer to Chapter 13 for more about high-altitude baking and methods for cakes and cookies.

This chapter will discuss the characteristics, preparation, and ingredient functions of the following:

- Shortened cakes
- Foam cakes
- Cookies
- Crackers

CONSUMPTION TRENDS AND NUTRITION

Cakes, cookies, and crackers are baked cereal-based products that provide energy, protein, and B vitamins. Formulas and ingredients ultimately determine the nu-trient content and energy levels. Wheat flour is used in majority of cakes, cookies, and crackers, but cereal grains may vary. Fat content may be high in shortened cakes, cookies, and crackers depending on the product and formulations. Other product formulations contain no fat, such as angel food cakes or matzos. Whole grain components and other ingredients can be used to boost nutrient composition in some products.

American concerns over "healthy eating" have increased demand for whole grain products and low-fat products. Fast-paced, on-the-go lifestyles have increased the demand for individual package serving sizes for cakes, cookies, and crackers. Demand for fewer ingredients, no trans fat, and no GMO ingredients has also forced a change in formulations and products. New flavor innovations including ethnic flavors are important in cookies, cakes, and crackers. Unique and gourmet brownies, colorful French style macarons, celebration cakes, and "indulgent" snacks such as cookies contribute to increased bakery purchases [65]. Breakfast-style cookie sandwiches called "biscuits" are trending in the breakfast offerings [66].

Crackers are typically considered a bread substitute with an extended shelf life. Cookies and cakes are traditionally considered a dessert item, but there is an increase with between-meal snack consumption. The average number of between-meal snacks consumed daily per person has increased from 1.9 in 2010 to 2.6 in 2015. In 2015, indulgent snacks outpaced the sale of healthy snacks [65]. Cookies, cakes, and crackers are often eaten as snacks between meals. Individual snack cakes are boosting cake offerings. Gluten-free crackers, cookies, and cakes are now readily available in the marketplace. The inclusion of ingredients such as ground pulses (dried beans, peas, lentils) in formulations is trending with plant proteins "super food" benefits; these plant protein inclusions can present challenging flavor issues in cakes and cookies [5].

Seasonal eating patterns reflect higher cookie consumption in fall, whereas brownies and cake consumption is highest in spring and summer. Individual serving size packaging, whole grain cereals, and new flavor combinations are trends in crackers, cakes, and cookies. The artisan bread trend has expanded to crackers with more artisan-style crackers and a variety of flavors, grains, and ingredients being marketed by manufacturers.

SHORTENED CAKES

Types and Characteristics

Shortened cakes contain fat; they are classified either as *pound cake, standard shortened cake,* or *high-ratio shortened cake.* Sometimes shortened cakes are called "butter cakes" since traditionally butter was used as the fat for making cakes.

Pound Cakes. Traditional pound cakes are prepared from one pound each of butter, sugar, flour, and eggs with no added leavening agent. Modern commercial

Figure 16–2

Pound cakes are often baked in a loaf pan and have a very fine, compact texture. Originally pound cakes contained about one pound each of the main ingredients: eggs, butter, flour, and sugar. (RoJo Images/Shutterstock)

pound cakes are lighter and less dense with better eating and keeping qualities compared to traditional pound cakes (**Figure 16–2**). A typical "modernized" commercial pound cake formula contains equal amount of sugar and flour and half the amount of fat and eggs with milk added for liquid while liquids (eggs and milk) are equal flour or sugar weights [58, 34].

Traditional pound cakes are leavened by air and steam. Air is incorporated during the creaming of fat and beating of eggs. Butter and eggs provide the moisture for the steam leavening. All baked products contain some moisture so steam is an important leavening agent. Steam is formed during baking as water from eggs, butter, and liquid ingredients vaporizes and expands in air cells that are trapped in the batter. The air cells form a network of starches and proteins that set during baking as flour starch gelatinizes and proteins set forming cake structure.

Characteristics of Pound Cake. Pound cakes should have small, fine, evenly distributed air cells with a tender crumb and thin crust (**Figure 16–3**). Pound cakes should not be heavy or soggy. The texture of pound cake is compact as it lacks the soft, light, velvety crumb of a well-made shortened cake. Taste should be sweet with a pleasant aroma and buttery flavor.

Standard Shortened Cakes. All standard shortened cakes are formula derivations of the traditional pound cake recipe. Over the years, bakers experimented with the basic pound cake recipe. Bakers balanced the recipe by reducing quantities of sugar, fat, and eggs compensating by adding milk. Standard shortened layer cake formulas also contain a leavening agent such as baking powder or baking soda plus an acid such as buttermilk. Leavening agents are

Figure 16–3

(Left) Improperly mixed pound cake with tunnels, irregular grain with large air cells, and low volume. (Right) Pound cake with fine texture and good volume. (Richard Embery/Pearson Education)

added to produce carbon dioxide gas that increases cake volume and improves crumb texture. The leavening agents must be used in a precise quantity to produce an excellent product. Air incorporated during the creaming of fat and beating eggs or egg whites also aids in mixture leavening. Milk or buttermilk is typically used as a liquid to provide moisture in shortened cakes. Flavor is enhanced with small amounts of salt and flavoring agents such as vanilla extract.

Cake formulas rely on precise ingredient measurement or weighing; formulas must be balanced so toughening effects of flour and egg are balanced with tenderizing impacts of sugar and fat. However, ingredient amounts can be manipulated within certain limits without producing undesirable results. Ingredients proportions vary widely in shortened cakes formulas.

Shortened cake mixtures may be classified as lean or rich depending on the relationship of fat and sugar to the ingredients that give structure varying from a one-egg layer cake to a rich pound cake. Changing ingredient proportions often requires a change in mixing methods. The mixing method is often adjusted to account for ingredient proportions. Shortened cakes can be defined by the mixing methods used to produce the batter, which will be discussed later. Shortened cake batter ingredients are balanced and mixed to produce and hold batter air cells, that when baked, yield a soft rigid structure and tender crumb with a pleasant flavor and sweet taste. Shortened cakes may be baked as loaves, layers, sheets, Bundt pans (**Figure 16–4**), cake pops, or cupcakes (**Figure 16–5**)

A satisfactory plain standard shortened cake formula is shown below.

Basic Standard Shortened Cake Formula.

Sugar: 1½ cups	Eggs: 2
Fat: ½ cup	Salt: ½ tsp
Milk: 1 cup	Baking powder: 3 tsp
Cake flour: 3 cups	Flavoring: 1 tsp

This cake formula uses measurements with one-third as much fat as sugar, two-thirds as much milk as sugar, and about three times as much flour as liquid. The ratio of egg to fat is typically 1:1 for a tender crumb; the toughening effect of egg protein must be balanced by tenderizing the level of fat. Eggs and milk are about a 1:1 ratio with combined weight equaling flour. Too little liquid will yield a dry crumb with low palatability; too much liquid will yield a weak crumb structure and cakes with low volume. Salt is used in cakes for flavor, and only small amounts are needed. Small amounts of flavoring, typically alcohol-based extracts, are added for additional flavor.

Figure 16–4

Shortened cake may be baked in Bundt pans or specialty molded cakelet pans. (© Amanda Frye)

Figure 16–5

Cupcakes are made from shortened cake batter. (Ruth Black/123RF)

Cake formulations can also be expressed as weighed ingredients typically in grams or ounces. Commercial bakers use what is known as "baker's percentage" to express ingredient proportions where each ingredient in the formula is expressed as a percentage of flour weight. The flour weight is always 100 percent. The percentage of each ingredient can be determined by ingredient total weight divided by flour weight multiplied by 100. Baker's formulas allow for precise ingredient measurement and recipes are easily adapted for any yield by scaling formula up or down.

High-ratio Cakes. These are modified shortened cakes. High-ratio cakes resulted from the development of shortenings containing emulsifiers and surfactants allowing higher liquid levels to be incorporated in the cake batter with finer more uniform dispersion of fat and air. Emulsified shortening, sometimes called high-ratio shortening, is essential in high-ratio cakes. The shortening contains emulsifiers so the batter can hold larger amounts of water compared to regular shortening. The emulsifier also plays an important role in high-ratio cake firmness, extending cake shelf life [58, 78]. As a result, high-ratio cakes are richer with a higher moisture content and extended shelf life. High-ratio cakes are high in sugar and have a thinner liquid batter.

High-ratio cakes have sugar-flour ratio greater than or equal to 1.0, so weight of sugar exceeds flour [17, 58]. Egg weight exceeds shortening, and weight of liquids (including eggs) should exceed the sugar [58].

Emulsified shortenings do not cream well so the mixing method is different. High-ratio cakes blend emulsified shortening with flour and other dry ingredients until smooth prior to adding liquids including eggs [27, 43]. Chlorinated flour is essential in high-ratio cakes as starch is modified during the chlorination process. The cell structure gains stability from the chlorinated flour's starch, which prevents the cake from collapsing in the oven [33]. Commercial bakeries typically use high-ratio cake formulas. These cakes have a relatively high volume with a fine, smooth, and moist crumb [43].

Characteristics of a Standard Shortened Layer Cake.
A good standard shortened cake should have a uniform shape with flat or slightly round top free from cracks. The crusts should be thin and tender. The crust color depends on ingredients but is typically golden brown. Top crusts should be smooth or slightly pebbly. The crumb should have texture that is a fine grain with evenly distributed air cells of uniform size and thin cell walls. The crumb should be tender, velvety, and moist but not sticky or crumbly. The cake should be light, moist, and sweet with a pleasant aroma and flavor.

Shortened Cake Ingredients and Functions

Flour, sugar, fat, egg, liquid, leavening agent, salt, and other flavorings are ingredients in standard shortened cake ingredients (**Figure 16–6**). The main cake

Figure 16–6

Ingredients to make a shortened cake include flour, sugar, eggs, fat, liquid (typically milk), chemical leavening agent, salt, and flavoring. (AKZ/123RF)

ingredients can be classified as tougheners (structure builders), tenderizers, moisteners, or driers. A cake formula must balance the tenderizing effects of sugar and fat with the toughening structural effects of flour and egg and the moistening effects of liquids must balance drying effects of flour and other dry ingredients like cocoa. Some ingredients have multiple roles in cakes, such as egg that provides moisture and structure. The transformation of the ingredients into cake involves a series of complex processes whose science is not fully understood [74].

Shortened cakes are a complex food system. The shortened cake batter is an oil-in-water emulsion (see Chapter 8). Incorporation of air into the system makes it also a foam. Large number of air cells incorporated into the cake batter during mixing is important to produce a cake with fine crumb texture and good volume. During baking, this cake batter emulsion foam is converted into a semisolid substance due to starch gelatinization, protein coagulation, carbon dioxide gas production, and air incorporation during mixing and the interaction of ingredients. The heat from baking stabilizes this mixture into an airy soft tender solid product that we call cake.

Flour. Flour contributes structure to shortened cakes. Flour functions as a drier and "toughener" absorbing liquid and contributing structural components in shortened cakes. The flour starch plays an essential role in providing cake structure. Flour starch and proteins absorb water during the batter mixing and increase batter viscosity. The batter starch and protein network entraps leavening air and gases. During baking, the flour starch gelatinizes around the air cells producing building blocks of the crumb and the cake structure [3]. The cake texture depends on how many air cells were entrapped and expanded before they rupture during baking. There is minimal gluten production during mixing of shortened cakes. Starch contributes to cake firmness with gluten proteins contributing to cell wall structure and springiness attributes of cakes [74, 75].

Too little flour produces a cake with a weak structure, coarse texture, and susceptible to collapse. Excess flour, on the other hand, produces a compact, dry cake in which tunnels form. However, tunnels may form in a cake of good proportions if the mixture is overmanipulated or is baked at too high a temperature (see Chapter 13). Tunnels may also develop if the cake is baked in too small a cake pan [68] (**Figure 16–7**).

All-purpose or cake flour may be used in cake formulas. Commercial bakers typically use only cake flour for bakery cakes. Cake flour is produced from soft wheat with lower protein content with smaller particle size and

Horizontal cross section of shortened cake shows tunnel patterns. (Trimbo, H. B., & Miller, B. S. (1973). The development of tunnels in cakes. *Bakers Digest*, 47(5), 24–26, 70–71.) (© Bakers Digest/Sosland Publishing Co.)

Tunnels are evident in this piece of cake. (Jesus Keller/ Shutterstock)

smooth texture, which is important in delicate baked goods. Cake flour is treated with chlorine bleach that lowers the pH and modifies the starch resulting in improved cake baking quality. Cake flours are low-gluten flours with a protein content of 8 percent versus all-purpose flour with a protein content of 11 percent.

Cakes made with all-purpose flour are generally lower in volume and have a coarser texture than similar cakes made with cake flour. Chlorinated cake flour is essential in high-ratio cakes. High-ratio cakes have a high proportion of sugar and water in relationship to flour and can collapse in the oven when cake flour is not used [58].

All-purpose flour can be substituted for cake flour in a cake formula that specifies cake flour. One cup of all-purpose flour minus 2 tablespoons can be used in place of 1 cup of cake flour [1]. Others suggest replacing the 2 tablespoons of flour removed from the cup of all-purpose flour with 2 tablespoons of cornstarch and then substituting this flour–starch blend for cake flour.

Sugar. White granulated sugar is a primary ingredient in shortened cakes. Sugar adds sweetness, flavor, and calories. It also has an effect on the texture and cake volume. Sugar also influences the color, texture, appearance, and keeping qualities of shortened cakes. Some color and flavor attributes are due to caramelization of sugar during the baking process.

Crumb texture and cake volume are influenced by sugar. Sugar weakens the cake structure by interfering with gluten development in the flour. Sugar affects gluten development by attracting and holding water, thereby preventing sufficient hydration of the flour proteins. Consequently, less gluten can be produced, and the cake is tender. However, if sugar content is too high, the cake will fall and have a coarse texture with thick cell walls. Both crust and crumb will be gummy. The crust may appear rough, sugary, and too brown.

Cake volume is influenced by sugar because of the (1) air trapped during creaming, (2) influence on starch gelatinization, and (3) reduction of cohesive forces. Granulated sugar, when creamed with shortening, traps small air bubbles, contributing to batter leavening. The temperature at which starch gelatinizes also affects volume. Sugar raises the temperature at which the starch gelatinizes and causes a decrease in the viscosity of the batter in the early stages of baking [33]. Thus, the cake has more time to increase in volume before the batter "sets."

During the cake batter mixing phase, granulated sugar can be creamed with shortening to facilitate the air incorporation causing small air bubbles (cells) to be formed and entrapped in batter. These air bubbles are essential points for leavening and volume. After the creaming stage, eggs are added; egg liquidity acts as a solvent for sugar. The sugar attracts and holds water from the egg and other liquid ingredients. Sugar's water binding property makes water unavailable for other components. Finer sugar granules dissolve more quickly. The sugar water binding prevents flour proteins (tougheners) from being sufficiently hydrated thus inhibiting gluten formation during mixing. Therefore, sugar acts as a tenderizer as it interferes with gluten formation by binding water. The less gluten produced in a shortened cake results in a tender cake crumb. As sugar is increased in a formula, there is a weakening effect on crumb structure.

A stretchable network, composed primarily of starch along with wheat and egg proteins, entraps air cells that are formed then expand during baking. Without this network, air cells would escape and the product would collapse. The protein and starch cake structures prevent the cake from collapsing when cooled, but too much gluten produces a tough cake [74]. Therefore, controlling gluten production is essential in shortened cakes.

Other tenderizing effects of sugar occur during baking. Sugar acts to delay both egg protein denaturation and starch gelatinization so more leavening gases are released before the cake structure is set. The most significant role of sugar is on starch gelatinization during the baking of shortened cakes [74]. Sugar binds water limiting the water available for the starch granules thus raising the temperature that the starch gelatinizes and cake "sets."

"Sets" is a term used to describe the phase change altering the physical state as the viscous cake batter transforms to a solid appearance during baking as protein and starch structures form solid air cell walls. Delaying the setting process allows more gas to be trapped before cell walls are "set" giving a more open cell structure essential for cake tenderness. Sugar acts by raising the temperature at which starch gelatinizes as it decreases batter viscosity in the early baking stages [37]. Thus, the cake has more time to increase volume before cells "set" during baking.

The starch gelatinization timing in the baking process is important for an open cell structure allowing leavening gases to expand before being trapped in the starch and protein matrix [13]. If starch gelatinization occurs too early, the cake will be compact with a lower volume. Therefore, air cells in batter with high levels of sugar expand more before batter sets. However, too high proportions of sugar can yield a cake with coarse and open texture [12]. Sugar's hygroscopic nature also aids in moisture retention of the baked shortened cake prolonging cake freshness and shelf life.

Another way in which sugar influences volume is by decreasing cohesive forces. It has been suggested that the resistance to movement of a cake batter during baking, referred to as *cohesive forces*, influences the development of the structure of the finished cake. Various ingredients affect these cohesive forces in different ways. An optimum quantity of sugar decreases the cohesive forces and allows the batter to move more freely. The volume of the cake therefore increases [54].

The many functional characteristics of sugar make it difficult to find a replacement in cake formulas. Sugar's functional, structural, and sensory characteristics cannot be replicated by any one product. Cakes made without sugar must use multiple ingredients to replace sweetening and non-sweet functions of sugar such as volume and bulk [23, 24].

When other types of sweeteners are used, quality attributes of the cake are affected. If glucose or fructose is substituted for sugar (sucrose), more fructose is required to attain the same starch gelatinization temperature [3]. Cakes made with fructose also tend to be darker because the Maillard browning reaction is more pronounced; also, cake volume is somewhat lower [47, 49].

High-intensity sweeteners require reformulations with bulking agents, emulsifiers, and gums to replace non-sweet role of sugar in order to produce something that resembles a shortened cake [25, 26].

Egg. Eggs in shortened cakes contribute moisture, structure, leavening, emulsifying effects, shortening action, flavor, and nutritional value. Eggs add air to cake batter when beaten and contribute to the structure of cakes by the protein coagulation during baking. The optimum amount of egg in a given cake mixture produces finer cells, thinner cell walls, and usually larger volume than obtained with a lower or higher percentage of egg.

A whole egg is 73 percent water. This water acts as a moistener for dry ingredients. Water from eggs must be calculated as liquid in egg formulations. Egg whites are 86 percent water versus egg yolk 49 percent water, so moisture level must be adjusted in the formula. So, if egg yolks are substituted for whole egg, more moisture would be needed in the formula. The size of the egg in recipes makes a difference too. A large egg weighs 50 grams compared to a medium egg which weights 45 grams. (**Figure 16–8**).

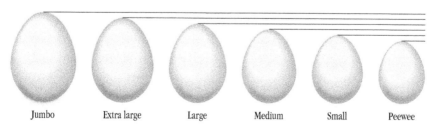

| Jumbo | Extra large | Large | Medium | Small | Peewee |

Figure 16–8

Egg sizes vary so the amount of egg in the recipe may need to be adjusted based on egg size.

Egg yolks contain natural emulsifiers that help emulsify fats and liquids. Egg yolk lipoproteins such as lecithin enhance the emulsion process by lowering the tension at the oil–water interface [74]. During mixing, the egg helps to create a stable emulsion in the cake batter. This emulsifying action contributes to smooth batters. The emulsifying effect also contributes an increased volume and better texture in shortened cakes.

During mixing, an egg foam is created. This egg foam adds air to cake batter when beaten. Egg whites are good foaming agents. The egg white proteins stabilize air cells and contribute to foam formation [76]. The presence of egg yolk does interfere with the egg white foaming properties as it displaces the stabilizing white's proteins, and yolk lipids decrease the foam membrane stability. Egg contributes the greatest amount of air incorporation when cakes are made by conventional method, especially when eggs are separated and beaten egg whites are folded into cake batter at the end.

Eggs also act as toughening agents. Both egg white and yolk proteins coagulate during baking contributing to the cake structure. The optimum amount of egg in a given cake mixture produces finer cells, thinner cell walls, and usually larger volume than are obtained with a lower or higher percentage of egg. The way the eggs are added in the batter may modify egg protein impacts. An excess of egg gives a rubbery, tough crumb. When beaten egg whites are added last, the effects of increased egg are less noticeable. The cohesive forces in a cake batter are increased as egg white is added in increasing amounts [54].

Egg yolks impart a yellow color to cakes and contribute to crust browning. White shortened cakes use only egg whites. Fresh egg whites are 85 percent water, so when separated from the yolks and used alone act as a moistener and the albumen proteins act to provide cell structure.

Egg whites contribute to cake viscosity and assist in air incorporation when whipped. Thinner egg whites foam quicker with greater volume than do thick viscous egg whites [58]. Dried egg products are sometimes used in commercial bakeries or boxed cake mixes; dried egg functions as a "drier."

Fat. Shortening, butter, and margarine are common fats used in shortened cakes. Fat is a major ingredient in shortened cakes. Fat has various functions in shortened cakes as it entraps air during the creaming process to increase volume. Fat coats protein and starch particles to disrupt gluten formation contributing tenderness. If emulsified shortening is used, the emulsified fat acts to emulsify liquid and fat.

Any fat in shortened cakes acts as a tenderizer by shortening gluten strands, contributing to a tender crumb. Shortening refers to solid fat described as "plastic fat" that is solid and spreadable at room temperature. Shortening may be made from vegetables oils,

animal fat, or both. Shortenings are 100 percent fat and contain no water. Butter and margarines are considered "water in fat emulsions." Butter and margarines contain 80 percent fat which is required by federal regulations. Note that products called "spreads" contain 60 percent fat and 40 percent water; they will not give the same results as butter in a shortened cake formula.

Emulsified fats are essential in high-ratio cake formulas. Emulsified shortenings can hold a large amount of water. Emulsified shortening in high-ratio cake formulas cannot be substituted. These emulsified shortenings do not cream well so are not appropriate to substitute in standard shorten cake formulas. Emulsified shortenings are mixed first with flour to coat flour particles, which inhibits gluten formation increasing tenderness.

Mixing methods and types of fat are important as shortened cake batters are considered a water-in-fat emulsion, a uniform mixture of water in fat. Cake batter should be smooth as water is held in tiny droplets surrounded by fat and other ingredients. When fat cannot keep water in the emulsion then "curdling" occurs, when the mixture changes into a "fat-in-water" emulsion with small particles of fat surrounded by water and other ingredients. Proper formulation, ingredients, temperature, and mixing methods are essential to produce a smooth batter that does not curdle. Different types of fats have different properties so cannot be easily interchanged in formulations without adjustments. Emulsions are best formed when the temperature of ingredients is 70°F at room temperature; ingredients too cold can cause curdling. Adding liquids too quickly, adding too much liquid, or not following proper mixing procedures can cause curdling [39].

Fat is a tenderizer in shortened cakes. Fat surrounds flour particles and prevents water absorption necessary for gluten formation. The fat coats the flour protein and starch particles disrupting the protein–starch matrix and preventing gluten particles from sticking together. This makes the cell walls more pliable allowing for gas expansion. This effect gives a more tender cake crumb. If the amount of fat is too high, the air cells will explode which decreases cake volume.

Fat aids in incorporating air into the batter. Most hydrogenated fats are marketed containing tiny air cells of inert gas distributed throughout, typically 10–12 times more gas by volume. Creaming fat and sugar together adds air bubbles to the cake batter. These air bubbles incorporated into fat act as the focal cells for the distribution of leavening gas (carbon dioxide) during mixing and baking.

The characteristics of the fat should be considered if substituting one type of fat for another in a shortened cake recipe. Since shortening contains 100 percent fat compared to butter or margarine, which contains approximately 80 percent fat, when substituting shortening for butter the amount of fat would be decreased by 20 percent and liquid increased by 20

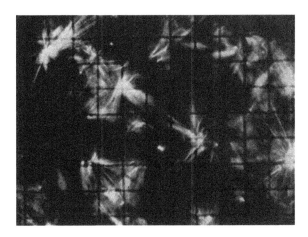

Figure 16–9

Fat crystals help to stabilize air incorporated in cake batter. (Moncrieff, J. (1970) Shortening and emulsifiers for cakes and icings. The *Bakers Digest*, 44(5), 60–65.) (© Bakers Digest/Sosland Publishing Co.)

percent. Butters or margarine spreads contain lower percentage of fat and consequently are not recommended for baking.

Different types of fat also will provide different results when creaming. All fats do not cream equally well. Fats with a wide plastic range where they maintain a solid but workable state over a wider temperature range are best for creaming. Butter and margarine have a narrow temperature range at which the fat is plastic. If the butter or margarine is too liquid or too hard, it will not cream as well. For example, butter can start melting at room temperature losing plasticity, whereas shortening will stay solid. Oils are liquid at room temperature and cannot be creamed with sugar. Fats of good creaming quality, such as shortening, will yield a cake of better texture than soft or liquid fats unless the methods of mixing are altered.

Fat crystals from solid fats stabilize air cells in the cake batter and contribute to the crumb texture (**Figure 16–9**). The air bubbles created during mixing are temporarily stabilized by egg proteins. The fat crystals are adsorbed onto air bubble surface creating a film around the protein stabilized air cell. Thus, the fat crystals coat the interfacial layer of proteins to stabilize the air cell. In all-in-one batters, the fat stabilization of air cells is a secondary process after the absorbed proteins have stabilized the air cells. The fat crystals interact with the fat–water and air–water interfaces so that each fat crystal is in direct contact with the air. The fat crystals stabilize the small air bubbles which expand without rupturing during baking. These fat crystals melt and leave behind an interface film in the bubble which aids in air cell expansion during baking [9]. Shortening with an emulsifier can stabilize more small air bubbles yielding finer crumb structure [52].

In comparing various fats, butter has been reported to make cakes that scored highest for tenderness and velvet-like texture, whereas hydrogenated shortening produced cakes with the highest rating for evenness of grain [48]. The finer the fat dispersion in a cake the softer the crumb. Shortenings with emulsifiers produce a larger number of small bubbles and softer cake crumb compared to plain shortening [9].

Butter produces a cake with a less even grain and lower volume compared to cakes made with shortening. Typically, butter has a higher cost than shortening. However, butter does have some major advantages. Butter is a natural product that imparts desirable cake flavor and mouthfeel. Butter melts in the mouth giving a desirable sensory effect compared to shortening which is sometimes said to leave a film in the mouth.

Reducing fat in a cake recipe can be desirable to reduce calories or fat content. Commercial formulas use a variety of fat replacers including bulking agents, fiber, modified starch products, gums, emulsifiers, and stabilizers. In home baking, a portion of cake fat replaced with applesauce or fruit puree has produced acceptable low-fat cakes.

Emulsifiers. A shortened cake batter is an emulsion as the liquid and fat ingredients are mixed into a smooth stable batter. The liquid and fat are naturally two immiscible substances which will separate when mixed together. Emulsifiers aid in the formation of the emulsion within the cake batter (**Figures 16–10a and b**). Cake batter with emulsifiers appears glossy, smooth, and not curdled. Emulsifying agents in shortened cake batter enable a fine fat distribution throughout the batter [49].

Egg yolk provides a natural emulsifier in shortened cakes. The yolk phospholipids such as lecithin help create smooth batters with stable emulsions. The importance of egg yolk in standard shortened cakes is demonstrated by the ratio of fat to egg in lean versus rich cake with no additional emulsifiers. Lean cakes use ¼ cup fat to 1 egg versus rich cake containing 1 ½ cups versus 6 eggs. However, the role of egg yolk emulsifiers in shortened cake is minimal compared to emulsifiers added to shortening and commercial cake formulas.

Additional emulsifiers are essential for high-ratio cake formulas which have high ratios of sugar and liquid to flour. High-ratio cakes use emulsified shortenings with higher amounts of eggs, liquids, and sugar in the formula. High-ratio cakes have a ratio of sugar to flour over one with sugar around 110–160 percent of flour weight. Without emulsifiers the high-ratio cake texture, flavor, and appearance would be compromised.

The function of additional emulsifiers in shortened cakes are summarized as follows: (1) decease surface tension of oil–water interface for a stable batter emulsion; (2) control fat to allow smaller and

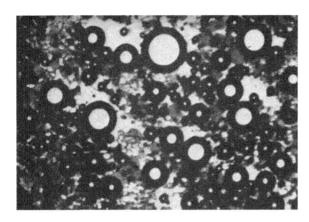

Figure 16-10a

Larger and fewer air cells in shortened cake batter without emulsifiers. (Moncrieff, J. (1970). Shortening and emulsifiers for cakes and icings. *The Bakers Digest, 44*(5), 60–65.) (© Bakers Digest/Sosland Publishing Co.)

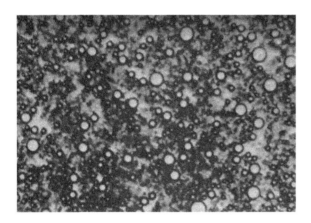

Figure 16-10b

Emulsifiers in cake batter decrease size of air cells and increase number of air cells leading to a finer grain, increased volume, and increased tenderness. (Moncrieff, J. (1970). Shortening and emulsifiers for cakes and Icings. *The Bakers Digest, 44*(5), 60–65.) (© Bakers Digest/Sosland Publishing Co.)

uniform air bubble size; (3) help more fine and uniform distribution of fat in the batter; (4) promote air incorporation in batter; (5) affect starch gelatinization resulting in a more tender crumb.

Emulsifiers are commonly added to shortenings. Most hydrogenated shortenings contain about 3 percent of emulsifiers typically mono- and diglycerides. Polysorbate 60 (about 1 percent) is also frequently used in commercial emulsified shortenings. A larger variety of emulsifiers are available to commercial bakers [19].

Optimum amounts of an emulsifier allow cohesive forces in the cake batter to be decreased resulting in a thinner, less viscous batter that moves or flows. Air is more finely dispersed in cakes with emulsifiers resulting in a finer texture of the baked cake. A less viscous batter during the early stages of the baking period allows more air bubble expansion before

structure sets. Baked shortened cake containing added emulsifiers have an increased volume with a fine and even texture [37].

Liquids. Liquids in shortened cakes act as moisteners and perform a number of functions. Milk and buttermilk are the primary liquids used in shortened cake, but other liquid may be used including water and fruit juices. Sometimes dried powder milk solids are added to dry ingredients and water is added as the liquid. Milk improves flavor and aids in development of browning and crust color [34]. Most boxed cake mixes use the addition of water and contain no milk solids. The water content from the egg and butter also contribute to the total water in a cake formula. Water has been classified as a tenderizer since it acts as a diluent to crumb structure components [50].

Liquids dissolve the sugar and salt into solution within the cake batter. Chemical leavening reactions of baking powder or baking soda are possible with the presence of a liquid. Liquids disperse the fat in the shortened cake's oil-in-water emulsion. Steam leavening in shortened cakes is the result of liquids. In early baking stages, cake liquids expand and evaporate producing steam which expands air cells trapped within the batter's protein and starch network. The steam vaporization causes air cell expansion which increases cake volume thus contributing to leavening.

Liquids also act to disperse flour particles in the cake batter. Flour can absorb and bind slightly more than one-fourth its weight in water [12]. Only water not bound by flour contributes to the cake batter fluidity during baking. Liquid acts as a moistener as it hydrates starch and protein flour components allowing both starch gelatinization and limited gluten formation. Water alone can control starch gelatinization temperature, cause the initial increase in batter viscosity, and affect the degree of starch gelatinization.

Water bound by flour proteins and starch increase the cake batter viscosity [74]. Water is absorbed by starch components which then swell, gelatinize, and set during baking. Flour gluten water absorption is limited because of the high sugar and fat levels in shortened cake. Therefore, the flour gluten proteins never fully develop during shortened cake batter mixing. Gluten in shortened cakes acts as a water binder rather than a major structural component. The exact role of flour protein in the cake structure is still the subject of research and discussions [74, 75].

Sufficient liquid must be available to allow for starch gelatinization which is essential for cake structure during baking and cooling. Without adequate starch gelatinization the cake will collapse upon cooling [33]. Too little liquid results in a cake with a sunken appearance whereas too much liquid yields a cake that is "peaked" [38]. Liquid is important for cake batter

FOCUS ON SCIENCE
CAKE BATTER SPECIFIC GRAVITY

Specific gravity = Weight of a substance (cake batter)/ Weight of an equal volume of water

Specific gravity refers to the weight of an ingredient or mixture such as cake batter in relation to the weight of water (1 pint water = 16 fl oz = 1 pound).

Cake batter specific gravity indicates how much air was incorporated during mixing which determines the finished cake volume and crumb texture. Too little air incorporated into the batter will yield a cake of low volume and dense grain. Too much air will produce a cake with a coarse grain

that may collapse. Specific gravity tests are important for food scientists and commercial bakers. The specific gravity test can be used in working with new or improved or substituted cake ingredients or optimizing cake formulas or to ensure consistent uniform products. Sometimes batters with inadequate specific gravity measurements will be discarded before being panned and baked. Lower specific gravity yields cake with high volume, thus an inverse relationship. Shortened cake batters have higher specific gravity measurement compared to foam cakes [43, 58].

aeration during mixing which directly influences volume, crumb texture and tenderness of baked cake.

Leavening Agents. Leavening involves the production or incorporation of gases in a shortened cake to increase volume and provide texture and lightness. Shortened cakes are leavened by steam, air incorporation during mixing, and carbon dioxide from chemical leavening agent reactions. Air is incorporated during creaming, formation of egg foam during beating, and mixing of batter, thus creating the air (gas) cells in the cake batter. These air cells eventually set and become the "grain" that provides texture of the baked cake. The air cells become the focal cells for collection of (1) steam formed during baking and (2) carbon dioxide produced from chemical leavening agents. When water turns to steam, it increases 1,100 times the original volume. Since shortened cakes contain moisture, steam leavening is an important leavening component.

A true pound cake is leavened by air and steam. Standard shortened cakes have the addition of chemical leavening agents such as baking powder or baking soda (sodium bicarbonate) and an acid that produces carbon dioxide. Amounts of chemical leavening agents used depends on how much air is incorporated during creaming of fat, the total number of eggs, and if eggs are used whole or separated with whites beaten and folded into batter. For example, a two-egg cake will need more leavening than a rich four egg cake with eggs separated then egg whites beaten folded into batter. The leavening action must be timed so gases are produced while the cake batter can still expand but not too early so gases escape batter. If gases are released too late the batter cannot expand and cake grain will collapse [34] (Figure 16-3).

Correct chemical leavening for the cake formula is important. Double acting powder is most commonly used in standard shortened cakes. However, other chemical leavening agents such as baking soda

plus an acid are used in shortened cakes. Baking powders are a more versatile leavening agents since they do not rely on an additional acid in the cake formulations.

Baking powders can be single acting baking powders that are activated by moisture that requires immediate baking. Double acting baking powders are most common in shortened cake formulas. They release some carbon dioxide with the liquid addition during the mixing process and then heat during baking releases a second wave of carbon dioxide.

Too little baking powder in a cake produces a compact, heavy product. Increasing amounts of chemical leavening agents increase cake volume until the optimum quantity is reached, but beyond that, volume decreases, the cake collapses, and undesirable flavors are created. A coarse texture and a harsh, gummy crumb may also result from an excess of baking powder. Cakes made using SAS-phosphate powder may be disagreeably bitter if large amounts are used. Less baking powder is needed to produce the best volume and texture when more air is incorporated into the cake by means of a creamed fat–sugar mixture or beaten egg whites. Adding baking soda without an acid or substituting baking soda for baking powder results in a coarse grain and produces a product with a soapy taste.

Baking soda is used in conjunction with an acid such as buttermilk, molasses, or fruit juices/purees. Cocoa is acidic, but generally does not provide enough acid to allow the use of only baking soda. Some chocolate cake recipes will use both baking soda and baking powder as leavening agents. Sometimes cream of tartar (tartaric acid) is used as the acid in cakes leavened by baking soda.

Baking soda requires moisture plus an acid to produce carbon dioxide. Heat is not necessary for this reaction so cakes leavened by baking soda must be baked immediately. Often baking soda for leavening is used with the addition of baking powder.

Shortened chocolate cake ready to be frosted. (Ffolas/ Shutterstock)

Chocolate. Chocolate cake is a popular cake flavor (**Figure 16–11**). Cocoa and chocolate contain starch and act as a drier as it absorbs moisture in the cake batter. Chocolate is added to cake batter in several ways. Cocoa may be added with dry ingredients when mixing or blended with shortening when using high-ratio shortening. When cocoa is added to a yellow cake formula to make a chocolate cake, a smaller percentage of flour is added to compensate for the cocoa starch. Flour should be reduced by 3/8 (37.5 percent) of weight of cocoa added. Failure to reduce the flour results in a dry cake with a cracked top [58].

Cocoa is the same as bitter chocolate without the cocoa butter so substitutions are possible. Shortening can be substituted for cocoa butter. However, shortening has twice the shortening power as cocoa butter so half shortening is needed to replace cocoa butter. Cocoa has a greater thickening effect than chocolate because the percentage of starch in cocoa is about 11 percent compared to 8 percent in chocolate [58].

The acidity of chocolate is not sufficiently high to necessitate the use of baking soda instead of baking powder unless buttermilk is used in the cake mixture. Chocolate cake color gradually changes from cinnamon brown to mahogany red as the acidity decreases and the alkalinity increases. *Devil's food cakes,* which are characteristically mahogany red, contain excess baking soda to produce an alkaline pH (7) in the batter that react with the cocoa/chocolate pigments. Devil's food cakes have a coarser grain due to higher levels of baking soda. The characteristic chocolate flavor, as well as the color, is changed with increasing amounts of soda [58].

Flavorings. Flavorings maybe divided into two categories: natural and artificial. Salt is a natural flavor used for taste and to enhance flavor in shortened cakes. Extracts can be natural or artificial flavorings. Extracts are flavorful oils dissolved in alcohol.

Vanilla and almond extracts are commonly found in shortened cakes.

Emulsions of flavorful oils mixed with water and emulsifiers are sometimes used as flavorings. Orange and lemon emulsions are most common. Emulsions produce stronger flavors than extracts requiring less to be used. Alcoholic beverages such as rum or brandy or other liqueurs are sometimes used as a flavoring agent in shortened cakes.

Mixing

Shortened cake mixing involves blending ingredients to obtain a smooth batter without overmanipulating ingredients. A variety of methods can be used to combine the ingredients in shortened cakes. The method depends on the cake ingredients and formula. The objectives of all mixing methods are as follows: (1) distribute salt and leavening agent (i.e., baking powder) evenly through the flour; (2) distribute fat evenly through batter; (3) aerate batter to incorporate air; and (4) manipulate batter to moisten all ingredients and dissolve sugar without releasing too much carbon dioxide or overmanipulating batter. Correct ingredient temperature and mixing speed are necessary for air cell formation. Fat creams best at room temperature [11]. Four commonly used methods to mix shortened cakes are described subsequently.

Conventional or Creaming Method. The conventional method consists of creaming a plastic fat such as butter or shortening (**Figure 16–12**). Sugar is gradually added to the fat with continued creaming until light and fluffy. Creaming produces an air in fat foam; the more the fat is creamed, the more air is incorporated. The initial creaming stage is an 8- to 10-minute process [14]. Eggs or egg yolks are added to the fat–sugar mixture, and beaten until the mixture is well blended and very light. At this point, a water-in-oil

Creamed butter and sugar are shown in this mixer bowl. (Richard Embery/Pearson Education)

emulsion has been created. The mixing of eggs into creamed mixture takes 5–6 minutes [14].

The dry ingredients are sifted together and added alternately with the milk in about four portions. Some recipes may direct that egg whites be beaten separately until stiff but not dry. The whipped egg whites are incorporated into the batter at the end of mixing by folding in to avoid loss of air from the whites. The mixing of dry ingredients and milk into creamed egg mixture should take another 5–6 minutes.

Flavoring extract may be added to the creamed mixture or to the milk or when the dry and liquid ingredients are being added. Total time to mix a cake using the creaming method is approximately 15–20 minutes [14]. The conventional method of mixing is more time consuming than the other methods described, but it produces a fine-textured cake and may be used for mixing cakes by hand.

Conventional Sponge Method. The conventional sponge method is used with lean cake mixtures in which the amount of fat is not sufficient to produce a light creamed mass when all the sugar is added to the fat. The conventional sponge modifies the conventional method by beating the egg or egg white with parts of the sugar, and this sugar egg foam is folded into the batter. A dry, crumbly character of the fat–sugar mixture is avoided by reserving about half of the sugar beaten with the eggs until this mixture is very stiff. The rest of the sugar is creamed with the shortening. The liquid and dry ingredients are added alternately to the fat–sugar mixture. The beaten egg–sugar mixture is then folded into the batter at the end of mixing. Note that a surprisingly large amount of sugar can be creamed with a small or moderate

amount of fat if the fat is at the most favorable temperature for creaming 75–85°F (24–29°C) and if the addition of sugar is gradual. A good cake can be made from oil by using the conventional sponge method.

Muffin Method. In the muffin method, the eggs, milk, and melted fat are mixed together and added all at once to the sifted dry ingredients. This method is simple and rapid and is particularly useful for lean formulas when the cake is to be eaten while still warm.

Quick-Mix Method. The quick-mix method is known by several other names, including the *single-stage, one-bowl,* or *one-mix* method. It requires a change in the proportions of ingredients from those that are satisfactory for the conventional method of mixing. Higher proportions of sugar and liquid are used with the quick-mix method, and the shortening should contain an emulsifying agent. High-ratio cakes are mixed by this method. All of the ingredients, particularly the fat, should be at room temperature so that the ingredients can be readily dispersed. Use of this method is difficult when mixing by hand. An electric mixer is desirable; however, commercial cake mixes, which are designed for the one-bowl method of mixing, may be mixed by hand if the number of mixing strokes, rather than time, is used as the measure. The quick-mix method used with an appropriate formula yields a fine-grained, tender, moist cake of good volume that remains fresh for a relatively long period.

The mixing of the batter can be completed in two stages. In stage one, sift all dry ingredients into the bowl used for mixing. Add all fat, *part* of the liquid, and flavoring or add all fat, liquid, and flavoring. Beat for a specified time. In stage two, add unbeaten

WHY USE CAKE FLOUR?

Cake flour produces tender and delicate cakes. High-ratio cakes, in particular, will fall or collapse in the oven when cake flour is not used.

Cake flours are finely milled from soft wheat, which is low in protein. Additionally, cake flours are treated with chlorine gas to improve baking quality for delicate cakes. Chlorine bleaches pigments in the flour, oxidizes flour proteins to reduce normal gluten-developing properties, and interacts with the starch to increase swelling capacity [27, 34]. Apparently, some of the lipids in the flour are also affected [27]. Because cake batter is a complex system, the chlorine-treated flour undoubtedly reacts with other formula components to produce the texture and volume of the final product [53]. In making cakes with cake flour, the gelatinized starch is probably more important to structure than the small amount of gluten developed. The

gelatinization of the starch helps to convert a fluid phase into a solid, porous structure.

Researchers have investigated methods and ingredients for cake making that will result in high-quality cakes without the use of chlorine-treated flour. Cakes prepared with heat-treated flour and the addition of xanthan gum to the formula were found to have slightly greater volumes and a crumb grain that was essentially equivalent to the control cake prepared with chlorinated flour [71]. Other researchers found that non–chlorine-treated flour could be used to produce white layer cakes with better quality characteristics compared to the control cakes prepared with chlorine-treated flour. The formula of the non–chlorine-treated flour cakes was modified to include starch, soy lecithin, xanthan gum, and a higher concentration of dried egg albumen [18]. ■

eggs or egg whites and the remaining liquid if part of the liquid was withheld in the first stage, then beat for a specified time.

In some recipes, the baking powder may be omitted from the first stage and stirred in quickly (all by itself) between the two stages. For uniformity of blending, both the sides and the bottom of the bowl should be scraped frequently during mixing. Total mixing time for single-stage method is 8–10 minutes [14, 15].

Effects of Under- and Overmanipulation. The amount of mixing needed to produce the best cake texture varies with the proportions of ingredients and the quantity of batter. Medium mixing speed is typically used in mixing shortened cakes except when egg whites are beaten which is typically done on high speed. The temperature of the ingredients is also a factor with fat and eggs at room temperature. The distribution and amount of the leavening agent is important.

The thoroughness of creaming the fat–sugar mixture affects the extent of subsequent mixing. Thorough creaming makes possible a wider range in the amount of mixing that produces a good texture. A good creamed mixture is light and fluffy but has enough body to prevent an oily, pasty, or frothy mass. When eggs are added to the creamed fat and sugar, the mass becomes softer but should retain enough air to remain light. When the fat–sugar mixture separates into large flecks or curds on the addition of eggs, the resulting cake usually has a coarser texture than a cake produced from an uncurdled batter (**Figure 16–13**). A more stable emulsion may result from adding eggs gradually to the fat–sugar mixture. The use of a shortening containing an emulsifier, such as mono- and diglycerides, also aids in forming a stable emulsion.

Mixing a cake batter barely enough to dampen the dry ingredients may yield a cake of good volume, but the texture is coarse and the cell walls are thick.

The optimum amount of stirring produces a cake of good volume, uniform texture, small cells, thin cell walls, and a slightly rounded top.

Overstirring tends to produce a compact cake of smaller volume. When cakes are greatly overstirred, they become heavy or soggy. As stirring is increased, peaks tend to form, and the side walls of the cake are not as high as those in cakes stirred the optimum amount. If cakes are cut or broken where the peaks occur, long tunnels will be found. Certain rich mixtures may show a concave surface as if they were understirred.

The fact that cake mixtures contain more sugar and fat than most other flour mixtures decreases the tendency for toughness to result from stirring. Gluten development is retarded by sugar and fat. Thus, cakes are generally mixed much more vigorously than muffins or pancake batter. Stirring more than the optimum amount can toughen cakes, however, especially those made from lean mixtures and from flours with strong gluten quality.

Preparation of Pans

Cake pans impact how the cake bakes. Dark dull pans cause cake to brown more readily and uniformly than bright shiny pans. Shiny pans tend to reflect heat, whereas the dull pans more easily absorb heat. Nonstick pans are popular choice, but are not necessary for cake baking.

Baking pans should be prepared before the cake batter is mixed so that the batter can be transferred into the pans immediately after mixing. Allowing the batter to stand prior to baking will allow leavening to be lost, thereby negatively affecting the volume and texture of the baked cake.

Bottom of cake pans are greased but generally sides are not greased allowing cake batter to cling to side for traction and better volume (**Figure 16–14**).

Figure 16–13

Curdled fat mixture will not hold air cells. (Richard Embery/Pearson Education)

Figure 16–14

Grease the bottom of the pan and dust with flour before beginning to mix the cake. (© Douglas and Barbara Scheule)

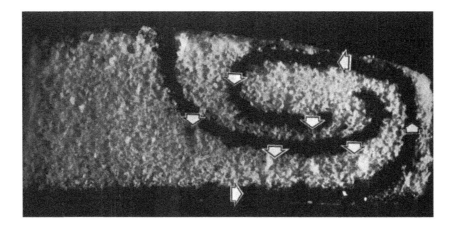

Figure 16–15

Partial cross section of cake shows cake batter flow pattern during baking. Movement of batter is by slow-moving convection currents. (Trimbo, H. B., & Miller, B. S. (1966). Batter flow and ring formation in cake baking. *Bakers Digest, 40*(1), 40–42, 44–45.) (© Bakers Digest/Sosland Publishing Co.)

Lightly flouring the greased bottom of the pan aids in removing the cake from the pan. An alternative procedure is to cut a piece of parchment or waxed paper to fit the bottom of the pan. After the paper is placed in the greased pan, it is greased on the surface which will come in contact with the cake. Pans should be filled approximately half full with batter allowing for batter expansion during baking.

Cupcakes are individual shortened cakes. They are typically made in parchment paper lined muffin tins and baked for a shorter time.

Baking

Changes in cake batter occur simultaneously when heat is applied during baking. During the early stages of baking, air bubbles are released into the aqueous (liquid) phase of batter. Carbon dioxide released from baking powder collects in these air bubbles and starts growing in size. Increasing temperatures melt fat and cause a decrease in batter viscosity, making a thinner batter with expanding air bubbles which becomes a foam. As the batter heats, convection currents set the expanding liquid batter filled with expanding air bubbles, fat, and swollen starch granules in a slow motion. **Figure 16–15** shows how batter bakes due to the direction of convection currents in cake batter. Batter convection currents are slow. The batter flows up from the bottom then to the outer edges of the pan then the currents turn inward toward the center of the pan. Batter on the bottom and sides of pans heat first and the top heats last. Steam and carbon dioxide cause a rise in cake volume as the batter heats and the gas cells move violently through the batter and the carbon dioxide starts escaping the batter. Air cells that are elastic and do not readily rupture letting gases escape are essential to yield a fine crumb and high-quality cake. At this point, the cake will collapse if the oven door is open and the temperature drops since the batter is not set.

During the late stages of baking, starch granules swell and gelatinize as egg proteins denature to form a network that causes the structure to set entrapping the expanded air cells. The top center is the last to bake. At this point, the cake is a solid foam. When the cake is removed from the oven to cool, the gases contract and structure strengthens. If the structure is not strong enough, the cake will collapse [11, 15, 74].

Baking Temperatures. The oven temperatures commonly used for baking shortened cakes range from 350 to 375°F (177 to 191°C). The oven should be preheated prior to placing batter-filled pans in the oven. The optimal temperature varies with the cake formula and the type of pan. High temperatures are sometimes not recommended because of excessive browning and humping of the cake top. An oven that is too slow (cool) will cause poor cake volume and texture because if the cake doesn't set fast enough, the cake structure collapses. Do not open oven or disturb cakes until they have finished rising and are partially brown. Disturbing cakes before they set may cause the structure to collapse. The cake browning is from caramelization of sugar in the hot oven and also the Maillard reaction.

Cooling the Cake Before Removal from the Pan. Cakes should not be removed from the pan until the interior reaches a temperature of about 140°F (60°C) so that the cake is firm enough to avoid damage. Cell walls are most fragile right out of the oven. Allowing the baked cake to stand about 10 minutes before removal from the pan is usually sufficient for this temperature to be reached (**Figure 16–16**). Shortened cakes should be cooled on wire racks to allow air circulation.

Microwave Baking. Flour mixtures do not form a brown crust when cooked by microwaves so flavor associated with browning is not developed. A browning

Figure 16–16

Steps for baking a perfect cake. (a) Pour the batter into prepared pans. The batter should be divided evenly between the layer pans. (b) Place the pans on the middle rack at least one inch from the sides of the oven. The pans should not touch. (c) After minimum baking time, touch the center lightly. If no imprint remains, the cake is done. Or insert a wooden pick in the center. If it comes out clean, the cake is done. (d) Allow cakes to cool 10 minutes on wire racks before removing them from the pans. If cakes are left in the pans too long, they will steam and become soggy. (e) The finished cake has a moist, velvety crumb and good volume. (© Barbara and Nathan Scheule)

FOCUS ON SCIENCE
MORE ABOUT CHOCOLATE CAKES AND LEAVENING AGENTS

Early research conducted on chocolate cake found that a combination of baking soda and baking powder had a positive effect on the crumb structure of the chocolate cake. Baking soda alone produces a coarse crumb, whereas baking powder produces a very fine crumb. All this has to do with how the carbon dioxide is evolved in the batter from the different leavening sources.

When a recipe contains a combination of baking powder and baking soda, the baking powder does most of the leavening. The baking soda is added to neutralize the acids in the recipe and to add tenderness and some leavening. Baking soda alone will produce a batter with a pH of 7, resulting in a red color or Red Devil's food. Increasing the amount of baking soda will darken the color but will also compromise the chocolate flavor with a soapy overtone. If baking powder is used alone, the pH will decrease below 7, producing a lighter brown color and a decrease in the chocolate flavor.

---

unit in the microwave oven may aid in browning the top surface of the cake. Cakes can be frosted to minimize lack of crust formation which impacts cake appearance.

Some cake mixes are specifically formulated to be cooked in a microwave oven. Microwave oven–safe pans packaged with the mix or available at home must be used. Because microwaved cakes rise higher than conventionally baked cakes, the pans should be filled no more than one-third to one-half full. The method of starting the cake at 50 percent power and finishing it at high power results in a more even top than cooking on high for the entire period. The top of a microwaved cake may be slightly moist when done, but the moisture will evaporate during standing time out of the oven.

FOAM CAKES

The proper incorporation and retention of air in whipped egg whites or eggs are critical to foam cakes for volume and texture. The foundation of foam cakes is an egg white foam. Egg whites are beaten or whipped incorporating air; viscous egg whites are transformed into a fine protein foam with many small air cells. Air trapped inside the protein-based foam is stabilized by flour proteins and starches. Sugar acts as a tenderizer.

The three basic ingredients found in foam cakes are egg whites, flour, and sugar. Foam cakes contain little or no fat and rely on beaten egg whites for their leavening and volume. Egg foam cakes are springier and tougher than shortened cakes. Foam cakes may or may not contain fat.

Unshortened foam cakes are of two types: white *angel food,* which is made from egg whites, and *yellow sponge,* which is made from the whole egg. Twinkies® are an example of a crème-filled yellow sponge cake (**Figure 16–17**).

Shortened foam cakes include chiffon. Chiffon cakes contain vegetable oil. Chiffon cakes were invented in California in 1927; it was touted to be "light as angel food cake and rich as pound cake." The chiffon cake recipe was later sold to General Mills® and the recipe used on their cake flour box [43] (Figure 16–17).

Figure 16–17a

Twinkies® are a crème-filled yellow sponge cake. (© Amanda Frye)

Figure 16–17b

Chiffon cake. (Richard Embery/Pearson Education)

Genoise are classic European-style foam cakes that may or may not contain fat. Genoise contain whole eggs which are whipped with sugar until light and fluffy. These cakes are rather dry so they are typically soaked with flavored syrup or liqueur for flavor and moisture.

Genoise and sponge cake are layered with frostings, fruit purees, jams, or fillings as the basis for many European tortes and desserts.

Figure 16–18

A good-quality angel food cake has large volume and thin cell walls. (© Barbara Scheule)

Angel Food Cake

Some may consider angel food cake the ultimate fat-free cake. Angel food cake is the simplest foam cake containing three basic ingredients—egg whites, sugar, and flour—with ratio of 42:42:15 [58]. Angel food cakes are a true egg foam cake with the sugar sweetened egg foam (a meringue) a functional component [70]. Angel food cake is leavened because of air trapped in whipped egg whites and steam. Air accounts for approximately half of the leavening in angel food cakes. Steam, formed from the vaporization of the water of egg white, causes the angel food cake to expand during baking. Steam is responsible for two to three times as much expansion as air [6]. Angel food cakes, like other cakes, may be made from scratch or from a mix.

Characteristics. A desirable angel food cake is porous or spongy with large volume, and has thin cell walls (**Figure 16–18**). The top is flat or slightly rounded. The top crust should look rough, but even and delicate brown. Angel food cake crumb should be snowy white; sponge cake yellow. Crumb should be tender and moist, not dry or sticky, but resilient and tender. Small uniform cells with thin cell walls are desired. The cake should be light, sweet with a delicate flavor and aroma.

Ingredients. Egg whites, sugar, cake flour, and cream of tartar are the primary ingredients in an angel food cake. The ratio of sugar to flour in the following cake formula is appropriate for tenderness yet not so high to cause the collapse of the cake:

Egg whites: 1 cup	Cream of tartar: 1 tsp
Sugar: 1¼ cup	Salt: ¼ tsp
Cake flour: 1 cup	Flavoring: 1 tsp

Egg Whites. Egg whites are the most important ingredient in angel food cakes. Egg whites incorporate air when beaten to form a foam. The mechanical forces of beating cause coagulation of egg proteins and stabilization of the foam (see Chapter 23 for a discussion of beating eggs). Egg white's ability to form a voluminous and stable foam is the result of complex interactions among the individual egg white proteins rather than a single egg protein component [72]. In addition, some proteins in egg whites are coagulated by heat and give structure to the baked cake.

Fresh eggs are preferable to older eggs for making angel food cakes because the pH of older eggs increases upon storage and maybe as high as 9.6. Egg white foams that produce the optimal angel food cake are 5.0 to 6.6 which is achieved by adding cream of tartar to egg whites at 1.5–1.7 percent per egg white weight basis. However, adding more cream of tartar to neutralize old egg whites has detrimental effects on the hydrolyzing egg white proteins [31, 35, 58].

Greater volume is also achieved if the egg whites are warmed to room temperature before beating. Eggs should be separated when cold and warmed to room temperature. The optimum whipping temperature of egg whites is 62–72°F (12–17°C) [58]. Care should be taken to avoid contaminating egg whites with fat or yolk as whipping and structural functionality will be compromised [72]. If the egg whites are overbeaten, they will break down and separate with liquid leakage. Eggs also act as the liquid to dissolve sugar and hydrate flour starch removing excess water from the batter [34] (**Figure 16–19**).

Good quality angel food cakes may also be prepared using frozen or dried egg whites [23]. Dried egg white solids must be reconstituted with six to seven parts water (weight based), then allowed to fully rehydrate [58]. Attempts to substitute part of angel food cakes' egg white with whey, xanthan gum, or wheat starch result in cake collapse and inferior product quality [22]. Egg white proteins are essential for the foam and stability of angel food cakes.

Flour. Cake flour produces a superior, delicate, and tender angel food cake because of the low protein content, weak quality of gluten, and fine granulation. The flour is folded into beaten egg whites so not to disturb the foam. Flour provides starch which is hydrated and gelatinized increasing the cake crumb strength and contributing to the structure. As the amount of sugar is increased, the flour must also be increased to provide a satisfactory ratio of sugar to flour so that sufficient structure is maintained in the cake. To avoid a tough cake, the proportion of flour should be less than half of the eggs on flour weight basis [11]. Angel food cakes made with all-purpose flour will be compact and have a small volume. All-purpose flour causes angel food cakes to shrink and pull away from the pan sides during later baking periods and cooling because of the cohesive gluten properties [6].

Sugar. Sugar stabilizes the egg white foam, sweetens, aids in browning, and promotes tenderness. Sugar allows more beating of the egg whites without overcoagulation of the egg proteins. A sugary crust can occur if the percentage of sugar in the formulation is too high. Sugar interferes with gluten development and therefore tends to produce a more tender and fragile cake when used in increasing amounts. Sugar elevates the coagulation temperature of egg proteins and, if used in excess, may result in the cake collapsing. In addition, the temperature for starch gelatinization is increased by sugar, which slows the setting of the structure attributed to the cake flour.

Cream of Tartar. Cream of tartar (tartaric acid) is an important constituent of angel food cake because of its beneficial effect on color, volume, and tenderness. Cream of tartar is added to improve the foaming capacity of the basic egg white. Cream of tartar, as an acid substance and whipping aid, reduces egg white pH, improving the whipping properties of the egg whites. Egg white stabilization occurs allowing heat penetration and egg white coagulation without collapse of the foam.

Cream of tartar additions produce a foam cake with white color and fine, even grain cells. Small air cells with thin walls are preferred since large air cells and thick cell walls cause a coarse grain from the effects of an unstable foam that has partially collapsed. Cakes omitting cream of tartar are yellowish in color with a coarse, tough crumb with thick cell walls [32]. Cream of tartar improves cake color. Flour anthoxanthin pigments are yellowish in an alkaline medium but are white in an acid or neutral medium. The Maillard or browning reaction between sugars and proteins is also less likely to occur in an acid than an alkaline medium. Therefore, the addition of cream of tartar (an acid salt) produces a cake that is more white than yellow or tan. The angel food cake has a lighter crust color than other cakes because the pH of the batter is lower due to the amount of cream of tartar used in the cake. The Maillard browning reaction, which is responsible for browning, proceeds at a lower rate because of the acidic pH, resulting in a "macaroon" color with a crust that is more crisp and sugary [14, 15]. Cream of tartar prevents extreme shrinkage of the cake during the last part of the baking period and during the cooling period. Angel food cakes containing cream of tartar produce a more tender cake than without.

Mixing. An angel food cake is mixed by (1) sifting flour or flour and partial amount of sugar, (2) beating room-temperature egg whites, (3) incorporating sugar into the egg whites, and (4) folding in of the flour or flour–sugar mixture. Some recipes specify that the cake flour and part of the sugar should be sifted together before folding into the egg whites in the final step. Sifting should be done in advance of beating the egg whites so that the flour is ready to use once the eggs are whipped. Sifting (1) blends the flour and sugar thoroughly, (2) lightens the flour and removes lumps, and (3) helps to reduce the amount of folding needed to blend the flour into the beaten egg whites.

Egg whites and cream of tartar are beaten with an electric mixer, a rotary beater, or a wire whisk. The whisk usually produces a somewhat larger volume of cake, but the cells also are larger. Many recipes suggest beating in some or all of the sugar once the egg whites have been beaten to the foam stage. Beating the sugar into the egg whites is known as the *meringue method* and is preferable if an electric mixer is used. Beating some sugar into the egg white foam seems to have a greater stabilizing effect on the cake than folding all of the sugar in with the flour. Regardless of the method used for adding sugar, about 2 tablespoons of sugar at a time are sifted over the surface of the egg whites. Adding the sugar too quickly results in loss of air.

Properly beaten egg whites should be stiff, but the peaks and tails that form should bend over slightly instead of standing rigid and upright. Excessively overbeaten egg whites will break down

FOCUS ON SCIENCE
CREAM OF TARTAR

Cream of tartar changes the pH of the egg white to an acidic range (pH of 5.6 to 5.7) by increasing the number of free-floating hydrogen ions (H^+) in the egg white. This pH range is near the isoelectric point of globulin G_2 and considerably below pH 8.0, at which the dissociation of ovomucin occurs. Both globulin G_2 and ovomucin are proteins found in egg whites.

At the more acidic pH range, the egg white foam becomes stable and is able to hold on to air whipped into the whites. During baking, this more stable foam reaches the temperature of coagulation before the foam collapses. Thus, the cake shrinkage during the last phase of baking and the cooling period is less likely to occur.

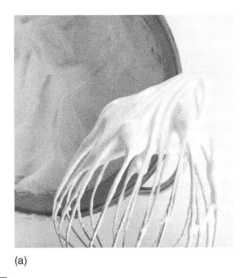
(a)

(b)

Figure 16–19

(a) Egg whites whipped to stiff peaks. (b) Overwhipped egg whites which are spongy and foam broken. (Richard Embery/Pearson Education)

and separate (**Figure 16–19**). Egg whites overbeaten but not separated will negatively impact cake quality by contributing to dryness and a lack of extensibility in the film surrounding the air bubbles. The air cells break and collapse, resulting in a cake of low volume, thick cell walls, and coarse texture. Egg whites contaminated with a small amount of yolk or fat will not properly whip. Egg whites should never be whipped in a plastic bowl or with a plastic whisk since these products can retain fat that will destroy the egg white foam [34].

The cake flour or cake flour and sugar mixture should be gently folded into the beaten egg whites in small increments with as little "mixing" as possible. A folding instead of a mixing motion helps to retain air in the egg whites (**Figure 16–20**). When folding by hand, use a spatula and cut down through the mixture. Then move the spatula along the bottom of the bowl and lift up and over. The folding action may also be done with an electric mixer on the lowest speed possible. Overmanipulation, whether when folding by hand or with a mixer, results in a loss of air and tenderness of the angel food cake. "Cupping" of the top crust can be corrected by slightly increasing flour in the recipe [58].

The flavoring extract may be added after the whites are partially beaten or when folding in the flour. Adding the extract at one of these stages allows it to become thoroughly distributed without the necessity for overmanipulation later. Extract should not be added at the end of mixing because either the extract is incompletely blended with the batter or extra manipulation is needed. Salt may be added toward the end of the beating of the foam and before the addition of flour. Salt may have a slight destabilizing effect on the egg white foam if it is added earlier.

Figure 16–20

To maintain air in egg whites, gently fold flour into the whites by cutting down through the whites with the edge of a spatula to the bottom of the bowl and then bringing ingredients up from the bottom and folding over the top. This process continues until the ingredients are blended. Folding flour into a chocolate angel food cake is shown here. (Richard Embery/Pearson Education)

Preparation of Pans. Pans are not greased for angel food or chiffon cakes. Angel food cake is typically baked in a tube pan with steep sides often with a removal bottom, but other pans such as loaf pans work too. It is desirable to have the mixture cling to the sides of the pan until it is coagulated by the heat of the oven. Tapping filled pans slightly before

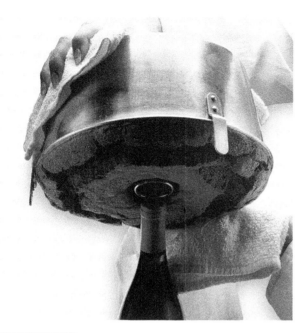

Figure 16–21

Angel food cake should be cooled upside down to protect the light, delicate structure until cool. (Richard Embery/Pearson Education)

placing in the oven or running a metal spatula gently through the filled pan can help eliminate large air pockets in the finished product [58]. Excessive crust browning can be corrected by slightly wetting the interior pan surface prior to filling. The pan moisture delays rise of surface temperature and caramelization, hence a lighter crust color [58]. After baking, the pan is inverted and allowed to stand until the cake is thoroughly cooled (**Figure 16–21**). This gives the delicate cake structure a chance to set with the least amount of strain placed on it.

Baking Temperatures. Baking at 350°F (177°C) has been found to result in a more tender and moist angel food cake of larger volume and thinner cell walls than baking at lower temperatures [2]. Cakes are done when lightly brown and a toothpick inserted into the center comes out clean. Overbaking tends to toughen the cake whatever the temperature, but greater toughening occurs with longer baking at higher temperatures.

Angel food cakes made from commercial mixes and baked at 350–375°F (177–191°C) scored higher in all quality characteristics than those baked at 400–425°F (204–218°C) [9]. Compact layers formed as a result of partial collapse of the structure after the cakes baked at 400–425°F (204–218°C) were removed from the oven. Higher temperatures cause premature

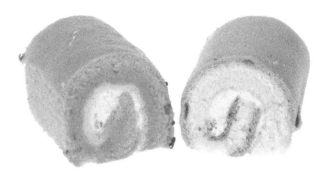

Figure 16–22

Sponge cake is the base cake for a rolled jelly roll or Swiss rolls. (Sunsetman/Shutterstock)

setting and thus lower volumes [43]. Angel food cakes made from commercial mixes, baking initially at 375°F (191°C) and then lowering the temperature to 350°F (177°C), 325°F (163°C), and finally 300°F (149°C) at 10-minute intervals, yield tender baked cakes of very high volume.

Sponge Cake

Sponge cakes, unlike angel food cakes, use both the egg whites and yolks (**Figure 16-22**). Toughening effect from whole egg must be balanced with tenderizing aspects of sugar. Sugar is typically equal or slightly more than egg. Some sponge cake recipes will also include cream of tartar to stabilize the egg white foam, a small amount of baking powder for leavening, and various flavorings. Traditional sponge cakes are leavened by air trapped in the whipped eggs and steam without the use of baking powder. Air incorporated during mixing contributes to leavening, but steam contributes more to batter expansion. Sponge cake structure develops during baking as gas bubbles expand, proteins coagulate, and starch gelatinizes. Gas bubbles expand early in baking leading to batter expansion. Further heating causes starch granules to swell and protein coagulate to form a gel-like structure and stop bubble expansion. End-stage baking causes structure to set as proteins coagulate [6] (**Figure 16–23**).

Ingredients and Formula The usual ingredients and proportions for yellow sponge cake are as follows:

Eggs: 6	Water: 2 Tbsp
Sugar: 1 cup	Lemon juice: 1 Tbsp
Cake flour: 1 cup	Grated lemon rind: 1 Tbsp
Salt: ¼ tsp or slightly less	

Figure 16–23

(Left) Poor-quality sponge cake with compact, low volume, irregular grain, and tunneling. (Right) Good-quality sponge cake with good volume, even grain, and texture.

(Richard Embery/Pearson Education)

Mixing. Sponge cake preparation involves more steps than angel food cake. There are multiple procedures to prepare sponge cake. Yellow sponge cakes can be made by (1) whole eggs, (2) separated eggs, or (3) meringue methods. In the whole-egg method, the eggs are beaten until they are foamy. The water, lemon juice, and lemon rind are then added, and the mixture is beaten until it is as stiff as possible. (This mixture can be made very stiff.) The sugar is added gradually and beaten into the mixture. The flour and salt are mixed together and then sifted over the surface, about 2 tablespoons at a time, and folded into the egg mixture until all is well blended.

In one separated-egg method, the egg yolks are partially beaten. The sugar, salt, water, lemon juice, and lemon rind are added, and the whole mass is beaten until very stiff. The flour is folded lightly into the mixture, after which the stiffly beaten egg whites are folded in [7]. Alternatively, the stiffly beaten mixture of yolks, sugar, water, lemon juice and rind, and salt is combined with the beaten egg whites before the flour is folded into the mixture.

In a meringue method, the sugar is boiled with about three-fourths the volume of water to 244°F (118°C). It is then poured gradually over the beaten egg whites with constant stirring until a stiff meringue is formed. The egg yolks, lemon juice, lemon rind, and salt are beaten together until very stiff. The yolk mixture is folded into the whites, and the flour is then gradually folded in.

Commercial bakers may use emulsifiers in shortened sponge cakes. Emulsifiers allow the use of a simplified one-stage mixing procedure and result in a lighter cake of uniform grain, greater tenderness, and longer shelf life.

Panning and Baking. Several types of pans may be used for a sponge cake, depending on the final use of the cake. Tube pans, standard round cake pans, or sheet pans may be used. Sponge cakes to be used for a jelly roll are baked in a sheet pan. The pan used to bake a sponge cake is usually not greased, but it may be lined with parchment. Baking temperatures for sponge cakes are similar to those used for angel food cakes. Sponge cakes are toughened by overbaking.

Genoise Cake

Ingredients. The usual ingredients in a classic genoise cake are cake flour, eggs, and sugar. Melted butter may or may not be included. The cake is leavened from air trapped with whipped whole eggs and steam. The usual ingredients and proportions for a classic genoise [18] are as follows:

Eggs: 7	Cake flour: 1⅓ cup
Sugar: 1⅓ cup	Butter, melted: 2 Tbsp

Mixing. A genoise cake is prepared by whisking the eggs and sugar together. Then this mixture is placed over warm water to heat the eggs to approximately 100°F (38°C) so that a greater volume may be obtained when beaten [43]. Care must be taken to not cook the eggs. Once warm, the egg–sugar mixture is beaten vigorously with a mixer until triple in volume. This whipped egg–sugar mixture is folded gently with presifted flour. If melted butter is used, it is folded in at the end.

Panning, Baking, and Finishing. The batter is spread into a parchment-lined sheet and baked at 350°F (180°C). This thin sheet of cake may then be used for layering with various icings, jellies, or fillings. Because this cake is relatively dry compared to other types of cakes, it may also be soaked with syrups, or liqueurs [43].

Chiffon Cake

Ingredients. Chiffon cakes share several similarities to angel food cakes. However, unlike angel food cakes, chiffon cakes include egg yolks and oil (Figure 16–17). The leavening is largely because of the air beaten into egg whites and steam; however, most recipes also include baking powder. If orange or lemon chiffon is being prepared, part of the water will be substituted with juice. Typical ingredients for a chiffon cake are the following:

Cake flour: 2¼ cups	Water: ¾ cup
Sugar: 1½ cups	Egg whites: 8
Vegetable oil: ½ cup	Baking powder: 1 Tbsp
Egg yolks: 6	Salt and flavoring extract

Figure 16–24

Folding whipped egg whites into chiffon cake batter to produce a cake with high volume. (Richard Embery/Pearson Education)

Mixing. A chiffon cake is mixed in several steps. First, the flour, baking powder, and salt are sifted together. The oil, egg yolks, water, and flavorings are beaten together, then mixed with the flour mixture. In a separate bowl, the egg whites are beaten until foamy, and then sugar is added gradually with continued beating until the egg whites are stiff. Part of the egg whites are folded with the batter to start, and then the remaining egg whites are incorporated by folding into the cake batter [43] (**Figure 16–24**).

Panning, Baking, and Finishing. Chiffon cakes are baked at 325°F (160°C) in an ungreased tube pan. Like an angel food cake, the cake is hung upside down to cool after removal from the oven. The cake may be lightly glazed or iced once cool. These cakes have similarities to the angel food cakes, but because of the fat in the yolks and the oil, these cakes are moister and richer [43].

Altitude Adjustments for Cakes

Cake ingredients and formulas need to be adjusted when baking at high altitudes since atmospheric pressure is much lower than at sea level. Exact adjustments depend on exact altitude and type of cake. Altitude modifications start being needed around 2,000 feet. At altitudes higher than 3,000 feet, a cake may become overinflated and collapse during baking without recipe modifications.

Leavening. At higher altitudes, leavening gases expand more since the atmospheric pressure is lower with less air pressure to overcome for the cake rising. Baking powder and baking soda need to be reduced. Baking powder should be reduced 20 percent at 2,500 feet, 40 percent at 5,000 feet, and 60 percent at 7,500 feet. Creaming and foaming procedures should be reduced so less air is incorporated.

Liquids. Waters boils at a lower temperature at higher altitudes so water evaporates more easily and liquids may need to be increased in cakes to prevent drying during and after baking. Increasing liquid amounts also help compensate for moisture loss from high altitude adjustments for the other ingredients—sugar, fat, and flour. Liquid increase guidelines are 2,500 feet increase 9 percent, 5,000 feet increase 15 percent, and 7,500 feet increase 22 percent.

Flour. Increased flour is needed at higher altitudes because more structural support is required. Flour increases start minimally at 3,000 feet at 5,000 feet increase of 4 percent and 7,500 feet 9 percent increase.

Eggs. Increase egg levels for structural support and increased liquid needs. Higher eggs do not toughen cakes at higher altitudes. Egg increases for 2,500 feet 2.5 percent, 5,000 feet 9 percent, and 7,500 feet 15 percent.

Sugar. Reduction in sugar is needed to provide for improved structural strength. Sugar concentration increase as water evaporation increases at higher levels. Decrease sugar 3 percent at 2,500 feet, 6 percent at 5,000 feet, and 9 percent at 7,500 feet.

Shortening. Fat should be decreased at very high altitudes, 9 percent at 7,500 feet due to fat's effect to weaken cake structure.

Baking Temperatures. Increasing baking temperatures 10–15°F will increase the rate cake sets by speeding protein coagulation and starch gelatinization for a stronger cake structure. Increase baking temperature 25°F above 3,500 feet.

Pan Greasing. Grease pans more heavily and remove cakes from pans as soon as possible as high-fat cakes have a tendency to stick to pans at higher altitudes.

Storage. Due to increased water evaporation rate at high altitudes wrap or ice cakes as soon as possible to prevent drying. Refer to Chapter 13 for more information on high-altitude baking.

COOKIES

Cookie originated from the Dutch word *Koekje* meaning a small cake [46]. Cookies come in a wide variety of flavors, shapes, sizes, and textures. Mixing and shaping procedures depend on ingredients ratios. Some characteristics that are desirable in one cookie are not desirable in another. For example, ginger snaps are meant to be crisp, whereas a chocolate chip cookie may be soft and chewy. Some cookies are formed to hold shape and others to spread during baking. Production methods of baking cookies vary widely based on the cookie. Home and commercial production offer even more variations. *Crispness, softness, chewiness,* and *spread* are terms used to describe cookies. These characteristics are derived from various ingredients, mixing methods, production process, baking methods, and storage methods. Understanding how these characteristics are produced in cookies is important.

Cookies are similar to cakes since they are typically high in sugar and fat and relatively low in moisture. Typically, cookie formulas are lower in liquid than cakes. This lower liquid level and high sugar concentration do not allow starch to gelatinize during the baking of cookies. Since the starch does not gelatinize, the cookie structure collapses compared to cake whose structure is set with starch gelatinization. Cookies are usually made from all-purpose flour at home or a specialty soft wheat flour for commercial production.

Cookie spread is an important quality standard. The cookie spread of dough is the increase in size "spread" caused by the viscous dough flow influenced by heat (**Figure 16–25**). Formulation, ingredients, production methods, and baking conditions all influence cookie spread [58]. The cracking characteristic pattern is important for certain cookies like gingersnaps and snickerdoodles. The "snap" may be an important characteristic of some cookies. Snap is independent of hardness. A small amount to no chemical leavening is used in cookie doughs [34].

Cookies in Europe and other parts of the world are called "biscuits." However, in the United States biscuits are a less sweet leavened individual size quick bread. There are also a number of products that are called cookies but do not fit a standard cookie definition and do not fit in any other categories.

Classification and Characteristics

Cookies formulations and methods fall into broad categories. There are six basic types of cookies that are produced by hand for small-scale production such as home, food service, or small bakery production. *Rolled cookies,* when baked, may form either a crisp or a soft cookie, depending on the proportions of the ingredients and the degree of doneness (**Figure 16–26**). *Dropped cookies* are made from a stiff batter that may be dropped or scraped from the spoon (**Figure 16–27**). *Bar cookies,* a cake-type mixture, are baked in a thin sheet and later cut into bars or squares (**Figure 16–28**).

Figure 16–26
Rolled, cut, and decorated cookies. (Richard Embery/Pearson Education)

Figure 16–25
Cookie spread of same recipe prepared altering creaming times shows effect on cookie spread. (Left) Normal amount of creaming with largest spread. (Middle) moderate spread. (Right) Minimal creaming and air incorporation (Richard Embery/Pearson Education)

Figure 16–27
Chocolate chip cookies are made from a drop cookie dough. (Nattika/Shutterstock)

Figure 16–28

Bar cookies may be made from cookie dough pressed or poured into individual serving pieces after baking. Brownies are a bar cookie; they may be cake-like (left) or dense and fudgy (right). Fudgy brownies are typically leavened only by the air incorporated during mixing. (Richard Embery/Pearson Education)

Figure 16–30a

Mexican Wedding Cookies (Polvorones) are molded by hand into the round balls prior to baking. (Richard Embery/Pearson Education)

Figure 16–29

Pressed cookies can be made with a cookie press. Interchangeable discs allow the creation of cookies with different shapes and designs. (© Amanda Frye)

Figure 16–30b

Peanut butter cookies are first molded into a ball and then flattened with fork tines, which forms the hatch pattern. Baked cookies cooling on a wire rack, which allows air circulation. (Charles Brutlag/123RF)

Pressed cookies are made from an extra-rich stiff dough that is pressed through a cookie press into various shapes (**Figure 16–29**). *Molded cookies* are made from a stiff dough that is shaped into balls, bars, or crescents and sometimes flattened before baking (**Figure 16–30**). *Icebox* or *refrigerator cookies* are made from a mixture so rich in fat that the dough is difficult, if not impossible, to roll; it is chilled in the refrigerator to harden the fat and is then sliced from the roll or molded and baked (**Figure 16–31**).

The characteristics of cookies vary with the type being prepared. Some are crisp, tender, chewy, or crisp on the outside and tender in the inside. Crisp cookies are usually made from a mixture that is rich in fat or sugar or both. Softer cookies should include a type of sugar with invert sugar (fructose and glucose). Honey, corn syrup, and brown sugar will contribute

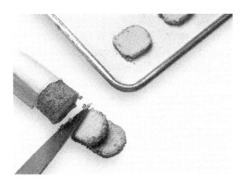

Slicing a roll of refrigerator cookies and placing on parchment lined baking sheet. (Richard Embery/Pearson Education)

to a softer cookie [43]. The length of baking will also have an impact on texture. To maintain a moist tender interior, the cookies should be removed from the oven when brown but still moist. See Chapter 9 for more about types of sugar, including invert sugar.

The spread of cookies is another important attribute. If cookies spread too much, they are thin and brittle. Cookies that spread too little can be humped and on cooling may be dry. Commercially consistent cookie size is extremely important from not only a cost standpoint, but also a packaging issue. Cookies must be able to fit in the box or carton in which they are sold.

The amount of spread can be influenced by a variety of factors. High-protein flour and limited liquid ingredients can result in a cookie that is too firm and spreads too little. To increase the spread, use granulated sugar, increase fat, increase moisture slightly, or use lower-protein flour. To reduce the amount of spread, add additional baking soda or powder or increase flour [43]. Higher altitudes increase cookie spread due to delayed starch gelatinization [5].

Ingredients

Formulas for cookies are varied. As with cakes, the function of the ingredients should be considered when making recipe adjustments.

Flour. All-purpose flour is used for most homemade cookies. Pastry flour, which is lower in protein, may be used in some food service operations to produce a crisp, but chewy-in-the-center cookie. Cake flour is not generally used for cookies because few cookies have a soft, velvety crumb or the texture of good sponge or shortened cakes. Cake flour can be useful in obtaining the desired tenderness in brownies [10]. Bread flours are generally too high in protein to produce an acceptable cookie. Commercial cookie flours are typically soft wheat long patent or straight grade flours with a protein content between 9 and 10 percent. Deposit-style cookies are typically made from soft white winter wheat with a protein content of 7.5–8.5 percent.

Sometimes stronger flours are used to prevent excessive spread or to preserve top designs from extruded doughs. Flour quality for cookies is often evaluated by American Association of Cereal Chemists (AACC) sugar snap cookie baking tests. Commercial cookie bakers do not use chlorinated flours since chlorination interferes with flour proteins and subsequently with cookie spread. High chlorinated flours will decrease cookie spread [58]. Malt, derived from flour, is often added to cookie dough as a flavor enhancer and humectant.

Flours other than wheat flour have also been used for cookies. Cookies can be prepared from a combination of flours such as wheat flour, rice flour, and defatted soy flour [30]. Gluten-free cookies use ingredients such as tapioca, potato, and corn starch; corn, rice, or soy flour; and xanthan gum.

Sugar. Cookie recipes usually include white granulated sugar, brown sugar, or a combination of both. Sugar is creamed with butter or shortening, thereby contributing to leavening. Professional bakers typically use fine granulated sugar for cookies since it dissolves rapidly during mixing. However, coarser sugar yields more tender cookies with greater spread. Powder sugar rapidly dissolves, but decreases cookie spread and tenderness [58].

Sugar adds sweetness and contributes to browning, because of caramelization when baked, as well as the flavors associated with caramelization. Sugar increases the flour starch gelatinization temperature. White granulated sugar promotes a crisp texture. As a cookie cools, it hardens due to sugar crystallization which makes a cookie crisp [58]. Soft cookies lose moisture during storage changing the texture. The cookie will remain soft as long as sugar stays dissolved or is in a supersaturated solution. If sugar crystallizes, the cookie will become brittle. High fructose corn syrup can be used as along as the water in the syrup does not exceed liquid in the formula. Invert syrups are sometimes used to produce a more tender softer cookie [58]. Sugar influences surface cracking. Surface cracking is reduced when fructose, high fructose corn syrup, or glucose syrups were substituted for 10 percent of the crystalline sucrose and no surface cracking occurs with complete substitution [34].

Brown sugar contributes flavor as well as a moist, chewy texture [36, 63]. Dark brown sugar will add more flavor than light. Selected cookies may include molasses or corn syrup; both will add moisture. Molasses also contributes a distinctive flavor and acid for leavening reactions.

Fat. Butter or shortening is often used in cookie recipes. Cookie formulas are typically between 10 and 30 percent fat with the average cookie formula around 15–20 percent fat total dough weight based on total dough/batter weight [44]. Vegetable oil is used in some recipes, but neither oil nor shortening will contribute the same flavor or mouthfeel as butter. Fat influences leavening when creamed with sugar as air is incorporated into dough. Shortening of gluten strands by coating flour proteins is another role of fat. Fat also inhibits interaction between flour structural protein and starch components [43]. It also has an impact on crispness, moistness, and the amount of spread in the oven. Some cookie recipes use several different fats to achieve a desired result. A two-part unsaturated fat to one-part saturated fat offers a tender, chewy cookie center [28]. Therefore, a blend of butter and vegetable oil may help to create the bite and texture desired [4]. When making substitutions, it should be noted that (1) butter and margarine are approximately 20 percent water, (2) shortening and oil are 100 percent fat, and (3) margarine spreads are not recommended for baking because of low fat content.

Shortenings are primarily used in commercial cookie production and play a critical role to produce a consistent dough for automated cookie production. Shortenings also are important for cookie shelf life and texture of the finished product. However, the shortening trans fat ban forced manufacturers to find alternative fats or modify formulas.

Fat substitutes have been tested in cooking recipes. In one study, oatmeal, peanut butter, and chocolate chip cookies were prepared with applesauce or prune puree to reduce the fat content [67]. The reduced-fat peanut butter cookies were the most difficult to prepare with acceptable quality attributes. Flavor acceptability was impaired when fruit purees were used. However, the sensory panel found the reduced-fat oatmeal and chocolate chip cookies to be acceptable. The use of pureed white beans as a fat substitute in oatmeal chocolate chip cookies was also found to prepare an acceptable cookie [61].

Eggs. Most cookie recipes use whole fresh egg, although some may use only the yolks or whites. As in cakes, eggs contribute to structure. Eggs are also a source of liquid in the recipe that wets other ingredients. Too high a proportion of eggs may make the cookies dry or more cake-like [36]. Commercial cookie production may use fresh or frozen liquid whole eggs or sometimes dried whole eggs [58].

Liquid. Cookie recipes are often prepared without a liquid such as milk or water. The ingredients are often moistened by the eggs and fat. When liquid is added, it may be as little as 1 to 3 tablespoons in a cookie batch yielding two dozen cookies. Including dairy products in cookies improves color, texture, taste, shelf life, and nutritional value of the products [58].

Leavening. Cookies may use baking powder, baking soda, or both as leavening ingredients. An acidic ingredient such as molasses, honey, or brown sugar is essential when baking soda is used. Some types of cookies use no added leavening ingredient. In this case, the leavening is mainly from air incorporated during the creaming of sugar and fat plus steam leavening.

Leavening agents affect the cookie grain and texture. No leavening gives a very dense grain and brittle hard-textured cookie. Rich cookie doughs high in fat and sugar typically require less leavening than a leaner dough. Surface cracking or checking results when leavening gases are released when interior dough is still "plastic" but exterior is set. Delayed release of soda will result in cracking or checking. Dough pH affects baked cookie color. Browning is accelerated in alkaline conditions, but retarded in acidic conditions. Formulations should strive for a neutral pH, but often an alkaline pH is used for chocolate products for color accentuation.

Mixing and Handling

The objective of cookie dough mixing is to produce a uniform mixture and incorporate air into the dough. The creaming or conventional method includes the following steps: (1) creaming fat and sugar, (2) beating in eggs, (3) addition of other liquid ingredients, and (4) mixing in flour and nuts or chips. This method is used for mixing most cookies. Butter, when used in the recipe, should be at room temperature so that it is a plastic consistency—not too brittle and not too soft. Because cookies are usually made with relatively rich dough that is high in fat and sugar, overmixing is less a concern than with other types of baked goods. However, excessive mixing should be avoided after the flour is added so gluten development is minimized.

Drop cookies are dropped from a spoon onto a cookie sheet (Figure 16–27). Most cookie doughs are too stiff to be dropped from the spoon and must be scrapped off. Small ice cream scoops make the task of dipping cookies faster and easier (**Figure 16–32**). Homemade bar cookies are poured, pressed, or spread into a pan with sides.

Pressed cookies, such as spritz, are pressed through discs in a cookie press or a pastry bag to create attractive shapes. The dough needs to be stiff enough to maintain shape when baked yet soft enough to be pressed through the cookie press (Figure 16–29).

Rolled cookies are soft enough to roll out yet stiff enough to be rolled and handled. To avoid tough, dry cookies, it is best to cut out the cookie shapes to avoid as much scrap dough as possible. Minimizing the amount of rerolling that is done in the process of using all of the dough is best. Flour will need to be added to the board or counter when rolling out the dough. The least amount of flour possible to avoid sticking should be used. The thickness of rolled dough ready for cutting is usually 1/8 or 3/16 inch. If the dough is to be used for cutouts, especially large ones, it is good to roll it to a ¼-inch thickness (**Figure 16–33**).

Baking

Proper baking is essential in making good cookies. Cookies must be baked at proper temperature for correct length of time for an excellent final product. Most

Figure 16–32
Drop cookies are quickly placed onto a pan by using a small disher or scoop as shown here. (Richard Embery/Pearson Education)

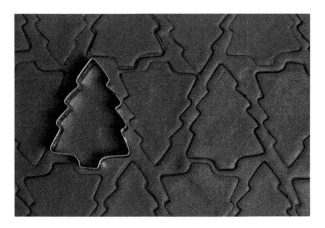

Figure 16–33
Cut-out cookie dough should be rolled 1/8–1/4 inch thick. Cut-outs should be done as close together as possible to avoid excess scrap dough. (Emilia Stasiak/Shutterstock)

cookies bake at a relatively high temperature for a short time. Good cookie quality can be summarized by (1) the cookie size width and height and (2) sensory qualities of appearance, cookie flavor, and cookie bite—a high-quality cookie must have tender bite [33]. Cookie size can be directly related to cookie spread. In commercial bakeries, errors in cookie spread can be costly as cookies that spread too much cannot be placed in packaging without breaking and too little spread will not fill the packaging container. Cookies no matter if crisp or chewy must not be tough or difficult to bite [33]. Failures in the baking stage can result in a cookie with poor flavor, diminished eating

qualities, and poor appearance even if a proper formula and high-quality ingredients were used [44].

Preparation of Pans

Cookies are baked on flat baking sheets for dropped and shaped cookies, whereas bar cookies such as brownies require baking pans with high sidewalls. Depending on the type of cookie, dough is placed on greased or ungreased cookie sheets or parchment paper lined pans. Pan preparation typically depends on richness of dough used. Lean doughs (15–20 percent fat or less by weight) must be baked on parchment line pans or greased pans for easy removal. Typically, richer cookies such as butter cookies or shortbreads (20 percent fat by weight) are baked on ungreased/unlined pans. Baking sheets rather than cake pans are more efficient for baking most cookies because there are no high sidewalls to interfere with the circulation of heat and the browning of the cookies.

Cookies may stick to pans if (1) pans are not clean; (2) pans are wet or have wet spots; (3) pans not properly greased or parchment paper not used; and (4) pans are warped or uneven on the bottom. Warped, battered, or dented pans cause uneven distribution of heat interfering with cookie baking [44]. Depending on the type of cookie, cookies are baked in an oven preheated to 350°F (177°C) to 400°F (204°C). Constant even heat is important and flash heat or sudden changes in heat should be avoided [44]. Double panning can be used where bottom oven heat is excessive or not controlled. Double panning is done by placing a second same size sheet pan under the pan with cookies. Convection ovens are useful in providing even heating for cookies during baking.

Commercial Cookies

Large-scale commercial bakeries group cookies based on the equipment used for production (**Figure 16–34**). The dough formulations, rheology, and consistency

Figure 16–34
Baked cookies being carried on a conveyor belt to be packaged. (Jordache/Shutterstock)

Figure 16–35

Jam filling deposited on cookie dough before baking.
(Lcarmen13/Shutterstock)

Figure 16–37

Animal crackers are an example of a wire cut cookie. (Louella938/ Shutterstock)

Figure 16–36

Ladyfingers are made from a deposited batter.
(Christianhaas/123RF)

are based on the equipment used in production. Commercial baked cookies have similarities and differences to handmade/homemade counterparts. Commercially, cookies are typically baked in long tunnel ovens with conveyor belt stainless steel bands that move the cookie dough at various rates through the oven (**Figure 16–35**). Commercial baking equipment is always changing to improve baking quality. The method in which commercial cookie dough is placed on the steel baking band falls into various categories.

Deposit or drop cookies are produced from a flour mixture with similar consistency as layer cake batter. Deposit cookie formulations are based on flour weight 35–40 percent sugar, 65–75 percent shortening, and 15–25 percent whole eggs (liquid). Dough/batter is deposited onto baking band. Ladyfingers and macaroons are an example of deposited dough cookies (**Figure 16–36**).

Wire cut cookies are more like hand-scooped dough such as homemade chocolate chip cookies

or rolled cookies such as handmade sugar cookies. The soft dough is extruded through an orifice then cut by a wire. These doughs are cohesive enough to hold together yet short enough (has enough fat) to separate from wires. Wire cut cookies rise and spread like a homemade drop cookie and have a homemade cookie appearance. Many commercial cookie products are produced by the wire cut method including such cookies as chocolate chip. These cookies per flour weight contain a high amount of sugar (50–70 percent) and fat (50–60 percent) and up to 15 percent egg to produce more cohesive soft dough. Different colored or textured doughs may be coextruded and cut to create dual textured or colored cookies. Dual texture doughs are created by use of different sweeteners with differing humectant qualities. One dough may contain crystalline sucrose for a crisp texture and the other dough may contain invert syrup or corn syrup to inhibit crystallization for a softer texture [58].

Cutting machine or rotary cut cookies are stamped (cut) into various shapes from a continuous sheet of dough. Animal crackers/cookies or gingerbread men are an example of cutting machine cookies (**Figure 16–37**). These cookies are typically lower in sugar [31].

Rotary mold cookies are made by placing dough in a cylinder whose surface is embossed molds engraved with designs [76] (**Figure 16–38**). Filled sandwich cookies like Oreos are produced by forcing dough into rotating cylinder with a series of embossed shallow molds (**Figure 16–39**). The mold's designs are imprinted on the cookie dough. The dough is extracted from the mold placed on baking band. The molded cookie dough cannot be disturbed before or during baking otherwise the design will be distorted. Rotary mold cookie dough formulas have high sugar and fat levels with low moisture content (less than 20 percent moisture based on flour weight). Similarly, homemade German *springerle* cookies are made by

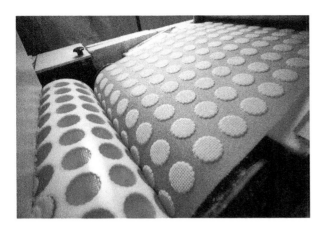

Figure 16–38

A commercial rotary mold for cookie production. (Pipicato/ Shutterstock)

Figure 16–40

Springerle molds and embossed rolling pin used to make homemade molded cookies. (Kathik/Fotolia)

Figure 16–39

These cream-filled sandwich cookies are made in embossed rotary molds which leave the design imprint on the cookie. (© Amanda Frye)

Figure 16–41

Gingersnap cookies are characterized by a cracking pattern on the surface caused by moisture loss of dough and sugar crystallization on surface during baking. (© Amanda Frye)

molding cookie dough using embossed rolling pins or carved wooden molds (**Figure 16–40**).

Commercial bar cookies are extruded through die slits on a baking band and cut with a guillotine before or after baking. These cookies are typically filled with fig or other jams. These cookies are high in egg (60 percent) to keep cookie soft after baking [58]. Fig Newton are a filled bar cookie.

Baking Effects

Many events occur as cookie dough is heated in the oven. First, the fat in the dough melts. Shortening helps give the dough some plastic character. During baking, the shortening melts. Dough containing melted shortening freely moves under the force of gravity [34]. Next sugar dissolves. During mixing only about half the sugar dissolves with the residual sugar remaining in crystalline form until heated which then dissolves in dough water giving more dough fluidity during heating. Increased batter fluidity causes cookie spread. The leavening system increases the spread and expansion in all directions. The cookie spread continues until melted dough becomes to thick or viscous. Minimal starch gelatinization occurs as the dough heats so cookie structure collapses.

Certain cookies, such as gingersnaps and snickerdoodles, have a cracking pattern on the surface. This cracking pattern develops during baking (**Figure 16–41**). The cracking pattern is due to moisture loss of dough and sugar that crystallizes on the surfaces of the dough. As the surface dries during baking the leaving system expands the cookie producing the cracked pattern [34]. The surface cracking patterns are determined by sugar levels [55].

When sugar crystallizes during baking, the sugar bound water is released. That sugar can either be bound by other ingredients or released into the hot oven. When water is released, sugar concentrates and recrystallizes contributing to the cracked pattern and snap of certain cookies when broken in two pieces [34, 55]. The development of a snap in a cookie takes one or two days to develop and is independent of hardness [6, 16]. High-fructose corn syrup cannot successfully be used for hard cookies [6]. Soft cookies can be achieved by using a sugar (brown sugar or honey) or other ingredient that interferes with the sugar recrystallization such as corn syrups.

The methods used to test for doneness of cakes are generally not effective for most cookies. Carryover cooking occurs when cookies are removed from ovens. There is enough heat contained in the pan to cause some continuation of baking when cookies are removed from oven [44]. Cookies should be lightly brown and should appear to be slightly moist when ready to be removed from the oven. Slightly undercooking cookies allows the carryover cooking so the cookies do not overbake and dry out. Overbaked cookies lose flavor and texture qualities [44]. Failure to take into account carryover cooking will result in cookies that are very crisp or hard after cooling. Fudge brownies and some other bar cookies can be especially difficult to assess. Brownies often do not contain baking powder which produces a less "fudgy" cake-like product. These bar cookies, unlike cakes, should be slightly moist when removed from the oven.

Cooling and Storage

Cookies should be cooled on racks to allow adequate air circulation. Cookies on ungreased or unlined baking pans should be removed while still warm to prevent sticking. Soft cookies should be removed once cool enough to handle. Cooling cookies completely before storing or packaging retains cookie shape and texture. Soft-textured cookies should be stored in closed containers to prevent drying. Crisp cookies may be affected by hygroscopic nature of sugar and humidity causing crisp cookies to soften when exposed to humid air. Cookies may be made crisp again by reheating in 300°F oven for 3–5 minutes [56].

Non-traditional Cookies

Wafers, Waffle Wafers, Syrup Waffles, Pizzelle, Fortune Cookies. Wafers, stroopwafels, waffle wafers, pizzelle, and fortune cookies are similar to cookies but are produced from thin flour-based batters baked on (0.3–0.8 mm) gridded or embossed two-sided metal-heated plates or irons which are hinged at one end [45].

Pizzelle cookies are traditional Italian thin round waffle-type cookies made from flour, eggs, sugar, butter, or vegetable oil, flavoring (anise is traditional), and usually a small amount of baking powder (**Figure 16–42**). Pizzelle means "small, flat, and round." They were said to have originated in Italy during the eighth century. These round sweet wafers are cooked on irons with shallow round batter molds which are embossed grooved with patterns such as snowflakes or other designs (**Figure 16–43**). Cannoli shells can be formed

Figure 16–42

Pizzelle are a traditional Italian thin wafer cookies. (Leungchopan/Shutterstock)

Figure 16–43

A pizzelle iron is a hinged two-sided hot plate that has embossed molds to cook this traditional Italian treat usually flavored with anise. (© Amanda Frye)

Figure 16–44

Fortune cookies are thin wafers baked on hinged molded iron plates. While warm the wafers are folded over a small piece of paper with a written "fortune." The wafer is then folded over a slender dowel to create the butterfly shape cookie. (DwaFotografy/Shutterstock)

by wrapping the warm pizzelle wafer around a small wooden cylinder. The shells are later filled with sweet ricotta cheese filling. A similar product is the Fortune cookie. Fortune cookies are made from a simple batter of flour, sugar, egg, oil, and vanilla that is poured on a two-sided hot iron with small round molded areas for batter (**Figure 16–44**). The batter is then quickly cooked, then while warm folded with "paper fortune" tucked inside and folded again over a small slender cylinder into the butterfly-shaped "fortune cookie."

Wafers are very thin, crispy flat dry products made from a thin flour-based batter cooked on two-sided small gridded irons (**Figure 16–45**). Wafers are usually unsweetened but may be sweetened. Wafers may be sold flat, as cream-filled sandwiches, dipped or as cones. Wafers used for Communion are "Holy Wafers." A typical wafer formula is made from flour 100 percent, water 135–140 percent, baking powder 0.4 percent, salt 0.2 percent, lecithin 0–0.5 percent, and small amount of coconut oil 0.5–1 percent [33]. Corn starch is used in some formulas for more tender wafers. The batter must not be overstirred to prevent stringy batter and prevent starch from settling to the bottom. Commercial mixing times are 2.5–6 minutes. Sometimes batter is run through screens to remove any lumps before it is deposited on the hot plates [45]. Steam is the primary leavener and quickly evaporates on the hot iron [58]. Baking time is 1.5–3 minutes. Moisture content of wafers is 1–2 percent [45]. Wafers may be flat or hollow. They may be made as gridded sheets filled and cut. Sugar wafers are layers of wafers filled with sweet cream fillings. It is typical to have three to four wafers with two or three layers of cream made into "books" which are cut into individual serving squares or rectangle by circular saws. KitKat ® candy bars are wafers layered and dipped in chocolate. Hollow rolled

Figure 16–45

Wafers come in various shapes with a wide variety of fillings. The thin waffle wafer is a slightly sweetened wafer cooked on a gridded iron. (© Amanda Frye)

wafer sticks are cooked on a cylinder drum and then filled with frosting. Wafer batter is used for unsweetened or sweetened ice cream cones. Sweetened cone batter has substantial amounts of sugar so the sheets are flexible when hot off the iron and can be easily changed into a cone shape. The cone becomes rigid upon cooling. Waffle wafers can be plain flat discs or filled. Syrup waffles or *Stroopwafels* are a Dutch product, which contains two small waffle wafers sandwiched with a sweetened syrup. These round waffle breakfast treats can be warmed over a cup of hot coffee making the filling warm, soft, and gooey [58] (**Figure 16–46**).

Some wafer batter can be baked into sweet delicate thin discs. This batter consists of equal weights of flour, butter, powder sugar, and egg whites. Often these thin wafers are rolled into slim cylinders for "Russian Cigarettes" or shaped into small cups called "tulipe cookies," which are filled with ice cream, cream fillings, or fruit [43] (**Figure 16–47**).

Biscotti. Italian biscotti are unique cookie products that are "twice baked" cookies (**Figure 16–48**). The stiff cookie dough is shaped into a log and baked, then logs are diagonally cut into individual pieces and baked again. Biscotti have a firm, dry, and crisp texture sometimes served with coffee and dunked [43, 58].

Figure 16–46

Stroopwafels are filled with a gooey syrup filling. Stroopwafels can be warmed on top of a hot cup of coffee. (© Amanda Frye)

Figure 16–47

Baked wafer cookies rolled warm around a dowel to make "Russian Cigarette" cookies. (Richard Embery/Pearson Education)

Figure 16–48

Biscotti means "twice baked." Above, a baked biscotti is sliced diagonally for a second baking. (Richard Embery/Pearson Education)

Figure 16–49

Macarons are colorful and made by folding finely ground almond flour into an egg white foam sweetened with sugar (meringue) which is piped in small discs and baked. The Macaron is a filled sandwich style macaroon cookie. (ksena2you/Shutterstock)

Macaroons. Macaroons are a unique cookie made from sugar-sweetened egg white foam (meringue). The egg white base is combined with other ingredients such as ground nuts, almond paste or coconut, or chocolate and baked. *Macarons* are a French-style macaroon that have gained popularity in recent years (**Figure 16–49**). These colorful festive macarons are made from the sugar sweetened egg white foam base (meringue) and finely ground almond flour folded into the batter until the batter becomes shiny and falls from the spatula in thick "ribbons." This procedure is called *macaronnage*. The batter is piped in small discs on to parchment paper and baked

at 325°F (160°C) until set but not browned. The cooled macarons are sandwiched together with a small amount of jam, buttercream, or curd [43].

Madelines. Madelines are unique cookies that are made from sponge cake or genoise batter. The batter is piped into special small fluted molds [43] (**Figure 16–50**).

Figure 16–50

Madelines are made from sponge or genoise batter piped into special molded fluted pans. (Richard Embery/Pearson Education)

Figure 16–51

Savory crackers made by hand using home pasta machine to "sheet" the dough into a thin even dough instead of rolling dough with a rolling pin. (Richard Embery/Pearson Education)

Sandwich Creme Fillings. Sandwich creme fillings are beyond the scope of this chapter but are included in sweet and savory cookie and cracker products. The sweet cream fillings are primarily sugar and fat in an approximate 2:1 ratio [58]. However, recipes vary with 30–40 percent fat and 40–70 percent sugar [42]. Powdered sugar is used to manufacture the fillings [58]. Savory cheese fillings are used in cracker sandwiches. The cheese fillings are around 40 percent fat, 35–40 percent cheese powders, and 10 percent whey powders. Flavorings, starch, salt, emulsifiers, and other ingredients make up the other components. Lecithin is typically included at low levels. These fillings are 40–75 percent of the cookie or savory sandwiches [45].

CRACKERS

The term *crackers* applies to a broad category of individual serving size cereal-based products that are baked. Cracker doughs start out with about 15–25 percent water and the final baked product has a moisture content of no more than 5 percent. The name "cracker" comes from the "cracking" sound when broken [45]. Crackers typically serve as a bread alternative but have the advantage of a longer shelf life. Wheat flour serves as the foundation cereal grain in most crackers, but many other grains are used for crackers. Most crackers are under 3 inches in size, but there are exceptions.

Crackers can be made at home or by hand (**Figure 16–51**) but are typically a commercial product. A wide variety of formulations exist for crackers. They may be sweet or savory. Crackers are steam leavened, chemical leavened or fermented, or a leavening combination. Crackers' flavors, shapes, and styles are numerous. Long narrow stick style crackers are typically produced by extrusion or rotary cut machines.

Crackers can be categorized based on the balance of flour, sugar, fat, and water. Typically, crackers have little to no sugar, and moderate to high amounts of fat (10–20 percent) with water levels of dough (20–30 percent). High ratios of sugar and fat to flour yield a more fluid dough with less gluten developed structure. High levels of water and flour with low levels of sugar and fat yield a dough that is a firm structure and more gluten development [34].

Cracker dough can be classified as (1) fermented dough such as soda/saltine crackers—sponge plus dough, (2) chemically leavened dough such as savory snack and butter crackers, or (3) sweet chemically leavened dough such as graham crackers.

Fermented dough used for soda/saltine crackers, which are typically firm and extensible but low in sugar and fat. Chemically leavened doughs are softer and more extensible with moderate sugar and fat. Sweetened chemically leavened doughs have higher sugar ratios that yield softer dough with gluten development.

Ingredients

Flour. Cracker flour are typically long patent or straight grade soft red or white winter wheat flours. Flour components vary using strong flours with protein content of 13–14 percent and weak flour with 8–9 percent protein content or a combination depending on desired gluten content and structure [34]. Bench top procedures to predict flour gluten functionality in chemically leavened crackers were recently developed [40, 41]. There is a wide variety of cracker products and classifications. Cracker flours typically have lower absorption capacity, less starch damage, and finer granulation [21, 58]. (See Chapter 13 for more discussion on flour).

Leaveners. Steam leavening is important leavening in cracker production. Low levels of yeast are used in fermented doughs, but it is the associated lactic acid bacteria that play the major leavening role in fermented crackers such as saltines [46, 34, 62]. Chemical leavening agents such as sodium bicarbonate and ammonium bicarbonate are used separately or in combination in many cracker formulas.

Fat. Shortenings are used in crackers primarily for flakiness, dough lubrication, and mouthfeel. Oils are sprayed at the end of baking for flavor, mouthfeel, and to adhere dry flavorings to crackers.

Sugar. Granulated sugar is primarily used at low levels in crackers. Graham crackers contain higher levels of sugar. Some cracker formulas do use low levels of corn syrup or high fructose corn syrup.

Salt. Salt is primarily a flavor enhancement agent. In fermented doughs, salt does act to control fermentation. Fine granulated salt called "flour salt" is used in cracker doughs. Coarser flake salts are used for cracker toppings because the size and rough edges adhere to cracker surface better [58].

Processing

Cracker dough is rolled into strong thin sheets of dough. These thin sheets are stacked together or folded over and pressed together in a process called *laminating*. This process creates a product with flaky layers. Holes are pricked in the dough by docking for uniform thickness and to keep layers together. Crackers are baked at a high temperature for a short time. Many crackers are sprayed with oil after baking to improve flavor, mouthfeel, and to adhere dry seasonings.

Commercial cracker production includes laminating, sheeting, gauging, cutting, and docking. Dough sheeting is basically the process of rolling dough into a smooth strong sheet. The sheeter is a series of rollers that process dough into a strong, smooth, continuous relaxed sheet of dough. Laminating dough is accomplished by layering sheets of dough together to develop a light, tender, flaky product. The dough must be strong extensible without tearing or crumbling. Laminating prepares an even dough that is then ready to be gauged, cut, and docked. Sweep laminators fold a continuous sheet of dough in layers. A cut-sheet laminator cuts individual sheets and dough, which are stacked on top of each other. After dough is laminated, one to three rollers compress and reduce laminated layers into a single sheet of dough [77]. Finally, the dough is gauged where it goes through a "gauge roller" to regulate the finished weight of the dough. A dough that is too heavy or too light will affect the final product. Cutting individual crackers may be done with a rotary cutter either tied or shaped cut. Tied cut yields a large solid perforated dough sheet and scrap cut yields individual cut dough

pieces that are then baked [51]. Docking is the process of imprinting "docker" holes in the cracker during cutting. Docker holes provide distinctive patterns in the crackers. The docking controls thickness of baked product by "pinning" laminated layers together. The docking reduces baked product blistering and helps achieve uniformity in product's baked interior [34, 58].

Baking

Cracker baking is typically done at high temperatures for a short time. During early stages of baking, the cracker structure starts to develop as starch gelatinizes and moisture evaporates, producing steam leavening. The chemical leavening agents start producing gases (ammonia and carbon dioxide depending on leavenings used). The ammonia odors are discharged through gas bubbles. Bottom heat allows cracker to heat up without drying the top surface too quickly. If top surface dries too quickly, moisture can become trapped inside the cracker center producing a high moisture content in the cracker interior. Also, the volume or stack height will be reduced due to lack of leavening in the cracker center.

During the middle stages of baking, "free water" continues to be removed and there is maximum gas expansion. The structure is set as gelatinized starch set and gluten proteins become denatured. The cracker crusting begins as product volume starts to "relax." If crusting begins too early, blisters may result.

Final baking stages produce color development due to sugar caramelization and Maillard browning. The structure is fully set and residual moisture is removed. Crackers may have undesirable crust checking which are hairline cracks in the baked product, which increase breakage upon packaging. Checking occurs during cooling so minimizing cold drafts of air is important [58, 51].

Cooled baked crackers are packaged. Goals in packaging include the following: (1) protect product from moisture in atmospheric air, (2) shield product from light and atmospheric air that would promote fat rancidity, and (3) protect product from breakage. Packaging must be food safe, easily sealed, grease resistant, puncture resistant, and have low odor to prevent odor transfer to the food. Manufacturing of packing and wrapping materials is a large industry that is constantly changing with new developments.

Matzos and Water Crackers

Matzos are only made from flour and water. Water crackers are similar to matzo with additional ingredients. These crackers are the most basic laminated crackers [45].

Matzos. Matzos are a Jewish unleavened bread important for Passover but eaten throughout the year and by non-Jewish populations too. Matzo is primarily a commercial baked product. Matzo is a water cracker

Figure 16–52

Matzo. (Oleg Lopatkin/Age fotostock /Alamy Stock Photo)

Figure 16–53

Saltine or soda crackers are an American invention. (© Amanda Frye)

made from only flour and water (**Figure 16–52**). Wheat flour must meet strict Kosher standards for Passover (See Chapter 13). A typical matzo recipe is 100 parts flour to 38 parts water. The ingredients are mixed into a crumbly dough which is rolled, laminated 2–6 times then sheeted, pressed, cut, and heavily docked. The docking allows only small blisters to form during baking. The matzo dough is baked for a very short time in a very hot oven. Baking time is about one minute. The baked matzo is pale with small darker blisters on the surface. Moisture content of matzo is around 3 percent [44, 45].

Water Crackers.   Crackers are similar to matzo with more variations. The recipe is simple flour, fat, salt, and water in a ratio of 100:6.5:1:29. The dough forms a firm ball or is crumbly after mixing. Sometimes dough undergoes a conditioning period after mixing to allow proteolytic activity to mellow gluten making it slightly more extensible during this "relaxation" period. Few varieties of water crackers are made with low levels of sugar, syrup, or malt extract, which undergo a short fermentation period. Laminating the dough is essential to yield some gluten. The laminated dough is strong and tough. The dough is sheeted, cut, docked, and baked in moderately hot oven for 4–5 minutes. Due to longitudinal dough shrinkage, the cutters are more oval shaped so a round cracker is produced upon baking. Water crackers have pale appearance with darker blistered surface like matzo. The water biscuits are thin, fairly hard, and crisp with a bland flavor [44, 45].

Soda (Saltine) Crackers

Soda crackers, also known as saltines or premium crackers, are an American invention produced since 1840. These crackers are primarily a commercial baked cracker but can be made at home. Soda crackers are typically square shape (**Figure 16–53**). Oyster crackers (soup crackers) are made from the same dough as saltine crackers but are cut into small rounded shapes [58].

Soda crackers are made by using two stages: sponge and dough method. The typical saltine recipe has a sponge with 65–70 percent flour, 30 percent water, and 0.125–0.2 percent yeast. The dough part is 30–35 percent flour, 8–11 percent fat, 1–1.5 percent salt, and 0.625–0.7 percent soda (sodium bicarbonate). Diastatic Malt syrup (containing alpha-amylase) (about 1.5 percent) is often used as a fermenting aid, which feeds yeasts as the alpha-amylase converts some of the starch to sugar and contributes flavor during the fermentation process [45, 58, 77]. The sponge stage has a long ferment time, 16–24 hours, in controlled conditions with temperatures 28°–30°C (82°–86°F) and relative humidity of 75–80 percent. The dough stage remixes the dough with the addition of soda, flour, and other ingredients. The dough stage is fermented for an additional 3–5 hours under controlled conditions.

The bacteria associated with the yeast, not the yeast itself, plays a major role in soda cracker fermentation. During the ferment time, the pH drops from around 6.0 to 4.0. A buffer, sometimes referred to as an inoculum, is often added to ensure the pH drops. The buffer is often part of an old sponge which also ensures bacteria are enabled [34]. Gluten formation is necessary for saltine crackers. Gentle handling of dough is essential. A mixture of flours has been found to yield the best soda crackers with laminated layers yet not too hard [60].

The fermented or "ripe" dough is sheeted, laminated, gauged, and cut into approximately 2 inch squares (50 × 50 mm). The flaky texture in soda crackers is achieved by laminating 4–8 layers of dough with six layers considered ideal [77]. The layers of dough go through a series of rollers to reduce the dough into one strong thin dough sheet before it is cut. Scrap dough is carefully reworked into the dough avoiding waste. A rotary cutter is typically used to tie-cut squares. Docking pins, typically dull with a blunt end (0.15 cm), punch holes in a pattern across each cut dough piece. After cutting and before baking, fine salt (2.5 percent by weight) can be added on top of dough pieces.

Baking time is between 2.5 and 3 minutes in a hot oven at a 450–575°F (230–300°C) During baking, water is vaporized yielding a puffed appearance in crackers due to the steam. The laminated layers contribute to the cracker's increased volume, crispness, and flakiness while decreasing blistering fragility. After baking, the crackers are slowly cooled to avoid "checking." Checking is the hairline cracks in the cracker that can lead to breakage during shipping. These micro-fractures occur with moisture equilibrium as the center shrinks and edges expand causing internal stress leading to tiny cracks that grow over time then become visible. Checking that starts immediately after baking may not be visible until up to three weeks later. Checking is not mechanical damage [51].

After cooling, cracker sheets are broken apart and individual crackers are packaged. The final moisture content of soda crackers is about 2 percent.

Standard Characteristics. Soda crackers should have even spring and puffiness between docking. Crackers should be pale with slight browning on blisters. A heavy gloss on baked products indicates too much moisture during baking and a green tinge is indicative of too much soda. A dull greyish appearance is indicative of too much flour being used with lamination or cutting equipment. The bottom of the cracker should be nearly flat with small blisters.

Snack (Savory) Crackers

The snack or savory group of crackers vary widely with formulas, variety, shapes, and sizes (**Figure 16–54**). They are typically salted, flavored, and fat sprayed after baking. This group is usually chemically not yeast leavened products with high levels of fat and flavoring. The texture of snack crackers is typically heavier than saltine crackers. Well-known crackers in this class are Ritz® and Goldfish® crackers (**Figure 16–55**).

Savory cracker dough is mixed once with all ingredients or in a two-stage process. In the two-step process, the first stage is sometimes called "cream up" where the goal is to uniformly distribute minor ingredients such as flavorings into fat, sugar, or water mixture. The second stage completes the mixing as the fat and water phases are combined along with the

Figure 16–54

Round savory cracker. (Andrej_sv/Shutterstock)

Figure 16–55

Goldfish crackers. (AGorohov/Shutterstock)

chemical leavening and any syrup. Ammonia bicarbonate is a common leavening used in snack crackers. Flour, enzymes, and remaining leavening agents such as sodium bicarbonate are added to develop the cracker dough. The dough is mixed to evenly distribute the ingredients. Mixing transforms ingredients into a cohesive extensible dough that can be rolled, sheeted, or laminated into a sturdy continuous sheet of dough. The dough generally has no ferment time.

The dough is then rolled, laminated, and sheeted. The dough is cut and docked. Cracker dough is either "tied cut" or "scrap cut." *Tied cut* refers to a large dough sheet where the cut pieces remain interlocked in a continuous sheet. Edges are trimmed and scraps recombined into the process when tied-cut (98–99 percent fresh dough and 1–2 percent scrap dough). The perforated sheet of dough is baked. The individual crackers are separated from the sheet after baking.

Scrap-cut is used for round or shaped crackers. The individual pieces are cut out of a dough sheet and docked. The dough between the pieces is called *scrap*, which are reworked into the sheeting process. Scrap-cut products have 30–40 percent trim in the reworked dough. The reworked scrap dough changes dough texture and rheology making a less extensible dough. Baking time is typically 5 minutes with high heat in beginning baking phase.

Often fat is added to reduce mouthfeel dryness and enhance flavor. The fat spraying on cracker surface is done after baking while product is hot. It also enhances appearance and flavor, or to add flavor ingredients such as flavored oils. Spray oils are susceptible to rancidity [58, 34].

Cheese Crackers. Flavorings such as cheese or cheese powder present baking challenges. Cheese incorporation contributes additional protein and moisture to the cracker dough, so formulations must account for these changes. Fermented doughs is often used with cheese crackers since it enhances the cheese flavor.

Color enhancement is necessary since cheese itself doesn't contribute enough color. This enhancement is achieved by use of paprika (0.25 percent) and sometimes cayenne pepper or use of food color additive Yellow No. 6. Adding natural cheese requires fine grating of cheese. Any cheese rind mold must be removed prior to grating so it is not incorporated into cracker dough. Dried out grated cheese will not incorporate well into the dough [58]. Cheese crackers can be difficult to bake as cheese causes a shorter dough with a baked open texture. Too hot an oven develops bitterness in the cracker [45, 46]. Cheese crackers have a greater propensity to checking [45].

Graham Crackers

Graham crackers are thin flat sweet crackers with a slightly nutty caramelized sweet taste derived from whole wheat flour, also called graham flour (**Figure 16–56**). There are many formulation variations for graham crackers. Chemical leaveners of sodium bicarbonate and ammonium bicarbonate are used in graham crackers. Basic graham cracker recipe has per flour weight 80 percent flour, 20 percent whole wheat flour, 25 percent sugar, 8 percent honey, 12 percent shortening, 20 percent water, 1 percent sodium bicarbonate, and 0.5 percent ammonium bicarbonate [58].

The crackers are often slightly sweetened with honey or molasses. Graham crackers are various shapes and sizes but are typically 2.5 × 5 inch rectangles containing center perforation that can be broken into smaller square or rectangular crackers. Sometimes graham crackers are made into small animal shapes. Chocolate flavored graham crackers are common in the marketplace as well as cinnamon graham crackers. Graham crackers are typically a commercial packaged

Figure 16–56
Graham crackers are sweet leavened cracker made from whole wheat (graham) flour. Sometimes graham crackers are classified as cookies. (© Amanda Frye)

Figure 16–57
Pretzel's deep rich color is from a lye bath before baking. (Jiri Hera/Shutterstock)

product but can be made at home or in commercial food service operations [43].

Other Cracker-Like Products

Pretzels. They are a baked, uniquely shaped snack food with a dark hard outer surface (**Figure 16–57**). Pretzels can be hard or soft. Pretzels are a fermented flour-based dough that are dipped in lye prior to baking. Hard pretzels have moisture content of 2–3 percent for a hard crunchy product with a six-month-long shelf life. Pretzels come in a variety of shapes including knots, sticks, rods, and even-filled nuggets. Soft pretzels have a moisture content of 15–25 percent. Soft pretzel has a bread-like texture with limited shelf

Figure 16–58

Crisp bread. (© Amanda Frye)

Figure 16–59

Granola bars are a type of cookie made from rolled oats. (Richard Embery/Pearson Education)

life but are sold fresh and as a frozen product [58]. Pretzels are generally topped with flake salt.

Soft wheat flour with a protein content around 9 percent is generally used in pretzels. Water levels in pretzel dough formulas are about 42 percent of flour weight, about two-thirds that of a typical yeast bread. The fermenting time for dough is short, about 30 minutes, which gives very little fermentation. The dough is mixed then shaped or extruded into a rope, cut into sticks, or twisted into a knot, or dough may be sheeted then cut or shaped into knots. The shaped pieces are proofed. The proofed shaped pieces are then transferred to a mesh band that passes through a hot lye bath 150–200°F (65–93°C) of 1–2 percent lye (sodium hydroxide) solution. The lye (sodium hydroxide) reacts with carbon dioxide in the air to form sodium bicarbonate. The bath gelatinizes starch on the outer surface of the pieces. Immediately after the bath, the pieces are dusted with coarsely flaked salt (2 percent). The lye bath is what gives pretzels the characteristic dark brown and shiny surface during baking. After salting the pretzels pieces are baked starting with high heat to caramelize the gelatinized starch on the outer surface yielding a rich brown surface. The baking temperature is decreased to allow moisture to escape

from the knot areas. If heating is too fast, the pretzels will check and fall apart during shipping [34].

Crisp bread.   This is a whole grain, often rye based, product from Northern Europe made from coarse ground meal (**Figure 16–58**). A traditional recipe would be rye flour (100 percent), salt (1.2 percent), and iced water (129 percent); some crisp breads contain around 1 percent yeast. The product is sheeted, cut into rectangular slab, docked, and baked to yield a cracker with a moisture content around 5 percent with extended shelf life [45, 46].

Cereal bars.   Cereal bars such as granola bars are typically oat-based snack foods with a coarse mixture of flour, oat flakes mixed with syrup, and nuts and fruit or chocolate (**Figure 16–59**). The bars may be soft or crisp. The sticky mass is baked in thick sheets on a steel band. The sheets are divided into strips. Crisp bars go through a drying period after baking. The strips are cut into individual sizes after baking then packaged [45].

STUDY QUESTIONS

Shortened Cakes

1. Name and discuss the distinguishing characteristics of the types of shortened cakes.

2. List main cake ingredients. Classify and discuss each ingredient roles as tougheners, tenderizers, moisteners, or driers.

3. Below is a Yellow Butter Cake formula expressed in ounces, grams, and Baker's percentage of weighed flour basis. Using Baker's percentage, adjust recipe for 500 g of flour.

Yellow Butter Cake Formula

Ingredients	U.S.	Metric	Baker's %
Cake Flour	13 oz	390 g	100
Sugar	15 oz	450 g	115
Butter	8 oz	240 g	61.5
Milk	8 fl oz	240 ml	61.5
Eggs	6.4 oz (4)	190 g	49
Baking Powder	0.4 oz (1 T.)	12 g	3
Salt	0.2 oz (1 tsp)	6 g	1.5
Vanilla Extract	0.3 fl oz(2tsp)	9 ml	2.3
Total	3 lb 3oz	1537 g	393.9

Recipe from *On Baking 3rd ed (update)* [43]

4. Describe the usual role and the effect of an excessive amount of each of the following ingredients in the production of a shortened cake:

    (a) Sugar

    (b) Egg

    (c) Fat

    (d) Baking powder

    (e) Liquid

    (f) Flour

5. What role is played by an emulsifier in a shortened cake batter? What effect does it have on the finished product?

6. Briefly describe each of the following methods for mixing a shortened cake. Explain the advantages or disadvantages of each method.

    (a) Conventional

    (b) Conventional sponge

    (c) Muffin

    (d) Quick-mix

7. Describe the effects of under- and overmixing a shortened cake batter. What factors affect the desirable amount of mixing to be done?

8. Why is it important to prepare the pans for a shortened cake batter before the batter is mixed? Explain.

9. Suggest an appropriate temperature for baking a shortened cake. Explain why this temperature is recommended.

10. Why should a shortened cake be allowed to stand for about 10 minutes after baking before removal from the pan?

Foam Cakes

11. Name and describe characteristics of the four types of foam cakes.

12. Describe the usual role of each of the following ingredients in angel food cake:

    (a) Egg whites

    (b) Sugar

    (c) Cream of tartar

    (d) Flour

13. (a) Describe appropriate methods for mixing angel food, sponge, genoise, and chiffon cakes.

    (b) Point out precautions that should be taken in mixing each type of foam cake to ensure finished cakes of good quality.

14. Suggest appropriate baking temperatures for angel food and sponge cakes.

15. How should angel food and sponge cakes be cooled after baking? Why?

Cookies

16. Describe the similarities and differences between cookies and cakes.

17. Describe six basic types of homemade/handmade cookies.

18. Compare and contrast the basic homemade cookie classification to commercial cookies.

19. Describe a cookie you ate, made, purchased, or saw. Describe classification and food science principles involved in the cookie. How could the cookie have been improved or modified?

20. Discuss the ingredients used in cookies and their impact on cookie quality characteristics.

21. Suggest some precautions that are necessary in the preparation of rolled cookies of good quality.

22. What types of baking pans are generally recommended for cookies? Why?

Crackers

23. Describe similarities and differences between four cracker groups. Discuss ingredients and leavening differences. Give examples of each.

24. Describe a cracker that you have recently eaten. How was this cracker leavened? Describe and justify the category of cracker.

25. Describe the unique process that pretzels undergo to give the shiny, dark, hard crust.

26. Discuss "checking" in crackers. How can it be prevented? What problems does it present to manufacturers?

17
Pies and Pastry

Pastry dough is a stiff dough consisting of flour, fat, water, and salt. The term *pastry* is derived from the word *paste* meaning a mixture of flour, liquid, and fat. Pastries cover both conventional pie pastry dough (**Figures 17–1** and **17–2**), laminated puff pastry, and puff dough. Puff doughs such as cream puffs and éclairs were discussed in Chapter 14. Sometimes meringue-based products are included in the pastry category; refer to egg cookery in Chapter 23. However, this chapter will focus primarily on plain conventional pastry dough principles, but other types of pastry dough and products will be briefly explored (Figure 17–1).

Plain (conventional or traditional) pastry dough contains moderate to large amounts of fat and is mixed in a manner to produce flakiness. Pastry dough contains only a few simple ingredients. The key to quality pastry dough is technique. Chilling ingredients and keeping ingredients and dough cold are important for successful pastry production.

Pastry dough is a steam-leavened product. The science of plain pastry dough will be the focus of this chapter. Miscellaneous pastry doughs, crusts, and products' similarities and differences will be briefly discussed. Danish pastries are laminated yeast doughs discussed in Chapter 15. In this chapter, the following topics on the making of plain pastry and related pastry products will be discussed:

- Consumption trends and nutritive value
- Types of pastry and crusts and applications

- Characteristics of plain pastry
- Ingredient functions
- Mixing, rolling, and baking plain pastry
- Fillings and specialty pastry products

CONSUMPTION TRENDS AND NUTRITION

Consumption Trends

According to the American Pie Council, pie origins can be traced to the ancient Egyptians in 2000 B.C. passing through Greek culture then to Roman culture. The pastry shell of these early pies served as an inedible covering, cooking vessel, or plate to hold and cook fish and meat fillings. Romans made the crust from a mixture of flour, water, and olive oil. The first published Roman pie recipe was for a rye-crusted goat cheese and honey pie. Romans were thought to have spread the "pie" concept as they traveled across Europe. "Pye" (pie) was a popular word in the fourteenth century. Early English pies were primarily meat pies and the crust was referred to as a "coffyn." These early pies were often made from fowl whose legs hung over the side which served as handles. Fruit pies or "pasties" were thought to be made in the 1500s. Pies have been political too. In 1644, Oliver Cromwell, an English military and political leader, banned pie eating as it was declared a pagan form of pleasure; pie production and eating went "underground" until the ban was lifted 16 years later.

Colonists brought pies to America. These colonial pies were baked in long narrow pans; they called them "coffyns" like the crusts in England. The term *pie crust* evolved during the American Revolution. Pumpkin pie was introduced at the Pilgrim's second Thanksgiving in 1623. Pie was commonly eaten for breakfast during the nineteenth century. The molasses "Shoo-fly pie" was originally invented to attract flies from the kitchen. Pie has evolved into an integral part of the American culture. Pie is said to be "the most traditional American dessert" with millions of Americans declaring apple pie as their favorite (Figure 17-2).

Frozen pies are consumed by a quarter of American households. Worldwide pastry demand has increased with fastest global growth in Asia, especially China. Single serve and individual portion pies are thought to encourage impulse purchases and encourage consumers to try different pie flavors. Growth is expected in single serve pies and exotic flavor pies. Households with children have the highest consumption of pies, tarts, and turnovers.

Pastry items are often consumed at breakfast including boxed and frozen toaster pastries (**Figure 17–3**). Highest traditional pie consumption occurs in the fall and winter months with most pies consumed on Sunday throughout the year. Pie consumption is strongly correlated to holidays.

Nutritive Value

Pastries and pies contain a high proportion of fat. Flour adds some nutrient value. Pastries and pies typically have a higher caloric value. Nutritive value of pastry products will vary depending on filling, fat used, and other ingredients.

PASTRY CRUSTS AND THEIR USES

Plain pastry is the basis of sweet or savory pies that are usually baked in a shallow round slope sided pan whose finished product is typically served in wedges. Tarts pans are typically short straight-sided pans in a variety of shapes, often with a removable bottom. Pies may have a single bottom crust (Figure 17–1) or covered with a top crust that is solid (Figure 17–2) or made from strips of pastry dough woven into a lattice design (**Figure 17–4**). Pie dough edges are sealed often in decorative crimped styles (**Figure 17–5a, b** and **c**). Tarts are similar to a pie but baked in straight-sided pan often with a fluted edge and often with a removal pan bottom. Tarts can be any

Figure 17–4

Lattice topped pie. (© Svetlana Foote/Shutterstock)

Figure 17–3

Toaster pastries are a popular breakfast pastry. (Endeavor/Shutterstock)

Figure 17–5a

Crimped edge for a single crust pie. Use the index finger and thumb and press dough with index finger of the other hand to create a crimped, scalloped edge. (Richard Embery/Pearson Education)

Figure 17–5b

Two crust pie. Seal top crust to the bottom crust with water or egg wash. Crimp edge as for single crust pie. (Richard Embery/ Pearson Education)

Figure 17–6

Open face fruit tart. (Eddy Van Damme/Pearson Education)

Figure 17–5c

Pie dough cut-outs overlapped on edge of pie crust. (Richard Embery/Pearson Education)

Figure 17–7

Pie crust baked "blind" prior to being filled with chocolate custard. (Richard Embery/Pearson Education)

shape and typically served open faced (**Figure 17–6**). Pie crust may be filled and baked or the pie crust may be baked completely before filling, sometimes referred to as "baked blind" (**Figure 17–7**). Some individual serving size pies are deep fat fried.

Plain pie crust is traditionally bland. A variety of fats maybe used to produce crusts with different attributes. The following briefly outlines different pastry crusts and their uses:

- Plain pastry or pie crust is used to make all types of tarts, turnovers, and dessert pies, including single- and double crust fruit pies (**Figure 17–8**); custard-type pies baked in the shell (**Figure 17–9**); and soft starch-thickened cream pies or gelatin-based chiffon pies in which the fillings are added after the pie shells are baked (**Figure 17–10**). Chiffon fillings are made by adding gelatin to stirred custard or pureed fruit, then folding in whipped egg whites.

- Plain pastry shells are also used as a carrier of high-protein savory foods to be served as a main

Figure 17–8

Brushing an egg white wash on free-form individual apple tarts. (Richard Embery/Pearson Education)

Figure 17–9

Pumpkin pie is a custard pie baked in unbaked pie shell.
(Bhathaway/Shutterstock)

Figure 17–10

Lemon meringue pie with meringue topping being placed on top of starch-based lemon filling that was poured into a baked pastry shell. (Richard Embery/Pearson Education)

Figure 17–11

French onion tart. (Richard Embery/Pearson Education)

Figure 17–12

Quiche Lorraine. (Richard Embery/Pearson Education)

dish or hors d'oeuvres. Savory tarts or pies include various types of meat, poultry, and fish pies with single or double crusts; and quiches, which are savory egg custard-based pies containing a variety of ingredients, such as bacon, ham, Swiss cheese, mushrooms, onions, and other vegetables (**Figure 17–11** and **Figure 17–12**). Spanish Empanadas, Portuguese Pastels, and Cornish Pasties are individual meat pies where filling is placed in small pastry circle that is folded, sealed, and baked. Variations of these individual meat pies are found throughout South America, Haiti, India, Belize, Italy, and Philippines. Individual sweet and savory pastries are found in many cultures (**Figure 17–13**).

Figure 17–13

Traditional Cornish Pasties. (Haddon Davies/Pearson Education Ltd)

• Puff pastry is a laminated dough with layers of butter rolled and folded into dough. Layers of light, buttery dough baked into rich flaky light crisp layers. Puff pastry is used to make sweet or savory foods. Sweet products include fruit turnovers (**Figure 17–14a** and **b**), Napoleons, and Palmiers (**Figure 17–15a, b,** and **c**).

Puff pastry can be used as shell for savory fillings such as chicken a la king, topping for chicken pot pie, or a savory wrap for products such as Beef Wellington (**Figure 17–16**). Many hors d'oeuvres and appetizers use puff pastry (**Figure 17–17a** and **b**). Puff pastry dough can be shaped into containers of various sizes and shapes. Small puff pastry shells filled for hors d'oeuvres or appetizers are called bouchées (boo-SHAY).

Figure 17–15a

Cream-filled Napoleon. (Richard Embery/Pearson Education)

Figure 17–14a

Puff pastry 5-inch (13 cm) square filled with thickened cherries about to be folded over for cherry turnover. (Eddy Van Damme/ Pearson Education)

Figure 17–15b

Puff pastry fan (top); Palmiers (bottom). (Richard Embery/Pearson Education)

Figure 17–14b

Turnover. (Eddy Van Damme/Pearson Education)

Figure 17–15c

Filled puff pastry cream horns. (Richard Embery/Pearson Education)

Figure 17–16

Beef Wellington. (Shutterstock)

Deeper shells are often filled with savory main course mixtures such as chicken a la king. These individual deep puff pastry shells are called vol-au-vents (vul-oh-vanz) (**Figure 17–18**). Feuilletés (fuh-yuh-TAY) are square, rectangular, or diamond-shaped puff pastry boxes filled with either sweet or savory mixtures (**Figure 17–19**).

• Sweet dough is a rich, sturdy, mealy, and non-flaky dough that typically contains egg yolks and is used for sweet tarts (**Figure 17–20**).

• Crumb crusts are a quick bottom crust usually made from sweetened finely ground graham crackers or

Figure 17–17a

Strips of puff pastry sprinkled with cheese and twisted into cheese straws. (Richard Embery/Pearson Education)

Figure 17–18

Vol-au-vent, a deep puff pastry shell made with two pieces of puff pastry. Base puff pastry is topped with puff pastry with interior cut-out to form a border ring of dough. Shells can be filled with sweet or savory mixtures. (Richard Embery/Pearson Education)

Figure 17–17b

Baked cheese straws. (Richard Embery/Pearson Education)

Figure 17–19

Feuilletés. (Eddy Van Damme/Pearson Education)

Figure 17–20

French apple tart with sweet dough crust. (Richard Embery/ Pearson Education)

Figure 17–22

Vegetable strudel. (Richard Embery/Pearson Education)

Figure 17–21

Key lime pie with graham cracker crumb crust. (Richard Embery/ Pearson Education)

Figure 17–23

Assorted pastries from kataifi and phyllo dough. (© Amanda Frye)

cookie crumbs that are moistened with butter then pressed into pan. Crumb crusts can be baked with their filling such as cheesecakes or set by brief baking or freezing then filled (**Figure 17–21**).

- Strudel dough is a traditional European pastry dough made from a strong flour, egg, water, oil, and salt. Strudel is a traditional pastry in areas of the former Austrian-Hungarian empire. Puff pastry dough and phyllo dough are sometimes substituted for strudel dough. Sweet strudel is filled with fruit or sweet cheese filling; savory strudel is filled with cabbage, sauerkraut, spinach, or meat fillings (**Figure 17–22**).

- Phyllo (Filo) dough and kataifi are used to make Middle Eastern pastries (**Figure 17–23**). Phyllo dough is made from semolina (durum wheat) flour and moderate amount of liquid and a small amount of oil. Kataifi looks like shredded phyllo dough but

is actually a poured batter that is drizzled on a griddle wheel to bake. Phyllo and kataifi are layered or filled with butter, sweet syrup, and nuts for sweet pastries such as Baklava or other pastries (**Figure 17–24**) or meats and cheese for savory dishes like Spanakopita (**Figure 17–25**).

- Danish pastry is a rich yeast dough layered with butter used to make sweet-filled pastries made from laminated yeast doughs. These laminated pastry doughs contain about 50 percent fat and often use higher protein flour. Careful handling of dough ensures a tender product. The dough is leavened by yeast but flakiness is due to steam (see Chapter 15 for yeast breads).

Figure 17–24

Baklava made from sheets of phyllo dough brushed with butter layered with sugared nut mixture. Product is scored prior to baking. Flavored syrup is poured over baked mixtures. (Richard Embery/Pearson Education)

Figure 17–26

Pia with duran fruit filling. (© Amanda Frye)

Figure 17–25

Spanakopita. Strips of phyllo dough filled with spinach and feta cheese mixture, folded into triangles that are cut then baked. (Richard Embery/Pearson Education)

Figure 17–27

Moon cake with salted duck egg. (123rf.com/Pearson)

- Meringues and éclair paste may be classified as pastries. Meringues and éclair paste products serve as the foundation for pastries, but were discussed in previous chapters as they are not a pastry dough.
- Pia is a unique Asian pastry made from two pastries. There is an outer "water dough" and inner "oil dough." These two doughs are layered, folded, and rolled then filled often with bean paste traditionally "mung bean" [3] (**Figure 17–26**).
- Asian moon cakes are made from an oil-based pastry dough that is pressed into a mold, then filled and baked. Moon cakes often contain a salted egg yolk to represent the moon (**Figure 17–27**).

CHARACTERISTICS OF PLAIN PASTRY

Good-quality pastry is tender, crisp, and flaky with a lightly golden brown color with a center that is less brown. Pastry should be tender, but not crumbly as it does not easily break when served yet is tender when cut with a fork. Good pastry is crisp and flaky with a blistered surface and is slightly crisp and pleasantly flavored.

There are two basic types of pie dough: (1) flaky and (2) mealy. The difference is the type of fat and how it is mixed with the flour. A flaky crust cuts the fat into the flour until flour-coated fats are pea-size particles. Flaky crusts rely on some gluten formation to achieve pastry layers. The moisture turns to steam during baking thus separating the layers during baking. Mealy dough has oil or fat coating more of the flour preventing water absorption by the flour, thus interfering with gluten formation. Fat can be cut into flour until the mixture resembles cornmeal. These pie crusts are more tender and crumbly, but not as flaky.

Flakiness

Flakiness is described as thin layers of baked dough separated by open spaces (**Figure 17–28**). Flakiness is thought to result from a process in which small particles of fat are coated with moistened flour or dough and then flattened into thin layers when the dough mixture is rolled out. On baking, the fat melts, is absorbed by the surrounding dough, and leaves empty spaces between thin layers of the baked dough. Some factors that have been found to affect flakiness are (1) the character of the fat used (solid versus melted or liquid oils), (2) the consistency of solid fat, (3) the type of flour used, (4) the proportion of water, (5) the degree of mixing, (6) the method of mixing, and (7) the number of times the dough is rolled.

Solid fats yield a flaky crust more easily than melted or liquid fats because a solid fat can be cut into the flour, resulting in flakes when the fat particles melt. Liquid fats mix more completely with flour. Oil and flour crusts yield a tender and crumbly crust that is not flaky (**Figure 17–29**). When oil is used in the same proportion as solid fats, crusts are tender but not flaky as those made with a solid fat, such as shortening or lard.

Solid fats that are warm and therefore softer will blend more fully with the flour during mixing and rolling of the crust. Therefore, if working in a warm kitchen, chilling the fat may be helpful to improve flakiness. Often pastry is rolled on a chilled marble slab. Some pastries use butter because of the flavor. When used, the temperature of the butter needs to be managed so that it is not too soft.

The type of flour, the amount of liquid, and mixing method will influence gluten development. Some gluten development is needed for flakiness. Too much gluten development, however, will result in a tough crust. The least amount of water needed to create moist dough is used; both mixing and handling when

Mealy pastry from three oil crusts stacked layers. (© Amanda Frye)

rolling dough should be minimized. Pastry flour contains less protein so it can tolerate more mixing and still yield a tender flaky crust.

Tenderness

Tenderness is one of the most desirable characteristics of good pastry. Tenderness is influenced by the type and quantity of fat. In general, shortenings and lard produce more tender pies than butter or margarine, which are not 100 percent fat as they contain water.

Tenderness in pastry is determined by the amount and distribution of gluten. The fat in the pastry dough inhibits gluten formation. It requires at least as much consideration as flakiness, yet some of the factors that produce flakiness tend to decrease tenderness and vice versa. Tenderness is at a maximum when the fat spreads over the flour particles, interferes with the hydration of gluten proteins in the flour, and thus decreases the formation of gluten strands. If the fat blends too thoroughly with the dough, the crust is too tender to handle and tends to be crumbly or mealy. Techniques of combining ingredients and manipulating the dough have a major impact on tenderness.

A mealy crust is caused by use of oil or warm plastic fat. Also, fat that is overcut into flour mixture can cause a mealy crust. Additionally, a mealy crust may be the result of using too little water and under manipulation of ingredients. Tough pastry is a result of too little fat, too much water, and insufficient cutting of fat into flour or over manipulating dough. Using excessive flour added during rolling will also cause a tough crust. Adjustments in both ingredients and techniques of mixing and handling must be made so that both flakiness and tenderness are achieved in the baked pastry. Pastry tenderness and crispness can be objectively measured by an instrument known as a "shortometer," which measures the force to break the pastry.

Figure 17–28

Flaky pastry layers visible in the three conventional stacked pastry layers. (© Amanda Frye)

Crispness

Pastry crispness results when enough water evaporates from dough layers during baking. Thickness of rolled dough and baking conditions will affect crispness. The lower crust and the upper crust typically have different crispness. Baking of crust prior to filling also affects crispness. Too much water in pie dough or too low oven temperature at the beginning of baking will result in a soggy crust. Allowing filled pie to stand prior to baking causes a soggy crust. Brushing pie crust surface with egg yolk and baking in a hot oven to form a coagulated egg protein water proof film prior to filling will decrease bottom crust sogginess. Fruit pie filling may be thickened prior to being poured into the unbaked pie crust prior to baking; this pre-thickened fruit filling helps to prevent a soggy bottom crust.

INGREDIENTS IN PLAIN PASTRY

Plain pastry contains only a few ingredients—flour, fat, salt, and water. Plain pastry is leavened primarily by steam produced when baking in a hot oven. Leavening in plain pastry is not extensive.

Flour

Flour is the main ingredient in pastry dough. Either pastry or all-purpose flour can be used; pastry flour requires less fat for optimum tenderness and is used primarily by commercial bakers. Pastry flour has enough gluten for a flaky structure that is tender when dough is properly handled. The stronger the flour, the more fat is needed for a tender product. Because of the larger amount of gluten formed with all-purpose flour, about ⅓ cup of fat per cup of flour may be needed to produce a tender crust. The proportion of fat needed also will vary with the type of fat used and the mixing methods.

Water

Water is the principal liquid used in pastry dough. Only a minimum amount of water should be used to produce a cohesive pie dough that yields a flaky, tender crust. Typically, 2 to 4 tablespoons of water are required for 1 cup of flour. The water should be very cold. Sometimes iced water is used but chunks of ice are not incorporated into pie dough. The liquid acts to moisten flour so as to bind the dough ingredients. Water is essential to steam production, which leavens pastry dough.

The amount of water required for plain pastry varies with the hydration capacity of the flour, the amount and type of fat, the temperature of the ingredients, and the individual technique of handling. There should be only enough water added so ingredients stick together. Two tablespoons of water per cup of flour are enough for flour hydration and some gluten production required for flakiness while minimizing risk of making the dough tough. An excessive amount of water added to pastry dough allows the flour protein hydration and development of more gluten than is desirable for optimum tenderness [4]. Even a small amount of excessive water has noticeable effects on pastry outcome.

Toughness of pastry is therefore increased by too much water in the dough. Too little water produces a dry dough that is crumbly, difficult to handle, and the pastry that falls apart. The amount of liquid should be sufficient to barely form a dough; the dough should not be wet and sticky [7]. Cold water 40°F (4°C) is important to maintain proper dough temperature.

Milk can be used for pie dough, but it will yield a crust that is tougher, browner, and of higher cost to produce.

Fat

Fat is responsible for pastry tenderness or shortness of baked pastry. The fat coats flour particles acting to waterproof the flour. This fat coating allows the fat to spread over the particles of flour and retard their hydration limiting starch hydration and gluten formation. The starch is partially responsible for pastry toughness. Fats such as butter or margarine containing water have less shortening power than a pure fat.

Plastic fats, in particular, also play an important part in the development of flakiness in pastry. The type of fat used will effect flavor, tenderness, and flakiness of finished product. Lard produces the flakiest pie crust but may have a noticeable taste. Lard is a pork source product so it may be objectionable to people who don't eat pork.

Fats vary in their tenderizing properties [6]. Liquid oils spread more than plastic fats and usually have greater tenderizing power, but do not produce pastry with flaky qualities. Softer plastic fats also spread more readily than harder fats. The fat should be cold enough to be firm rather than pasty or oily but plastic enough to be measured accurately and to cut into the flour. In warm weather, some chilling of fat may be necessary. Likewise, chilling of water may be desirable or rolling out pastry on a cold marble slab may be necessary to produce a high-quality product.

Butter and margarine contain 80 percent fat and 20 percent water; therefore, they have less tenderizing power than 100 percent fats such as lard and hydrogenated shortening when substituted on a weight basis. Lard is solid fat and has no inert air incorporated as shortening. A cup of lard weighs more than a cup of hydrogenated shortening because the shortening has been pre-creamed and contains an inert gas to make it lighter. Oil coats flour particles preventing gluten formation and will only produce a crumbly, but tender, crust.

The proportion of fat to flour varies but customarily ¼ cup to ⅓ cup fat to one cup flour is standard. More fat yields a greasy and crumby crust; less fat causes the potential for increased gluten formation and toughness.

Salt

Salt acts primarily as a flavoring ingredient in pastry dough. However, salt does have some minor effect on tenderizing and conditioning effect on gluten. Salt can be added to the water to assure even distribution or mixed with flour prior to cutting in the fat. Omitting salt in pastry dough has little effect on pastry outcome except for taste. Pastry without salt tastes flat. One half teaspoon of salt per cup of flour is recommended.

TECHNIQUES OF MIXING

Even though pastry dough contains simple ingredients, skill is required to transform these ingredients into dough for a flaky and tender pastry crust. Correct proportion of ingredients, and the way and how much the dough is manipulated will determine if the crust is tender or tough and flaky or mealy. The secret is properly distributing ingredients and manipulating the dough. Gluten toughens pastry yet is essential in producing a flaky crust. Two pie crusts may have the same amount of gluten yet tenderness can differ. If flakes are large and exist only in a few thick layers, the pastry will be tough; thin numerous layers will yield a crisp and tender pastry. Traditional mixing method involves (1) cutting the fat into the flour, (2) adding water and stirring dough, and (3) rolling and shaping dough.

An interrelationship between ingredients, the characteristics of ingredients, their proportions, and the extent to which the ingredients are manipulated are important to produce a pastry dough with desired characteristics. Different conditions may necessitate adjustments in temperature controls, manipulation, and water levels. Type of fat and flour, proportion of water and fat, and the extent to which fat is cut into flour all have interacting effects on pastry outcome. Controls at each step are essential for pastry outcome.

Traditional (Conventional) Mixing Method

A standard plain pie crust may be prepared by cutting in the fat, then adding water with a minimum amount of mixing. Flour and salt are sifted together to evenly distribute salt. A plastic fat such as lard or shortening is then evenly distributed through flour mixture through a process called "cutting." Cutting the fat into the flour mixture can be achieved by using a pastry blender, or a pastry fork, or two knives that are manipulated in a scissor-like motion, or kitchen scissors, or by using the fingers (**Figure 17–30**). Using fingers to cut in fat causes heat transfer from hand to mixture heating up the fat, plus there can be sanitation issues, so this method is not the first choice. If fingers are used, the process must be fast to minimize heat transfer. Cutting fat into the flour coats the flour particles, and subdivides and distributes fat in the flour. The finer the fat is cut into flour, the more waterproof the flour and less likely for excessive gluten

Figure 17–30

Fat may be cut into flour with a pastry cutter, knives, or by hand as shown here. (Richard Embery/Pearson Education)

formation or starch hydration. However, cutting the fat in too fine for distribution does not allow the proper gluten formation and will just yield a crumbly and mealy crust. The flour will appear to have pea-size to cornmeal-size particles when fat is properly cut and distributed. Fat acts to coat flour particles like a raincoat so water cannot come in contact and hydrate the flour for starch gelatinization and gluten formation. Fat distribution is essential for a tender and flaky pastry.

When mixing pie crust by hand, cold water is typically sprinkled over the flour–fat mixture dough to evenly distribute water over the mixture. The water should be sprinkled over the flour–fat mixture, and with a few quick light whisking motions the flour mixture is lightly tossed using a fork between water additions (**Figure 17–31**). Quick and light motions are important in mixing the water. After water is distributed in the flour, the dough should be stirred at once with only a few wide circular motions, typically with a fork, so that the dough does not have wet, sticky, and dry spots. The dough can be overmanipulated, if there is attempt to thoroughly mix or moisten all the dry ingredients. Stirring should be discontinued when the dough comes together in a ball. The dough is then gathered into a ball, covered (plastic wrap works well), and refrigerated for 15 to 30 minutes before rolling into the crust. During this period of holding, the water migrates throughout the dough, and the fat is chilled.

A reasonably uniform blending of fat with flour produces a more uniformly tender crust, sometimes called a *mealy crust*, yet one that is flaky. Fat particles may vary in size. Cutting of the fat into particles the size of peas is generally suggested for a flaky crust. Those

(a) First measure flour and salt into a bowl. Then the shortening or butter is cut into the flour until the "fat" is about the size of green peas.

(b) Sprinkle cold water about a tablespoon at a time over the flour-fat mixture and mix very lightly with a fork to moisten the dry flour. Mixing as little as possible will promote a flaky, tender pie crust.

(c) When the pie dough is moist, press together into a ball. Refrigerate the dough for about 30 minutes to chill the fat before rolling out.

(d) To roll out the dough, lightly flour the surface and partially flatten the dough ball with your hands. Then start rolling out with a lightly floured rolling pin. Roll the dough from the center to the edges of the dough. As you roll out the dough, periodically move the dough and lightly flour underneath to prevent sticking of the dough to either the rolling surface or the rolling pin. Roll out the dough until it is about 2 inches larger than the pie pan to be used.

(e) To place the dough in the pan, the dough can be rolled onto the rolling pin or folded into quarters to lift into the pie pan. The dough pictured here was folded into quarters and then unfolded into a half for final placement of the dough.

(f) The dough is pushed into place in the pie pan taking care to ease dough down into the pan instead of stretching it to fit. Stretched doughs may shrink when baked. To complete this crust, trim excess dough and add a decorative edge as desired.

Figure 17–31

Preparation of conventional pastry dough. (© Doughlas and Barbara Scheule)

who favor a relatively coarse division of fat in the flour–salt mixture do so on the theory that flakiness is increased by rolling larger fat masses into thin layers.

Electric mixers or *food processors* can also be used both to cut the fat into the flour and to mix the liquid with the flour–fat mixture in the final stages of dough preparation. Flour and salt are mixed together. Cold chilled fat is cubed into ½-inch squares, scattered over flour mixture, then processed until the mixture has a pea-size crumb appearance. Half the amount of iced cold water is sprinkled directly over fat–flour mixture, then barely mixed. Remaining water is added to moisten. Proper dough moisture can be assessed by squeezing a marble-sized ball of dough in the hand. If the dough holds together firmly, no additional water is needed. Additional water is incorporated a tablespoon at a time, so dough is moist enough to form a smooth ball when pressed together. However, care must be taken to avoid overmixing. Excessive mixing when adding the water will toughen the crust.

Alternative Pastry-Mixing Methods

Puff Pastry Method. Pastry can also be made by a modified puff pastry method sometimes referred to as "rough puff pastry." About 2 tablespoons of the flour–fat mixture are removed before the liquid is added. After the pastry has been rolled out, this flour–fat mixture is sprinkled over the dough. The dough is rolled up like a jelly roll and cut into two pieces. One piece is placed on top of the other, and they are then rerolled for the pie pan. This method tends to increase flakiness in pastry.

Modified Mixing Method. A modified method of mixing pastry has been developed in which ¼ cup of a 2-cup portion of flour is reserved to be mixed with liquid to form a paste. After the fat has been cut into the remaining flour, the paste is added all at once and blended with the flour–fat mixture.

Oil Method. The nontraditional oil method produces a crumbly, tender, non-flaky crust [1]. The oil and water are stirred into the flour and salt. Alternatively, the oil can be sprinkled over the flour–salt mixture followed by stirring to disperse the oil. The water can then be added as in the traditional method. Oil pastries are often patted into pie pans.

Hot Water Method. Hot water pastry method is a British method for making pie dough. Hot water pastry is typically used for savory meat pies such as pork pie, game pies, and sometimes kidney steak pie or other "pasties" (**Figure 17–32**). The fat in the hot water method is typically animal fat such as lard, suet, or meat drippings. This hot water pastry crust is often molded around a filling and baked free form rather

Figure 17–32

Pork pie made with hot water crust. (Stargatechris/123RF)

than in a pie dish. The pliable and somewhat sticky nature of the crust allows for the crust to be easily molded as it does not tear. The hot water pastry mixing method melts cut-up fat by stirring fat pieces into boiling water to form an emulsion. The emulsion is then stirred into the flour and salt. Pastry made with this method is tender, mealy, but usually less flaky than pastry made by traditional methods.

ROLLING PASTRY

Pastry can be rolled as soon as it has been mixed, but allowing the dough to stand for a few minutes increases the extensibility or elasticity of the dough, making it easier to handle and to roll. When the work area is warm, refrigeration of the dough before rolling helps to maintain flakiness.

When rolling out a pie dough, use a minimal amount of flour on the board to keep the crust from sticking without toughening the pastry. Occasional lifting of the crust while rolling also tends to prevent sticking. The dough can be rolled on a lightly floured canvas-covered board or between two layers of parchment, wax paper or plastic film or a chilled marble slab. The pie dough is rolled from the center of the

---

FOCUS ON SCIENCE

WHY DOES A PLASTIC FAT PERFORM BETTER THAN OTHER KINDS OF FAT IN PASTRY DOUGH?

A fat that is plastic covers the largest surface area and has the greatest "shortening power." A plastic fat contains both liquid and solid phases of fat. Depending on the fatty acid composition and distribution, at room temperature as much as 70 to 85 percent of the glycerides may be liquid with only 15 to 30 percent crystallized in solid form. Both chemical composition and physical structure affect the liquid/solid ratio and thus the plasticity of the fat.

dough to the edges multiple times by lifting the rolling pin back to the center with each pass, instead of rolling dough in a back-and-forth motion, to obtain a thickness of about 1/8 inch (Figure 17-31). Crusts that are rolled very thin become too brown when baked as pie shells and break when handling or serving. If used for fruit pies, thin crusts may break during baking and allow juices to flow out.

Crusts are rolled into a circular shape. If the dough tears or breaks, it can be pressed back together to patch the tear with or without a small amount of water. The dough for a lower crust or a pie shell should be about 1 to 2 inches greater in diameter than the top of the pan, this allows for variable pan depth (Figure 17–31). Typical pie pan size is 9–10 inches diameter and 1 ¼ inches high, with deep-dish pie pans up to 2 inches in height. The standard 9-inch pie plate has a 4 ½ cup capacity and the standard 10-inch pie pan a 6 cup capacity. A standard 9-inch pie plate will require approximately 8 oz (225 g) of pie for the bottom crust and 6 oz (170 g) for the top crust. Rolled dough is carefully folded into quarters and lifted to the pie pan (pie plate). Place folded dough in the center of the pie plate; gently unfold dough letting extra pie dough hang-over the edge. Pie dough is placed in pan with overlapping edges and trimmed later. Excessive rolling and re-rolling of dough should be avoided as it toughens the pastry. Each crust is rolled one at a time. For future use, the rolled pastry can be frozen before baking [2] or the baked shells can be frozen.

Although pie shells tend to shrink somewhat in baking, excessive shrinkage can be prevented if the dough is not stretched when it is fitted into the pan. Preparing enough dough to make a rim or a frilled edge is also an advantage if shrinking occurs. Overdevelopment of the gluten by rerolling may result in greater shrinkage during baking than occurs when gluten is not developed to an appreciable extent.

Formation of large blisters or steam pockets in pastry shells during baking can be prevented by forcing air out from under the dough while putting the dough into the pan and by pricking the dough adequately with a fork before baking or using pie weights. Pricking the pie crust is called docking. Pie crusts are sometimes baked prior to filling so they retain their shape, which is sometimes referred to as "baked blind." The pie crust would be lined with parchment or greased foil then pie weights or beans would be placed in the lining to prevent steam pockets from forming (**Figure 17-33**). Crusts in which fillings are to be cooked are never pricked or docked.

Top crusts for fruit pies are less likely to break under the pressure of steam if small openings called steam vents are made near the center for the escape of

Cover plated pie dough with liner of parchment paper, greased aluminum foil (greased side down) or heat resistant food-grade plastic. Press liner against the pie dough shell extending above the pan. Fill with pan with baking weights, or dried rice or beans. (Richard Embery/Pearson Education)

steam. Large gashes should be avoided because they are unattractive and permit the loss of juices. Making the air vents into a decoration results in an attractive pie (Figure 17–2). Sometimes ceramic "pie birds" are placed in the pie center peeking out through the top crust and baked in the pie. These pie birds allow the steam to be vented through the top crust (**Figure 17–34**). A lattice top crust is made by half inch strips of dough that are woven to form a lattice for the top crust (**Figure 17–35**). Top crusts adhere more closely to lower crusts if edges are moistened with water before the crusts are pressed together. Pie edges are crimped between fingers to form an attractive edge. Streusel filling is sometimes used as an alternative top crust on fruit pies (**Figure 17–36**).

Figure 17–34

Ceramic pie bird baked in pie as a steam vent for double crusted pie. (© Amanda Frye)

Figure 17–35

Preparing a lattice top crust for a fruit pie. Pastry dough is rolled out and cut into even ½-inch (1.2 centimeter) strips. Strips of dough are woven in an over-under-over pattern for an attractive top crust. Lattice strips and bottom crust are crimped together to seal before baking. (Richard Embery/Pearson Education)

Figure 17–36

Single-crust apple-cranberry pie with streusel topping. (Richard Embery/Pearson Education)

BAKING

Plain pastry that is baked prior to the addition of the filling is baked at a hot oven temperature 425–450°F (218–232°C). If a lower temperature is used, then baking time is extended. Foil can be placed around the crust edges if they become too brown during baking.

The oven heat allows rapid production of steam, which separates the layers of dough formed as the fat particles melt. Baking is continued until the surface is delicately browned, which probably occurs chiefly as a result of the **Maillard reaction**. Crust browning can be increased by brushing dough prior to baking with egg wash, milk, or cream.

For pies such as apple or pumpkin, the crust is baked with the filling. Baking temperatures are adjusted according to the type of filling in pastry shells. The filling must be adequately cooked before the crust becomes too brown. Soaking of bottom crusts by fruit and custard fillings can be a problem and results in a soggy or soft bottom crust.

Preventing Soaked Crusts

Many methods have been suggested and tried for preventing a soaked crust in fruit, custard, and pumpkin pies. Some methods—partially baking the crust, coating the crust with raw egg white, or heating the crust until the egg white is coagulated—have no value. A partially baked crust becomes more soaked than one that is not baked. It also tends to be heavy or soggy. Raw egg white, being soluble in water, blends with the filling, thus offering no protection against the soaking of the crust.

So how can the crusts be protected? For fruit pies, you can coat the upper surface of the lower crust with melted butter, use a hot oven temperature for the first 15 minutes of baking, and thicken the filling before placing it in the pastry-lined pan. Thickening the filling gives you the added advantage of knowing the precise consistency of the juice before the pie is baked.

For custard and pumpkin pies, the problem of soaked crusts is even more difficult to solve. The lower baking temperatures required for egg mixtures prolong the baking time and permit increased soaking before the pie is done. A method that has been suggested to improve the crusts of custard pies is chilling the pastry for 1 hour before adding the filling and using a high oven temperature 450°F (232°C) for the first 10 minutes of baking. Increasing the percentage of egg in the mixture (three eggs per pint of milk) lowers the coagulation temperature of the egg proteins and increases the ease of coagulation for the mixture. Scalding the

---

FOCUS ON SCIENCE
HOW DOES FLAKINESS FORM IN A BAKED PIE CRUST?

Some of the plastic fat forms discrete particles with flour adhering to them. These particles are flattened when rolled, thus creating layers of fat and dough. When the pie crusts are baked, steam is formed, the dough gelatinizes, and the fat melts into the dough, thereby leaving an empty space and flakiness. It is important that the fat has a high melting point such that it remains solid until the dough gelatinizes.

milk used for the filling also shortens coagulation time. Coagulated custard does not penetrate the crust as readily as an uncooked mixture. An overcooked custard may exude water to produce a wet crust. This process is called syneresis, sometimes referred to as "weeping."

Using a Microwave Oven

Microwaved pastry is tender, flaky, and puffy, but it does not brown. A few drops of yellow food coloring can be added to the dough, or the pastry can be brushed with egg yolk before microwaving. A one-crust pastry shell is cooked on high power for about 6 or 7 minutes, the dish being rotated one-half turn after 3 minutes. Alternatively, the pastry shell can be baked in a conventional oven and the filling cooked in a microwave oven.

The bottom crust of a two-crust pie can be cooked by microwave on a medium setting for 5 to 6 minutes, the uncooked filling added, the top crust put in place, and the pie cooked again. The pie should be turned midway in the cooking period. If a broiling unit is not available for browning, the pie can be finished by baking for 10 to 15 minutes in a hot conventional oven. Meringues can be cooked by microwaves but must be browned in a conventional heating unit.

Prepared Pie Crust

Homemade pie crusts can be frozen baked or unbaked and then used later. Alternatively, partially prepared pie crust may be purchased in several forms. Frozen ready-to-bake pie crust in aluminum pie pans, refrigerated rolled sheets of dough, or pie crust mixes are all available.

OTHER PASTRY CRUSTS, DOUGHS, AND FILLINGS

Crumb, Cookie, and Sweet Tart Crusts

The bottom crust on pies as well as some other desserts such as cheesecakes may be made from crumbs (Figure 17–21). Graham cracker crumbs are frequently used; sugar cookies, chocolate sandwich cookies, gingersnaps, and other cookies may be crumbed and used. The typical ratio of ingredients in crumb crusts is one part melted butter, two parts sugar, and four parts crumbs [5]. When cookies are used instead of graham cracker crumbs, the amount of sugar may need to be decreased.

The preparation of crumb crusts is generally quick and easy. The crumbs, sugar, and melted butter are blended. If the mixture is too dry to stick together, additional melted butter may be slowly added until the desired consistency is achieved.

Then the crumbs are pressed into the bottom of the pan to a depth between $\frac{1}{8}$ and $\frac{1}{4}$ inch. This crust may be refrigerated and filled after the butter has firmed, or it can be baked in an oven preheated to 350°F (177°C) for about 10 minutes or until lightly browned and then filled. Baked crusts will be firmer and will provide a stronger crust.

Mealy Dough

Mealy dough is used when a soggy crust may be a problem since it yields a sturdier pie crust. The term *mealy* refers to the cornmeal-like appearance when fat is cut into the flour mixture. The fat is blended in thoroughly in a mixing procedure similar to making cookies as opposed to the mixing procedure for standard pie pastry. The more complete coating of flour makes a more tender crust that is short and has less gluten development. Less water is needed for a mealy dough. The baked pie crust is less likely to absorb filling water; therefore, the pie is not soggy.

Enriched Pie Dough (Sweet Pie Dough or Shortbread Pie Dough)

Enriched pie dough or sweet pie dough or shortbread pie dough is essentially a mealy pie dough with the addition of egg yolk and sugar. These sweet dough crusts generally are not flaky like other pie crusts, but they have the advantage of being crisp and sturdy. The creaming method is typically used to make enriched pie dough. Enriched or sweet pie dough is used for sweet tarts shells. Butter is typically used for the fat. Egg yolk proteins contribute to a sturdier crust. Fat coats flour particles more readily yielding less gluten formation, thus producing a tender, crumbly crust. A stronger flour such as all-purpose or bread flour is needed for a stronger crust. The type of sugar used affects the final product as powdered sugar produces a finer-texture dough compared to granulated sugar. Sometimes cocoa powder and nut flour are used to make a chocolate tart dough. These characteristics are desirable for stand-alone tarts, which are usually made in a shallow, straight-sided pan (Figure 17–20). Tartlet pans are used for individual serving-size tarts.

Puff Pastry

Puff pastry is a rich dough that separates into many light, crisp layers when baked. Steam is the leavening agent in this dough, and rolling a sheet of butter into the dough results in the flaky layers that are characteristic of puff pastry (**Figure 17–37**). Puff pastry is made by rolling chilled butter in a well-kneaded flour-and-water dough, then folding and rerolling several times to make many thin layers of dough separated by thin layers of butter (**Figure 17–38**).

Figure 17–37
Puff pastry (top right) is properly laminated puff pastry that can rise six times the original volume with many visible even layers. Puff pastry (bottom left) is compact with low volume and lacks layers that is a result of poor laminated puff pastry. (Richard Embery/Pearson Education)

Figure 17–38
Chocolate puff pastry dough highlights the visible layers of butter. (Richard Embery/Pearson Education)

(a)

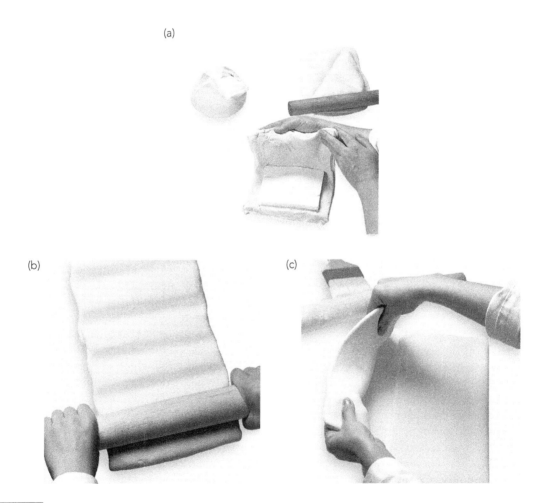

(b)

(c)

Figure 17–39
Steps for incorporating fat to make puff pastry. Photo (a) Roll butter (fat) to a slab to be placed on prepared dough. Place butter slab on prepared dough folding over to wrap dough. Use fingertips to seal edges of dough to secure rolled-in fat. (b) Roll out dough by first making ridges with rolling pin; then, roll dough smooth and each ridge is double in size. (c) Fold dough in thirds. (© Richard Embery/Pearson Education)

During baking, the butter melts and permeates the dough. Laminated dough procedures are also discussed in Chapter 15.

Making puff pastry from scratch requires skill and patience, as the chilled dough must be rolled multiple times to create the layers from the butter that has been folded and rolled into the dough. Alternatively, commercial frozen puff pastry is available frozen for use in creating a number of desserts and other dishes.

Phyllo Dough

Phyllo (Filo or Fillo) dough is a paper-thin pastry dough that is bland in flavor. It is used in Mediterranean, Balkan, Middle Eastern, and Central Asian dishes (**Figure 17–40**) [5]. Phyllo dough is made from semolina flour (durum wheat). Phyllo dough is commercially produced and generally purchased frozen because of the time and skill required to make this dough. Sheets of phyllo are brushed with butter and layered and stacked; these are used as a base for a variety of sweet desserts, and savory dishes. Phyllo dough may be layered into custard cups, baked, and then filled with a custard or cheese filling and topped with fruit (**Figure 17–41**). Phyllo dough is also used for the classic Greek dessert called *baklava*. Frozen phyllo dough should be thawed slowly in the refrigerator because attempts to thaw phyllo dough quickly create difficulties in separating and handling the sheets. While working with phyllo dough, cover it with plastic wrap to prevent it from drying out. Many recipes will call for the dough to be lifted one sheet at a time and placed in the pan and brushed with butter before adding another sheet and repeating the process. Phyllo dough pastries create a flaky crust by directly adding fat between the prepared flour-based dough layers.

Kataifi is sometimes referred to as shredded phyllo dough although it is drizzled onto a hot round

Figure 17–41a

Kataifi. (Richard Embery/Pearson Education)

Figure 17–41b

Making kataifi on a traditional spinning hot plate. Batter dispenser is in background attached to the wall. (Turgay Koca/123RF)

griddle to make noodle-like strands (Figure 17–41b). These kataifi strands are filled or wrapped with nuts and sweet buttery mixtures for Middle Eastern specialties (Figure 17–41a).

Strudel Dough

Traditional strudel dough is a specialty European pastry dough made from a strong flour (bread flour), eggs, water, and small amount of oil. This dough is

Figure 17–40

Phyllo dough. (Richard Embery/Pearson Education)

unyeasted and needed for an extended period to develop gluten. The dough is stretched by hand into a very thin nearly transparent sheet. Strudel dough is stretched over the backs of the hands to avoid poking holes in the dough. The dough stretches best if slightly warm. Stretched strudel dough is filled with sweet fillings such as apple, cheese, or poppy seed or savory fillings (Figure 17–22), then rolled and baked. Baked roll is sliced into individual pieces. Strudel dough is similar to, but different from, phyllo dough. Strudel is traditionally from areas of the former Austrian–Hungarian Empire.

Pia Dough

Pia is a traditional individual serving size Chinese pastry with variations found throughout Asia. Pia dough is made with two doughs: Outer dough (water dough) and inner dough (oil dough). The two pia doughs are layered with the rich inner dough placed on top of the outer dough. The fat in each dough performs different functions. Fat in the inner crust is responsible for the layering and puffiness specific to pia. The outer dough provides structure and stability from gluten [3]. The two doughs are folded and rolled to create flaky layers. Individual dough pieces are filled, then the dough is wrapped encasing the filling. The encased product is baked. Traditionally mung bean (conserve) paste is used as the filling, but many filling variations exist such as durian fruit. The individual *pia* is baked often with an egg white wash (Figure 17–26).

Asian Moon Cake

Vietnamese and Chinese moon cakes are actually a pastry served during the mid-autumn festival celebrating harvest and the brightest moon (Figure 17–27). These pastries are an oil-based (sometimes part sesame oil) pastry traditionally mixed with golden syrup (invert syrup from cane sugar) and alkaline water. The pastry dough is pressed into a deep carved mold. The filling can be a variety of ingredients such as rich fruit, nut, lotus, or red bean paste mixtures. The moon cake mixture often surrounds a steamed salted egg yolk (often duck egg yolk) that represents the moon when cut open. The pastry shell completely encases the filling and is baked (**Figure 17–42**).

Vegan mooncake with nuts, fruit, and seed filling (© Amanda Frye)

Sweet Pie Fillings

Sweet pie fillings can fall into four broad categories: (1) cream-based starch, (2) fruit, (3) custard, and (4) chiffon. Stabilizing and thickening agents are standard in most pie fillings. Stabilizing and thickening agents are typically starch, egg, or gelatin. Starches must be combined with cold liquid or sugar prior to heating or adding hot liquid to avoid lumping. Starch and liquid must be heated to a point that fully gelatinizes the starch giving the thickening power. Flour has less thickening power than other starches and produces a cloudy (not clear) filling. Flour is sometimes used in fruit pies. Used less frequently in place of flour are tapioca, potato starch, and rice starch.

Cornstarch produces a firm, clear (uncloudy) gel, but gel strength is lessened by sugar and acid. Adding acid and sugar after starch has thickened helps to prevent lessening of gel strength. Typically, cornstarch is used for cream-based fillings since it holds a firm shape, but may be used in fruit pies. Cornstarch gel separates and breaks during freezing.

FOCUS ON SCIENCE
HOW DOES THE TYPE OF PIE PAN HAVE AN IMPACT ON COLOR AND THE POTENTIAL SOAKING OF CRUSTS?

For well-baked golden bottom crusts, use pans made of heat-resistant glass, dull anodized aluminum enamel, or darkened metal. These types of pie pans absorb heat, thereby ensuring the crusts brown perfectly. Shiny pans reflect heat, so bottom crusts are more likely to be soggy. Therefore, the selection of the pan is essential.

Tapioca starch freezes well, gelatinizes at a lower temperature than cornstarch, and cooks to a clear gel. Frozen pies should use a waxy maize or modified starch. Waxy maize or modified starches work best for a clear, but soft gel which is desired with fruit pies. Instant or pregelatinized starch requires no heating for fillings. Eggs are also used as a thickening agent in custard and cream fillings. Gelatin is the thickener in chiffon fillings. Many aspects of these filling components are discussed in other chapters.

Cream Fillings

Cream fillings are basically a pudding or flavored starch thickened egg custard base. Cream fillings are usually made with cornstarch or sometimes with a cornstarch/flour combination. Lemon filling is derivation of a cream filling that uses lemon juice instead of milk. The starch custard mixture must be cooked enough to gelatinize the starch. Eggs are added to the cooked gelatinized starch paste. Eggs are tempered when adding to the hot starch mixture to prevent curdling. Then egg starch thickened mixture is slowly heated to a point to prevent food-borne illness, coagulate egg proteins for further thickening, and deactivate egg alpha amylases that can cause thinning of cream fillings upon standing. Often only egg yolks are used. Starch gelatinizes at a higher temperature. Cream fillings are completely cooked on the stove top and poured into a prebaked pie crust or crumb crust warm or chilled. Pies with cream fillings should be refrigerated.

Fruit Fillings

Fresh fruit, canned fruit, frozen fruits, and rehydrated dried fruits can be used in fruit pie fillings (Figure 17-1). Fruit fillings are typically suspended in a starch thickened gel. Sometimes fresh fruit is coated with flour or other starch, sugar, and seasonings and placed directly into an unbaked pie shell. As the pie bakes, water from fruit combines with the thickening starch agent which thickens the fruit juice. Also, water exits from the fruit cell structure and fruit size shrinks as it bakes. Modified starches give a soft clear gel and are usually preferred for fruit pie fillings. Traditional fruit fillings combine fruit, sugar, flavorings, and flour or starch that is then placed in an unbaked pie shell. Most traditional fruit pies are two-crusted pies (Figure 17-2), but some are one-crust pies. In some pies, fruit and pie shells are baked together. Some fruit pies substitute a strudel mixture for top crust. For other fruit pies, a thin gel glaze is prepared often from fruit juice. Thin gel glaze is mixed with fresh fruit to coat fruit and then placed in a baked pie shell.

Figure 17-43
Pumpkin pie custard filling being poured into unbaked pie shell. (Richard Embery/Pearson Education)

Custard Fillings

Custard pies are a flavored egg custard base that is poured into an unbaked pie shell and baked together (**Figure 17-43**). Pumpkin, pecan, and custard pies are examples of the custard fillings. When egg proteins coagulate, the filling firms. Custard pies present challenges of baking a custard without having a soggy crust or overcooking the custard. Overcooked custard gel breaks causing syneresis, or weeping. Typically, custard filled pies start the baking temperature at a high temperature around 400°F (200°C) for a short time, about 10 minutes, prior to reducing heat to 325-350°F (160-180°C) to finish cooking the custard. The custard filling should no longer be liquid at the end of the cooking period and a thin knife inserted in the middle of the custard filling should come out clean. Custard pies require refrigeration.

Chiffon Fillings

Chiffon fillings are a fruit puree or stirred custard mixture thickened by adding gelatin. The gelatin must be completely dissolved and thoroughly distributed throughout the mixture. Never use gelatin with raw pineapple or papaya. Whipped egg whites are folded into the gelatin custard mixture. The egg whites create a light fluffy mixture and texture. Pasteurized egg whites should be used for food safety reasons. The mixture is poured into a baked pie shell and chilled.

Tart Glaze (Mirror Glaze)

Tart glaze is a thin, shiny, transparent coating applied to fruit-filled tarts. The glaze is spooned over the filled tart and makes it shiny and prevents drying. Some glazes are flavored, others contain liquors, and still others are unflavored, called *neutral* glazes. Fruit preserves are sometimes used in place of a glaze.

STUDY QUESTIONS

Types of Pastry and Crusts and Applications

1. Discuss various pastries and crusts used throughout the world. Describe the applications of various crusts used with various pastries.

2. Using your knowledge of food science, discuss the similarities and differences of various crust forms and methods used for variations of conventional pie dough.

Consumption Trends and Nutrition

3. Discuss how pie crusts have evolved.

4. How has food science knowledge been used in pastry and pie crust trends?

Characteristics of Plain Pastry

5. Describe desirable characteristics of good-quality pastry.

Ingredient Functions

6. Describe the role of each of the following ingredients in the preparation of good-quality pastry:
   (a) Flour
   (b) Fat
   (c) Water

7. (a) Suggest an appropriate ratio of fat to flour for making pastry.
   (b) Explain how the type of fat and the type of flour used might affect these proportions.

Mixing, Rolling, and Baking Plain Pastry

8. (a) Describe several procedures for mixing pastry.

(b) What techniques of mixing are likely to produce the most flaky pastry? Why?

(c) Describe how different crusts, methods, and fillings are interrelated.

9. Describe a satisfactory procedure for making pastry with oil. How does this pastry compare with one made using a solid fat?

10. What is the effect of each of the following on tenderness of pastry?
    (a) Type of fat used
    (b) Type of flour used
    (c) Technique of mixing and handling

11. Some people have suggested that alcohol such as vodka (60 percent alcohol) can be substituted for the liquid to make a "fool proof" pie dough.
    (a) How would this effect the pie dough and baked crust?
    (b) What might be the reasoning behind such substitution?
    (c) How are these claims supported or not supported by peer-review research?

12. Suggest an appropriate temperature for baking plain pastry. Explain why this temperature may be recommended.

13. What can be done to prevent or minimize the soaking of bottom crusts of custard and fruit pies during baking?

14. Discuss the similarities and differences of conventional pie dough, oil pie dough, puff pastry, phyllo dough, and pia dough.

18
Vegetables and Vegetable Preparation

What exactly is a vegetable? We can define vegetables broadly as plants or parts of plants that are used as food. The term *vegetable*, however, has come to apply in a more narrow sense to plants or parts of plants that are served either raw or cooked as part of the main course of a meal. Sweet corn, a cereal, is often used as a vegetable at the table.

Regardless of how we define vegetables, we value them for their unique contributions to color, flavor, and texture in our menus. In addition, vegetables are an important part of our daily food intake because of their nutritional merit, particularly in regard to their content of vitamins, minerals, and fiber.

In this chapter, the following topics will be discussed:

- Consumption trends and nutritional value
- Kinds of vegetables
- Purchasing
- Storage
- Preparation and quality considerations
- Cooking methods

CONSUMPTION TRENDS AND NUTRITION

Consumption Trends

Food supply data showed an increase in the availability of vegetables in the United States from 328 pounds per person in 1970 to 381 pounds per person in 2015 [65]. However, consumption is concentrated among a small number of vegetables. The 2015 average per capita availability data from the U.S. Department of Agriculture (USDA) show that potatoes and tomatoes account for large amount of the total vegetable availability [63] (**Figure 18–1**). The average daily per capita cup-equivalents of vegetables are 1.7 cups after adjustment for spoilage and other waste. Americans of all ages are consuming less than the amount of vegetables recommended by the U.S. Dietary Guidelines [67] (**Figure 18–2**). Using phone interview data, 22 percent of adults report eating less than one serving of vegetables daily

[55]. Overall, in 2015 only 9 percent of Americans ate enough vegetables [52].

Low-income individuals (income below 185 percent of the poverty level) consumed fewer tomatoes, potatoes, and other vegetables as compared with those with higher incomes [30]. Education level also appears to influence vegetable intake. College-educated adults eat more "other" vegetables, tomatoes and more vegetables overall as compared to adults with a high school diploma or less than a high school diploma. Those with less than a high school diploma consumed comparatively the least amount of other vegetables, potatoes, and tomatoes [30]. Researchers have found that among individuals and families experiencing food insecurity (see Chapter 1), the disliking of health food taste and cost is associated with a lower vegetable consumption [38]. For all respondents in this study, being too busy to prepare food was associated with reduced vegetable and fruit consumption.

Nutritive Value

Vegetables offer a number of beneficial qualities to our diets. Vegetables and fruits probably do more than any other group of foods to add appetizing texture, color, and flavor to daily meals. From a health perspective, vegetables have been associated with a reduced risk of certain cancers, type 2 diabetes, stroke, and, potentially, cardiovascular disease and hypertension [49, 74]. In 2003, the U.S. Food and Drug Administration (FDA) issued a dietary guidance statement that may be used in product labels and other print materials. This statement is, "Diets rich in fruits and vegetables may reduce the risk of some types of cancers and other chronic diseases" [68].

The *2015 U.S. Dietary Guidelines for Americans* recommend the daily consumption of 2½ cups of a variety of vegetables for a reference 2,000-calorie intake [67]. The ChooseMyPlate graphic that replaced the USDA Food Guide Pyramid in 2011 recommends that half of the food on our plates should be fruits and vegetables (**Figure 18–3**). More vegetables should be consumed by those with higher caloric needs. Variety in vegetable consumption is encouraged and may be accomplished by including all five vegetable subgroups in meals or snacks several times each week: dark green, orange,

Vegetable Availability: 2015

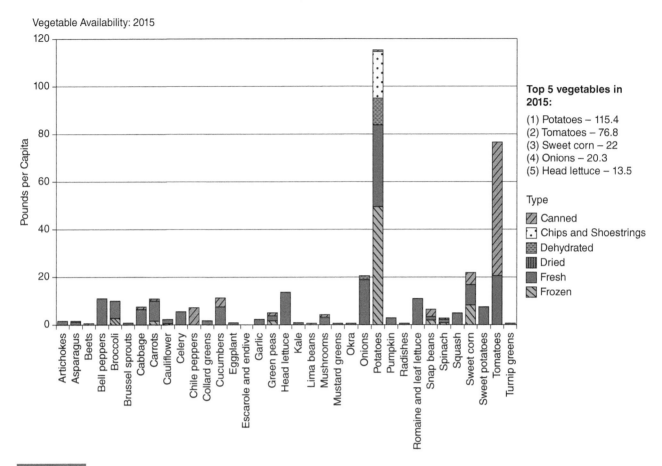

Top 5 vegetables in 2015:

(1) Potatoes – 115.4
(2) Tomatoes – 76.8
(3) Sweet corn – 22
(4) Onions – 20.3
(5) Head lettuce – 13.5

Type

- Canned
- Chips and Shoestrings
- Dehydrated
- Dried
- Fresh
- Frozen

Figure 18–1

This bar chart provides data from the USDA Economic Research Service showing Food Availability data. Potatoes and tomatoes account for the largest amount of vegetable use in the United States. Potatoes are largely consumed frozen or fresh, but tomatoes are most often consumed as canned tomatoes. (USDA, Economic Research Service)

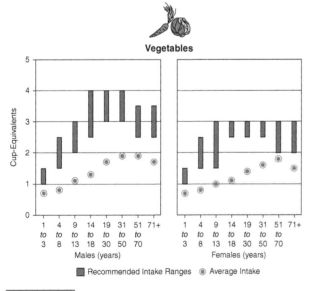

Figure 18–2

Males and females of all ages consume less than the recommended servings of vegetables. The orange dots represent the typical number of cups consumed at the ages listed. The blue bar is the recommended number of cups (or cup equivalents) of vegetables that are recommended on a daily basis depending on individual needs at each age. (USDA)

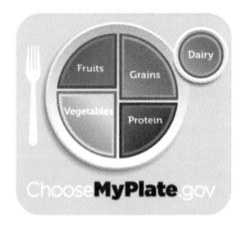

Figure 18–3

Choosing fruits and vegetables for half of your plate is recommended by the USDA for a healthy diet. (USDA Center for Nutrition Policy and Promotion)

legumes, starchy vegetables, and other vegetables [56]. Examples of vegetables in these five groups are provided in **Table 18–1**. Individualized food consumption recommendations can be obtained from www.choosemyplate.gov.

Table 18–1
VEGETABLE SUBGROUPS BASED ON NUTRIENT CONTENT (EACH GROUP SHOULD BE INCLUDED SEVERAL TIMES EACH WEEK IN MEALS)

Vegetable Group	Examples
Dark green	Bok choy, broccoli, collard greens, dark green leafy lettuce, kale, mesclun, mustard greens, romaine lettuce, spinach, turnip greens, watercress, green herbs (parsley, cilantro)
Red and orange	Acorn squash, butternut squash, carrots, hubbard squash, pumpkin, red peppers (hot and sweet), sweet potatoes, tomatoes
Dry beans and peas (may be purchased dried or canned)	Black beans, black-eyed peas, garbanzo beans (chickpeas), kidney beans, lentils, lima beans (mature, dried), navy beans, pinto beans, soybeans, edamame (green soybeans), split peas, white beans (See Chapter 19)
Starchy	Cassava, corn, green peas, lima beans (green), potatoes, water chestnuts, plantains
Other vegetables	Artichokes, asparagus, avocado, bean sprouts, beets, Brussels sprouts, cabbage, cauliflower, celery, cucumbers, eggplant, garlic, green beans, green peppers, iceberg (head) lettuce, mushrooms, okra, onions, olives, parsnips, turnips, wax beans, zucchini

Source: References 56, 67.

Table 18–2
EXCELLENT AND GOOD VEGETABLE SOURCES OF SELECTED NUTRIENTS

Nutrients	Vegetable Sources
Fiber	*Excellent sources:* Navy beans, kidney beans, black beans, pinto beans, lima beans, white beans, soybeans, split peas, chickpeas, black-eyed peas, lentils, artichokes
Folate	*Excellent sources:* Black-eyed peas, cooked spinach, Great Northern beans, asparagus
Potassium	*Good sources:* Sweet potatoes, tomato paste, tomato puree, beet greens, white potatoes, white beans, lima beans, cooked greens, carrot juice, prune juice
Vitamin A	*Excellent sources:* Sweet potatoes, pumpkin, carrots, spinach, turnip greens, mustard greens, kale, collard greens, winter squash, red peppers, Chinese cabbage
Vitamin C	*Excellent sources:* Red and green peppers, sweet potatoes, kale, broccoli, Brussels sprouts, tomato juice, cauliflower

Note: Excellent sources provide 20 percent or more of the Daily Value per reference amount. Good sources provide 10 to 19 percent of the Daily Value per reference amount.

Source: U.S. Centers for Disease Control and Prevention Reference 53.

Nutritionally, vegetables provide fiber, potassium, vitamin A, vitamin C, vitamin B_6, vitamin E, vitamin K, folate, thiamine, niacin, choline, copper, magnesium, iron, manganese, and other nutrients [67]. The nutritive value of vegetables may be found from the USDA Nutrient Data Laboratory online (see Appendix C). Examples of excellent and good vegetable sources of nutrients are provided in **Table 18–2**. Many vegetables, as well as fruits (See Chapter 20 on fruits), also are rich in **phytochemicals**. Phytochemicals such as carotenoids (including lycopene), flavonoids, glucosinolates, phytoestrogens, phenols, sulfides, capsaicin, anthocyanins, tannins, and more have been found to function as antioxidants or anticancer agents [74]. Phytonutrient intake is higher when adults consume the recommended amount of fruits and vegetables [39].

In addition to many vegetables having a high nutrient content, most vegetables are low in calories and thus may be beneficial in maintaining a healthy weight. To promote vegetable consumption among consumers, the Fruits and Veggies—More Matters[TM] health initiative was launched in March 2007 (**Figure 18–4**) and offers a web page to assist consumers in consuming more

Figure 18–4

Logo for Fruit and Veggies—More Matters™. (Produce for Better Health Foundation)

vegetables and fruits. Along with the *2015 Dietary Guidelines for Americans,* this national initiative by the Produce for Better Health Foundation, the Centers for Disease Control and Prevention, and other government and national partners has been designed to help Americans overcome common barriers to eating fruits and vegetables.

KINDS OF VEGETABLES

Various parts of plants are used as vegetables. One grouping by plant part is shown in **Table 18–3**. Technically, some vegetables might be placed under more than one heading.

Leaf Vegetables

Many different types of greens are available for the consumer to purchase or grow in a garden. Although iceberg lettuce is one of the most widely consumed greens, consumers are increasingly choosing romaine, leaf lettuce, and other specialty greens, such as radicchio, arugula, and red oak (**Figure 18–5**). A description of selected leaf vegetables is provided in **Table 18–4**. Leafy greens are discussed further in Chapter 21.

Leaf vegetables may be generally characterized as being high in water and low in carbohydrate and calories, with only small amounts of protein and little or no fat. These vegetables' chief nutritive contribution is providing vitamins and minerals, especially iron, vitamin A value, riboflavin, folate, and vitamin C. Leafy greens that are darker green have a higher vitamin A value. Green leaves also contain calcium, but most of the calcium in spinach, chard, and beet greens is bound with **oxalic acid** in the plant and is not available for absorption from the digestive tract.

To preserve quality, leafy greens should be stored under refrigeration away from ethylene-producing fruits and vegetables, such as tomatoes or apples. Ethylene-producing fruits and vegetables will promote premature spoilage. High humidity conditions are preferable to avoid wilting of the lettuce leaves. All leafy lettuce and greens should be washed thoroughly. Submerging the leaves under cool water and then lifting out of the water to drain and repeating in fresh water two or three times until thoroughly washed is recommended. A salad spinner is helpful to adequately dry wash lettuce and greens.

Vegetable-Fruits

Tomatoes, cucumbers, peppers, squash, and several other vegetables are classified as **vegetable-fruits** (**Figure 18–6**). Although typically served as vegetables, these vegetable-fruits are botanically classified as fruits because each one develops from a flower.

Table 18–3
PARTS OF PLANS COMMONLY USED AS VEGETABLES

Leaves	Beet, Collard, Dandelion, Mustard, and Turnip Greens Bok choy, Brussels sprouts, Cabbage, Chard, Chinese cabbage, Endive, Escarole, Kale, Lettuce, Parsley, Romaine, Spinach, Watercress
Vegetable-Fruits	Cucumber, Eggplant, Okra, Pepper, Pumpkin, Snap beans, Squash, Sweet corn, Tomato
Flowers	Artichoke, Broccoli, Cauliflower
Stems, Shoots	Fennel, Asparagus, Celery, Kohlrabi
Roots	Beet, Carrot, Celeriac, Jicama, Parsnip, Radish, Rutabaga, Salsify, Sweet Potato, Turnip
Tubers	Ginger root, Potato, Sunchoke
Bulbs	Chives, Garlic, Leek, Onion, Shallot
Seeds	Beans, Lentils, Peas (See Chapter 19)

Red Leaf Lettuce

Radicchio

Dandelion

Red and Green Cabbage

Bok Choy

Arugula

Figure 18–5
Several examples of leafy green vegetables are shown here. (Richard Embery/Pearson Education)

Table 18–4
LEAF VEGETABLES

Description

Brussels Sprouts
Very small heads (often 1 inch across or less). Dark green, compact leaves. Firm texture. Usually cooked before consumption.

Lettuce (See also Chapter 21)
Arugula. Small, flat leaves with long stems and a peppery taste. Often mixed with other salad greens.

Belgian Endive. Elongated head with white compact leaves and creamy yellow tips. Crisp texture, mild and slightly bitter flavor.

Boston and Bibb. Loose heads, buttery texture, and mild flavor.

Chicory or Curly Endive. Narrow leaves with very curly edges. May be dark green on outer leaves to yellow-white in center. Mild to slightly bitter flavor.

Escarole. Loosely bunched, large heads, and slightly crumbled green leaves. Milder taste than curly endive.

Frisee. Ivory-yellow, very thin, and ruffled leaves.

Iceberg. Crisp texture and very mild flavor. Pale green leaves on compact head. Least nutritious of the salad greens.

Looseleaf (Oak Leaf, Red Leaf, Green Leaf). Leaves are joined at stem and do not form a head. Oak leaf has a similar shape of the leaves on an oak tree. Red and green leaf lettuce varieties are characterized by color. Texture is crisp but tender.

(Continued)

Table 18–4
LEAF VEGETABLES (*CONTINUED*)

Description

Radicchio. Maroon-red leaves on a small compact head. Slightly bittersweet distinctive flavor. Usually expensive.

Romaine or Cos. Elongated leaves. Dark green. Strong flavor and crispy texture. Often used for Caesar salads.

Cabbage

Green. Light green compact leaves. Round head.

Red. Purple-red leaves. Round, compact head. Sweeter flavor than green cabbage.

Savoy. Pale green color and crinkled leaves. Round to oblong head with loose, compact leaves.

General Tips. Select firm heads, heavy for size. Precut cabbage is best avoided because of reduced vitamin C content. May be eaten raw or cooked.

Chinese Cabbage

Bok Choy. Thick white stalks and large green leaves. Mild flavor and tender-crisp texture. Often stir-fried but may be used raw.

Napa Cabbage or Chinese Cabbage. Tightly packed oblong head. Leaves are pale green and crinkled. Tender crisp with a mild flavor. May be used fresh or cooked.

Cactus Pads or Napales

Broad green pads with tiny thorns. Tender texture. Flavor is a cross between fresh green beans and bell pepper.

General Tips. Dry, limp, or soggy pads should be avoided when purchasing. May develop bronze discoloration if exposed to temperatures that are too cold. Best stored at 41°F (5°C). Remove thorns or eyes before preparing and rinse under water. May be eaten raw or cooked by lightly steaming or sautéing.

Greens

Beet. Flat, green leaves with thin red stems and red ribs.

Broccoli Rabe. Dark green leaves on slender stalks topped with small clusters of tiny buds. Bitter pungent flavor. Used in Italian and Chinese cuisines. Entire plant is consumed. Flavor is best when cooked.

Collard Greens. Loaf-shaped, flat, green leaves

Dandelion. Narrow, dark green, ragged-edged leaves. Thin, white stems. Mild cabbage-like flavor.

Kale. Depending on variety, may have blue-green or yellow-green leaves. Leaves have curly edges and flat centers. Is typically cooked.

Mustard Greens. Large green, curly-edged leaves. Long narrow stems. Have a pungent, peppery flavor.

Swiss Chard. Large dark green leaves with red veins. Thick, white stems. Flavor is mild and sweet with a slight bitterness.

Turnip. Flat, green, slightly fuzzy leaves. Long, narrow green stems.

Spinach

Flat or Smooth Leaf. Dark, green, slightly crinkled leaves.

Savoy. Dark, green, crinkled leaves.

General Tips. Wash thoroughly to remove sand and dirt. Tear off the stems. May be consumed raw or cooked.

Watercress

Dark-green, heart-shaped leaves. Long, thin stalks. Spicy flavor. Soft to slightly crunchy texture.

Source: References 43, 54.

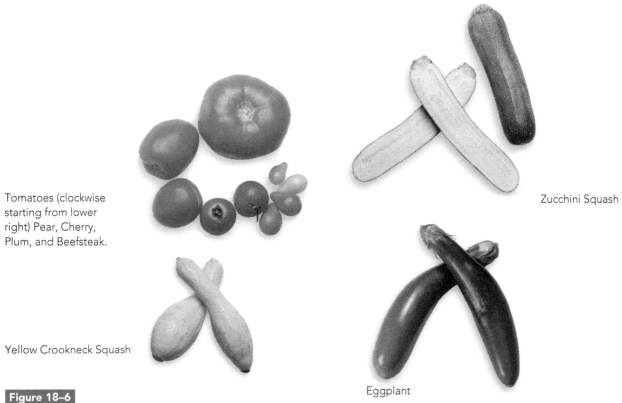

Tomatoes (clockwise starting from lower right) Pear, Cherry, Plum, and Beefsteak.

Zucchini Squash

Yellow Crookneck Squash

Eggplant

Figure 18–6

Several examples of vegetable "fruits" are shown here. (Richard Embery/Pearson Education)

People often do not think of these vegetables as fruits, because they do not taste sweet and are generally prepared in combination with other vegetables. Although green and red peppers, string beans, and okra can be classified as vegetable-fruits, they are also seed pods.

Tomatoes may be consumed raw or cooked and are used by food processors for catsup, tomato sauces, and other tomato products. Peppers can be mild or hot and used in many different kinds of foods. See Chapter 6 for a discussion of the types of peppers used for seasoning. A description of selected vegetable-fruits is provided in **Table 18–5**.

Most of the commonly eaten vegetable-fruits are relatively high in water content (92 to 94 percent), with small amounts of carbohydrate. Winter squash is an exception to the usually high water content of this group; it contains only about 85 percent water and 12 percent carbohydrate in the raw state, comparable in carbohydrate content with many of the sweet, fleshy fruits. Cucumbers are particularly low in carbohydrate content and high in water content—about 97 percent. Tomatoes and green peppers are vegetable-fruits that are important sources of vitamin C. Pumpkin and yellow squash, tomatoes, and green peppers contain **carotenoid** pigments, some of which are **precursors** of vitamin A.

Flowers and Stems

Flowers and stems (**Table 18–6**) are, in general, high in water and low in carbohydrates. Broccoli has been shown to be a particularly nutritious green vegetable in terms of its vitamin and mineral content and also as a source of phytochemicals. It is one of the richest vegetable sources of vitamin C; even the stems contain this vitamin, so, when possible, the stems should be pared and used. Broccoli also provides vitamin A value and contributes some riboflavin, calcium, and iron. Cauliflower and kohlrabi are good sources of vitamin C, and green asparagus has vitamin A value. **Figure 18–7** depicts preparation techniques for artichokes.

Roots, Bulbs, and Tubers

Root vegetables include beets, carrots, turnips, rutabagas, and parsnips (**Table 18–7**). Examples of bulbs, which are enlargements above the roots, are onions, leeks, and shallots. The potato is a **tuber**, which is an enlarged underground stem. Potatoes are the most commonly consumed vegetable by Americans at 64 retail pounds per capita annually [64]. Forty percent of the potato consumption is frozen potatoes [64] such as French fries, and other similar potato products. Idaho and Washington state are the leading growers of potatoes in the United States [66].

Table 18–5
VEGETABLE-FRUITS

Name and Description	Selection and Preparation Pointers
Cucumber Dark green skin and firm. Interior is a pale green and moist with seeds running through the center. Often treated with edible wax to reduce moisture loss.	Store under refrigeration in high humidity away from ethylene-producing fruits and vegetables. Wash. Peeling and removal of the seeds is optional, depending on preference and recipe. Often consumed raw by simply slicing; may be made into pickles. Cucumber variety is often selected for intended use—fresh or pickled.
Eggplant Usually large (1 to 5 pounds) with a shiny dark purple skin. Interior is a creamy colored. May be oval or elongated in shape. Excessively large eggplants may be tough and bitter.	Select eggplants with smooth, uniformly colored skin. Store under refrigeration with high humidity away from ethylene-producing fruits and vegetables. Will bruise easily, so handle with care. To prepare, wash and slice off ends. To reduce moisture and bitterness, lightly salt sliced eggplant and drain for 30 minutes. May be cooked with or without skin; however, if skin is tough, peeling is preferable. A variety of cooking methods may be used.
Okra An elongated, lantern-shaped vegetable that is 2 to 7 inches in length. The skin is green and slightly fuzzy. Rows of tiny seeds and a sticky texture are evident when sliced open. Several different varieties are available.	Store under refrigeration with high humidity away from ethylene-producing fruits and vegetables. May be steamed, boiled, pickled, or sautéed. The more it is cut, the stickier it becomes. Is used as a thickener in some recipes due to this quality. Do not cook in iron, copper, or brass pans to avoid darkening of okra.
Pepper Bell peppers may be green, red, or yellow. The red bell peppers are sweeter, milder, and have 11 times more beta carotene than green bell peppers.	Look for firm, fresh-looking, and brightly colored peppers. Shriveled peppers should be avoided. May be consumed raw or cooked in a variety of dishes. To prepare, slice off ends of pepper, remove seed core, and slice off the light colored spines. Cut remaining pepper as desired with knife contact being from the interior of the pepper to the exterior skin. Peppers may be "roasted" by holding over a flame or near a heat element until the skin is blackened. Alternatively, peppers may be roasted under a broiler. Wrap roasted pepper in plastic to "sweat" briefly. Scrape off blackened skin and use pepper as desired.
Pumpkin May range in size from 1 to 25 pounds. Smaller pumpkins are generally preferred for cooking purposes. Often purchased canned, rather than fresh for use in recipes.	Best stored at 60 to 65°F (16 to 18°C) with a humidity of 65 to 70 percent for long-term storage. Higher humidity levels are acceptable for short-term storage. To cook fresh pumpkin, slice in half, remove seeds, pulp, and stringy parts. Cut into smaller segments and peel. Steam or boil until tender and mash or purée in a food processor. The pureed pumpkin then may be used for pies and other recipes. The seeds may be rinsed to remove pulp, then dried with a paper towel. Next toss seeds with seasonings and butter or oil, then roast. The browned and crunchy seeds may be enjoyed as a snack.
Snap or String Beans *Green.* Long straight pods, should snap easily when bent. *Yellow Wax.* Long straight pods. Creamy to yellow in color.	Best if stored at 45 to 50°F (7 to 10°C) in high humidity away from ethylene-producing fruits and vegetables. In home setting, refrigeration will require storage under colder conditions than ideal; thus, store for minimum length of time. Cold-damaged beans may develop pitting or russeting (browning).

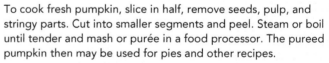
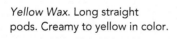

Table 18–5 (CONTINUED)

Name and Description	Selection and Preparation Pointers
Summer Squash *Pattypan.* Round, squat, small squash with scalloped edges. Yellow or light green color with white flesh. *Yellow Crookneck.* Cylindrical shape. Bulb-shaped end. Creamy yellow rind and white flesh. *Zucchini.* Cylindrical, dark green squash with light speckles. Flesh and seeds are white.	Squash should be firm with shiny rinds. Pitting or dull rinds are indications of age and damage. Smaller summer squash are generally higher quality—more tender and better flavor. Ideally should be stored at 45°F (7°C) or warmer. Store away from ethylene-producing fruits and vegetables. May be consumed raw or cooked. The skin, flesh, and seeds may be used.
Winter Squash *Acorn.* Acorn shape. Green to yellow-gold hard rind. Flesh is yellow and slightly sweet. *Banana.* Large cylindrical-shaped. Creamy yellow, hard rind. *Butternut.* Dark green hard rind with gray flecks or strips. Slightly sweet, orange flesh. *Hubbard.* Large round squash. Ends taper inward. Rind may be orange, golden, green, or blue-gray. *Spaghetti.* Yellow, semihard rind. Large and oblong shape. Yellow flesh separates into spaghetti-like consistency after cooking.	Most winter varieties of winter squash should be stored slightly cooler than room temperature. The rinds should be hard and not tender. Generally consumed cooked, the rind may be removed before or after cooking. Typically, only the flesh of winter squash is used.
Tomato *Cherry.* Small round tomatoes. *Grape.* Small oblong shape. Concentrated flavor. *Roma.* Oblong shape, medium size. Shiny red skin and firm flesh. *Round or Globe.* Round with shiny red skin and firm flesh. Variety commonly used for slicing.	Avoid soft or mushy tomatoes with blemishes. Tomatoes should not be refrigerated. Should be stored above 50°F (13°C) to avoid flavor and quality loss. Handle with care to avoid bruising. May be consumed fresh or cooked. To peel, place cut small "x" at base of tomato and heat in boiling water briefly. Plunge in ice water. The skin will wrinkle and remove very easily.

Source: References 27, 43, 54.

Bulb, root, and tuber vegetables (**Figure 18–8**) are generally higher in carbohydrate and lower in water content than leaves, stems, and flowers. Most of the carbohydrate in potatoes is in the form of starch. Sweet potatoes also contain a fairly large amount of starch but have more sugar than white potatoes. Potatoes are significant sources of vitamin C, whereas the yellow carotenoids in sweet potatoes contribute vitamin A value. Selected roots, tubers, and bulbs are described in Table 18–7 and **Table 18–8**.

Characteristics of Potato Varieties. Many different varieties of potatoes are available in the marketplace, and most can be classified into five basic types: russet, long white, round red, round white, and yellow flesh.

Mealiness and waxiness are qualities ascribed to cooked potatoes. A mealy potato separates easily into fluffy particles that feel dry. A type of potato exhibiting this quality to a marked degree is the russet Burbank, which is excellent for baking, mashing, frying, and roasting. On the other hand, a waxy potato is more compact and moist, or almost soggy, and does not separate easily into fluffy particles. Waxy potatoes are therefore not the best choice for mashed or french-fried potatoes. The round reds and round whites are generally regarded as waxy potatoes and are especially good for boiling and

Table 18–6
FLOWERS, STEMS, AND SHOOTS

Names and Description	Selection and Preparation Pointers

FLOWERS

Artichoke
Shape and color will vary by variety. Generally green, although some may have a tinge of purple. Globe or conical shape with flared petals.

Overmature artichokes will appear woody. Should be stored under refrigeration with high humidity to avoid wilt or mold.

Wash under running water. Outer, lower petals should be pulled off. Cut stem close to base. Snip off tips of petals if desired. Cook by boiling, steaming, sautéing, or microwaving until a leaf near the center will pull out easily.

Serve hot or cold. To eat, pull each leaf from the choke. Hold the pointed end and pull the leaf between your teeth to enjoy the edible portion. Discard the leaf. Once all leaves are consumed, scoop out the fuzzy center and discard. The remaining base of the artichoke is edible.

Broccoli
Compact bud clusters on light green stalks. Bud clusters are a dark green with a purple tinge. Clusters should not be open showing yellow flowers.

Store under refrigeration in high humidity (90 to 98 percent). Avoid storage with ethylene-producing fruits and vegetables.

Wash thoroughly. May be consumed raw or cooked. Stems are more tender if peeled.

Cauliflower
White. Creamy white compact heads with jacket leaves that are bright green and fresh. Heads have appearance of curds.

Green and Purple. Green is a hybrid of broccoli and cauliflower. Purple is actually a type of broccoli that has an appearance like cauliflower. Purple cauliflower turns green when cooked.

Gray-brown discoloration or softening suggests potential freeze injury.

Store under refrigeration in high humidity away from ethylene-producing fruits and vegetables.

Wash thoroughly. May be consumed raw or cooked.

STEMS AND SHOOTS

Asparagus
Green. Spears should be fresh and firm. Tips should be compact and may have a purple tinge.

White. Spears are thicker and more tender than the green variety. Tips are smooth and rounded.

Select fresh, firm asparagus with compact tips.

Store under refrigeration with high humidity. May stand asparagus butt-end down in water. Alternatively, may be stored in a plastic bag for short periods.

To prepare, wash and snap off ends at the natural breaking point. White asparagus is frequently peeled with a peeler. Green asparagus may be cooked without peeling.

Celery
Green or pascal is primary variety sold. Light green with long, crisp stalks.

Select celery with compact stalks, firm and crisp ribs, and green and not wilted leaves.

Store under refrigeration with high humidity away from ethylene-producing produce. Store away from onions to avoid odor absorption.

Wash thoroughly. May be consumed raw or cooked.

Fennel
Pale green, feathery top. Celery-like stems and bulblike base.

Select fennel with green leaves and firm straight stalks. The bulb should be compact and not spreading. Cut stalks off the bulb and store separately under refrigeration.

Stalks may be used in soups. Feathery leaves may be used as an herb. The bulb should be washed and trimmed. Bulbs may be used raw, grilled, steamed, or sautéed.

Table 18–6 (CONTINUED)

Names and Description		Selection and Preparation Pointers
Kohlrabi Light green or purple with a globe-shaped root. Leaves and root portion are edible. Bulb flavor is somewhat similar to turnips. Leaves taste like collard greens or kale.		Choose kohlrabi with fresh leaves and smooth bulbs free of cracks. Should be stored under refrigeration in high humidity conditions. Leaves are typically cooked. Bulb may be used raw or cooked.

Source: References 27, 53, 68.

(a)

(b)

Figure 18–7

To prepare globe artichokes, (a) using kitchen shears, clip off the thorny tip or barbs on top of each leaf; (b) using a chef's knife cut away the top of the artichoke as shown and also the stem. Additional preparation includes pull off any heavy loose leaves around the bottom; and drop into boiling, salted water. Season by adding a small clove of garlic, a thick slice of lemon, and one tablespoon of olive or salad oil for each artichoke. Cover and boil until a leaf can be pulled easily from the stalk or until the stub can be easily pierced with a fork (20 to 45 minutes). Remove carefully from the water. (Richard Embery/Pearson Education)

Table 18–7
ROOTS AND TUBERS

Name and Description		Selection and Preparation Pointers
Beet Roots are dark purple-red and round. Tops have green leaves with purple-red stems and veins.		Select smooth, hard, uniformly round beets. Young beets are more tender and may be eaten raw. Medium or large beets are best cooked. Excessively large beets will be undesirably woody. Store under refrigeration with high humidity without tops. Store tops separately, then eat as soon as possible. Wash and scrub beets before use. Peel after cooking to minimize color loss.
Carrot Firm, smooth exterior, and crunchy texture. Are orange or orange-red.		Select firm, brightly colored carrots. Avoid soft or wilted roots.

(Continued)

Table 18–7
ROOTS AND TUBERS (CONTINUED)

Name and Description	Selection and Preparation Pointers
	Bunched carrots are more perishable when topped; thus, if purchased with tops, remove before storage. Store under refrigeration with high humidity away from ethylene-producing fruits or vegetables or foods with strong odors.
	May be used raw or cooked. Often peeled but scrubbed peels may be consumed.

Celeriac or Celery Root
Bulb-shaped, knobby root. Skin is brown and rough. Texture is crisp and flavor is nutty and celery-like. May be used cooked or uncooked.

Select firm, not spongy roots.

Store under refrigeration with high humidity.

Scrub, trim top and bottom, quarter, and peel before eating. May be used cooked or uncooked. Overcooked celery root will become mushy.

Ginger Root
Gnarled light brown rhizome. Rhizomes are underground stems and in the case of ginger are typically referred to as a *root*. Golden to white flesh. Sweet yet woodsy smell. Sweet, peppery flavor.

Choose roots with fairly smooth light brown skin with minimum knots. Avoid soft or shriveled roots.

Store at 60 to 65°F (16 to 18°C) in relatively high humidity. If stored under refrigeration, may soften or shrivel.

Peel skin from root. May be sliced, grated, or minced. Often used as a flavoring in Asian cuisines.

Jicama
Round, slightly squat shape resembling a turnip. Light brown skin and ivory flesh. Subtle and sweet flavor. Texture is crunchy and juicy.

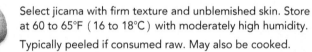

Select jicama with firm texture and unblemished skin. Store at 60 to 65°F (16 to 18°C) with moderately high humidity.

Typically peeled if consumed raw. May also be cooked.

Parsnip
Similar in appearance to a carrot but is creamy beige.

Select medium-sized roots that are fresh and crisp. Store under refrigeration with high humidity away from ethylene-producing produce items.

Like carrot, may be peeled or cooked with the skin. May be consumed raw or cooked and may be mashed.

Potato
Russet. Oblong shape with netted brown skin. White flesh. A mealy, high-starch potato that is good choice for baking, roasting, mashing, and frying. Will be light and fluffy when cooked. Varieties include Burbank, Centennial, and Norgold.

Select firm and smooth potatoes. Avoid potatoes with excessive soil or with green skins which is evidence of exposure to light. Green areas, if present, must be removed before use.

Preferably store at 60 to 65°F (16 to 18°C) in a dark, well-ventilated area. Refrigerated storage is not recommended because starch in the potato will turn to sugar, affecting flavor and browning when cooked. Sugar will revert to starch when returned to warmer storage.

Scrub and cook as desired. May be peeled or consumed with the peel.

Long White. Oval shape. Thin light-tan skin and firm waxy texture. Medium starch, good all-purpose potato. Good choice for boiling, salads, stews, soups, and roasting. Major variety is White Rose.

Round Red. Rosy red skin. Low in starch and sweet flavor. Often known as "new potatoes." Best for boiling, roasting, or potato salads. Major varieties include La Rouge, Red La Soda, and Red Pontiac.

Table 18–7
ROOTS AND TUBERS (CONTINUED)

Name and Description	Selection and Preparation Pointers

Round White. Smooth, light-tan skin. Waxy-textured, low-starch potato. Good for scalloped potatoes, roasting, and potato salads. Major varieties include Katahdin, Superior, and Chippewa.

Yellow Flesh. Oval to round shape. Buttery flavor. Dense and creamy texture. Good for baking, mashing, and roasting. Major varieties include Yukon Gold and Yellow Finn.

Purple or Blue. Deep purple or blue skin and flesh. Have a subtle nutty flavor. Major varieties include Purple Peruvian and All Blue.

Fingerlings. Heirloom potatoes. Small, oblong potatoes. Firm, flavorful, waxy potatoes.

Radish

Red Globe. Red and white radish that is small, round, or oval shaped. Usually about 1 inch in diameter.

Black. Turnip-like size and shape. Often about 8 inches in length. Dull black or dark brown skins. Flesh is white and pungent.

Select radishes that are hard and solid. Leaves, if attached, should be crisp and green. Radishes with a pithy or spongy texture are old.

Store under refrigeration with high humidity.

Usually consumed raw but may be cooked for some dishes. Daikons are often pickled.

Daikons. Large carrot-shaped radish that is up to 18 inches long. White, juicy flesh is hotter than red globe radishes but milder than black radish. They are often pickled.

Rutabaga

Round with shape like a top. Creamy white to pinkish-red skin with creamy flesh. A cross between a turnip and cabbage.

Select rutabagas that are clean, fairly smooth, without growth cracks or shriveling. Smaller rutabagas are sweeter.

Store under refrigeration with high humidity away from ethylene-producing produce.

Often sold waxed, so wash and peel before cooking. A variety of cooking methods may be used. Overcooking will develop a strong, potentially undesirable flavor.

Salsify or Vegetable Oyster

Black. Stick-like root. Has black skin and cream-colored flesh.

White. Parsnip-shaped root. Skin has tiny rootlets. Tan skin and off-white flesh.

General Information. Both types have a mild oyster flavor with some flavor components similar to artichokes. Texture is crisp like carrot.

Select firm roots that are not soft or flabby. Store under refrigeration with high humidity.

Trim tops and bottoms. Is generally used cooked. Will become mushy if overcooked.

Sweet Potato

Oblong root vegetable with generally smooth skin. Color may be pale yellow, deep purple, or orange depending on variety. Flesh color will be light yellow, pink, red, or orange.

Should not be confused with yams, which are large starchy roots grown in Africa and Asia.

Select firm, dark orange sweet potatoes without evidence of sprouts, bruises, or decay.
Store in a cool (60–65°F/16–18°C), dry location away from ethylene-producing fruits and vegetables. Do not store in the refrigerator to prevent development of an off-flavor.
Wash thoroughly. Cook whole when possible and peel after cooking.

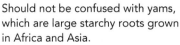

(Continued)

use in salads or dishes such as scalloped potatoes. The long whites are a good all-purpose potato and function quite well in both boiling and baking.

Potatoes with higher starch content are denser. A higher-**density** potato tends to be mealier. The density of potatoes may be tested by placing a potato in a brine solution of 1 cup salt to 11 cups water. If the potato floats, indicating low solids content, it may be a waxy potato best for boiling; if it sinks, it may be a mealy potato best for baking. Not all researchers, however, have found a correlation between specific gravity and textural characteristics of potatoes [35].

It has been suggested that the swelling of starch causes the separation of plant cells that occurs in mealy potatoes. The starch granules swell markedly when potatoes are cooked, and water tends to be absorbed when they are boiled. Mealy potatoes that are high in starch content tend to slough off their outer layers when boiled. Storage at temperatures between 50 and 70°F (10 and 21°C) seems to decrease the tendency of the potato to slough during cooking. Also, if the cooking water contains enough calcium salt to maintain or slightly increase the calcium content of the potato, sloughing can be partially controlled.

Seeds

Although corn is a cereal product, sweet corn is commonly used as a vegetable in the United States. Dent corn, discussed in Chapter 12, is used as a grain. Corn is relatively high in carbohydrate, chiefly in the form of starch. **Legumes** are seeds of the *Leguminosae* family and include many varieties of beans, peas, soybeans, and lentils. Legumes will be discussed in more detail in Chapter 19 on alternative proteins. Selected seed vegetables are described in **Table 18–9**.

Mushrooms

Mushrooms are fungi and not technically vegetables. However, mushrooms are served and used like vegetables and thus will be discussed in this chapter. There is a variety of different kinds of mushrooms, not all of which are edible. Only well-trained experienced individuals (mycologists) should harvest mushrooms from the wild. Poisonous mushrooms growing in the wild can be easily mistaken for edible mushrooms. Selected varieties of edible mushrooms are described in **Table 18–10**.

Mushrooms that are clean and not soft or do not show evidence of spoilage should be selected. Store mushrooms in the original container in the refrigerator with high humidity away from foods with strong odors. Mushrooms should be gently cleaned prior to use. Many recommend gently wiping mushrooms with a brush or damp cloth. Others suggest that rinsing mushrooms under cool, running water is acceptable. Soaking or submerging in water when cleaning is not recommended. Mushrooms may be served raw or cooked [27, 43].

Table 18–9
SEEDS

Name and Description		Selection and Preparation Pointers
Corn Plump tender yellow, white, or white and yellow kernels. Corn on the cob should have green husks.		Select corn on the cob with fresh, green husks, consistently sized kernels, and silk ends free of decay or worms. Store under refrigeration.
Peas *Snow.* Flat green pods with immature peas in interior. Entire pod is edible. *Green.* Large, bulging, bright green pods. Mature peas are inside pod. Only the peas are consumed. *Snap.* Similar in appearance to green peas. Entire pod is edible but should be destringed.		Select green, fresh pods. Green peas should be bulging as evidence of mature peas. Store under refrigeration with high humidity away from ethylene-producing fruits and vegetables. A variety of cooking methods may be used. Snap and snow peas may be consumed raw or cooked. Green peas are typically cooked.

Source: Reference 43.

Table 18–10
MUSHROOMS

Description

Agaricus or White or Button

Most common variety. Creamy white to light brown in color and ranging in size from small to jumbo. Mild, woodsy flavor when raw. May be used raw or cooked.

Chanterelle

Trumpet-shaped. Golden to yellow-orange color with rich, meaty, slightly almond flavor. Should be cooked.

Crimini or Italian Brown

Similar in appearance to agaricus mushroom but is a light tan to brown color. Flavor is earthier than agaricus. May be used raw or cooked.

Enoki

Fragile and flower-like. Grows in clusters with long, slender stems, and tiny, creamy caps. Light fruity taste. Often used raw.

Morel

Sponge-like cap with a short, thick stem. Dark brown color and meaty flavor. Used cooked.

Oyster

Large fluted cap that may be brown to gray. Subtle oyster flavor. Are best when cooked but may be used raw.

Porcini

White to red-brown cap. Meaty texture and nutty flavor. Used cooked.

Portabello

A large mushroom that may be 3 inches or more in diameter. Is similar to the agaricus and crimini with a meaty texture. Often grilled or roasted.

Shiitake

Large, black-brown, umbrella shaped mushrooms. Rich woodsy flavor. Meaty texture when cooked. Usually used cooked.

Woodgear

Brown, with a floppy cap and short stem. Mild, rich flavor. Usually used cooked.

Source: Reference 43.

PURCHASING

Considerations when purchasing vegetables include the overall quality, cost, and preferences for graded, organic vegetables, or value-added pre-prepared products. Fresh vegetables selected for purchase should be firm, crisp, and bright in color. Size, shape, gloss, color, absence of defects, and freshness are considered. In making selections, distinguish between defects that affect appearance only and those that affect edible quality. Consumer preferences for "perfect" vegetables and fruits have been identified as one issue causing excessive food waste [7].

In-season and locally grown vegetables may offer the highest quality and lowest price. However, growing conditions, supply, and demand can all have an impact on price and availability along with transportation distance. The availability of frozen and canned vegetables offers additional ways to enjoy vegetables throughout the year.

Many fresh vegetables are highly perishable and thus are best used as fresh as possible. Consequently, when purchasing, the amount of vegetables that can be stored and used while still at peak quality should be considered. The use of frozen and canned vegetables enables longer storage periods than possible with fresh vegetables. Quality characteristics for specific vegetables may be found in Tables 18–4 through 18–10.

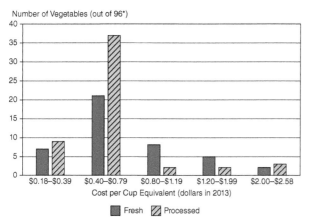

Number of Vegetables (out of 96*)

Cost per Cup Equivalent (dollars in 2013)

■ Fresh   ▨ Processed

Notes: *Three of the fresh vegetables were priced in their both raw and cooked forms. A cup equivalent is the edible portion of a vegetable that will fit in a 1-cup measuring cup; 2 cups for lettuce and other raw leafy greens.

Figure 18–9

A large number of vegetables can be purchased for below $0.79 per cup or cup equivalent. The number of fresh versus processed (such as canned or frozen) vegetables at each price grouping is also shown.

Economic Considerations

When purchasing vegetables and fruits, (see Chapter 20) price can be a factor in the selection process. One argument used by some for the limited consumption of fruits and vegetables is cost. One group of researchers examined the cost of 153 different forms of vegetables and fruits. The average cost per edible cup equivalent was 50 cents. In 2013, Americans could purchase the quantity of fruits and vegetables recommended for a 2,000-calorie diet (2½ cups of vegetables and 2 cups of fruit or equivalents) for between $2.10 and $2.60 per day [50]. Sixteen vegetables were identified that cost less than $0.40 per cup or equivalent (**Figure 18–9**). Fresh potatoes and dried pinto beans were the least expensive.

The decision to purchase frozen, canned, or fresh is another factor influencing prices. In this study canned or frozen fruits and vegetables were not consistently more or less expensive than fresh [50]. A wide variety of fruits and vegetables (fresh and processed) could be purchased by a family of four following the USDA Thrifty Food Plan and Dietary Guidelines [10, 50] (**Figure 18–10**). Researchers have also examined the nutrients per unit cost and concluded that fruits and vegetables provide more nutrients per cost than many other foods [13].

The allocation of household budgets for the purchase of fruit and vegetables is not unique to low income households, in fact all households spend proportionally a similar amount on various food groups (**Figure 18–11**). For Americans to consume more

Examples of how a consumer on a 2,000-calorie diet could satisfy fruit and vegetable recommendations over one day

	Cup equivalents	Cost
Apples, fresh	1	$0.42
Oranges, fresh	1	$0.58
Romaine lettuce	0.5	$0.20
Carrots, fresh	0.5	$0.11
Roma tomatoes	0.5	$0.26
Corn, canned	0.5	$0.25
Green beans, frozen	0.5	$0.20
	4.5	$2.10

	Cup equivalents	Cost
Raisins	1	$0.58
Banana	1	$0.29
Broccoli florets, boiled	0.5	$0.44
Sweet potato, boiled	1	$0.50
Mixed peas and carrots, frozen	0.5	$0.21
Black beans, canned	0.5	$0.29
	4.5	$2.31

	Cup equivalents	Cost
Grapefruit juice, ready-to-drink	1	$0.60
Fruit cocktail, packed in juice	1	$0.80
Romaine lettuce	0.5	$0.20
Carrots, baby	0.5	$0.20
Green beans, frozen	1	$0.55
Cucumber, fresh	0.5	$0.18
	4.5	$2.53

	Cup equivalents	Cost
Orange juice, ready-to-drink	1	$0.60
Strawberries, fresh	1	$0.80
Broccoli florets, boiled	0.5	$0.44
Carrots, boiled from frozen	0.5	$0.24
Potato, boiled from fresh	0.5	$0.09
Cucumber, fresh	0.5	$0.18
Pinto beans, canned	0.5	$0.26
	4.5	$2.61

Figure 18–10

Although food prices do change over time, ideas for the economic inclusion of vegetables and fruits are offered. (USDA)

Percent of At-Home Household Food Expenditures, Four-Person Households

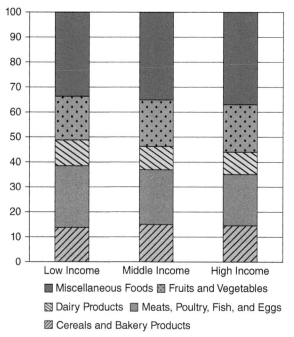

Low income = household income of $20–29,999,
Middle income = household income of $50–69,999,
High income = household income of $70,000 and above.

Figure 18–11

Low-income, middle-income, and high-income Americans spend similar proportions of their food expenditures on each food group. (USDA, ERS)

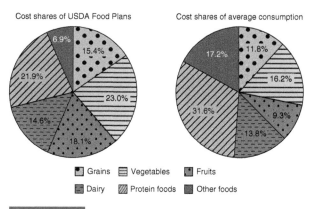

Figure 18–12

Americans can fit more fruits and vegetables into their diets and food budget by increasing the expenditures on fruits and vegetables and decreasing expenditures on protein foods, and other foods such as sweetened beverages. (USDA)

fruits and vegetables and overall align their diets with the Dietary Guidelines, less money should be spent on "other foods" such as fats, oils, sweets, sugar sweetened beverages, and other similar foods. Additionally, food expenditures for protein foods should reduce from 32 to 22 percent of the household food dollar while then increasing expenditures for vegetables and fruits [9] (**Figure 18–12**).

Grades

Fresh, frozen, and canned vegetables and fruits (See Chapter 20 for fruits) may be graded, thus providing an identifiable standard of quality for consumers and foodservice managers to make purchase decisions and price comparisons. Grades specify such characteristics as size, shape, color, texture, general appearance, uniformity, maturity, and freedom from defects. A common language is thus provided for wholesale trading and aids in establishing prices based on quality. The USDA has established grades for a many food products. Food processors may develop their own grading system, but manufacturers' grades may represent different quality levels than USDA grades of the same name. Thus, when purchasing a "Fancy" or "No. 1" grade, it is important to know whether it is a USDA or a manufacturer grade designation.

USDA grading is not required by law. USDA grading is voluntary and is provided by request of the food processor or grower. The producer or distributor pays a fee for the USDA grading but can then benefit by the ability to market its product with the USDA grade.

Fresh Vegetable and Fruit Grades. The USDA uniform grade terms for fresh vegetables and fruits are U.S. Fancy, U.S. No. 1, U.S. No. 2, and U.S. No. 3. Only a few vegetables or fruits are packed as the top-quality grade U.S. Fancy. The grade most often found is U.S. No. 1. Vegetables with this grade will be tender and fresh-appearing, have good color, and be relatively free from decay and bruises [59]. The top grade for potatoes is U.S. Extra No. 1, and the second grade is U.S. No. 1. The grade most often found on consumer packages of potatoes is U.S. No. 1 [60].

Because fresh vegetables are perishable, the quality may change between the time of grading and the time of purchase, thereby limiting the usefulness of grades on fresh produce. (See Chapter 3 for a general discussion of grading.)

Canned Vegetable and Fruit Grades. USDA grades of quality have been established for many canned and frozen vegetables and fruits, based on color, uniformity of size, shape, tenderness or degree of ripeness, and freedom from blemishes. The label may designate U.S. Grade A or Fancy, U.S. Grade B or Choice, and U.S. Grade C or Standard [57, 58]. Availability of graded products allows the buyer to select the quality that will be most satisfactory for the intended use. Lower grades of vegetables and fruits are still good and wholesome, although they are less perfect than Grade A in color, uniformity, and texture.

When a product has been officially graded under continuous inspection by a USDA inspector, it may carry the official grade name and the statement "Packed under continuous inspection of the U.S. Department

Figure 18–13

USDA shield for products packed under continuous inspection. (U.S. Department of Agriculture)

Figure 18–14

The USDA Organic shield may only be used if more than 95 percent of the ingredients are organic. Most products will need to be "certified" to use the organic shield or to make any organic claims. (U.S. Department of Agriculture)

of Agriculture" (**Figure 18–13**). The grade name and the statement may also appear within a shield-shaped outline. Most canned and frozen vegetables and fruits are packed according to grade, whether or not that fact is indicated on the label, and are generally priced according to their quality. Most products marketed are at least Grade B quality, which is quite good. As with fresh produce, the use of the USDA grades is voluntary and is paid for by the packer. The specific brand name of a frozen or canned vegetable or fruit may be an indication of quality because the packers set quality standards for their brand names.

Organic

National standards for organic foods were set in place by the USDA in 2002 to provide consumers the choice of organic foods in the marketplace. Organic foods must be produced without most conventional pesticides, synthetic fertilizers, sewage sludge,

bioengineering, or ionizing radiation [61]. For a product to be labeled as organic, the farm is inspected to certify the farmer is following the USDA organic standards (**Figure 18–14**). Companies that handle and process organic foods also must be certified. "Natural" and "organic" do not have the same meaning. Only foods with the organic label have been certified as meeting the USDA standards. For more information about USDA organic food labeling, refer to Chapter 3.

No claims are made by the USDA that organically produced food is safer or more nutritious [61]. However, it is clear that there is a consumer demand for such foods, and the USDA certification provides a uniform standard for consumers who prefer organic foods. Consumers may choose organic foods because of environmental concern, perceived nutritional benefits, perceived flavor, or other reasons. In one study, several types of vegetables were grown conventionally

KEEPING IT SAFE
BEAN SPROUTS

The technique of sprouting soybean and mung bean seeds was developed by the Chinese centuries ago. Sprouts from many different seeds have become popular and are particular favorites at fresh salad bars. The sprouts of some seeds provide significant sources of vitamin C, thiamin, riboflavin, and several minerals [15]. However, due to food safety concerns, current recommendations from the FDA suggest that raw bean sprouts, including alfalfa sprouts, should be avoided, especially by individuals at high risk for foodborne illness. Scientists have been exploring methods of destroying pathogenic bacteria on seeds without damaging the ability of the seed to sprout. ■

and organically and then compared by consumers in a sensory analysis [82]. The consumer sensory assessment of the conventional and organically grown vegetables did not reveal differences in liking or flavor between the vegetables except for tomatoes. The conventional tomatoes were rated more favorably; however, the researchers noted a potential difference in tomato ripeness may have had an impact on the ratings.

Organic foods do appear to be lower in pesticide residues than conventional foods, but the risk posed by consuming conventional foods may be insignificant [79]. Some studies have found higher nutrient levels in organic foods, although other studies report no differences. Researchers have stated that evidence is lacking for nutritional benefits associated with organic food consumption [12]. Thus, additional research is needed to understand this issue. Overall, in the Institute of Food Technologists' Scientific Status Summary, it was stated that to conclude either conventional or organic food systems to be superior was premature [79].

Biotechnology and Vegetable Production

For centuries, humans have exploited the genetic diversity of living systems for improvement of the food supply. Traditional **biotechnology** works with plant and animal breeding for the selection of desired characteristics. A new biotechnology, often called *genetic engineering*, produces genetic modification at the molecular level. Biotechnology provides a set of tools for improving the variety and efficiency of food production in less time and with more precision and control than with traditional methods [24]. There are 10 genetically engineered plant foods in use in the United States as of 2018 [47]. These include soybeans, corn, papaya, squash, sugar beet, cotton, canola, apple, potato, and alfalfa.

How does genetic engineering work for vegetable crops? It allows controlled insertion of one or two genes into a plant without transferring undesirable characteristics as would likely occur in traditional cross-fertilization methods. Through genetic engineering, soybeans, cottonseed, and corn have been made to tolerate herbicides used to kill weeds and to avoid pests, thus reducing the need for pesticides. Squash, potatoes, and papaya resist plant diseases as the result of genetic engineering.

The development, testing, and sale of genetically modified plants are regulated by the USDA, the FDA, the Environmental Protection Agency (EPA), and most state governments. The goal of these agencies is to ensure the safety of genetically engineered foods for consumption by people and animals. These foods must also be judged by government regulators to not have a harmful impact on the environment when grown. Researchers publishing in the *Journal of Academy of Nutrition and Dietetics* concluded that based on the current available studies of genetically engineered foods and human consumption, there were no clear adverse impacts on humans with regard to allergenicity, nutrient adequacy, or disease association [47]. See Chapters 2 and 12 for additional information about biotechnology and food safety.

Partially Processed, Value Added, or Fresh Cuts

Convenience is another factor to consider when purchasing produce. Fresh vegetables and fruits can be pretrimmed, peeled, cut, sliced, and so on for direct use by consumers in the home or restaurants and other food service establishments. Prepared salad mix and peeled baby carrots are examples of these partially processed, **value-added**, or fresh-cut foods. Fresh, sliced, packaged apples, offered in a number of quick-service restaurants, is another example of these products.

HOT TOPIC
WHAT ABOUT PESTICIDES?

Some people have expressed concern about pesticide residues on vegetables and fruits. Government monitoring of actual pesticide residue levels in foods as prepared and consumed have shown no pesticide residues in 71 percent of the domestic food samples and 53 percent of the import food samples. Ninety-nine percent of domestic samples and 88 percent of import samples were below the EPA tolerances [70]. Independent researchers have reported that consumer exposure to detected pesticides on apples, celery, and strawberries is 20,000 to 6,000,000 times lower than the doses that do not affect lab animals [78, 80]. These researchers point out that the detectable presence of pesticides on produce at such very low levels should not be of concern to consumers, contrary to the recommendations of the Environmental Working Group in their "Dirty Dozen" list [78, 80]. The FDA regularly monitors pesticide residues on foods. The USDA organic guidelines provide another option for consumers. Refer to Chapters 2 and 3 for more information about food safety and the regulation of pesticides, as well as organic labeling guidelines and rules. ■

Food manufacturers are using a variety of technologies to produce minimally processed vegetables and fruits [4, 6], including refrigeration, **modified-atmosphere packaging** in combination with refrigeration, and heat treatment in combination with **hermetic packaging**, which is packaging that is completely sealed. Custom-tailored packaging films can help to slow the natural degradative changes due to cell respiration by controlling the oxygen, carbon dioxide, and moisture levels inside the package (See Chapter 28 for more on packaging). Some fresh-cut vegetables have a refrigerated shelf life of up to 21 days because of modified-atmosphere technologies [6].

These minimally processed vegetables and fruits are perishable compared to unprocessed foods because the degradative changes related to senescence, or aging, are enhanced by the physical actions of cutting and slicing. Respiration by the cells increases in response to the injuries [76]. Therefore, partially processed fruits and vegetables must be refrigerated and handled in a sanitary manner to ensure microbiological safety.

Methods of reducing spoilage in partially processed produce foods continue to be investigated. Fresh-cut iceberg lettuce treated with hydrogen peroxide and mild heat was found to maintain a higher level of sensory quality over 15 days of storage as compared to the control [36]. In another study, the effect of low-dose irradiation was compared to acidification, blanching, and chlorination as methods of maintaining the quality of diced celery. The irradiated samples were preferred in sensory tests and maintained color, texture, and aroma longer than the conventionally treated diced celery samples [42].

STORAGE

Fresh vegetables and fruits are perishable and have a limited shelf life. The short storage life of many vegetables is due to their rapid **respiration** or metabolism. Vegetables and fruits are composed of living, respiring tissue that is also **senescing** and dying [23]. Thus,

when storing vegetables, storage conditions and the length of storage should be considered so that foods may be enjoyed and waste avoided. See Tables 18–4 through 18–10 for storage recommendations for various types of vegetables.

General Conditions

Fresh vegetables of high water content, if allowed to stand long after harvesting without low temperature and high humidity controls, wilt and toughen through loss of moisture, or loss of *turgor* [28]. The flavor is also impaired, mainly because of enzyme actions in the tissues. Leafy greens, in particular, benefit by storage in high-humidity conditions. However, excessive moisture can promote spoilage. When vegetables are washed before storage, thorough draining is advised.

Where vegetables are stored is also important. Vegetables stored near strongly flavored foods, such as onions, may absorb unintended flavors. A number of vegetables will spoil more rapidly when stored with other vegetables and fruits that produce ethylene gas. Cucumbers, okra, tomatoes, and a wide variety of fruits, such as apples, pears, bananas, berries, pineapples, and plums, produce ethylene gas naturally. Ethylene gas can work to your advantage when trying to ripen a vegetable or fruit more rapidly. Placing vegetables or fruits in a paper bag will help to concentrate the ethylene gas.

Temperature

The ideal storage temperature varies from vegetable to vegetable. Several kinds of roots, tubers, and winter squash are typically not refrigerated. Potatoes are generally not stored in the refrigerator to avoid an increase in sugar content because of changes in the metabolism of the plant tissue. Holding at room temperature for several days after refrigeration brings down the elevated sugar content. Thus, when storing for longer periods of time, cold storage can delay sprouting and decay, but warmer storage conditions are necessary before use.

FOCUS ON SCIENCE
WHAT IS MEANT BY LOSS OF TURGOR?

Turgor is pressure that full vacuoles (composed of water and various solutes) exert on cell walls. This results in a rigid, crisp texture. Turgor is controlled by osmosis in living cells. Osmosis is the flow of water across a membrane into or out of a cell, depending on the concentration of solids, such as sugar and salts, inside of a cell. Solutes are present inside the cell (vacuole); therefore, pure water flows into the cell. In plant cells, water enters the cell until the inside and outside water potential is equal; however, the cell wall prevents the cell from bursting, resulting in pressure on the cell wall from within. The pressure of each cell wall against its neighbor results in stiffness that allows the plant to stand upright. When vegetables become dehydrated and limp, they will crisp if soaked in water or sprayed with water, as is done in many grocery stores.

Tomatoes are best stored at room temperature prior to being sliced or otherwise prepared. If tomatoes are picked before being fully ripened, the quality and vitamin value will be better if the tomatoes are ripened at room temperature or a little below (59 to 75°F/15 to 24°C) and kept in a lighted place unwrapped. Although the refrigeration of ripe tomatoes has been commonly recommended, researchers found that a trained sensory panel rated the flavor and aroma of tomatoes significantly lower when stored under refrigeration for two days [33]. These researchers concluded that the storage of ripe tomatoes under refrigeration could be an important contributing factor to consumer complaints about tomato flavor.

Many vegetables, such as leafy lettuce and greens, cucumbers, asparagus, celery, beets, carrots, peas, broccoli, cauliflower, and more, are best stored under refrigeration. It is interesting to note that refrigeration is useful in conserving vitamin content [3]. Vegetables vary, however, in the extent of change in vitamin C content, even when kept under refrigeration. In one study [14], fresh broccoli did not lose vitamin C when stored up to seven days, although other researchers found a loss of 18 percent within this length of storage [16]. Green beans have been found to lose as much as 88 percent when stored for six days at 36°F (2°C) and 95 to 100 percent relative humidity [14].

Methods to Extend Storage

A thin coating of a vegetable-oil **emulsion** on snap beans and other fresh vegetables has been found to decrease the respiration process [46]. When stored at 40°F (4°C), the waxed beans were generally in better condition than the unwaxed beans. Using this procedure to extend storage life and maintain product quality is common in the marketing of fresh vegetables, such as cucumbers, and many fruits. In practice, the vegetable or fruit is first washed thoroughly and rinsed, which removes the natural protective wax coating along with dust and dirt. A synthetic edible wax is then applied to restore nature's own coating and extend the shelf life of the product.

Lettuce may be stored in a **controlled atmosphere** to extend its shelf life [45]. In an atmosphere containing 2.5 percent carbon dioxide and 2.5 percent oxygen, lettuce heads can be stored up to 75 days. The controlled atmosphere, combined with polyethylene packaging, reduces the rate of respiration in the lettuce tissues. (See Chapter 20 for a discussion of controlled atmosphere storage of fruits.)

VEGETABLE PREPARATION AND QUALITY CONSIDERATIONS

Many people decide what to eat with their eyes. Vegetables therefore must be prepared to preserve pleasing colors. Flavor and texture are also important factors that determine whether we will eat and enjoy a particular vegetable. With the emphasis on the important nutritional contributions of vegetables, preparation techniques that preserve the nutrient value should be used. Both raw and cooked vegetables should retain their attractive and appetizing characteristics until they are served. Food safety is also an important consideration.

Food Safety and Preparation

Vegetables may be contaminated by various microorganisms present in the soil, by postharvest handling, or by improper storage. Furthermore, because not all vegetables are cooked before consumption, pathogenic organisms will not be destroyed by heat, thus cleanliness is of particular importance during preparation.

Spores of *Clostridium perfringens* or *Clostridium botulinum* may be present in dirt that clings to some vegetables. Contamination of spinach, romaine lettuce, and other greens by *Escherichia coli* 0157:H7 has also occurred and resulted in foodborne illness [8, 69]. From the farm to your fork, many have responsibility for the food safety of produce. The FDA has provided recommendations for good agricultural and manufacturing practices to minimize food-safety hazards common to growing, harvesting, packing, and transporting raw vegetables and fruits [71].

As a first food-safety step, produce with minimal damage or decay should be selected. Fresh-cut vegetables and fruit must be refrigerated or iced before and after purchase. Vegetables should not come in contact with raw meat, cleaning chemicals, or other items during shopping or storage in the refrigerator to prevent contamination with pathogenic organisms or poisonous chemicals. Hands, sinks, counters, cutting boards, and knives must be clean before preparing vegetables [72]. A cutting board previously used for raw meat and then used to prepare salad ingredients has caused many foodborne illnesses.

Most vegetables grow near or in the ground; therefore thorough washing is needed to remove soil and sand. Even portions of the plant not consumed should be washed to avoid cross-contamination with that to be consumed. In washing, the vegetables should be lifted out of the wash water so that the heavier particles of dirt remain in the water (**Figure 18–15**). More than one washing is recommended, especially for those vegetables such as leafy greens to be consumed raw. Pods, such as lima bean and pea pods, should be washed well before being shelled. The removal of all spoiled and discolored portions of vegetables is another part of the preliminary preparation. Leafy vegetables should have all undesirable leaves and coarse stems removed. Some vegetables such as carrots and potatoes may be peeled, or, alternatively, the skins may be thoroughly washed and

(a)

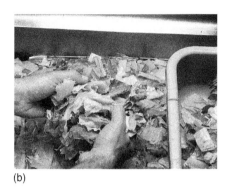
(b)

Figure 18–15

(a) By filling a clean sink with cold water and stirring the greens, they can be efficiently washed. (b) Lift the greens out of the water leaving the dirt at the bottom. *(Richard Embery/Pearson Education)*

consumed. Preparation tips for several kinds of vegetables are provided in Tables 18–4 through 18–10.

A firm brush is helpful for washing of some vegetables. Other vegetables, such as celery and leeks, need to be cut apart to allow the wash water to fully contact inner surfaces that may be trapping soil. At this time, the FDA is not recommending the use of vegetable washes or other cleaning chemicals. Finally, once vegetables have been cut or cooked, refrigeration is necessary [72].

Potatoes with green pigmentation must be peeled. Potatoes become green from exposure to sunlight or artificial light. Greening is accompanied by the formation of solanine, a bitter alkaloid substance that is toxic if consumed in relatively large amounts [60]. Food safety was discussed further in Chapter 2.

Edible Portion and Yield

Some fresh vegetables, depending partly on the way they are trimmed for marketing, may have a relatively high percentage of refuse or waste parts that are thrown away. In quantity food preparation, recipes will note if the ingredient weight or measure has been provided for *edible portion* (EP) or *as purchased* (AP). Edible portion is the amount of the product remaining after cleaning, and as purchased is the amount prior to peeling and cleaning. Whether preparing food at home or in a professional kitchen, an understanding of the amount of waste generated when cleaning vegetables is important because it will affect the quantity of food available for consumption after preparation as well as the cost of the food consumed. **Table 18–11** shows the percentage of refuse from some vegetables. The amount of refuse, or waste, will vary, depending on the condition of the vegetable and how much is trimmed. For example, lettuce with a refuse of 5 percent when the core is removed would yield 95 percent. If outer leaves are damaged and also need to be removed, then the refuse may be 24 to 25 percent leaving a yield of only 75 to 76 percent [37].

Why Cook Vegetables?

Many vegetables are improved in palatability and more easily and completely digested when they are cooked. Some valuable vegetables, such as dried legumes, could not be masticated (chewed) or digested in the raw state. The flavors of cooked vegetables are different from those of raw vegetables, adding variety to their use.

Heating improves the utilization of protein from dried legumes, and some of the minerals and vitamins, particularly of soybeans, are more available after the beans are heated [29]. Cooking also causes **gelatinization of starch** and increases its digestibility. Microorganisms are destroyed by the heating process. Red navy beans must be brought to a boil to destroy natural toxins found in the raw bean. Moreover, the bulk of leafy vegetables is greatly decreased, as they wilt during cooking.

Plant Pigments

Much of the appeal of vegetables and fruits is due to their bright colors, which result from the presence of various pigments in the plant tissues. Under appropriate temperatures for postharvest storage, green vegetables have been reported to undergo little change in color over a 12-day period [17]. Other vegetables also retain color well when stored properly. One challenge of cooking vegetables is to retain these bright colors because heat and the various conditions of preparation may produce pigment changes that make them dull and less attractive.

Vegetable and fruit pigments include the following:

- Chlorophyll—green pigments
- Carotenoids—yellow and orange (some are pink or red)
- Anthocyanins—red, purple, and blue
- Betalains—purplish red (some are yellow)
- Anthoxanthins—creamy white to colorless

Table 18–11
REFUSE FROM VEGETABLES

Vegetable	Source of Refuse	Refuse (%)
Artichokes	Stem and inedible parts of flowers	60
Asparagus	Butt ends	47
Beans, snap	Ends, strings, trimmings	12
Beets, without tops	Parings	33
Broccoli	Leaves, tough stalks, trimmings	39
Brussels sprouts	Outer leaves	10
Cabbage	Outer leaves, core	20
Carrots, raw	Crown, tops, scrapings	11
Cauliflower, raw	Leaf stalks, core, and trimmings	61
Celery	Root and trimmings	11
Chard, Swiss, raw	Tough stem ends, damaged leaves	8
Corn, sweet, raw	Husk, silk, trimmings	35
	Cob	29
Cucumber, pared*	Parings, ends	27
Eggplant, raw	Ends, parings, and trimmings	19
Garlic, raw	Knob and skin	13
Ginger root	Scrapings	7
Lettuce, iceberg	Core	5
Lettuce, Romaine	Core	6
Potatoes	Parings, trimmings	19
Boiled, cooked in skin	Skin and eyes	9
Baked, fresh only	Skin and adhering flesh	23
Shallots, raw	Skins	12
Spinach, raw	Leaves, stems, and roots	28
Squash, summer	Ends	5
Squash, winter, all others, raw	Seeds, rind, and stem	29
Sweet potato, raw	Parings and trimmings	28
Turnip greens, raw	Root, crown, tough stems, and discarded leaves	30
Tomato	Core and stem ends	9

*Refuse will be less when the vegetable is not pared or scraped or may be greater when additional trimming or cleaning of damaged parts is needed. Refuse percentages may be subtracted from 100 for a yield percentage.
Source: Reference 62.

The yellow-orange and red-blue pigments predominate in fruits. Anthocyanins and anthoxanthins have many similarities in chemical structure. They are called **flavonoid pigments** and are increasingly being recognized as nutritionally valuable.

Chlorophyll. Chlorophyll plays an important role in photosynthesis, in which the plant uses the energy of the sun's rays with gases from the air to synthesize carbohydrates (See Chapter 11). Chlorophyll is concentrated in the green leaves, where it is present in tiny bodies called *chloroplasts* [21]. It is mostly insoluble in water. Exposure to acids, alkalies, overcooking, or extended hot holding will chemically change chlorophyll (see **Table 18–12**).

Heat. Initial heating of green vegetables results in an intensified green color. This brightening of the color is explained in part by the removal of air from the tissues when the green vegetable is heated by steam or boiling water. The removal of air permits greater visibility of the underlying chlorophyll. The bright green color of frozen green vegetables is a result of blanching.

Green beans, broccoli, and other green vegetables will become increasingly olive green in color due to the degradation of chlorophyll to *pheophytin* within as little as 5 minutes of overcooking. Vegetables should therefore be cooked for the minimum amount of time necessary to tenderize. The hot holding time for vegetables should also be minimized because the same undesirable color changes will occur.

Table 18–12
CHLOROPHYLL AND RELATED COMPOUNDS

Compound	Color	Factors Promoting Chlorophyll Degradation
Chlorophyll	Green	
Pheophytin	Dull-olive green	Caused by overcooking, extended hot holding, or contact with acids.
Pyropheophytin	Dull-olive green or olive-brown	Along with pheophytin, is common in canned vegetables. Canned vegetables are heated at high temperatures for extending periods during the canning process.
Chlorophyllin	Bright-green	Caused by exposure to an alkaline, such as baking powder. Use of an alkaline to maintain bright color is not recommended to avoid alkaline-induced nutrient losses.

Canned vegetables have been subjected to high heat for extended periods to destroy botulism spores and other microorganisms. This extended cooking causes essentially all of the chlorophyll to degrade to an olive green or olive brown color. *Pyropheophytin* is apparently the major degradation product of chlorophyll in canned vegetables [44]. The differences in color can be readily observed by comparing frozen or fresh green beans or peas with canned.

Acid and Alkalies.   Acid contact, like extended exposure to heat, will cause green vegetables to become a dull-green color due to *pheophytin*. Green vegetables may come in contact with acids because of the liberation of acids present in vegetables during cooking or because of the use of an acidic vinaigrette. The length of time vegetables are marinated in a vinaigrette therefore should be kept to minimum. To reduce contact with volatile acids during cooking, remove the pan cover during the first few minutes of cooking to allow some volatile acids to escape.

Alkalies, such as baking soda, have the opposite effect on color. A small amount of baking soda added to green vegetables during cooking will change the chlorophyll to a bright green, more water-soluble pigment called *chlorophyllin*. The use of baking soda in cooking vegetables is not recommended, however, because the flavor, texture, and vitamin content of the vegetables can be adversely affected. Thiamin and vitamin C are particularly susceptible to destruction when baking soda is added. Texture can become undesirably soft because soda has a disintegrating effect on the hemicelluloses.

Carotenoids.   Carotenoids, like chlorophyll, are insoluble in water and are present in the chloroplasts of green leaves. In the autumn, when the chlorophyll disappears, the yellow color can usually be seen. Carotenoids constitute a group of similar pigments, some of which are called *carotenes*. Three of the carotene pigments—α-, β-, and γ-carotene—are found in relatively large amounts in carrots. Other carotenoids, which contain some oxygen in addition to carbon and hydrogen, are called *xanthophylls*. Cryptoxanthin is a xanthophyll that is found in many yellow vegetables. The red pigment of tomatoes, named lycopene, is a carotenoid. Lycopene is also found in watermelon and pink grapefruit and is believed to be an antioxidant that when consumed in the diet correlates with a reduced incidence of cancer and possibly heart attacks [2]. Some of the carotenoid pigments—including α-, β-, and γ-carotene and cryptoxanthin—are changed into vitamin A in the body and therefore contribute substantially to the vitamin A value of the diet.

Carotenoid pigments may lose some of their yellow color when exposed to air because they are susceptible to **oxidation**. This reaction may occur in vegetables such as carrots when they are dehydrated. The carotenoid pigments are quite stable during ordinary cooking procedures. The presence of alkali has little effect on the color. With longer heating, especially with overcooking, the pigments may undergo some chemical change by a process called **isomerization** in the presence of acid so that the orange color becomes somewhat more yellow.

Anthocyanins.   The flavonoid pigments are water soluble and found in the cell sap. Common vegetables and fruits colored by anthocyanins include red cabbage, radishes, blackberries, and black raspberries [81].

The pigments in the anthocyanin group of flavonoids are usually red in an acid medium and change to blues and purples as the pH becomes more alkaline. Not all plant anthocyanins behave in the same way with changes of acidity and alkalinity, perhaps as the result of the presence of other pigments or of substances that modify the reactions.

Red cabbage easily changes color, especially during cooking. The German custom of cooking red cabbage with an apple and adding a small amount of vinegar when served helps to retain the red color.

When cut with a non–stainless-steel knife, red cabbage reveals another property of anthocyanins—the ability to combine with metals to form salts of various colors. The use of **lacquered tin** for canning red fruits and vegetables prevents the bluish red or violet that results from the combination of anthocyanin pigment with tin or iron. The salts of iron combined with anthocyanins are bluer than those formed with tin.

Betalains. The pigments in the root tissue of red beets are not chemically similar to those of anthocyanins; they contain nitrogen and are called *betalains* [75]. Some of these pigments are purplish red (red beets), whereas others are yellow (yellow cactus pear). Betalains are stable between pH 3 and 7 [18]. Beets lose pigment and become pale when they are pared and sliced before cooking because the betalains are very soluble in water and leach from the tissues. If beets are not peeled and 1 or 2 inches of the stem are left intact, they may be cooked in boiling water with a minimal loss of pigment. Beets should therefore be peeled after cooking.

Anthoxanthins. The anthoxanthin pigments change from white or colorless to yellowish as the **pH** increases from acidic to alkaline ranges. These pigments are widely distributed in plants and often

occur with anthocyanins. Vegetables containing anthoxanthins include potatoes, cauliflower, turnips, and white onions. They may combine with some metals, such as iron, to form a dark complex. Some combinations with aluminum produce a bright yellow. The anthoxanthin pigments are generally quite stable to heating. If the cooking water is alkaline, however, the pigments may appear yellow. If heating is excessive or prolonged, the pigments also darken. **Table 18–13** summarizes the effect of various factors on the color of plant pigments.

Enzymatic Oxidative Browning

Some pared vegetables, including potatoes and sweet potatoes, as well as avocados and artichokes darken or discolor on exposure to air. The darkening results from the oxidation of **phenolic compounds** in the vegetable when oxygen from the air is available; the reaction is catalyzed by oxidizing enzymes, called **oxidases**, present in the plant tissue. (See Chapter 7 for a discussion of enzymes.) Unattractive, brown pigments are the end products of this enzymatic oxidative reaction.

Methods to Control Browning. The prevention or control of enzymatic darkening is desirable because it is aesthetically unappealing in fresh, frozen, canned, or dried foods. Lemon juice, which is highly acidic, interferes with enzyme activity and can be used to coat fruit surfaces to reduce discoloration. Pineapple juice accomplishes the same purpose, although it is less acidic

Table 18–13
SOLUBILITY IN WATER AND EFFECT OF VARIOUS FACTORS ON THE COLOR OF PLANT PIGMENTS

Name of Pigment	Color	Solubility in Water	Effect of Acid	Effect of Alkali	Effect of Prolonged Heating	Effect of Metal Ions
Chlorophylls	Green	Slightly	Changes to olive green *pheophytin*	Intensifies green *chlorophyllin*	Olive green *pheophytin* and *pyropheophytin*	
Carotenoids	Yellow and orange; some red or pink	Slightly	Less intense color	Little effect	Color may be less intense*	
Anthocyanins	Red, purple, and blue	Very soluble	Red	Purple or blue	Little effect	Violet or blue with tin or iron
Betalains	Purplish red; some yellow	Very soluble	Little effect	Little effect	Pale if pigment bleeds from tissues	
Anthoxanthins	White or colorless	Very soluble	White	Yellow	Darkens if excessive	Dark with iron; bright yellow with aluminum

*Heating *usually* produces little effect.

than lemon juice. Pineapple juice contains a **sulfhydryl compound** that seems to act as an **antioxidant** in retarding browning. Vitamin C (ascorbic acid) also aids in reducing discoloration because of its ability to act as an antioxidant. It may be used alone or as an ingredient with citric acid in a product such as Fruit-Fresh®. Commercially, sulfur dioxide is sometimes used to inhibit enzyme activity before fruits are dehydrated. Some vegetables, such as potatoes, may be submerged in water or saltwater to prevent browning.

Sulfites. Sulfites are able to control browning on peeled raw potatoes and other fresh fruits and vegetables. They also have been used for other purposes, such as preventing "black spot" on shrimp and lobster and conditioning doughs. However, some people are sulfite sensitive. The FDA estimates that this sensitivity involves one in a hundred persons in the general population and 5 percent of those with asthma.

In 1982, in response to numerous consumer reports, the FDA contracted with the Federation of American Societies for Experimental Biology (FASEB) to examine the link between sulfites and reported health problems. FASEB concluded in 1985 that, although sulfites are safe for most people, they pose a hazard of unpredictable severity to asthmatics and others who are sensitive to them. In 1986, the FDA prohibited the use of sulfites to maintain color and crispness on vegetables and fruits meant to be eaten raw, such as those served in salad bars. They also required that the presence of sulfites be disclosed on labels of packaged food. Consumers sensitive to sulphites need to read labels of packaged foods and check carefully, when eating away from home [41]. Vitamin C derivatives and citric acid can replace sulfites in retarding undesirable enzymatic browning in fresh fruits and vegetables.

Discoloration in Potatoes after Cooking

Some potatoes darken after cooking, the degree varying with the variety, the locality or soil where grown, the season, and differences in chemical composition. Discoloration is usually found at the stem end of the potato and apparently results from the formation of a dark complex of **ferric iron** and a polyphenol, probably chlorogenic acid. Addition of a small amount of cream of tartar (about 1 teaspoon per quart of water) to make the cooking environment more acidic appears to retard the development of after-cooking darkening in susceptible varieties of potatoes.

FOCUS ON SCIENCE
CHEMICAL STRUCTURES OF PLANT PIGMENTS

Chlorophyll

Chlorophyll consists of four pyrrole groups in a porphyrin ring with a magnesium molecule in the center chelated to the nitrogens of the pyrroles. The green color of chlorophyll is produced through the resonance of electrons along its conjugated double-bond system. The porphyrin ring can have several different side chains, usually including a long phytol chain. There are a few different forms that occur naturally, but the most widely distributed in terrestrial plants are chlorophyll a (contains methyl groups; bright blue-green color) and chlorophyll b (contains aldehydes; yellow-green color). The ratio of chlorophyll a to chlorophyll b is two to one.

Carotenoids

Carotenoids are defined by their chemical structure. Carotenoids are responsible for many of the red, orange, and yellow hues of plant leaves, fruits, and flowers as well as the colors of some birds, insects, fish, and crustaceans. Carotenoids are derived from a 40-carbon polyene chain that could be considered the backbone of the molecule. The chain may be terminated by cyclic end groups (rings) and may be complemented with oxygen-containing functional groups. The hydrocarbon carotenoids are known as carotenes, whereas oxygenated derivatives of these hydrocarbons are known as xanthophylls. Beta-carotene, the principal carotenoid in carrots, is a familiar carotene, and lutein, the major yellow pigment of marigold petals, is a common xanthophyll. A conjugated double-bond system is responsible for the yellow to red color due to the movement of electrons along the unsaturated chain. Intensity of color is affected by the length of the unsaturated chain along with which the electrons can oscillate and by the shape of the chain, which is influenced by the cis and trans configuration of the bonds.

Anthocyanin

Anthocyanins are water-soluble glycosides of polyhydroxyl and polymethoxyl derivatives of 2-phenylbenzopyrylium or flavylium salts. Individual anthocyanins differ in (1) the number of hydroxyl groups present in the molecule; (2) the degree of methylation of these hydroxyl groups; (3) the nature, number, and location of sugars attached to the molecule; and (4) the number and nature of aliphatic or aromatic acids attached to the sugars in the molecule. Cyanidins and their derivatives are the most common anthocyanins present in vegetables, fruits, and flowers. Anthocyanins share a basic carbon skeleton in which hydrogen, hydroxyl, or methoxyl groups can be found in six different positions. In fruits and vegetables, six basic anthocyanin compounds predominate, differing both in the number of hydroxyl groups present on the carbon ring and in the degree of methylation of these hydroxyl groups.

Flavor

A wide variation occurs in the flavor of vegetables—some are mild, and others, such as asparagus and parsnips, have relatively strong, distinctive flavors. The sugar content is high enough to produce a definite sweet taste in carrots and sweet potatoes, whereas the flavor of spinach includes a slightly bitter component. Onions, garlic, broccoli, and cabbage have distinctive aromas. Vegetables of the cabbage and onion families are sometimes described as strong flavored. The natural flavors that make each vegetable distinctive probably result from mixtures of many compounds, most of them present in tiny amounts. These compounds include **aldehydes**, **alcohols**, **ketones**, **organic acids**, **esters**, and sulfur-containing compounds.

When preparing vegetables, the impact on flavor needs to be considered. Overcooking changes the flavor of many vegetables. An "overcooked" vegetable flavor is generally undesirable. For example, compare the differences in flavor among canned, frozen, and fresh vegetables. The amount of water used for cooking also has an influence. When cooking in a large amount of water, more flavor substances will be extracted and thereby lost. Sugars, acids, and some minerals that contribute to flavor are water soluble and easily extracted from the tissues. Although methods of cooking will be discussed later in the chapter, the method of cooking—boiling, steaming, roasting, or stir-frying—will have an influence on the flavor.

Cabbage Flavors. Vegetables of the cabbage or mustard family, called *Cruciferae*, include cabbage, cauliflower, broccoli, Brussels sprouts, kale, kohlrabi, mustard, rutabaga, and turnips. These vegetables are relatively mild when raw but may develop strong flavors or odors when improperly cooked because of extensive decomposition of certain sulfur compounds [31].

Vegetables of the cabbage family have a milder flavor when cooked (1) until just tender to the fork; (2) in open, uncovered pan; and (3) with enough water to almost cover. Hydrogen sulfide and other volatile sulfur compounds may produce a strong, pungent, sulfurous flavor and odor in overcooked cabbage-family vegetables. Vegetable acids also may aid in the decomposition of the sulfur compounds; therefore, leaving the lid off for the first part of cooking to allow some volatile acids to escape may help to control these changes. A large amount of water dilutes the natural flavors of the vegetables, usually to a substantial degree. The desirability of a milder flavor or stronger natural flavor is a matter of personal preference, however, so preparation techniques may be adjusted to accomplish the desired flavor.

Onion Flavors. The onion family includes onions, leeks, garlic, and chives (Figure 18–8). These vegetables are usually strong flavored in the raw state but tend to lose some of their strong flavors when cooked in water. Raw vegetables of the onion family contain derivatives of the sulfur-containing amino acid, cysteine. These compounds are acted on by enzymes in the tissues when the vegetables are peeled or cut to produce volatile sulfur compounds that irritate the eyes and cause tearing or produce biting sensations on the tongue.

The sharp flavor of onions as well as garlic is reduced on cooking. The flavor of onions can be mild when cooked in a large amount of water with the lid of the pan loose or off. The flavor can be sweeter and more concentrated when cooked in a small amount of water with the lid on. Onions generally tend to increase in sweetness on cooking. Personal preference may determine the cooking method.

Texture

Tender-crisp is often recommended as a desirable end-point texture when cooking vegetables. There are exceptions, of course; a baked potato is expected to be cooked until tender. As with color, the extent to which a particular vegetable is enjoyed will be influenced by texture. **Fiber** components in vegetables are an important contributor to the texture of vegetables.

Fiber Components. Cellulose, a long-chain **polymer** of glucose, is the main structural component of plant cell walls. Other structural compounds include

---

FOCUS ON SCIENCE
CABBAGE FAMILY CHEMICAL SUBSTANCES

Chemical substances in vegetables of the cabbage family include *thioglucosides*—compounds that contain a sugar molecule with a sulfur-containing portion. *Sinigrin* is the thioglucoside found in cabbage. When cabbage tissues are damaged by cutting or shredding, an enzyme (a thiogluco-sidase called *myrosinase*) breaks down the sinigrin to produce a mustard oil, chemically called *allyl isothiocyanate*.

This compound gives a sharp, pungent flavor that is typical of shredded raw cabbage. An amino acid, *S*-methyl-L-cysteine sulfoxide, is also present in raw cabbage and several other members of the cabbage family. On cooking, this compound produces dimethyl disulfide, which contributes to the characteristic and desirable flavor of the cooked vegetable, along with a number of other volatile compounds [31].

hemicelluloses and *pectins.* All of these substances are complex carbohydrates called **polysaccharides** and, because they are not broken down or hydrolyzed by enzymes in the human digestive tract, make up a major part of dietary fiber [1, 22].

Pectins are found not only in the cell walls but also between the cells, where they act as a cementing substance to bind cells together. Pectic substances include *protopectin,* the insoluble "parent" molecule; *pectinic acid* or *pectin;* and *pectic acid. Betaglucans,* which also are fiber components, are glucose polymers with linkages somewhat different from cellulose that make them more soluble in water. They appear to increase cholesterol excretion from the bowel, thus aiding in the prevention of heart disease [1]. A complex noncarbohydrate molecule, *lignin,* is present in woody parts of plants. Various *gums* and *mucilages* are also found in plants as fiber components but are nonstructural polysaccharides.

Influence of Cooking. There appears to be no great loss of **fiber** when vegetables are prepared by typical kitchen methods or commercial processing [83]. Cellulose is somewhat softened by cooking but indigestible for humans. When calculated on a dry-weight basis, cellulose content seems to increase somewhat when vegetables are boiled, which may result from the liberation of cellulose from the cell walls, making it more available for analysis [19, 20, 32].

The pectic substances, which are part of the intercellular cementing material in plant tissues, may be **hydrolyzed** to a certain extent during cooking, resulting in some cell separation; however, the total pectin content appears to be well retained [83]. In the canning of many vegetables, the solubilization and hydrolysis of pectin apparently contribute to excessive softening. During prolonged cooking at approximately neutral pH, **de-esterification** and de-polymerization (hydrolysis) occur [73].

Alkalies, Acids, and Calcium Salts. Neither baking soda nor acid should be added during the cooking of vegetables or legumes. Sodium bicarbonate (baking soda) added to cooking water tends to cause the hemicelluloses to disintegrate, producing a soft texture in a short cooking period. Acid, on the other hand, prevents softening of vegetables.

Calcium salts, as calcium chloride, make vegetable tissues firmer, probably by forming insoluble calcium salts with pectic substances in the plant tissue. Commercially, traces of calcium are added during canning to help preserve the shape and firmness of tomatoes. The FDA allows calcium chloride to be added up to 0.07 percent. It can also be used to make melon rinds firm and brittle for pickling.

Prevention of Nutrient Losses

Nutrient loss can occur during storage, preparation, and cooking. Vitamins may be destroyed by oxidation, lost by leaching into cooking water, or adversely affected by heat.

Storage Losses. Vegetables prepared and used as close to the time of harvest as possible will have higher nutrient levels. Vitamin C losses during storage can vary with losses ranging from 15 percent in green peas and 77 percent for green beans stored under refrigeration for seven days [3]. In one study, 18 percent of vitamin C was lost in broccoli stored under refrigeration for seven days [16]. Losses in B vitamins also occur during storage.

How Cooking Losses Occur. Cooking losses can occur (1) through the dissolving action of water or dilute salt solutions; (2) by chemical decomposition, which may be influenced by the alkalinity or acidity of the cooking medium; (3) by oxidation of specific molecules such as vitamins; (4) by the mechanical loss of solids into the cooking water; and (5) by volatilization. Mechanical losses of nutrients in vegetable cookery are the result of paring, rapid boiling (agitation), and overcooking. Loss of starch and other nutrients occurs from cut surfaces. Losses are greater when parings are thick and when overcooking results in marked disintegration. The chief volatile loss is water, although volatilization of other substances may cause loss of flavor.

Cooking Losses—Water-Soluble Nutrients. Water-soluble vitamins and some minerals are lost when vegetables are cooked in a large volume of water [40]. Therefore, when cooking in a liquid, the use of as little water as possible is suggested. Vitamin C is easily oxidized and hence tends to be better retained if conditions favoring oxidation can be eliminated. The more alkaline the cooking water, the faster the rate of oxidation of several vitamins, particularly thiamin and vitamin C. Covering pans during cooking can have a negative effect on the color and flavor of some vegetables; however, a covered pan hastens cooking, reduces air contact, and thus can be beneficial for nutrient retention. Researchers examining vitamin C losses in broccoli found that microwave and pressure cooking did not appreciably affect the vitamin C content. Steaming or boiling, however, was associated with 22 and 34 percent loss of vitamin C, respectively [16].

Thiamin is more unstable to heat than riboflavin and niacin, and it appears to be less stable when heated in a water medium than when heated in the dry state. The extent of destruction increases with rising temperature. Riboflavin and niacin are stable to heat even at temperatures above 212°F (100°C).

Cooking Losses—Fat-Soluble Nutrients. Vitamins A and E and the carotenoids, including lycopene, are sensitive to heat, light, oxygen, and pH [3]. These fat-soluble nutrients do not leach into the cooking water like the water-soluble nutrients and appear to be well retained during preparation.

Cooking Losses—Antioxidants. A study of cooking conditions on lycopene levels in tomatoes found losses of 50 percent or more, depending on the method and length of cooking [34]. Researchers who examined the antioxidant activity of 20 different vegetables prepared by boiling, pressure cooking, baking, microwaving, griddling, or frying concluded that microwave cooking or griddling (cooking in a heavy frying pan without fat) resulted in the smallest loss of antioxidant activity [26]. Boiling and pressure cooking resulted in the greatest loss of activity. There was variability among the vegetables, with antioxidant activity losses greater in some vegetables as compared to others.

Influence of Food Production Systems. A comparison was made of vitamin C and folate (a B vitamin) retention in a cook/chill system and cook/hot-hold system. Vegetables reheated after one day of chilled storage had greater losses of both vitamins than those held hot at 162°F (72°C) for 30 minutes. However, the cook/chill vegetables had better vitamin retention than those cooked and held hot for 2 hours [77]. Holding vegetables hot after cooking causes loss of flavor and nutritive value.

Cooking in batches in food service is an important strategy that results in food with higher nutritional value as well as better sensory qualities because the texture and color are less likely to deteriorate when food is freshly cooked and holding is kept to a minimum. For cooking vegetables in a food service operation, convection steaming retained vitamin C well with losses of only 6 to 12 percent. However, when broccoli and cauliflower were held an additional 30 minutes at 145°F (63°C) after cooking, the total loss was 36 to 45 percent [11]. Holding of whipped potatoes before service in a simulated conventional food service system resulted in loss of 36.2 percent of the vitamin C present [48].

Other Changes during Cooking

Other changes that occur during the cooking of vegetables may have an impact on the water content or starch granules. The water content of vegetables is altered during cooking. Water may be absorbed if the vegetable is cooked submerged in water or, to a lesser extent, in steam. Removal of water occurs during baking. The gelatinization of starch, described as the swelling of starch granules in the presence of moisture, occurs during the cooking of vegetables. This gelatinization may be partial or complete.

SPECIFIC METHODS OF COOKING VEGETABLES

Vegetables may be cooked in a variety of ways. As discussed in the preceding pages, color, texture, flavor, and nutrient retention should be considered when preparing vegetables. The choice of cooking method is often influenced by personal preferences.

Broiling and Grilling

High heat is used to cook vegetables when broiled or grilled. Both baking or roasting and grilling result in flavorful vegetables in part due to caramelization. Also, flavors are not diluted by water with these dry-heat cooking methods.

Vegetables may be grilled over hot charcoal by cutting into pieces large enough not to drop through the grates or placing on skewers (**Figure 18–16**). Lightly brushing the vegetable with an oil and then seasoning with an herb before broiling or grilling will contribute delicious flavors.

(a)

(b)

Figure 18–16

(a) Toasted breaded can be topped with fresh tomatoes, and other vegetables drizzled with olive oil to create the appetizer bruschetta. (b) Grilled garden kabobs are a summertime treat that adds excitement to eating your vegetables. (Richard Embery/Pearson Education)

Roasting and Baking

Baking or roasting vegetables can be accomplished by the direct heat of the oven, or the vegetable can be pared, sliced, or diced and placed in a covered casserole. In the casserole, however, a moist atmosphere surrounds the vegetable as it cooks. Potatoes, sweet potatoes, and winter squash are often baked, but many other vegetables are also baked or roasted. Some vegetables are commonly baked in the skin. Corn on the cob may be shucked and wrapped in foil before baking, or the corn may be baked unshucked. In this case, the silk should first be removed and the ear soaked in water so that the shucks will not burn during the baking process.

Moderately hot oven temperatures, which form steam quickly within the vegetable, give better texture to starchy vegetables than is obtainable at low temperatures. Starchy vegetables; such as potatoes, dry out if overbaked or get soggy if the skin of the vegetable is not opened when baking is finished.

Panfrying and Deep-Fat Frying

Both *panfrying* (cooking to doneness in a small amount of hot fat) and *deep-fat frying* (cooking submerged in hot fat) are methods of frying. Potatoes are frequently fried, but many kinds of vegetables can be fried.

Onion rings, eggplant, and zucchini are often battered before being fried in deep fat (**Figure 18–17**). Carrots, green peppers, parsnips, and mushrooms should be parboiled before being covered with batter and fried in deep fat. There appears to be little loss of vitamins and minerals in the frying of vegetables. **Table 18–14** gives approximate temperatures and time periods for deep-fat frying some vegetables and vegetable mixtures. Frying was discussed in more detail in Chapter 8.

Sautéing

Vegetables may be sautéed as a preliminary cooking step in a recipe or as the cooking method for a side dish. The light browning of vegetables such as diced onions, carrots, or celery in a small amount of fat at a moderately high temperature enhances flavor and appearance. Thus, lightly sautéed vegetables are desirable when preparing them for soups and sauces.

Vegetables may be sautéed from the raw state when prepared for a vegetable side dish. For more rapid sautéing, vegetables such as carrots may be blanched first and then sautéed to finish. When cooking vegetables with differing cooking times together, the vegetables that will take the longest to cook

(a)

(b)　　　(c)

Figure 18–17

Onion rings may be made from scratch: (a) dredging the onion rings in flour, (b) dipping in batter, and (c) frying. (Richard Embery/Pearson Education)

Table 18–14
APPROXIMATE TEMPERATURES AND TIMES FOR FRYING VEGETABLES IN DEEP FAT

Food	Temperature of Fat		Time (min)
	°F	°C	
Croquettes (cooked mixtures)	375–390	190–199	2–5
French-fried onions, potatoes, and cauliflower	385–395	196–202	6–8
Fritters	360–375	182–190	3–5

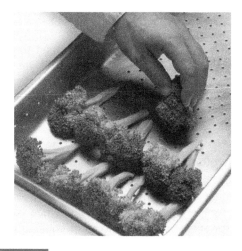

Figure 18–18

These broccoli spears are placed in a perforated pan to be steamed in a commercial foodservice steamer. In the home, small, perforated liners are used by placing above boiling water in a saucepan. (Richard Embery/Pearson Education)

should be started earlier than the quick-cooking vegetables. Sautéed vegetables should be slightly firm or tender-crisp when done. Vegetables may be sautéed and seasoned with a variety of herbs and sauces for a tasty vegetable dish.

Boiling

Vegetables may be boiled either by partially or completely submerging in water. As a result of extensive water contact, soluble substances in vegetables such as water-soluble vitamins, relatively soluble mineral salts, organic acids, flavor substances, and sugars may be lost in the cooking water. Less soluble material loss occurs if vegetables are boiled in their skins.

Blanching. Blanching is the partial cooking of foods in boiling water for a very brief period. Vegetables may be blanched for several different purposes. Blanching can be used to loosen skins on vegetables, such as tomatoes, or as a method to set color or soften firm vegetables. Vegetables may also be blanched prior to an additional cooking step, such as breading and frying. In this case, blanching will partially cook the vegetable, so less cooking is needed during frying, allowing the breading to remain a golden brown. Vegetables to be frozen are blanched to inactivate enzymes that will result in undesirable changes during frozen storage.

Parboiling. Parboiling is similar to blanching, except the cooking time is longer. Parboiling often is used to shorten the final cooking step for vegetables such as broccoli, cauliflower, winter squashes, and root vegetables.

Steaming

Steaming consists of cooking in steam, with the vegetable suspended over boiling water in a perforated container (**Figure 18–18**). Although some tender young vegetables may cook quickly in steam, most vegetables cooked in an ordinary steamer take somewhat longer to cook than those that are boiled. The fact that the vegetable is not actually in water favors the retention of water-soluble constituents.

Pressure Cooking

Cooking in a pressure saucepan involves cooking in steam, but the steam is confined in the tightly closed pan, and a high pressure is created. The cooking temperature rises as the steam pressure rises. Many models of pressure saucepans are adjustable for 5, 10, and 15 pounds of pressure. At 15 pounds of pressure, the temperature is 250°F (121°C), and thus the cooking time is less than if cooked by boiling in a standard pan. Small, lightweight pressure saucepans can conveniently be used to cook a variety of foods (**Figure 18–19**), especially roots, tubers, and legumes.

Figure 18–19

A pressure saucepan may be used to cook a variety of foods. (© okinawakasawa/Fotolia)

With young, tender vegetables such as spinach, the pressure saucepan may easily result in overcooking, with accompanying loss of color and flavor. The fact that acids released from the vegetable are trapped in the pressure saucepan also contributes to a loss of green color. To test for doneness, pressure cookers must be cooled down and the pressure released before opening the lid.

Microwave Cooking

Generally, both fresh and frozen vegetables can be satisfactorily cooked in a microwave oven. For many vegetables, the nutrient losses are less when cooked in the microwave as compared to other cooking methods [16, 26]. Some vegetables have better color and/or flavor when cooked by microwaves, whereas others have higher-quality characteristics when boiled in a saucepan or cooked by other conventional methods [5, 51]. Whole vegetables or pieces should be of uniform size for the microwave oven to allow more even cooking. Large pieces take longer to cook than small pieces, and microwaving time increases with the amount of food being cooked. Vegetables cooked in their skins should be pricked or cut to allow excess steam to escape. Standing time outside the microwave oven should be considered in the cooking of large vegetables. Microwaving is a good method for cooking corn on the cob. Each cob of corn may be wrapped in waxed paper or left in the husk before microwaving. General principles of microwave cookery were discussed in Chapter 5.

Cooking Times for Vegetables

When preparing vegetables, a variety of recipes books can provide guidance for pre-preparation and cooking times. It is best to cook for the minimum time suggested by a recipe and then test for doneness with a fork before continuing to cook. Variations in the maturity of samples of vegetables, the sizes of whole vegetables or cut pieces, the variety, the temperature of the vegetable, and the cooking method selected will affect the amount of preparation time.

Cooking of Frozen Vegetables

Essentially, the cooking of frozen vegetables is no different from the cooking of fresh vegetables. The cooking time of frozen vegetables is about half that required for fresh vegetables because they have been blanched before freezing. Frozen green soybeans are an exception, as they require almost as long to cook as fresh. Frozen vegetables are often cooked from the frozen state, but vegetables frozen in a block are likely to cook more evenly if defrosted first. Frozen corn on the cob is generally thawed before cooking because the cob will not fully thaw in the brief time needed to heat the corn kernels.

Cooking of Canned Vegetables

Canned vegetables are already overcooked in the processing; hence, a relatively short reheating time is desirable to avoid further softening of the vegetables. A short heating period is safe for commercially canned foods; however, it is recommended that low-acid, home-canned vegetables be boiled for at least 10 minutes before tasting to destroy **botulinum toxin**, if present [25]. Boiling should be extended by one additional minute for each 1,000-foot increase in elevation. Commercially canned vegetables may be easily heated in the microwave oven or by conventional methods.

STUDY QUESTIONS

Consumption Trends

1. Discuss the trends in vegetable consumption based on USDA availability data and survey data.

Nutritional Importance of Vegetables

2. Discuss the USDA Dietary Guidelines for Americans with regard to vegetables.

3. Explain why vegetables are nutritionally important for health in our diets.

4. Identify each of the different types of vegetables from a nutritional perspective and discuss why each type should be included in the diet weekly (for example red/orange vegetables).

Kinds of Vegetables

5. Identify what foods are vegetables. Give definitions.

6. List eight classification groups of vegetables based on the parts of the plant that are used as food. Give examples of vegetables in each category.

7. Describe characteristics of mealy potatoes and waxy potatoes and, explain why one variety may be best for some dishes.

8. Explain why mushrooms are not technically considered vegetables.

Purchasing

9. (a) Describe the usual characteristics of fresh vegetables of good quality.

   (b) Suggest important factors to consider in purchasing fresh vegetables.

10. Discuss the economic considerations of including fruits and vegetables in the diet? Are vegetables affordable? Explain why or why not based on data and information provided or additional information researched.

11. Both fresh and processed vegetables and fruits may be graded.

    (a) What advantages result from the use of grades on fresh fruits and vegetables?

    (b) What factor most limits the use of consumer grades for fresh fruits and vegetables?

    (c) List three USDA grades that may be used on canned and frozen vegetables and fruits.

    (d) Discuss the value to the consumer of grading these products.

12. Discuss the regulations and labeling guidelines that are in place to enable consumers who purchase organic vegetables and fruits to know what they are purchasing?

13. Discuss if all conventionally grown vegetables have pesticide residuals detectable. Also identify if there is a difference in the pesticide residuals on produce based on whether the food domestic or imported.

14. Define biotechnology and genetic engineering, and identify the plants currently grown in the United States that have been genetically engineered.

15. Using scientific data and research, debate the pros and cons of food grown using genetic engineering.

16. Discuss the role of "value added" vegetables in foodservice and home kitchens.

Storage

17. Suggest appropriate methods for storing various types of fresh vegetables to retain quality.

18. Identify vegetables best refrigerated before use and vegetables best not refrigerated. Explain.

19. Describe controlled atmosphere storage and how it has an impact on the rate of respiration and senescence of vegetables.

Preparation and Quality Considerations

20. Explain why it is important to cleanse fresh vegetables thoroughly as a first step in their preparation?

21. Explain why the green pigmentation that sometimes develops on potatoes exposed to light should not be eaten.

22. Define EP and AP.

23. Discuss vegetable yield. Specifically explain why if you purchase a pound of a vegetable, why may you not have a pound to serve after pre-preparation and preparation?

24. Why cook vegetables?

25. The color of fruits and vegetables is due to their content of certain pigments.

    (a) List five groups of plant pigments. Describe the color for each group.

    (b) Explain how the pigments and/or colors change in the presence of acid and alkali and with prolonged heating?

    (c) Explain why it is important to preserve the natural colors of vegetables and fruits during cooking.

    (d) What is the impact on some of these plant pigments on health and nutrition?

26. Explain enzymatic oxidative browning and how it may be controlled.

27. Identify reasons why sulfites may be used with some produce items and why it can be a problem for some consumers.

28. Discuss why potatoes may discolor after cooking and methods to suppress this discoloration.

29. Flavor varies from one vegetable to another, and many substances contribute to the characteristic flavors.

    (a) List two different families of vegetables that are considered to be strong flavored and indicate what types of compounds are responsible for these flavors.

    (b) Explain how cooking procedures may change these flavors.

30. Explain how texture may impact the desirability of a vegetable when being consumed.

31. Discuss the fiber components found in plants.

    (a) List at least three plant polysaccharides that are components of dietary (indigestible) fiber.

    (b) Name three pectic substances. What roles do these play in plant structure? Which pectic substance is important in making fruit jellies and jams?

32. Explain the implications of alkalies, acids, and calcium salts on vegetable texture.

33. Describe several ways in which nutrient losses may occur during the cooking of vegetables.

34. In the following list, check the items that describe what may happen when vegetables are cooked. Correct any incorrect statements.

    (a) Starch swells and gelatinizes.

    (b) Cellulose fibers harden.

    (c) Volatile flavors are trapped inside the cells.

(d) Leafy vegetables become limp.

(e) Cellulose fibers soften slightly.

(f) Intercellular cement is hardened.

(g) Vitamins go off in the steam.

(h) Some vitamins and minerals dissolve in the cooking water.

(i) Texture becomes softer.

(j) Some vitamins are lost by oxidation.

(k) Some volatile flavors are lost.

(l) Chlorophyll may be changed to anthocyanins.

(m) Carotenes may become white.

(n) Some volatile acids are released.

(o) Pheophytin, an olive green pigment, may be produced from chlorophyll.

(p) Proteins are coagulated.

(q) Pectic substances are hydrolyzed or broken down.

Cooking Methods

35. Outline an appropriate procedure for cooking each of the following vegetables. Explain why you would use the procedure in each case.

    (a) A green vegetable such as broccoli

    (b) Cabbage

    (c) Onions

    (d) Beets

36. Describe eight appropriate methods for cooking vegetables.

37. Describe an appropriate method for preparing frozen vegetables and canned vegetables.

38. Explain why frozen vegetables require less time for cooking than similar fresh vegetables.

19
Alternative Proteins

Throughout history and around the world, people have consumed alternative proteins to meet or supplement their biological need for protein and energy. As with many of our food choices (see Chapter 1), the choice of protein is influenced by the region one lives in and the foods available; family, cultural, and religious factors; and economics. Today, the choice of protein is also increasingly being impacted by environmental sustainability concerns and preferences for a protein source that is low fat and low cholesterol.

Alternative proteins, within the context of this chapter, and as also understood by those in food science, nutrition, and food fields, include: legumes, pulses, high-protein grains and seeds, nuts, seaweed and algae, and insects. Although many of these alternative proteins are choices acceptable to those consuming a vegan diet because they are plant-based foods, insects are included here, not as a vegan choice, but as a protein viewed by many as an "alternative." Some also view eggs and dairy milk as alternative proteins because they can serve as alternatives to red meats, poultry, and seafood. However, these proteins will not be discussed in this chapter; dairy and eggs are instead discussed in Chapters 22 and 23.

In this chapter the alternative proteins will be presented, as also their use for food as prepared at home or foodservices, or as offered as ingredients and products by the food industry. The following topics will be discussed:

• Consumption trends
• Nutritive value
• Vegetarian diets
• Legumes and pulses
• Grains
• Seeds
• Nuts
• Seaweed and algae
• Insects

CONSUMPTION TRENDS AND NUTRITION

Consumption Trends

Consumption trends of alternative proteins are impacted by the number of people who consume vegetarian diets, and also by those who periodically choose vegetarian meals. Several alternative protein foods are prevalent in multicultural cuisines and can also be menu choices enjoyed by those who eat meat, poultry, or seafood. For example, consider those who drink soy or almond milk substitutes, eat beans and legumes such as refried beans or hummus, include quinoa as a side dish, eat nuts and seeds as a snack or baking ingredient, and enjoy sushi often wrapped in seaweed. Insects, in much of the United States are never or rarely consumed, and, if consumed, are a novelty. Worldwide about 2 billion people consume insects on a regular basis [13].

A 2016 Harris poll found 3.3 percent of Americans are vegetarians [8]. Of these, about half are vegans and eat only plant-based foods. However, about 37 percent of Americans order vegetarian food when eating out, even though they may not be vegetarian. Furthermore, about 36 percent of Americans report eating a vegetarian meal at least once per week. Millennials seem to lead this trend, with 12 percent identifying themselves as vegetarians. Additionally, 60 percent of millennials consume alternative proteins [8]. Meatless Monday could be helping to drive some of this interest in alternative proteins among those who typically consume meat. Meatless Monday was practiced because of rationing during World War I; however, today it is gaining traction again as both

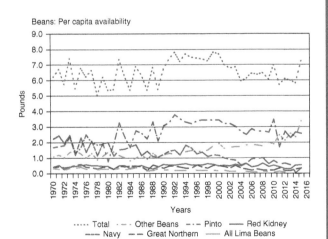

Figure 19–1

Legume consumption by Americans has recently increased, but is lower than that consumed, as measured by USDA availability data, than the 1990s. (USDA, ERS)

a healthy and sustainable choice. Today, as in years past, it is usually an economical choice as well.

USDA availability data for several legumes are provided in **Figure 19–1** [41]. Over nearly 40 years, the availability of these beans has increased and decreased, but does not reveal a steadily increasing trend. Both total bean and other bean (includes black, small red, pink, cranberry, garbanzo, and blackeye) consumption has increased in recent years. However, with 7.3 pounds per capita of these beans available in 2015, it is evident that as compared to other foods Americans' consumption of these legumes is modest. The USDA availability data for tree nuts, including peanuts, which are technically classified as a legume, are provided in **Figure 19–2** [41]. The use of tree nuts and peanuts by Americans has increased in recent years. The accessibility of almonds has increased notably since 2005, most likely in part fueled by the popularity of almond milk substitute.

Nutritive Value

Alternative proteins are identified as such because nutritionally these foods offer high protein content as compared to many other foods, and thus can serve as a valuable source of protein in the diet (**Table 19–1**). However, many of these foods can also offer other important nutrients such as dietary fiber, iron, zinc, folic acid, thiamine, potassium, manganese, and calcium. The position of the Academy of Nutrition and Dietetics

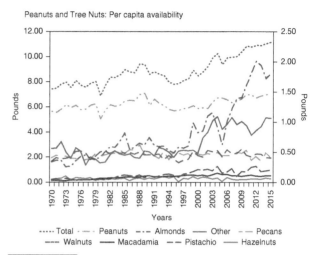

Figure 19–2

Americans eat more peanuts (botanically a legume) than tree nuts. Left scale for Total and Peanut chart data. Right scale is for all other nuts that are consumed much less. (USDA, ERS)

on vegetarian diets is that "appropriately planned vegetarian, including vegan, diets are healthful, nutritionally adequate, and may provide health benefits in the prevention and treatment of certain diseases" [1]. The USDA Dietary Guidelines for Americans also identifies vegetarian diets as a healthy eating pattern. In these guidelines a vegetarian eating pattern is provided with adjustments for those following a vegan diet [42].

Table 19–1
ONE OUNCE EQUIVALENT OF PROTEIN FOODS

Protein	Portion Size
Meats, poultry, seafood	1 ounce cooked
Eggs	1 egg
Legumes and pulses	¼ cup cooked beans: kidney, pinto, black beans, chickpeas (garbanzo beans), and others ¼ cup cooked blackeye or cow peas ¼ cup cooked lentils
Prepared legume and pulses	¼ cup or 2 ounces of tofu 1 ounce cooked tempeh ¼ cup roasted soybeans 2 tablespoons of hummus ½ cup of split pea, bean, or lentil soup
Grains	About 1 cup of cooked amaranth, hulled barley, buckwheat, Khorasan wheat, rolled oats, quinoa, sorghum, spelt, wheat, wild rice 1 ounce of seitan (prepared wheat gluten)
Seeds	½ ounce hulled and roasted pumpkin, sunflower or squash seeds 1 tablespoon of hemp seeds
Nuts	½ ounce nuts (12 almonds, 24 pistachios, 7 walnut halves) 1 tablespoon of peanut butter 1 tablespoon of almond butter
Notation on recommendations	5 to 6 ounces or equivalent of protein are suggested daily for adult men and women, depending on age, activity and other individual differences.

Source: References 35, 39.

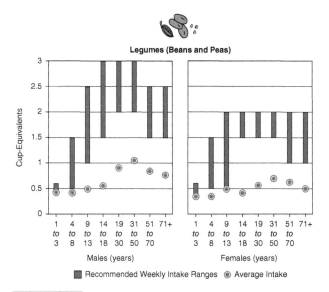

Legumes (Beans and Peas)

Males (years)

Females (years)

■ Recommended Weekly Intake Ranges ◉ Average Intake

Males and females at age 4 and older consume less than the recommended servings of legumes. The orange dots represent the typical number of cups consumed at the ages listed. The blue bar is the recommended number of cups (or cup equivalents) of legumes that are recommended depending on individual needs at each age. (USDA)

Notably, the Dietary Guidelines for Americans encourages all Americans to eat more legumes by including legumes at least weekly. Americans are under-consuming nearly all types of vegetables (see Chapter 18). **Figure 19–3** shows the gap between Dietary Guideline recommendations for legume consumption and Americans' consumption. Legumes offer health benefits when consumed because they are rich in complex carbohydrates, dietary fiber, and protein and are low in fat. Researchers have suggested that an increased consumption of dry beans and peas by Americans would be likely to increase the intake of fiber, folate, zinc, iron, and magnesium while lowering fat intake [20]. Plant-based diets have been shown to be associated with a lower body mass, reduction in cardiovascular disease, lower risk of type 2 diabetes, and overall lower risk of cancer [1].

Protein

In the past, a discussion of plant proteins emphasized the need for vegetarians to carefully plan food choices to include all the essential amino acids in the diet (see Chapter 7). There are nine essential amino acids that must be provided in our diet. Although plant foods generally contain all of the essential amino acids, some alternative proteins are higher in some essential amino acids and lower in others [28]. For example, cereal grains are low in the essential amino acid lysine, but supply sufficient methionine. Legumes are low in methionine, but supply adequate amounts of lysine. Soy, tofu, tempeh, and seitan are all high in lysine [28]. The

idea of "complementary" proteins was discussed extensively in years past from a perspective that incomplete proteins must be combined at meals. The Academy of Nutrition and Dietetics states the terms complete and incomplete proteins can be misleading and points out that a variety of plant proteins, consumed throughout the day, will provide all the essential amino acids when calorie needs are also met [1]. The USDA MyPlate tips for vegetarians also states it is not necessary to combine different protein (complementary) sources at the same meal [40], as was once recommended.

In addition to understanding protein quality by the essential amino acid content in the food, the protein digestibility-corrected amino acid score (PDCAAS) examines proteins by the amount of essential amino acids and also digestibility [28]. The PDCAAS was first published by the Food and Agriculture Organization and the World Health Organization of the United Nations in 1991. The FDA began to use the PDCAAS for nutrition labeling in 1993. Soybeans are the highest of the plant foods with a PDCAAS of 0.99 [28]. Another method of scoring protein quality, digestible indispensable amino acid score (DIAAS), has been introduced. The DIAAS uses different methods to assess digestibility [28].

Fatty Acids

Vegetarians usually consume less long-chain omega-3 fatty acids like eicosapentaenoic acid (EPA) and docosahexaenoic acid (DHA) than those who eat animal foods, and vegans generally do not consume these fatty acids at all [1]. Seafood is the predominant source of these omega-3 fatty acids in the diet, though some omega-3s are available through non-seafood sources. The intake of the omega-3 fatty acid α-linolenic (ALA), for example, is similar in vegetarians and vegans to those who consume animal proteins.

ALA is converted to EPA and DHA in the body, but this conversion can be inefficient and variable based on individual factors. ALA is found in flax, chia, camelina, canola, and hemp seed. It is also found in walnuts. Microalgae-based DHA supplements in low doses can be beneficial for vegetarians and vegans with specific needs, such as during pregnancy [1].

Minerals

Iron, zinc, iodine, and calcium are minerals needed in the diet, and often discussed with regard to vegetarian diets. Hemoglobin and other measures of iron status in vegetarians are similar to those of nonvegetarians [1]. Vegetarians generally consume similar levels of iron as those who consume animal products, and although the iron in plants (nonheme iron) is not absorbed as effectively, the absorption varies widely and appears to increase if they are iron deficient. Zinc status similarly does not appear to be a concern for vegetarians. Soy, legumes, grains, seeds, and nuts all provide zinc in the diet. Iodine can be low in vegetarian diets. Iodized salt and sea vegetables can help to increase iodine levels. Sea salt and kosher salt are usually not iodized [1]. Supplementation may be advised for some vegans such as pregnant women.

Calcium intake can be variable among vegans in particular. However, fortified plant-based milk substitutes such as soy or almond will provide the same level of calcium as cow's milk. It should be noted that the term "milk" is generally reserved for milk that comes from cows, and therefore "milk substitute" will be used in this chapter. Tofu made with calcium salt is also a good option [1]. Several vegetables do contain modest amounts of calcium, although the absorption, depending on the vegetable, can be poor.

Vitamins

Many plant foods are an important part of the diet because of their vitamin content. However, two vitamins of potential concern for vegetarians are vitamin D and vitamin B_{12} [1]. Vitamin D can be obtained by sunlight, but for those who live at high latitudes, exposure to sunlight can be low during certain seasons. Supplementation with vitamin D or the consumption of fortified foods may be needed [1].

Vitamin B_{12} is generally not provided by plant foods. Although fermented foods such as tempeh, and also nori, spirulina, chlorella algae, and unfortified nutritional yeast, can offer some vitamin B_{12}, it is usually inadequate to meet nutritional needs. Breakfast cereals and some other foods are fortified with vitamin B_{12} or alternatively a supplement should be used to avoid deficiency [1].

VEGETARIAN DIETS

The adoption of a vegetarian diet may be motivated by a variety of factors, including ecological and sustainability concerns, religious beliefs, animal welfare, chronic disease risk reduction, philosophical or ethical values, taste preferences, and economic considerations. The following general classifications of vegetarians have been suggested by the Institute of Food Technologists. The Vegetarian Resource Group does not identify semivegetarians and pesco-vegetarians in their list of vegetarian types because these two include foods derived from animal flesh.

Semivegetarian: Eats dairy products, eggs, chicken, and fish but no other animal flesh.

Pesco-vegetarian: Eats dairy products, eggs, and fish but no other animal flesh.

Lacto-ovo-vegetarian: Eats dairy products and eggs but no animal flesh.

Lacto-vegetarian: Eats dairy products but no animal flesh or eggs.

Ovo-vegetarian: Eats eggs but no dairy products or animal flesh.

Vegan: Eats no animal products of any type.

Increasingly, the term "flexitarian" is also being used. A flexitarian eats vegetarian or vegan meals, but may also periodically consume meat, poultry, or seafood. This approach may be attractive to those moving from a diet with animal products to a plant-based diet. "Lesstarian" is another term being used to describe those consuming less red meat, poultry, and seafood than in the past.

At this time, insects are consumed little in the United States. Many vegans do not eat honey because it is a product of bees. Consequently, it would be anticipated that vegans, as well as other vegetarians, would be unlikely to eat insects.

LEGUMES AND PULSES

Legumes are plants with an edible seed enclosed in a pod [35]. Botanically, legumes are fruits; but from a culinary perspective, they are consumed as vegetables or alternative proteins. They are part of the *Leguminosae*

UP CLOSE
SUSTAINABILITY AND THE FUTURE OF FOOD

In the year 2050, it is estimated that more than 9 billion people will be populating the planet. The world's food supply will need to increase by 70 percent. The sustainability of water-intensive crops (such as almonds, walnuts, and soybeans) and other foods such as meat and animal products [33] is being questioned. Overfishing, the amount of land being used for agriculture, deforestation, and the reality of the volume of food needed in the future are all prompting the examination of other food sources.

Alternative protein sources have to some extent been at the front of this sustainability movement. The amount of feed, water, and land necessary to produce protein foods has led some to look to the oceans for alternatives such as seaweed and algae [33]. On the land, pulses are a relatively high-quality protein and high-nutrient food source that replenish the soil with nitrogen and require less water as compared to many other crops [14].

The Institute of Food Technologists launched a webpage "Future Food 2050" to offer scientific perspectives and research on the future of food. ■

plant family. Legumes and pulses have been the heart of many traditional cuisines for thousands of years. Legumes are relatively inexpensive, but high in protein, fiber, folate, and polyphenols [35]. Legumes include soybeans, peanuts, fresh peas, fresh beans, and pulses.

The Food and Agricultural Organization (FAO) declared 2016 the year of the pulse. Pulses are from the *Fabaceae* or *Leguminosae* family [14]. Common pulses include dry beans, dry peas, chickpeas, and lentils. There are 11 major types of pulses grown in the world recognized by FAO. Pulses are high in protein and fiber, but low in fat. Soybeans and peanuts, both legumes, are not classified as pulses because of their high fat content. Although peanuts are legumes, within this chapter they will be discussed with other nuts because their common usage is similar to that of other tree nuts. Fresh peas and beans (see Chapter 18) are also not pulses because they are fresh and not dried seeds.

Soybeans

Soybeans, a legume, are a good source of protein of high biological value and have been used for centuries in various forms as a food staple by millions of people. Soybean products can play an important role in vegetarian and nonvegetarian diets. These beans were first grown on a large-scale basis in the United States in the twentieth century. They are the second most planted field crop after corn [38]. Most of the soybean crop is grown in the upper Midwest and is commonly rotated with corn (**Figure 19–4**). Soybeans are largely used for soybean oil, but are important for many other soy food products. **Table 19–2**

Figure 19–4

Soybeans growing in a field. (Oticki/Shutterstock)

Table 19–2
SOY-BASED FOODS

Name	Description and Use
Edamame	Green vegetable soybeans are harvested when the beans are still green. They may be served as a vegetable dish after cooking. They may be purchased in the pod or shelled.
Natto	Natto is traditionally served in Asian countries as a rice topping, in miso soups, or with vegetables. It is made from fermented, cooked whole soybeans.
Okara	Okara can be baked, added as fiber in granola and cookies, or made into sausage. It is a pulp-fiber by-product of soy plant-based milk substitute.
Miso	This salty condiment is used in Japanese cooking. It may be used to season soups, sauces, and other foods. This smooth paste is made from soybeans, rice (or another grain), salt and a mold culture. It is aged for one to three years.
Soybeans	Fully ripened beans are hard and dry. They can be cooked whole and used in a variety of recipes. Soaked beans can be also cooked by roasting until brown and eaten as "soynuts."
Soy "Milk"	Soy milk substitute is produced from soaked, finely ground, and strained soybeans. It is often fortified with calcium.
Soy Sauce	Soy sauce is a liquid made from soybeans that has been fermented. There are three common kinds of soy sauce. Shoyu made from a blend of soy and wheat. Tamari is made from soybeans as a by-product of making miso. Teriyaki sauce also includes sugar, vinegar, and spices.
Tofu (Soybean Curd)	This soft food is made by curdling fresh, hot soy "milk." Firm tofu is solid and can be cubed. Soft tofu worked well for recipes when blending the tofu is desirable. Silken tofu is creamy and can be used as a sour cream replacement.
Tempeh	Soybeans may be mixed with rice or millet and then fermented. Tempeh, originating from Indonesia, has a smoky or nutty flavor and can be marinated, grilled, or otherwise incorporated into recipes.
Yuba	A thin layer forming on the surface of hot soy "milk" is lifted and dried to produce yuba. It can be found fresh, half dried, or as dried bean curd sheets.
Additional Soy Products	Flavored or fruit soy beverages, soy-based whipped toppings, soy infant formulas, soynut butter, soy yogurt, and nondairy soy frozen desserts are additional products made from soy available in the marketplace.

Source: Reference 12.

(a)

(b)

Figure 19–5

Soybeans can be used in a number of ways. (a) Edamame are fresh soybeans that may be eaten in the pod, (Natu/Shutterstock) and (b) Yuba (soybean skin) is a soybean curd sheet.

(© Amanda Frye)

provides an overview of several kinds of foods prepared from soybeans, and some are shown in **Figure 19–5**.

Tofu. Tofu originated in China in the second century B.C. In the United States, tofu has been made since the twentieth century but is consumed at relatively low levels [17]. Tofu is high in protein, low in saturated fat, and is a good source of calcium.

Tofu is made by soaking the beans for four to ten hours depending on the temperature of the water or if the beans are ground before soaking. The soybean hulls may be removed before grinding

to improve color and reduce the beany flavor. The addition of sodium bicarbonate can further reduce beany flavors and increase smoothness of the tofu. After grinding of the soybeans, the ground slurry is cooked for less than 10 minutes to denature the soy protein and remove volatile beany flavors [17].

Using filtration or a centrifuge, the soy milk substitute is removed from the solid soy pulp (fiber), also called okara (Table 19–1). The soy milk substitute may be concentrated before the next step—coagulation. Coagulation is accomplished by the use of salts, acids, and/or enzymes. Calcium sulfate is a traditional coagulant. Finally, the tofu curds are pressed when making firm or extra firm tofu to release excess liquid. Soft and silken tofu is not pressed. Tofu is often pasteurized to extend the shelf life of the product [17].

Firm or extra firm tofu can be sautéed, fried, or incorporated into pasta or stir-fry dishes. Firm tofu will hold its shape (**Figure 19–6**). Tofu is mild flavored and takes on the flavor of the dish being prepared, thus it is a flexible recipe ingredient. Soft and silken tofu can be used in dips, sauces, and desserts like cheese cake to replace other ingredients such as cream cheese or sour cream.

Soy Flour, Protein Concentrate, and Isolated Soy Proteins. Soy flour may be made from dehulled soybeans that contain the oil normally present in this product (about 18 percent) or by grinding soy flakes from which soybean oil has been pressed. Soy flour is one of the flour options used by those who are avoiding gluten (see Chapter 13).

Soy protein concentrate is produced when soluble carbohydrates are extracted from defatted soy flour. It contains 70 percent or more protein. On further removal of nonprotein substances, *isolated soy proteins* remain, containing 90 percent or more protein.

Texturized Soy Proteins. Textured soy protein, or the protein from other legumes, can be desirable when making foods with a texture similar to meats or poultry. Extrusion and fiber spinning are the most common methods used [9]. In the fiber spinning method, the protein isolate is spun into long fibers by a process similar to the spinning of textile fibers. Although this method creates a meat-like fiber structure, it is not often used commercially because of its complexity [9].

Extrusion is more commonly used as the method for producing texturized vegetable protein to be used in meat analogs (**Figure 19–7**). Soy, pulse, and other alternative proteins can all be extruded. In this procedure, soy flour or protein concentrate is blended with desired ingredients and then fed into a cooking extruder that works the material into a dough. As the dough flows within the channels of an extrusion screw and moves through the small openings of a die, the large protein molecules lose their original structure and form layered masses that cross-link with

(a)

(b)

Figure 19–6

(a) Whole soybeans, soy sauce, soy plant-based "milk," firm tofu, texturized soy protein, and soy analogs are shown. (Igor Dutina/123RF) (b) Black pepper soybean slices can be purchased and consumed like jerky or incorporated in a dish. (© Amanda Frye)

Figure 19–7

This vegan sandwich is made with soy cheese, soy "burger," tomatoes, and sprouts. (Stockstudios/Shutterstock)

each other. These masses resist disruption on further heating or processing. The release of pressure as the protein mixture is extruded causes expansion, with tiny air pockets being uniformly dispersed throughout the mass. Texturized soy or vegetable protein can be combined with other foods in various dishes.

Soybeans and Flavor. Some object to the beany flavor of soybeans. These differences in preferences may be because of cultural experiences with consuming soybeans and soybean foods. The flavors in soybeans that are characterized as being off-flavors are largely because of **lypoxygenases** [36]. The undesirable flavors can be managed by inactivating these enzymes or by using different varieties of soybeans.

Soybeans and Nutrition. Soybeans are a source of *phytoestrogens*, which are isoflavonoid compounds that have a weak estrogenic activity in the body [10]. For this reason, there is some question about the consumption of soy by women with hormone-positive breast cancer. Research at this time suggests there is a reduced cancer recurrence and mortality among breast cancer patients who consume soy [25]. With regard to other health issues, soy has been associated with a reduced risk of type 2 diabetes and has a favorable impact on blood lipid profiles to lower cardiovascular risks.

Pulses

Pulses are legumes, but pulse refers to only those dried seeds that are also low fat. Dry beans, dry peas, chickpeas, and lentils are all pulses (**Table 19–3**) (**Figure 19–8**). Of those, there are several different varieties under each grouping. In the United States, pulses are grown most commonly in the Northern Plains (North Dakota, Montana, and South Dakota), and in the Palouse area of the Pacific Northwest (Washington, Idaho, and Oregon) [4].

Pulses grow easily in many different climates throughout the world. Pulses, as well as soybeans, are nitrogen-fixing crops that can use nitrogen in the air, thus they enrich the soil. They also require very little water. For these reasons, pulses are viewed as a sustainable crop.

Harvest and Processing. Pulses are generally harvested with a combine that cuts the plant from the field and then separates the seeds. The plant residue is distributed across the field. Harvesting when the pulses are dry, but not too dry, is important for storage, yield, and quality [37].

Prior to use in food, pulses are usually dried, cleaned of dust or stones, and sorted for size. Next legumes and pulses may be dehulled by (a) sun drying; (b) the addition of an edible oil, then sun drying; (c) soaking in water, then sun drying; or (d) soaking alone. Pulses, such as split peas, may be split along with the dehulling process [37].

Table 19–3
VARIETIES OF PULSES

Type	Description and Use
Dry Beans	
Adzuki	These deep red beans, common in Asian cooking, have a nutty flavor. They can be used in casseroles, ground into flour, or used in a sweet paste filling in Chinese mooncakes.
Black beans	Sometimes called *black turtle-soup beans*; used in thick soups and in Oriental and Mediterranean dishes
Broad beans	These strong nutty flavored beans include fava, pigeon, horse, and Windsor beans.
Cannellini beans	These white beans are popular in Italian dishes such as minestrone or pasta e fagioli soup.
Garbanzo beans	Also known as *chickpeas*; they originated in Turkey and can be used in a variety of dishes. In Middle Eastern dishes, falafel (ground, shaped into balls and fried) and hummus (cooked and ground into a paste) are popular. In India they may be ground into flour for flatbreads. They may also be pickled in vinegar and oil for salads. Two main varieties are desi and kabuli.
Great Northern beans	Larger than but similar to pea beans; used in soups, salads, casserole dishes, and baked beans
Kidney beans	Large, red, and kidney shaped; popular for chili con carne; used also in salads and many Mexican dishes
Lima beans	Broad, flat, and in different sizes; used as a main-dish vegetable and in casseroles. These beans may also be called butter beans.
Mung beans	Small, oval, and olive colored. Often found in India, China, and Southeast Asia. May be eaten in the sprouted form as bean sprouts
Navy beans (Haricot)	Broad term that includes navy bean, haricot, white pea bean, or pea bean.
Pinto beans	Beige and speckled; of the same species as kidney beans and red beans; used in salads, chili, and many Mexican dishes. These beans are often mashed and used as refried beans in Mexican cuisine.
Red and pink beans	Pink beans are more delicate in flavor than red beans; both used in many Mexican dishes and chili.
Urid Beans	Also known as black gram, matpe beans, or black lentils, they are widely consumed in Southeast Asia.
Dry Peas	
Black-eyed peas	Also called *black-eyed beans* or *cowpeas*; small, oval shaped, and creamy white with a black spot on one side; often used as a main-dish vegetable. It is also used in Creole cuisine and Indian curries.
Split peas	These are soft when young, and are dried. Split peas, as often sold, are split in half and often disintegrate into a puree when cooked. Two main varieties are the green and the yellow split peas.
Lentils	
Lentils	Unlike other legumes, lentils do not need to be soaked before cooking. Varieties include yellow, puy, red, green and brown, and Umbrian. They are disk shaped and about the size of a pea; require a short cooking time (about 30 minutes); and combine well with many different foods.

Source: Reference 14.

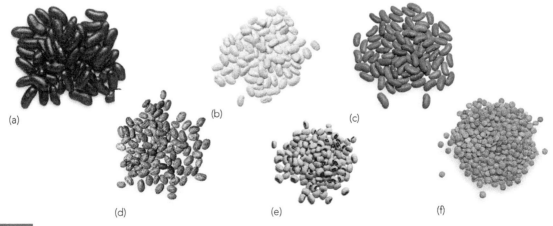

(a)   (b)   (c)   (d)   (e)   (f)

Figure 19–8

Many different pulses are available (a) black beans, (b) Great Northern beans, (c) red kidney beans, (d) pinto beans, (e) black-eyed peas, and (f) lentils. (Richard Embery/Pearson Education)

Forms for Pulses. In their whole form, pulses may be sold dried in packages or canned. Pulses may also be found fried or roasted. Pulses are increasingly being milled into flour in the United States (see Chapters 12 and 13). There are various milling processes that can be used depending on the desired final product. These pulse flours can be useful in gluten-free baking applications [37] or for thickening soups and sauces [35]. Various types of pulse flours can be used to make high-protein, high-fiber pastas, and a variety of other foods and snacks [22, 23].

Pulses may also be fractionated to produce starch or protein particles. Pea protein concentrates and isolates can be a favorable alternative to soy flour [37]. Fractionated pea starch, produced when fractionating protein, offers excellent gel strength [37]. The starch in yellow peas is high in amylose content and therefore gels (see Chapter 11 more about starch and types of starch). Pea protein concentrates and isolates have also been used as egg replacers and can be an ingredient in vegan mayonnaise.

Hummus. Hummus is made from mashed chickpeas (garbanzo beans) that are blended with tahini (sesame seed paste), olive or sesame seed oil, lemon juice, and other desired seasonings [15]. This thick dip or spread is a staple in Middle Eastern cuisine that likely originated in Cairo in the thirteenth century. Currently, about 26 percent of Americans purchase hummus (**Figure 19–9**). Two-thirds of the chickpeas in the United States are grown in Washington state and Idaho.

The manufacture of hummus starts with cleaned, dry chickpeas. Next, they are soaked for 10 to 14 hours in water that may also contain sodium bicarbonate (baking soda) to help loosen the skins. Following soaking, the skins are removed and the chickpeas are cooked. Once drained, the chickpeas are ground into a smooth paste. The other ingredients, including

tahini, are mixed into the chickpea paste with part of the cooking water reincorporated to obtain desired consistency. Pasteurization is often utilized as a final step [15]. Hummus may be made in the home or in the foodservice setting.

Some similar products may be found with the name hummus made with ingredients other than chickpeas. Edamame, white bean, and yellow lentil are examples of these alternative types of hummus [15]. Hummus, whether made with chickpeas or other ingredients, is generally low in fat and high in protein and fiber.

Preparation of Legumes

Legumes require cooking before eating. When they are cooked, proteins are made more available, starch is at least partially gelatinized [11], flavor is improved, and some potentially toxic substances found in some raw forms of beans are destroyed. As discussed in Chapter 2, kidney beans that are raw, undercooked, or cooked at a low temperature (slow cooker) should not be consumed. A toxin, believed to be phytohaemagglutinin, must be destroyed by high-heat cooking to prevent illness.

When purchased as dry legumes, they are hard and the cellulose and other fiber components are well developed. Therefore, dried beans, soybeans, and chickpeas are generally soaked in water, followed by cooking in water to soften them (**Figure 19–10**). The ease of softening depends somewhat on how readily the legumes absorb water. Split peas and lentils because of their small size can be cooked in water without soaking. The cooking time required for split peas and lentils is also much less than the other legumes.

Soaking of Beans. Prior to cooking, dried legumes are soaked in water. Two main methods may be used: (1) overnight soaking in cold water or (2) soaking for 1 hour in water that was brought to a boil briefly. The rate of hydration is faster in hot water than at room temperature or by the method of soaking all night in cold water [6]. When soaking is started by boiling the beans for 2 minutes, dry beans absorb as much water in 1 hour as when soaked in cold water for 15 hours. Additional water is absorbed during the cooking process, making a gain in weight of 150 to 160 percent (about 4 cups of water per cup of dry beans for both soaking and cooking).

Soft or Hard Water. Soft water is preferable for both soaking and cooking dry beans because the calcium and magnesium salts in hard water may form insoluble salts with pectic substances in the cell walls and between cells in the bean tissue and inhibit proper hydration. There is more water absorbed and fewer hard beans remaining at the end of cooking when soft water rather than hard water is used.

Figure 19–9

Hummus, made from chickpeas, can be eaten with pita.

(Elena Elisseeva/Shutterstock)

(a)

(b)

(c)

Alkali and Acid. Alkali in the form of baking soda has been used to hasten the softening of dried beans during cooking. The use of baking soda, however, is not necessary and can be undesirable. Alkali increases water absorption, but it is destructive to the thiamin content of legumes. The use of baking soda may also cause the bean texture to become too soft. If baking soda is used, the amount of soda needs to be carefully regulated ($\frac{1}{8}$ teaspoon per pint of water) to prevent

an unappealing flavor, texture, and appearance of the cooked beans. In small amounts, baking soda can serve as an aid in softening the seed coats when hard water is used to cook the beans.

In contrast, acids will reduce the softening of dried beans and other vegetables. For this reason, acidic ingredients such as tomatoes, lemon juice, vinegar, and so forth should be added after the beans have satisfactory softened (see Chapter 18).

Canned Beans. One constraint limiting the use of dried beans is the length of preparation time required. Canned beans are convenient and save time in preparation because they are ready to consume in only the time required to heat. They, however, may be softer than desired and may not be as bright in color as a bean prepared from dried beans. For example, black beans may be a richer black color when prepared from dried beans because some of the black color may be lost in the liquid used in the canning process.

Raffinose and Stachyose. Legumes contain appreciable amounts of the oligosaccharides raffinose and stachyose, which are not digested by enzymes in the intestinal tract. It is assumed that the flatulence resulting from the ingestion of legumes results from the degradation of these carbohydrates by intestinal microorganisms. It has been suggested that the soaking and cooking water be discarded to maximize the removal of these gas-forming carbohydrates.

GRAINS

Grains are used in a variety of ways in our menus: breads and other baked goods, side dishes (rice), and salads (pasta, rice, or a Tabouli salad) (see Chapters 12 and 13). As used in these ways, protein may not be the focus; instead, fiber and the benefit of whole grains may be a greater consideration or simply the functionality in the dish being prepared. However, within a predominately plant-based diet, the protein in these grains can be appreciable. About one cup or less of some grains can contain the protein equivalent to one ounce of meat or cheese, or one egg. Amaranth, barley, Kamut or Khorasan wheat, millet, oats, quinoa, sorghum, spelt, wheat (including bulgar), wild rice, and buckwheat are among the grains identified as having comparatively high protein [27, 35]. Quinoa, although technically a seed, is generally used more as a grain and thus is discussed within grains (**Figure 19–11**) [29]. Chapter 12 discusses grains in greater detail.

Wheat gluten can be a meat substitute. Wheat gluten, not unlike soy products such as tofu and tempeh, has been used by the Chinese, Japanese, Koreans, and Vietnamese, and other Asian cultures, for many years. The term "seitan" is of Japanese origin and often used

FOCUS ON SCIENCE
MORE ON THE PREPARATION OF LEGUMES

Acidic Ingredients, Salt, and Softening of Legumes

Ingredients such as tomatoes, catsup, molasses, and brown sugar contain organic acids. These ingredients are added to many dishes containing legumes to boost flavor, but at the same time, they have to be added after the legume has softened. This is because of the pectin content of the legume. If the legume has not softened and the acid ingredient is added too soon, the legume will remain hard. Salt may also cause toughening of beans and therefore should be added near the end of cooking.

Rancidity and the Influence of Lipoxygenase

Lipoxygenase is an enzyme that is specific to linoleic (18:2) and linolenic (18:3) fatty acids. The enzyme supplies the oxygen to the fatty acid and causes rancidity, which produces off-flavors. This enzyme is particularly found in fresh peas. Thus, it is important that fresh peas are blanched immediately—especially if they are to be frozen—so that lipoxygenase activity is prevented.

HEALTHY EATING
ALLERGIES AND ALTERNATIVE PLANT PROTEINS

Some people seek out alternative proteins because of allergies to other kinds of proteins. Milk, eggs, fish, crustacean shellfish, tree nuts, peanuts, wheat, and soybeans are identified as the eight major allergens responsible for 90 percent of food allergic reactions [43]. Among the alternative proteins, tree nuts, peanuts, wheat, and soybeans should be noted, and those allergic to crustaceans could also be allergic to some insects.

Pulses, seaweed, and algae are other available options that are not known as allergens. The pulses in particular have a distinctive advantage as a non-allergen food source [14].

Figure 19–11

Quinoa is a high-protein pseudo grain that can be consumed as a hot dish or cold, as shown here, with beans, avocado, tomatoes, corn, and parsley. (Bonchan/Shutterstock)

in the United States to describe this wheat gluten food; however, each culture has a name for this food. Seitan can mimic the taste of meat [35]. From a protein perspective, three ounces can contain 20 grams [35] or between one-third and one-half of daily protein needs depending on the individual. Seitan can be purchased in the marketplace or made in the kitchen (**Figure 19–12**).

SEEDS

More traditionally, seeds such as sunflower and pumpkin seeds have been consumed as a snack food or an extra crunch on a salad or other kind of dish. In some cultures, such as Vietnamese, melon seeds are also commonly consumed much like sunflower seeds. Flaxseed, chia, and hemp seeds have gained popularity in the marketplace for their protein content as well as other nutrients. There are many seeds used for food, but sunflower, pumpkin, flax, chia, hemp, and sesame seeds will be discussed here.

Sunflower Seeds

Sunflower seeds (*Helianthus annuus*) can be enjoyed salted and still in the shell (**Figure 19–13**). It is native to North American and has likely been used for food

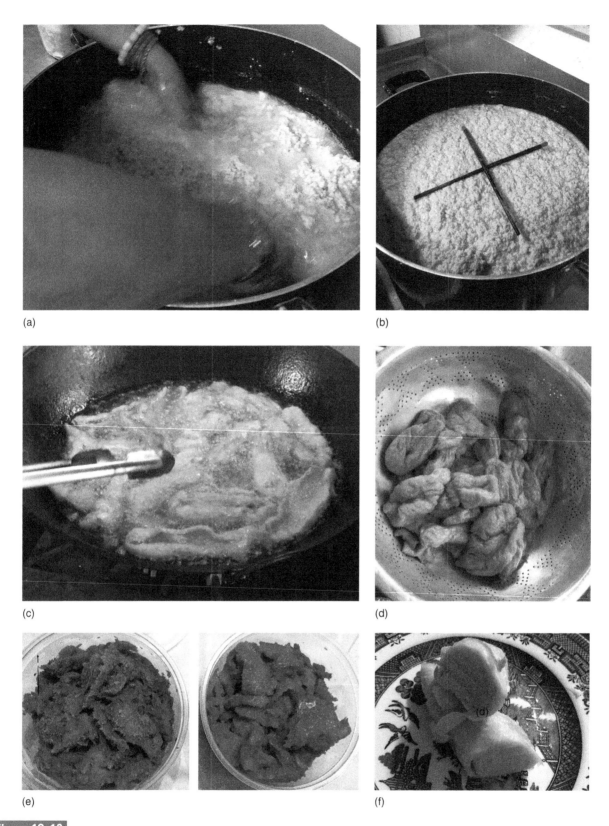

(a)

(b)

(c)

(d)

(e)

(f)

Figure 19–12

Seitan is a high-protein food made from gluten. It may be prepared or purchased. (a) Using high-protein wheat flour or gluten prepare a dough using water or other flavored liquids. Once a firm dough is mixed, manipulate under water to rinse out the starch. (b) Allow the gluten to rest for several hours. (c) Seitan can be cut into bite-size pieces or rolled into a baguette shape before frying (shown here) or boiling. (d) Fried seitan, ready to enjoy, is shown here. (e) Several seasoning options are possible for cooked seitan. (f) Ready-prepared seitan "sausages" are also available for purchase as shown here. (© Amanda Frye)

UP CLOSE
BURGERS AND BBQ

Burgers and BBQ for many are an American tradition. For vegans and vegetarians, some very good plant-based burgers and BBQ are now available.

Impossible Burger

The impossible burger, with its pink color in the raw state, debuted in New York in 2016. It is now offered in restaurants all across the United States. Gas chromatography/mass spectrometry was initially used to analyze the taste and aroma of ground beef. Heme was determined to be an essential component. Next, soy-root nodules were found to have a plant-based similar compound to heme. A small piece of the soy DNA was inserted into standard yeast strains [9]. The yeasts produce the red heme that is used in the impossible burger. Other ingredients include textured wheat protein, coconut oil, potato protein, flavors, yeast extract, salt, soy protein isolate, konjac gum, and xanthan gum [9]. Reviews of this impossible burger indicate its flavor and other characteristics compare very favorably with beef burgers.

Beyond Burger

The beyond burger has also captured the distinctive color of beef in their burgers, crumbles, and other meat analog products. This burger is composed of predominately pea protein isolate with beet juice for the red color. Other ingredients include vegetable oils, yeast extract, plant fiber, binders, and flavoring [9].

Classic Burger

The classic burger by Upton's Natural is made from vegan meat analogs. Its ingredients include seitan (wheat gluten), tofu, and eggplant. The seitan offers protein and a meat-type mouthfeel [9].

BBQ

With only about 2 grams of protein per serving (or essentially a ⅓ ounce protein equivalent), jackfruit is not a particularly significant source of protein. However, this large fruit (up to 100 pounds) offers a stringy texture that lends itself well to plant-based meat substitutes. The Upton's Natural company offers BBQ, Chili Lime Carnitas, and Thai Curry jackfruit along with additional options. Legume and pulse side dishes can increase the protein content of a jackfruit BBQ meal [8]. ∎

Figure 19–13

Sunflower seeds are high in protein. They can be enjoyed as a snack, or purchased as a seed without the shell to be used as recipe ingredient. (Bergamont/Shutterstock)

as early as 900 B.C. Native Americans used it as an energy source. In the 1950s, it became an important crop in North Dakota and Minnesota. Sunflower seeds are used for oils with high-polyunsaturated oils.

Sunflower seeds are a popular snack food offering a mild taste and nutty texture. They are high in protein, fiber, iron, potassium, and vitamin E. Sunflower seeds can be used as a crunchy topping on salads, yogurt, or coating for other foods. They may also be incorporated into stir-fry vegetables, used in baked goods, and consumed with breakfast cereal. A sunflower butter, similar to peanut butter, is also available [29].

Pumpkin Seeds

Pumpkin seeds can be roasted at home for a snack after carving a pumpkin. Pumpkin seeds (also called pepitas) are popular in Mexican cuisines for moles, or in Indian cuisine used with garam masala spice blend [29]. Other squash seeds may also be roasted and consumed.

Flax Seeds

Flax (*Linum usitatissimum*) was cultivated as far back at 10,000 years ago in Mesopotamia. Flax can be brown or yellow. Like other seeds, it is also used for seed oil (see Chapter 8 for more on oil processing). Flaxseed oil is high in polyunsaturated fats and alpha linoleic oil, an omega-3 fatty acid. The seed is high in protein, fiber, folate, B_6, and several minerals.

Flaxseed has a mild nutty flavor and crunchy texture. It, like many other seeds, can be used in a wide variety of foods. It can be purchased whole, milled, roasted, or as a flour. In food products, it can be used as a replacer for guar gum that helps to provide texture in some food products [29].

Chia Seeds

Chia seed (*Salvia hispanica)* is part of the sage family. It is native to Mexico and Central America. Around 2,000 years ago chia seeds provided energy for the Incan, Mayan, and Aztec cultures. The seeds may be a mottled brown, gray, black, or white (Figure 12–33). It can be used whole, ground, or as a flour. Chia seeds offer a slightly nutty taste. They contain a high level of omega-3 fatty acids, and are rich in protein, fiber, antioxidants, vitamins, and minerals.

When chia seeds are soaked in a liquid, a gel is created with the seeds suspended. In 10 minutes chia seeds can swell to 12 times their weight in a liquid. This gelatinous or mucilaginous characteristic of chia seeds in a liquid can make this mixture an alternative to eggs or oils in salad dressings, porridges, or puddings. Chia seed beverages and milk substitute can be made from this small seed. It can also be made into a spread or nut butter. Like many other seeds it can be incorporated into a wide variety of dishes, including baked goods, either as a seed or as a flour [29].

Hemp Seeds

Hemp plants have been used for food, fiber, and fuel for more than 5,000 years in Asia and Europe [29]. Although hemp and marijuana come from the same species of plant, they are different varieties. Furthermore, hemp seeds have no "drug" properties with none of the psychoactive substances found in marijuana.

Hemp seeds are high in protein and both omega-3 and omega-6 fatty acids along with other important vitamins and minerals. These seeds have a nutty flavor with similarities to sunflower seeds. They may be used raw, toasted, or as a recipe ingredient in salads, smoothies, baked goods, or other recipes. Flour, hemp milk substitute, and hemp seed butter can be made from hemp seeds [29].

Sesame Seeds

Sesame seeds are a well-recognized decoration on hamburger buns. These seeds, however, like other seeds, can be used in a variety of ways, including as sesame seed oil. Sesame seeds may be white, yellow, brown, or black. They offer a delicate nutty flavor and crunch when toasted, and are a valued ingredient in Asian, Middle Eastern, and Mediterranean cuisines [29].

Sesame seeds are the key ingredient to tahini, one of the ingredients used when making hummus [15]. Tahini is made with unhulled, hulled, or toasted sesame seeds. Sesame seeds are first soaked in water for about a day. They are then crushed to separate the bran from the kernels. Next, they are soaked in saltwater to further separate the seeds from the skin. Roasting at 350°F (177°C) usually follows, although tahini may be made from raw seeds. Grinding the seeds into an oily paste is the final step in making tahini. It is rich in vitamins, minerals, and omega-3 and omega-6 fatty acids (see Chapter 8 for a discussion of fats in food).

NUTS

Nuts have historically been well recognized as an excellent protein source. They also contain various other nutrients, including polyunsaturated fats. Peanuts, as well as some of the seeds, can become rancid because of their high fat content. Rancidity is characterized by off-flavors and odors, thus making the rancid food undesirable. Chapter 8 discussed factors associated with rancidity and its prevention.

Peanuts are used within our diets like a nut, and will therefore be discussed with the tree nuts even though botanically they are legumes. California grows nearly 90 percent of the tree nuts used in the United States [18]. Peanuts are grown predominately in the southern United States.

Tree Nuts

Many types of tree nuts grow throughout the world (**Figure 19–14**). They are called tree nuts because they grow in trees. These nuts can be eaten whole, chopped, or roasted. Tree nuts can also be processed into flours, nut butters, or nut milk substitute. Almond milk substitute has become one of the most popular plant-based milks in the marketplace, exceeding the sale of soy milk substitute. A vegan gelato is available that is made from cashews [7].

Types. There are many different tree nuts grown. Relatively popular and high-protein tree nuts are discussed here.

Almonds. Almonds are among the most popular of the tree nuts. California produces more than 80 percent of the world's almonds [18]. Almonds are harvested by shaking the trees and collecting the nuts. Almonds have a tough outer hull covering a hard shell. The hull and shell are removed through vibration and rollers. Nutritionally, almonds offer a high level of polyphenols, which are predominately tannins and flavonoids [3]. They are also high in protein, vitamin E, and calcium, in addition to having a favorable fatty acid profile.

Brazil Nuts. Grown in the Amazon and collected wild, Brazil nuts are consumed raw, roasted, and salted. Interestingly, a by-product of the Brazil nut oil is used in hair-care products [5].

Cashews. Cashews are believed to have originated in Brazil. They are grown in Sri Lanka, India, Tanzania, Mozambique, Brazil, and Venezuela. Cashews are a valuable tree nut with only about 10 pounds produced per tree per year [5]. They must be steamed or roasted before consumption to destroy the naturally present toxic resin urushiol.

Hazelnuts. Hazelnuts are currently grown in Oregon, Turkey, Spain, and Italy. They are believed to have originated in Asia. They are also known as filberts, and are

Figure 19–14

There are many different tree nuts that are high in protein: (a) almonds, (b) Brazil, (c) cashews, (d) hazelnuts, (e) macadamias, (f) pecans, (g) pine nuts, (h) pistachios, and (i) English walnuts. They can be used as a nut, or as paste, flour, or milk. (Richard Embery/Pearson Education)

often used in chocolate candies [5]. They are also a key ingredient in Nutella spread, but the protein contribution of this product is less than half that of peanut butter. Hazelnuts have been associated with improving plasma lipid profiles of those consuming a hazelnut-rich diet [24, 25].

Macadamias. Macadamia nuts originated in Australia [5]. Within the United States, Hawaii is a major producer. These nuts are predominately consumed as snacks. As compared to other nuts, macadamias are lower in protein.

Pecans. These tree nuts are native to North America. Pecans are grown in the southeast (Georgia, New Mexico, and Texas), thus the popularity of pecan dishes in the southern United States [5]. Pecans contain multiple vitamins and minerals. One ounce of these pecans provide about 10 percent of the daily value for fiber [24].

Pine Nuts. Pine nuts are also called pignoli and often used in Italian, Greek, and Spanish cuisines. They are a key ingredient in pesto. Pine nuts are gathered from pine trees in the Mediterranean and dried [5].

Pistachios. These green tree nuts most likely originated in the Middle East. They are grown in California, Iran, and Turkey. Pistachios, unlike other nuts, require little to no processing. They dry naturally and crack on their own [5]. Like some of the other tree nuts, the consumption of pistachios has been associated with more favorable cholesterol levels [24].

Walnuts. California also produces about 99 percent of the English walnuts grown in the United States. English walnuts, black walnuts, and white walnuts are three common varieties [5]. More than half the crop is exported [18]. Walnuts are harvested by shaking trees once the green outer husk begins to split. Postharvest, the hulls are removed and, if desired, the shells are also removed. Walnuts are usually air dried to a moisture level of 8 percent to reduce deterioration. Walnuts are also believed to have a favorable impact on heart health [24, 26].

Tree Nut Processing. Many of the tree nuts are mechanically shaken from the trees for harvest (**Figure 19–15**). Most tree nuts are dried before cracking, followed by separation by size, removal of the shells or shell fragments, and then packaging. Some nuts are moistened and then dried later to prevent the nut meat from breaking. Tree nuts, consumed as snacks, is a high-value market, but tree nuts are also used to produce edible oils or nut butters. The nut snacks are prepared by oil cooking, dry roasting, or simply drying. The nut shells are a by-product that can be made into charcoal or used for cleaning surfaces when sand would be too gritty [5, 18].

Peanuts

Unlike tree nuts, peanuts grow underground (**Figure 19–16**). As a legume, they are part of the *Leguminosae* plant family. Peanuts are believed to have originated in South America. Dr. George Washington Carver is credited as the father of the peanut industry in the United States because of his research and promotion of the rotation of peanuts with cotton crops. Like other legumes, peanuts enrich the nitrogen in the soil. In the United States, the southern states, the Carolinas, Virginia, Texas, Georgia, Alabama, Mississippi, Oklahoma, New Mexico, and Florida are leading producers. Of the nuts, peanuts are the most popular in the United States (Figure 19–2). Peanuts are consumed in 73 percent of households [31].

Types. There four varieties of peanuts: Virginia, runner, Spanish, and Valencia. The Virginia peanuts are known as cocktail nuts. The runner peanuts are popular for use in peanut butter. Spanish peanuts are small with a reddish skin. They are often used in peanut candies, snacks, and peanut butter. Valencia are usually served roasted in the shell or boiled. There are several nuts per shell.

Harvesting, Processing, and Peanut Butter. Peanuts are planted in the spring, and then harvested in the fall. A digger-shaker uproots the plants. Shells and other foreign materials are then removed from the peanuts before shipping to a processor [16].

To make peanut butter, the peanuts are dry roasted in ovens. The peanuts are rapidly cooled to stop cooking and reduce the oil loss from the skins. Blanching with heat or water follows to loosen and crack skins to facilitate removal. A final sorting for color and potential imperfections occurs before grinding the nuts. Typically, the nuts are first ground coarsely with salt, then ground to a fine consistency. During the grinding process, vegetable oil and sugar

(a)

(b)

(c)

Figure 19–15

Tree nuts grow in trees: (a) almonds (Nito500/123RF), (b) cashews (Bannerwega/123RF), and (c) pecans. (Viktoriya Field/Shutterstock)

(a)

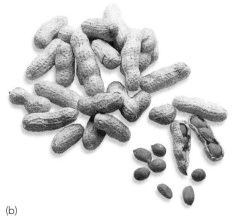
(b)

Figure 19–16

Peanuts are a legume, even though we use them as a nut in our diets. (a) A peanut plant dug from the ground shows the peanuts that grow underground. ((Wilaiwanphoto/123RF)) (b) Peanuts in and out of the shell are pictured here.   (Richard Embery/Pearson Education)

may be added for flavor and to stabilize the consistency of the peanut butter. The peanut butter may be heated again during this phase to improve food safety. To produce chunky peanut butters, peanut pieces are added into the smooth peanut butter or the grinding is performed to allow for chunky nuts. As a final step, the peanut butter is cooled and packaged [16]. Similar processes are used in the production of other nut butters such as almond and cashew.

Peanut butter, as discussed with regard to tree nuts, may also be made into oil, flour, and other products. Peanut oil is known for having a high smoke point, and therefore it is a good choice for frying applications (see Chapter 8).

Nutrition. Peanuts provide protein, are an excellent source of niacin, and are a good source of folate, vitamin E, and fiber [21, 25]. Peanuts also include multiple functional ingredients that may reduce cardiovascular disease, cancer, and diabetes [30]. Roasted peanuts

with the skins are higher in total phenolics as compared to blueberries, red wine, tea, and cocoa milk. One of the types of phenolic compounds found in roasted peanuts is resveratrol. Roasted peanuts are an important food source of resveratrol after red wine, red grape juice, and dark chocolate [30].

SEAWEED, ALGAE, AND DUCKWEED

Seaweed has been consumed in Japanese, Chinese, and Korean cultures for thousands of years (**Figure 19–17**). Europeans and Canadians living in coastal areas have used seaweed as part of their diet for hundreds of years. American consumption of sea plants is limited. Americans eat seaweeds when consuming nori-wrapped sushi rolls, miso soup, or most predominately as an ingredient in processed foods [33].

(a)

(b)

Figure 19–17

Seaweeds provide protein and other nutrients. (a) Green seaweed,   (JIANG HONGYAN/Shutterstock) (b) brown seaweed.
(Antoni halim/Shutterstock)

Many varieties of seaweed, algae, and duckweed are high in protein and rich in multiple vitamins and minerals [33]. Algae are a diverse group of predominately aquatic plants. They generate more oxygen than other plants, and by utilizing solar energy they convert carbon dioxide into their food. Thus, algae play a role in removing excess carbon dioxide from the environment [35]. Collectively, these water and sea vegetables are considered to be a sustainable food source. Researchers in Maine, Oregon, and other coastal areas are further researching these sea plants already being harvested and cultivated [32, 34].

Seaweed and Macroalgae

Macroalgae are visible to the eye and include seaweed as well as other multicellular algae. They grow in lakes, rivers, ponds, and oceans. Macroalgae are classified as brown, red, and green algae. Among seaweeds, the red seaweeds are especially high in protein, and although called "red," they may be purple, bluish, or brownish red in color [33].

Nori.   Nori, commonly used to wrap sushi rolls, is a red seaweed species called *Porphyra*. Its protein content is comparable to sunflower seeds with an amino acid profile similar to legumes. Unlike other plant foods, it contains vitamin B_{12}, and also the EPA omega-3 fatty acid commonly found in seafood [35]. Nori can also be found in untoasted dry sheets, as a snack made from toasted nori (**Figure 19–18**), or it can be sprinkled onto soup and noodle dishes.

Dulse.   Another type of red seaweed is known as dulse. It is of the seaweed species *Palmaria palmata* [35]. Dulse is not as high in protein as nori, but it is rich in multiple vitamins and has a very high level of the EPA omega-3 fatty acid [35]. Different counties around the world use dulse in different ways. In Iceland, it is consumed as a dried snack and added to salads, bread, and curds. Dulse in the form of seafood parsley is used to season and add a salty flavor to foods in Nova Scotia. In Wales, it is served as a purée to serve with toast and other foods, or rolled in oatmeal and fried [35]. A rapidly growing strain of dulse at the Oregon State University tastes like bacon when fried and has been developed for use in peanut brittle and a rice cracker [32].

Kelp.   Kelp is brown seaweed that is widely consumed in some cultures [33]. A type of kelp called kombu is used in miso soup. Wakame, another brown seaweed, is also often used in miso soup (**Figure 19–19**).

Seaweed in Processed Foods.   The **hydrocolloids** called carrageenan, agar, and alginate are used in processed foods [33]. They are made from red and brown seaweed. The function of these hydrocolloids is to thicken, stabilize, or suspend foods. They have been used since the 1600s in foods.

Agar and carrageenan may be used for a plant-based gelatin alternative (see Chapter 21). Carrageenan is often used in chocolate, ice cream, pudding, whipped cream products, yogurt, and meat products such as deli meats. Agar is used in breads, processed cheese, mayonnaise, icing, and frozen dairy products. Alginate is found in salad dressings, gravies, puddings, and pie fillings [33].

Microalgae

There are thousands of varieties of microalgae. Microalgae are single-celled microorganisms visible when viewed through a microscope. When millions are growing together in what is commonly called an algae bloom, they can be seen with the naked eye [35]. Not all algae may be consumed. Those algae that can serve as a source of food will be discussed here.

Figure 19–18

Nori is often used to wrap sushi, but it can also be dried and used as a snack or in other types of dishes. (Jeehyun/Shutterstock)

Figure 19–19

Miso soup includes seaweed. This soup also has sesame seeds. (Yasuhiro Amano/123RF)

Microalgae are especially high in protein. They also contain both DHA and EPA omega-3 fatty acids that can otherwise be lacking in vegan and vegetarian diets.

Types. Three types of microalgae—*Dunaliella*, *Chlorella*, and *Arthrospira*—have been most often used for food. *Dunaliella* are a saltwater microalgae. They are green, high in protein, and the richest source of beta-carotene on the planet. They are typically used as powders mixed into beverages. *Chlorella* is a freshwater microalgae. They are also high in protein in the dried form. At this time they are used as powders and extracts to be added to foods. Finally, *Arthrospira* (also called *Spirulina)* grows in salty lakes and ponds. It is blue-green, high in protein, and similarly used as powders and liquid extracts [35].

Use in Foods. Currently, the microalgae are not often used in foods. One of the challenges with using microalgae is that they often taste fishy and are green. However, a South Korean company has *Chlorella* noodles, and Malaysian and Italian manufacturers have *Spirulina* noodles and pastas. A company in Austin, Texas, has produced cold-pressed hemp milk substitute with blue-green algae included [35]. The Naked Juice company has a beverage with spirulina and the seaweed dulse as ingredients [2].

Duckweed

Duckweeds grow rapidly in ponds and slow-moving water. A member of the duckweed family called water lentils is also part of this water-plant group. Duckweeds are the smallest flowering plant found in the world. They are high in protein and provide additional vitamins and minerals. They are also considered to be beneficial for the environment [35]. Although not often consumed in much of the world, they have been a food in Laos, Thailand, Vietnam, and Africa for centuries.

Two products, relatively new in the marketplace are *Lentein plus* and *Mankai*. Lentein plus is made from water lentils and is sold as a green powder that can be added to beverages and a variety of other foods. It was developed in Florida. Mankai is produced in Israel from duckweed. It can be obtained fresh or dried and then used in bakery products, beverages, pasta, or sprinkled on salads.

INSECTS

Insects are a part of the traditional diets of about 2 billion people. The consumption of insects is called entomophagy. More than 1,900 species are believed to be used as food (**Figure 19–20**). Around the world, the most commonly consumed insects are beetles (Coleoptera); caterpillars (Lepidoptera); bees, wasps, and ants (Hymenoptera); grasshoppers, locusts, and crickets (Orthoptera); cicadas, leafhoppers, planthoppers, scale insects, and true bugs (Hemiptera); termites (Isoptera); dragonflies (Odonata); flies (Diptera); and other insect orders [13].

Insects are distinguished by their notched body with three parts—head, thorax, and abdomen. They have an exoskeleton, are cold-blooded, and reproduce quickly. Insects can undergo metamorphosis to adapt to seasons. They are found in most environments.

Insects are consumed in the African continent, especially caterpillars during the rainy season when they offer important dietary protein. In Asia, as many as 200 different species of insects are consumed. Red palm weevils are a delicacy in some areas. The insects may live and be gathered from aquatic, ground

Figure 19–20

A platter of cicadas ready to be enjoyed. (Wxin/123rf)

(such as crickets) or tree, bush, and shrub (grasshoppers) habitats. Availability varies by the season and therefore influences the choice of insect for the diet. Similarly, in Latin America, a wide variety of insects are consumed depending on the time of year and location [13]. Notably, insects in the tropics are larger, tend to congregate in large groups, and are available year round. These factors may suggest why insects are consumed more in temperate regions.

The domestication of plants and animals in history may offer a perspective on the reasons that Western cultures usually do not eat insects, and furthermore may find insects disgusting. From an agricultural view, insects can be pests. As cultures evolved, the "gathering" of food, including insects, may also have been viewed as more primitive and therefore unappealing. Native Americans, in what is now Utah, were known to eat grasshoppers, locusts, and crickets. The Western aversion of insects as a food and valuable protein in the diet has at times had unfortunate consequences when Westerners have provided aid, or traveled in Africa and Latin America and discouraged insect consumption. Without alternative protein sources, people in these areas then lacked adequate dietary protein.

How Are Insects Consumed?

Insects may be consumed whole; ground or as a paste; or as an extract of protein, fat, or chitin (the exoskeleton composed of polysaccharides) for use in foods. When consumed whole, the legs and wings are often removed before roasting, frying, or boiling (**Figure 19–21**). When used ground or as a paste, it can be used as a flour or powder to add to other foods and thereby increase the protein content of the food. To make powder, the insect is dried and ground. Because of expense, protein extraction of insects in not often done at this time [13].

Cricket powder is being produced and sold in protein bars, protein shakes, and tortilla chips in the United States and elsewhere. About 25 companies in the United States and Canada are producing products with cricket powder from farm-raised crickets [19]. Several cookbooks are available with recipes featuring insects.

Figure 19–21

Crickets being eaten with a dipping sauce. (Hasloo Group Production Studio/Shutterstock)

Whole insects such as grasshoppers, crickets, mealworms, and ants can be seasoned with curry, garlic, sriracha, or other choices of your preference. In 2017, the Seattle Mariners Baseball team added chili-lime salted grasshoppers to their ballpark menu offerings [22].

Why Use Insects for Food?

Many insects are a high-protein, low-fat, renewable, and sustainable food source that are also high in other vitamins and minerals. As the world population grows, 9 billion forecasted in 2050, a wider choice of foods is anticipated to be necessary to feed the world. Many people in the world currently eat insects by choice. Cultures have embraced this food choice for thousands of years, and thus, insects can be enjoyed like many other foods [13].

From a sustainability perspective, insects have high-feed conversion efficiency. Thus compared to meat, seafood, and poultry, it takes little feed to produce insects for consumption on a comparative basis. Insects emit fewer greenhouse gases and produce less ammonia than livestock. Insects can also be beneficial in the environment through pollination, waste biodegradation or the clean up of dead organic matter, and the control of other harmful pests [13].

STUDY QUESTIONS

Consumption Trends

1. Discuss the trends in the legume, peanut, and nut consumption using USDA data.

2. Identify demographic trends and other trends that may change the consumption of alternative proteins in the future.

Nutrition

3. Develop a menu using only alternative proteins that would include recommended protein amounts based on a reference 2,000 calorie adult diet.

4. Discuss implications of a vegan diet with regard to nutritional recommendations for (a) protein, (b) fatty acids, (c) vitamins, and (d) minerals.

Vegetarian Diets

5. Divide into groups, one group to debate that all of the classifications are vegetarians and a second group to debate that not all of the classifications are vegetarians.

6. Identify multiple reasons that individuals are vegetarians or consuming red meats, poultry, and seafood less frequently.

Legumes and Pulses

7. Define (a) legumes and (b) pulses, then compare and contrast.

8. Discuss several benefits to the use and consumption of legumes and pulses.

9. Describe how tofu and hummus are made.

10. Describe several (a) soy products and (b) pulses.

11. Explain how to prepare dried beans.

12. Identify the pros and cons of using dried beans as compared to canned beans.

Grains

13. Identify and describe grains that are comparatively high in protein.

14. Identify the protein source in seitan.

Seeds

15. Identify and describe several seeds that may be used as alternative proteins.

16. Explain how seeds may be incorporated into the diet either as seeds or in other forms.

Nuts

17. Botanically speaking, identify the differences between peanuts and tree nuts.

18. Identify and describe several nuts that may be used as alternative proteins.

19. Explain ways nuts may be incorporated into the diet.

20. Describe how peanut butter is made.

Seaweed, Algae, and Duckweed

21. Define macro- and microalgae.

22. Describe different kinds of seaweeds and how they are used in food.

23. Identify potential advantages to using seaweeds and algae as alternative proteins.

24. Explain some nutritional benefits to the consumption of microalgae.

25. Discuss food uses for duckweed.

Insects

26. Identify areas in the world where insects are used as a protein source.

27. Discuss reasons that the consumption of insects can be a valuable protein source today and in the future.

28. Explain several ways that insects can be consumed either as intact insects or as insect-based products.

20

Fruits and Fruit Preparation

What are fruits? To answer this question, we might begin by saying that all fruits are produced from flowers and are the ripened **ovaries** and adjacent tissues of plants. In this respect, from a botanical point of view, some foods used as vegetables, nuts, or grains are fruits of the plants from which they were harvested. However, the foods usually designated and used as fruits in food preparation have some common characteristics in addition to the botanical similarity—they are fleshy or pulpy, often juicy, and usually sweet, with fragrant, aromatic flavors.

Thus, the definition of fruits according to botanical characteristics does not always agree with the classification of common usage. Several fleshy botanical fruits, including tomatoes and squash, are not sweet and are used as vegetables. Cereal grains, nuts, and legumes are dry fruits (not fleshy) and have been classified into separate groups for practical use. Rhubarb, which is not a fruit in the botanical sense, is often used as a fruit in meal preparation.

Fruits, like vegetables, are valued for the color, flavor, texture, and valuable nutrition they bring to our menus. Many, although not all fruits, offer sweetness and therefore can provide a nutritious and sweet snack or dessert. Fruits are an important part of our daily intake because of their nutritional merit.

In this chapter, the following topics will be discussed:

- Consumption trends and nutrition
- Types of fruit
- Selection of fresh fruit
- Changes during ripening
- Purchasing
- Storage of fruits
- Preparation
- Cooking with fruits

CONSUMPTION TRENDS AND NUTRITION

Consumption Trends

According to U.S. loss-adjusted food availability data, Americans consume only 0.8 cups of fruit per day [45]. In 2016, 117 pounds of fruit (adjusted for loss) were available annually per capita as compared to 106 pounds in 1970 [45]. The top five fruits consumed in descending order are oranges, apples, bananas, grapes, and watermelon [44] (**Figure 20–1**). Americans are increasingly choosing fresh fruit, instead of processed fruits, or fruit juices [24] (**Figure 20–2**).

Although food availability data from the U.S. Department of Agriculture (USDA) reveal a modest increase in fruit availability over the years, fruit consumption is nevertheless below recommendations by the U.S. Dietary Guidelines for all age groups except children under eight years and younger [46] (**Figure 20–3**). Individualized recommendations for fruit and other food intake can be found at http://www.choosemyplate.gov.

Nutritive Value

Two cups of fruit each day are recommended for those consuming a reference 2,000-calorie diet in the 2010 Dietary Guidelines for Americans [46]. Fruits provide several important nutrients in our diet, and along with vegetables (see Chapters 18 and 19), are associated with a reduced risk for several chronic illnesses. In 2003, the U.S. Food and Drug Administration (FDA) issued a dietary guidance statement that may be used in product labels and other print materials. This statement is, "Diets rich in fruits and vegetables may reduce the risk of some types of cancers and other chronic diseases" [47].

The handling practices, methods of processing, storage temperatures, and length of storage of fruits may result in the loss of vitamin values. With regard to fresh versus frozen produce, researchers examining the retention of ascorbic acid, riboflavin, α-tocopherol, and β-carotene in strawberries, blueberries, and selected vegetables found the vitamin content of frozen fruits and vegetables was comparable or at times higher than the fresh counterparts [6]. Another group of researchers concluded for blueberries, strawberries, and selected vegetables that for vitamin C, provitamin A, and total folate there were no significant differences between fresh-stored and frozen produce [23]. Furthermore, if these fruits and vegetables are stored under refrigeration for five days after purchase, the nutrient content was more frequently higher in the frozen than the fresh.

Fruit Availability: 2015

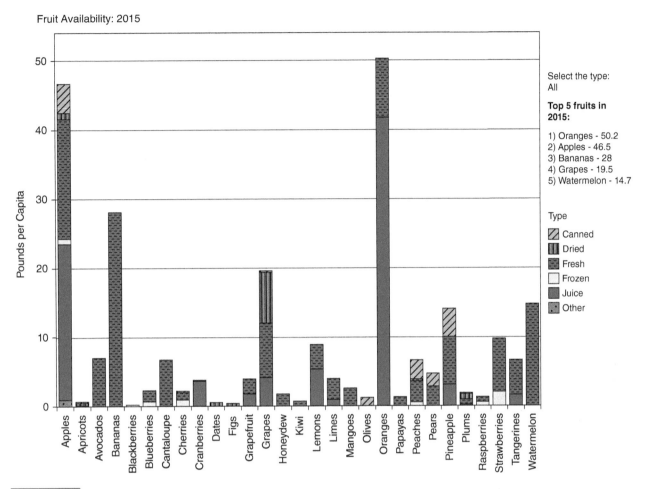

Figure 20–1

This bar chart provides data from the USDA Economic Research Service showing food availability data. Oranges and apples are the two most frequently used fruits. Oranges are predominately consumed as juice, whereas apples are consumed most often fresh or as juice. (USDA/ERS)

Pounds Available per Capita

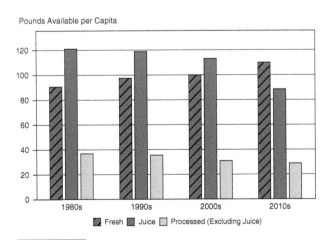

Figure 20–2

Consumers are favoring more fresh fruit than other purchase forms such as juice or processed (canned, frozen, or other). (USDA/ERS)

Ripeness and the method of ripening also influence the vitamin content of fruits. For example, the vitamin C content of bananas is greatest in fully ripe fruits, although the total amount present is relatively small. Vine-ripened tomatoes also have a higher vitamin C value than tomatoes picked green and ripened off the vine (see Chapter 18).

Key nutrients found in fruits are provided in **Table 20–1**. The composition and vitamin content of fruits and fruit juices may be found from the USDA Nutrient Data Laboratory online as explained in Appendix C.

TYPES OF FRUITS

Fleshy fruits may be classified as simple, aggregate, or multiple, depending on the number of ovaries and flowers from which the fruit develops. *Simple fleshy fruits* develop from a single ovary in one flower and include citrus fruits, drupes, and pomes. Oranges, grapefruit, lemons, and limes are examples of citrus fruits (**Figure 20–4**). Drupes are fruits in which a stone or pit encloses the seed and include apricots,

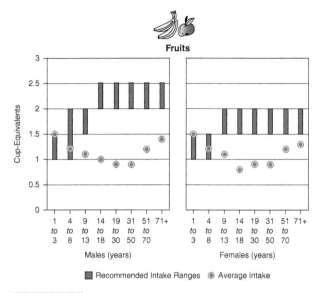

Fruits

Figure 20-3

Males and females at age nine and older consume less than the recommended servings of fruits. The orange dots represent the typical number of cups consumed at the ages listed. The blue bar is the recommended number of cups (or cup equivalents) of fruits that are recommended on a daily basis depending on individual needs at each age. (USDA)

cherries, peaches, and plums. Pomes are fruits that have a core. Apples and pears are pomes. *Aggregate fruits* develop from several ovaries in one flower and include raspberries, strawberries, and blackberries.

Pineapple and figs are examples of *multiple fruits* that have developed from a cluster of several flowers.

Although fruit is the focus of this chapter, other parts of plants that produce fruits also have culinary uses. Consider, for example, stuffed grape leaves in the Mediterranean dish *dolma*. Banana leaves are also edible, and can be used to wrap or steam foods in many different cultures.

SELECTION OF FRESH FRUITS

An abundance of fresh fruits is available in U.S. markets year-round. In making selections, the consumer should look for signs of good quality, which are generally evident from the external appearance of the product. These signs include the proper stage of ripeness, good color, freedom from insect damage, and the absence of bruises, skin punctures, and decay. Quality may be better and prices lower when fruit is in season in the local area. In any case, when the fruit harvest is plentiful, the prices are lowest. **Table 20-2** summarizes some points to consider in selecting various fruits.

Apples

Apples are among the most widely used fruits. They rank second in U.S. per capita fruit consumption behind citrus fruits. Apples are grown on trees in most parts of the United States in many varieties that differ in

Table 20-1
NUTRIENTS FOUND IN FRUITS

Nutrient	Fruit Sources and Additional Notations
Carbohydrates	The sources of calories found in fruits are carbohydrates present predominately as sugar (often fructose).
Fat	Few fruits contain fats. Coconut (35 percent fat) and avocado (17 percent fat) are exceptions.
Vitamin C	Citrus fruits are a reliable source of vitamin C. Tomatoes (botanically a fruit), strawberries, cantaloupe, kiwi, and guava are additional fruits high in Vitamin C.
Vitamin A	Apricots, cantaloupe, mangoes, and persimmons all contain appreciable amounts of vitamin A value. Nectarines, peaches, star fruit, grapefruit, guavas, mandarin oranges, plantains, plums, and watermelon are examples of other fruits that contain vitamin A, although to a lesser amount than those previously noted.
Calcium and Iron	Fruits are not generally considered excellent sources of these minerals. However, blackberries, raspberries, strawberries, dried apricots, prunes, dates, and figs contribute iron to the diet. Of the fruits available year-round, oranges, grapefruit, and figs provide a fair source of calcium.
Fiber	Whole fresh fruits are better sources of fiber than other forms. For example, a whole apple, with peel, has 2 grams of fiber. One-half cup of applesauce provides 0.65 gram of fiber, and ¾ cup of apple juice supplies only 0.25 gram of fiber [32].
Phytochemicals and Antioxidants	Along with vegetables, fruits appear to provide a protective effect against various types of cancer when consumed in recommended amounts [33, 51]. Phytochemicals, present in many fruits and vegetables, have been identified as being health protective [51]. Both watermelon and tomatoes are rich in the phytochemical lycopene. It is a red pigment with antioxidant properties [2]. Blueberries are rich in anthocyanins, another natural pigment, that also functions as an antioxidant [27].

characteristics and seasonal availability. However, six states—Washington, New York, Michigan, California, Pennsylvania, and Virginia—account for more than 85 percent of the U.S. apple crop. Washington State is the leading producer of apples. Controlled-atmosphere storage (discussed later in this chapter) has lengthened their seasons of availability. According to the U.S. Apple Association, the top 10 varieties sold in the United States are Gala, Red Delicious, Fuji, Granny Smith, Honeycrisp, Golden Delicious, McIntosh, Pink Lady®, Braeburn, and Jazz®.

Apples have many culinary uses. They may be served fresh in salads or as desserts and cooked in sauces, pies, and cobblers. Varieties differ in their suitability for being cooked or eaten fresh. **Table 20–3** gives some suggestions for use, and **Figure 20–5** shows several different varieties of apples.

Avocados

The bland flavor and smooth texture of avocados blend well with many foods including avocado toast, salads, and guacamole. Avocados are unique fruits in that they contain about 17 percent fat. Avocados are available all year, grown in California, Florida, and other countries, such as Mexico and Chile [30]. There are nearly 500 different kinds of avocados. The Hass avocado is most commonly available in the United States and accounts for 95 percent of the market.

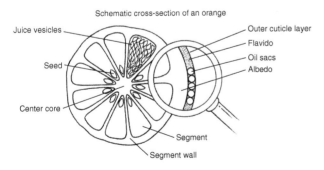

Figure 20–4

A cross section of an orange shows the various parts of the fruit. (Reprinted from Matthews, R. F., and Braddock, R. J. Recovery and applications of essential oils from oranges. *Food Technology*, 41(1), 57. 1987. Copyright by Institute of Food Technologists)

Figure 20–5

Varieties of apples. (Richard Embery/Pearson Education)

Table 20–2
SELECTION OF FRESH FRUITS

Quality Characteristics to Look for During Selection

Fruits

Apple	Firm, crisp, well colored; mature when picked; varieties vary widely in eating and cooking characteristics (see Table 20–3)
Apricot	Plump, firm, golden yellow; yield to gentle skin pressure when ripe
Avocado	Shape and size vary with variety; may have rough or smooth skin but no dark, sunken spots; yield to gentle skin pressure when ripened and ready for use
Banana	Shipped green and ripened as needed at 60–65°F (16–18°C); refrigerate only after ripened; firm, yellow, free from bruises
Blueberry	Dark blue, silvery bloom, plump, firm, uniform size; discard green berries
Cherry	Very delicate; handle carefully; fresh, firm, juicy, well matured, well colored
Citrus	Firm, well shaped, heavy for size, reasonably smooth-textured skin. Consider variety with intended use
Cranberry	Plump, firm, deep red to red-maroon color
Dates	Select plumb, glossy fruit; consume fresh or dried
Figs	Moist, small, pear-shaped seeded fruit; Calimyrna, mission, white adriatic, and kodota varieties
Grape	Well colored, plump, firmly attached to stem
Guava	Skin color green to yellow, depending on variety; flesh white to deep pink; round, firm, but yielding to slight pressure when ripe
Kiwifruit	Chinese gooseberry renamed kiwifruit; light brown, furry, tender soft skin
Mango	Vary in size and shape; yellowish; firm, smooth skin; ripen at room temperature until yields to slight pressure; soft, aromatic flesh
Nectarine	Plump, rich color, slight softening along "seam," well matured
Papaya	Well shaped; well colored, at least half yellow and not green; smooth, unbruised
Peach	Fairly firm, yellow between red areas, plump, well shaped, "peachy" fragrance
Pear	Firm, well shaped, color appropriate for variety
Pineapple	Well shaped, heavy in relation to size; greenish-brown to golden-brown color, fragrant odor
Plum	Fairly firm to slightly soft; good color for variety; smooth skin
Pomegranates	Unbroken, hard rind covering many seeds; varies in color from yellow to deep red; heavy for size; large sizes juicier; only seeds are edible
Strawberry	Full red color, bright luster, firm flesh, cap stem attached, dry, clean

Variety Fruits

Atemoya	Small, green, rough skinned; creamy, soft, sweet pulp; large black seeds
Breadfruit	Oval or round, 2–15 pounds; yellowish-green rind with rough surface; white to yellow fibrous pulp; important food in South Sea Islands
Carambola (star fruit)	Waxy, yellow; five fluted sides; tart, sweet-sour flavor
Cherimoya (custard apple)	Almost heart shaped; uniform green when ripe; no mold or cracks at stem end; fresh pineapple-strawberry-banana flavor
Passion fruit (granadilla)	Size and shape of an egg; tough, purple skin; yellowish meat with many black seeds
Kumquat	Small, football shaped, yellow, firm; sweet skin and tart flesh
Loquat	Small, round or oval; pale yellow or orange; somewhat downy surface; thin skin; firm, mealy flesh
Persimmon	Bright orange; Hachiya variety slightly pointed and soft when ripe; Fuyu variety more firm when eaten (like an apple); smooth, rich taste
Plantain	Greenish looking bananas with rough skins and blemishes; frequently used as a cooked vegetable; never eaten raw
Ugli fruit	About the size of a grapefruit; spherical; extremely rough peel, badly disfigured, with light green blemishes that turn orange when fruit is mature; very juicy with orange-like flavor

Source: References 29, 30.

Table 20–3
DESIRABILITY OF APPLE VARIETIES FOR DIFFERENT USES

Variety	Flavor and Texture	Fresh and in Salads	Pies	Sauces	Baking	Freezing (Slices)	Main Season
Braeburn	Sweet, tart, firm	Excellent	Good	Good	Good	Good	October to July
Cortland	Mild, tender, resists browning	Excellent	Excellent	Very good	Good	Very good	September to April
Empire	Sweet-tart, crisp	Excellent	Good	Good	Good	Good	September to July
Fuji	Sweet, spicy, crisp	Excellent	Good	Good	Good	Excellent	Year-round
Gala	Sweet, crisp	Excellent	Fair	Excellent	Fair	Excellent	August to March
Ginger Gold	Sweet, tart, crisp	Excellent	Good	Good	Good	Good	October
Golden Delicious	Sweet, semifirm	Excellent	Very good	Good	Very good	Very good	Year-round
Granny Smith	Tart, crisp	Excellent	Excellent	Excellent	Excellent	Good	Year-round
Gravenstein	Tart, crisp	Good	Good	Good	Good	Good	July to September
Honeycrisp	Sweet, tart, crisp	Excellent	Excellent	Excellent	Excellent	Excellent	September to February
Idared	Sweet, tart, tangy, firm	Excellent	Excellent	Excellent	Excellent	Excellent	October to August
Jonagold	Sweet, tart, crisp	Excellent	Very good	Excellent	Very good	Very good	October to May
Jonathan	Tart, tender	Very good	Very good	Very good	Poor	Very good	September to January
McIntosh	Slightly tart, tender	Excellent	Excellent	Good	Fair	Good	September to July
Red Delicious	Sweet, mellow, crisp	Excellent	Poor	Fair	Poor	Fair	Year-round
R. I. Greening	Slightly tart, firm	Poor	Excellent	Excellent	Very good	Excellent	October to March
Rome Beauty	Slightly tart, firm	Good	Very good	Very good	Excellent	Very good	October to April
Stayman	Tart, semifirm	Excellent	Good	Good	Good	Good	October to March
Winesap	Slightly tart, firm	Excellent	Good	Good	Good	Very good	October to June
Yellow Transparent	Tart, soft	Poor	Excellent	Good	Poor	Poor	July to August
York Imperial	Tart, firm	Fair	Good	Very good	Good	Good	October to May

Source: Reference 4.

Avocados may be purchased slightly underripe and ripened at room temperature in a paper bag with an apple or banana to speed ripening if desired. When ready for use, they should yield to gentle pressure on the skin. The skin of a ripe Hass avocado will be dark when ripe, but the skin of other varieties will remain green. Avocados should be refrigerated only after ripening. **Figure 20–6** provides suggestions for avocado preparation.

Bananas

Banana plants grow in tropical areas, and bananas of many different varieties are produced. As the plant blooms, a cluster of tiny blossoms emerges, each blossom producing one banana. The fruits grow together on a stem of about 300 bananas (**Figure 20–7**). After harvest, the stem is divided into hands, each of which contains 10 to 12 individual bananas. Bananas are picked green and ripen best after harvesting. As they ripen, the skin gradually turns yellow.

The United States imports bananas primarily from Costa Rica, Guatemala, Ecuador, Colombia, and Honduras [31]. Until they are fully ripe, they should be kept at room temperature; they do not ripen normally if chilled. Bananas with gray or darkened skins have been cold damaged.

Bananas should be washed before peeling. They are often consumed raw, but are also used cooked in dishes such as bananas foster, or baked in banana bread. A yellow banana with green tips is often preferred when consuming raw or when sauteing. Fully ripe bananas with brown speckled skins offer the most flavor for baked products. Bananas and banana flakes have been used to reduce fat in baked products.

Berries

Blueberries, strawberries, cranberries, raspberries, and blackberries are some of the varieties of berries available in the marketplace. Blueberries are available from May through September. Large blueberries are cultivated varieties, and the small berries are wild.

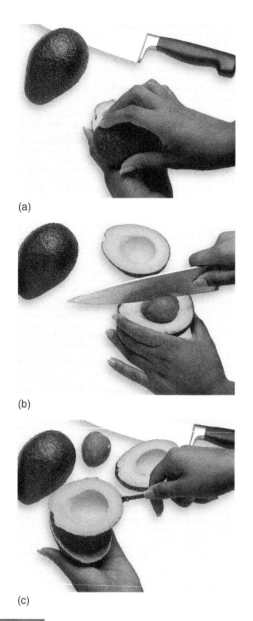

(a)

(b)

(c)

To prepare avocados (a) Cut avocado in half lengthwise working around pit, and then twist to separate halves. (b) Tap chef's knife on pit and then twist pit to remove. (c) Separate the avocado flesh from the skin by running a spoon between the flesh and skin. (Richard Embery/Pearson Education)

Green bananas are growing and will be ready for harvest.
(Anan Kaewkhammul/Shutterstock)

High-quality blueberries should be a dark blue color with a silvery bloom, which is a natural protective coating. Blueberries should be washed immediately before use, not before storage. Cranberries are sold primarily from September through January and are a seasonal favorite in many homes over the fall and winter holidays.

Strawberries should have a full red color, firm flesh, and the cap stem attached. Like other berries, strawberries should also be washed just before use. Washed berries will mold rapidly during storage. Strawberries are most readily available in May and June, although with transportation from warmer U.S. climates and imports, strawberries can be purchased nearly throughout the year. Blackberries, raspberries, dewberries, and loganberries are similar to each other in structure. These berries should be plump and tender but not mushy when purchased.

FOCUS ON SCIENCE
PECTIN DEVELOPMENT IN FRUIT

$$\text{Protopectin} \xrightarrow[\text{Protopectinase}]{} \text{Pectin (or Pectinic Acid)} \xrightarrow[\text{Pectin methyl esterase}]{} \text{Pectic Acid}$$

During ripening, protopectinase converts protopectin to colloidal pectin (able to gel) or water-soluble pectinic acid. Pectin methyl esterase (pectinase) cleaves the methyl esters from pectin to produce poly D-galacturonic acid or pectic acid, and this substance is partially degraded to monomeric D-galacturonic acid by polygalacturonase. These enzymes act in concert during maturation in determining fruit and vegetable texture. Pectic acid causes a soft, mushy, and mealy texture.

Figure 20–8

Cherries may be pitted for use in a pie, cobbler, or fruit cup by using a cherry pitter. Remove the stem, then put the cherry with the indent facing the metal bar that will press out the pit once the handles are squeezed together. (Richard Embery/Pearson Education)

Navel

Blood Oranges

Figure 20–9

Varieties of oranges. (Richard Embery/Pearson Education)

Cherries

Cherries may be sweet or tart. Tart cherries are generally used for cooking and baking (**Figure 20–8**). Sweet cherries include the dark red Bing and Lambert varieties and the yellowish Royal Anne. Cherries do not ripen off the trees, and they decay rapidly. Domestic cherries, depending on the variety, may be purchased from May to August.

Citrus Fruits

Oranges, lemons, grapefruit, limes, tangerines, mandarins, clementines, kumquats, pomelos, and tangelos (which are a cross between a tangerine and a grapefruit) are included in the citrus fruit classification. The chief producing areas of these fruits in the United States are Florida, California, Texas, and Arizona. Citrus fruits are a valuable and reliable source of vitamin C in the diet and are also noted for the tart and appetizing flavor they contribute to fruit desserts and salads.

Size and Quality. Citrus fruits can be classified on the basis of size, depending on the quantity of fruit required to fill certain standard-size containers (refer to Chapter 18 for more about USDA grading of produce). Cartons holding 40 pounds are often used. Large oranges may be 56 count (56 oranges per carton), medium oranges may be 88 count, and small oranges may be 113 or even 138 count. Large oranges are usually about 4⅜ inches in diameter, medium ones about 3½ inches, and small ones about 2½ inches.

The selection of citrus fruits is influenced by the intended use, personal preferences, and the growing season. USDA grading standards indicate high quality

citrus should be mature, firm, and well colored without evidence of hard or dry skins, mushiness, or damage. The thickness of the skin can vary by growing conditions as well as the location grown. Russeting, which is a tan, brown, or blackish mottling or speckling on the skin of some Florida and Texas oranges and grapefruit, has no effect on eating quality.

Varieties of Oranges. Two principal market varieties of oranges are the Valencia and the Navel. Blood and Cara Cara oranges are additional types of oranges. Blood, also called moro oranges, have a deep-red interior because of anthocyanin (**Figure 20–9**). Cara Cara oranges have a pink-red interior and a sweet, tangy flavor.

Valencia oranges are most often used for making juice but may also be used for sectioning. They are available over the summer months in contrast to other oranges generally available in the winter. Valencia oranges have a tendency late in the season to turn from a bright orange to a greenish tinge, particularly around the stem end. This change in color affects only the outer skin and is not an indication of maturity. All Valencias have seeds, but the California Valencia has only a few.

The Navel orange is distinguished by the formation of a navel at the apex or blossom end of the fruit. This formation appears to be a tiny orange within a larger one. The Navel orange is available in California and Arizona from November until early May and has no seeds, less juice, and a thicker, somewhat more pebbled skin than the Valencia. Navel oranges are easy to peel and are often consumed as wedges or slices.

Grapefruit.   Some varieties of grapefruit are classed as seedless, although they often contain a few seeds, and some are seeded. Some grapefruit varieties have white flesh, whereas others have pink or red flesh. Although Florida is the main producer of grapefruit, it is also supplied by Texas, California, and Arizona. Grapefruit is available all year but is most abundant from January through May.

Grapes

Many different kinds of grapes are grown. Table grapes are consumed as fruit for a meal or snack. Wine grapes (for example, pinot noir and chardonnay) are important in the production of wine. Juice and jelly grapes (concord) are used predominately for making juice or jelly.

California produces most of the table grapes in the United States. Grapes are also grown in Arizona. Over half of all the grapes grown in the United States are used to make wine [32]. Some types of grapes, which are firm fleshed and very sweet, include Thompson seedless (an early green grape), Red Flame Grapes, Tokay and Cardinal (early, bright red grapes), and Emperor (late, deep-red grape). The blue-black Concord variety is also commonly marketed and is unexcelled for juice and jelly making (**Figure 20–10**).

Grapes are picked ripe and thus do not ripen in storage. Like many other fresh fruits, grapes should not be washed until ready to use [30]. When selecting, look for grapes that are well colored, plump, and firmly attached to the stem. Stems should be green and pliable [30].

Melons

Melons (**Figure 20–11**) are among the most difficult of fruits to select. No absolute guide for selection is available, but desirability is indicated by such qualities as ripeness, heaviness in relation to size, usually a characteristic aroma, characteristic color, and freedom from abnormal shape, decay, and disease. The ripeness of some melons, such as honeydew, crenshaw, casaba, and cantaloupe, is indicated by color and a slight yielding to thumb pressure on the bud end or on the surface. If the melon was mature when picked, it usually shows a round dent where the stem broke away from the melon.

Most cantaloupes are firm and not completely ripe when first displayed in markets. Holding them a few days at room temperature allows the completion of ripening. The color of uncut watermelons is probably the best key to ripeness. A yellowish underside, regardless of the green color of the rest of the melon, is a good sign. Other guides in selection might be a relatively smooth surface, a slight dullness to the rind, and ends of the melon that are filled out and rounded. In cut watermelons, desirable characteristics include firm, juicy flesh with a good red color, dark brown or black seeds, and no white streaks.

(a)

(b)

(c)

Figure 20–10

Three varieties of grapes: (a) Red flame, (b) Thompson seedless grapes, and (c) Concord grapes used for jelly or juice making. (Richard Embery/Pearson Education)

Melons can be a source of foodborne illness. Measures to prevent or reduce the risk of foodborne illness include (1) thorough washing of the melon before cutting, (2) use of good personal hygiene and kitchen sanitation practices, and (3) refrigeration of prepared melons. Foodborne outbreaks of salmonellosis are most common; however, outbreaks of Listeria and *Escherichia coli* have also occurred. Careful washing of melons before cutting reduces the chance of cross contamination of the fruit with microorganisms on the rind. In 2016, only about one-half of Americans reported rinsing or washing cantaloupe before preparing it to eat [48].

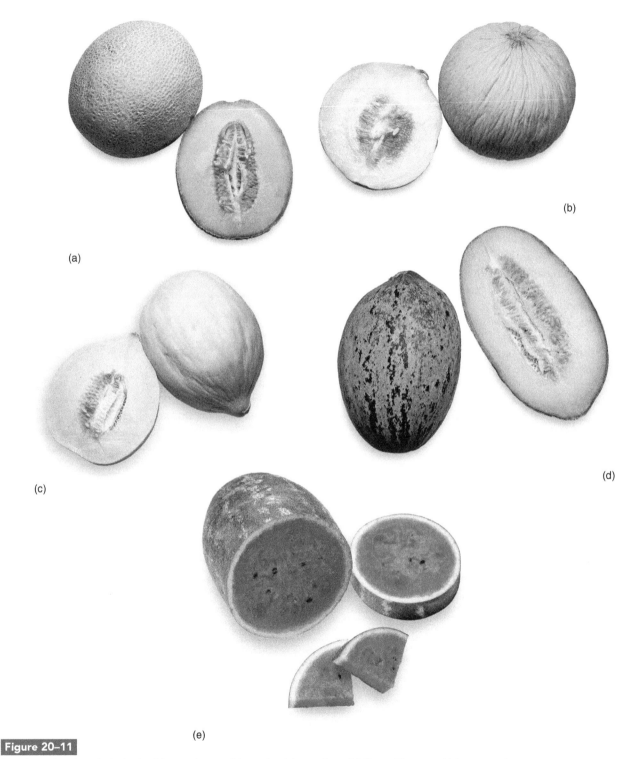

Figure 20–11

A variety of melons include the (a) cantaloupe, (b) casaba, (c) crenshaw, (d) Santa Claus, and (e) watermelon. (Richard Embery/Pearson Education)

Growers also need to follow recommended practices to reduce contamination. An outbreak of listeriosis associated with cantaloupe occurred in 2011 that was traced to a single farm [40]. Hands and kitchen preparation areas need to be clean. Outbreaks of *E. coli* 0157:H7 have been associated with cantaloupe from salad bars. In this case, the

melon may have been inoculated with *E. coli* by cross contamination from another product, such as beef, during kitchen preparation. The refrigeration of prepared melons is also important because microbes will multiply on cut melon if temperatures are suitable for growth [38]. Food safety was discussed in Chapter 2.

(a)   (b)

Figure 20–12

(a) Peaches have a fuzzy skin. (b) Nectarines are smooth skinned. (Richard Embery/Pearson Education)

Peaches and Nectarines

Both nectarines and peaches originated in Asia thousands of years ago. California is the largest producer of these fruits in the United States [20]. Although peaches and nectarines are similar, they each are distinct fruits (**Figure 20–12**). Nectarines do not have the fuzzy coat of peaches but will have a strong "peachy" fragrance even when only partially ripe. Nectarines and peaches may be freestone or clingstone. The flesh of freestone varieties will separate readily from the flesh and are used most commonly for eating fresh or freezing. The flesh clings to the pit of clingstone varieties. Clingstones are used primarily for canning.

An important factor in peach quality is the stage of maturity at harvest. Peaches will ripen off the tree. Once picked, they are immediately dipped in ice water to remove the field heat and stop the ripening process. Then they are stored at 34–40°F (1–5°C) to keep ripening at a minimum and retard decay. If peaches are picked too soon, they will never ripen after cold storage, and they will lack flavor [28].

The best-quality peaches have a good yellow undercover and yield slightly to finger pressure. The appearance of a peach does not always indicate the

Figure 20–13

Santa rose plums. (Richard Embery/Pearson Education)

flavor, however. Peaches should be eaten at optimum ripeness. To avoid chill injury (brown flesh, lack of juice, and poor flavor), a peach that is not fully ripened should not be refrigerated until after it has been held at room temperature and ripened [30].

Plums

Many varieties of plums are available (**Figure 20–13**). The peak season for domestic plums is June through September [30]. Plums from Chile are available during the winter months. Plums are highly perishable and thus must be purchased and used at peak quality, or spoilage will occur. Plums should range from firm to slightly soft when purchased. Plums that are not fully ripened should not be refrigerated but instead should be held at 55–70°F (13–21°C) [30]. Once ripened, the plums may be refrigerated but should be used within a few days.

Pears

The most popular type of pear is the Bartlett. Other varieties of pears, grown primarily in Washington, Oregon, and California, are Anjou, Bosc, Winter Nellis, and Comice (**Figure 20–14**). Pears are generally firm when purchased but will soften at room temperature. Fully ripe pears will be sweet and juicy.

Anjou   Bosc   Red d'Anjou

Asian Pears   Bartlett

Figure 20–14

A variety of pears. (Richard Embery/Pearson Education)

Pineapple

The pineapple plant bears its first fruit 18 to 22 months after planting. Each plant produces a single 4- to 5-pound fruit. The fruit is harvested when the appropriate stage of sweetness is reached. The optimum flavor is a balance between sweet and tart. The sweetest flavor and brightest yellow color are found at the base of the pineapple fruit.

A ripe pineapple has a rich fragrance. It springs back slightly when touched. Color may vary from green through brown to golden and is not an indication of ripeness [30]. A hard pineapple should be kept at room temperature until it becomes fragrant and springy. Once ripe, it can be refrigerated.

Pineapple is a popular canned fruit. It may be processed as chunks, cubes, slices, or crushed. The preparation of pineapple is shown in **Figure 20–15**.

Variety Fruits

Many uncommon fruits have appeared on the market throughout the United States in recent years. As consumers become more familiar with these fruits and learn to use them, their market share increases.

Kiwifruit. Kiwifruit, or Chinese gooseberries, grown in New Zealand and California, have become a widely accepted fruit in a relatively short time. Californian kiwifruit is marketed from October through May. Although the furry skin is edible, most prefer to peel the skin to reveal the bright green flesh (**Figure 20–16**). Ripe kiwifruit should yield slightly to the touch.

Coconuts. Coconuts are familiar to American consumers as packaged flaked coconut. However, fresh coconuts may be preferred in some recipes due to their flavor. Fresh coconuts are prepared by puncturing the shell through one of the eyes with an ice pick or a knife, then draining out the coconut milk. Next, the shell is baked in a 350°F (177°C) oven for approximately 15 minutes and placed in the freezer until cool but not frozen. This heating and cooling process will

(a)

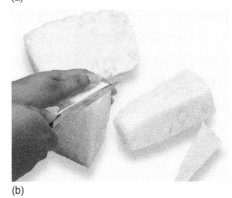
(b)

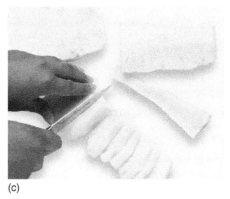
(c)

Figure 20–15

Fresh pineapple may be quickly prepared. (a) Slice off leaves and stem end, then stand fruit upright and cut the peel off in vertical strips. (b) Cut the fruit in quarters, then remove the woody core as shown. (c) Cut the flesh into wedges or chunks as desired. (Richard Embery/Pearson Education)

THINKING GREEN
HONEYBEES: POLLINATOR OF OUR FRUITS AND VEGETABLES

The common honeybee provides essential "services" for nearly one-third of the U.S. food supply. Honeybees pollinate about 130 different crops in the United States, including almonds, pumpkins, watermelons and other melons, grapefruit, sunflowers, tomatoes, blueberries, and macadamia nuts [13]. These little workers are important not only to the United States but also to our world environment.

Honeybee colony collapse disorder is now affecting many bee colonies throughout the world. Honeybee pathogens are varied but can include viruses, bacteria, fungi, and parasites. In short, we need healthy bee colonies to continue enjoying many of our favorite fruit and vegetables. Stay tuned as scientists seek ways to promote and protect the health of our bees.

Figure 20–16

Kiwifruit has a brown, fuzzy skin on the exterior and bright green flesh and small black seeds on the interior. (Richard Embery/Pearson Education)

(a)

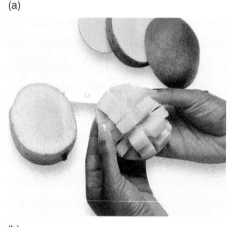

(b)

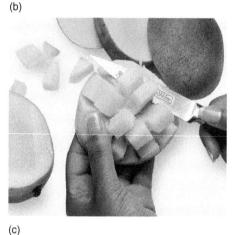

(c)

allow the flesh to separate easily from the shell. Any brown skin remaining on the coconut may be pared or peeled off. The coconut milk and the shredded coconut may be used in many dishes.

Mangoes.   Mangoes have become popular with the interest in Caribbean and Mexican cuisines. Mangoes have a spicy, sweet flavor with an acidic note. These fruits are grown primarily in Florida, Mexico, Haiti, and Puerto Rico [29]. Ripe mangoes should have yellow, orange, or red skins and should yield to gentle pressure [30]. The preparation of mangoes is shown in **Figure 20–17** [20].

Papayas.   Papayas are available year-round, with supplies peaking in May through September (**Figure 20–18**). A ripe papaya should yield to gentle pressure [30]. Papayas may be eaten raw or used for sauces, sorbets, pickles, or chutneys [20]. The seeds are edible, providing a peppery flavor with a crunch.

Other.   Other exotic fruits include *passion fruit*, a small egg-shaped fruit with an intense and tart flavor that goes well in fruit punches and juices. The pulp can be used in desserts such as sherbets, ice creams, and parfaits. The *prickly pear*, or *cactus pear*, can be chilled, the spines and peel cut away, sliced, and served raw. The *cherimoya* can be chilled, cut in half, and eaten with a spoon. The *carambola*, or star fruit, is recognized by the star shape of a slice. It is very tart, with a sweet-sour flavor, and is often cooked. *Figs* are small, soft, pear shaped fruits that may be consumed raw out of hand or in salads. Alternatively they may be baked or used to make jams or compotes. The *jackfruit* (**Figure 20–19**) is the largest fruit. It is grown in tropical climates, and has the flavor of banana, melon, and mango. Only the sweet, juicy seeds of *pomegranates* are consumed. To prepare, bend back the rind and pull out the seeds from the surrounding white membrane [30]. Other variety fruits may be explored at https://www.fruitsandveggiesmorematters.org and https://www.friedas.com/ and are listed in Table 20–2 and pictured in **Figure 20–20**.

Figure 20–17

A mango can be pitted and cut as follows: (a) Cut along each side of the pit. (b) Cube each section by making crosswise cuts through the flesh, just to the skin. Press up on the skin side to expose the cubes. (c) Cut the cubes off for use in salads and other dishes. (Richard Embery/Pearson Education)

CHANGES DURING RIPENING

Fruits are living systems. Respiration occurs in the cells of the fruit as they carry on normal metabolic processes involving growth, maturation, and eventual ripening. **Ethylene** gas is a ripening hormone produced in small amounts by the cells after the fruit is mature. Without ethylene, the fruit does not ripen. Distinct changes

MULTICULTURAL CUISINE
EXOTIC FRUITS AND FRIEDA'S SPECIALITY PRODUCE

As our world becomes more global, so has our food supply. Kiwi was introduced to the United States by Frieda of Frieda's Specialty Produce in 1962. Today, kiwi is found in grocery stores and on menus throughout the United States. She has been credited with introducing over 200 new exotic fruits for consumers and restauranteurs to enjoy. Her business is now led by her daughters.

Go to www.friedas.com and learn about a wide variety of specialty and exotic fruits and vegetables. ■

Figure 20–18

This papaya has golden to reddish-pink flesh with dark silver black seeds. Other varieties may be reddish. (Richard Embery/ Pearson Education)

Figure 20–19

Jackfruit is a large fruit that may be 15 pounds (7 kilograms) to 80 pounds (36 kilograms) or more. They are dark olive green when ripe. In addition to the sweet fruit, the seeds may also be roasted or boiled. (Annrapeepan/Shutterstock)

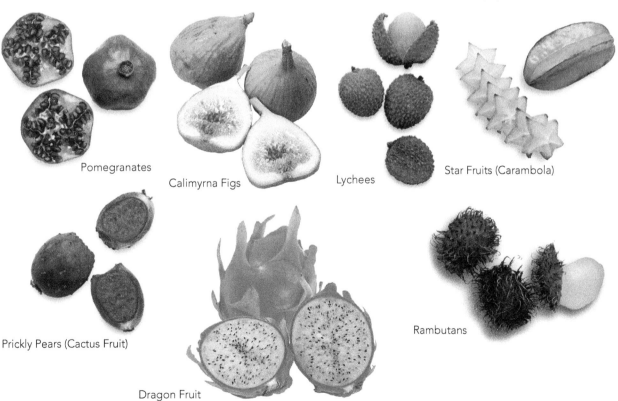

Pomegranates

Calimyrna Figs

Lychees

Star Fruits (Carambola)

Prickly Pears (Cactus Fruit)

Dragon Fruit

Rambutans

Figure 20–20

Exotic fruits. (Richard Embery/Pearson Education)

occur in fruits during ripening: (1) a decrease in green color and development of yellow-orange or red-blue colors, (2) a softening of the flesh, (3) the development of characteristic pleasant flavors, and (4) changes in soluble solids, such as sugars and organic acids.

Role of Ethylene Gas in Ripening

Ethylene gas, produced naturally by many fruits and vegetables, promotes ripening. Fruits that have been harvested well before ripening has started may be stored in an atmosphere that contains ethylene gas to speed up the ripening process. Bananas are generally ripened in this way. This is the same concept that is being applied when fruit is placed in a closed bag to promote ripening. Because apples and bananas emit ethylene gas, an apple or banana is sometimes placed in the bag with the fruit to be ripened. Ethylene gas, produced naturally by the fruit, builds up in the closed bag. Alternately, fruit that is fully ripe should not be stored in a closed bag or near apples and other highly ethylene-producing fruits and vegetables to reduce ethylene gas exposure. In general, there is no material difference in the gross composition (protein, fat, and carbohydrate) of fruits that ripen naturally and those that ripen by ethylene gas in a controlled atmosphere.

Ethylene production is stimulated when plant tissues are injured. Preparation of fruits and vegetables involves peeling, slicing, and cutting, which injure tissues and induce ethylene production. When these products are placed in sealed containers, the ethylene accumulates and accelerates undesirable changes in quality, such as a decrease in firmness and loss of the pigment chlorophyll. Researchers found that when an absorbent for the ethylene gas (charcoal with palladium chloride) was placed in a small paper packet and enclosed in the package containing the processed fruit, the accumulation of ethylene was deterred, thereby preventing the softening of fruits such as kiwifruits and bananas [1]. Researchers are also exploring the use of an ethylene-inhibiting chemical, 1-methylcyclopropene, to extend the shelf life of fruits and vegetables [11].

Color

The change in color during ripening is associated with both synthesis of new pigments and breakdown of the green pigment chlorophyll. Chlorophyll may mask yellow carotenoid pigments in the immature fruit. Anthocyanins are probably synthesized as ripening proceeds.

Softening

Involved in the softening of fruits are the pectic substances (see Chapters 7 and 18 for more about the structural components in fruit and vegetables). During ripening, the complex insoluble protopectin is degraded to pectin (also called *pectinic acid)*. Gel-forming properties are characteristic of pectin, making it important in the preparation of jams and jellies. Further softening in ripening fruit changes pectin to pectic acid. Pectin has gelling ability, but pectic acid does not, so gelling ability is lost. The breakdown of pectic substances found between plant cells may cause separation of cells as part of the softening process. Many fruits soften faster when the temperature of the surrounding air is increased [5].

Flavor

The development of a characteristic pleasant flavor in ripened fruit involves a decrease in acidity and an increase in sugar, along with the production of a complex mixture of volatile substances and essential oils. Thus, fruit that is not fully ripe may be tart and lack sweetness. In some fruits, such as bananas, the increase in sugar is accompanied by a decrease in starch; however, sugar content increases even in such fruits as peaches, which contain no appreciable amount of starch at any time. Some cell wall polysaccharides may decrease as the sugar content increases. In addition, the phenolic compounds, with their astringent properties, seem to decrease.

PURCHASING

The overall quality, seasonal availability, cost, preferences for graded, organic fruits, and the form in which fruits are purchased are all considerations when purchasing fruits. Consumers should assess their intended use of the fruit. Perfection is not necessary if preparing banana bread, apple cobbler, and other dishes where any blemishes can be removed without any perceptible impact on the final dish. It is estimated by the Department of Agriculture, Economic Research Service that about 31 percent of the food supply (141 trillion calories) in the United States is not consumed, and thus wasted. The desire for "perfection" in the purchase and use of our fruits and vegetables is one of several reasons for the high amount of waste [8].

Economic Considerations

Price can be a factor in the selection process for fruits and vegetables (see Chapters 1 and 18). Researchers found fruit and vegetable recommendations in the U.S. Dietary Guidelines (2 cups of fruit and 2½ cups of vegetables in a 2,000 calorie diet) could be met for between $2.10 and $2.60 per day [34]. Nine fruits (three fresh and three processed) were found that cost less than $0.40 per cup equivalent. Watermelon and frozen concentrated apple juice could be purchased for less than $0.30 per serving, whereas apples, oranges, and grapes could be purchased for less than $0.75 per serving [34] **(Figure 20–21)**. The nutrients per unit cost is another way of considering cost. Fruits and vegetables offer more nutrients per cost than many other foods [14].

The price of fruit is influenced by seasonality, grade, and organic preferences. Fresh fruits in season are generally less expensive than fruits purchased out of season when supply is limited or the fruit is transported

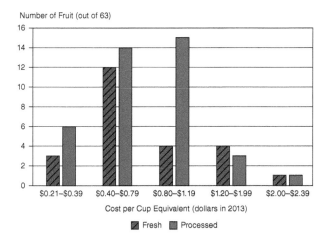

Number of Fruit (out of 63)

Cost per Cup Equivalent (dollars in 2013)

■ Fresh ■ Processed

Figure 20–21

A number of fruits can be purchased for less than $0.79 per cup or cup equivalent. (USDA/ERS)

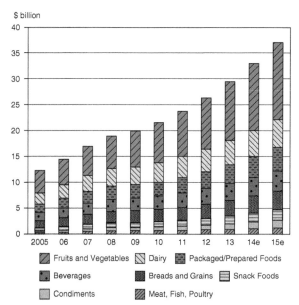

$ billion

☑ Fruits and Vegetables ☐ Dairy ▦ Packaged/Prepared Foods
⦙ Beverages ▦ Breads and Grains ▤ Snack Foods
☐ Condiments ▨ Meat, Fish, Poultry

Figure 20–22

The sales of organic foods have increased since 2005. Organic fruits and vegetables in particular are purchased by consumers. (U.S. Department of Agriculture, Economic Research Service.)

for long distances. Fifty-three percent of the fresh fruit in the United States is imported [24]. "Country-of-Origin" labeling enables consumers to know where their fruits or vegetables were grown. Direct-to-consumer sales of produce through farmer's markets and roadside stands have increased, and appear to be resulting in greater demand for fruits and vegetables [35]. Weather and environmental conditions such as drought, freezing temperatures, insects, or blight and other diseases can also influence the supply, and thus the prices.

Fruits and vegetables may be graded by the USDA to offer a consistent understanding between the supplier and the purchaser of the quality. The U.S. grade standards are voluntary. More information about the USDA grading standards can be found in Chapter 3, Chapter 18, and the USDA web pages [42].

Increasingly, consumers are selecting and purchasing organic fruits and vegetables [18] (**Figure 20–22**). More than half of millennials report seeking organic products. Some organic foods command premium prices in light of the higher cost of farm production. The price premiums for several organic fruits and vegetables are more modest as compared to other foods [9]. More information about organic fruits and vegetables, and organic regulations overall may be found in Chapters 18 and 3, respectively.

Purchase Forms

Fruits may be purchased fresh, dried, frozen, canned, or as fruit juices. The preferred form may be influenced by price, preference, convenience, or the intended use of the fruit. More than half (55%) of available fruit in the United States is consumed fresh, but nearly half (45%) is processed [45]. Of processed fruits (juice, canned, frozen, dried, and other), the majority is used as fruit juice. Candied fruit, jams, and jellies are additional options. All of these processed forms of fruits enable longer storage, reduce waste of perishable fresh produce, and offer dietary variety throughout the year. Fruit juices, and dried, frozen, and canned fruits will be discussed here.

Fruit Juices. Fruit juices are an important means of utilizing fresh fruits. After the commercial introduction of frozen orange concentrate in 1945 and 1946, this product became the leader among processed fruits in terms of fresh-weight equivalent

HOT TOPICS
FRUIT AND VEGETABLE IMPORTS AND COUNTRY-OF-ORIGIN LABELING

The variety of fresh fruit in the food supply is supported by the growth of imports. Imported fresh fruit permits Americans to enjoy tropical fruits and fresh fruits that are out of season domestically. Mexico, Canada, Chile, Brazil, China, and Argentina are leading sources of fruit imports into the United States [43]. Nearly half of the fresh fruit consumed in the United States is imported. Bananas represent half of the fresh fruit import volume.

Imported fruits, vegetables, and other foods are now labeled with the country of origin. In March 2009, mandatory country-of-origin labeling for fruits and vegetables took effect [25, 41].

consumed. A large share of the Florida orange crop is used to produce juice. Although frozen concentrated orange juice continues to be produced, single-strength, not-from-concentrate juice is the most popular for consumer use [12].

Fruit Juice and Vitamin C. Some edible material is lost when juices are extracted and the juice is strained, resulting in the total nutritive value of the whole fruit being somewhat higher than the juice. Regardless, little loss of vitamin C occurs during preparation and processing of citrus juices. The freezing and subsequent storage of orange juice at 0°F (18°C) or below does not cause a significant loss of vitamin C, especially if aeration before freezing is avoided.

Apple, cranberry, grape, pineapple, and prune juices and apricot nectar contain little vitamin C unless they are fortified with the added vitamin. Vitamin C is added to some juices, partly to increase the nutritive value and partly to improve their appearance, flavor, and stability during storage. The added vitamin C in noncitrus juices may be less stable than the vitamin naturally present in citrus juices. In opened containers stored in a refrigerator, the vitamin C in canned orange juice was found to be more stable, up to 16 days, than that in vitamin C–fortified canned apple juice [26]. Additional vitamin C, calcium, and other nutrients are added to some orange and other juices.

Pasteurization or Treatment of Juice for Safety. Juices are commonly pasteurized or treated with high pressure, ozone, UV irradiation, or surface treatment of the fruit to reduce pathogens that may result in foodborne illness. Juices not treated by any of these methods may be sold but must be labeled to warn the public that they have not been pasteurized and may contain harmful bacteria. The treatment of juice to kill pathogens is important for safety, as illustrated by the outbreak of *E. coli* 0157:H7 illness in 1996 that was linked to the consumption of unpasteurized apple juice. Additional foodborne outbreaks have occurred since 1996 [39].

Pasteurization is a short, high-heat treatment used to kill potential pathogens in fruit juice. About 98 percent of the juice sold in the United States is pasteurized. Juices treated with ozone, UV irradiation, surface treatment of the fruit, or high-pressure treatment may be marketed as fresh squeezed. These juices will not be labeled as "pasteurized," but unlike unpasteurized and untreated juices, these treated juices are not required to use the warning label [39]. See Chapters 2 and 28 for more information on food safety and preservation.

Orange Juice Processing. In preparing orange juice concentrate, the fruit is graded, washed, and sanitized before it enters the juice extractors. Juice may be extracted using a machine similar to a kitchen juicer that cuts the fruit in half, then presses the half against a rotating burr. In another commonly used method of extraction, the fruit is penetrated by a porous tube and then crushed. Next, the juice is processed to remove the seeds and membranes. During this step, the amount of pulp can be controlled to produce high- or low-pulp juice [12].

Single-strength, not-from-concentrate juice is pasteurized to reduce pathogenic or spoilage organisms and eliminate enzymes that can promote the separation of the pulp [12]. It is then rapidly chilled at about 35°F (1.7°C) before packaging. The package may be lined with a special material that prevents loss of volatile flavor substances in the packaging [15]. Some processors may use **aseptic** bulk storage in the marketing of chilled, pasteurized, single-strength orange and grapefruit juices.

Frozen, concentrated orange juice is heated to a greater extent than single-strength pasteurized juice. Thermally accelerated short-time evaporators are

HEALTHY EATING
FRUIT JUICE OR FRUIT DRINK—WHAT IS THE DIFFERENCE?

To be labeled "fruit juice," the product must contain 100 percent juice. When a beverage contains less than 100 percent juice, the name of the product must include the term *drink, beverage,* or *cocktail.* Furthermore, any product with a name, label, or flavoring that suggests that the product is made with fruits or vegetables must provide a statement of the total percent of juice. Therefore, a product that appears to contain juice but does not must indicate "contains no juice."

A product labeled "orange juice" is a "juice," and a statement indicating 100 percent juice will be found on the label. In contrast, a grape juice drink or cranberry juice cocktail uses the term *drink* or *cocktail*; these products will be less than 100 percent juice. Some of these drinks, beverages, and cocktails may contain only 10 or 20 percent juice. Although fruit drinks, beverages, and cocktails may contain 100 percent of the daily value of vitamin C because of fortification, consider the other nutrients contained in a juice that will be absent from a drink. Read the ingredient labels, which often show that water and added sugar are key ingredients. It should be noted that cranberry juice cocktail is often sold as a cocktail or blend because of the very tart nature of cranberries.

So what's the difference between a juice and a drink? It is all in the percentage of actual juice!

Source: References 49, 50.

commonly used to concentrate orange juice. With this process, water is removed until the soluble solids are about 65 percent [12]. To produce the standard three-parts-water-to-one-part juice sold frozen in the marketplace, the juice may be diluted to 42 percent

Noncitrus Juice Concentrates. Noncitrus juices may be sold as concentrates. One major advantage of fruit juice concentrates is that the volume is greatly reduced and shipping and handling costs are less. Concentrated juices and fruit purees may be dehydrated by roller or drum drying, spray drying, or foam mat drying. Although some flavor loss occurs in drying, the final product is acceptable.

Cloud or Haze in Fruit Juice. Cloud or haze is a desirable characteristic of citrus juices but not in other juices, such as apple or grape, which are preferred clear. Haze is a complex mixture of cellular organelles (specialized subunits with cells), color bodies, oil droplets, flavonoids, and cell wall fragments that include pectic substances, cellulose, and hemicelluloses. Pectic substances play an important role in stabilizing the cloudy appearance and also contribute a characteristic body or consistency. Present in cell walls and between cells, pectic substances are released into the juice when extracted. In citrus juices, this cloud may be stabilized by flash heating to a temperature higher than usual pasteurization temperatures to destroy **pectin esterase** enzymes that destabilize the cloud by allowing calcium ions to link de-esterified pectin molecules into aggregates that settle out.

Apple and grape juices are processed differently so that they are clear. Pectin-degrading enzymes (-**pectinases**) may be added so that the juice is less viscous and can be easily filtered. This process is called *clarification*. The color and flavor of the clarified juices are also stabilized. To increase yield while still maintaining or improving the quality and stability of the final juice product, enzyme preparations that contain **cellulase and hemicellulase** activity, as well as pectinase, may be used. These additional enzymes act on the fruit tissue to macerate and further liquefy in order to extract more soluble solids [16]. Haze formation in apple juice may also commonly be the result of a protein–tannin haze [3].

Dried Fruits. The term *dried fruit* is commonly applied to all fruits in which the water content has been reduced to 30 percent or less. In the **vacuum drying** of fruits, the water content is reduced to very low levels, about 2.5 to 5 percent. Dried fruits with 28 to 30 percent water are examples of intermediate-moisture foods that are plastic (or flexible), easily chewed, and do not produce a sensation of dryness in the mouth but are microbiologically stable. Because dried fruits are greatly reduced in water content and consequently have increased sugar content, they are resistant to

microbial spoilage. Dried fruits should be stored in tightly closed plastic, glass, or metal containers to protect against insect infestation and to maintain their low moisture levels.

In dried fruits, the removal of water results in carbohydrate, caloric, and mineral values being higher by weight than those of the corresponding fresh fruits. The flavor of dried fruits is also more concentrated than that of fresh fruit. The vitamin content of dried fruits may be impacted, depending on the drying and sulfuring methods used. Some fruits, such as apricots and peaches, are subjected to the fumes of sulfur dioxide gas or are dipped in a sulfite solution to prevent darkening of color and to kill insects. Sulfuring aids in the preservation of vitamins A and C but adversely affects thiamin. Individuals sensitive to sulfites (discussed in Chapter 18) may also be sensitive to sulfur-treated dried fruits.

Dried Fruit Methods and Storage. Fruits may be dried by sun-drying, by artificial heat, under vacuum, or by freeze-drying. Sun-drying uses the sun as a source of heat to cause the evaporation of water. Dehydration can also be accomplished by artificial heat under well-controlled humidity, temperature, and air circulation conditions. Sanitation may be more easily controlled with drying fruits under artificial heat. Physical properties, such as color, texture, and flavor, in heated dehydrated fruits may also be better controlled as compared with sun-dried fruits.

Vacuum drying results in fruit with very low moisture levels, although relatively low temperatures are used in the process. Under vacuum, water evaporates at a lower temperature. These fruits usually have excellent eating quality, and they rehydrate quickly and easily. Fruits may also be **freeze-dried**.

Some fruits, such as dates, figs, currants, raisins (dried grape), pears, and peaches, may be dried to a water content of only 15 to 18 percent. As sold, these fruits usually contain 28 percent or more moisture; therefore, they may be partially rehydrated before being packaged for the consumer.

Dried Prunes /Dried Plums. Prunes are varieties of plums that can be dried without fermenting while still containing the pits. Two main varieties are the French plum, grown chiefly in California and France, and the Italian plum, grown chiefly in Oregon. These fruits are blue or purple on the outside, with greenish yellow to amber flesh. They have a high sugar content, so they produce a sweet-flavored prune when dried.

Before drying, plums are dipped in lye to puncture the skin and make it thinner, thus permitting rapid drying and improving the texture of the skin. Careful washing removes the lye before further processing. Some packaged prunes have been sterilized and packed hot in a package lined with aluminum foil. The residual heat in the pits seems to be sufficient to sterilize the package and also to tenderize the prune fiber to some extent, thus giving the prune its quick-cooking quality.

Prunes are classified according to size, that is, the approximate number to the pound. It is generally conceded that large prunes of the same variety and quality as small prunes have no better flavor than the small fruit. Because larger fruit may be more expensive, prices of edible portion for the various sizes and the intended use should be considered when determining the best size to purchase.

The laxative value of prunes is the result of their fiber content and of a water-soluble extractive, *diphenylisatin*, that stimulates intestinal activity. Prune juice also contains the active laxative agent.

Canned Fruit. Canned fruit is essentially cooked fruit that has been sealed and processed for keeping and, as such, represents a widely used convenience food. Flavors and textures are somewhat altered by cooking or canning, and vitamin values may be slightly reduced. The vitamins and minerals that go into solution are conserved because juices are usually eaten with the fruit.

Canned fruits lose nutrients and flavor less readily when stored at relatively low temperatures. If stored for prolonged periods above 72°F (22°C), they deteriorate in quality at a relatively rapid rate.

Fruits may be canned in heavy syrup, light syrup, or fruit juice. Fruits packed in fruit juice or light syrup provide less added sugar than fruits packed in heavy syrup, which has a high sugar level. Thus, from a nutritional standpoint, light syrup or fruit juice canned fruits are recommended. The grading of commercially canned fruits was discussed in Chapter 18, and general government regulations on packaged (including canned foods) were presented in Chapter 3. Home canning is explained in Chapter 28.

Frozen Fruits. The fruits that are most commonly frozen are cherries (both sour and sweet), strawberries (both sliced in sugar and whole), boysenberries, loganberries, red and black raspberries, blueberries, and sliced peaches. Frozen mixed fruits, rhubarb, plums, black mission figs, cranberries, pineapple, apple slices, and some varieties of melon are also available in some markets. Most frozen fruits are not heated during processing but are often frozen in a sugar syrup. Commercially, small whole fruits may be frozen quickly in liquid nitrogen without added sugar. Vitamin C (ascorbic acid) prevents browning by preventing oxidation and is often used to prevent the browning of frozen fruits, such as apples and peaches.

Frozen apples, cherries, and some other fruits used for pies should be partially defrosted to facilitate their use and to drain some of the juice. Otherwise, they are used in the same manner as fresh fruit.

If the fruit has been frozen with some sugar or syrup and is to be used in recipes, the amount of added sugar in the recipe may need to be adjusted. Rhubarb should be cooked without defrosting. Blueberries and other fruits frozen dry can be used either frozen or thawed in cooked dishes. All frozen fruits to be used raw should be barely defrosted before use. If all the crystals have thawed, the fruit tends to become flabby, particularly when using berries or peaches in shortcake, which is often warm when served.

Frozen fruits need to be kept frozen throughout the market channels and from the store or supplier to your home or business. Partial thawing and refreezing lowers quality. For best quality, frozen fruits need to be stored at a temperature of 0°F (18°C) or lower.

STORAGE OF FRUITS

Temperature and Storage Conditions

The storage conditions necessarily depend on the kind of fruit or fruit product. Canned fruits and vegetables may be stored at room temperature. Use within a year is generally recommended, although canned foods can be stored for more than one year. Frozen fruits and vegetables may be stored in the freezer at or below 0°F (−18°C) for a few months. Dried fruits will often provide a "best by" date on the label. In general, dried fruits may last for up to one year at best quality.

Fresh fruits are perishable and most, but not all, require refrigeration. Soft fruits such as berries keep better when spread out on a flat surface. Citrus fruits, except lemons, which keep best at a temperature of 55–58°F (13–15°C), should be refrigerated and covered to avoid drying out. Avocados and bananas should be stored at room temperature. They are damaged by chilling resulting in discoloration and the inability to ripen even if later held at warmer temperatures. In fact, bananas are injured when held at temperatures lower than 55°F (13°C) *before* ripening. If these and other tropical fruits must be held for any time, they should be ripened before being stored at colder temperatures. After ripening, avocados hold best at about 40°F (4°C). Similarly, peaches, nectarines, and plums should not be refrigerated until after fully ripened because these fruits can also be cold damaged and fail to ripen properly.

Several fruits, such as grapes and berries, should not be washed until just before use. Grapes and blueberries have a natural protective bloom that should not be washed off prior to storage. Berries, in general, tend to mold more rapidly if washed too far ahead of consumption. Apples are not necessarily damaged by advanced washing; however, many apples are marketed with a light coat of wax that will become hazy in appearance if the apples are washed and then stored [30].

Methods to Extend Storage of Fresh Fruits

Controlled Atmosphere. Fruits are actively metabolizing tissues and, even after harvesting, continue to respire—to take in oxygen and give off carbon dioxide. Cold temperatures reduce the rate of metabolism and retard ripening but do not completely stop these processes. An additional aid in controlling metabolic changes and thus lengthening the possible storage period, or extending the shelf life, for certain fruits is *controlled-atmosphere storage* [22].

In controlled-atmosphere storage, the oxygen in the atmosphere is reduced below the usual 21 percent level to as low as 2 to 3 percent. This lowers the rate of cell metabolism and aging in the fruit. Changes that would normally occur are delayed, and storage life is prolonged. For example, changes in pigments, decrease in acid, loss of sugars, and breakdown of pectic substances are retarded in apples stored at 38°F (4°C) in an atmosphere containing 5 percent carbon dioxide and 3 percent oxygen [19].

Each stored fruit has a critical oxygen level below which injury to the tissues occurs. Relatively high carbon dioxide levels are sometimes used with the low-oxygen atmosphere. However, the atmosphere is carefully monitored, and excess carbon dioxide, produced by the fruit during respiration, is removed so that a desirable level of carbon dioxide is constantly maintained. Temperature and humidity are also carefully controlled. Apples that have been stored in a controlled atmosphere are commonly marketed as controlled-atmosphere apples. Controlled-atmosphere apples offer a level of freshness and quality not otherwise available in the spring and the summer months.

Modified-Atmosphere Packaging. Another preservative technique closely related to controlled-atmosphere storage is *modified-atmosphere packaging*. This technique involves a modification of the oxygen, carbon dioxide, and water vapor levels in the air surrounding a product in a package. A semipermeable film used for packaging allows the natural process of respiration by the fresh or minimally processed fruit to reduce the oxygen and increase the carbon dioxide content of the atmosphere around the fruit. As modified-atmosphere packaging systems have become more sophisticated (see Chapter 28), the package can allow oxygen in while allowing the escape of excess carbon dioxide, water, heat, or ethylene gas [7]. A low storage temperature must still be maintained because changes in temperature may affect the gas concentrations in the package [37]. The initial microbial load on the fruit or vegetable should be as low as possible because the modified atmosphere does not stop the growth of microorganisms [21].

Irradiation. Irradiation of fresh fruits, at controlled dosages, can delay senescence, reduce mold growth, and extend shelf life. It may be used in combination with modified-atmosphere treatment. Irradiation was discussed further in Chapter 2. Another way irradiation may be used in fresh fruits is to kill insects on specific types of imported fruits, instead of using fumigation.

PREPARATION

Food safety, yield, plant pigments, and flavor chemistry should all be considered in the preparation and use of fruits and vegetables. Fruits, like vegetables, are grown in nature. Thus, thorough washing is needed to remove dirt (see Chapter 18 for more on food safety of fruits and vegetables). Cross-contamination and proper temperature control must also be taken into account through good food handling practices (see Chapter 2). One half of the consumers surveyed in 2016 reported not washing cantaloupe before use in spite of serious foodborne illnesses associated with cantaloupe [48].

Many fruits also do not yield 100 percent. For example, once the rind and seeds of cantaloupe are removed, only about 50 percent of the purchase weight remains. Consider also the peels of oranges, or the core or pits of fruits such as apples, pears, mangoes, avocadoes, and others. Thus, the edible portion (EP) is usually less than the as purchased (AP) weight. Recipes, as well as the nutritional analysis of recipes, need to take into account the necessary amount to purchase versus the amount anticipated in useable

---

FOCUS ON SCIENCE
COATINGS ON FRUIT TO PRESERVE QUALITY

Different materials have been used and researched to preserve quality of fruit and vegetables. Wax, parafilm, hydrocolloids, lipids, and protein materials have been explored and researched for use on fruits and vegetables to extend shelf life. A thin coating of the aforementioned materials is applied on the fruit's surface to decrease the respiration rate (senescence), thereby delaying the ripening process and at the same time maintaining quality and freshness and extending shelf life.

fruit or consumed fruit from a nutritional analysis perspective. See Chapter 18 for more about edible portion and yield.

Plant Pigments

The pigments that give fruits their characteristic colors are the same as those in vegetables:

- Chlorophyll (green)
- Carotenoids (primarily yellow and orange)
- Anthocyanins (red, purple, and blue)
- Betalains (primarily purple-red)
- Anthoxanthias (creamy white to colorless)

In fruits, the predominant pigments are the yellow-orange carotenoids and the red-blue anthocyanins. Enzymatic oxidative discoloration is also similar for fruits and vegetables. Chapter 18 provided a more in-depth discussion of these topics. **Table 20–4** offers an overview of methods to prevent oxidative browning.

Mixing various colored fruit juices may sometimes produce surprising, often unattractive results. The tin or iron salts present in canned juices can explain some of the reactions that occur. Metals combine with the anthocyanin pigments to produce violet or blue-green colors. Pineapple juice contains a small amount of iron from the equipment used in its processing, and when added to red or purple fruit juices, reds may change to blue, or the blues may be more intense. Usually acid, in the form of lemon juice, intensifies the red color of red or blue fruit juice mixtures. Orange juice is best omitted from combinations of red or blue fruit juices because it often produces a brownish color when present in a fairly large quantity. Nevertheless, some very tasty and attractive juice blends, punches, and smoothies can be prepared.

The color of canned fruits containing anthocyanin pigments tends to deteriorate on storage, whether the container is tin or glass. This deterioration is greater in the presence of light and warm temperatures. Canned or bottled shelf-stable cranberry juice cocktail is an example of a fruit product that will exhibit an unattractive reddish-brown color with extended storage.

Flavor

The flavor of fruits may be described as tart, fragrant, and sweet—these characteristics blending together in a pleasant and refreshing flavor bouquet (see Chapter 1 for a discussion on taste, aroma, and flavor). The flavor of each fruit is characteristic of that fruit. A ripe banana, for example, is readily identified by its odor and taste, which result from a specific complex combination of flavor components. Fruit flavors are the product of naturally found chemical compounds in fruit. In chemistry, some of the compounds contributing to flavor are classified as **esters**, **aldehydes**, **alcohols**, and **organic acids**.

The flavors we experience are also influenced by other ingredients. Aspartame, a high-intensity sweetener, appears to enhance the fruitiness of natural fruit-flavored systems, such as orange and strawberry. The addition of sucrose or table sugar does not produce a similar enhancement of fruit flavor [52]. Salt is also known to intensify sweetness, and is the reason some lightly salt watermelon or cantaloupe before consumption.

Aromatic Compounds.   Fruits owe their characteristic flavors largely to certain **aromatic compounds** that are present in them. Many of these compounds are **esters**. For example, the ester methyl butyrate is responsible for the typical odor and flavor of pineapple. Other compounds include aldehydes, such as benzaldehyde derivatives, and various alcohols that have been found to be responsible for the floral and fruity part of the aroma of apricots [10]. In each fruit, many different compounds contribute to flavor. At least 32 different substances have been identified in the aroma of apricots. In loquat fruit—a tropical or subtropical fruit with a flavor described as being mild, subacid, and apple-like—researchers have identified 80 aromatic substances. Benzaldehyde (an aldehyde) was a

---

Table 20–4
METHODS TO PREVENT ENZYMATIC OXIDATIVE BROWNING

Method	Explanation
Acid pH	Fruit may be dipped in acid solutions composed of ascorbic acid (vitamin C), citric acid, or cream of tartar. Diluted orange, lemon, or pineapple juice may be used for this purpose.
Reduce oxygen contact	Coat or sprinkle fruit with sugar or submerge in a sugar solution. A salt solution may be used to prevent oxidative browning of potatoes because the salty flavor imparted would be acceptable for potatoes.
Heat (blanching)	Heat will denature the enzymes that cause browning. Thus, fruits or vegetables are often blanched prior to freezing.

THE CHEMISTRY OF ENZYMATIC BROWNING

Enzymatic browning takes place when the enzyme poly-phenoloxidase (PPO) or other enzymes catalyze the oxidation of phenols in the fruit to form compounds called *quinones*. The quinones can polymerize to form *melanins*, which cause the brown pigments.

Chemical Reaction

Phenolic Compound → Diphenol → Quinone → Melanin
(discoloration)

Chlorogenic Acid PPO; Oxygen; Copper (Cu^{+2}) [cofactor]

Treatments That will Prevent Enzymatic Browning

- Lemon juice and other acids are used to preserve color in fruit, particularly apples and avocados, by

lowering the pH and removing the copper site necessary for the enzyme to function.
- Ascorbic acid can inhibit browning by reducing the quinones back to the original phenol compounds.
- Sulfites react with quinones. Therefore, no color pigment is formed.
- Heat will inactivate the enzyme.
- Honey contains short-chain proteins that interact with quinones.

Beneficial and Detrimental Aspects of Enzymatic Browning

Enzymatic browning can be beneficial because of color and flavor development in tea and dried fruits such as figs and raisins. Discoloration in cut fresh fruits and vegetables, as well as seafood such as shrimp, is detrimental.

major aromatic compound [17]. Some of the fruit flavor compounds can be synthesized in the laboratory, thus helping to improve the quality of artificial flavorings.

Acids. Also contributing to flavor are **organic acids**, occurring in fruits in the free form or combined as **salts** or esters. Although mixtures of acids may occur, one component usually predominates in each fruit. Malic and citric acids are most commonly present in fruits. Tartaric acid is a prominent constituent of grapes, and cream of tartar, used in cooking, is a by-product of wine making. Fruits of the plum family and cranberries contain some benzoic acid that cannot be used by the body but is excreted as hippuric acid. Rhubarb contains variable amounts of oxalic acid, depending on the maturity of the plant. Oxalic acid usually binds with calcium in the plant to form insoluble calcium oxalate, which is not absorbed from the digestive tract.

Fruits vary in acidity; some of this variation depends on variety and growing conditions. Scores for flavor have been positively correlated with pH in fruits such as peaches and raspberries [36]. Thus, acidity is a desirable characteristic in some fruits.

Essential Oils. Some fruits, as well as other plants, contain essential oils (see Chapter 6). Oil of lemon and oil of orange, well-known examples of such oils, occur in the leathery skin of the fruit. They may be expressed and used as flavoring or as the basis of extracts, which are made by combining the oil with alcohol.

Other Compounds. Sugars, some mineral salts, and a group of **phenolic compounds** also contribute to fruit flavor. Acid salts may affect flavor when fruits are cooked in metal containers and acid salts are formed. Tin or iron salts in canned fruits may result in a metallic flavor, but these salts are not harmful. Phenolic compounds usually impact the flavor and sensations experienced when consuming immature fruits. Phenolic compounds impart a bitter taste and produce an astringent or puckery feeling in the mouth.

COOKING WITH FRUITS

Most fresh fruits are generally considered to be at their best in the raw, ripened state and are thus served without cooking when possible. Fresh fruits, including

WHY DO THE BLUEBERRIES IN MUFFINS TURN GREEN AFTER BAKING?

The next time you make blueberry muffins, read the recipe carefully. If the muffin batter contains buttermilk and baking soda, you may want to reconsider the recipe. Baking soda neutralizes the acid in the buttermilk and makes the pH of the batter alkaline. Therefore, when the blueberries

are added to the batter and baked, a green color will develop around the blueberries.

Blueberries contain the anthocyanin pigment. This pigment requires an acidic pH to maintain its blue color. An alkaline pH will turn anthocyanin green. A muffin made with milk and baking powder should give better results.

those with rinds, such as melons, should always be washed before preparation or consumption. The cleanliness of hands and all work surfaces are also critical to avoid cross contamination. See Chapters 2 and 3 for more information on food safety and food regulation.

If fruits that brown easily, such as bananas, avocados, and apples, are to be peeled and cut, they should be dipped in or covered with lemon juice, pineapple juice, or solutions of vitamin C mixtures so that discoloration does not readily occur (Table 20–4). The acids and/or antioxidants in these solutions retard the enzyme activity and/or tie up oxygen to prevent brown compounds from forming. Placing the fruit in a sugar syrup or even immersing it in water retards browning to some degree by excluding air.

Citrus fruits are generally peeled, sectioned, sliced, or wedged. When peeling oranges, it is desirable to remove as much of the white membrane between the peel and the fruit as possible because this membrane is bitter and may be tough. The peel may be removed with a knife (**Figure 20–23**), or oranges may be placed in boiling water briefly and then peeled by hand. This method is best if several oranges are to be peeled because the oranges will peel more easily and quickly when heated.

Some recipes call for orange or lemon zest. Zest is the colored portion of the rind, excluding the white part of the rind. Zest may be prepared using a tool that cuts thin strips of the rind or by using a fine grater (**Figure 20–24**).

For some fruits, including green apples and rhubarb, cooking is sometimes desirable or necessary because they are more palatable and digestible when cooked. Cooking is also one way to add variety as fruits are included in daily menus. Overripe fruits may be further preserved by cooking.

Effect of Cooking Medium

The softening and breakage of pieces of fruit or vegetable during cooking is influenced by the cooking medium. If it is desirable to have fruits retain their shape, they may be cooked in a sugar syrup. If sauce is the expected end product, cooking in water hastens disintegration of the tissues.

The reason for these differences lies with the imbalance between sugar concentrations inside the fruit and in the cooking liquid. In uncooked fruit tissue, the cell walls act as *semipermeable membranes*, allowing

(a)

(b)

Figure 20–23

Oranges may be segmented by hand peeling and pulling apart the segments and leaving the membranes intact. Alternatively, (a) the peel and white pith may be removed by slicing off with a knife followed by (b) carefully cutting alongside each membrane to produce the fruit segment. (Richard Embery/Pearson Education)

passage only of water. If there is a difference in sugar concentration within and outside the cells, such as when sugar is sprinkled on fresh strawberries, water exits the cells in an attempt to dilute the concentrated sugar solution that has formed on the surface of the fruit. Thus, juice forms when strawberries are left to stand with sugar. The reverse occurs, that is, water enters fruit cells when fruit is placed in plain water because the concentration of sugar within the cells is greater than in the

Figure 20–24

A fine grater or a five hole zester (as shown here) may be used to remove fine strips of rind from citrus fruits, such as limes, lemons, and oranges. (Richard Embery/Pearson Education)

water outside the fruit. This movement of water through a semipermeable membrane is *osmosis.*

As fruit is heated, however, the permeability of the cell walls changes to allow not only the passage of water but also the movement of sugar and other small molecules. Simple **diffusion** then occurs as sugar and water move into or out of tissues. Therefore, in fruit slices cooked in a sugar syrup more concentrated than the 12 to 15 percent sugar solution found naturally in most fruits, sugar moves into the cells, and water moves out into the cooking liquid in an attempt to equalize the sugar concentration throughout (**Figure 20–25**). Because fruits shrink slightly, they appear shiny and translucent, and the tissue is firm.

A desirable proportion of water to sugar for most fruits is about two to one by measure. When the shape of the fruit pieces is to be retained, the fruit should not be stirred during cooking.

Conversely, when fruit is cooked in water alone, sugar moves from the more concentrated solution within the cells to the plain surrounding water, and some water moves back into the tissues (Figure 20–25). Fruits that are to be cooked to a smooth pulp are stewed in water until they attain the desired softness, after which sugar is added. These fruits may be stirred during cooking. Contrary to these general principles, some varieties of fruits do not cook to a smooth pulp in any circumstance. Furthermore not every type of fruit holds its shape well when cooked in syrup. The final product obtained is therefore partly a matter of the type of fruit being prepared.

General Cooking Recommendations for Fruits

Cooking of fruits will proceed most evenly when the pan is covered during cooking. The heat source should be regulated so that the liquid in the pan simmers or boils slowly.

Rhubarb is easily overcooked. Using a small amount of water and careful, slow cooking, only until the pieces are tender and partially broken, produces a desirable sauce from rhubarb. Apples sliced for cooking may sometimes include the skin for added color, flavor, and nutritive value. After cooking, the fruit may be run quickly through a strainer or food mill to increase the smoothness of the pulp if applesauce is being prepared.

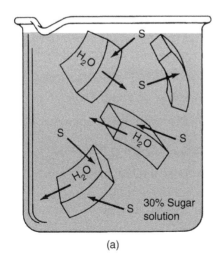
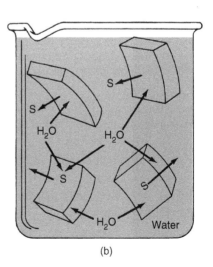

(a)   (b)

Figure 20–25

Cooking of fruit. (a) Apple slices cooked in a sugar solution will retain their shape. Sugar (S) moves into the fruit cells, and some water (H_2O) comes out into the surrounding sugar solution in an attempt to dilute it. (b) Apple slices cooked in plain water tend to break up more as water moves into the cells, expanding them.

Excess sugar in fruit sauces overwhelms the delicate flavor of many fruits. The desirable amount is often difficult to determine, especially when fruits are made into pies and other products in which the amount of sugar may not be added gradually until the desired amount is determined. The same variety of apple or other fruits varies in acidity from season to season and at different times during the storage period.

Cooking Dried Fruits

Dried fruits are used in various recipes. In some cases, it is desirable for the dried fruit to be softened or plumped by rehydrating the fruit. When dried fruits are soaked in water, then cooked, the tissues are softened. Soaking dried fruit in hot water for a short time results in good water absorption. The dried fruit, covered with water, may be brought to a boil, immediately covered and removed from the heat source, and then left to stand for 20 to 30 minutes (no longer than 1 hour). After soaking, the fruit is simmered until the desired degree of softness is achieved.

The higher sugar content of dried fruits reduces the need for additional sweetening. The small amount of sugar that is sometimes used is added at the end of the cooking period. The degree of acidity of the fruit determines the amount of sugar to be used. For example, dried apricots, being much more tart, require more sugar than dried plums.

Baking

Some fruits, such as apples, pears, bananas, and rhubarb, lend themselves well to baking. The aim is to have the fruit hold its form but be cooked until tender throughout. Apples and pears are often baked in their skins (cores removed) to hold in the steam that forms within the fruit and cooks the interior. Pared slices or sections may be baked in a covered casserole (350–400°F/177–204°C oven temperature). Rhubarb will keep its shape when baked.

Glazing

A range-top method known as *glazing* can be satisfactorily used to cook apples. The apples are cored as for baking, and a slit is cut in the skin all around the apple at right angles, or parallel, to the core. The apples are then placed in a saucepan with ¼ cup of water and ⅛ cup of sugar for each apple in the pan. They are covered and cooked over low heat. The apples are turned once while cooking and are cooked until tender. The cover is removed for the last minute before the apples are done.

Broiling or Grilling

Bananas, grapefruit halves, and pineapple slices are some of the fruits that can be satisfactorily broiled or grilled. Often a glaze or sauce may be used to add flavor.

Sautéing

Apples, bananas, and pineapple slices may be prepared by sautéing, or cooking quickly in a small amount of fat. A flavorful fat such as butter is preferred.

STUDY QUESTIONS

Consumption

1. Examine the consumption of fruit trends and then poll individuals you know to explore reasons for the limited consumption of fruit by Americans.

Nutrition

2. Discuss the nutritional implications of selecting fresh, or frozen, fruit as the form for the consumption of fruit.

3. Explain the reasons why nutritionally fruits are important in the diet.

4. (a) Identify the type of carbohydrate that usually predominates in ripe fruits.
   (b) List fruits that are good sources of vitamin C and vitamin A.
   (c) Identify other nutrients found in fruits.
   (d) Identify fruits that contain fat.

5. Discuss the value of phytochemicals in the diet, and identify sources of phytochemicals in fruits and vegetables.

Types of Fruit

6. Define a fruit.

7. Explain the difference between different types of fruits such as pome, drupe, aggregate, and multiple. Provide examples.

Selection of Fresh Fruit

8. Discuss the selection of several kinds of fruit.

Changes During Ripening

9. Describe the major changes that occur during the ripening of fruit.

10. Explain the role of ethylene gas in ripening and additional implications of storage.

11. Discuss how fruit changes in color, softening, and flavor during ripening.

Purchasing

12. Assess the economics of purchasing of fruits. Use information presented in other chapters in the text (Chapters 1, 18) and additional research to explain how U.S. Dietary Guidelines for fruit consumption may be accomplished at various budget levels.

13. Describe country-of-origin labeling and why consumers may find this information useful.

14. Discuss the reasons why organic produce may be more expensive to purchase?

15. Identify groups of consumers who tend to prefer organic fruits.

16. Identify several forms in which fruits may be purchased.

17. (a) Describe the major steps in the production of orange juice concentrate.

(b) Discuss contributors to the stability of the hazy cloud characteristic of orange juice.

(c) Explain how juice may be processed to reduce cloud formation, and why this treatment is effective.

(d) What special processing that involves enzyme action may be used to produce a sparkling clear fruit juice? Describe and explain.

18. Explain the difference between fruit juice and fruit drinks.

19. Explain why some fruits are treated with sulfur before drying, and discuss how sulfur influences nutritive value.

20. Discuss the different options for packing syrup with canned fruits and offer nutritional recommendations.

21. Provide suggestions for the use of frozen fruits.

Storage of Fruits

22. Discuss storage recommendations for several different types of fruit.

23. Compare and contrast controlled atmosphere storage and modified atmosphere packaging.

24. Identify the time of year when controlled atmosphere storage apples are sold in the marketplace and explain why.

Preparation

25. Provide instruction for consumers on the food safety considerations associated with preparing fruit.

26. (a) Identify the pigments often present in fruits.

(b) Explain why pigment content should be considered when mixing various fruit juices to make a fruit drink.

(c) Suggest ways to avoid a green color in blueberry muffins.

27. Identify and discuss the compounds that impact flavor and aroma of fruits.

Cooking with Fruits

28. (a) Compare the general effects of cooking fruits in water and in sugar syrups. Explain what is happening in each case.

(b) Suggest an appropriate procedure for cooking dried fruits. Explain why you would recommend this procedure.

(c) Describe several additional methods for cooking fruits.

29. Describe common characteristics of fruit flavor. List four types of chemical substances that contribute to the flavor of fruits.

30. (a) Describe the usual characteristics of fruits of good quality and suggest appropriate storage conditions to maintain quality.

(b) What factors are generally monitored during controlled-atmosphere storage of fruits and vegetables? Why is this type of storage effective for some fruits?

(c) Explain what is involved in modified-atmosphere packaging.

21
Salads, Gelatin Salads, and Table Olives

At one time, the term *salad* may have applied only to green leaves or to stalks that were eaten raw (**Figure 21–1**). Although today we often refer to green leafy vegetables, such as lettuce, endive, and romaine, as *salad greens*, the term *salad* has a much broader meaning. It includes mixtures of meat, fish, poultry, cheese, nuts, seeds, grains, legumes, and eggs as well as all kinds of vegetables and fruits. Often, salads are made with raw or uncooked foods, but they are certainly not limited to these items. A salad may be composed entirely of cooked or canned products, or mixtures of raw and cooked items. A dressing is usually served either mixed with or accompanying the salad. The dressing may be rich and elaborate, or it may be as simple as lemon juice or oil and vinegar. Congealed salads, prepared with gelatin, which contain a variety of ingredients are yet another type. Gelatin is also used in other recipes including desserts.

Table olives are an important food throughout the world, dating back to early civilizations. Throughout the world, olives are consumed with meals including breakfast, also as a snack, hors d'oeuvre, or added to salads, pasta, and many other foods. Olives are made edible through curing. Olives may be whole or pitted. They can be further processed by stuffing, chopping, or made into items such as tapenade that is eaten as a dip or used as a condiment.

The salad may be served at numerous points in a meal. It often accompanies the main course as a side dish. Salads are also served as a separate course before the main course or between the main course and the dessert. Some salads, especially those with fruits and nuts that are dressed with a rich or somewhat sweet dressing, are appropriately served for dessert. For lunch or dinner, the salad may be the main course, with the remainder of the menu being built around it (**Figure 21–2**).

The type of salad served depends on its use or position in the meal. The dinner salad is usually a light, crisp, tart accompaniment to the meat or other entrée. Heavier high-calorie salads, such as macaroni and tuna fish or meat and potato, are not appropriately included in a meal already composed of filling high-protein foods. Instead, meat, poultry, fish, egg, cheese, and potato salads that are combined with some crisp vegetables and relishes are suitable for use as a main course. Some small fish salads of high flavor, such as crab, shrimp, lobster, and anchovy, may serve as an appetizer, similar to cocktails and canapés made with these fish. Usually, the amount of fish used is not large, and it is combined with crisp, flavorful foods.

Potato salad may be an accompaniment to a meal. Used in this way, the starchy potato functions as it does in the dinner menu. Potato salad is sometimes served hot, as was the original German potato salad.

Figure 21–1

Mixed salad greens with balsamic mustard vinaigrette is simple yet flavorful. The greens in this salad include watercress, romaine, and Bibb lettuce. (Richard Embery/Pearson Education)

Figure 21–2

Salad can be served as a main entrée or side dish. (Gayvoronskaya_Yana/Shutterstock)

Figure 21–3

Traditional Caesar salad. (Daniel Korzeniewski/123RF)

The fruit salad is particularly suitable as an appetizer or dessert. If kept tart and not too large, it may also be appropriately used as an accompaniment in the dinner menu. A fruit salad can be a popular choice for refreshments at an afternoon or evening party. Fruit salads may also be served with a cheese plate and crisp crackers or a sweet creamy yogurt dressing.

The salad is an appealing food form using fresh fruits and vegetables. The element of crispness, which most salads introduce, provides an opportunity for greater variation in texture for many menus. Tartness and appetizing, fresh flavors are easily added to the meal in the form of salads.

In this chapter, the following topics will be discussed:

- Consumption trends and nutritive value
- Salad preparation and ingredients
- Salad dressings
- Vinegar
- Table olives
- Gelatin structure and characteristics
- Effect of temperature, concentration, and other factors on gelation
- Gelatin gels, salads and desserts

CONSUMPTION TRENDS AND NUTRITION

The eating of greens dressed with vinegar, oils, and herbs can be traced back to Ancient Romans and Greeks. This dressed greens custom was first adopted throughout Europe then in America [3]. In the early 1900s, ice shipping helped expand shipping range and the popularity of lettuce.

Consumption Trends

Consumption of salads continues to grow [7, 30]. In 2015, 24.5 pounds of lettuce were consumed per

person, of which 55 (13.5 pounds per person) percent was head lettuce according to the Agricultural Marketing Resource Center. Fresh spinach consumption in 2014 was 1.7 pounds per person. Nearly half of U.S. consumers claim to eat green salad at least once every three days with 46 percent claiming their consumption has increased in the past year. Nearly 90 percent of restaurant menus offer salads, as customers look for healthier options [30]. Classic Caesar salads (**Figure 21–3**) are found on half of the menus with house salads, garden salads, and Greek salads as popular menu options [30]. Kale salad is the fastest growing menu trend, and Brussel sprouts and wedge salads are gaining popularity. Salad variety with exotic ingredients along with high protein and high fiber are other consumer trends [30].

Pre-packaged, ready-to-eat salad greens have increased consumer demand for salads [49]. Agricultural Marketing Resource Center estimates about one-fourth of all iceberg lettuce is destined for pre-packaged salads. Head lettuce and romaine lettuce continue to be large drivers in fresh vegetable production [9]. Per capita availability of fresh dark-green and leafy vegetables including salad greens of escarole, romaine, leaf lettuce, kale, and spinach increased from 1.4 pounds per person in 1970 to 22.1 pounds in 2014. Romaine and leaf lettuce more than tripled from 1985 of 3.3 pounds per person to 10.8 pounds per person in 2014. However, the availability of head lettuce dropped to 14.5 pounds per person in 2014 [7]. Historic head lettuce patterns are shown in **Figure 21–4**. Popularity and availability of other salad greens maybe explain decrease in head lettuce demand.

Table olive consumption has been increasing worldwide over the past two decades according to the International Olive Council. See **Figure 21–5** for global table olive consumption trends.

Flavored gelatin is available in a wide variety of flavors. Single-serve, prepared gelatin options in grocery shelves and the refrigerated section continue to meet consumer demand for such products.

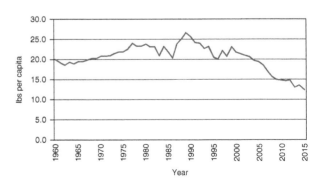

Figure 21–4

Retail availability of head lettuce. (Data from U.S. Department of Agriculture/Economic Research Service/graphics Sam Frye)

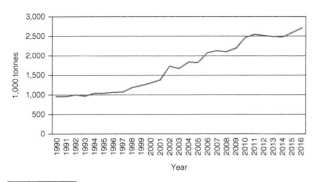

Figure 21–5

World table olive consumption has risen over the last two decades. (Data source: International Olive Council and graph by Sam Frye)

Non-protein gel options expand needs of vegan, kosher, and halal consumers. These non-protein gel products are often polysaccharide and gum-based products. Individual serving sizes and shelf-stable gel products are still popular options.

Nutritive Value

Increased salad consumption can help meet *2015–2020 Dietary Guidelines for Americans* goals to increase fruits and vegetables consumption. Two cups of leafy salad greens is considered an equivalent of a 1 cup vegetable serving [7]. The majority of salads prepared from fresh fruits and vegetables are comparatively low in kilocalories (not including the dressing, of course), but are important sources of minerals, vitamins, and fiber. Fruit and vegetable salads are an excellent source of **phytochemicals** that appear to function as antioxidants or anticancer agents [57]. Studies have shown red pigments in lettuce have higher antioxidant properties and are rich in phenolic acids [41]. The green leafy vegetable salads are especially valuable for iron, vitamin A, vitamin C, and beta-carotene. Spinach is an excellent source of folic acid and vitamin K, C, A, E, and B6. It is a good source of iron, magnesium, and potassium. Lettuce and other greens have some calcium. Iceberg lettuce has the least amount of vitamins because most of the edible portion of head lettuce is the interior leaves that are somewhat "bleached" [19]. Darker leaves like those found in romaine and leaf lettuce have more vitamins and minerals [19].

Starchy salads, such as potato, are higher in kilocalories than salads made with fruits and succulent vegetables. Meat, fish, egg, and cheese salads furnish chiefly protein, although some crisp vegetables often form a part of such mixtures.

The final caloric value of salads, as consumed, is greatly influenced by the type and quantity of dressing used. The amount of fat, usually contained in the salad oil or cream, is the major factor influencing the caloric content of dressings. Cooked dressings, particularly those made with water or milk, have a lower caloric value than mayonnaise, creamy, and vinaigrette dressings. A variety of commercial salad dressings average 60 to 80 kilocalories per tablespoon. Mayonnaise contains about 100 kilocalories per tablespoon. There are, however, many reduced-fat dressings on the market. Special fat-free dressings may furnish as little as 6 kilocalories per tablespoon. See Chapter 8 for information about the preparation of salad dressings including mayonnaise.

For centuries, olives have had a long history of nutritional and medicinal benefits [25]. Consumption of table olives has been associated with many health benefits including decreased cardiovascular and cancer risks attributed to the antioxidant properties of phenolic compounds [60]. Tocopherols (a form of vitamin E) and monosaturated fatty acids are also considered a nutritional benefit [56]. Recently, the oleuropeins were found to increase insulin secretion [61].

Gelatin is a protein food derived from animal sources, yet it is a protein of low biologic value. It lacks several essential amino acids, particularly tryptophan. Regardless of the quality of protein, the amount of gelatin required to form a gel is so small (1 tablespoon per pint of liquid) that its nutritive contribution is insignificant. One tablespoon of granulated gelatin

UP CLOSE
SALADS—SERVED THROUGH THE AGES

The salad is not a modern preparation. Green leaves were used by the ancient Romans. Other nationalities from the fifteenth century onward favored the use of flavorful herbs and raw vegetables. The introduction of salads into England was apparently made by Catherine of Aragon, one of the wives of Henry VIII and a daughter of Ferdinand and Isabella of Spain. The origin of present-day meat and fish salads was probably the salmagundi of England, used for many years as a supper dish. This meat dish made use of numerous garnishes that are used today, such as hard-cooked eggs, pickles, beets, and anchovies.

The influence of southern France is apparent in the use of French dressing for salads. The original dressing was made of olive oil and was seasoned to perfection. Spain has made the pepper a popular salad vegetable, and the Mediterranean countries introduced garlic flavor. The original German potato salad has many variations today. ■

furnishes about 30 kilocalories and 9 grams of protein. Some gelatin desserts and salads may provide the means by which significant amounts of fresh fruits and vegetables are incorporated into the diet, but it is the added foods rather than the gelatin that are nutritionally valuable.

SALAD INGREDIENTS

Salad Greens

Sometimes the term salad greens or leafy greens are misleading as not all salad greens are the color green; some are red, brown, yellow, or white [31]. Salad greens vary in size, shape, texture, color, flavor, and nutritional quality [19]. Many greens are lettuces or part of the chicory family [31]. Salad greens are sold fresh, lightly processed, and in bulk for restaurants or as pre-packaged, ready consumer packages or ready-to-eat individual salads [19].

Lettuce is the best known salad plant. Lettuce is a leafy vegetable. Multiple types and varieties of lettuce exist. Cultivation of lettuce is thought to have started in the Mediterranean basin. Written accounts of lettuce being served to Persian royalty date back to 500 B.C. prior to ancient Greek and Roman writings. Lettuce was thought to have spread to Northern Europe by the Roman soldiers. Lettuce was one of the first vegetables brought to the United States [19]. Lettuce is produced year round in the United States, but is a cool season crop that thrives in moderate temperatures with cool nights.

California is the largest lettuce producer in the United States, growing 70–75 percent of all lettuce, with Arizona being the second-largest producer, growing 18–20 percent of lettuce [19]. In California, most specialty greens are grown in beds or in the open under plastic-covered tunnels for multiple harvest or "ratooning" [12].

Food Safety Concerns

Lettuce and salad green processing leads to potential contamination entry points especially with pre-shredded, chopped, and packaged items [8]. Contamination of leafy greens with foodborne illness pathogens can occur in the field, cooling facilities, packing houses, processors, transportation vehicles, or food establishments. Direct and indirect microbial contamination is a concern from field to table [34]. Issues and concerns about food safety have risen with processed and bagged salad lettuce/greens as fresh cut produce increases risk of contamination since natural barriers are broken. The plant cellular components, once released, provide a nutritive medium for pathogens. Downy mildew is a fungus that is the biggest problem in lettuce production [29, 37]. Downy mildew is thought to create openings for foodborne disease pathogens such as *E. Coli* to enter lettuce tissues [29]. Microbial growth prevention is the goal to prevent foodborne illness [8]. New lines of lettuce resistance to downy mildew are being developed [37]. Scientists continue to research how to improve food safety of salad greens. Industrial scale washing procedures, lettuce treatments, and bagging material have undergone a great deal of research as demonstrated in **Figure 21–6** [8, 34]. Sanitizing leafy greens before processing and controlling atmospheric conditions and processing times can help reduce microbial contamination and growth [23, 34]. Packaging that allows plants to breathe slowly after bagging and creates a barrier against pathogen introduction, plus storage at the

---

HEALTHY EATING
ADD A SALAD AND REAP NUTRITIONAL BENEFITS

Salads can help us to consume more fruits and vegetables and gain the benefit of more vitamins, fiber, and phytochemicals in our diet. Others suggest that consuming a high-volume but low-calorie salad, such as green salad with a low-calorie dressing, can help decrease calorie intake. But does it really work?

A group of researchers, using the Third National Health and Nutrition Examination Survey, which included 9,406 women and 8,282 men, found that the consumption of salads and raw vegetables was positively associated with higher serum levels of folic acid, vitamins C and E, lycopene, and α- and β-carotene [46].

Another group of researchers examined the influence of salad consumption on satiety and how the consumption of a salad as a first course affected food consumption during the remaining meal. Forty-two women participated in this study. These researchers found that consuming a low-energy dense salad as a first course reduced intake during the entire meal [42]. Choose the first course wisely, however; a high-calorie but small salad may result in an overall increase in calories at the meal.

Figure 21–6

A USDA microbiologist withdraws a gas sample from bagged lettuce stored under modified atmosphere packaging in a film that restricts oxygen transmission. (Peggy Greb/USDA ARS)

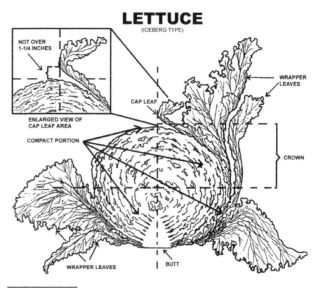

Figure 21–7

Iceberg lettuce parts. (USDA/Agriculture marketing service)

correct temperature during handling and transport are all important in controlling microbial pathogens in processed greens [8, 11, 20].

The FDA 2009 Food Code defines "cut leafy greens" as fresh leafy greens whose leaves have been cut, shredded, sliced, chopped, or torn. "Leafy greens" does not include herbs. Lettuce or other leafy greens that are cut from their root in the field with no other processing are considered a raw agricultural commodity. The FDA guidance is that storage of greens should be at less than 41°F (5°C) to minimize bacterial pathogen growth. New lettuce lines are being developed by scientists to improve eating, shipping, and growing qualities plus disease resistance [20].

Lettuce Categories

Lettuce can be subdivided into four broad categories of crisphead lettuce, butterhead, leaf lettuce, and romaine (cos) [19].

Crisphead Lettuce.

Iceberg Lettuce. This is the most well-known crisphead lettuce type. It is the most popular of the salad greens. Heads are compact, very firm, and spherical with crisp texture [53]. **Figures 21–7** and **21–8** show the part of a head lettuce. The leaves are broader than they are long [19]. Outer leaves are dark green with inner leaves a whitish or creamy yellow pale green. Heads are firm, compact with crisp texture,

Figure 21–8

This head lettuce with wrapper leaves is Iceberg lettuce from USDA Agriculture Research Service (ARS) breeders. Most Iceberg lettuce is grown in the Salina Valley of California, the world's largest lettuce growing region. (Scott Bauer with U.S. Department of Agriculture/Agriculture Research Service)

and mild flavor. Rust can be a problem with iceberg lettuce, especially in the months of January through April (**Figure 21–9**). Rust, bruising, discoloration, dirt, and pink rib are all grading defects. Head lettuce is graded U.S. Fancy, U.S. No. 1, and U.S. No. 2, depending on head defects based on USDA grading standards [53]. Lettuce is shipped packed in cartons as "naked," "wrapped," or "film bags" described as follows: [53]

Naked—Heads are not individually wrapped and generally have wrapper leaves attached (see **Figure 21–10**).

Figure 21-9

Rust spots on head lettuce. (USDA/Agriculture Marketing Service)

Figure 21-10

A crate of "naked" head lettuce. (Scott Bauer/ United States Department of Agriculture/ Agriculture Research Service)

Wrapped—Wrapper leaves have generally been removed and heads are wrapped with a film covering.

Film bags—Wrapper leaves have generally been removed and the heads are placed in film bags. Bags may have three to five heads per bag, placed in cartons.

Batavia (French Batavia). This is a subtype of crisphead lettuce and is similar to iceberg, except it is smaller, less dense, and more flavorful. Batavia is popular in Europe and is found in farmers' markets or is home grown [11].

Butterhead. Butterhead types, including Bibb and Boston, have smooth leaves and a delicate, buttery flavor (**Figure 21-11**). They have soft, pliable leaves and the inner leaves have an oily feeling to touch [53]. The heads are considerably smaller and looser than crisphead lettuce. Since the head is loose, it is difficult to distinguish between wrapper leaves. All leaves of butterhead are considered head leaves, even those leaves that do not form around a compact head portion.

Boston and Bibb. Boston is larger and paler than Bibb [31]. Leaves form cups and are broader than long. The heads have light to dark-green leaves on the outside with creamy yellow leaves inside. Some varieties may have red pigmentation [19, 31, 41]. The same grading of iceberg lettuce applies except there is "No established U.S. grade" for red Boston type lettuce.

Roman or Cos. Romaine or cos is characterized by elongated leaf shapes that are longer than broad, with heads that are either closed or relatively open at the top and more narrow at the base [19, 53]. Leaves appear coarse yet are actually tender, sweet, and more flavorful than iceberg lettuce. Outer leaves are typically darker green and inner leaves yellowish [19]. Romaine hearts are the tender inner portion of the romaine head [53]. An elongated seedstem is a grading defect and is shown in **Figure 21-12.**

Leaf Lettuce. Leaf lettuce or cutting lettuce occurs in many sizes, shapes, and colors, but is characterized by the fact that it does not form heads (see Figure 21-11). Leaf lettuce grows in bunches or rosettes of leaves that may be long or broad, round, spatulate, or lobed with smooth or frilled margins and dark to light green or red [19, 31]. It grows more open than head lettuce, so there are fewer bleached leaves compared to other lettuce. Leaf lettuce is grown in greenhouses, hot houses, or open fields [53]. The flavor is slightly strong but still mild in tender leaves [19, 31]. Good quality lettuce should have nicely shaped leaves that are free from breaks, tears, bruises, or brown spots. Leaf lettuce that has grown a long time may have coarse stems that are tough and fibrous [53]. Baby lettuces are miniature versions of more matured varieties of leaf lettuce. They have a more delicate and subtle flavor. Smaller size, variety, and flavor works well for salads and garnishes. *Mesculum* is French for a mixture of these baby lettuces [31]. A mix of young specialty greens that is sold in the United States is known as *California Salad* [12].

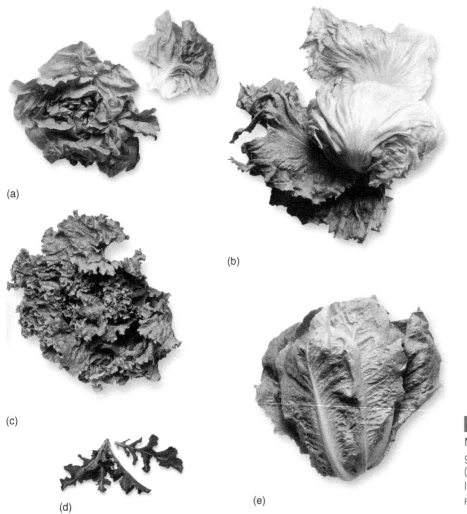

Figure 21–11

Many different kinds of lettuce greens are available: (a) Boston, (b) iceberg, (c) leaf, (d) red oak leaf, (e) romaine. (Richard Embery/ Pearson Education)

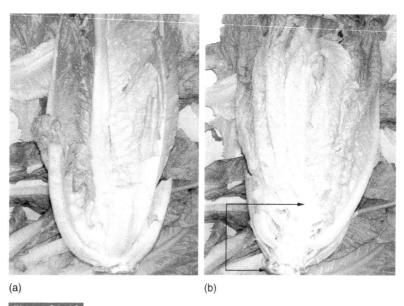

Figure 21–12

(a) Standard Romaine or cos lettuce. (b) The black arrows demonstrate seedstem defect in the Romaine lettuce. (USDA/Agricultural Marketing Service)

Figure 21–13

Belgium endive or witloof. (Richard Embery/Pearson Education)

Figure 21–14

Curly endive. (Richard Embery/Pearson Education)

Figure 21–15

Escarole. (Richard Embery/Pearson Education)

Figure 21–16

Radicchio or red chicory. (Richard Embery/Pearson Education)

Chicory. Two types of chicories are grown for leaf salads. One is large-rooted chicory that has broad-leafed tops of upright, spreading growth with leaves that may or may not be bleached [53]. The other type is known as witloof or Belgian/French endive, that is always bleached and resembles a Chinese cabbage. Chicories are slightly bitter. Their shape, color, and size are numerous.

Belgian Endive. Belgian endive or witloof is actually the shoot of a chicory root [31]. The heads are small, tight with elongated pointed leaves as shown in **Figure 21–13**. The leaves are white at the base with yellow fringes and tips. There are purple-tipped Belgian endives too. The leaves, cut or whole, can be used as salads. Sometimes endive heads are served grilled or braised. Originally from Belgium, this endive is now grown in California although a great deal is imported from Europe, where it is an important winter vegetable [31, 53].

Large Root Chicories.

Curly Endive or Frisée. This is a chicory with dark-green outer leaves that are sturdy, deeply frilled, and pointed with slightly bitter taste, which is shown in **Figure 21–14**. The inner leaves are more yellow, tender, and less bitter. Curly endive is strong flavored and often mixed with other greens for texture and flavor [31].

Escarole. This is a broadleaf endive with thick, flat leaves that are slightly bitter. The outer leaves are dark and pale green with yellow leaves in the center as shown in **Figure 21–15**. Escarole is often mixed with

other greens for added texture. Its strong flavor pairs with full, robust dressings [31].

Radicchio or Red Chicory. This is a reddish and white chicory that resembles a small red cabbage as shown in **Figure 21–16**. The bitter flavor is strong, so it is often mixed with other greens for color, texture, and flavor in a salad. The leaves form cups when separated and can be used to hold salad mixtures. Radicchio is less readily available and sometimes rather pricey [31].

Other Salad Greens and Ingredients

There are many other greens that may be used as salad greens, offering yet another dimension to the flavor, taste, and appearance of a salad. Purslane, amaranth, collards, beet greens, turnip greens, mustard greens, pea shoots, baby bok choy, tatsoi, broccoli rabe, and Chinese cabbage or celery cabbage are also highly acceptable as salad plants [43]. Sprouts, edible flowers, and fresh herbs are also used in salads.

Spinach. Spinach is a quick maturing, cool season, leafy green vegetable crop used in salads, which is shown in **Figure 21–17a**. It is a member of the goosefoot family (*Chenopodiaceae*) like beets and Swiss chard [54]. The popularity of spinach has grown with increased consumption as fresh (salads) and

Figure 21–17a

Flat leaf spinach. (Richard Embery/Pearson Education)

Figure 21–17b

Wilted spinach salad with hot bacon dressing. (Richard Embery/ Pearson Education)

processed spinach. The principal commercial types of spinach are "savoy" (crinkly leaf type) and "flat leaf."

Spinach has a deep-green color with rich flavor and tender texture. It is marketed as clipped and bagged and fresh market bunched. The fresh bagged spinach contains very small young leaves referred to as "baby spinach." Bunched spinach leaves are much larger. Good quality spinach should be crisp not wilted or yellowed [31]. A popular spinach salad is one that is tossed with hot bacon dressing **Figure 21–17b**. Spinach is graded as U.S. Extra No. 1, U.S. No. 1, and U.S. Commercial [54].

Sprouts.   Sprouts are not a salad green but are often used as or in salads (**Figure 21–18**). These sprouts

Figure 21–18

Sprouts. (Richard Embery/Pearson Education)

are young plants from sprouted seeds, such as alfalfa, daikon, mung bean, or mustard plants. Other sprouted seeds include red clover, broccoli, wheat, radish, soybean, and other vegetables or grains. Alfalfa sprouts have a fine texture with mild sweet flavor and taste. Daikon and mustard sprouts have a peppery flavor [31].

However, sprouts represent a food-safety concern because the conditions for producing sprouts (time, temperature, water activity, pH, and available nutrients) are also ideal for pathogen growth such as *Salmonella* or *E. coli* [14] (**Figure 21–19**). In the United States, between 1996 and 2016, sprouts were responsible for approximately 46 foodborne illness outbreaks accounting for 2,474 illnesses, 187 hospitalizations, and three deaths, including two documented outbreaks of *Listeria monocytogenes* [52]. The FDA has been working on industry guidance for safeguards to prevent foodborne illness associated with sprouts [52].

Edible Flowers.   Flowers are grown specifically for eating. Nasturtiums, calendulas, and pansies can add color to a salad or a plate when used as a garnish as shown in **Figure 21–20**. Squash blossoms are sometimes sliced into julienne strips and added to salads. Chive blossoms can also add flavor and color to a salad. Only edible flowers that are pesticide free should be used. Some flowers and blossoms are toxic. Flowers used in salads should be purchased directly from a food purveyor [31].

Fresh Herbs.   Herbs such as cilantro, basil, dill, oregano, marjoram, mint, sage, savory, tarragon, and rosemary may be added in small quantities to mixed greens for flavor. The leafy herbs can be cut in slivers or chiffonade. Other herb leaves are picked from stems or chopped, and then mixed with greens [31].

Watercress.   Watercress has a peppery flavor and adds spicy flavor to a salad. The small dime-size leaves are usually picked from the thick stems (see **Figure 21–21**). Watercress should be dark green with no yellowing. The leaves are often packed in ice to preserve freshness [31].

Kale.   There are over 50 varieties of kale. Kale is a thick coarse green with flat or ruffled curly leaves ranging in color from deep-dark green to purple to yellowish green (see **Figure 21–22**). Kale leaves are removed from the thick stems and prepared much like spinach. Kale has a pungent somewhat bitter peppery flavor and some varieties have a sweeter, more nutty, flavor. Red Russian kale with reddish stems and green leaves is described as the sweetest kale. Young tender leaves are less bitter and more suited for salads. Ancient Greeks and Romans enjoyed kale and it was popular during the Middle Ages. Kale was introduced

Figure 21–19

Microbiologists observe the display of a confocal microscope being used to examine an alfalfa sprout root that has been experimentally contaminated with salmonella. The microbes show up green or blue on the computer screen.
(Scott Bauer/United States Department of Agriculture)

Figure 21–22

Kale. (Barbro Bergfeldt/Shutterstock))

Figure 21–20

Edible flowers can add color to salads or be used as a garnish. (Richard Embery/Pearson Education)

Figure 21–23

Raw kale salad has become a popular salad choice. This kale salad with avocado, carrots, and raisins with lemon dressing is full of vitamins and minerals. (Richard Embery/Pearson Education)

Figure 21–21

Watercress. (Richard Embery/Pearson Education)

to the United States in the 1600s. Kale is a valuable crop in Africa and Turkey [1]. It is easy to grow and nutritionally rich. Kale has been labeled a "superfood" being rich in vitamin C, vitamin K, calcium, folic acid, and magnesium; it is high in fiber but low in oxalates

[6, 27]. Kale salad popularity has soared over the last decade (**Figure 21–23**). It is sold as leaves, bundles, and bagged and individual salads.

Arugula. Documents record arugula use by ancient Greeks in the first century [38]. Arugula or *rocket* (English), *roquette* (French), *rucola* or *rughetta* (Italian), is a collective name for several species that are members of the mustard family [38]. Arugula leaves are dull green with deep cut edges with stems that may be

Figure 21–24

Arugula pumpkin salad. (NADKI/Shutterstock)

Figure 21–25

Dandelion greens. (Richard Embery/Pearson Education)

light or reddish. It has a pungent peppery spicy flavor. Arugula can be used alone or mixed with other salad greens [38]. Arugula is best 2–4 inches (5–10 cm) long [31]. The tiny white arugula flowers can also be added to salads [43] (see arugula salad in **Figure 21–24**).

Dandelion.   Dandelion leaves can be used for salad greens. The long, thin leaves with jagged edges that look like "arrows" are shown in **Figure 21–25** [43]. Dandelion salad greens are best with small leaves as they are more tender and less bitter [31].

Mâche.   Mâche is also known as lamb's lettuce or corn salad (lettuce), since it is found in corn fields. Mâche is a delicate, tender, mildly nutty-flavored green, shown in **Figure 21–26**. It has small, curved pale to dark-green leaves. It is typically combined with other mild greens such as Boston or bibb lettuce and served with a light dressing [31].

Mizuna.   Mizuna is of Asian origin. The feathery dark green has fringed leaves as shown in **Figure 21–27**, which are tangy in flavor. Baby mizuna is essential in mesclun [11, 43].

Figure 21–26

Mâche. (Richard Embery/Pearson Education)

Figure 21–27

Mizuna. (Mr. Pawin Pummarin/123RF)

Figure 21–28

Sorrel. (Richard Embery/Pearson Education)

Sorrel.   Sorrel or sourgrass has the appearance similar to spinach (see **Figure 21–28**). The flavor of sorrel is tart and lemony. It is usually combined with other greens in a salad [31].

Salad Purchasing, Pre-Preparation, and Preparation

Purchasing fresh salad greens that are free from brown spots and yellowing greens and that are crisp and not limp or wilted is the first step toward making a salad. While shopping or storing, greens should be kept separate from other groceries especially raw meat [11]. Greens should be used as soon as possible after purchase. Unwashed greens will keep three to four days in the refrigerator [43]. Greens should be stored between 35 and 40°F (1.6 and 4.4°C) [11]. Greens should be handled carefully to avoid bruising and tearing, which activates enzymes and starts plant decay and deterioration.

Pre-chilling all salad ingredients, including dressings, canned items such as canned tuna or olives, and vegetable ingredients, is a beneficial pre-preparation step. As a food-safety practice, salads will chill more rapidly after preparation, if ingredients have been pre-chilled.

Cleanliness of hands and work areas is of prime importance, when preparing salads. Many salads are consumed raw, and therefore ingredients will not be cooked to destroy pathogenic organisms introduced through poor sanitation. Once the preparation area is sanitary and clean, ingredients should be carefully and thoroughly washed.

For maximum retention of freshness and nutritive value, many salad ingredients should be prepared shortly before the salad is to be made and served. Some vegetables, such as green leaves and celery, however, will be crisp and fresh if they are washed, wrapped, and chilled in the refrigerator for several hours. All excess water should be removed from the vegetables before storage to decrease the likelihood of spoilage.

Salad Green Preparation. The initial preparation of salad greens includes (1) removal of damaged outer leaves, (2) removal of the core, and (3) thorough washing. Removing the core/butt from an iceberg lettuce head speeds the absorption of water and simplifies separation of the leaves from the head. Firmly striking the head lettuce core on a hard surface loosens the core for easy removal (**Figure 21–29**).

When washing greens, submerge in cool water, then lift the greens out of the water away from the soil. Repeat with fresh water and give extra care to those greens, such as endive and savoy spinach, which may easily trap dirt. Spinach has a stem and midrib that may be removed simply by folding the leaf along the stem and then tearing it out (**Figure 21–30**).

For romaine lettuce, the leaf tips may be damaged and can be cut or torn off. Some prefer also to remove part or all of the rib on romaine by either tearing or cutting it from the leaf. Although hand tearing of greens is recommended to reduce bruising of the leaves, greens may also be satisfactorily cut or chopped with a chef's knife (**Figure 21–31**).

Salad greens should be dried after washing. Drain thoroughly in a colander. A salad spinner is preferred to remove excess moisture (**Figure 21–32b**). Alternative method of drying greens is blot with clean towel or paper towels. Oil-based dressing will not adhere to wet greens; dressing is diluted on wet greens [31].

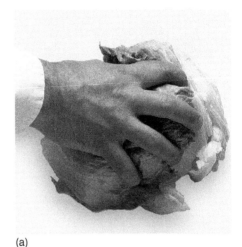

(a)

(b)

Figure 21–29

To remove a core from iceberg lettuce, (a) firmly strike the head of lettuce, core side down, against a cutting board or countertop and (b) remove the core that is now broken free from the head. (Richard Embery/Pearson Education)

Figure 21–30

The stem and rib of spinach may be removed by folding the spinach leaf in half as shown, then tearing the stem and rib away. (Richard Embery/Pearson Education)

(a)   (b)   (c)

(d)   (e)

Figure 21–31

Preparing romaine lettuce: (a) Remove wilted leaves and cut off discoloration or bad spots. (b) Trimmed head. (c) Trim outer leaves and damaged tips, then split the head lengthwise. (d) Cut lengthwise, then across the head into bite-size pieces. Or (e) Cut rib out of individual leaves and cut into bite-size pieces. (Richard Embery/Pearson Education)

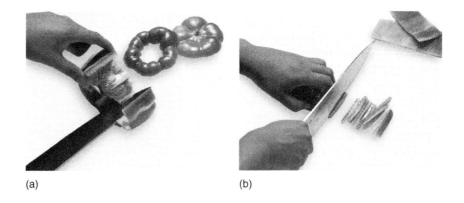

(a)   (b)

Figure 21–32a

Prepare green peppers by (a) cutting off the ends followed by removing the seed core and white ribs. Then the pepper (b) may be cut into julienne strips, as shown, or into other cuts as desired. (Richard Embery/Pearson Education)

Figure 21–32b

Salad spinner is the preferred method for drying greens. (Richard Embery/Pearson Education)

Salad green pieces should be small enough to spear with fork and be placed easily in the mouth, uniform pieces approximately 1½–2 inches across. Small leaves can be left whole. Iceberg lettuce and cabbage can be shredded [43]. Prewashed ready-to-eat bagged salads are readily available for ease in salad green preparation (**Figure 21–33b**). Some bagged salad greens are complete with dressing and salad condiments.

Dressing green salads should be done immediately before serving. Greens are combined in a large bowl and the dressing is placed on top and mixed gently with tongs, oversized fork and spoon, or even clean hands. The tossing action is from the bottom of the bowl, gently lifting the greens upward so that the topmost greens fall to the bottom. The greens are gently tossed until the dressing is distributed evenly. Greens should have just enough dressing to enhance the flavor and not overpower them [43].

Vegetables. A wide variety of vegetables are used in salads. Potatoes, greens beans, corn, cabbage, celery, cucumbers, green and red peppers, broccoli, cauliflower, and carrots are examples of a few of the vegetables commonly found in salads. Because vegetables were discussed in Chapter 20, the discussion here will be limited to preparation considerations for salads.

Cabbage is often shredded to be used in coleslaw. The cabbage may be shredded with a manual shredder, mixer, or food processor or by slicing thinly with a chef's knife on a cutting board. Likewise, carrots may be shredded for use in salads or alternatively may be diced or cut into coins with a knife. Green, red, and yellow peppers are prepared by removing the ends and then the stem and seeded core (**Figure 21–32a**). Many also recommend the removal of the pale-colored ribs, although they are

edible. Using a chef's knife and cutting board to cut from the interior flesh to the exterior skin of the peppers avoids the knife's slipping on the tough skin. Depending on intended use, peppers are often sliced or diced for use in salads. Raw turnip is another interesting ingredient for salads. It can be used in thin slices (often allowed to curl in cold water), sticks, or fine shreds.

Tomatoes may be sliced or diced for use in salads. For some salads, it may be preferable to remove the seeds and juicy pulp. To do this, cut the tomato in half, then gently squeeze out the seeds and pulp (**Figure 21–33a**). Broccoli and cauliflower are often

Figure 21–33a

The seeds and pulpy juice may be removed from tomatoes by cutting the tomato in half and squeezing. (Richard Embery/ Pearson Education)

Figure 21–33b

Bagged salads are one of the most popular items in the fresh produce section of supermarkets today. (Keith Weller/USDA/ARS)

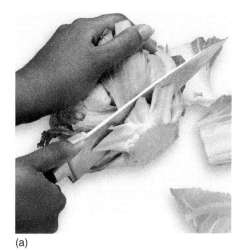

(a)

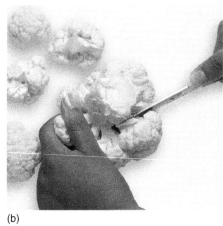

(b)

Figure 21-34

Cauliflower florets are prepared by (a) cutting off the core and (b) cutting the florets, as shown. (Richard Embery/Pearson Education)

cut into florets for use raw in salads (**Figure 21-34**). Other vegetables, such as green beans or asparagus tips, are blanched and then chilled for use in a salad with a marinade and other ingredients. Cooked beets have a desirable texture and flavor for some types of salads; however, because of the soluble red pigment (betalain) present, they may "bleed" red color onto the other salad ingredients.

Potatoes used for salad should be of a variety that holds its form when diced (see Chapter 18). Mealy potatoes, such as russets, tend to form a starchy mass when made into salad; therefore, most consider waxy potatoes to be a better choice (see **Figure 21-35**). Potatoes may be diced before or after cooking; however, dicing before boiling will reduce the amount of handling that is needed after the potatoes are cooked. Sometimes potatoes are cooked in their "jackets" meaning with skins on; then skin is removed from the cooked potato, sometimes while still warm.

In general, vegetables in most mixed salads should be cut into bite-size pieces so that the use of

a knife is not needed when eating the salad. The preferred size of vegetables will vary, however, depending on preferences and the recipe. In most cases, salad ingredients should not be finely minced because soft foods that are too finely cut tend to form a paste when mixed with salad dressings. Cabbage, regardless of how it is used, is better seasoned if it is finely shredded. Coarse shreds of cabbage are difficult to chew, particularly if it is a variety that does not become crisp easily (**Figure 21-36**).

Fruit Preparation. Many different fruits may be used in salads in a variety of ways. Some fruits provide a sweet contrast in vegetable salads. For example, mandarin oranges, peaches, or apples may be found in green, leafy salads. Other fruit salads use fruit as the focus and then add flavor and interest with complementary vegetables. Waldorf salad is an example

Figure 21-35

Potato salad. (Richard Embery/Pearson Education)

Figure 21-36

Asian coleslaw. (Richard Embery/Pearson Education)

of this. It has diced apples with celery, nuts, grapes or raisins, and optional marshmallows plus a dressing to bind the mixture together. Other fruit salads are simply fruit cups with several types of fruits mixed together with or without a dressing.

The preparation of fruits for salads will depend on the recipe and salad being prepared. Sections of citrus fruits can be prepared well in advance without significant quality loss. Citrus fruit sections used in salads are usually left whole, but many fruits are cut into bite-size pieces. Fresh fruits, such as apples, bananas, pears, peaches, and nectarines, will need to be dipped into an acidic fruit juice, such as diluted orange juice, or lightly sugared to prevent enzymatic oxidative browning unless cut immediately prior to consumption. Refer to Chapter 20 for more information about fruits and their preparation. Enzymatic oxidative browning and methods to control it were discussed in greater detail in Chapters 18 and 20.

Pasta and Grains. Pasta salads are not limited to macaroni salad. Penne, spaghetti, tortellini, orzo, bowties, and many others may be used for salad (**Figure 12–38b**). Most recipes call for the pasta to be cooked and then marinated in a vinaigrette, creamy, or mayonnaise-based dressing. Keep in mind that the pasta will absorb more moisture from the marinade; therefore, it should be cooked only until al dente. Overcooked pasta that is then marinated will likely become excessively soft.

Grains such as couscous (made from durum wheat), bulgur (parboiled and dried whole wheat), and rice are also featured ingredients in several recipes. Couscous and rice are usually cooked before finishing the salad with other vegetables, fruits, herbs, and dressings (see **Figure 21–37**). Tabouli (also called tabbouleh) is made from uncooked bulgur

Figure 21–38a
Tabouli salad. (Richard Embery/Pearson Education)

Figure 21-38b
Pasta salad. (Travellight/Shutterstock)

that is soaked in cold water to soften. Flavor is developed with tomatoes, onions, fresh parsley, olive oil, and other ingredients (see **Figure 21–38a**). Some of the grain-based salads, such as tabouli, are a tasty way to incorporate whole grains into a meal. Refer to Chapter 12 for more information about types of pasta and grains, as well as preparation recommendations.

Legumes. Black, cannellini, and kidney beans are examples of just a few types of beans that can be used for delicious salads. These and other beans may be used from a can, or, alternatively, dried beans may be cooked and chilled. Ingredients such as onions, green peppers, parsley, olive oil, red wine vinegar, or lime juice add contrasting textures, colors, and flavors that complement the beans. The preparation of beans was discussed in Chapter 19.

Meat, Poultry, Fish, and Eggs. Meats and chicken used in salads are usually diced, but fish is most often coarsely flaked with a fork. Small shellfish, such as shrimp, may be left whole or diced. Canned salmon and tuna fish are difficult to prepare in a way that retains the form of pieces, although tuna is more firm

Figure 21-37
Couscous salad. (Richard Embery/Pearson Education)

Figure 21-39

Cobb salad. (Richard Embery/Pearson Education)

Figure 21-40

Caprese salad. (Barbara Dudzinska/Shutterstock)

than salmon. Fish canned with a considerable amount of oil can be washed off with hot water before being chilled. Thus, water-packed fish is preferable, or, alternatively, the oil may become part of the dressing.

Eggs, for egg salad or as an ingredient in potato salad, are first hard cooked and then peeled. Depending on the recipe, the eggs may be finely or coarsely chopped. Care should be taken not to overcook eggs to avoid the dark olive green ring around the yolk. Refer to Chapter 23 for more information about eggs. The Cobb salad shown in **Figure 21-39** has julienne turkey, bacon, avocado, diced eggs, and crumbled Roquefort cheese.

Cheese

Cheese is often used in or on salads. Cheese may be shredded, grated, crumbled, sliced, or cubed. Blue (bleu) cheese and feta cheese are popular cheeses that are crumbled onto salads. Roquefort and blue cheese dressings contain the crumbled cheese in the dressing. Shredded or grated parmesan cheese is an ingredient in Caesar salad or may be sprinkled on top of the salad. Cottage cheese is sometimes served stuffed in a tomato as a salad. Tomatoes are layered with sliced mozzarella garnished with fresh basil and olive oil in Caprese salad (**Figure 21-40**). Cobb salads typically contain Roquefort or blue cheese crumbles. Strips of cheese are standard fare with Chef salads.

Marinated Salads and Salad Dressings

Marinated.   Meat, fish, starchy vegetables, and whole firm pieces of more succulent vegetables may be improved by *marinating*, which is the process of coating food lightly with a dressing or oil (a *marinade*) and letting the mixture stand in the refrigerator for an hour

or more before being made into a salad. The major purpose of marinating most salads is to improve the flavor. Many flavorful marinades can be prepared using specialty oils, vinegars, wines, fruit juices, herbs, and spices.

Some pasta salads are marinated overnight in the refrigerator. As previously discussed, it is important to cook the pasta only until "tender to the bite," or the pasta will be too soft. Leafy vegetables generally cannot be marinated because they wilt. The color of the vegetables in the salad also should be considered. For example, a fresh green bean or broccoli salad will not maintain a bright green color if marinated in an acidic marinade for more than a few hours (see Chapter 18). Excess marinade is drained off when the salad is served to avoid a pool of marinade on the plate.

Salad Dressings.   A wide variety of salad dressings are available. Dressings may be cooked or uncooked and the emulsions maybe temporary or permanent. Leafy green salads may be served with a dressing tossed into the salad just before serving. Dressing a green salad well in advance of serving is not recommended because extended contact of the greens and the dressing will cause the greens to wilt. Alternatively, the dressing may be passed for individuals to serve themselves. Most salad dressings are examples of **emulsions**, either temporary (most vinaigrette or French dressings) or permanent (mayonnaise). Types of dressings and their preparation were discussed in Chapter 8.

Certain types of salads, including potato, macaroni, meat, chicken, and fish and some fruit salads, are improved by being left to stand in the refrigerator for a time with the dressing. These salads are often mixed with the dressing and chilled for several hours before serving. Shredded cabbage, as in coleslaw, is improved by brief contact with the dressing. In contrast to

(a)

(b)

Figure 21–41

(a) This salade Niçoise was prepared by carefully arranging cherry tomatoes, sliced cucumbers, green beans, wedged hard-cooked eggs, sliced fingerling potatoes, blanched red peppers, artichoke hearts, and fresh tuna over a colorful bed of greens. (b) An attractively arranged Greek Salad creates a light and juicy summer salad. (Richard Embery/Pearson Education)

marinated salads that may be drained before serving, dressed salads usually incorporate only the amount of dressing that is needed to lightly coat the ingredients.

Presentation and Garnishes

Whether elaborate or simple, salads should be attractively arranged (**Figure 21–41**). Whole stuffed tomatoes, halves of peaches or pears, slices of pineapple, and gelatin molds necessarily take on a more fixed appearance than combination salads made from cut pieces. Color can be added by mixing a colorful ingredient in the main body of the salad or by adding a bed of greens and a garnish. The use of contrasting colors and shapes is especially effective. However, some colors may not combine attractively—for example, the clear red **lycopene**

KEEPING IT SAFE
FOOD SAFETY AND FRESH FRUITS AND VEGETABLES

Eating fruits and vegetables is associated with a healthy lifestyle, so what hazards could possibly be connected to these favored foods? Actually, there are several points in the production of fruits and vegetables at which contamination could occur. Potential concerns can include contamination with pathogens directly from improperly treated manure fertilizer or irrigation water that is microbiologically unsafe. In addition, postharvest operations, such as packing, can present potential contamination [40].

In 2006, a foodborne illness outbreak involving fresh spinach occurred. Although in this outbreak no specific error could be identified, it was evident that the field had become cross contaminated with a cattle operation in the local area. The need to examine and further improve agricultural practices to minimize the risk of *Escherichia coli* 0157:H7 outbreaks has been identified by the U.S. Food and Drug Administration [48].

Fresh-cut produce, which has become very popular in the marketplace, can present special food-safety considerations. The process of cutting up fruits and vegetables removes the protective skin and increases the surface area available for contamination. Also, the living tissues begin to respire more rapidly when cut, decreasing the period of peak quality. Modified-atmosphere packaging helps to control these changes if done properly, and these foods must be kept under refrigeration.

Various washing and sanitizing processes are used in the packing of fresh vegetables and fruits, and newer technologies are being studied. Methods to remove pathogens include physical removal, chlorine dioxide, acidified sodium chlorite, acidic compounds, and ozone. Use of irradiation is another possibility [18], and good manufacturing practices and Hazard Analysis and Critical Control Points programs continue to be the primary pathogen control strategy [40].

Not to be overlooked is your role in the safety of produce. A number of consumers report not washing produce before use, rarely washing melons before preparation, and storing their produce below raw meats in the refrigerator [33]. All of these are hazardous practices that have resulted in foodborne illness. So do your part and follow good food-safety practices when preparing your fresh fruits and vegetables.

pigment of tomato may clash with the purplish red pigment of beets.

Garnishes are not used solely as decorations but are also edible salad components. Ripe or stuffed green olives, radishes, and small cheese-stuffed celery stalks can also function as garnishes. Sprigs of watercress or parsley, which introduce a darker green color and an interesting leaf design, add appeal to many vegetable salads. Overgarnishing should be avoided, however, so that it complements and does not detract from the salad. Edible flowers, as well as fresh herbs, may be used as salad garnishes and ingredients.

Croutons add a crunchy texture and salad garnish. Add croutons immediately before serving so they do not become soggy. Nuts, seeds, bacon bits are other items used as garnishes to add texture and crunch to a finished salad [43].

Salads and Food Safety

Sanitary food-handling practices and good temperature control are important when preparing and serving salads. The cutting, dicing, and arranging of salads must be done in a way to minimize cross contamination from hands, cutting boards, kitchen sinks, or other sources. All fruits and vegetables, including melons, need to be stored at or below 41°F (4°C) once peeled, sliced, or otherwise broken apart.

The hot summer months and the popularity of picnics combine to encourage the holding of meat and starchy salads with mayonnaise or creamy salad dressings for extended periods without chilling. Any salad composed of high protein, neutral pH, and high-moisture foods will spoil readily if temperature abused. Thus, salads have caused outbreaks of food poisoning when held too long without adequate refrigeration. This is why it is particularly important that salads be refrigerated or iced in a cooler, if taken to a picnic, to prevent the growth of any undesirable microorganisms (see Chapter 2). Although mayonnaise has historically been implicated in the outbreak of foodborne illness in some salads, commercial mayonnaise, which is acidic, is not the culprit—rather, it is the lack of cleanliness during preparation and temperature control that are to blame. Keep salads at 40°F (4.4°C) or below.

VINEGAR

Vinegar is an ingredient commonly used in salad dressings and marinades [15]. Since ancient times, vinegar has been used throughout the world as a cooking ingredient, condiment, food preservative, pickling agent, cleaning agent, and for medicinal purposes [17, 28, 31]. Vinegar (Fr. *vinaigre*) literally means sour wine.

Vinegar is produced by a two-step fermentation process involving yeast and acetic acid bacteria. Fermentation can be the traditional slow method taking months to years or a faster process that is completed in weeks. The first stage uses yeast to convert a carbohydrate source to alcohol. The second stage is acetous fermentation where the alcohol is almost completely converted to acetic acid by *Acetobacter* bacteria [15, 32]. Acetic acid is responsible for the tart, pungent, biting characteristics of vinegar. The vinegar fermentation process requires oxygen with an optimal temperature around 80−85°F (26.6−29.4°C).

Any fermentable carbohydrate such as apples, wine, rice, molasses, or malt can be made into vinegar. Each sugar source yields a unique vinegar characteristic flavor and color as shown in **Figure 21−42**. Common vinegar categories are cider, distilled, wine, and malt. Other vinegars such as balsamic, rice, and flavored vinegars have become popular and prevalent in retail stores. Many fruit and other flavored vinegars are available in specialty shops. Different countries use fermentable carbohydrate sources readily available in the area. Vinegars from pineapple, raspberries, pomegranate, date, sugarcane, and coconut are found in regions that grow these products. The vinegar's chemical and organoleptic properties reflect the starting carbohydrate material [28]. **Table 21−1** describes some common vinegars and their characteristics and uses.

Vinegar must contain a minimum of 4 percent acetic acid (4 grams of acetic acid per 100 milliliters) [50]. Natural vinegars after fermentation often contain acetic acid in excess of 4 percent. Some vinegars may have acetic acid content as high as 15 percent [32]. When the vinegar is diluted with water, the label must state "diluted with water to ____ percent acid strength" [50].

Vinegar contains a number of volatile components that contribute to the vinegar aroma and other properties. Thus, pure acetic acid is not vinegar and cannot be labeled as such. Acetic acid should not be substituted in pickled or other products customarily expected to be prepared with vinegar [51].

FOCUS ON SCIENCE
ACIDIC MARINADES AND CHLOROPHYLL

The addition of an acid to a marinated salad containing a green (chlorophyll) vegetable will turn the chlorophyll to an olive-green color (pheophytin). A portion of the chlorophyll compound undergoes a chemical change because of the acid quantity and contact time with the acidic ingredient.

Figure 21–42

Balsamic vinegar, raspberry vinegar, and cider vinegar. (Richard Embery/Pearson Education)

Vinegar in the Supreme Court

Vinegar was the subject in a landmark court decision under the Food and Drug Act of 1906. The Supreme Court case of *United States v. 95 Barrels, More of Less,* *Alleged Apple Cider Vinegar* (285 U.S. 438, 1924) ruled that vinegar made from dried apples was not the same as vinegar that would have been produced from apples without dehydration. Vinegar made from dehydrated apples could not be labeled as "Apple Cider Vinegar."

Today's labeling guidelines state vinegars made from dried apples, apple cores, or apple peels must be labeled as "vinegar made from ____" where the blank is filled in with the name of apple product(s) used as the fermented source [50].

Mother of Vinegar and Vinegar Eels

Mother of vinegar is a non-toxic, thick, slimy, firm layer of cellulose formed by acetic acid bacteria *Acetobacter* during traditional vinegar fermentation [63, 28, 5] (**Figure 21–43**). Fermenting wine that has gone bad will produce a mother of vinegar or mat. Sometimes the mother of vinegar has been described as an acetic acid producing "organism" [32]. The mother of vinegar can act as a starter culture to introduce acetic acid

Table 21–1
SOME COMMON VINEGARS AND CHARACTERISTICS

Type of Vinegar	Carbohydrate Source	Characteristics	Notes
Cider vinegar Vinegar Apple vinegar	Unpasteurized apple juice or cider	Pale brown color Mildly acidic Fruity aroma	Popular in the United States
Wine vinegar Grape vinegar Sherry vinegar Champagne vinegar	Grape juice/wine	Maybe red or white grape Color and flavor depends on wine or grape juice used	Preferred in French and Mediterranean cuisines
Malted vinegar	Malted barley or cereal grain whose starch has been converted to malt	Dark brown Slightly sweet Mild flavor	Common in the United Kingdom as a condiment Used as condiment with fried foods especially fried fish
Distilled vinegar Spirit vinegar Grain vinegar	Distilled grain alcohol	Clear Strong vinegar flavor High acid content	Used for pickling and preserving
Rice vinegar	Rice wine	Slightly sweet Clean flavor Color depends on rice used may be clear, light yellow, pinkish, or light brown	Used in Asian cuisines Dipping sauce Works well in a variety of salads and other dishes
Balsamic vinegar (It. *Aceto balsamico*)	Produced from white *Trebbiano* or red *Lambrusco* grapes	Dark reddish brown (red) Light color (white) High acidity Sweet and tart Mellow	Traditionally aged in wooden barrels for 4–50 years Condiment and seasoning especially tomatoes and strawberries Sometimes used as bread dipping condiment with olive oil

Figure 21–43

Mother of vinegar. (© Amanda Frye)

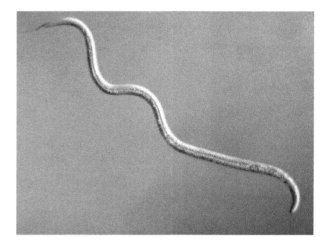

Figure 21–44

Vinegar eel. (Eric Grave/Science History Images/Alamy Stock Photo)

bacteria during acetous fermentation. It converts alcohol to acetic acid yielding vinegar [58].

The mother of vinegar typically develops like a skin on top of the fermenting brew. Sometimes the mother of vinegar becomes so heavy it falls to the bottom. The mother of vinegar can be saved from a previous vinegar and then used to produce more vinegar. If the mother of vinegar is left too long in the vinegar it can lead to negative effects.

Some vinegars are sold "with the mother of vinegar." However, most commercial vinegar is filtered and pasteurized prior to bottling to eliminate the mother of vinegar. A mother of vinegar may form in vinegar that has been opened and stored. The mother of vinegar is harmless and can be filtered out and discarded [39].

Vinegar eels are not eels or worms; they are live nematodes *Turbatrix aceti* feed on organisms in fermenting vinegar. Vinegar eels may be used in or found during vinegar production [64] (**Figure 21–44**). Vinegar eels are spread by fruit flies (*Drosphila*). Some vinegar makers believe that vinegar eels scavenge dead and dying *Acetobacter*, and so consider them as important in keeping the fermentation clean and active [32]. Other vinegar makers believe vinegar eels affect bacterial count and are harmful. However, federal policy states that finding vinegar eels in finished bottled product would be considered objectionable and the vinegar

would be considered a filthy substance. Thus, the bottled vinegar containing a vinegar eel would be classified as adulterated according to the federal code [50].

TABLE OLIVES

The olive tree has been part of Mediterranean civilization since before recorded history (**Figure 21–45**). For over 6,000 years, humans have consumed olives [56]. The olive tree is one of the oldest cultivated trees in the world with a 1,300-year-old tree growing in Mut, Turkey [2]. Olives are an important part of the Mediterranean diet. Many olive varieties are grown throughout the world [36]. Table olives are olives that are eaten versus olives that are made into oil. Only 10 percent of the olives worldwide are used as table olives, as 90 percent is made into olive oil [36].

Franciscan monks from Spain planted olive trees at the California missions starting in the 1700s [36, 62]. Today, California produces more than 95 percent of U.S. olives, but only 0.5 of 1 percent of the worldwide olives [36]. California table olive crop increased 9 percent in 2017 to 73,000 tons [13]. The United States also imports many olives with strict standards and inspections by the USDA Agricultural Marketing Service [22, 36]. International table olives codex standards were revised in 2013 to align with other international

Figure 21–45

Green unripe olives on the tree. (© Amanda Frye)

olive standards [36, 60]. More than 90 percent of the California crop is processed as black, ripe olives and the rest as specialty styles or olive oil [36]. Spain is the largest producer of olives in the world with about 30 percent, followed by Italy and Greece [55]. Other countries with significant table olive production include France, Portugal, Slovenia, Egypt, Turkey, Syria, Argentina, and Morocco [36]. **Table 21–2** lists some of the different varieties, characteristics, and origins of table olives. **Figure 21–46** shows some common olives.

Olive fruit is a drupe with a fleshy fruit and pit with shapes ranging from almost round to oval or elongated with pointed ends [56]. The unripe olive is pale green that turns to purple then black as it ripens [56]. Compared to other drupes, olives have low sugar content (2.6–6 percent) and a high oil content (12–30 percent), depending on the phase in the ripening stage and the olive variety. Olive is an alternate or biennial fruit-bearing tree, producing a large crop one year and a smaller one the next [36]. Most table olives are harvested in autumn when olives change from green to yellowish-green [56]. Naturally black olives are harvested in California starting in mid-November

Table 21-2
SOME COMMON VARIETIES OF OLIVES AND OLIVE ORIGIN CHARACTERISTICS

Manzanillo	California Originated in Spain	Most common in California Medium to large size Rounded and oval
Mission	California Originated in Spain	Brought to California missions by Spanish Franciscan monks Medium to large size, ovate or oblique
Sevillano (Gordal or Spanish queen)	California Originated in Spain	Very large fruit Popular olive for stuffing
Ascolano	California Originated in Italy	Medium to large fruit
Barouni	California Originated in Tunisia	Very large fruit Green and black ripe olives
Kalamata/Kalamon	Small scale orchards California Originated in Greece	Ripe, elongated Greek olive
Picholine	Small scale orchards California, originated in Morocco and grown in France	Unripe, green, small to medium size Creamy, nutty, chewy
Hojiblanca	Originated in Spain	Slight sweet taste and bitter notes with almond aftertaste mainly used as ripe black olives
Niçoise	Originated in southern France	Black, nutty, fragrant, firm
Amphissa (Amfissa)	Originated in Greece	Small, round with buttery notes Harvested green or black
Oblitza	Originated in former Yugoslavia	Large apple and heart shaped
Gemlik	Originated in Turkey	Black table olives

(a) Jumbo Spanish olive, (b) Black ripe California olive, (c) Kalamata olive, and (d) Niçoise olive. (Richard Embery/Pearson Education)

continuing into December [62]. Olives may be picked green, semi-ripe, or ripe. Ripe olives are picked when they are red to ripe purplish black.

Olives are not edible directly from the tree and must be processed to remove the bitter, water soluble phenolic *oleuropein* components [36]. The processing that transforms the olive into a delicious food varies by region and customs. Basic olive processing or curing methods involve lye (sodium hydroxide) treatment or salt or brine treatment followed by water rinsing to remove the bitter components [62]. An exception is the Greek *Thrubolea* that is ripened on the tree by fermentation.

The fermentation process converts the sugar in the fruit to lactic and acetic acids [62]. Fermentation also breaks the chemical bond between the bitter oleuropein and sugars in the olive allowing the bitter component to be leached from the fruit [62]. The natural yeast found on the olive is thought to play a minor role during fermentation [4]. Natural olive fermentation (without the use of lye) takes a long time with the edible stage reached after six to nine months [21]. During fermentation the pH of olives decreases and the fruits fade in color [21].

More than 90 percent of the California olive crop is processed as black olives; over 70–80 percent of U.S. consumed ripe olives are from California. The remaining California olive crop is processed into oil or specialty olives. Table olive varieties are based on olive volume, shape, flesh to pit ratio, taste, firmness, and ease of detachment from pit, which makes them suitable to process. Olives are cured in lye, brine, water, dry salt, or lye-fermented [62]. They are sorted

by size prior to processing [21]. Similar-sized olives are processed in batches, since chemical reaction and fermentation differs with size [21]. Table olives vary in color, shape, and flavors, based on curing methods and olive varieties. Naturally processing olives without lye yields olives with higher total phenols that have been associated with health benefits [21, 25, 61]. Commercially canned olives are sterilized and hermetically sealed. Home-canned olives are always pressure canned for a long period of time (50 to 60 minutes), due to high pH level [62].

Brine-cured olives are processed in a concentrated salt solution, called a brine, where they undergo fermentation. Brine curing is simple and requires water and salt (pure pickling salt) for bitter extraction, washing, and fermentation. However, brine cure takes at least three months and maybe six months or longer depending on fruit variety, temperature, salt concentration, and brine acidity [59]. Green-ripe olives take longer than naturally black ripe olives to brine cure [62]. Greek-style black olives and Sicilian-style green olives are examples of brine-cured olives. Salt concentration is important as it also acts as a preservative. Brine-cured olives can be stored in brine for one year [62].

Dry salt-cured olives use fully ripe, mature oil rich fruit that is dark red to black. Mission olives are common in the United States for this method. Smaller olives are used in dry cure since large olives will soften too much during the process [62]. Olive salting dehydrates the olive flesh causing a soft, moist, shriveled olive after five to six weeks of processing. Dry salt olives are salty and more bitter, since the dry salt curing removes less oleuropein than other methods [62]. Dry salt olives can be stored for six months and refrigerated or frozen up to a year [62]. Olives become rancid with longer storage. If desired, dry salt olives can be dipped in boiling water to remove the salt, then air dried and rubbed with olive oil and herbs such as rosemary before serving [62].

Lye cured olives, sometimes referred to as California-style curing, is a rapid curing method using lye. Olives are placed in a lye solution to remove bitter compounds; once curing is complete, the olives are washed with a series of water rinses to remove the lye before brining. Progressive lye-solution treatments are used until the lye penetrates to the pit. Then lye-processed olives are rinsed to remove all lye and bitter components. There is no fermentation step in lye-cured olives. The lye breaks the chemical bond between oleuropein and sugars [62]. Lye curing is used for both green and black ripe olives that use green ripe fruit [62]. The black-brown olive color in dark ripe olives is developed when olives are exposed to air during the lye-curing process. Natural phenolic compounds in the olives react with air to create the black color [62]. Commercially, air is bubbled through lye-curing olive vats to oxidize them. Iron salts (ferrous gluconate, ferrous sulphate, or ferrous lactate) are sometimes added to fix the dark brown-black color of ripe black olives [36, 16]. Lye-curing olives is the most common method for commercial olive production including green ripe olives and dark ripe olives. Olives are ready to eat, process, or brine in about two weeks.

Lye-cured fermented olives undergo an initial lye treatment and then are fermented in brine for several months [36]. The lactic acid bacteria produced during the fermentation phase give these olives a distinctive flavor and aroma [62]. Even though fresh olives naturally contain lactic acid, a lactic acid starter culture is generally added for the fermentation phase since natural lactic acid levels may not be high enough after lye treatment. Sometimes sugar (2 teaspoons per gallon of brine) is added to the brine to increase fermentation and develop greater acidity in the olives. Manzanillo and Mission olives are often augmented with sugar for fermentation [62]. Lye-cured fermented olives can be stored up to a year in brine or preserved by commercial or home pressure canning methods. Spanish-style green olives are lye-cured fermented olives.

Common Olive-Curing Styles
Spanish-Style Green Olives. These are cured in a short time (8–10 hours) in dilute lye (NaOH solution), rinsed, and then fermented in brine (changed regularly) for three months. Fermentation is by lactic

acid and yeast naturally present in olives. Citric acid may be added at the end of processing to control microbes. The processed olives are then sealed and pressure canned. Around 60 percent of world's olives are processed by this method [36].

Sicilian-Style Green Olives. These are cured by water or brine, with no lye treatment. Sicilian-style green olives are cured in brine seasoned with herbs such as pickling spice, fennel seed, dill, garlic, peppercorns, or whole dried chili peppers [62]. Green ripe Servillano olives are typically used [62]. Olives must be green ripe for olives with any color soften and do not hold up during the curing process [62]. These olives are similar to the Spanish-style cocktail olives but more bitter since they have only been fermented in a seasoned brine. Commercially prepared cocktail olives are typically seasoned in lye to remove more bitterness [62]. Unripened green olives are placed in water or brine for natural fermentation. The salt concentration increases every week. Curing takes from two or three weeks up to four months. Olives can be kept up to one year in brine [62].

Greek-Style Ripe Black Olives. These are cured in brine or by dry salt curing with no lye treatment. Mature, fully colored (dark red to purplish black) olives must be used. Any variety can be used but in the United States most common are Manzanillo, Mission, or Kalamata varieties [62]. Olives are placed in brine to

FOCUS ON SCIENCE
LYE

Lye, also known as sodium hydroxide (NaOH) or caustic soda, must be handled carefully since it is a highly reactive and corrosive chemical. Lye reacts with metals such as aluminum, zinc, tin, or galvanized metals; hence, lye cannot be used in the curing process since the metal will corrode. Zinc galvanized metals are dissolved by lye and thus cause the olives to be poisonous. However, stainless steel can be used for processing along with wooden barrels, food earthenware, glass, and food-grade plastics [62]. Lye used must be 100 percent pure sodium hydroxide (NaOH). Lye is available in flake or granular form (2 ounces (weighed) of lye = 4 tablespoons flake or 3 tablespoons granular lye). Lye is added to cold water; never add cold water to lye. A great deal of heat (chemical energy) is generated when lye is added to cold water, therefore, the mixture must be cooled to 65 to 70°F prior to olive curing as the hot lye solution will soften and discolor the olives [62]. Careful handling and disposal of lye-processing solutions is essential [62].

FOCUS ON SCIENCE
CONCENTRATED BRINE FOR CURED OLIVES

Cured olives can be preserved in concentrated brine and stored at room temperature in this brine for eight to nine months [62]. This concentrated brine is composed of 2½ pounds (4 cups) of pickling salt per gallon of water. Olives are covered with brine for two days before an addition of 10 ounces (1 cup) pickling salt for each gallon of brine is mixed into the brine and olive mixture. An additional 10 ounces (1 cup) of pickling salt per gallon of brine is again mixed into the brine and olives before they are covered and stored. These heavy-brined olives are typically soaked in fresh water and rinsed multiple times to remove excess salt [62].

ferment or, alternatively, washed and packed in salt for a month or more. Dry cure draws out moisture, which may cause olives to shrivel [62]. After curing and some fermentation, olives are rinsed and allowed to dry. Olive coloring may fade during curing, but oxidation through air exposure causes darkening again [62]. Oil-cured olives are dry salt-cured olives softened in oil [36]. The finished product has fruity and bitter flavors.

Kalamata-style/Mediterranean-style Crack Olives. These are cured in water or brine. Kalamata are made with ripe olives (dark red to purplish black) and Mediterranean-style olives are made with green unripened olives [62]. Kalamata or Mission olives, which are oil rich, are used for this method as other olives such as Servillo become too soft during curing [62]. The olives are packed in brine after curing [36]. Mediterranean-style cracked olives are often seasoned with oregano, garlic, or lemon slices during the final brine phase [62].

California-style Ripe Black Olives. These are lye cured. Green and black olives can be cured by this process. The process uses horticulturally immature fruits. The harvest begins when olive skin changes from green to pale green or straw color [44]. Olives are soaked in a lye solution (1–2 percent NaOH, pH 13) for 2–24 hours for 3–7 days. Lye is very caustic and extreme caution must be used in handling the chemical [62]. Lye treatment is considered complete when lye reaches the pit turning the olive flesh to a yellowish-green color. Olives where lye has not penetrated to the pit have a milky whitish flesh radiating out from pit until it meets the point of lye-penetrated discolored flesh [62].

California-style ripe black olives are a product of oxidization. Air is bubbled through the solution to turn the olives to black color. Iron (typically ferrous gluconate) is sometimes added to set (fix) the color. Studies have shown that darker olives can be achieved with the single-lye method and reuse of preservation liquid, yielding higher amounts of the "healthy" phenolic compounds [10]. Acrylamide formation, which is primarily formed during sterilization, is reduced in lye-treated olives [16].

Green olives are not exposed to air or iron. Both green and black olives cure in about a week; then they can be sealed, canned, and heat sterilized in brine or further processed. Further processing may involve pitting, slicing, chopping, or stuffing [36].

GELATIN AND GELS

Gelatin is sold in sheets, granular, and pulverized forms that may be flavored or unflavored. Fine division of flavored pulverized gelatin allows it to be easily dispersed in hot water. Gelatin mixes, which include sugar, acid, coloring, and flavoring substances, usually contain pulverized gelatin. Unflavored gelatins usually will need to be first dissolved in cold water. A good-quality unflavored gelatin should be as nearly flavorless and odorless as possible. The other ingredients in recipes using unflavored gelatin will provide the desired flavors.

Edible gelatin is used to form a basic gel structure. Flavored gelatins may be consumed without other ingredients, or the gel structure formed may carry fruits, vegetables, cheese, meats, whipped cream, nuts, and other appropriate foods as various salads and desserts are prepared (**Figure 21–47**). Gelatin may also act as a foam stabilizer in whipped products and as a thickener in some puddings and pies. It is used in the making of certain candies, such as marshmallows, and in some frozen desserts in which it acts to control crystal size. *Gelatina de leche* is a Mexican favorite prepared with boiling milk instead of water (**Figure 21–48**).

Manufacture of Gelatin

Gelatin is obtained by the hydrolysis of **collagen**, which is found in the connective tissues of animals. Since gelatin is derived from animal collagen, it is properly classified as a "derived protein" [24]. The chief sources of commercial gelatin are animal hides, skins, and bones. The most significant raw material source for edible gelatin in North America is pork skin [24]. Kosher gelatin made from beef is available. The conversion of collagen to gelatin is, in fact, a fundamental part of the cookery of less tender cuts of meat. As cooked meat cools, the formation of a gel from the

---

FOCUS ON SCIENCE

WHAT IS THE DIFFERENCE BETWEEN GEL FORMATION CAUSED BY EGGS AND THAT CAUSED BY PECTIN?

Eggs	Pectin
Eggs form a gel based on the sequence of amino acids that are present on the protein chain. Heat allows the chain to denature (unravel), and liquid is trapped. Calcium enhances the mechanism to occur, as observed in baked custard.	Pectin, because of its chemical makeup, requires both a particular amount of sugar (at least 55 percent) and an acidic pH (3.0 to 3.2) for the chain mechanism to occur to trap liquid and form a gel.

Figure 21–47

Gelatin is often served plain or with fruit. (© Amanda Frye)

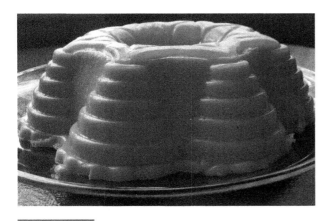

Figure 21–48

Gelatina de leche is gelatin prepared with milk instead of water. (© Amanda Frye)

gelatin produced in the meat juices is often visible. Collagen gelatin solutions can be hydrolyzed by proteolytic enzymes to yield its peptide and amino acid components [24].

The industrial manufacture of gelatin comprises three basic stages: (1) the raw material is treated to separate the collagen from the other components present; (2) the purified collagen is converted into gelatin; and (3) the gelatin is purified, refined, and recovered in dry form [59]. The conditions for manufacturing edible gelatin include an acid and a lime treatment, followed by washing and sterilization, to ensure a product of high sanitary quality (**Figure 21–49**) [24]. The dry form in which gelatin is marketed also favors a low bacterial count. When gelatin is hydrated, however, and used to make a gel, the moist product is a favorable medium for bacterial growth and should be refrigerated as are other perishable foods.

Guidance has been provided to the industry regarding the sourcing and processing of gelatin to reduce potential risks of bovine spongiform encephalopathy (BSE). BSE is sometimes called "mad cow disease." BSE is a progressive neurological disorder of cattle that was first found in Great Britain in the late 1980s. Epidemiological and laboratory evidence has suggested a causal relationship between a variant form of Creutzfeldt-Jakob disease in Great Britain and BSE.

Gelatin as a Gel Structure

Gelatin is a highly efficient, tasteless, and odorless, faint, yellow gelling agent [24]. Although we discuss gelatin as a single product, it is actually a mixture of amino acid fractions joined by peptide linkages to form various polymers [24]. As little as 1 to 3 parts of gelatin in 97 to 99 parts of water produces a moldable gel. A gel is a special kind of structure that might be described as something between a solid and a liquid. Gels are sometimes described as mixtures that hold the shape of the container after they are removed from it; however, gels vary from being soft to fairly rigid [47]. Most food gels are relatively soft but are

---

HOT TOPIC
FISH GELATIN AND PLANT-BASED GELATIN SUBSTITUTES

Some individuals may prefer to use gelatin derived from sources other than pork or beef. Those who follow a vegetarian diet or who avoid pork or beef for religious reasons avoid foods prepared with gelatin or seek other options. Gelatin may be made from fish. Gelatin derived from fish usually has lower melting and gelling temperatures compared to conventional gelatins [26]. These differences are more pronounced when the type of fish used is a cold-water fish as opposed to a warm-water fish. In general, fish gelatins can be more similar to gelatins made with pork skin if the concentration of fish gelatin is increased [65].

Agar and carrageenan are additional options for those who prefer to avoid gelatin made from meat as well as fish. Agar and carrageenan are derived from seaweed and thus are plant based (Compared to other gels, agar and carrageenan gels melt at higher temperatures [65]).

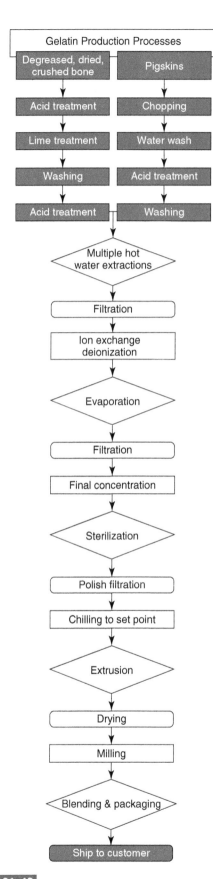

Figure 21-49

Gelatin production process. (Pearson Education. Based on Gelatin Manufacturers Institute of America, Reference 24)

resilient or elastic. Industry measures gelatin gelling strength by gelatin bloom. The higher the bloom number, the stiffer the gel [24].

Gels occur in a variety of food products in addition to those salads and desserts made with gelatin. Other examples of gels include most starch-thickened puddings and pie fillings, egg custards, and fruit jellies. For more about starch-thickened mixtures, see Chapter 11. Egg custards are discussed in Chapter 23.

There are certain characteristics common to all gels, including those formed with gelatin. Gels are composed mainly of fluid, but they behave much like rigid solids. These interesting characteristics appear to be the result of their special type of structure. Gels contain long, thin chainlike molecules called **polymers** that are joined or cross-linked at random spots to produce a three-dimensional structure, something like a pile of dry brush (**Figure 21-50**). These polymers create a network to trap the liquid.

Different polymers form gels, depending on the food. Examples of these polymers and the foods with which they are associated are as follows:

* The linear protein molecules of gelatin (gelatin gels)
* The **amylose** fraction of starch with its long chain of glucose molecules linked together (starch-thickened puddings)

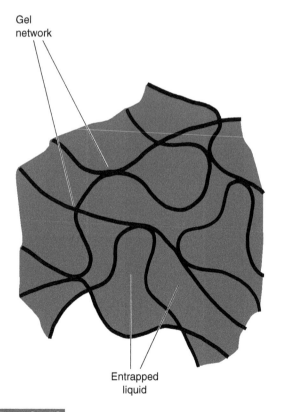

Figure 21-50

When a gel is formed, a network of long, thin molecules traps liquid in its meshes.

- The large protein molecules of egg, composed of long chains of **amino acids** (egg custards)
- **Pectin** molecules, responsible for the "setting" of jellies and jams, which are long chains of **galacturonic acid** and its **methyl esters** (fruit jellies and jams)

The polymer network that is responsible for gel formation is immersed in a liquid medium to which it is attracted. In a sense, it traps the liquid in its chain-like network. The liquid and the polymer network then work together—the liquid keeps the polymer network from collapsing into a compact mass, and the network keeps the liquid from flowing away.

Environmental conditions affect the characteristics of many gels. Some gels shrink or swell with changes in temperature. Many food gels liquefy or melt over a relatively narrow temperature range. The melting and solidifying constitute a reversible process in such gels as gelatin mixtures. Gels may also be affected by pH, becoming softer with greater acidity. Some gels exhibit **syneresis**. This may occur in overcooked egg mixtures and in some starch and gelatin gels stored in the refrigerator for a few days.

Gelatin Hydration, Swelling, and Dispersion

The methods to hydrate gelatin will vary, depending on the type of gelatin being prepared. Gelatin granules soaked in cold water hydrate into discrete swollen particles [24]. When gelatin is hydrated with hot water the particles dissolve into a solution. Hot water is preferred when high gelatin concentration is desired [24]. Flavored gelatins may be hydrated with hot water. Unflavored, plain gelatin should be first soaked in cold water to hydrate the gelatin. The water molecules are attracted to the gelatin molecules and form a water shell around them. This aids in later dispersion of the unflavored, plain gelatin in hot water.

The ease, rapidity, and extent of swelling depend on several factors. If the gelatin is finely granulated or pulverized, more surface is exposed to the water. Consequently, the rate of swelling is increased. The degree of acidity or alkalinity, the kinds of salts present, and the presence of sugar all influence the swelling of gelatin. Sugar and certain salts inhibit swelling, whereas other salts accelerate it. Plain, unflavored gelatin does not have sugar or other ingredients to interfere with swelling. When plain gelatin is used in a recipe, any flavoring ingredients, such as fruit acids and sugar, are usually not added until the unflavored gelatin has swelled and been dispersed.

When preparing flavored gelatin, the first step is to add hot water to disperse and dissolve the gelatin. However, when using unflavored, plain gelatin, the first step is to soak in cold water. Plain, unflavored gelatin molecules will separate or disperse following the soaking period when the temperature of soaked gelatin is elevated to 95°F (35°C) or higher. For either flavored or unflavored gelatin, only part of the required water is added hot. The remaining water is added cold. Adding part of the liquid cold enables the gelatin to cool and form a gel (gelatin) more quickly.

Gelation

Gelation means gel formation or the stiffening of a gelatin dispersion. Gelation does not occur at a fixed or clearly defined point but rather is a gradual process. It involves the joining or linking of gelatin molecules in various places to form the three-dimensional "brush-heap" structure that is typical of gels (see Figure 21–50). Gelation was also discussed in Chapter 11 in relation to starch mixtures. Gelatin granules can be stored for long periods of time in airtight containers at room temperature [24]. However, gelatin loses its ability to swell when exposed to temperatures above 45°C and high relative humidity above 60 percent [24]. Gelatin solution behavior is influenced by temperature, pH, ash content, method of manufacturing, thermal history, and concentration [24].

Effect of Temperature. Gelatin has a unique property to form thermoreversible gels [24]. Different gelatins set at different temperatures, but all require cooling below the temperature of dispersion, which is 95°F (35°C). Gelatins that require a low temperature to solidify tend to liquefy readily when brought back to room temperature. Gelatin dispersions that have set quickly because they were subjected immediately to very low temperatures also melt more readily at room temperature than similar gelatin mixtures that set at somewhat higher temperatures.

A gelatin dispersion may remain liquid at temperatures that would ordinarily be low enough for gelation, if rapidly cooled. Adding ice cubes to cold water to speed the setting process and then refrigerating is an example of rapid cooling that is sometimes used to set gelatin quickly. The gel is typically softer. If more time is allowed, however, and ice is not used, gelation occurs at a higher (warmer) temperature and results in a firmer gel.

Gelation also occurs more quickly at a cold temperature if the gelatin dispersion stands at room temperature for a specific time before being chilled. Temperatures required for the solidification of a gelatin dispersion vary from less than 50°F (10°C) to approximately 58 to 60°F (14 to 16°C).

Prolonged heating of gelatin solutions above 104°F (40°C) weaken gel strength. Sterile gelatin solutions keep indefinitely in cold storage, but elevated temperatures cause hydrolysis of the gelled solutions [24].

Concentration.   The concentration of gelatin affects not only the firmness of the gel but also the rate of setting. The higher the concentration, the firmer the gel and the faster the rate of setting. The usual percentage of gelatin in a gelatin mold of good texture is about 1.5 or 2 percent, depending on the ingredients used in the mixture. One tablespoon (7 grams) of unflavored gelatin per 2 cups of liquid gives a gelatin concentration of about 1.5 percent.

Beating the gelatin dispersion to a **foam** or sponge increases the volume sufficiently to decrease the firmness of the gel. A higher concentration of gelatin is thus required to produce a firm texture in whipped products. Very weak dispersions of gelatin, such as those used in ice creams, eventually set if given a long time and a low temperature. If excess gelatin is used in ice cream, gumminess increases with longer storage.

Gels become stiffer with longer standing. Unless a relatively high concentration of gelatin is used, it is usually desirable to allow gelatin mixtures to stand several hours or overnight at a low temperature to develop optimum stiffness.

Degree of Acidity.   Gelatin gel strength is affected by pH. Decreasing pH also decreases gel strength [24]. Fruit juices, wines, and vinegar that may be added to gelatin mixtures used for desserts and salads increase the acidity of the dispersions. Too high a concentration of acid can prevent gelation or cause the formation of a soft gel, even when a fairly high concentration of gelatin is present.

Lemon juice and vinegar have a more pronounced effect on gelation than tomato juice and some other fruit juices of lower acidity. Two tablespoons of lemon juice as part of 1 cup of liquid is usually enough for good flavor unless the dispersion is to be beaten to a foam. In this case, the flavor is diluted. This dispersion forms a more tender gel than one made without acid yet is usually satisfactorily stiff even when no extra gelatin is added.

Diced fruits added to a gelatin mixture mechanically break up the gel and may prevent its setting into a sufficiently firm mass. If, in addition, preparing an unflavored gelatin to which orange juice or lemon juice is added for flavor, these acidic juices may result in a weak gel that is too tender to be molded. Use of a somewhat higher concentration of gelatin may be necessary in such circumstances. The time required for acid gelatin dispersions to set is greater than that required for neutral ones.

Effect of Salts, Sugar, and Enzymes.

Salts.   Gel strength is increased when milk is used as a liquid in gelatin mixtures, probably as a result of the salts present in milk. Even hard water that contains minerals produces a firmer gel than distilled water.

Addition of Sugar.   Sugar weakens a gelatin gel and retards the rate of setting. Usual recipes for gelatin mixtures have been adjusted so that the weakening effect of sugar is counterbalanced by the firming effect of increased gelatin concentration.

Effect of Enzymes.   The proteolytic enzyme, bromelain, found in fresh pineapple hydrolyzes gelatin protein. Other tropical fruits, including kiwi and papaya, also contain proteases. If these enzymes are not destroyed by heat before the fruit is added to a gelatin dispersion, they will break down gelatin molecules so that they cannot form a gel. Because the heat of processing has destroyed the enzyme in canned pineapple pieces or juice, these products can be satisfactorily used in gelatin mixtures. Freezing does not affect the activity of the enzyme, however, and thus frozen pineapple cannot be used in a gelatin gel.

Gelatin Salads and Desserts

Fruit, Vegetable, Meat, and Fish Jellies.   Before fruits, vegetables, or other solid food materials are added to a gelatin mixture, they should be thoroughly drained of juices. The juices of fruits and some vegetables may be added as part of the liquid required

---

FOCUS ON SCIENCE
GELATIN: A SOL AND A GEL

Gelatin contains amino acids joined in a sequence to form a polypeptide chain called a *primary structure*. When coarse dry gelatin hydrates and swells when soaked in cold water, it is known as a *sol* (solid in a liquid). Hot liquid is then added to dissolve and disperse the gelatin. As the liquid cools, the gelatin chains come together to form a *gel* (liquid trapped in a solid).

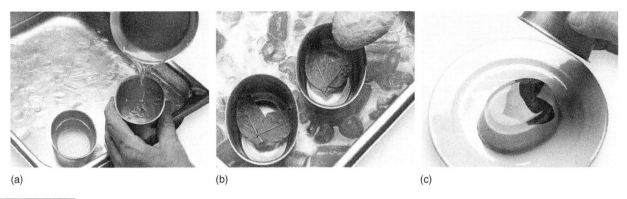

(a)   (b)   (c)

Figure 21–51

(a) Cool, liquid aspic jelly is poured into the mold. (b) Mold is garnished with vegetable leaves, then filled with a cold mousse. (c) After refrigeration, the mold is dipped in warm water, then inverted onto a plate. (Richard Embery/Pearson Education)

to disperse the gelatin. Gelatin mixtures should stand until they are thickened and just ready to form a gel before solid food materials are added to them. If the gelatin mixture is not partially set, the added pieces will float. Waiting until the mixture is thickened allows the added materials to be dispersed more evenly throughout the mixture.

Aspics. Aspic is usually a beef-flavored gelatin mixture, although fish and poultry flavors may also be used. Tomato aspic salad is made with unflavored gelatin and seasoned tomato juice. Chopped celery may be added to a tomato aspic salad. As a variation of this salad, avocado slices can be placed in the salad mold before the tomato aspic mixture is poured over them, or the aspic can be layered with a cottage cheese and sour cream mixture to which unflavored gelatin has been added. Aspic is often used to make fancy canapés that may be part of buffet platters (**Figure 21–51**).

Foams and Sponges. A gelatin dispersion can be beaten to form a foam. It increases two or three times its original volume, depending largely on the stage at which the dispersion is beaten. If beating is not started until the gelatin begins to set, the volume obtained is small, and finely broken bits of solidified gelatin are evident throughout the mass. The best stage for beating is when the dispersion is about the consistency of whipping cream or thin egg whites. The gelatin mixture is elastic and stretches to surround the air bubbles. Beating is continued until the mass is very stiff, to avoid the formation of a clear layer in the bottom of the mold. However, it may be necessary to stop and chill the beaten mixture again in the middle of beating. Just the friction of continued beating can warm the mixture enough to thin it. On standing, the gelatin sets and stabilizes the foam. An increase in gelatin, sugar, and flavoring is required if the gelatin dispersion is to be beaten to a foam because the increased volume of a foam dilutes these ingredients.

To form a sponge, whipped egg white is beaten into the mixture after the syrupy gelatin mixture is beaten until it is thick and foamy. The sponge can be poured into molds and should be refrigerated until it solidifies. There is a danger of salmonella organisms being present in raw egg white. For safety, the egg whites should be pasteurized. Frozen or refrigerated pasteurized eggs or pasteurized egg-white powder can be purchased.

Bavarian and Spanish Creams. Gelatin mixtures that have stood long enough to be thickened and syrupy may have fruit pulp added and whipped cream folded into them to make Bavarian creams. Charlottes are similar to Bavarian creams, but may contain a large proportion of whipped cream, and are usually molded

FOCUS ON SCIENCE
MY GELATIN IS SET. HOW CAN I ADD THE OTHER FOOD INGREDIENTS?

As long as no excessive acidic ingredients were added to the gelatin mixture, gelatin can be melted by setting it over boiling water, then chilled to reset. Recall that acid weakens the gelatin strands, which is why resetting a gelatin with acidic ingredients may be less successful. The ability for the gelling mechanism of gelatin to be reversible is very unique to gelatin; it cannot be done to starch or pectin.

Figure 21–52

A Charlotte with Bavarian cream base. (Richard Embery/Pearson Education)

Figure 21–53

Lime chiffon. (Richard Embery/Pearson Education)

with ladyfingers. Whipped evaporated or dried milk is sometimes substituted for whipped cream in gelatin desserts.

Fillings for chiffon pies have gelatin as a basic foam stabilizer. In the preparation of most chiffon fillings, a cooked custard mixture containing egg yolk and sugar is thickened with gelatin. Whipped pasteurized egg whites and possibly whipped cream are folded into the mixture. The gelatin sets and stabilizes the egg and/or cream foam.

Spanish cream is a soft custard made with egg yolks that is set with gelatin. The egg whites are beaten to a stiff foam and folded into the mixture after it is partially set. A danger of salmonella organisms is also present in the making of chiffon pie and Spanish cream if raw egg white rather than pasteurized egg white is used. These products should not be made unless pasteurized egg whites are available (see **Figures 21–52** and **21–53**).

Unmolding the Gel. Gelatin may be poured in a decoratively shaped mold and allowed to gel. To unmold a gelatin gel, the mold containing the gel should be dipped for a few moments in lukewarm (not hot)

Figure 21–54

Agar gels molded and sliced hearts. (© Amanda Frye)

water. One side of the gel should then be carefully loosened with a knife to allow air to come between the gel and the mold. Place a plate over the bottom of the mold and then flip, similar to how a cake could be removed from a pan. The gel should slide easily from the mold. The mold can be very lightly oiled before the gelatin mixture is placed in it to facilitate removal of the gel (**Figures 21–54**).

STUDY QUESTIONS

Consumption Trends and Nutrition

1. Discuss salad consumption trends and nutritional contributions.

2. **(a)** Describe four or five ways in which salads may be used in a meal.
   (b) Describe 10 or 12 different salads. Suggest appropriate uses for them in a menu.

Salad Preparation and Ingredients

3. **(a)** Describe several leafy plants that can be appropriately used as salad greens.
   (b) Suggest a satisfactory way to prepare these greens for use in salads. Explain why this procedure is effective.

4. Identify several considerations in the use of various vegetables, fruits, pasta, grains, legumes, meats, poultry, fish, and eggs when preparing salads.

5. Identify and explain several food-safety practices to be observed when preparing and serving salads.

6. Marinating may be appropriate for what types of salads? Explain why.

7. Give several appropriate suggestions for arranging salads as they are served.

Vinegar and Salad Dressings

8. Discuss the process of making vinegar.

Table Olives

9. Discuss why table olives must be cured.

10. Describe the basic olive-curing processes.

11. Explain why lye is used in curing olives.

Gelatin Structure and Characteristics

12. Gels of various types have common characteristics.
   (a) Give several examples of food products that are gels.
   (b) Describe the theoretical structure of a gel.
   (c) Discuss why gelatin is considered a thermoreversible gel.

13. What is *gelatin*? What is its source commercially?

14. In what forms is gelatin usually sold on the market?

15. How should unflavored gelatin be treated—and why—as it is used in the preparation of gelatin gels?

16. Describe what happens as gelatin forms a gel.

Effect of Temperature, Concentration, and Other Factors on Gelation

17. What is the effect of each of the following on the gelation of gelatin gels?
   (a) Temperature
   (b) Concentration of gelatin
   (c) Addition of acid
   (d) Addition of sugar
   (e) Addition of raw pineapple

Gelatin, Gels, Salads, and Desserts

18. Describe major characteristics of each of the following gelatin mixtures:
   (a) Aspics
   (b) Foams
   (c) Sponges
   (d) Bavarian creams
   (e) Spanish creams

22
Milk, Cheese, and Other Milk Products*

Humans have consumed milk from domesticated animals, such as the cow, goat, sheep, buffalo, and camel, since the "agricultural revolution" around 10,000 B.C. In the United States, only cow's milk is of commercial importance. A small amount of goat milk is sold or used in cheese production. Other animal milk such as sheep and water buffalo may also be found in some cheeses.

Milk is a versatile and unique food. It is consumed as a beverage in fresh fluid form, used in cooking, or made into other milk products (**Figure 22–1**). The milkfat components such as half-and-half, light cream, and whipping cream may also be consumed in beverages or used in cooking. Milk can be manufactured into other food products. Milk manufacturing involves turning fluid milk into products such as cheese, butter, sour cream, ice cream, and frozen desserts or cultured products such as buttermilk, yogurt, kefir, or other probiotic drinks. Fluid milk can also be manufactured into dried milk solids or its constituents. Some of these manufactured milk products are sold to consumers and others are used by the food industry for processed foods.

All milk in the United States is cow's milk unless another animal source is named. "Milk" in the United States is legally defined in the Code of Federal

Figure 22–1

Milk is a versatile food. It can be consumed as a beverage, used in cooking, or made into other products. (Volff/123RF)

Figure 22–2

Black-and-white Holstein dairy cows grazing in a pasture. Holsteins are the most common dairy breed in the United States. (Chris Elwell/123RF)

Regulations as the "lacteal secretion...from one or more healthy cows" [28]. Without the cow there would be no "milk" (**Figure 22–2**).

The most common dairy cow breeds found in the United States are Holstein (Black/White and the recessive gene Red/White), Jersey, Brown Swiss, Guernsey, Ayrshire, Milking Shorthorn, and Dutch Belted. In the United States, 86 percent of all dairy cows are Holsteins, less than 8 percent are Jerseys, and other breeds make up the remaining 6 percent [114]. Each breed has unique characteristics and varying milk attributes. Holsteins are typically the overall best milk producers and Jersey produce the highest milkfat between 4.5 to 5.5 percent. Milk production, protein, and fat percentage are affected by cow breed, genetics, season, feed, health, stage of lactation, and age of animal [1, 22].

For a cow to produce milk, the cow must have calved (given birth to a calf). Dairy cows require a nutritious high-energy diet from grain, silage (a stored and fermented fodder), and forage (grass and hay) that the rumen processes into the nutrients needed for milk production [22]. The mammary gland uses the nutrients that enter via the blood; then, the mammary gland turns these nutrients into milk. The lactation cycle is when the cow can produce milk; it is the time

*"Milk products" in the title of this chapter refers to those other than butter and ice cream.

between one calving and the next. The lactation cycle is approximately 300 days. About one to two months after calving cows go in estrus and are impregnated. The pregnancy lasts nine months. The cow needs a dry period, average about 60 days, where it is not milked before it can lactate again. During the dry period the milk tapers off because of maternal needs for the fetus and the udder needs time to prepare for next lactation cycle. This cycle repeats five to six lactations or with some breeds much longer.

Cows are milked two to three times a day. Udders and teats are cleaned and are milked typically with automatic milking machines (**Figure 22–3**). Some cows are milked by robots on a voluntary basis as determined by the cow. On average, the cow produces 70 pounds or 8 gallons of milk per day. U.S. dairy cows produce over 21 billion gallons of milk every year [109] (See **Figures 22–4** and **22–5**). According to the USDA National Agricultural Statistics Service, milk production has increased 14 percent and the pounds of milk per cow have increased over 13 percent between 2007 and 2013 (see **Figure 22–6**).

The *Grade "A" Pasteurized Milk Ordinance* [120] and state regulations provide the standards and guidance for assuring milk in the United States is of the safest and highest quality. Milk is obtained from the cow under sanitary conditions (**Figure 22–7**). Within two hours of milking, the milk must be cooled to 45°F (7°C). The milk is picked up by a "handler" who delivers the milk to a dairy processing plant in a

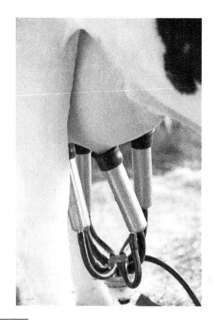

Figure 22–3

The cows' udders and teats are cleaned and sanitized before attaching the milking machine. (2bears/Shutterstock)

tanker. The processing plant tests the milk, which then is typically processed and pasteurized within 24 hours.

The traditional dairy philosophy is minimal milk modification as it is preserved and handled through the market channels. Relatively simple processes and physical separations are used in manufacturing various dairy products, preserving their natural properties. These

2016 U.S. Milk Cow Population

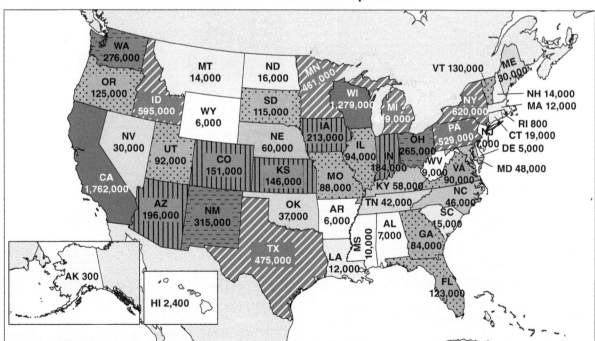

Figure 22–4

Dairy cow population per state. (Cartographer Charle Frye/© Amanda Frye)

Milk Production per Cow (in Pounds) in 2016, United States

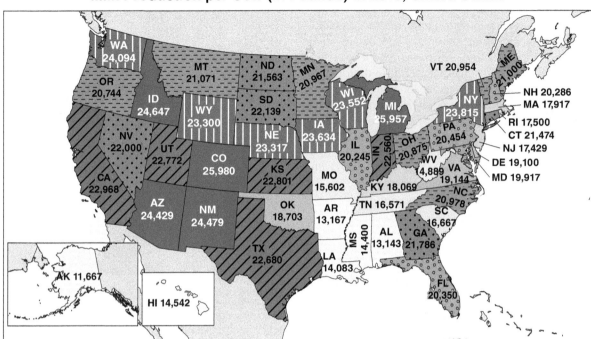

Figure 22–5

Dairy cows produce an average of 22,774 pounds of milk per year. (Cartographer Charlie Frye/© Amanda Frye)

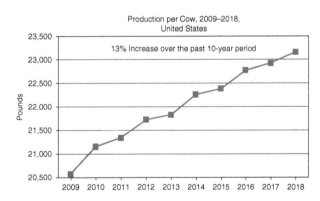

Figure 22–6

Cow milk production has risen 13 percent over the last decade. (United States Department of Agriculture, National Agriculture Statistics Service)

Figure 22–7

Cows are milked under sanitary conditions. (IdeaStepConcept Stock/Shutterstock)

dairy products are used in our diets as beverages, food and ingredients in a wide array of products. Although butter and ice cream are dairy products, these dairy products were discussed in Chapters 8 and 10.

In this chapter, the following topics will be discussed:

• Consumption trends and nutritive value
• Composition and milk properties
• Sanitation, grades, and processing
• Types of milk and cream products
• Food preparation with milk and cream

• Cheese manufacturing and cheese types
• Food preparation with cheese

CONSUMPTION TRENDS AND NUTRITION

Milk and milk drinks contribute calories, nutrients, and fluid (water intake) in the diet. Milk, cheese, and other dairy products are a cornerstone in the traditional American diet.

Consumption Trends

According to the U.S. Department of Agriculture (USDA) food availability data, the annual consumption of fluid milk, including whole, 2 percent, 1 percent, nonfat milk, and buttermilk, has decreased from 31 gallons per person in 1970 to 22 gallons per person in 2010 to 19 gallons per person in 2016 (see **Figure 22–8**). In 2015, fluid milk sales were down 5.6 percent in one year [91]. Alternative plant-based "milk"-like beverage products

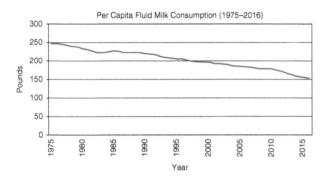

Figure 22–8

Milk consumption has been decreasing steadily since 1975. This corresponds with the fact that Americans' dairy intake is below dietary guidelines. (USDA/ERS)

have been competing with fluid milk at the consumer and retail level. Some decline has also been attributed to consumer experiences with low-quality fresh milk [91].

The kind of milk consumed has changed considerably over the years (see **Figure 22–9**). Whole-milk consumption has decreased since 1975 while the use of fat-reduced milk has increased. In 2015, trends changed direction as whole-milk consumption began to increase and the low-fat milk trend began to decrease. Flavored milk has also increased since 1975, but preference has switched from whole flavored milk to less-fat flavored milks.

In contrast to the downward trend in milk consumption, Americans are consuming record-high levels of sour cream and cheese (see **Figure 22–10**) with annual growth predicted through 2025. Sour cream use has increased from 350 million pounds in 1975 to 1,373 million pounds in 2016. American cheese consumption has increased from 8.1 pounds per person in 1975 to 14.3 pounds in 2016. However, cottage cheese consumption has decreased from 4.6 pounds in 1975 to 2.2 pounds in 2016 (see **Figure 22–11**). In 2015, specialty cheeses represented a 4 billion dollar industry with 15 percent growth in two years [2]. U.S. natural cheese sales have continued to increase with 2018 sales reaching $12.9 billion. There has also been an increase in other cow's

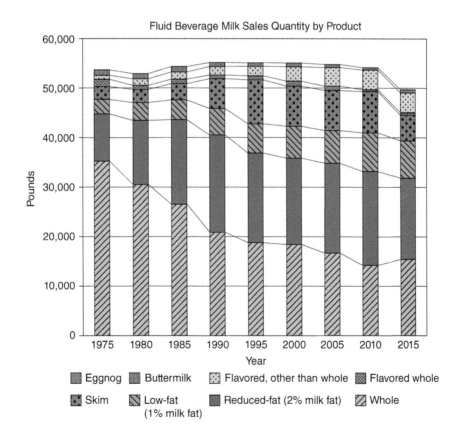

Figure 22–9

The type of milk consumed has changed from 1975 to 2015 as there was a gradual decline in whole milk and increase in low fat milk. This trend started reversing in 2015. (Graph Sam Frye/ Data USDA ERS)

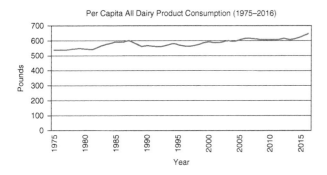

Figure 22–10

Although fluid consumption has decreased since 1975, there has been an increase in total dairy consumption primarily due to the increase in sour cream and cheese intake. (Graph Sam Frye/ Data USDA ERS)

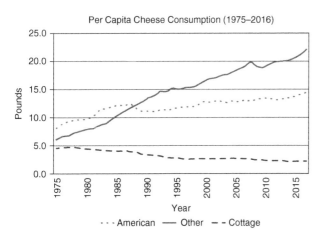

Figure 22–11

American cheese intake has increased over the past four decades, but cottage cheese consumption has decreased. (Graph Sam Frye/ Data USDA ERS)

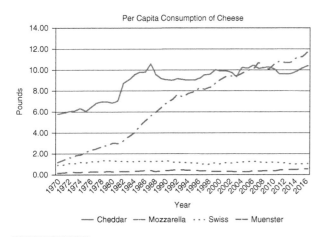

Figure 22–12

Cheddar and mozzarella cheese consumption has increased since 1970, while Swiss and Muenster consumption has remained unchanged. (USDA/ERS)

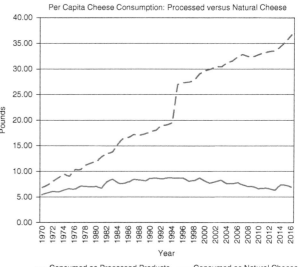

Figure 22–13

Consumption trend of natural cheeses have increased since the 1970s, while consumption of process cheese has remained steady. (Graph Sam Frye/ Data USDA ERS)

milk cheese including mozzarella, Swiss, blue, Muenster, brick, and cream cheese (see **Figures 22–12**, **22–13**, and **22–14**). Hispanic cheese consumption has also risen from 14.98 pounds per person to 22.03 pounds per person in 2016. Other cow's milk cheese imports have remained fairly constant at around a quarter pound per person from 1995 to 2016. Processed cheeses have slightly decreased in consumption from 8.7 pounds per capita to 6.98 pounds in 2016 and the decreasing trend continues [113]. Americans are increasingly choosing foods containing cheese such as pizza, cheeseburgers, nachos, and an array of Mexican and Italian foods that feature cheese [102] (see **Figure 22–15**).

Yogurt is a large global dairy market topping over $69 billion in 2014. China is the fastest expanding yogurt market where drinkable yogurt dominates consumption. The highest per capita yogurt consumers are found in France and Turkey with over half the populations regularly consuming yogurt [73]. Yogurt consumption in the United States has risen from 2.0 pounds per person in 1975 to 13.7 pounds in 2016, which is slightly off the high of 14.9 pounds in 2014 [113] (see **Figure 22–16**). This is still far less than the European per capita yogurt consumption of 40 pounds per year [73]. In the United States, a reported 20 percent of the population consume yogurt daily. Yogurt in the United States is typically eaten at breakfast whereas in Europe yogurt is typically eaten midday or in the evening [73].

Current intakes of dairy foods including fluid milk are far below recommendations for healthy U.S.-style dietary patterns. The only group that met recommended needs was the young 1–3 year olds. Age-related decline in milk consumption starts in childhood and

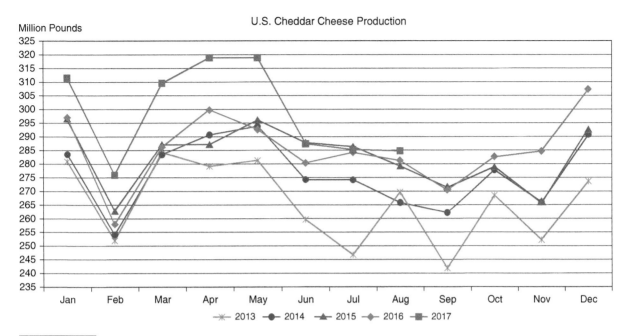

Figure 22–14

Cheddar cheese production has increased between 2013 and 2017 with variances between months. (Graph Sam Frye/ Data USDA ERS)

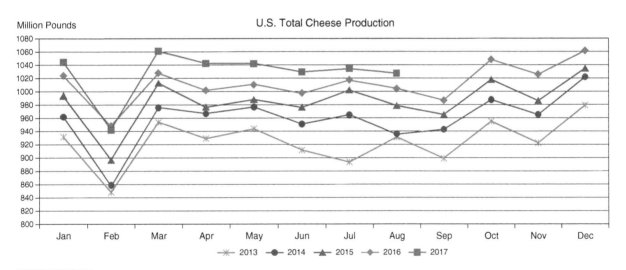

Figure 22–15

Total cheese production has risen. Monthly variation remains about the same year to year. (USDA-NASS)

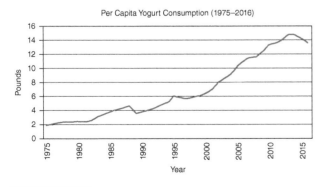

Figure 22–16

Yogurt consumption in the United States has grown significantly over the past four decades. (Graph Sam Frye/ Data USDA ERS)

persists through all adult age groups. Only approximately 25 percent of adults are reported to drink milk daily and that consumption was only ½ cup [62]. For adults, milk consumption as a beverage at meals and snack times is low, as its consumption is only 8 percent at breakfast, 5 percent at lunch, 9 percent at dinner, and 5 percent as a snack [62]. The *2015–2020 Dietary Guidelines for Americans* reported that the Americans consume dairy as fluid milk (51 percent), cheese (45 percent), and yogurt (2.6 percent) [118]. The *Dietary Guidelines* recommend choosing fat-free and low-fat milk products. Many cheese products are concentrated dairy sources high in salt and fat, which can lead to excessive calories, sodium and fat if over-consumed.

Nutritive Value

The *2015–2020 Dietary Guidelines for Americans* recommends the consumption of three cups of dairy equivalents per day in from age nine through adulthood depending on caloric needs and age levels [118]. As a beverage, milk provides calories, and a significant source of fluid, calcium, vitamin D, magnesium, riboflavin, and potassium [62]. Milk products are the major source of calcium in the diets of most Americans. Calcium intake is associated with higher bone density, which is desirable for healthy bones (see **Figure 22–17**). The Surgeon General of the United States reported that an estimated two million Americans suffer an osteoporosis-related fracture annually, and these numbers are anticipated to double or triple by the 2020 without positive changes in food consumption and other health habits [10, 23, 59, 122]. The consumption of milk is also associated with reduced risk of cardiovascular disease, lower blood pressure in adults, and a reduced risk of type 2 diabetes. Sour cream, cream cheese, and cream are not considered dairy equivalents because of their low calcium content [118].

Milk provides many nutrients in addition to calcium. The protein in milk is a complete protein, providing all essential amino acids. Milk is a good source of the amino acid tryptophan. Tryptophan is a precursor to niacin; 60 mg of tryptophan is needed to make 1 mg niacin. Milk also provides significant levels of vitamin B6, vitamin D (when fortified), vitamin A, phosphorus, potassium, iodine, thiamine, riboflavin, and vitamin B12 [47]. The Daily Values for a reference 2,000-calorie diet for several nutrients found in milk are presented in **Table 22–1**.

The intake of dairy foods is associated with statistically significant increases in the intake of calcium, magnesium, potassium, zinc, iron, vitamin A, riboflavin, and folate [130]. Although milk is not particularly high in iron and folate, those who consume more dairy

Table 22–1

DAILY VALUES FOR NUTRIENTS FOUND IN 8 OUNCES OF MILK BASED ON A REFERENT 2,000-CALORIE DIET

Nutrient	Daily Value (percent)
Calcium	30
Riboflavin	26
Vitamin D (fortified)	25
Phosphorus	25
Vitamin B$_{12}$	22
Protein	16
Potassium	11
Vitamin A	10
Niacin equivalent	10

Source: National Dairy Council.

foods apparently consume higher levels of other high-nutrient foods such as fortified cereals. Individuals who consume limited amounts of dairy foods do not appear to compensate with other calcium-rich foods, and thus, have a low calcium intake. The consumption of dairy foods was not found to be associated with higher fat and cholesterol intakes [130] (**Figure 22–18**).

Milk contains little vitamin D, but is fortified with vitamin D of 400 IU per quart for retail sale in the United States [47]. U.S. milk fortification was started in the 1930s to prevent rickets [15]. Most milk in the United States is fortified with vitamin D. The FDA requires the actual amount of vitamin D be at least equal to the amount declared on the label with good manufacturing practice range of 100–150 percent of declared content. Over the past two decades, studies have found wide variability of vitamin D actually in

Osteoporosis

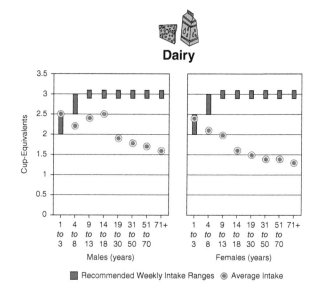

Healthy bone   Osteoporosis

Figure 22–17

Osteoporosis rates are expected to triple with low dairy intake levels. Healthy bone on the left versus a thinning bone matrix with osteoporosis. (Alila Medical Media/Shutterstock)

Dairy

Figure 22–18

Milk consumption is far below the recommended three cups. equivalents per day. (USDA)

milk and milk products some greatly below stated label values [89]. In 2001, over half the 2 percent milk samples were found to be below 400 IU levels, but resampling in 2007 found improvement with 12.5 percent not meeting requirements [89, 90]. Quality control problems during processing have been cited for these variances in vitamin D values [90].

Cheese is a highly concentrated food; 1 pound of cheese may contain the protein and fat of 1 gallon of milk. The protein is of high biologic value, and the fat is largely saturated. Vitamin A is carried in the fat. Cheese is a high-sodium food since salt is added for flavor and preservation; milk does contain some sodium too. Two ounces of many cheeses can provide 40–50 percent of daily calcium needs [131].

COMPOSITION AND PROPERTIES OF MILK

Milk is a unique and complex food. As a food system, milk is an oil-in-water **emulsion** with the aqueous phase whose constituents are a **solution** and **colloidal** dispersion. The oil-in-water *emulsion* is the milkfat dispersed as fat globules throughout the aqueous milk plasma. The milk plasma makes up the milk constituents minus the milkfat globules. The *colloidal dispersion* is formed as colloidal size proteins as well as citrates, calcium and magnesium phosphates are dispersed throughout the aqueous milk serum. The milk serum refers to the milk components minus casein micelles and fat globules. Lactose, minerals, and vitamins are dissolved in the milk aqueous to form a *solution* [17].

The average composition of whole cow's milk is 88 percent water, 3.4 percent protein, 3.7 percent fat, 4.7 percent carbohydrate, and 0.7 percent ash [16] (**Figure 22–19**). Milk composition varies somewhat in response to several physiological and environmental factors. The cow breed, the milking time, the feed consumed, the environmental temperature, the season, and the age and health of the cow are all factors that can affect the composition of milk [65] (**Figure 22–20**).

Milk properties including protein and milkfat content vary between dairy cow breeds. Holsteins produce the lowest milkfat between 2.5–4 percent, and Jerseys the highest milkfat averaging 4.6–5.5 percent. Milking Shorthorn breeds have a high protein to fat ratio. Guernsey cows produce a golden-colored milk because of the high levels of beta carotene. Brown Swiss milk is often used in cheese production with high cheese yield of 16 percent. Ayrshire cows produce milk with a small fat molecule; the milk produces a high cheese yield that has a rich, creamy texture. Protein content varies between breeds with levels of 1.57–4.66 percent. The average milk protein content is around 3 percent. Some cow breeds are preferred for their milk components rather than overall milk output. The Dutch Belted, sometimes referred to as the "Oreo Cookie Cow" due to the black-and-white markings, produce milk with small finely dispersed almost naturally homogenized fat globules, which is good for cheese production. The Jersey's high milkfat content is desirable for cream and butter.

The most variable component of milk is the fat, followed by protein. Both ash, which is the mineral content, and carbohydrate (lactose) vary only slightly. The fat content of pooled market milk is adjusted to a desired level by the dairy processor. The average milkfat produced in 2016 was 3.79 percent [113]. The composition of milk products may be found from the USDA National Nutrient Database (see Appendix C).

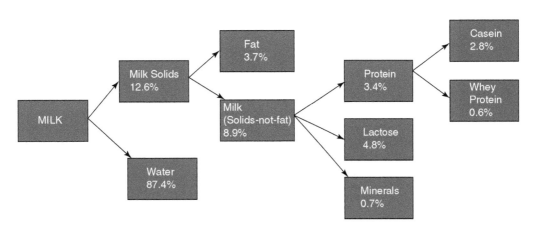

Figure 22–19

Composition of milk. (Reference 16)

Composition of milk varies by dairy cow breeds. Jersey cows produce milk with the highest fat content of around 5 percent. (John Young/123RF)

Casein molecules can be precipitated during cheesemaking. Casein molecules form the curd that separates from the liquid portion called the whey, which contains the whey proteins. (Paya Mona/Shutterstock)

Protein

Casein and whey are the two primary proteins found in milk. Casein and whey are not single proteins but rather complexes of many closely related protein molecules (**Table 22–2**). Very small amounts of other proteins are also present in milk. Most of the proteins are synthesized in the mammary gland [68]. Casein and whey function differently in food preparation and cheesemaking, as will be explained later in the chapter. See Chapter 7 for a more in-depth discussion of proteins.

Casein. About 80 to 82 percent of the protein in milk is *casein*. Casein is dispersed in the watery portion of milk, called *milk serum*. Casein precipitates and forms curds when (1) an acid such as lemon juice is added to lower the pH to about 4.6, (2) an enzyme called rennet is added, or (3) when age gelation occurs affecting shelf stable, concentrated and aseptic UHT milk products [106]. Long-term shelf stable milks are subject to gel formation due to irreversible micelle aggregation [106, 18]. Rennet used in cheesemaking causes casein to precipitate curd and will be discussed later in the chapter. The precipitation of casein produces cheese "curds" (see **Figure 22–21**).

Casein is classified as a phosphoprotein because of the phosphoric acid that is contained in its molecular structure [25]. At the normal acidity of fresh milk (about pH 6.6), casein is largely combined through the phosphoric acid part of its structure with calcium, as calcium caseinate. Kappa (κ) casein (Table 23–2) plays an important role in stabilizing the tiny casein particles or micelles in a **colloidal** dispersion. The casein micelle surface has a "hairy layer" from κ-casein segments giving a "brush like" appearance extending into the solvent [111, 71].

The casein molecules are linked into tiny **micelles** with the help of colloidal calcium phosphate. The casein micelle biologically functions as a carrier of calcium and phosphate [99] to the young mammal being fed. These micelles are apparently responsible for the whiteness of milk.

Whey. Whey proteins make up about 20 percent of milk protein. The whey proteins are more water soluble than caseins and dispersed in the milk serum. It is made up principally of *lactalbumin* and *lactoglobulin* (Table 22–2). Whey proteins are not precipitated by acid or rennet, but can be denatured and coagulated by heat. These proteins seem to be chiefly responsible for the precipitate that usually forms on the bottom and sides of a container in which milk is heated. The beta lactoglobulins make up about half of total whey proteins; alpha lactalbumin, bovine serum albumin, and immunoglobulins are the remaining whey proteins.

The (sweet) whey is the by-product of cheesemaking, which consists of the fluid drained off after curd formation including whey proteins. Acid whey is a by-product of Greek yogurt production. The sweet and acid wheys are about 95 percent water. Whey was traditionally thought of as a waste product, but scientists are continually researching ways to recycle whey

Table 22–2
CASEIN AND WHEY PROTEINS IN MILK

Casein	Whey
α_{S1}-casein	β-lactoglobulin
α_{S2}-casein	α-lactalbumin
β-casein	Serum albumin
κ-casein	
γ-casein	

Source: Reference 48.

UP CLOSE
A2 VERSUS A1 BETA CASEIN

Beta (β) casein genetic variants of A1 and A2 proteins have been studied and implicated for dairy intolerance, gastrointestinal inflammation, and other disease states [110, 36, 49, 19]. The A2 beta casein has been determined to be the original beta casein since it existed prior to the A1 genetic mutation that happened 5,000 to 10,000 years ago in northern European dairy cow herds. Dairy cow breed's genetics dictate A1 and A2 beta casein protein production. Guernsey produce 90 percent A2 beta caseins. Jersey cows produce a high percentage of A2 beta casein. Holstein's milk is about an equal mix of A1 and A2 beta casein.

The difference between A1 and A2 beta caseins is in the 209 amino acid chain at position number 67. The A2 beta casein contains the amino acid proline, while the A1 beta casein has the amino acid histidine substituted in its place. Although the milk is nutritionally and functionally the same, difference in the digestion of the A2 and A1 variants have been implicated in gastrointestinal inflammatory response and other disease states. The digestion of A1 beta casein results in proteolysis that uniquely yields beta-casomorphin-7 (BCM-7), which is said to exert a pro-inflammatory response; it is said to be an immunosuppressant that may disrupt digestive processes and may mimic lactose intolerance symptoms [110] (see **Figure 22–22**). A1 beta caseins have been demonstrated to cause gastrointestinal inflammation and response compared to digestion of A2 beta casein [36, 49, 110, 19]. Milk sold as "A2" features milk from cows producing only A2 beta casein. ∎

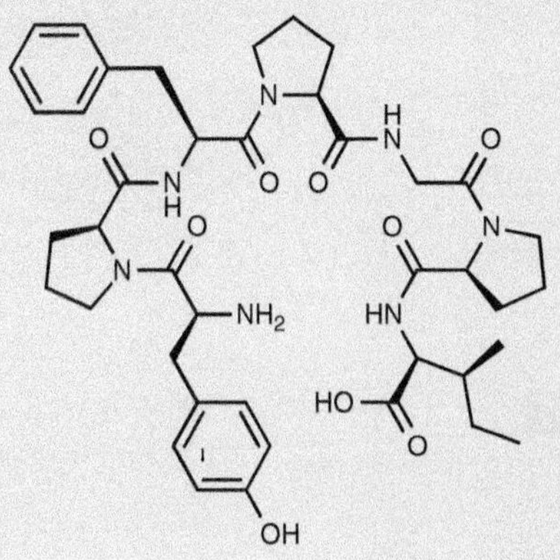

beta-casomorphin 7

Figure 22–22

Beta-casomorphin-7 (BCM-7) is the unique compound formed during the digestion of A1 beta casein. This compound produced by proteolysis during digestion is thought to cause symptoms that mimic lactose intolerance in some people consuming milk containing high proportions of A1 casein. (Molekuul/123RF)

for value. Whey proteins can be transformed into food products and used in a variety of food products such as high-protein beverages, "sport supplement whey protein powders," or substances with salt enhancement characteristics to lower sodium content in food and beverages [94]. Acid whey is difficult to work with and has less protein than sweet whey from cheesemaking. Acid whey has some protein, lactose, calcium, phosphorous, galactose, and lactic acid. The galactose and lactic acid turn sticky when dried. High-tech membrane filtration is being used to extract lactose and other components from acid whey for a value-added food product turns waste into value for the food producers [3]. The whey products are often labelled as "dairy product solids" or used as "milk protein concentrates."

Fat

The fat in milk is commonly called milkfat, butterfat, or cream. The fat in milk exists as small droplets called fat globules. These fat globules typically are between 0.2 and 15 μm with these native fat globules averaging about 4 μm [9, 71]. The milkfat globules may differ in size by 2.5 to 5.7 μm depending on the cow [70]. This difference may affect processing, texture, and product yields [70]. Each native fat globule is covered by a thin fat globule membrane [4].

Milkfat is a complex lipid composed primarily of **triglycerides** (98.3 percent), but also **phospholipids** (0.8 percent), and some **sterols**. The sterols are mainly cholesterol (0.3 percent). The triglycerides are characterized by the presence of 11 percent short-chain (C4–C10), **saturated fatty acids**, such as butyric (C4) and caproic (C6), caprylic (C8), and capric (C10) fatty acids. Major intermediate fatty acids (C12–C16) include 11 percent myristic (C14) and 26 percent palmitic (C16); long-chain fatty acids of 20 percent stearic (C18), and 20 percent oleic (C18:1). Half the fatty acids in milk are synthesized by the mammary gland and the other half are derived directly from the blood. Milk globule size maybe partly regulated by feed [133]. Butyric acid (C4) is only found in ruminant animal milkfat [9, 68]. Butyric acid is responsible for the rancid flavor as it is cleaved from glycerol by lipase. A large array of fatty acids are found in milkfat; they are saturated and unsaturated, *trans* and *cis* forms, odd- and even-number carbons [67]. The fatty acids are responsible for the relatively low melting point (98.6°F and 37°C) and, therefore, the soft-solid consistency of butter. Milkfat may appear solid at refrigerated temperatures 41°F (5°C), but it still contains 50 percent liquid fat. The milkfat alpha crystals

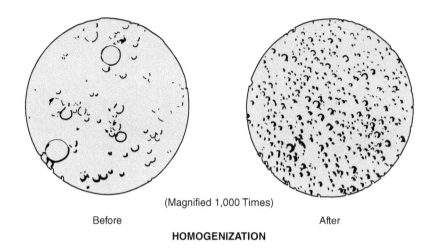

(Magnified 1,000 Times)

Before   After

HOMOGENIZATION

Figure 22–23

Homogenization of milk decreases the distribution and size of the dispersed fat globules as shown in this photomicrograph of evaporated milk.

persist longer than in other fats before morphing into more stable crystalline forms. (See fat crystal and milkfat discussion in Chapter 8.)

The native fat globule membrane is made up of phospholipids. The fat globule membrane wraps around lipids. The fat globule membrane is important to food manufacturing. This membrane prevents coalescence of fat globules and protects the fat from enzymes. The fat globule membrane has a polar hydrophilic side and a non-polar lipid side. The triglycerides are in the core of the fat globule. The fat globule membrane acts as an emulsifier suspending the fat in the milk serum [71].

Heat treatment and homogenization both alter milkfat globule plasma membrane [71]. Thus, the native fat globular membrane is modified during heating and processing. The new recombined fat membrane is much different than the native fat globule membrane. The "new" fat globules are smaller in diameter with increased surface area. After processing such as homogenization, the recombined globule membrane is made up of casein micelles and membrane fragments, which surrounds the fat. The milkfat may have different properties and interactions after processing due to difference in composition and structure of the fat interface [71, 4]. These changes in the fat globule due to heat or processing have an influence on sensory perceptions and functional properties.

Butter spoilage is the result of triglyceride **hydrolysis**. The disagreeable odor and flavor is from the triglycerides release of free butyric and caproic acids. Refer to Chapter 8 for a more extensive discussion on lipids in foods.

Milkfat exists in whole homogenized milk as tiny droplets dispersed in the milk serum (watery portion); thus, milk is an oil-in-water **emulsion**. The fat globules vary in size, but most are minute, yet easily visible under the microscope (see **Figure 22–23**). The fat globules remain dispersed in an emulsified form because they are surrounded by a thin film or membrane called the *milkfat globule membrane*. This membrane is composed of a lipid-protein complex and a small amount of carbohydrate [54]. The lipid portion includes **phospholipids**, **triglycerides**, and **sterols**.

Fat globules in fresh, unprocessed milk are loosely grouped in small clusters. When non-homogenized milk stands, the fat globules tend to *flocculate* forming larger and larger clusters. *Creaming* occurs because fat is less dense than the watery portion of milk so the fat clusters rise to the surface as cream.

The size of the dispersed fat globules in milk is decreased by the process of homogenization. The dispersion is therefore more stable, and the cream no longer rises to the surface on standing. Homogenization is discussed later in the chapter.

Carbohydrate

The primary carbohydrate found in milk is lactose, also called milk sugar. Lactose is a disaccharide. On hydrolysis, lactose yields the monosaccharides glucose and galactose (see Chapter 9 for the chemical structures of disaccharides and monosaccharides). The biological function of lactose in milk is to regulate water and osmotic content maintaining equilibrium so thus lactose is a stable 4.7 percent constituent in milk. Therefore, it stands to reason that it is the rate of lactose synthesis that regulates water and ultimately milk yield [68].

In food systems, lactose serves as a fermentable sugar for lactic acid bacteria. Thus, lactose is the fermentable substrate in many fermented dairy products. Lactose is the least sweet and less soluble of sugars.

Because of its low solubility, it may crystallize and give some food products a sandy texture when present in too large an amount. For example, when too much nonfat dry milk, which is high in lactose, is added to ice cream, the less soluble sugar may produce sandiness at the low temperature required for freezing. When separated, the milk lactose has many uses in the food industry. It may be an ingredient in such products as cooked sausages and hams, confections, and infant formulas.

Other minor carbohydrate components existing in fractional amounts include small amounts of free glucose and galactose, the sugar alcohol myoinositol and a few other oligosaccharides, sugar phosphates, and sugar nucleotides.

Lactose Intolerance. The enzyme *lactase* is normally produced in the small intestine. Lactase breaks down lactose into the monosaccharides glucose and galactose. In some people, however, the lactase enzyme is present in insufficient quantity for them to consume more than a very small amount of milk sugar without discomfort. People with a lactase deficient do not properly digest lactose. The lactose remains in the intestine and is broken down by microorganisms, producing gas, cramping, and diarrhea. A deficiency of lactase causes what is known as lactose intolerance. People with lactose intolerance may be able to tolerate some fermented milk products, such as yogurt and buttermilk, because much of the lactose in these products has been broken down. Aged cheese may also be tolerated [41].

Lactase enzymes are commercially available. The dairy industry has produced "reduced lactose" fluid milks that have been treated with enzymes to reduce lactose 70 percent [41]. These milks are sweeter tasting because the lactose has been broken down to the sweeter sugars—glucose and galactose. Lactase is also available for home use in liquid and tablet or capsule form. The lactase can be consumed directly or added to regular milk.

Minerals and Vitamins

Calcium, phosphorus, magnesium, potassium, chloride and sodium are some of the minerals found in milk. Milk, in particular, is valued for its calcium content. One 8-ounce glass of milk provides approximately 300 milligrams of calcium. Jersey cows produce milk with the highest calcium and phosphorus content. Three cups of milk contains about 95 percent of the phosphorus recommended daily for adults 19 years and older [76].

Water- and fat-soluble vitamins are found in milk. The fat-soluble vitamins A, D, E, and K are carried in the fat globules. Vitamin A, a fat-soluble vitamin, is removed with the cream when reduced-fat milk products are produced. Thus, reduced-fat milk is fortified to replace vitamin A. Vitamins D, E, and K are found in low levels in milk. Milk is commonly fortified with vitamin D to provide 25 percent of the daily recommendation for this nutrient in an 8-ounce serving [76]. Milk is also a good source of B vitamins—thiamine, riboflavin, niacin, vitamin B6 (pyridoxine), vitamin B12, and pantothenic acid.

Milk Enzymes

Milk contains enzymes that include lipoprotein lipase, plasmin, and alkaline phosphatase. Lipoprotein lipase (LPL) is a lipid enzyme found in milk plasma and is associated with casein micelles. It splits glycerol from the fatty acids. It can attack the lipids in the fat globular membrane causing lipolysis. Plasmin is a proteolytic enzyme that splits proteins. It attacks both beta alpha-2 caseins. It is heat stable and responsible for the bitterness in pasteurized milk.

Alkaline phosphatase (ALP) is an enzyme present in all raw milk, although the levels present may vary in the raw milk. The heat stability of alkaline phosphatase is greater than that of pathogens that maybe found in milk. Complete pasteurization destroys alkaline phosphatase and thus pathogens. Testing for ALP is often used to ensure proper pasteurization and product safety.

UP CLOSE
CASEIN AND WHEY IN FOOD PRODUCTS

Both casein and whey may be isolated and then used in a variety of food products. Isolated casein and caseinate products may be found in such products as imitation cheese, coffee whiteners, dessert toppings, and bakery items.

Sweet whey is a by-product of cheesemaking and may be further processed by a procedure involving ultrafiltration to produce whey protein concentrate (WPC). WPC may be made to contain about 35, 50, or 80 percent protein. Further processing may produce whey protein isolate, which contains greater than 90 percent protein. These whey products, in dried form, may be used in a wide range of food applications, including the formulation of high-protein beverages that are popular with athletes, and used in bakery products, prepared mixes, soups, confectionery, and margarines [39, 45]. On heating, dispersions of WPC can act as gelling agents. β-lactoglobulin accounts for about 50 percent of total whey proteins and is apparently the principal gelling protein in whey [72, 80].

Color

The white appearance of milk is due to the reflection of light by the colloidally dispersed casein micelles and by the calcium phosphate salts. The fat-soluble carotenes are found in the milkfat and contribute to a yellow, creamy color. The breed of the cows and their diet influence milk carotenes. Depending on the concentration of carotenes, the intensity of color in milk varies. The water-soluble vitamin riboflavin is responsible for milk's greenish-yellow fluorescent color, which is particularly noticeable in liquid whey.

Flavor

The flavor of milk is bland, but also slightly sweet because of lactose content. A major flavor sensation of milk is thought to be its particular mouthfeel, which results from the emulsion of milkfat, as well as from the **colloidal** structure of the proteins and some of the calcium phosphate. The slight aroma of fresh milk is produced by several low-molecular-weight compounds, such as acetone, acetaldehyde, dimethyl sulfide, methyl ketones, short-chain fatty acids, and lactones. Some of the volatile compounds contributing to the flavor of milk are unique to the fatty portion of milk.

Heat Processing. Heat processing may affect the flavor of milk, the change in flavor being dependent on the time and temperature of heating. The pasteurization of milk, including the use of ultrahigh temperatures for very short periods, has minimal impact on flavor, and if flavor changes occur, they tend to disappear during storage. Milk sterilized at ultrahigh temperatures tastes much like conventionally pasteurized milk, although some may notice a slightly cooked flavor [84].

Other Factors Influencing Flavor. The off-flavors that sometimes occur in milk may result from the feed consumed by the cow, the action of bacteria, chemical changes in the milk, or the absorption of foreign flavors after the milk is drawn. Feed and weed flavors can be transferred to milk. Even "barny" flavors can be transmitted to milk if ventilation is poor in the milking barn. One chemical off-flavor is called *oxidized* flavor [2]. This flavor can result from the oxidation of phospholipids in the milk. Because traces of copper accelerate the development of oxidized flavor, copper-containing equipment is not used in dairies.

An off-flavor may also be produced when milk is exposed to light. As little as four hours of light exposure can change flavor [91]. Light exposure from the dairy case can be responsible for flavor changes of milk. Low-level LED lights have less effect initiating flavor oxidation compared to fluorescent lights, which can be important in retail dairy cases or point of sale displays [91].

The light oxidation off-flavor, which develops rapidly, involves both milk protein and riboflavin. The amount of riboflavin, in milk decreases as the off-flavor develops. Vitamin A, lipids, and proteins are also affected by this oxidative process. Waxed cartons and opaque plastic containers help to protect milk from light, thus reducing riboflavin loss and the development of off-flavors.

pH

Fresh milk has a pH of about 6.6, which is close to the neutral pH of 7. As milk stands exposed to air, its acidity decreases slightly because of the loss of carbon dioxide. Raw milk ordinarily contains bacteria that ferment lactose and produce lactic acid, thus gradually increasing acidity. The natural "souring" of the raw milk and the development of curds are produced by the lactic acid bacteria process; a clean, acidic taste is characteristic. Natural soured raw milk is known as "clabbered milk." Pasteurized milk does not sour in this way. The heat of pasteurization destroys most of the lactic acid bacteria responsible for the souring process. Instead, pasteurized milk spoils by the action of putrefactive bacteria, which breaks down the proteins in milk and results in a bitter, unpleasant flavor.

FOCUS ON SCIENCE
CAUSES OF OFF-FLAVORS IN MILK

Action of Copper in Milk

Copper is a metal that will cause a "clipping" action on the triglyceride producing free fatty acids in the milk. Once there are free fatty acids, especially if the fatty acids are unsaturated, they will undergo oxidative rancidity—a procedure that will cause off-flavor and aroma in the milk.

Since Riboflavin Is a Vitamin, How Can It Produce an Off-Flavor in the Milk?

When exposed to light, riboflavin decomposes to *lumiflavin*. Lumiflavin is a stronger oxidizing agent than riboflavin and can catalyze destruction of a number of vitamins, particularly ascorbic acid. When milk was sold in bottles, this reaction sequence caused a significant problem with loss of nutrients and the development of undesirable flavor known as "sunlight" off-flavor. Opaque milk containers prevent this problem by reducing the light exposure [100].

SANITATION, GRADING, AND PROCESSING

Milk is among the most perishable of all foods because it is an excellent medium (high protein, moist, and neutral pH) for bacterial growth. Some bacteria that grow in milk are harmless, but some may be pathogenic to humans. Various controls over the production, processing, and distribution of milk have been instituted to ensure quality and safety in dairy products. However, the consumer trend in organic and natural foods has increased consumption of raw unpasteurized dairy products such as raw milk and unpasteurized fresh cheese. About 3.2 percent of the population consumes raw unpasteurized dairy milk and cheese, which is responsible for 96 percent of illnesses from contaminated dairy products [13, 20]. These raw dairy products cause illnesses from *Salmonella spp., Listeria monocytogenes*, and *Campylobacter spp.* and Shiga toxin producing *Escherichia coli* (STEC) [20].

Grade "A" Pasteurized Milk Ordinance

The Grade "A" Pasteurized Milk Ordinance is a set of recommendations made by the U.S. Public Health Service and the Food and Drug Administration (FDA). This ordinance describes the steps necessary to protect the milk supply. It outlines sanitary practices, which include the following:

- Inspection and sanitary control of farms and milk plants
- Examination and testing of herds
- Employee instruction on good manufacturing practices
- Proper pasteurization and processing
- Laboratory examination of milk
- Monitoring for chemical, physical, and microbial adulterants
- Provides guidelines for Grade "A" milk from goat, camel, water buffalo, and other hooved mammals
- Includes guidance for whey products, condensed, and dry milk products
- Incorporates provisions governing packaging and the sale of Grade "A" milk, buttermilk, and other milk products

The Grade "A" Pasteurized Milk Ordinance was formulated as a guide to states and other jurisdictions responsible for milk quality. This ordinance has been voluntarily adopted by many state and local governments and is revised periodically [121, 120]. The majority of people in the United States live in areas where the guidelines of this ordinance are in effect.

Grading

Sanitary codes generally determine the grading of milk. Grades and their meanings may vary according to local regulations. In areas where the pasteurized

Figure 22–24

USDA shields indicate quality in dairy products. (U.S. Department of Agriculture)

milk ordinance has been adopted, the grading standards are uniform. The most rigid control is placed on the production and processing of Grade A market milk, which is the grade most sold to consumers. The *Grade A Pasteurized Milk Ordinance* recommends that state health or agriculture departments have programs to regularly monitor the milk supply for the presence of unintentional microconstituents, such as pesticide residues, antibiotics, and radioactivity. In addition, the FDA regularly conducts surveys and other monitoring activities.

The U.S. Department of Agriculture (USDA) has set quality grade standards for nonfat dry milk, butter, and some cheeses. In addition, a Quality Approved rating is available for products with no established grade standard (**Figure 22–24**). If a manufacturer uses the USDA grade or Quality Approved shield on product labels, the plant must operate under the continuous inspection of USDA agents. The grades for regular nonfat dry milk are U.S. Extra and U.S. Standard. For the instantized product, the grade is U.S. Extra. Grading is a voluntary, fee-for-service program.

Pasteurization

Low bacterial count and high standards of production do not always ensure a milk supply that is free from pathogenic organisms. Even under the best sanitary practices, disease-producing organisms may contaminate raw milk [76]. Therefore, milk is pasteurized as a safeguard for consumers. Pasteurization is required by law for all Grade A fluid milk and milk products that enter interstate commerce for retail sale [13]. The sale of raw milk is legal within some states in spite of the risks associated with its consumption. The FDA has stated that consumers are 160 times more likely to contract a Listeria infection from soft-ripened cheese made from raw milk compared to pasteurized milk [58] (**Figure 22–25**).

The pasteurization process involves heating raw milk in properly approved and operated equipment at a sufficiently high temperature for a specified length of time to destroy pathogenic bacteria, thereby preventing serious illnesses. Pasteurization generally destroys

HOT TOPICS

WHAT IS RBST AND BST? WHY ARE SOME DAIRY PRODUCTS LABELED "FROM COWS NOT TREATED WITH RBST?"

Cows produce a natural nonsteroidal hormone in their pituitary gland that influences the cow's milk production. This hormone is known as bovine somatotropin (bST). The bST is only produced by cows and is only effective in cows. This protein hormone can be synthetically manufactured with biotechnology into "rbST" [114]. When rbST is given to cows, it increases their milk production by 10 percent. The FDA evaluated research and found that milk and meat from rbST-treated animals is safe for human consumption. Therefore, in 1993, the FDA approved the use of rbST [12]. A second review of rbST in 1998 affirmed the safety of this protein hormone.

Dairy processors realized consumer demand for dairy foods produced from cows not treated with rbST, so these products are marketed as "From Cows Not Treated with rbST." Whether or not milk produced without the use of rbST is different is another issue because the label also reads, "No significant difference has been shown between milk derived from rbST-treated cows and non-rbST-treated cows." The organic milk category does not allow synthetic hormones [26].

However, safety questions about rbST linger in part due to misinformation often posted on the Internet. The FDA based its assessment on the scientific literature. Scientific journals are *refereed*, which means that a scientific research study, published in a refereed journal, has undergone a *blind* review by other scientists. A research paper based on inadequate research methodology or inappropriate statistical analysis will be rejected for publication. In contrast, anything can be posted on the Internet.

What does this have to do with rbST? The reason that product labels must state that there is no difference between cows treated with rbST and those not treated is because the findings reported in refereed scientific journals do not reveal differences. Some points to consider follow:

- The National Institute of Health, the World Health Organization, and the *Journal of the American Medical Association* are among those in the scientific community who have reviewed the rbST data and concluded that milk and meat from rbST cows are safe.
- bST and rbST are protein hormones; thus, like insulin, which is a protein hormone, bST and rBST have no activity when taken by mouth.
- bST appears to be species specific and was shown not to influence growth, even when injected into humans.
- bST is a normal hormone for cows that naturally fluctuates in levels over the period of lactation. The milk produced from an rbST-treated cow contains no higher hormone levels than that produced from nontreated cows.
- A variety of factors influences the incidence of mastitis in cows, and rbST can be one factor. However, milk from both rbST-treated and rbST-nontreated cows is tested for antibiotic residues. If antibiotic residues are found, the milk is discarded [8].

95 to 99 percent of nonpathogenic bacteria as well. The main two milk pathogens of concern are *Coxiella burnetii* and *Mycobacterium tuberculosis/M. bovis*. The Pasteurized Milk Ordinance and the International Dairy Federation consider pasteurization adequate if these two pathogens are destroyed.

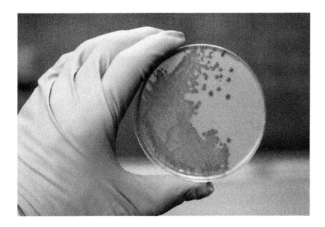

Figure 22–25

Listeria germs growing on an agar plate. (Ggw1962/Shutterstock)

Although milk is not completely sterilized by pasteurization, its keeping quality is greatly increased over that of raw milk. Various time and temperature relationships that can be used in pasteurization are provided in **Table 22–3**. Milk products that are condensed, have added sweeteners, or have a fat content above 10 percent, will need increased processing temperatures and time. Eggnog is a milk product that requires increased pasteurization time and temperatures.

The most common pasteurization method is high temperature short time (HTST) continuous process. The continuous process method pumps the raw milk from a holding tank through a continuous pasteurization system where milk flows through series of thin plates that heat milk to an appropriate temperature for an appropriate time before flowing into the cooling area and onto bottling or processing. The continuous flow process is either high temperature short time (HTST) or higher-heat shorter time (HHST). Vat or batch pasteurization is where the milk is pumped into a vat heated to an appropriate temperature and held for at least 30 minutes, then cooled and pumped out. Today, vat pasteurization is primarily used in the dairy industry for

Table 22–3
TIMES AND TEMPERATURES THAT MAY BE USED FOR THE PASTEURIZATION OF MILK

Name of Process	Time and Temperature	Comments
Batch (Vat) Pasteurization	145°F (63°C) for 30 minutes	These time and temperature combinations are identified in the Grade A Pasteurized Milk Ordinance. 145°F (63°C) for 30 minutes is often called low-temperature, long-time pasteurization.
Continuous Flow (HTST) Pasteurization	161°F (72°C) for 15 seconds	161°F (72°C) for 15 seconds is a high-temperature, short-time pasteurization process.
Continuous Flow Pasteurization (HHST)	191°F (89°C) for 1.0 seconds 194°F (90°C) for 0.5 second 201°F (94°C) for 0.1 second 204°F (96°C) for 0.05 second 212°F (100°C) for 0.01 second	
Ultra Pasteurization	280°F (138°C) for 2 or more seconds	Product may be stored under refrigeration for an extended period (14 to 28 days).
Sterilization	280° to 302°F (138° to 150°C) for 1 to 2 seconds 240°F (115.6°C) for 20 minutes	Sterilizes the milk. When in **aseptic packaging** in presterilized containers, this milk may be kept on the shelf without refrigeration for at least three months. After it is opened, however, it must be refrigerated. Canned products such as evaporated milk
Ultra high-temperature (UHT)	Depends on equipment and products processed	Aseptic processing operations must file with FDA's "Process Authority," which determines and validates processing times and temperatures.

Source: References International Dairy Foods Association, 76,120.

preparing milk for cheeses, fermented dairy products, or for ice cream mixes or by smaller dairy operations. Extended shelf life products are processed by various thermal methods. Continuous Ultra Pasteurization (UP) is used for refrigerated milk and cream with an extended shelf life. Room temperature shelf stable milk products use Ultra heat treatment (UHT) for aseptic packaging and sterilization for canned evaporated milk. Shelf storage guarding against light and heat are essential. Once these shelf-stable products are opened they must be refrigerated. *Aseptic processing and packaging* is defined by the Code of Federal Regulations 21 §113.3 as "the filling of a commercially sterilized cooled product into presterilized containers, followed by aseptic hermetical sealing, with a presterilized closure, in an atmosphere free of microorganisms." The FDA's "Process Authority" establishes and validates proper aseptic processing times and temperatures based on equipment and products processed. **Figure 22–26** shows a single-serve, aseptic UHT packaged milk.

Milk pasteurization can be ascertained by various tests such as the measurements of alkaline phosphatase. This enzyme, naturally present in milk, is completely inactivated if the milk has been heated sufficiently to destroy any pathogenic microorganisms. The temperatures

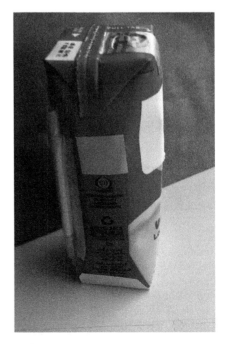

Figure 22–26

Aseptic UHT pasteurized milk is shelf stable.
(© Amanda Frye)

FOCUS ON SCIENCE
MORE ABOUT PASTEURIZATION

Bacteria Found in Milk

Pasteurization is important to destroy pathogenic bacteria that are inherent in milk. *Salmonella dublin*, *Listeria monocytogenes*, *E. coli*, and *Campylobacter jejuni* are bacteria that can pose a problem and are under constant surveillance.

Why Is Alkaline Phosphatase Pinpointed When Evaluating the Effectiveness of Milk Pasteurization?

Alkaline phosphatase is an enzyme that may not be irreversibly destroyed but only reversibly inactivated by high-temperature, short-time pasteurization. This creates a dilemma for the processor when, for example, milk properly pasteurized by a high temperature short time method exhibits a positive phosphatase test (indicative of improper pasteurization) only because of regeneration of this enzyme.

homogenizer. The native fat membrane is disrupted by homogenization. New small fat globules are created. A recombined membrane film of adsorbed protein or lipoprotein immediately surrounds each of the new globules, acting as an **emulsifier**, and prevents them from reuniting. It is estimated that about one-fourth of the protein of milk is adsorbed on the finely dispersed fat particles of homogenized milk.

The increased dispersion of fat imparts a richer flavor and increased viscosity to the milk. Because light is scattered more effectively by the greater number of fat globules, homogenized milk is white. Homogenized milk is also less likely to develop an oxidized flavor and produces a softer curd in the stomach, thereby aiding digestion.

Homogenization reduces milkfat globules into a small size (1.0 μm) so the fat stays dispersed and evenly distributed in the milk. Thus, many small fat globules are created. If milk was not homogenized, the cream would rise. Sometimes non-homogenized milk is called "creamline" milk since the fat globules will rise and separate to form a cream layer. This phenomenon is changed by homogenization since fat globules are divided into such small particles that they are dispersed permanently in a very fine emulsion throughout the milk serum (Figure 22–23). Most of the milk marketed in the United States is homogenized.

and times for pasteurization do not significantly alter the milk constituents or properties. Whey proteins are denatured only slightly, and minerals are not appreciably precipitated. Vitamin losses range from 0 to 10 percent [13]. Changes in digestion of milk due to homogenization and heat treatment have been found to be useful in dairy products' nutrient bioavailability [134]. Pasteurization yields finer curd when milk is digested. Non-thermal pasteurization methods of dairy products such as pulsed electric field treatment and electron beam (eBeam) processing are being explored [66, 136].

Homogenization

Homogenization consists of pumping milk or cream under pressures of 2,000 to 2,500 pounds per square inch through tiny openings in a machine called a

Fortification

Fortification is the addition of certain nutrients to milk as a means of improving the nutritional value. The principal form of fortification is the addition of about 400 international units (IUs) of vitamin D per quart. Vitamin D helps the absorption and utilization of calcium and phosphorus in the body. Since the milk is an outstanding source of these minerals, milk is generally regarded as a logical food to fortify with vitamin D. Although the addition of vitamin D is very common, according to the standards of identity for milk vitamin D fortification is optional. Some milk products also may be fortified with

HEALTHY EATING
RAW MILK—WHAT ARE THE RISKS?

The consumption of raw milk or cheese produced from unpasteurized (raw) milk caused 2,659 illnesses, 269 hospitalizations, and three deaths, six stillbirths, and two miscarriages from 1987 to 2010. These illnesses and deaths were the result of 133 foodborne illness outbreaks identified by the Centers for Disease Control and Prevention in which raw milk was implicated. The CDC statistics show increasing trends with 2016 statistics related to raw milk and cheese consumption as 3,109 outbreaks, 85,096 illnesses, 1,743 hospitalizations and 95 deaths. Not all foodborne illnesses are reported, and thus the actual numbers of consumers

who became ill as the result of consuming raw milk during this time period is likely much higher. These illnesses and deaths are mostly preventable with proper pasteurization.

Claims on the Internet about the safety and superior quality of raw milk are **not** supported by science [13]. One such claim is that pasteurized milk must be fortified by vitamin D because of pasteurization. However, milk, whether raw or pasteurized, is not high in vitamin D. Milk is a logical choice for vitamin D fortification because this vitamin works with calcium to promote healthy bones. See also Chapter 3 for more about food safety. ■

nonfat dried milk solids, which will increase the protein and calcium content of the milk.

Fat-reduced milk, such as 2 percent milk or nonfat milk, must be fortified with vitamin A. Vitamin A fortification of reduced-fat milk is mandatory because vitamin A, a fat-soluble vitamin, is present only in the fatty portion of milk. Thus, removal of the cream results in the loss of the vitamin A. It is particularly important that nonfat dry milk sent to other countries be fortified with vitamin A, because vitamin A deficiencies are common in some developing countries.

Ultrafiltration

Ultrafiltration (UF) is a mechanical filtration technology used for milk processing. The milk is passed over a series of semipermeable membranes with various pore sizes. The milk that passes through the membrane is the *permeate* and the portion that does not pass through the membranes is the *retentate*. Ultrafiltration retains macromolecules and particles greater than about 0.001–0.02 micrometers. Dairy processing uses ultrafiltration to retain all protein components of milk including casein and whey proteins, while some of the milk lactose, minerals, and water soluble vitamins are drained off with the water. UF may be applied to raw or pasteurized dairy products. Ultrafiltration is also used to produce whey protein concentrates. The Food and Drug Administration amended the standard of identity for cheese and related cheese products to allow ultrafiltration for cheese production [126]. Food labels must contain the words "ultrafiltered milk" [126].

TYPES OF MILK PRODUCTS

Milk is sold in several different forms to appeal to the varied tastes and desires of the consuming public from refrigerated to shelf-stable products. Packaging of milk in individual milk "chugs" has promoted milk as a grab-and-go beverage. Glass bottles, plastic jugs, waxed cartons, aseptic packages, and cans are all used to package milk. Cost variations among different forms of milk depend on such factors as supply and demand, production and processing costs, and governmental policies.

Federal standards of identity have been set for a number of milk products that enter interstate commerce. These standards define the composition, the kind and quantity of optional ingredients permitted, and the labeling requirements. (Refer to Chapter 3 for more information about food labeling.) State and local agencies are encouraged to adopt the federal standards to enhance uniformity. Tests to quickly detect fraud and mislabeling in milk and dairy products have been developed [27].

Fluid Milk

Fresh fluid milk is commonly labeled according to its content of milkfat. Beginning January 1, 1998, the labeling of fat-reduced milk followed the same requirements that the FDA established several years ago for the labeling of most other foods that are reduced in fat. Therefore, skim milk may be labeled "skim," "fat-free," "zero-fat," or "no-fat" milk. The regulations were also changed to give dairy processors more freedom to devise new formulations, for example, "light" milk with at least 50 percent less fat than whole milk and reformulated milks with reduced-fat content but increased creaminess [60, 85]. The names for milk and fat content are summarized in **Table 22–4**.

Whole Milk. The term *milk* usually refers to whole milk. According to federal standards, whole milk packaged for beverage use must contain not less than 3.25 percent milkfat and not less than 8.25 percent milk-solids-not-fat, which are mostly protein and lactose [117]. At milk-processing plants, the milk from different suppliers is standardized to one fat level by removing or adding milkfat as necessary.

Table 22–4
NAMES FOR MILK

Old Name	New Name	Total Fat per 240 mL or 1 Cup	Kilocalories per 240 mL or 1 Cup
Milk	Milk	8.0 grams	150
Low-fat 2 percent milk	Reduced-fat or less-fat milk	4.7 grams	122
Low-fat 1 percent milk	Low-fat milk	2.6 grams	102
Skim milk	Fat-free, skim, zero-fat, no-fat, or nonfat milk	Less than 0.5 gram	80

Source: Reference 60.

Figure 22–27

Eggnog is a specialty milk beverage most likely sold at stores during the winter holidays. It is often garnished with nutmeg or cinnamon. Raw eggs should never be used in this product. (William Berry/Shutterstock)

Figure 22–28

Canned evaporated and sweetened condensed milk are shelf stable. (© Amanda Frye)

Fat-Reduced Milks. Milks may be modified in fat content as listed in Table 22–4. The nutrients that lower-fat milk products provide, other than fat, must be at least equal to full-fat milk before vitamins A and D are added. The word *skim* is allowed in the labeling of nonfat milk because skim milk has been a traditional name that is familiar to consumers. *Skim* or *nonfat milk* is milk from which as much fat has been removed as is technologically possible. The fat content is less than 0.5 percent. All of these milks contain at least 8.25 percent milk-solids-not-fat. Addition of vitamin A to low-fat and skim milk is required for milk shipped in interstate commerce.

Flavored Milk and Eggnog. Milk flavored with chocolate, strawberry, or other flavors is available. These dairy products have the same nutritional value as unflavored milk, but may have a moderately or significantly higher caloric content due to the added ingredients. Eggnog includes milk, egg yolk, sweeteners, and flavors, such as nutmeg and vanilla. It is most often sold as a specialty milk during the Thanksgiving and Christmas holiday seasons (see **Figure 22–27**).

Concentrated Fluid Milk

Evaporated Milk. Evaporated milk contains about 60 percent of the water found in regular milk and is usually purchased in cans (see **Figure 22–28**). In the production of evaporated milk, water is removed in a vacuum pan at 122 to 131°F (50 to 55°C). A prewarming period of 10 to 20 minutes at 203°F (95°C) is usually effective in preventing coagulation of the protein casein during sterilization. The heat sterilization process occurs after the product is homogenized and canned. In another process, the concentrated milk may be heated in a continuous system at ultrahigh temperatures and then canned aseptically. This product is less viscous and whiter and tastes more like pasteurized milk than evaporated milk processed by the traditional method. Evaporated milk is fortified with 400 IUs of vitamin D per quart.

Federal standards require that evaporated milk contain not less than 6.5 percent milkfat and not less than 23 percent total milk solids. Evaporated skim milk must contain not less than 20 percent milk solids. In this case, both vitamin A and vitamin D must be added [123].

Figure 22–29

Sweetened condensed milk has sugar added and less water than fluid milk, giving increased viscosity. (Oleg Malyshev/Shutterstock)

FOCUS ON SCIENCE
SWEETENED CONDENSED MILK AND LIME JUICE—WHY DOES IT THICKEN?

Key lime pie sometimes uses lime juice and sweetened condensed milk mixed together. Why will this mixture thicken?

When the protein casein is concentrated in a product such as sweetened condensed milk, the proteins show a high water-holding capacity by thickening and forming a gel when (1) heated or (2) in contact with an acid. In traditional Key lime pie recipes, sweetened condensed milk and lime juice are mixed together, and a gel is formed because of the acid contact when it is allowed to chill.

Sweetened Condensed Milk. Sweetened condensed milk also has less water than found in regular milk, and it is sweetened (see **Figure 22–29**). To prepare sweetened condensed milk, about 15 percent sugar is added to whole or skim milk, which is then concentrated to about one-third of its former volume. Because the 42 percent sugar content of the finished product acts as a preservative, the milk is not sterilized after canning. Federal standards require 28 percent total milk solids. Whole sweetened condensed milk must contain 8 percent milkfat, whereas the skim milk product must have not more than 0.5 percent fat.

Storage and Quality. Sterilized canned evaporated milk should keep indefinitely without microbiologic spoilage; however, other changes affect its quality, so storage beyond one year is not recommended. If allowed to stand for a long time, the homogenized fat particles tend to coalesce, thus breaking the emulsion. The solids begin to settle, and the product may thicken and form curds or clots. To retard these changes, stored cans of evaporated and condensed milk should be turned every few weeks. The vegetable gum carrageenan is often added to evaporated milk as a stabilizer.

Both sweetened condensed milk and evaporated milk may show evidence of browning. Browning of condensed milk and evaporated milk is probably due to the **Maillard reaction** and occurs during both sterilization and storage. The rate of browning is greater when stored at room temperature and for a longer storage time. See **Figure 22–30**.

Dry Milk

Dairy products may be dried to allow extended storage without the need for refrigeration. Nonfat dried milk is commonly available, but other dried milk products are also available. Whole or low-fat milk, when dried, has a shorter shelf life than nonfat dried milk because the fat is subject to oxidation, resulting in rancid or other off-flavors. Dried buttermilk is available through retail and food distribution channels. It is widely used in commercial flour mixtures. Dried churned buttermilk is an excellent ingredient for use in baked products because it contains phospholipids that function as emulsifiers.

Figure 22–30

Browning and other quality changes are evident in these cans of evaporated and sweetened condensed milk that are several months past the best use-by dates. (© Amanda Frye)

Nonfat dry milk powder is usually made from fresh pasteurized skim milk by removing about two-thirds of the water under vacuum and then spraying this concentrated milk into a chamber of hot filtered air. This process produces a fine powder of very low moisture content, about 3 percent. Nonfat dry milk may also be produced by spraying a jet of hot air into concentrated skim milk (foam spray-drying).

The method of processing has an impact on how easily a dried milk product will reconstitute. Instant nonfat dry milk disperses readily in cold water. To make the instant product, regular nonfat dry milk is remoistened with steam to induce agglomeration of small particles into larger, porous particles that are creamy white and free flowing. The lactose may be in a more soluble form, particularly on the outside of the particles.

To reconstitute instant dried milk, add the powder to water and then shake or stir. For use in flour mixtures and some other products, the dry milk can be mixed with dry ingredients and the water added later. Warm water and agitation are helpful when reconstituting dried milk that is not instant because it will not dissolve as readily as instant dried milk. The quantity of instant milk powder needed to make 1 quart of fluid milk is usually $1\frac{1}{3}$ cups.

FOCUS ON SCIENCE
TEMPERATURE ABUSE OF MILK AND SPOILAGE

Why Does Milk Spoil If I Pour Any Milk That Was Held at Room Temperature Back into Its Original Carton?

After pasteurization, very little bacteria is left in the milk. Any bacteria that may be introduced may thrive and proliferate if held at room temperature for any length of time because there are few "competitors" in the milk. Additionally, because milk is a source of proteins and nutrients such as minerals and vitamins, it provides a good environment for

bacterial growth. Buttermilk and sour cream have a longer shelf life because their pH (acidic) is low enough to prevent microbes from thriving.

Thus, when milk is temperature abused by being left at room temperature, any bacteria present or incidentally added to the milk will grow rapidly. Adding this contaminated milk into the original carton will essentially inoculate the entire carton with bacteria that are likely to cause spoilage.

FOCUS ON SCIENCE
DRY MILK AND SHELF LIFE

Whole dried milk can become rancid and, like nonfat dried milk, can turn a tan or brown color with extended storage. Why does this occur?

Rancidity

Water activity will have an effect on rancidity in dried whole milk. In dried foods with very low moisture content, oxidation proceeds very rapidly. Thus, nonfat dried milk is preferred because there is no fat in the product to become rancid.

Browning

Dried milk, however, will undergo browning due to a Maillard reaction. Maillard browning requires protein (amino acid) and carbohydrate (sugar). In dried milk, the presence of lactose and amino acid (lysine) will cause Maillard browning. Additionally, the nutrient content is compromised because lysine, an essential amino acid, may be lost in the browning reaction.

Cultured Milk Products

Cultured or **fermented** milks are one of the oldest preserved foods, having been used for centuries. Several hundred different cultured milk products are consumed worldwide [59]. Yogurt, buttermilk, and sour cream are among some of the available cultured dairy products. Sour cream will be discussed with other types of creams.

Cultured milk products are prepared by the addition of appropriate bacterial cultures to the fluid milk. The bacteria ferment lactose to produce lactic acid. Lactic acid production lowers the pH of the product to between 4.1 and 4.9 and thus discourages the growth of undesirable microorganisms. Acids, such as lactic and citric acid, may also be added directly to milk, either with or without the addition of microbial cultures. The development of acidity is responsible for several physical and chemical properties that make the fermented products unique. Each bacterial culture produces its own characteristic flavor components. Some protein hydrolysis occurs, apparently contributing to a softer, more easily digested curd.

Yogurt. Yogurt is a cultured milk product with a "custard like" consistency made from whole, low-fat, and skim milk or even cream. Although the use of

cow's milk is common in the United States, the milk from other animals may also be used for yogurt. Yogurt standard of identity is given in the U.S. Code of Federal Regulations [24]. In yogurt production milk is pasteurized prior to adding cultures. The required mixed culture of *Lactobacillus bulgaricus* and *Streptococcus thermophilus* is added to preheated pasteurized milk. These mixed cultures are typically a ratio of 1:1 [73]. *Lactobacillus acidophilus* or other strains may also be added to the culture. Pasteurization is important since it kills microorganisms that might interfere with fermentation and it denatures whey proteins [73]. The milk and the culture are then incubated at 108 to 115°F (42 to 46°C) until the desired flavor, acidity, and consistency are attained. During this time, the bacterial culture causes an increase in acidity, causing the casein to coagulate. After yogurt has reached the desired flavor and consistency, further bacterial activity is retarded by chilling. Lactic acid level (or pH) determines when yogurt is ready to cool. Current minimum standards for yogurt in United States require pH of 4.4 or 0.9 percent acidity [73]. All yogurt must contain 8.25 percent solids not fat. Full-fat yogurt must contain not less than 3.25 percent fat. Stabilizers may be used in yogurt to improve the body and texture increasing the firmness and preventing syneresis. Common yogurt stabilizers include alginates (carrageenan gum), gelatin, locust bean gum or guar gum, pectin, or starch. See **Figure 22–31** for basic yogurt (or yoghurt) processing steps.

A sharp, tangy flavor is characteristic of yogurt. Several types of yogurt are manufactured, including a set style with a firm gel, stirred yogurt with a semi-liquid consistency, liquid yogurt that is drinkable, and Greek yogurt. Greek yogurt is prepared like other yogurts, but after it is cultured, it is strained through a cloth or small strainer to allow some of the whey to drain off. Greek yogurts are usually creamier, higher in protein, and lower in lactose compared to other types.

Many yogurts contain fruit to sweeten the otherwise tangy yogurt. Swiss-style yogurt has flavors added to the chilled fermented yogurt [73]. These yogurts may be fruit flavored or have fruit mixed throughout or have sweetened fruit on the bottom as sundae-style yogurt. Some yogurt products are labeled to inform the consumer that a significant level of live, active cultures is present. Other yogurts may be heat treated after fermentation to extend shelf life and consequently do not contain live cultures.

The nutrient composition of yogurt reflects the nutrient composition of the milk used, the added fruit or other ingredients, or the type of yogurt, such as Greek yogurt. The lactose content of yogurt is reduced during fermentation because some lactose is hydrolyzed to the monosaccharides glucose and galactose. The lactose level of Greek yogurt is even lower because of how it is prepared. Thus, yogurt may be a good choice for those who are lactose intolerant. Drinkable yogurt is also available. Skyr is an Icelandic yogurt made from skim milk with thicker consistency

than regular or Greek-style yogurts [135]. Yogurts are the most common probiotic [29]. Some manufacturers offer multiple probiotic cultures in their yogurt.

Kefir.   Kefir is a fermented milk beverage that may be made with the milk of cows, sheep, or goats. Kefir is popular in Russia and the Caucasus Mountain region were it originated [135, 29]. The fermentation of Kefir involves bacteria and cultures from grain producing yeasts [135]. Kefir is a probiotic drinkable yogurt like drink, but it contains more cultures than yogurt plus some beneficial yeasts [29, 97]. "Soymilk" kefir has also been produced [69]. Kefir grains are used to inoculate the milk with a wider number of cultures than typically found in yogurt. Kefir is tart, slightly carbonated, and mildly alcoholic due to the fermentation process. Like yogurt, kefir may be tolerated by adults that are lactose intolerant [33].

Buttermilk.   The term *buttermilk* was originally used to describe the low-fat liquid remaining after cream is churned to produce butter. This liquid is still used for the production of dried buttermilk, a baking ingredient, or if purchased in the liquid form, it is called sweet cream buttermilk. Most buttermilk sold in stores is a cultured milk. Cultured buttermilk is usually made from pasteurized low-fat or skim milk, with nonfat dry milk solids added. It can also be made from fluid whole milk or reconstituted nonfat dry milk. In the process of manufacturing, a culture of *Lactococcus lactis* (formerly called *Streptococcus lactis*) is added to the milk to produce the acid and flavor components. The product is incubated at 68 to 70°F (20 to 22°C)

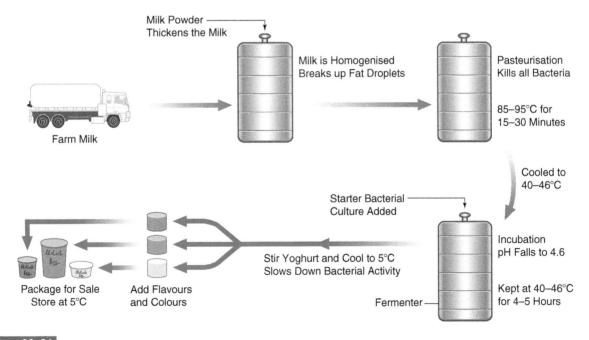

Figure 22–31

Yogurt production. (Oxford Designers & Illustrators Ltd./Pearson Education Ltd.)

HEALTHY EATING
PROBIOTICS

Probiotics are live microbial food ingredients that are alleged to have beneficial effect on the gastrointestinal tract. Milk products are easy ways to deliver these active cultures. Probiotics include fermented milk products such as yogurt, kefir, and buttermilk. Evidence suggesting the positive health benefits of probiotics in the diet and the cultured dairy food market is growing [40, 56, 86]; *Lactobacillus acidophilus*, *Lactobacillus reuteri*, and bifidobacteria are normal inhabitants of the intestinal tract, contributing to increased acidity and deterrence of undesirable microbial growth (see **Figure 22–32**). Probiotics are said to have a "symbiotic relationship" in the intestinal "microbial ecosystem" although the mechanisms are mostly speculative [95]. However, animal studies show that the probiotics positively alter gene expression [129]. The addition of safe and suitable microbial organisms to milk products is allowed by the Pasteurized Milk Ordinance. Additional research is necessary, however, to provide sufficient proof for the FDA to approve label claims for nutritional benefits of [42, 43, 103]. The United Nations Food and Agriculture Organization (FAO) and the World Health Organization (WHO) have jointly drafted guidelines for probiotics [51]. ∎

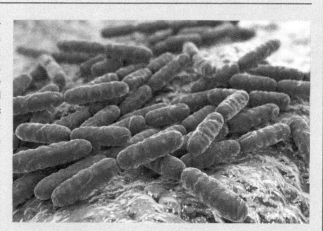

Figure 22–32

Lactobacillus bacteria are used in cultured milk products and probiotics. (Kateryna Kon/Shutterstock)

---

until the acidity is 0.8 to 0.9 percent (pH 4.6), expressed as lactic acid [84]. Butter granules or flakes, salt, and a small amount of citric acid may be added to enhance the flavor.

Acidophilus Milks.   Low-fat or skim milk may be cultured with *L. acidophilus* and incubated at 100°F (38°C) until a soft curd forms. This formulation is then called *acidophilus-cultured milk*. It has an acidic flavor. In another process, a concentrated culture of *L. acidophilus* is grown and then added to pasteurized milk to produce *sweet acidophilus milk*. This product is not acidic in taste, and its consistency is similar to that of fluid milk. Acidophilus milk introduces acidophilus bacteria into the intestine, where it may help to maintain a proper balance of microorganisms.

Crème Fraîche.   A cultured cream product that is richer and thinner than sour cream. It has a tart and tangy flavor. Crème fraîche is popular in French cuisine [61].

Filled and Imitation Milks

Filled and imitation milks do not meet the standard of identification for milk, but are instead substitute products. Filled and imitation milks are subject to variable state regulations, but are not governed by the same rigid sanitation and composition requirements as pasteurized Grade A milk and milk

products. Filled and imitation milks are subject to the federal nutrition labeling requirements.

Some dairy processors use a special seal on their products to emphasize that their dairy products are real, not imitation, products. **Figure 22–33** shows this seal, which consists of the word "Real" enclosed in a symbolic drop of milk. It has also been suggested by some that filled and imitation milks not be allowed to continue to use the term "milk" in their title to further distinguish these products from milk in the minds of consumers.

Figure 22–33

Sometimes dairy processors put on their packaged products a special symbol containing the word Real. This emphasizes that these products are not imitation but meet the government standards of identity for "milk" or "dairy." (National Milk Producers Federation)

Filled Milk. Filled milk is a substitute product that can be made by combining a fat other than milkfat with water, nonfat milk solids, an emulsifier, color, and flavoring. The mixture is heated under agitation and then homogenized. The resulting product appears to be very much like milk [21]. Cheese and cultured milk products may be produced from filled milk. This process creates dairy-like products that do not contain butterfat or cholesterol. In the past, coconut oil has been the main source of fat in filled milk because of its desirable flavor, even though it is a highly saturated fat. Other sources of fat for filled milk are partially hydrogenated soybean, corn, and cottonseed oils containing approximately 30 percent linoleic acid.

Imitation Milk. Imitation milk resembles milk but usually contains no milk products. Thus, imitation milk is a nondairy product. Ingredients such as water, corn syrup solids, sugar, vegetable fats, and a source of protein are most often used in imitation milk. Derivatives of milk, such as casein, casein salts, and whey, may be used as the protein source; soy proteins may also be used. The vegetable fat is often coconut oil.

Types of Cream Products

Cream is the liquid high-fat milk product that can be separated from milk containing not less than 18 percent milkfat as defined by the Code of Federal Regulations Title 21 §131.3. Cream adds richness and body to foods that are prepared with it and, when whipped, provides a creamy yet airy delicacy.

Fluid Cream. Several liquid cream products are defined by the Code of Federal Regulations. Milkfat content defines the cream; the "heavier" the cream the higher the proportion of milkfat. These products are subject to pasteurization (**Figure 22–34**). The marketed liquid cream products include *light cream* or coffee cream containing 18 to 30 percent milkfat,

Figure 22–34

Light whipping cream has a milkfat content between 30 and 36 percent. (Ericlefrancais/Shutterstock)

light whipping cream with 30 to 36 percent milkfat, and *heavy cream or heavy whipping cream* with not less than 36 percent milkfat [84]. If cream is to be whipped, a minimum of 30 percent milkfat is necessary. Whipped cream produces a fat foam which was discussed in Chapter 8. *Half-and-half* is a mixture of milk and cream containing not less than 10.5 percent milkfat but less than 18 percent. This product is commonly used in place of light cream or coffee cream.

The thickness of cream is related to its fat content; it is generally thicker at higher fat levels. Other factors also affect thickness. Cream at room temperature is thinner than cream at refrigerator temperature because chilling makes the fat globules firmer, thereby increasing the **viscosity** of the cream. When chilled to a temperature of 41°F (5°C) and held at that temperature for 24 to 48 hours, cream gradually increases in thickness.

Sour Cream. Commercial sour cream is a cultured or an acidified light cream. A culture of *Lactobacillus lactis* organisms is added to cream, and the product is held at 72°F (22°C) until the acidity, calculated as lactic acid, is at least 0.5 percent [84]. Nonfat milk solids and stabilizing vegetable gums such as carrageenan may be added to sour cream, which can also be produced from half-and-half. If manufacturers use food-grade acid instead of bacteria to make sour cream, the product must be labeled as "acidified sour cream" [117].

Dried Cream. Dried cream is available that may be used reconstituted to liquid form. An instant dry creamed milk made from modified skim milk (calcium reduced), light cream, and lactose has also been manufactured. When it is sprinkled on the surface of a beverage, it disperses quickly. Federal code requires dried cream to milkfat content to be not less than 40 percent, but less than 75 percent by weight of milkfat. It must have a moisture level of less than 5 percent by weight of milk-solids-not-fat basis.

Nondairy Products. Many nondairy products for whipped toppings, coffee whiteners, sour cream-type mixtures, and snack dip bases have been developed and marketed. Initially, these were promoted as low-cost substitutes for the more-expensive natural dairy products. Many of them, particularly whipped toppings and coffee whiteners, have been accepted on their own merits rather than as substitutes and have taken over much of the market. One advantage of whipped toppings is their stability. Whipped toppings will tolerate overmixing to a greater degree than real whipped cream and will maintain quality during storage for a longer period of time.

Nondairy whipped toppings often contain sugar, hydrogenated vegetable oil, sodium caseinate, and emulsifiers. Whipped toppings are available in a dry form that is added to cold milk before whipping and also in a frozen, whipped form. The foam is stable and requires only defrosting before use. Nondairy products resembling whipped cream that contain water, vegetable fat, sugar, sodium caseinate, emulsifiers, and vegetable gums are also available in pressurized cans. These products must be refrigerated. Nondairy coffee whiteners are widely used in hot beverages. They usually contain corn syrup solids, vegetable fat, a source of protein such as sodium caseinate or soy protein, emulsifiers, and salts.

Although nondairy whipped toppings, coffee whiteners, and other products are termed "nondairy," these products often contain casein or whey. Thus, those who are allergic to dairy products often must avoid these nondairy foods as well.

FOOD PREPARATION WITH MILK AND CREAM

Milk and milk products are used to prepare a variety of dishes, including salads, soups, entrees, side dishes, desserts, and beverages. When used in cooking, the prevention of curdling is desired. High temperatures, extended hot holding or cooking, and acidic or salty ingredients can all contribute to curdling. The tendency for milk to curdle is diminished by the use of low or moderate temperatures. You may already have observed less curdling of the milk on scalloped potatoes cooked in a low or moderate oven than when a higher temperature is used. In addition, higher-fat milk products, such as cream or whole milk, are more stable than low-fat or nonfat milk and thus are less likely to separate.

Milk foams are important in food systems. In Chapter 8, milkfat foams were discussed. However, milk foams in food preparation can be desirable and undesirable. Milk foams in infant formula are not desirable. However, frothing milk for a cappuccino or hot cocoa are desirable milk foams.

In the following section, the general effect of heat, acid, enzymes, phenolic compounds, salt, freezing, and whipping on milk during usual food preparation practices is considered. Preparation of milk-based sauces, soups, and puddings was discussed in Chapter 11, and preparation of hot chocolate containing milk is covered in Chapter 27.

Heat

Heating milk during cooking results in several changes. Proteins coagulate, calcium is less dispersed, fat globules coalesce, surface films may form, and the sugars and protein may brown due to the application of heat (see **Figure 22–35**).

Protein Coagulation. On heating, the whey proteins lactalbumin and lactoglobulin become insoluble, or **precipitate**. Lactalbumin begins to **coagulate**

Figure 22–35

Can you identify elements of heated milk in this pan? Scorched proteins? Precipated lactalbumin? Calcium phosphate? Surface film formation? (© Amanda Frye)

at a temperature of 150°F (66°C). The amount of coagulum increases with rising temperature and time of heating. The coagulum that forms appears as small particles rather than a firm mass and collects on the bottom of the pan in which the milk is heated. This collection of particles contributes to the characteristic scorching (burning) of heated milk. You can stir the milk while it heats to lessen the amount of precipitate on the bottom, but some scorching may still occur, particularly if a large quantity of milk is heated at one time. One way to prevent scorching is to heat milk over hot water in a double boiler rather than with direct heat. Heating milk in a thick-bottom saucepan also helps to prevent the scorching.

Casein, the protein found in the largest amount in milk, does not coagulate at the usual temperatures and times used in food preparation. Although some of its properties may change slightly, it coagulates only when heated to very high temperatures or for a long period at the boiling point. In fact, as long as 12 hours may be required for casein to coagulate when heated at a temperature of 212°F (100°C).

Heating periods that produce casein coagulation are shorter when the concentration of casein is increased above that in regular fluid milk. For example, in the sterilization of canned evaporated milk, it is necessary to take certain measures to prevent coagulation of the casein. One such measure is to prewarm the milk prior to its sterilization.

The coagulation of milk proteins by heat is accelerated by an increase in acidity. This can be observed when preparing cream of tomato soup, which curdles easily when heated. Milk protein coagulation is also influenced by the kinds and concentrations of salts present. The salts in such foods as ham and vegetables are partly responsible for casein coagulation when cooked with milk.

Mineral Changes. The dispersion of calcium phosphate (a common form for calcium) in milk is decreased by heating, and a small part of it is precipitated. Some of the calcium phosphate collects on the bottom of the pan with coagulated whey proteins, and some is probably entangled in the milk surface film.

Coalescence of Fat Globules. A fat layer may form on boiled milk, which results from the breaking protein film membrane surrounding fat globules in the unheated milk. The globule membrane rupture then permits the fat globule coalescence.

Surface Film Formation. The composition of the surface film on heated milk is variable. It may contain coagulated protein, with some precipitated salts and fat globules entangled in the mesh of coagulated matter.

The formation of a film or scum on the surface of heated milk is often troublesome and contributes to milk boiling over the pan. A certain amount of pressure develops under the film, forcing the film upward and resulting in the milk boiling over. A slight film may form at relatively low temperatures, but it may be prevented by a cover on the pan, by dilution of the milk, or by the presence of fat floating on the surface. As the temperature is increased, a tough scum forms that is insoluble and can be removed from the surface, but as soon as film is removed another film forms.

Sometimes, to break up the film, the heated milk is beaten with a rotary-type egg beater. This has limited usefulness because of the continuous formation of fresh film; however, foam formation at the surface appears to aid in preventing a tenacious film from forming. Often hot chocolate or cocoa is whipped with a rotary beater to form a milk foam to prevent surface film formation. Whipped cream placed on the surface of hot chocolate or cocoa is one another method used to discourage surface film formation.

Browning. When certain sugars and proteins are heated together, browning occurs. This particular nonenzymatic browning is of the Maillard type. Concentrated milk products, such as evaporated milk, contain substantial amounts of both protein and the sugar lactose and develop some brown color on heating. This reaction may also occur in dried milk stored for long periods.

Heating sweetened condensed milk in a can that has been placed in a pan of water for several hours results in browning. The milk also develops a thickened consistency and sweet caramel flavor. It may be consumed like a pudding for dessert.

Acid Coagulation

Although the protein casein is hardly susceptible to coagulation by heating, it is highly sensitive to precipitation on the addition of acid. The acid may be an added ingredient, or it may be produced by bacteria as they ferment milk sugar. Recall that in cultured milk products, lactic acid is produced, making the product more acidic. The acid curdling of milk is a desirable reaction in making such products as cultured buttermilk, yogurt, sour cream, and some cheeses.

Prevention of casein coagulation or curdling, however, is fundamental to the success of such products as cream of tomato soup. Fruit–milk mixtures may also curdle, as you may have noticed when putting cream on fresh fruits or making fruit–milk beverages or sherbets (**Figure 22–36**).

Enzyme Coagulation

A number of enzymes from plant, animal, and microbial sources are capable of clotting milk or producing a curd. A **protease** called *chymosin* is often used in cheesemaking. It is found in the stomachs of young

Dairy products such as frozen yogurt may be blended with fruits to make delicious smoothies. If the fruit is highly acidic, a curdled appearance may occur after standing a short time because of casein coagulation. (Liv friis-larsen/Shutterstock)

animals, and its function is to clot milk prior to the action of other protein-digesting enzymes. The name *chymosin* is derived from the Greek word *chyme*, meaning "gastric liquid," and is used in the recommended international enzyme nomenclature [105]. The crude chymosin enzyme is called *rennet*. Rennet has been used for many years in the preparation of most varieties of cheeses. When the sources of rennet became limited, several other non-rennin milk-clotting enzymes were used as rennet substitutes [31]. The FDA has affirmed that use of the chymosin preparation derived by fermentation from the genetically modified *Aspergillus* mold is **GRAS** (generally recognized as safe). This was one of the first genetically engineered food products to be approved.

Because rennet is an enzyme preparation, it requires specific conditions of temperature and acidity for its action. The optimum temperature is 104 to 108°F (40 to 42°C). Refrigerator temperatures retard its action. No action occurs below 50°F (10°C) or above 149°F (65°C). Rennet acts best in a slight acid medium, and action does not occur in an alkaline environment.

When casein is precipitated by the action of rennet, the calcium is not released to the whey but remains attached to the casein. Therefore, cheese made with rennet is a much better source of calcium than cheese made by acid precipitation alone. Cottage cheese is often made by acid precipitation.

Other enzymes act on milk. The action of the enzyme bromelin from raw or frozen pineapple in preventing the setting of gelatin is well known. This enzyme digests proteins and hence changes the gelatin to smaller compounds that do not form a gel. The enzyme bromelin also clots milk, but later digests the clot. Other enzymes in fruits are probably responsible for some of the curdling action that occurs when milk or cream and certain fruits are combined. All fruits contain some organic acids, but not always in sufficient concentration to cause the curdling of milk. Destroying the enzymes before combining fruit with milk will, of course, prevent curdling caused by enzyme action.

Coagulation by Phenolic Compounds

Some phenolic-type compounds are present in fruits and vegetables. In fruits, these compounds are found chiefly in the green stages and are present in a greater amount in some varieties than in others. Seeds and stems may contain significant amounts of phenolic substances. Among vegetables, the roots, pods, some seeds, and woody stems are likely to contain more **phenolic compounds** than other parts of the plant, although distribution is general throughout the plant. Curdling of milk may occur if phenolic-containing foods, such as potatoes, are cooked in the milk; however, the time and temperature of heating also influence curdling. Low levels of organic acids in potatoes also contribute to curdling.

Coagulation by Salts

Salt also may cause the coagulation of casein. The salt can be present in the milk or in the food combined with the milk or because of added sodium chloride.

FOCUS ON SCIENCE
WHAT HAPPENS WHEN ACID IS ADDED TO MILK?

Observe the impact of acid by adding vinegar or lemon juice to milk. Curdling quickly becomes evident. The curdling of milk can be explained scientifically.

The pH of milk is normally about 6.6. When the pH reaches about 4.6, the colloidally dispersed casein particles become unstable. These casein proteins adhere and form a coagulum or curd. This probably occurs because the usual negative charge on the casein particles, which causes them to repel each other and remain apart, is neutralized by the acidic hydrogen ion (H^+). A considerable amount of calcium is also released from the casein molecules to the liquid whey. The calcium was bonded through the phosphoric acid groups of casein. The curd then traps the whey in its meshes. The whey, which contains the whey proteins, most of the lactose, and many minerals, is released when the curd is cut or stirred and heated. These processes occur in the manufacture of cheese (see **Figure 22–37**).

Figure 22–37

Casein proteins coagulate to form curds when an acid such as lime juice is added to the heated milk. (Richard Embrey/Pearson Education)

Of the meats commonly cooked in milk, ham usually causes more coagulation than chicken, veal, or pork, although these may vary in their effect. The high sodium chloride content of ham may be responsible for the excessive curdling that occurs when ham is cooked in milk. Processed shrimp can also contain sodium levels that may cause curdling in a milk-based dish.

Freezing

When milk or cream is frozen at a relatively slow rate, the film of protein that acts as an emulsifying agent around the fat globules, is weakened or ruptured. As a result, the fat globules tend to coalesce. The oily masses that float on top of hot coffee when previously frozen cream is added demonstrate the cohesion of fat particles that results from freezing. The dispersion of protein and calcium phosphate is also disturbed by freezing. Both constituents tend to settle out on thawing and standing, thus reducing the whiteness of milk. The effects of freezing are not harmful and do not affect nutritional value.

Foam Formation by Mechanical Agitation and Gas Injection

A foam is a dispersion of a gas in a liquid. Foam formation requires gas, liquid, a surfactant, and energy applied to the system. A surfactant is required to lower surface tension between the gas and liquid allowing the formation of small gas bubbles in the liquid. Energy must be applied to create the foam. In cream (milk-fat) and milk foams the gas is typically air. The liquid is water-based milk or cream. The surfactant in milk/cream foams is protein. Proteins form a viscoelastic film around the air bubbles stabilizing the foam and reducing interfacial tension [107]. Foamability (foam capacity) reflects the time to gain a specified foam volume. Foam stability is related to the time the foam maintains it properties often reflected as the foam liquid drained over time [107]. Energy such as whipping, steam injection, or propellant in pressurized aerosol cans is typical in milk/cream foam formation. Milkfat foams, i.e., whipped cream foams were also discussed in Chapter 8.

Steam-injected milk foams are used in the *frothing of milk* in coffee beverages, i.e., cappuccino (see **Figure 22–38**). Milk steam injection is the process of foaming liquid milk via the incorporation of steam. Steam (a gas) is injected into the liquid milk through a small opening (nozzle) resulting in air bubbles being formed in the milk [46]. The steam is typically injected into cold milk until the temperature reaches approximately 149°F (65°C) [46]. These milk foams are viscoelastic, but unstable and deteriorate rapidly over time or with force such as stirring [50]. Steam-injected milk foams have been found to be stronger and more stable compared to mechanically

Figure 22–38

A milk foam being made by steam injection. (Kondor83/ Shutterstock)

aerated (whipped) milk foams [30]. Skim milk produces the best steam-injected milk foams [30]. Thicker foam layers were found in lower layers of steamed foams [30]. Reconstituted skim milk was found to produce a foam with the greatest strength [30].

Mechanical agitation to produce a milk or milk-fat foam can be achieved by simply shaking milk in a closed container such as a bottle and infant formula or by using a household whisk or rotary beater. The energy is transferred from the gas–liquid interface forming air bubbles in the liquid [46]. These milk foams may be undesirable in baby formula. However, milk foam is desirable if done to prevent the milk skin on the surface of hot cocoa. Agitation intensity and duration along with milk temperature and type of milk will affect the stability and strength of milk foams. These foams are typically less stable than other milk foams.

Milk Foams

Milk foams are a protein foam formed by steam injection, mechanical agitation, or aeration. Milk proteins whey and casein contribute to foaming properties. The globular proteins have good surface activity. The whey α-lactalbumin and β-lactoglobulin are adsorbed at the air–liquid interface and the casein micelles secondarily attach [14]. In milk foams, fat is a destabilizing force causing decreased foam formation and stability [46, 30]. Thus, skim milk produces voluminous and stable milk foam [46, 76]. Whole-milk foams produce smaller bubbles that rupture due to coalescence compared to skim milk foams [53]. The most stable milk foams are formed at 113°F (45°C) [53]. However, milk foams are far less stable than milkfat foams such as whipped cream. UHT processed milk produces inferior milk foams and has been shown to adversely affect milk foaming capacity [30]. Milk has a neutral pH between 6.0 and 7.0, but reducing pH to 5.6 was found to increase skim milk foamability, which was thought to be dissociation of beta casein from the casein micelle. Modified pH dried skim milk powders with added citrate have been shown to increase milk foam and stability due to disassociation of casein micelles [6]. However, if pH is lowered to the 4 to 5 range then caseins precipitate, yielding poor foaming properties [46].

Milk foam stability is related to the changes in air bubbles due to coalescence, disproportionation of gas bubbles, and liquid drainage from foams. Coalescence decreases the number of gas bubbles and increases the size of foam bubbles. The spreading of the bubble surface agents, such as proteins, causes thinning of the surface layer and the bubbles are joined together, eventually, leading to foam collapse [46].

Disproportionation results from the gas (air) transporting from smaller to larger bubbles. There is higher pressure inside small bubbles. When bubbles of difference sizes are separated by a liquid layer, the gas diffuses from the small bubbles to the larger bubbles; the small bubbles become smaller until they disappear and the large bubbles become larger, which evidently results in bubble surface thinning and the foam eventually collapses [46]. Milk foam bubbles are typically spherical, separated by layers of milk liquid. When the liquid drains, the bubbles come in contact changing shape and becoming more unstable. Liquid is drained by gravity from the foam [46, 57].

Evaporated Milk. When evaporated milk is chilled to the ice crystal stage, it will whip to about three times its original volume. This ability to whip is evidently the result of the higher concentration of milk solids in evaporated milk than in fresh whole milk. The protein in the milk acts as a foaming agent and aids in stabilizing. This foam, however, is not stable on standing. The addition of acid, such as a small amount of lemon juice (about 1 tablespoon per cup of undiluted milk), helps to stabilize the protein and makes a more lasting foam.

Nonfat Dry Milk. A light and airy whipped product may be produced by whipping reconstituted nonfat dry milk. Equal measures of dry milk and very cold water are normally used, with the dry milk being sprinkled over the surface of the water before whipping. Foam stability may be increased somewhat by adding small amounts of an acid substance, such as lemon juice, before whipping.

Whipped Cream

Whipped cream is a milkfat foam. During whipping, air bubbles are incorporated and surrounded by a thin liquid film that contains protein. The foam cells are stabilized by coalesced fat globules. The fat globules apparently coalesce because much of the milkfat globule membrane surrounding them and keeping them separated has been removed in the whipping

process [64]. At the cold temperature of the whipping cream, the fat globules are solid. Whipping is the first stage of churning cream. If whipping is continued too long there is an emulsion inversion and butter is formed. Air bubbles in whipped cream must be surrounded by protein films. The air bubbles are held in a matrix of partially coalesced fat globules that act as bridges between the air bubbles [104]. If homogenized cream is used, there is an increased number of fat globules; and, so much protein is used to surround each globule, then little protein remains to surround air bubbles formed in whipping. Therefore, whipping cream is usually not homogenized. Several factors, including temperature, affect cream whipping properties. Milkfat foams were discussed in more detail in Chapter 8.

Temperature and Viscosity. Cream held at a cold temperature (45°F/7°C or below) whips better than cream held at warmer temperatures. Above 50°F (10°C), agitation of cream increases the dispersion of the fat instead of decreasing it. The cream, beater, and bowl should be chilled. In whipping cream, the aim is to increase clumping of fat particles; at low temperatures, agitation results in clumping. Lower temperatures increase viscosity, which increases the whipping properties of cream. Higher fat content also increases viscosity and furnishes more fat globules for clumping. Because viscosity increases with aging, the whipping property improves with the aging of cream. Commercial stabilizers increase whipping cream viscosity and thus, the whipped cream stability [104].

Fat Content. A fat content of about 30 percent is the minimum for cream that will whip with ease and produce a stiff product. Increasing the fat up to 40 percent improves the whipping quality of cream because more solid fat particles are available to stabilize the foam.

Amount of Cream Whipped. In whipping large amounts of cream, it is better to do successive whippings of amounts tailored to the size of the whipper used rather than to whip a large amount at one time. If a very small amount of cream is to be whipped, a small, deep bowl should be used so that the beaters can adequately agitate the cream.

Effect of Other Substances. Increased acidity up to the concentration required to produce a sour taste (0.3 percent) has no effect on whipping quality. If sugar is added before whipping, it decreases both foam volume and stiffness while increasing the time required to whip the cream. If sugar is to be added, add after the cream is stiff or just prior to serving. If sugar is added just before serving, powdered sugar should be used because granulated sugar needs more time to dissolve (**Figure 22–39**).

Figure 22–39

This crème Chantilly was made by first whipping chilled heavy cream until thickened. Powdered sugar and vanilla were added, and the mixture was whipped until the consistency shown here. (Richard Embery/Pearson Education)

Pressurized Aerosol-Whipped Cream and Whipped Topping. Instant foams are produced from pressurized aerosol-canister whipped cream and non-dairy whipped toppings (see **Figure 22–40**). The foam is produced by releasing pressure in the pressurized aerosol canister containing the whipping cream or whipped topping mixture. *Supersaturation* is the principle used to form these instant foams. This involves dissolving gas in a liquid under pressure. When pressure is released, the solubility of the gas is reduced causing air bubbles to form in the liquid

Figure 22–40

Instant foams are created by nitrous oxide dissolved under pressure in sweetened cream. When the nozzle is pressed, pressure is released producing a cream foam. This is an unstable cream foam. (© Amanda Frye)

yielding a foam [46]. The propellant (gas) is usually the soluble food-grade nitrous oxide sometimes referred to as laughing gas. The nitrous oxide is dissolved in the liquid cream due to the pressure in the aerosol can. Nitrous oxide is 50 times more soluble than air [132].

Foam formation occurs when the pressurized canister nozzle is opened, causing a decrease in pressure that allows the gas to escape from the cream causing bubbles to form in the liquid causing a whipped cream foam. Aerosol-whipped cream has a high overrun (400–600 percent) [132]. These instant aerosol-whipped cream foams are less stable than mechanical-agitated (whipped) whipping cream foams. The high solubility of the gas in the aerosol increases the disproportionation process [132]. Thus, there is more gas diffusion from smaller to larger bubbles decreasing foam stability [132]. Instant whipped cream foams typically collapse within 15 minutes [132]. The canister nozzle should be rinsed and dried after each use.

The processing of the aerosol whipped cream is as follows. The unfoamed whipping cream undergoes UHT pasteurization then is homogenized to reduce fat globule size. The cream typically is sweetened with sugar and flavorings, plus it often contains emulsifiers, stabilizers, and antioxidants. The processed cream mixture is placed in aerosol metal containers that have a valve to control pressure. The propellant nitrous oxide gas is added through the valve under pressure, which dissolves the gas in the liquid cream.

Shaking the can before dispensing the foam is recommended to evenly distribute the dissolved gas and any fat globules in the cream [132]. The higher the pressure, the more the dissolved gas. Excessive pressure inside the can will cause the can to explode. The can should not be exposed to heat. Aerosol-whipped cream is perishable and must be kept under 45°F (7.2°C).

MILK HANDLING AND STORAGE

Fundamentals in the care of fluid milk, whether by producer or by consumer, are cleanliness, cold temperature, and the prevention of contamination by keeping the milk covered. Milk, being very perishable, should be stored at 41°F (5°C) or below immediately after purchase [83]. It should be returned to the refrigerator immediately after use to prevent warming and bacterial growth. Milk that has been poured but not used should never be returned to the original container because it may contaminate the rest of the milk. Milk that has been properly refrigerated should remain fresh for approximately three to five days [117]. The absorption of other food odors should be avoided by keeping the milk container closed during storage.

Containers or storage conditions that protect milk from exposure to light should be used. Light exposure produces an oxidized off-flavor and reduces riboflavin and vitamin A content. Riboflavin is very unstable in ultraviolet light, meaning that milk exposed to light may lose large amounts of this vitamin. Because approximately 38 percent of the riboflavin in the American diet comes from milk and dairy products, it is important to protect the riboflavin in milk. The retention of riboflavin in skim milk placed in blow-molded polyethylene containers and held in a lighted chamber for five days has been reported to average 58 percent at the top of the containers compared with 92 percent at the bottom of the containers [87].

Nonfat dry milk should be stored in moisture-proof packages at a temperature no higher than ordinary room temperature. Dry milk takes up moisture and becomes lumpy and stale when exposed to air during storage. Because of the fat content, whole dry milk is not as stable to storage as nonfat. Powdered milk will keep up to six months if stored in a cool place. Once the package is opened, it should be used within one month. Reconstituted milk should be treated the same as fluid milk and be refrigerated and used within three days.

Unopened cans of evaporated milk or UHT shelf-stable milk can be stored at room temperature. Once opened, they are perishable and must be refrigerated. Store unused portions in clean, opaque, airtight containers in the refrigerator; use within three days of opening. UHT and canned milk found in the non-refrigerated aisle are perishable, once opened. Opened UHT and canned milk must therefore be refrigerated. After opening canned milk, immediately transfer any unused portions to a clean, opaque, and airtight container. These milk products should be used within three days of opening.

Milk can be frozen for up to six weeks without any impact on its flavor and nutritional content. Thawing can cause separation and loss of smooth texture. Skim milk freezes better than whole milk. Thaw milk in the fridge. If separation upon thawing occurs, beat the milk with an electric mixer or an immersion blender with the whip attachment. Leftover evaporated milk can be frozen in an airtight container for up to six weeks with no adverse effects. When cans of evaporated milk are stored for several months, they should be turned over periodically to retard the settling out of milk solids.

GOAT MILK AND SHEEP MILK

Some of the world has more access to goat and other non-bovine milk than cow's milk. Non-bovine milk throughout the world includes goats, sheep, buffalo, Zebu, mare, camel, reindeer, and yak. Goat and sheep were the first domesticated animals occurring in the Middle East [7]. Goat's milk is sometimes substituted for cow's milk. Goat's milk accounts for 2.3 percent and sheep's 1.4 percent use

in world non-bovine milk production. The world's largest producer of sheep milk is China. Many areas of the Mediterranean, Middle East, Near East, Eastern Europe, Northern African, Asia, and South America produce substantial quantities of goat and sheep milk. Portugal, Greece, France, Romania, and Italy are top producers of sheep milk. Non-bovine milk is often used by home consumers, specialty gourmet markets including cheese, for medical needs, or in regions where cow's milk is not accessible. In the United States, goat milk production is a small, but a growing industry (**Figure 22–41**). The U.S. dairy goat breeds include Nubian, Toggenburg, LaMancha, Alpine, Saanen, Oberhasli, Sable, and Nigerian Dwarf. In the United States, there are under 250 dairy sheep producers with only two dairy sheep breeds Lacaune and East Friesian. There are many cheese varieties that use goat or sheep milk [88, 125]. Most sheep milk is used for fine cheese varieties, yogurt, and whey cheeses [7]. Dairy goats can produce 6 to 8 pounds (3 to 5 quarts) per day [124]. Sheep are not as good of milk producers, so sheep milk is immediately quick frozen at −13 to −17°F (−25 to −27°C) for storage; frozen shelf life is around 12 months [7]. Frozen milk will be delivered to or used at a later date by processors.

Goat and sheep milk is regulated through guidance of the Grade "A" Pasteurized Milk Ordinance and state regulations. Goat's milk must not have less than 2.5 percent milkfat and not less than 7.5 percent milk-solids-not-fat [120]. The basic composition of goat milk is similar to cow's milk with 3.8 percent fat, 3.5 percent protein, 4.1 percent lactose, 0.8 percent ash and total solids of 12.2 percent [88]. Sheep's milk is higher in protein and fat. Sheep milk composition is 5.9 percent protein, 4.8 percent lactose, 7.4 percent fat, and total solids of 19.0 percent. Most sheep milk produced is used for cheese production. Current production of sheep milk is around 9.4 million pounds produced annually in the United States.

Figure 22–41

Fresh goat cheese. (Cjung/123RF)

Goats and sheep produce milk differently than cows. The sheep and goat milk have different quality standards than cow's milk. Differences include somatic cell count, short-chain fatty acid ratio, casein content, fat content, alkaline phosphatase content, vitamin D, and freezing point.

Goat's milk taste is different than cow's milk and has a different mouthfeel compared to cow's milk. There is a slight caprine "goaty" flavor and texture is normal and desirable in goat's milk [98]. Sheep's milk is described as having a "sheepy" flavor. These flavors are from volatile branched fatty acids [52]. The fat globule in goat milk is 0.73 to 8.58 μm, which is slightly smaller than cow's milk 0.92 to 15.75 μm [5, 1]. Sheep's milk also has small fat globules similar to goat's milk [7]. Sheep's milk is high in casein (4.2 g/1000 g) and whey (1.02 to 1.3 g/100 g) proteins. Casein makes up about 80 percent of sheep's milk making it ideal for cheese production [7]. The goat and sheep's milk higher content of calcium-mineralized caseins micelles allows for more cross-linking during rennet cheese production [7]. Sheep's milk needs less rennet to make cheese [7]. Research has found that HTST pasteurization (74°C for 16 seconds) of goat's milk retains maximum nutrient value and best practice for processing goat's milk [63].

CHEESE

Cheesemaking dates back at least 4,000 years to when nomadic tribes would store milk in vessels made from sheep and goat stomachs. These stomach lining naturally contained rennet that along with wild natural bacteria and warm sunlight caused milk caseins to coagulate and separate, producing some of the first cheese. Milk is a perishable item, so for centuries people have been converting excess milk to cheese as a way to transform milk into a nutrient dense food for longer storage. Cheese makers have relied on local natural microflora, enzymes and different domesticated animal milks to produce cheeses of different styles, types, traits, textures and flavors [127]. The USDA *Agriculture Bulletin 54* describes over 400 varieties of cheeses [125]. Many cheese names are derived from locations or landmarks in those locations [125]. There are over 300 cheese varieties now produced in the United States [131]. Today, modern cheese makers are going beyond traditional methods and varieties to produce even more cheese variations [82, 38]. Total U.S. retail cheese sales are estimated to exceed $27 billion dollars in the United States [108]. Over the next decade, per capita cheese consumption is expected to climb to 36.5 pounds per person in the United States [73].

Cheese is a concentrated food high in protein and, often, fat. Cheese can be loosely defined as the fresh or matured product obtained by draining the

Cheese and fruit can be served as either a snack or a dessert. These natural cheeses make a wonderful selection when mixed with crusty breads, grapes, pears, apples, or guava. (Richard Embery/Pearson Education)

whey after coagulation of casein although there are whey cheeses. The four basic cheese ingredients involved in cheesemaking are milk, salt, cultures (microflora, wild or synthesized), and rennet (rennin). Most cheese in the United States is made from cow's milk; the milk from other animals, such as goats, sheep, and water buffalo are also used. Many different kinds of cheese may be produced with soft or firm textures, mild, pungent, or sharp flavors. Cheese may be enjoyed as part of a cheese, fruit, and cracker board or as a component of a recipe (see **Figure 22–42**).

Composition

The main ingredient in cheese is milk. One pound of cheese may contain the same amount of protein and fat as a gallon of milk. There are many varieties of cheeses. Standards of identities define the composition of most common cheeses sold in the United States (21 CFR 133). The standards of identity define type of milk used for each cheese variety along with other ingredients that can be used in processing. Milkfat, milk solid, and moisture levels for different cheeses are also regulated. Processing and labeling requirement are also given by federal code. The composition of the cheese depends on the variety and type of cheese.

Cheese may be classified as ripened or unripened [115, 116]. Unripened cheeses are eaten immediately after processing. Cottage cheese is an example of an unripened cheese. Ripened cheeses are "aged"; cheddar is an example of a ripened cheese. Cheese maybe "natural" or "process". Natural cheese is a cheese made directly from milk such as Swiss cheese. Process cheese is made using natural cheese and other ingredients that are cooked together to change texture and/or melting properties such as cheese spread (see **Figure 22–43**).

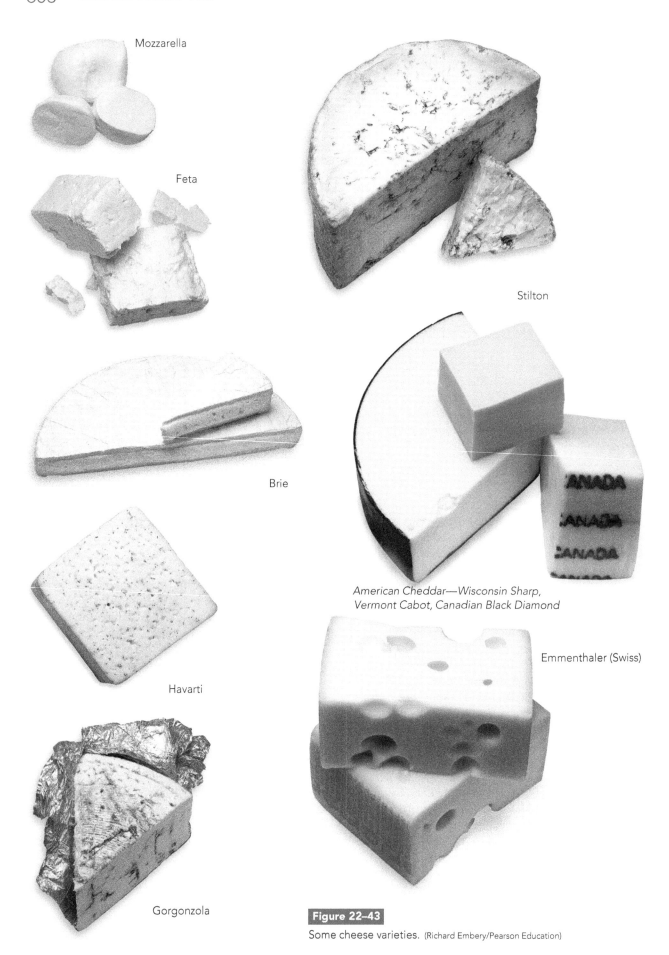

Mozzarella

Feta

Stilton

Brie

Havarti

American Cheddar—Wisconsin Sharp, Vermont Cabot, Canadian Black Diamond

Emmenthaler (Swiss)

Gorgonzola

Figure 22–43

Some cheese varieties. (Richard Embery/Pearson Education)

Gruyère

Parmigiano-Reggiano
(Parmesan)

Asiago

Figure 22–43
Some cheese varieties. *(Continued)*

American cheddar cheese averages, roughly, one-third water, one-third fat, and one-fourth protein. It also contains about 4 percent ash and less than 1 percent carbohydrate, including lactic acid. Cheese made from low-fat milk or skim milk is lower in fat content than cheese made from whole milk. Cheese containing vegetable oil instead of milkfat is available for those who want to decrease their intake of animal fat.

The moisture content of soft cheese varies from 40 to 75 percent, whereas hard cheeses tend to contain a more nearly uniform amount of water—from 30 to 40 percent. High moisture content is a factor in the perishability of cheese, those with a large amount of moisture being more perishable.

The casein and fat are the basic milk components used for cheesemaking. Milk is coagulated to form curds. The watery whey portion is removed leaving the fat and casein curds. The composition of cheese varies widely with milk used and the amount of moisture retained. When cheese is made from whole milk, the fat remains with the curd when the whey is drained off. Much of the milk sugar, the soluble salts, and the water-soluble vitamins are drained off in the whey, although even in hard cheeses the whey is never entirely removed. Whey cheeses and concentrated whey are added to cheese spreads, cheese foods, or incorporated into other food products.

Cheese made by rennet coagulation is an excellent source of calcium and phosphorus; however, cheese coagulated by acid alone contains less calcium. The reason for this difference in calcium content is that the lower pH or greater acidity produced by adding acid causes the release of more calcium ions (Ca^{2+}) from the phosphate groups in the casein molecule. Much of this released calcium goes into the whey and is not retained in the curd. Cheddar-type cheese, made chiefly by rennet coagulation of the milk, may retain up to 80 percent of the original milk calcium. Soft cheeses made by acid precipitation, such as cottage cheese, may retain not more than one-fourth to one-half of the milk calcium.

Types of Cheese

More than 2,000 names have been given to cheeses with somewhat different characteristics, but there are only about 10 distinct types of natural cheese. **Table 22–5** describes the characteristics of some popular varieties of natural cheeses. Cheese can be grouped by (1) the amount of moisture in the finished cheese and (2) the kind and extent of ripening. Based on moisture content, cheese may be classified as soft, semihard, or hard. Based on the kind and extent of ripening, cheese may be classified as unripened, mold ripened, or bacteria ripened.

Table 22-5
CHARACTERISTICS OF SOME POPULAR VARIETIES OF NATURAL CHEESES

Kind or Name (Place of Origin)	Kind of Milk Used in Manufacture	Ripening or Curing Time	Flavor	Body and Texture	Color	Retail Packaging	Use
Soft, Unripened Varieties							
Cottage, plain or creamed (unknown)	Cow's milk skimmed; plain curd, or plain curd with cream added	Unripened	Mild, acid	Soft, curd particles of varying size	White to creamy white	Cup-shaped containers, tumblers, dishes	Salads, with fruits, vegetables, sandwiches, dips, cheese cake
Cream, plain (United States)	Cream from cow's milk	Unripened	Mild, acid	Soft and smooth	White	3- to 8-oz. packages	Salads, dips, sandwiches, snacks, cheese cake, desserts
Neufchatel (Nû-shä-tĕl') (France)	Cow's milk	Unripened	Mild, acid	Soft, smooth, similar to cream cheese but lower in milkfat	White	4- to 8-oz. packages	Salads, dips, sandwiches, snacks, cheese cake, desserts
Ricotta (rĭc ō´-ta) (Italy)	Cow's milk, whole or partly skimmed, or whey from cow's milk with whole or skim milk added; in Italy, whey from sheep's milk	Unripened	Sweet, nutlike	Soft, moist or dry	White	Pint and quart paper and plastic containers, 3-lb metal cans	Appetizers, salads, snacks, lasagna, ravioli, noodles and other cooked dishes, grating, desserts
Firm, Unripened Varieties							
Gjetost* (Yĕt´ôst) (Norway)	Whey from goat's milk or a mixture of whey from goat's and cow's milk	Unripened	Sweetish, caramel	Firm, buttery consistency	Golden brown	Cubical and rectangular	Snacks, desserts, served with dark breads, crackers, biscuits, or muffins
Mysost (mü sôst), also called Primost (prē´m-ôst) (Norway)	Whey from cow's milk	Unripened	Sweetish, caramel	Firm, buttery consistency	Light brown	Cubical, cylindrical, pie-shaped wedges	Snacks, desserts, served with dark breads
Mozzarella (mō-tsa-rel´la) (Italy)	Whole or partly skimmed cow's milk; in Italy, originally made from buffalo's milk	Unripened	Delicate, mild	Slightly firm, plastic	Creamy white	Small round or braided form, shredded, sliced	Snacks; toasted sandwiches; cheeseburgers; cooking, as in meat loaf; or topping for lasagna, pizza, and casseroles

Table 22-5
CHARACTERISTICS OF SOME POPULAR VARIETIES OF NATURAL CHEESES (CONTINUED)

Kind or Name (Place of Origin)	Kind of Milk Used in Manufacture	Ripening or Curing Time	Flavor	Body and Texture	Color	Retail Packaging	Use
Soft, Ripened Varieties							
Brie (brē) (France)	Cow's milk	4–8 weeks	Mild to pungent	Soft, smooth when ripened	Creamy yellow interior; edible thin brown and white crust	Circular, pie-shaped wedges	Appetizers, sandwiches, snacks, good with crackers and fruit, dessert
Camembert (kăm ĕm-bâr) (France)	Cow's milk	4–8 weeks	Mild to pungent	Soft, smooth, very soft when fully ripened	Creamy yellow interior; edible thin white or gray-white crust	Small circular cakes and pie-shaped portions	Appetizers, sandwiches, snacks, good with crackers and fruit such as pears and apples, dessert
Limburger (Belgium)	Cow's milk	4–8 weeks	Highly pungent, very strong	Soft, smooth when ripened; usually contains small irregular openings	Creamy white interior; reddish-yellow surface	Cubical, rectangular	Appetizers, snacks, good with crackers, rye, or other dark breads, dessert
Bel Paese* (bĕl pä-ă´-ze) (Italy)	Cow's milk	6–8 weeks	Mild to moderately robust	Soft to medium firm, creamy	Creamy yellow interior; slightly gray or brownish surface sometimes covered with yellow wax coating	Small wheels, wedges, segments	Appetizers, good with crackers, snacks, sandwiches, dessert
Brick (United States)	Cow's milk	2–4 months	Mild to moderately sharp	Semisoft to medium firm; elastic, numerous small mechanical openings	Creamy yellow	Loaf, brick, slices, cut portions	Appetizers, sandwiches, snacks, dessert
Muenster (mün stĕr) (Germany)	Cow's milk	1–8 weeks	Mild to mellow	Semisoft; numerous small mechanical openings; contains more moisture than brick	Creamy white interior; yellow-tan surface	Circular cake, blocks, wedges, segments, slices	Appetizers, snacks, served with raw fruit, dessert
Port du Salut (por dü să´ü) (France)	Cow's milk	6–8 weeks	Mellow to robust	Semisoft, smooth, buttery; small openings	Creamy yellow	Wheels and wedges	Appetizers, snacks, served with raw fruit, dessert

(Continued)

Table 22–5

Characteristics of Some Popular Varieties of Natural Cheeses

Kind or Name (Place of Origin)	Kind of Milk Used in Manufacture	Ripening or Curing Time	Flavor	Body and Texture	Color	Retail Packaging	Use
Firm, Ripened Varieties							
Cheddar (England)	Cow's milk	1–12 months or longer	Mild to very sharp	Firm, smooth; some mechanical openings	White to medium-yellow-orange	Circular, cylindrical loaf, pie-shaped wedges, oblongs, slices, cubes, shredded, grated	Appetizers, sandwiches, sauces, on vegetables, in hot dishes, toasted sandwiches, grating, cheeseburgers, dessert
Colby (United States)	Cow's milk	1–3 months	Mild to mellow	Softer and more open than Cheddar	White to medium-yellow-orange	Cylindrical, pie-shaped wedges	Sandwiches, snacks, cheeseburgers
Caciocavallo (kä´cho-kä-val´lō) (Italy)	Cow's milk; in Italy, cow's milk or mixtures of sheep's, goat's, and cow's milk	3–12 months	Piquant, similar to Provolone but not smoked	Firm, lower in milkfat and moisture than Provolone	Light or white interior; clay or tan surface	Spindle- or 10-pin-shaped, bound with cord, cut pieces	Snacks, sandwiches, cooking, dessert; suitable for grating after prolonged curing
Edam (ē´dăm) (Netherlands)	Cow's milk, partly skimmed	2–3 months	Mellow, nutlike	Semisoft to firm, smooth; small irregularly shaped or round holes; lower milkfat than Gouda	Creamy yellow or medium yellow-orange interior; surface coated with red wax	Cannon ball–shaped loaf, cut pieces, oblongs	Appetizers, snacks, salads, sandwiches, seafood sauces, dessert
Gouda (gou´-dá) (Netherlands)	Cow's milk, whole or partly skimmed	2–6 months	Mellow, nutlike	Semisoft to firm, smooth; small irregularly shaped or round holes; higher milkfat than Edam	Creamy yellow or medium yellow-orange interior; may or may not have red wax coating	Ball shaped with flattened top and bottom	Appetizers, snacks, salads, sandwiches, seafood sauces, dessert
Provolone (prō-vō-lō´-nĕ), also smaller sizes and shapes called Provolette and Provoloncini (Italy)	Cow's milk	2–12 months	Mellow to sharp, smoky, salty	Firm, smooth	Light creamy interior; light brown or golden yellow surface	Pear shaped, sausage and salami shaped, wedges, slices	Appetizers, sandwiches, snacks, soufflé, macaroni and spaghetti dishes, pizza, suitable for grating when fully cured and dried

Table 22-5
CHARACTERISTICS OF SOME POPULAR VARIETIES OF NATURAL CHEESES (CONTINUED)

Kind or Name (Place of Origin)	Kind of Milk Used in Manufacture	Ripening or Curing Time	Flavor	Body and Texture	Color	Retail Packaging	Use
Swiss, also called Emmenthaler (Switzerland)	Cow's milk	3–9 months	Sweet, nutlike	Firm, smooth, with large round eyes	Light yellow	Segments, pieces, slices	Sandwiches, snacks, sauces, fondue, cheeseburgers
Parmesan (pär´-mē-zǎn´), also called Reggiano (Italy)	Partly skimmed cow's milk	14 months–2 years	Sharp, piquant	Very hard, granular; lower moisture and milkfat than Romano	Creamy white	Cylindrical, wedges, shredded, grated	Grated for seasoning in soups, vegetables, spaghetti, ravioli, breads, popcorn, used extensively in pizza and lasagna
Romano (rō-mā´-nō), also called Sardo Romano and Pecorino Romano (Italy)	Cow's milk; in Italy, sheep's milk (Italian law)	5–12 months	Sharp, piquant	Very hard granular	Yellowish-white interior, greenish-black surface	Round with flat ends, wedges, shredded, grated	Seasoning in soups, casserole dishes, ravioli, sauces, breads, suitable for grating when cured for about 1 year
Sap Sago* (săp´-sä-gō) (Switzerland)	Skimmed cow's milk	5 months or longer	Sharp, pungent, cloverlike	Very hard	Light green by addition of dried, powdered clover leaves	Conical, shakers	Grated to flavor soups, meats, macaroni, spaghetti, hot vegetables; mixed with butter, makes a good spread on crackers or bread

Blue-Vein Mold-Ripened Varieties

Kind or Name (Place of Origin)	Kind of Milk Used in Manufacture	Ripening or Curing Time	Flavor	Body and Texture	Color	Retail Packaging	Use
Blue, spelled "Bleu" on imported cheese (France)	Cow's milk	2–6 months	Tangy, peppery	Semisoft, pasty, sometimes crumbly	White interior, marbled or streaked with blue veins of mold	Cylindrical, wedges, oblongs, squares, cut portions	Appetizers, salads, dips, salad dressing, sandwich spreads, good with crackers, dessert
Gorgonzola (gôr-gän-zō´-lä) (Italy)	Cow's milk; in Italy, cow's milk or goat's milk or mixtures of these	3–12 months	Tangy, peppery	Semisoft, pasty, sometimes crumbly, lower moisture than blue cheese	Creamy white interior, mottled or streaked with blue-green veins of mold; clay-colored surface	Cylindrical, wedges, oblongs	Appetizers, snacks, salads, dips, sandwich spreads, good with crackers, dessert
Roquefort* (rōk´-fẽrt) or (rōk-fôr´) (France)	Sheep's milk	2–5 months or longer	Sharp, slightly peppery	Semisoft, pasty, sometimes crumbly	White or creamy white interior, marbled or streaked with blue veins of mold	Cylindrical wedges	Appetizers, snacks, salads, dips, sandwich spreads, good with crackers, dessert
Stilton† (England)	Cow's milk	2–6 months	Piquant, milder than Gorgonzola or Roquefort	Semisoft, flaky; slightly more crumbly than Blue	Creamy white interior; marbled or streaked with blue-green veins of mold	Circular, wedges, oblongs	Appetizers, snacks, salads, dessert

*Italian trademark—licensed for manufacture in United States; also imported.
†Imported only.
Source: Reference 115.

Ripened cheese may be strong and sharp or mild. There are many terms associated with cheese. These are broad terms and cheese classifications [115, 116].

Turophile is a cheese connoisseur, cheese fancier, or lover of cheese.

Specialty cheese has limited production. It is produced from all types of milk and may include special flavorings, herbs, spices, fruits, and nuts.

Artisan cheese or *artisanal* implies the cheese has been produced in a small batch by hand in a particular traditional cheesemaking style using minimal mechanization (see **Figures 22–44** and **Figure 22–45**).

Farmstead cheese is cheese made from a farmer's own herd or flock on the farm where the animals are raised. Milk for production may not be obtained from any outside sources.

Fresh cheese has not been aged or ripened and undergoes a slight to no curing process. These cheeses are eaten immediately after production. Fresh cheeses have a high moisture content and are mild with a creamy texture. They can be made from all kinds of milk, but in the United States pasteurized milk is required for production. These cheeses are highly perishable. Fresh cheeses include mascarpone, ricotta, chevre, Feta, cream cheese, quark, and cottage cheese (see **Figure 22–46**).

Figure 22–45

Artisan cheese maker with freshly molded goat cheese.
(RossHelen/Shutterstock)

Soft-ripened cheese describes cheeses that are ripened from the outside in, very soft, and even runny at room temperature. It is common for soft-ripened cheese to have a white, "bloomy" rind that is flecked with red or brown. The edible rind is produced by spraying the cheese surface with a special mold called *Penicillium candidum* before a brief aging period. U.S. soft-ripened cheeses are typically made from pasteurized milk. Soft-ripened cheeses include Brie and Camembert and triple crème styles (see **Figure 22–47**).

Semisoft cheese describes cheeses that have a smooth creamy interior and little or no rind. These cheeses are high in moisture with a range of mild to pungent flavors. Pasteurized or raw milks are used depending on aging requirements and the cheese

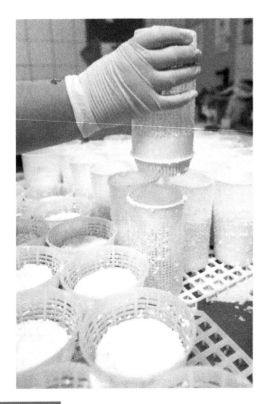

Figure 22–44

Artisan goat cheese being drained leaving only the curds placed in the cheese molds.   (Operafotografca/Shutterstock)

Figure 22–46

Fresh homemade ricotta cheese in cheese cloth draining the whey.   (Magnago/Shutterstock)

maker. Many washed rind cheeses are in this category. Semisoft cheeses include many blue cheeses, Colby, Fontina style, Havarti, and Monterey Jack (see Figure 22–43).

Firm/hard cheese describe a broad range of cheeses whose taste range from very mild to sharp and pungent. Their textures range from elastic to hard and they need to be grated when used. These cheeses may be made from pasteurized or raw milk. Firm/hard cheeses include Gouda, Cheddar, dry Jacks, Swiss (Emmenthaler) styles, Gruyere styles and "tomme" styles (small, round French-style cheeses with creamy interior and dark earthy rind), and Parmesan style (see Figure 22–43).

Blue (Bleu) cheese describes cheeses with the distinctive blue/green veining created by mold exposed to air. Mold is added during the cheesemaking process and provides a mild to pungent distinct flavor. Blue cheeses can be found in all categories except fresh cheese and may be made from pasteurized or raw milk depending on aging requirements, cheese, and cheese maker. Blue cheeses include Roquefort (French), Gorgonzola, (Italian), and Danish blue (bleu) style (see **Figure 22–48**).

Pasta filata cheese refers to a family of Italian cheeses. These cheeses are cooked, kneaded, or "spun." They can be very fresh to hard grating depending on cheese and producer. Pasta filata cheeses include Italian mozzarella, Provolone, and Scamorza (see **Figure 22–49**).

Natural rind cheeses have self-formed rinds acquired during the aging process. Generally, no molds, microflora, or washes are added. Natural rind mold

and microflora may exist from the environment. Many natural rind cheeses are from raw milk since they age for an extended period of time. Natural rind cheeses include many "tomme style," which describes the origin location such as French Tomme de Svoie and Mimolette, English Stilton, and Lancashire (see **Figure 22–50**).

Washed rind cheese are those cheeses whose surface has been ripened by washing the cheese throughout the aging period with brine, beer, wine, brandy, or a mixture of ingredients that encourages bacterial growth. Exterior rinds may vary from bright orange to brown with flavor and aroma profiles that are pungent and the interior of the cheese is semisoft and creamy. These cheeses are made from pasteurized

Figure 22–50

Tomme cheeses are an example of natural rind cheeses that form as a result of dehydration during aging. (Funlovingvolvo/123RF)

Figure 22–51

Taleggio has been produced since the tenth century in Italy. Made from cow's milk, this cheese contains 48 percent fat and is aged for one to two months. It has an orange-color washed edible rind that has a pungent flavor. It is molded in an approximate 8-inch square and is 2-inches thick. Taleggio is often served as a dessert cheese. (Richard Embrey/Pearson Education)

Figure 22–52a

Process cheese includes American cheese slices and these "spreadable cheese wedges." (© Amanda Frye)

Figure 22–52b

Milk is the essential ingredient in cheese. Making cheese is a way to preserve excess milk. (Kubais/Shutterstock)

and raw milks depending on cheese and cheese maker. Washed rind cheeses include tomme style, triple crème style, semisoft cheese similar to Epoisses, Livarot, and Taleggio (see **Figure 22–51**).

Natural cheese imply cheeses made directly from milk.

Cold-pack cheese or *club cheese* or *crock cheese* is made by grinding and mixing together one or more varieties of cheese without the aid of heat. Acid, water, salt, coloring, and spices may be added, but the final moisture content must not exceed that permitted for the variety of natural cheese from which it was prepared. The cheese is packaged in jars or in moisture-proof packages in retail-size units.

Cold-pack cheese food is prepared in the same manner as cold-pack cheese, but it may contain other ingredients, such as cream, milk, skim milk, nonfat dry milk, or whey. It may also contain pimientos, fruits, vegetables, or meats and sweetening agents, such as sugar and corn syrup.

Process cheese is produced by blending natural cheese with emulsifiers, stabilizers, cream, butter, and other dairy and non-dairy ingredients, followed by heating and continuous mixing to form a homogenous product with extended shelf life. Process cheese often is a way to recycle, rework, and profit from natural cheese trimming waste. Natural cheese left overs, scraps, waste cheese, or edible but damaged natural cheese blocks or wheels are "reworked" to make process cheese [55]. Process cheese is a stable oil-in-water emulsion. Process cheese includes American cheese, processed cheese spreads, and "cheese" flavored spreads.

Cheese Ingredients

The essential ingredients to produce cheese are milk, coagulant, bacterial cultures, and salt (**Figure 22–53**).

Milk. Milk is the essential main ingredient in manufacturing cheese. Casein and fat are the most important milk components for cheese production. Cheese can be made using raw or pasteurized milk.

The composition of the milk influences cheese quality, characteristics, and yield. The casein and fat components are crucial ones. The amount of fat is limited to the amount of casein that keeps the fat stable in the cheese system; therefore, the casein (protein)-to-fat ratio is critical. The ideal milk for cheddar cheese would have a 4.2 percent fat and 3.6 protein with 14 to 15 percent total milk solids and a casein-to-fat ratio of 0.7 [101]. However, the "ideal" milk doesn't always exist, so cheese makers standardize their milk through various processes. Fat is altered by cream separation or adding cream; protein can be increased by adding protein through nonfat milk solids, ultrafiltered concentrate, or condensed skim milk. The type of cheese and final cheese composition will dictate milk component casein-to-fat ratio needs. The ideal casein-to-fat

ratio for cheddar cheese is 0.70 compared to Parmesan, which is 1.10, or Swiss, which is 0.85 [101]. The size of the "native" fat globule has been found to have an impact on the cheese's physical and sensorial properties. Smaller fat globules resulted in moister cheese with better melting qualities [75]. Cheese makers look for milk that best matches their needs for the best quality of cheese and cheese yields. The calcium content, pH, and color are often adjusted [101].

Raw milk imparts different quality traits such as aroma, flavor, and texture to the finished cheese. There are an estimated 60 enzymes in raw milk yet only about 20 have been characterized [127]. The numerous enzymes, "indigenous microflora," substrates along with their interactions, and by-products impart unique characteristics and qualities to the finished cheese. The diverse enzymes and cultures that act on milk components provide the cheese's unique sensorial experiences. Proteolysis and lipolysis of the raw milk enzymes degrade cheese structure matrix imparting favorable textural changes. Often cheese makers use commercial dairy cultures to control spoilage and conditions.

High-quality raw Grade "A" milk from healthy animals is essential for raw milk cheese production [127]. For some cheese varieties, raw milk is given a heat shock treatment (60 to 65°C for 15 seconds, which is below pasteurization requirements) prior to cheese production. The heat shock kills spoilage pathogens, but keeps active enzymes and beneficial bacteria providing a better environment for cheese cultures [127]. Raw milk cheese must be aged for a minimum of 60 days at temperatures above 35°F (1.6°C). If more than two hours lapses between time of receipt or heat treatment and setting, milk should be cooled to 45°F or lower until time of setting (7 CFR 58.439). These raw milk regulations help reduce pathogen exposure. Extended aging beyond the 60 days is required for some cheeses. Fresh raw milk cheese that is not aged cannot be sold in the United States, since raw milk cheese requires minimum 60 day aging [127]. It is estimated that in the United States, less than 1 percent of cheese is made from raw milk [127]. However, 30 of 72 cheeses defined in the federal code can be made with raw milk [127].

Cultures. Starter cultures may be natural or "wild" in milk or they may be added as a commercially produced starter. Commercial starter cultures originated from the natural "wild" bacteria originally found in milk that was successful in making cheese. A small part of whey or cream from the successful cheesemaking was saved much like starters for bread dough. In cheese production this is called "back slopping" [77]. Eventually, the successful cultures were isolated, selected, and grown for commercial cheese production; the commercial starter cultures allow for better control throughout the cheesemaking process [77].

Figure 22–53

Cheese maker checking cheese curd. (Giuseppe Parisi/Shutterstock)

Cheesemaking cultures are lactic acid bacteria (LAB), since milk lactose is the energy source. Lactic acid bacteria turns lactose into lactic acid during fermentation. Different bacterial cultures provide the distinct cheese flavors and textures. Homofermentive bacteria produce only lactic acid during fermentation [73]. The homofermentive bacteria are used in cheeses where a "clean acid flavor" is desired such as in cheddar cheese. Heterofermentive bacteria produce lactic acid plus other compounds such as alcohol, aldehydes, ketones, and carbon dioxide, which yield a wide range of flavors including fruity flavors [73]. Starter cultures are added early in the cheesemaking process to lower the pH to around 5. Starter cultures are used in small amounts at a level of 1.5 to 2 percent [73]. Cultures are added 30 to 60 minutes prior to rennet addition to assist with coagulation, depending on the cheese being produced. The starter culture contributes desirable flavors and textural changes and aid in preservation to help prevent spoilage pathogens [78].

Adjunct cultures or nonstarter lactic acid bacteria (NSLAB) are added to provide and enhance cheese flavors and texture. They are added in low levels of 0.1 to 1 percent [44]. Some adjunct flavors such as *Propionibacterium freudenreichii* are added for the eye formation in Swiss cheese. Some adjunct cultures are used as a "smear" for "washing" the outside of formed cheeses; *Brevibacterium linens* is used on Gruyere, brick, and Limburger cheeses.

Yeasts and molds (fungi) are used to provide certain cheese characteristics and flavors. Brick and Limburger cheese are ripened with a smear of *torula yeast*. Mold spores are added to mold-ripened cheeses. Mold provides mild to pungent flavors and also characteristic colors. Molds used include *Penicillium roqueforti* in blue cheeses to provide the blue/green veining and *Penicillium camemberti* or *Penicillum candidum* can be used in Camembert and Brie to provide distinctive soft rind.

In cheesemaking, the starter culture destruction by unwanted bacterial phages can be a problem. These bacteriophages (viruses that infect bacteria) destroy the starter culture through lysis (rupturing of cell membranes) [35]. If starter cultures are destroyed the pH will not be lowered or production will be slowed or ruined leading to loss of entire batches of milk or cheese [79].

Coagulants (Acid or Rennet)

All cheese is made by coagulating the milk proteins to form the curd. Coagulation of casein forms a protein gel that entraps fat within its protein network. Cheese can be produced by the addition of acid, enzymes, or acid plus heat used for milk protein coagulation. Whey cheese can also be made.

Acid Coagulation. Many fresh unripened cheese use acidification for production. Acidification can be achieved by direct addition of a food-grade acid or by the use of lactic acid bacterial culture. In the United States, pasteurized milk is required for fresh cheeses. There is no ripening phase. The cheese is ready to eat immediately after processing. Direct acid-coagulated cheeses such as cottage cheese, cream cheese, and quark (European-style cottage cheese or farmer's cheese) are made adding lactic acid bacteria to milk. The shelf life of fresh cheese is limited to two to three weeks. Fresh cheese is produced with addition of acid and little or no rennet to coagulate curd at around 86 to 90°F (30 to 32°C.) Typically acid coagulation is achieved around pH 4.6 to 4.8 [35]. The cheese curd is typically heated to 52°C to inactivate bacteria then the curd is often washed to reduce acidity before salting. Sometimes enzymatic rennet is added with or without acid to increase pH level (6.5 to 6.7) for fresh cheese coagulation [35]. Most fresh cheese is high moisture, around 50 to 70 percent water.

Italian mascarpone cheese is made by adding citric or acetic acid to cream to reduce pH to 5.0 then whey is drained. Cottage cheese is made by coagulating milk lactic acid bacteria fermentation or direct addition of lactic acid, which lowers pH to form curds. Sometimes rennet is also used. Whey is drain and curd recovered, salted, and sometimes creamed.

Cream cheese is made by acidifying pasteurized homogenized whole milk to form an oil-in-water emulsified gel structure. This protein emulsion holds fat within its coagulated network; whey is separated by centrifuging or other means. The acid-coagulated gel mixture is typically pasteurized again to inactivate the lactic acid bacteria and then homogenized again before packaging and sealing. Cream cheese mostly have less than 55 percent moisture and less than 30 percent milkfat [44].

Hispanic white unripened cheeses (*queso blanco*), "white cheese," use either acid or rennet to coagulate casein depending on the variety of the cheese made [119]. The cheese has a creamy white appearance and must be made from pasteurized cow's milk. Queso blanco cheeses have been produced and sold illegally as "bathtub" cheeses in an underground markets leading to foodborne illness outbreaks from *Listeria* and *Salmonella* [11, 20].

Queso blanco is slightly acidic, firm, salty curd that is sliceable. It is sometimes referred to as "frying cheese" and does not melt when heated. It is typically used on enchiladas, burritos, or combined with fruit for dessert [119].

The direct-acidified fresh cheeses use lime juice, vinegar, or fruit juice to form curd [128]. These direct-acidified Hispanic cheeses are *queso del pais, queso de la tierra, queso de cincho,* and *queso sierra*.

Enzymes (Rennet). Rennet is the milk-clotting enzyme. About 75 percent of cheese varieties are produced by rennet coagulation. Enzyme coagulation uses rennet with the protease enzymes. Traditional rennet is protease enzyme chymosin. Rennet can be derived from several sources: animal rennet, microbial rennet, or thistle flower rennet. Traditionally, rennet enzymes were retrieved from calf stomach lining. Now rennet is mostly synthesized by fungus or bacteria or bioengineered, which is much less expensive. Thistle flower-based rennet called *Cynzime* is an aspartic acid protease [82]. Wild thistle flower (cardoon) extracts have been used to coagulate milk for cheese in the Roman Empire as well as Spain and Portugal [82]. *Cynzime* rennet cleaves all casein bonds including κ-, α-, β- and γ-casein compared to other sources that only cleave κ-casein. Since *Cynzime* is plant based, it can be used for kosher- and halal-certified cheeses. *Cynzime* requires increased mixing and reaction times compared with the other rennet. *Cynzime* is used to coagulate Portuguese sheep milk cheeses and Spanish goat milk and sheep milk cheeses [82].

Rennet forms curds by cleaving the κ-casein that destabilizes the casein micelle. The destabilized casein micelles move closer together, then coagulate through calcium phosphate bridges between micelles. This network of linked casein micelles tighten and trap fat, forming the curd expelling the whey. Calcium content is important in coagulation and curd strength. Sometimes calcium salts (calcium chloride) are added to increase curd strength and formation.

Hispanic rennet fresh cheeses *queso blancos* are known as *queso fresca, queso de prensa, queso de puna, queso de hoja, queso de matera, and queso pasteurizado.* A Mexican sweet cheese dessert called *chongos zamoranos* is made by using rennet enzyme to curdle whole milk with sugar and cinnamon [93].

Acid Plus Heat. Heat-acid precipitated cheese forms coagulum of milk proteins by using both heat and acid. This method is typically used for whey products such as Italian ricotta and Indian cheeses Chhena and Paneer. Ricotta cheese is traditionally made from the whey of mozzarella cheese. Whey is heated to denature protein then acidified by direct addition of food-grade lactic, acetic, or citric acid to denature casein and whey proteins. Sometimes the curd is described as a "foam type curd." High moisture content of up to 80 percent is due to whey's high water-holding capacity [35]. Whey cheeses are often "frying cheeses" [35].

Salt. Food-grade salt (NaCl) is added to cheese during the cheesemaking process. Salt is added for taste and flavor accentuation. Salt also promotes syneresis of whey, but also for food safety to control pathogenic growth. Salt is added at about 2.5 percent weight basis. Salt does contribute sodium along with sodium naturally occurring in milk. Some cheese contains more salt than others. Natural cheeses are typically lower in sodium ranging between 100 to 200 mg sodium per ounce [131]. Feta has 317 mg sodium/ounce and Roquefort has 500 mg sodium/ounce [131]. Processed cheese and cheese foods contain more sodium around 300 to 450 mg sodium per ounce [131].

Color. Annatto is a natural yellow coloring derived from annatto seed extracts. The annatto seeds are from the "Lipstick tree," *Bixa orellana.* Annatto is used to enrich cheese color. Most cheddar cheese color is enhanced by annatto.

Cheese Manufacturing

The objectives of cheesemaking are to produce cheese with (1) composition that has optimal moisture, pH (acidity), fat to protein ratio and calcium (2) high-quality texture and structure, and (3) that is ripened for optimal aroma, flavor, taste, and physical characteristics. Cheese manufacturing procedures depend on the type of cheese being processed. Type of milk, times, temperatures, coagulant, acidification, pH, block formation, and aging can vary.

Most cheese production begins with pasteurized milk and follows steps that include (1) promoting curd formation with acid produced by lactic acid-producing bacteria (a starter culture) and/or a coagulating enzyme; (2) cutting the curd into small pieces to allow the whey to escape; (3) heating the curd to contract the curd particles and hasten the expulsion of whey; (4) draining, knitting or stretching, salting, and pressing the curd; and (5) curing or ripening [84]. Some cheeses, including cottage cheese, cream cheese, and mozzarella, are not ripened.

Basic Cheesemaking Steps

These are general cheese production steps. Some steps may be modified, altered, or omitted depending on cheese being produced or the cheese maker.

1. **Standardize milk.** Optimize protein to fat ratio for good quality cheese with good yield.

2. **Pasteurize/homogenize/heat treat milk.** Destroy spoilage pathogens and improve environment for starter culture. Raw cheese may or may not be heat treated, but must be aged for 60 days. Milk is homogenized to evenly distribute small fat globules.

3. **Cool milk to 90°F (32°C).** A Temperature of 90°F (32°C) is needed for starter growth. Raw milk may need to be heated this temperature.

4. **Inoculate with lactic acid bacteria starter culture and nonstarter adjunct cultures. Incubate 15 to 60 minutes.** Starter culture and ripening

decreases pH to about 5.0 for curd formation to occur. Adjunct culture adds flavoring enzymes.

5. **Add rennet and form curd.** Rennet enzymes are added to form curds. Curd is allowed to develop undisturbed for 30 minutes (see Figure 22–53).

6. **Cut curd or coagulum (the mass of coagulated matter).** Final pH (typically between 5.0 and 6.5) reached. Coagulum is cut with "cheese" knives or wires. Large processing plants cut cheese both vertically and horizontally with large, sharp multi-bladed wire knives. Soft cheeses are cut in large chunks and hard cheeses are cut in small chunks [73]. Allow curd to set. Some cheese curds are slowly and gently agitated.

7. **Heat curd.** Temperature of heating depends on cheese being made. Curd chunks slowly heated to around 100°F (38°C) to help separate curd and whey (see **Figure 22–54**). Heating may vary from 91.4°F (33°C) to 170°F (80°C depending on type of cheese). Heating deactivates proteolytic enzymes that destroy elastic qualities of cheese. Each curd has a thin membrane film form that traps fat but allows whey to escape. Salt is sometimes added to promote syneresis for whey removal. Failure to remove whey causes lactose retention, increased acidity, and other defects, which may occur during ripening. Too much acid production leads to brittle and crumbly cheese. If temperature is raised too quickly the curd will become excessively firm on the outside known as *case hardening*. Case hardening causes excessive moisture and lactose retention.

8. **Drain whey.** Whey is drained from the vat leaving a curd "mat." Whey can be drained by multiple methods. Curds can be scooped out of whey and placed in molds. Curds and whey can be pumped to the drain table so whey drains off and curds remain. Soft cheese curds are transferred to perforated molds (see **Figure 22–55a**). Perforated screens can be used to drain whey. Cheese curds "knit" together so individual curds are no longer distinct. Lactic acid is further developed. Draining time is about 20 minutes.

"Cheddaring" for cheddar cheese involves cutting curd mat and piling sections on top of each other and flipping, turning, and repiling to achieve desired texture.

9. **Washing.** In some cheeses, washing curds is done to remove remaining lactose. The type of cheese determines water temperature. Not all cheese production involves washing. Hot water is used for Gouda to dry curd and develop moisture [35]. Colby and Brick cheeses are other common washed cheeses. Washing also removes excess whey that is replaced by water in cheese.

Figure 22–54

Cheese maker checking temperature while heating cheese coagulum. (Olaf Speier/Shutterstock)

Figure 22–55a

Cheese maker places curds in perforated molds to drain whey. (Anistidesign/Shutterstock)

Figure 22–55b

Mozzarella cheese is formed into small loaves before being dipped in brine solution. (Giuseppe Parisi/Shutterstock)

Figure 22–56

At this French Cheese factory the cheese has been placed in wooden hoops for shaping and covered with cloth. (Prochasson frederic/Shutterstock)

Figure 22–57

Cheese placed on wooden shelves to ripen. (Maxim Golubchikov/Shutterstock)

10. **Dry salt or brine.** Salting improves flavor, texture, and suppresses bacterial growth improving cheese-keeping quality. Dry salt can be sprinkled on curd and mixed. Curd can be formed into small loaves and dipped in brine (see **Figure 22–55b**). Dry salt can be rubbed on the outside of cheese.

11. **Form cheese into blocks.** Salted cheese curds are placed in cheese "hoops," forms, or cloth bags and then pressed to give characteristic shape (see **Figure 22–56**). Pressing also compacts texture and removes more whey. Often external weights may be used. Curds of medium- and low-moisture cheeses require pressing, but high-moisture cheeses do not require pressing. Special treatment of surface mold smearing is applied to some cheeses.

12. **Cheese ripening.** The "ripening" or aging/maturing of cheese is essential to develop flavor and other qualities. The French term *affinage* describes the aging and maturing of cheese. The *affineur* is the person who is responsible for aging the cheese. Each cheese has unique requirements for temperature, humidity, and treatments so that the cheese will develop the proper flavor and desired characteristics. Cheese may be ripened for several months to a year in a cheese "cave" under control temperature and humidity. Cheese may be placed on mats or wooden slabs and periodically turned, wrapped in cloth, washed, or rotated (see **Figure 22–57**). Some cheeses develop rinds naturally via dehydration. Brine curing is a unique curing method for Feta cheese that takes two to three months [44].

Freshly made curds have a bland flavor. Cheese ripening is a complex transformation to alter the physical and chemical properties, which lead to the aroma, flavor, texture, composition, and appearance of the final cheese product. Cheese proteins, fatty acid, and lactose serve as the substrate for complex biochemical changes. The ripening is the result of microbiological, enzymatic, and metabolic processes from lipolysis, proteolysis, and glycolysis and secondary changes from their by-products. The final texture, flavor, and compositional changes result from the formation of carbon dioxide, amines, thioesters, hydrogen sulfide, keto acids, ammonia, fatty esters, phenylesters, alcohols, aldehydes, thiols, lactones, acetic acids, lactic acid, propionic acid, ethanol, and carbon dioxide [81]. All compounds that developed during ripening give cheese its flavor. The presence of salt delays bacterial growth and therefore alters the rate of ripening.

Swiss cheese owes its large holes to special gas-forming organisms that produce carbon dioxide gas during the early stage of ripening while the cheese is soft and elastic. Limburger cheese owes its characteristic odor to the development of putrefactive bacteria that are allowed to act over a considerable period. Cheddar cheese varies widely in flavor and texture, depending on the organisms that predominate and the length of time of ripening. Both *Lactobacilli lactis* and *S. lactis* organisms play major roles in the ripening of good Cheddar cheese.

The length of ripening depends on cheese being produced. Mild cheeses, such as brick and Monterey Jack, are allowed to ripen for a shorter period than strong cheeses, such as Parmesan. Blue cheese is usually aged three to four months but may be aged up to nine months for more pronounced flavor. Mild cheddar is ripened for a shorter length of time than sharp cheddar. Acid-coagulated cheese is usually not ripened. Ripening is an expensive process for the cheese industry; the cheese industry constantly searches for ways to reduce ripening time.

Natural protein breakdown during ripening is called "putrification" [35]. Some excessive protein breakdown during cheese ripening yields undesirable off notes such as bitterness, stringent, "brothy," or "putrid" [35, 37].

13. **Packaging.** Cheese is cut or packaged in blocks sealed in plastic. It may be sealed in waxes or wrapped in cloth or paper (see **Figure 22–58**). Single-serving packaging of cups, cubes, sticks, and slices are popular with consumers.

Grades

USDA grade standards, U.S. Grade AA and U.S. Grade A, have been developed for Swiss, Cheddar, Colby, and Monterey cheese [121]. Cheese bearing these grades must be produced in a USDA-inspected and approved plant under sanitary conditions. Graders evaluate the flavor and texture of the cheese. Some cheese and cheese products not covered by a U.S. grade standard may be inspected and bear a USDA Quality Approved inspection shield on the label. This shield indicates that the cheese has been manufactured in a plant meeting USDA sanitary specifications and is a cheese of good quality [116].

Process Cheese

A significant part of the cheese produced in the United States today is made into pasteurized process cheese and related products. Process cheese is made by grinding and mixing together different natural cheese trimmings with the aid of heat and an emulsifying agent, such as sodium salts of phosphoric acid. A selected blend of cheese or portions of the same variety selected at different stages of ripeness are used, and the product is pasteurized before packaging.

After the cheese is melted, it is run into molds that may be jars, glasses, or metal foil-lined cardboard boxes. As the cheese hardens, it clings closely to the jar or foil, thus preventing molds from attacking the surface. Pasteurization of the cheese destroys bacteria and enzymes, thus stopping all ripening. Process cheese is also sold in individual slices and can be purchased with individual slices separately wrapped. Low-fat pasteurized process cheese products are also available and may contain skim milk cheese, water, emulsifier salts, flavorings, and a preservative (sorbic acid).

The quality and flavor of process cheese depends on the cheese used to make it. Several varieties of cheese are made into pasteurized process cheeses, including cheddar, Swiss, and brick. Convenience, ease of blending in cooked dishes, and the protection offered by the package against spoilage are factors influencing the consumer's choice to use process cheese. The blend of cheeses is chosen to retain as far as possible the characteristic flavor of the type of cheese used; however, the flavor of the process cheese is seldom, if ever, equal to that of the original product. The characteristic differences in texture of the original cheeses tend to be lost, as the texture of process cheese is more or less uniform and soft. The moisture content of process cheese may not exceed 40 percent.

Process Cheese Foods and Spreads. Pasteurized process cheese food is produced in a manner similar to process cheese except that it contains less cheese. Cream, milk, skim milk, nonfat milk solids or whey, and sometimes other foods, such as pimientos, may be added to it, resulting in a product that is higher in moisture than process cheese. Cheese food is more mild in flavor, melts more quickly, and has a softer texture than process cheese because of its higher moisture content. Pasteurized process cheese spread generally has a higher moisture and lower milkfat content than process cheese food. A stabilizer is added to prevent separation of ingredients. It is generally more spreadable than process cheese food.

Low-Fat Cheese. Fat-free, "part skim," and low-fat cheeses are available. Low-fat milk is used to make many low-fat cheeses. Reduced-fat cheeses are generally perceived to be less desirable than full-fat cheeses from a sensory perspective. Researchers have found that reduced-fat cheeses have a texture that is more hard, waxy, chewy, and springy than full-fat cheeses [32]. In addition, reduced-fat cheeses may be less sticky, cohesive, meltable, and smooth.

Researchers are exploring methods of producing higher-quality low-fat cheeses. One process involves the removal of fat from a full-fat Cheddar cheese through

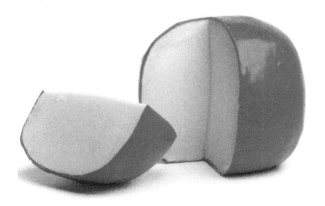

Figure 22–58
Dutch Edam with red wax coating. (Pauliene Wessel/123RF)

FOCUS ON SCIENCE
MORE ABOUT RENNET

Where does Rennin (Rennet) Come from?

Until 1990, rennet was produced the old-fashioned way from abomasums (the last of the four chambers of the stomach of a ruminant animal) and from various "vegetable" rennets (some of which, called *microbial coagulant*, are made from the microorganism *Mucor miehei*). Today, at a cost of one-tenth of that before 1990, chymosin (or rennet) is produced by genetically engineering bacteria into which the gene for this enzyme has been inserted. When the bacteria are grown in large vats, they secrete rennin, which is then purified for cheese-making. Rennin is available commercially in tablet or in liquid form.

(Martin Sanders. Beehive Illustration/Pearson Education Ltd.)

How Does Rennet Work?

Rennet is an enzyme; therefore, there are specific requirements for its activity—temperature, pH, substrate, and amount. Rennet is specific for its operation in milk to convert it to a gel. Before the addition of rennet, the temperature of the milk should be 104 to 108°F (40 to 42°C). Because rennet needs a substrate, which is calcium, and because some calcium may be lost from the solution during pasteurization, a small amount of calcium chloride is added. The calcium chloride aids coagulation and ensures a firm curd that does not fall apart when cut. Lactic acid bacteria also may be added to acidify the milk. One rennet tablet will set 5 gallons of milk.

Source: Reference 7.

---

centrifugation. A high-quality Cheddar cheese with about 16 percent fat, compared to 34 percent fat in full-fat cheese, can be produced using this method [92]. The choice of culture also appears to be important in the production of a flavorful and functional low-fat cheese.

Cheese Storage

All cheese is best kept cold. Soft and unripened cheeses have limited keeping quality and require refrigeration. To prevent the surfaces from drying out, the cheese should be well wrapped in plastic wrap or metal foil or kept in the original container if it is one that protects the cheese. In the refrigerator, strong cheeses that are not tightly wrapped may contaminate other foods that readily absorb odors.

Soft fresh cheese such as cottage cheese, cream cheese, and goat cheese must be refrigerated for food-safety reasons. Hard natural ripened cheeses will keep longer in the refrigerator, but does not necessarily need refrigeration. Refrigeration will extend shelf life of process cheese although it does not require refrigeration.

Refrigerated storage times for natural hard cheese are six months, unopened, or three to four weeks after opening. Shredded natural cheeses can be stored for one month after opening. Soft cheeses can be stored for one week and cream cheeses for two weeks. The shelf life of cottage cheese may be extended two or three times the usual period by adding carbon dioxide gas and packaging the product in high-barrier material [74].

Molds are used to make some kinds of cheeses and thus will be found on the exterior or interior of Roquefort, blue, Gorgonzola, Stilton, Brie, and Camembert. Molds used to produce cheese are safe to eat. Wild molds that are not part of the manufacturing process are undesirable when growing on the surface of cheeses. Wild molds may be safely cut off of hard cheeses, such as Cheddar. However, if soft or shredded cheeses mold, the cheese will need to be discarded because the mold cannot be completely removed.

Freezing is not recommended for most cheeses because, on thawing, they tend to be mealy and crumbly; however, some varieties of cheese can be frozen satisfactorily in small pieces (one pound or less, not more than 1 inch thick). These varieties include Brick, Cheddar, Edam, Gouda, Muenster, Port du Salut, Swiss, Provolone, Mozzarella, and Camembert. Freezing cheese works for most cheese except ricotta, cottage, and cream cheeses. Other cheeses may be frozen for six months. When frozen cheese is to be thawed, it may be taken from the freezer and placed in the refrigerator for several days before using it. This so-called *slow thawing* helps to avoid the detrimental effects of freezing and aids in preserving the original flavor, body, and texture.

Cheese usually exhibits its most distinctive flavor when served at room temperature. The amount of

Figure 22–59

Cheese, wine, and, sometimes, other seasonings such as garlic are melted over low heat in a fondue pot. Chunks of bread on long fondue forks are dipped into the hot cheese mixture. (stockcreations/Shutterstock)

Figure 22–60

Cheese soufflé is an egg dish prepared with whipped egg whites, a thickened milk-based sauce, and cheese. (Richard Embrey/Pearson Education)

cheese to be used should be removed from the refrigerator about 30 minutes prior to serving [84]. An exception is cottage cheese, which should be served cold.

Cheese in Cooked Foods

Cheese adds flavor, color, and texture to a variety of cooked foods. Many casserole mixtures use cheese, either as a basic component or as a topping. And what would pizza be without cheese? In addition, a cheese tray combined with fresh fruits and/or vegetable relishes makes an easy snack or a colorful dessert.

A hard cheese, such as Cheddar, softens and then melts when it is heated at low to moderate temperatures (see **Figure 22–59**). Overheating the cheese or using too high of a temperature results in the separation of fat; development of a tough, rubbery curd; stringiness; and the tendency to harden on cooling. Finely dividing the cheese by grating or grinding before

combining it with other ingredients facilitates melting without overheating. Cheese sauces should be cooked in a double boiler or over low heat with continuous stirring. Well-ripened cheese and process cheese blend better in heated mixtures than mild (less aged) natural cheese and are less likely to produce stringiness.

Welsh rarebit (sometimes called Welsh rabbit) is a thickened savory cheese sauce. It may also contain egg and is usually served over toast. Cheese soufflé is a combination of white sauce and whipped egg whites with grated cheese to give it flavor (**Figure 22–60**). The white sauce (see Chapter 11) used as a basis may vary in consistency or in amount, but soufflés made with a thick sauce base are usually easier for the inexperienced person to make and tend to shrink less after baking. The baking dish containing the soufflé should be placed in a pan of water during baking to avoid overcooking.

STUDY QUESTIONS

Milk Consumption Trends

1. Describe present trends in the consumption of dairy products in the United States.

2. Discuss the nutritive value of milk and milk products. How do milk and milk products fit into a healthy dietary plan.

Milk Composition and Properties

3. What is the average percentage composition of whole cow's milk?

4. Name the following items and discuss their role in milk and milk products:

   (a) Protein found in milk in largest amount

   (b) Two major whey proteins

   (c) Major carbohydrate of milk

   (d) Two minerals for which milk is considered to be a particularly good source

   (e) Vitamin for which milk is a good source that is easily destroyed when milk is exposed to sunlight

5. Explain why milk is classified as an emulsion, solution, and colloidal dispersion. Describe role of milk components.

Sanitation, Grading and Processing

6. How do opaque containers help to protect milk against the development of off-flavor? Explain.

7. Describe the purpose, process, and resulting product when milk is
   (a) Pasteurized
   (b) Homogenized
   (c) Fortified

8. Briefly describe the major characteristics of each of the following processed milk products:
   (a) Whole fluid milk
   (b) Skim milk
   (c) Reduced-fat milk
   (d) Low-fat milk
   (e) Ultrahigh-temperature processed milk
   (f) Evaporated milk
   (g) Sweetened condensed milk
   (h) Nonfat dry milk, regular, and instant
   (i) Dried buttermilk (churned)
   (j) Buttermilk (cultured)
   (k) Filled milk
   (l) Yogurt

9. Discuss proper milk handling and storage.
   (a) Explain why it is so important that milk be handled properly, both in processing and in the kitchen.
   (b) What does the USDA Quality Approved shield mean when it is placed on certain dairy products?
   (c) What is the Grade A Pasteurized Milk Ordinance?

Food Preparation with Milk

10. (a) What causes milk to scorch when it is heated over direct heat?
    (b) Which milk proteins coagulate quite easily with heating? Which do not?

11. Suggest ways to prevent or control the formation of a film or scum on the surface of heated milk.

12. (a) Which milk protein coagulates easily with the addition of acid?
    (b) Give examples illustrating when the acid coagulation of milk is desirable and when it is undesirable.

13. Compare and contrast the difference between a milkfat foam and a milk foam.
    (a) Describe what happens when cream is whipped.
    (b) What conditions should be controlled, and why, if cream is to whip properly?
    (c) Suggest effective procedures for whipping evaporated milk and nonfat dry milk.

14. What kind of milk is best to use for milk frothing for a cappuccino? Discuss why.

Goat and Sheep Milk

15. Compare and contrast properties of cow, sheep, and goat milk.

Cheese

16. (a) What is *rennet*? What does it do to milk?
    (b) What role does rennet play in cheesemaking?
    (c) What is *chymosin*? List two sources.

17. Discuss acidification and coagulation.

18. Describe the general steps usually followed in the manufacture of cheese.

19. (a) What is meant by *ripening* cheese?
    (b) Describe general changes that may occur during the ripening process.

20. Give examples of each of the following types of cheese:
    (a) Soft, unripened
    (b) Firm, unripened
    (c) Soft, ripened
    (d) Semisoft, ripened
    (e) Firm, ripened
    (f) Very hard, ripened
    (g) Blue-vein mold-ripened

21. Describe the major characteristics of the following:
    (a) Cold-pack cheese
    (b) Process cheese
    (c) Process cheese food
    (d) Process cheese spread

22. (a) Describe what happens when cheese is heated too long or at too high of a temperature.
    (b) Suggest an appropriate way for preparing a cheese sauce. Explain why this method should be effective.

23
Eggs and Egg Cookery

Eggs are a versatile food ingredient used alone or in combination with other foods. As a major protein source, eggs may be the main dish for a meal. Eggs are an essential and functional ingredient in other food products such as cakes, cookies, meringues, sauces, or mayonnaise. The egg is an inexpensive high-quality protein and nutritive source. Eggs contribute color, viscosity, moisture, richness, and flavor. They can act as a binding and adhesion ingredient or coagulating agent. Eggs can be used as a wash or to adhere seeds to bread crust during baking. The ability of eggs to be aerated, form a foam structure, and contribute in structural integrity makes eggs an essential ingredient in many products. Egg whites can even be made into edible packaging. Eggs play a variety of roles in foods and the cookery processes.

Lipoproteins in the yolk makes the egg yolk especially valuable in **emulsion** formation as discussed in Chapter 10. The egg white protein **surface activity** makes the egg useful in the production of films that hold air and thus create a **foam**, such as found in meringues and angel food cake. The leavening of a variety of food mixtures results from this characteristic. An egg white foam used in certain candies also improves the texture by controlling crystallization of sugar.

The ability of egg proteins to **coagulate** when heated, resulting in thickening or **gel** formation, contributes much to the characteristic properties of such dishes as custards, puddings, and various sauces. Coagulation of egg protein, along with the viscosity of the uncooked egg, is the basis for the use of egg as a binding agent and as a coating to hold crumbs together for crust formation on breaded foods. Rigidity of cell walls and of crusts in numerous doughs and batters is increased by coagulation of egg.

Use of the egg as a **clarifying** agent also depends on the coagulation of egg proteins. Broths and coffee may be clarified with eggs. Adding eggs improves the color and flavor of most dishes. Plain eggs—cooked in the shell, scrambled, and fried—also provide eating enjoyment. The egg is an inexpensive source of protein and an excellent source of many essential vitamins and minerals.

All bird eggs may be eaten; quail, duck, guinea, goose, and other eggs are delicacies in many cultures (**Figure 23–1**). However, chicken eggs are the most commonly consumed so thus are the focus in this chapter.

Figure 23–1

All eggs may be eaten and some eggs are considered delicacies. Eggs come in different colors and sizes. Eggs of (left to right) quail, chicken, duck, and goose. The chicken egg is the most commonly consumed egg. (CatMicroStock/Shutterstock)

In this chapter, the following topics will be discussed:

- Consumption trends and nutrition
- Composition
- Structure
- Quality and sizing
- Food safety of eggs
- Preservation and processing
- Coagulation of eggs in food preparation
- Preparation methods for eggs

CONSUMPTION TRENDS AND NUTRITION

Consumption Trends

Poultry is a term for domesticated fowl such as chickens (*Gallus domesticus*). The domesticated chicken descended from the Red Jungle Fowl (*Gallus gallus*) and is native to Asia. The Red Jungle Fowl and waterfowl were thought to be domesticated about 5,000 years ago in Asia. Ancient Egyptians and Chinese were credited for raising egg-producing birds in 1400 B.C. and Europeans by 600 B.C. Christopher Columbus is

Figure 23–2

White chicken eggs are the most common in the United States. (Akiyoko/Shutterstock)

Figure 23–3

White Leghorns are commonly used as commercial egg layers since they are good egg producers. The Leghorn is a breed of chicken with origins in Tuscany, central Italy. Different breeds of chicken lay different color eggs. Commercial laying hen breeds are selected because of their high egg production. (Mariusz S. Jurgielewicz/Shutterstock)

said to have introduced the first chickens to America on his second voyage in 1493. Today, there are around 200 breeds and varieties of chickens in the world. Different breeds and varieties of chickens lay eggs of different colors and sizes. However, in the United States, the white eggs from the White Leghorns chickens are the most common (**Figure 23–2**). The White Leghorn breeds are used as commercial laying hens since the breed is considered to be "good layers" with high egg production averaging 280 eggs per year and sometimes producing 300–320 eggs a year (**Figure 23–3**). Average commercial egg-laying hens produce approximately 250–300 eggs a year with proper feed and conditions [5].

Figure 23–4

Chickens laying eggs at a commercial poultry farm. (MENATU/Shutterstock)

Egg production has evolved over the years. In the United States during 1800s and early 1900s, most eggs were produced in small backyard flocks which expanded into bigger flocks during the early part of the 1900s. In the 1940s, research helped to improve egg production and hen health. Ventilated chicken houses with wire cages improved sanitary laying conditions. Egg collection was made easier and more automated technology with decreased egg contamination. During the 1960s, large commercial egg farms replaced the backyard smaller laying flocks with improved machinery and technology. Today large egg producing states have farms with flocks of 100,000 to 1 million layers [4]. There is a trend of egg farm consolidation and larger laying flocks. The American Egg Board reports that in 2017 there were 63 egg producers with 1 million layers per flock and 15 companies with 5 million layers. There are about 201 egg producers with flocks of 75,000 hens.

Shell eggs is the term used for eggs that are still in their shell. Most eggs that are purchased or sold are shell eggs. Egg products are "broken" eggs whose contents are removed from the shell, pasteurized, and sold in various forms such as liquid, frozen, or dried whole, yolk, or whites.

White eggs are predominant in the United States and preferred in countries such as Austria, Germany, Switzerland, Spain, and Australia [31]. Some brown eggs are produced in the United States with predominance in the Northeast. Brown eggs are popular in Europe including the United Kingdom, France, Ireland, and Portugal [31] (**Figure 23–4**).

According to the USDA Economic Research Service, the highest per capita egg consumption was in 1945 with 402 eggs consumed per person per year (**Figure 23–5**). Egg consumption in the United States was on a downward slide between the 1940s to

Figure 23–5

Brown chicken egg. (Picsfive/Shutterstock)

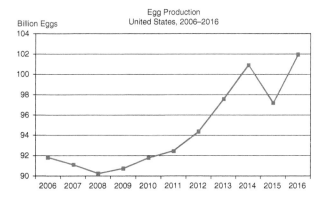

Figure 23–6

An increase in egg production from 2006 to 2016. (USDA-NASS)

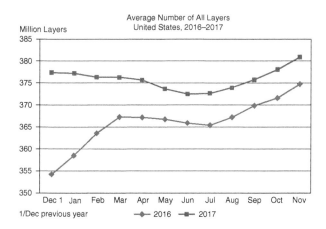

Figure 23–7

The number of chickens laying impacts the number of eggs produced. (USDA-NASS)

the 1990s. In 1950, per capita egg consumption was 389 eggs per person. In 1967, Americans were eating about 320 eggs per person per year. As concerns about fat and cholesterol in the diet increased, however, the

high cholesterol content of egg yolk made it a target. The low per capita egg consumption was in 1995 with 232 eggs per person. Egg consumption rose slightly to 237 per person in the next year [43]. The new century ushered in an increase in egg consumption with 256 eggs consumed per person per year in 2004. Egg production has been increasing since 2006 with 105.7 billion eggs produced in the United States in 2017 [1] (**Figures 23–6** and **23–7**). In 2010, 242 eggs were available in the food supply per person [55]. Egg consumption per capita was estimated to be 252.9 eggs per person in 2015 (**Figure 23–8**). According to the USDA Economic Research Service, retail egg prices are among the most "volatile retail food prices" as they can be affected by seasonal demand and region. The USDA tracks holiday egg sales in the month leading up to major egg consuming holidays such as Easter, Christmas, and Thanksgiving, which impact egg consumption and demand. The restaurant trend of serving "all day breakfast" has increased the number of egg menu items with 61 percent restaurants having a breakfast sandwich which typically includes eggs.

Egg cost ranges from approximately 9 to 25 cents a piece [60]. The avian flu impacted laying hens production in the spring of 2015 and egg farmers had to rebuild flocks, thereby affecting egg supplies [23]. In 2017, more egg-laying hens and an increased number of eggs per hen caused a decrease in the retail price (9 to 8 percent in 2017) and expected to decrease 1 to 0 percent in 2018 (**Figure 23–9**).

Iowa is the largest egg-producing state. **Figure 23–10**. Today about 60 percent of the eggs are going to retail operations to be used by consumers, 8 percent are used by food service operations, and the remaining 30 percent are used or processed into egg products for commercial food processing. The American Egg Board reports a small amount of eggs (2 percent) are exported to Mexico, Canada, Japan, and Hong Kong and small imports from Canada, the Netherlands, and Spain. The United Egg Producer general U.S. egg statistics from May 2017 gave the rate of egg layers as 76.7 eggs per 100 layers.

Specialty eggs include USDA certified organic, Omega-3 nutritionally enhanced, cage-free, and vegetarian fed eggs. Specialty eggs are a growing segment of the retail shell eggs. Organic eggs sold retail fetch prices that are double to triple that of comparable conventional USDA Grade AA or A extra large or large eggs [60, 61]. Brown eggs prices typically sell for more than white eggs. Omega-3 eggs are also selling for approximately double conventional USDA graded eggs. Cage-free eggs retail for double the price of conventional eggs and vegetarian eggs sell for a higher premium than conventional USDA graded eggs

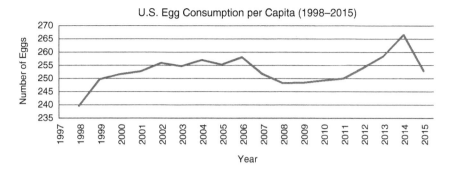

Figure 23-8

Egg consumption increasing since 1998. (Data United Egg Producers Graph by Sam Frye)

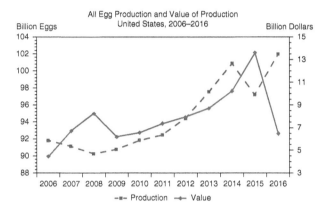

Figure 23-9

The graph shows egg production and value from 2006 to 2016. (USDA-NASS)

[60, 61]. Specialty eggs are increasing in the United States with organic and cage-free shell egg production about 13.2 percent of egg layers. The certified organic cage-free layers is estimated to be 4.7 percent or 14,300,000 eggs with estimated laying rate of about 75 percent with weekly egg production of 208,542 eggs (**Figure 23-11**). There are more nonorganic cage free layers—33,500,000 with estimated laying rate of 75 percent yielding more eggs at 488,542 (30-dozen cases) [62]. On average, cage-free brown eggs retail for more as compared to white eggs [62, 61].

In 2012, European Union laws banned battery cages egg-laying hens. In California, voters approved the 2008 Prevention of Farm Animal Cruelty Act that went in effect in 2015 requiring egg producers to increase space in hen layers battery cages that allow the chickens to be able to stand up and turn around and extend limbs in the cage. Critics claim the law decreased hen productivity by 35 percent and increased egg prices by 22 percent [41]. Perhaps other issues not analyzed are responsible for the change in numbers.

Research indicates that dietary cholesterol has less effect on serum cholesterol than previously thought, and eggs are getting better press [2]. Furthermore, recent nutrient analysis found that cholesterol levels were lower than previously analyzed. Eggs have several nutritional and economic advantages and are readily available.

Nutritive Value

Eggs are a high-quality protein source, easily accessible, nutrient dense, and affordable. The 2015–2020 Dietary Guidelines for Americans (DGA) support regular consumption of eggs along with other nutrient-rich whole foods such as fruits, vegetables, and whole grains [26, 56]. These guidelines reversed previous recommendations to limit daily cholesterol intake. A recent meta data analysis showed that daily egg intake does not appear to be associated with coronary heart disease [2].

One egg provides 13 essential vitamins and minerals plus a high-quality protein providing all essential amino acids [54]. The nutritive content of a large egg is 70 kilocalories, 6.3 g protein, 0.6 g carbohydrates, and 5.0 g of fat including 0.186 to 0.21 g of cholesterol [58]. Egg protein contains all the essential amino acids and is easily digestible [58]. The fat in the egg is concentrated in the yolk. Eggs are the least expensive source of high-quality protein per standard USDA serving.

The yolk is nutrient rich. It is a good supply of iron and vitamin A. Eggs also are a good source of choline needed by all cells and is important during pregnancy for fetal brain development. Eggs contain antioxidants lutein and zeaxanthin, which are believed to reduce the risk of cataracts and macular degeneration. Eggs are one of the few foods that naturally contain vitamin D. USDA recently changed the nutrition database on eggs increasing vitamin D content 41 IU and lowering cholesterol to 186 mg for a large egg [57]. Egg whites contain protein, riboflavin, and selenium. Riboflavin is responsible for the slight greenish tint in egg whites. **Table 23-1** and **Figure 23-12**.

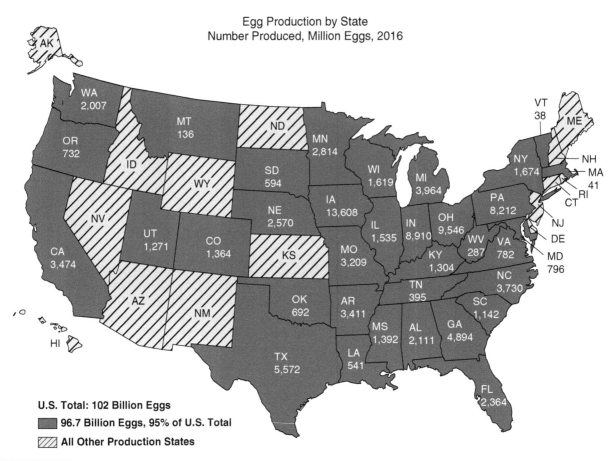

Egg Production by State
Number Produced, Million Eggs, 2016

AK

WA 2,007
OR 732
MT 136
ID
ND
MN 2,814
WI 1,619
MI 3,964
VT 38
ME
NH
MA 41
RI
CT
NY 1,674
PA 8,212
NJ
DE
MD 796
SD 594
WY
IA 13,608
NE 2,570
NV
UT 1,271
CO 1,364
KS
MO 3,209
IL 1,535
IN 8,910
OH 9,546
WV 287
VA 782
KY 1,304
NC 3,730
CA 3,474
AZ
NM
OK 692
AR 3,411
TN 395
SC 1,142
HI
TX 5,572
LA 541
MS 1,392
AL 2,111
GA 4,894
FL 2,364

U.S. Total: 102 Billion Eggs
■ 96.7 Billion Eggs, 95% of U.S. Total
▨ All Other Production States

Figure 23–10

Shows the egg production by state. In 2016, 102 billion eggs were produced. (USDA-NASS)

Figure 23–11

Crates of brown eggs. (Chainfoto24/Shutterstock)

EGG FORMATION

It takes a hen approximately 24–26 hours to produce one egg [48]. Once the hen lays the egg, the process starts all over again after about 30 minutes. The egg-making process is complex. An appreciation for the hen and the egg can be gained with a basic understanding of the egg cycle (**Figure 23–13a**). Without the hen, there would be no eggs.

Commercial shell eggs sold for retail food are infertile. However, it is important to remember that the egg contains all the nutrients for a baby chick to grow and hatch, which is part of the reason the egg is such a good nutritional source. The term *hatching eggs* applies to fertilized eggs that are for agriculture breeding purposes. Our discussion focuses only on commercial shell eggs and egg products.

In commercial egg-laying hens, only the left **ovary** and left oviduct develop [48]. A hen is born with about 4,000 tiny yolks or ovas in her ovary [58]. The first step in the egg-making process is the ovulation of the mature yolk (ovum). Each ovum is enclosed in a thin-walled sac [58]. Once the ovum (egg yolk) reaches full size, it is released by the ovary into the oviduct [15]. The oviduct is a 25–27 inch (63.5–68.6 cm.) tube-like organ that connects from the ovary to the tail vent; this is where the egg is made. The oviduct can be divided into five areas with specific roles in egg production discussed below [53] (**Figure 23–13b**).

Table 23-1
CHEMICAL COMPOSITION OF EGG WITHOUT SHELL

	Amount	Weight (g)	Water (%)	Energy (kcal)	Protein (g)	Fat (g)	Cholesterol	Iron (mg)	Vitamin A (IU)	Vitamin D (IU)	Thiamin (mg)	Riboflavin (mg)
Whole egg, large	1	50	76	72	6.28	4.76	186	0.88	270	41	0.02	0.22
Egg white	1	33	86	15	3.6	0	0	0.03	0	0	trace	0.145
Egg yolk	1	17	52	60	2.7	4.51	184	0.46	245	37	0.03	0.090

Source: U.S. Department of Agriculture (2012), National Nutrient Database for Standard Reference (Release 24). Washington, D.C.; U.S. Government Publishing Office.

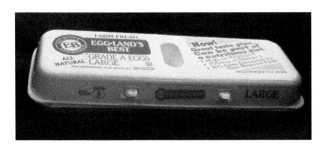

Figure 23-12

These Grade A large eggs marketed by Eggland are high in vitamin E and omega-3 fatty acids and have 25 percent less saturated fat than regular eggs. (U.S. Department of Agriculture)

The yolk is captured in the first part of the oviduct called the *infundibulum*, which is a 3–4 inch (7.62–10.16 cm) long funnel shaped tube [48, 15]. Commercial shell eggs are not fertilized, but if fertilized eggs are desired for hatching, the infundibulum is where fertilization occurs since it serves as the reservoir for sperm [58]. The egg remains in the *infundibulum* for about 14–15 minutes where there is formation of the *perivitelline membrane* (the transparent membrane that encloses the yolk) [48]. The forming egg then moves by peristaltic action to *magnum*, the second section of the oviduct, where the egg white albumen 40 proteins are produced. The egg remains in the 13–15 inch (33–38.1 cm) magnum, the longest part of the oviduct, for about three hours developing the thick white layer of albumen known as the egg white. The albumen surrounds the yolk acting as mechanical and bacterial protection for the yolk [48]. The albumen is about 67 percent of the egg weight [58]. The albumen contains more than half the egg proteins, niacin, riboflavin, magnesium, potassium, sodium, chloride, and sulfur [58]. The chalaziferous layer forms here. The *chalazae* (pronounced kah-lay-za) appears like two twisted membrane rope like structures that anchors the yolk from each end in the center of the egg [53].

The developing egg passes into the *isthmus* for the next 1.25 hours. The isthmus is the 4 inch (10.16 cm) constricted area of the oviduct. This is where the fibers develop for the inner and outer shell membrane. Keratin, like found in hair, is a shell membrane component. Some water and mineral salts are added at this stage. The first crystals of the shell begin; these are the mammillary core [49, 58]. The inner most shell membrane provides for the exchanges of gas and water. As the egg ages, the membranes separate forming the air sac cell.

The egg next enters the 4 inch (10.16 cm) *shell gland (uterus)* for the next 20 hours. In the shell gland, the egg undergoes a process called "plumping" for the next five hours. This is where water and electrolytes are added to the albumen and the formation of the mammillary core for the shell takes place. The mammillary core serves as the foundation for the shell development and is important in shell strength [51, 49]. The egg spends the next 15 hours in the egg gland pouch getting its shell [48]. In the shell gland, calcium deposits attach to the shell membrane forming interconnected calcium columns. The tiny holes left in the shell are called pores. There are approximately 17,000 tiny pores in an eggshell [58]. The eggshell is primarily made of about 2–2.5 grams of calcium carbonate crystals. At the end of the process, the shell receives its pigment or color, determined by the hen's breed. The hen adds a protective lipid coating called the *egg bloom* or *waxy cuticle* on the outside of the egg. The coating seals the shell pores and prevents bacteria from entering the shell and reduces moisture loss from the egg. The egg travels to the vagina (2 inch or 5.1 cm) and cloaca (the juncture for digestive, urinary, and reproductive systems) for oviposition known as egg laying. The newly formed shell egg exits via the *vent* located under the hen's tail. About 30 minutes later the hen will start to make another egg.

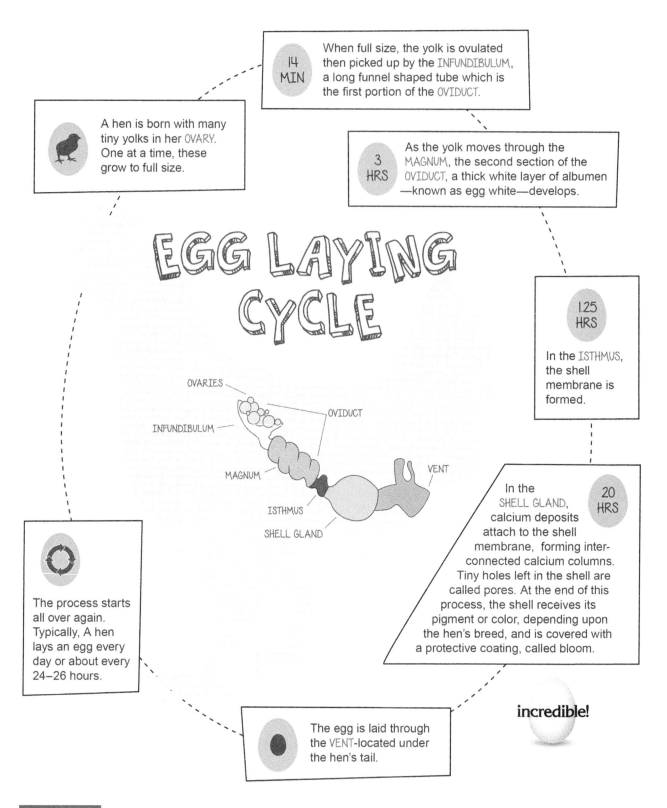

When full size, the yolk is ovulated then picked up by the INFUNDIBULUM, a long funnel shaped tube which is the first portion of the OVIDUCT.

14 MIN

A hen is born with many tiny yolks in her OVARY. One at a time, these grow to full size.

As the yolk moves through the MAGNUM, the second section of the OVIDUCT, a thick white layer of albumen —known as egg white—develops.

3 HRS

EGG LAYING CYCLE

OVARIES
OVIDUCT
INFUNDIBULUM
MAGNUM
ISTHMUS
SHELL GLAND
VENT

1.25 HRS

In the ISTHMUS, the shell membrane is formed.

The process starts all over again. Typically, A hen lays an egg every day or about every 24–26 hours.

In the SHELL GLAND, calcium deposits attach to the shell membrane, forming inter-connected calcium columns. Tiny holes left in the shell are called pores. At the end of this process, the shell receives its pigment or color, depending upon the hen's breed, and is covered with a protective coating, called bloom.

20 HRS

The egg is laid through the VENT-located under the hen's tail.

incredible!

Figure 23–13a

The hen's egg cycle takes about 24 hours. This illustration shows the cycle as it moves through the oviduct. (© American Egg Board)

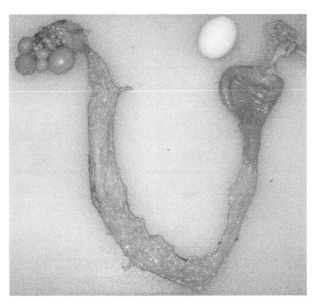

Figure 23–13b

The hen ovary and oviduct where the egg is produced. Each of the egg yolks clustered at the ovary will become an egg upon its release. (© Jacquiline Jacob)

The quality of the egg interior and shell are very important for the food industry. Temperature and conditions can allow bacteria to penetrate the egg defenses. Egg products must meet strict federal codes throughout processing (9 CFR 590) [58]. Egg quality issues can cost the industry millions of dollars and affect egg supplies. Eggshells must be strong to prevent breakage and hens must be supplied calcium carbonate in their feed to assure strong eggshells [48]. Shell eggs must be "clean and sound" free from leaks, cracks or dirt, and strong odors. Housing, conditions, health, stress, and feed all affect egg quality [48]. Rodent control is important as they can spread diseases such as *Salmonella*.

Shell color makes no difference in the nutritional quality of the egg. All color in the eggshells are applied in the shell gland after the yolk and white have been formed so nutrient content of egg is not affected by shell color. Eggshell pigment may be brown, rose, white, or blue to green. The breed of chicken determines the egg color. Araucana chickens lay the blue and green eggs. Brown eggshell contain protoporphyrin pigments and blue eggshell contain biliverdin pigments [73].

COMPOSITION

Whole egg contains about 75 percent water, 12 percent protein, 10 percent fat, 1 percent carbohydrate, and 1 percent minerals. The white and the yolk are very different from each other in composition, however, as shown in Table 23–1. Essentially all the fat of the egg is found in the yolk; the white contains a larger percentage of water. The shell makes up about

9 to 12 percent of the total weight of the egg and is composed of approximately 95 percent calcium carbonate in crystal form [45].

Although the ratio of white to yolk varies in individual eggs, the white is usually about two-thirds by weight of the total edible portion, and the yolk is approximately one-third. In general, the yolk has higher nutrient density than the white, containing more minerals and vitamins relative to its weight. The average egg weighs about 2 ounces (57 grams) of which the edible nutritive interior is about 50 grams [58].

Proteins

Egg proteins are of excellent nutritional quality, having the highest **protein efficiency ratio** of any of the common foods.

Egg Whites (Albumen). The major protein in egg white is *ovalbumin*, a protein that contributes to foaming. Ovalbumin is easily denatured by heat [3, 58]. The *ovomucin* gives the viscous gel properties to the white. Ovomucin, although present in a comparatively small amount, is a very large molecule with a filamentous or fiber-like nature. The ovomucin helps to give egg foams stability so they can retain shape of air cells [58]. Some of the other egg white proteins are *ovotransferrin* (also called *conalbumin*), *ovomucoid*, *ovomucin*, and *lysozyme*. Albumen pH of a newly laid egg is 7–8.5 and will gradually rise during storage due to the loss of carbon dioxide [53].

Egg Yolks. The major proteins in egg yolk are **lipoproteins**, which include *ovovitellin or lipovitellin* since it is associated in a lipoprotein complex. Also, in small amounts is the aqueous protein *ovolivetin*. *Ovovitellin* is about three-fourths of the yolk proteins. The lipoproteins are responsible for the emulsifying properties of egg yolk when used in such products as hollandaise sauce or mayonnaise. The preparation of mayonnaise was discussed in Chapter 8.

Lipids

The fat or lipids in egg yolk include triglycerides, phospholipids, and cholesterol and account for about one-third of the weight of fresh yolk. One large egg yolk contains about 186 milligrams of cholesterol; the egg white has no cholesterol [54]. Because of the high level of cholesterol in the yolk, the egg was at one time considered an **atherogenic** food, but that concept has changed. The fatty acid composition of egg yolk may be altered by changing the hen's diet. For example, an increased level of omega-3 fatty acids have been reported to result from the addition of small amounts of menhaden fish oil or special mixtures to the laying hen's diet [64]. Eggs have been introduced into consumer markets that have 175 milligrams of cholesterol per egg, 25 percent less saturated fat, and double the amount of omega-3 fatty acids as a result of a patented all-vegetarian feed program.

Pigments

Because certain yellow carotenoid pigments can be converted into vitamin A in the body, the question has been raised of whether more highly colored egg yolks are a better source of vitamin A than pale yolks. The predominant yellow pigment of egg yolk is a *xanthophyll*, which is not changed to vitamin A in the body. Deep-colored yolks, however, are high in vitamin A content because the same rations that produce color in the yolks also contain more provitamin A, which the hen converts into vitamin A and deposits in the yolk. Hens that do not have access to green or yellow feed and that produce pale yolks may be given vitamin A—supplemented rations. The pale yolks are then high in vitamin A. The vitamin A content of egg yolk, therefore, cannot be predicted solely based on the depth of the yellow color. In practice, egg producers usually feed chickens either green vegetation or xanthophyll pigments to yield a yolk of medium color intensity.

STRUCTURE

Eggshell

The eggshell is porous and allows exchange of gases and loss of moisture from the egg. It is brown or white, depending on the breed of the hen. The color of the shell has no effect on the flavor, quality, or nutritive value of the contents. An air cell formed at the large end of the egg is produced on cooling by the separation of two thin, fibrous protein membranes that are present between the shell and the egg white (**Figure 23–14**).

It has been suggested that the protective dull waxy coat on the outside of the egg, referred to as the *cuticle* or the *bloom*, should not be washed off. When eggs are washed, the porous shell may then more easily permit bacteria, molds, and undesirable flavors or odors to enter the egg. There also may be a greater evaporation of moisture from the egg. However, because dirt or soil on shells is probably the most prominent cause of the bacterial invasion of eggs, in commercial practice dirty eggs are washed. The eggs are usually washed in automatic washers using alkaline cleaning compounds. After washing, the eggs may be rinsed with a sanitizing agent. When eggs are washed properly, the undesirable effects of washing are kept at a minimum [27]. Then to replace

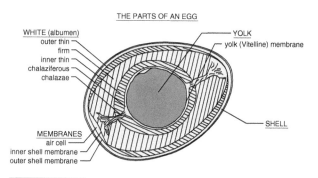

Figure 23–14

The parts of an egg.

the natural cuticle, some producers use edible mineral oil to coat the eggs before packaging [5].

Albumen, Chalazae, and Membranes

The albumen, usually called the *egg white*, consists of four layers of thin and thick portions [5]. The proportions of thin and thick white vary widely in different eggs and change during storage under varying conditions. It has been estimated that about 20 to 25 percent of the total white of fresh eggs (1 to 5 days old) is thin white. Thick white is characterized by a higher content of the protein ovomucin than is found in thin white [13].

Immediately adjacent to the *vitelline membrane*—the thin membrane that surrounds the egg yolk—is a *chalaziferous* or inner layer of firm white. This chalaziferous layer gives strength to the vitelline membrane and extends into the *chalazae*. The chalazae appear as two small bits of thickened white, one on each end of the yolk, and anchor the yolk in the center of the egg. Chalazae appear to have almost the same molecular structure as ovomucin [25]. Two more membranes are found in eggs. These membranes are called shell membranes and are found adjacent to the shell.

Yolk

The yolk is composed of tiny spheres of various sizes and shapes, closely packed in the vitelline membrane. Protein granules and oil droplets exist within the spheres [40]. Commercial eggs are usually infertile, and the germinal disc on the surface of the yolk does not develop. No difference in nutritive value is noted between infertile and fertilized eggs, but fertile eggs may tend to deteriorate more rapidly.

Occasionally, a blood spot may be found on a yolk. It is not because the egg has been fertilized but instead is the result of the blood vessel rupture on the surface of the yolk. Blood spots are primarily a cosmetic defect and thus are safe to eat. Meat spots are thought to be older blood spots or other sloughed-off tissue from the hen's reproductive organs. Blood and meat spots are found in less than 1 percent of eggs [58]. Sometimes a double yolk will appear in the egg. Other egg anomalies would be an egg with no yolk, an egg with no outer shell, an egg within an egg, or abnormally shaped or wrinkled egg.

EGG QUALITY AND SIZING

Physical Characteristics of Fresh and Deteriorated Eggs

Most eggs reach the stores only a few days after being laid and thus exhibit the characteristics of fresh eggs. A very fresh egg, when broken onto a flat plate, stands up in rounded form largely because of the viscosity of the thick portion of the egg white. Very fresh eggs may also exhibit a cloudy or milky-appearing white that is caused by dissolved carbon dioxide in the white shortly after laying [3].

As eggs age, quality deterioration is observable by (1) thinner whites, (2) a flatter yolk, (3) weaker chalazae, (4) a larger air cell, and (5) greater alkalinity. The proportion of thick white decreases in older eggs, resulting in mainly thin whites that allow an egg to spread significantly when broken from the shell. The thinning of the thick white appears to involve some changes in the filamentous protein ovomucin. Lysozyme also may be involved.

With aging, the yolk takes up water from the white, and the yolk membrane stretches. When broken out, the egg yolk does not stand high and round but instead is somewhat flattened. If the yolk membrane is stretched excessively by movement of water into the yolk, it may break when the egg is removed from the shell. Separation of the yolk from the white is thus difficult or impossible. The chalazae start to disintegrate and no longer hold the yolk in the center of the eggshell. As an egg ages, especially in a warm, dry atmosphere, moisture escapes through the shell. The air cell, which is very small in a fresh egg, increases in size.

The yolks of fresh eggs are slightly acid (pH 6.0–6.2), whereas the whites are alkaline (pH 7.6–7.9). A loss of carbon dioxide from the egg in storage results in increased alkalinity of both white and yolk. The white may eventually reach a pH of 9.0–9.7, which, among other changes, results in more transparent whites. This increase in pH or alkalinity of eggs during storage may be slowed to an appreciable degree by coating the eggshells with a thin layer of oil on the day the eggs are laid. It has been suggested that damage to some egg white proteins by a very alkaline pH results in angel food cakes of decreased volume [37]. These changes in eggs because of age are summarized in **Table 23–2**.

Flavor and Odor Deterioration

The flavor and odor of fresh eggs are affected by the feed, the individuality of the hen, and storage conditions. During storage, off-flavors may be produced in eggs by contamination with microorganisms or by the absorption of flavors from the environment. One study of the **headspace** over scrambled eggs reported the presence of 38 volatile substances, including alcohols, aldehydes, ketones, esters, benzene derivatives, and sulfur-containing compounds [36]. A comparison with the volatile compounds of polystyrene packaging materials, commonly used in egg cartons, suggested that some migration of volatile compounds from the packaging into the

Table 23–2
PHYSICAL CHANGES IN EGGS DUE TO INCREASING AGE

Component	High-Quality Fresh Eggs	Poor-Quality Older Eggs
Air cell	Small.	Larger.
Albumin (egg whites)	Egg whites adjacent to the yolk are noticeably thick. Whites of very fresh eggs may appear cloudy.	Egg white is thin, runny, and relatively transparent.
Yolk	Yolk stands high and round when broken out onto a plate.	Membrane around yolk weakens. Yolk appears more flattened when broken onto a plate.
Chalazae	Chalazae are strong and hold yolk in center of whites within the shell.	Chalazae weaken, and yolk is no longer "centered" in the shell.
pH	Slightly acidic yolks (pH 6.0–6.2). Alkaline egg whites (pH 7.6–7.9).	Increased alkalinity of whites and yolks (pH of 9.0–9.7).

eggs may have occurred during storage. Further studies of cooked egg flavors will be interesting and useful.

Purchasing Fresh Eggs

Consumers can gauge the freshness of eggs by the pack or expiration date on the egg carton. The "pack date" must be displayed on eggs cartons using the U.S. Department of Agriculture (USDA) grade shield [53]. The pack date is generally provided using the *Julian date*, which is a three-digit code representing the day of the year; thus, January 1 is 001, and December 31 is 365. Eggs may also provide an optional "exp" (expiration date) on the carton. According to the USDA, expiration dates may be no more than 45 days from the date of packing [53]. In general, properly refrigerated eggs should maintain good quality for 3 to 5 weeks after purchase or 4 to 5 weeks after the Julian date [5]. Some eggs are stamped with ink that must be approved by the USDA. The USDA grades are discussed later in the chapter.

Measuring Quality

Candling is the method used to determine the interior quality of eggs that go into trade channels. Hand candling, shown in **Figure 23–15**, is rarely used in present commercial grading operations, having been replaced by automated mass-scanning devices. Candling may still be used for spot-checking, however, and is useful for teaching and demonstrating quality determination or determining if an egg is fertile. When candling by hand, the egg is held to an opening behind which is a source of strong light. As the light passes through the egg, it shows the quality of the shell, the size of the air cell, the position and mobility of the yolk, blood spots, meat spots, molds, and a developing embryo, if one is present. As eggs deteriorate and the chalazae weaken, the yolk tends to settle toward the shell rather than remain suspended in the firm white. In such circumstances, the yolk is more fully visible when the egg is candled, in part because the yolk is no longer centered. Dark yolks also cast a

(a)

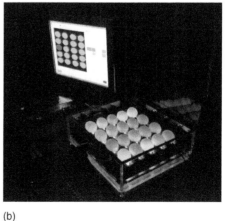

(b)

Figure 23–15

(a) Eggs are held to a bright light during hand candling. (b) Mass scanning devices speed candling process. (USDA)

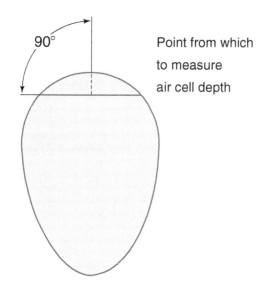

90°
Point from which
to measure
air cell depth

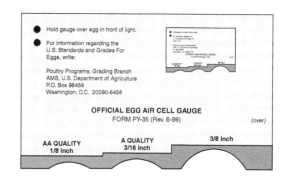

Figure 23–16

Official air cell gauge and method for measuring candled air cell depth. (USDA)

Figure 23–17

A micrometer is used to evaluate the quality of an egg that has been removed from the shell. This is done by measuring the height of the thick white. This instrument gives a direct reading in Haugh units. (U.S. Department of Agriculture)

more distinct shadow than light yolks. USDA grades for eggs are based on their candled appearance. In Grade AA eggs, the air cell is about $\frac{1}{8}$ inch in depth and the diameter of a dime. Grade A eggs may have an air cell up to $\frac{3}{16}$ inch (**Figure 23-16**) [53].

Although candling is the best method available for rating unbroken eggs, it may not always be reliable in indicating the quality of the egg when it is opened. Some tests done on the broken-out egg include measurement of the height of the thick white in relation to the weight of the egg (Haugh unit) and measurement of the height of

the yolk in relation to the width of the yolk (yolk index). **Figure 23–17** shows the operation of an instrument for measuring Haugh units in a broken-out egg.

Inspection and Grading

Egg inspection for wholesomeness is mandatory, but egg grading for quality is voluntary.

Inspection. The Egg Products Inspections Act (Chapter 15 Title 21 Code of Federal Regulations) was enacted in 1970 to protect public interest and consumer health, safety, and welfare. Eggs and egg products were recognized for being an important source of food and used in various forms in food. The act was to assure eggs and egg products are wholesome, unadulterated, and properly labelled and packaged. The act applies to eggs of domesticated chickens, turkey, duck, goose, or guinea.

In 2009, the U.S. Food and Drug Administration (FDA) implemented new "Egg Rule" regulations that require shell egg producers to implement measures to prevent *Salmonella enteritidis* (SE) from contamination on the farm, storage, and transportation. These FDA regulations known as Prevention of *Salmonella enteritidis* in Shell Eggs During Production, Storage and Transportation is codified at 21 CFR part 118 [16]. The section below on food safety and government regulations provides information in more details. States may have additional egg safety laws.

The USDA Shell egg surveillance program is part of the Agricultural Marketing Service (AMS) and the inspection for wholesomeness. Shell eggs sold to consumers can have no more restricted eggs than permitted in U.S. Consumer Grade C. Restricted eggs are ungraded eggs defined as eggs with cracks or checks in the shell, dirty eggs (dirties), incubator rejects, and inedible leaker or loss eggs. *Cracks* are breaks in the eggshell that goes through the shell and shell membranes. *Checks* are shell cracks that have not gone through the shell membrane. *Dirties* have dirt and conspicuous stains on more than one-fourth of the egg. *Inedibles* are moldy, musty, sour, rot, blood rings, green whites, stuck yolks, or embryo chicks. *Leakers* have a crack in both shell and shell membranes so that the contents are leaking. *Loss eggs* are leakers, "inedibles," and any eggs that have been cooked, frozen, or contaminated. *Incubator rejects* are unhatched eggs that have been incubated.

Only eggs designated "checks" and "dirties" may be sold or shipped to official USDA egg product processing plants for processing and pasteurization into egg products for human consumption. These processing plants are often referred to as "breakers" or "breaking plants" since they break the eggs and process and pasteurize these eggs. The Egg Products Inspection Act (EPIA) controls the disposition of restricted eggs to prevent them from being used by consumers as shell eggs.

Egg products are eggs that are removed from their shell for processing at breaking plant facilities. Egg product processing includes breaking eggs, filtering, mixing, stabilizing, blending, pasteurizing, cooling, freezing, or drying then packaging. USDA Food Safety and Inspection Service inspects all breaker processing plants; egg products must be wholesome. The FDA is responsible for inspection of egg substitutes, imitation eggs, and similar products. Egg products then processed and pasteurized include whole eggs, whites, yolks, and blends with or without non-egg ingredients such as salt.

Restricted eggs must be processed or destroyed; the eggs cannot be given away for free for human use. Products unfit for human consumption are the leakers, loss and inedible eggs may be processed into animal food, processed into industrial products or destroyed by intermingling with refuse and discarded. Incubator rejects, which were incubated eggs that did not hatch and cannot be removed from their shell, must be crushed or denatured and destroyed.

Grading. Eggs are graded for quality using standards developed by the USDA. These standards only apply to shell eggs that are products of domesticated chickens. The interior qualities are based on candling and occasional corroborating Haugh unit values from broken-out eggs [59]. These grading standards are summarized in **Table 23–3**.

In grading, the candled appearance of the eggshell, air cell, white, and yolk are considered. According to the results of the candling inspection, the eggs are assigned one of three consumer grades: U.S. Grade AA, U.S. Grade A, or U.S. Grade B. These grades are illustrated by photographs of broken-out eggs in **Figure 23–18a, b and c**, and the grade marks are shown in **Figure 23–19**.

Table 23–3
SUMMARY OF U.S. STANDARDS FOR QUALITY OF INDIVIDUAL SHELL EGGS BASED ON APPEARANCE OF CANDLED EGG

Quality Factor	AA Quality	A Quality	B Quality
Shell	Clean Unbroken Practically normal shape	Clean Unbroken Practically normal	Clean to slightly stained Unbroken Somewhat abnormal
Air cell	$1/8$ in. or less in depth Unlimited movement and free or bubbly	$3/16$ in. or less in depth Unlimited movement and free or bubbly	Over $3/16$ in. in depth Unlimited movement and free or bubbly
White	Clear Firm	Clear Reasonably firm	Weak and watery. Small ($1/8$ in. in diameter or smaller) blood and meal spots may be present. Small blood and meat spots may be present.
Yolk	Outline slightly defined Practically free from defects	Outline fairly well defined Practically free from defects	Outline plainly visible Enlarged and flattened Clearly visible germ development but no blood

Source: Reference 53.

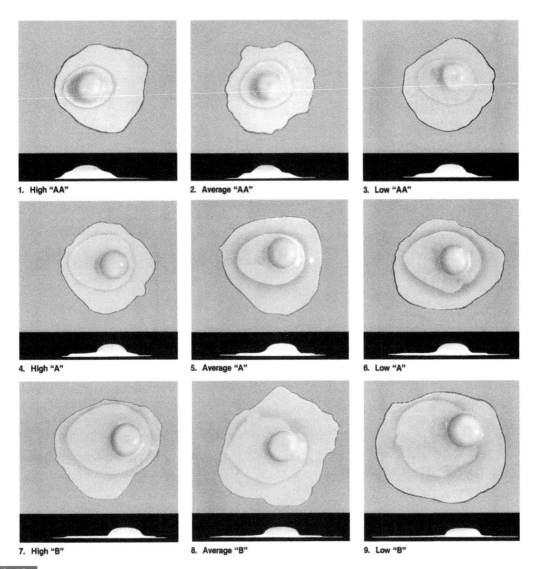

1. High "AA" 2. Average "AA" 3. Low "AA"
4. High "A" 5. Average "A" 6. Low "A"
7. High "B" 8. Average "B" 9. Low "B"

Figure 23–18a

Characteristics of egg quality, with the yolk standing highest on the thick white of the U.S. Grade AA eggs, are evident in broken-out eggs and in poached eggs. (U.S. Department of Agriculture)

Figure 23–18b

Wrinkled eggshell and irregular pigment shell coloring are grading defects. (© Amanda Frye)

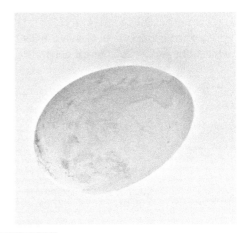

Figure 23–18c

Stained egg would be restricted egg. (© Amanda Frye)

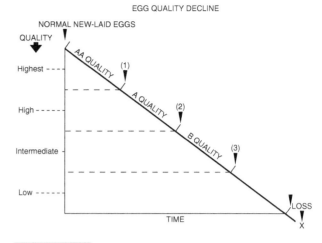

Figure 23–20

The graded quality of eggs declines with the time of holding. (U.S. Department of Agriculture)

Figure 23–19

Three grade marks for eggs graded under federal and state supervision. The marks show both grade and size. (U.S. Department of Agriculture)

Grades AA and A eggs have a large proportion of thick white that stands up around a firm, high yolk. These eggs are especially good for frying and poaching, when appearance is important. Grade B eggs have thin, runny whites but are acceptable for general baking and cooking. Grade B eggs are generally not found in retail stores. The nutritional value for all grades is similar.

Eggs must be held under refrigeration, preferably in a closed carton, to maintain quality. Storing eggs under refrigeration slows aging and bacterial growth. Keeping eggs in the carton reduces moisture loss and the absorption of odors. **Figure 23–20** indicates how egg quality decreases with the time of holding. With proper care, however, this decline in quality can be minimized.

Sizing

Separate from the process of grading, eggs are sorted for size into six weight classes, as shown in **Figure 23–21**. This separation is based on weighing individual eggs. The commercial weighing and packaging of eggs may be automated, as illustrated in **Figure 23–22**. Within each grade are several sizes usually available on supermarket shelves.

Size relative to cost per dozen is a factor to consider when buying eggs. Most eggs are sold in cartons, on which the minimum weight per dozen, in ounces, is usually listed. This weight can be divided into the price

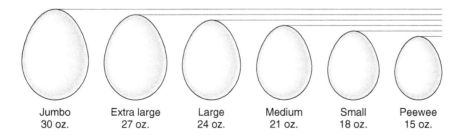

Jumbo 30 oz. · Extra large 27 oz. · Large 24 oz. · Medium 21 oz. · Small 18 oz. · Peewee 15 oz.

Figure 23–21

When purchasing eggs, you should be aware of both size (an indication of quantity) and grade (an indication of quality). There are six sizes shown. The weights shown in the illustrations represent ounces per dozen eggs. (*Source:* Reference 30)

Figure 23-22

Eggs are handled and weighed by automatic in-line scales. Eggs of different sizes are weighed and ejected from the line at different points. (U.S. Department of Agriculture)

per dozen to determine the cost per ounce of egg. The cost per ounce of each of the sizes of eggs can then be compared to determine which is the best buy. Minimum weight per dozen are Jumbo—30 ounces, Extra Large—27 ounces, Large—24 ounces, Medium—21 ounces, Small—18 ounces, and Peewee—15 ounces.

Another point to consider in buying eggs is the use for which they are purchased. Most recipes are standardized for large eggs. Recipes may need to be adjusted based on egg size. One large egg provides about 3 tablespoons with large egg white equal to 1 ounce or 2 tablespoon and one large egg yolk about ½ ounce or 1 tablespoon. Reduce the number of eggs by one-fourth to one-third if substituting jumbo and extra-large eggs. Alternatively, increase the number of eggs by one-fourth to one-third when substituting small and peewee eggs in a recipe. Calculation of egg quantity by weight is most accurate and is often used in recipes for commercial food services. For other uses of eggs, there is no one best size to buy. Medium or large eggs may be preferred for table use, but for other purposes, the price per ounce may be a more important consideration.

Commercial food service and food processors purchase eggs in large quantities. Detailed specifications for large volume of eggs will assure consistent product and quality. The USDA Agricultural Marketing Services have guidelines and regulations to assist volume buyers [63].

FOOD SAFETY OF EGGS

Unbroken shell eggs may contain *Salmonella* bacteria because of (1) infection of the chickens' reproductive system or (2) contamination on exterior of cell. *Salmonella enteritidis* may infect the reproductive system of laying hens, which then results in the contamination of the egg in advance of shell formation. These eggs are laid already contaminated with the organism inside the intact shell. Eggs also may become infected from pathogens carried in fecal and dirt contamination

on the shell exterior that then moves through the shell pores to the white and yolk [72]. Washing of eggs during processing and a light oil coating to seal the shell reduce this risk. However, because the interior of shell eggs without visible cracks may be contaminated with *Salmonella*, it is important to cook, handle, and consume eggs with this in mind. The consumption of raw eggs is not recommended unless they are pasteurized.

Government Regulation

The FDA and the USDA share federal responsibility for egg safety. A 1999 Egg Safety Action Plan developed by the FDA and the USDA Food Safety and Inspection Service (FSIS) seeks to reduce and eventually eliminate eggs as a source of *S. enteritidis*. In 2009, additional regulations took effect requiring egg producers to (1) acquire only *Salmonella*-free chickens, (2) refrigerate laid eggs within 36 hours, (3) conduct testing for *Salmonella* in poultry houses, and (4) establish rodent, pest control, and biosecurity controls [38]. Egg producers under 3,000 chickens or those who sell directly to the public are not covered by these regulations.

In 2000, the FDA finalized regulations to require safe food-handling instructions on cartons and new refrigeration requirements. Shell eggs are required to have the following statement: "Safe Handling Instructions: To prevent illness from bacteria: keep eggs refrigerated, cook eggs until yolks are firm, and cook foods containing eggs thoroughly." The refrigeration requirements, effective in 2001, specify that untreated shell eggs sold at stores, roadside stands, and so forth must be held and displayed at or below 45°F (7°C).

Federal, state, and local governments work with the egg industry and scientific community to improve egg safety and monitoring. Multiple agencies within the USDA cooperate with the FDA, local, and state governments to ensure a safe egg supply. The Center for Disease Control (CDC) tracks and monitors cases of foodborne illnesses. The egg industry and scientists work with government agencies to try to eliminate *Salmonella* in eggs through careful monitoring, inspections, research, better flock management guidance, plus better food handling protocol and laws.

The USDA FSIS, USDA Agricultural Marketing Service (AMS), USDA Agricultural Research Service (ARS), and USDA Animal and Plant Health Inspection Service (APHIS) work with the FDA, state, and local government agencies to ensure elimination of *Salmonella* in eggs and ensure safe shell eggs and egg products for the consumer. The USDA and FDA have overlapping jurisdiction on commercial egg and egg products. US Commerce Department ensures trucks only for food transport eggs and egg products through the 1990 Sanitary Food Transportation Act.

Processing and Storage Considerations

If *Salmonella* are present in an egg, the bacteria count would likely be small at the time of laying and would probably not create a problem if the egg was eaten immediately. *Salmonella,* however, can grow rapidly if the eggs are warm at any place along the production line from the hen to the consumer. One bacterium can multiply to more than one million in six hours, which is why eggs should always be properly refrigerated.

A cryogenic system of cooling eggs has been developed to cool eggs quickly from the "just-laid" temperature of 110°F (43°C) down to 45°F (7°C) in 80 to 90 seconds [38]. Eggs are conveyed into a cooling tunnel in which liquid CO_2 is piped, creating a vapor–snow mixture that rapidly chills the eggs. Eggs can take as long as 7 to 14 days to cool from 110°F (43°C) to 45°F (7°C) under normal processing and packaging conditions. Quickly cooled eggs are fresher, and microbial testing has shown lower levels of *S. enteritidis.* Rapid cooling with CO_2 has also been shown to maintain Grade AA quality for up to 12 weeks [9].

Shell Egg Pasteurization

According to USDA FSIS calculations, pasteurization of shell eggs in the United States could reduce egg-related illness by 85 percent [18, 44]. Under 3 percent of the 74 billion fresh commercial shell eggs are currently pasteurized [18, 44]. A new egg pasteurization technology has been developed using radio frequency (RF) waves to kill *Salmonella* and other pathogens without damaging egg whites [44]. This new patented device using radio frequency energy to heat eggs and kill the *Salmonella* while ensuring the yolk gets more heat than albumen [44] (**Figure 23–23**). The two-step process involves using hot water and radio frequency energy to pasteurize eggs in under 30 minutes, which kills *E. coli* in eggs too [18]. Eggs are connected to electrodes then immersed in warm water and heated with RF for 3.5 minutes. The eggs are rotated during processing to prevent hot spots and ensure even heating. The eggs then are placed in a hot water bath to give yolks additional processing time. This RF treatment reduces pathogen level by 99.999 percent in 23 minutes [44]. The process provides a fast and low-cost solution to pasteurize shell eggs.

Shell egg pasteurization by hot water immersion takes about an hour and add $1.50 to retail price per dozen eggs [44]. The process controls time and temperature (130–140°F) to result in a **5-log reduction** in *Salmonella* [39]. However, the hot-water immersion pasteurization also can have detrimental effects on egg white proteins causing proteins to denature and coagulate [44].

Microwave energy has been used to pasteurize eggs in South Africa [18, 68]. The microwave shell egg pasteurization takes about 30 to 40 minutes. Some

Figure 23–23

USDA Agricultural Research Service chemical engineer David Geveke and colleagues developed radio frequency equipment to kill *Salmonella* and *E. coli* in fresh eggs. (USDA/ARS Photo by Joseph Sites)

changes occur in egg white protein along with decreased whipping ability [18, 68]. In South Africa, the pasteurized shell eggs are marketed as "Safe Eggs" [68].

High hydrostatic pressure (HHP) processing is being studied as a potential treatment to eliminate egg contamination [42]. A high-moisture and hot-air method of pasteurization is also being studied. Both methods maintain the desirable characteristics of shell eggs, including the whippability of the white. In 2000, the FDA approved use of ionizing radiation on eggs in the shell to reduce *Salmonella*. Although irradiation is effective, the white may become slightly opaque and lose some of the whipping ability [39].

Purchasing and Storage Recommendations

Buy eggs at retail from refrigerated cases only; for food service, use only eggs delivered under refrigeration. Buy clean eggs with uncracked shells. Refrigerate eggs immediately, in cartons or cases, at 40–45°F (4.4–7°C) or slightly below. Do not wash eggs unless they are to be used immediately. Use shell eggs within 3 to 5 weeks. Shell eggs do not freeze well, but if eggs are accidently frozen, thaw and use immediately. Raw egg whites and yolks should be used within 2 to 4 days. Frozen egg whites will keep for up to 12 months. Raw egg yolks do not freeze well. Leftover egg dishes should be stored in small enough containers so cooling down to 40°F (4°C) is rapid and used within 3 to 4 days. Hard-cooked eggs should be stored for no longer than one week. Quiche, pumpkin, or custard-based pies should be refrigerated and used within 3 to 4 days. See Chapter 2 for more about recommended cooling procedures for foods.

Backyard chickens are popular, but strict guidelines should be followed for home use of eggs. Eggs should be picked up at least twice a day. Cracked eggs should be discarded. Eggs should be refrigerated immediately. Any dirty eggs should be cleaned or discarded. Wash hands after handling eggs. Housing conditions should be clean. County extension agents and other government agencies should be able to provide more information.

Handling and Preparation Recommendations

Procedure to Break Eggs. Wash hands, utensils, equipment, and work surfaces before or after contact with eggs. Use only clean fresh eggs. Discard any cracked, checked, or leaking eggs. Individually break each egg into small custard cup, ramekin, or bowl then transfer to bowl or cooking vessel. To break egg, take egg in hand and hit the center of the egg firmly on the edge of a clean counter to cause a cracked area in the middle of the egg. Using your thumbs separate the cracked eggshell to open the egg up (**Figure 23–24**). The egg contents are carefully emptied into the bowl or ramekin trying not to break the yolk. Inspect the egg; remove blood spots, meat spots, or eggshell fragments with spoon. Do not contaminate egg with exterior shell since the shell is a source of contaminants. Each egg should be broken individually then cooked or combined with other eggs or ingredients. Breaking eggs individually allows removing any undesirable eggs or components without contaminating other eggs or ingredients. Eggs can be separated by cracking and allowing the egg white to be poured into a small ramekin or bowl while not puncturing egg yolk and contaminating egg white as shown in **Figure 23–25**. Discard shells. Wash hands, utensils, counter tops, and other surfaces in which egg may have come in contact to avoid cross-contamination. Utensils and work surface may be sanitized with bleach solution.

Egg Storage. Store eggs in refrigerator at 40–45°F (4.4–7°C). Never store eggs at room temperature. Store shell eggs in their case. Store eggs away from foods with strong odors such as onions, cabbage, garlic, fish, etc. Do not keep eggs out of the refrigerator for more than two hours since they start "sweating" which can spread any shell contaminants to the inside of the egg. Break only the number of eggs that are needed to accommodate the cooking or baking need. Quickly refrigerate or dispose of unused egg portions. Shelled liquid eggs not used immediately should be refrigerated at 40°F (4.4°C) or below and used within eight hours. Do not add shelled liquid egg to containers broken on a different day. Cooked eggs for a picnic should be packed in a cooler with enough ice to keep cool.

Raw and Cooked Eggs. Do not eat raw eggs, including foods such as milkshakes, smoothies, Caesar salad, ice cream, or eggnog made from recipes in

Figure 23–24

Breaking egg with thumbs placed on each side of the crack and pulling shell apart to release egg. (Paul Cowan/ Shutterstock)

Figure 23–25

Carefully separating white and yolk. Must keep yolk whole to avoid contamination of egg whites. (Iva/Shutterstock)

which the raw egg ingredients are not cooked. Foods such as ice cream and eggnog should be prepared from a cooked base heated to 160°F (71°C). Prepare other foods, such as Caesar salad, with pasteurized or irradiated eggs or precook the egg, yolk, or white, as described in **Table 23–4**.

Cook eggs slowly over moderate or medium heat to avoid shrinking and toughening proteins. An end-point cooking temperature of 145°F (57°C) is acceptable for eggs that will be immediately consumed. In general, cook at least until the whites are completely coagulated and the yolks are firm. Scrambled eggs should not be runny. Cook eggs in small batches. Those especially at risk, such as infants, pregnant women, immunocompromised, the elderly, or the

Table 23–4
COOKING OF WHOLE EGG, EGG YOLKS, OR EGG WHITES FOR USE IN RECIPES CALLING FOR RAW OR LIGHTLY COOKED EGGS

Egg Type	Cooking Instructions
Whole	Mix one whole egg with at least ¼ cup of the sugar, or liquid in the recipe. Cook over low heat while stirring constantly to cook until 160°F (71°C). Place pan in ice water and stir until cool. Continue with recipe to be prepared. **Recipes:** Eggnog, ice cream, or others
Yolk	Mix together one egg yolk with at least 2 tablespoons of the liquid in the recipe. Cook over low heat while stirring constantly to cook until 160°F (71°C). Place pan in ice water and stir until cool. Continue with recipe to be prepared. **Recipes:** Hollandaise sauce, Caesar salad dressing, chilled soufflés, mousses, and others
Egg white	Mix together the two egg whites with (a) at least 4 tablespoons of sugar, (b) 2 teaspoon water, and (c) 1/8 teaspoon cream of tartar. Cook over low heat or a double boiler while beating with a mixer. Cook until the whites reach 160°F (71°C). Continue to beat until soft peaks and then proceed with recipe. **Recipes:** Icing recipes calling for raw egg white

Note: Ingredient amounts are given for one or two eggs. Increase as needed for recipes.
Source: Reference 6.

ill, should avoid eating soft-cooked or runny eggs. Pasteurized shell eggs or egg products should be used for these individuals at a high risk for foodborne illness. In food service, only pasteurized eggs must be used in dishes such as scrambled eggs if a large number of eggs will be **pooled** and cooked.

Never leave eggs at room temperature including preparation and service for more than one hour. For buffet lines and institutional food service operations cooked eggs should be held at 140°F (60°C) or higher for no longer than 30 minutes. Always use fresh steam table pan when changing egg pans. Do not combine eggs that have been held in steam table pans with a fresh batch of eggs.

Casseroles and other dishes containing eggs should be cooked to 160°F (71°C) and checked by thermometer. Divinity candy and 7-minute frosting are safe when prepared by combining hot sugar syrup with the beaten egg whites. Meringue-topped pies should be prepared by placing the meringue on a hot filling and baking at 350°F (177°C) for about 15 minutes until an internal temperature of 160°F (71°C) is obtained. Cooked eggs and egg-rich foods, such as custards, puddings, and pumpkin pie, should be served immediately after cooking or refrigerated at once for use within 3 to 4 days.

PRESERVATION AND PROCESSING

Processed Egg Products

"Egg products" is the name for eggs that are removed from their shells for processing at USDA-inspected facilities called "breaker plants." Liquid eggs, frozen eggs, and dried eggs in various forms are processed and pasteurized into various egg products. Commercial egg drying started in 1880, frozen whole eggs in 1903, and separated eggs in 1912. The first commercial egg breaking machines were used in 1951. Egg products are convenient and easy to store and handle with a higher level of food-safety assurance because of pasteurization.

Egg breaking, separation, and pasteurization in preparation for freezing or drying are done by egg-processing plants. After washing and candling, the eggs go to egg-breaking machines. Completely automated equipment processes the eggs, removing them from filler flats, washing and sanitizing the outside shells, and breaking and separating the eggs into white, yolks, and mixture of white and yolk. The liquid egg product is then filtered and chilled before further processing. Scrupulous cleanliness must be maintained throughout the process. All egg products are monitored for pathogenic organisms, and tests for *Salmonella* are made regularly by the egg products industry and the USDA. Only products negative for *Salmonella* organisms can be sold.

Pasteurized. Pasteurization involves the application of heat to destroy pathogenic microorganisms. It is required by the federal government for all processed eggs, whether frozen, dried, or liquid. Egg pasteurization is a way to kill bacteria while maintaining the functional properties (whipping and baking performances) of the eggs [28]. The USDA regulates the minimum temperature and holding time for the pasteurization of egg products. A summary of pasteurization temperatures is provided in **Table 23–5**.

Table 23–5
PASTEURIZATION TEMPERATURES FOR EGG WHITES, YOLKS, AND WHOLE EGGS

Type of Egg Product	Pasteurization Temperatures and Conditions
Liquid whole egg	140°F (60°C) for not less than 3½ minutes
	Note: Whole egg blends must be heated to a higher temperature.
Egg whites	134°F (57°C) for 3.5 minutes or 132°F for 6.2 minutes (without addition of acid)
	Note: Egg whites become denatured with a loss of foaming ability when pasteurized at temperatures used for whole eggs. Increasing acidity of the whites before pasteurization reduces denaturation.
Egg yolks	140°F (60°C) for 6.2 minutes or 142°F for 3.5 minutes
	Note: The pasteurization temperatures for egg yolks with sugar or with salt added are slightly different.

Source: Reference 12.

Frozen. Many different types of egg products are frozen for use by consumers and food services. The functional properties of raw egg whites are not altered by freezing and thawing. However, frozen egg yolks become viscous and gummy on thawing unless they are mixed with sugar, salt, or syrup before freezing. (See Chapter 28 for directions on freezing eggs at home.) It has been suggested that the freezing process destabilizes the surface of the tiny lipid-protein particles (lipoproteins) in egg yolk. The fragments that are liberated then aggregate on thawing to form a mesh-type structure or gel [29]. Whole mixed eggs are often frozen without added salt or sugar but may retain their culinary qualities better when a stabilizer is added. Cooked egg white is not stable to freezing and thawing. The gel structure of the coagulated protein is damaged by ice crystal formation, and **syneresis** occurs on thawing.

Egg-processing firms design and produce several specialty egg products, many of which are frozen. Hard-cooked, chopped, and peeled eggs are used for salad bars. Frozen or refrigerated hard-cooked egg rolls, or *long eggs*, offer the advantage of providing consistently sized sliced eggs for salad garnishes. To make these long eggs, albumen is cooked around a center core of egg yolk that may be approximately 10 inches in length, thus the name. Frozen, precooked products, such as egg patties, fried eggs, crêpes, omelets, French toast, quiche, and egg breakfast sandwiches, are also available in grocery stores and for food service use.

Dried. Muffin and cake mixes that need only water added usually contain dried eggs. Drying is a satisfactory method for preserving eggs, either whole or as separated yolks or whites. Spray-dried egg whites and egg yolks have long shelf lives and are used in many food product formulations. To retain their functional properties, good color, and flavor and to help control the **Maillard reaction** during storage, dried whites require treatment to remove the last traces of glucose. Dried eggs keep best if the initial moisture content is low and if they are kept in a tightly sealed container. Low storage temperatures are also important in maintaining the quality of the dried products.

USDA Dried Egg Mix was developed for the militaries during the 1930s and is distributed through food banks, Indian reservations, and disaster feedings. USDA Dried Egg Mix is a blend of dried egg, nonfat dried milk, soybean oil, and salt. This can be reconstituted by blending 2 tablespoons of dried egg mix with ¼ cup of water to make the equivalent of one egg. A similar product is USDA All Purpose Egg Mix with a greater proportion of eggs and is reconstituted with one part egg mix and two parts water. All Purpose Egg Mix is available to schools for the school lunch and breakfast programs.

Dried eggs can be reconstituted before use, or they can be sifted with dry ingredients prior to adding the liquid ingredients. Dried whites, reconstituted with water, are beaten very stiff for most, if not all, uses. Dried egg whites are commonly found in angel food cake mixes.

Liquid. Liquid eggs, broken out of the shell, are available to food service operators and food processors as whole eggs, egg whites, egg yolks, or blended egg products, such as scrambled egg mix. Liquid refrigerated egg products offer advantages for use in food service operations and food-processing facilities. They may be easily poured, the need for thawing is eliminated, functional properties and quality are maintained, there is no need to dispose of eggshells, and they are pasteurized. Furthermore, quantity food service operations would not be able to serve menu items such as scrambled eggs without the use of pasteurized egg products because food-safety regulations prohibit the pooling of shell eggs in quantity.

Liquid refrigerated eggs are pasteurized, so any *Salmonella* or other pathogenic organisms that could be present are destroyed. However, the product is not sterile and thus must be stored under refrigeration

HOT TOPICS
CAGE-FREE, CAGED, FREE-RANGE EGGS—WHAT DOES IT MEAN?

How chickens are housed has become an important consideration for some consumers and businesses that use eggs. Eggs may be identified by one of the following descriptions, each with its own pros and cons:

- *Conventional.* Hens live in cages with access to feed and water in small groups. Some are concerned about limited space per hen, whereas others point out that the birds may be carefully monitored for health. Eggs are potentially cleaner because of the egg collection and manure management systems.

- *Free-Range.* Hens live in large "barns" with access to the outside. Hens have floor space, nesting space, and perches. Proponents believe that it is a better environment for the hens. Others point out that the hens may experience greater stress living in large social groups where pecking and other bullying behaviors may occur.

Furthermore, litter and manure management in this housing may result in more dust, which has negative health implications for the birds and the employees.

- *Cage-Free.* Hens live under circumstances similar to free-range hens. Cage-free hens may or may not have access to the outdoors.

- *Organic.* Organic eggs are from hens fed rations that meet the USDA organic guidelines.

- *Enriched Colony.* This housing system is American Human Certified. Hens have perch space, can dust bathe, and have scratch areas and nest space. Birds are housed in colonies instead of small or very large (10,000 hens) groups prevalent in other housing systems. ■

Source: Reference 4.

FOCUS ON SCIENCE
WHAT IS A 5-LOG REDUCTION?

At present, FDA regulations cover the pasteurization of eggs, milk, juice, and seafood. In all cases, FDA talks of achieving zero pathogen levels through pasteurization. In practice, what is meant by "zero pathogen level" or "destruction or elimination" of a "[heat resistant] microorganism" is reducing the offending pathogenic microorganism by at least five orders of magnitude, for example, a 100,000-fold reduction, also known as 5-log reduction.

and used or discarded by the "use by" or expiration dates. An ultra-pasteurization process, with heating to 154°F (68°C) and subsequent aseptic packaging, has been developed for homogenized liquid whole eggs [10, 19]. These products must be refrigerated but have an extended shelf life of 6 to 7 weeks [12].

Egg Substitutes
The food industry has responded to the desire of some consumers to have a low-cholesterol egg product by marketing egg substitutes in both liquid and dry forms. Most of the available egg substitute products contain no egg yolk, but have a high concentration of egg white (over 80 percent). To provide yolk-like properties to the egg white mixture, various ingredients are used. These include, in different products, corn oil and nonfat dry milk; soy protein isolate, soybean oil, and egg white solids; and calcium caseinate, nonfat dry milk, and corn oil. A few products on the market contain small amounts of egg yolk. Because egg

substitutes often use vegetable oils to replace the yolk, they contain (1) little, if any, cholesterol, (2) less fat overall, and (3) less saturated fat.

When compared with fresh whole eggs, egg substitutes may have somewhat less desirable flavor, aroma, and overall acceptability [17]. Custards made from egg substitute products have been reported to have less sag and spread than those made with whole eggs. One study found that custards prepared with nonfat, lactose-reduced milk produced less desirable custards when made with egg substitutes as compared to whole eggs [71]. Yellow cakes prepared with egg substitutes were higher in volume than those made with whole eggs, but were less desirable in flavor and overall acceptability.

Commercial Cold Storage
In the past, some eggs produced in the United States were placed in commercial cold storage during periods of higher production. Eggs were stored at 29–32°F (−1.5–0°C), which is just above their

freezing point. Only eggs of original high quality were stored. These eggs remained in desirable condition when the storage room was well controlled for humidity (85–90 percent), circulation of air, and freedom from objectionable odors. A controlled atmosphere of carbon dioxide or ozone was advantageous in maintaining quality. Eggs stored under these conditions could be maintained at Grade A quality for as long as six months. However, extended commercial cold storage is rarely used today because modern breeding and flock management have virtually eliminated seasonal differences in production [5].

COAGULATION OF EGG PROTEINS

Heat Coagulation of Egg Proteins

Both egg white and yolk proteins coagulate when heated and can therefore be used for thickening or gel formation. On heating, the egg proteins are **denatured** and then gradually aggregate to form a three-dimensional gel network. Protein denaturation involves breaking hydrogen bonds, unfolding the protein structure, and exposing the reactive groups such as –SH sulfhydryl groups. Denatured proteins interact to form physical and chemical bonds. The network is stabilized by cross bonds that include **disulfide linkages** and hydrogen bonding [35]. Egg white proteins are more sensitive to heat than egg yolk proteins. Egg whites begin coagulation at 140°F (60°C) and the yolk coagulate near 149°F (65°C). Heating egg proteins beyond this point shrinks and toughens proteins. When egg proteins are diluted or are mixed with sugar, the protein coagulation temperature is raised. The denaturation of proteins is important in food products such as cakes, custards, puddings, etc. Egg yolk proteins and lipoproteins are denatured

starting 140°F (60°C). There is increased viscosity due to protein–lipoprotein complexes.

Egg functions best as a thickener when it is beaten only enough to blend the egg smoothly. If too much air is incorporated during beating, the egg foam may float on the surface of the mixture to be thickened. The following factors affect the heat coagulation of egg proteins.

Concentration and Part of Egg Used. The temperature at which egg proteins coagulate and the time required for coagulation depend in part on the proportion of egg in any mixture (**Table 23–6**). Coagulation does not occur instantaneously but rather proceeds gradually. Egg yolk proteins require a slightly higher temperature for coagulation than those of egg white. Egg white loses its transparency and becomes opaque white on coagulation. Because little color change occurs in egg yolk at the beginning of coagulation, the exact temperature at which thickening starts is more difficult to judge than is the case with egg white. Dilution of egg with an ingredient such as milk increases the temperature at which coagulation occurs.

The texture of coagulated egg yolk, when cooked intact, is crumbly and mealy but solid. When the yolk membrane is ruptured and the stirred yolk is heated, however, the texture of the resulting gel is firm and rubbery. This difference in texture of intact and stirred egg yolk may result from changes that occur in the intricate microstructure of egg yolk with stirring. The tiny discrete granules of the intact yolk may form a highly cross-linked protein network when disrupted [70].

Time and Temperature. The rate and amount of coagulation within a given time period will increase with increasing temperature. The character

---

Table 23–6
COAGULATION TEMPERATURE OF EGG PROTEINS IN EGG WHITES, YOLK, WHOLE EGGS, AND EGG MIXTURES

Portion of the Egg	Temperature Range for Coagulation
Egg white, undiluted	140°F (60°C)—Coagulation begins, and whites begin to become opaque
	158°F (70°C)—Whites are coagulated and fairly firm
Egg yolk, undiluted	149°F (65°C)—Beginning of coagulation
	158°F (70°C)—Yolk loses its fluidity
One whole egg, diluted with 1 cup of milk	176°F (80°C)—Approximate temperature of coagulation
	Temperature for coagulation of diluted eggs will vary with the amount of dilution and whether other ingredients are included.

of the coagulum formed when egg white is heated at high temperatures is firm, even tough, compared with the soft, tender, more evenly coagulated product obtained when coagulation takes place at lower temperatures.

The toughness and greater shrinkage of the protein coagulated at a high temperature are the basis for the recommended use of low or moderate temperatures for egg cookery. The temperatures used need not be as low as 158°F (70°C), although that temperature, maintained for a sufficient length of time, eventually brings about complete coagulation of egg proteins. If eggs are cooked in water, the water should not boil. Water at a temperature of about 185°F (85°C) will produce a texture that is tender yet firm. Oven temperatures from 300°F to 350°F (149–177°C) have been found to be satisfactory for cooking eggs and egg dishes, although there are indications that somewhat higher temperatures also are satisfactory if time is carefully controlled. Placing egg dishes, such as custard, in a pan of water when baking in an oven will help to protect the egg product from becoming overcooked.

Effect of Rate of Heating. Rapidly heated egg mixtures such as custards coagulate at a higher temperature than similar mixtures that are slowly heated. The fact that the coagulation temperature with rapid heating is very close to the curdling temperature means that a rapidly cooked custard is more likely to curdle than one that is slowly heated. A slowly heated custard can, nevertheless, curdle if it is heated to a temperature that is too high.

Effect of Added Substances. Sugar, acids, and salts have an impact on the coagulation of eggs. Egg mixtures containing sugar coagulate at a higher temperature. Sugar affects the temperature of coagulation by increasing the heat stability of the proteins. Custards are a typical egg dish that is sweetened. In contrast, slightly acidic whole egg mixtures coagulate more quickly at a lower temperature. Examples of acidic egg mixtures include those with added dates or raisins, omelets made with tomato or orange juice, and hollandaise sauce containing lemon juice. The coagulum formed in an acidic egg mixture is also firmer than that of less acidic mixtures. The hardness and cohesiveness of egg white gels have been reported to be minimal at pH 6 and increased as the pH was either decreased to 5 or increased to 9 [69]. Too much acid in egg mixtures may cause curdling. Salts, such as chlorides, phosphates, sulfates, and lactates, promote coagulation or gel formation in cooked egg mixtures.

Coagulation by Mechanical Beating and Egg Foams
Whole eggs, egg whites, and egg yolks may be beaten to form a foam. Of these, egg whites increase in volume significantly. Egg whites will increase six to eight times in volume as compared to egg yolks, which may double or triple [3]. A small increase in volume is evident with beaten whole eggs.

Egg White Proteins in Foam Formation
Egg whites have excellent foaming capacity. The egg white (albumen) proteins are responsible for the ability to surround air bubbles and stabilize the bubbles in the foam network. Egg whites are a mixture of proteins and each protein plays a different role in foam formation and stability. The globulin proteins are thought to be responsible for the high foamability acting at the air bubble interface. The ovomucoids and globulins increase viscosity and slow foam drainage. The lysozymes and ovomucins act to give strength to the protein film around the air bubbles [32].

Proteins unfold and surround air cells as a viscoelastic film around the bubbles [65]. The first step in egg foam formation involves the protein rapidly adsorbed at the hydrophobic surface of the air bubble [33]. The protein content and whipping time affect foam bubble size and density of air bubbles with more proteins unfolding on the air bubble surface as whipping time increases [32]. Egg white protein ovalbumin contains four sulfhydryl groups –SH which are located internally in the folded protein structures [33]. Egg white protein unfolding exposes these groups allowing for S–S disulfide linkages to form. The protein unfolding is increased with moderate lowering of pH. Lowering pH also increases egg albumen hydrophobicity resulting in better foaming properties. There is improved egg white protein ovomucin foaming stability with weak acid treatment and decreased pH around 5 [50]. Cream of tartar is often used to decrease pH in egg white foams such as angel food.

Egg white pasteurization has been found to have a positive effect on egg white foams [65] probably due to partial unfolding of egg proteins. Moderate spray drying of egg whites also increases egg white foaming and stability [7]. Egg albumen foaming properties are a complex interaction of hydrophobicity, protein unfolding exposing sulfhydryl (–SH) groups, and disulfide interaction (S–S) to give increased foaming capacity and stability [65]. Good egg white foaming properties rely on protein migrating to the bubble air water interface, unfolding then rearranging to form a stable foam [50].

Egg yolk contamination of egg whites with yolk decrease foaming capacity and are detrimental to foam formation [65]. Even a small amount of egg yolk contamination has adverse effects on egg white foams. One drop of egg yolk in 30 ml of egg white decreases foaming capacity [65]. Egg yolk contamination is not only an issue with the home cook, but also egg product processors. Heating and shearing forces during egg white processing are not responsible for decreased foaming capacity, but yolk contamination has the most significant impact on egg white foam production in processed egg white products [65].

Egg White Foam. Egg white foams are a conversion of the green tinged translucent viscous liquid egg white into a voluminous stiff white opaque foam. As egg whites are beaten, they first become foamy and then form soft moist peaks. With additional beating, the peaks become stiffer. Eventually, with overbeating, the foam becomes dry and may appear to be **flocculated (Figure 23–26)**. Part of the protein in the thin films surrounding each of the air bubbles or cells that make up the structure of a beaten egg white foam is coagulated in the beating process. This provides some rigidity and stabilizes the foam. If the protein becomes overcoagulated, however, the foam takes on a dry, lumpy appearance because of loss of flexibility in the films and the breaking of many air cells. Undesirable effects on both foam volume and stability can be expected when whites are overbeaten. Overbeaten egg whites are brittle and inelastic and will not blend well with other ingredients. On standing, liquid will separate from the foam.

Egg whites, beaten to form moderately stiff peaks, are used in many dishes, such as soufflés, soft meringues, puffy omelets, and angel food cakes. When a beater is withdrawn from the beaten whites and the tips fall over, the egg whites are described as moderately stiff. The foam should retain a shiny, smooth surface, and the mass should flow very slowly if the bowl is partially inverted. Air cells should be quite fine and of even size. Reconstituted dried egg whites, such as those in angel food cake mixes using a two-stage mixing method, are beaten to a very stiff stage, as indicated in the package directions. Stiff peaks will remain standing tall when the beater is removed from the beaten whites. More about egg white foams is discussed in Angel Cakes in Chapter 16.

Other Factors Affecting Egg Foams. The freshness of eggs and temperature, as well as the type of beater and bowl, will affect the whipping quality of eggs.

Thin and Thick Whites. The foam produced from the beating of thin whites is more fluffy and has less body than the foam created from thick, viscous whites.

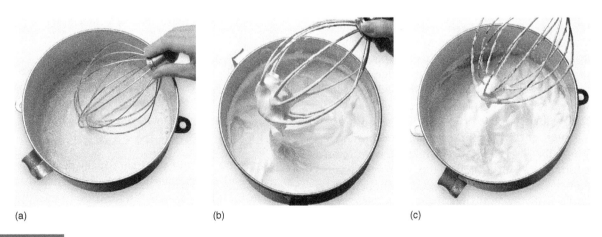

(a)   (b)   (c)

Figure 23–26

(a) Eggs properly whipped to soft peaks. (b) Eggs properly whipped to stiff peaks. (c) Spongy, overwhipped eggs. (Richard Embery/ Pearson Education)

Thick whites seem to produce a more stable foam even though thin whites may initially beat to a larger volume. The volume of cooked products, such as angel food cake and meringues, is greater when thick whites are used rather than thin whites. Thus, fresher eggs are preferable when beating egg whites to produce a foam.

Temperature. Eggs at room temperature whip more easily and quickly and to a larger volume than eggs at refrigerator temperature. This may be due to the lower **surface tension** at air–water interface at room temperature. Thus, eggs should be removed from the refrigerator before beating or warmed to room temperature in a bowl of warm water.

Type of Beater Used. The type of beater used and the fineness of the wires or blades of the beater can affect the size of the air cells that are obtained and the ease with which the eggs are beaten. Thick blades or wires do not divide egg whites as easily as fine wires, and the resulting air cells are therefore larger. All cells become smaller with longer beating regardless of the type of beater used.

Type of Container in Which Eggs Are Beaten. Bowls with small rounded bottoms and sloping sides are preferable if using a mixer or eggbeater so that the beater can pick up and beat the eggs. The size of the bowl must obviously be adapted to the amount of egg to be beaten. If a whisk is used for hand beating of egg whites, a large, wide bowl will allow rapid, vigorous whipping. Some chefs will use copper bowls to beat egg white foams. Egg whites beaten in a copper bowl have increased resistance to foam breakdown due to a copper–conalbumin complex [11].

Effect of Added Substances. Fat, salt, acid, and sugar will affect egg foams by interfering with whipping, decreasing volume, increasing stability, or increasing the whipping time.

Fat. Fat interferes with the development of high-volume egg white foams. The source of fat can be the result of yolk contamination in the whites, the use of oily beaters or bowls, or the use of plastic bowls that cannot be fully cleaned to be completely oil free. Thus, plastic bowls should not be used when beating egg whites. Refined cottonseed oil has been shown to interfere with whipping of egg whites when present to the extent of 0.5 percent or more. The presence of small amounts of yolk in egg white likewise retards foam formation, so separating the whites and yolks should be done with care. This effect is thought to be the result of the fat, probably the lipoproteins, in the egg yolk, which may form a complex with proteins in the white [34, 47].

Salt. The addition of a small amount of salt to egg whites (1 gram salt to 40 grams egg white) has been reported to decrease the volume and stability of the foam and to increase the whipping time [21]. Egg white foams are less elastic when they are beaten with salt than when no salt is added.

Acid. The addition of acid or acid salts to egg white decreases the alkalinity of the white and increases the stability of the egg white foam. A stiff and large volume foam results from the addition of an acid, such as cream of tartar. Because the addition of an acid will increase the whipping time, it is often added before or shortly after the whites begin to foam.

Sugar. Sugar retards the denaturation and coagulation of egg proteins and increases the beating time required to attain maximum volume. The presence of sugar in an egg white foam stabilizes the foam as it forms, greatly decreasing the possibility of overbeating. The texture of the sweetened egg white foam is also very fine, with many small air cells, and the surface has a shiny, satiny appearance.

The beating time of egg whites can be prolonged excessively if sugar is added too early. Therefore, it is generally recommended that the sugar be added in small increments (1 to 2 tablespoons at a time) to the egg whites once the eggs have begun to foam or soft peaks are forming. The whites should be beaten between additions of the sugar. Adding sugar in too large of increments or too quickly may result in the loss of air from the foam.

Beaten Whole Eggs. Whole eggs can be beaten to a less stiff foam. The foam can be beaten much stiffer than might be expected if beating is continued for a long enough time. The presence of the fat from the yolk, which retards foam formation, ensures little danger of overbeating the whole egg. As air is incorporate the color changes to an opaque pale yellow. The whole egg foam lacks stability and volume.

Beaten Egg Yolks. Egg yolks can be converted into a foam. Yolks increase modestly in volume when air is incorporated. Yolks change to a pale lemon color as air is incorporated and may become thick and full of fine cells. Yolks proteins are not denatured so foam lacks stability as air bubbles rise to top of the foam as liquid drains to the bottom [66].

ROLE OF EGGS IN COOKING

Eggs can be cooked used as a main dish. They may act to bind ingredients together in prepared dishes such as in meatloaf. Eggs can function to introduce air into a product such as puffy omelet or sponge cake. They can provide emulsifying properties in items such as cakes or mayonnaise. Eggs can serve as a thickener such as puddings. The egg can act as a gelling agent to provide a 3-D structure as in custard. Eggs add liquid to batters. Eggs are a source of leavening such as air and steam leavening. They can provide structural component and rigidity to a product such as muffins or cakes. Egg can also act as a tenderizer in baked goods. Eggs can add color, flavor, and nutritional value to processed food [30].

Egg's Emulsifying Functions

The egg yolk itself is an example of a "natural" emulsion so it is no surprise that the yolk contains components that can emulsify and stabilize emulsions. Phospholipid components serve to stabilize egg emulsion. Lecithin (phosphatidyl choline) and lysolecithin make up about 79 percent of egg yolk [11]. Lecithin promotes formation of oil-in-water emulsions and cholesterol promotes water-in-oil emulsions. Eggs as an emulsifier were discussed in previous chapters.

SPECIFIC METHODS OF EGG PREPARATION

Eggs Cooked in the Shell

Eggs may be cooked in the shell to varying degrees of firmness. The difference between the hard-cooked and soft-cooked egg is the cooking time and amount of protein coagulation that has occurred. Cooking an egg in a shell is a simple process. The objective is to coagulate proteins to the degree of doneness desired. The eggs should be cooled as quickly as possible after cooking to stop the cooking process. Eggs prepared for those who are pregnant, elderly, very young, or ill should be thoroughly cooked. The temperature of the yolk should be minimum of 160°F (71°C) to destroy any *Salmonella* organisms present.

Hard- and soft-cooked eggs involve covering and cooking eggs in simmering water, not boiling water. The term *hard* or *soft boiled eggs* is misleading. Boiling

eggs results in overcooked proteins which are tough and rubbery. The egg white proteins of eggs that have been boiled may turn brown due to a chemical reaction between egg white amine and glucose components. The more alkaline the egg white and longer the exposure to excessive heat, the greater the reaction.

Cracked shells can occur when cooking shell eggs, causing egg to leak into cooking water. Heating water too high which causes eggs to move into each other can cause shell cracking. Too little water can also cause egg cracking while cooking.

Overcooked egg yolks may have a green-grey ring around the yolk (**Figure 23–27**). This ring is the result of a reaction between the iron in the yolk and the sulfur in the white. A more alkaline egg white will make this reaction more severe because the loss of carbon dioxide yields more hydrogen sulfide (H_2S). Higher cooking temperatures and longer cooking times cause hydrogen sulfide to be liberated from the whites. Slow cooling time also causes this problem. After hard-cooked shell eggs have finished cooking, immediately drain hot water and run eggs under cool water to stop the cooking process. Eggs should be cooked in a single layer using about one pint water per egg; less water can be used with more eggs to cover eggs with 1 inch of water.

Soft-cooked eggs. are cooked to until the egg white is soft and coagulated and the yolk is thickened. Select fresh eggs of high quality for the preparation of soft-cooked eggs. The temperature of the water in which the eggs are cooked should be maintained below the boiling point, and the time of cooking should be no longer than is required to coagulate both the white and the yolk.

Soft-Cooked Egg Cooking Method. Soft egg cooking water is brought to a boil then shell eggs are gently

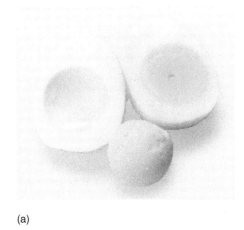
(a)

(b)

Figure 23–27
(a) Hard-cooked egg is properly cooked with uniform coloring of yolk. (b) The green gray discoloration around the yolk reflects an overcooked egg. (Richard Embery/Pearson Education)

lowered into water using a slotted spoon or other utensil. The water will immediately stop boiling and heat should be maintained until the water returns to boil. Once the water returns to a boil, the heat is immediately lowered and water reduced to a simmer and then the timing of the egg cooking starts. Soft-cooked eggs are cooked in simmering water for 3–5 minutes. Traditional egg timers (**Figure 23–28**) are three minutes. Soft-cooked eggs that are to be refrigerated are cooked for five minutes. Typically, soft-cooked eggs are immediately removed and served at the time. Soft-cooked eggs are typically served in egg cups with large egg end in the cup. The narrow egg end is cut or "topped" then scooped or eaten from the shell. Figure 23–28. A knife, egg topper, or spoon can be used to remove the egg top. Soft-cooked eggs are typically seasoned with salt and pepper prior to eating. Soft-cooked eggs will be more like a soft gel.

Hard-cooked eggs. Hard-cooked eggs are cooked longer until the white is tender, coagulated, and opaque white; the yolk is pale yellow dry and mealy. Heat is transferred from the hot water to egg white and yolk by conduction. The egg white will be heated above coagulation temperature so the yolk proteins coagulate. If the surface of the yolk is green, it is most likely overcooked (Figure 23–27). Water maintained at a boiling temperature for the entire cooking period has toughening effect on the white. Cooling hard-cooked eggs in cold water immediately after cooking stops the cooking process and facilitates the removal of the shell. Even so, very fresh eggs (less than 48 hours old) are difficult to peel without considerable

Figure 23–28
Shown above are egg topper scissors, a three minute egg timer and soft cooked egg in egg cup with top cut ready to eat.
(© Amanda Frye)

white adhering to the shell; the air sac is smaller in a fresh egg and white is less alkaline. Eggs should be shelled immediately after cooking and refrigerated. Hard-cooked eggs can also be stored in the eggshell for 1 week.

Hard-Cooked Egg Cooking Methods. Two methods for hard-cooking eggs can be used to produce hard-cooked eggs with tender whites and thoroughly cooked yolks without over cooking.

Method 1. Place eggs in a single layer in a saucepan and add water until the eggs are covered. Cover and bring just to boiling, then turn off heat. For hard-cooked eggs, allow the eggs to remain in water for 15 minutes for large eggs. At the end of the designated time for either hard- or soft-cooked eggs, place the eggs in cold or ice water until cool enough to handle.

Method 2. Add eggs to a pot of water at a simmering but not boiling temperature of about 185°F (85°C). Water must cover eggs. Cover pan and maintain this temperature for at least 25–30 minutes for hard-cooked eggs. Plunge eggs into cold water then remove shells.

One group of researchers [24] compared hard-cooked eggs prepared in two ways: (1) by placing the eggs in cold water in a covered pan, bringing the water to a boil, and then removing the pan from heat and holding for 25 minutes or (2) by placing eggs in boiling water, reducing heat to a simmer at 185°F (85°C), and then cooking for 18 minutes. The researchers reported that the eggs placed in boiling water and then simmered were easier to peel and rated higher in all criteria than those prepared by starting in cold water and bringing to a boil.

Poached Eggs

Poaching consists of cooking the edible portion of an egg in hot water, milk, cream, or other liquids (**Figure 23–29**). Use fresh, high-quality eggs since otherwise the cooked eggs will spread the yolk off center. The use of a double boiler will guard against scorching when eggs are poached in milk or cream. A simmering liquid with a temperature of about 185°F (85°C) is recommended when poaching eggs. Higher water temperatures will promote toughening of the proteins, and lower temperatures will take more time. Eggs poached in 185°F (85°C) liquids will cook in about 5 to 8 minutes. Because the addition of cold eggs to hot liquid immediately lowers the temperature of the liquid, it is possible to have the temperature of the liquid at the boiling point when the eggs are added. The heat can then be regulated to keep the liquid simmering. If the

Add eggs that have been broken in an individual dish to simmering water. After eggs have cooked 5–8 minutes remove with slotted spoon serve immediately or place in ice water to cool then refrigerate. (Richard Embery/Pearson Education)

water is not hot enough when the egg is added, the egg white will spread throughout the liquid in filmy and fragmented layers rather than set quickly and hold its original shape.

The liquid in the pan used for poaching should be deep enough to cover the eggs so that a film of co-agulated white may form over the yolk. Both salt and acid added to the cooking water aid in coagulation, but are not necessary. If used, however, 2 teaspoons of vinegar and ½ to 1 teaspoon of salt per pint of water can be effective. Eggs poached in salted water have a more opaque white and are less shiny than eggs poached in unsalted water. The eggs may appear puckered or ruffled as also occurs when poached in boiling water.

There is a wide range of individual preference regarding the desirable characteristics of poached eggs. Many people enjoy a poached egg that is rounded, with a film of coagulated white covering the yolk. The white is completely coagulated but jelly-like and tender and the yolk is thick enough to resist

flowing. For safety, as discussed earlier in the chapter, the yolk should be thickened and not runny.

The freshness of eggs and thickness of whites have considerable influence on the poached prod-uct. For example, older eggs with thin whites tend to spread out in thin layers and may fragment into pieces when placed in the hot liquid. The technique of adding the egg to the water also is important to the quality of the cooked egg. It is usually desirable to remove the egg from the shell and place it in a small, flat dish from which it can be slipped easily and quickly into the poaching water. Use slotted spoon to remove egg after poaching.

Fried Eggs

Fried eggs may be *sunny side up* (not flipped), *over easy* (flipped with a runny yolk but firm white), or *over hard* (flipped with a hard yolk and white). Basted eggs are another variation of fried eggs. Basted eggs are not flipped. The top surface of basted eggs is cooked by either basted fat spooned over the eggs or water added to a pan that is then covered with a lid to create steam. The preparation of over-easy eggs is shown in **Figure 23–30**.

Eggs are fried by heating a small amount of oil or clarified butter in a sauté pan. Only the amount of fat needed to prevent sticking of the eggs is rec-ommended. The pan and fat should be hot enough that the egg begins to fry when added to the pan but not so hot that the fat begins to smoke or brown. Temperatures that are too high will toughen the egg. If the underside of a fried egg is brown and the edges are crisp and frilled, the pan and fat were probably too hot, unless, as is true for some people, crispness in a fried egg is preferred.

Scrambled Eggs

The whites and yolks are mixed together in the preparation of scrambled eggs. If they are thor-oughly mixed, the product has a uniform yellow

(a)

(b)

(c)

(a) Pouring eggs into a nonstick sauté pan. (b) Eggs are flipped with a quick movement of the wrist. (c) Eggs are slid onto a plate. (Richard Embery/Pearson Education)

color. Some people like the marbled effect that is produced by mixing yolks and whites only slightly. About 1 tablespoon of milk or water is added per egg, with salt and pepper. The mixture is then poured into a warm skillet containing a small amount of oil, melted butter, or margarine. As the mixture begins to set under moderate heat, a heat-resistant spatula or an inverted pancake turner may be gently drawn across the bottom, forming large soft curds (**Figure 23–31**).

To reduce the risk of foodborne illness, large numbers of broken-out eggs should not be pooled. Thus, in the food service setting, frozen or refrigerated pasteurized scrambled egg mixes are used. Scrambled eggs can be dressed up for lunch or supper by adding other ingredients.

Shirred Eggs

Shirred eggs are cooked and served in the same dish. The dish is coated with butter or margarine, the eggs are broken into it, and the dish is placed in a 325°F (160°C) oven to bake. Additional ingredients, such as ham or cheese, can be baked with the eggs (**Figure 23–32**). Care must be taken not to overcook and thus toughen shirred eggs.

Omelets and Frittatas

The two basic types of omelets are plain or French and foamy or puffy. Frittatas are essentially an open-faced omelet with a comparatively high proportion of other ingredients as fillings.

French Omelets.   Small amounts of liquid may be added to the French omelet. The liquid used in omelets can be water, milk, cream, or acid juices, such as

Figure 23–32

Shirred eggs are baked in a ramekin. This egg has been baked with ham and topped with cheese. (Richard Embery/Pearson Education)

tomato and orange. Omelets can be filled with cheese, a mixture of vegetables, or fruits.

To make French omelets, whole eggs are beaten to blend white and yolk, then diluted slightly with liquid and seasoned. The mixture is cooked in a lightly greased pan until it is coagulated, after which the omelet is folded (**Figure 23–33**). To produce more rapid coagulation, a spatula can be used to carefully lift the edges of the egg mass as it coagulates, thus allowing the liquid portion on top to flow underneath, so it comes in contact with the pan. Another aid is to cover the pan to furnish steam to cook the top surface of the omelet. The omelet should be cooked at a medium-high heat for the minimum time needed to avoid over-cooking and toughening the eggs.

PROPORTIONS FOR A FRENCH OMELET	
4 eggs	½ tsp (3 g) salt
4 Tbsp (59 mL) liquid	A few grains of pepper

Puffy Omelets.   Puffy or foamy omelets may also be called soufflé omelets. These omelets are light and fluffy because they are made with whipped egg whites.

PROPORTIONS FOR A PUFFY OMELET	
4 eggs	½ tsp (3 g) salt
2 to 4 Tbsp (30 to 59 mL) liquid	A few grains of pepper
⅛ tsp cream of tartar	

Figure 23–31

Scrambled eggs should be slowly stirred forming large "curds" by slowly lifting cooked portions and allowing liquid raw egg to flow to bottom of skillet. Cook until eggs are still moist and shiny but cooked. (Richard Embery/Pearson Education)

FOCUS ON SCIENCE
WHAT IS CLARIFIED BUTTER?

Clarified butter also is known as *drawn butter*. The butter has been slowly melted, thereby evaporating most of the water and separating the milk solids from the golden liquid on the surface. The milk solids sink to the bottom of the pan. After any foam is skimmed off the top, the clear (clarified) butter is poured or skimmed off the milky residue and used in cooking. Milk solids burn easily when heated. Therefore, clarified butter has a higher smoke point than regular butter because the milk solids have been removed. See Chapter 8 for more about types of fat and smoke points.

(a)

(b)

(c)

(d)

Figure 23–33

The preparation of a folded omelet is shown here. It is similar to a French omelet, except the fillings are added before the omelet is folded. (a) Lifting the egg from the pan's edges to allow raw egg under the cooked eggs. (b) Adding filling. (c) Folding the omelet. (d) Placing omelet onto a plate. (Richard Embery/Pearson Education)

To make a puffy omelet, cream of tartar is added to the egg whites, which are beaten until moderately stiff. The liquid, salt, and pepper are added to the egg yolks, and the mixture is beaten until it is lemon colored and so thick that it piles. The beaten yolk mixture is folded into the beaten whites carefully to blend the mass evenly and yet avoid too much loss of air.

The puffy omelet mixture is poured into a lightly greased pan preheated to a moderately high temperature. The omelet is cooked moderately slowly until it is light brown underneath (**Figure 23–34**). To cook the top layer of this thick, puffy omelet, it may be baked for about 15 minutes in a 350°F (177°C) oven. Alternatively, a lid may be placed on top of the pan while it still cooks on the range top. This method is less desirable because the top of the omelet will not brown.

Frittatas. Like plain or French omelets, frittatas are made by beating whole eggs until well blended. However, frittatas often have a high proportion of filling ingredients. Recipes may call for as much as 1 cup of filling ingredients for four eggs. Some recipes will suggest cooking the eggs in a preheated sauté pan and then, when nearly cooked, adding fillings ingredients, such as

Figure 23–34

A puffy omelet is prepared by beating separated eggs whites until fluffy. Next, beaten eggs yolks are folded in. The omelet is poured into a preheated, oiled pan then cooked range-top until brown on the bottom. To finish, the puffy omelet is baked in the oven until brown on top and cooked throughout. The omelet pictured here is ready to eat.
(© Douglas and Barbara Scheule)

Figure 23–35

Frittata made with asparagus, goat cheese garnished with radish and parsley. (Richard Embery/Pearson Education)

Figure 23–36

Crepes can be filled with many different ingredients from asparagus and cheese as shown here to fruits (cherry cheese blintzes) or meats (chicken or tuna cheese crepes). (Janmika/123RF)

precooked meat, vegetable, and cheese ingredients, on top (**Figure 23–35**). Other recipes suggest sautéing the meat and vegetables and then pouring the egg mixture into these "filling" ingredients. In both cases, if the frittata is relatively thick, it may be helpful to finish cooking under the broiler or by placing in the oven. Frittatas are usually served by cutting into wedges.

Crêpes

Crêpes are thin, tender pancakes containing a relatively high proportion of egg. They can be filled with a variety of sweet or savory items, including fish, meats, poultry, eggs, cheese, vegetables, and fruits (**Figure 23–36**). Crêpes can also be served with sweet, dessert-type fillings.

The thin crêpe batter is cooked on medium heat in a seasoned slope-sided omelet or crêpe pan. Enough batter is poured in to cover the bottom of the pan, then the pan is tipped or tilted to allow the batter to move quickly over the bottom, forming a thin layer. Any excess batter is poured off. The crêpe is cooked until it is lightly browned on the bottom and dry on the top.

Soufflés

The word *soufflé* is French for *puff*. A soufflé is thus a dish that puffs up spectacularly in the oven. Soufflés are similar to foamy or puffy omelets, except that they have a thick, white sauce base and contain additional ingredients, such as grated cheese, vegetables,

or ground meats. Dessert soufflés are sweet and may contain lemon, strawberry, and chocolate.

In the preparation of a soufflé, beaten egg yolks are added to the thick white sauce base. Cheese or other ingredients are then added. A stiffly beaten egg white foam is folded into the white sauce base. The high proportion of egg in the soufflé provides structure as the egg proteins coagulate, and basic principles of egg cookery require moderate cooking temperatures. Soufflés are usually baked, although they can be steamed. When they are baked, the dish containing the soufflé mixture is typically a high sided ceramic dish. It is often baked by placing dish in a pan of hot water to protect against excessive heating. Soufflés will shrink or deflate after removal from the oven and should therefore be served immediately. **Figure 23–37** is a cheese soufflé.

Figure 23-37

Cheese Souffle. (Richard Embery/Pearson Education)

Custards

A true custard consists only of eggs, milk, sugar, and flavoring without a starch ingredient. Custards are of two types: the stirred or soft custard, which is given a creamy consistency by being stirred while it is cooking, and the baked custard, which is allowed to coagulate without stirring, thereby producing a gel. There must be enough egg in the baked custard to produce a firm consistency when cooked, particularly if the custard is to be unmolded when served. The proportion of egg to milk is often the same for baked and stirred custards; however, less egg is used in stirred custard when a thin consistency is desired.

Custard dishes can be served as simple egg desserts or can be elegant dishes. Flan, popular in Mexican cuisine, is similar to baked custard. It is a custard baked over a layer of caramelized sugar. Flans are generally unmolded, and the caramelized sugar flows over the top for a delicious and beautiful dessert. Crème brûlée is another type of custard that can be prepared as either a baked or a stirred custard. Crème brûlée is a very rich custard generally composed of egg yolks and heavy cream rather than whole eggs and milk, as in other baked custards (**Figure 23-38**). This custard is generally topped with brown or white sugar that is caramelized either under a broiler or with a torch. A description of basic baked and stirred custards follows. Quiche involves an egg custard and savory filling baked in a pastry shell.

PROPORTIONS FOR CUSTARDS	
1 c (237 mL) milk	2 Tbsp (25 g) sugar
1 to 1½ eggs or 2 to 3 yolks	¼ tsp vanilla or ¹⁄₁₆ tsp nutmeg

Figure 23-38

Crème brûlée, traditional French vanilla cream dessert, made with egg yolks and heavy cream rather than whole eggs and milk with caramelized sugar on top. (Robyn Mackenzie/Shutterstock)

(To measure ½ egg, mix together white and yolk of whole egg, then divide into two equal portions by measuring 1 Tbsp at a time.)

Baked Custard. Because the egg is used for thickening, it is beaten only enough to blend the white and yolk well. Sugar can be added to the egg or dissolved in the milk. Milk is usually scalded before being added to the egg mixture. Scalding hastens the cooking and helps retain a mild, sweet flavor, but it does not produce a smoother custard. Flavoring must be added when the mixture is prepared for cooking.

The custard cups should be placed in a pan of hot water as a protection against overheating, even though a moderate oven temperature may be used (about 350°F [177°C]). Custards placed in a pan of very hot water can be baked in a 400°F (204°C) oven for a much shorter time than in a 350°F oven. However, care must be exercised to remove the custard from the oven as soon as it is coagulated to avoid undesirable overcooking.

The baked custard is done when the tip of a knife inserted halfway between the center and outside comes out clean (**Figure 23-39**). When custard is overcooked, some clear liquid separates from the gel structure; that is, syneresis occurs. In addition, the custard may appear porous and contain holes, especially on the outer surfaces, when it is unmolded.

Figure 23–39

Baked custard cups are cooked in a pan with hot water to prevent overcooking of the outer edges of the custards. To test doneness, insert a knife into the center of the custard to see if it comes out clean. (© Barbara Scheule)

The top surface may be concave and browned. In an overcooked custard, the egg proteins that form the meshlike gel structure shrink and squeeze out some of the liquid that was held in the mesh.

Soft or Stirred Custard. The mixture of egg, milk, and sugar is prepared in the same manner as for baked custard. The vanilla, because of its volatility, is added after the other ingredients are cooked. Custards that are cooked more slowly coagulate more completely at a lower temperature than custards that are cooked rapidly. There is less danger of curdling, and both consistency and flavor are better in stirred custards cooked relatively slowly. The total cooking time, in a double boiler, should be 12 to 15 minutes, heating more rapidly at first and then more slowly near the end of the cooking period.

Constant stirring is necessary to prevent lumping. Stirring separates the coagulated particles, resulting in a creamy consistency regardless of the amount of egg used. The tendency is to cook a soft custard until it appears as thick as is desired, but caution should be exercised. The custard will be thicker when it is cold. When the custard coats the spoon well, it should be removed from the heat and cooled immediately by either pouring it into a cold dish or suspending it, in the pan used for cooking, in cold water.

Overheating a stirred custard results in curdling. A very slightly curdled custard may be improved if it is beaten with a rotary beater, but this treatment is of no value for excessively curdled custards. In an overcooked custard, the coagulated proteins shrink and separate out from the more liquid portion of the mixture, giving the appearance of curds. Also, the flavor of an overcooked custard tends to be strong and sulfury.

A stirred custard can be used to create some interesting and delicious desserts. For example, hard meringue shells can be filled with crushed or whole sweetened strawberries or other fruit and the custard poured over the fruit. This can then be crowned with a bit of whipped topping. Or the custard can be flavored with caramelized sugar and poured into individual serving dishes. Small soft meringues that have been previously baked can be placed on top of the custard.

Meringues

Meringues are of two types: the soft meringue used for pies and puddings, and the hard meringue generally used as a crisp dessert base or as a cookie. Pavlova

---

FOCUS ON SCIENCE
WHY DO EGGS TURN GREEN?

Usually eggs turn green because of overcooking. Eggs held hot for too long will also turn green. Therefore, hard-cooked eggs should be cooled quickly in cold water to prevent continued cooking. Scrambled eggs held hot in an oven or warmer may also start to develop an olive-green shade. Although safe to eat, green eggs are typically considered unattractive. Refrigerated, pasteurized egg products often contain citric acid. Citric acid will make the eggs resistant to turning green even if overcooked.

The science behind green eggs is as follows. Reaction of iron in the yolk with hydrogen sulfide from the white produces the greenish ferrous sulfide (FeS) deposit. Most of the iron in an egg is present in the yolk. Sulfur occurs in about equal amounts in yolk and white, but the sulfur compounds in the white are more labile to heat than those in the yolk. Hydrogen sulfide (H_2S) is therefore easily formed from the sulfur compounds in the white during prolonged heating and forms even more readily when the pH of the egg is markedly alkaline, as in an older egg.

Ferrous sulfide forms very slowly until the yolk reaches about 158°F (70°C) and seldom occurs in fresh eggs cooked 30 minutes at 185°F (85°C). The green color is less likely to form in rapidly cooled eggs because the hydrogen sulfide gas is drawn to the lowered pressure at the surface of the cooling egg and thus combines less readily with iron at the surface of the yolk. However, if an egg is cooked 30 minutes in boiling water, the ferrous sulfide will probably form regardless of cooling. Also, in older eggs that are very alkaline, the green color may be produced despite the precautions taken during cooking [8].

is a meringue dessert that is thought to originate in New Zealand and Australia in honor of the Russian ballerina Anna Pavlova. Typically, the large meringue is made with vinegar and topped with whipped cream and kiwi or berries as shown in **Figure 23–40**.

Pavlova is made with meringue base topped with whipped cream and berries. Popular dessert in New Zealand. (Bonchan/ Shutterstock)

PROPORTIONS FOR SOFT MERINGUES	
1 egg white	1/16 tsp cream of tartar (optional)
2 Tbsp (25 g) sugar	1/8 tsp flavoring (if desired)

To produce a soft meringue that is fine textured, tender, cuts easily without tearing, and shows neither syneresis nor **beading** on top of the baked meringue, each of the following items should be considered carefully:

1. When the egg whites are partially beaten (to a soft foam), sugar is gradually added, ½ to 1 tablespoon at a time, and the beating is continued until the mixture is stiff but with soft peaks that still tip over.
2. The meringue should be placed on a *hot* filling.
3. The meringue should be baked at 350°F (177°C) for 12 to 15 minutes until it is 160°F (71°C).

Heating must be sufficient throughout the soft meringue to destroy any *Salmonella* organisms that may be present in the eggs. Meringues baked at moderate oven temperatures may be slightly sticky compared to those baked at high oven temperatures, but the moderate temperature produces an attractive, evenly browned product. Two problems that may be encountered in making soft meringues are weeping, or leaking of liquid from the bottom of the meringue, and beading [20, 22]. Weeping, or syneresis, apparently results from undercooking the meringue. It can also occur from underbeating the egg whites. Placing the meringue on a hot filling helps to achieve complete coagulation of the egg proteins. Beading is usually attributed to overcooking or overcoagulation of the egg white proteins. It can also result from a failure to dissolve the sugar sufficiently when it is beaten into the meringue.

PROPORTIONS FOR HARD MERINGUES	
1 egg white	1/16 tsp cream of tartar
1/4 c (50 g) sugar	A few grains of salt
1/8 tsp vanilla	

In the preparation of hard meringues, cream of tartar is added to the egg white, which is beaten until a soft foam begins to form. Flavoring may be added at this point. Sugar is added gradually and beating continued until the mass is very stiff. Portions of the meringue are dropped onto a baking sheet, which may be covered with parchment paper, and shaped into small shells.

Meringues are baked at a low oven temperature (about 250°F [121°C]) for 50 to 60 minutes, depending on the size of the meringues, and then left in the oven with the heat turned off for another hour. If a temperature lower than 250°F (121°C) can be maintained for a longer time, the effect is one of drying instead of baking the meringue and produces even better results. Well-insulated ovens that hold the heat for several hours can be preheated and then turned off entirely.

Desirable hard meringues are crisp, tender, and white in appearance. It is important that they do not show gumminess or stickiness, which results from underbaking. This may occur from either an oven temperature that is too high or a baking time that is too short. When the baking temperature is too high, the meringues are browned on the outside before the interior is dry enough, and the residual moisture produces stickiness.

Microwave Cooking

Because the egg yolk contains more fat than the egg white, it attracts more energy and cooks faster. If an egg is microwaved until the white is completely coagulated, the yolk may toughen. One thing that the microwave oven does not do successfully is cook an egg in its shell. Steam builds up inside the egg, and it bursts. However, eggs can be satisfactorily cooked in several other ways by microwaves. They can be poached in liquid. The liquid is first brought to a boil in a custard cup. Then the broken-out egg is added and cooked for a short time on medium power. The egg should be cooked until the white is opaque but not set. During a standing period of 2 to 3 minutes, the cooking is completed. Broken-out eggs can also be cooked in individual custard cups without liquid, as shirred eggs are cooked. The yolk membrane should be first pierced with a toothpick to help prevent bursting from steam pent up during cooking.

Scrambled eggs are prepared for the microwave by mixing melted butter, eggs, and milk and cooking on high power for about half the cooking time before breaking up the set parts and pushing them to the center of the dish. The eggs are stirred once or twice more while the cooking is completed. Again, standing time after cooking is important to finish the cooking without toughening the eggs. Scrambled eggs prepared by microwaves are fluffier and have more volume than conventionally scrambled eggs. Omelets, including puffy omelets, can also be prepared in the microwave oven.

For fried eggs, a browning dish is necessary. The browning dish is preheated on high, and then the eggs are added. The browning dish absorbs enough energy and produces a hot enough surface to brown the eggs lightly. Egg dishes such as quiche can also be prepared using microwaves.

In hospital food service, microwaves are often used to reheat food at the point of serving; however, some questions have been raised concerning the lack of uniformity in heating, which results in lack of confidence in the ability of this heating process to destroy microorganisms sufficiently. It has been found, when reheating scrambled eggs in a microwave oven under actual food service operating conditions, that temperature variability in the eggs could be controlled within 9°F (5°C) if voltage to the oven and temperature of the food before heating were rigidly controlled [9]. Careful attention to these factors that affect heating is necessary to ensure safety of the food for service to clients [14].

DUCK EGGS AND EGG DELICACIES

Duck eggs are an important part of Asian ethnic cuisines. Ducks were domesticated in Asia thousands of years ago for their eggs and meat. Duck eggs are 50 percent larger than jumbo chicken eggs. Duck eggs are higher in calories, fat, cholesterol, iron, folate, potassium, vitamin A, vitamin E, and vitamin B-12 than chicken eggs [52]. Ninety percent of commercial duck eggs are produced in Asia with China producing 65 percent of duck eggs sold worldwide. Historically duck eggs were preserved and transformed into a unique food not common in Western cultures [67]. Some of these ethnic egg

delicacies are briefly discussed below. These eggs are not included in FSIS inspection; they are subject to other rules and import laws enforced by the USDA and FDA.

Century Egg or Thousand Year Egg or Millennium Egg

These are duck eggs preserved in a mixture of clay, salt, quicklime, and rice hulls for weeks to months [67]. The egg is converted into a unique food which is popular in China, Vietnam, and Thailand. Variations of these preserved duck eggs include "Hulidan" which results when eggs are individually coated in a mixture of salt and wet clay or ash for a month. This process darkens and partially solidifies the yolk giving the egg a salty taste. "Dsaudan" eggs are described as having a wine-like flavor. They are packed in cooked rice and salt for six months which softens the shell, thickens the membranes and coagulates egg proteins. "Pidan" is made by covering eggs with lime, salt, wood ashes, and a tea infusion for five months or more. The egg yolks turn greenish gray and the egg white transforms into a coffee-brown jelly. Pidan eggs are described to have an ammonia-like smell and a taste of lime.

Salted duck eggs

Salted duck eggs are another Asian specialty popular in China and Vietnam. The salted yolks are often used in mooncakes as discussed in Chapter 17. Raw eggs are soaked in a brine or packed in salted charcoal to cure for 4–6 weeks. Filipinos use what is described as the "Pateros" method which involves dipping raw eggs in a clay batter with salt and water then wrapping them in newspaper to cure for approximately two weeks. These eggs are often dyed red. Salted eggs are boiled, peeled, and steamed prior to eating. The eggs have hard firm orange-red yolks. Salted yolks are often used in traditional moon cakes [67].

Balut

Balut are popular street food in the Philippines, China, and Vietnam. Balut are incubated, fertilized duck eggs boiled for 30 minutes when embryos are at least 16–21 days old. The Balut egg eating ritual involves cracking a hole in the wide end of the shell in order to sip the warm broth before eating the yolk and young duckling [67].

Pickled Eggs

Pickled eggs can be made from any marinated hard-cooked egg. Marinades include vinegar and pickling spices, spicy cider, pickle juice, or pickled beet juice. The pickling juice eggs in various colors. Commercial pickled eggs will keep for several months on the shelf and should be refrigerated after opening and eaten within a week. Home-prepared pickled eggs should be refrigerated and used within seven days.

STUDY QUESTIONS

Consumption Trends and Nutritive Value

1. Discuss consumption trends for eggs. How have consumption trends changed? What factors have impacted these changes?

2. Discuss the nutritive value of eggs and how eggs can fit into a healthy meal plan.

Egg Composition and Structure

3. Discuss why the hen and her health are important for egg production.

4. **(a)** Compare the chemical composition of whole egg, egg white, and egg yolk, indicating major differences.

   (b) What major protein is found in egg white?

   (c) What types of proteins predominate in egg yolk?

5. Describe the following parts of an egg and indicate the location for each.

   (a) Cuticle or bloom

   (b) Shell

   (c) Outer membrane

   (d) Inner membrane

   (e) Air cell

   (f) Thin white

   (g) Thick white

   (h) Chalazae

   (i) Vitelline membrane

   (j) Yolk

Egg Inspection and Grading

7. Discuss the difference between egg inspection and egg grading. What government departments and agencies oversee these activities?

8. **(a)** Compare the major characteristics of fresh and deteriorated eggs.

   (b) How can freshness best be maintained in eggs during storage?

9. **(a)** List the USDA consumer grades for eggs and describe the major characteristics of each grade.

   (b) Describe the process by which eggs are graded.

Food Safety

10. **(a)** Explain why shell eggs can be a potentially hazardous food. How has the government responded?

    (b) Give several suggestions for the safe handling and preparation of shell eggs.

Egg Preservation and Processing

11. **(a)** Explain why eggs are pasteurized before freezing or drying.

    (b) What special problem is usually encountered in the freezing of egg yolks? How can this problem be solved?

Eggs in Food Preparation

12. List several different uses for eggs in food preparation.

13. Egg proteins coagulate on heating and can therefore be used for thickening purposes in cooking. Describe the effect of each of the following factors on the temperature of coagulation:

    (a) Source of egg protein (white or yolk)

    (b) Rate of heating

    (c) Dilution

    (d) Addition of sugar

    (e) Addition of acid

14. Describe the various changes or stages that occur as egg white is mechanically beaten to a very stiff, dry foam.

15. Describe the effect of each of the following on the volume and/or stability of egg white foam:

    (a) Thickness of the white

    (b) Temperature of the white

    (c) Type of beater used

    (d) Type of container used

    (e) Addition of salt

    (f) Addition of acid

    (g) Addition of sugar

Preparation Methods for Eggs

16. Describe and explain an appropriate procedure for preparing each of the following food items:

    (a) Poached eggs

    (b) Eggs cooked in the shell

    (c) Fried eggs

    (d) Scrambled eggs

    (e) Omelets, plain or French, foamy or puffy, and frittata

    (f) Shirred and poached eggs cooked by microwaves

17. (a) Describe appropriate procedures for preparing stirred custard and baked custard. Explain why each step in the procedures is important.

    (b) Why should precautions be taken to avoid overheating custards during preparation? Explain.

18. Describe major differences in the preparation and use of soft and hard meringues.

24
Meat and Meat Cookery

Meat is defined as "the flesh of animals used for food." Cattle, swine, and sheep are the chief meat animals in the United States. Small amounts of rabbit and venison are also consumed in the United States; in other parts of the world, horse, dog, llama, and camel are used as meat.

This chapter will focus on meat from cattle, swine, and sheep. In this chapter, the following topics will be discussed:

- Consumption trends and nutrition
- Composition and structure
- Classifications
- Meat production and marketing
- Purchasing meat
- Tenderness and flavor
- Cured and processed meats
- Safe storage and preparation of meats
- Methods of preparing and cooking meat
- Stock, broth, consommé, gravy, and sauces
- Carving meat

CONSUMPTION TRENDS AND NUTRITION

Consumption Trends

For many, meat, poultry, and fish play an important role in meal planning. Changes have occurred, however, over the past two decades in the amounts of these protein-rich foods consumed by Americans. The current trend is toward the consumption of less red meat and more poultry [78] (**Figure 24–1**). According to U.S. Department of Agriculture (USDA) food accessibility data, Americans ate, on an annual per capita basis, 132 pounds of red meat (beef, veal, pork, lamb, and mutton) retail weight in 1970, but only 100 pounds in 2016. At the same time, the consumption of poultry increased from 34 pounds per person in 1970 to 76 pounds in 2016. The total consumption of meat, poultry, and fish increased from 178 pounds per person per year in 1970 to 192 pounds in 2016.

Nutritive Value

Meat is composed of approximately 75 percent water, 20 percent protein, and 5 percent representing fat, carbohydrate, and minerals [92]. The percentage of these components varies depending on the kind of meat and the cut. The protein in meat is of high biological value, including all of the essential amino acids.

The USDA Dietary Guidelines recommend 5½ ounces (or equivalent) of protein foods for a 2,000 calorie reference diet. These protein needs can be met with plant sources (see Chapter 19) or with meats, dairy, poultry, and seafood [96]. Many Americans overconsume protein foods or are consuming adequate amounts of protein foods [96] (**Figure 24–2**).

Lean meats are a good source of thiamin, riboflavin, and niacin as well as other members of the B complex. Lean pork is particularly rich in thiamin. Liver and kidney are good dietary sources of riboflavin and are richer in niacin than most other tissues. All meats furnish tryptophan, the amino acid that serves as a **precursor** of niacin for the body. Liver is a variable but excellent source of vitamin A and iron. Meat is an excellent source of iron, zinc, selenium, and phosphorus. Twenty-three percent of the iron in the U.S. food supply is supplied by meat, poultry, fish, and meat alternatives [23]. Some copper and other trace minerals are also supplied by meat.

The **monounsaturated**, **saturated**, and **polyunsaturated** fats are found in meats (refer to Chapters 7 and 8). Meat also contains cholesterol. The amount of fat in meat can vary significantly by the cut, amount of fat trim, and preparation method. For example, a 3-ounce serving of eye of round beef roast contains 1.7 grams of saturated fat and 4.8 grams of total fat. This cut of beef is therefore considered lean. Ground

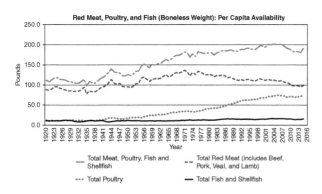

Figure 24–1

U.S. per capita availability of meat. (U.S. Department of Agriculture, Economic Research Service)

HEALTHY EATING

WHAT DOES IT MEAN IF THE LABEL STATES "LEAN"?

Nutrition claims are regulated by the government. Therefore, terms such as *lean* and *extra lean* have standardized definitions. There are many different cuts of red meats and poultry that are lean. While not all lean meats are labeled "lean," if you see these terms on a package of meat, here is what they mean:

Lean—100 grams (3.5 ounces) of beef with

• less than 10 grams of fat,

• 4.5 grams or less of saturated fat, and

• less than 95 milligrams of cholesterol.

Extra Lean—100 grams (3.5 ounces) of beef with

• less than 5 grams of fat,

• less than 2 grams of saturated fat, and

• less than 95 milligrams of cholesterol.

Source: Reference 94.

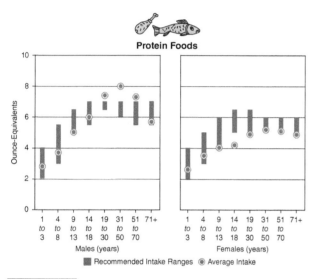

Protein Foods

Recommended Intake Ranges ▮ Average Intake ⊙

Males (years) 1 to 3, 4 to 8, 9 to 13, 14 to 18, 19 to 30, 31 to 50, 51 to 70, 71+

Females (years) 1 to 3, 4 to 8, 9 to 13, 14 to 18, 19 to 30, 31 to 50, 51 to 70, 71+

Figure 24-2

Most Americans are consuming adequate amounts of protein. Some age groups of males are consuming more protein than suggested by the USDA Dietary Guidelines. The orange dots represent the typical number of ounces (or equivalent) consumed at the ages listed. The blue bar is the recommended number of ounces (or ounce equivalents) of protein that are recommended on a daily basis depending on individual needs at each age. (USDA)

beef is sold with fat content ranging from 70 to 95 percent lean. A 3-ounce serving of 95 percent lean ground beef that has been pan-broiled will contain 5.5 grams of fat, or about 8 percent of the daily value of total fat based on a 2,000-calorie intake. In contrast, 75 percent lean ground beef will have 14 grams of fat, or about 21 percent of the daily value of total fat intake [77]. See Appendix C for information about the USDA National Nutrient Database.

COMPOSITION AND STRUCTURE

As purchased, meat is composed of muscle, connective tissue, and fatty or adipose tissue. Muscle is composed of as much as 75 percent water, which is held by the proteins in a gel-type structure. The connective tissue is distributed throughout muscle, binding cells and bundles of cells together. It is also present in tendons and ligaments.

Some cuts of meat include bone, and although it is not eaten, it is an important aid in identifying various cuts of meat. Pigments in meat influence our perceptions of quality as well as the type of meat. Beef, pork, and lamb, while all considered red meats, vary in color.

Muscle

Muscle has a complex structure that is important to its function in the living animal, where it performs work by contracting and relaxing. Muscle fibers are the basic structural units of muscle. It is important to pay attention to how muscles are put together because it affects the quality and cooking characteristics of meat.

Muscle Fibers. The muscle fiber is a long, threadlike cell that tapers slightly at both ends (**Figure 24–3**). It is tiny, averaging about 1/500th inch in diameter and 1 to 2 inches in length. Inside the muscle fiber or cell is an intricate structure including contractile material called *myofibrils* (**Figure 24–4**). The myofibrils are surrounded by a **cytoplasmic** substance called *sarcoplasm*. There is also a system of tubules and **reticulum** around each myofibril that plays a key role in initiating muscle contraction. In addition, many **mitochondria** act as powerhouses to provide energy for the cell in the form of the high-energy compound adenosine triphosphate (ATP).

Myosin, Actin, and Actomyosin. If you could look further into the structure of the tiny myofibrils, about 2,000 of which are present in each muscle cell, you would see special proteins. These proteins form thick filaments and thin filaments that are set in an orderly array (**Figure 24–5**). If you visualize a transverse section cut through the center of a myofibril, it would be similar to that shown in **Figure 24–6**. The thick filaments are composed primarily of the protein *myosin*, whereas the thin filaments are made up of another protein, *actin* [20].

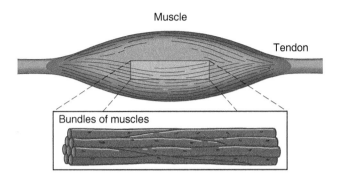

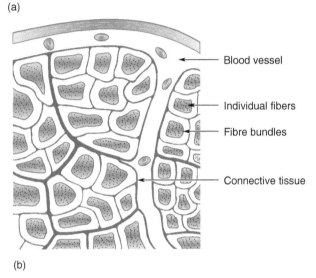

Figure 24–3

(a) Tiny muscle fibers or cells are combined to make small bundles that are then part of the muscle. (b) This cross-cut illustration of meat shows the fiber bundles, and additional structural components.

Figure 24–4

The muscle fiber or cell consists of many tiny myofibrils held together by the cell membrane. Each myofibril is made up of contractile proteins in a special ordered array, as shown in Figure 24–5.

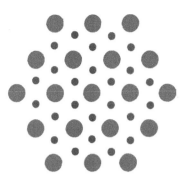

Figure 24–6

Transverse section through a cylindrical myofibril. The large dots represent the thick filaments composed of myosin molecules. The smaller dots represent the thin filaments composed of actin.

It is thought that when a muscle contracts, the thick and thin filaments slide together, something like a telescope, thus shortening the length of the muscle. As the thick and thin filaments slide together, they apparently form cross bridges with each other, thus making a new protein in the shortened myofibril called *actomyosin*. Energy for this process is provided from chemical changes in ATP.

The parallel alignment of the thick and thin filaments in all the myofibrils of a cell produces a pattern of dark and light lines and spaces when viewed under a microscope (**Figure 24–7**). The thick filaments are present in the dark bands, and the thin filaments extend into the light bands. The striated pattern continues to repeat itself along the length of the myofibril.

Muscle Structure. Let us now return to the basic unit—the muscle fiber or cell—and see how these units are built into larger bundles and muscles. Each cell or fiber is surrounded by a fine membrane called the *sarcolemma*. Small bundles of the fibers, surrounded by thin sheaths of connective tissue to hold them together, form primary bundles (each containing 20 to 40 fibers). The primary bundles are then bound together with sheets of

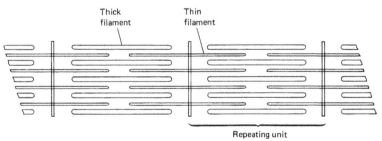

Figure 24–5

Thick and thin, rodlike components or filaments inside the myofibril are composed of protein molecules. Myosin is the protein found in the thick filaments; actin makes up the thin filaments. They are systematically arranged in a cylindrical shape. When muscle contracts, the thin filaments in each repeating unit push together, thus shortening the length of the muscle.

FOCUS ON SCIENCE
MOIST- OR DRY-HEAT COOKING METHOD? LOOK AT THE BONES

The bones in a cut of meat can provide a good indicator of whether to use moist- or dry-heat preparation methods. The guesswork of "How should I prepare this cut of meat?" can be removed by knowing where a retail cut (e.g., sirloin) is located on the carcass. The type of bone corresponds with specific retail cuts.

Dry Heat
    T-bone (short loin)
    Rib bone (rib section)
    Pin, flat, and wedge bones (sirloin)

Moist Meat
    Round bone (round)
    Blade bone (chuck)

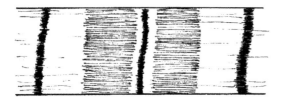

Figure 24–7

Representation of a striated muscle showing light and dark bands on the myofibrils (enlarged about 20,000 diameters).

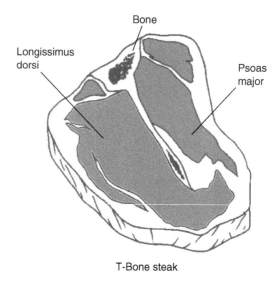

T-Bone steak

Figure 24–8

The major muscles in a T-bone steak are shown in this drawing. The cut of meat, known as the "tenderloin," is the psoas major muscle. In a Porterhouse steak the psoas major muscle is larger than in the T-bone, thus making a Porterhouse steak a more expensive cut. "Strip steaks" are a cut of meat predominately from the longissimus dorsi muscle shown opposite the psoas major muscle.

connective tissue to form secondary bundles. Secondary bundles bound together by connective tissue form major muscles. The primary bundles comprise the grain of the meat, which may appear to be fine or coarse.

Each major muscle in the animal body has been named. **Figure 24–8** shows two of the major muscles in a T-bone steak—the *longissimus dorsi*, which runs along the back of the animal, and the *psoas major* or *tenderloin* muscle, which is particularly valued for its tenderness.

Connective Tissue

Muscle tissue does not occur without connective tissue that binds the muscle cells together in various-size bundles. It also makes up the tendons and ligaments of an animal body. Generally, connective tissue has few cells but a considerable amount of extracellular background material called *ground substance*. Running through and embedded in this matrix of ground substance are long, strong fibrils or fibers. Many of these fibrils contain the protein *collagen*.

Types of Connective Tissue. Collagen, elastin, and reticulin are three kinds of connective tissue found in meat. Collagen-containing connective tissue is white. Connective tissue that contains another protein, called *elastin*, is yellow. Although collagen fibers are flexible, they do not stretch as much and are not as elastic as elastin fibers. Very little elastin seems to be present in most muscles, particularly those of the loin and round regions, but a considerable amount of elastin may be present in the connective tissue of a few muscles, including some in the shoulder area. A third type

of connective tissue fibril, *reticulin*, consists of very small fibers. This type of connective tissue forms a delicate network around the muscle cells.

Tenderizing Connective Tissue. When connective tissue is heated with moisture, some collagen is **hydrolyzed** to produce the smaller gelatin molecule. This change accounts for much of the increase in tenderness that occurs in less tender cuts of meat cooked by moist heat. Heating causes only slight softening of elastin, however. If elastin is present in relatively large amounts, it should be trimmed out or tenderized by cutting or cubing (as in the preparation of minute steaks).

Connective tissue tends to develop more extensively in muscles that are used by an animal for locomotion, such as those in the legs, chest, and neck. Less tender cuts of meat usually contain more connective tissue than tender cuts, although this is not the only factor affecting meat tenderness.

Fatty Tissue

Special cells contain large amounts of fat for storage in the body. These cells are embedded in a network of connective tissue to form adipose or fatty tissue. Some hard fats, such as beef suet, have visible sheets of connective tissue separating layers or masses of fat cells. Fat called suet is the hard fat found in the inside loin, near the kidneys, of cattle and sheep. Fat is generally colorless, but in older animals, it becomes yellowish instead of white as **carotenoid pigments** accumulate. The type of cattle feed may also affect the color of the fat.

Fats from different species and from different parts of the same animal differ to some extent in composition. The more brittle, hard fats of beef and mutton contain higher percentages of **saturated fatty acids**. Softer fats contain more **unsaturated fatty acids**. The high melting point of lamb fat causes it to congeal when served unless the meat is very hot. Lard extracted from the fatty tissue around the glandular organs has a somewhat higher melting point than that produced from back fat.

There are three major kinds of fat in meat: *intra*muscular, *inter*muscular, and subcutaneous. Intramuscular fat also is called **marbling**. It is observed as very small streaks of fat between muscle fibers and bundles (**Figure 24–9**). Marbling is associated with juiciness, flavor, and tenderness [20]. Intermuscular fat is found between individual muscles and may be either a small or a relatively large seam of fat. Subcutaneous fat is the fat found under the skin and, if excessive, may be trimmed from the exterior of the muscle before sale to the consumer.

Bone

Long shafts of bone consist chiefly of compact bony tissue. A center canal is filled with yellow marrow. Other bones may be spongy in character and may contain red marrow, which has many blood vessels. Bones or pieces of bone that appear in retail cuts of meat aid in the identification of the cut, giving clues to its location on the carcass. The condition of the backbone, or *chine* bone, also provides an indication about the age of the animal. Relatively young animals will have backbones that are redder and less hard than backbones from mature animals.

Pigments

The color of meat comes chiefly from the pigment *myoglobin*. Although *hemoglobin* is a red pigment in the blood, it contributes little to the color of meat because much of the blood is drained from the carcass. Myoglobin and hemoglobin are similar in chemical structure. Both contain the protein globin and the iron-containing pigment heme, but myoglobin is smaller. Hemoglobin carries oxygen in the bloodstream, whereas myoglobin holds it in the muscle cells.

The quantity of myoglobin in muscle increases with age; thus, beef has a darker color than veal. The color of

Figure 24–9

This beef rib-eye steak is well marbled. Fat is distributed throughout the muscle of this beef ribeye steak. The large fat streak, also shown in this cut, is an example of intermuscular fat that divides two muscle groups. (The Beef Checkoff www.BeefItsWhatsForDinner.com)

meat also varies with the species of animal from which it is obtained. Pork muscle generally contains less myoglobin than beef muscle and appears lighter in color. Different muscles of the same animal may also differ in color.

Forms of Myoglobin. Myoglobin exists in three primary forms: *oxymyoglobin, deoxymyoglobin,* and *metmyoglobin*. Each of these forms is responsible for a different color; thus, meat may appear cherry red, purple-red, or brown. These forms of myoglobin are affected by the presence of oxygen and exposure to light. The form of myoglobin also has an impact on the final appearance of cooked meat. Thus, temperature, not color, is the best indicator of doneness of meats. **Table 24–1** provides an overview of each of these forms of myoglobin, and **Figure 24–10** depicts the chemical changes associated with each pigment.

Factors Influencing Myoglobin. Other factors that influence myoglobin are pH, meat source, packaging, freezing, fat content, and added ingredients [36]. The appearance of the meat when raw as well as when cooked can be influenced by these additional factors (**Table 24–2**). Thus, although color is often used as an indication of quality or cooking doneness, it is not reliable. A thermometer is the only safe and reliable way to assess doneness, especially when preparing meats such as ground beef, which may result in a foodborne illness if undercooked (see Chapter 2).

CLASSIFICATION

Beef

Beef is the meat from full-grown cattle (bovines). Cattle are generally slaughtered at a weight of 1,200 pounds, often around 2 years of age. Beef carcasses

Table 24–1
FORMS OF MYOGLOBIN AND DESCRIPTION OF CHARACTERISTICS

Forms	Color	Description of Characteristics
Oxymyoglobin	Bright cherry red	Easily formed in presence of oxygen. The plastic overwrap, often used for retail meatpacking, allows oxygen to permeate the wrap, thereby resulting in bright red meat.
		Easily denatured when cooked and may denature to a brown color prematurely before the meat is a safe temperature for consumption.
Deoxymyoglobin	Purple-red	Chemically reduced form. Often observed when packaged in *cryovac*, which is a vacuum-sealed, airtight, plastic package. Exposure to oxygen on opening of the package will cause the color to "bloom" to a bright red (oxymyoglobin). Also may be observed in an oxygen-permeable package where the exterior of the meat is bright red but the low oxygen interior of the meat is still purple-red. This form is least sensitive to heat denaturation; thus, meats cooked when purple-red may still appear reddish-pink when at a safe temperature for consumption.
Metmyoglobin	Brown	Formed after a period of storage with exposure to oxygen. **Reducing substances** are no longer produced in the tissues over time, and this oxidized form of myoglobin is produced, resulting in a brown color. Fluorescent light accelerates the formation of metmyoglobin. Is not necessarily an indication of spoilage. Denatures rapidly when cooked and is likely to appear brown when undercooked.

Source: References 36, 90.

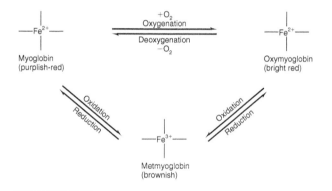

Figure 24–10
This diagram depicts the change in meat pigments because of naturally occurring chemical reactions.

are classified on the basis of age and sex. A *steer* is a male castrated when young, a *heifer* is a young female that has not yet borne a calf, a *cow* is a female that has borne a calf, a *stag* is a male castrated after maturity, and a *bull* is a mature male that has not been castrated.

Steer carcasses are generally preferred by meat handlers because of their heavier weight and the higher proportion of meat to bone, but steer and heifer carcasses of the same grade are of equal quality. A steer weighs about 1,000 pounds at 2 years and yields about 450 pounds of meat [94]. The quality of meat from cows is variable, depending on maturity, but is usually inferior to both steer and heifer meat, and thus is not eligible for the USDA Prime grade. Stag meat is not normally marketed in the United States, and bull carcasses generally are used in processed meats.

Veal

Veal is meat from immature bovines (cattle). In the wholesale market, veal carcasses are usually from animals of either sex that are at least 3 weeks but generally less than 20 weeks of age [56]. They are fed largely on milk or milk products. The term *calf* or baby beef is applied to animals slaughtered between 5 months and about 10 months of age with a maximum weight of 450 pounds [91]. The older animals have passed the good veal stage but do not yet possess the properties of good beef.

Lamb and Mutton

Sheep carcasses are classified as lamb, yearling mutton, and mutton according to the age of the animal. Lamb is obtained from young animals of either sex that are less than 12 months of age, although the exact age at which lamb changes to mutton is somewhat indefinite. Yearling mutton is approximately 12 months of age but shows evidence of greater maturity than the established standards for lamb. Mutton carcasses are those that have passed the lamb stage. The usual test for a lamb carcass is the break joint. The feet of a lamb, when broken off sharply, separate from the leg above the regular joint. The break shows four distinct ridges that appear smooth, moist, and red with blood. In mutton, the break comes in the true joint, which is below the break joint.

Most of the meat from sheep is marketed as lamb. Relatively little older mutton is sold. The flesh of all carcasses in the mutton class is darker in color than

Table 24–2
ADDITIONAL FACTORS THAT INFLUENCE MYOGLOBIN IN MEATS

Factors	Description
pH	Normal muscle pH is around 7, whereas fresh meat pH is 5.4 to 5.6. The pH drops after slaughter due to the breakdown of glycogen to lactic acid. Animals that are active or stressed shortly before slaughter will use glycogen; as a result, the meat will have a higher pH (6.2 or higher). High-pH meat will be darker in color and is commonly called dark, dry, firm meat.
	Although the effect is variable, high-pH meat tends to brown prematurely when cooked.
Meat source	Higher myoglobin concentrations are found in male animals, extensively used muscles in either sex, and more mature animals.
Modified-atmosphere packaging	80 percent oxygen and 20 percent carbon dioxide modified-atmosphere packaging promotes *oxymyoglobin* and will stabilize the red color.
	0.4 percent carbon monoxide and 30 percent carbon dioxide with the balance as nitrogen forms *carboxymyoglobin*. This pigment is a stable cherry red color.
	Meat packaged in a modified atmosphere may brown prematurely when cooked.
Freezing	Color may fade or darken with frozen storage. Color changes of meat cooked from frozen or previously frozen meats is variable, but premature browning is common.
Fat content	Lean ground meats tend to appear redder in the raw state due to less "white" fat mixed into the meat. The influence of fat content on browning is apparently limited.
Added ingredients	Salt will cause faster browning of meat. Nitrate, used in cured meats, will result in a heat-stable pink color as is commonly observed in ham or smoked turkey.

Source: References 36, 90.

IN DEPTH
IRIDESCENT COLORS AND MEAT

The surface of meat may have shiny, rainbowlike colors. This physical phenomenon is called *iridescence*. It also may be observed in the rainbow of colors in soap bubbles and fish scales. Consumers may conclude that meat with green, red, orange, and yellow iridescence is spoiled; however, iridescence is not caused by spoilage or chemical additives.

So what do we know about iridescent colors and meat? Iridescence is associated primarily with light diffraction and the surface microstructure. Meat may be more likely to be iridescent under the following conditions:

- When the meat is from the *semitendinosus* muscle found in the round
- When fibers are more perpendicular to slicing surface
- When the meat is hydrated and has a moist surface
- When the meat is sliced with a very sharp blade, such as a very sharp meat slicer

Source: Reference 38.

lamb. It is also less tender and has a stronger flavor when it is from animals beyond 2 years of age.

Pork

Pork is the meat of swine. Good-quality pork is obtained from young animals usually 6 to 7 months of age and 175 to 240 pounds [86]. In young animals, there is no distinction in quality or grade because of sex, whereas sex differences in older animals are pronounced. Most of the pork sold in the United States comes from young animals.

MEAT PRODUCTION AND MARKETING

Livestock is raised on farms across America as well as throughout the world. Livestock are used for meat, however, their hides and fat are used for other purposes (see rendering in Chapter 8). Some cattle are grass-fed. These cattle often take longer to gain weight thus increasing costs. The consumer demand for grass-fed beef is growing [68]. About three-fourths of the cattle are "finished" in feedlots [94] the last 4 to 6 months before slaughter. The feed in feedlots consists

MULTICULTURAL CUISINE
BISON

Huge, shaggy animals once roamed the land from Canada to Mexico, grazing the Great Plains and the mountain areas. These animals—the scientific species bison—were the center of life for many Native Americans, who used them for food, shelter, and clothing. Buffalo are of the bovine family, as are domestic cattle. During the "Wild West" years, buffalo were hunted extensively. From an estimated 60 million animals in earlier times, by 1893 there were only slightly more than 300 bison left in the United States.

Today, however, the bison are coming back, with an estimated 200,000 heads in North America [85]. In addition to bison found in public parklands, many are privately owned, raised on the open range, and grain-fed 90 to 120 days before they are slaughtered for food. About 20,000 are slaughtered *each year* in the United States, compared to approximately 125,000 cattle *per day*. In contrast to other meats, USDA inspection of bison is voluntary.

As meat, is bison different from beef? Bison is lower in fat and calories as compared to beef. Three and a half ounces (100 gram) of raw bison (meat only) contains about 109 calories and 1.8 grams of fat compared to 291 calories and 24 grams of fat for raw beef. Some say that bison has a sweeter, richer flavor than beef.

What do you do with bison once you have made the decision to try it? Handle bison meat as you would any other type of meat—always following safe food-handling practices. Because bison is very lean and lacks marbled fat, it should generally be cooked using low heat and long cooking times. Braising or other moist cooking methods are recommended for roasts and steaks, although broiling or panfrying may be used on thin-sliced bison. Ground bison should always be cooked to 160°F for safety reasons [85].

As you continue your experiences with new foods, you might like to try "beefalo," a cross between bison and domestic cattle. It has taken years of research to develop this breed because the natural result of bison–domestic bovine crossbreeding is sterile offspring. Beefalo is also an excellent high-quality protein source with relatively low fat content. Enjoy your journey as you explore more red meat varieties.

Courtesy of Michael Einspahr

of a balanced mix of grass, hay, and grains such as corn. Lamb is often finished in feedlots as well [88].

Antibiotics and Hormones

Antibiotics may be used to treat illnesses in livestock. As of 2017, the FDA banned the use of medically important antibiotics for growth promotion, and is requiring a prescription from a veterinarian for these antibiotics to treat sick livestock [68]. A growing concern regarding antibiotic resistance and the ability to treat illnesses in humans and animals is prompting these changes [49].

Antibiotic residues may not be present in the meat or dairy when sold. Therefore, the USDA's Food Safety and Inspection Service (FSIS) randomly samples animals at slaughter and also tests for residues [94]. An animal that has been given antibiotics must be off the antibiotics for a specified period of time before it is legal to slaughter the animal.

Hormones may be used in cattle and lambs to promote growth [68, 88, 94]. Three natural hormones and two synthetic hormones have been approved for use in cattle. One hormone has been approved for use in lamb. These hormones are used as an implant in the animal's ear and must be used in accordance with regulations. Hormones are not permitted for use in veal, pork, or poultry [86, 91].

Animal Welfare and Slaughter

The care for animal well-being includes housing, nutrition, disease prevention, and treatment. Animals must be handled humanely and slaughtered in accordance with the Humane Methods of Slaughter Act of 1978 [79, 80, 87] and the 2011 updates to directives on the Humane Handling and Slaughter of Livestock [87]. For example, livestock must have access to water, access to feed if held for more than 24 hours, and enough space to lie down. Appropriate methods of moving animals and the construction of the pens are given within the regulations.

During slaughter, livestock must be insensible to pain by stunning before being shackled, hoisted, or cut. Shortly after stunning, when the animal is unconscious, a sharp instrument is used to cut the carotid arteries and jugular veins or the blood vessels closer to the heart to bleed the animal [98]. Approximately 50 percent of the blood is drained from the animal. The only exception to the stunning requirement is ritual slaughter in accordance with the Jewish (Kosher slaughter) or Islamic (Halal slaughter) religious faiths [80].

Postmortem Changes

The muscles are soft and pliable before an animal is slaughtered. The metabolism in the cells is interrupted on death, beginning processes that lead to a stiffening of the carcass known as *rigor mortis*. Postmortem metabolic changes include (1) the accumulation of lactic acid in the muscles, resulting in a decrease in pH, and (2) the disappearance of ATP, which is the high-energy compound produced in metabolism in the living animal. As a result of these postmortem changes, the muscle becomes contracted. The muscle proteins (actin and myosin), which form the thin and thick filaments of the myofibrils in the muscle cell, slide or telescope on each other and bond together, forming actomyosin. Thus, the muscle is no longer extensible.

The time required after the death of the animal for occurrence of the stiffening process is affected by various factors. Both colder and warmer temperatures speed the development of rigor [26, 99]. The species of animal, its age, and its activity just before slaughter also affect the time of onset of rigor. In large animals, such as cattle, rigor begins more slowly and lasts longer than in smaller animals. In beef, the softening of the muscles, signaling the resolution of rigor mortis, occurs within 24 to 48 hours. If meat is separated from the carcass immediately after slaughter and cooked rapidly before rigor has a chance to develop, it will be tender. If the cooking is slow, however, rigor may develop during heating and increase toughness in the cooked meat [26, 32].

If the supply of glycogen in the muscle is low at the time of death, as is the case when much activity occurs just before slaughter, less lactic acid is produced from glycogen. As discussed in Table 24–2, when the pH of the muscle remains high, the meat is an undesirable dark color [36]. This dark muscle tissue has an increased water-binding capacity, resulting in firm meat with a dry, sticky texture because the water is so tightly bound in the muscle [17, 36].

Aging

If meat is allowed to hang under refrigeration for 1 or 2 days after slaughter, it will gradually begin to soften as rigor mortis passes. If it is held still longer, a process of ripening or aging occurs. The aging of meat results in an increase in tenderness, improvement of flavor and juiciness, better browning in cooking of both lean and fat, and a loss of red interior color at a lower cooking temperature [33]. Aging too long may result in a strong flavor or development of an off-flavor and off-odor. A major reason for the increase in tenderness during aging appears to be a breakdown of proteins in the myofibrils by enzymes [37]. Aging of beef may also produce some change in **mucoprotein**, which is a component of connective tissue [47].

Two different methods—dry aging and wet aging—can be used by meat processors for the postmortem aging of meat. Dry aging is aging meat "as is" under refrigeration, whereas wet aging involves packaging the meat in a vacuum bag and holding it under refrigeration. Dry-aged beef sold today may be dry aged after having been initially vacuum packed. Researchers found that previously vacuum-packed beef that was removed from the bag and then dry aged for an additional 14 or 21 days (1) was more tender, (2) had a dry-aged flavor (beefy and brown roasted flavors), and (3) was more juicy than vacuum-aged beef [11]. The additional storage time associated with dry aging, coupled with greater shrink and trim loss, makes dry-aged beef more expensive than wet-aged beef.

Beef is the only type of meat that is commonly aged, although some consumers also prefer lamb when it is aged. Many cuts of beef are tender after 11 to 14 days of aging; however, other cuts benefit by a longer aging period. Veal is not improved by aging, and the lack of fat on the carcass results in excessive surface drying. Pork is usually obtained from a young, tender animal; thus, toughness is not generally a problem. Aging of pork for more than 3 or 4 days may be complicated by the tendency of relatively rapid development of rancidity in the fat during holding.

Packaging

Many supermarkets as well as food service operations receive much of their fresh meat in reduced-oxygen barrier bags (*cryovac* packaging). Beef packaged in vacuum barrier bags will be a purplish-red and will not "bloom" to a bright cherry red color until the package is opened. It is this same packaging that is used when beef is wet aged. Most beef sold in supermarkets is a bright red because the oxygen barrier bags have been opened and the meat is portioned and repackaged on a Styrofoam tray with an oxygen-permeable plastic wrap (**Figure 24–11**).

Case-ready meat is sold in some retail markets and grocery stores. Case-ready meat is packaged centrally and then delivered to the retail market ready for the display case. Centralized packaging removes the cutting and packaging steps from the supermarket meat departments into centralized operations. Costs can be reduced, shelf life extended, and microbiological quality improved [6, 7, 8]. Some of the case-ready meat packaging systems are described in **Table 24–3**.

Labeling

The FSIS approves labels for meat and poultry products. Each meat or poultry label must contain the following information: (1) product name, (2) producer or distributor name and address, (3) inspection mark (round stamp), (4) ingredient list in order from highest to lowest amounts, (5) net weight, (6) establishment number indicating the plant where the product was processed, and

Figure 24–11

Two types of meat packaging can be observed in this photo. Starting at the right side of the photo is the meat packaged in a tray with an air space above the meat and plastic wrap. This is an example of modified atmosphere packaging. In the middle of the picture is the traditionally packaged ground beef in Styrofoam trays with oxygen-permeable plastic wrap directly over the meat.   (USDA)

(7) handling instructions for products that require special handling to remain safe. Refer to Chapter 3 for more about government regulation and labeling requirements.

In 1994, the USDA mandated a safe-handling label for raw or partially cooked meat and poultry

products that are packaged in USDA- or state-inspected processing plants and retail stores (**Figure 24–12**). These instructions are designed to decrease the risk of foodborne illness attributable to unsafe handling, preparation, and storage of meat and poultry products both at food service facilities and in private kitchens by educating the consumer. The language and format for the label are specified [42].

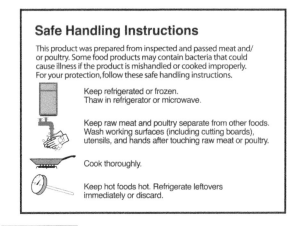

Figure 24–12

The USDA requires safe-handling instructions on packages of all raw or partially cooked meat and poultry products. (USDA)

Table 24–3
TYPES OF CASE-READY MEAT PACKAGING SYSTEMS

Type of Packaging	Description	Meat Color
Vacuum packaged, reduced oxygen	Heavy plastic bag (cryovac) with reduced oxygen levels. Will maintain a relatively long shelf life.	Purplish-red color until the package is opened.
High-oxygen modified atmosphere	Oxygen and carbon dioxide are added to the package atmosphere. The package often is a solid plastic tray covered with a barrier clear film. The package volume is approximately double that of the meat to allow adequate headspace for the modified atmosphere. The high oxygen levels promote oxidation, and thus antioxidants may be used.	Bright red. High oxygen level converts the pigment to brown metmyoglobin over time.
Carbon monoxide, low-oxygen modified atmosphere	Up to 0.4 percent of carbon monoxide is added to the package atmosphere. Carbon dioxide levels are also elevated. The package volume is approximately double that of the meat. Shelf life for meat packaged in this way is typically longer than for other methods. The modified atmosphere in this package retards oxidation and the growth of spoilage organisms.	A stable red color is produced by the low level of carbon monoxide. "Use by" dates and other spoilage indicators must be followed because this product will retain a bright red color and appear fresh for extended periods.

Source: References 7, 8, 65.

As of 2012, meat and poultry must also provide nutrition labeling either on the package or on a poster at the point of sale [83]. Raw meats and poultry were previously exempt from the nutrition labeling requirements. Like other products, meat and poultry are now provided country-of-origin labeling (COOL) [81].

Some meat is labeled as "natural." Products labeled "natural" may not contain artificial color or flavor, preservatives, or other artificial ingredients [94]. Additionally, a statement on the package should explain to the consumer what is meant by the term *natural*. Some companies identify their meat as natural to indicate that no hormones or antibiotics were used or that the animals were raised in grass and not finished in a feedlot. The terms *natural* and *organic* should not be used interchangeably because specific governmental guidelines have been established for the use of the term *organic*. See Chapter 3 for information about organic food regulations.

Government Regulation, Inspection, and Grading

Regulation. Several laws have been passed and regulations published at the national and local levels to protect and inform the consumer on the purchasing of meat and poultry products. The aim of these regulations is to protect the public not only from obvious abnormalities and animal disease but also from the hazards of pathogenic microorganisms that may be present on carcasses or in processing plants. The USDA has the responsibility at the federal level for the inspection, grading, setting of standards, and labeling of all meat and poultry products. The Wholesome Meat Act of 1967 requires that state governments have local programs of meat inspection equal to those of the federal government for meat that is sold within state boundaries. Otherwise, the federal government will assume the responsibility for inspection. State programs are periodically reviewed to see that satisfactory standards are maintained. The Federal Meat Inspection Act also requires that all meat imported into the United States comply with the same standards of inspection applied to meat produced in the United States.

Much of the slaughtered meat and poultry goes into processed items, including sausages, ham, pizza, frozen dinners, and soups. The federal inspection program is also responsible for the safety of these products. An in-plant inspector monitors the processing operations (**Figure 24–13**).

Inspection. The inspection for the wholesomeness of all meats entering interstate commerce by qualified agents of the USDA's FSIS is required. If meat carcasses pass the inspection process, the inspector's stamp (**Figure 24–14**) is placed on each wholesale cut of the carcass. This stamp carries numbers to indicate the packer and identify the carcass. If the meat is unsound, it is not permitted to enter retail trade. Consumers should, however, always use safe food-handling practices to protect against foodborne illness (see Chapter 2).

Figure 24–13

An USDA inspector is checking the temperature of lamb carcasses that already have the blue inspector stamp. (U.S. Department of Agriculture)

Figure 24–14

Federal meat inspection stamps are stamped on meats using a food-safe (edible) dye to indicate inspection by the USDA. (U.S. Department of Agriculture)

Traditionally, the inspection system relied largely on sight, touch, and smell, which was appropriate in an era when the goal was to protect the public against obvious abnormalities and animal disease. Animals are inspected alive and at various stages of the slaughtering process. The cleanliness and operating procedures of meatpacking plants are also supervised. However, certain hazards cannot easily be observed, particularly contamination of the animals or processing plants with pathogenic microorganisms—bacteria, parasites, fungi, and viruses—that can cause human illness. Because of the danger of illness for the meat-consuming public, the USDA revised many aspects of the inspection system to detect and reduce the microbial hazards while providing greater assurance that meat and meat products are safe for human consumption. Four essential elements make up the modernized inspection process [10]:

1. All state and federally inspected meat and poultry slaughter and processing plants must have a Hazard Analysis and Critical Control Points plan (see Chapter 2).
2. Each of these meat and poultry plants must develop written sanitation standard operating procedures to show how they will meet daily sanitation requirements.
3. The federal agency tests for *Salmonella* on raw meat and poultry products to verify that pathogen reduction standards for *Salmonella* are being met.
4. Slaughter plants test for generic *Escherichia coli* on carcasses to verify that the process is under control with respect to preventing and removing fecal contamination.

E. coli. Regulations designed to reduce the incidence of *E. coli* 0157:H7 have been strengthened [25]. The incidence rate was 0.9 illness per 100,000 people in 2010 [71], which is down from 2.1 cases per 100,000 in 1997. Data from the CDC's FoodNet continues to show a drop in incidence of *E. coli* 0157:H7 [72, 84], and furthermore several of these outbreaks in recent years have been in produce items (such as romaine, alfalfa sprouts) and not meat [73]. Nevertheless, all those who handle raw meat must use safe food-handling and cooking practices to further protect against a potential foodborne illness. See Chapter 2 for a discussion on foodborne illness.

Bovine Spongiform Encephalopathy. Federal agencies, including the USDA and the U.S. Department of Health and Human Services, have worked to prevent bovine spongiform encephalopathy (BSE) from entering the United States. BSE, also sometimes called *mad cow disease*, has been found in a total of five U.S. animals, the first in 2003 and the most recent in 2017 [29, 75, 76]. Meat from these animals did not enter the food supply.

BSE was first reported in the United Kingdom in 1986. Since 1989, the United States prohibited the importation of cattle and edible animal products from countries with cases of BSE [58]. Additional preventive measures have included (1) regulations prohibiting the use of most mammalian protein in feeds manufactured for **ruminants**, (2) U.S. Food and Drug Administration (FDA) inspection of feed mills and rendering facilities, (3) USDA examination of all cattle before approval for food and prohibition of the use of all cattle with neurological diseases, and (4) USDA examination of cattle brains for the presence of BSE [24, 58].

Following the identification of the first two U.S. cattle that tested positive for BSE, more protective regulations were added. These include the banning of the following from the human food supply: (1) nonambulatory or downer cattle; (2) specific risk materials, such as brain (from cattle older than 30 months), spinal cord, nerves attached to spinal cord, and so forth; and (3) beef processed with **mechanical separation** [29].

Trichinella Spiralis. There is no practical means of inspecting for the presence of the small parasite *T. spiralis*, which may be found in the muscle of pork carcasses. When consumed, this organism causes trichinosis. Regulations for the inspection of meat products containing pork that are usually eaten without cooking require treatment of such products in a way that destroys any live trichinae that may be in the pork muscle tissue. This process can be accomplished in one of three ways: (1) heating uniformly to a temperature of $137°F$ ($59°C$), (2) freezing for not less than 20 days at a maximum temperature of $5°F$ ($-15°C$), or (3) curing under special methods prescribed by the USDA. Products such as dried and summer sausage, bologna, frankfurter-style sausage, cooked hams, and cooked pork in casings are among those requiring this treatment.

Grades and Grading. A program separate from the inspection service is the USDA system of grading meat. Whereas inspection of meat for wholesomeness is mandatory for all meat as it is slaughtered, grading is voluntary. Although it is not required that meat be graded to be marketed, grading provides a national uniform language for use in the buying and selling of meat. Grades are also useful to the consumer in knowing what quality to expect from purchased meats. The grading program is administered by the USDA, but the cost of the service is borne by those meatpackers who use it.

Two types of USDA meat grading are done: one for yield and another for quality. In 2009 an electronic instrument grading system has increased the uniformity of yield and quality grading assessments [53]. A picture of the meat cut allows a computer to analyze the grading standards (**Figure 24–15**).

Yield Grades. Yield grades are based on cutability, which indicates the proportionate amount of salable retail cuts that can be obtained from a carcass. Yield

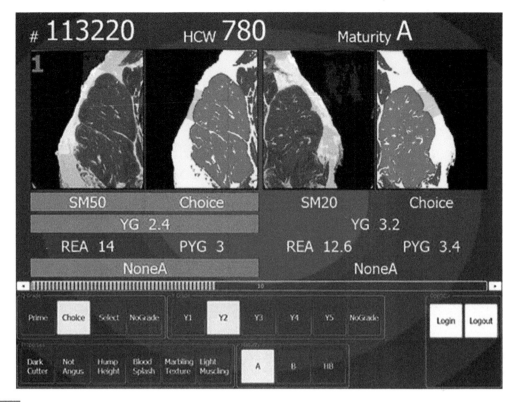

The yield and quality grading of meat can now be accomplished by taking a photo that a computer analyzes. On the left side we see the meat photo and the computer illustration where the amount of muscle and fat is measured. This cut is a yield grade 2, quality grade choice. (U.S. Department of Agriculture)

U.S. yield grades identify carcass differences in cutability: the percentage yields of boneless, closely trimmed retail cuts from the high-value parts of the carcass. (U.S. Department of Agriculture)

Grade 1 is for the highest yield; Yield Grade 5, the lowest (**Figure 24–16**). A large proportion of edible meat is indicated by a relatively large ribeye area, a thin layer of external fat, and a small amount of fat around the internal organs. The dual system of grading, for both quality and yield, attempts to offer the consumer high-quality meat without excess fat. Both quality and yield grades must be used when beef and lamb are federally graded. Conformation, or shape and build of the animal, is reflected to some degree in the yield grade. A stocky, muscular build usually represents a relatively high proportion of salable meat and receives a high yield grade.

Quality Grades. Quality grades have been established for beef, veal, lamb, and mutton. In pork, the grade is determined by class (barrow, gilt, sow, stag, or boar) and consideration of quality and yield [56]. Barrow (castrated male swine) and gilt (young female swine that have not reproduced) are graded. Meat from boars (males not castrated) may have an objectionable odor or flavor called *boar taint* and are not eligible for grading. Factors considered in determining the quality grades are associated with palatability or eating quality.

Marbling and maturity are the two major considerations in evaluating the quality of beef. Marbling refers to the flecks of fat within the lean muscle (**Figure 24–17**). An optimum thickness of surface fat layer also appears to contribute to palatability [16, 69]. The maturity of an animal affects the lean meat texture—the grain generally becoming more coarse with increasing maturity. Fine-textured lean is usually slightly more tender than

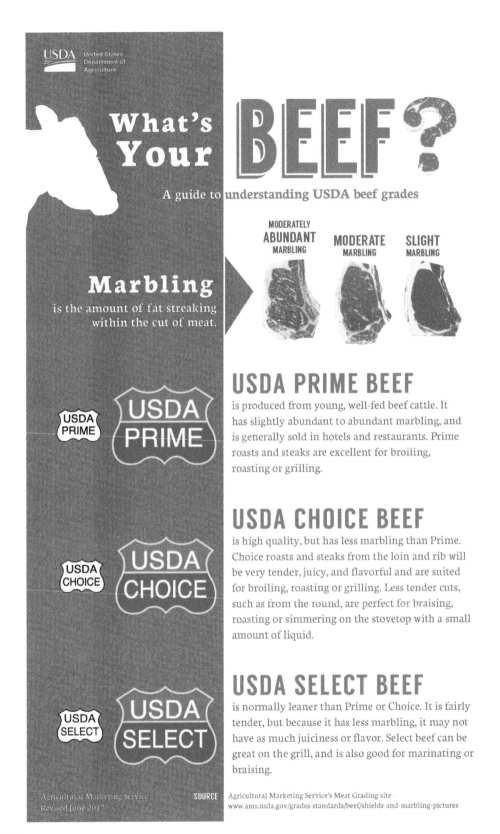

USDA United States Department of Agriculture

What's Your BEEF?

A guide to understanding USDA beef grades

Marbling
is the amount of fat streaking within the cut of meat.

MODERATELY ABUNDANT MARBLING

MODERATE MARBLING

SLIGHT MARBLING

USDA PRIME

USDA PRIME BEEF
is produced from young, well-fed beef cattle. It has slightly abundant to abundant marbling, and is generally sold in hotels and restaurants. Prime roasts and steaks are excellent for broiling, roasting or grilling.

USDA CHOICE

USDA CHOICE BEEF
is high quality, but has less marbling than Prime. Choice roasts and steaks from the loin and rib will be very tender, juicy, and flavorful and are suited for broiling, roasting or grilling. Less tender cuts, such as from the round, are perfect for braising, roasting or simmering on the stovetop with a small amount of liquid.

USDA SELECT

USDA SELECT BEEF
is normally leaner than Prime or Choice. It is fairly tender, but because it has less marbling, it may not have as much juiciness or flavor. Select beef can be great on the grill, and is also good for marinating or braising.

Agricultural Marketing Service Revised June 2017

SOURCE Agricultural Marketing Service's Meat Grading site · www.ams.usda.gov/grades-standards/beef/shields-and-marbling-pictures

Figure 24–17

Marbling in cuts of meat and the corresponding USDA grade shields for beef are shown. The meat grading program is administered by USDA, but the cost of the service is borne by the meat packagers. (U.S. Department of Agriculture)

lean with a very coarse texture. A mature animal develops changes in connective tissue that contribute to decreased tenderness. Characteristics of quality for different kinds of meat are given in **Table 24–4**.

Table 24–5 shows USDA quality grades for beef, veal, lamb, and mutton. The pork grades are yield and quality designations. Utility and lower grades of meat are rarely, if ever, sold as cuts in retail stores but instead are used in processed meat products. The appropriate USDA quality grade mark is applied to meat with a roller stamp that leaves its mark on the full length of the carcass.

Table 24–4
INDICATORS OF QUALITY IN BEEF, VEAL, LAMB, AND PORK

Meat Classification	Indicators of Good Quality	Indicators of Poor Quality
Beef	Bright red color of lean muscle after the cut surface is exposed to air for a few minutes (meat will be a purplish-red color before exposure to air).	Darker red color and coarse grain. Lacks smooth, satiny surfaces when cut.
	Fine grained and smooth to the touch. Firm fat.	Fat is oily or soft in texture.
	Chine, or backbone, is soft, red, and spongy and shows considerable cartilage.	Bones are white, hard, and brittle and show little or no cartilage.
Veal	Grayish-pink flesh and a texture that is fine grained and smooth to the touch.	Either a very pale or a dark color of the lean.
	Interior fat is firm and brittle. Bones are red, spongy, and soft and have an abundance of cartilage.	Little or no fat distributed throughout the carcass.
Lamb	Pinkish-red color, fine-grained, and smooth-cut surfaces of the flesh.	Darker color of the lean, heavier fat layers, and a stronger flavor.
	Firm, flaky, and brittle fat.	
	Bones are soft, red, and spongy and show cartilage.	
Pork	Grayish-pink color.	Excess fat distributed in the lean tissues and on the exterior.
	Fine grained. Very firm fat but not brittle as in other types of meats.	Color of the lean is darker, the grain is coarser, and the bones may appear less red and spongy—usually because it is from an older animal.
	Soft, red, and spongy bones.	

Source: References 40, 56.

Table 24–5
USDA QUALITY GRADES FOR MEAT

Beef	Veal	Lamb	Mutton	Pork* (Excludes Stag and Boar Classes)
Prime	Prime	Prime	Choice	U.S. No. 1
Choice	Choice	Choice	Good	U.S. No. 2
Select	Good	Good	Utility	U.S. No. 3
Standard	Standard	Utility	Cull	U.S. No. 4
Commercial	Utility			U.S. Utility
Utility				
Cutter				
Canner				

* Pork designations include yield and quality.

Note: Standard and commercial beef grades may be sold as "ungraded" meat. Utility, cutter, and canner grades may be used for ground beef or processed products.

Source: Reference 56.

Because beef can vary so much in quality, it has eight designated grades, with USDA Prime beef being the highest quality. Only about 7 percent of marketed beef is likely to be graded Prime, and most of this beef is purchased for use in commercial food service. USDA Choice grade beef has slightly less marbling than Prime but is still of very high quality. USDA Select and Standard grades lack the juiciness and quality of the higher grades, but because meat from these grades comes from animals younger than 30 to 42 months, it may be fairly tender. USDA Commercial, Utility, and Cutter grade beef comes from mature animals that are older than 42 months. Thus, slow cooking with moist heat is needed to tenderize these lower grades.

PURCHASING MEAT

As with other foods, your needs and preferences should be evaluated when making meat purchasing decisions. Your preference for organic (discussed earlier in the chapter and in Chapter 2), grass-fed, types of cuts, kinds of meat, nutrition, budget, and your intended use of the product all need to be considered. Meat is often one of the more expensive per pound food purchases.

Meat Primal and Retail Cuts

An understanding of primal and retail cuts of meat cuts is useful when purchasing meat. Primal or wholesale cuts are first major division of the carcass. Price, tenderness, and recommended preparation methods can in large part be predicted when the location of the primal cut on the carcass is known. Primal cuts are then further divided into smaller retail cuts. Primal or wholesale and retail cuts of beef, pork, and lamb are shown in **Figures 24–18, 24–19,** and **24–20**, respectively. A cut of meat named a steak or chop is one from a primal that is cut relatively thin—an inch or less usually. Roasts are cuts that are larger. The use of steak, chop, or roast does not offer guidance on whether a meat will be tender.

Division into cuts is made in relation to bone and muscle structure. Muscles found together in any one retail cut generally have similar characteristics of tenderness and texture. The shapes and sizes of bones and muscles in retail cuts act as guides to identification (**Figure 24–21**). Because the skeletal structure is similar for all meat animals, the basic cuts are similar for beef, pork, veal, and lamb; however, each type of meat carcass is divided into a somewhat different manner.

The industry-wide Cooperative Meat Identification Standards Committee, organized by the meat industry, has developed standards for the retail meat trade and provided a master list of recommended names for retail cuts of beef, pork, veal, and lamb. The recommended retail package label information includes the species or kind of meat, the primal cut name, and the specific retail name from the master list (**Figure 24–22**). A typical label reads "Beef Chuck—Blade Roast." When purchasing meat for food service, Institutional Meat Purchase Specifications (IMPS) provide standardized meat cuts by number. Photographs and written descriptions of the IMPS items are provided in the North America Meat Processors Association's *Meat Buyer's Guide* [56]. This guide can in particularly be helpful because some meat cuts are known by different names in various parts of the country. For example, boneless beef top loin steaks are commonly called Delmonico, Kansas City, New York, or strip steaks; flank steak may be called London broil or minute steak. Thus, the standard IMPS numbers in the *Meat Buyer's Guide* enables those purchasing meat for food services to be clear in identifying the intended cut to be purchased.

Beef. Cuts of beef are sometimes classified by most tender, medium tender, and least tender cuts. In general, those muscles that are little used are the most tender. Thus, meat from the rib, loin, and sirloin primals are the most tender and also typically cost more per pound than other cuts. **Table 24–6** lists the primal cuts by tenderness. There are some exceptions to these general rules. The top five muscles, in order of tenderness, are given in **Table 24–7** and include two individual muscles from the chuck primal. Although the chuck primal in general is not considered to be tender, these two individual muscles are exceptions.

Several popular steaks are cut from the loin (also called short loin) and the sirloin. The loin and sirloin are cut into steaks as follows: top loin (nearest the rib) then T-bone, porterhouse, and sirloin. The tenderloin muscle, which lies on the underside of the backbone (between the backbone and kidney fat), forms one eye of meat in the loin steaks. It is very small or even nonexistent in the top loin steak area but increases in size farther back, having maximum size in the porterhouse steaks. The tenderloin may be purchased as a boneless cut suitable for roasting or cutting into steaks. Because of its tenderness, tenderloin commands a high price.

Veal, Lamb, and Pork. Veal, lamb, and pork carcasses, being smaller than those of beef, are divided into fewer primal and retail cuts. The loin of pork is a long cut including both the rib and loin sections. The rib and loin sections of veal, lamb, and pork are cut into chops or roasts. The hind legs are also tender enough for roasts. The individual cuts are identical in

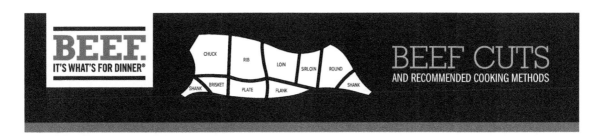

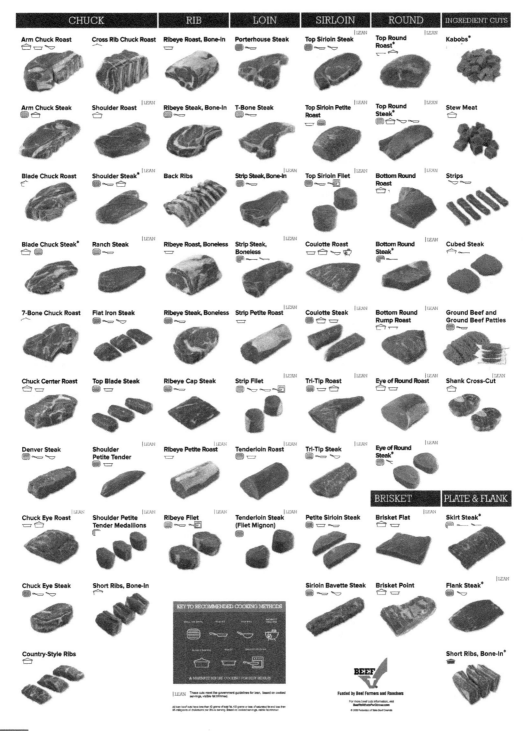

Figure 24–18

Primal and retail cuts of beef. (The Beef Checkoff www.BeefItsWhatsForDinner.com)

Figure 24–19

Primal and retail cuts of pork. (National Pork Board)

Figure 24–20

Primal and retail cuts of lamb. (American Lamb Board)

Bones Identify Seven Groups of Retail Cuts

Shoulder Arm Cuts		Arm Bone
Shoulder Blade Cuts (Cross Sections of Blade Bone)	Blade Bone (near neck)	Blade Bone (center cuts) — Blade Bone (near rib)
Rib Cuts		Back Bone and Rib Bone
Loin Cuts		Back Bone (T-Shape) T-Bone
Hip (Sirloin) Cuts (Cross Sections of Hip Bone)	Pin Bone (near loin) — Flat Bone* (center cuts)	Wedge Bone† (near round)
Leg or Round Cuts		Leg or Round Bone
Breast, or Brisket Cuts		Breast and Rib Bones

*Formerly part of "double bone" but today the back bone is usually removed leaving only the "flat bone" (sometimes called "pin bone") in the sirloin steak.
†On one side of sirloin steak, this bone may be wedge shaped while on the other side the same bone may be round.

Figure 24–21

Basic bone shapes aid in meat cut identification.

general shape and characteristics to similar cuts from beef, but less variation exists in the tenderness of cuts from different sections of the animal. All cuts of young

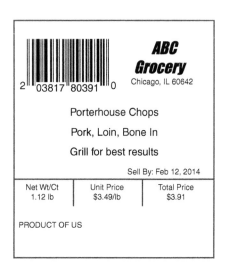

Figure 24–22

Meat labeled for sale in grocery stores identify the type of meat (such as beef or pork), the primal (such as chuck, rib, or loin), and the cut (such as steak, chop, or roast). In addition, the retailer may add a common or popular name, such as filet mignon or London broil. Price per pound and "sell by" dates are also provided.

Table 24–6
LEVEL OF TENDERNESS ASSOCIATED WITH BEEF CUTS

Most Tender Cuts	Medium Tender Cuts	Least Tender Cuts
Rib	Chuck	Flank
Loin (short loin)	Round	Plate
Sirloin		Brisket
		Neck
		Shanks

pork of good quality, both fresh and cured, are tender. However, like beef, the cuts from the loin primal, such as pork chops and pork tenderloin, are often preferred.

Lamb and veal are similar to beef in that neck, shoulder or chuck, breast, and shanks may require some moist heat in cooking for tenderness. Even the most tender cuts of veal may be improved by some application of moist heat to hydrolyze the collagen in connective tissue. The lack of fat marbling in veal may also affect its tenderness. Larding, which involves inserting strips of fat into lean meat, supplies fat and enhances the flavor. The leg, loin, and rib sections of good-quality veal may be satisfactorily roasted.

Restructured Meat

The market demand for boneless meat that can be prepared rapidly cannot always be met with existing high-quality meat supplies at prices desired by consumers. One way to help supply this potential market is with

Table 24–7
THE TOP FIVE BEEF MUSCLES IN ORDER OF TENDERNESS

Name of Muscle	Location of Muscle	Retail Name
Psoas major	Beef loin, tenderloin	Tenderloin or filet mignon
Infraspinatus	Chuck, beef shoulder, top blade	Flat iron steak
Gluteus medius	Top sirloin center-cut	
Longissimus dorsi	Beef rib, ribeye and beef loin strip steak, center-cut	Ribeye steak or strip steak
Triceps brachii	Chuck, beef shoulder, arm	Ranch steak

Source: Reference 56.

the production of restructured meats. *Restructuring* is changing the form of soft tissues, including lean, fat, and connective tissue [44]. The process generally begins with flaking, coarse grinding, dicing, or chopping the meat to reduce the particle size. Following this reduction process, it is mixed with small amounts of such substances as salt and phosphates to solubilize muscle proteins on the surface of the meat pieces and to aid in binding the particles together. The meat pieces are then formed into the desired shape and size. Through restructuring, less valuable pieces of meat, including lean trimmings, are upgraded. They are used to produce boneless, uniformly sized steak or roast products that resemble fresh intact muscle in flavor, color, and texture [13].

There are a variety of restructured meats in the marketplace. Canadian-style bacon may be sold as a whole muscle or a restructured product. Other examples of restructured meat and poultry products include some ham or turkey deli meat and breaded chicken nuggets. These items may also be purchased as whole muscle, but they will be more expensive than their restructured counterparts.

Variety Meats

Included in the category of variety meats are sweetbreads, tripe, heart, tongue, liver, kidney, brains, pork rinds, pickled pigs feet, and oxtail. Sweetbreads are the thymus gland of the calf or young beef. This gland disappears as the animal matures. The thymus gland of lamb is sometimes used for sweetbreads but is too small to be of practical value. The thymus gland has two parts—the heart sweetbread and the throat, or neck, sweetbread. It is white and soft.

Tripe is the smooth lining from the first beef stomach, the honeycombed lining from the second stomach, and the pocket-shaped section from the end of the second stomach. It is used in the Mexican dish menudo, as well as many other regional and ethnic dishes. The heart and tongue are much-exercised muscles and therefore are not tender. They, as well as tripe, require relatively long, slow cooking for tenderization.

Liver is a fine-textured variety meat. Veal or calf liver, because of its tenderness and mild flavor, is usually preferred to other kinds of liver and for that reason is more expensive. Livers from all meat animals are high in nutritive value. Kidneys from beef and veal consist of irregular lobes and deep clefts. Kidneys from veal are more tender and delicate in flavor than those from beef.

Ground Beef and Hamburger

Both ground beef and hamburger are made from beef that has been ground. However, beef fat may be added to "hamburger," but not to "ground beef" [82]. A processor may add fat to hamburger if the meat being ground is particularly lean and a higher fat level is desired. A

IN DEPTH

HOW TO BUY A HAM

The first step in purchasing a ham is to understand the terminology. *Fresh ham* or *leg* refers to the meat from the pork primal called "leg" that has not been cured. The leg primal (previously called ham) is the rear leg of the pork. The USDA defines a *cured ham* as meat from the leg pork primal.

In common usage, a variety of pork cuts may be cured and called "ham." Curing may be dry or wet. Ingredients used in curing include salt, sodium or potassium nitrate, and other seasonings. Not all hams are fully cooked; therefore, the label must be checked for the statement "cook before eating" to know if the ham needs further cooking or may be consumed as purchased.

There are a variety of hams available in the marketplace. Those hams produced from primal cuts other than the leg primal do not meet the USDA definition for ham and usually have a qualifying term, such as *cottage*. Some of the terminology used for hams includes the following:

- *Capocolla ham.* Usually made from the pork shoulder. Should always be labeled with "cooked" in product name.

- *Cottage ham.* Usually not cooked. Is cured pork from the shoulder primal and thus does not meet the USDA definition for ham.

- *Country ham.* Uncooked, cured, dried pork from the leg (previously ham) primal or the pork shoulder. Prepared by a dry application of salt and other curing-ingredients.

- *Ham.* Cured leg of pork.

- *Ham shank end.* From the lower, slightly pointed part of the leg.

- *Ham, Smithfield.* Aged, dry-cured ham made exclusively in Smithfield, Virginia.

- *Ham, water added.* At least 17 percent protein with 10 percent added solution.

- *Ham, with natural juices.* At least 18.5 percent protein.

- *Hickory-smoked ham.* Cured ham smoked over burning hickory wood chips in a smokehouse.

- *Prosciutto.* Italian-style dry-cured ham that is raw. Because of the dry-curing process, it may be consumed without cooking unless otherwise labeled. Prosciutto, Cooked, refers to a dry-cured ham that is cooked.

Source: Reference 95.

maximum fat content of 30 percent by weight has been set for both ground beef and hamburger ground in federally inspected plants. Most ground beef, however, is prepared in local supermarkets to maintain freshness. The percentage of lean is often provided on the label.

Cooking yields of ground beef increase with decreasing fat content in the raw product, but tenderness and juiciness generally decrease [15]. Ground chuck must come specifically from the chuck area of the carcass, and ground round must come only from the round.

E.coli 0157:H7 has been associated with both ground beef and hamburger. Irradiated ground beef or hamburger may be purchased as one method of avoiding *E. coli* 0157:H7. Cooking ground meats (ground beef or other ground meats) to recommended temperatures is an important protective step (see Chapter 2). Microbiological product testing has resulted in meat recalls. However, because a small number of organisms can cause illness, irradiation can provide a high level of safety [3, 59]. This extra level of protection may be especially important when serving populations at a high risk for foodborne illness, such as children, or when preparing ground beef in situations where careful and consistent temperature control may be difficult. In one study, consumers rated irradiated and control ground beef patties equally for overall liking, toughness, flavor, and texture. The irradiated beef patties were rated as juicier than the nonirradiated [97]. See Chapter 2 for a more extensive discussion on food safety.

Economic Considerations

American families tend to spend a substantial percentage of their food money on meats. Balancing expense with the USDA Dietary Guidelines should be taken into account [96]. The USDA Choose My Plate website (www.choosemyplate.gov) offers menu-planning advice on a budget as well as individualized nutrition guidance. Other sources of protein, such as dried beans, are economical and can help to stretch the food dollar (see Chapter 19).

There are many economical cuts of meat, such as selected cuts from the beef chuck or round, that, when prepared with the use of marinades or moist cooking methods, are delicious and tender. Retail prices are influenced by demand for such factors as tenderness, general appearance, and ease or convenience in cooking. The consumer tends to buy on the basis of these qualities to so great an extent that the loins and ribs, which represent only about one-fourth of the beef carcass, are about one-half of the retail cost. The food value is similar in both tender and less tender lean meat cuts. Thus, consumers have many opportunities to save money when selecting meat cuts.

Considerable variation exists in the percentage of bone, muscle meat, and visible fat among retail cuts. **Table 24–8** provides information about the yield of boneless cooked meat from various cuts. Ground beef yields the largest number of 3-ounce servings per pound of beef; short ribs, bone-in, yield the smallest number of servings. In general, the cost per pound of an edible portion is greatest in those cuts that command the highest prices and vice versa, but several exceptions occur because of differences in the percentage of bone and fat in the cuts. For example, at the same price per pound (as purchased or AP), the rump (bone-in) may cost almost double the price of round per pound of edible portions (edible portion or EP) because only about 43 percent of the rump is edible compared with about 76 percent of round. Therefore, it is important to recognize that cost per pound of meat as purchased is not the only consideration. The cost per pound of edible meat yield should also be taken into account.

The usual amount to buy per serving is 4 ounces of meat with little or no bone and ¾ to 1 pound of meat with a high refuse content. One average pork chop is a serving, as is one to two lamb chops, depending on the size and thickness of the chops. In recent years, however, portion sizes have increased and have resulted in higher meal costs while not necessarily improving dietary quality. The USDA Choose My Plate website (www.choosemyplate.gov) recommends that meat take up only about one-fourth of your plate.

TENDERNESS AND FLAVOR

Tenderness

One of the most valued attributes of meat is tenderness. There are a variety of factors that influence beef tenderness, including animal maturity, postmortem aging, muscle type, marbling, marinating when prepared, mechanical tenderization, proper cooking methods, degree of doneness, and carving techniques. The grading of meat by USDA standards does not directly measure tenderness, although the probability that a beef carcass will be tender is greater in a higher grade than in a lower grade. Pork and lamb are usually tender because they are relatively young when slaughtered as compared to beef.

Much of the research on tenderness has been on beef because of its greater variability. The U.S. Meat Animal Research Center in Nebraska has developed a testing system to identify beef carcasses with rib and loin cuts of above-average tenderness [27]. Under this system, a rib steak from a chilled carcass is cooked, then measured for tenderness with an electronic testing machine that provides computer data (**Figure 24–23**). Research at the Meat Animal Research Center has shown that marbling accounts for only 10 percent of the variation in beef ribeye tenderness [27].

Table 24–8
YIELD OF BONELESS COOKED MEAT FROM 1-POUND RETAIL CUTS OF BEEF AND VEAL*

Kind and Cut of Meat	Number of 3-Ounce Servings	Volume, Chopped or Diced (Cups)
Beef		
Brisket		
Bone-in	2	1–1½
Boneless, fresh or corned	3	1½–2
Chuck roast, arm		
Bone-in	2½–3	1½–2
Boneless	3½	2
Chuck roast, blade		
Bone-in	2½	1½
Boneless	3–3½	2
Club or T-bone steak, bone-in	2	—
Flank steak, boneless	3½	—
Ground beef	4	—
Porterhouse steak, bone-in	2–2½	—
Rib roast		
Bone-in	2½	1½
Boneless	3	1½–2
Round steak		
Bone-in	3–3½	—
Boneless	3½–4	—
Bottom round (rump) roast		
Bone-in	2½	1½
Boneless	3½	2
Short ribs, bone-in	1½	1
Sirloin steak		
Bone-in	2–2½	—
Boneless	2½–3	—
Veal		
Breast		
Bone-in	2	1–1½
Boneless	3	1½–2
Cutlet		
Bone-in	3½	—
Boneless	4	—
Leg roast		
Bone-in	2½	1½
Boneless	3½	2
Loin chops, bone-in	2½–3	—
Loin roast		
Bone-in	2½	1½
Boneless	3½	2
Rib chops, bone-in	2½	—
Rib roast		
Bone-in	2–2½	1–1½
Boneless	3½	2
Shoulder roast		
Bone-in	2½	1½
Boneless	3½	2

* These figures allow no more than 10 percent fat on a cooked bone-in cut and no more than 15 percent fat on a cooked boneless cut.
Source: Used by permission of the U.S. Department of Agriculture.

Figure 24–23

A food technologist uses a computer program to predict tenderness and beef carcass composition based on test results. (Keith Weller/U.S. Department of Agriculture)

Figure 24–24

This beef chuck seven-bone steak has more connective tissue than cuts from the rib and loin. Take note of the distinctive seven-shaped bone at the picture. (The Beef Checkoff www. BeefItsWhatsForDinner.com)

Taste panels, in studying the tenderness of meat, have described (1) the ease with which teeth sink into the meat, or softness; (2) the crumbliness of the muscle fibers; and (3) the amount of connective tissue or the amount of residue remaining after the meat is chewed for a specified time. Each of these components of tenderness may be influenced by various factors operating in the production and preparation of beef and other meats.

Connective Tissue. Larger amounts of connective tissue in a cut of meat cause decreased tenderness (**Figure 24–24**). The least-used muscles of an animal, particularly those in the rib and loin sections, contain less connective tissue than muscles that are used for locomotion. The muscles of the rib and loin, for example, are more tender than the muscles of the legs and shoulders.

As animals mature and become older, more and stronger connective tissue usually forms in muscle tissues. The cross-links between collagen monomers that make up the fibrils in connective tissue appear to become less soluble and more resistant to heat as an animal ages. This factor is important in explaining the difference in tenderness between younger and older animals.

The tenderloin muscle, which is not used in locomotion and has little connective tissue, remains tender in animals up to 48 months of age, whereas other muscles with strong connective tissue triple in toughness [66]. The case of veal is different, however. Although it is a very young animal, there is still a relatively high percentage of connective tissue in the muscles because of the lack of time for development of the muscle itself.

Fat and Marbling. The fattening of animals has long been thought to improve the tenderness of meat. It has been suggested that a layer of subcutaneous fat on a carcass delays chilling of the meat, thereby

FOCUS ON SCIENCE
HOW DOES THE WARNER-BRATZLER SHEAR MEASURE THE TENDERNESS OF MEAT?

The Warner-Bratzler shear test has been used to determine the tenderness of meat. Sensory scores have been found to correlate with shear readings. This agreement in tenderness scoring may be because the dull edge that is used to shear the meat simulates the grinding surfaces of the teeth, which also are dull.

The following procedure is used:

- A core piece of meat (0.5 to 1 inch in diameter) is placed on the triangular opening of the guillotine fixture.
- An initial rise in the measurement chart is due to the compression of the sample by the blade prior to shearing.
- The tenderness is measured by the final reading as the meat is cut.

allowing postmortem metabolic changes that result in greater tenderness [16]. The USDA quality grade standards for beef include an estimation of the amount of marbling (the distribution of fat throughout the muscle). Small but statistically significant decreases in tenderness have been found in beef by expert judging panels as marbling decreased from moderately abundant to practically devoid [67]. Juiciness and flavor also decreased. Untrained consumers in San Francisco and Kansas City gave slightly lower scores for overall desirability of top loin beef steaks as the marbling level decreased. In the same study, consumers in Philadelphia rated the steaks with lesser marbling considerably lower than those well marbled, indicating regional differences [64]. Marbling would appear to have an impact on the eating quality of beef steaks, including tenderness, but sometimes this effect on tenderness may be small.

Ground beef and hamburger are popular meat products in the United States. When cooked ground beef/hamburger patties made from raw meat containing 5, 10, 15, 20, 25, and 30 percent fat were compared, it was noted that the low-fat patties (5 and 10 percent) were firmer in texture, less juicy, and less flavorful than the patties with 20 to 30 percent fat [70]. Objective measurements with the Warner-Bratzler and Lee-Kramer shear instruments also showed decreasing tenderness with decreasing fat content.

Other Tenderness Factors. Carcasses of beef are sometimes subjected to low-voltage electrical stimulation immediately after slaughter to increase tenderness [31]. The beneficial effects may result from an increase in the rate of postmortem metabolism and a disruption of the myofibrils with accelerated enzymatic breakdown of the muscle proteins [18]. Electrical stimulation and 48 hours of aging were reported to have the same tenderizing effect on both steer and bull carcasses as a six-day aging period [22].

The hereditary background of the animal, the management of its feeding, and the size of muscle fibers are other factors that affect meat tenderness. Many of these factors are undoubtedly interrelated, and more research is needed to clarify the whole picture of tenderness in meat. For example, pronounced differences in tenderness are apparent among various muscles of the beef carcass. The tenderloin, or psoas major, and the longissimus dorsi muscles in the rib and loin sections are the most tender; muscles of the round and chuck sections are generally less tender. These differences in tenderness cannot be completely explained by differences in connective tissue, fat content, or state of muscle contraction [48].

Tenderizing. Because of the lower cost of certain less tender cuts of meat in comparison with more tender pieces, attempts have been made to tenderize the less tender cuts. Grinding and cubing break up the connective tissue and make meat more tender.

Meat tenderizers can be applied to the surface of meats prior to cooking. Tenderizing compounds containing various enzymes, usually **proteinases**, hydrolyze some of the proteins in meat. Enzymes used as tenderizers may include papain and chymopapain from the green papaya fruit, bromelin from pineapple, ficin from figs, and actinidin from kiwifruit. Most of these enzymes act primarily on the muscle cell proteins; bromelin is more active on the collagen of connective tissue. Enzymatic action occurs mostly during cooking and not so much at room temperature. The optimal temperature for papaya enzyme activity is 140°–160°F (60°–70°C). Excessive action of meat tenderizers on the meat fibers can result in the development of a mealy or mushy texture.

Flavor

The flavor of meat involves responses from taste and smell and also sensations from pressure-sensitive and heat-sensitive areas of the mouth. Flavor of meat is developed primarily by cooking; raw meat has little aroma and only a bloodlike taste. The flavor of boiled meats differs from that of roasted meats in part because of the flavor produced by caramelization on the surface of roasted meats.

The chemistry of meat flavor is highly complex, as many compounds contribute to the characteristic flavor of the cooked product. Some of these flavor compounds are volatile and give rise to odor. One study of the volatile flavor components of fresh beef stew identified 132 different compounds [61].

Although volatile components are possibly the most important part of meat flavor, non-volatile compounds stimulate taste buds and contribute to the overall flavor complex. The most important taste compounds are inorganic salts, producing a salty taste; sugars, producing a sweet taste; hypoxanthine, contributing some bitterness; organic acids, producing a sour taste; and some nitrogen-containing compounds, including nucleotides, amino acids, and peptides. In addition to volatile and non-volatile components of meat flavor, other substances called *flavor potentiators* and *synergists* contribute to taste. Although these substances have no distinctive flavor of their own, they enhance the flavor of other compounds. Flavor potentiators (see Chapter 6) in meat include some amino acids, such as glutamic acid, and certain 5'-nucleotides, such as inosinic acid [51].

The feeding management of beef cattle affects the flavor of the meat, particularly the flavor of the fatty portions. Grass- or forage-fed steers have flavors characterized as grassy, gamey, and milky-oily as compared to animals finished on grain [45, 50].

Serving temperature also affects perceived meat flavor. Beef steaks tasted at 122°F (50°C) are more flavorful and juicy than similar samples tasted at 72°F (22°C) [57]. Not only the temperature but also the time that a meat product is held before serving can affect flavor. Freshly cooked meat sauce with spaghetti was found to be more flavorful and generally more acceptable to a taste panel than a similar product held hot on a cafeteria counter for 90 minutes [2]. Irradiation of ground beef to reduce foodborne pathogens does not affect the aroma, taste, aftertaste, or texture of ground beef either immediately after irradiation or after frozen storage [19].

Warmed-over flavor is an off-flavor of meats commonly present when meats have been cooked, held under refrigerated or frozen storage, and then reheated. Warmed-over flavor is characterized as "cardboardlike," "painty," or "rancid." These flavors are the result of oxidation. Polyunsaturated fatty acids oxidize more readily than saturated fats; thus, those meats with higher levels of polyunsaturated fatty acids are more likely to develop warmed-over flavors. Most prevalent meats with warmed-over flavors are fish, poultry, pork, beef, and lamb in descending order. Oxidation can be reduced by vacuum packaging or covering with a sauce to reduce oxygen exposure. Light exclusion and ingredients such as vitamin E, butylated hydroxyanisol (BHA), citric acid, ascorbic acid, nitrites, and certain spices can also be useful. Oxidation reactions were discussed further in Chapter 7.

CURED AND PROCESSED MEATS

For centuries, curing has been an important method for preserving meat. At one time, salt (sodium chloride) in comparatively large amounts was the substance used in curing. Today, curing ingredients include sodium nitrite, sugar, and seasonings in addition to salt. Nitrite reacts with myoglobin, the red pigment of meat, producing nitrosylmyoglobin, which later changes to the characteristic pink color of cured meats while heating during the curing process. The heated pink pigment is nitric oxide hemochrome.

Nitrite and Nitrate

Sodium nitrite alone, or used with sodium nitrate, fixes the characteristic pink color in cured meats, contributes to the development of characteristic flavor, and inhibits the growth of the bacterium *Clostridium botulinum*. It also slows the development of rancidity. The control of *Clostridium botulinum* is essential, because under anaerobic conditions, it produces a deadly toxin (see Chapter 2). Sodium nitrite and sodium nitrate are listed on package labels and regulated as food additives (see Chapter 3 on regulations).

Nitrite is toxic when consumed in excessive amounts. It is present, however, in small amounts in a variety of dietary sources including some vegetables, and cured meats. Untested well water can also be a source. Vegetables are estimated to account for 80 percent of the nitrate and nitrites in the human diet [74]. In addition, it has been shown that certain cancer-producing substances, called *nitrosamines*, can be formed in food products or in the acid environment of the stomach by reactions between nitrite and **secondary amines**.

The FDA has limited the amount of nitrite that can be present in a finished cured product. A 1997 report of analysis for nitrite in cured meats obtained from the marketplace indicated that the current residual nitrite level is approximately one-fifth the level of 25 years earlier [12]. The risks from nitrites are considered to be very low at this time, although research is ongoing. Ascorbic acid (vitamin C) and tocopherol (vitamin E) have been found to reduce levels of nitrosamines in bacon and other nitrite-cured products [93]. Some manufacturers of cured meats have completely eliminated the use of nitrites through product formulation changes.

Salt

Salt in the curing mixture inhibits the growth of undesirable microorganisms during curing and adds flavor. Salt, in sufficient quantities with or without other curing agents, also causes the development of a heated pink pigment. This change in color can occur accidentally and undesirably in products such as meatloaf if the salt content is high enough and the product is not cooked shortly after mixing. Raw, processed turkey breasts may also show this color defect if the amount of salt used in processing was too high. Both of these products will remain pink even if thoroughly cooked. In processed meats, such as ham or smoked turkey, this pink color is expected.

Some processed meats are being produced with lower salt content because of the interest in decreasing the sodium levels in the American diet. Phosphates may also be used in curing solutions to decrease shrinkage in meat by retaining moisture.

Cured Products

Ham, bacon, smoked pork-shoulder picnic, and Canadian bacon are commonly cured pork cuts. Corned beef is the cured brisket of beef. Frankfurters or hot dogs and a variety of sausages are also cured. Smoked turkey is another example of a cured product.

Meats may be cured by (1) rubbing the curing mixture dry on the outside of the meat, (2) submerging the meat in a solution of the curing ingredients, or (3) injecting the curing solution into the meat. When the curing mixture is dry rubbed, the rate of diffusion of the ingredients into the meat is slow. The curing ingredients are much more rapidly and uniformly distributed throughout the meat when they are injected. Pumping the curing solution into meat increases the weight of the meat. Federal regulations require that a ham must be "shrunk" back to at least its original fresh weight by the time heating and/or smoking is completed. If not, the ham must be labeled "ham, water added" if it contains up to 10 percent added moisture.

Ham

Prior to the widespread use of refrigeration, hams were cured for preservation purposes. Today, hams are cured to create desired flavors and other characteristics. In contrast to "ham, water-added," hams labeled "country-style" are processed by using a dry-cure, slow-smoking, and long-drying process. They are firm textured, relatively low in moisture (about 85 percent of the original weight), and always require cooking before eating.

After treatment with the curing solution, hams are heated or smoked. Hams that are only heated or smoked to an internal temperature of 140°F (60°C) will need additional cooking before serving. Hams labeled "fully cooked" are heated to an internal temperature of about 150°F (66°C) and may be consumed cold or heated. Canned hams that have been processed at sterilizing temperatures are also available. All processed products containing pork must be treated so that any trichinae present are destroyed to prevent trichinosis in humans.

Sausages and Luncheon Meats

More than 200 varieties of sausages and luncheon meats are available in the United States (**Figure 24–25**). These are made from chopped or ground meat (**comminuted**) with various seasonings and often contain curing ingredients. Sausages are usually molded in casings, either natural or manufactured, or in metal molds. Many casings are edible, but some, such as the casings used for summer sausage, are not edible and should be removed prior to use. Sausages can be classified as follows:

1. Uncooked
   a. Fresh pork sausage in bulk or encased as links
   b. Fresh bratwurst
   c. Bockwurst

FOCUS ON SCIENCE

MORE ABOUT THE CAUSES OF WARMED-OVER FLAVOR

Warmed-over flavor is caused by unsaturated fatty acids that are found in meat, such as beef, lamb, pork, poultry, and fish. The more unsaturated the fatty acid, the more susceptible it is to degradation during cooking to smaller compounds (aldehydes and ketones). Initially, no flavor changes are evident, but when the food is reheated, the compounds that were formed "volatize" and produce off-flavors in the food. Research has shown that certain spices, such as rosemary, sage, and thyme, contain certain antioxidants that prevent warmed-over flavor. Covering the food with gravy also acts as a "blanket" to prevent oxidation.

FOCUS ON SCIENCE

HOW DO PHOSPHATES WORK IN CURED MEATS?

The addition of appropriate phosphates increases the water-holding capacity of raw and cooked meats. Therefore, phosphates are used in the production of sausages, in the curing of ham, and in poultry and seafoods to decrease drip losses. Sodium tripolyphosphate ($Na_5P_3P_{10}$) is the phosphate most commonly added to processed meat, poultry, and seafood. It often is used in blends with sodium hexametaphosphate ($[NaPO_3]_n$, $n = 10-15$) to increase tolerance to calcium ions that exist in brines used in meat curing.

Uncertain of the mechanism, researchers believe that phosphate anions interact with divalent cations and myofibrillar proteins. Binding of polyphosphate anions to proteins and simultaneous cleavage of cross-linkages between actin and myosin result in increased electrostatic repulsion between peptide chains and a swelling of the muscle system. If exterior water is available, it can be taken up in an immobilized state within the loosened protein network.

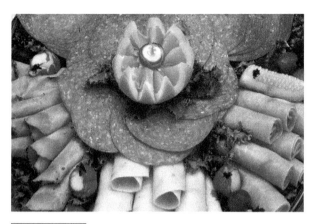

Figure 24–25

Agricultural research scientists study the source of flavor differences in deli meats, bologna, and sausages. Consumers have a wide variety of meats from which to choose. (Scott Bauer/U.S. Department of Agriculture)

2. Cooked
   a. Bologna (small, medium, and large)
   b. Frankfurters (wieners or hot dogs)
   c. Knockwurst
   d. Liver sausage or Braunschweiger
   e. Miscellaneous loaves

3. Semidry or dry fermented
   a. Salami
   b. Cervelat
   c. Pepperoni

   Comminuted emulsion-type products, such as wieners, sausages, and bologna, can be produced with reduced-fat levels (See Chapter 8 for more about emulsions). The maximum allowable level of binders, individually or collectively, is 3.5 percent. Turkey, pork, and beef are used in the production of a variety of sausages, frankfurters, and luncheon meats, including bologna.

Cured Meat Pigments

Cured meat pigments tend to be oxidized and to discolor when exposed to the lighting of display cases in supermarkets. Vacuum packaging in oxygen-impermeable material prevents oxygen from coming in contact with the meat. Such packaging increases the shelf life of processed products such as bacon and luncheon meats by controlling the oxidation of pigments and the development of oxidized off-flavors.

SAFE STORAGE AND PREPARATION OF MEATS

Safe Storage and Handling

Fresh meats are highly perishable. A cold storage temperature that is at or below 40°F (4.5°C) is

Table 24–9
SUGGESTED STORAGE PERIODS TO MAINTAIN HIGH QUALITY IN BEEF AND VEAL

Product	Storage Period	
	Refrigerator (35°– 40°F [2°– 4°C])	Freezer (0°F [– 18°C])
Fresh meat		
Chops and cutlets	3–5 days	3–4 months
Ground beef or veal	1–2 days	2–3 months
Roasts		
Beef	3–5 days	8–12 months
Veal	3–5 days	4–8 months
Steaks	3–5 days	8–12 months
Stew meat	1–2 days	2–3 months
Variety meats	1–2 days	3–4 months
Cooked meat and meat dishes	1–2 days	2–3 months

Source: Used by permission of the U.S. Department of Agriculture.

required. Coolers for meat in food service operations should be set at 36°F (2°C) or colder. Meats should not be placed above other foods in the refrigerator to avoid cross-contamination of other foods, such as fruits and vegetables, that may not be cooked before consumption. When handling meat, everything should be kept clean—hands, utensils, counters, cutting boards, and sinks. In particular, wash, rinse, and sanitize utensils that have touched raw meat before using for cooked meats. Refer to Chapter 2 for more about recommended food-safety practices.

Suggested storage times for some meats are given in **Table 24–9**. Many packages also provide "use by" dates. For freezing, meat should be wrapped tightly in moisture-/vapor-proof material (**Figure 24–26**). The meat may be divided into serving-size portions before freezing. It should be kept frozen at 0°F (−18°C) until used. Frozen ground meat should be defrosted (1) in the refrigerator, (2) in the microwave and cooked immediately after thawing, or (3) in cold, running water. Thawing meats at room temperature is not recommended because it provides an opportunity for the growth of pathogenic bacteria.

Preparation and Food Safety

Knowledge of and adherence to the recommended end-point cooking temperatures of meat is necessary to prevent foodborne illness. The use of a thermometer is the only reliable way to know that a safe temperature

Wrapping Instructions

Choose a moisture/vapor-proof freezer wrap to seal out air and lock in moisture. Heavy duty, pliable wraps such as freezer paper or aluminum foil, or heavy plastic wrap are good choices for bulky, irregular-shaped meat cuts since they can be molded to the shape of the cut.

1. Place meat cut in center of wrapping material. When several cuts are packaged together, place a double thickness of freezer wrap between them for easier separation.

2. Bring edges of wrap together over meat. Fold over at least twice, pressing wrap closely to meat to force out air.

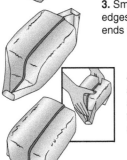

3. Smooth ends of wrap, creasing edges to form triangles. Double-fold ends toward package to seal out air.

4. Fold ends under package as shown and seal with continuous strip of freezer tape. Label tape with name of cut, number of servings and date of freezing.

Figure 24–26

Wrapping instructions for meat that is to be frozen.

has been reached. All raw meats are potentially contaminated with pathogenic microorganisms or parasites that are likely to cause foodborne illness, especially if the food is mishandled or undercooked.

Ground Beef and Hamburger. *E. coli* 0157:H7 caused concern after several outbreaks of hemorrhagic colitis resulting in some deaths were traced to ground beef patties in the early 1990s. Ground beef must be cooked to at least 155°F (68°C) for 15 seconds in food service operations and 160°F (70°C) in home kitchens to destroy any *E. coli* 0157:H7 that may be present (**Figure 24–27**). The ground beef temperature guidelines should also be applied to beef products that have been punctured, such as blade-tenderized or minute steaks, because bacteria can be in the center of these meats also.

One important contributing factor in *E. coli* 0157:H7 outbreaks associated with ground beef has been undercooking [9]. For safety, ground meat should always be cooked to the recommended internal temperature and checked with a properly calibrated thermometer (see Chapter 2). In the early 1990s, consumers

were told to cook their ground beef until the juices ran clear; however, starting in 1997, the FSIS began recommending the use of a food thermometer [62]. This change was made because research conducted at Kansas State University and later confirmed by the USDA's Agricultural Research Service found that some meat appears to be brown before reaching a safe endpoint temperature. One group of researchers found that nearly 50 percent of the patties tested showed premature browning [35]. This study supported other research [30] that found that patties were more likely to brown before reaching a safe internal temperature if the ground beef contains mainly oxymyoglobin (cherry-red) or metmyoglobin (brown) pigments. Alternatively, some lean ground beef or ground beef that contains spices and spice extractives may remain pink at temperatures well above 160°F (70°C). Thus, color is not a reliable indicator of doneness.

Beef Steaks, Pork, and Lamb. Beef steaks and roasts may be cooked to lower temperatures (145°F [63°C]) because these solid muscle meats will be heated to high enough temperatures to kill bacteria that could be present on the surface. Pork steaks and roasts must be cooked to 145°F (63°C) to destroy *T. spiralis*. Ground pork, like ground beef, must be cooked to 155°F (68°C). Although the infection rate of pork with *T. spiralis* has declined considerably over the years, cooking to recommended temperatures is still advisable. Lamb should be cooked to an end-point temperature of 145°F (63°C). When cooking any meat in a microwave oven, an end-point temperature of 165°F (74°C) is recommended [54]. All previously cooked products should be reheated to 165°F (74°C) [54]. **Table 24–10** summarizes recommended endpoint cooking temperatures for meats. See Chapter 2 for additional guidance on safe cooking temperatures.

METHODS OF PREPARING AND COOKING MEAT

Meat may be prepared in a variety of ways for consumption. The cut of meat, food preferences, and cuisine will influence the method of cooking. As an initial preparation step, fat and connective tissue may be trimmed from the cut. Safe vegetable dyes are used for the government inspection and grade stamps. Thus, unless preferred, these stamps do not need to be trimmed off. Occasionally, bone splinters may be present and should be removed.

Dry, Moist, and Combination Cooking Methods

Conventional cooking of meat is divided into dry-heat and moist-heat methods (see Chapter 5).

Figure 24–27

The USDA reminds consumers through the "Is it done yet" campaign that a thermometer should be used to test doneness of foods. (USDA)

Dry Heat. Dry-heat cookery traditionally includes roasting or baking, broiling, and pan-broiling. Frying can also be included in this classification because fat, not moisture, comes in contact with the surface of the meat during cooking.

Moist Heat. Moist-heat methods are stewing or cooking in water and pressure cooking. Simmering temperatures for stewing are sometimes specified on the assumption that the boiling temperature toughens meat; however, boiling temperatures do not appear to result in less tenderness (**Figure 24–28**).

Combination. Braising is often called a combination method of cooking because both dry- and moist-heat methods are used. The braising of large pieces of

Table 24–10
FDA FOOD CODE MINIMUM INTERNAL END-POINT COOKING TEMPERATURES FOR MEAT

Product	Minimum Internal Cooking Temperature
Ground meat (ground beef, pork, and other meat)	155°F (68°C) for 15 seconds
Pork, beef, veal, lamb	Steaks/chops: 145°F (63°C) for 15 seconds Roasts: 145°F (63°C) for 4 seconds
Injected meats (brined ham or flavor-injected roasts)	155°F (68°C) for 15 seconds
Meat cooked in microwave	165°F (74°C)

Source: Reference 54.

Figure 24–28

This savory beef stew with roasted vegetables is prepared by lightly browning the beef in oil and then simmering until tender. (Olga Miltsova/Shutterstock)

meat is sometimes called *pot roasting*. When meats are braised, the surfaces may first be browned using dry heat by pan-broiling or frying before finishing the cooking process with a moist method involving potentially a sauce or steam heat. The term *fricassee* may be applied to braised meats cut into small pieces before cooking.

Selection of Cooking Method. For many years, dry-heat methods of cooking were generally applied only to tender cuts of meat, whereas moist-heat methods were thought to be necessary to tenderize all less tender pieces. However, roasting less tender cuts with dry heat can be satisfactorily accomplished using very low oven temperatures and long periods of time [39]. The flavors developed in beef during roasting and broiling seem to be favored by most people over those developed in braising or pot roasting.

Not all cuts of meat respond similarly to various cooking methods. Beef loin, a tender cut of meat usually cooked with dry heat, becomes tougher if cooked thoroughly with moist heat [14]. In contrast, bottom round steaks, which are less tender, become more tender when braised well done. Thus, moist-heat cooking methods may be unsuitable for some tender cuts. Dry heat can be appropriate for tender and less tender cuts, provided that the temperature is reduced and the length of cooking is extended for the less tender cuts. Apparently there is enough water in the meat itself to provide for the hydrolysis of connective tissue during slow cooking of less tender cuts.

Effect of Heat on Meat

Heat produces many changes in meat. Fat melts, myoglobin is denatured, and tenderness changes. Fat melts when meat is heated, and the capacity of the muscle proteins to hold water is lessened, thus causing reduced juiciness and tenderness and increased weight loss. The volume of the meat decreases on cooking.

Redness decreases as internal temperature increases. The meat pigment myoglobin appears to be denatured around 140°F (60°C), and denaturation of other proteins seems to be complete by 176°F (80°C) [5]. However, as previously discussed, a brown color is not a reliable indicator of the doneness of ground beef.

Heating causes a decrease in tenderness when the meat reaches 104°–140°F (40°–60°C). This is followed by a gradual increase in tenderness above 140°F (60°C) or even above 122°F (50°C) in young animals. The original toughening appears to be the result of a shortening of the fibers accompanied by hardening as the proteins **denature** and **coagulate**. The later tenderizing evidently results from the softening of connective tissue and the hydrolysis to gelatin of some collagen in this tissue [4, 41, 46].

The response of an individual muscle to heating is influenced by the amount of connective tissue; however, the muscle fibers from different muscles may also react differently toward heat. In one study, researchers heated a tender muscle (longissimus dorsi) and less tender muscles (semitendinosus and semimembranosus) of beef to three different internal temperatures. They found that the tender muscle did not change in tenderness with increasing degrees of doneness, but the two less tender muscles increased in tenderness with higher internal temperatures [63]. The less tender muscles contained more connective tissue, which was evidently softened with increased temperatures. A different balance between the hardening of muscle fibers and the softening of connective tissue was achieved in the less tender muscles than in the tender muscle.

Cooking Losses

Cooking losses, including loss of weight and loss of nutrients, increase gradually with increasing internal temperatures [5]. Meat weight loss results from the formation of drippings, evaporation of water, and evaporation of other volatile substances. When meat is roasted in an open pan, considerable evaporation of water from the meat surface occurs, but nutrients and flavor substances are better retained when using dry-heat instead of moist-heat cooking methods. As water evaporates, minerals and extractives are deposited on the surface of the meat, which may account in part for the pronounced flavor of the outer brown layer of roasted meat.

Fat. Fat losses are inconsistent, probably because of the unequal distribution of fat throughout most pieces of meat. Fat on or near the surface is lost to a greater extent than fat in the interior because of the slowness of heat penetration. Not all fat that liquefies is lost because some of it penetrates to the interior. The fat layer on the outside of meat aids in decreasing water loss by preventing evaporation. Researchers have found that the degree of fat trim on raw beef loin steaks did not significantly affect the sensory characteristics of the cooked meat. However, the fat content of cooked steak was lower when the fat was completely trimmed off [1]. In cooking ground beef, fat losses are greater when the fat content of the raw meat is higher [43].

Weight. Total weight losses of cooked meat are influenced by the final internal temperature and the cooking method. Weight loss increases with increasing internal temperature. Thus, if preparing two identical beef roasts, the one cooked to rare or medium rare will weigh more when removed from the oven than the roast cooked to well done. The use of moist-heat cooking methods will usually also result in a greater weight loss compared to dry-heat methods. Top round steaks showed total cooking losses of 27.5 percent when they were cooked by moist heat compared with 20.6 percent when they were cooked by dry heat [52].

Vitamins. Although some losses of B vitamins, including thiamin, riboflavin, and niacin, occur during cooking, cooked meats are still good sources of these vitamins. Greater vitamin losses occur during braising and stewing than during roasting and broiling, but many are retained in the cooking liquid. Vitamin retention in meats during cooking in water depends on the cooking time, with greater losses occurring as cooking continues. Riboflavin and niacin are more resistant to destruction by heat than thiamin.

Shrinkage

Shrinkage in cooked meats begins at 122–140°F (50–60°C) because of the shortening of muscle fibers and coagulation of proteins. There is loss of water and melting of fat. The amount of shrinkage increases with higher internal end-point cooking temperatures. Less shrinkage usually occurs in meats roasted at 300–350°F (149–177°C) than in meats roasted at higher oven temperatures. Meats roasted for the whole cooking time at a high oven temperature may shrink as much as 40 to 60 percent compared with 15 or 20 percent at low temperatures. It is wise to consider excess shrinkage in economic terms, as fewer servings can be obtained from meats that have been allowed to shrink excessively during cooking. Particularly in quantity cookery, the yield of the meat can have a very noticeable impact on the number of servings available after cooking.

Flavor

Salt is not the only option when adding flavor to meats. The U.S. Dietary Guidelines suggest Americans reduce their consumption of salt, and therefore other methods of seasoning meat can be beneficial from a health perspective. Various herbs, spices, seasonings (see Chapter 6), and sauces can be used to enhance flavor while creating unique and tasty dishes. The cooking medium selected, broths or seasoned fats, can also add flavor.

Salt. If using salt, when should meat be salted? As common practice, many cooks salt roasts before placing in the oven; however, salting during or after preparation is also acceptable. Salt will penetrate the meat generally no more than about ½ inch. The use of too much salt on the surface of a roast will create a crusty outer layer and result in meat or drippings that are too salty and therefore unsatisfactory for use. When seasoning stews, the salt as well as other spices are added to the water during cooking. The loss of moisture or juice from meats salted prior to or during cooking does not appear to be significant.

Rubs. Rubs used to season meats may be wet or dry [40]. The dry rubs may include ingredients such as pepper, paprika, sugar, garlic, oregano, orange peel, and lemon pepper. Wet rubs or pastes have many of the same ingredients but have a small amount of a moist ingredient, such as oil, vinegar, crushed garlic, or one of many different kinds of mustard. Rubs, either wet or dry, are applied to the surface of the meat just before cooking or up to 2 hours in advance. If applying the rub well in advance of cooking, return the meat to the refrigerator until ready to cook.

Marinades. Marinades may be used to flavor meats or tenderize them. When the goal is flavor, 15 minutes to 2 hours of contact with the marinade may be satisfactory. However, if tenderization is desired, the meat should be in contact with the marinade for 6 to 24 hours. Marinades may contain a variety of ingredients, including some of the same spices found in rubs. However, marinades contain much more liquid. Typical liquids found in marinades are vinegar, steak sauce, lime or orange juice, soy sauce, honey, olive oil, and Italian dressings.

Usually ⅓ to ½ cup of marinade per pound of meat is sufficient. The meat should be placed in a sealable plastic bag or in a glass or plastic container with the marinade and then stored under refrigeration until ready to cook the meat. If any of the marinade is to be used for basting or a sauce, then some should be reserved without contact with raw meat. Marinade used on raw meat or poultry should not be reused unless it is boiled first to destroy any bacteria introduced from the raw meat.

Basting. Pouring or spooning liquids such as meat drippings or a marinade over the surface of meat while it is roasting is called *basting*. The major purpose of basting is to keep the surface moist, but the use of a savory liquid also enhances the flavor of the cooked meat. If meats are placed in the roasting pan with the fat layer on top, the melted fat flows over the surface of the roast as it cooks, and self-basting occurs.

Juiciness

Juiciness is a highly desirable characteristic in cooked meats. The interior temperature to which meats are cooked affects juiciness, with meats cooked to the rare and medium-done stages being juicier than well-done meats. In fact, it is difficult to cook meats to a brown interior color without a substantial loss of juiciness.

Meats that are cooked for a long time in moist heat to develop tenderness reach an interior temperature so high that they lose moisture. If meats are cooked in moisture and are served in the cooking liquid, as Swiss steak is, they may appear to be moist, but that moistness is not juiciness within the meat itself.

Tenderization

Proper cooking and carving or the use of marinades and meat tenderizers contributes to the development of the desirable trait of tenderness in less tender meat or to its preservation in already tender cuts. Meat tenderizers contain enzymes that increase the tenderness of meat through enzymatic hydrolysis of proteins in the tissue as the meat is heated [21]. Enzymes were discussed earlier in the chapter under "Tenderness and Flavor."

Cooking and Carving. Tender cuts of meat do not contain large amounts of connective tissue, which may need to be softened by long cooking. Therefore, overcooking of tender cuts should be avoided. For less tender cuts containing connective tissue, tenderization of collagen in particular generally occurs with either the application of moist heat or the use of dry heat for long cooking periods at low temperatures. These cooking methods promote tenderization because of the hydrolysis of the collagen to produce gelatin. A firming effect that may take place in muscle fibers subjected to long cooking is more than counterbalanced by the softening of connective tissue.

Meat should be carved across the grain, producing short muscle fiber segments to promote tenderness. Especially when meat has been cooked using moist heat or an extended low-temperature dry heat to tenderize the connective tissue, carving technique is important. Long intact muscle fibers, separated because of connective tissue disintegration, may contribute to apparent toughness as the meat is eaten. Proper carving of meat thus contributes to tenderness by the shortening of the muscle fibers.

Marinades. Less tender cuts of beef can be tenderized to some extent by soaking the meat in an acid-containing marinade for 24 or more hours before cooking [28, 60]. The tenderizing effect depends on the concentration of acid present. Marinated beef muscles with a pH of 3.25 have been found to be significantly more tender than those with a pH of 4.25 [60]. At the lower pH, the water-binding capacity of the muscle is increased, the total collagen content is reduced, and cooking losses are decreased.

Specific Cooking Methods

Roasting or Baking. Historically, the term *roasting* was applied to the cooking of large cuts of meat before an open fire. Today the terms *roasting* and *baking* are often used synonymously and apply to the method of placing meat on a rack in an open pan and cooking by the dry heat of an oven. Baking is actually more commonly used with portion cuts and roasting with large pieces of meat (**Figure 24–29**). Meats may be baked or roasted in conventional or convections ovens. Because the circulating air in a convection oven causes more rapid cooking, the temperature and cooking time should be reduced. Convection heat was discussed in Chapter 5.

The oven temperature generally recommended for roasting tender cuts of meat is 325°F (177°C). As the oven temperature is increased from 300 to 450°F (149° to 232°C), the cooking time for meats cooked to the same internal temperature is decreased, total cooking losses are increased, and the uniformity of doneness throughout the meat is decreased. Adequate browning for good flavor and

Figure 24–29

This roast is being checked for doneness with an instant-read thermometer. Notice that the temperature is taken in the center of the roast. (Richard Embery/Pearson Education)

attractive appearance occurs at low constant oven temperatures, particularly if temperatures between 325 and 350°F (163 and 177°C) are used. A high temperature at the beginning of roasting does not seal in juices.

Cuts of Meat for Roasting.   Tender and less tender cuts of meat may be roasted. Less tender cuts of beef are tender and acceptable when roasted at low oven temperatures of 225–250°F (107–121°C) [55] for a longer length of time. The less tender cuts have been found to be more moist and juicy than similar cuts that are braised.

Length of Cooking Time.   The length of cooking time may be estimated by minutes per pound guides found in many cookbooks and also in **Table 24–11**. Assessment of doneness is best done by a thermometer near the end of the estimated cooking time because the actual time needed can vary by the (1) shape, thickness, and the proportion of meat to bone and (2) oven load. A standing rib roast cooks in less time than a rolled rib roast because the latter is made more compact by boning and rolling. Large roasts of the same general shape as small roasts require fewer minutes per pound. Additionally, if an oven is heavily loaded or frequently opened, the temperature of the oven may drop and result in a longer cooking time.

Carryover Cooking and Standing Time.   After a relatively large roast is removed from the oven, it continues to cook as heat continues to penetrate to the center. This effect may be referred to as *carryover* cooking. The rise in temperature may continue for 15 to 45 minutes or longer and may be from 5° to 10°F (3° to 6°C). Roasts will have a greater rise in temperature when removed from the oven when (1) the oven temperature is higher, (2) the roast is larger, and (3) the internal temperature of the roast is lower (such as rare or medium rare). Thus, to avoid overcooking, medium and large roasts should be removed from the oven at a lower temperature than the desired end point to allow for the rise in temperature. Small, thin roasts may show little or no rise in temperature because of the rapid cooling from the surface.

Thermometer Use.   To accurately measure the doneness of meat, a meat thermometer or an instant-read thermometer should be used. The thermometer is inserted in the thickest portion of the meat (Figure 24–29). Meat thermometers may remain in the roast while it is cooking. Instant-read thermometers may be used to check the internal temperature at the end of the cooking period but are not designed to be left in the oven. The recommended internal temperatures for solid, muscle (not ground) fresh beef or lamb cooked to various stages of doneness are as follows [88, 94]:

> Medium rare 145°F (63°C)
>
> Medium 160°F (71°C)
>
> Well done 170°F (77°C)

Broiling.   In broiling, meats are cooked with a direct heat source, such as a gas flame, live coals, or an electric element, that emits radiant energy (see Chapter 5). Broiling is used for relatively thin cuts of meat, such as steaks and chops. It is usually done using the broil setting on a range, with the door closed for a gas range and open for an electric range. A rack for holding the meat out of the drippings is essential both to keep the meat from stewing in its juices and to prevent burning of the fat.

The source of heat used for broiling is usually constant, with variation in temperature achieved through regulating the distance of the surface of the meat from the source of radiant heat. The distance of the meat surface from the broiling unit is usually 2 to 5 inches. Thicker cuts are placed farther from the heat source than thin cuts to allow more uniform cooking.

The relatively high temperatures normally used in broiling do not seem to toughen the meat, possibly because cooking times are relatively short or because tender cuts of meat are used. Broiling may be used for relatively thin, less tender cuts of meat if they have been marinated or treated with meat tenderizers.

Table 24–12 gives the approximate broiling time for some typical cuts. Like the timetable for roasting, it is strictly a guide, not a precise statement of time. The doneness of steaks can be tested in various ways. To avoid cutting the steak or otherwise damaging the appearance, test doneness by using a thermometer (see Chapter 2 for thermometer recommendations) or by assessing the firmness of the meat as a guide. Rare meat will be soft, but well-done meat will be firm when pressed with a utensil. With experience, the firmness of meat can become a good indication of doneness for steaks. Unlike ground beef, which must be tested with a thermometer for doneness, steaks that may be contaminated with *E. coli* 0157:H7 will have contamination only on the surface; thus, an internal temperature lower than 155°F (68°C) is acceptable because the external temperature will exceed that necessary to destroy *E. coli*.

Pan-Broiling.   A variation of broiling is pan-broiling. In this case, heat is applied by means of direct contact with a hot surface, such as a heavy pan or a grill. The surface of the pan is lightly oiled to prevent the muscle tissue from sticking. As fat accumulates in the pan during cooking, it should be poured off to avoid frying the meat in its own fat.

Table 24–11
**APPROXIMATE ROASTING TIME AND INTERIOR TEMPERATURE FOR SOME
TYPICAL MEAT CUTS***

Cut	Weight (lb)	Oven Temperature	Interior End-Point Cooking Temperature of Meat	Approximate Time per Pound (Minutes)
Beef				
Rib roast, bone-in	5–6	325°F (163°C)	145°F (63°C) medium rare	23–25
			160°F (71°C) medium	27–30
			170°F (77°C) well done	32–34 (if boneless, add 5–8 minutes per pound)
Round or rump roast	2½–4	325°F (163°C)	145°F (63°C) medium rare	30–35
			160°F (71°C) medium	35–40
Tenderloin, whole	4–6	425°F (218°C)	145°F (63°C) medium rare	45–60 minutes total
Half			160°F (71°C) medium	35–45 minutes total
Veal				
Rib roast	4–5	325°F (163°C)	160°F (71°C) medium	25–27
			170°F (77°C) well done	29–31
Loin	3–4	325°F (163°C)	160°F (71°C) medium	34–36
			170°F (77°C) well done	38–40
Pork, fresh				
Loin roast, bone-in or boneless	2–5	350°F (176°C)	145°F (63°C) medium	20–25
Boston butt	3–6	350°F (176°C)	145°F (63°C) medium	40
Tenderloin	½–1½	425°F (218°C)	145°F (63°C) medium	20–27 minutes total
Leg (fresh ham), whole, bone-in	12–16	350°F (176°C)	145°F (63°C) medium	22–25
Pork, cured and fully cooked				
Whole, bone-in	10–14	325°F (163°C)	140°F (60°C)	15–18
Spiral cut, whole or half	7–9	325°F (163°C)	140°F (60°C)	14–18
Arm picnic shoulder, boneless	5–8	325°F (163°C)	140°F (60°C)	25–30
Lamb				
Lamb leg, bone in	5–7	325°F (163°C)	145°F (63°C) medium rare	20–25
			160°F (71°C) medium	25–30
			170°F (77°C) well done	30–35
Lamb leg, boneless rolled	4–7	325°F (163°C)	145°F (63°C) medium rare	25–30
			160°F (71°C) medium	30–35
			170°F (77°C) well done	35–40
Shoulder roast or Shank leg half	3–4	325°F (163°C)	145°F (63°C) medium rare	30–35
			160°F (71°C) medium	40–45
			170°F (77°C) well done	45–50

* If higher or lower temperatures are used for roasting, the times will obviously be somewhat shorter or longer, respectively.

Table 24–12
APPROXIMATE BROILING TIMES FOR SOME TYPICAL MEAT CUTS

Cut	Average Weight (lb)	Time (Minutes)		
		Rare	Medium	Well Done
Beef				
Club steak (top loin)				
1 in.	1	14–17	18–20	22–25
1½ in.	1¼	25–27	30–35	35–40
Porterhouse				
1 in.	2	19–21	22–25	26–30
1½ in.	2½	30–32	35–38	40–45
Sirloin				
1 in.	3	20–22	23–25	26–30
1½ in.	4½	30–32	33–35	36–40
Ground beef patty 1 in. thick by 3½ in. diameter			18–22	24–28
Lamb				
Loin chops				
1 in.	$^3/_{16}$		10–15	16–18
1½ in.	$^5/_{16}$		16–18	19–22
Rib chops				
1 in.	$^1/_8$		10–15	16–18
1½ in.			16–18	19–22
Ground lamb patty 1 in. thick by 3½ in. diameter			18–20	22–24

Source: USDA, FSIS, National Pork Board

Tender beef steaks, lamb chops, and ground beef patties are satisfactorily pan-broiled. Veal, because of its lack of fat, may be somewhat dry when broiled or pan-broiled. Pork chops are tender enough for dry-heat methods of cooking but should be cooked to an internal temperature of 145°F (63°C).

Sautéing and Frying. Sautéing and frying are additional methods that may be used for cooking tender cuts of meat (**Figure 24–30**). Sautéing and frying are similar, but sautéing uses less fat and a higher temperature compared to frying. Also, pan-fried foods are often lightly dredged in flour or crumbs. In panfrying, only a small amount of fat (enough to form a layer of melted fat ¼ to ½ inch deep) is used. The type of fat, which may include a vegetable oil or clarified butter, varies with the recipe being prepared; however, a fat with a high smoke point is needed so that the fat does not burn. Smoke points were discussed in Chapter 8.

Foods may also be deep-fat fried. In deep-fat frying, the melted fat (usually hydrogenated vegetable oil or liquid vegetable oil) is deep enough to cover the food. Fried food should be drained on a rack or on

Figure 24–30

The initial preparation on this beef and vegetable dish would have involved sautéing the beef in a small amount of oil.
(Joshua Resnick/Shutterstock)

absorbent paper to remove excess fat. Meats may be dipped in flour or in egg and crumbs before frying to produce a brown crust on the meat. Frying can also be used to brown meats that are to be braised.

Microwave Cooking. The flavor of microwaved meats may be somewhat different from that of meat cooked by conventional methods. Foods do not brown in microwave ovens unless special browning dishes are used and thus the flavor is affected. Frequent turning and basting with a sauce ensure full flavor and color development of the surface.

Microwaving can be useful for reheating cooked meat and meat dishes not only because it is rapid but also because it results in minimal warmed-over flavor and aroma [34]. Another convenient use of the microwave oven is for the rapid thawing of frozen meats. Because microwaves do not heat uniformly, a higher end-point cooking temperature is recommended for meats cooked by microwave for food-safety reasons. Cooking all meats to a minimum of 165°F (74°C) is recommended when using a microwave oven [54]. See Chapter 5 for more about microwave cooking.

Braising. Braising is a combination method of cooking that is usually applied to less tender cuts of meat, such as beef chuck or round. It may also be used for a variety of meats. Browning of the meat surface develops flavor and can be accomplished by first sautéing, frying, pan-broiling, or broiling. Next, the meat is cooked in a covered pan and simmered with a small amount of added liquid or with only juices from the meat.

Braising can be done either on the top of the range or in the oven. The cooking time is longer in the oven, using more energy. Cooking in a tightly covered pan, whether in the oven or on the range top, creates a moist atmosphere that hydrolyzes collagen. The time of cooking depends on the character of the meat and the size of the cut, but braised meat is always cooked well done. The term *pot roasting* is often used to refer to the braising of large cuts of meat, such as beef chuck roasts. Swiss steaks are braised beef steaks.

Stewing. Stewing is cooking in liquid at simmering or slow boiling temperatures (**Figure 24–31**). Stewing differs from braising by the use of a greater amount of liquid. For brown stew, part or all of the meat may be browned before stewing to help develop flavor and color in the stew. If vegetables are used, they should be added at an appropriate time during cooking to allow them to be cooked but not overcooked.

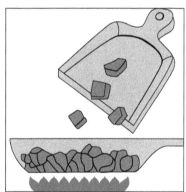

STEP 1. Coat beef with seasoned flour, if desired. Brown on all sides in small amount of oil, if desired.

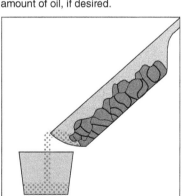

STEP 2. Pour off excess drippings.

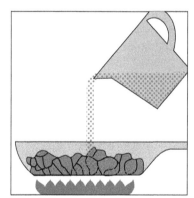

STEP 3. Cover with liquid. Season with additional herbs, if desired.

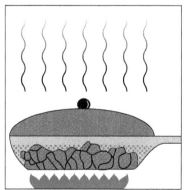

STEP 4. Cover utensil and simmer on top of range or in oven until tender. Add vegetables to meat and liquid just long enough before serving to cook through, or until tender.

Figure 24–31

Less tender meat may be tenderized by cooking in a liquid.

Pressure Cooking. Cooking meat in a pressure saucepan is a moist-heat method generally used for less tender cuts. Only a relatively short cooking time is necessary because heating produces a temperature higher than that of the usual boiling point of water, which is the temperature used for braising and stewing. The retention of steam within the cooking vessel, which increases the vapor pressure of the water, is responsible for the high temperature. Meats prepared in a pressure saucepan are commonly cooked to a well-done stage. A distinctive steamed flavor can usually be recognized.

Crockery Slow Cooking. Various types of crockery slow-cooking pots are available and are often used for meat cookery. These electric appliances have a low-temperature setting that allows meat and other foods to be cooked for long periods without constant watching. For example, a beef roast can be placed in the cooker with no added liquid, covered, and cooked on the lowest setting for 10 to 12 hours. Meat dishes with added liquid, such as beef stew or Swiss steak, are also satisfactorily cooked in crockery slow cookers. The low setting usually represents a temperature of about 200°F (93°C). The direct heat from the pot, lengthy cooking, and steam created within the tightly covered container combine to destroy bacteria and make this method of cooking meat safe, however the meat should always be thawed first [89].

Cooking in these covered pots is achieved by moist heat. The long cooking period allows the breakdown of the connective tissue to gelatin in less tender meats, thus increasing tenderness (see chapter 21 for more about gelation and gelatin structures).

Cooking Variety Meats

The choice of a cooking method for variety meats is influenced by the tenderness of the various parts. Heart, kidney, tongue, and tripe require cooking for tenderness and are braised or simmered. Beef liver may also require tenderizing by braising. Calf or veal liver and sweetbreads are tender and may be cooked by dry-heat methods, such as broiling or frying. These variety meats may also be cooked by moist-heat methods. Sweetbreads are delicate tissues that are made more firm and white when they are precooked for about 20 minutes at a simmering temperature in salted, acidulated water. After this preliminary treatment, they can be prepared in various ways. **Table 24–13** provides suggestions pertinent to the preparation of variety meats.

Cooking Frozen Meats

Frozen meats can be either thawed and cooked or cooked without thawing first. The cooking temperature must be lower, and the time of cooking must be increased if the meat is frozen when cooking begins. If pieces of frozen meat are large, the cooking time may be considerably longer than for similar thawed or fresh cuts. Frozen roasts require up to 1.5 times as long to cook as unfrozen roasts of the same size. If frozen meats are braised, they may be browned at the end of the braising period rather than at the beginning.

There are no appreciable differences in palatability or nutritive value in meats cooked from the thawed or frozen state. Thawed meats are cooked in the same way as fresh meats. Thawing of frozen meat, particularly large pieces of meat, should be done in the refrigerator for microbiological safety. Meats may also be thawed under cold running water or in the microwave if cooked immediately after thawing.

STOCK, BROTH, CONSOMMÉ, GRAVY, AND SAUCES

Stock and Broth

Stocks and broths are flavored liquids used in the making of soups or sauces. Beef is the most commonly used red meat for stock. Veal produces a very mild stock that may be desirable in some dishes. Lamb and mutton produce excellent broth, but they should be used only when lamb or mutton flavor is desired. The bones and meat from poultry make desirable broth. Stock may also be made from fish.

Stocks are generally prepared using the meat bones. Broths are prepared using similar steps to those for stocks, but browned meat and meat bones are used. Seven principles should be followed to produce high-quality stocks: (1) start with cold water, (2) simmer gently, (3) skim frequently, (4) strain carefully, (5) cool quickly, (6) store properly, and (7) degrease [40]. When making a meat-based stock, bones are covered with cold water and then simmered for 6 to 8 hours. Bones from younger animals are generally preferred because they contain more collagen [40]. During simmering, scum that forms on the surface should be skimmed off frequently. Vegetables (such as onions, carrots, and celery) and various spices (such as peppercorns, bay leaves, parsley, and thyme) may be added later in the cooking process. Once finished, the bones and vegetables are strained out, and then the stock must be cooled rapidly to prevent the stock being in the temperature danger zone (see Chapter 2 for more on food safety). Once cooled, the layer of hard fat that forms on the surface may be skimmed off.

The major difference between brown and white stock is that, in the making of brown stock, about one-third of the bones are first browned in a skillet or in a pan in the oven. The vegetables also may be caramelized in the oven or on top of the range for additional

HEALTHY EATING
GRILLED MEATS AND YOUR HEALTH

Heterocyclic amines (HCAs) and polycyclic aromatic hydro-carbons (PAHs) may be produced when meats are grilled. Both of these chemicals have been associated with a higher potential risk of cancer. HCAs are produced on meats when cooked at high temperatures when grilled, broiled, or fried. PAHs are usually formed when fat drips onto coals or hot stones, producing smoke or flare-ups.

Meat cooked well done, burnt, or charred appears to be the most problematic. Consequently, here are some ways to reduce exposure to heterocyclic amines:

- Grill fruits or vegetables because these foods do not produce HCAs or PAHs.

- Marinate meats because these appear to produce lower levels of these chemicals when grilled.

- Trim the fat from meats and remove the skin from chicken to reduce the amount of fat dripping onto the coals.

- Precook meats in the oven or microwave, and then finish on the grill.

- Flip frequently to cook evenly and reduce formation of HCAs

- Do not consume burnt or blackened parts of the meat.

- Do not allow flames from the grill near the meat.

Source: American Cancer Society and American Institute for Cancer Research.

Table 24–13
VARIETY MEATS

Name	Preliminary Preparation	Cooking Methods
Liver	Liver from young animals should be sliced ½ in. thick for best results in retaining juiciness. Remove outside membrane, blood vessels, and excess connective tissue. Wash large pieces before removing membrane.	Broil or pan-broil young liver. Fry or bread young liver. Braise whole piece of older beef liver. Grind and make into liver loaf. (Liver is easier to grind if first coagulated in hot water.)
Kidney	Wash kidneys and remove outer membrane. Lamb kidneys may be split in half and veal kidneys cut into slices. Cook beef kidneys in water for tenderness, changing the water several times.	Young kidneys may be broiled, pan-broiled, made into stew or kidney pie, or ground and made into loaf. Beef kidneys, after being cooked for tenderness, may be cooked in the same way, except that they should not be broiled or pan-broiled.
Sweetbreads	Soak in cold water to remove blood. Remove blood vessels and excess connective tissue. Parboil in salted, acidulated water to make firm and white using 1 tsp salt and 1 Tbsp vinegar per quart of water.	Sweetbreads may be creamed, dipped in egg and crumbs and fried in fat, combined with cooked chicken and creamed or scalloped, or dipped in melted fat and broiled.
Heart	Heart is a muscular organ that is usually cooked by moist-heat methods for tenderness. Wash in warm water and remove large blood vessels.	Stuff with bread dressing and braise until tender. May be cooked in water seasoned with salt, onion, bay leaf, celery, and tomato and served hot or cold.
Tongue	Tongue is a muscular tissue that requires precooking in water for tenderness. After cooking, remove the skin and cut out the roots. Smoked or pickled tongue is usually soaked for several hours before cooking.	May be cooked in water and seasoned with salt, onion, bay leaf, and celery. If it is to be served cold, it is more moist when allowed to cool in the water. After it is cooked in water, the tongue may be covered with brown or tomato sauce and braised in the oven. The cooked tongue may be reheated in a sweet pickling solution. For this method, the tongue is best precooked in plain salted water.
Tripe	Fresh tripe is cooked before selling but requires further cooking in water until tender (1 or more hours).	Serve precooked tripe with well-seasoned tomato sauce. Dip in batter and fry in deep fat. Brush with flavorful fat and broil.

flavor and color. The pan is deglazed by adding water to dissolve the brown material from the pan, which is then added to the stockpot with the browned bones, meat, and water.

Because of the time that is required to make stock from scratch, many use purchased meat broths or soup bases. The meat broths sold canned or in cartons are ready to use in recipes. Soup bases are added to water to create the stock. When purchasing a soup base, look for the meat as the first ingredient. Soup base or bouillon cubes may list salt as the first ingredient. These will offer less meat flavor for the soup, gravy, or sauce.

Consommé

A *consommé* is made from a clarified broth or stock. Start with 1 quart of broth or stock and add one egg white and one crushed shell. Heat the stock or broth to simmering to coagulate the egg and trap impurities. Pour the stock or broth through several thicknesses of cheesecloth to strain out the coagulated egg with its adhering particles. The impurities removed from the soup stock by clarifying is mainly coagulated protein.

Gravies and Sauces

Gravies or sauces are commonly used as accompaniments to enhance the flavor of meat. The drippings from fried, pan-broiled, or roasted meat and the cooking liquid from stewed or braised meats or poultry can be used to make gravy or a variety of different sauces.

When meats are cooked at moderately high temperatures, browned particles of meat or vegetables may be stuck to the pan. By adding a liquid and heating, the browned particles will loosen and create a flavorful liquid. This process is called *deglazing*. If the pan also contains fat, the fat should be drained off before adding water or other liquids. Meats cooked at a low temperature will result in very few browned particles. Meat cooked at very high temperatures may result in browned particles that are burnt and therefore undesirable.

The liquid produced from deglazing a pan may be used as a base for gravies and sauces. *Au jus* is not thickened and goes naturally with roast beef. When preparing a pan gravy, the reserved fat or butter is combined with flour to create a roux. This roux in then whisked into the deglazed pan with added liquid or to a broth. Heating is continued, with stirring, until the starch **gelatinizes**, resulting in thickening.

Alternatively, the liquid produced when deglazing the pan or a broth may be thickened with a slurry. A slurry is a mixture of starch (often cornstarch) and cold liquid. The slurry is whisked in to the deglazed pan or a broth/stock while heating. Chapter 11 provides additional information about the preparation and use of a roux and slurry for the thickening of sauces and gravies.

The liquid used in sauces and gravies may be water, milk, meat stock, tomato juice, wine, vegetable juice, or other liquids. The gravy will be best if the drippings are rich and flavorful. Gravies should be tasted before serving to make certain that the proper blending of flavors has been achieved.

A great variety of sauces can be served with meats. Sauces may be made from drippings but are often made without any meat components. White sauce (discussed in Chapter 11) may be the basis for some sauces served with meats. Tomato sauces go with meatballs and spaghetti, and mushroom sauce is often served with Swiss steak. Brushing broiled lamb chops with melted butter containing parsley, lemon juice, and white pepper produces a sauce called *maître d'hôtel butter*. Hollandaise sauce, which is an emulsified sauce, consisting of egg yolk, oil, butter, lemon juice, vinegar, and cayenne pepper, may also be used as a sauce for meats. Hollandaise also serves as the base for other sauces, such as Béarnaise. Pesto, salsa, coulis (a pureed fruit or vegetable sauce), mole, and many other kinds of sauces may also be prepared to accompany meats.

CARVING MEAT

Successful carving of meat partly depends on some knowledge of the anatomy of the cut to be carved. It is important to know something of the location of the joints and the direction in which the muscle fibers run. Insofar as possible, meats should be carved across the grain (**Figure 24–32**). Knives for carving should be well sharpened and of good-quality steel that will hold an edge well.

Before carving meat, it should generally be allowed to rest at room temperature after removing from the source of heat. Roasts should rest for about 20 to 30 minutes. Steaks should rest for about 5 minutes. This

Figure 24–32

This pork loin is being carved across the grain into individual servings. (Richard Embery/Pearson Education)

resting time reduces the amount of juice lost from the meat when it is carved. Carving should be done rapidly so that the meat stays warm. Neatness and economy of cutting are also important. If some parts of the meat are better than others, such parts should be divided among those at the table rather than given to the first ones served. Enough meat to serve all at the table should be carved before the host starts to serve the plates. The slices are arranged neatly on the platter. Before inviting guests to be served a second time, the host should be sure that some meat is carved and ready.

Beef Steak

Steak is carved by lying the steak flat on the platter, then inserting the fork in a suitable position for holding the steak firmly. To separate the bone from steaks from the loin (top loin, T-bone, porterhouse, and sirloin), allow the knife to follow the bone closely until the meat is completely separated. Then cut the meat into pieces of a suitable size for serving. Porterhouse and T-bone steaks are usually carved so that each person receives some tenderloin and some outer muscle. In this case, steaks are cut with the grain of the fiber because the steak is already cut across the grain by the butcher.

Standing Rib Roast

Place the standing rib roast on a cutting board with the rib side to the left. Insert a fork between two ribs. Pass the knife from the outer edge toward the ribs to remove a slice of meat. Slices may vary in thickness, but ¼ to ⅜ inch is desirable. After several slices are carved, use the knife to separate the slices from the bone.

Pot Roasts

Slices of pot roasts should be cut across the grain to the extent possible. Some cuts used for pot roasts may have fibers running in several directions, in which case it is difficult to carve across the fibers. If the muscles are separated first, cutting across the grain is easier.

Ham

Place the shank bone of the ham toward the right if right handed. Slice the larger muscles of the ham by cutting straight down from the outer edge to the leg bone. After several slices are carved, insert the knife in the last opening and allow it to follow the bone, thus separating slices from the bone. Lift slices out of the ham.

Loin Roasts

Carve a loin roast of pork by cutting slices from the end of the roast. As purchased, the rib section should have the backbone sawed loose from the ribs. Remove the backbone in the kitchen before placing on a platter. Cut close along each side of the rib bone. One slice contains the rib, the next is boneless, and so on.

Leg of Lamb

The cushion of a leg of lamb, which is the most meaty portion, lies below the tail. Insert a fork to bring the cushion into an upright position. Slices may then be carved as from ham.

STUDY QUESTIONS

Consumption

1. Identify the trends in the consumption of red meats versus poultry and fish.

Nutrition

2. Describe why meat is considered to be a complete protein of high biological value.

3. Identify the vitamins and minerals found in significant amounts in meat.

4. Discuss the types of fat found in meats and explain why this is significant from a nutritional perspective.

5. Describe what "lean" and "extra lean" means on a food label for meat.

Composition and Structure

6. Meat is basically muscle tissue containing some fat and bone. Describe what meat is like in structure, including each of the following components in your explanation:
   - (a) Muscle proteins—myosin and actin
   - (b) Myofibrils
   - (c) Muscle fibers
   - (d) Bundles of muscle fibers (making the grain of the meat)
   - (e) Muscles (such as tenderloin and ribeye)
   - (f) Connective tissue
   - (g) Connective tissue proteins—collagen and elastin
   - (h) Fat cells, fatty tissues, and marbling
   - (i) Bone

7. Explain how to tenderize meat with predominately (a) collagen or (b) elastin connective tissue.

8. Identify the name of the forms of meat pigments.

9. Explain why the color of meat may change from a purplish-red to a bright red when exposed to air.

10. Explain why meat may turn a brownish color when held too long.

11. What is responsible for the typical cured meat color?

12. Explain several reasons that color is not a reliable indication of the temperature of doneness of meat from a food-safety perspective.

Classifications

13. Identify three kinds of meat that are from "bovines."

14. Identify the difference between a steer and a heifer.

15. Describe veal.

16. Compare and contrast mutton and lamb.

17. Compare and contrast bison, beef, and beefalo.

18. Identify the type of meat that is produced from swine.

Meat Production and Marketing

19. Discuss what is permitted in livestock: (a) antibiotics or (b) hormones.

20. Explain *rigor mortis*. Discuss why rigor mortis is important in a study of meat.

21. Explain why is beef aged and discuss the changes that occur during the aging of meat.

22. Compare and contrast wet and dry aging.

23. Describe the various packaging methods for meat and discuss pros and cons for each.

24. Identify what must be included on a meat or poultry label.

25. Explain what nutrient content claims can be made on meat labels.

26. Explain what the round inspection stamp on meat carcasses implies.

27. Discuss why are meats graded, and by whom are they graded.
  a. Is this a mandatory or a voluntary program?
  b. Explain the difference between quality grades and yield grades for meat.

28. From the following list of quality grade names, indicate which apply to beef, to veal, and to lamb.

(1)	Prime	(6)	Choice
(2)	Select	(7)	Cutter
(3)	Standard	(8)	Canner
(4)	Commercial	(9)	Cull
(5)	Utility	(10)	Good

29. Compare and contrast yield versus quality grades.

30. Define marbling in meat and explain how marbling influences the grading of beef.

Purchasing Meat

31. Explain the value of knowing where a primal is located when purchasing meat for home or for food service in relationship to (a) tenderness, (b) cooking methods likely to be appropriate, and (c) cost.

32. Define IMPS numbers and explain how they are useful when purchasing meat for food service.

33. Identify what information is presented on a meat label that helps when purchasing to know exactly what you are buying.

34. Label the primal cuts on an unmarked drawing of beef and pork. Identify several cuts of meat that are from each primal cut.

35. Identify the primals on both beef and pork that are typically most expensive.

36. Define variety meats.

37. Define *restructured meats* and explain the advantages they offer.

38. Compare and contrast ground beef and hamburger.

39. Identify several different types of ham available for purchase and discuss quality implications of each choice.

40. Discuss economical choices and considerations when buying meat.

41. Explain factors that impact meat yield and the cost of edible meat. In your response, include fat content, bone-in versus boneless, and cooking losses.

Tenderness and Flavor

42. List several factors that may affect tenderness of meat.

43. Discuss flavor attributes of meat and factors that influence the flavor of meat.

Cured and Processed Meats

44. Name several cuts of meat that are commonly cured.

45. Identify ingredients usually used in the curing process.

46. Discuss advantages and disadvantages of the use of nitrite as a curing ingredient.

Safe Storage and Preparation of Meats

47. Describe appropriate storage conditions for meat in the kitchen.

48. Explain reasons for using a thermometer and why ground beef and intact meat such as roasts and texts have different endpoint cooking temperature requirements.

49. Identify the recommended end point temperature for ground meat and explain why the color of meat is not a reliable indicator for doneness from a food-safety perspective.

50. Identify the recommended endpoint cooking temperature for (a) ground beef, (b) beef, pork, veal, and lamb steaks and roasts, and (c) minute steaks

Methods of Preparing and Cooking Meats

51. Describe dry, moist, and combination methods of cooking meat and discuss why each may be preferable depending on the cut and type of meat.

52. Discuss several ways to add flavor to meats.

53. Describe methods of cooking or preparing meat that can (a) reduce cooking losses, (b) improve juiciness, and (c) improve tenderness.

54. Define carryover cooking and why it is important when cooking roasts.

Stock, Broth, Consommé, Gravy, and Sauces

55. Describe appropriate procedures for the preparation of the following:

    (a) Stock, broth, or consommé

    (b) Gravy or sauce prepared with a roux or a slurry

Carving Meat

56. Compare and contrast cutting with the grain of meat and across the grain of meat.

57. Describe how meat should be carved.

25
Poultry

The term *poultry* is used to describe all domesticated birds that are intended for human consumption, including chickens, turkeys, ducks, geese, guinea fowl, squab (young pigeons), quail, ostrich, pheasant, and pigeons. Chickens and turkeys are by far the most commonly consumed poultry items in the United States. Poultry is marketed throughout the year in a wide variety of forms, many of which are convenience foods. In this chapter, the following topics will be discussed:

- Consumption trends and nutrition
- Composition
- Classification and market forms
- Poultry production and marketing
- Government inspection, grading, and oversight of labeling
- Purchasing
- Safe storage, handling, and preparation
- Cooking methods

CONSUMPTION TRENDS AND NUTRITION

Consumption Trends

Chicken (63 pounds per capita) is the most commonly consumed meat in America. While "red meat" (beef, veal, pork, lamb, and mutton) was overall larger at 100 pounds per person in 2016 [26], Americans consumed less beef (53 pounds) and pork (47 pounds) than chicken. Between 1970 and 2016, annual per capita poultry consumption more than doubled; 76 pounds of poultry were available in the food supply in 2016 compared to 34 pounds in 1970. According to data available in 2019 from the U.S. Department of Agriculture (USDA) food supply data, chicken accounted for 63 pounds per capita compared to 13 pounds of turkey per capita (**Figure 25–1**). Like chicken, turkey consumption has doubled since 1970. The popularity of poultry has been influenced by the consumer's perception that it is low fat, inexpensive, and convenient to prepare compared to other meat.

Nutritive Value

Chicken and turkey meat provides high-quality protein to the diet. When consumed without the skin and prepared with little or no added fat, a 3½ ounce serving of chicken or turkey breast meat will have less than 2 grams of fat per serving [25]. The cholesterol content of poultry is similar to that found in lean red meats. Like other meats, poultry provides B vitamins and iron. The iron content of poultry white

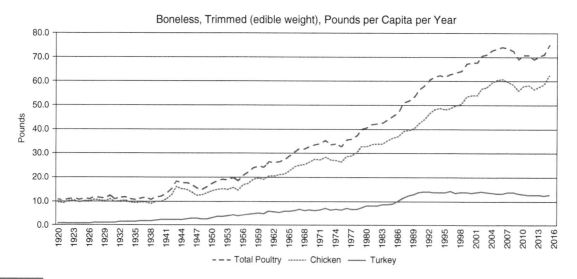

Figure 25–1

U.S. per capita availability of poultry. (U.S. Department of Agriculture, Economic Research Service)

meat is lower than that in the dark meat, such as legs or thighs. Goose and duck are high in fat.

COMPOSITION

Poultry, like other meats (see Chapter 24), is composed of muscle, connective tissue, and fat. Chicken muscle contains about 66 to 69 percent water naturally, in addition to protein (about 20 percent), and about 5 percent of fat, carbohydrates, and minerals [31]. Like red meats, the pigment responsible for color is myoglobin. The light meat of poultry, particularly the breast, has shorter, tenderer fibers that are less firmly bound together with connective tissue than those of dark meat. As in mammals, the amount of connective tissue in poultry varies with age; it is more abundant in old birds, especially males.

The fat of poultry is deposited in layers under the skin, in the abdominal cavity, and to a lesser degree in the muscle tissue. Because fat is deposited under the skin, consuming poultry without the skin will lower the fat content considerably. The fat content of the meat is similar if the skin is removed before or after cooking as long as the skin is not consumed. The fat of all types of poultry has a softer consistency and lower melting point than the fat of other meats. **Capons** have more fat and a more uniform distribution of fat in the flesh than other chickens. Goose and duck are higher in fat than chicken or turkey. Geese, particularly, have a distinctive flavor that may be objectionable in older birds.

Like other meats, myoglobin is responsible for the color of the meat in poultry. Muscles that are used to a greater extent, such as the legs and thighs, have a higher level of myoglobin and will therefore be dark. Birds that fly, such as duck, have only dark meat. The skin of chicken can range in color from a creamy white to yellow. This color difference is due to the feed provided to the bird and is not an indication of differences in nutritional value or flavor [32]. Refer to Chapter 24 for a more in-depth discussion of myoglobin in meat.

CLASSIFICATION AND MARKET FORMS

The market forms of poultry have changed over the years, from the early 1960s, when whole dressed chicken accounted for over 80 percent of chicken sales, to the present day, when the largest share of chicken is marketed as cut-up parts, some of them

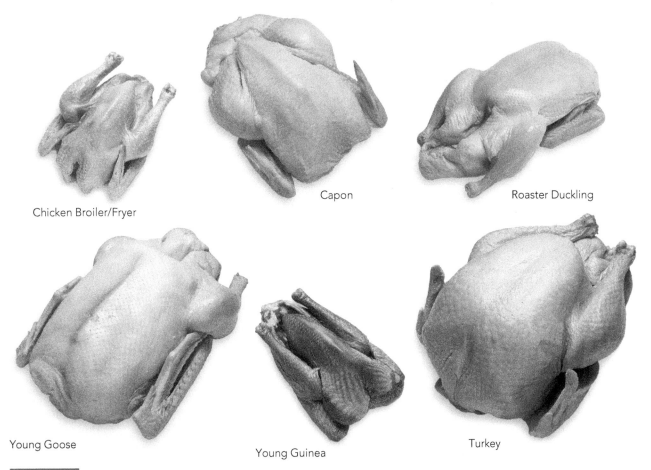

Chicken Broiler/Fryer

Capon

Roaster Duckling

Young Goose

Young Guinea

Turkey

Figure 25–2

Several different types of poultry. (Richard Embery/Pearson Education)

Table 25–1
POULTRY CLASSIFICATION

Type	Description	Age	Weight
Young chicken	*White and dark meat. Is low fat without skin. Cook with a variety of methods.*		
Broiler-fryer	Either sex; tender	9–12 weeks	2½–4½ pounds
Roaster	Either sex; tender	3–5 months	5–8 pounds
Capon	Castrated male; very meaty and tender	16 weeks–8 months	4–10 pounds
Poussin	Small immature birds	<24 days	<1 pound
Rock Cornish game hen	Cross of Cornish chicken with another breed. Either sex; immature; tender	4–7 weeks	<2 pounds
Older chicken	*Flavorful but less tender. Prepare with moist heat.*		
Baking or stewing hen	Mature laying hen; less tender	>10 months	5–6 pounds
Young turkey	*White and dark meat. Low fat without skin.*		
Fryer-roaster	Either sex, tender	10–12 weeks	4–8 pounds
Young hen	Female; tender	5–7 months	8–16 pounds
Young tom	Male; tender	5–7 months	>16 pounds
Duck	*A dark-meat bird. Pekin duck is the most common variety. High percent of bone and fat.*		
Duckling	Either sex; tender	6–8 weeks	3–6 pounds
Roaster duckling	*Either sex; younger than mature duck*	<16 weeks	4–7 pounds
Goose	*A very fatty dark-meat bird. Usually roasted.*		
Young	Either sex; tender	10–16 weeks	10–16 pounds
Mature		<25 weeks	
Domestic game birds			
Guinea fowl or guinea hen	Tender light and dark meat with little fat	11 weeks	2–3 pounds
Pigeon	Squab the most common form; dark, tender meat with little fat	28–30 days	12–16 ounces
Partridge	Usually coarse-textured meat; best cooked with moist heat	<1 year	
Pheasant	Mild-flavored meat; hen is tenderer than the cock		1¾–4 pounds
Quail	A small lean bird; related to the pheasant		3–7 ounces

Source: References 18, 28, 32.

boneless and skinless. No longer just for holidays, turkey has become popular year-round. The proliferation of quick-service restaurants that sell chicken fillet sandwiches, chicken nuggets, and turkey deli sandwiches, along with a wide variety of frozen and fresh convenience foods such as turkey pot pies, chicken enchiladas, and chicken fettuccini, has contributed to these changing market trends.

Although chicken and turkey are the most commonly consumed types of poultry, duck, goose, and game birds may also be prepared (**Figure 25–2**). Chickens used for meat production are a different breed than those used for laying eggs (see Chapter 23). Poultry, as sold in grocery stores and other markets, is classified on the basis of age and weight. Younger birds are tenderer than mature birds. Various types and classifications of poultry are provided in **Table 25–1**.

POULTRY PRODUCTION AND PROCESSING

Production

Georgia, Alabama, and Arkansas produce the greatest number of broiler chickens for meat [15]. Chickens are raised by farmers under contract with integrated poultry companies [16]. Chickens are housed in *grow-out houses* where they are free to roam about the house with access to feed and water. Guidelines are in place for the square footage necessary per chicken in the house. If poultry is labeled as *free range*, access to a yard outside the house is provided [33]. Turkey is raised in similar conditions.

Poultry feed generally consists of corn and soybean meal with added vitamins and minerals. Antibiotics may be used to treat illness or to increase the efficiency of the feed; however, a withdrawal period is required so that the birds are free from antibiotic residuals prior to slaughter [30, 32]. Hormones are not permitted for use in poultry.

Processing

Birds are slaughtered after first being anesthetized with an electric current. Many of the processes, such as feather removal and evisceration, are automated.

Slaughtered, eviscerated poultry are washed with water and chilled immediately, usually by immersion of the carcasses in chilled water at less than 36°F (2°C) to control the growth of microorganisms. USDA inspectors monitor the processes and test for **Salmonella** organisms as a measure of the plant's effectiveness in controlling contamination.

A certain number of chickens will leave processing plants with some detectable *Salmonella* bacteria. Some of these bacteria may be firmly attached to or entrapped in poultry skin when they first arrive at the processing plant. The USDA's Food Safety and Inspection Service has approved the use of trisodium phosphate (TSP) to reduce microorganisms [32]. TSP can significantly reduce microbial levels of poultry without affecting flavor, texture, or appearance.

Raw poultry and poultry products may be treated with ionizing radiation to control and reduce the population of pathogens such as *Salmonella, Campylobacter,* and *Listeria monocytogenes.* Irradiation of poultry has been approved by the USDA and by the Food and Drug Administration (FDA). Packages must bear an irradiation logo and the statement "Treated with radiation" or "Treated by irradiation." The shelf life of irradiated chicken has been reported to be as long as 15 days compared with about 6 days for unirradiated carcasses, as evidenced by the bacterial counts [13].

GOVERNMENT REGULATIONS

Inspection

The Wholesome Poultry Products Act, similar to the Wholesome Meat Inspection Act, was enacted in 1968. It requires that all poultry marketed in the United States be inspected for sanitary processing and freedom from disease. This inspection is performed either by agents of the federal government or by adequate state systems. The inspection process in a poultry-production plant is illustrated in **Figure 25–3**. The handling of both poultry and meat inspection at the federal level is the responsibility of the Food Safety and Inspection Service of the USDA.

All poultry-processing plants must operate under a Hazard Analysis and Critical Control Points (HACCP) plan (see Chapter 2). The processor must also have written sanitation standard operating procedures for daily operation and must test for certain microorganisms. Pathogen reduction is a major goal of the program.

Figure 25–4 shows the USDA inspection mark. Poultry bearing the official mark, sometimes printed on a tag attached to the wing, must come from a healthy flock, be processed under specified sanitary conditions, and be properly packaged and labeled. Only processed poultry products, not fresh poultry, may contain additives such as a basting solution, salt, or other approved ingredients [30]. Prepared poultry products, such as canned, boned poultry, frozen dinners and pies, and specialty items, must also be produced with USDA inspection.

(a)

(b)

Figure 25–3

(a) A federal inspector examines the poultry in the production room. (b) An Agricultural Research Service engineer is developing a computer-directed scanning system to speed the inspection of the nearly 8 billion chickens processed annually through federally inspected plants in the United States. (U.S. Department of Agriculture, Keith Weller/U.S. Department of Agriculture)

POULTRY 101

A guide to understanding USDA poultry grades, terms & cooking recommendations

USDA GRADE A is the most common grade of poultry available in retail stores. Grade A whole birds and parts are plump and meaty. They have significant fat under the skin, which provides moisture during cooking. The birds are symmetrical, with good bone structure, and parts are properly cut, with no broken bones.

USDA GRADE A BONELESS POULTRY PRODUCTS

are free of bone, cartilage, tendons, bruises and other defects. You may also see cooked or prepared foods labeled "Prepared from USDA Grade A."

THE USDA INSPECTION SEAL

refers to the safety and wholesomeness of poultry products and the accuracy of their labels. All poultry products are USDA inspected.

THE USDA GRADE SHIELD

is an added assurance of quality based on official USDA standards. Only poultry products examined for quality by USDA graders bear the USDA grade shield.

TIP #1

For breast meat, cook with the skin on to keep meat moist and flavorful. Just remove it before serving to reduce fat and calories.

cook to 165°

140 150 160 170 180 190

TIP #2

Try a dark meat cut, such as legs or thighs, when grilling. The slightly higher fat content will help the meat stay moist.

Figure 25–4

USDA poultry grade and inspection descriptions. (U.S. Department of Agriculture)

FOCUS ON SCIENCE
MORE ABOUT TRISODIUM PHOSPHATE (TSP)

At present, the mechanism of TSP is not well understood. However, at the cell membrane level, TSP helps to remove fat films and exerts surfactant and detergent effects when at a high pH level (pH = 12). Research also has indicated loss of cell viability and membrane integrity and disruption of cytoplasmic and outer membranes of *Salmonella enteritidis* strains treated with concentrations of TSP at pH 10 to 11.

Source: Reference 20.

Grading

In addition to inspecting for wholesomeness, the USDA has developed voluntary standards for quality grades. These grades—A, B, and C—are placed on the label in a shield-shaped mark (**Figure 25–4**). Many states participate in a grading program, and in such states the official stamp reads, "Federal–State Graded." Signs of quality that are evaluated in grading include conformation or shape of the bird, fleshing, distribution and amount of fat, and freedom from pinfeathers, skin and flesh blemishes, cuts, and bruises. Grade A birds will be nearly free from defects [30].

Labeling

Many aspects of the food label are regulated to provide useful and accurate information to consumers (see Chapter 3). As consumer preferences and priorities change over time, those packaging foods add additional information to the label that then may need further clarification and potential regulation to prevent misleading labeling information impacting consumers. Specialty label claims often result in a higher price per pound [11] (**Figure 25–5**).

Natural or Organic. The term *natural* has become a popular marketing term favored by many consumers when selecting foods. However, natural has limited meaning and should not be confused with organic which is regulated under the USDA organic program. The organic label and associated regulations provide many of the attributes consumers purchasing "natural" may be seeking [11] (**Figure 25–6**). **Table 25–2** offers guidance on the meaning of these terms.

No Hormones or Raised Without Antibiotics.
Hormones may not be used in chickens. However, some consumers find this labeling to be attractive, and then may be willing to pay an additional premium per pound even though a poultry package without this label is not different in terms of hormone use.

Antibiotic use in the raising of meat and poultry, as well as misuse in human health, has become a concern with the increase of antibiotic-resistant infections. If antibiotics are used, USDA tests for and requires that no residuals are found in the meat.

The majority of broiler (Table 25–1 provides terminology) producers report not using antibiotics in flocks except in case of illness [22]. Labels stating

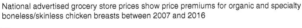

National advertised grocery store prices show price premiums for organic and specialty boneless/skinless chicken breasts between 2007 and 2016

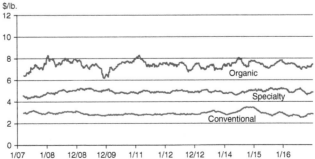

Figure 25–5

Poultry prices are higher if the product includes specialty labeling or if it is organic as compared to conventionally raised poultry. (U.S. Department of Agriculture)

USDA's Organic Seal reflects regulatory standards for many of the "single-trait" practice claims on food products

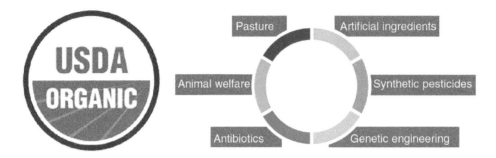

Figure 25–6

Foods, including poultry, may be labeled as "organic" when organic regulations are followed for a variety of attributes.

(U.S. Department of Agriculture)

"raised without antibiotics" are a voluntary label that can be useful for some consumers, but at the same time can be misleading. One poultry company was required by USDA to remove the "raised without antibiotics" label when further review determined antibiotics had been used in the eggs used to hatch the chickens [2].

Fresh and Frozen. The terms *fresh* and *frozen*, as applied to poultry products, were defined in 1997.

Fresh poultry must have never been below 26°F (−3°C). Raw poultry held at 0°F (−18°C) or below must be labeled as "frozen" or "previously frozen." A third category of poultry is referred to as *hard chilled* or *previously hard chilled*. Hard-chilled poultry has been held below 26°F (−3°C) but above 0°F (−18°C). Poultry that has been hard chilled is not required to have any descriptive label on the product, but it should not be labeled as "fresh" or "frozen" because neither of these categories applies [29, 33].

Table 25–2
POULTRY LABELING TERMS

Basted or self-basted	Products injected or marinated with a solution containing butter or other edible fat, stock or water plus spices, flavor enhancers, and other approved substances. A maximum added weight of 3 percent for bone-in poultry and an added weight of 8 percent for boneless poultry.
Chemical free	This term is not allowed on labels.
Free range or free roaming	Poultry has been allowed access to outside.
Halal or Zabiha Halal	Prepared in federally inspected plants and handled according to Islamic rule under Islamic authority.
Kosher	Prepared in federally inspected plants and handled under rabbinical supervision.
Mechanically separated poultry	Effective 1996, poultry product that has been separated from the bone through a sieve or similar device under pressure must be labeled as "*mechanically separated chicken*" or "*turkey.*"
No hormones	Hormones are not allowed in the raising of poultry; therefore, if this statement is used on a label, it must be followed by the statement "Federal regulations prohibit the use of hormones."
No antibiotics	May be used if poultry was raised without antibiotics.
Oven prepared	Fully cooked and ready to eat.
Oven ready	Product is ready to cook.
Organic	Specific guidelines under USDA's National Organic Program must be followed in the production and processing of the product. Feed used for the birds must also be organic.
Natural	Contains no artificial flavors, coloring, chemical preservatives, or other artificial or synthetic ingredients. The term *natural* must be explained on the label.

Source: References 30, 33.

Absorbed and Retained Water. Under new regulations effective in 2002, poultry products must label the percentage of absorbed or retained water in any raw poultry product as a result of carcass washing, chilling, or other postslaughter processing unless the amount of water retained can be demonstrated to be unavoidable due to meeting food-safety requirements [31]. Poultry has been traditionally chilled using water immersion, which may result in water retention. This new regulation came into effect because of a suit brought by poultry consumers and red-meat producers alleging that poultry products containing absorbed water were adulterated (in an economic sense) and misbranded under the 1957 Poultry Products Inspection Act.

Nutrition Labeling. The 1990 Nutrition Labeling and Education Act mandates nutrition labels on processed poultry products. As with meat, as of 2012, poultry must also provide nutrition labeling either on the package or on a poster at the point of sale [35]. Raw meats and poultry were previously exempt from the nutrition labeling requirements. Like other products, meat and poultry also have "country-of-origin labeling."

Other Labeling Requirements. As with meat, raw or partially cooked poultry must carry a safe-handling label. The other requirements for a poultry label include the product name, name and address of the producer or distributor, inspection mark, ingredients and net weight, establishment number identifying the plant where the product was processed, and handling instructions. After the product leaves the processing plant, it comes under the jurisdiction of the FDA, which is responsible for preventing the sale of adulterated food, including poultry. Additional information and terms that may appear on a poultry label are provided in Table 25–2.

PURCHASING POULTRY

Quality and Characteristics of Age

Age. Most poultry sold in retail markets are young, tender birds. In a young bird, the end of the breastbone is pliable, and the wing offers little resistance when bent into an upright position. The skin of a young bird is pliable, soft, and tears easily. An older bird has a hard, calcified breastbone and may show an abundance of long hairs. The skin of older birds is tougher, and the flesh is less tender. Weight varies by breed and is not necessarily an indication of age. In young birds, sex differences are not significant; however, with increase in age, male birds are inferior in flavor to female birds.

Color. The color of chicken skin can be a creamy-white to a yellow. The color is influenced by the feed given to the chicken. It does not indicate differences in nutrition, tenderness, or other characteristics of the bird. Some areas in the United States prefer a more yellow bird and therefore growers adjust the feed to provide this color [32].

Quality Defects. Three defects have appeared globally in poultry: white stripping, woody breast, and spaghetti meat. White stripping is characterized by several white lines, usually in the breast meat, that can be seen running parallel to muscle fibers [10]. It should not be mistaken from a natural fat line also in a chicken breast. Woody breast is evident by a raw breast being firmer than normal. If particularly severe then a prominent bulge or ridge may also be apparent [10]. Muscle fibers separate excessively in spaghetti meat. All of these conditions appear to be more prevalent with the increased growth rate of birds, but are not fully understood.

Researchers found chickens with white stripping or woody breasts had a lower water holding capacity. Cooking moisture losses were greater and when marinated, less marinade was absorbed [24].

Amount to Buy and Economic Considerations

The quantity of raw, bone-in poultry to be purchased per person is greater than other types of meat because poultry has a relatively high proportion of waste from the raw carcass to the cooked bird. Skin, fat, and bone accounted for about 50 percent of the weight of the cooked chicken. Cooking of poultry, as well as other meats, results in lost moisture and fat, which will affect the cooked yield of the meat. The yield of cooked weight for young chickens has been reported to be 65 percent of the raw weight for those that were baked and 73 percent for those that were simmered [17]. Thus, the yield of cooked edible meat from the raw chicken carcass was about 35 percent. Cooking losses vary with the temperature and method of cooking and with the percentage of fat. The high fat content of ducks and geese results in particularly high cooking losses.

General guidelines for the amount of poultry to purchase have been developed [28, 34]:

- Fresh or frozen whole turkey—1 pound per person
- Fresh or frozen whole chicken—½ pound per person
- Duck or goose—1 to 1½ pounds per person

Table 25–3 gives the estimated number of servings from a pound of ready-to-cook poultry for additional types of poultry products. To satisfy individual preferences for various poultry parts, pieces of all one kind, such as chicken breasts or drumsticks, are often packaged together and marketed. As Table 25–3 indicates, more poultry is needed per serving when such pieces as wings or thighs are purchased than when breasts, which contain less bone, are bought.

Table 25–3
NUMBER OF SERVINGS FROM A POUND OF READY-TO-COOK (RTC) POULTRY

Kind and Class	Size of Serving	Approximate Servings of Cooked Meat	
		Number of Servings per Pound RTC	Approximate Yield of Cooked, Diced Meat (Cups)
Chicken			
Whole			
Broiler-fryer	3 oz without bone	2	$1\frac{1}{4}$
Roaster	3 oz without bone	$2\frac{1}{4}$	$1\frac{1}{2}$
Stewing hen	3 oz without bone	2	$1\frac{1}{4}$
Pieces			
Breast halves (about 5¾ oz each)	1, about 2¾ oz without bone	$2\frac{3}{4}$	
Drumsticks (about 3 oz each)	2, about 2½ oz without bone	$2\frac{1}{2}$	
Thighs (about 3¾ oz each)	2, about 3 oz without bone	$2\frac{1}{4}$	
Wings (about 2¾ oz each)	4, about 2¾ oz without bone	$1\frac{1}{2}$	
Breast quarter (about 11 oz each)	1, about 4½ oz without bone	$1\frac{1}{2}$	
Leg quarter (about 10¾ oz each)	1, about 4¼ oz without bone	$1\frac{1}{2}$	
Turkey			
Whole	3 oz without bone	$2\frac{1}{4}$	$1\frac{1}{4}$
Pieces			
Breast	3 oz without bone	$2\frac{3}{4}$	$1\frac{3}{4}$
Thigh	3 oz without bone	$2\frac{3}{4}$	
Drumstick	3 oz without bone	$2\frac{1}{2}$	
Wing	3 oz without bone	$1\frac{3}{4}$	
Ground	3 oz	$3\frac{3}{4}$	
Boneless turkey roast	3 oz	$3\frac{1}{4}$	
Duckling	3 oz without bone	1	
Goose	3 oz without bone	$1\frac{3}{4}$	

Source: Courtesy of the USDA.

When considering what form of poultry offers the best value, the price per serving rather than the price per pound should be considered. Bone-in chicken will generally cost less than a boneless chicken breast, but the boneless chicken breast will yield more meat per pound. If purchasing a whole chicken versus a whole cut-up chicken, the additional cost per pound for the cut-up chicken reflects convenience. With practice, cutting up a bird can be done easily and will save money. There are a number of good videos online demonstrating how to quickly and easily cut a whole chicken into breasts, wings, legs, and thighs.

SAFE STORAGE AND PREPARATION

Safe Storage and Handling

Chilled, raw poultry is a highly perishable product and should be stored at a refrigerator temperature of 40°F (4°C) or below. Even at refrigerator temperatures, storage time is usually limited to a few days. If poultry must be stored longer than one to two days, wrap it in moisture-proof packing to help prevent **freezer burn** and freeze. Frozen storage should be at or below 0°F (−18°C).

All surfaces, such as countertops and cutting boards, which come into contact with raw poultry during its preparation should be thoroughly cleaned and sanitized before other foods are placed on them. One tablespoon of household bleach in 1 gallon of water may be used to sanitize cutting boards and other work surfaces. Cutting boards made of wood should be sanitized with 3 tablespoons of bleach per gallon of water and then rinsed with a standard disinfection solution of 1 tablespoon of bleach per gallon of water. These precautions are necessary to avoid cross-contamination of cooked poultry and other foods prepared on the same surfaces because raw poultry may be contaminated with *Salmonella* or *Campylobacter* bacteria when brought into the kitchen. A retail study conducted in Minnesota found that 88 percent of the poultry sampled from local supermarkets tested positive for *Campylobacter* [7]. *Salmonella* and *Campylobacter* foodborne illnesses were discussed in Chapter 2.

Washing or rinsing of poultry before cooking is not recommended [32]. Washing of poultry prior to preparation does not affect the safety of the bird after cooking but may result in contamination of other areas in the kitchen, posing a safety risk [32, 36]. Any bacteria that may be present on the bird will be destroyed by proper cooking.

Thawing of Frozen Poultry

Poultry products, like other highly perishable foods, should be thawed in one of three ways: (1) under refrigeration; (2) in clean, cold water that is changed every 30 minutes; or (3) in the microwave [30]. Birds thawed under cold water or in the microwave should be cooked immediately after thawing. Birds thawed under refrigeration may be stored in the refrigerator for one to two days prior to cooking. Thawing on the kitchen counter or in warm water is an unsafe practice because part of the bird may be in the **temperature danger zone**, thereby allowing microorganisms to grow.

When thawing under refrigeration, allow a minimum of 24 hours per 4 to 5 pounds. The bird should be placed at the bottom of the refrigerator in a leak-proof container so that raw juices from the thawing bird do not contaminate other foods. Birds thawed in water should be in a leak-proof package and submerged in cold tap water that is changed every 30 minutes so that the water remains clean and cold. Warm water should not be used to thaw a bird because the outer areas of the bird will be exposed to temperatures favorable for rapid bacterial growth. When thawing under cold water, approximately 30 minutes per pound should be adequate.

Safe End-Point Cooking Temperatures

Poultry should always be cooked to a minimum 165°F (74°C) to destroy any pathogenic organisms that may be present. The temperature of whole birds should be checked in (1) the innermost part of the thigh and

---

HOT TOPICS

SCIENTISTS AND CHICKENS—PARTNERS?

It takes a tough scientist to make a tender (and juicy) chicken! Thus says the Agricultural Research Service of the USDA [5]. Brenda Lyon is a food scientist at its research center in Athens, Georgia, where she focuses on the relationships between sensory attributes (eating quality) of poultry meat and production practices (growing and processing the birds).

For over 20 years, Lyon has studied the characteristics of poultry meat. We like our chicken to be tender and moist, but there are many components that affect these characteristics. The amount of force it takes to cut through a piece of poultry—called *shear value*—can be easily measured with a machine. But human subjects, with their senses of smell, taste, touch, and sight, are essential in evaluating aroma, appearance, juiciness, texture, and so on. And it doesn't stop there. For example, characteristics such as mouthfeel, springiness, chewiness, compaction of the meat after chewing, and ease of swallowing all play a part in creating a sensory texture profile.

To be a sensory evaluator in these research projects requires intensive training in order to identify the various characteristics of poultry meat and assign intensity values to them. In Lyon's laboratory, she is a tough trainer. Just how tender is tender and how juicy is juicy—on a scale monitored by a computer?

What is the ultimate goal of this food technology research? It is to assist the poultry producers in bringing to the marketplace a nutritious product that consumers will buy and enjoy. For example, it has been found that the amount of time the breast muscles remain on the bone after processing affects the texture and tenderness of the boned meat. It seems that the best timing for acceptable

Food technologists discuss the fiber orientation of a chicken breast sample. (U.S. Department of Agriculture, Agricultural Research Service; photo by Peggy Greb)

tenderness is 4 to 6 hours postmortem. Rigor mortis occurs and is dissipated by this time period. Sensory panels found that meat left on the bone for less than 4 hours was tougher than meat left on the bone longer. This 4- to 6-hour period must be integrated into the inspection, chilling, and cutting processes in a poultry plant. Reducing the chilling time to accommodate the deboning process interfered with rigor mortis and made the cooked breast meat tough. The sensory panels were key in determining the real effects of the production processes.

Thus, the food scientist and the poultry processor need to work together as partners in order to produce the kind of chicken we all enjoy. Eating quality is the ultimate deciding factor in whether a process is successful. ■

wing and (2) the thickest part of the breast. Higher temperatures of 170 to 180°F (77 to 82°C) may be recommended by some sources to ensure that an acceptable temperature has been reached throughout the bird or because of personal preferences for a more well-done bird. Color of the meat and juices and looseness of the joints when wiggled are suggestive of doneness but are not reliable indicators from a food-safety perspective.

Whole turkeys and some roasting chickens may have "pop-up" temperature indicators. These temperature indicators are usually set for a temperature of 185°F (85°C). However, because these indicators are in only one location of the bird, it is still recommended that a thermometer be used to check other areas of the bird to assess doneness [34].

To Stuff or Not to Stuff

Stuffing a bird before roasting is not generally recommended. Bacteria can survive in stuffing that has not reached the safe temperature of 165°F (74°C), potentially resulting in foodborne illness. If a bird is stuffed, the following precautions should be taken. First, stuff the bird loosely immediately before placing in the oven. Do not stuff the bird the night or even hours ahead. Second, check the temperature of the dressing and see that it is at 165°F (74°C) or higher throughout before removing from the oven to serve. The bird is likely to be well above 165°F (74°C) when the dressing is adequately cooked but should be checked in several locations to be certain.

Although prestuffed fresh birds may be purchased in the marketplace, these are not recommended by the USDA [34]. Frozen, prestuffed birds may also be purchased and are considered safe when cooked from the frozen state. Manufacturer's directions should be followed. The temperature in the center of the stuffing, as measured with a thermometer, should reach 165°F (74°C).

Handling Leftovers

Cooked poultry products are ideal for the growth and/or toxin production of any microorganisms with which they may have been contaminated during handling and serving; therefore, maintaining proper temperature control is essential. Poultry products should always be refrigerated promptly and used within a few days. When a large bird has been prepared, the meat should be removed from the bone, cut into smaller pieces, and refrigerated so that the meat cools rapidly. If cooked poultry will be kept longer than a few days, it should be placed in a moisture- and vapor-proof wrapping or container and frozen. Like meat, **warmed-over flavor** can occur in poultry (see chapter 24). Longer storage periods are possible when raw or cooked poultry is frozen. Better flavor and texture are maintained in the uncooked than in the cooked frozen product when they are to be stored for a few months.

COOKING POULTRY

The fundamental principles of cooking poultry do not differ from those for other meats. Dry-heat methods (broiling, frying, baking, and roasting) are applicable to young, tender birds. Moist-heat methods should be applied to older, less tender birds to make them tender and palatable (see Chapter 5 for more on dry and moist heat cooking methods). Most of the poultry sold on the market today is young and tender and can be cooked by dry-heat methods.

Roasting

All kinds of young, tender poultry can be roasted or baked (**Figure 25–7**). Poultry may be roasted in an oven or in an electric roaster. Before roasting, birds may be **trussed** by tying the legs together as well as the wings with thread or butcher's twine to create a more compact shape if desired (**Figure 25–8**).

Figure 25–7

A roasted chicken can be presented on a platter before carving.
(Elisanth/Shutterstock)

Figure 25–8

Two examples of trussed birds are shown. To truss a bird, the legs are tied together, and then the twine is pulled up and tied above the neck. The first joint of the wings may be folded back behind the bird, or, as shown on the bird to the bottom right, the first and second joints may be removed. (Richard Embery/Pearson Education)

KEEP IT SAFE
HANDLING PRECOOKED POULTRY PRODUCTS SAFELY

Processed poultry products are popular for use in the food service industry because they are uniform in weight, shape, yield, composition, and cooking requirements. Some of these are distributed in a precooked form that requires only refrigeration rather than freezing. The raw poultry product may be vacuum packaged in a multilaminate film, cooked, and then marketed in the same package. When vacuum packaged, uncured precooked turkey breast rolls were evaluated for microbiologic stability past 30 days of storage at 40°F (4°C), no colonies of **psychrotrophic** aerobic bacteria were detected; however, some **mesophilic** anaerobic bacteria were present. These findings indicate that precautions should be taken when serving these precooked poultry products to ensure that they are not temperature abused. Thus, they should not be held at higher than refrigerator temperatures for any period that would allow bacteria to multiply, and they must always be refrigerated [21]. ■

Poultry may be roasted with little pre-preparation or after brining (see the "How Does Brining Work" feature). Although not ideal, turkey and chicken may be roasted from the frozen state; however, the time required for cooking will be 50 percent more. Finally, duck and goose are roasted with consideration of their high fat content.

Traditional Roasting. To roast a whole chicken or turkey, the bird should be placed in a relatively shallow roasting pan to allow contact of the hot oven air with the bird. Many sources recommend that half cup of water be added to the bottom of the pan. The oven temperature for roasting poultry should be no lower than 325°F (163°C) [30]. An aluminum foil tent is sometimes used to cover the breast of turkeys at either the beginning or the end of roasting to prevent overbrowning. Alternatively, the whole bird can be wrapped in foil, although lower palatability for foil-wrapped turkeys versus open pan-roasted birds has been reported [4]. Palatability is probably similar for birds roasted with the breast either up or down in the roasting rack. Birds may be **basted** during cooking using juices from the roaster pan.

When a minimum end-point temperature of 165°F (74°C) has been reached, the bird should be removed from the oven and allowed to stand for approximately 20 minutes before carving. This resting period will allow the juices to more readily remain in the meat when sliced. **Table 25–4** gives approximate cooking times for unstuffed turkeys. The internal temperature of turkey meat, both whole birds and light- or dark-meat roasts, appears to be a good guide in cooking. The yield and juiciness of cooked meat decrease as the internal temperature increases from 104 to 194°F (40 to 90°C). At the same time, the scores for odor, flavor, and mealiness increase with increasing temperature [8]. **Figure 25–9** shows the suggested steps for the carving of a turkey.

Electric Roaster Ovens. Poultry may be roasted in a large electric roaster. The roaster should be preheated to 325°F (163°C). The lid should remain on throughout cooking to maintain adequate temperature levels.

Brining Before Roasting. Poultry can be soaked in a mixture of salt and water, which is called *brine*. About 2 cups of salt for 2 gallons of water is suggested. Other seasonings, such as bay leaves, garlic, and peppercorns, may be added for additional flavor. To brine a bird, submerge it in the salt-and-water mixture in a large container for 6 to 8 hours while keeping it at or below 40°F (4°C). After brining, remove the bird from the liquid and roast. The bird may cook more rapidly when brined, so temperatures should be monitored to avoid overcooking.

Roasting of Duck and Goose. Duck and goose contain a relatively high level of fat under the skin. Therefore, when these birds are roasted, it is recommended that the skin be scored in a crisscross pattern with a knife so the fat can drain off during roasting. Higher oven temperatures are often used to encourage the rendering of the fat from the bird.

Table 25–4
TIMETABLE FOR ROASTING FRESH OR THAWED TURKEY

Purchased Weight (lb)	Approximate Roasting Time at 325°F (Hours)*
8–12	2¾–3
12–14	3–3¾
14–18	3¾–4¼
18–20	4¼–4½
20–24	4½–5

* These times are approximate and should always be used in conjunction with a properly placed thermometer.
Source: Courtesy of the USDA.

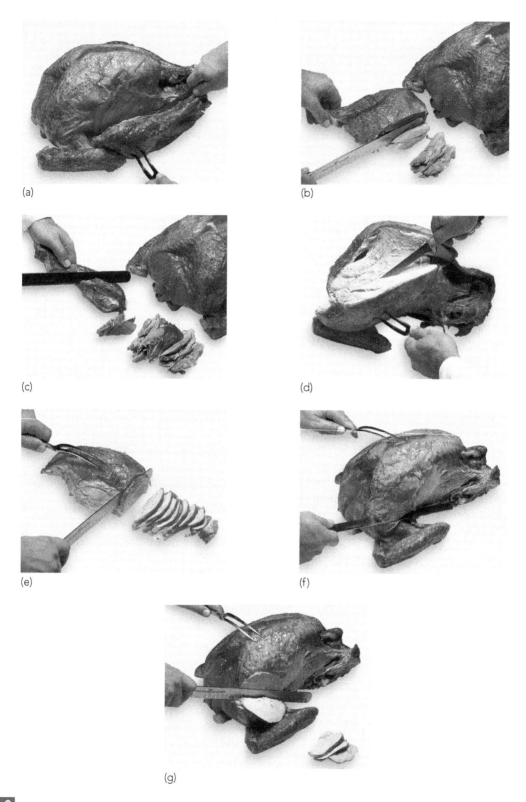

(a)

(b)

(c)

(d)

(e)

(f)

(g)

Figure 25–9

Steps on carving turkey. (a) Allow turkey to rest for 20 minutes after roasting to avoid loss of juices when carving. Start by pulling the leg and thigh outward. Cut through the cartilage between the joint. (b) Repeat on other side of the bird, then slice meat from the thigh by slicing parallel to the bone. (c) Separate the thigh from the leg by cutting through the joint cartilage (between leg and thigh). Slice meat parallel to the bone. (d) Separate the breast from the ribs by cutting along the bone. (e) Place the half breast (just removed from the carcass) on a cutting board and slice across grain as shown. (f) Alternatively, the breast may be carved on the bird. Start by cutting horizontally just above the wing toward the rib. (g) Next slice the breast meat as shown, while watching to slice across the meat grain. (Richard Embery/Pearson Education)

Broiling and Grilling

For broiling or grilling, young tender birds are cut into halves, quarters, or smaller pieces. Small young chickens and small fryer-roaster turkey pieces all may be appropriately broiled or grilled. The pieces are placed on a slotted grid or rack on the broiler pan or on grates over hot coals. Joints may be snapped so that pieces lie flat. With the broiler rack placed 5 to 6 inches from the flame or heating element, chicken pieces broiled for 20 to 25 minutes on each side should be cooked well done. Turkey pieces require 30 to 35 minutes on each side. Tongs should be used to turn the poultry pieces during broiling.

Poultry to be broiled or grilled may be marinated or flavored with a paste of seasonings (**Figure 25–10**). Poultry picks up the flavors of a marinade fairly rapidly, generally in 2 hours.

Figure 25–10

These chicken legs and thighs are being cooked on a grill after being rubbed with Jamaican Jerk seasonings. (Richard Embery/Pearson Education)

Extended contact with acid in the marinade may cause the texture of the meat to soften excessively and thus should be avoided [12]. For food safety, leftover marinade should be discarded. The flavor and color of broiled and grilled poultry may also be enhanced by basting during broiling or by applying a coating or breading mixture before cooking. Coating greatly reduces cooking losses not only with broiling but also with other cooking methods [19].

Grilling and Smoking of Whole Turkeys or Chickens

Whole birds may be grilled on a covered gas or charcoal grill. Smaller turkeys, less than 16 pounds, are recommended because a larger bird may take too long to cook and food safety could be compromised [27]. A grill or appliance thermometer should be used to monitor the temperature inside the grill. A temperature of around 300°F (149°C) is desirable.

The bird is cooked by indirect heat inside the grill. With charcoal, the hot coals should be pushed evenly around the edge, and a drip pan with water should be placed in the center. The bird is then placed on the grates above the drip pan, and the lid is placed on the grill. New briquettes must be added every hour to maintain temperature. For a gas grill with more than one burner, place the turkey to the side away from burners that are turned on. If the grill has only one burner, place a pan of water under the grate to create indirect heat and place the bird on top of the grate in a roasting pan. Likewise, the lid of the grill should be closed to raise the heat within the grill.

Panfrying

Pieces of young chickens are frequently fried. The pieces are first coated by being rolled in seasoned flour mixtures, batters, or egg and crumbs [3, 23]. Slow, careful cooking is necessary when panfrying to prevent overbrowning before the birds are done. Usually, 40 to 60 minutes is required to cook the flesh thoroughly, part of this time with the frying pan covered.

FOCUS ON SCIENCE
HOW DOES BRINING WORK?

Starting at the molecular level, poultry and other meats are made up of cells. Within these cells are membranes that allow for the movement of substances in and out. Water is the only substance able to move freely in and out across these borders. Additionally, inside these cells are dissolved solutes (solids), such as salts, potassium, and calcium. If there is only water outside, the balance of solids will be off; some water will go in, and salt will come out.

When the raw poultry is submerged in the brine solution, some of the water will be drawn out of the meat, thereby diluting the brine solution and resulting in the brine solution entering into the meat. The salt in the brine solution, once absorbed into the meat, will cause the proteins to unravel or denature into loose coils. During cooking, these proteins will trap water almost like a gel. Therefore, a moist finished product will be the result.

FOCUS ON SCIENCE
MORE ON THE DEEP-FAT FRYING OF WHOLE TURKEYS

The first step in deep-fat frying a turkey is to determine the correct amount of oil to be used in the fryer. Place the turkey into the pot that will be used for frying and add water just until it barely covers the top of the turkey. The water level should be at least 4 to 5 inches below the top of the pot. Remove the turkey from the pot and mark where the water line is. This will be the amount of oil to be used for frying. This precaution will prevent the overflow of the hot oil when the turkey is placed in the fryer, which could lead to fire and severe burning. If the pot is too small to allow a 4- to 5-inch headspace, use a larger pot and measure using the same procedure.

Select a fat with a high smoke point. Peanut oil is usually suggested because it contains a fatty acid of 22 carbons and a high smoke point, making it a good choice for frying. Heat the fat to the desired temperature, approximately 350°F (177°C), using a thermometer made for deep-fat frying. The temperature of the oil will drop when the turkey is added, so start timing when the temperature again reaches 350°F (177°C). The cooking time can be estimated by calculating a cooking time of 3 minutes per pound and then adding another 5 minutes to the total. Therefore, for a 12-pound turkey, the cooking time is calculated as $12 \times 3 = 36 + 5 = 41$ minutes. Check doneness with a thermometer.

Young chickens may be oven-fried at about 400°F (204°C). The pieces are first coated and then placed in a baking pan containing a small amount of oil. The chicken is turned midway through the baking process.

Deep-Fat Frying

To deep-fat fry, the food is submerged in hot oil. Pieces of chicken to be deep-fat fried may be steamed almost done before being dipped in flour, batter, or egg and crumbs and then browned in the heated fat. Deep-fat fried chicken may also be coated and fried from the raw state. It is cooked at 325 to 350°F (165 to 175°C) for 20 to 30 minutes, depending on the size of the chicken piece. Pressure deep-fat fryers have been developed especially for the frying of poultry in the food-processing and food service industries (see Chapter 8).

Deep-fat frying of whole turkeys has gained in popularity. Safety should be of prime importance when deep-fat frying a large bird because hot oil can cause severe burns and can catch fire if overheated. Deep-fat frying of turkey in the home setting should be done outdoors. Storage and subsequent disposal of oil must also be considered.

To deep-fat fry a turkey, select a bird that is 12 pounds or less [27]. The cooking oil should be maintained at a temperature of 350°F (175°C) by monitoring with a thermometer designed for deep fat. The length of cooking time is approximately 3 to 5 minutes per pound. The turkey is done when the internal temperature of the bird is at a minimum of 165°F (74°C) as measured with a thermometer.

Braising

The method of braising involves cooking poultry in steam in a covered container. The term *fricassee* is often applied to cut pieces of chicken that are braised, usually in a white or cream-based sauce. The pieces are browned by first frying in a small amount of fat. Then moisture is added, and the poultry is simmered in a covered skillet until tender and well done. Alternatively, the poultry can be cooked until tender and then fried until brown. A sauce or gravy made from the pan drippings is often served over the poultry pieces. Braising tenderizes older, less tender poultry but also is an appropriate method for cooking young birds.

Stewing

For stewing, birds are usually cut into pieces, although whole birds may be cooked in water seasoned with spices, herbs, and vegetables. The poultry should be simmered in a relatively large amount of water until tender.

Microwave Cooking

Poultry may be cooked in a microwave oven [27]. However, for a variety of reasons, many do not recommend the microwave cooking of poultry. Microwave energy is not as effective as conventional cooking for destruction of microorganisms in whole turkeys, in chicken halves, and probably in pieces. In one study, turkeys that had been inoculated with food-poisoning bacteria before cooking were baked in the microwave oven. Roasting to an internal breast temperature of 170°F (77°C) did not completely eliminate the microorganisms [1]. Although the turkeys in this study contained abnormally high numbers of bacteria, it is possible that pathogenic microorganisms present in more usual numbers will survive. In another study, cooking chicken halves in the microwave oven to an internal temperature of 185°F (85°C) was not sufficient to destroy, in more than 50 percent of the chickens, all *Salmonella* organisms with which the birds had been inoculated [14].

Cooking and Color Changes

Discoloration of Poultry Bones. The bones of frozen young birds are often very dark in color after the birds are cooked. Freezing and thawing break down the blood cells of bone marrow and cause a deep red color to appear [6, 32]. During cooking, the red color changes to brown, although this color change does not affect flavor. Cooking directly from the frozen state has been shown to result in less darkening than rapid or slow thawing [6].

Pink Flesh. At times the meat of poultry can be a pink color even though it is fully cooked. Reasons for this "pinking" vary. Cured poultry such as smoked turkey is expected to be pink (see chapter 24 for more on curing and smoking). Some of the reasons why uncured poultry can be pink include (1) genetics, feed, and preslaughter handling; (2) incidental nitrite or nitrate exposure through feed or the environment; (3) carbon monoxide exposure in gas ovens; and (4) smoke exposure during grilling [9]. Pink poultry is safe to eat, provided that it has been cooked to a minimum of 165°F (74°C).

STUDY QUESTIONS

Consumption Trends and Nutrition

1. Using USDA food availability data, identify the kind of meat or poultry that is consumed the most in the United States. Discuss potential reasons for this trend.

2. Identify important nutrients found in poultry.

Composition

3. Describe the composition of poultry, including protein, fat, connective tissue, and pigments.

Classification and Market Forms

4. Describe each of the following classes of chickens and turkeys.

Chickens	Turkeys
Broiler-fryer	Fryer-roaster
Roaster	Young hen
Capon	Young tom
Rock Cornish hen	
Baking hen	
Stewing hen or fowl	

5. Suggest satisfactory methods of cooking each type of poultry listed in question 4. Explain why each method is appropriate?

Poultry Production and Marketing

6. Identify the states with the highest broiler production in the United States.

7. Describe ways that may be used to reduce the bacterial contamination of poultry during processing.

Government Inspection, Grading, and Oversight of Labeling

8. Explain what the round USDA inspection mark means when placed on poultry.

9. List the USDA grades that may be used on poultry and describe the qualities that are considered in grading.

10. Discuss the information and the terminology that are found on the labels of poultry products.

Purchasing

11. Provide suggestions on how much poultry to purchase if a "bone-in" bird.

12. Discuss several quality characteristics associated with poultry.

Safe Storage, Handling, and Preparation

13. Explain why it is so important to handle poultry properly, both in the raw and in the cooked state.

14. Identify the safe end point cooking temperature for poultry.

15. Explain why it is *not* recommended to wash raw poultry.

16. Describe three acceptable ways to thaw poultry.

Cooking Methods

17. Describe an appropriate method for roasting turkeys. Explain why you would suggest this procedure.

18. Describe general procedures for broiling, frying, braising, and stewing poultry. Explain why the microwave cooking of poultry is often not recommended.

26
Seafood

There are thousands of different species of fish worldwide, about 300 of these being within the United States or in the coastal waters surrounding it. Fish live in freshwater or in the seas and oceans. Seafood comes to the United States from all over the world.

More than 80 percent of the seafood consumed in the United States is estimated to be imported, either from seafood caught or raised in other countries, or as seafood caught domestically but exported for processing and then re-imported into the United States [28]. The leading nations in commercial fishery landings were China (38.5 percent), Indonesia (6.3 percent), India (5.9 percent), Vietnam (3.5 percent), and the United States (3.2 percent) [28]. In the United States, the greatest volume of fish landings comes from Alaska, Louisiana, Washington, Virginia, and Mississippi. Although not on the top five list of states for volume, Maine and Massachusetts are among the list of top five states for dollar value of landings. Recreational anglers in the United States landed an estimated 182 million pounds of fish [28].

In this chapter, the following topics will be discussed:

- Consumption trends and nutrition
- Composition
- Classification
- Seafood harvest and aquaculture
- Government regulations and grading
- Purchasing fish and shellfish
- Safe storage and handling
- Preparation

CONSUMPTION TRENDS AND NUTRITION

Consumption Trends

Compared to the annual per capita consumption of red meats and poultry in the United States, the consumption of fish and shellfish is modest but increasing (**Figure 26–1**). According to U.S. Department of

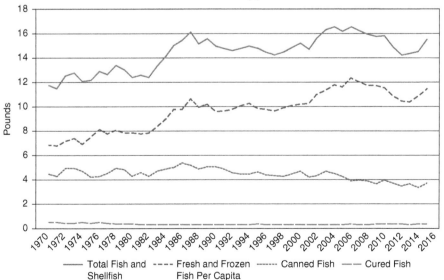

Figure 26–1

U.S. per capita availability of seafood. (U.S. Department of Agriculture, Economic Research Service)

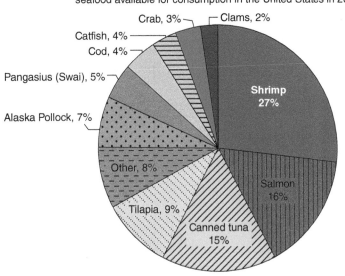

Shrimp, salmon, and canned tuna made up more than half of the seafood available for consumption in the United States in 2014

Clams, 2%
Crab, 3%
Catfish, 4%
Cod, 4%
Pangasius (Swai), 5%
Alaska Pollock, 7%
Other, 8%
Tilapia, 9%
Canned tuna 15%
Salmon 16%
Shrimp 27%

Figure 26–2

USDA availability data for seafood in United States provides an indication of consumption patterns. (U.S. Department of Agriculture)

Agriculture (USDA) food availability data, 14.9 pounds of fish and shellfish—fresh, canned, and frozen—were available per capita in 2016 compared to 11.7 pounds in 1970. In contrast, USDA data reveal much higher quantities of other meats per capita. In 2016, 63 pounds of chicken, 53 pounds of beef, and 47 pounds of pork were available per capita in the United States [24, 25].

Shrimp, salmon, and canned tuna represent more than half of the seafood consumed in the United States (**Figure 26–2**). The remaining top species available for consumption in the United States in descending order are tilapia, Alaska pollack, pangasius (a type of imported freshwater catfish), cod, catfish, crab, and clams [9].

Nutritive Value

The U.S. Dietary Guidelines recommend that Americans consume seafood twice each week totaling at least 8 ounces because of the health benefits associated with seafood consumption [26, 29]. Americans' intake of seafood is 2.7 ounces per week [9] (**Figure 26–3**); thus, most will need to more than double their seafood consumption to meet the U.S. Dietary Guidelines (**Figure 26–4**).

Pregnant and breast-feeding women or women who want to become pregnant should consume at least 8 to 12 ounces per week. An important reason for the recommendations for seafood consumption for all Americans is the health benefits associated with omega-3 **polyunsaturated fatty acids** (PUFA), eicosapentaenoic acid (EPA), and docosahexaenoic acid (DHA) consumption. Seafood is the main source of omega-3 fatty acids in the American diet.

The consumption of one to two servings of fish per week with reasonably high levels of EPA and DHA

has been associated with a reduction in coronary death [1, 18, 19, 29, 43]. DHA also appears to be beneficial for early neurodevelopment, which explains the recommendations of seafood consumption for women who want to become pregnant and for pregnant and breast-feeding women [7, 26]. The fat in many common fish contains 8 to 12 percent EPA and 30 to 45 percent total **omega-3 PUFA** [8], which makes fish an important source of these nutrients. The grams of omega-3 fatty acids found in a 3-ounce serving of some commonly consumed kinds of fish are provided in **Table 26–1**.

Seafood is also an important source of minerals, with oysters being particularly rich in zinc, iron, and copper [43]. Oysters, clams, and shrimp also contain a somewhat higher percentage of calcium than other fish and meats, which are notably low in calcium. Canned fish, such as sardines that are consumed with the bones, are a good source of calcium. Marine fish are a dependable source of iodine. Oysters, clams, and lobsters are the highest in iodine of all seafood. Shrimp ranks next, with crab and other ocean fish last in order.

Fat fish contain more vitamin A than lean varieties. Canned salmon is a fair source of vitamin A and a good source of riboflavin and niacin. The presence in raw fish of the enzyme *thiaminase*, which destroys thiamin, may make the vitamin unavailable if fish is held in the raw state.

COMPOSITION

The gross composition of seafood is similar to that of lean meat. Seafood, like red meat and poultry, is a valuable source of good-quality protein. Fish average 18 to 20 percent protein. Many varieties of fish are

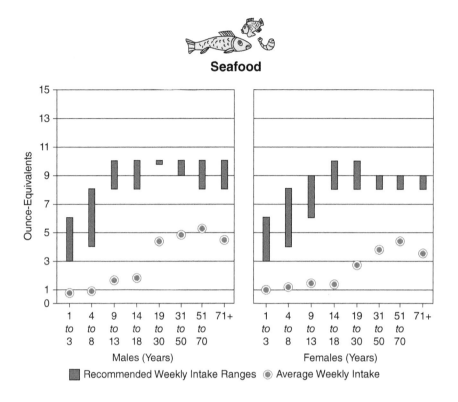

Figure 26-3

Americans are consuming less seafood than recommended by the USDA Dietary Guidelines. The orange dots represent the typical number of ounces (or equivalent) consumed at the ages listed. The blue bar is the recommended number of ounces (or ounce equivalents) of seafood that are recommended on a daily basis depending on individual needs at each age. (U.S. Department of Agriculture)

lower in fat and cholesterol compared to other meats, and the small amount of fat present in most kinds of fish is highly unsaturated. As noted, seafood is an important source of omega-3 fatty acids in the diet.

All shellfish have some carbohydrate in the form of **glycogen**. Lobsters have less than 1 percent, but abalone, clams, mussels, oysters, and scallops have from 3 to 5 percent. The sweet taste of various shellfish is

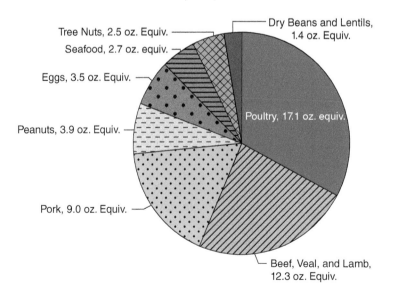

Figure 26-4

USDA food availability data reveals Americans consume only 2.7 ounces of seafood weekly as compared to a higher use of poultry, red meats (beef, veal, and lamb), pork, peanuts, and eggs. (U.S. Department of Agriculture)

Table 26–1
GRAMS OF OMEGA-3 FATTY ACIDS IN SELECTED KINDS OF SEAFOOD

Seafood Name	Milligrams of Omega-3 Fatty Acids (EPA + DHA) per 4-Ounce Serving
Anchovies, herring, and shad	1,200–2,400
Tuna: bluefin and albacore	1,700
Oysters: Pacific	1,500
Mackerel: Atlantic and Pacific (not king)	1,350–2,100
Salmon: Atlantic, Chinook, coho	1,200–2,400
Sardines: Atlantic and Pacific	1,100–1,600
Trout: freshwater	1,000–1,100
Tuna: white (albacore) canned	1,000
Mussels, blue	900
Salmon: pink and sockeye	700–900
Squid	750
Pollock: Atlantic and walleye	600
Flounder, plaice, and sole	350
Crab: blue, king, snow, queen, and Dungeness	200–550
Clams	200–300
Cod: Atlantic and Pacific; scallops: bay and sea; haddock; hake; and crayfish	200
Tuna: skipjack, yellowfin, and light canned	150–350
Tilapia	150
Catfish	100–250
Shrimp	100

Note: 1,750 milligrams of EPA and DHA is recommended per week and may be met by consuming two servings of fish each week that are moderately high in these omega-3 fatty acids.
Source: Reference 26.

FOCUS ON SCIENCE
EICOSAPENTAENOIC ACID (EPA) AND DOCOSAHEXAENOIC ACID (DHA)

Both EPA and DHA are highly unsaturated fatty acids with five and six double bonds, respectively. They also are classified as omega-3 fatty acids, which contribute health benefits to the diet. However, because they are highly unsaturated, they are susceptible to rancidity, which will lead to off-aromas and off-flavors if the fish is not handled properly. Fish should be chilled immediately when brought home by keeping it on ice in the refrigerator before cooking.

due to the glucose formed by enzyme action from the glycogen. Shrimp are high in cholesterol compared to beef, chicken, and other seafood products. However, shrimp are very low fat.

CLASSIFICATION

Two major categories for the classification of fish are vertebrate fish with fins and shellfish or invertebrates. The Food and Drug Administration (FDA) provides two useful online resources, the *Seafood List* and the *Regulatory Fish Encyclopedia*, available at www.fda.gov [35, 36].

Information about many different kinds of fish as well as acceptable market names are provided. The National Oceanic and Atmospheric Administration (NOAA) also provides *FishWatch* (www.fishwatch.gov), which gives pictures of seafood, profiles, and nutrition information. The *Seafood Handbook* is another excellent resource that is especially useful for those who purchase seafood in food service organizations [22].

Finfish

Finfish are usually covered with scales and may be further divided into two types: flat and round fish

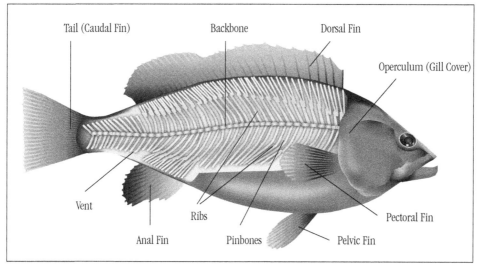

(a)

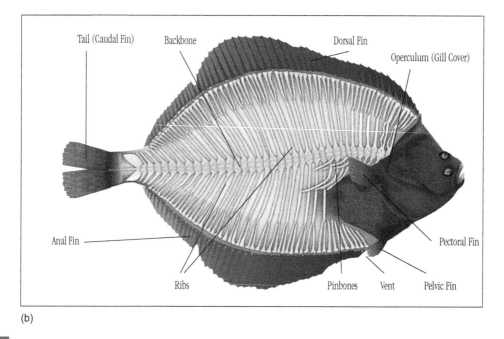

(b)

Figure 26–5

The bone structure of round fish and flatfish. (a) Round fish swim vertically and have eyes on each side of the body. (b) Flatfish swim horizontally and have both eyes on the top.

(**Figure 26–5**). Round fish swim vertically, whereas flatfish swim in a horizontal position (**Figure 26–6**). Some examples of round fish include bass, catfish, cod, haddock, pollock, grouper, mahimahi, orange roughy, red snapper, salmon, shark, swordfish, tilapia, trout, tuna, and whitefish. Fish classified as flatfish include flounder, sole, and halibut [10]. Some of the most commonly consumed finfish are described in **Table 26–2**.

Fish are also categorized according to whether they live in *fresh* or *salt* waters. Freshwater fish come from lakes and rivers instead of the oceans. Saltwater fish usually have more distinctive flavor than freshwater fish. Fish with vertebrae are further classified on the

basis of their fat content as *lean* or *fat*, lean fish having less than 5 percent fat in their edible flesh. Oily fish, such as salmon, usually have more flavor than lean fish. Examples of lean and fat fish are found in **Table 26–3**.

Shellfish

Shellfish are of two types: mollusks and crustaceans. The shellfish most commonly marketed in the United States are clams, crab, lobster, oysters, scallops, and shrimp.

Mollusks. Mollusks have a soft structure and are either partially or wholly enclosed in a hard shell that is largely of mineral composition. Mollusks may be further

Striped Bass

Chinook or King Salmon

Atlantic Cod

Halibut

Lemon Sole

Figure 26–6

Examples of round (Bass, Salmon, Cod) and flat fish (Halibut, Sole). (Richard Embery/Pearson Education)

Table 26–2
DESCRIPTION OF SELECTED POPULAR FINFISH IN THE UNITED STATES

Name of Fish	Description
Tuna	Albacore, bluefin, yellowfin, and skipjack are all varieties of tuna. Tuna may be purchased fresh, frozen, or canned. Bluefin and yellowfin are used in the raw market as sashimi and sushi. "Canned" tuna may be sold in cans or pouches with a water or oil pack. Albacore is known as "white meat tuna." Most of the light-meat canned tuna is skipjack, although some may be yellowfin. Light-meat tuna is low in mercury compared to albacore.
Salmon	Atlantic, Chinook, chum, coho, pink, and sockeye are all kinds of salmon. Salmon may be purchased fresh, frozen, smoked, or canned. Atlantic salmon is successfully "farmed" in floating net pens in open bays. Chinook salmon are found in the Pacific Ocean and are known for a buttery, rich taste and red flesh. Chum salmon are also found in the Pacific Ocean and have a lower oil content than other varieties with orange, pink, or red flesh. Coho has a relatively high fat content and a mild flavor. Pink salmon is generally lean and mild flavored. It is often canned.
Pollock	Alaskan pollock is in the cod family. It is a mild, delicate fish that produces a white flesh when cooked. Pollock fillets may be prepared by baking or grilling. It is often used to produce surimi or breaded and battered fish.
Tilapia	Tilapia is commonly farm raised. It is lean, mild, and sweet tasting. After cooking, the flesh is white with tender flakes. It may be purchased fresh, frozen, or as breaded fillets. Poor-quality tilapia may have an off-flavor.
Catfish	Catfish is farmed, raised with much of the U.S. catfish produced in the Mississippi Delta. The meat is moist and dense. The cooked meat is white and opaque.
Cod	Cod may be harvested from the Pacific and Atlantic oceans. Atlantic and Pacific cod are used interchangeably, although there are subtle differences between them. Cod is lean and cooks quickly. The flavor is neutral. The cooked flesh is white.

Source: Reference 22.

Table 26–3
SOME SPECIES OF FISH

Species	Weight Range (lb)	Usual Market Form	Suggested Preparation Method
Lean saltwater fish			
Bluefish	1–7	Whole and drawn	Broil, bake, fry
Cod	3–20	Steaks and fillets	Broil, bake, fry, steam
Flounder	¼–5	Whole, dressed, and fillets	Broil, bake, fry
Haddock	1½–7	Drawn and fillets	Broil, bake, steam
Hake	2–5	Whole, dressed, and fillets	Broil, bake, fry
Halibut	8–75	Steaks	Broil, bake, steam
Rosefish	½–1¼	Fillets	Bake
Snapper, red	2–15	Drawn, steaks, and fillets	Bake, steam
Whiting	½–1½	Whole, dressed, and fillets	Bake, fry
Fat saltwater fish			
Butterfish	¼–1	Whole and dressed	Broil, bake, fry
Herring	¾–1	Whole	Bake, fry
Mackerel	¾–3	Whole, drawn, and fillets	Broil, bake
Salmon	3–30	Drawn, dressed, steaks, and fillets	Broil, bake, steam
Shad	1½–7	Whole and fillets	Bake
Lean freshwater fish			
Brook trout	¾–8	Whole	Broil, bake, fry
Yellow pike	1½–10	Whole, dressed, and fillets	Broil, bake, fry
Fat freshwater fish			
Catfish	1–10	Whole, dressed, and skinned	Bake, fry
Lake trout	1½–10	Drawn, dressed, and fillets	Bake, fry
Whitefish	2–6	Whole, dressed, and fillets	Broil, bake

subdivided into univalves (abalone), bivalves (clams, oysters, and mussels), and cephalopods (squid and octopus).

Univalves.   As the name suggests, univalves have a single shell. Abalone are harvested in California and are characterized by a flavor somewhat like lobster [22]. Overcooked abalone will become very tough. Conch provide a firm, lean meat similar in flavor to abalone or clam. They are found in the Caribbean and off the Florida Keys. In the United States, commercial harvesting is banned because conch are endangered in domestic waters [22].

Bivalves.   Oysters, clams, mussels, and scallops are all examples of bivalves (**Figure 26–7**). Bivalves have two shells connected by a hinge. Oysters can be purchased live in the shell, fresh or frozen, shucked (removed from the shell), or canned. Live oysters have a tightly closed shell. Gaping shells indicate that they are dead and therefore no longer usable. Shucked oysters should be plump and have a natural creamy color, with clear liquor.

Several species of clams are used for food. They are marketed live in the shell, fresh or frozen shucked,

IN DEPTH
WHAT IS FISH ROE?

Roe is the mass of eggs from finfish and consists of sacs of connective tissue enclosing thousands of small eggs. It is important that the sacs remain intact because the eggs cannot otherwise be held together. Although roe is of minor importance in the marketing of fish, available only during spawning season and very perishable, fresh fish roe is well liked by some people. The most highly prized for flavor is shad roe. In the Great Lakes area, whitefish roe is also popular. Roe from most fish that are commonly consumed can be eaten. Caviar is sturgeon roe preserved in brine. It is expensive and is used mainly for making appetizers.

A method of cooking that intensifies flavor is preferable for fish roe. It is usually parboiled for 2 to 5 minutes, after which it is dipped in cornmeal or in egg and crumbs and fried. Parboiling aids in thorough cooking of the roe without its hardening by being fried too long.

SEAFOOD 729

Figure 26–7

Bivalve Mollusks. (Richard Embery/Pearson Education)

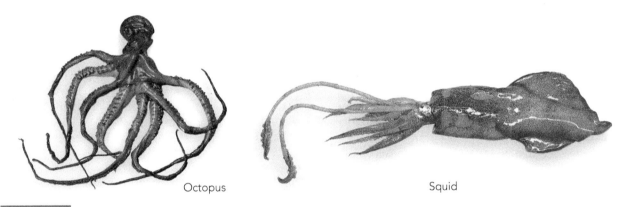

Figure 26–8

Cephalopods. (Richard Embery/Pearson Education)

or canned. Shucked clams should be plump, with clear liquor, and free from shell particles. Mussels have a distinctive taste that is a blend of clams and oysters. Mussels have "beards" or byssus threads that should be removed just before cooking [22]. Tightly closed shells of clams and mussels indicate that they are alive and therefore usable.

Scallops are mollusks similar to oysters and clams except that they swim freely through the water by snapping their shells together. The oversize adductor muscle that closes the shell is the only part of the scallop eaten by Americans. Both bay and sea scallops may be found in the marketplace, although only the bay scallop may be found whole and live [22]. Usually both kinds of scallops are sold shucked and cleaned.

Cephalopods. Octopus and squid are cephalopods (**Figure 26–8**). Both are characterized by a head with a number of arms attached near the head. Neither has an external shell, but instead both have an internal shell called a cuttlebone [10]. Squid often is called *calamari* on menus. To tenderize, octopus must be cooked by simmering or another slow-cooking method. In contrast, squid should be cooked quickly because overcooking will make it tough [22].

Crustaceans. Crustaceans are covered with a crustlike shell and have segmented bodies. Common examples are lobster, crab, shrimp, and crayfish (**Figure 26–9**).

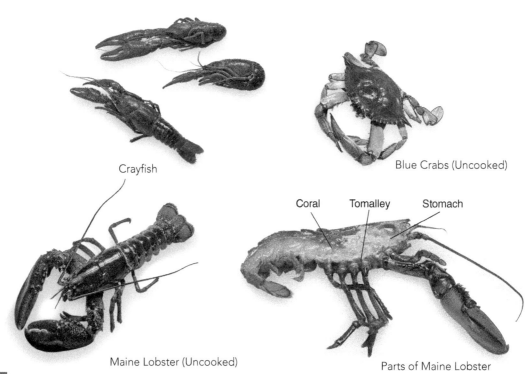

Crayfish

Blue Crabs (Uncooked)

Coral   Tomalley   Stomach

Maine Lobster (Uncooked)

Parts of Maine Lobster

Figure 26–9

Crustaceans.   (Richard Embery/Pearson Education)

Shrimp. Shrimp include the common or white shrimp, which is greenish-gray when caught; the brown or Brazilian shrimp, which is brownish-red when raw; the pink or coral shrimp; and the Alaska and California varieties, which vary in color and are relatively small. Despite the differences in color in the raw state, cooked shrimp differ little in appearance and flavor. Raw shrimp in the shell are often called *green shrimp* (**Figure 26–10**). Shrimp are usually sold with the head and thorax removed. The sand vein should be removed in larger shrimp.

Shrimp are designated by the count per pound as jumbo, large, large medium, medium, and small. The largest size has 15 or fewer shrimp to the pound; the smallest size has 60 or more to the pound. Breaded shrimp, which have been peeled, cleaned, and breaded for frying, are available. Prawn are shrimplike crustaceans that are usually relatively large in size.

Lobster. The true lobster, or northern lobster, is found near the shores of Europe and North America in the cold waters of the North Atlantic Ocean. The spiny or rock lobster is nearly worldwide in its distribution. The spiny lobster may be distinguished by the absence of large, heavy claws and the presence of many prominent spines on its body and legs.

Lobsters are dark bluish-green when taken from the water but change to a "lobster red" during

cooking. Lobsters and crabs must be alive at the time of cooking to ensure freshness. The tail should curl under the body when the live lobster is picked up. Lobsters cooked in the shell are available. They should be bright red in color and have a fresh odor. Frozen lobster tails can be purchased in some markets. The cooked meat, picked from the shells of lobsters and crabs, is marketed fresh, frozen, and canned.

Crawfish and Crayfish. *Crawfish* and *crayfish* are terms often used interchangeably in the United States to refer to freshwater crustaceans that are similar to lobster. *Crawdad* is another term that may be used. Crawfish, like spiny lobster, have small claws. The majority of crawfish in the United States are raised using aquaculture in Louisiana.

Figure 26–10

Raw shrimp with the head removed are shown here and often called "green headless shrimp."   (Richard Embery/Pearson Education)

Crab. Several types of crabs are harvested in the waters surrounding the United States. The crabs include blue, Dungeness, Jonah, king, Kona (Hawaii), snow, and stone crabs. Blue crabs represent about 50 percent of all crab marketed in the United States [28]. They come from the Atlantic and Gulf coasts. Blue crabs, if harvested right after molting, are called "soft shell" crabs. Because the shell is so tender, the shell and meat of soft shell crabs are consumed. Fresh-cooked meat from blue crabs may be packed in several grades: lump meat, or solid lumps of white meat from the body of the crab; flake meat, or small pieces of white meat from the rest of the body; lump and flake meat combined; and claw meat, which has a brownish tinge.

Dungeness crabs are found on the Pacific Coast from Alaska to Mexico. Fresh-cooked meat from both the body and claws of Dungeness crabs has a pinkish tinge and is packed as one grade. Jonah crabs are found off New England in the United States and are a less expensive crabmeat compared to blue and Dungeness crabs [22]. King crab is harvested in Alaska and is usually sold as frozen legs and claws (**Figure 26–11**). Snow crab is also harvested in Alaska. It is smaller than king crab but is known for its white, sweet meat. Stone crabs are found in Florida and the Gulf of Mexico. Only the claw may be harvested. The crabs will regenerate another claw when returned to the ocean [40]. Stone crab claws are generally sold as cooked frozen claws.

(a)

(b)

Figure 26–11

(a) King crab legs are larger than snow crab legs that are otherwise similar. (b) Stone crab claws. (Richard Embery/Pearson Education)

SEAFOOD HARVEST AND AQUACULTURE

Wild Caught

Seafood are harvested from oceans, rivers, and lakes by commercial fishing operations for sale to the public or by those who fish for sport and personal enjoyment. Commercially, fish may be harvested by trawling, trolling, purse seining, gill-netting, longlining, pot fishing, or dredging [22]. Trawling is accomplished by dragging a large cone-shaped net through the water. When baits or lures are dragged behind the fishing vessel, it is called *trolling*. Salmon may be caught in using this method. Purse seining is used for schools of fish that are encircled with a net, then "pursed" at the bottom. Gill nets catch fish by trapping the fish in the net sized to catch certain varieties and sizes of fish. A long line with baited hooks placed either near the surface or near the bottom, depending on species, is called *longlining*. Crabs and lobsters are harvested by trapping them in a pot or trap placed on the bottom of the ocean. Clams, oysters, mussels, and scallops are caught by dredging a metal rake along the ocean bottom.

Aquaculture

Aquaculture, or fish farming, is not new. It was apparently practiced in China as early as 2000 B.C. Extremely rapid growth has occurred in this industry since the mid-1980s. China, India, Indonesia, Vietnam, Bangladesh, Norway, Egypt, and Chile lead the world in aquaculture production. The United States is ranked 16th in total global aquaculture production. In the United States, the top aquaculture species by dollar value are oysters, clams, Atlantic salmon, shrimp, and mussels. Most of the seafood consumed by Americans is imported. Of this imported seafood, nearly half of it is farmed [32].

Sustainability

The farming and harvesting of seafood with consideration for the long-term health of the ecosystem promote the sustainability of our seafood supplies. Darden Restaurants, operators of Red Lobster restaurants, is an example of one company that has been including sustainability into its purchasing decision-making process [22]. Within the U.S. government under NOAA, *FishWatch* (www.fishwatch.gov) provides information about various seafood species to help consumers make informed decisions about what species may be at risk because of overfishing [39]. The Monterey Bay Aquarium Seafood Watch also provides pocket and mobile guides to assist consumers in selecting sustainable seafood (www.montereybayaquarium.org).

GOVERNMENT REGULATIONS AND GRADING

Food and Drug Administration Inspection and Regulatory Oversight

The FDA maintains an Office of Seafood as part of its regulatory responsibilities, and is responsible for wholesomeness and accurate labeling of domestic and imported seafood [38]. Since December 1997, seafood processors, packers, and warehouses—both domestic and foreign exporters to this country—have been required to follow a Hazard Analysis and Critical Control Points (HACCP) system (see Chapters 2 and 3). The HACCP system focuses on identifying and preventing hazards that could cause foodborne illness rather than relying on random sampling of finished seafood products and occasional plant inspections.

The FDA also sets standards for seafood contaminants, such as pesticide residues and mercury; administers the National Shellfish Sanitation Program with shellfish-producing states and other countries; and analyzes fish and fishery products for toxins, chemicals, and other hazards in agency laboratories. The FDA regularity oversight also extends to imported seafood and aquaculture, including the feed and drugs that may be used in raising seafood [37]. Imported seafood found to contain substances not allowed may be placed on an import alert. The FDA inspects domestic and foreign seafood processors, and has offices in international locations (**Figure 26–12**).

This FDA inspector is examining seafood imported at the Los Angeles International Airport. In addition to examination by sight, touch, and smell, samples will be tested in a lab. (FDA)

U.S. Department of Commerce, NOAA Fisheries Grading and Inspection

NOAA in the U.S. Department of Commerce operates a voluntary seafood inspection and grading program for vessels, processing plants, and retail facilities in the United States and foreign countries. A fee for the voluntary service is paid by the processor. Fish products meeting the official standards may carry U.S. inspection and grade labels [42] (**Figure 26–13**).

Quality grades are determined largely on the basis of appearance, uniformity, absence of defects, character (mainly texture), and flavor and odor of the product. Grades for breaded items also consider the amount of edible fish as compared with the amount of breading and the presence of bone in fish sticks.

NOAA has also established a regulatory program for aquaculture in federal waters. Specifically, a permitting system for the Gulf of Mexico was created to manage and expand seafood farming. In part the goals are to protect the environment and create economically sustainable methods [27]. Additional areas of NOAA oversight include the Magnuson-Stevens Act and Endangered Species Act.

Mark using red, white, and blue   Shield with white background

(a)

U.S. Grade A/PUFI Mark

(b)

PUFI Mark

(c)

NOAA under the U.S. Department of Commerce conducts voluntary grading and inspection of seafood. (a) Shield showing Grade A. (b) Grade A also indicating product was under continuous inspection. (c) Product processed under federal inspection. (U.S. Department of Commerce)

Traceability

The traceability of our food supply has become an important issue. Product tracing enables a product to be traced throughout the food supply system and enables the identification of the food, and the originating source for the food in the case of foodborne illness or other issues such as illegally harvested fish (see Chapter 3). NOAA is involved in establishing rules for the tracking of seafood. The FDA and USDA are similarly involved with developing food traceability requirements with other high-risk foods. The CDC works collaboratively with these agencies when a foodborne illness occurs and tracing of the food to the source is necessary [16].

Environment

Seafood and fish live in lakes, rivers, and oceans. If the water is unclean because of natural or human contamination (including plastics and microplastics), the safety of the seafood can be affected. FDA leads the National Shellfish Sanitation program. Fish and shellfish advisories are maintained by the EPA [31]. Recreational fishers can obtain information about potential water advisories for their nearby lakes and rivers from the EPA National Listing of Fish Advisories [30]. These advisories will let those catching and consuming recreationally caught fish know if the waters and fish may be contaminated. Depending on potential contamination, advisory recommendations indicate if fish caught in that location should (1) be consumed no more than twice per week, (2) be consumed no more than once per week, or (3) not be consumed.

PURCHASING FISH AND SHELLFISH

The first step in purchasing seafood is to assess your retailer. The fresh seafood counter should be clean and without a strong "fishy" odor. Fresh fish does not smell, and thus a strong odor is suggestive of old fish or poorly cleaned display cases. Fresh fish should be in a refrigerated case, preferably displayed on ice to maintain a temperature just above freezing. Shellfish should have tags that identify the certification number of the processor and the location of harvest. This information should also be printed on the label.

Identification

Seafood offers some unique challenges for identification once it is cut into fillets, steaks, or other common market forms. Unlike beef, pork, and lamb, the fish flesh of one species can look very similar to that of another. Thus, foodservice operators and consumers have at times paid for a higher price type of fish when what was sold was in fact another much less expensive type of fish. As with any food purchased, learn about the food and its distinguishing characteristics to better protect yourself from deception.

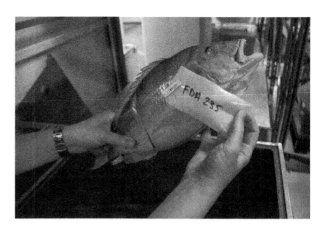

Figure 26–14

This fish was tested for DNA and has a bar code identification number that can be used to identify other fish with the same DNA. This identification system will reduce the selling of fish improperly identified. (FDA)

The FDA is creating DNA barcodes to provide definitive identification for fish species [34]. It is a massive project when one considers that there are an estimated 15,000 species of fish sold in the United States out of 30,000 species thought to exist worldwide. The DNA barcodes can be thought of as a universal barcode [15] that will enable the detection of mislabeled fish. FDA scientists are obtaining fish samples that are then tested for DNA. With this information, a public database of barcodes are being made available through the FDA website (**Figure 26–14**). The Federal Food, Drug, and Cosmetic Act (Section 403) prohibits the misbranding of foods.

Freshness

Fish generally live in relatively cold environments, which is a contributing factor to the limited amount of time that fresh fish remain fresh. Fresh finfish have firm flesh, a stiff body, and tight scales. The gills are red, and the eyes are bright and unsunken. Pressure on the body does not leave an indentation in the flesh except in the case of fish that has been frozen and thawed. The exterior of fresh fish has little or no slime. Fresh seafood should not smell "fishy" but rather like a "fresh ocean breeze." Stale fish, on the other hand, are flabby, and the eyes are dull and sunken. The scales are easily brushed off, the gills are no longer bright red, and the odor is stale, sour, or strongly fishy.

Frozen fish should be solidly frozen when purchased, with no discoloration unexpected for the variety of fish. It should have little or no odor and should be wrapped in a moisture- and vapor-proof material. Frozen fish with frost, ice, or large amounts of ice crystals may have been thawed and refrozen and should not be purchased.

Mollusks in the shell should always be alive when they are purchased. The shells of live mollusks will be tightly closed or will close when tapped lightly or iced. Any mollusks that do not close tightly, and thus are dead, should be thrown away. Seafood should be bought only from reputable dealers. The area of harvest for shellfish is an important factor influencing the safety of the shellfish, and reputable dealers will provide product from approved sources. When selecting fresh lobster, only lobsters that move when handled and thus are alive should be purchased.

Market Forms

Several varieties of finfish, fresh or frozen, are marketed as (1) whole or round fish, (2) drawn, (3) dressed, (4) butterfly fillets, (5) fillets, (6) steaks, and (7) wheel or center-cut (**Figures 26–15**). Shellfish are marketed in the shell, shucked (removed from the shell), headless (shrimp and some lobster), or already cooked.

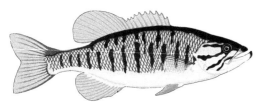

(a) Whole or Round

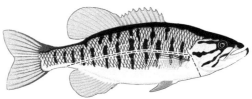

(b) Drawn

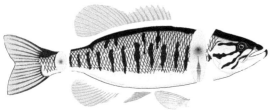

(c) Dressed or Pan-Dressed

(d) Butterflied Fillets

(e) Fillets

(f) Steaks

(g) Wheel or Center-Cut

Figure 26–15

Market forms of fish. (a) Whole or round fish are sold just as they come from the water. (b) Drawn fish have had only the entrails removed. (c) Dressed or pan-dressed fish are scaled and eviscerated and usually have the head tail and fins removed. (d) Butterflied fish are pan dressed and then opened so that they lie flat. (e) Fillets are sides of the fish cut lengthwise away from the backbone. (f) Steaks are cross-cut sections of the larger sizes of dressed fish. (g) Wheel or center-cut is cut through large fish, such as swordfish and sharks, producing a round wheel, as shown.

Fish Products

Many value-added fish products are available from which consumers and food service establishments can choose.

Minced Fish Products and Surimi. Minced fish may be used to produce frozen minced fish blocks that are cut into fish sticks and portions. These products can be found on the market in a variety of forms, including crunchy breaded pieces, seafood nuggets, and fish loaf. These products provide an economical way to enjoy fish as compared to sticks cut from fillets.

A raw material called *surimi* (from the Japanese) offers opportunities for the production of several food items. To prepare surimi, minced fish (including heat) is first washed to remove fat, blood, pigments, and other undesirable substances, leaving only the myofibrillar proteins of the fish flesh. This material is then frozen with the addition of **cryoprotectants**, such as sucrose and sorbitol or possibly maltodextrins and polydextrose, to protect the myofibrillar proteins of fish, which are labile to denaturation on freezing [13].

Further processing and fiberizing produce an elastic and chewy texture in the product that can be made to resemble that of shellfish [11]. Surimi-based fiberized simulated crab legs are shown in **Figure 26–16**. Japanese techniques in the production of surimi are used to produce surimi and similar products in the United States.

Cured Fish. Although fish may be cured for preservation purposes, the cure often imparts a distinctive flavor of its own that is appreciated for variety. Some hardening and toughening of the outer surface occur when fish is salted, dried, or smoked. Common examples of cured fish are salt cod, mackerel, finnan haddie, and kippered herring and lox. Finnan haddie is haddock that has been cured in brine to which carotene pigment has been added and later smoked. It is preferred lightly cured but does not keep long with a light cure. If finnan haddie is to be kept for some time or shipped long distances, the cure must be stronger. Kippered herring is also lightly brined and smoked. It is often canned to preserve its typical flavor rather than being cured in a heavier brine.

Figure 26–16

Surimi is made by a special process from mechanically deboned fish flesh. It is used for a variety of fabricated seafood products. (Richard Embery/Pearson Education)

Canned Fish. The principal kinds of canned fish are salmon, tuna, sardines, shrimp, crab, lobster, and clams. Five principal varieties of salmon are packed, depending on the locality. Five common varieties are red salmon or sockeye; Chinook; coho, medium red or silverside; pink; and chum.

In the United States, 14 species of tuna may be labeled "tuna" when canned. Yellowfin, skipjack, albacore, bluefin, bigeye, and slender tuna are some of the varieties allowed [6]. Albacore may be labeled "white meat"; the other species are labeled "light meat." Three different styles of packing for canned tuna are fancy or solid pack, chunk style, and flake or grated style. Each style can be packed in either oil or water. The normal color of precooked or canned tuna is pinkish. Some fish do not develop the pink color but take on a tan or tannish-green color and then are rejected. These fish are referred to in the industry as *green* tuna.

Tuna is also sold in flexible retort packaging as an alternative method of providing the consumer with "canned" tuna. The flexible pouches are packed with very little oil or water, and thus the product is ready to use without draining. (See Chapter 1 for more about retort packaging.)

Breaded or Battered Fish Products. A variety of seafood products ranging from shrimp, fillets, fish sticks, and more are available that have been breaded or battered. Breaded and battered products should be evenly covered and should separate from other portions easily. If products appear to be frozen together or exhibit excessive amounts of frost, poor temperature control is the likely cause, and the product should be avoided. Breaded and battered fish should remain frozen until cooked [22]. In general, the amount of fish in relation to the amount of breading or batter should be assessed in relation to price. Breaded seafood that contains less than 50 percent by weight of seafood must be labeled "imitation" [22].

SAFE STORAGE AND HANDLING

Seafood Safety

Seafood is the most perishable of flesh foods and does present potential hazards if not produced and handled properly (**Table 26–4**). The primary causes of foodborne illness associated with seafood include (1) bacteria or viral contamination, (2) parasites, and (3) shellfish or finfish toxins.

In particular, the consumption of raw shellfish may result in a death rate as high as 35 percent among those with impaired health if contaminated with *Vibrio vulnificus*. Illness can occur from any raw fish consumed including sashimi, poke, tartare, lox, and ceviche. The lime juice used in ceviche recipes does not actually "cook it" even though it may visually appear cooked.

Table 26–4
SEAFOOD FOOD-SAFETY HAZARDS

Hazard	Type of Seafood Affected	Description	Safeguards
Bacteria			
Vibrio vulnificus and *Vibrio parahaemolyticus*	Raw or improperly cooked oysters	Naturally found in warm coastal waters. Most prevalent during months of April to October.	Individuals with liver disease, diabetes, suppressed immune system, or other significant health concerns are at highest risk for serious illness and potentially death as the result of *V. vulnificus*. Anyone in a high-risk group should not eat raw oysters. Cook oysters before consumption. Purchase from approved, reputable suppliers.
Virus			
Hepatitis A and norovirus	Shellfish contaminated by sewage or by food handler	Primarily found in feces of people infected with these viruses. Thus, sewage-contaminated waters or food handlers are the usual cause.	Cook shellfish. Purchase from approved reputable suppliers. Use good personal hygiene when handling food and, if ill, do not prepare food for others.
Parasites			
Anisakiasis	Raw and undercooked: herring, cod, halibut, mackerel, and Pacific salmon	Worm-parasite that is found in the environment of certain fish.	Cook fish to 145°F (63°C). If serving undercooked, purchase sushi-grade fish that has been frozen for the approved time and temperature required to destroy this parasite. Purchase from approved suppliers.
Fish toxins			
Scombroid or histamine poisoning	Most commonly found in tuna, bonito, mackerel, and mahimahi	Found on certain fish when the fish has been temperature abused.	Not destroyed by cooking, freezing, curing, or smoking. Avoid temperature abuse. Purchase from approved, reputable suppliers.
Ciguatera fish poisoning	Most commonly found in predatory reef fish, including barracuda, grouper, jacks, and snapper	Found on predatory reef fish that have eaten smaller fish who have consumed toxic algae. The algae are naturally found in the environment.	May not be smelled or tasted. Not destroyed by cooking or freezing. Purchase from reputable suppliers who sell fish from safe waters.
Shellfish toxins			
Paralytic shellfish poisoning	Shellfish found in colder waters, including clams, mussels, oysters, and scallops	This toxin, *saxitoxin*, is found on certain toxic algae found in cold waters.	None of the shellfish toxins may be smelled or tasted and are not destroyed by cooking or freezing.
Neurotoxic shellfish poisoning	Shellfish found in warmer waters, including mussels, clams, and oysters	This toxin, *brevetoxin*, is found on certain toxic algae found in warm waters.	Harvesting of shellfish is closed in areas with toxic algae blooms. Some, although not all, algae blooms may be called "red tide."
Amnesic shellfish poisoning	Shellfish found in coastal waters of the east coast of Canada and the Pacific Northwest	This toxin, *domoic acid*, is found in certain toxic algae in cooler coastal waters.	Purchase shellfish from approved, reputable suppliers.

Source: Reference 5.

Bacteria have been shown to survive the lime juice treatment. Freezing at specific temperatures can eliminate parasite contamination but not bacteria, viruses, or toxins (see Chapter 2).

Chemicals such as mercury may also be present in some fish. The FDA has released a consumer advisory for pregnant women over the years. In this advisory, the avoidance of shark, swordfish, king mackerel, and tilefish by pregnant women is suggested to reduce mercury exposure [33] (**Figure 26–17**). A general recommendation of eating an average of 12 ounces of fish per week is provided. Local fish advisories should also be checked to assess the risk of mercury contamination from recreationally caught fish. This information may be obtained from the Environmental Protection Agency (www.epa.gov) or state and local health departments.

These recommendations should be interpreted with a realization most Americans consume far less than 12 ounces of fish per week. Furthermore, the consumption of long-chain omega-3 fatty acids has been associated with health benefits including improved cognitive function in infants [7, 17]. Continuing research into mercury contamination of fish, the potential protective role of selenium, and environmental cleanup is needed [20].

Spoilage of Fish and Storage Recommendations

Fresh fish are extremely perishable and spoil rapidly. In addition to the delicate structure of fish, which makes bacterial invasion easy, it has been shown that rapid spoilage is partly the result of the high degree of activity of the enzymes present in fish. The low temperatures of the natural environment of some fish may account for the unusual activity of the body enzymes. Thus, to maintain quality, fish are stored in flaked ice (cubed ice may bruise the fish) or in a frozen salt solution to achieve a somewhat lower temperature until the fish are ready for sale [12].

When fish spoils, bacteria decompose fish tissue, and a volatile substance called *trimethylamine* is released. Measurement of trimethylamine levels

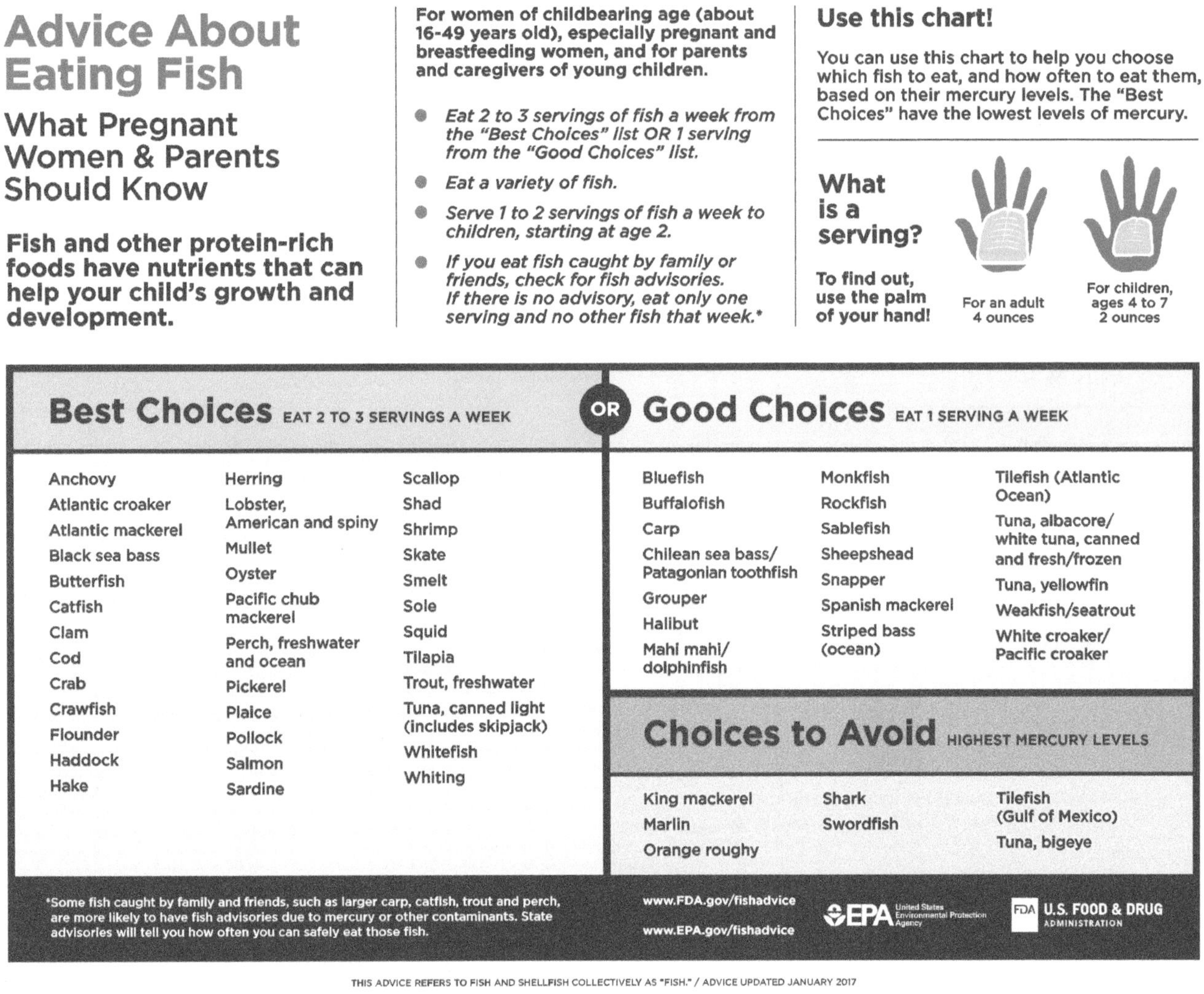

Advice About Eating Fish

What Pregnant Women & Parents Should Know

Fish and other protein-rich foods have nutrients that can help your child's growth and development.

For women of childbearing age (about 16-49 years old), especially pregnant and breastfeeding women, and for parents and caregivers of young children.

- *Eat 2 to 3 servings of fish a week from the "Best Choices" list OR 1 serving from the "Good Choices" list.*
- *Eat a variety of fish.*
- *Serve 1 to 2 servings of fish a week to children, starting at age 2.*
- *If you eat fish caught by family or friends, check for fish advisories. If there is no advisory, eat only one serving and no other fish that week.**

Use this chart!

You can use this chart to help you choose which fish to eat, and how often to eat them, based on their mercury levels. The "Best Choices" have the lowest levels of mercury.

What is a serving?

To find out, use the palm of your hand!

 For an adult 4 ounces — For children, ages 4 to 7 2 ounces

Best Choices EAT 2 TO 3 SERVINGS A WEEK | **Good Choices** EAT 1 SERVING A WEEK

Anchovy, Atlantic croaker, Atlantic mackerel, Black sea bass, Butterfish, Catfish, Clam, Cod, Crab, Crawfish, Flounder, Haddock, Hake, Herring, Lobster (American and spiny), Mullet, Oyster, Pacific chub mackerel, Perch (freshwater and ocean), Pickerel, Plaice, Pollock, Salmon, Sardine, Scallop, Shad, Shrimp, Skate, Smelt, Sole, Squid, Tilapia, Trout (freshwater), Tuna (canned light, includes skipjack), Whitefish, Whiting

Bluefish, Buffalofish, Carp, Chilean sea bass/Patagonian toothfish, Grouper, Halibut, Mahi mahi/dolphinfish, Monkfish, Rockfish, Sablefish, Sheepshead, Snapper, Spanish mackerel, Striped bass (ocean), Tilefish (Atlantic Ocean), Tuna albacore/white tuna (canned and fresh/frozen), Tuna yellowfin, Weakfish/seatrout, White croaker/Pacific croaker

Choices to Avoid HIGHEST MERCURY LEVELS

King mackerel, Marlin, Orange roughy, Shark, Swordfish, Tilefish (Gulf of Mexico), Tuna bigeye

*Some fish caught by family and friends, such as larger carp, catfish, trout and perch, are more likely to have fish advisories due to mercury or other contaminants. State advisories will tell you how often you can safely eat those fish.

www.FDA.gov/fishadvice
www.EPA.gov/fishadvice

 EPA United States Environmental Protection Agency

FDA U.S. FOOD & DRUG ADMINISTRATION

THIS ADVICE REFERS TO FISH AND SHELLFISH COLLECTIVELY AS "FISH." / ADVICE UPDATED JANUARY 2017

Figure 26–17

The FDA and EPA provide guidelines for pregnant women and parents on the consumption of seafood to minimize exposure to mercury. (FDA and EPA)

gives an indication of the microbiologic quality of fish [44]. Researchers are developing methods of packaging fish for sale in supermarkets to enhance safety and shelf life. Packaging structures may incorporate antimicrobial compounds or package surfaces that provide spoilage indicators by measuring ammonia, trimethylamine, and dimethylamine [3]. Storage recommendations for seafood are provided in **Table 26–5**.

Table 26–5
STORAGE RECOMMENDATIONS FOR SEAFOOD

Kind of Seafood	Storage Recommendations
Fresh finfish	
Whole, fresh caught	Store at 32°F (0°C). Ice with shaved ice to maintain cold temperatures. Should not sit in water as a result of the melting ice. Alternatively, may be wrapped in moisture-proof packaging and refrigerated. Should be used or frozen within two days. Rapid freezing is desirable to prevent large ice crystals that will contribute to drip loss when thawed.
Fillets and steaks	Store at 32°F (0°C). Wrap in moisture-proof packaging and use within 2 days or freeze (0°F/[18°C]) in vapor-barrier freezer packaging for longer storage. Icing is not recommended unless in moisture-proof packaging because fillets will easily absorb melted water.
Shellfish	
Live clams, oysters, mollusks, lobsters, and crabs	Store at 41°F (5°C) in high humidity. May store with seaweed or damp paper. Do not put in freshwater because these saltwater shellfish will perish. Storage in plastic bags and icing is not recommended. Under good conditions, shellfish may be kept alive for several days. Dead shellfish will need to be discarded.
Shucked oysters, clams, and scallops	Maintain cold temperatures. Set in container on ice to lower temperature. Do not allow direct contact with ice because melting water will be absorbed.

Source: Reference 10.

HOT TOPIC
SUSHI

Sushi, common is Japan, has become a popular choice for many Americans. Sushi is a vinegared rice with raw, cooked, or marinated fish [2]. It may also include shellfish, vegetables, eggs, and fish roe. Nori, a type of seaweed, may be used shredded or in sheets in which to roll the sushi. Wasabi may be included as a seasoning accompaniment.

What about food safety of sushi? The Massachusetts Department of Public Health [14] and University of Florida Extension [23] recommend the following:

- As with all foods, sourcing foods from approved sources and maintaining these foods under proper storage temperature and conditions is of great importance (see Chapter 2) and all work surfaces must be clean, and sanitized.

- Risks associated with fish include live parasites, and other foodborne illness concerns discussed in Table 26–4 should be understood and risks reduced.

- Large tuna to be consumed raw (yellowfin, bluefin, blackfin, bigeye, and albacore) do not pose a significant

risk for parasites, and therefore do not require freezing prior to use in sushi.

- Raw fish, at risk for parasites, must be cooked to 145°F (63°C) for 15 seconds or if to be consumed raw should be frozen. The required temperatures and length of freezing time include (1) at –4°F (–20°C) for 7 days or (2) –31°F (–35°C) or below for 15 hours.

- Consumers should be informed of the risk of consuming raw food because freezing of the fish will kill parasites, but will not impact other types of contamination that could be present. Pregnant women and others at high risk for foodborne illness are advised not to consume raw fish.

- Sushi rice must be cooked and acidified with vinegar (often rice vinegar) to a pH of below 4.6 to enable the rice to be held at room temperature so that it can be handled for making sushi.

- Bamboo mats used for rolling sushi should be wrapped in plastic replaced at least every 4 hours.

- Bare hand contact with foods to be consumed without cooking should not occur.

PREPARATION

Cooking Finfish

General Recommendations. To lend variety to menus, fish may be cooked by either dry- or moist-heat methods. Fish have very little connective tissue, and it is of a kind that is easily hydrolyzed. The structure of fish is delicate and tender, even in the raw state; therefore, the use of moist heat for tenderization purposes is not necessary. In fact, a big problem in fish cookery is retention of the form of the fish, which is done by careful handling. If fish is cooked in water, such as poaching, it may be necessary to tie the piece of fish in cheesecloth or wrap it in parchment paper to prevent it from falling apart during cooking. Because extractives are low in fish, a method that develops flavor, such as frying, broiling, and baking, or the use of herbs and other seasonings is often preferred. When poaching, the liquid used as the cooking medium can add flavor with the use of wine, citrus, or other ingredients.

Although overcooking is to be avoided, for optimum food safety, fish must be cooked to a minimum safe temperature of 145°F (63°C). A visual indication of doneness is evident when the flakes separate easily. It should be tested with a fork in a thick portion, as the outer, thin edges cook more readily than the thicker muscles. About 10 minutes of cooking time per 1 inch of thickness is generally suggested for fish fillets.

If frozen, individual steaks or fillets may be cooked either thawed or frozen. If to be thawed, then thaw in the refrigerator and allow about a day for defrosting, depending on the size of the fish. If two or more fish fillets have been frozen in a package, it is necessary to partially defrost them to separate them for cooking. For partially or wholly frozen fish, the cooking temperature must be lower and the time of cooking longer than for defrosted fish to permit thawing as the fish cooks. Otherwise, ice may remain in the center of the cut even when the outside is thoroughly cooked.

Cooking Methods to Preserve Fatty Acids—DHA and EPA. Fish is valued in the diet in part because of its contribution of the omega-3 fatty acids, DHA and EPA. Researchers found pan-fried and grilled fatty fish maintained about 85 percent of the DHA and EPA present in the raw fish. However, less than 60 percent was maintained in fatty fish that was deep-fat fried [4].

Broiling and Grilling

Fish to be broiled may be in the form of fillets, steaks, or boned or unboned whole fish (head removed). Unboned whole fish is cut through the ribs along the backbone, allowing it to lie flat. If the skin has been left intact, the fish is placed skin-side down on the broiler rack. It may later be turned, but turning large pieces of fish is difficult and tends to break the fish apart. Using a relatively low broiling temperature to prevent overbrowning and basting the top surface with olive oil or butter to keep it moist usually make it possible for fish to be broiled until done without turning.

Fish may also be cooked on a barbeque grill. Delicate fish can easily drop between the grates; therefore placing the fish on aluminum foil or in a specially designed seafood grate will allow getting the fish on and off the grill intact. Foil or grates should be lightly oiled to prevent sticking of the fish. Small slices in the foil will allow dry heat to rise from the coals to the fish.

Baking

Fish fillets may be used for baking (**Figure 26–18**). Whole stuffed fish can also lend itself nicely to baking. The fish are usually placed in a shallow, open pan and

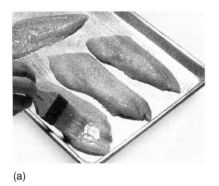
(a)

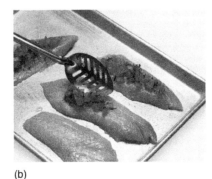
(b)

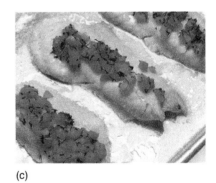
(c)

Figure 26–18

(a) Brushing fillets with butter or another desired flavored oil, (b) topping snapper with tomato *concassée*, and (c) the baked fish. (Richard Embery/Pearson Education)

can be basted to keep the skin from becoming hard and dry. Sour cream, yogurt, and a variety of toppings can be placed on top of the fish while baking to add flavor and maintain moistness. Oven temperatures can vary from moderate to hot depending on the size of the fish fillet and whether it is stuffed.

Frying

Small whole fish, fillets, or steaks may be pan-fried or deep-fat fried. Pieces of a suitable size for serving may be dipped in water, milk, or egg mixed with milk, then in a dry ingredient, such as corn meal, flour, planko bread crumbs, or other types of crumbs. Some prefer first dipping the fish in flour, then milk, followed by crumbs. Each component should be seasoned. If the fish is to be deep-fat fried, the temperature of the fat should not exceed 385 to 395°F (196 to 202°C) so that the fish will be fully cooked by the time it is browned.

Steaming and Simmering

Fish may be cooked by steaming, simmering, or poaching (**Figure 26–19**). These are closely related methods of cookery, varying in the amount of the cooking liquid used. Fish to be steamed may be placed on a rack over a boiling liquid with a tight cover on the pan and cooked until done. Steaming may also be done in the oven in a covered pan, or the fish may be wrapped tightly in parchment paper or aluminum foil. The foil retains moisture, and the fish cooks in an atmosphere of steam.

When poaching, the fish is cooked in a liquid that may not fully cover the fish. The temperature of a poaching liquid is often slightly lower than that for simmering. Fish that are simmered are covered with a liquid and cooked just below the boiling point.

Figure 26–19

This paella is a classic dish originated from Spain. This dish, prepared in part by steaming, includes poultry, meats, shellfish, vegetables, and rice. (Richard Embery/ Pearson Education)

Depending on the variety of fish, it may hold form better if tied in cheesecloth or wrapped in parchment paper. The fish may be seasoned by adding white wine, lemon juice, or vinegar and salt as desired. Fish cooked in moist heat may be served with a sauce, or a complementary vegetable or fruit salsa.

Microwave Cooking

Fish can be prepared in a variety of ways using the microwave oven, including soups and chowders, appetizers, and main dishes. Generally, fillets or steaks are arranged in a baking dish, with the thickest portions toward the outside of the dish. Special care should be taken to avoid overcooking of the fish.

FOCUS ON SCIENCE
SPOILAGE INDICATORS FOR FISH

Some of the visual indicators of fish spoilage can vary with the kind of fish. For example, depending on the species of the fish, the eyes of the fish may be dark. The aroma of the fish, however, is a strong indicator of freshness.

Most marine fish contain a substance called trimethylamine oxide (TMAO). Certain types of bacteria that occur naturally on the skin and in the gut of fish and in seawater can break down TMAO to trimethylamine (TMA). The amount of TMA produced is a measure of activity of spoilage bacteria in the flesh and therefore an indicator of degree of spoilage.

Bacteria can also generate small amounts of ammonia in spoiling fish, mainly from free amino acids. The amount of ammonia can give an indication to the extent of spoilage. Shellfish may develop more ammonia than most marine fish and at an earlier stage.

Cooking Shellfish

Shellfish, the flesh of which appears to differ in structure from that of finfish, are much firmer and are easily toughened by high temperatures. Whether the differences are due to the amount and kind of connective tissue is not certain. Nevertheless, in cooking most shellfish, high temperatures and long cooking should be avoided. Moist-heat methods are generally satisfactory, but if the shellfish are cooked in a liquid medium, as in the making of oyster stew, a simmering temperature of 181–185°F (82–85°C) should be used.

Lobster. Live lobsters may be steamed or boiled in water. If cooking in boiling water, a vigorous, rolling boil is best before adding the lobster. Once the lobster has been added, keep the water at a low boil or simmering until fully cooked. Fresh lobster must be alive before cooking, but many recommend the lobster be placed in the freezer for 20 minutes before cooking then killed just before adding to the boiling water. The lobster may be killed quickly by running a knife between the head and body, or by turning the lobster over and slitting the main body section in half.

If boiling, start timing when the water returns to a boil after adding the lobster. A one and half pound lobster will require 7 to 9 minutes. If steaming, bring only 2 to 3 inches of water in a large pot to a boil. Add the lobster and cook 8 to 10 minutes, timing once the water has returned to a boil after adding the lobster. Overcooking lobster toughens the flesh and should therefore be avoided.

Shrimp. Shrimp may be breaded and fried, sautéed, or simmered depending on the recipe and your planned use for the shrimp after cooking. When cooking shrimp you may wish to peel the shrimp before or after cooking. If using for chilled cocktail shrimp, then leave the shell on and simmer until the shrimp begins to curl and turn pink. Ice the shrimp to cool quickly. For both fried and sautéed shrimp, the shrimp should be peeled before cooking so it can simply be enjoyed once done. Shrimp may be breaded before frying using similar methods to that used for other types of fish and breaded or battered foods.

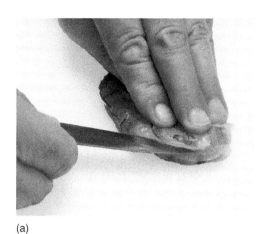

(a)

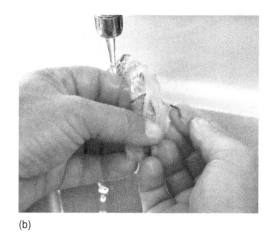

(b)

Figure 26–20

(a) To remove the sand vein (or digestive track) on shrimp, first make a shallow cut along the back, (b) then remove the dark sand vein as shown. (Richard Embery/Pearson Education)

On larger shrimp the sand vein should be removed before cooking (**Figure 26–20**). The sand vein is the intestinal tract located just under the outer curved surface. Slicing along this vein will enable its removal. Alternatively, shrimp can be purchased that already has the sand vein removed.

Clams, Mussels, and Oysters. Mollusks should be thoroughly rinsed to help remove sand. Like lobsters, fresh clams, mussels, and oysters should be alive before cooking. Any shells that are open and do not close when lightly tapped indicate the mollusk is dead and therefore must be discarded and not cooked. Bring a kettle with a few inches of water to a brisk boil and then add the mollusks. The water may be seasoned with seafood seasonings, beer, wine, or other options. Cook for about 5 to 9 minutes at which point the shells will be wide open (**Figure 26–21**).

Figure 26–21

Mussels shells open after cooking. (Richard Embery/Pearson Education)

STUDY QUESTIONS

Consumption Trends

1. Identify where most of the seafood in the United States comes from.

2. Describe the current seafood consumption trends.

Nutrition and Composition

3. Explain from a nutritional perspective why has there been an emphasis in recent years on increasing the consumption of fish in the American diet.

4. Identify key nutrients provided by seafood.

Classification

5. Explain how flat fish and round fish are different from each other.

6. Describe mollusks and crustaceans, and provide several examples of each.

Seafood Harvest and Aquaculture

7. Compare and contrast seafood harvested and raised by aquaculture.

8. Identify and describe some tools to use when purchasing seafood for foodservice or home use that will assist in making decisions about sustainability.

Government Regulations and Grading

9. Discuss the role of each of the following governmental agencies or departments in the regulatory or grading oversight of seafood:
   (a) The Food and Drug Administration
   (b) The Department of Commerce and NOAA
   (c) The Environmental Protection Agency

Purchasing Fish and Shellfish

10. Discuss potential challenges with identifying seafood when you purchase it and how FDA is developing methods to assist with these issues.
11. Describe the characteristics of high-quality fresh fish.
12. Identify and describe the market forms for the purchasing of fresh and processed seafood.

Safe Storage and Handling

13. Identify how several kinds of seafood should be stored and explain why.
14. Describe food-safety hazards that may be associated with fish and seafood.
15. Describe the potential hazards of consuming raw fish or seafood.
   (a) Identify members of the population who should not eat raw seafood because of potential health risks.
   (b) Explain the steps taken to reduce food-safety risks with sushi.
16. Identify the members of the population who should be particularly cautious with seafood high in mercury.
17. Identify seafood with low, medium, and high levels of mercury.
18. Identify the end point cooking temperature recommended for seafood and explain why.
19. Describe food-safety considerations when catching and consuming fish caught recreationally.

Preparation

20. Explain why it is appropriate to cook fish with either dry- or moist-heat methods.
21. Describe satisfactory procedures for cooking fish by each of the following methods:
   (a) Broiling
   (b) Baking
   (c) Sautèing
   (d) Frying
   (e) Steaming and poaching
   (f) Microwaves
22. Describe methods for cooking shellfish.

27

Beverages

A wide variety of commercially produced beverages are on the market. This market continues to diversify, with beverage production increasingly being targeted to specific market segments. This trend toward diversification can be observed even with a basic beverage such as coffee. No longer do we simply ask, "Coffee—black or with cream?" Today, there are flavored coffees, espresso, and more. Unique beverages are available to satisfy and interest consumers with varied preferences and needs.

This chapter provides an overview of the basic characteristics of several beverages and describes the preparation of coffee, tea, and cocoa. The following topics will be discussed:

• Consumption trends and nutrition
• Water
• Carbonated beverages
• Functional beverages
• Noncarbonated fruit and vegetable beverages
• Alcoholic beverages
• Coffee
• Tea
• Cocoa and chocolate

CONSUMPTION TRENDS AND NUTRITION

Consumption Trends

Over the years, the beverages we choose have changed. In the 1940s, 45 gallons of milk were available in the food supply per person compared to only 18 gallons per person in 2016 as documented by the U.S. Department of Agriculture food accessibility data sets [67]. Although our consumption of coffee has been relatively stable in the last 20 years, our current level of consumption (36 gallons) is down from the 1940s, when 40 to 45 gallons were reported per capita annually. The consumption of soft drinks and bottled water has increased over the years. According to industry data, Americans consumed 39 gallons of bottled water per person and 38.5 gallons of carbonated beverages in 2016 [4]. Overall, carbonated beverages appear to be declining in popularity. Much of the water is consumed in individual serving plastic bottles, raising questions about environmental impact. Data, tracked from alcohol beverage sales by the National Institute on Alcohol Abuse and Alcoholism, indicates that the per capita consumption of beer, wine, and spirits has increased over the years [71] (**Figure 27-1**). Sports drinks,

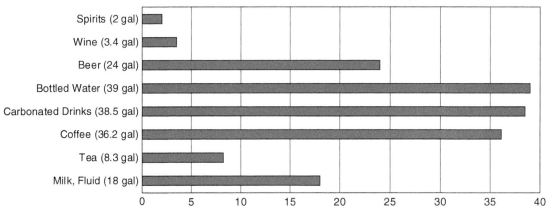

Gallons per capita of selected beverages per year: Data for 2015 (coffee, tea, milk) and 2016 (water, carbonated drinks, and alcoholic beverages)

Figure 27-1

The data for this figure came from three sources and should be interpreted with this in mind. (References 4, 67, 71)

energy drinks, soy or almond substitute milks, fruit and vegetable juices, and fruit drinks are some of the additional beverage options enjoyed by consumers.

Nutritive Value

The nutritional impact of beverages varies widely with the choices we make. Beverages can add a significant number of calories to our daily intake through sugar or added fats from cream. Sweetened beverages, such as carbonated beverages, sports drinks, sweet tea or coffee, and various fruit drinks, contribute added sugars with little other nutrient value. On the other side of the spectrum, milk and soy milk substitute contribute calcium and other needed nutrients, and 100 percent fruit and vegetable juices contribute various vitamins and phytonutrients (including flavonols), depending on the type of fruit or vegetable. Flavonols are also found in coffee, tea, and cocoa [72]. Ongoing research is pointing to the health benefits of consuming coffee and tea because of their antioxidant content [64].

Water

Water is critically important to enable the body to maintain an appropriate temperature, lubricate joints, protect the spinal cord and other body tissues, and enable waste removal through urination, perspiration, and bowel movements [65]. Especially during exercise or when in hot weather, the lack of water can result in cramps, heat exhaustion, heat stroke, or death. Those exercising should replace any pound loss during that period of activity (jogging, playing tennis, or outdoor work in the heat) by drinking a pint (pound) of water per each pound lost during exercise as a guide to maintain hydration. Other types of beverages can also help to replace fluid.

Sugar-Sweetened Beverages

Sugar-sweetened beverages include regular carbonated beverages (soda or pop), fruit drinks (fruit-flavored beverages with added sugar), sport and energy drinks, sweetened tea and coffee, and other sugar-sweetened beverages. Among youth aged 2 to 19 years, 64 percent consumed at least one sugar-sweetened beverage

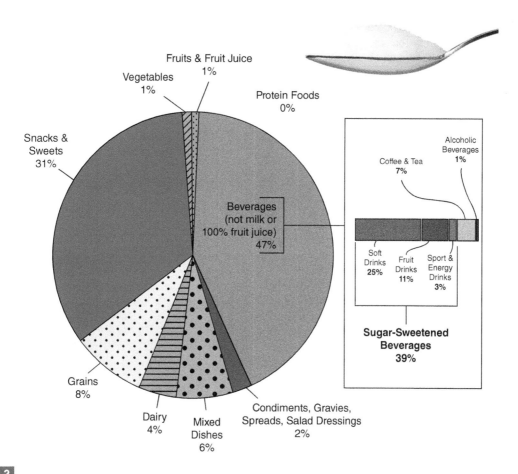

Figure 27–2

Sugar-sweetened beverages account for 39 percent of the added sugars in American's diets. The contribution of other foods to added sugars in the diet are also shown. (U.S. Department of Agriculture)

daily [56]. On average, sugar-sweetened beverages accounted for 7 percent of children's daily caloric intake. Among adults (age 20 and older) about one-half consumed a sugar-sweetened beverage daily, and on average, consumed nearly 7 percent of their total calories from sugar-sweetened beverages [55].

The USDA Dietary Guidelines recommend that Americans consume no more than 10 percent of their daily calories in "added sugars" [69]. Sugar-sweetened beverages account for nearly half of the added sugars in the diets of Americans [69] (**Figure 27–2**). Beverages and foods that are high in added sugars often offer little nutritional value while providing a high number of calories.

Energy Drinks and Alcohol

The consumption of energy drinks, high in caffeine, especially with alcohol, is a significant public health concern because of increased toxicological consequences [54]. Caffeine and alcohol alone or together are also dehydrating because they have a diuretic effect. Additionally, the combination of high-caffeine beverages, such as energy drinks, has been associated with binge drinking. Binge drinking is defined as four or more drinks per occasion for women and five or more for men. Consuming an energy drink with alcohol can mask the level of impairment, but does not reduce blood alcohol combinations [66]. The FDA does not permit the sale of alcoholic beverages with the addition of caffeine.

Alcoholic Beverages

The consumption of alcoholic beverages is associated with an increase in the risk of cancer. Higher consumption is associated with a greater risk [45]. Cancers most associated with alcohol consumption include head and neck, esophageal, liver, breast, and colorectal [70]. Because of alcohol's dehydrating effects, it is not recommended during high heat or vigorous exercise [66]. Red wine contains phytochemicals and could therefore potentially offer health benefits when consumed in moderation.

For those who choose to consume alcoholic beverages, the USDA Dietary Guidelines define moderate drinking as up to one drink daily for women and up to two drinks daily for men [69]. Consuming more than three drinks per day, or seven per week for women or 14 drinks per week for men is considered to be heavy drinking. Pregnant and nursing women should not consume alcohol.

Coffee

The health implications of coffee consumption have been studied by many researchers. In a paper reviewing of 1,277 studies on coffee and health, researchers concluded that moderate, regular coffee drinking by healthy individuals is without harm or mildly beneficial [49]. Health conditions such as cancer, cardiovascular

disease, metabolic health, neurological disorders, gastrointestinal conditions, liver disorders, and overall mortality were considered in this review. Like tea, coffee contains phytochemicals that are beneficial.

Acrylamide (see Chapter 8) is a by-product of roasting beans. It is also present in French fries, potato chips, and cereal-based foods cooked at high temperatures. Acrylamide was discovered in 2002 and has been found to cause cancer in high doses in laboratory animals, thus there is a possibility it also may cause cancer in humans [68]. More research is needed to understand acrylamide levels in coffee. Dark roast coffee results in less acrylamide because it is destroyed with continued roasting. Also, acrylamide appears to decline with storage [68].

Tea

Tea is rich in polyphenols, including theoflavins, thearubigins, and catechins [25, 48]. Polyphenols are naturally occurring compounds found in fruits, vegetables, cereals, and beverages [48]. Flavonoids, often associated with plant pigments (see Chapter 18) are one of the most studied (**Figure 27–3**). Polyphenols in the diet are considered to be protective against cancer, cardiovascular disease, diabetes, osteoporosis, and neurodegenerative diseases.

The method of brewing and type of tea can have an impact on polyphenol content. Black tea had the highest levels in a short-time, hot-water brewing. Green tea had higher antioxidant levels when brewed in cold water for a prolonged period. Prolonged hot water produced the best result for antioxidants in white tea [25].

Chocolate

Cocoa has been widely studied for potential health benefits. Cocoa offers a higher antioxidant level per serving than red wine or tea [1]. A number of studies

Figure 27–3

This Agricultural Research Service scientist is using high-performance liquid chromatography to measure flavonoids in black tea and other beverages. (U.S. Department of Agriculture, ARS. Photograph by Keith Weller)

Figure 27–4

Bottled water has become one of the leading beverages purchased. The volume of plastic bottles has caused some to be critical of this trend. (Gemenacom/Shutterstock)

Table 27–1
WATER TREATMENT METHODS

Water Treatment Methods	Description
Distillation	Water is turned into vapor and then condensed into water again. Minerals are too heavy to vaporize and thus are left behind.
Reverse osmosis	Water is forced through membranes to remove minerals and other substances.
Absolute 1-micron filtration	Filters are used to remove particles larger than 1 micron.
Ozonation	Ozone gas (O_3) is used as an antimicrobial agent for disinfection purposes. Bottlers often use this method instead of chlorine that may leave a chlorine taste and odor. Ozone may be produced with action of electricity on oxygen.

Source: References 6, 11.

suggest a positive relationship between cocoa and dark chocolate consumption and cardiac and neurological health. Research is ongoing; the polyphenols found in cocoa appear to be the primary contributors to the health benefits observed [1].

WATER

Only 1 percent of the water on the earth is available for drinking and other uses [63]. Our water comes from surface water (lakes and rivers) or groundwater (wells). Surface water supplies 74 percent of the water used in the United States. The Environmental Protection Agency regulates public water systems under the Safe Water Drinking Act. Water quality is also regulated by the Clean Water Act. This federal law governs the control of water pollution.

Compared to other beverage choices, water is calorie free yet thirst quenching. Consumers drink water from the tap and bottled water (**Figure 27–4**). Bottled water is convenient to carry and may be perceived by some consumers as "better than" tap water. Increasing concerns, however, have been expressed about the volume of plastic bottles used for bottled water—not all of which are recycled. *Enhanced waters*, containing functional ingredients such as vitamins and calcium or superoxygenation of water, are also sold [31].

Around 75 percent of the water bottlers use groundwater, although the municipal water system is the source of water for other companies [63]. Generally, the water is further filtered and treated to offer the quality desired by consumers. Filtering and water treatment methods include distillation, reverse

osmosis, absolute 1-micron filtration, and ozonation (**Table 27–1**). However, filtering systems at this time cannot remove all possible contaminants. Like other foods, the U.S. Food and Drug Administration (FDA) regulates bottled water (21CFR129). The FDA definitions for types of bottled water are provided in **Table 27–2**. Seltzer, soda, tonic, and some sparkling waters are considered to be soft drinks and thus will be discussed later in the chapter.

CARBONATED BEVERAGES

Carbonation is the process of saturating the beverage with carbon dioxide, giving unique zest to the drink. The carbonation also provides protection against bacterial spoilage during storage [22]. Home beverage carbonation machines have come onto the market. These machines basically have a cartridge of carbon dioxide and a valve system to enable carbonation of the desired liquid. Restaurants are similarly creating their own craft carbonated beverages.

The first step in the production of commercial carbonated soft drinks is the preparation of a syrup for sweetening. Flavoring, coloring, acid, and a preservative are added with continuous mixing. Finally, the syrup is diluted to the finished beverage level and carbonated [22]. Many carbonated drinks are made

<table>
<tr><td colspan="2">

Table 27–2

FDA Standard Definitions for Types of Bottled Water
</td></tr>
<tr><td>

Types of Bottled
Water
</td><td>

Definitions
</td></tr>
<tr><td>Artesian</td><td>Water from a well that taps a confined aquifer. When tapped, pressure in the aquifer often pushes the water to the surface. Artesian well water may be more pure; however, there is no guarantee artesian waters are cleaner than water from an unconfined aquifer.</td></tr>
<tr><td>Mineral</td><td>Water from an underground source with at least 250 parts per million of total dissolved solids. Minerals and trace elements must be present in the water and not added later.</td></tr>
<tr><td>Purified</td><td>Water treated to meet the U.S. Pharmacopeia definition of pure water.</td></tr>
<tr><td>Spring</td><td>Water from an underground formation that flows naturally to the earth's surface. May be collected through a borehole if the water obtained is the same as that feeding the spring. Must be collected in the spring.</td></tr>
<tr><td>Well</td><td>Water from a hole bored or drilled into an aquifer.</td></tr>
<tr><td>Sparkling</td><td>Water that contains the same amount of carbon dioxide as present when it emerged from source. Carbon dioxide may be replaced to obtain the original carbon dioxide levels.</td></tr>
</table>

Source: References 2, 6, 63.

Table 27–3

Caffeine Content of Selected Foods and Beverages

	Caffeine (mg)
Coffee (5-oz cup)	
Drip method	110–150
Percolated	64–124
Instant	40–108
Decaffeinated	2–5
Instant decaffeinated	2
Tea (5-oz cup)	
1-minute brew (black)	21–33
3-minute brew (black)	35–46
5-minute brew (black)	39–50
Instant	12–28
Iced tea (12-oz can)	22–36
Chocolate products	
Hot cocoa (6-oz cup)	2–8
Milk chocolate (1 oz)	1–15
Soft drinks (12-oz can)	
Pepsi One	57.1 ± 3.3
Mountain Dew	54.8 ± 2.5
Tab	48.1 ± 1.9
Diet Coke	46.3 ± 1.7
RC Cola	45.2 ± 4.1
Dr. Pepper	42.6 ± 2.0
Sunkist Orange	40.6 ± 0.2
Pepsi	38.9 ± 1.0
Coca-Cola	34.4 ± 1.5
Barq's Root Beer	22.4 ± 1.4

Source: References 7, 10, 23, 61.

without sugar, using alternative sweeteners such as **aspartame**. Refer to Chapter 9 for more information about high-intensity, alternative sweeteners.

Sparkling water beverages contain carbon dioxide and a low level of sweetener, which is often fructose, and flavoring. Enticing names such as *summer strawberry* and *wild mountain berry* are often attached to these flavored waters. Club soda is carbonated water with sodium bicarbonate and potassium carbonate added. The original seltzer is simply carbonated water, but seltzers are also sold with sweetener and flavor ingredients added. Tonic water is a carbonated water flavored with quinine.

Many carbonated beverages contain caffeine, including cola drinks, pepper products, and many citrus products. The labeling of caffeine content of beverages is not mandated at this time but has been recommended. Researchers analyzing 56 national-brand and 75 private-label, storebrand carbonated beverages found that the caffeine content of beverages varied widely, from 4.9 to 74 milligrams of caffeine per 12 ounces of beverage [10]. The caffeine level for the national-brand beverages was found to be more consistent compared to the store brands, which could vary by production lot. Caffeine content of some carbonated drinks is shown in **Table 27–3**.

FUNCTIONAL BEVERAGES

Functional beverages include energy drinks and shots, some isotonic (sport) beverages, herbal and green teas, fortified waters, enhanced smoothies, and others [21, 29, 39, 62]. Functional beverages in today's marketplace refer to beverages (or foods) that have been designed to offer specific health benefits through components that are typically above the quantity usually associated with basic nutritional needs [14]. Consumers are interested in functional beverages for a variety of reasons, including the desire to make up for unhealthy eating, to supplement healthy habits, to avoid empty calories, to add energy, or to address a specific health issue [39].

Calcium, antioxidants, vitamins, minerals, omega-3 fatty acids, fiber, and green tea are ingredients desired by today's consumers [62]. Protein is another sought after attribute. Some drinks contain substances such as herbal extracts (ginseng, ginkgo leaf, and ma huang), **guarana**, amino acids, vitamins, minerals, and other ingredients that may stimulate energy and alertness. Some of these ingredients are untested and their short- and long-term effects are controversial.

Food processors are faced with some challenges in the formulation of functional beverages. Calcium can result in a chalky mouthfeel, iron and potassium may leave a metallic aftertaste, and other nutrients likewise can cause undesirable flavors [19]. Successful functional beverages will overcome objectionable sensory attributes to result in a pleasing as well as healthful beverage.

Sports or Isotonic Beverages

Sports beverages are designed to prevent dehydration during vigorous exercise and to give a quick energy burst. They should have the same osmotic pressure as human blood to allow for rapid absorption. Typically, sports beverages have a low level of carbonation and a carbohydrate content of 6 to 8 percent (compared with soft drinks, which have 10 to 12 percent). The sweeteners added to sports drinks are usually glucose, maltodextrins, and sucrose. For electrolyte replacement, sports drinks contain ingredients such as monopotassium phosphate, sodium chloride, sodium citrate, and potassium chloride [22]. The preferred beverage for fluid replacement in athletes during training and competition appears to be one that tastes good, does not cause gastrointestinal discomfort when consumed in large volumes, promotes rapid fluid absorption and maintenance of extracellular fluid volume, and provides energy to working muscles [8, 15].

Energy Drinks

The term *energy drinks* has also been used to describe beverages with high levels of caffeine and potentially also sugar. Like other kinds of functional beverages, the popularity of energy drinks has grown considerably. Energy shots, often 2 to 4 ounces, have grown significantly in popularity since their introduction in 2004 [21]. Some of these energy drinks report increased energy and endurance in their advertisements. Ingredients may include caffeine, B vitamins, botanicals such as ginseng and guarana, D-ribose, L-carnitine, taurine, and peptides [47].

Peer-reviewed research is needed on the ingredients found in energy drinks [35]. Some of energy

beverages have been banned or restricted in European countries. The high levels of caffeine in these beverages can cause a rapid heart rate, hypertension, and tremors and can increase the risk of dehydration during exercise [35].

NONCARBONATED FRUIT OR VEGETABLE BEVERAGES

Fruit or vegetable beverages that contain less than 100 percent juice must be labeled with a qualifying name, such as *beverage*, *drink*, or *cocktail*, such as grape juice beverage, orange juice drink, or cranberry juice cocktail [3]. To be called *juice* without a qualifying term, 100 percent of the fruit or vegetable, such as orange juice, must be included (**Figure 27–5**).

Fruit and vegetable beverages, drinks, and cocktails often have added water as well as sweeteners, flavoring, coloring, and preservatives. These beverages can be either low calorie or high calorie. Acidulants may be added. Acidulants contribute to flavor and may act as preservatives to restrict microbial growth by lowering the **pH**. The addition of flavoring substances strengthens and deepens the flavor of the fruit or vegetable juice in the drink. Juice drinks may also contain various vegetable gums, cellulose derivatives, and starch in small amounts to add body and affect the mouthfeel of the beverage [52]. See also chapter 20 for a discussion about juice processing.

For orange "juice" to be called "juice," it must be composed of 100 percent juice. If less than 100 percent juice, then the term used on the bottle, package, or menu must be beverage, drink, or cocktail. Orange juice is pictured here.
(U.S. Department of Agriculture)

Figure 27–6

Smoothies may be made from a variety of fruit and vegetable ingredients such as berries (shown here) or kale. When made from whole fruits and vegetables, smoothies can contribute favorably to nutritional intake. (Liv friis-larsen/Shutterstock)

Fruit and vegetable beverages are susceptible to microbial spoilage and **fermentation**. Therefore, protection by **pasteurization** or added preservatives is required. Pasteurization is accomplished by heat or microfiltration, with the product often being heated in-line and then placed in **aseptic** packaging. The approval of hydrogen peroxide as a packaging sterilant in 1984 made possible the packaging of many beverages in laminated boxes, which are available in various sizes. Alternatively, the beverage may be pasteurized by filling the package, closing, and then heating it [22].

Fruit smoothies have become a popular beverage that may be prepared with a blender at home or purchased when eating out. Smoothies are a blended beverage composed of fruit, fruit juices, vegetables, vegetable juices, yogurt, or other dairy ingredients (**Figure 27–6**). In the commercial market, a variety of functional ingredients may be added to create a unique beverage [51].

ALCOHOLIC BEVERAGES

Three general classifications of alcoholic beverages exist: wines, beers, and spirits. Alcoholic beverages are consumed as a drink but may also be used as a flavoring in cooking. Depending on the recipe and method of cooking, residual alcohol may be present in the prepared dish. A brief overview of alcoholic beverages follows.

Wine

Wine is usually made from the juice of grapes. However, other fruits, such as pears, apples, or cherries, may also be used to make wine. The process of making wine involves the chemistry of fermentation, as does the making of all alcoholic beverages. The process of fermentation is simple in that yeast acts on sugar, converting it into alcohol and carbon dioxide gas [36]. Finished wines usually contain 10 to 14 percent alcohol.

In wine production, the grapes are crushed to release the juice. If making white wine, the juice is separated from the skins. Next, the wine is fermented in tanks through the action of either natural yeast found on the grape skins or added yeast. During fermentation, other microorganisms may grow and either positively or negatively affect the characteristics of the wine. Once fermentation is complete, red wines are separated from the grape skins. Whether making white or red wines, the yeast and other solids are allowed to settle. These solids are called the *lees* [36]. Additional impurities may be removed from the wine before it is bottled by a process called *fining*. Some wines may undergo a second fermentation to produce desired characteristics. After fermentation, wines are aged to develop the flavor and aroma. Red wines are usually aged longer than white wines. Some wines are aged in oak to add an oaky flavor [38]. Other wines are fortified with a spirit such as brandy. Port, sherry, and Madeira are examples of fortified wines.

Beer

The making of beer has a long history, first being traced to about 9500 B.C. [41]. The United States is the second-largest producer of beer behind China. Craft breweries are growing significantly in popularity.

FOCUS ON SCIENCE
WHAT IS BRIX?

The brix scale is a standard measurement of the concentration of sugar in a sugar solution. Degrees brix is shown as °Bx. Brix is commonly used to measure the concentration of sugar in wines, fruit juices, and sugar syrups. For example, one crop of oranges may be naturally sweeter than another, and therefore, when different oranges are blended, the desired level of sweetness in a 100 percent orange juice may be measured and produced. The sugar content of wine also varies, and brix is used to measure these differences.

Figure 27–7

Hops used in the brewing of beer are shown here.
(Václav Mach/123RF)

Beer is made from water, hops (**Figure 27–7**), and traditionally malted barley (see Chapter 12 for more about malted barley) [38]. Other grains can be used in some beers such as wheat, rye, corn, rice and oats to produce different qualities in flavor, body, and texture [43]. Like wine, beer is fermented by yeast to produce an alcohol content of 2 to 6 percent. A vine, called *Humulus lupulus*, produces the small flowers that are the hops used in beer [38].

The first step in brewing beer is to malt the barley by steeping it in water until it begins to germinate, a process that can continue for six or more days [41]. Next, the malt is heated and dried in a process called *kilning*. The dried malt is then cracked in a mill, and hot water is added. The steeping of the malt in the hot water is called *mashing*. During this step, a sweet liquid called *wort* is produced. *Lautering* is the separation of the wort from the spent grains.

Brewing is the boiling of the wort, to which the hops have been added. Following brewing, the wort is cooled and strained. Yeast is added to the wort to begin fermentation (converting sugars into alcohol and carbon dioxide) and produce the beer. The beer is conditioned during storage to develop flavor and filtered to remove particles causing cloudiness.

Beers to be bottled or canned are pasteurized. Draft beers are not pasteurized and therefore must be kept refrigerated to protect flavor and slow yeast activity [41]. The type of beer, ales or lagers, as well as the unique qualities of an individual beer, is affected by variations to the basic brewing process described.

Craft Hard Cider

Craft hard cider is a fermented apple beverage [43]. Although an age-old beverage, it has gained in popularity in recent years. The type of apple, the kind of barrel used for aging, and variety of yeast all impact the characteristics of the final cider. Some producers use wild yeast found naturally in the apple orchard.

Spirits

Spirits or liquors are alcoholic beverages, such as gin, rum, tequila, vodka, whisky, and brandy, that have a high alcohol content. These beverages are made by distilling the liquid from grains, vegetables, or other ingredients, such as molasses that has been first fermented. Commonly grains are used for whisky and gin; pale grain, beets, or potatoes for vodka; fruit for brandy; sugarcane and molasses for rum; and agave for tequila. Additionally juniper berries and other botanicals are use in gin. Like those producing craft beers, craft distillers are experimenting with new flavors and methods to create unique beverages [43].

Distillation concentrates the alcohol. In the United States, spirits are classified by proof. A spirit that contains 40 percent alcohol by volume would be labeled 80 proof.

COFFEE

The coffee plant has been traced back to Ethiopia and other parts of tropical Africa. It was introduced into the Middle Eastern countries in the fifteenth century, and, later, both the growing of the plant and the custom of coffee drinking spread throughout the Eastern Hemisphere. Coffee was introduced into Java by the Dutch in the seventeenth century and later into South America. Since that time, Brazil has become the largest coffee-producing country in the world. Central America, Colombia, Hawaii, Africa, and Puerto Rico also have climatic conditions favorable to the growth of a fine grade of mild coffee.

The Coffee Plant

The coffee plant grows 6 to 20 feet high, depending on the species, the country in which it is grown, and the local custom of pruning. There are many varieties of coffee, but only a few are grown for commercial use. The original species native to Ethiopia, and the one most commonly grown is *Coffea arabica*, but when grown in different soils, altitudes, and climates, this species takes on different characteristics. Arabica, which is now grown chiefly in Central and South America, has a fine full flavor and aroma. A second hardy variety commonly grown in Africa, but also in South America, is *Coffea robusta.* Robusta coffee shrubs are best suited to low elevations (about 1,000 feet), and the beans are not as flavorful or as acid tasting as those from Arabica coffee plants.

The evergreen coffee plant bears white flowers from which the fruit develops. When ripe, the fruit resembles a small cherry with the dark red pulp covering two oval beans, growing with the flat sides together (**Figure 27–8**). Botanically, coffee beans are not beans but rather seeds. Nevertheless, the term *coffee bean* is commonly used. It is the coffee "bean" that is used to make the coffee beverage.

Harvest and Processing of Beans

Ripe coffee fruit is picked. However, several steps must occur to turn this ripe coffee fruit into coffee beans or ground coffee. First, the fruit covering the coffee beans must be removed. Three methods—dry, wet, or semidry—are used to remove the fruit, skin, and pulp surrounding the coffee bean.

Dry Method. In the dry method, the coffee fruit is put in the sun to dry for 10 days to three weeks. Once dried, machines are used to strip off the fruit husk. Although high-quality coffee beans can result from the dry method, poor-quality coffee can occur if the process is poorly controlled and the fruit begins to mold or rot.

Wet Method. The wet method is used for most of the fine coffee beans sold. In the classic wet method, the fruit is removed from the beans before drying. Once the outer skin is removed, the beans are still covered with a sticky fruit residue. Next, the sticky beans are either wet or dry fermented. Water is added in the wet fermentation process but not in the dry fermentation. During fermentation, natural enzymes and bacteria digest the sticky residue. After fermentation, the coffee beans, still covered with one last layer of parchment, are washed and then dried. The parchment skin, once dried, is easily removed.

Semidry Method. The semidry or natural pulped method is used in only limited coffee production areas. The fruit is removed using the wet process. The fruit residue remaining after the wet process, however, is removed by allowing the beans to dry in the sun.

Cleaning, Sorting, and Shipping

Following the removal of the skin, pulp, parchment, and silverskin, the cleaned beans are light green or bluegreen. The green beans are classified into different sizes and graded. Unripened and discolored beans, sticks, small stones, and other foreign matter are eliminated. Next, the beans are packed into jute or fiber bags and shipped to various markets. Green coffee may be stored for prolonged periods with no adverse effects.

(a)

(b)

Figure 27–8

(a) Fruit surrounding the coffee "bean" is ripening. (Hvoya/ Shutterstock) (b) Roasted coffee beans. (Miguel G. Saavedra/ Shutterstock)

Each variety of coffee has its own flavor and other characteristics. Coffee that is available to the consumer may be a blend of as many as five or six different varieties of coffee beans. The blends are controlled for flavor, aroma, color, and strength or "body" of the beverage from the roasted bean. Blending is done by "creative artists" of the coffee world who choose beans that combine to produce desirable brews that are not too expensive. Once a blend combination has been developed, it is continuously produced so that one brand of coffee always has the same flavor and aroma.

Roasting

Green coffee beans have little flavor and aroma until they are roasted. Roasting is the main odor and taste determinate for a given green bean coffee blend; thus, a precise control of time and temperature is required to reach the desired flavor profile [58].

Naturally occurring sugars, plant acids (including **chlorogenic acid**), proteins, and other minor nitrogen-containing compounds react at roasting temperatures to form a majority of the desirable flavor constituents [32]. The beans expand to 1.5 times their original size and become more porous. The dull green changes to brown. Coffee roasts are classified according to the color of the roasted bean into light roast, medium roast, dark roast, and Italian or French roast, which is very dark.

Moisture is lost during roasting, carbon dioxide gas is formed, and sugar is decomposed. Changes in the sugar, possibly in combination with other substances, contribute much to the color of the beverage produced from the roasted beans. Modern roasting equipment allows careful control of time and temperature so that the flavor is constant from batch to batch.

Carbon dioxide gas appears to be lost gradually from roasted coffee on standing but is better retained in the bean than in ground coffee. Carbon dioxide is a desirable constituent of coffee from the standpoint of both the keeping quality and the retention of flavor and aroma substances. Flavor and aroma substances may be in some way tied up with the gas, or the presence of the gas may tend to prevent undesirable oxidation reactions on certain coffee constituents. The loss of carbon dioxide is closely associated with loss of flavor and aroma.

Composition of Coffee

The constituents of coffee of significance in the making of the beverage include acids, volatile substances, bitter substances, and caffeine. Caffeine is desired by some for increased alertness. It is not desirable for others who enjoy the flavor but not the stimulating effect of coffee.

Organic Acids. Several organic acids are present in aqueous coffee extracts, including acetic, pyruvic, caffeic, chlorogenic, malic, citric, and tartaric acids. The predominant acid is chlorogenic, which is somewhat sour and slightly bitter. It has been suggested that, in general, the more acid tasting the coffee, the better the aroma and flavor [61]. Coffee acidity is apparently affected by many factors, including variety, the altitude at which the plant is grown, the processing of the fruit, the age of the beans, and the degree of roasting of the beans.

Volatile Substances. Almost 700 volatile compounds have been identified as contributing to the aroma of coffee [57]. The most desirable aroma comes from a delicate balance in composition of volatiles. Sulfur compounds and **phenolic compounds** are among the main contributors to the characteristic aroma. Many of the flavor substances in a coffee beverage are lost or changed by heat. Therefore, an extended heating period at a high temperature can remove or destroy the desirable aroma and flavor. Long heating even at a low temperature may have the same effect. Reheating a coffee beverage has been shown to decrease organoleptic acceptance by a judging panel at the same time that a loss of volatile substances was shown by gas chromatographic techniques [60].

Bitter Substances. Bitterness in coffee becomes more pronounced as the **polyphenol** content increases. Polyphenol solubility apparently increases with temperature, and a boiling temperature releases polyphenols readily from the coffee bean. Caffeine contributes to bitterness. Coffee also contains other substances that produce distinctly bitter tastes.

Caffeine. Pharmacologists classify caffeine as a mild stimulant of the central nervous system and consider it one of the world's most widely used drugs [33]. Caffeine is one of a group of chemical compounds called *methylxanthines*, which occur naturally in the parts of many species of plants, including coffee beans, tea leaves, cocoa beans, and cola nuts. Theobromine, a somewhat milder stimulant than caffeine, is also a methylxanthine and is found in chocolate and cocoa. Table 27–3 gives the caffeine content of some common foods and beverages.

Kinds of Coffee Beverages

Decaffeinated Coffee. Some people want the flavor of the coffee beverage without caffeine. Most of the caffeine can be removed from the green coffee beans to yield decaffeinated coffee. Although decaffeinated coffee generally has good flavor, there is a slight loss of the usual coffee flavor during processing.

HOT TOPICS
FAIR TRADE

Fair trade certified products include tea, coffee, cocoa, vanilla, and others. In part, the goals of fair trade are to pay a fair price to farmers in Central and South America, Africa, and Asia to promote environmentally sound and socially just methods of production. The World Fair Trade Organization and Fair Trade USA are two organizations that certify fair trade products and in the process enable consumers to make informed choices when purchasing products produced in economically disadvantaged areas of the world. ■

Several processes are available for use in accomplishing decaffeination. These extraction processes primarily employ (1) water, (2) steam, (3) carbon dioxide, (4) ethyl acetate, (5) methylene chloride, or (6) coffee oils. The FDA regulates the level of solvent residue that may remain in the decaffeinated bean.

Instant Coffee Products. Instant or soluble coffee is convenient either for use as a beverage or to add coffee flavor in a recipe. The dry, powdered, water-soluble coffee is produced by dehydrating very strong, brewed coffee. The flavor of instant coffee is similar to freshly brewed coffee, but the aroma is usually lacking in comparison with the fresh-brewed. Instant coffee flavor can be improved by capturing desirable aroma compounds in coffee oil and adding them back to the coffee powder [28].

Some soluble coffees are freeze-dried. In this process, the strong, brewed coffee is first frozen and then dried by vaporization in a vacuum. Like instant coffees produced by other methods, the freeze-dried products are reconstituted by adding boiling water according to directions on the package. Soluble coffees should be kept packaged in water- and airtight containers because they are **hygroscopic**.

Specialty Coffee Beverages. How Americans drink coffee has changed over the years. The growth of premium, upscale coffee shops has resulted in the popularity of a wide variety of coffee beverages, many of which are based on espresso [30]. *Espresso* coffee is prepared from a French roast coffee and heated by steam. Espresso is a strongly flavored, rich beverage prepared with special equipment (**Figure 27–9**).

Figure 27–9

Espresso coffee machines have become common in many coffee shops. Home-sized espresso machines are also available. (PondPond/Shutterstock)

Figure 27–10

Cappuccino and caffé latte have become popular coffee beverages. (Richard Embery/Pearson Education)

Espresso machiatto is espresso with a small amount of steamed milk. *Cappuccino* is prepared with one-third espresso, one-third steamed milk, and one-third foamed milk (**Figure 27–10**). *Caffé latte* is composed of one-third espresso and two-thirds steamed milk without the foam. A strong coffee with steamed milk is called *café au lait* [38]. Additionally, a variety of flavored coffees, such as hazelnut and French vanilla, may be purchased, or coffee beverages may be prepared from sweet, icy, blended coffees.

Iced Coffee. Iced coffee is made by pouring a freshly made, strong coffee infusion over crushed ice in a glass. Strong infusions, whether combined hot or cold with ice, are made with a larger-than-usual amount of coffee per cup of water and a typical infusion period. Long infusion periods are not recommended because flavor and aroma decrease and bitterness increases.

Coffee Substitutes. Parched ground cereals and/or roots are used as coffee substitutes. Their flavor is due largely to various products formed during the heating process. Coffee substitutes do not generally produce a stimulating effect as does the caffeine in coffee.

Chicory is sometimes added to coffee substitutes for a somewhat bitter taste, or it may be blended with coffee. Chicory is the roasted root of endive, which is a type of lettuce. Coffee with chicory is darker with less coffee flavor and aroma. However, because of its distinctive characteristics, it is enjoyed on its own merit by many.

Purchasing and Storing Coffee

Purchasing. Coffee may be purchased ground, whole beans, or single service pods. The kind of bean and roast should be considered in relation to your coffee preferences. Whole beans provide a level of freshness difficult to obtain when purchasing a ground coffee. If ground, coffee should be vacuum sealed to reduce exposure to oxygen. Once opened, however, the coffee will begin to lose flavor and quality. Good grades of coffee are characterized by a sharp, more desirable flavor compared with the flat, neutral flavor of poor grades. Poor-grade coffee, although less expensive, may not result in the anticipated cost savings because a larger amount of coffee may be required for an acceptable flavor compared to a high-quality coffee.

The single service pods are used by 28 percent of coffee drinkers in the United States [20]. Although convenient, these single service pods have been criticized because of contributing to plastic trash. Some of the plastic pods are recyclable, but it is unclear how many will be placed in recycling bins by consumers.

Storage. The freshness of coffee is an important factor affecting the quality of the coffee beverage. Coffee is best when it is freshly roasted. Thus, for best flavor, whole-bean coffee should be stored for about a week or less in an airtight container. Although coffee beans can be used for several weeks after purchase, the flavor will be less desirable. If a longer storage time is needed, freezer storage is preferable to refrigerated storage because the moisture and odors present in refrigerators will promote quality deterioration. Ground coffee becomes flat or stale more rapidly than coffee in the bean.

The chief cause of staleness has been assumed to be the oxidation of certain coffee constituents. Because ground coffee has a high level of oxygen exposure, it is not surprising that it deteriorates more quickly as compared to whole beans. The effect of oxygen on roasted coffee is rapid during the first three weeks and is thought to affect mainly the flavor constituents. Coffee apparently does not become rancid in the short time required for coffee to become stale. The oxygen probably combines with the oils of the coffee, resulting in the development of true rancidity after several months.

Moisture has a pronounced effect in decreasing the storage life of coffee. Tests on volatile substances extracted from coffee show that if the substances are sealed in a vacuum tube, changes are retarded; if the substances are exposed to air, changes occur rapidly; and if the substances are exposed to moisture, the changes are still more pronounced.

Proper sealing of roasted—especially ground—coffee is fundamental. The vacuum type of package from which air is removed before sealing affords more protection than other types of packages. Flavor deterioration in vacuum-packed coffee depends on the extent to which air is removed from the container. Carbon dioxide gas may be added to vacuum-packed coffee to help maintain quality.

Grind and Quality

For the best coffee flavor, whole beans should be ground immediately prior to brewing. Coffee grinders are available for home or food service use. Coffee may be ground to differing degrees of fineness. Any grind, however, contains particles of many sizes.

Alternately, ground coffee may be purchased. Ground coffees differ basically in the proportion of each size of particles. A *regular grind* contains a higher proportion of coarse particles than a *drip* or *medium grind*; a *fine grind* contains no coarse particles. Consistency in the grind is important in maintaining consistent quality.

FOCUS ON SCIENCE
HOW ARE COFFEES FLAVORED?

Hazelnut, Irish cream, French vanilla, and other flavors of coffee are available. Flavors may be added to whole or ground coffee. The coffee chosen for flavoring should be a low-acid, full-flavored bean that is a light or medium roast. Espresso, a dark roast, is also sometimes flavored. The amount of flavor added to the beans or ground coffee is usually 2 to 3 percent by weight. So how it is added?

Whole Bean Coffee

- The flavors are suspended in a liquid system composed of propylene glycol or vegetable oil.
- The flavors are atomized—sprayed on or applied in a rotating mixer.

- The beans are likely to have a glossy sheen from the addition of the flavor.

Ground Coffee

- The beans may be flavored before grinding, but the flavor tends to stick to the grinders. Later batches of beans may be contaminated with unintended flavors.
- The addition of dried flavors to ground coffee appears to be a preferable flavoring method to avoid cross contamination.

Source: Reference 37.

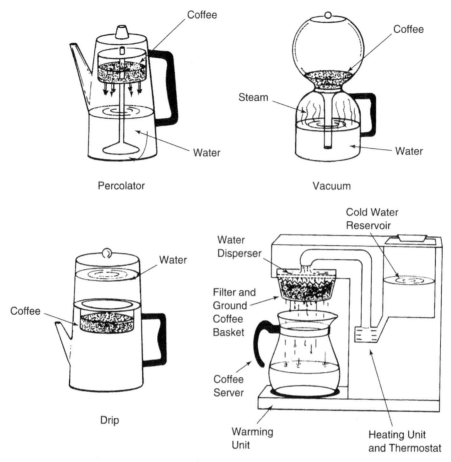

Figure 27–11

Types of coffee makers.

As the percentage of large particles in the coffee grind is increased, the brewed beverage is weaker. A food service manager should know if the supplier measures and controls consistency of the grind.

Methods of Making Coffee

Good coffee may be brewed by several methods (**Figure 27–11**). In each method, important factors include (1) clean equipment to avoid off-flavors and (2) control of the water temperature and the time that the coffee is in contact with the water. The temperature of the water should be at least 185°F (85°C) to extract a desirable amount of soluble solids; however, it should not be hotter than 203°F (95°C) to avoid extraction of excessive amounts of bitter substances and loss of many volatile flavor substances.

The amount of coffee used in relation to the water determines the initial strength of the brew. Measures of 1 to 3 tablespoons of coffee per cup (8 ounces) of water yield brews ranging from weak to very strong. Because coffee "cups" included with many dish or china services are actually only 5 to 6

ounces, many coffeemakers are gauged for this size of "cup." One to 2 tablespoons per 6-ounce "cup" of coffee is often recommended but should be adjusted depending on desired strength.

Drip or Filtration. In the drip or filtration method, the water filters through the coffee into the lower compartment of the coffeemaker. In food service, an urn is used to make drip or filtered coffee. The upper part of a drip coffeemaker is perforated and holds the coffee grounds, and the lower compartment receives the filtered beverage. The perforations of the upper compartment are covered with thin filter paper or a metal mesh basket to prevent the passage of coffee grounds into the beverage. If the perforations are too small, the rate of filtration is too slow to yield a desirable beverage.

The drip method extracts less of the bitter substances than other methods. If it is not allowed to boil and is not kept hot too long, coffee made by the drip method retains more of the flavor constituents than coffee made by other methods.

Vacuum Filtration. Another type of pot for the filtration method is the vacuum coffeemaker. The upper compartment, which holds the coffee, has an open tube that extends almost to the bottom of the lower compartment. Coffee is usually prevented from passing into the lower compartment by a cloth-covered disk that is held in place over the tube opening. In some models, a glass rod that fits the tube opening is used instead of the disk. Water is placed in the lower compartment, and the pot is heated until most of the water rises into the upper compartment. The pot is then removed from the source of heat until the water filters through the coffee and passes back into the lower compartment. The upper compartment is removed, and the beverage is carefully reheated to a desirable temperature for serving. The chief difficulties in the use of this method are that the coffee may not be hot when served, or, if kept hot, it may boil and lose much of the flavor and aroma.

French Press. To make coffee in a French press, a coarse grind is best. Water is brought to a boil, then poured over the coffee grounds in the vessel. After about 4 minutes, the coffee grounds are "pressed" to the bottom, and the coffee may be served. Some describe the flavor of coffee prepared with a French press as more flavorful; others comment that the coffee can have less clarity. One drawback to this method is that many French press coffeemakers do not have a heat source, and thus the coffee must be served immediately, as it will become cold.

Percolation. When coffee is percolated, heated water is forced upward through a tube into the coffee compartment. The water filters through the coffee several times before the beverage is of desirable strength. The water is probably not at the boiling point when it is in contact with the coffee, but the beverage is close to the boiling point when it is ready to be served. Unless the construction of the pot is good and the time of percolating is carefully controlled, flavor and aroma may be lost by this method. The time required varies with the speed of percolation and with the quantity of coffee made. Four to 6 cups of coffee may be percolated in about 6 to 8 minutes. More time is required when a greater quantity is prepared.

Steeping. Although steeped coffee is sometimes described as *boiled*, the flavor is more desirable if the coffee and water are heated together at a temperature below boiling. Steeping (extracting flavor below the boiling point) extracts much less of the bitter substances from coffee than boiling. Coffee boiled for 1 minute is distinctly more bitter than coffee heated from 185 to 203°F (85 to 95°C). The length of steeping varies with the temperature of the water that is mixed with the coffee and with the fineness of the coffee grind. Heating the water before adding the grounds is preferable because less time is required to steep the coffee than if using cold water. Short infusion periods usually yield better-flavored coffee than longer periods.

Steeped coffee may be convenient for use on picnics and camping excursions. If egg white is mixed with the coffee before the water is added, the temperature must rise high enough to coagulate the dilute solution of eggs to clarify the beverage. Boiled coffee made with egg is more bland than that made without egg because of the combination of egg albumin with the polyphenol compounds.

Other Factors Affecting Coffee Quality

The Coffeepot. Pots made of glass, earthenware, or enamelware are good choices for coffee making. Some metals form compounds with caffeine as well as potentially other constituents of coffee and thus are best avoided. Metallic pots may impart a metallic flavor. Stainless steel is resistant to attack, and therefore its effect on the flavor of coffee is negligible. Chrome and nickel plating show no staining or corrosion when used in a coffeepot.

A clean coffeepot is essential to making a good coffee beverage. The pot should be washed with hot soapy water and rinsed thoroughly to remove the oily film that collects on the inside. A pot that retains a stale coffee odor is not clean and will mar the flavor of the best-made coffee. Regular cleaning schedules should be employed for coffee-making equipment used in foodservice establishments.

Water. The water used to brew coffee should be free of any undesirable elements picked up in pipelines, boilers, or water tanks. Coffee should not be brewed with water you would not drink. Soft water or water of low hardness gives coffee a more desirable flavor than very hard or alkaline water. Water having a high carbonate or bicarbonate content and water that has passed through an ion-exchange softening system (and thus is high in sodium ions) will not filter through coffee in a drip or vacuum pot as rapidly as naturally soft water. This means an increase in both the time of contact with the coffee and the amount of material extracted, which can be objectionable.

Temperature and Time. The optimum temperature for brewing a good coffee beverage is 185 to 203°F (85 to 95°C). Boiling produces a distinctly bitter beverage in part because polyphenol substances are more soluble at boiling than at 203°F (95°C). At 185 to 203°F (85 to 95°C), nearly all the caffeine is dissolved, and not as many flavor substances are lost than as at higher temperatures. Boiling water may be used to start the preparation of coffee because the temperature drops on (1) removal from the heat and (2) contact with the coffee and the pot.

In addition to temperature, the length of brewing is also important. The longer the heating period, even at lower temperatures, the higher the percentage of bitter substances dissolved and the greater the loss of flavor substances.

TEA

A legend tells us that one day in 2737 B.C., the Chinese emperor Shen Nung was boiling drinking water over an open fire [42]. He believed that drinking boiled water was a healthy practice. Some leaves from a nearby *Camellia sinensis* plant floated into the pot. The emperor drank the mixture and declared that it gave him vigor of body, contentment of mind, and determination of purpose. Today that potion—tea beverage—is the second most consumed beverage in the world, following water [42]. Tea played an important role in American history with the 1723 Boston Tea Party that has been cited as an important event leading to the American Revolution.

Twenty-three percent of Americans currently drink tea daily, with about 80 percent of that tea consumed as iced [42]. Millennials, in particular, favor tea as a beverage. Countries that produce the largest volumes of tea are China, India, Sri Lanka, Kenya, Turkey, Indonesia, Vietnam, Japan, Iran, and Argentina. Teas vary according to the age of the leaf, the season of plucking, the soil, and climatic conditions as well as the method of processing.

The Tea Plant

Tea comes from the leaves of *Camellia sinensis*, a white-flowered evergreen (**Figure 27–12**). There are three major varieties of this plant, and additional regional varietals produced through hybridization [44]. The plant is pruned and cultivated to produce many young shoots. Tea leaves are picked from the bushes up to four times each year [42]. When the terminal bud and two leaves are plucked by hand, the highest quality of tea is produced. Clippers may be used for coarse plucking or machine harvesters can also be used. Machine-harvested tea is often of a lesser quality because of additional cellulose and wood structures included in the harvest [42].

After processing, tea leaves are sorted into sizes by a screening procedure. Grades refer to the leaf size and have nothing to do with the quality or flavor of tea. The largest leaves are orange pekoe, pekoe, and pekoe souchong. The smaller or broken leaves are classified as broken orange pekoe, broken pekoe souchong, broken orange pekoe fannings, and fines (also called "dust") [59].

Processing

Three principal types of tea, differentiated by the method of leaf processing, are black, green, and oolong (**Figure 27–13**). A fourth type, white tea, is

(a)

(b)

Figure 27–12

(a) Tea leaves are often harvested by hand. (Awei/Shutterstock)
(b) This close-up picture shows the first few tea leaves shortly after harvest. (Joannawnuk/123RF)

also produced. Withering is the first step in the processing of tea. The leaves wilt shortly after picking and are allowed to further wilt by spreading out on fabric or bamboo mats [42]. During withering, moisture levels can drop by 50 percent, and proteins in the leaves break down into free amino acids and the caffeine availability increases.

Black Tea. About 75 percent of the tea consumed in the United States is black tea [42]. In the traditional method of black tea production, the leaves are first withered to remove moisture. The leaves are then

White Tea.   White tea is made from the white buds or the buds and first few leaves under the buds. These buds and leaves are then withered, air dried, then packaged. This very limited processing of young tea leaves and buds results in a pale colored tea with a delicate flavor [44]

Composition

The stimulating characteristic of tea comes from its caffeine content. The tea beverage contains less than half as much caffeine as coffee (see Table 27–3). The actual content of caffeine depends on the method of brewing. Longer brewing results in higher caffeine content.

Tea has been reported to contain a significant amount of folacin [9]. A person could obtain up to 25 percent of the Recommended Dietary Allowance for folacin by drinking 5 cups of tea per day. Tea appears to have a negative effect on iron absorption when consumed with a meal [17].

The flavor of tea is influenced by the presence of considerable quantities of polyphenolic substances, which are particularly responsible for **astringency**. Some of the polyphenols are changed in the **oxidation** process that takes place when black tea is fermented. They contribute to the characteristic aroma and flavor of this tea. Degradation of other substances, including **linolenic acid**, amino acids, and **carotenes**, during the manufacture of black tea may also contribute to flavor and aroma.

Market Forms

A wide variety of teas are available on the market. A large amount of tea prepared in the United States is prepared using tea bags. Loose tea is another option, preferred by some. The use of instant tea mix has declined in popularity while the purchase of ready-to-drink tea has increased.

Many scented and flavored teas are marketed. These teas contain such flavorings as oils of peppermint, strawberry, orange, or lemon; spices such as cinnamon or cloves; blackberry leaves; almond; and licorice root. As with coffee, decaffeinated tea is also available and may be flavored.

A variety of herbal teas are on the market. These "teas" contain dried leaves of various plants other than tea, and therefore are not actually tea. Often they are a mixture of several dried plant materials, such as strawberry leaves, apples, hibiscus flowers, rose hips, peppermint, ginger, nutmeg, cinnamon, chamomile, and alfalfa. Herbal teas contain no caffeine but often contain substances that are soothing or stimulating.

Considerations for Tea Making

High-quality teas are brewed under similar conditions as those best for the brewing of coffee. Water is preferably soft and just under boiling temperature. Glass,

Figure 27–13

Tea and tea leaves are shown here. Left to right are black, green, and oolong tea. (U.S. Department of Agriculture)

rolled in machines that release enzymes and juices from the leaves. Next, the leaves ferment and are allowed to oxidize in a room with controlled temperature and humidity. During oxidation the chlorophyll breaks down enzymatically and tannins are released [42]. Finally, they are dried in ovens.

Green Tea.   Green tea has gained in popularity with consumers. Green tea is produced by allowing the leaves to wither followed by steaming or firing the leaves to inactivate the enzymes. Steamed green leaves have more of a vegetable and green flavor and aroma. Leaves pan-fired or roasted in a wok have more of a toasted flavor [42, 44]. After one of these heat treatments, the leaves are rolled, dried, and then packaged.

The leaf retains much of its original green color, especially the finer leaves. Older leaves often are a blackish-gray color. The beverage made from green tea is greenish-yellow and is distinctly bitter and astringent. It has little aroma and flavor as compared to black tea because the preliminary steaming destroys the enzymes that produce flavor substances during the fermentation of black tea.

Oolong Tea.   Oolong tea is a partially fermented/oxidized tea. The fermentation period is too short to change the color of the leaf completely; it is only partially blackened. To end the oxidation process, these leaves are either steamed or roasted (fired) in a wok. The flavor of oolong tea can vary from more floral with minimal oxidation to fruity and woody with greater oxidation [44]. Comparatively, the flavor and aroma of this beverage are intermediate between those produced from green and black teas.

earthenware, enamelware, or other vitrified ware is recommended because metallic pots impart a metallic taste.

Water Quality and Temperature. Soft water is preferable to hard alkaline water for making tea because the polyphenol substances in tea may interact with certain salts in hard water to produce an undesirable precipitate.

Water just under boiling temperature is generally best for brewing black tea. Boiling water may volatilize flavor and aroma substances. Lower water temperatures (about 185°F [80°C]) are suggested for white tea or oolong teas that may be scorched by higher temperatures. Water should be freshly boiled with enough oxygen still in it to prevent the flat taste that results from the loss of dissolved gases by boiling.

Quantity of Tea and Length of Infusion. The aim in making tea is to extract the maximum flavor with a minimum of polyphenol compounds, which are bitter.

Flavor substances and caffeine are readily extracted by short infusion periods of 3 to 7 minutes. Green tea may be brewed to a desirable flavor in as little as 1 minute. Strong beverages of good flavor require a larger quantity of tea instead of a longer infusion period. The usual proportion of tea per cup of water is about 1 teaspoon.

Effect of Lemon Juice. Tea is lightened by the addition of lemon because the oxidized polyphenolic compounds change color in an acid medium. These substances tend to be dark in an alkaline medium.

Tea-Making Methods

Tea may be made with the use of a tea bag or loose tea. This beverage then may be consumed hot or can be iced to make iced tea. Milk added to tea is another way to enjoy tea. It may be added cold, or steamed for a tea latte.

MULTICULTURAL CUISINE
MORE BEVERAGES!

Bubble Tea

Bubble tea is reported to have originated in Taiwan. While it can be made in a variety of ways and with various flavors, it is at a basic level cooked or soaked tapioca pearls (boba) sweetened with sugar, brewed tea, and milk or cream. The liquid ingredients are shaken together with ice, and then the tapioca pearls are added. Often consumed with a straw, the tapioca offers a chewy treat to the beverage.

Kombucha

Kombucha is a slightly acidic and sweet fermented tea. Tea leaves, usually black tea, are infused and fermented with bacteria and yeasts called "tea fungus." Kombucha is believed to have originated in northeast China during the Tsin Dynasty, about 220 B.C. [34]

Yerba Mate Tea

Also known as "mate," this herbal tea beverage has been widely consumed in South America. It is made from an infusion of the leaves of the tree *Ilex paraguariensis*, and has a distinctly bitter taste [26]. In the United States it can be found packaged in tea bags. Mate leaves are blanched, dried, and aged. Unlike black tea, there is very little fermentation with mate. Furthermore, mate is dried slowly and often with wood smoke instead of high temperature air drying as is usually done with green tea. Mate is high in antioxidants, yet there has been some association with increased cancer risk by those who consume this beverage. More research is needed to understand these contradictory health implications.

Matcha

Matcha is a tea made from particular tea plant varieties in Japan [44]. It was originally consumed by Buddhist monks in Japan. Close to harvest, the plants are covered with nets to increase the shade which then results in higher levels of amino acids and chlorophyll. After harvest the leaves are steamed, slowly dried, and then ground into a green powder. The powder is whisked into water producing a green, grassy beverage with sweetness and umami.

Lassi

Lassi is from India and Pakistan. It is a traditional mildly sweet yogurt beverage made by mixing with water and spices such as cumin. It can also be flavored with rosewater or fruit pulp or juices, and milk. It is increasingly being served in American restaurants.

Horchata

It is a beverage when made in Mexico and Guatemala is prepared by cooking, then pureeing a rice mixture. This mixture is strained, mixed with sugar, chilled, and dusted with cinnamon before serving. Other variations exist in regions of the world that may use ground sesame seeds, ground almonds, barley, or tiger nuts.

Chicha Morada

This Peruvian beverage is prepared from purple corn and spices. The corn is boiled with pineapple, cinnamon, clove, and sugar. Some recipes also include apples, limes, and lemons for additional tartness. Chicha morada is served cold. ∎

Tea Bags. The tea bag is placed in hot water (just under boiling for black tea) and remains in contact with the water until the desired strength is achieved.

Steeping of Loose Tea. To steep tea, the measured tea is placed in a preheated pot, and boiling water is poured into the pot. The pot is then covered and allowed to stand in a warm place until the desired strength is obtained. Steeping periods usually range from 3 to 7 minutes, depending on the type of tea, temperature, and desired strength. The leaves are strained out of the beverage.

Iced Tea. Iced tea is best made from a larger proportion of tea to water than is normally used for hot tea because it is diluted with cold water and melting ice. Lengthy steeping to brew a beverage strong enough to stand dilution extracts too many polyphenol substances. It is believed that a cloudy beverage may result from a complex formed between caffeine and some of the polyphenol substances. This complex may form more readily in iced tea than in hot tea. Its formation is encouraged when larger amounts of polyphenol substances are present. Diluting strong infusions while hot helps to prevent cloudiness.

For sweetening iced tea with sugar, an extrafine granulation that is quickly soluble is desirable. If mint flavor is desired in iced tea, the mint leaves can be crushed and added to the tea leaves before the boiling water is added, or a sprig of mint can be served in the glass of iced tea. Southern sweet tea is made by adding sugar to the hot brewed tea, then icing.

Iced tea dispensers may be used in food service establishments. Care should be taken to daily dismantle, clean, and sanitize these dispensers, as recommended by the FDA, to avoid microbial buildup.

COCOA AND CHOCOLATE

The history of chocolate can be traced back 3,000 years to a beverage in Central and South America. The Aztecs used chocolate for a bitter dark chocolate beverage. Chocolate found its way to Europe with the Spanish who sweetened it with sugar or honey. In Jamaica, milk was added to create the first milk chocolate in 1689 [40]. Although chocolate started predominately as a beverage, today it is used and consumed widely in chocolate candy, baked goods, and in beverages (see Chapters 9 and 16). The United States consumes about 20 percent of the world's chocolate, and about 20 percent of that is consumed as dark chocolate. Europe consumes nearly 50 percent of the world's chocolate [40].

Cacao Tree

The cacao tree (*Theobroma cacao*) requires very exacting growing conditions. It is cultivated only in an area within 20 degrees latitude of the equator, generally under a canopy of tropical rain forests [40]. The cacao tree produced fruits that are pods containing 35 to 50 seeds in a mucilaginous pulp [1] (**Figure 27–14**). There are thousands of varieties of *Theobroma cacao*. Forastero, Criollo, Trinitario, and Nacional are the most common. The Criollo, Trinitario, and Nacional types are considered to be "fine" cocoas and are used predominately to make dark chocolate. The Forastero and sub-varieties are classified as bulk, or basic cocoa grade, representing about 90 percent of the world's cocoa. These varieties are used for cocoa powder, cocoa butter, milk, and dark chocolate [1]. Beans of different varieties may be blended [12].

Seventy percent of the cocoa comes from Western Africa. The Republic of Côte d'Ivoire, also known as the Ivory Coast, is the largest producer. Ghana is the second largest producer, followed by Indonesia, Nigeria, Cameroon, Brazil, Ecuador, the Dominican Republic, and Malaysia [1]. About 80 to 90 percent of the crop is raised by small, family-run farms. The average cacao farmer makes $1.90 per day [27], and thus farming methods to increase yield, while at the same time preventing child labor and deforestation are important issues to be addressed to support a sustainable future.

Harvest and Processing

Cacao beans ripen on the tree until the pods are a golden-orange or red color. Harvest is accomplished predominately by hand. The pods are then split open to expose the beans and pulp. The stages that follow, fermentation, drying, and roasting, are critically important to the quality and flavor of the chocolate.

Fermentation and Drying. Fermentation is a chemically complex process that removes the pulp, forms flavor precursors, reduced bitterness, and develops color. Yeasts, bacteria, and fungi all play a role. Fermentation is accomplished over a five to seven day period by piling the beans and pulp on platforms, heaps, trays, or boxes [1]. During fermentation, the fruit pulp is digested as the temperature rises, and cocoa flavor begins to develop. The bean becomes dark brown [1, 40].

Following fermentation, the beans are dried either in the sun or with dryers [40]. Sun drying is preferred because it results in a better chocolate flavor. The drying process continues the process of reducing bitterness, astringency, and acidity that initiated during fermentation and reduced the moisture level to about 7 percent [1]. At this point the beans can be cleaned, sorted, and bagged.

Roasting. Roasting is accomplished at temperatures of 221°F (105°C) to 302° F (150°C) for 20 to 30 minutes [40]. It is a very important process that further develops flavors, results in nonenzymatic Maillard reactions, and further reduces the moisture levels to 1 to 2 percent [1]. Roasting is often thought of the roasting of whole beans, but nib roasting or liquor roasting can alternatively also be performed [1].

(a)

(b)

Figure 27–14

(a) A cocoa pod in the trunk of a cacoa tree growing in the southern Caribbean. (© Barbara Scheule) (b) The split cocoa pods with seeds in the pulp are shown along with beans held in a hand to provide a perspective on size. (Aedka Studio/Shutterstock)

Winnowing, Grinding, Milling, and Refining. A winnowing machine cracks the beans and separates the shell from the bean, leaving cracked inner beans [40]. The cracked beans are called *nibs*. These nibs contain about 53 percent cocoa butter.

Next the nibs go to grinders that are similar in design to older flour mills. Heat from the friction produced during grinding melts the fat, converting the nibs into a suspension of cocoa solids in cocoa butter called *chocolate liquor* [18]. Chocolate liquor may also be called a chocolate mass. The term liquor does not refer to alcohol, instead the liquid nature of the cocoa solids in the cocoa butter.

Further Processing and Kinds of Chocolate. Several kinds of chocolate, cocoa, bittersweet and semi-sweet, and milk chocolate are produced from the chocolate liquor. If the liquor is pressed to remove the cocoa butter, a dry press cake remains that can be ground into cocoa. If simply solidified, then unsweetened chocolate is formed. With additional grinding between metal drums the particle size is further reduced.

The addition of sugar results in bittersweet or semisweet chocolate. Semisweet has more sugar than bittersweet, but these two types may be used interchangeably in many recipes. Milk chocolate is produced with the addition of milk and sugar. White chocolate is the cocoa butter without the chocolate liquor [40].

Conching and Tempering. If a smooth, velvety chocolate candy is to be produced from the roasted nibs, the ground liquid mass is subjected to a process called *conching*. Conching involves heating the liquid chocolate at a carefully controlled temperature while constantly stirring for a period of four hours to three days [40]. The mixture is aerated during the conching, some volatile acids and moisture are driven off, and flavor is developed [12]. Additional cocoa butter, emulsifiers, sugar, milk solids, and flavorings may be added at this stage before the liquid mass is molded.

Chocolate must be carefully tempered at a controlled temperature while it cools, to ensure that a desirable texture results from the proper type of crystallization of the fat in the finished product (see Chapter 8). Improperly tempered chocolates can have different sizes of crystals and a white coating or fat bloom. The best chocolate has type V crystals, a uniform glossy appearance, and a texture that will crisply snap when broken [40].

Natural- and Dutch-Processed Cocoa. As previously discussed, cocoa is produced from pressing the chocolate liquor to remove the chocolate butter. Cocoas may be divided into two main classes: natural processed and Dutch processed. Some chocolate is also Dutch processed.

Dutch processing consists of treating the cocoa mass, liquor, or powder with alkali, thereby increasing the pH. Bitterness decreases, a dark brown reddish color is produced, and the solubility of the cocoa is increased [1, 40]. Dutch-processed cocoa is also lower in polyphenols [1]. The pH of Dutch-processed cocoa is 6.0 to 8.8, and that of natural-processed cocoa is usually 5.2 to 6.0. The color a chocolate cake made with Dutch-processed cocoa may range from cinnamon brown to deep mahogany red as the pH changes from acid to alkaline (see Chapter 16).

Composition

Fat. According to the FDA standard of identity, bitter chocolate contains not less than 50 percent and not more than 58 percent by weight of cocoa fat or cocoa butter. The high-fat content of chocolate produces a beverage richer than that made from cocoa. Cocoas vary in fat content. Breakfast cocoa is a relatively high-fat cocoa and must contain at least 22 percent cocoa fat [5]. When baking cocoa is substituted for chocolate, particularly in baked products, approximately 3 tablespoons of cocoa plus 1 tablespoon of fat are considered to be equivalent to 1 ounce of chocolate. Recall that in the production of cocoa, the butter fat was removed.

The fat of chocolate contributes much to its eating quality because it has a sharp melting point that is close to body temperature. This results in rapid melting of the chocolate in the mouth with a smooth, velvety feel. The cocoa butter also contributes to enhancing flavor release in the mouth [73].

Starch. Cocoa contains about 11 percent starch and chocolate about 8 percent starch. In preparing a beverage from cocoa and chocolate, a method that cooks the starch results in a more homogeneous beverage. Cocoa or chocolate tend to settle out of the beverage when prepared without heating of the chocolate.

The thickening effect of starch must also be taken into account when cocoa and chocolate are used in flour mixtures such as cakes (see Chapter 16). For example, when modifying a white cake recipe to make chocolate cake, the amount of flour must be reduced. Furthermore, if cocoa is substituted for chocolate in a recipe on the basis of weight, the recipe with cocoa will be thicker.

Flavor. Chocolate, like many foods, contain non-volatile and volatile components that are responsible for cocoa flavor. Among the non-volatile compounds are chemical components such as alkaloids (methylxanthines), polyphenols, proteins, and carbohydrates (sugar and polysaccharides) that are responsible for cocoa flavors [1]. Volatile compounds make up a large part of the flavor bouquet. Over 600 volatiles have been identified [1]. Many of these compounds are developed during fermentation and drying and include alcohols, aldehydes and ketones, esters, pyrazines, acids, and others [1]. Marked changes in the flavor of chocolate and cocoa can occur when these products are heated to high temperatures, especially in the absence of water. Bitter, disagreeable flavors develop, and scorching occurs easily.

Theobromine and Caffeine. Considerably more theobromine than caffeine is found in cocoa and chocolate. Both substances are methylxanthines, but theobromine is a milder stimulant than caffeine. The theobromine and caffeine contents of various foods containing cocoa or chocolate are listed in **Table 27–4**.

Table 27–4
THEOBROMINE AND CAFFEINE CONTENT OF COCOA PRODUCTS

	Theobromine (mg/serving)	Caffeine (mg/serving)
Dark sweet chocolate, 1 oz	123.5	15.1
Milk chocolate, 1 oz	38.1	5.4
Chocolate fudge topping, 2 Tbsp	62.7	3.5
Brownies, 1 oz	29.4	2.8
Chocolate chip cookies, one serving	17.6	2.1
Chocolate cake with chocolate frosting, 1/12 cake	161.2	15.8
Chocolate pudding, 1/2 cup	87.5	7.0

Source: Reference 16.

FOCUS ON SCIENCE
PUTTING THE SHINE ON SOLID CHOCOLATE

Cocoa butter has a characteristic melting behavior that gives it properties that are significant in chocolate. At ambient temperatures, it is hard and brittle, giving chocolate its characteristic snap, but it also has a steep melting curve that allows for a complete melting at mouth temperature. The melting behavior is related to the chemical composition of cocoa butter: rich in palmitic (24 to 30 percent), stearic (30 to 36 percent), and oleic (32 to 39 percent) acids. The palmitic and stearic acids are found on the 1 and 3 positions on the triacyglycerol. These positions and the amount of fatty acids make it predictable and account for its sharp melting point. When the chocolate melts and solidifies, because of its fatty acid makeup, it can form crystals in many different forms or positions (I through VI). Form V is required for the characteristic chocolate shine that is achieved through a series of cooling and heating processes that have been found to optimize the production. When the fatty acids change position or into another form (VI), white crystals of fat (bloom) appear on the surface of the chocolate. This is because of the fluctuation of temperature during storage or migration of liquid oils from nut centers.

Source: Reference 24.

Bloom and Storage Recommendations

Bloom. A grayish-white haze, called *bloom*, may sometimes develop on the surface of chocolate. In addition to the appearance defect, the mouthfeel of solid sweetened chocolate may be granular when bloom develops. Because bloom is a quality defect, preventing bloom is an important consideration for both manufacturers and retailers of chocolate. There are two types of bloom. One type arises from changes in the fat crystals with an accumulation of large fat crystals or agglomerates of fat crystals on the surface of the chocolate. These reflect light, creating the appearance that is called *bloom*. Another type of bloom results from the action of moisture on the sugar ingredients in the chocolate [50].

Bloom may occur for a variety of reasons, including incorrect cooling methods, warm or fluctuating storage temperatures, the addition of fats that are incompatible with cocoa butter, and abrasion or finger marking, particularly under warm conditions. The use of proper tempering temperatures and time periods during the manufacturing process and the use of emulsifiers and modifiers retard bloom formation. See Chapter 8 to read more about chocolate bloom and fat.

Storage. The avoidance of high storage temperatures is essential in maintaining the quality of chocolate and avoiding the development of bloom. Moisture is also detrimental and encourages lumping in cocoas. Both chocolate and cocoa are best stored at a temperature no higher than 65 to 70°F (18 to 21°C) and 50 to 65 percent relative humidity [73]. Milk chocolate absorbs flavors and odors and should be stored where this cannot occur.

Cooking with Chocolate

Chocolate Melting. When chocolate is melted, care must be used to avoid overheating, which may produce a firm, lumpy mass that does not blend with other ingredients. A low to moderate temperature should be applied to chocolate that has been shaved or chopped into pieces. Heating the chocolate over hot water lessens the danger of overheating. However, care should be taken to avoid getting water into the melting chocolate because the chocolate can seize (suddenly harden), thereby becoming stiff rather than smooth throughout. Chocolate can also be easily melted in the microwave oven. The use of chocolate in coating confections was discussed in Chapter 9.

Methods for Making Cocoa Beverage. Cocoa or hot chocolate can be made by a quick method or a syrup method. In the quick method, the hot milk is poured over a cocoa–sugar mixture in the cup. A disadvantage of the quick method is that the starch is not cooked sufficiently to prevent the cocoa from settling out.

In contrast, preparation of the beverage by either a syrup or a paste method produces more desirable body and flavor than usually results from the quick method. In both the syrup and the paste method, a portion of the chocolate is cooked with water and sugar to form a syrup or a paste. The cooking of the mixture cooks the starch found in the cocoa or, in the case of the paste method, cooks the starch in the cocoa and the added starch. The purpose of the cornstarch is to produce a beverage with more body and to prevent any tendency of the cocoa to settle. With instant cocoa mixes, the addition of a stabilizer or emulsifier may help to keep the particles dispersed. Proportions and instructions for the syrup and paste methods are provided in **Table 27–5**.

Because milk is a prominent constituent of cocoa or chocolate beverages, scum formation may occur. It can be retarded by covering the pan or by beating the mixture to produce a light foam. Alternatively, the surface of the cocoa can be covered with whipped topping or marshmallows to prevent scum formation. High temperatures, which may scorch both milk and chocolate, should be avoided (see Chapter 22).

Table 27–5
SYRUP AND PASTE METHODS FOR THE PREPARATION OF HOT COCOA AND HOT CHOCOLATE

Syrup Method for Hot Cocoa or Hot Chocolate

Make a syrup by boiling the ingredients in either of the cocoa or chocolate ingredient lists for one minute. Evaporation will reduce the volume. Add 3/4 cup of hot milk. The syrup can be made in quantity and stored in the refrigerator, then mixed with hot milk when desired.

Cocoa Recipe	Chocolate Recipe
2 tsp to 1 Tbsp cocoa	$1/3$ oz chocolate, shaved fine
2 tsp to 1 Tbsp sugar	1 to $1\frac{1}{2}$ Tbsp sugar
$1/4$ cup water	$1/3$ cup water

Paste Method for Hot Cocoa or Hot Chocolate

Boil all listed ingredients for 1 to 2 minutes. Combine with 2 cups of hot milk.

$1/2$ Tbsp corn starch	1 oz chocolate (or 3 Tbsp cocoa)
$1/3$ cup water	2 Tbsp sugar

STUDY QUESTIONS

Consumption Trends

1. Discuss trends in beverage consumption in the United States.

Nutrition

2. Discuss the nutritional and health implications associated with the consumption of several beverages.

3. Explain the health importance of water as a beverage.

Water

4. Identify the source for much of the bottled water sold in the marketplace.

5. Discuss advantages and disadvantages of bottled water consumption.

6. Compare the various ways water can be treated before bottling.

7. Identify the differences in the FDA standard definitions for types of bottled water.

Carbonated Beverages

8. Explain how carbonated beverages are made.

9. Identify the differences in club soda, seltzer, and tonic water.

10. Identify what is added to carbonate a beverage.

Functional Beverages

11. Define functional beverages.

12. Discuss pros and cons to the consumption of sports drinks and energy drinks.

Noncarbonated Fruit or Vegetable Beverages

13. Identify what must be true to call a fruit or vegetable "juice."

Alcoholic Beverages

14. Describe the production of wine, beer, hard cider, and spirits.

15. Provide the percent of alcohol in a 60 proof spirit.

Coffee

16. Discuss the plant that produced coffee beans.

17. Summarize the steps necessary to process a coffee crop into coffee beans ready to be ground and used for coffee.

18. List the constituents of coffee that contribute to its quality as a beverage.

19. Describe conditions that will aid in preserving freshness in coffee, both in the bean and in the ground.

20. Describe three methods for preparing coffee and identify the methods most likely to produce the least or most bitter beverage.

21. Explain why coffee generally should not be boiled.

22. Identify the type of water preferable for preparing coffee.

23. Explain why freshly brewed coffee and coffee that has been sitting for a period of time may taste different.

Tea

24. Describe differences in processing and characteristics of black, green, oolong, and white teas.

25. Describe two appropriate procedures for the preparation of tea.

26. Discuss several factors that are important in the preparation of good quality tea and iced tea.

27. Compare and contrast tea and herbal tea.

Cocoa and Chocolate

28. Identify the plant source and growing regions of chocolate and cocoa?

29. Summarize the harvesting and processing of chocolate.

30. Define chocolate liquor, nibs, cocoa butter, and conching.

31. Describe cocoa, bittersweet, semisweet, milk chocolate, and white chocolate

32. Explain the differences between natural-processed and Dutch-processed cocoa.

33. How do chocolate and breakfast cocoa differ in fat and in starch content?

34. Explain how to substitute cocoa for chocolate in a recipe.

35. Describe *bloom* on chocolate and give possible explanations for its development.

36. Explain how chocolate and cocoa be stored, and explain why.

37. Suggest a satisfactory method for preparing cocoa beverage, and explain your recommendation.

Food Packaging and Preservation

Count every food item consumed during a day that has been packaged in some way, or preserved for longer storage. Bottles, wrappers, bags, boxes, and cans protect and enable the transportation and storage of much of the foods we consume. The functionality of these packages are important, but the impact on the environment once the package is no longer needed also needs consideration. As discussed in Chapter 1, convenience is important to consumers and foodservice operators, and packaging has a role in this convenience.

Food preservation is also critical, and an important aspect of packages. Many of the food packaging systems are designed to preserve foods and reduce food waste. Also discussed in Chapter 1 was the large amount of food waste (about one-third of our food supply) that occurs for a wide variety of reasons from the farm to the home or foodservice and then the ultimate consumer.

Food preservation has been practiced for thousands of years, but today's technology has enabled food to be stored at excellent quality for longer periods of time. In early historic times, people dried their supplies of fresh meat and fish in the sun. Later, they smoked and salted perishable foods to extend the time that the foods remained edible.

Canning was discovered in France about 1810. This allowed the storage of fruits, vegetables, and meats through the seasons of the year. It was not until 1920 that frozen food industry was developed. Consider for a moment what our food choices would be throughout the year without the technology enabling frozen and canned foods. Today, much of the processing and initial treatment for the preservation of foods in Western countries is done by the food industry. Consumers, as well as food service managers, are accustomed to purchasing canned, frozen, fermented, dried, portioned, and packaged foods. Despite these trends in commercial preservation and packaging of foods, many enjoy raising their own food in home or community gardens, and the excess produce is canned, frozen, or dried for future use. Thus, a brief discussion of techniques for canning and freezing in the home is provided at the end of this chapter. In this chapter, the following topics will be discussed:

- Food Packaging
- Food Spoilage Causes
- Food Preservation Basics
- Freezing
- Canning

FOOD PACKAGING

There are many types of packages for food and beverages. These packages perform a number of different functions and are also made from several different materials. Today, plastics are used for the majority of food packaging. The technology of packaging continues to evolve at a rapid rate to provide convenience for consumers; reduce spoilage and food waste; enable various processing treatments such as heat, cold, or high pressure; and address environmental concerns. Intelligent, active, and responsive packages are all important developments [5] (**Figure 28–1**).

Functions of Food Packaging

The main functions of food packaging are to protect the food from contamination, contain the food, and provide information [45, 5].

Protection. Food packaging provides protection from chemical, biological, and physical influences that may cause deterioration of the product. Tamper-resistant packaging has been developed to protect consumers from willful tampering and adulteration of foods and other products [45].

Shelf-Life Stability. A variety of chemical changes in food can be controlled or prevented by the type of packaging. Appropriate packaging minimizes reactions that affect the stability or the shelf life of the food products. Water vapor and oxygen are always present in the environment around foods and can affect the stability of packaged food products. The package may provide a barrier to these gases. It acts in some cases to keep moisture in the food and thus prevent drying or desiccation. In other cases, it prevents moisture from entering the package and being absorbed by the food. Certain packages control migration of atmospheric oxygen. The permeability of the package to light may also affect the stability of the food. For example, excessive light can promote the greening of potatoes or off flavors in milk.

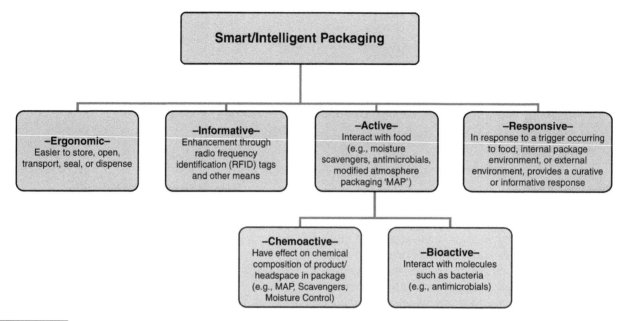

Figure 28–1

Smart and intelligent packaging can include many different aspects as shown and described in this figure. Responsive packaging is on the leading edge of research. (Reference 5)

The development of new "active" packaging technologies enable the package to offer ways to manage or regulate the conditions inside the package that can impact the chemical or the biological aspects, thereby protecting the food safety and quality. The majority of meat jerky packages have oxygen absorbing packets to help keep the jerky fresh [22]. Other packages can offer scavenger technology to absorb the build-up of ethylene gas, a natural plant hormone that promotes ripening and can therefore result in faster spoilage [5].

Contamination Protection. Proper packaging keeps biological contaminants at a minimum by providing a barrier to microbes, insects, rodents, or other animals [45]. Packaging can also provide an environment not conducive to the growth of microorganisms (such as moisture control) and thus reduces microbial decomposition of foods.

Physical Protection. Physical protection of the foods helps to prevent breakage, crushing, and other forms of damage that would cause the food to be undesirable or unusable [45]. For example, fresh eggs are protected by egg cartons.

Containment. Food containers hold and separate foods into units of a particular size and weight. Containers provide ease in handling and convenience. From a packaging-waste perspective, large containers, as compared to individual serving-size containers, result in less environmental waste. Individual or small containers may result in less food waste, however, if the larger container of food cannot be used before quality has deteriorated.

Flexible packaging has become very common in the marketplace. Flexible packaging was historically made from paper, thin tin, or aluminum foil [13]. Today an estimated three-fourths of our food is in contact with flexible packaging, most of which is plastic. Fresh greens and salads are packaged in flexible packaging.

Marketing and Information. The package provides information about the product for the consumer. The food facts nutrition label, package contents, product use, and even recipes may be provided on the label. Innovative packaging can boost sales [45]. The "intelligent or smart" packaging of today and tomorrow can and will be offering even more information. Time temperature sensors can indicate the temperature a package of food has experienced throughout the distribution system so consumers know before purchase if the food was maintained at a safe temperature [55]. Other intelligent packages can allow the consumer to swipe the package with a smartphone to gain additional product information with regard to ingredients or nutrition. This information may also be linked to fitness and calorie trackers or inform the consumer if the package is recyclable [55]. Radio frequency identification (RFID) allows packaging to be tracked and scanned [5].

RFID or unique codes on package labels also enable traceability of the product throughout the distribution process. If a food recall occurs, the products affected by the recall can be traced and therefore identified.

Packaging of the Future. All aspects of smart intelligent packaging are continuing to evolve (Figure 28–1). Responsive packaging is a focus of much current research, but is limited in current use. This type of packaging can respond to conditions either in the package or in the external environment, and then respond with information or a solution. External reactions can be to address thermal or mechanical issues. A mechanical concern could be the dropping of a package that is detected by a sensor, and then communicated so that the product is not sold or used. Internal responses could be to address biological or non-food chemical changes within the food or the atmosphere within the headspace of the package [5].

Regulatory Requirements

The FDA considers the compatibility of food and its packaging to be a safety issue. The package is a potential source of chemical substances for the food product [54]. Migration of substances from packaging materials does occur and cannot be completely

eliminated; thus, the packaging materials are legally considered to be food additives and require premarket safety evaluation and approval by the FDA [28].

The FDA also oversees the regulation of food labels and specific requirements regarding nutrition, ingredients, health claims (see Chapter 3). Labeling and packaging to reduce the likelihood of product misrepresentation are additional areas of FDA oversight. Slack-fill, or the amount of space allowed in the product beyond that needed for the food, is another regulatory packaging concern. Slack-fill may be functional if it (a) protects the ingredients; (b) is needed to seal package; (c) occurs because of product settling; (d) is needed for specific in-package preparation space; (e) is a package

---

FOCUS ON SCIENCE
FOOD PRESERVATION AND PACKAGING IN SPACE

A unique way to illustrate the main points in this chapter is to identify the particular food preservation and packaging techniques utilized in NASA's astronaut program. In space, food is individually packaged and stowed for easy handling in a zero-gravity environment space. An oven is provided in the space shuttle and the space station to heat foods to their proper temperature. Depending on the mission, there may be no refrigerators in space, so food must be stored and prepared properly to avoid spoilage, especially on longer missions.

Food Packages

On earth, the disposal of food packages is often done without a thought. In space, astronauts throw their food packages away in a trash compactor or inside the space shuttle when they are done eating. Some packaging actually prevents the food from flying away. The food packaging is designed to be flexible, to be easy to use, and to maximize space when stowing or disposing food containers.

Rehydratable Food

A variety of foods and beverages may be rehydrated in space travel. Some of these foods include soups, macaroni and cheese, chicken and rice, shrimp cocktail, scrambled eggs, and cereals. Breakfast cereals are prepared by packaging in rehydratable package with nonfat dry milk and sugar, if needed. Water is added to the package just before eating.

Thermostabilized Food

Food is heat processed to destroy undesirable microorganisms and enzymes. Individual servings of thermostabilized foods are available in aluminum or bimetallic cans, plastic cups, or in flexible retort pouches. Cans are easy open with full-panel, pullout lids. Most of the entrees are packaged in flexible retort pouches that may be heated, cut open with scissors, and eaten directly.

Intermediate Moisture Food

Intermediate moisture foods are preserved by restricting the amount of water available for microbial growth. Water

is removed or restricted with water-binding substances such as sugar or salt. The moisture level of intermediate moisture foods ranges from 15 to 30 percent.

Natural Form Foods

A variety of natural form, ready-to-eat foods, such as nuts, granola bars, and cookies, are available. These foods are packaged in flexible pouches and require no further processing.

Irradiated Meat

Beef steaks are cooked, packaged in flexible foil-laminated pouches, and sterilized by exposure to ionizing radiation. These steaks are stable at ambient temperature.

Condiments

Several condiments are provided and include commercially packaged individual packets of catsup, mustard, mayonnaise, taco sauce, and hot pepper sauce. Pepper is dissolved in oil, and the salt is dissolved in water, then packaged in polyethylene dropper bottles. The salt and pepper, as sold on earth, would float around at zero gravity.

Shelf-Stable Tortilla

Tortillas are served instead of bread because the crumbs would float around and go into the equipment. However, tortillas became moldy on long flights. Shelf-stable tortillas were developed that are stabilized by a combination of modified atmosphere packaging, pH (acidic), and water activity. Mold growth is prevented by removing oxygen from the package. This is accomplished by packaging in a high-barrier container in a nitrogen atmosphere with an oxygen scavenger. Water activity is reduced to less than 0.9 in the final product by dough formulation. Reduced water and lower pH inhibit growth of pathogenic clostridia, which could be a potential hazard in the anaerobic atmosphere created by modified atmosphere.

Source: NASA, Food for Space Flight, www.nasa.gov

also used as a reusable container; and (f) the package size reduces pilfering, allows for labeling space, or offers tamper resistance. Non-functional slack-fill, which is a container larger than necessary, may mislead the consumer, and is regulated in 21 CFR §100.100 [54].

Packaging Materials

Packaging materials are chosen with their ability to protect, contain, and offer information to facilitate sale. Food quality, food processing methods, consumer wants, packaging costs, and environmental impact are all issues to be considered.

Food flavors can be adversely affected by the type of packaging. Direct contact of food with packaging materials may result in migration of volatile compounds from the package into the packaged food. The loss of desirable content constituents in the plastic packaging is referred to as *scalping* [10]. Plastic materials such as polyethylene and polypropylene in particular have been implicated in flavor absorption into the plastic [10].

Particular types of packaging materials are needed for **aseptic-packaged**, hot-filled, dry-filled–no process, frozen, and retorted foods [14]. Stand-up flexible pouches have gained in popularity as one way to reduce the amount of packaging materials [7]. Plastics, glass, paper and paperboard, and metals are commonly used for packages.

Plastics. Plastics are **organic polymers** with variable chemical compositions and physical properties. Many different fabrication processes are used to produce the many types and shapes of both rigid and flexible packages used by the packaging industry. Several different kinds of plastics are described in **Table 28–1**.

Table 28–1
KINDS OF PLASTICS COMMONLY USED FOR FOOD PACKAGING

Name	Characteristics	Examples
Polyolefin Polyethylene (PE) Polypropylene (PP)	Most widely used food packaging plastics. Flexible, light, strong, stable, resistant to moisture and chemicals. May be recycled or reused.	Milk, juice, and water bottles. Cereal box liners. Margarine tubs and yogurt containers. Trash and grocery bags.
Polyesters Polyethylene terephthalate (PETE) or (PET) Polycarbonate (PC) Polyethylene naphthalate (PEN)	PETE/PET is the most widely used food packaging polyester. Provides good barrier to gases and moisture. Does not have good resistance to bases. Polycarbonate is clear, heat resistant, and durable. Harsh chemicals may release a potentially hazardous chemical, and additional risk assessment has been suggested. PEN performs well at high temperatures but is more expensive than PETE.	PETE is used for plastic carbonated beverage containers, food trays, and thin-oriented films such as used for snack food wrappers. Polycarbonate is often used for returnable or refillable water bottles and sterilizable baby bottles. PEN is well suited for beer and other beverage containers.
Polyvinyl chloride (PVC)	Heavy, stiff, with excellence resistance to chemicals. Is difficult to recycle and should not be incinerated because of chlorine content.	Bottles and packaging films.
Polyvinylidene chloride (PVdC)	Heat sealable and excellent barrier to many substances. Should not be incinerated because of high chlorine content.	Packaging of poultry, cheese, snack foods, tea, coffee, and confections.
Polystyrene (PS)	Clear, hard, and brittle. Has a low melting point. May be recycled or incinerated.	Egg cartons, disposable plastic silverware, cups, plates, bottles, and food trays.
Polyamide (nylon)	Good chemical resistance, toughness, and gas permeability.	Boil-in-the-bag packaging.
Ethylene vinyl alcohol (EVOH)	Excellent barrier to oil, fat, and oxygen. Is moisture sensitive.	Multilayered films when not in direct contact with foods.
Laminates and coextrusions	Lamination is the process of bonding two or more plastics together or bonding a plastic to another material such as paper or aluminum. Coextrusion is the combination of two or more layers of molten plastics during film manufacturer. Because laminates and coextrusions include multiple materials, recycling is difficult.	

Source: Reference 45.

Plastics are used for many food-related purposes in our daily world. (Nils Z/Shutterstock)

Polyethylene (PC), polypropylene (PP), polystyrene (PS), polyvinyl chloride (PVC), polyethylene terephthalate (PET), phenolic resin, melamine resin, polyester resin, and polycarbonate (PC) are the predominant plastics used for food and other consumer packaging [3]. Worldwide, plastic production has increased from 1.5 metric tons in 1950 to over 300 million metric tons currently (**Figure 28-2**).

Safety. The safety of plastic and plastic additional ingredients used to make the plastic flexible, soft, or colored are under increasing scrutiny by the public. Some of these plastic additives are under examination as endocrine-disruptors with implications for health. Bisphenol A (BPA) is one of these additives. The scientific evidence for the safety or, alternatively, risk of some of these various plastic additives is not clear [3]. With stronger risk evidence, the U.S. Consumer Product Safety Improvement Act banned six phthalates in children's products. Those banned permanently are benzyl butyl phthalate (BBP), di-butyl phthalate (DBP), and di-ethylhexyl phthalate (DEHP). Banned temporarily pending more evidence are di-isodecyl phthalate (DIDP), di-isonoyl phthalate (DINP), and di-n-octyl phthalate (DnOP) [3].

A review of nearly 200 research studies suggests at this time that PE, PET, and PP synthetic plastics are considered safe. BPA, used in the manufacture of plastics, has been banned in some countries; however, BPA, phthalates, and styrene are believed to be in the safe range. DEHP, DBP, DIDP, and DINP warrant further risk assessment and because of the extent of migration from the package to the food, may be of concern [3].

Biobased Plastics. Biobased plastics are produced from materials that are renewable. These materials can be made from a starch or components such as corn or sugar beets that are also biodegradable. These containers are generally best used or low moisture foods. Biobased, but not biodegradable containers, have the functionality of plastics made from natural gas and can be used for liquids. They are made through the fermentation of carbohydrates [51]. The PET PlantBottle™ was developed by Coca-Cola company. Through a partnership with Heinz it is also being used for ketchup bottles. This container has up to 30 to 100 percent plant based materials derived from molasses with a blend of petrochemical ingredients [51, 56]. In examining the full lifecycle of various plastics, petro-based or biobased, each have their pros and cons; however, the biobased, but not biodegradable may be the plastic of the future [51].

Glass. Glass offers the advantage of being chemically inert and thus does not affect flavor. However, compared to other kinds of packaging, glass is heavy and costly to transport. It also is breakable, which is a significant disadvantage for some packaging needs. Glass offers a variety of shapes and sizes, and can be clear, allowing the consumer to see the product (**Figure 28-3**). Glass is fully recyclable.

Glass is used to package some foods such as tomato and spaghetti sauces. (Tom Baker/123RF)

Figure 28–4

Paper and cardboard is used for pizza boxes, sandwich wrappers and boxes, food bags, cereal boxes, cups, and more. (Anna Hoychuk/Shutterstock)

Paper and Paperboard. A variety of paper and paperboard packages are used (**Figure 28–4**). Corrugated boxes, milk cartons, folding cartons, bags, sacks, and wrapping paper are examples of paper and paperboard packages. Paper and paperboard are produced from cellulose fibers derived from wood [45]. Any additives used in the processing of paper intended for food use are regulated by the FDA. Because paper has poor barrier properties, it is treated, coated, laminated, or otherwise processed [45].

Paper and paperboard packages are used for several different types of food products. Paperboard trays, developed for microwave use, may also withstand up to 400°F (204°C) in conventional ovens. A heat-resistant plastic resin is applied to solid, bleached sulfate board that is formed into trays of various shapes and sizes. These containers can be used for **shelf-stable foods**, refrigerated foods, and frozen foods. Orange juice and milk cartons of paperboard may have resealable caps for easier opening and pouring.

Rectangular paperboard cartons, laminated with aluminum and/or polyethylene, can be used for the aseptic packaging of products such as fruit juices and drinks [36]. These containers are made in various sizes. An assortment of products, including dry cereals, cake mixes, rice mixes, macaroni and cheese, and so on, are packed in paperboard cartons. In some cases, inner linings hold the product.

Metals. Metals used for packaging include aluminum, aluminum foil, tinplate, and tin-free steel [45]. Aluminum is lightweight, resistant to corrosion, and easily recycled. However, because it cannot be welded, it is used only for seamless containers. Tinplate is produced by coating thin sheets of steel in molten tin. These containers may be heat treated and sealed and thus are useful for sterilized products. Tinplate can be recycled and is less expensive than aluminum. Tin-free

steel must be coated with an organic material for corrosion resistance. It cannot be welded. Tin-free steel is used for food cans, trays, and bottle caps.

Metal cans may be flat rectangles, tall and thin, squat, potbellied, and many other configurations. The bodies may be three- or two-piece and fabricated from steel or aluminum [11]. Likewise, many different styles of closure may be used. The traditional metal can is made of steel with a thin coating of tin. It generally is cylindrical and is made of three pieces (**Figure 28–5**). The two ends are attached to the cylinder, which has a soldered seam. Two-piece cans, with the base and cylinder in one piece, are manufactured; these cans have fewer seams, are more durable and lighter in weight, stack better on shelves, and can be produced more inexpensively than the traditional three-piece cans.

Combinations of Materials. A combination of two or more materials can provide improved functional properties for food packages. Several films can be laminated together, each layer contributing specific characteristics. For example, containers for aseptic packaging may be fabricated with aluminum foil as a barrier material and polypropylene or polyethylene as heat-sealing and food-contact surfaces. Because foil must be protected from mechanical damage, paperboard is often utilized as the outer layer of this laminate. These packages act as barriers to moisture, oxygen, light, and microorganisms and have the necessary strength and heat sealability [57]. Individually portioned fruit drinks are often marketed in such packages.

Figure 28–5

Cans package foods and can be two-piece or three-piece cans. They may be opened with can openers or pull-off tabs. The cans pictured here are three-piece cans with separate tops and bottoms connected to the center of the can. (Jesus Keller/Shutterstock)

The flexible retort pouch is another example of a package using a combination of materials. It typically consists of three laminated materials held together by adhesives. The outer layer is polyester, which provides strength; the middle layer is aluminum foil, which provides a barrier to moisture, gas, and light; and the inner layer is polyolefin (polyethylene or polypropylene), which provides a good heat seal.

The retort pouch is thin and permits sterilizing temperatures to be reached more quickly throughout the contents than the traditional can. Thus, the processed product is fresher and firmer. The sealed pouch can be stored at room temperature. Tuna was introduced in retort packaging in 2000 and is now widely available [11].

Edible Films and Coatings. An edible film is defined as a thin layer of edible material formed on a food as a coating or placed (preformed) on or between food components [34]. Edible coatings and films are not meant to replace nonedible, synthetic packaging materials for prolonged storage of foods. They can, however, act as adjuncts for improving overall food quality and extending shelf life. They may inhibit migration of moisture, oxygen, carbon dioxide, aromas, lipids, and so on; carry food ingredients such as antioxidants, antimicrobials, or flavor; and/or improve mechanical integrity or handling characteristics of the food.

The desired characteristics of the edible film depend on the food product and its primary type of deterioration. For example, if the food is a manufactured product high in polyunsaturated fat, a film extremely resistant to the entrance of oxygen would be desirable to avoid the early development of rancidity. If the product is a fresh fruit or vegetable, however, the film would need to retard moisture loss but allow some permeability of oxygen and carbon dioxide gases as the plant cells continue to respire [32]. Edible films can also offer a natural plant source of antimicrobial agents as an edible coating [1].

Potential edible films include polysaccharides such as starch, high amylose starch, methyl cellulose, **alginate**, **carrageenan**, and low-methoxyl pectin; proteins such as collagen, gelatin, wheat gluten, zein from corn, soy protein isolate, whey proteins, and casein; edible waxes; and combinations of these substances [34].

Packaging and Processing

Aseptic Packaging. Aseptic processing involves sterilization of the food product, sterilization of the package or container in which the food will be placed, filling the sterilized container with the sterilized food in an environment in which sterility is maintained, and sealing the container to prevent subsequent contamination [9]. Aseptic processing was developed in the 1940s. Superheated steam or dry hot air may be used to sterilize aseptic packages, as can hydrogen peroxide in combination with heat or ultraviolet light [30]. Hydrogen peroxide together with heat or ultraviolet radiation treatment is commonly used for the sterilization of paper-based packaging. Magnetic resonance imaging inspection of aseptically packaged foods has been developed as a technique for the 100 percent inspection of products, at production line speeds, to ensure product quality and safety [47].

Food products to be aseptically packaged are pumped through heat exchangers of various types, then into a holding tube, and finally into a cooling section before being packaged. Aseptic packaging of low-acid foods containing particulates requires demonstration of sterility at the center of the food particles, based on a defined microbiological procedure and a mathematical model. Destruction of any **Clostridium botulinum** spores present must be ensured. Aseptic sterilization and packaging has several advantages over in-container sterilization, the process used in conventional canning. Processing conditions are independent of container size, and therefore very large containers can be used. The process is highly automated, resulting in higher productivity. It is also more energy efficient and less expensive. Packaging costs are lower for many container types. Aseptic processing yields higher-quality foods than traditional procedures requiring longer heating. Transport and storage costs are also less than those for frozen foods, as refrigeration is unnecessary [57].

Modified Atmosphere Packaging. Modified atmosphere packaging (MAP) may be defined as the enclosure of food products in gas-barrier materials, in which the gaseous environment has been changed or modified (**Figure 28–6**). The modification may slow respiration rates of fresh produce, reduce microbial spoilage, retard deterioration due to enzymatic

Figure 28–6

Precut lettuce is often sold in modified atmosphere packaging. (U.S. Department of Agriculture)

Table 28–2
Gas Mixtures for Selected Food Products

Product	Temperature (°C)	Gas Concentration (%)		
		Oxygen	Carbon Dioxide	Nitrogen
Fresh meat	0–2	70	20	10
Cured meat	1–3	0	50	50
Cheese	1–3	0	60	40
Apples	4–6	2	1	97
Tomatoes	5–10	4	4	92
Baked products	Room temperature	0	60	40
Pizza	Room temperature	0	60	40

Source: Reference 58.

reactions, and slow oxidation of unsaturated fats in snack foods [26, 53, 58]. The gaseous atmosphere within the package usually contains a reduced amount of oxygen and increased amounts of carbon dioxide and nitrogen. MAP is very often applied to fresh-cut produce; however, sandwiches, pastas and sauces, meats and poultry, lunch kits, and snacks also use MAP. MAP may be of two types: high gas permeable or low gas permeable. Respiring products such as fresh produce are packaged in high-gas-permeable MAP; while pasta and other prepared dishes are placed in low-gas-permeable MAP [8].

Modification of the gas mixture may be accomplished by two different methods: vacuum packaging and gas packaging. Vacuum packaging involves packaging the product in a film with low oxygen permeability, removing air from the package, and sealing it **hermetically**. Oxygen in the headspace is reduced to less than 1 percent. Carbon dioxide, if it is produced from tissue and microbial respiration, eventually increases to 10 to 20 percent within the headspace. Low oxygen and elevated carbon dioxide extend the shelf life of fresh meat by inhibiting the growth of aerobic microorganisms. The meat must be kept refrigerated. Although this works well for fresh and processed meat products, it cannot be used for crushable items such as pizza, pasta, and baked products [58].

The technique in gas packaging involves removing air from the package and replacing it with a mixture of nitrogen, oxygen, and carbon dioxide. The pressure of gas inside the package is maintained approximately equal to the external pressure. Nitrogen is an inert gas that does not affect the food and has no antimicrobial properties. It is used chiefly as a filler to prevent package collapse in products that can absorb carbon dioxide. Oxygen is generally avoided except for products that continue to respire after packaging, such as fruits and vegetables. Carbon dioxide is bacteriostatic and fungistatic. Its effect depends on several

factors, including the microbial load, gas concentration, temperature, and packaging film permeability. **Table 28–2** gives some examples of gas mixtures for selected foods [58].

Sous Vide. *Sous vide* is a French term meaning "under vacuum." *Sous vide* processing technology involves the slow, controlled cooking of foods in sealed, evacuated, heat-stable pouches or trays so that the natural flavors are retained, followed by quick chilling, and cold storage at 32 to 37°F (0 to 3°C). These refrigerated products with extended shelf life can be reheated in a boiling water bath or in a microwave oven. The major microbiological hazard associated with this processing technology is the potential growth and toxin production of *Clostridium botulinum*. Other organisms of public health concern include pathogenic strains of *Escherichia coli*, *Salmonella*, *Staphylococcus*, *Listeria*, and *Yersinia* species. All these organisms should be destroyed during the heating process; however, a Hazard Analysis and Critical Control Points approach at all stages of *sous vide* processing and handling is essential to promote a reasonable degree of confidence in product safety [58]. The risks involved in temperature abuse continue into the kitchen. Refrigerator temperatures should always be 40°F (4°C) or lower.

Microwave Assisted Thermal Sterilization (MATS™). MATS™ uses steam and microwave to rapidly sterilize foods. The processing time required to sterilize the food, excluding cooling, can be as little as 10 minutes, thereby producing food not overcooked or otherwise affected by high heat. The food is packaged in hermetically sealed flat barrier plastic trays with a high surface-to-volume ratio. This allows the rapid conduction of heat. (See Chapter 5 for more about heat transfer.) The sealed food moves through hot water, under pressure, with the applications of microwave energy [12].

High-Pressure Processing. High-pressure processing can be used for a number of food products to reduce vegetative cells of bacteria that could cause foodborne illness. Fruit juices sold as raw, that do not also have a warning labeling on food-safety risk, are generally processed with high pressure. The pressures can be 800 Mega Pascals applied in equipment capable of producing these pressures typically in water [16]. High-pressure processing does not impact enzymes or nutrients, thus offering a fresh taste, without the use of preservatives. Packaging is generally flexible and adapt to the pressure well. Bottles used for juices must be able to handle the pressure while maintaining the seal of the bottle cap [16].

Packaging Waste Management

As we evolve into a "throwaway" society, we are producing waste from packaging, as well as from other sources, at a faster rate than we are finding solutions to deal with it. Landfills are quickly being filled up (**Figure 28–7**), and news reports highlight the plastic marine debris in what some have called the ocean garbage patches [65, 66] (**Figure 28–8**).

Plastics and microplastics (less than 5 mm in length), are now infiltrating the food chain through zooplankton and other marine life. Industries and legislatures alike are facing the challenge of handling solid waste in an economical and environmentally attractive manner. Packaging and food waste together are responsible for nearly 45 percent of the materials in U.S. landfills [64].

Some strategies include source reduction or eliminating unnecessary packaging and using lighter-weight materials; reusable plastic containers and pallets; recycling (**Figure 28–9**), which provides another source of raw materials and decreases the waste going to landfills; incineration, burning waste properly without causing air pollution; and landfilling—the least desirable

Figure 28–7
Nearly half of the trash in landfills is wasted food and food packaging. Source reduction, reuse, and recycling are all important strategies to reduce trash. (Huguette Roe/Shutterstock)

method but the most commonly used. **Table 28–3** provides data about some of these strategies. The success of these strategies will depend on communication between industry and government, the creation of markets for recycled goods, the development of effective disposal systems, public support of recycling programs, and individual efforts in appropriate handling of trash.

FOOD SPOILAGE CAUSES

When foods spoil, they become inedible or hazardous to eat because of chemical and physical changes that occur within the food. The two major causes of food spoilage are the growth of microorganisms, including bacteria, yeasts, and molds, and the action of **enzymes** that occur naturally in the food. Additional causes of food spoilage are nonenzymatic reactions such as oxidation and, mechanical damage such as bruising, undesirable drying, and damage from insects and rodents.

Microorganisms

Although microorganisms can cause food spoilage, they also have important advantageous roles in food preservation and processing. For example, certain cheeses, such as Roquefort and Camembert, are ripened by molds; other cheeses are ripened by bacteria. Production of some Oriental foods, including soy sauce, requires fermentation by molds. Yeast is an essential ingredient in bread and is needed by the brewing industry. Buttermilk, yogurt, sauerkraut, and fermented pickles owe their special desirable flavors to bacterial action. (Some basic characteristics of molds, yeasts, and bacteria were described in Chapter 2.)

Enzymes

Enzymes are present in any food that has been living tissue, such as meat, fish, fruits, vegetables, milk, and eggs. Unless undesirable enzyme action is controlled or the enzymes are destroyed (often by heating), they may be responsible for unwanted chemical changes in preserved foods. (General characteristics of enzymes were discussed in Chapter 7.)

Drying, Bruising, and Oxidation

Proper packaging of food plays an important role in controlling food spoilage resulting from **desiccation** (severe drying), bruising, and damage by insects and rodents. Oxidation of fats may also be retarded to some degree by appropriate packaging as well as by the control of environmental conditions and the addition of antioxidants. Biodegradable polymer films offer alternative packaging without the environmental problems produced by plastic packaging [34].

Edible films or coatings composed of lipids, resins, polysaccharides, proteins, or combinations of

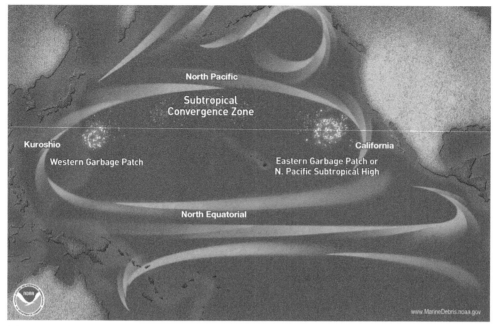

(a)

(b)

Figure 28–8

(a) Some of our trash ends up in lakes, rivers, and then ocean. This NOAA figure shows the location of ground-up plastic particles in the ocean. The location of this plastic is influenced by ocean currents. Seafood and other sea creatures are negatively impacted by this plastic. (NOAA)

(b) Everyone has a responsibility to prevent trash from getting into our waterways. (David W. Leindecker/Shutterstock)

these substances are used on a variety of food products. On fresh fruits and vegetables, for example, films and coatings are (1) moisture barriers and (2) oxygen and carbon dioxide barriers to control respiration in the tissues and reduce postharvest decay [4].

FOOD PRESERVATION BASICS

All methods used for preserving foods are based on the general principle of preventing or retarding the causes of spoilage—microbial decomposition, enzymatic and nonenzymatic chemical reactions, and damage from

Figure 28–9

Recycling is one part of the solution to reducing trash in the landfills and water. (Auremar/123RF)

unfavorable to microbial growth, whereas sufficiently high temperatures destroy spoilage agents.

Cold Temperatures. Cold temperatures inhibit the growth of microorganisms, although some destruction of microbial cells occurs at very low temperatures. With chilling, the length of time that the food remains wholesome varies with the storage temperature and with the type of food being chilled. It also depends on the type of packaging, including modified atmosphere packaging and vacuum cooking–packaging, which extend the effective period of refrigerated storage for food. Refrigerated foods with extended shelf life have generally received precooking or minimal processing. The chief microbiological concern for refrigerated extended shelf life foods is the growth of **psychrotrophic** and **mesophilic** pathogens that might occur during extended refrigerated storage or temperature abuse [46].

Refrigeration and Controlled-Atmosphere Storage. In most refrigerators, maintenance of a temperature of 41° (5°C) or lower preserves many foods for only a few days. In cold-storage warehouses, the time is increased. Here the temperature is lower and the humidity controlled, both conditions favoring preservation. Control and monitoring of gases in the atmosphere of the cold-storage facility (controlled-atmosphere storage) are also used in some cases to retard ripening or maturation changes that decrease the storage life of fresh produce. Apples are often stored in controlled-atmosphere storage to maintain quality for extended periods after harvest (see Chapter 20).

Freezing. Freezing can preserve foods for long but not indefinite periods of time provided that the quality

mechanical causes, insects, and rodents. When the growth of microorganisms is only retarded or inhibited, preservation is temporary. When spoilage organisms are completely destroyed and the food is protected so that no other microorganisms are permitted to reinfect it, more permanent preservation is achieved.

No method of food preservation improves the original quality of a food product. If a preserved food is to be of satisfactory quality, then the starting material must be fresh, flavorful produce at an optimal stage of ripeness or maturity.

Preservation by Temperature Control

Either cold or hot temperatures can be used to preserve foods. Cold temperatures produce an environment

Table 28–3
PACKAGING WASTE MANAGEMENT STRATEGIES

Strategy	
Pay-as-you-throw programs	Waste reductions of 14 to 27 percent in communities where consumers pay for trash removal based on amount of trash.
Source reduction	Manufacturers are "lightweighting" packages by making more lightweight containers. Glass containers decreased 50 percent in weight (1992–2002). Aluminum decreased 26 percent in weight (1975–2005). Steel cans decreased 40 percent in weight since 1970. 1-gallon milk jugs decreased 30 percent in last 20 years.
Reuse	Refillable containers are being produced.
Recycle	30 million tons of containers and packaging recycled in 2005, representing 40 percent of the packaging generated.
Combustion	Controlled burning of waste in designated facility. Heat can be recovered from combustion to produce energy. Air emissions must be controlled.
Landfills	New landfill technologies are being developed to improve the degradation of waste. Air emissions and potential ground water contamination must be controlled.

Source: Reference 45.

of the food is initially good and the temperature of storage is well below the actual freezing temperature of the food. For the highest retention of both flavor and nutritive value in frozen foods, the freezer should be maintained at no higher than 0°F (−18°C) [27]. Care must be exercised in the marketing of frozen foods to ensure that they are held at freezing temperatures at all times as they move through the various market channels to the consumer.

The action of enzymes already present in the tissues is retarded at freezing temperatures. In certain products such as vegetables, however, enzyme action may still produce undesirable effects on flavor and texture during freezer storage. The enzymes, therefore, must be destroyed by heating the vegetables in hot water or steam, a process called *blanching*, before they are frozen.

Hot Temperatures/Thermal Processing. Hot temperatures preserve by destroying both microorganisms and enzymes. Yeasts, molds, and enzymes are readily destroyed at the boiling temperature of water. The heating must be maintained long enough to permit all parts of the food to reach the necessary temperature. Heat penetration is sometimes slow in such foods as pears or peaches.

Bacteria are less readily destroyed than yeasts, molds, and enzymes. The vegetative or active cells are more easily destroyed than **spore** forms. Many bacterial spores, including spores of *Clostridium botulinum*, are highly resistant to heat, especially in a low-acid environment. Care must be exercised in the heat processing of canned food to ensure destruction of bacterial spores. **Botulism** in the United States can occur because of the consumption of inadequately processed home-canned foods, usually low-acid vegetables or meats. *Clostridium botulinum* may also be found in home-prepared garlic-seasoned oils that have been improperly handled (see Chapter 2).

Canning. Canning as a method of food preservation involves essentially the complete destruction of microorganisms and their spores, as well as enzymes, by the use of high temperatures, followed by sealing of the container to prevent recontamination of the food (**Figure 28–10**). The food in this case is essentially sterilized.

Retort pouches or packages have been developed as flexible packaging for thermoprocessed foods. Lightweight pouches with a relatively thin cross section of a food improve the quality of sterilized packaged food because less time is required for complete heat penetration. Energy savings also result. Because the weight of the packages is much less than that of metal cans and lids, the ease of transporting is increased, and the expense is decreased [61]. Tuna in retort packaging made its debut in 2000 [11]. Chapter 1 discussed the use of retort packaged foods in military rations.

Bottled green beans, cooked in a home pressure canner, are sealed so that recontamination by microorganisms cannot occur. Bottles and lids designed for home "canning" must be used. (© Douglas and Barbara Scheule)

Pasteurization. **Pasteurization** of food products involves the use of temperatures lower than required for **sterilization**. Foods that are often pasteurized include milk, fruit juices, and eggs that are to be frozen or dried. All pathogenic microorganisms—but not all other microorganisms present—are destroyed by pasteurization. Thus, pasteurization results in a more limited or temporary preservation period than sterilization and canning.

New and Emerging Thermal Processing Methods. Infrared heating is accomplished by the release of energy through electromagnetic waves from 0.75 μm to 1,000 μm. (See Chapter 5 for more about the electromagnetic spectrum.) The absorption of the infrared heat by water, organic compounds, and biological polymers in food increases molecular vibration, and thus can enable thermal processing of food [44]. Infrared energy has a limited penetration and is therefore most effective for thin foods.

Radio frequencies can used to pasteurize and apply thermal heat for other thermal processing purposes. Radio frequency processing uses electromagnetic waves of the frequencies 13.56 MHz, 27.12 MHz, or 40.68 MHz (see Chapter 5). The energy is applied via a pair of electrodes that causes dielectric molecules in food to vibrate, and thus generate heat [40]. As compared to microwaves, the radio frequency direction can be controlled, and also is capable of penetrating deeper into bulky foods thereby enabling faster heating.

Microwaves have been used to process food for a number of years (see Chapter 5). Drying, cooking, and tempering have all been accomplished with microwaves. Microwaves in the electromagnet spectrum at frequencies of 2,450 MHz and 915 MHz are used in the United States. Most foods are dielectric, and thus the molecules fibrate when in an electromagnetic field and heat is generated. Microwave heat is used on a limited base for the pasteurization and sterilization of foods [38]. However, microwave heat retains nutrients, uses less energy, and causes less damage to the food from extended heat application, and therefore may be used more for sterilization and pasteurization in the future.

Solar heat has been used for centuries to dry foods for preservation. It is considered to be likely the first form of food processing used by people. Solar heat is a renewable source of thermal heat. It is increasing being used for food processing and researched for new approaches to enable the large-scale cooking, baking, and drying of foods [43].

Preservation by Moisture Control

Drying. One of the oldest methods of preserving foods involves the removal of moisture until the product is dry. As practically applied, the food is dried in the sun or by air currents and artificial heat until the moisture content of the food is reduced to a level that inhibits the growth of microorganisms. The actual percentage of moisture varies but is usually under 30 percent. Some dehydrated foods such as dried potato slices contain only 2 to 3 percent moisture. Many commercially dried fruits, with intermediate moisture content of about 15 to 35 or 40 percent, have water activity (see Chapter 2) low enough for preservation yet are pleasant to eat directly without rehydration [23]. Osmotic drying is used in some commercial products such as *craisins*. In osmotic drying, a strong syrup is used to draw water from the food and then the food is finish dried with air [15].

Some foods can be easily dried at home, including most garden vegetables, fruits, and garden herbs, such as parsley and oregano. Drying can be done in driers especially designed for this purpose, in the oven, or, in sunny climates, in trays placed in the sun. Vegetables, with few exceptions, should be **blanched** before drying to stop the action of enzymes that produce undesirable changes in texture and flavor during storage. Dried vegetables that have been blanched also dry more easily and retain more vitamins. Light-colored fruits, such as apples, apricots, and peaches, are of better quality when they are treated to prevent enzymatic browning. The use of ascorbic acid (vitamin C), citric acid, or lemon juice (a source of citric acid) can all be used. Various powdered products, such as Fruit-Fresh®, can be purchased as the source of citric acid or vitamin C. Alternatively, sulfur and sulfites have been used in the past, but can cause serious asthmatic reactions [17]. Chapter 20 offers more information about enzymatic browning.

Freeze-Drying. There are three components to freeze drying, (1) freezing, (2) sublimation drying, and (3) desorption. The freezing process needs to be rapid to avoid the formation of large ice crystals that will result in an inferior final food quality. Large crystals will damage the texture of the food product. Next during drying, the pressure is lowered with a high vacuum and mild heat is applied. Under the reduced pressure of the vacuum, the ice in the frozen food changes directly to water vapor (sublimes) and is carried away by the circulating heated air. This phase can require several hours to two days during which about 95 percent of the water is removed [41]. The final stage is a secondary drying at a higher temperature to vaporize water molecules (desorption). Pressure may or may not be lowered in this phase.

Freeze dried foods ultimately contain only 1 to 4 percent moisture. They are of superior quality as compared to other dehydrated foods [41]. Freeze dried food remains frozen through most of the drying period; it does not get warm as does food that is subjected to ordinary drying processes. Fresh flavors and textures are therefore better preserved by freeze-drying than by sun-drying or other procedures of artificial drying without vacuum.

Freeze-dried foods do not require refrigeration and offer the advantage of being light when transported. Sir Edmund Hillary took 300 pounds of freeze-dried items on his Himalayan mountain-climbing expedition. The products reconstituted to 1,200 pounds and included ham, chicken, chops, steaks, fruits, and vegetables. Although refrigeration is not required, freeze-dried products do tend to deteriorate with long storage unless they are properly packaged.

Use of Preservatives

Adding chemical preservatives to a food product is another method of inhibiting the growth of undesirable microorganisms. Common preservatives, sometimes called *household preservatives,* include acids, salt, sugar, spices, and smoke. It is the phenols in wood smoke that seem to exert the major preservative action.

Acids and Sugar. Vinegar contains acetic acid and is commonly used, along with salt, to pickle vegetables (**Figure 28–11**). In pickle and sauerkraut fermentations, lactic and other organic acids are produced over time by friendly bacteria present on the vegetables. Not only does the acid prevent unwanted microbial growth, but additional flavor substances are produced by the desirable bacteria. Sugar in large amounts is used in the production of jellies, jams, and preserves (**Figure 28–12**). It acts as a preservative by binding the moisture necessary for microbial growth and activity.

Spices. Spices inhibit bacterial growth to some degree but vary in their effectiveness. Ground cinnamon and cloves are more valuable than nutmeg and allspice in quantities that can be used without negatively impacting flavor. However, spices themselves are often

responsible for introducing bacteria into foods. Oils of spice are sterile and have a more inhibitory effect on microbial growth than ground spices.

Other Preservatives. Numerous preservatives are used as food additives and must be approved for use by the U.S. Food and Drug Administration (FDA). Thorough testing for safety is required before approval is given. (Food additives were discussed in Chapter 6.) Sodium benzoate, used in very small amounts in some margarines, and sodium propionate, used to retard molding in bread, are examples of preservatives that may be added

to foods. An antioxidant is a special type of preservative that inhibits the spoilage of fats that may occur from a nonenzymatic oxidative process (see Chapter 8). The FDA has approved nisin, or *bacteriocin*, a polypeptide antibacterial substance, for use in some pasteurized cheese spreads. It is active only against gram-positive bacteria and is approved for use to inhibit the growth of *Clostridium botulinum* spores. The bacterium *Streptococcus lactis* produces this antibiotic [21, 24].

Preservation by Irradiation

Food is exposed to ionizing radiation to (1) reduce microbial levels, (2) destroy pathogens, (3) extend shelf life, and (4) remove insect infestation [42, 59]. Irradiation has been found to be safe through more than 50 years of research. It has been approved for use in several foods by the FDA and the U.S. Department of Agriculture (USDA) (**Table 28–4**). The World Health Organization, the UN Food and Agricultural Organization, and the International Atomic Energy Agency have concluded that irradiated food is safe. Additionally, it has been endorsed by the American Medical Association [63]. Irradiation of half of all ground beef, poultry, pork, and processed meat has been estimated by experts at the Centers for Disease Control and Prevention to reduce foodborne illnesses by one million cases [60]. More than 40 food products are irradiated in over 37 countries [63].

Irradiation has been called "cold" pasteurization by some because it destroys microorganisms without heating the food. Sources of radiation energy allowed for food processing include **gamma rays** (produced from cobalt-60 and cesium-137), beta rays generated by electron beams, and X-rays [59]. Electron beams are produced with electricity [42]. Ionizing radiation, produced by one of these methods, has energy high enough to change atoms in the irradiated food by removing an electron to form an **ion**. These freed electrons break chemical bonds in the microbial DNA, thereby killing the microbe. Ionizing radiation does not have enough energy to split atoms in the food and cause it to become **radioactive**. Thus, irradiated foods are not radioactive.

Irradiated foods marketed for consumers must be labeled with an official logo (**Figure 28–13**) and the statement "treated with radiation" or "treated by irradiation." Consumer acceptance is important for commercial application of food irradiation. It is important for consumers to know that irradiation of food can effectively reduce or eliminate pathogens and spoilage microorganisms while maintaining wholesomeness, sensory quality, and nutrient content [59].

Preservation by Other Methods

A variety of additional methods for food preservation are in use or being explored.

Table 28–4
FOOD IRRADIATION IN THE UNITED STATES

Product	Purpose of Irradiation	Dose Permitted (kGy)**	Date
Wheat and wheat powder	Insect disinfestations, mold control	0.2–0.5	1963
Pork carcasses or fresh noncut processed cuts	Control of *Trichinella spiralis*	0.3–1.0 max.	1985
White potatoes	Sprout inhibition, extend shelf life	0.05–0.15	1964
Herbs, spices, and dry vegetable seasoning	Microbial control, decontamination, or disinfestation of insects	30.0 max.	1986
Dry or dehydrated enzyme preparations	Control of insects and microorganisms	10.0 max.	1986
Fruits and vegetables, fresh	Disinfection, delay maturation	1.0 max.	1986
Poultry, fresh or frozen	Control of illness-causing microorganisms such as *Salmonella*	3.0 max.	1990
Poultry, fresh or frozen (USDA)	Microbial control	1.5–4.5	1992
Meat, frozen, packaged*	Sterilization	44.0 min.	1995
Animal feed and pet food	*Salmonella* control	2.0–25.0	1995
Meat, uncooked, chilled	Microbial control	4.5 max.	1997
Meat, uncooked, frozen	Microbial control	7.0 max.	1997
Meat, uncooked, chilled (USDA)	Microbial control	4.5 max.	2000
Meat, uncooked, frozen (USDA)	Microbial control	7.0 max.	2000
Shell eggs, fresh	*Salmonella* control	3.0 max.	2000
Seeds for sprouting	Microbial control	8.0 max.	2000
Molluscan shellfish, fresh or frozen	*Vibrio, Salmonella, Listeria* control	5.5 max	Approved
Uncooked meat, meat by-products, and certain meat food products	Pathogen control and shelf life extension	4.5 max.	Approved
Fresh iceberg lettuce and fresh spinach.	Pathogen control and shelf life extension	4.0 max	Approved
Chilled or frozen raw, cooked, or partially cooked crustaceans or dried crustaceans (water activity less than 0.85)	Pathogen control and shelf life extension	6.0 max	Approved

*For meats used solely in National Aeronautics and Space Administration (NASA) space flight programs.
**The amount of radiation energy absorbed is measured in units of grays (or kilograms, meaning 1,000 grays (kGy)). One gray equals 1 joule of absorbed energy per kilogram.

Source: References 59, 29.

Figure 28–13
An irradiated food on the retail market should bear the international radura symbol along with either of the statements "treated with radiation" or "treated by irradiation." (U.S. Department of Agriculture)

High Pressure. High-pressure processing, as discussed earlier in the chapter, is the application of high pressure to food. It is a nonthermal, batch process inside equipment able to raise pressure up to 120,000 psi. It has been commonly used for raw juices because it can destroy pathogens without imparting a cooked flavor to the juice. High-pressure processing can also be used for ready-to-eat meats, seafood, and a variety of prepared salads and other foods [16]. High-pressure processing does not destroy spores, such as those formed by *Clostridium botulinum*. However, a combination process using heat to at least 250°F (121°C) with high-pressure processing, called pressure assisted thermal sterilization (PATS) can effectively destroy these spores at a milder heat treatment as compared to traditional canning processes [16].

Ozone. Ozone has been used as a disinfectant for bottled water for a number of years. In 2001, it was approved for direct contact with food under the FDA Final Rule 21 CFR Part 173.336 [37]. Ozone is a strong oxidizer capable of killing microorganisms. It is a gaseous form of oxygen, composed of three oxygen atoms. It leaves no harmful chemical residuals and therefore is environmentally friendly. Foods may be treated with ozone in a gaseous or liquid form [37].

Ultrasound. Ultrasound is an emerging technology that is nonthermal, and it is considered to be an environmentally green choice. It can be used to inactivate microorganisms and enzymes to preserve foods. Ultrasound works through the rapid creation and collapse of bubbles by the ultrasonic waves. Wave frequencies of 20 to 600 kHz are typically used [39].

FREEZING

Clarence Birdseye, a food technology pioneer, began development of the frozen food industry in the 1920s with the production of frozen fish. He applied his engineering skills to develop plate freezers and blast freezers not unlike those used today. Although interrupted by World War II, the infant frozen food industry grew rapidly during the late 1940s and 1950s [6]. Equipment for rapid freezing and widespread availability of freezers in both home and institutional kitchens contributed importantly to this growth. Since the early days, there have been many improvements in freezing technology. Researchers have studied the freezing process itself in an attempt to understand and minimize the effects on food quality at each stage in the production of frozen foods. A large assortment of frozen foods is marketed. The popularity of the microwave oven for reheating frozen foods has also contributed to growth in the frozen food industry.

The frozen food industry continues to work at improving the quality of their products. Some areas of research include air-impingement, pressure shift, and extrusion freezing methods. Air-impingement freezing uses thin, high-velocity jets of air directed at the food to accomplish fast cooling rates, resulting in reduced moisture loss and formation of smaller ice crystals [50]. Pressure-shift freezing uses an increase of pressure to depress the freezing point of water, thereby allowing the product to be cooled to −4°F (−20°C) without the water freezing. When the pressure is released, the water freezes rapidly, and smaller, uniform ice crystals are formed. Extrusion freezing is a way to freeze ice cream to −4°F (−20°C) directly from the freezer. Traditionally, ice cream is frozen to 19°F (−7°C), then placed in a hardening room to complete the freezing process. Extrusion freezing has been shown to produce a more uniform crystal size [50].

Producers of frozen foods are also concerned with maintaining quality as the food moves through the transport and distribution systems, where it must consistently be held at low temperatures. Time-temperature indicators are a means of monitoring and controlling critical temperatures during the storage, handling, and distribution of frozen and refrigerated foods.

The freezing of foods in the home can be advantageous to enable the preservation of produce from home gardens or to extend the storage of purchased foods. Larger quantities of a variety of foods may also be prepared at home and then frozen for later use. For example, cookies, lasagna, or chili may be readily frozen for later use. The home freezer contributes to efficient management in meal planning and preparation, and it has the advantage of allowing quantity buying on a less frequent basis.

The Freezing Process

Freezing is the change in physical state from liquid to solid that occurs when heat is removed from a substance. When foods are frozen, they undergo a phase change of liquid water into solid ice. The water molecules reduce their motion and form an organized pattern of crystals. The three stages in the freezing process are as follows:

1. The temperature of the food is lowered to freezing.
2. Ice crystals begin to form as the liquid reaches the freezing point; the temperature required varies with the product to be frozen. For pure water, the freezing temperature is 32°F (0°C), whereas for water that contains dissolved solutes, that freezing point is depressed. As ice crystals form, the remaining water becomes more concentrated with solute, lowering the freezing point still further. This process is continuous, but the zone of maximum crystal formation in frozen foods is 25 to 31°F (−4 to −0.5°C). See **Figure 28–14**.
3. After ice formation ceases, the temperature of the frozen product is gradually lowered to the necessary storage temperature.

In a frozen food product, the activity of microorganisms is negligible; however, upon thawing these microorganisms can become active again. (See Chapter 2 on food safety.) Enzymatic processes may continue although at a reduced rate. Fast freezing and low storage temperatures are favorable for holding enzyme activity to a minimum and for the best retention of nutrients. Most vegetables are **blanched** before freezing to destroy enzymes so that enzymatic

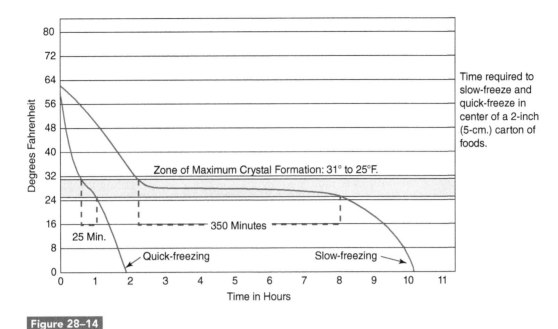

Figure 28–14

Diagram showing differences in the time and temperature between quick and slow freezing.

action does not produce off-flavors and undesirable texture changes during frozen storage. When the secondary changes in flavor and texture resulting from blanching are unacceptable, as with freezing strawberries or other fresh fruits, vitamin C (ascorbic acid) may be added to control some of the enzymatic reactions [50]. After thawing, the growth of microorganisms may occur at a rapid rate.

The first commercial method of freezing foods was the slow-freezing process sometimes called *sharp freezing*. In this method, foods are placed in refrigerated rooms ranging from 25 to −20°F (−4 to −29°C), but large pieces of food or large containers of food require many hours or days to freeze. Quick-freezing methods use lower temperatures, −25 to −40°F (−32 to −40°C), so the time of freezing is greatly reduced relative to that achieved in sharp freezing. Other factors that aid in hastening the freezing process are small masses of foods, contact with freezing coils or metal plates, and rapidly moving currents of frigid air. Figure 28–14 shows the relative differences in time of freezing by quick- and slow-freezing methods. The freezing of food in most home freezers is a relatively slow process.

The process of freezing rapidly at very low temperatures (−76°F [−60°C] or lower) is called *cryogenic freezing*. In cryogenic freezers, which use liquid nitrogen or carbon dioxide, the food is cooled so quickly that many tiny ice crystals form simultaneously, producing a much smaller number of large crystals. Tiny ice crystals have a less damaging effect on plant and animal cells than large crystals.

Changes during Freezing, Storage, and Thawing

Changes may occur in many foods that are to be frozen as they are held before freezing. Careful handling, transportation, and storage procedures must be used before and during preparation for freezing to minimize quality loss [50]. Crops should be harvested at the optimal stage of maturity and the produce frozen before the sugar content is reduced or undesirable enzyme activity develops. Such care results in high-quality frozen produce. Changes in food also occur during freezing, holding frozen, and then thawing.

Formation of Ice Crystals. The texture of many frozen foods may be affected by ice crystal formation, changes in those crystals during frozen storage, and later thawing. The effects of freezing depend partly on the nature and state of the material that is frozen. Vegetable and fruit tissues, in particular, decrease in firmness with freezing and thawing. Whether plant tissues are blanched may affect how ice crystals form in the tissues. For example, in unblanched tissue, the cell walls are intact, and the exchange of water through **osmosis** is possible. If the freezing rate is slow, significant amounts of water may translocate from within cells into the extracellular medium. The formation of ice crystals in extracellular spaces causes injury to the cells. On thawing, not all of the moisture is reabsorbed by the cells.

With rapid freezing, more and smaller ice crystals are formed within cells. These small ice crystals also cause damage to cell structures, although the damage is less than that caused by large crystals. The loss of water held in the cells (turgor) as the cells are ruptured during freezing is probably responsible for much of the loss of firmness in frozen and thawed plant tissues.

As the temperature is reduced during freezing and more ice crystals form, the concentration of dissolved substances in the unfrozen medium increases, and the viscosity of this unfrozen portion increases. At some temperature, depending on the composition of the system, the viscosity of the unfrozen matrix becomes so high that molecular motion is greatly inhibited. Unfrozen water molecules can then no longer migrate to join ice crystals. Other reaction rates become slowed. The temperature at which this transformation takes place is called the *glass transition temperature* (T_g). The transition state can be detected by observing changes in various dielectric, mechanical, and thermodynamic properties [52]. Frozen storage stability is greatest at or below T_g temperature. This information can be valuable in optimizing storage conditions for particular frozen products as researchers develop methods of modifying T_g [50].

Enzyme Action. Enzymes are present in all living tissue. Respiration, catalyzed by many enzymes, continues in fruits and vegetables after they are severed from the growing plant. These metabolic reactions reduce sugar content, which accounts for the loss of sweetness in such vegetables as peas and corn. Other enzymatic changes also occur. Unless the enzymes responsible for undesirable chemical changes are destroyed before foods are frozen, the foods may show various undesirable color, flavor, and texture changes during freezing, storage, and thawing. Freezing inhibits enzyme action, but it neither destroys the enzymes nor entirely stops their actions.

Vegetables are blanched before freezing to inactivate enzymes that may cause browning, destruction of chlorophyll and carotenoid pigments, or development of unpleasant flavors during storage [4, 49]. In addition, blanching shrinks the vegetable tissues so that they pack more easily, expels air so that the potential for oxidation is lessened, and decreases the microbial load. From the standpoint of both overcooking and loss of soluble nutrients, blanching should be as short as possible.

Light-colored fruits, such as peaches and apples, are particularly susceptible to **enzymatic oxidative browning** in both the fresh and frozen states. The addition of sugar or syrup to the fruit before freezing aids in the retention of color, although some darkening may occur if the fruits are held too long. Sugar also aids in preventing marked flavor changes and loss of the natural aroma. The addition of vitamin C to the syrup is effective in preventing browning; it acts as an **antioxidant**. Citric and other organic acids may also be effective agents for some fruits by lowering the pH enough to interfere with the activity of the browning enzymes.

Nonenzymatic Oxidation. The process of **nonenzymatic oxidation** of fat in frozen foods may occur. Residual oxygen is usually present in frozen foods. The fat of pork is particularly susceptible to oxidation and the development of rancidity. Bacon, for example, does not keep well in frozen storage. Antioxidants may be added to some products commercially to control unwanted oxidation.

Freezer Burn. If food products to be frozen are not properly packaged with **moisture- and vapor-proof material**, they tend to lose moisture by **sublimation**. In this process, some of the ice changes directly to water vapor without going through the liquid state, and the water vapor collects to form frost inside the package and/or inside the freezing compartment. **Desiccation** or dehydration thus occurs.

The term *freezer burn* as applied to frozen foods refers to dehydration resulting in discoloration, change in texture, and off-flavors. This condition is often observed in frozen poultry and other flesh foods as white or brownish dehydrated areas. The dehydrated areas are also generally tough or leathery. Freezer burn may occur in other foods as well. Proper packaging is important in the control of freezer burn.

Activity of Microorganisms. Usually present in frozen foods, microorganisms' activity is negligible as long as the storage temperature remains below 16 to 10°F (−9 to −12°C). The microorganisms become

---

FOCUS ON SCIENCE
WHY ARE VEGETABLES BUT NOT FRUITS BLANCHED BEFORE FREEZING?

Vegetables have different characteristics compared to fruits and, as a result, can be blanched prior to freezing. Fruits will turn mushy after defrosting if blanched. This change in texture is not a problem for fruits that are going to be cooked after defrosting. However, if frozen fruits are to be used without cooking, they should not be blanched. Instead, the fruit should be treated with an antioxidant, such as citric acid or ascorbic acid, to prevent discoloration.

active at warmer temperatures. They may begin to multiply rapidly as soon as defrosting occurs. It is important that frozen foods be held at optimal, nonfluctuating storage temperatures and be used as soon as they are defrosted.

Selection of Foods for Freezing

Success in freezing depends to a considerable degree on the kinds and varieties of foods selected for freezing. Local agricultural experiment stations (or state extension offices) can provide advice concerning the locally grown fruits and vegetables that are best adapted to freezing preservation. The fruits that are least changed by freezing preservation include red tart cherries, cranberries, currants, gooseberries, blueberries, and raspberries. Strawberries and peaches yield frozen products superior to those preserved by other methods. Loganberries, boysenberries, blackberries, dewberries, pineapples, melons, apples, and plums also yield good frozen products.

Although citrus fruits do not freeze well, their juices freeze quite satisfactorily, as do apple cider and other fruit juices. Some fruit juices are concentrated by partial freezing, with the ice crystals being removed by straining. Some vegetables do not freeze satisfactorily, including green onions, lettuce and other salad greens, radishes, and raw tomatoes.

Fruits and vegetables should be frozen at the peak stage of maturity and quality. Meats and poultry to be frozen should be of high quality. Fish deteriorates so rapidly that it is best frozen as soon as possible after it is caught.

Techniques for Freezing

Fruits. Detailed instructions for the freezing of fruits and vegetables are provided in the Cooperative Extension Service, University of Georgia/Athens [2], and the *Ball Blue Book* [31].

Mixing juicy fruits with dry sugar draws out the juices to form a syrup. Alternatively, the fruit can be covered with a sugar syrup. Most fruits require either sugar or syrup treatment to protect against enzymatic changes during freezing and storage. As noted, blanching changes the fresh flavor and texture characteristics of fruits and is, for this reason, not commonly used. Blueberries and cranberries yield satisfactory products when frozen without sugar or syrup or scalding. Strawberries can be frozen whole, but they retain their best color and flavor in sliced form in sugar or syrup packs.

When syrups are used, they are prepared and chilled prior to packing. Vitamin C (ascorbic acid) may be added to the syrup to control browning of the fruit—approximately ½ teaspoon of crystalline vitamin C per quart of syrup. Commercial products containing vitamin C are also available for use in retarding the browning of frozen fruit. Syrup concentrations usually vary from about 30 to 70 percent sugar, although lower concentrations may be preferred from both a flavor and nutritive standpoint.

Vegetables. Most vegetables yield products of the best quality and flavor when frozen on the day they are harvested. If immediate freezing is impossible, adequate refrigeration is necessary for the interim. The speed at which the vegetables go from garden to freezer is one of the most important factors affecting quality in frozen products. The stage of maturity is also important. For those vegetables that change rapidly in maturity, such as peas, corn, snap beans, lima beans, soybeans, and asparagus, one or two days may mean the difference between a young tender vegetable and one that is tough and of poor quality.

Washing, draining, and sorting of the vegetables usually precede trimming and cutting. To avoid undesirable enzyme-related changes, most vegetables require blanching to inactivate the offending enzymes. Blanching can be done in boiling water, in steam, or by the application of microwaves. Water-soluble constituents are better retained in steam blanching, but efficient steaming equipment is sometimes difficult to obtain for home use. A tightly closed container is needed, one that holds enough rapidly boiling water to form steam, and a rack to hold the vegetables above the water level. If boiling water is used, enough water should be used so that the boiling does not stop when the vegetables are placed in the water. Wire racks are ideal containers to hold the vegetables. At least 1 gallon of water per pound of vegetables is needed, and more might be desirable.

Important as the blanching process is, it should not be overdone. The shortest possible time needed to inactivate enzymes should be used to avoid both actual cooking and the loss of water-soluble nutrients. Small quantities of a vegetable are blanched at one time so that all pieces will be quickly, thoroughly, and uniformly heated. After blanching, the vegetables must be cooled quickly to about 50°F (10°C) in cold running water or ice water. Chilling is necessary to avoid overheating and to maintain quality. Prompt freezing is very important in the freezing preservation of foods, particularly vegetables. The sooner vegetables are frozen after blanching, the better the product is likely to be.

Meat, Fish, and Poultry. Meats to be frozen are usually cut into pieces of a suitable size for cooking. The pieces may be steaks, chops, roasts, ground meat, cubes for stews, or other forms. While not required, removal of the bone conserves freezer space. Fish can be boned and packed as fillets or steaks. Poultry can likewise be frozen. Only high-quality fresh meat, poultry, and seafood products should be frozen.

Careful wrapping or packaging with recommended packaging materials is essential in protecting the products from oxidation and desiccation. More information on the freezing of meat, fish, and poultry is found in the *Ball Blue Book* [31] and in bulletins obtained from county agricultural extension agents [2].

Eggs. Frozen egg whites seem to lose none of the quality needed for culinary uses; however, yolks become gummy and gelled on thawing because of an irreversible change involving the lipoproteins. To be usable, a stabilizer such as sugar, syrup, or salt must be added to yolks before freezing. Mixed whole eggs usually have a small amount of stabilizer added because they contain the yolk, but they have been successfully frozen without a stabilizer.

When freezing eggs at home, about 1 tablespoon of sugar or corn syrup or ½ teaspoon of salt can be blended with 1 cup of egg yolk before freezing. Defrosted eggs may have a relatively high bacterial count and deteriorate rapidly after defrosting.

Prepared Foods. On the market are many different frozen prepared foods and meals that simply require reheating. Packaging technologies that allow direct heating in the microwave oven or boiling in the bag in which the product was frozen contribute to the wide variety of available choices. Prepared foods that require only thawing, including a variety of baked products, are usually brought into the kitchen for short-term storage only.

Many prepared foods can also be frozen in the kitchen for convenience and efficiency. Various casseroles, main dish items, and plated meals can be prepared in quantity and frozen for future use.

Baked products can be frozen either before or after baking. The storage life of unbaked batters and doughs is usually less than that of the baked products. If frosted or iced cakes are to be frozen, they might be frozen first without wrapping to prevent the wrapping material from sticking to the frosting and then wrapped and returned to the freezer.

Frozen bread doughs can be made from the usual formulations, provided that the amount of yeast is increased by 4 or 5 percent. A short fermentation period is desirable before freezing. If a satisfactory product is to result, sufficient yeast viability must be maintained during freezing and freezer storage to produce adequate amounts of carbon dioxide gas necessary for leavening (see Chapter 15).

Certain foods do not freeze well at home. For example, cooked egg whites toughen and become rubbery, mayonnaise tends to separate as the emulsion breaks, starch-thickened sauces tend to weep as starch retrogradation occurs, and fried foods often

change in flavor when reheated. See Chapter 11 for information about types of starch that may be used in products to be frozen.

Containers

Containers for freezing foods can be made of metal, plastic materials, paper or fiberboard, and certain moisture- and vapor-proof transparent materials, and they should have tight-fitting lids or closures. Although glass containers may be used for freezing, the risk of breakage should be considered. A container that is ideal for freezer use has been described as one that is both airtight to prevent oxidation and moisture- and vapor-proof to prevent dehydration. Cube-shaped containers permit the most efficient use of storage space. It is obvious that rigidity in a container prevents crushing of the products. If containers are made of a material that can be thoroughly cleaned, they may be reused. Moisture- and vapor-proof bags are satisfactory if little handling is required.

Pliable moisture- and vapor-proof bags should have as much air as possible removed from them and should be twisted and tightly closed. Immersing the lower part of the bag and its contents in water while packaging such irregularly shaped items as whole poultry may aid in removing air by the pressure of the water on the bag. Boil-in-the-bag containers and vacuum-packaging systems are available for home use in freezing prepared foods.

The size of the container used is important because many frozen foods should be used very shortly after defrosting (see **Table 28–5**). Containers larger than ½ gallon or 5 pounds are also not recommended because of the slow rate of freezing.

For dry packs, the cartons can be almost completely filled before freezing. Syrup packs, or juicy products such as sliced strawberries mixed with sugar, should have about 10 percent headspace to allow for expansion of the contents during freezing.

Use and Management of the Home Freezer

A freezer can be a convenience in many ways, but careful planning should go into its selection and use. The needs in each situation differ, and freezer use

Table 28–5
SIZE OF CONTAINER IN RELATION TO NUMBER OF SERVINGS

Servings	Size of Container
1 or 2	½ pint
4	1 pint
8	1 quart

should be adapted to individual conditions and preferences. A freezer is an investment and should be kept full or nearly full at all times to minimize the operating cost per unit of food stored. However, the quality of frozen foods is not maintained indefinitely—it decreases with time. Suggested maximum storage periods for maintaining good quality in commercially frozen foods that are stored in home freezers are provided in **Table 28–6**.

Time can be saved by doubling or tripling recipes when they are being prepared if they are suitable for freezing. The frozen products can be conveniently served on busy days. Advance planning in meal preparation and entertaining may be simplified with the use of a freezer. An accurate inventory of frozen foods should be kept.

All foods should be stored no higher than 0°F (−18°C) to maintain palatability and nutritive value. Accurate and effective temperature control is therefore important. If a freezer stops running and remains off for an extended period, several alternatives are possible to keep the food from spoiling. If it is available, enough dry ice may be added to the freezer to maintain below freezing temperatures for a few days. Or the food may be put into insulated boxes or wrapped in newspapers and blankets and rushed to a freezer-locker plant. If the freezer will be off only a few hours, it should simply be kept tightly closed.

Sometimes frozen foods are partially or completely thawed before it is discovered that the freezer is not operating. Although partial thawing and refreezing reduce the quality of most foods, partially thawed foods that still contain ice crystals or foods that are still cold (about 40°F or 4°C) can usually be safely refrozen. Ground meats, poultry, and seafood should not be refrozen if they have thawed completely because bacteria multiply rapidly in these foods. Each package of meat, vegetable, or cooked food should be carefully examined. If the food is thawed or the color or odor is questionable, the food should be discarded because it may be dangerous.

CANNING

Canning involves two processes: (1) the application to foods of temperatures high enough to destroy essentially all microorganisms present, both vegetative cells and spores, and (2) the sealing of the heated product in sterilized airtight containers to prevent recontamination. The degree of heat and the length of heating needed vary with the type of food and the kinds of microorganisms likely to occur. Fruits and tomatoes that are sufficiently acidic are successfully canned at the temperature of boiling water. The time of boiling depends on the degree of acidity, the consistency of the product, the method of preparation, and other factors.

Vegetables, including some low-acid tomatoes, and meats, which are relatively low in acid, must be heated to temperatures higher than that of boiling water at atmospheric pressure. This method involves the use of a pressure canner. Because bacterial spores that may be present are more resistant to heat under conditions of low acidity, the time of heating necessary to destroy them at the temperature of boiling water would likely be several hours. The food would be rather unpalatable after such a prolonged cooking period. Moist heat can destroy microorganisms by coagulating proteins, and it destroys enzymes in a similar manner.

Historical Highlights

The history of canning began about 1795, when the French government offered a prize for the development of a new method of preserving food from one harvest to the next. Nicolas Appert, a Parisian confectioner, worked many years on such a process, and finally, in 1809, he successfully preserved some foods by sealing them with corks in glass bottles and heating them for various lengths of time [18]. Appert received financial support from the French government, including an initial cash award (12,000 francs) for his accomplishment.

With contributions from many workers along the way, the canning industry gradually developed until today cans of food are being filled, sealed, and processed by the millions. The tin canister was first developed in England about 1810. Peter Durand, a broker, was granted a patent in London, possibly as an agent or middleman for a French inventor, Philippe de Girard [19, 20]. Canned foods were produced in England for the British navy in the early 1800s. The retort for pressure canning was developed in Philadelphia around 1874 [25]. Pasteur's work with microorganisms about 1860 began a study of the true causes of food spoilage, opening the door to a scientific approach to the process of canning beginning around the turn of the twentieth century.

Retort is the name of equipment used in commercial canning to obtain the time and temperatures necessary for food preservation. Various types of batch and continuous **retorts** are used in commercial canning [33]. Some retorts agitate or rotate the cans during processing to increase the rate of heat penetration and to aid in heat distribution. Commercial canning also includes methods that employ higher temperatures and shorter time periods than are used in traditional commercial canning. **Aseptic canning** is also practiced, preserving a fresher flavor for many food products. The variety of equipment available for commercial canning provides the industry with the flexibility it needs to develop and produce unique food products and to select various packaging options. Semirigid and flexible packages, such as the **retort pouch**, can be

Table 28–6
SUGGESTED MAXIMUM HOME-STORAGE PERIODS TO MAINTAIN GOOD QUALITY IN COMMERCIALLY FROZEN FOODS

Food	Approximate Holding Period at 0°F (–18°C) (Months)	Food	Approximate Holding Period at 0°F (–18°C) (Months)	Food	Approximate Holding Period at 0°F (–18°C) (Months)
Fruits and vegetables		Pies (unbaked)		Cooked chicken and turkey	
Fruits		Apple	8		
Cherries	12	Boysenberry	8	Chicken or turkey dinners (sliced meat and gravy)	6
		Cherry	8		
		Peach	8		
Peaches	12			Chicken or turkey pies	12
Raspberries	12			Fried chicken	4
Strawberries	12			Fried chicken dinners	4
Fruit juice concentrates		**Meat**			
Apple	12	Beef			
Grape	12	Hamburger or chopped (thin) steaks	3		
Orange	12				
Vegetables				**Fish**	
Asparagus	8	Roasts	12	Cod, flounder, haddock, halibut, pollock	6
Beans	8	Steaks	12		
Cauliflower	8	Lamb			
Corn	8	Patties (ground meat)	3	Mullet, ocean perch, sea trout, striped bass	3
		Roasts	12		
Peas	8	Pork, cured			
Spinach	8	Pork, fresh	2	Pacific Ocean perch	2
		Chops	4	Salmon steaks	2
Frozen desserts		Roasts	8	Sea trout, dressed	3
Ice cream	1	Sausage	2	Striped bass, dressed	3
Sherbet	1			Whiting, drawn	4
		Veal			
Baked goods		Cutlets, chops	4	**Shellfish**	
Bread and yeast rolls		Roasts	8	Clams, shucked	3
White bread	3	Cooked meat		Crabmeat	
Cinnamon rolls		Meat dinners	3	Dungeness	3
Plain rolls	3	Meat pie	3	King	10
Cakes		Swiss steak	3	Oysters, shucked	4
Angel	2			Shrimp	12
Chiffon	2	**Poultry**			
Chocolate layer	4	Chicken	9		
Fruit	12	Cut up	3	**Cooked fish and shellfish**	
Pound	6	Livers	12	Fish with cheese sauce	3
Yellow	6	Whole	6	Fish with lemon butter sauce	3
		Duck, whole	6		
Danish pastry	3	Goose, whole	6	Fried fish dinner	3
Doughnuts		Turkey	12	Fried fish sticks, scallops, or shrimp	3
Cake type	3	Cut up			
Yeast Raised	3	Whole			
				Shrimp creole	3
				Tuna pie	3

Source: U.S. Department of Agriculture.

readily handled to produce shelf-stable foods. Tuna is an example of a food product often sold in a retort pouch. For reasons of safety and compliance, in all cases of commercial canning, careful written documentation of temperature distribution during processing must be maintained [48].

Although much of our canned food is now produced commercially, some people still can or jar foods at home for various reasons, including palatability, economy, and the satisfaction derived from do-it-yourself projects. For those who must restrict their intake of salt and sugar, products may be canned without the addition of these substances. The canning of tomatoes from backyard gardens appears to be one of the more popular home food preservation activities.

Methods for Home Canning

High-quality products should always be selected for canning, and recommended procedures should be followed to ensure safe products that do not spoil on storage. Detailed steps to be followed in home canning are given in the Cooperative Extension Service, University of Georgia/Athens, *So Easy to Preserve* [2], the *Ball Blue Book* [31], and the *USDA Complete Guide to Home Canning* [62].

Packing. Only glass jars, specifically designed for safe home canning, are available. Foods can be packed into the jars either raw or hot in preparation for the canning processing step (**Figure 28–15**).

In the raw-pack method of canning, the uncooked food is packed into the container, and the container is filled with boiling liquid. Some headspace should be left in the top of the container before sealing; usually ½ to 1 inch is suggested. This space allows for the expansion of the jar contents during heating. Glass jars are only partially sealed before processing at the necessary temperature for the recommended time.

In the hot-pack method of canning, the food is heated in syrup (heavy, medium, or light), water, steam, or extracted juice before being packed into containers. With this method, the temperature of the food should be at least 170°F (77°C) when packed into the container.

The raw-pack method may have an advantage over the hot-pack method in that large pieces of fruit, such as peach halves or fragile berries, can be placed in jars so that they present an attractive appearance and are closely packed. The hot-pack method may be advantageously used for some foods because it helps to drive out air, wilts or shrinks plant tissues (thereby allowing closer packing), and slightly shortens the processing time. The initial temperature of the food is relatively high, and heat penetration is more rapid when the food is packed hot. Pears, apples, and pineapples have a more attractive translucent appearance when prepared by the hot-pack rather than by the raw-pack method. Also, more fruit can be fit into the container.

Processing. The processing of canned fruits, vegetables, and meats is done after these foods have been

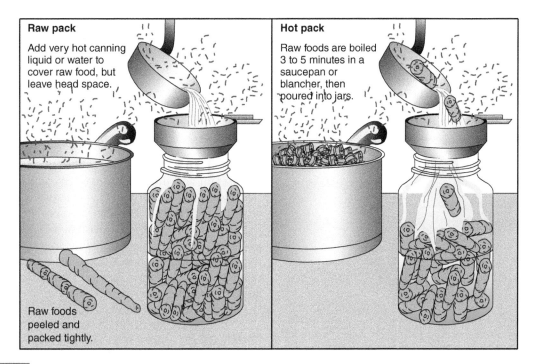

Figure 28–15

Bottles (canning jars) can be filled by either the raw-pack or the hot-pack method, as illustrated. (U.S. Department of Agriculture)

packed into containers by either the hot- or the raw-pack method as described previously. The processing may be accomplished in a boiling water bath for acidic fruits and acidic tomatoes. Acidic foods have a pH of below 4.6. For vegetables, meat, fish, and poultry, which are low in acid (pH of 4.6 or higher), the use of a pressure canner is essential. A higher temperature is required with these products for the complete destruction of bacterial spores. Of particular concern is the destruction of the spores of *Clostridium botulinum*. These spores can vegetate and, under the anaerobic conditions that are found in the sealed cans, may produce a deadly toxin that causes **botulism** when consumed, even in tiny amounts. In low-acid foods such as vegetables and meats, the temperature of boiling water is not sufficient to ensure spore destruction. A pressure canner, in which higher temperatures can be attained, must be used in the canning of these products.

Boiling Water Bath.   Acidic (high pH) foods may be processed by a boiling water bath. Processing by means of a boiling water bath requires a large boiling water canner (**Figure 28–16**). The canner must be deep enough so that at least one inch of briskly boiling water will be above the tops of the jars during processing. A fitted lid covers the canner. A rack keeps jars one inch or less above the bottom, thus avoiding breakage and allowing for even circulation of heat underneath the jars. Unless the bath has a removable holder for jars, a lifter of some kind is necessary for placing jars into and removing them from the boiling water.

The canner should be filled halfway with water. For raw-packed foods, preheat the water to 140°F (60°C) and for hot-packed foods to 180°F (82°C). Load the filled jars, fitted with lids, into the canner rack and use the handles to lower the rack into the water or fill the canner one jar at a time. Add more

Figure 28–16

The boiling water should extend two inches above the jars in a boiling water canner. A rack in the canner promotes proper water circulation around the jars and allows for easy removal of the jars.   (© Douglas Scheule)

boiling water so that the water level is at least one inch above the jar tops. Heat on high until the water boils vigorously. Cover the canner and lower the heat to maintain a gentle boil (212°F [100°C]) throughout the processing period [31, 62].

Some varieties of tomatoes now being grown in the United States are lower in acid content than those commonly produced in previous years. These tomatoes are likely to have pH values above 4.6 and are considered to be low-acid foods. If they are to be canned as acid foods in a boiling water canner, they must be acidified with lemon juice or citric acid to a pH of less than 4.6. Two tablespoons of bottled lemon juice or ½ teaspoon citric acid per quart of tomatoes will ensure a safe level of acidity [31, 62]. Properly acidified tomatoes can be processed in a boiling water canner. Alternatively, low-acid tomatoes, not treated with lemon juice or citric acid, must be processed in a pressure canner, as are other vegetables and meat products.

Pressure Canning.   Low-acid foods, with a pH of higher than 4.6, must be canned with a pressure canner to achieve temperatures higher than 212°F (100°C) [31]. The boiling point of a liquid, such as water, varies with the atmospheric pressure over its surface. As the atmospheric pressure is decreased with higher altitudes, the boiling point of the liquid is decreased. In a pressure canner, the water vapor or steam that is produced when the water is heated to its normal boiling point is captured inside the canner with its tightly sealed cover, thus increasing the pressure over the surface of the water in the pressure canner. This raises the boiling point of the water, and temperatures higher than the usual boiling point of water can be achieved.

Pressure canners in the past were constructed of heavy metal with clamp-on or turn-on lids. They had a dial gauge to indicate pressure. Most pressure canners of today are lightweight, thin-walled kettles with turn-on lids (**Figure 28–17**). Their essential features are a *rack* to hold jars off the bottom, a *vent port* (steam vent or petcock) that is left open for a few minutes to drive out air and fill the compartment with steam and then closed with a *counterweight*, or *weighted gauge*, and a *safety fuse* or *valve* through which steam may escape if pressure becomes too high within the canner (**Figure 28–18**). As noted, the pressure canner is used primarily to provide a high temperature for the destruction of heat resistant microorganisms and their spores, and it achieves this goal in a shorter time than is possible at the unpressurized boiling temperature of water.

To operate the pressure canner, put 2 to 3 inches of water in the canner and then place filled jars on the rack, using a jar lifter. Space the jars to permit circulation of steam. Fasten the canner lid securely, making sure that the gasket is clean and in place. Leave the

Figure 28–17

A pressure canner is necessary to obtain temperatures higher than 212°F (100°C). Pressure canners are heated on top of the range to achieve the necessary pressure for the canning of low-acid foods such as green beans. (B Brown/Shutterstock)

the weight on the vent port. The steam drives air out of the canner as completely as possible, or *exhausts* the canner. If the air is not removed, the air in the canner contributes a partial pressure along with the steam, and the temperature inside the canner will not be as high as when all the pressure comes from steam. The food may therefore be underprocessed. Canners are not equipped with thermometers that show the exact interior temperature, so it is important that the canner be properly exhausted. **Table 28–7** shows temperatures that are obtainable in a pressure canner at different pressures, provided that no air remains in the canner.

Pressure will build up during the first 3 to 5 minutes after closing the vent port. Start the timing process when the pressure gauge shows the desired pressure or when the weighted gauge begins to wiggle or rock. Regulate the source of heat to maintain a steady pressure on the gauge. Rapid and large fluctuations in pressure during processing will cause liquid to be lost from the jars. Weighted gauges should jiggle periodically or rock slowly throughout the process. They allow the release of tiny amounts of steam each time they move and thus control the pressure precisely. Constant watching is not required.

petcock open or the weight off the vent port and heat on high until steam flows from the port or petcock. Allow a steady stream of steam to exit from the canner for 10 minutes before closing the petcock or placing

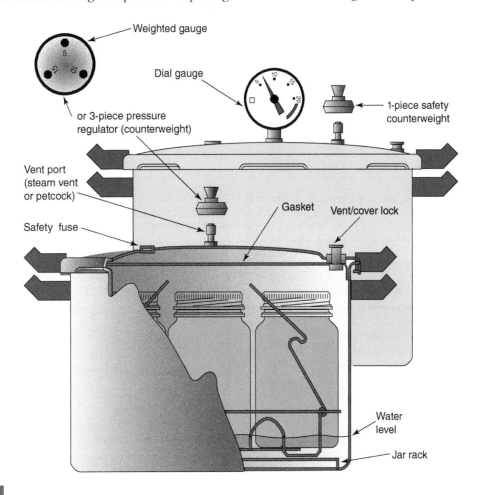

Figure 28–18

The essential parts of a pressure canner are shown with the correct water level for canning. (U.S. Department of Agriculture)

Table 28–7
TEMPERATURES OBTAINABLE AT DIFFERENT PRESSURES IN A PRESSURE COOKER AT SEA LEVEL

Pressure (lb)	Temperature °F	°C
5	228	109
10	240	116
15	250	121
20	259	126
25	267	131

When the processing time is completed, turn off the heat and remove the canner from the heat source, if possible. Let the canner depressurize. *Do not force the cooling process.* Cooling the canner with cold water or opening the vent port or petcock before the canner is depressurized will cause loss of liquid from the jars and the seals may fail. After the canner is depressurized, remove the weight from the vent port or open the petcock, unfasten the lid, and open the canner carefully.

Immediately after processing in either the boiling water canner or the pressure canner, jars not tightly closed before processing, as is proper when using self-sealing lids, should now be tightly closed.

Sealing occurs automatically with cooling through the vacuum that is gradually produced as the jars cool. A tight seal will be apparent by the jar lids now being slightly concave downward, a status that should be confirmed following processing and cooling.

The temperature most commonly used for home canning of low-acid foods is 240°F (116°C), corresponding to a pressure of 10.5 pounds per square inch at sea level. However, it has been reported that a higher pressure (15 pounds), and thus a shorter processing time, also gives satisfactory results in terms of texture, color, and flavor of vegetables. Asparagus, peas, and strained squash were the vegetables tested [35].

Internal canner temperatures are lower at higher altitudes. Adjustments must therefore be made to compensate. If the pressure canner has a pressure gauge, the canner should be checked for accuracy at the beginning of each season. Checking is often done locally through the county cooperative extension service or the home service department of a utility company. The amount and direction of error in the pressure gauge should be noted on a tag tied to the canner. An adjustment should then be made when the canner is used. Weighted-gauge canners cannot be adjusted for altitude. Therefore, at altitudes above 1,000 feet, they must be operated at canner pressures of 10 instead of 5 pounds per square inch or 15 instead of 10 pounds, and processing times may need to be lengthened as indicated in the *Ball Blue Book* [31] and *USDA Home Canning Guide* [62].

FOCUS ON SCIENCE
CANNING AT HIGH ALTITUDES

When canning at high altitudes using the boiling water bath or a pressure canner, modifications must be made to the processing times and pressure levels for the food to be safe. Some of the basic differences for high altitude canning are noted below.

Boiling Water Bath—High-Acid Foods

The boiling point of water is lower at high altitudes (at high altitudes, water boils *below* 212°F [100°C]). Therefore, the processing time must be increased at higher elevations. Canning guides, such as the *USDA Complete Guide to Canning*, must be followed.

Pressure Canner—Required for Low-Acid Foods

All low-acid foods must be heated at 240°F (115°C) for the appropriate time in order to destroy heat-resistant bacteria and the spores formed by bacteria. To achieve these temperatures, a steam pressure canner must be used. At sea level, 10 pounds of steam pressure will produce 240°F (115°C), but at altitudes of 2,000 feet and above, the number of pounds of steam pressure must be increased to reach this temperature. For safe canning at high altitudes, the pressure must be increased as illustrated in the following:

Altitude	Pressure Required
Sea level	10.0 lb
2,001–4,000 feet	12.0 lb
4,001–6,000 feet	13.0 lb
8,001–10,000 feet	15.0 lb

Source: Colorado State University Cooperative, Extension Resource Center. Prepared by Pat Kendall, professor of Food Science and Human Nutrition, Colorado State University Cooperative Extension.

Containers for Canning

Commercial Canning.   Containers for commercially canned foods are usually made of tin-plated steel (tin cans), aluminum, or glass. Tin-free steel cans have also been produced. Tin cans are of two types: plain and lacquered. The type of lacquer used varied with the type of food, its acidity, pigments, and other characteristics. Commercial canning in metal has several advantages over glass: Breakage is eliminated, cans are always sealed before processing, heat penetration is more rapid than with glass, the cans may be rapidly cooled after processing by being plunged into cold water, and the cans are generally less expensive. Flexible packages, such as retort pouches, may also be used for commercial canning to produce shelf-stable foods not requiring refrigeration.

Home Canning.   The jars generally available in the United States for home canning are heat-resistant glass jars with self-sealing lids (**Figure 28–19**). The self-sealing closure for a canning jar has a composition ring in the lid that becomes soft when heated and then hardens, forming a seal on the edge of the jar top when it has cooled. New lids are required for self-sealing jars each time the jars are used, but the screw bands may be reused over a long period. The lids are placed in simmering but not boiling water for at least 10 minutes prior to use according to the manufacturer's directions [31].

For low-acid vegetables and for meats, jars no larger than quart size are recommended because of the danger of poor heat penetration in larger jars. The pint size is usually advised for corn, shell beans, and lima beans, in which heat penetration is slow.

Heat Penetration

Heat penetration during canning is affected by such factors as the size of the container, the material from which the container is made, the initial temperature of the food when the processing is started, the temperature used for processing, the fullness of the pack, and the character of the food. Heat penetration is more rapid in smaller containers and is more rapid in tin than in glass. Starchy vegetables and closely packed leafy vegetables transmit heat poorly. Colloidal starch solutions retard heat penetration more than concentrated sugar solutions. Heat penetration is more rapid if the food is hot when the processing is started and if a higher temperature is used for processing. In general, the higher the processing temperature, the shorter the required heating time.

Obtaining a Partial Vacuum

A partial vacuum in the sealed jar is important in the canning of food because it helps to maintain an effective seal and it inhibits oxidative changes. A partial vacuum is created when the air within the jar exerts less pressure outward than the atmosphere exerts on the outside of the jar. This vacuum is produced as a result of several events that occur during the canning process. First, food is heated. The application of heat causes internal gases to expand. When the food is heated in a glass canning jar, the gases escape through the partially sealed lid. Formation of an effective vacuum depends largely on this process of *venting.*

After processing is completed and the jar is removed from the canner, sealing occurs. With self-sealing devices, the complete sealing takes place automatically as the softened sealing compound hardens on cooling. During cooling, the contents of the jar contract, leaving a space in the top that is less dense than the atmosphere pressing down on the outside of the lid. Thus, a partial vacuum forms, aiding in keeping the seal tight.

Obtaining an Effective Seal

A good seal is essential in canned foods. All jars should be examined for nicks or rough places on the sealing surfaces that might interfere with a good seal. Lids must fit well. Care should be taken to remove small bits of food from the top of the jar before closing the container because they interfere with the formation of a complete seal.

After the jars have cooled for 12 to 24 hours, the screw bands may be removed and the jars tested for a complete seal. If the center of the lid is either flat or bulging, it is probably not sealed. It should be concave, that is, pulled down slightly in the center. Try to gently lift the lid off with your fingertips. If the lid does not flex up and down and the lid is tightly attached, then the lid has a good seal [31].

Handling after Processing

Proper handling and storage of canned food are important in maintaining its quality. When glass jars with self-sealing lids are thoroughly cool and have sealed,

Figure 28–19

The most commonly used closure for canning jars is the metal screw band and metal self-sealing lid. Sealing occurs on the top edge of the jar. (U.S. Department of Agriculture)

the screw bands should be removed and rinsed clean so that they can be used again. If they are left on the jars they may stick or rust, making removal difficult. The outside of the jars should be wiped clean of any residual syrup or other material. Containers should be labeled to show the contents and date of processing.

Canned foods should be stored in a cool, dry, dark place. At cool storage temperatures, the eating quality and nutritive value are better maintained. Glass jars, particularly, should be stored in a dark place because light causes fading and discoloration of plant pigments. Properly canned foods may be safely stored for several years, but the quality of the food gradually decreases, especially if storage temperatures are relatively high. Therefore, use of canned foods within a year is generally recommended.

All canned products should be inspected before use to ensure that the vacuum seal is present. Check for signs of mold, gassiness, cloudiness, spurting liquid when the jar is opened, seepage, yeast growth, fermentation, sliminess, and disagreeable odors [31]. All of these are indications of spoilage, and the food should not be used. Steps to avoid cross-contamination with potentially spoiled foods should be followed as suggested by the USDA Canning Guide [62] or other reliable sources.

STUDY QUESTIONS

Food Packaging

1. Describe several functions of food packages.
2. Explain why the FDA considers food-packaging materials to be food additives.
3. Briefly describe and give examples of how each of the following materials can be used in packaging:
   (a) Paper
   (b) Plastics
   (c) Metals
   (d) Combinations of materials
   (e) Edible films and coatings
4. Describe *aseptic packaging*, and discuss the advantages it has for food products.
5. Explain how *modified atmosphere packaging* helps to preserve foods.
6. Identify types of foods that may benefit from a modified atmosphere and explain why.
7. Identify two methods that may be employed for the modification of the gaseous atmosphere in a package.
8. Describe the *sous vide* processing of food and discuss precautions to be used for food safety.
9. Describe several ways to reduce and manage packaging waste.

Food Spoilage Causes

10. Describe several basic causes of food spoilage.

Food Preservation Basics

11. Explain why enzymes are of concern in preserving foods.

12. For each of the following general principles of food preservation, describe a specific method of preserving food:
    (a) Use of low temperatures
    (b) Use of high temperatures
    (c) Reduction of moisture
    (d) Addition or development of acid
    (e) Addition of large amounts of sugar
13. Explain the use of *ionizing radiation* in preserving foods.
14. Discuss the safety, and advantages offered by irradiation of foods.
15. Describe briefly several additional methods for the preservation of foods.

Freezing

16. Discuss differences in methods used, rate and time of freezing, and size of resulting ice crystals between slow freezing and quick freezing.
17. Describe several undesirable changes that may occur during freezing, frozen storage, or thawing of frozen foods.
18. Explain why vegetables should be blanched before freezing.
19. Provide several suggestions for carrying out the blanching process to ensure that it will accomplish its purpose satisfactorily.
20. Define *freezer burn*, and explain how it can be prevented in frozen foods.
21. Explain how freezing controls the causes of food spoilage and thereby preserves foods.

22. Discuss several points that should be considered in selecting foods for freezing.

23. Identify two important roles, in addition to sweetening, that are played by sugar or syrup packs in freezing fruits.

24. Describe general procedures to follow in the freezing of meat, fish, and poultry.

25. Identify differences that exist between the procedures for freezing egg whites and egg yolks.

26. Explain why containers and wrappers used on frozen foods should be moisture- and vapor-proof.

27. Provide reasons that a headspace should be left in containers when freezing foods.

28. List several factors that should be considered to make the most effective use of a freezer.

Canning

29. Describe some pertinent events in the history of canning that are associated with each of the following names and dates.

    (a) Appert, 1809
    (b) 1810
    (c) 1874
    (d) Pasteur, 1860s

30. Distinguish between the raw-pack and the hot-pack methods of packing canned foods, and discuss advantages of each.

31. Explain why fruits and high-acid tomatoes can be safely canned in a boiling water bath, but vegetables and meat products must be canned in a pressure canner. Address the issue of botulism in your explanation.

32. Describe the essential parts of a pressure canner and explain their functions.

33. Explain why is it important to completely exhaust a pressure canner before closing the petcock and building pressure.

34. Suggest a possible explanation for the loss of liquid from jars processed in a pressure canner.

35. Identify what materials are "tin" cans, and explain why their inside surfaces are sometimes lacquered.

36. Describe self-sealing lids commonly used on home canning jars or bottles, and explain how they work.

37. Identify the steps to ensure that an effective seal is formed in home canned jars or bottles.

38. List several factors that may affect the rate of heat penetration as canned foods are processed.

39. Explain how a partial vacuum is formed in canned foods, and discuss why it is important that this occurs.

A
Weights and Measures

ABBREVIATIONS FOR MEASUREMENTS

tsp	= teaspoon	cc	= cubic centimeter
Tbsp	= tablespoon	mL	= milliliter
fg	= few grains	L	= liter
fl oz	= fluid ounce	oz	= ounce
c	= cup	lb	= pound
pt	= pint	μg	= microgram
qt	= quart	mg	= milligram
gal	= gallon	g	= gram
		kg	= kilogram
		mm	= millimeter
		cm	= centimeter
		m	= meter

EQUIVALENTS

		Common Use
1 gram	= 0.035 ounce	
1 ounce	= 28.35 grams	30 grams
4 ounces	= 113.40 grams	125 grams
8 ounces	= 226.80 grams	250 grams
1 kilogram	= 2.2 pounds	
1 kilogram	= 1,000 grams	
1 pound	= 0.454 kilogram	
1 pound	= 453.59 grams	450 grams
1 liter	= 1.06 quarts	
1 liter	= 1,000 milliliters	
1 quart	= 0.946 liter	0.95 liter
1 quart	= 946.4 milliliters	950 milliliters
1 cup	= 236.6 milliliters	240 milliliters
½ cup	= 118 milliliters	120 milliliters
1 fluid oz	= 29.57 milliliters	30 milliliters
1 tablespoon	= 14.8 milliliters	15 milliliters
1 teaspoon	= 4.9 milliliters	5 milliliters
1 inch	= 2.54 centimeters	2.5 centimeters
1 centimeter	= 0.4 inch	
1 yard	= 0.914 meter	

COMMON MEASUREMENTS USED IN FOOD PREPARATION

3 tsp	= 1 Tbsp	$10\frac{2}{3}$ Tbsp = $\frac{2}{3}$ c	
16 Tbsp	= 1 c	2 c	= 1 pt
4 Tbsp	= $\frac{1}{4}$ c	4 c	= 1 qt
8 Tbsp	= $\frac{1}{2}$ c	4 qt	= 1 gal
12 Tbsp	= $\frac{3}{4}$ c	2 Tbsp	= 1 fl oz or $\frac{1}{8}$ c
$5\frac{1}{3}$ Tbsp	= $\frac{1}{3}$ c	8 fl oz	= 1 c or $\frac{1}{2}$ pt

APPROXIMATE NUMBER OF CUPS IN A POUND OF SOME COMMON FOODS

$2\frac{1}{4}$ c granulated sugar

4 c all-purpose flour

2 c butter or margarine

4 c grated cheese

WEIGHTS AND MEASURES FOR SOME FOOD INGREDIENTS

All-purpose flour, sifted	1 lb = 4 c	115 g per c
Whole wheat flour, stirred	1 lb = $3\frac{1}{3}$ c	132 g per c
SAS-phosphate baking powder	14 oz = $2\frac{1}{2}$ c	3.2 g per tsp
Baking soda	1 lb = 2 c	4 g per tsp
Granulated sugar	1 lb = $2\frac{1}{4}$ c	200 g per c
Brown sugar, packed	1 lb = $2\frac{1}{4}$ c	200 g per c
Salt	1 lb = $1\frac{1}{4}$ c	288 g per c
Margarine	1 lb = 2 c	224 g per c
Hydrogenated fat	1 lb = $2\frac{1}{3}$ c	188 g per c
Oil	1 lb = $2\frac{1}{6}$ c	210 g per c
Eggs, fresh whole	1 lb = $1\frac{3}{4}$ c	248 g per c

STANDARD CAN SIZES

Can Size	Contents (c)	Average Net Weight
8 oz	1	8 oz
Picnic	$1\frac{1}{4}$	11 oz
No. 300	$1\frac{3}{4}$	15 oz
No. 303	2	16 oz
No. 2	$2\frac{1}{2}$	1 lb 4 oz
No. $2\frac{1}{2}$	$3\frac{1}{2}$	1 lb 13 oz
No. 3 cylinder	$5\frac{1}{2}$	46 fl oz
No. 10	13	6 lb 10 oz

Source: American Home Economics Association. (1993). *Handbook of Food Preparation* (9th ed.). Washington, DC: American Home Economics Association.

SOME INGREDIENT SUBSTITUTIONS

For:	Substitute:
1 tablespoon flour (thickener)	$\frac{1}{2}$ tablespoon cornstarch, potato starch, or arrowroot starch or 1 tablespoon quick-cooking tapioca
1 cup sifted all-purpose flour	1 cup unsifted all-purpose flour minus 2 tablespoons
1 cup sifted cake flour	$\frac{7}{8}$ cup or 1 cup minus 2 tablespoons sifted all-purpose flour
1 cup sifted self-rising flour	1 cup sifted all-purpose flour plus $1\frac{1}{2}$ teaspoons baking powder and $\frac{1}{2}$ teaspoon salt
1 cup honey	$1\frac{1}{4}$ cups sugar plus $\frac{1}{4}$ cup liquid
1 cup corn syrup	1 cup sugar plus $\frac{1}{4}$ cup liquid
1 cup butter	1 cup margarine or $\frac{7}{8}$ cup hydrogenated shortening or $\frac{7}{8}$ cup lard
1 ounce baking chocolate	3 tablespoons cocoa plus 1 tablespoon fat
1 ounce semisweet chocolate	$\frac{1}{2}$ ounce baking chocolate plus 1 tablespoon sugar
1 cup buttermilk	1 cup plain yogurt
1 teaspoon baking powder	$\frac{1}{4}$ teaspoon baking soda plus $\frac{5}{8}$ teaspoon cream of tartar or $\frac{1}{4}$ teaspoon baking soda plus $\frac{1}{2}$ tablespoon vinegar or lemon juice

METRIC CONVERSIONS

		Multiply by:
Length	inches to centimeters	2.5
	feet to centimeters	30
	yards to meters	0.9
Volume or capacity	teaspoons to milliliters	5
	tablespoons to milliliters	15
	fluid ounces to milliliters	30
	cups to liters	0.24
	cups to milliliters	237
	quarts to liters	0.95
	gallons to liters	3.8
Mass or weight	ounces to grams	28
	pounds to grams	454
	pounds to kilograms	0.45

B
Temperature Control

OVEN TEMPERATURES

Temperatures for cooking can be most accurately controlled when a thermostat or a thermometer is used. Ovens generally have thermostat-controlled heat. They may be checked occasionally with a portable oven thermometer if there is some question about the accuracy of the thermostatic control.

Temperature Range for Ovens

Very low	250–275°F	121–135°C
Low	300–325°F	149–163°C
Moderate	350–375°F	177–191°C
Hot	400–425°F	204–218°C
Very hot	450–500°F	232–260°C

THERMOMETERS FOR OTHER USES

Thermometers are available for reading the temperature of deep fats, sugar syrups, and meats. In taking the temperature of hot fats or of boiling sugar syrups, the bulb of the thermometer should be fully submerged but should not touch the bottom of the utensil. In reading the scale, the eye should be level with the top of the mercury column.

Meat thermometers have a short scale, up to about 212°F (100°C). The bulb is small, and the thermometer is inserted so that the bulb rests in the center of the roast or the muscle being roasted.

CONVERTING FAHRENHEIT AND CELSIUS TEMPERATURES

Formulas

$$1.8 \times °C = °F - 32$$

or

$$°C = (°F - 32) \times 5/9$$

$$°F = (°C \times 9/5) + 32$$

The first formula given for temperature conversion can be used for changing either Celsius to Fahrenheit or Fahrenheit to Celsius simply by inserting the known temperature in the appropriate place in the formula and then solving the equation for the unknown.

Conversion Table			
°F	°C	°F	°C
50	10.0	200	93.3
60	15.6	210	98.9
70	21.1	212	100.0
80	26.7	215	101.7
90	32.2	220	104.4
100	37.8	230	110.0
110	43.3	235	112.8
120	48.9	240	115.6
130	54.4	245	118.3
140	60.0	248	120.0
150	65.6	250	121.1
160	71.1	252	122.2
170	76.7	255	123.9
180	82.2	260	126.7
190	87.8	270	132.2

C

Nutritive Value of Foods

The nutritive value of foods is determined through laboratory analysis. The nutritive value of thousands of foods is readily available through the U.S. Department of Agriculture (USDA) National Nutrient Database for Standard Reference. This database can be accessed by searching for (a) FoodData Central, (b) USDA National Nutrient Database or (c) USDA food composition from an Internet search engine or going to https://fdc.nal.usda.gov/ or https://ndb.nal.usda.gov/ndb/search/list?home=true. Web pages change overtime, therefore a search using the names indicated may be necessary.

Periodically, the database is updated. As of April 2018, the most recent database is the USDA National Nutrient Database for Standard Reference, Legacy Release and the USDA Branded Food Products Database. The FoodData Central includes additional data sources to these, including experimental foods.

references

Chapter 1

1. Academy of Nutrition and Dietetics. (2014). Position of the Academy of Nutrition and Dietetics: Nutrition guidance for healthy children ages 2 to 11 years. *Journal of the Academy of Nutrition and Dietetics, 114,* 1257–1276. http://dx.doi.org/10.1016/j.jand.2014.06.001

2. Academy of Nutrition and Dietetics. (2017). Position of the Academy of Nutrition and Dietetics: Food insecurity in the United States. *Journal of the Academy of Nutrition and Dietetics, 117,* 1991–2002. https://doi.org/10.1016/j.jand.2017.09.027

3. American Dietetic Association. (2001). Position of the American Dietetic Association: Dietetic professionals can implement practices to conserve natural resources and protect the environment. *Journal of the American Dietetic Association, 101,* 1221–1227.

4. Anundson, K., Sisson, S. B., Anderson, M., Horm, Soto, & Hoffman., L. (2017). Staff food-related behaviors and children's tastes of food groups during lunch at child care in Oklahoma. *Journal of the Academy of Nutrition and Dietetics* [online]. http://dx.doi.org/10.1016/j.jand.2017.07.023

5. Ayala, G. X., Baquero, B., & Kinger, S. (2008). A systematic review of the relationship between acculturation and diet among Latinos in the United States: Implications for future research. *Journal of the American Dietetic Association, 108,* 1330–1344. doi:10.1016/j.jada.2008.05.009

6. Barrett, A., Froio, D., & Richardson, M. (2015). Vitamin stabilization for long-term space flight. *Food Technology, 69*(4), 44–51.

7. Bartelme, M. Z. (2017). Inside the evolving food retail landscape. *Food Technology, 71*(10), 40–51.

8. Berge, J. M., Wall, M., Neumark-Sztainer, D., Larson, N., & Story, M. (2010). Parenting style and family meals: Cross-sectional and 5-year longitudinal associations. *Journal of the American Dietetic Association, 110,* 1036–1042. doi:10.1016/j.jada.2010.04.011

9. Bergman, E. A., Buergel, N. S., Englund, T. F., & Femrite, A. (2004, Fall). The relationship between the length of lunch period and nutrient consumption in the elementary school setting. *Journal of Child Nutrition and Management,* Issue 2. Retrieved from http://docs.schoolnutrition.org/newsroom/jcnm/04fall/bergman/bergman2.asp

10. Bergman, E. A., Buergel, N. S., Englund, T. F., & Femrite, A. (2004, Fall). The relationship of meal and recess schedules to plate waste in elementary schools. *The Journal of Child Nutrition and Management,* Issue 2. Retrieved from http://docs.schoolnutrition.org/newsroom/jcnm/o4fall/bergman/bergman1.asp

11. Blackburn, G. L. (2001). Feeding 9 billion people—A job for food technologists. *Food Technology, 55*(6), 106.

12. Bosley, G. C., & Hardinge, M. G. (1992). Seventh-Day Adventists: Dietary standards and concerns. *Food Technology, 46*(10), 112.

13. Bourland, C. T., Fohey, M. F., Rapp, R. M., & Sauer, R. L. (1982). Space shuttle food package development. *Food Technology, 36*(9), 38.

14. Brody, A. L. (2003). The return of the retort pouch. *Food Technology, 57*(2), 76–79.

15. Brody, A. L. (2004). An astronautical food odyssey. *Food Technology, 58*(3), 64–66.

16. Brody, A. L. (2006). Retort pouches and trays: A growing market. *Food Technology, 60*(4), 82–85.

17. Brody, A. L. (2008). Feeding astronauts. *Food Technology, 62*(1), 66–68.

18. Brucker, D. L., & Coleman-Jensen, A. (2017). Food insecurity across the adult life span for persons with disabilities. *Journal Disability Policy Studies, 28*(2), 109–188. doi: 10.1177/1044207317710701

19. Buss, D. (2018). New drivers for food delivery. *Food Technology, 72*(3), 36–45.

20. Bustillos, B., Sharkey, J. R., Anding, J., & McIntosh, A. (2009). Availability of more healthful food alternatives in traditional, convenience, and nontraditional types of food stores in two rural Texas counties. *Journal of the American Dietetic Association, 109,* 883–889.

21. Buzby, J. C., Wells, H. F., & Aulakh, J. (2014, June). Food loss – Questions about the amount and causes still remain. *Amber Waves.* Retrieved from https://www.ers.usda.gov/amber-waves/2014/june/food-loss-questions-about-the-amount-and-causes-still-remain/

22. Caranfa, M., & Morris, D. (2009). Putting health on the menu. *Food Technology, 63*(6), 29–36.

23. Carlson, A., Dong, D., Stewart, H., & Frazão, E. (2015, September 8). Following dietary guidance need not cost more – but many Americans would need to re-allocate their food budgets. *Amber Waves.* Retrieved from https://www.ers.usda.gov/amber-waves/2015/september/following-dietary-guidance-need-not-cost-more-but-many-americans-would-need-to-re-allocate-their-food-budgets/

24. Chapman, N. (2005). Securing the future for monitoring the health, nutrition, and physical activity of Americans. *Journal of the American Dietetic Association, 105,* 1196–1200.

25. Clauson, A. (2008). Despite higher food prices, percent of U.S. income spent on food remains constant. *Food Review, 6*(4), 5.

26. Coleman-Jensen, A., & Nord, M. (2013, May). Disability is an important risk factor for food insecurity. *Amber Waves.* Retrieved from https://www.ers.usda.gov/amber-waves/2013/may/disability-is-an-important-risk-factor-for-food-insecurity/

27. Cooper, M., Douglas, G., & Perchonok, M. (2011). Developing the NASA food system for long-duration missions. *Journal of Food Science, 76,* R40–R48. doi:10.1111/j.1750-3841.2010.01982.x

28. Costacou, T., Levin, S., & Mayer-Davis, E. J. (2000). Dietary patterns among members of the Catawba Indian nation. *Journal of the American Dietetic Association, 100,* 833–835.

29. Davis, D. E., & Stewart, H. (2002). Changing consumer demands create opportunities for U.S. food system. *Food Review, 25*(1), 19–23.

30. DeRovira, D. (1996). The dynamic flavor profile method. *Food Technology, 50*(2), 55.

31. DeWolf, M. (2017, March 1). 12 stats about working women. *U.S. Department of Labor Blog.* Retrieved from https://blog.dol.gov/2017/03/01/12-stats-about-working-women

32. Dizon, F., Costa, S., Rock, C., Harris, A., Husk, C., & Mei, J. (2016). Genetically modified (GM foods and ethical eating. *Journal of Food Science, 81*(2), R287–R291. doi:10.1111/1750-3841.13191

33. Doris, C. (2017). Plant-based eating evolves. *Food Technology, 71*(2), 26–37.

34. Escobar, A. (1999). Factors influencing children's dietary practices: A review. *Family Economics and Nutrition Review, 12*(3–4), 45–55.

35. Flores, J. D., Newsome, R., Fisher, W., Barbosa-Cánovas, G. V., Chen, H., Dunne, P.,… Ziegler, G. R. (2010). Feeding the world today and tomorrow: The importance of food science and technology: An IFT scientific review. *Comprehensive Reviews in Food Science and Food Safety, 9*, 572–599. doi:10.1111/j.1541.4337.2010.00127

36. Fu, B., & Nelson, P. E. (1994). Conditions and constraints of food processing in space. *Food Technology, 48*(9), 113.

37. Gable, S., & Lutz, S. (2001). Nutrition socialization experiences of children in the Head Start program. *Journal of the American Dietetic Association, 101*, 572–577.

38. Greene, C., Ferreira, G., Carlson, A., Cooke, B., & Hitaj, C. (2017, February 17). Growing organic demand provides high-value opportunities for many types of producers. *Amber Waves.* Retrieved from https://www.ers.usda.gov/amber-waves/2017/januaryfebruary/growing-organic-demand-provides-high-value-opportunities-for-many-types-of-producers/

39. Guthrie, J., Lin, B-H., Okrent, A., & Volpe, R. (2013, February 21). Americans' food choices at home and away: How do they compare with recommendations. *Amber Waves.* Retrieved from https://www.ers.usda.gov/amber-waves/2013/february/americans-food-choices-at-home-and-away/

40. Hackes, B. L., Shanklin, C. W., Kim, T., & Su, A. Y. (1997). Tray service generates more food waste in dining areas of a continuing-care retirement community. *Journal of the American Dietetic Association, 97*, 879.

41. Hampl, J. S., & Sass, S. (2001). Focus groups indicate that vegetable and fruit consumption by food stamp–eligible Hispanics is affected by children and unfamiliarity with non-traditional foods. *Journal of the American Dietetic Association, 101*, 685–687.

42. Harlander, S. K. (1991). Biotechnology: A means for improving our food supply. *Food Technology, 45*(4), 84.

43. Hoch, G. J. (1997). Flavor technology report: Reaction flavors. *Food Processing, 58*(4), 57.

44. Hollingsworth, P. (2001). Supermarket trends. *Food Technology, 55*(3), 20.

45. Horning, M. L., Fulkerson, J. A., Friend, S. E., & Story, M. (2017). Reasons parents buy prepackaged, processed meals: it is more complicated than "I don't have time." *Journal of Nutrition Education & Behavior, 49*(1), 60–66.e1. doi:10.1016/j.jneb.2016.08.012

46. Huang, Y., & Ang, C. Y. W. (1992). Vegetarian foods for Chinese Buddhists. *Food Technology, 46*(10), 105.

47. Institute of Food Technologists' Expert Panel on Food Safety & Nutrition. (1989). Food flavors. *Food Technology, 43*(12), 99.

48. Institute of Food Technologists' Expert Report on Biotechnology and Foods. (2000). Benefits and concerns associated with recombinant DNA biotechnology-derived foods. *Food Technology, 54*(10), 61–80.

49. Jackson, M. A. (2000). Getting religion: For your products, that is. *Food Technology, 54*(7), 60–66.

50. Kenney, B. F. (1990). Applications of high-performance liquid chromatography for the flavor research and quality control laboratories in the 1990s. *Food Technology, 44*(9), 76.

51. Kittler, P. G., & Sucher, K. P. (2001). *Food and culture* (3rd ed.). Belmont, CA: Wadsworth.

52. Kuchler, F., Greene, C., Bowman, M., Marshall, K. K., Bovay, J., & Lynch, L. (2017, November). Federal nutrition and organic labels paved the way for single-trait label claims. *Amber Waves.* Retrieved from https://www.ers.usda.gov/amber-waves/2017/november/federal-nutrition-and-organic-labels-paved-the-way-for-single-trait-label-claims/

53. Kuhn, M. E. (2014). Today's supermarket special: Transforming the store. *Food Technology, 68*(9), 24–37.

54. Kuhn, M. E. (2016). Decoding the science of taste. *Food Technology, 70*(5), 18–29.

55. Kuhns, A. (2018, May 1). Households purchase more produce and low-fat dairy at supermarkets, supercenters, and warehouse club stores. *Amber Waves.* Retrieved from https://www.ers.usda.gov/amber-waves/2017/may/households-purchase-more-produce-and-low-fat-dairy-at-supermarkets-supercenters-and-warehouse-club-stores/

56. Kuhns, A., & Saksena, M. (2017, December 29). Millennials devote larger shares of their grocery spending to prepared foods, pasta, and sugar and sweets than other generations. *Amber Waves.* Retrieved from https://www.ers.usda.gov/amber-waves/2017/december/millennials-devote-larger-shares-of-their-grocery-spending-to-prepared-foods-pasta-and-sugar-and-sweets-than-other-generations/

57. Leland, J. V. (1997). Flavor interactions: The greater whole. *Food Technology, 51*(1), 75.

58. Liebtag, E. S. (2005). Where you shop matters: Store formats drive variation in retail food prices. *Amber Waves, 3*(5), 13–18.

59. Liebtag, E. S. (2008). Retail food prices vary significantly across U. S. regions. *Amber Waves, 6*(1), 40.

60. Lin, B-H., & Guthrie, J. (2012, December) Nutritional quality of food prepared at home and away from home 1977-2008. EIB-105, U.S. Service. Retrieved from https://www.ers.usda.gov/webdocs/publications/43698/34513_eib-105.pdf?v=41270

61. Madsen, M. G., & Grypa, R. D. (2000). Spices, flavor systems, and the electronic nose. *Food Technology, 54*(3), 44–46.

62. Mancino, L., Guthrie, J., Ver Ploeg, M., & Lin, B-H. (2018, February). Nutritional quality of foods acquired by Americans: Findings from USDA's national household food acquisition and purchase survey, EIB-188, U.S. Department of Agriculture, Economic Research Service. Retrieved from https://www.ers.usda.gov/webdocs/publications/87531/eib-188.pdf?v=43151

63. Martinez, S. W. (2010). Varied interests drive growing popularity of local foods. *Amber Waves, 8*(4), 10–17.

64. Meade, B., & Thome, K. (2017, June). *International food security assessment, 2017–2027,* GFA 28, U.S.

Department of Agriculture, Economic Research Service. Retrieved from https://www.ers.usda.gov/webdocs/publications/84128/gfa-28.pdf?v=42914

65. Mermelstein, N. H. (2001). Military and humanitarian rations. *Food Technology, 55*(11), 73–75.

66. Morrison, R. M., Smith, T. A., & Link, B. H. (2009). Got data? Multiple data sources track U.S. food consumption. *Amber Waves, 7*(1), 39–41.

67. Moshfegh, A., Goldman, J., & Cleveland, L. (2005). *What we eat in America*, NHANES 2001–2002: Usual nutrient intakes from food compared to dietary reference intakes. U.S. Department of Agriculture, Agricultural Research Service.

68. Nachay, K. (2013). Moving forward on sodium reduction. *Food Technology, 67*(5), 34–44.

69. Nachay, K. (2016). Global inspiration: Cuisines of Europe and the Americas. *Food Technology, 7*(8), 53–61.

70. Nachay, K. (2017). Clean label approaches to food safety. *Food Technology, 71*(11), 53–62.

71. National Aeronautics and Space Administration. (2016, July). Space food. Retrieved from https://www.nasa.gov/aeroresearch/resources/artifact-opportunities/space-food

72. National Restaurant Association. (2017). *Pocket handbook: 2017 restaurant industry*. Retrieved from http://www.restaurant.org/Downloads/PDFs/News-Research/Pocket_Factbook_FEB_2017-FINAL.pdf

73. Nordin, S. M., Boyle, M., & Kemmer, T. M. (2013). Position of the Academy of Nutrition and Dietetics: Nutrition security in developing nations: Sustainable food, water, and health. *Journal of the Academy of Nutrition and Dietetics, 113*, 581–595. doi:10.1016/j.jand.2013.01.025

74. Norton, V. P., & Martin, C. (1991). Plate waste of selected food items in a university dining hall. *School Food Service Research Review, 15*(1), 37.

75. Office of Disease Prevention and Health Promotion. (2018, March). Healthy people 2010: Homepage. Retrieved from https://www.healthypeople.gov/

76. Ollberding, N. J., Wolf, R. L., & Contento, I. (2010). Food label use and its relation to dietary intake among US adults. *Journal of the American Dietetic Association, 110*, 1233–1237. doi:10.1016/j.jada.2010.05.007

77. Popper, R., & Kroll, B. J. (2003). Food preference and consumption among the elderly. *Food Technology, 57*(7), 32–38.

78. Pszczola, D. E. (1997). Lookin' good: Improving the appearance of food products. *Food Technology, 51*(11), 39.

79. Rabbitt, M. P., Coleman-Jenson, A., & Gregory, C. A. (2017, September). Understanding the prevalence, severity, and distribution of food insecurity in the United States. *Amber Waves*. Retrieved from https://www.ers.usda.gov/amber-waves/2017/september/understanding-the-prevalence-severity-and-distribution-of-food-insecurity-in-the-united-states/

80. Regenstein, J. M., Chaudry, M. M., & Regenstein, C. E. (2003). The Kosher and Halal food laws. *Comprehensive Reviews in Food Science and Food Safety, 2*, 111–127.

81. Rhone, A., Ver Ploeg, M., Dicken, C., Williams, R., & Breneman, V. (2017, January). Low-income and low-supermarket-access census tracts, 2010-2015. EIB-165, U.S.

Service. Retrieved from https://www.ers.usda.gov/webdocs/publications/82101/eib-165.pdf?v=42752

82. Robson, S. M., Couch, S. C., Peugh, J. L., Glanz, K., Zhou, C., Sallis, J. F., & Saelens, B. E. (2016). Parent diet quality and energy intake are related to child diet quality and energy intake. *Journal of the Academy of Nutrition and Dietetics, 116*, 984–990. http://dx.doi.org/10.1016/j.jand/2016.02.011

83. Samuelsson, M., (2006). *The soul of a new cuisine: A discovery of the foods and flavors of Africa*. Geneva, IL: Houghton Mifflin Harcourt.

84. Sloan, A. E. (2001). More on ethnic foods: Move over, BBQ, Cajun, and Caesar. *Food Technology, 55*(11), 18.

85. Sloan, A. E. (2006). What, when, and where America eats. *Food Technology, 60*(1), 18–27.

86. Sloan, A. E. (2007). Converting demographics into dollars. *Food Technology, 61*(7), 27–45.

87. Sloan, A. E. (2010). U.S. consumers have a taste for world cuisines. *Food Technology, 64*(6), 19.

88. Sloan, A. E. (2010). What's on the menu post-recession? *Food Technology, 64*(10), 29–42.

89. Sloan, A. E. (2014). Guys and groceries: A look at how men shop and cook. *Food Technolgy,68*(6), 22.

90. Sloan, A. E. (2015). Cooking behaviour close-up. *Food Technology, 69*(12), 15.

91. Sloan, A. E. (2016). A role reversal for ethnic foods. *Food Technology, 70*(2), 15.

92. Sloan, A. E. (2016). Eating responsibly. *Food Technology, 70*(12), 12.

93. Sloan, A. E. (2017). Easy eats: the new wave of meal solutions. *Food Technology, 71*(9), 17.

94. Sloan, A. E. (2017). Top 10 food trends. *Food Technology, 71*(4), 35.

95. Sloan, A. E. (2018). What, when, and where America eats. *Food Technology, 72*(1), 22–33.

96. Sobal, J., & Hanson, K. (2014). Family dinner frequency, settings and sources, and body weight in US adults. *Appetite, 78*(1), 81–88. https://doi.org/10.1016/j.appet.2014.03.016

97. Stewart, H. (2018, March 5). Shopping at farmers' markets and roadside stands increases fruit and vegetable demand. *Amber Waves*. Retrieved from https://www.ers.usda.gov/amber-waves/2018/march/shopping-at-farmers-markets-and-roadside-stands-increases-fruit-and-vegetable-demand/

98. Szczesniak, A. S. (1963). Classification of textural characteristics. *Journal of Food Science, 28*, 385.

99. Szczesniak, A. S. (1990). Texture: Is it still an overlooked food attribute? *Food Technology, 44*(9), 86.

100. Todd, J. E., & Leibtag, E. S. (2010). New database shows substantial geographic food price variation. *Amber Waves, 8*(3), 52–53.

101. Tsung, T., Schmitt, V., & Isz, S. (2001). Electronic tongue: A new dimension in sensory analysis. *Food Technology, 55*(10), 44–50.

102. Tuttle, C., & Kuhns, A. (2016, September 6). Percent of income spent on foods falls as income rises. *Amber Waves*. Retrieved from https://www.ers.usda.gov/amber-waves/2016/september/percent-of-income-spent-on-food-falls-as-income-rises/

103. U.S. Centers for Disease Control and Prevention. (2010, September 1). U.S. obesity trends: Trends by State

1985–2009. Retrieved from http://cdc.gov/obesity/data/trends.html#State

104. U.S. Department of Agriculture. (2016, October). Dietary intake data: What we eat in America: NHANES 2013-2014. Retrieved from https://www.ars.usda.gov/ARSUserFiles/80400530/pdf/1314/wweia_2013_2014_data.pdf

105. U.S. Department of Agriculture. (2017, May). Ag and food statistics: Charting the essentials: Agricultural trade. Retrieved from https://www.ers.usda.gov/data-products/ag-and-food-statistics-charting-the-essentials/agricultural-trade/

106. U.S. Department of Agriculture. (2018, January). Choose my plate: My plate. Retrieved from https://www.choosemyplate.gov/MyPlate

107. U.S. Department of Agriculture. (2018, March). USDA food plans: Cost of food. Retrieved fromhttps://www.cnpp.usda.gov/USDAFoodPlansCostofFood

108. U.S. Department of Agriculture, Economic Research Service. (2017, May). Agricultural trade. Retrieved from https://www.ers.usda.gov/data-products/ag-and-food-statistics-charting-the-essentials/agricultural-trade/

109. U.S. Department of Agriculture, Economic Research Service. (2018, January). Food availability: Documentation. Retrieved from https://www.ers.usda.gov/data-products/food-availability-per-capita-data-system/food-availability-documentation/

110. U.S. Department of Agriculture, Economic Research Service. (2018, February). Food expenditures. Retrieved from https://www.ers.usda.gov/data-products/food-expenditures.aspx

111. U.S. Department of Agriculture, Economic Research Service. (2018, March). Food dollar application. Retrieved from https://data.ers.usda.gov/reports.aspx?ID=17885

112. U.S. Department of Agriculture, Economic Research Service. (2018, March). Outlook for U.S. agricultural trade. Retrieved from https://www.ers.usda.gov/topics/international-al-markets-us-trade/us-agricultural-trade/outlook-for-us-agricultural-trade/

113. U.S. Department of Agriculture, Economic Research Service. (2018, March). Retail food price inflation closely in line with economy-wide inflation. Retrieved from https://www.ers.usda.gov/data-products/chart-gallery/gallery/chart-detail/?chartId=58350

114. U.S. Department of Health and Human Services, & U.S. Department of Agriculture. 2015–2020 Dietary Guidelines for Americans. 8th Edition. (2015, December). Retrieved from http://health.gov/dietaryguidelines/2015/guidelines/

115. U.S. Statistics. (2016, October). High-income households spent half of their food budget on food away from home in 2015. *The Economics Daily*. Retrieved from https://www.bls.gov/opub/ted/2016/high-income-households-spent-half-of-their-food-budget-on-food-away-from-home-in-2015.htm

116. U.S. Department of Labor, Bureau of Labor Statistics. (2016, December). Average minutes per day men and women spent in household activities. Retrieved from https://www.bls.gov/tus/charts/household.htm

117. U.S. Food and Drug Administration. (2018, March). Food facts: How to cut food waste and maintain food safety. Retrieved from https://www.fda.gov/downloads/food/resourcesforyou/consumers/ucm529509.pdf

118. van Buren, S. (1992). Analyzing time–intensity responses in sensory evaluation. *Food Technology, 46*(2), 101.

119. Ver Ploeg, M. (2010). Access to affordable nutritious food is limited in "food deserts." *Amber Waves, 8*(1), 20–27.

120. Weicha, J. M., Fink, A. K., Wicha, J., & Herbert, J. (2001). Differences in dietary patterns of Vietnamese, White, African-American, and Hispanic adolescents in Worchester, Mass. *Journal of the American Dietetic Association, 101*, 248–251.

121. Wintraub Austin, E. W., Austin, B. W., French, B. F., & Cohen, M. A. (2018). The effects of a nutrition media literacy intervention on parents' and youths' communication about food. *Journal of Health Communication, 23*(2), 190–199. doi:10.1080/10810730.2018.1423649

122. Yi-Ling, P., Dixon, Z., Himburg, S., & Huffman, F. (1999). Asian students change their eating patterns after living in the United States. *Journal of the American Dietetic Association, 99*, 54–57.

Chapter 2

1. Academy of Nutrition and Dietetics. (2014). Position of the Academy of Nutrition and Dietetics: Food and water safety. *Journal of the Academy of Nutrition and Dietetics, 114*, 1819–1829. http://dx.doi.org/10.1016/j.jand.2014.08.023

2. Altrekruse, S. F., Yang, S., Timbo, B. B., & Angulo, F. J. (1999). A multistate survey of consumer food-handling and food-consumption practices. *American Journal of Preventive Medicine, 16*(3), 216–221.

3. American Dietetic Association. (2006). Position of the American Dietetic Association: Agricultural and food biotechnology. *Journal of the American Dietetic Association, 106*, 285–293.

4. Anderson, J. B., Shuster, T. A., Hansen, K. E., Levy, A. S., & Volk, A. (2004). A camera's view of consumer food-handling behaviors. *Journal of the American Dietetic Association, 104*, 186–191.

5. Anderson, J. B., Shuster, T. A., Gee, E., Hansen, K., & Mendenhall, V. T. (2000). *A camera's view of consumer food handling and preparation practices.* Final report prepared for the U.S. Food and Drug Administration. North Logan, UT: Spectrum Consulting.

6. Balasubramaniam, V. M., Yousef, A E., Wan, J., & Husain, A. (2016). Kinder, gentler food processing. *Food Technology, 70*(12), 20–28.

7. *Ball Blue Book of Preserving.* (2005). Muncie, IN: Jarden Home Brands.

8. Bennett, G. A., & Richard, J. L. (1996). Influence of processing on *Fusarium* mycotoxins in contaminated grains. *Food Technology, 50*(5), 235.

9. Blackburn, G. L. (2001). Feeding 9 billion people—A job for food technologists. *Food Technology, 55*(6), 106.

10. Borchgrevink, C. P., JaeMin, C., & SeungHyun, K. (2013). Hand washing practices in a college town environment. *Journal of Environmental Health, 75*(8), 18–24.

11. Bren, L. (2004). Got milk? Make sure it's pasteurized. *FDA Consumer Magazine, 38*(5).

12. Bruhn, C., & Mason, A. (2002). Community leader response to educational information about biotechnology. *Journal of Food Science, 67*, 399–403.

13. Cates, S. C., Kosa, K. M., & Karns, S. (2009). Food safety knowledge and practices among older adults: Identifying

causes and solutions for risky behaviors. *Journal of Nutrition for the Elderly, 28*, 112–116. doi:10.1080/01639360902949986

14. Centers for Disease Control and Prevention, Division of Parasitic Diseases. (2012, August). Parasites: Trichinellosis (also known as Trichinosis). Retrieved from https://www.cdc.gov/parasites/trichinellosis/index.html

15. Centers for Disease Control and Prevention. (2014, June). *Campylobacter*. Retrieved from https://www.cdc.gov/foodsafety/diseases/campylobacter/index.html

16. Centers for Disease Control and Prevention. (2015, February). vCJD: Variant Creutzfeldt-Jakob disease (vCJD). Retrieved from https://www.cdc.gov/prions/vcjd/index.html

17. Centers for Disease Control and Prevention. (2015, February 10). Bovine spongiform encephalopathy (BSE), or mad cow disease: BSE in North America. Retrieved from https://www.cdc.gov/prions/bse/bse-north-america.html

18. Centers for Disease Control and Prevention. (2016, February). CSTE Botulism surveillance summary 2014. Retrieved from https://www.cdc.gov/nationalsurveillance/pdfs/botulism_cste_2014.pdf

19. Centers for Disease Control and Prevention. (2016, March 18). Foodborne outbreak tracking and reporting. Retrieved from https://www.cdc.gov/foodsafety/fdoss/index.html

20. Centers for Disease Control and Prevention. (2016, June). Harmful algal bloom (HAB) – Associated illness: Marine environments. Retrieved from https://www.cdc.gov/habs/illness-symptoms-marine.html

21. Centers for Disease Control and Prevention. (2016, October). Staphylococcal food poisoning. Retrieved from https://www.cdc.gov/foodsafety/diseases/staphylococcal.html

22. Centers for Disease Control and Prevention. (2016, October). Yersinia. Retrieved from https://www.cdc.gov/yersinia/

23. Centers for Disease Control and Prevention. (2016, December 12). Listeria (Listeriosis): People at risk: Pregnant women and newborns. Retrieved from https://www.cdc.gov/listeria/risk-groups/pregnant-women.html

24. Centers for Disease Control and Prevention (CDC). (2017). Surveillance for foodborne disease outbreaks, United States, 2015 Annual Report. Atlanta, Georgia: US Department of Health and Human Services. Retrieved from https://www.cdc.gov/foodsafety/fdoss/data/annual-summaries/index.html

25. Centers for Disease Control and Prevention. (2017, January). Clostridium perfringens. Retrieved from https://www.cdc.gov/foodsafety/diseases/clostridium-perfringens.html

26. Centers for Disease Control and Prevention. (2017, March 2). Foodborne Diseases Active Surveillance Network (Foodnet). FoodNet 2016 Preliminary data. Retrieved from https://www.cdc.gov/foodnet/reports/prelim-data-intro-2016.html

27. Centers for Disease Control and Prevention. (2017, March 17). Variant Creutzfeldt-Jacob Disease (vCJD): vCJD cases reported in the US. Retrieved from https://www.cdc.gov/prions/vcjd/vcjd-reported.html

28. Centers for Disease Control and Prevention. (2017, June). Food safety: Raw milk questions and answers. Retrieved from http://www.cdc.gov/foodsafety/rawmilk/raw-milk-questions-and-answers.html

29. Centers for Disease Control and Prevention. (2017, June 1). Salmonella. Retrieved from https://www.cdc.gov/salmonella/index.html

30. Claeys, W. L., Cardoen, S., Daube, G., De Block, J., Dewettinck, K., Dierick, K., … Herman, L. (2013). Raw or heated cow milk consumption: Review of risks and benefits. *Food Control, 31*(1), 251–262. doi:10.1016/J.FOODCONT.2012.09.035

31. Clark, J. P. (2005). Allergen-safe processing. *Food Technology, 59*(2), 63–64.

32. Clark, J. P. (2014). Irradiation close-up. *Food Technology, 68*(10), 77–79.

33. Clark, J. P. (2014). Putting on the pressure. *Food Technology, 68*(1), 73–75.

34. Condayan, C. (2010, September 13). Don't get caught dirty handed. *American Society for Microbiology*.

35. Crocco, S. (1981). Potato sprouts and greening potatoes: Potential toxic reaction. *Journal of the American Medical Association, 245*, 625.

36. Cross, H. R. (1996). HACCP: Pivotal change for the meat industry. *Food Technology, 50*(8), 236.

37. Donelan, A. K., Chambers, D. H., Chambers IV, E., Godwin, S. L., & Gates, S. C. (2016). Consumer poultry handling behaviour in grocery store and in-home storage. *Journal of Food Protection, 79*(4), 582–588.

38. Douglas, L. C., & Sanders, M. E. (2008). Probiotics and prebiotics in dietetics practice. *Journal of the American Dietetic Association, 108*, 510–521. doi:10.1016/j.jada.2007.12.009

39. Duxbury, D. (2004). Keeping tabs on *Listeria*. *Food Technology, 58*(7), 74–76, 80.

40. Food and Drug Administration. (2012). *Bad Bug Book, Foodborne Pathogenic Microorganisms and Natural Toxins* (2nd ed.). Retrieved from www.fda.gov

41. Food and Drug Administration. (2015, July 2). Food Code 2013. Retrieved from https://www.fda.gov/Food/GuidanceRegulation/RetailFoodProtection/FoodCode/ucm374275.htm

42. Food and Drug Administration. (2015, September). The dangers of raw milk: Unpasteurized milk can pose a serious health risk. Retrieved fromhttps://www.fda.gov/Food/resourcesForYou/consumers/ucm079516.htm

43. Food and Drug Administration. (2015, November). Food facts: Food and water safety during power outages and floods. Retrieved from https://www.fda.gov/downloads/food/recallsoutbreaksemergencies/ucm076962.pdf

44. Food and Drug Administration. (2016, March). Food safety for moms-to-be: P While you're pregnant–Listeria. Retrieved from https://www.fda.gov/Food/ResourcesForYou/HealthEducators/ucm083320.htm

45. Food and Drug Administration. (2016, April). Total diet study. Retrieved from https://www.fda.gov/food/foodscienceresearch/totaldietstudy/default.htm

46. Food and Drug Administration. (2017, January). Eating fish: What pregnant women and parents should know. Retrieved from https://www.fda.gov/Food/FoodborneIllnessContaminants/Metals/ucm393070.htm

47. Food and Drug Administration. (2017, January 13). FDA Food Safety Modernization Act (FSMA). Retrieved from http://www.fda.gov/Food/GuidanceRegulation/FSMA/default.htm

48. Food and Drug Administration (2017, April). Food allergies: What you need to know. Retrieved from https://www.fda.gov/food/ingredientspackaginglabeling/foodallergens/ucm079311.htm

49. Food and Drug Administration. (2017, May). Pesticide monitoring program: Fiscal year 2014 pesticide report. Retrieved from https://www.fda.gov/Food/FoodborneIllnessContaminants/Pesticides/ucm546327.htm

50. Formanek, R. (2001). Food allergies: When food becomes the enemy. *FDA Consumer, 35*(4).

51. Formanek, R. (2001). Highlights of FDA food safety efforts: Fruit juice, mercury in fish. *FDA Consumer, 3*(2).

52. Formanek, R. (2001). Proposed rules issued for bioengineered foods. *FDA Consumer, 35*(2).

53. Fox, J. A. (2002). Influence on the purchase of irradiated foods. *Food Technology, 56*(11), 34–37.

54. Greger, J. L. (2000). Biotechnology: Mobilizing dietitians to be a resource. *Journal of the American Dietetic Association, 100*, 1306–1308.

55. Greger, J. L., & Baier, M. (1981). Tin and iron content of canned and bottled foods. *Journal of Food Science, 46*, 1751.

56. Institute of Food Technologists' Expert Report on Biotechnology and Foods. (2000). Human food safety evaluation of rDNA biotechnology-derived foods. *Food Technology, 54*(9), 53–61.

57. Institute of Medicine (US) and National Research Council (US) Committee to Ensure Safe Food from Production to Consumption. Ensuring Safe Food: From Production to Consumption. Washington, D.C.: National Academies Press (US). (1998). C, Food Safety from Farm to Table: A National Food-Safety Initiative. A Report to the President, May 1997. Retrieved from https://www.ncbi.nlm.nih.gov/books/NBK209117/

58. Jackson, G. J. (1997). *Cyclospora*—Still another new foodborne pathogen. *Food Technology, 51*(1), 120.

59. Killinger, K. M., Hunt, M. C., Campbell, R. E., & Kropf, D. H. (2000). Factors affecting premature browning during cooking of store-purchased ground beef. *Journal of Food Science, 65*, 585–587.

60. Kosa, K. M., Cates, S. C., Bradley, S., Godwin, S., & Chambers, C. (2015). Consumer shell egg consumption and handling practices: Results from a national survey. *Journal of Food Protection, 78*(7), 1312–1319.

61. Lusk, J. L., Fox, J. A., & McIlvain, C. L. (1999). Consumer acceptance of irradiated meat. *Food Technology, 53*(3), 56–59.

62. Maheshwari, A., Fischer, M., Gambetti, P., Parker, A., Ram, A., Soto, C…. Hussein, H. M. (2015). Recent US case of Variant Creutzfeldt-Jakob disease—Global Implications. *Emerging Infectious Diseases, 21*(5), 750–759. https://dx.doi.org/10.3201/eid2105.142017.

63. Marder, E. P., Cieslak, P. R., Cronquist, A. B., Dunn, J., Lathrop, S., …. Geissler, A. L. (2017, April 21). Incidence and trends of infections with pathogens transmitted commonly through food and the effect of increasing use of culture-independent diagnostic tests on surveillance—Foodborne Diseases Active Surveillance Network, 10 U.S. Sites, 2013–2016. *Morbidity and Mortality Weekly Report (MMWR), 66*(15), 397–403.

64. McHugh, T., & Carswell, L. (2017). Illuminating e-beam processing. *Food Technology, 71*(1), 64–66.

65. Meadows, M. (2004). The FDA and the fight against terrorism. *FDA Consumer Magazine, 38*(11).

66. Meer, R. R., & Misner, S. L. (2000). Food safety knowledge and behavior of expanded food and nutrition education program participants in Arizona. *Journal of Food Protection, 63*, 1725–1731.

67. Mermelstein, N. H. (1993). Controlling *E. coli* 0157: H7 in meat. *Food Technology, 47*(4), 90.

68. Mermelstein, N. H. (2000). E-beam irradiated beef reaches the market, papaya and gamma-irradiated beef to follow. *Food Technology, 54*(7), 88–92.

69. Mermelstein, N. H. (2001). Sanitizing meat. *Food Technology, 55*(3), 64–68.

70. Mungai, E. A., Behravesh, C. B., & Gould, H. (2015). Increased outbreaks associated with nonpasteurized milk, United States, 2007-2012. *Emerging Infectious Diseases, 21*(1), 119–122. doi:http://dx.doi.org/10.3201/eid2101.140447

71. Murphy, P. A., Hendrich, S., Landgren, C., & Bryant, C. M. (2006). Food mycotoxins: An update. *Journal of Food Science, 71*, R51–R65.

72. National Center for Home Food Preservation. (2015). *USDA complete guide to home canning, 2015 revision*. Retrieved from http://nchfp.uga.edu/publications/publications_usda.html

73. National Institute of Diabetes and Digestive and Kidney Diseases (NIH), U.S. Department of Health and Human Services. (2014, August). Hemolytic uremic syndrome in children. *NIH Publication No. 14-4570*. Retrieved from https://www.niddk.nih.gov/health-information/kidney-disease/children/hemolytic-uremic-syndrome

74. National Restaurant Association. (2016). News and research: Facts at a glance. Retrieved from http://www.restaurant.org

75. National Restaurant Association Educational Foundation. (2014). *ServSafe coursebook* (6th ed.). Chicago: Author.

76. Nayga, R. M., Jr., Poghosyan, A., & Nichols, J. (2004). Will consumers accept irradiated food products? *International Journal of Consumer Studies, 28*(2), 178–185.

77. Newsome, R. (2006). Understanding mycotoxins. *Food Technology, 60*(6), 51–58.

78. Orlandi, P. A., Chu, D. M. Y., Bier, J. W., & Jackson, G. J. (2001). Scientific status summary: Parasites and the food supply. *Food Technology, 56*(4), 72–81.

79. Park, J., & Brittin, H. C. (1997). Increased iron content of food due to stainless steel cookware. *Journal of the American Dietetic Association, 97*, 659.

80. Patil, S. R., Cates, S., & Morales, R. (2005). Consumer food safety knowledge, practices, and demographic differences: Findings from a meta analysis. *Journal of Food Protection, 68*, 1884–1894.

81. Production, Storage, and Transportation of Shell Eggs, 21 C.F.R.§118 (2009, July 29).

82. Public Law 107-188. Public Health Security and Bioterrorism and Response Act of 2002. Retrieved from http://www.fda.gov/oc/bioterrorism/PL107-188.html

83. Ralston, K., Starke, Y., Brent, P., & Riggins, T. (2000). Awareness of risks changing how hamburgers are cooked. *Food Review, 23*(2), 44–50.

84. Scallon, E., Griffin, P. M., Angulo, F. J., Tauxe, R. V., & Hoekstra, R. M. (2011). Foodborne illness acquired in

the United States—Unspecified agents. *Emerging Infectious Diseases, 17*(1), 16–22.

85. Scallon, E., Hoekstra, R. M., Angulo, F. J., Tauxe, R. V., Widdowson, M. A., Roy, S. L., Jones, J. L., & Griffin, P. M. (2011). Foodborne illness acquired in the United States—Major pathogens. *Emerging Infectious Diseases, 17*(1), 7–15. https://dx.doi.org/10.3201/eid1701.P11101

86. Shah, N. P. (2001). Functional foods from probiotics and prebiotics. *Food Technology, 55*(11), 46.

87. Shiferaw, B., Yang, S., Cieslak, P., Vugia, D., Marcus, R., Koehler, J., Deneen, V., & Angulo, F. (2000). Prevalence of high-risk food consumption and food handling practices among adults: A multistate survey, 1996–1997. *Journal of Food Protection, 63*, 1538–1543.

88. Siuta-Cruce, P., & Goulet, J. (2001). Improving probiotic survival rates. *Food Technology, 55*(10), 36.

89. Smith, J. S., & Pillai, S. (2004). Irradiation and food safety. *Food Technology, 58*(11), 48–55.

90. Tarver, T. (2016). University of Nebraska allergy researchers fight foreign invasions. *Food Technology, 70*(8), 21–25.

91. Taylor, S. L., & Hefle, S. L. (2001). Food allergies and other sensitivities. *Food Technology, 55*(9), 68–83.

92. Taylor, S. L., & Hefle, S. L. (2005). Allergen control. *Food Technology, 59*(2), 40–43, 75.

93. Trautman, T. (2005). Labeling food allergens. *Food Technology, 59*(2), 92.

94. U.S. Department of Agriculture. (2017, June). Protect your baby and yourself from listeriosis. Retrieved from https://www.fsis.usda.gov/wps/portal/fsis/topics/food-safety-education/get-answers/food-safety-fact-sheets/foodborne-illness-and-disease/protect-your-baby-and-yourself-from-listeriosis/CT_Index

95. U.S. Department of Agriculture. (2017, July). USDA detects a case of atypical bovine spongiform encephalopathy in Alabama. Retrieved from https://www.aphis.usda.gov/aphis/newsroom/stakeholder-info/sa_by_date/sa-2017/sa-07/bse-alabama

96. U.S. Department of Agriculture, Food Safety and Inspection Service. (2013, August). Molds on foods—Are they dangerous? Retrieved from https://www.fsis.usda.gov/wps/portal/fsis/topics/food-safety-education/get-answers/food-safety-fact-sheets/safe-food-handling/molds-on-food-are-they-dangerous_/CT_Index

97. U.S. Department of Agriculture, Food Safety and Inspection Service. (2016, December). Is it done yet? Retrieved from http://www.fsis.usda.gov/is_it_done_yet

98. U.S. Environmental Protection Agency. (2016, September). Basic information about mercury. Retrieved from https://www.epa.gov/mercury

99. U.S. Environmental Protection Agency. (2017, May). Choose fish and shellfish wisely: Fish and shellfish advisories and safe eating guidelines. Retrieved from https://www.epa.gov/choose-fish-and-shellfish-wisely/fish-and-shellfish-advisories-and-safe-eating-guidelines

100. U.S. Federal Government: Foodsafety.gov. (2017, January 16). Who's at risk. Retrieved from https://www.foodsafety.gov/risk/index.html

101. Young, A., Taylor, J., & Fix, J. L. (1999, August). A killer in our food. *Detroit Free Press.*

102. Zhao, C., Ge, B., De Villena, J., Studler, R., Yeh, E., … Meng, J. (2001). Prevalence of *Campylobacter* spp., *Escherichia coli*, and *Salmonella* Serovars in retail chicken, turkey, pork, and beef from the Greater Washington, D.C., area. *Applied Environmental.*

Chapter 3

1. Barrows, J. N., Lipman, A. L., & Bailey, C. J. (2003). Color additives: FDA's regulatory process and historical perspectives (reprint from *Food Safety Magazine*, October/November 2003). Retrieved from https://www.fda.gov/ForIndustry/ColorAdditives/RegulatoryProcessHistoricalPerspectives/default.htm

2. Bliss, R. M. (2012, January). Nutrient data in time for the New Year. *Agricultural Research*, 20–21.

3. Brecher, S. J., Bender, M. M., Wilkening, V. L., McCabe, N. M., & Anderson, E. M. (2000). Status of nutrition labeling, health claims, and nutrient content claims for processed foods: 1997 food label and package survey. *Journal of the American Dietetic Association, 100*, 1056.

4. Burrows, A. (2009). Palette of our palates: A brief history of food coloring and its regulation. *Comprehensive Reviews in Food Science and Food Safety, 8*(4), 394–408. doi:10.1111/j.1541-4337.2009.00089.x 1111/j.1541-4337.2009.00089.x

5. Buzby, J. C., & Crutchfield, S. R. (1997). USDA modernizes meat and poultry inspection. *Food Review, 20*(1), 14.

6. Carlson, A. (2016, May 24). Investigating retail price premiums for organic foods. *Amber Waves*. Retrieved from https://www.ers.usda.gov/amber-waves/2016/may/investigating-retail-price-premiums-for-organic-foods/

7. Cody, M. M., & Stretch, T. (2014). Position of the Academy of Nutrition and Dietetics: Food and water safety. *Journal of the Academy of Nutrition and Dietetics, 114*(11), 1819–1829. doi:http://dx.doi.org/10.1016/j.jand.2014.08.023

8. Cohen, S. M., Fukushima, S., Gooderham, N. J., Hecht, S. S., Marnett, L. J. Rietjens, I. M. C. M., Smith, R. L., Bastaki, M., McGowen, M. M., Harman, C., & Taylor, S. V. (2015). GRAS 27 flavoring substances. *Food Technology, 69*(8), 40–59.

9. Final determination regarding partially hydrogenated oils. 80 F.R. § 34650. (2015, June 17).

10. Fisher, C., & Carvajal, R. (2008). What is natural? *Food Technology, 62*(11), 24–31.

11. Food labeling; Gluten-free labeling of foods, 21 C.F.R, § 101 (2013, August 5).

12. Food labeling: Revision of the nutrition and supplement facts labels, 21 C.F.R §101 (2016, May 16).

13. Food labeling: Serving sizes of foods that can reasonably be consumed at one eating occasion; dual-column labelling; updating, modifying, and establishing certain reference amounts customarily consumed; serving size for breath mints; and technical amendments. 21 C.F.R §101 (2016, May 27).

14. Food standards: Amendment of standards of identity for enriched grain products to require addition of folic acid. 61 F. R. § 8781 (1996, March 5).

15. Francis, F. J. (1985). Pigments and other colorants. In Owen Fennema (Ed.), *Food Chemistry* (p. 580). New York: Marcel-Dekker.

16. Giese, J. (2000). Pesticide analysis. *Food Technology, 54*(12), 64–65.

17. Griffiths, J. C. (2005). Coloring foods and beverages. *Food Technology, 59*(5), 38–44.

18. Hilts, P. J. (2006). The FDA at work: Cutting-edge science promoting public health. *FDA Consumer, 40*(1), 29–35, 39–41.

19. International Food Information Council and U.S. Food and Drug Administration. (2010, April). Overview of food ingredients, additives and colors. Retrieved from https://www.fda.gov/Food/IngredientsPackagingLabeling/FoodAdditivesIngredients/ucm094211.htm#why

20. Liu, R., Hooker, N. H., Parsidis, E., & Simons, C. T. (2017). A natural experiment: Using immersive technologies to study the impact of "all-natural" labeling on perceived food quality, nutritional content, and liking. *Journal of Food Science, 82*(3), 825–833. doi:10.1111/1750-3841.13639

21. Looney, J. W., Crandall, P. G., & Poole, A. K. (2001). The matrix of food safety regulations. *Food Technology, 55*(4), 60–76.

22. Meadows, M. (2006). A century of ensuring safe foods and cosmetics. *FDA Consumer, 40*(1), 7–13.

23. Mermelstein, N. H. (1993). Nutrition labeling in foodservice. *Food Technology, 47*(4), 65.

24. Mermelstein, N. H. (2001). Terrorism spurs renewed call for single food safety agency. *Food Technology, 55*(11), 32.

25. Mermelstein, N. H. (2011). Testing for gluten in foods. *Food Technology, 65*(2), 74–80.

26. Mermelstein, N. H. (2015). Determining the GRAS status of flavors. *Food Technology, 69*(2), 76–78.

27. Mermelstein, N. H. (2016). Coloring food and beverages. *Food Technology, 70*(1), 67–72.

28. Morrison, R. M., Mancino, L., & Variyam, J. N. (2011). Will calorie labeling in restaurants make a difference. *Amber Waves, 9*(1), 10–17.

29. Newsome, R. (1997). Codex, international trade, and science. *Food Technology, 51*(9), 28.

30. Ohr, L. M. (2004). Nutrition in a nutshell. *Food Technology, 58*(1), 55–59.

31. Regenstein, J. (2002). A single food safety agency is not the answer. *Food Technology, 56*(3), 104.

32. Smith, J. S., & Pillai, S. (2004). Irradiation and food safety. *Food Technology, 58*(11), 48–55.

33. Staff. (2006). FDA milestones. *FDA Consumer, 40*(1), 36–38.

34. erally recognized as safe. 81 F. R. § 54959. (2016, August 16).

35. Swann, J. P. (2014). FDA's origin. Retrieved from https://www.fda.gov/AboutFDA/WhatWeDo/History/Origin/ucm124403.htm

36. Tauxe, R. V. (2001). Food safety and irradiation: Protecting the public from Food borne infections. *Emerging Infectious Diseases, 7*(97), 516–521. https://dx.doi.org/10.3201/eid0707.017706.

37. Turner, R. E. (2002). Organic standards. *Food Technology, 56*(6), 24.

38. U.S. Department of Agriculture. (2015, March). U.S. Codex and Codex Alimentarius. Retrieved from https://www.fsis.usda.gov/wps/portal/fsis/topics/international-affairs/us-codex-alimentarius

39. U.S. Department of Agriculture. (2016, December). Irradiation and food safety answers to frequently asked questions. Retrieved from https://www.fsis.usda.gov/wps/portal/fsis/topics/food-safety-education/get-answers/food-safety-fact-sheets/production-and-inspection/irradiation-and-food-safety/irradiation-food-safety-faq

40. U.S. Department of Agriculture. (2017, July). USDA seeks input in developing a proposed bioengineered food disclosure rule. Retrieved from https://www.ams.usda.gov/content/usda-seeks-input-developing-proposed-bioengineered-food-disclosure-rule

41. U.S. Department of Agriculture. (n.d.). Agricultural biotechnology glossary. Retrieved on August 19, 2017 from https://www.usda.gov/topics/biotechnology/biotechnology-glossary

42. U.S. Department of Agriculture. (n.d.). Regulation of biotech plants. Retrieved on August 19, 2017 from https://www.usda.gov/topics/biotechnology/how-federal-government-regulates-biotech-plants

43. U.S. Department of Agriculture. (n.d.) Roles of USDA agencies in biotechnology. Retrieved on August 19, 2017 from https://www.usda.gov/topics/biotechnology/roles-usda-agencies-biotechnology

44. U.S. Department of Agriculture, Agricultural Marketing Service. (n.d.). National Organic Program. Retrieved from https://www.ams.usda.gov/about-ams/programs-offices/national-organic-program

45. U.S. Department of Agriculture, Food Safety Inspection Service. (2010, April). Country of origin labeling for meat and chicken. Retrieved from http://www.fsis.usda.gov/Fact_Sheets/COOL_Meat_and_Chicken/index.asp

46. U.S. Department of Agriculture, Food Safety Inspection Service. (2015, March). FSIS history. Retrieved from https://www.fsis.usda.gov/wps/portal/informational/aboutfsis/history

47. U.S. Environmental Protection Agency. (2017, June). EPA's regulation of biotechnology for use in pest management. Retrieved from https://www.epa.gov/regulation-biotechnology-under-tsca-and-fifra/epas-regulation-biotechnology-use-pest-management#role

48. U.S. Food and Drug Administration. (2013, January). A food labeling guide: Guidance for industry. Retrieved from www.fda.gov/FoodLabelingGuide

49. U.S. Food and Drug Administration. (2013, January). Guidance for industry: A food labeling guide (9. Appendix A: Definitions of nutrient content claims. Retrieved from https://www.fda.gov/Food/GuidanceRegulation/GuidanceDocumentsRegulatoryInformation/LabelingNutrition/ucm064911.htm

50. U.S. Food and Drug Administration. (2015, July). Background on the FDA Food Safety Modernization Act (FSMA). Retrieved from https://www.fda.gov/newsevents/publichealthfocus/ucm239907.htm

51. U.S. Food and Drug Administration. (2015, July 2). Food Code 2013. Retrieved from https://www.fda.gov/Food/GuidanceRegulation/RetailFoodProtection/FoodCode/ucm374275.htm

52. U.S. Food and Drug Administration. (2015, October). Consumer info about food from genetically engineered plants. Retrieved from https://www.fda.gov/Food/IngredientsPackagingLabeling/GEPlants/ucm461805.htm

53. U.S. Food and Drug Administration. (2016, April). Dietary supplements. Retrieved from http://www.fda.gov/Food/DietarySupplements/default.htm

54. U.S. Food and Drug and Administration. (2016, May). The importance of public comment to the FDA. Retrieved from https://www.fda.gov/drugs/resourcesforyou/consumers/ucm143569.htm

55. U.S. Food and Drug Administration. (2016, July). Guidance for industry: Voluntary labeling indicating whether foods have or have not been derived from genetically engineered plants. Retrieved from https://www.fda.gov/Food/GuidanceRegulation/GuidanceDocumentsRegulatoryInformation/ucm059098.htm

56. U.S. Food and Drug Administration. (2016, August). Nutrition facts label better informs your food choices. Retrieved from https://www.fda.gov/forconsumers/consumerupdates/ucm387114.htm

57. U.S. Food and Drug Administration. (2016, November). Food Allergen Labeling and Consumer Protection Act of 2004 (FALCPA). Retrieved from https://www.fda.gov/Food/GuidanceRegulation/GuidanceDocumentsRegulatoryInformation/Allergens/ucm106187.htm

58. U.S. Food and Drug Administration. (2017, January). How FDA regulates food from genetically engineered plants. Retrieved from https://www.fda.gov/Food/IngredientsPackagingLabeling/GEPlants/ucm461831.htm

59. U.S. Food and Drug Administration. (2017, January). Labeling of foods derived from genetically engineered plants. Retrieved from https://www.fda.gov/food/ingredientspackaginglabeling/geplants/ucm346858.htm

60. U.S. Food and Drug Administration. (2017, May). Calorie labeling on restaurant menus and vending machines: What you need to know. Retrieved from https://www.fda.gov/food/ingredientspackaginglabeling/labelingnutrition/ucm436722.htm

61. U.S. Food and Drug Administration. (2017, May). Pesticide monitoring program: Fiscal year 2014 pesticide report. Retrieved from https://www.fda.gov/Food/FoodborneIllnessContaminants/Pesticides/ucm546327.htm

62. U.S. Food and Drug Administration. (2017, June). Changes to the nutrition facts label. Retrieved from https://www.fda.gov/Food/GuidanceRegulation/GuidanceDocumentsRegulatoryInformation/LabelingNutrition/ucm385663.htm#dates

63. U.S. Food and Drug Administration (2017, July). About FDA: Fact sheet: FDA at a glance. Retrieved from https://www.fda.gov/aboutfda/transparency/basics/ucm553038.htm

64. U.S. Food and Drug Administration. (2017, July). Laws enforced by FDA. Retrieved from https://www.fda.gov/RegulatoryInformation/LawsEnforcedbyFDA/

65. U.S. Food and Drug Administration. (2017, August). FSMA final rule for mitigation strategies to protect food against intentional adulteration. Retrieved from https://www.fda.gov/Food/GuidanceRegulation/FSMA/ucm378628.htm

66. U.S. Food and Drug Administration. (2017, August). Seafood. Retrieved from https://www.fda.gov/food/populartopics/ucm341987.htm

67. U.S. Food and Drug Administration, Center for Food Safety and Applied Nutrition. (2006). *Trans* fat now listed with saturated fat and cholesterol on the Nutrition Facts label. Retrieved from http://www.cfsan.fda.gov/~dms/transfat.html

68. U.S. organic food sales totaled $43 billion in 2016. (2017, May 30). *Food Technology News*.

69. White chocolate: Establishment of a standard of identity. 21 CFR § 163. (2002, October 4).

70. Winter, C. K. (1993). Pesticide residues and the Delaney clause. *Food Technology, 47*(7), 81.

71. Wodicka, V. O. (1996). Regulation of food: Where have we been? *Food Technology, 50*(3), 106.

Chapter 4

1. American Association of Family and Consumer Sciences. (2001). *Food: A handbook of terminology, purchasing, and preparation* (10th ed.). Alexandria, VA: American Association of Family and Consumer Sciences.

2. American Standards Association. (1963). *American standard dimensions, tolerances, and terminology for home cooking and baking utensils.* New York: American Standards Association, Inc.

3. Arlin, M. L., Nielsen, M. M., & Hall, F. T. (1964). The effect of different methods of flour measurement on the quality of plain two-egg cakes. *Journal of Home Economics, 56*, 399.

4. Labensky, S. R., Damme, E. V., & Martel, P. A. (2009). *On baking: A textbook of baking and pastry fundamentals* (2nd ed.). Upper Saddle River, NJ: Pearson Prentice Hall.

5. Labensky, S. R., Martel, P. A., & Hause, A. M. (2011). *On cooking: A textbook of culinary fundamentals* (5th ed.). Upper Saddle River, NJ: Pearson Prentice Hall.

6. Lawless, S. T., Gregoire, M. B., Canter, D. D., & Setser, C. S. (1991). Comparison of cakes produced from computer-generated recipes. *School Food Service Research Review, 15*(1), 23–27.

7. Matthews, R. H., & Batcher, O. M. (1963). Sifted versus unsifted flour. *Journal of Home Economics, 55*, 123.

8. Molt, M. (2018). *Food for fifty* (14th ed.). Upper Saddle River, NJ: Pearson Prentice Hall.

9. Randal, J. (1994). Going metric: American foods and drugs measure up. *FDA Consumer, 28*(7), 23–26.

10. U.S. Department of Agriculture. (2013, June). Deep fat frying and food safety. Retrieved from https://www.fsis.usda.gov/wps/portal/fsis/topics/food-safety-education/get-answers/food-safety-fact-sheets/safe-food-handling/deep-fat-frying-and-food-safety/ct_index

Chapter 5

1. American Association of Family and Consumer Sciences. (2001). *Food: A handbook of terminology, purchasing, and preparation* (10th ed.). Alexandria, VA: Author.

2. Barber, N., Boyce, J., Binkley, M., Broz, C. (2007). How do silicone muffin pans compare to traditional metal pans? *Journal of Foodservice, 18*, 218–226.

3. Barber, N., Scarcelli, J., Almanza, B. A., Daniel, J. R., & Nelson, D. (2007). Silicone bakeware: Does it deliver a better product? *Journal of Foodservice, 18*, 43–51.

4. Bowers, D. E. (2000). Cooking trends echo changing roles of women. *Food Review, 23*(1), 23–29.

5. Brody, A. L. (2001). The return of microwavable foods. *Food Technology, 55*(3), 69–70.

6. Brody, A. L. (2011). Advances in microwave pasteurization and sterilization. *Food Technology, 65*(2), 83–85.

7. Carroll, L. E. (1989). Hydrocolloid functions to improve stability of microwavable foods. *Food Technology, 43*(6), 96.

8. Cipra, J. S., & Bowers, J. A. (1971). Flavor of microwave- and conventionally-reheated turkey. *Poultry Science, 50,* 703.

9. Clark, J. P. (2009). Getting to the heart of heat transfer. *Food Technology, 63*(9), 82–86.

10. Clark, J. P. (2013). Shedding light on UV radiation and pulsed light processing. *Food Technology, 67*(10), 65–67.

11. Dahl, C. A., & Matthews, M. E. (1980). Effect of microwave heating in cook/chill foodservice systems. *Journal of the American Dietetic Association, 77,* 289.

12. Decareau, R. V. (1992). *Microwave foods: New product development.* Trumbull, CT: Food & Nutrition Press, Inc.

13. Galgano, F., Favati, F., Caruso, M., Pietrafesa, A., & Natetlla, S. (2007). The influence of processing and preservation on the retention of health-promoting compounds in broccoli. *Journal of Food Science, 72*(2), S130–S135.

14. Giese, J. H. (1992). Advances in microwave food processing. *Food Technology, 46*(9), 118.

15. Gregoire, M. B. (2017). *Foodservice organizations: A managerial and systems approach* (9th ed.). Upper Saddle River, NJ: Pearson Prentice Hall.

16. Jiménez-Monreal, A. M., García-Diz, L., Martínez-Tomé, M., Mariscal, M., & Murcia, M. A. (2009). Influence of cooking methods on antioxidant activity of vegetables. *Journal of Food Science, 74*(3), H97–H103.

17. Labensky, S. R., Hause, A. M., & Martel, P. A. (2011). *On cooking: A textbook of culinary fundamentals* (5th ed.). Upper Saddle River, NJ: Pearson Prentice Hall.

18. Lindsay, R. E., Krissinger, W. A., & Fields, B. F. (1986). Microwave vs. conventional oven cooking of chicken: Relationship of internal temperature to surface contamination by *Salmonella typhimurium. Journal of the American Dietetic Association, 86,* 373.

19. Mandigo, R. W., & Janssen, T. J. (1982). Energy-efficient cooking systems for muscle foods. *Food Technology, 36*(4), 128.

20. McHugh, T. (2016). Microwave processing heats up. *Food Technology, 70*(10), 63–65.

21. McHugh, T. (2017). Sous vide: Cooking under vacuum. *Food Technology, 71*(12), 79–81.

22. McManus, L. (2010, September/October). The best cheap nonstick skillet. *Cooks Illustrated, 106,* 26–27.

23. Mermelstein, N. H. (1999). Microwave processing of food. *Food Technology, 53*(7), 114–116.

24. Miller, R. A., & Hoseney, R. C. (1997). Method to measure microwave-induced toughness of bread. *Journal of Food Science, 62,* 1202.

25. Molt, M. (2018). *Food for fifty* (14th ed.). Upper Saddle River, NJ: Pearson Prentice Hall.

26. National Restaurant Association Educational Foundation. (2014). *ServSafe coursebook* (6th ed.). Chicago: Author.

27. Ramesh, M. N., Tevini, D., & Wolf, W. (2002). Microwave blanching of vegetables. *Journal of Food Science, 67*(1), 390–398.

28. Ryynanen, S., & Ohlsson, T. (1996). Microwave heating uniformity of ready meals as affected by placement, composition, and geometry. *Journal of Food Science, 61,* 620.

29. Sierra, T. (2010, April/March). Re-evaluating large saucepans. *Cooks Illustrated, 103,* 28–29.

30. Sloan, A. E. (2010). Consumers are big fans of small appliances. *Food Technology, 64*(5), 18.

31. Tang, J. (2015). Unlocking potentials of microwaves for food safety and quality. *Journal of Food Science, 80*(8), E1776–E1793.

32. USDA Food Safety and Inspection Service. (2013, August). Microwave ovens and food safety. Retrieved from https://www.fsis.usda.gov/wps/portal/fsis/topics/food-safety-education/get-answers/food-safety-fact-sheets/appliances-and-thermometers/microwave-ovens-and-food-safety/ct_index

33. U.S. Food and Drug Administration. (2016, September). 5 tips for using your microwave oven safely. Retrieved from https://www.fda.gov/forconsumers/consumer-updates/ucm048953.htm

34. U.S. Food and Drug Administration. (2017, December). Microwave oven radiation. Retrieved from https://www.fda.gov/radiation-emittingproducts/resourcesforyouradiationemittingproducts/ucm252762.htm

Chapter 6

1. ASTM International. (2009). Standard terminology relating to sensory evaluations of materials and products, E253-09a. West Conshohocken, PA: ASTM International.

2. Augustin, J., Augustin, E., Cutrufelli, R. L., Hagen, S. R., & Teitzel, C. (1992). Alcohol retention in food preparation. *Journal of the American Dietetic Association, 92,* 486.

3. Bartelme, M. Z. (2017). Pathogen removal may affect spices: Better-for-you snacks. *Food Technology, 71*(6), 14.

4. Batenburg, M., & van der Velden, R. (2011). Saltiness enhancement by savory aroma compounds. *Journal of Food Science, 76*(5), S280–S288. doi:10.1111/j.1750-3851.2011.02198.x

5. Bosland, P. W. (1996). Capsicums: Innovative uses of an ancient crop. In J. Janick (Ed.), *Progress in new crops* (pp. 479–487). Arlington, VA: ASHS Press.

6. Brown, A. (2004). The parts department. In *I'm just here for more food* (p. 78). New York: Stewart, Tabori, and Chang.

7. Decker, K. J. (2008). Umami and beyond. *Food Product Design, 18*(2), 36–43.

8. Drake, S. L., & Drake, M. A. (2011). Comparison of salty states and time intensity of sea and land salts from around the world. *Journal of Sensory Studies, 26*(1), 25–34. doi:10.1111/j.1745-459X.2010.00317.x

9. Dresser, K. (2010, November/December). Making the most of salt. *Cook's Illustrated, 107,* 16–17.

10. Duncan, S. E., Moberg, K., Amin, K. N., Wright, M., Newkirk, J. J., Ponder, M. A., Acuff, G. R., & Dickson, J. S. (2017). Processes to preserve spice and herb quality and sensory integrity during pathogen inactivation. *Journal of Food Science, 82*(5), 1208–1215.

11. Dziezak, J. D. (1989). Spices. *Food Technology, 43*(1), 102.

12. Ejaz, A., Wu, W., Kwan, P., & Meydani, M. (2009). Curcumin inhibits adipogenesis in 3T3-L1 adipocytes and angiogenesis and obesity in C57/BL mice. *Journal of Nutrition, 139*(5), 919–925. doi:10.3945/jn.108.100966.

13. Edris, A., & Bergnstahl, B. (2001). Encapsulation of orange oil in a spray dried double emulsion. *Nahrung/Food*, *45*(2), 133–137.

14. Frye, A. M., & Setser, C. S. (1993). Ch.11. Bulking agents and fat substitutes. In A. M. Altschul (Ed.), *Low-calorie foods handbook* (pp. 211–251). New York, NY: Marcel Dekker, Inc.

15. Food and Drug Administration, Department of Health and Human Services. (2015). *Guidance for industry: Colored sea salts*. College Park, MD: Office of Food Additive Safety, HFS-200 Center for Food Safety and Applied Nutrition Food and Drug Administration.

16. Furth, P., & Cox, D. (2004). The spice market expands. *Food Technology*, *58*(8), 30–34.

17. Geha, R. S., Beiser, A., Clement, R., Patterson, R., Greenberger, P. A., Grammer, L. C. et al. (2000). Supplement—Review of alleged reaction to monosodium glutamate and outcome of a multicenter double-blind placebo-controlled study. *Journal of Nutrition*, *130*, 1058S–1062S.

18. Gillette, M. (1985). Flavor effects of sodium chloride. *Food Technology*, *39*(6), 47.

19. Griffiths, J. C. (2005). Coloring foods & beverages. *Food Technology*, *59*(5), 38–44.

20. Hatae, K., Takeutchi, F., Sakamoto, M., Ogasawara, Y., & Akano, H. (2009). Saltiness and acidity: Detection and recognition thresholds and their interaction near the threshold. *Journal of Food Science*, *74*(4), S147–S153. doi: 10.1111/j.1750-3841.2009.01116.x

21. Hayes, J. E., Sullivan, B. S., & Duffy, V. B. (2010). Explaining variability in sodium intake through oral sensory phenotype, salt sensation and liking. *Physiology & Behavior*, *100*(4), 369–380. doi:10.1016/j.physbeh.2010.03.017

22. Henney, J. E., Taylor, C. L., Boon, C. S. (Eds.). (2010). Institute of Medicine (US) Committee on Strategies to Reduce Sodium Intake. Washington, D.C.: National Academies Press (US).

23. Huang, X., Tang, L., Cal, H., Pan, Y., He, Y., Dai, C., Chen, A., Yu, X., Chen, M., Zou, L.,& Wan, L. (2015). Anti-inflammatory effects of monoammonium glycyrrhizinate on lipopolysaccharide-induced acute lung injury in mice through regulating nuclear factor-kappa B signaling pathway. *Evidence-Based Complementary and Alternative Medicine*, 2015, 272474. doi:10.1155/2015/272474

24. Institute of Food Technologists' Expert Panel on Food Safety and Nutrition. (1987). Monosodium glutamate (MSG). *Food Technology*, *41*(5), 143.

25. Institute of Medicine (US) Committee on Strategies To Reduce Sodium Intake. Spear, G (ed.) (2016). Taste and flavor roles of sodium in foods: A unique challenge to reducing sodium intake. In *Strategies to Reduce Sodium Intake in the United States*. Bethesda, Md: National Library of Medicine.

26. Jafari, S. M., Assadpoor, E., He, Y., & Bhandari, B. (2008). Encapsulation efficiency of food flavours and oils during spray drying. *Drying Technology*, *26*(7), 816–835.

27. Jo, M. N., & Lee, Y. M. (2008). Analyzing the sensory characteristics and taste-sensor ions of MSG substitutes. *Journal of Food Science*, *73*(5), S191–S198.

28. Jung, A. (2017). Kimchi: Salt and spice and everything nice – or not? *Food Technology*, *71*(4), 13.

29. Katz, B., & Williams, L. A. (2010). Salt reduction gains momentum. *Food Technology*, *64*(5), 25–32.

30. Kramer, S., Mojet, J., & Shimojo, R. (2009). Salt reduction in foods using naturally brewed soy sauce. *Journal of Food Science*, *75*(6), S255–S263. doi:10.1111/j.1750-3841.2009.01232.x

31. Kuhn, M. E. (2010). Strategies for reducing sodium in the U.S. *Food Technology*, *64*(5), 34–36.

32. Labensky, S. R., Damme, E. V., & Martel, P. A. (2009). *On baking: A textbook of baking and pastry fundamentals* (2nd ed.). Upper Saddle River, NJ: Pearson Prentice Hall.

33. Labensky, S. R., Hause, A. M., & Martel, P. A. (2015). *On Cooking* (5th ed. *update*). Upper Saddle River, NJ: Pearson Education, Inc.

34. Leung, Angela M., Lewis E. Braverman, and Elizabeth N. Pearce. (2016). History of U.S. iodine fortification and supplementation. *Nutrients*. MDPI, November 2012. Web. December 19, 2016.

35. Lindsay, R. C. (1985). Flavors. In O.R. Fennema (Ed.), *Food chemistry* (2nd ed.). (pp. 585–628). New York, NY: Marcel Dekker, Inc.

36. Lindsay, R. C. (1985). Food additives. In O.R. Fennema (Ed.), *Food chemistry* (2nd ed.). (pp. 629–687). New York, NY: Marcel Dekker, Inc.

37. Lioe, H. N., Selamat, J., & Yasuda, M. (2010). Soy sauce and its umami taste: A link from the past to the current situation. *Journal of Food Science*, *75*(3), R71–R76. doi: 10.1111/j.1750-3841.2010.01529.x

38. Marcus, J. B. (2005). Culinary applications of umami. *Food Technology*, *59*(5), 24–30.

39. Marcus, J. B. (2009). Unleashing the power of umami. *Food Technology*, *63*(11), 22–36.

40. Meadows, M. (2003). MSG: A common flavor enhancer. *FDA Consumer Magazine*, *31*(1), 1.

41. Mermelstein, N. H. (2016). Coloring foods and beverages. *Food Technology*, *70*(1), 67.

42. McGregor, R. (2004). Taste modification in the biotech era. *Food Technology*, *58*(5), 24.

43. Miller, M. A., Mills, K., Wong, T., Drescher, G., Lee, S. M., Sirimuangmoon, C., Scahefer, S., Langstaff, S., & Minor, B. (2014). Flavor-enhancing properties of mushrooms in meat-based dishes in which sodium has been reduced and meat has been partially substituted with mushrooms. *Journal of Food Science*, *79*(90), S17975–S1804. doi:10.1111/1750-3841.12549

44. Molt, M. (2011). *Food for fifty* (13th ed.). Upper Saddle River, NJ: Pearson Prentice Hall.

45. Nachay, K. (2016). Nine flavor and color developments for product formulators. *Food Technology*, *71*(6), 83–98.

46. Nachay, K. (2017). Ingredient development takes cues from research insights. *Food Technology*, *62*(3), 26–35.

47. Nachay, K., & Bartelme, M. Z. (2017). Game-changing ingredient innovations. *Food Technology*, *71*(8), 66–94.

48. Neta, E. R. D., Johanningsmeier, S. D., Drake, M. A., & McFeeters, R. F. (2009). Effects of pH adjustment and sodium ions on sour taste intensity of organic acids. *Journal of Food Science*, *74*(4), S165–S169. doi:10.1111/j.1750-3841.2009.01127.x

49. Ortiz, E. L. (1992). *The encyclopedia of herbs, spices, and flavorings: A cook's compendium*. New York: DK Publishing.

50. Pangborn, R. M. (1962). Taste interrelationships: Supra threshold solutions of sucrose and sodium chloride. *Journal of Food Science, 27*(5), 495–500. doi:10.1111/j.1365-2621.1962.tb00133.x

51. Porzio, M. (2004). Flavor encapsulation: A convergence of science and art. *Food Technology, 58*(7), 40–47.

52. Porzio, M. (2004). Flavor encapsulation: A convergence of science and art. *Food Technology, 58*(7), 40–47.

53. Porzio, M.A. (2007). Flavor Delivery and Product Development. *Food Technology, 61*(1), 22–29.

54. Porzio, M. (2012). Advances in Flavor Encapsulation. *Food Technology, 66*(6), *52–64.*

55. Pszczola, D. E. (1997). Salty developments in food. *Food Technology, 51*(10), 79.

56. Pszczola, D. E. (2001). 2001: A spice odyssey. *Food Technology, 55*(1), 36–44.

57. Pszczola, D. E. (2004). Flavor enhancement: Taking the mask off. *Food Technology, 58*(8), 58–69.

58. Pszczola, D. E. (2008). Craving condiments. *Food Technology, 62*(4), 67–89.

59. Pszczola, D. E. (2008). Sniffing out emerging ingredients. *Food Technology, 62*(7), 53–61.

60. Pszczola, D. E. (2009). Rediscovering ingredients of antiquity. *Food Technology, 63*(10), 43–57.

61. Pszczola, D. E. (2010). Flavor marriages say "I do." *Food Technology, 64*(3), 49–57.

62. Raghavan, S. (2004). Developing ethnic foods and ethnic flair with spices. *Food Technology, 58*(8), 35–42.

63. Riley, K. A., & Kleyn, D. H. (1989). Fundamental principles of vanilla/vanilla extract processing and methods of detecting adulteration in vanilla extracts. *Food Technology, 43*(10), 64.

64. Rosengarten, F., Jr. (1969). *The book of spices.* Wynnewood, PA: Livingston Publishing Company.

65. Santibañez, R. (2007). *Rosa's New Mexican table.* New York: Artisan: Workman Publishing Company.

66. Sloan, A. E. (2001). Eastern influence. *Food Technology, 55*(3), 18.

67. Sloan, A. E. (2001). Ethnic foods in the decade ahead. *Food Technology, 55*(10), 18.

68. Sloan, A. E. (2001). More on ethnic foods: Move over BBQ, Cajun, and Caesar. *Food Technology, 55*(11), 18.

69. Sloan, A. E. (2010). U.S. consumers have a taste for world cuisines. *Food Technology, 64*(6), 19.

70. Sloan, A. E. (2011). Not too basic. *Food Technology, 65*(2), 21.

71. Sloan, A. E. (2011). Spices, seasonings come on strong. *Food Technology, 65*(5), 20.

72. Strom, B. L., Yaktine, S. L., & Oria, M. (Eds.). (2013). *Sodium Intake in Population Assessment of Evidence Committee on the Consequences of Sodium Reduction in Populations* Food *and* Nutrition Board on *Population* Health *and* Public Health Practice *Institute of* Medicine *(U.S.) Of The National Academies.* Washington, D.C.: The National Academies Press.

73. Tarver, T. (2010). Desalting the food grid. *Food Technology, 64*(8), 45–50.

74. U.S. Department of Agriculture, Economic Research Service. (2009, August). U.S. food import patterns, 1998–2007: Outlook report no. (FAU-125). Washington, D.C.

75. U.S. Government Publishing Office. (2017). Electronic Code of Federal Regulations. Washington, D.C.: U.S. Government Publishing Office.

76. U.S. Department of Health and Human Services, U.S.. Department of Agriculture. (2016). What We Eat in America. NHANES 2013-2014. Washington, D.C.: USDA: Agricultural Research Service.

77. U.S. Department of Health and Human Services and U.S. Department of Agriculture. (2015). *2015–2020 Dietary Guidelines for Americans* (8th ed.). Washington, D.C.: U.S. Government Publishing Office.

78. U.S. Food and Drug Administration. (2017). Compliance Policy Guides (CPG) Sec. 525.750 Spices-Definition. U.S. Department of Health and Human Services. FDA/Office of Regulatory Affairs. Washington, D.C.: Government Publishing Office.

79. U.S. Food and Drug Administration U.S. Department of Health and Human Services (2016). Manual of Compliance Policy Guides. Washington, D.C.

80. Waddell, W. J., Cohen, S. M., Feron, V. J., Goodman, J. I., Marnett, L. J., Portoghese, P. S., Rietjens, I. M. C. M., Smith, R. L., Adams, T. B., Gavin, L C., McGowen, M. M., & Williams, M. C. (2007). GRAS flavoring substances. *Food Technology, 61*(8), 22–49.

81. Webb, D. (2016). Herbs and spices: Holiday spices. *Today's Dietitian, 18*(11), 14.

Chapter 7

1. American Association of Cereal Chemists. (2001). The definition of dietary fiber. *Cereal Foods World, 46*(3), 112–126.

2. American Association of Family and Consumer Sciences. (2001). *Food: A handbook of terminology, purchasing, and preparation* (10th ed.). Alexandria, VA: Author.

3. American Dietetic Association. (2002). Position of the American Dietetic Association: Health implications of dietary fiber. *Journal of the American Dietetic Association, 102*, 993–1000.

4. Bower, J. (1992). *Food theory and application.* New York, NY: MacMillan Publishing Co.

5. Buswell, A. M., & Rodebush, W. H. (1956). Water. *Scientific American, 194*(4), 2.

6. Carr, J. M. (1993). Hydrocolloids and stabilizers. *Food Technology, 47*(10), 100.

7. Charley, H. (1982). *Food science.* New York, NY: John Wiley & Sons.

8. Doell, D., Folmer, D., Lee, H., Honigfort, M., & Carberry, S. (2012). Updated estimate of *trans* fat intake by the US population. *Journal Food Additives & Contaminants: Part A, 29*(6), 861–874.

9. Dziezak, J. D. (1991). A focus on gums. *Food Technology, 45*(3), 116.

10. Gordon, D. T. (2002). Intestinal health through dietary fiber, prebiotics, and probiotics. *Food Technology, 56*(4), 23.

11. Hicks, K. B., & Moreau, R. A. (2001). Phytosterols and phytostanols: Functional food cholesterol busters. *Food Technology, 55*(1), 63–67.

12. Hollingsworth, P. (2001). Margarine: The over-the-top functional food. *Food Technology, 55*(1), 59–62.

13. Katz, E. E., & Labuza, T. P. (1981). Effect of water activity on the sensory crispness and mechanical deformation of snack food products. *Journal of Food Science, 46*, 403.

14. U.S. Department of Agriculture. (1991). *Nutritive value of foods.* Home and Garden Bulletin No. 72. Washington, D.C.: Author.

15. Ohr, L. M. (2002). Circulating heart smart news. *Food Technology, 56*(6), 109–115.

16. Pszczola, D. E. (1999). Starches and gums move beyond fat replacement. *Food Technology, 53*(8), 74–80.

17. Sanderson, G. R. (1996). Gums and their use in food systems. *Food Technology, 50*(3), 81–84.

18. Shah, N. P. (2001). Functional foods from probiotics and prebiotics. *Food Technology, 55*(11), 46.

19. U.S. Department of Agriculture, Agricultural Research Service. (2017). USDA National Nutrient Database for Standard Reference. Washington, D.C.: U.S. Government Publishing Office.

20. U.S. Department of Health and Human Services, U.S. Food & Drug Administration. (2013). Tentative determination regarding partially hydrogenated oils; Request for comments and for scientific data and information; Extension of comment period. *Federal Register, 78*(217), 67169–67175. Washington, D.C.: U.S. Government Printing Office.

21. U.S. Department of Health and Human Services, U.S. Food & Drug Administration. (2015). Final determination regarding partially hydrogenated oils. *Federal Register, 80*(16), 34650–34670.

Chapter 8

1. Agriculture Marketing Service, U.S. Department of Agriculture. (1995, February). How to buy dairy products. *Home and Garden Bulletin, 201.*

2. Akoh, C. C. (1998). Fat replacers. *Food Technology, 52*(3), 47.

3. Allen, K. E., Dickinson, E., & Murray, B. (2006). Acidified sodium caseinate emulsion foams containing liquid fat: A comparison with whipping cream. *LWT-Food Science and Technology, 39*, 225–234.

4. Allman-Farinelli, M. A., Gomes, K., Favaloro, E. J., & Petocz, P. (2005). A diet rich in high-oleic-acid sunflower oil favorably alters low-density lipoprotein cholesterol, triglycerides, and factor VII coagulant activity. *Journal of the American Dietetic Association, 105*, 1071–1079.

5. American Dietetic Association. (2005). Position of the American Dietetic Association: Fat. *Journal of the American Dietetic Association, 105*, 266–275.

6. Bentley, J., & Ash, M. (2016). Butter and Margarine Availability over the last Century. *Amber Waves (online).* Washington, D.C.: United States Department of Agriculture, Economic 7. Research Service.

7. Bentley, J. (2017). U.S. Trends in Food Availability and a Dietary Assessment of Loss-Adjusted Food Availability, 1970-2014. Economic Information Bulletin No. (EIB-166) USDA Economic Research Service.

8. Bentley, J. (2017). U.S. Diets Still out of Balance with Dietary Recommendations. *Amber Waves (online).* Washington, D.C.: United States Department of Agriculture, Economic Research Service.

9. Berger, K. (1986). Palm oil products. *Food Technology, 40*(9), 72.

10. Berger, K. G., & Idris, N. A. (2005). Formulation of zero-*trans* acid shortenings and margarines and other food fats with products of the oil palm. *Journal of American Oil Chemists Society, 82*(11), 775–7782.

11. Bimbo, A. (2017). *Marine oils. AOCS American Oil Chemists Society.* (online). Urbana, IL: AOCS Lipid Library.

12. Binkoski, A. E., Kris-Etherton, P. M., Wilson, T. A., Mountain, M. L., & Nicolosi, R. J. (2005). Balance of unsaturated fatty acids is important to a cholesterol-lowering diet: Comparison of mid-oleic sunflower oil and olive oil on cardiovascular disease risk factors. *Journal of the American Dietetic Association, 105*, 1080–1086.

13. Blumenthal, M. M. (1991). A new look at the chemistry and physics of deep-fat frying. *Food Technology, 45*(2), 68.

14. Brooker, B. E. (1993). The stabilization of air in foods containing fat-A review. *Food Structure, 12*(1), 115–122.

15. Buldo, P., Wiking, L. (2012). The role of mixing temperature on microstructure and rheological properties of butter blends. *Journal of the American Oil Chemists' Society, 89*, 787–795.

16. Caponio, F., & Gomes, T. (2004). Examination of lipid fraction quality of margarine. *Journal of Food Science, 69*, 63–66.

17. Charley, H. (1982). *Food science.* New York, NY: John Wiley and Sons.

18. Clark, P. (2004). Crystallization is key in confectionery processes. *Food Technology, 58*(12), 94–96.

19. Clark, J. P. (2005). Fats and oil processors adapt to changing needs. *Food Technology, 59*(5), 74–76.

20. Clark, J. P. (2013). Emulsions when oil and water do mix. *Food Technology, 67*(8), 80–82.

21. Clark, J. P. (2013). Spins and wrinkles on frying foods. *Food Technology, 67*(12), 89–91.

22. Conlon, B. A., & Colpaart, A. M. (2014). Substituting palm oil for trans fat. *Today's Dietitian, 16*(7), 20.

23. Coughlin, J. R. (2003). Acrylamide: What we have learned so far. *Food Technology 57*(2), 100.

24. Crandall, L. (2006). Mother Nature's nearly perfect food. *Inform, 17*(5), 276–277.

25. Deffense, E. (2017). Chemical Degumming. *AOCS Lipid Library (online).* Urbana, IL: American Oil Chemists Society.

26. Deman, J. M., & Beers, A. M. (1987). Fat crystal networks: Structure and rheological properties. *Journal of Texture Studies,* 18, 303–318.

27. Deman, L., & Deman, J. M. (1983). Trans fatty acids in milk fat. *Journal of the American Oil Chemists' Society, 60,* 1095–1098.

28. Deman, L., Shen, C. F., & Deman, J. M. (1991). Composition, physical characteristics of soft (tub) margarines. *Journal of the American Oil Chemists' Society, 68,* 70–73.

29. Dickinson, E. (2009). Food emulsions and foams: Stabilization by particles. *Current Opinion in colloid & interface science, 15,* 40–49.

30. Dijkstra, A. J. (2017). Hydrogenation mechanism. *AOCS Lipid Library (online).* Urbana, IL: American Oil Chemists Society.

31. Dijkstra, A. J. (2017). Chemical interesterification. *AOCS online Lipid Library (online)*. Urbana, IL: American Oil Chemists Society.

32. Dorko, C. (1994). Antioxidants used in foods. *Food Technology, 48*(4), 33.

33. Dresser, K. (2011). Butter 101. *Cook's Illustrated, 109*, 16–17.

34. Drewnowski, A. (1997). Why do we like fat? *Journal of the American Dietetic Association, 97*, S58.

35. Duxbury, D. (2005). Omega-3s offer solutions to *trans* fat substitution problem. *Food Technology, 59*(4), 34–39.

36. Dziezak, J. D. (1986). Preservatives: Antioxidants. *Food Technology, 40*(9), 94.

37. Dziezak, J. D. (1989). Fats, oils, and fat substitutes. *Food Technology, 43*(7), 66.

38. Eckel, R. H., Kris-Etherton, P., Lichtenstein, A. H., Wylie-Rosett, J., Groom, A., Stitzel, K. F., & Yin-Piazza, S. (2009). Americans' awareness, knowledge, and behaviors regarding fats: 2006–2007. *Journal of the American Dietetic Association, 109*, 288–296. doi:10.1016/j.jada.2008.10.048

39. Eisner, M. D., Jeelani, S. A. K., Bernhard, L., & Windhab, E. J. (2007). Stability of foams containing proteins, fat particles and nonionic surfactants. *Chemical Engineering Science, 62*, 1974–1987.

40. Erickson, M. D., & Frey, N. (1994). Property-enhanced oils in food applications. *Food Technology, 48*(11), 63.

41. Farfan, M., Alvarez, A., & Bouchon, P. (2015). Comparison of chemical and enzymatic interesterification of fully hydrogenated soybean oil and walnut oil to produce a fat base with adequate nutritional and physical characteristics. *Food Technology & Biotechnology, 53*(3), 361–366.

42. Fitzpatrick, M. P., Chapman, G. E., & Barr, S. J. (1997). Lower-fat menu items in restaurants satisfy customers. *Journal of the American Dietetic Association, 97*, 510.

43. Fulton, L., & Hogbin, M. (1993). Eating quality of muffins, cakes, and cookies prepared with reduced fat and sugar. *Journal of the American Dietetic Association, 93*, 1313.

44. Gadelha, I. C., Fonseca, N. B., Oloris, S. C., Melo, M. M., Soto-Blanco, B. (2014). Gossypol toxicity from cottonseed products. *Scientific World Journal, 2014*, 231635.

45. García-Closas, R., Berenguer, A., Tormo, M. J., Sánchez, M. J., Quiros, J. R., Navarro, C., & Ardanaz, E. (2004). Dietary sources of vitamin C, vitamin E and specific carotenoids in Spain. *British Journal of Nutrition, 91*(6), 1005–1011.

46. Goh, K. T., Ye, A., & Dale, N. (2006). Characterisation of ice cream containing flaxseed oil. *International Journal of Food Science and Technology, 41*, 946–953.

47. García-González, D. L., & Aparici, R. (2017). Olive oil, *AOCS Lipid Library (online)*. Urbana, IL: American Oil Chemist Society.

48. Gertz, C., & Klostermann, S. (2002). Analysis of acrylamide and mechanisms of its formation in deep-fried products. *European Journal of Lipid Science and Technology, 104*, 762–771.

49. Ghanbari, R., Anwar, F., Alkhardy, K. M., Gilani, A. H., & Saari, N. (2012). *International Journal of Molecular Sciences, 13*, 3291–3340.

50. Giese, J. H. (1993). Alternative sweeteners and bulking agents. *Food Technology, 47*(1), 114.

51. Giese, J. (1996). Fats, oils, and fat replacers. *Food Technology, 50*(4), 78.

52. Giese, J. (2002). Acrylamide in foods. *Food Technology, 56*(10), 71–74.

53. Goff, H. D. (2017). *Dairy chemistry and physics. Dairy Education E-book*. Ontario Agriculture College, University of Guelph, Canada.

54. Goff, H. D. (1997). Instability and partial coalescence in whippable dairy emulsions. *Journal of Dairy Science, 80*, 2620–2630.

55. Goff, H. D. (1997). Colloidal aspects of ice cream-A review. *International Dairy Journal, 7*, 363–373.

56. Granda, C., Moreira, R. G., & Tichy, S. E. (2004). Reduction of acrylamide formation in potato chips by low-temperature vacuum frying. *Journal of Food Science, 69*, E405–E411. doi:10.1111/j.1365-2621.2004.tb09903.x

57. Haney, M. M., Sneider, R., Sheiman, J., Losh, S. (2005). Ibuprofen-like activity in extra-virgin olive oil. *Nature, 43*(71), 45–46.

58. Hearn, T. L., Sgoutas, S. A., Hearn, J. A., & Sgoutas, D. S. (1987). Polyunsaturated fatty acids and fat in fish flesh for selecting species for health benefits. *Journal of Food Science, 52*, 1209.

59. Hernandez, E. M., & Kamal-Eldin, A. (2013). *Processing and nutrition of fats and oils*. New York, NY: John Wiley & Sons Ltd.

60. Hicks, K. B., & Moreau, R. A. (2001). Phytosterols and phytostanols: Functional food cholesterol busters. *Food Technology, 55*(1), 63–67.

61. Himawan, C., Starov, V. M., & Stapley, A. G. F. (2006). Thermodynamic and kinetic aspects of fat crystallization. *Advances in Colloid and Interface Science, 122*(1), 3–33.

62. Hollingsworth, P. (2001). Margarine: The over-the-top functional food. *Food Technology, 55*(1), 59–62.

63. Kinsella, J. E. (1981). Functional properties of protein: possible relationships between structure and function in foams. *Food Chemistry, 7*, 273–288.

64. Kostas, G. (1997). Low-fat and delicious: Can we break the taste barrier? *Journal of the American Dietetic Association, 97*, S88.

65. Kris-Etherton, P. M., & Hill, A. M. (2008). n-3 fatty acids: Food or supplements. *Journal of the American Dietetic Association, 108*, 11251130. doi:10.1016/j.jada.2008.04.025

66. L'Abbe', M. R., Stender, S., Skeaff, M., Ghafoorunissa, R., & Tavella, M. (2009). Approaches to removing trans fats from the food supply in industrialized and developing countries. *European Journal of Clinical Nutrition, 63*, S50–S67.

67. Labensky, S. R., Hause, A. M., & Martel, P. A. (2015). *On cooking: A textbook of culinary fundamentals* (5th ed. update). Upper Saddle River, NJ: Pearson Education Inc.

68. Lawson, H. W. (1985). *Standards for fats and oils*. Westport, CT: Avi Publishing.

69. Lee, S., & Inglett, G. E. (2006). Functional characterization of steam jet-cooked β-glucan-rich barley flour as an oil barrier in frying batters. *Journal of Food Science, 71*(6), E308–E313.

70. List, G. R. (2004). Decreasing *trans* and saturated fatty acid content in food oils. *Food Technology, 58*(1), 23–31.

71. Maier, C., Reichert, C. L., & Weiss, J. (2016). Characterization of chemically and thermally treated oil-in-water

heteroaggregates and comparison to conventional emulsions. *Journal of Food Science, 81*, E2484–E2491. doi:10.1111/1750-3841.13437

72. Marshall, R. T., & Goff, D. (2003). Formulating and manufacturing ice cream and other frozen desserts. *Food Technology, 57*(5), 32–45.

73. McComber, D., & Miller, E. M. (1976). Differences in total lipid and fatty acid composition of doughnuts as influenced by lecithin, leavening agent, and use of frying fat. *Cereal Chemistry, 53*, 101.

74. McHugh, T. (April 2016). How dark chocolate is processed. *Food Technology, 70*(4), 134–136.

75. Mendez-Velasco, C., & Goff, H. D. (2011). Enhancement of fat colloidal interactions for the preparation of ice cream high in unsaturated fat. *International Dairy Journal, 21*, 540–547.

76. Mensink, R. P., Sanders, T. A., Baer, D. J., Hayes, K. C., Howles, P. N., & Marangoni, A. (2016). Increasing use of interesterified lipids in the food supply and their effects on health parameters. *Advances in Nutrition, 7*(4), 719–729.

77. Mermelstein, N. H. (2010). Improving soybean oil. *Food Technology, 64*(8), 72–76.

78. Michels, R., Foschum, F., & Kienle, A. (2008). Optical properties of fat emulsions. *Optics Express, 16*(8).

79. Mozaffarian, D., & Clarke, R. (2009). Quantitative effects on cardiovascular risk factors and coronary heart disease risk of replacing partially hydrogenated vegetable oils with other fats and oils. *European Journal of Clinical Nutrition, 63*, S22–S33.

80. Mozaffarian, D., Aro, A., & Willett, W. C. (2009). Health effects of trans-fatty acids: Experimental and observational evidence. *European Journal of Clinical Nutrition, 63*, S5–S21.

81. Mozaffarian, D. (2011). The great fat debate: Taking the focus off of saturated fat. *Journal of the American Dietetic Association, 111*, 665–666. doi:10.1016/j/jada.2011.03.030

82. Murrary, B. S. (2007). Stabilization of bubbles and foams. *Current Opinion in Colloid & Interface Science, 12*, 232–241.

83. Nachay, K. (2015). The skinny on fats and oils. *Food Technology, 69*(5), 52–63.

84. Nachay, K. (2017). Bolstering the bakery aisle. *Food Technology, 71*(2), 51–60.

85. Nawar, W. W. (1985). Lipids. In Fennema, O. (Ed.), *Food chemistry* (2nd ed., pp. 139–244). New York, NY: Marcel Dekker, Inc.

86. Needs, E. C., & Huitson, A. (1991). The contribution of milk serum proteins to the development of whipped cream structure. *Food Structure*, 10, 353.

87. Nettleton, J. (2005). Omega-3 fatty acids in foods and health. *Food Technology, 59*(9), 120.

88. Neuhouser, M. L., Kristal, A. R., & Patterson, R. E. (1999). Use of food nutrient labels is associated with lower fat intake. *Journal of the American Dietetic Association, 99*, 45–50.

89. Nishida, C., & Uauy, R. (2009). WHO Scientific Update on health consequences of trans fatty acids: Introduction. *European Journal of Clinical Nutrition, 63*, S1–S4.

90. Oh, K., Hu, F. B., Manson, J. E., Stampfer, M. J., & Willett, W. (2005). Dietary fat intake and risk of coronary heart disease in women: 20 years of follow-up of the nurses health study. *American Journal of Epidemiology, 161*, 672–679.

91. Ohr, L. M. (2004). Controlling cholesterol. *Food Technology, 58*(11), 73–76.

92. Ohr, L. M. (2008). Not all fats are bad. *Food Technology, 62*(6), 101–106.

93. *Pocket Information Manual A Buyer's Guide to Rendered Products*. (2008). Alexandria, VA: National Renderers Association, Inc.

94. Pszczola, D. E. (2001). Antioxidants: From preserving food quality to quality of life. *Food Technology, 55*(6), 51–59.

95. Pszczola, D. E. (2001). Salad days? Not for these dressings. *Food Technology, 55*(4), 78–86.

96. Pszczola, D. E. (2004). Fats: In *trans*-ition. *Food Technology, 58*(4), 52–63.

97. Pszczola, D. E. (2006). Future strategies for fat replacement. *Food Technology, 60*(6), 61–84.

98. Pszczola, D. E. (2009). Separating fats from fiction. *Food Technology, 64*(9), 47–60.

99. Pszczola, D. E. (2011). Emulsifying excellence. *Food Technology, 65*(12), 50–67.

100. Tiffany, T. (2007). Oil options for deep-fat frying. *Food Technology, 61*(7), 46–56.

101. Reshma, M. V., Saritha, S. S., Balachandran, C., & Arumughan, C. (2008). Lipase catalyzed interesterification of palm stearin and rice bran oil blends for preparation of zero trans shortening with bioactive phytochemicals. *Bioresource Technology, 99*(11), 5011–5019.

102. Reidiger, N. D., Othman, R. A., Suh, M., & Mghadasian, M. H. (2009). A systemic review of the roles of n-3 fatty acids in health and disease. *Journal of the American Dietetic Association, 109*, 668–679. doi:10.1016/j.jada.2008.12022

103. Remig, V., Franklin, B., Margolis, S., Kostas, G., Nece, T., & Street, J. C. (2010). Trans fats in America: A review of their use, consumption, health implications, and regulation. *Journal of the American Dietetic Association, 110*, 585–592. doi:10.1016/j/jada.2009.12.024

104. Rønholt, S., Mortensen, K., & Knudsen, J. C. (2013). The effective factors on the structure of butter and other milk fat-based products. *Comprehensive Reviews in Food Science and Food Safety, 12*, 468–482. doi:10.1111/1541-4337.12022

105. Rousseau, D., & Marangoni, A. G. (2002). Chemical interesterification of food lipids. In C. C. Akoh & D. B. Min (Eds.), *Food lipids* (p. 303). New York, NY: Marcel-Dekker.

106. Ruíz-Méndez, M. R., & Dobarganes, M. C. (2017). Oil refining. *AOCS Lipid Library*. doi:10.21748/lipidlibrary.39212

107. Schmidt, E., & van Hooydonk, A. C. M. (1980). A scanning electron microscopical investigation of the whipping of cream. *Scanning Electron Microscopy II, 644*, 653.

108. Shin, J. -A., Lee, M. -Y., & Lee, K. -T. (2016). Oxidation stability of O/W emulsion prepared with linolenic acid enriched diacylglycerol. *Journal of Food Science, 81*, C2373–C2380. doi:10.1111/1750-3841.13421

109. Skeaff, C. M. (2009). Feasibility of recommending certain replacement or alternative fats. *European Journal of Clinical Nutrition, 63*, S34–S49.

110. Škevin, D., Rade, D., Štrucelj, D., Mokrovčal, Ž., Nederal, S., & Benčić, D. (2003). The influence of variety and harvest time on the bitterness and phenolic compounds

of olive oil. *European Journal of Lipid Science and Technology*, *105*, 536–541.

111. Smouse, T. H. (1979). Review of soybean oil reversion flavor. *Journal of the American Oil Chemists' Society*, *56*, 747A.

112. Sproston, M. J., Ifeduba, E. A., & Akoh, C. C. (2017). Structured lipids for food and nutraceutical applications. *AOCS Lipid Library*. doi:10.21748/lipidlibrary.41522

113. Stanley, D. W., Goff, H. D., & Smith, A. K. (1996). Texture-structure relationships in foamed dairy emulsions. *Food Research International*, *29*, 1–13.

114. Strayer, D. (2016). *Food fats and oils* (10th ed.). Washington, D.C.: Institute of Shortenings and Edible Oils.

115. Stender, S. (2006). High levels of industrially produced trans fat in popular fast foods. *New England Journal of Medicine*, *354*, 1650–1652.

116. Szafranski, M., Whittington, J. A., & Bessinger, C. (2005). Pureed cannelloni beans can be substituted for shortening in brownies. *Journal of the American Dietetic Association*, *105*, 1295–1298.

117. Szczesniak, A. S. (1990). Texture: Is it still an overlooked food attribute? *Food Technology*, *44*(9), 86.

118. Talati, R., Sobieraj, D. M., Makanji, S. S., Phung, O. J., & Coleman, C. I. (2010). The comparative efficacy of plant sterols and stanols on serum lipids: A systematic review and meta-analysis. *Journal of the American Dietetic Association*, *110*, 719–726. doi:10.1016/j/jada.2010.02.011

119. Tarrago-Trani, M. T., Phillips, K. M., Lemar, L. E., & Holden, J. M. (2006). New and existing oils and fats used in products with reduced *trans*-fatty acid content. *Journal of the American Dietetic Association*, *106*, 867–880.

120. Tarver, T. (2016). A big fat dispute. *Food Technology*, *70*(8), 27–35.

121. Tarver, T. (2017). Rutgers researchers explore the wonderful world of lipids. *Food Technology*, *71*(10), 18–23.

122. Thalheimer, J. C. (2015). Heart healthy oils: They're not all created equal. *Today's Dietitian*, *17*(2), 24.

123. Tiffany, T. (2007). Oil options for deep-fat frying. *Food Technology*, *61*(7), 46–56.

124. Uauy, R., Aro, A., Clarke, R., Ghafoorunissa, R., L'Abbe´, M., Mozaffarian, D., Skeaff, M., Stender, S., & Tavella, M. (2009). WHO Scientific Update on trans fatty acids: Summary and conclusions. *European Journal of Clinical Nutrition*, *63*, S34–S39.

125. United States Department of Agriculture. What We Eat in America, NHANES 2007-2010 for average intakes by age-sex group. Healthy U.S. Style Food Patterns, which vary based on age, sex and activity level, for recommended intake ranges. Washington, D.C.: Government Publishing Office.

126. U.S. Department of Agriculture and U.S. Health and Human Services. (2015). *2015-2020 Dietary guidelines for Americans*. Washington, D.C.: Government Publishing Office.

127. U.S. Department of Agriculture, Economic Research Service. (2010, February). *Data sets: Nutrient availability*. Washington, D.C.: Government Publishing Office.

128. United States Department of Agriculture National Agriculture Statistics Service. (2017). *Fats and oils: Oilseed crushings, production, consumption and stocks 2016 summary report*. Washington, D.C.: U.S. Government Publishing Office.

129. U.S. Department of Health and Human Services, The U.S. Food and Drug Administration Center for Food Safety and Applied Nutrition. (2016). *Guidance for industry acrylamide in foods*. HFA-305. College Park, MD: FDA and Government Publishing Office.

130. Visioli, F., Belleomo, G., & Galli, C. (1998). Free radical-scavenging properties of olive oil polyphenols. *Biochemical and Biophysical Research Communications*, *24*, 60–64.

131. Wang, F. C., Gravelle, A. J., Blake, A. I., & Marangoni, A. G. (2016). Novel *trans* fat replacement strategies. *Current Opinion in Food Science*, *7*, 27–34.

132. Wardlaw, G. M., & Kessel, M. W. (2002). *Perspectives in nutrition* (5th ed.). New York, NY: McGraw-Hill.

133. West, R., & Rousseau, D. (2017). Understanding the chemistry and evolution of chocolate flavor. *Food Technology*, *71*(6), 71–81.

134. Wright, A. (2003). Spreading the word on butter. *Inform*, *14*(10), 612–613.

135. Wright, A. J., Hartel, R. W., Narine, S. S., & Marangoni, A. G. (2000). The effect of minor components on milk fat crystallization. *Journal of the American Oil Chemists' Society*, *77*(5), 463–475.

136. Wu, R., Blend, A., Hackett, M., Masuda, T., & Zeng, T. (2015). Major fats and oils: Industry overview. In *Chemical Economics Handbook*, IHS Chemical.

137. Zelman, K. (2011). The great fat debate: A closer look at the controversy—Questioning the validity of age-old dietary guidance. *Journal of the American Dietetic Association*, *111*, 655–658. doi:10.1016/j.jada.2011.03.026

138. World Health Organization. (2017). Worldwide trends in body-mass index, underweight, overweight, and obesity from 1975 to 2016: a pooled analysis of 2416 population-based measurement studies in 128·9 million children, adolescents, and adults. *Lancet (online October 10, 2017)*.

Chapter 9

1. Altschul, A. M. (Ed.). (1993). *Low-calorie foods handbook*. New York, NY: Marcel Dekker, Inc.

2. Anonymous. (2017). Restructured Sugar enables 40% less usage in candy. *Food Technology*, *71*(1), 21.

3. Academy of Nutrition and Dietetics. (2012). Position of the Academy of Nutrition and Dietetic Association. Use of nutritive and nonnutritive sweeteners. *Journal of the Academy of Nutrition and Dietetics Association*, *112*(5), 739–758.

4. Awad, A., & Chen, A. C. (1993). A new generation of sucrose products made by cocrystallization. *Food Technology*, *47*(1), 146.

5. Bailey, R. L., & Barr, S. I. (2017). Introduction: Sweet taste perception and feeding toddlers. *Nutrition Today*, *52*(2), S3–S5.

6. Ballinger, R. (1978). History of Sugar Marketing since 1974. U.S. Department of Agriculture, Economics, statistics and cooperative services Agricultural economic report no. 382. Washington, D.C.

7. Bartoshuk, L. M. (1991). Sweetness: History, preference, and genetic variability. *Food Technology*, *45*(11), 108.

8. Bell, J. (1993). High intensity sweeteners—A regulatory update. *Food Technology*, *47*(11), 136.

9. Blankers, I. (1995). Properties and applications of lactitol. *Food Technology, 49*(1), 66.

10. Bowers, J. (1992). *Food theory and applications.* New York, NY: MacMillan Publishing Co.

11. Carr, J. M., Sufferling, K., & Poppe, J. (1995). Hydrocolloids and their use in the confectionery industry. *Food Technology, 49*(7), 41.

12. Charley, H. (1982). *Food science* (2nd ed.). New York, NY: John Wiley & Sons, Inc.

13. Cohen, S. M. (1986). Saccharin: Past, present, and future. *Journal of the American Dietetic Association, 86,* 929.

14. Coulston, A. M., & Johnson, R. K. (2002). Sugar and sugars: Myths and realities. *Journal of the American Dietetic Association, 102,* 351–353.

15. Dziezak, J. D. (1986). Sweeteners and product development. *Food Technology, 40*(1), 112.

16. Dziezak, J. D. (1989). Ingredients for sweet success. *Food Technology, 43*(10), 94.

17. Hardy, S. L., Brennand, C. P., & Wyse, B. W. (1979). Fructose: Comparison with sucrose as sweetener in four products. *Journal of the American Dietetic Association, 74,* 41.

18. Hess, D. A., & Setser, C. S. (1986). Comparison of aspartame- and fructose-sweetened layer cakes: Importance of panels of users for evaluation of alternative sweeteners. *Journal of the American Dietetic Association, 86,* 919.

19. Hoch, G. J. (1997). Sweet anticipation. *Food Processing, 58*(12), 45.

20. Hollingsworth, P. (2002). Artificial sweeteners face sweet 'n sour consumer market. *Food Technology, 56*(7), 24–27.

21. Hollingsworth, P. (2002). Developing and marketing foods for diabetics. *Food Technology, 56*(10), 38.

22. Jamieson, P. (2016). Reducing Added Sugars with Polyols. *Food Technology, 70*(11), 42–48.

23. Johnson, R. K., & Yon, B. A. (2010). Weighing in on added sugars and health. *Journal of the American Dietetic Association, 110,* 1296–1299. doi:10.1016/j.jada.2010.06.013

24. Kaya-Celiker, H., & Mallikarjunan, K. (2012). Better nutrients and therapeutics delivery in food through nanotechnology. *Food Engineering Reviews, 4*(2), 114–123.

25. Kavey, R. W. (2010). How sweet it is: Sugar-sweetened beverage consumption, obesity, and cardiovascular risk in childhood. *Journal of the American Dietetic Association, 110,* 1456–1460. doi:10.1016/j.jada.2010.07.028

26. Koivistoinen, P., & Hyvönen, L. (1980). *Carbohydrate sweeteners in foods and nutrition.* New York, NY: Academic Press.

27. Kroger, M., Meister, K., & Kava, R. (2006, April). Low-calorie sweeteners and other sugar substitutes: A review of the safety issues. *Comprehensive Reviews in Food Science and Food Safety, 5,* 35–47.

28. Labensky, S. R., Martel, P. A., & Van Damme, E. (2016). *Ono baking* (3rd ed. Update). Upper Saddle River, NJ: Pearson Education, Inc.

29. Mermelstein, N. H. (2015). More than a spoonful of sugar. *Food Technology, 69*(11), 67–71.

30. McManus, L. (2009, January/February). What should you put on your pancakes? *Cook's Illustrated, 96,* 26–27.

31. McNutt, K. (2000). What clients need to know about sugar replacers. *Journal of the American Dietetic Association, 100,* 466–469.

32. McQuate, R. S. (2011). Ensuring the safety of sweeteners from stevia. *Food Technology, 65*(4), 42–49.

33. McWilliams, M. (2008). *Foods: Experimental perspectives* (6th ed.). Upper Saddle River, NJ: Pearson Prentice Hall.

34. Muhammad, A., D'Souza, A., Meade, B., Micha, R., & Mozaffarian, D. (2017). The Influence of Income and Prices on Global Dietary Patterns by Country, Age, and Gender, Economic Research Report No. (ERR-225), USDA/ ERS, Washington, D.C.: Government Publishing Office.

35. Nabors, L. O. (2002). Sweet choices: Sugar replacements for food and beverages. *Food Technology, 56*(7), 28–34, 45.

36. *National Center for Health Statistics. Health, United States, 2015: With Special Feature on Racial and Ethnic Health Disparities.* Hyattsville, MD. 2016.

37. O'Donnell, K. (2012). Aspartame, Neotame and Advantame. *Sweeteners and Sugar Alternatives in Food Technology, 6,* 117.

38. Patrick, J. H., Botha, F. C., & Birch, R. G. (2013). Metabolic engineering of sugars and simple sugar derivatives in plants. *Plant Biotechnology Journal, 11,*142–156.

39. Phillips, K. M., Carlsen, M. H., & Blomhoff, R. (2009). Total antioxidant content of alternatives to refined sugar. *Journal of the American Dietetic Association, 109,* 64–71. doi:10.1016/j.jada.2008.10.014

40. Prakash, I., Corliss, G., Ponakala, R., & Ishikawa, G. (2002). Neotame: The next-generation sweetener. *Food Technology, 56*(7), 36–40, 45.

41. Pszczola, D. E. (1987). American fructose unveils new technologies in HFCS plant. *Food Technology, 41*(10), 50.

42. Pszczola, D. E. (1997). Ingredient developments for confections. *Food Technology, 51*(9), 70.

43. Pszczola, D. E. (1999). Sweet beginnings to a new year. *Food Technology, 53*(1), 70.

44. Pszczola, D. E. (2003). Sweetener + sweetener enhances the equation. *Food Technology, 57*(11), 48–61.

45. Pszczola, D. E. (2006). Synergizing sweetness. *Food Technology, 60*(3), 69–79.

46. Pszczola, D. E. (2008). Sweeteners for the 21st century. *Food Technology, 62*(11), 49–57.

47. Pszczola, D. E. (2009). The quest for innovation. *Food Technology, 63*(7), 42–55.

48. Pszczola, D. E. (2010). Trying to keep diabetes under control. *Food Technology, 64*(7), 54–63.

49. Pszczola, D. E., & Nachay, K. (2009). IFT plants a rich crop in Anaheim. *Food Technology, 63*(5), 47–91.

50. Rapaille, A., Gonze, M., & Van der Schueren, F. (1995). Formulating sugar-free chocolate products with maltitol. *Food Technology, 49*(7), 51.

51. Sadiki, M., Lagacé, L., & Perkins, T. D. (2013). Sulfite concentration in pure maple syrup. *Maple Syrup Digest, 25A*(3), 12–14.

52. Staff. (1987). Crystalline fructose: A breakthrough in corn sweetener process technology. *Food Technology, 41*(1), 66.

53. Staff. (1996). Thaumatin—The sweetest substance known to man has a wide range of food applications. *Food Technology, 50*(1), 74.

54. Staff. (2006). Artificial sweeteners: No calories–sweet! *FDA Consumer, 40*(4), 27–28.

55. O'Donnell, K., & Kearsley, M. W. (Eds.). (2012). *Sweeteners and sugar alternatives* (2nd ed.). West Sussex, UK: John Wiley & Sons, Ltd.

56. United States Standards for Grades of Maple Syrup. (2015). Washington, D.C.: U.S. Department of Agriculture.

57. United States Standards for Grades of Extracted Honey. (1985). Washington, D.C.: U.S. Department of Agriculture.

58. Van den Berg, A. K., Perkins, T. D., & Isselhardt, M. L. (2015). Chemical composition of five standard grades of pure maple syrup. *Maple Syrup Digest, 53*(1), 7–13.

59. Webb, D. (2017). Sugar industry cover-up? *Today's Dietitian, 19*(1), 20–23.

60. Woodruff, S., & Van Gilder, H. (1931). Photomicrographic studies of sucrose crystals. *Journal of Physical Chemistry, 35,* 1355.

61. Zhu, Y. J., Komor, E., & Moore, P. H. (1997). Sucrose accumulation in the sugarcane stem is regulated by the difference between the activities of soluble acid invertase and sucrose phosphate synthase. *Plant Physiology,* 115, 609–616.

Chapter 10

1. Berry, D. (2017). Little extras add flavor, color and fun. *Dairy Business News.* May 10, 3627.

2. Buck, J. S., Walker, C. E., & Pierce, M. M. (1986). Evaluation of sucrose esters in ice cream. *Journal of Food Science, 51,* 489.

3. Byer, J. (2002). Effect of a starch-lipid fat replacer on the rheology of soft-serve ice cream. *Journal of Food Science, 67,* 2177–2182.

4. Code of Federal Regulations. (2017). *Definitions and standards under the Federal Food, Drug, and Cosmetic Act: Frozen desserts. Title 21, Volume 2, Part 135.* 21CFR135. U.S. Government Publishing Office.

5. Charley, H. (1982). *Food science.* New York, NY: John Wiley & Sons.

6. Carper, J. (2017). Making ice cream to a tea. *Dairy Foods, 118*(3), 40–44.

7. Carper, J. (2017). Johnny Pops. *Dairy Foods, 118*(5), 36.

8. Jimenez-Flores, R., Klipfel, N. J., & Tobias, J. (1993). Ice cream and frozen desserts. *New York: VCH Publishers,* 57–159.

9. Güven, M., & Karaca, O. B. (2002). The effects of varying sugar content and fruit concentration on the physical properties of vanilla and fruit ice-cream-type frozen yogurts. *International Journal of Dairy Technology, 55*(1), 27–31.

10. Goff, H. D. (1997). Colloidal aspects of ice cream—A Review. *International Dairy Journal, 7,* 363–373.

11. Halford, B. (2004). Ice cream: The finer points of chemistry and flavor release make this favorite treat so sweet. *Chemical and Engineering News, 82*(45), 51–53.

12. Hatchwell, L. C. (1994). Overcoming flavor challenges in low-fat frozen desserts. *Food Technology, 48*(2), 98.

13. Keller, S. E., Fellows, J. W., Nash, T. C., & Shazer, W. H. (1991). Application of bulk-free process in aspartame-sweetened frozen dessert. *Food Technology, 45*(6), 100.

14. Keller, S. E., Fellows, J. W., Nash, T. C., & Shazer, W. H. (1991). Formulation of aspartame-sweetened frozen dairy dessert without bulking agents. *Food Technology, 45*(2), 102.

15. Kurtzweil, P. (1998). Skimming the milk label: Fat-reduced milk products join the food labeling fold. *FDA Consumer, 32*(1), 1.

16. Marshall, R. T., Goff, H. D., & Hartel, R. W. (2003). *Ice cream* (6th ed.). New York, NY: Kluwer Academic/Plenum Publishers.

17. Souza, D. (2011, July/August). The best vanilla ice cream. *Cook's Illustrated, 111,* 21–23.

18. Tharp, B. W., & Gottemoller, T. V. (1990). Light frozen dairy desserts: Effect of compositional changes on processing and sensory characteristics. *Food Technology, 44*(10), 86.

19. Tharp, B., & Young, S. (2017). On ice cream. *Dairy Foods 118*(40), 28.

20. Thomas, E. L. (1981). Structure and properties of ice cream emulsions. *Food Technology, 35*(1), 41.

21. *Thomas Jefferson, no date, Ice Cream Recipe.* [Manuscript/Mixed Material] Retrieved from the Library of Congress, https://www.loc.gov/item/mtjbib025779/.

22. U.S. Department of Agriculture, Economic Research Service. (2017). Data sets: U.S. per capita food availability: Dairy Products Per Capita consumption.

23. Wittinger, S. A., & Smith, D. E. (1986). Effect of sweeteners and stabilizers on selected sensory attributes and shelf life of ice cream. *Journal of Food Science, 51,* 1463.

Chapter 11

1. Atwell, W. A., Hood, L. F., Lineback, D. R., Varriano-Marston, E., & Zobel, H. F. (1988). The terminology and methodology associated with basic starch phenomena. *Cereal Foods World, 33,* 306.

2. Bean, M. M., & Yamazaki, W. T. (1978). Wheat starch gelatinization in sugar solutions. I. Sucrose: Microscopy and viscosity effects. *Cereal Chemistry, 55,* 936.

3. BeMiller, J. N. (2007). *Carbohydrate chemistry for food scientists* (2nd ed.). St. Paul, MN: AACC International, Inc.

4. Biliaderis, C. G., & Juliano, B. O. (1993). Thermal and mechanical properties of concentrated rice starch gels of varying composition. *Food Chemistry, 48*(3), 243–250.

5. Bird, A. R., Brown, I. L., & Topping, D. L. (2000). Starches, resistant starches, the gut microflora and human health. *Current Issues in Intestinal Microbiology, 1*(1), 25–37.

6. Bowers, J. (1992). *Food theory and applications* (2nd ed.). New York, NY: Macmillan Publish Co.

7. Buléon, A., Colonna, P., Planchot, V., & Ball, S. (1998). Starch granules: structure and biosynthesis. *International Journal of Biological Macromolecules, 23*(2), 85–112.

8. Charley, H. (1982). *Food science* (2nd ed.). New York, NY: John Wiley & Sons.

9. Conde-Petit, B., & Escher, F. (1992). Gelation of low concentration starch systems induced by starch emulsifier complexation. *Food Hydrocolloids, 6*(2), 223–229.

10. Fannon, J. E., Hauber, R. J., & BeMiller, J. N. (1992). Surface pores of starch granules. *Cereal Chemistry, 69*(3), 284–288.

11. García-González, C. A., Uy, J. J., Alnaief, M., & Smirnova, I. (2012). Preparation of tailor-made starch-based aerogel microspheres by the emulsion-gelation method. *Carbohydrate Polymers, 88*(4), 1378–1386.

12. Hanes, C. S. (1932). Studies on plant amylases: the effect of starch concentration upon the velocity of hydrolysis by the amylase of germinated barley. *Biochemical Journal, 26*(5), 1406.

13. Hansuld, M. K., & Briant, A. M. (1954). The effect of citric acid on selected edible starches and flours. *Food Research, 19*, 581.

14. Hegenbart, S. (1996). Understanding starch functionality. *Food Product Design, 1*, 1.

15. Hoch, G. J. (1997). The starch search. *Food Processing, 58*(5), 60.

16. Holmes, Z. A., & Soeldner, A. (1981). Effect of heating rate and freezing and reheating of corn and wheat starch–water dispersions. *Journal of the American Dietetic Association, 78*, 352.

17. Holmes, Z. A., & Soeldner, A. (1981). Macrostructure of selected raw starches and selected heated starch dispersions. *Journal of the American Dietetic Association, 78*, 153.

18. Homesey, C. (2000). Starch: Stabilizer solutions. *Food Product Design, 9*, 1.

19. Hosney, R. C. (1990). *Principles of cereal science and technology*. St. Paul, MN: American Association of Cereal Chemists, Inc.

20. Hsu, S., Lu, S., & Huang, C. (2000). Viscoelastic changes of rice starch suspensions during gelatinization. *Journal of Food Science, 65*(2), 215–220.

21. Izuka, K., & Aishima, T. (1999). Starch Gelation Process Observed by FT-IR/ATR Spectrometry with Multivariate Data Analysis. *Journal of Food Science, 64*(4), 653–658.

22. Karim, A. A., Norziah, M. H., & Seow, C. C. (2000). Methods for the study of starch retrogradation. *Food Chemistry, 71*(1), 9–36.

23. Kuntz, L. A. (2005). Ingredient insight: A starch that's hard to resist. *Food Product Design, (9)*, 1.

24. Labensky, S. R., Hause, A. M., & Martel, P. A. (2011). *On cooking: A textbook of culinary fundamentals* (5th ed.). Upper Saddle River, NJ: Pearson Prentice Hall.

25. Lehmann, U., Rössler, C., Schmiedl, D., & Jacobasch, G. (2003). Production and physicochemical characterization of resistant starch type III derived from pea starch. *Molecular Nutrition & Food Research, 47*(1), 60–63.

26. Luallen, T. E. (1994). The use of starches in frozen food formulation. *Food Technology, 48*(5), 39.

27. McGrane, S. J., Mainaring, D. E., Cornell, H. J., & Rix, C. J. (2004). The role of hydrogen bonding in amylose Gelation. *Starch/Stärke, 56*, 122–131.

28. Merchant, A. T., Vatanparast, H., Barlas, S., Dehghan, M., Shah, S. M. A., De Koning, L., & Steck, S. E. (2009). Carbohydrate intake and overweight and obesity among healthy adults. *Journal of the American Dietetic Association, 109*, 1165–1172.

29. Messenger, B. (1997). Going native. *Food Processing, 58*(1), 48.

30. Miles, M. J., Morris, V. J., & Ring, S. G. (1985). Gelation of amylose. *Carbohydrate Research, 135*(2), 257–269.

31. Peabody, E. (2005). Going with the Grain. *Ag Research Magazine, 53*(2), 20–21.

32. Miles, M. J., Morris, V. J., Orford, P. D., & Ring, S. G. (1985). The roles of amylose and amylopectin in the gelation and retrogradation of starch. *Carbohydrate Research, 135*(2), 271–281.

33. Pszczola, D. E. (1996). Native starches offer functionality comparable to modified starches. *Food Technology, 50*(12), 75.

34. Pszczola, D. E. (2006). Which starch is on first? *Food Technology, 60*(4), 51–64.

35. Sajilata, M. G., Singhal, R. S., & Kulkarni, P. R. (2006). Resistant starch: A review. *Comprehensive Reviews in Food Science and Food Safety, 5*, 1–18.

36. Sandhu, K. S., & Singh, N. (2007). Some properties of corn starches II: Physicochemical, gelatinization, retrogradation, pasting and gel textural properties. *Food Chemistry, 101*(4), 1499–1507.

37. Shamai, K., Bianco-Peled, H., & Shimoni, E. (2003). Polymorphism of resistant starch type III. *Carbohydrate Polymers, 54*(3), 363–369.

38. Spies, R. D., & Hoseney, R. C. (1982). Effect of sugars on starch gelatinization. *Cereal Chemistry, 59*, 128.

39. Svegmark, K., & Hermansson, A. M. (1993). Microstructure and rheological properties of composites of potato starch granules and amylose: a comparison of observed and predicted structures. *Food Structure, 12*(2), 6.

40. U.S. Department of Health and Human Services & U.S. Department of Agriculture. (2015). *2015-2020 Dietary guidelines for Americans* (8th ed.). U.S. Government Printing Office.

41. Van Der Maarel, M. J., Van Der Veen, B., Uitdehaag, J. C., Leemhuis, H., & Dijkhuizen, L. (2002). Properties and applications of starch-converting enzymes of the α-amylase family. *Journal of Biotechnology, 94*(2), 137–155.

42. Waniska, R. D., & Gomez, M. H. (1992). Dispersion behavior of starch. *Food Technology, 46*(6), 110.

43. Wheeler, M. L., & Pi-Sunyer, F. X. (2008). Carbohydrate issues: Type and amount. *Journal of the American Dietetic Association, 108*, S34–S39. doi:10.1016/j.jada.2008.01.024

44. Wiesenborn, D. P., Orr, P. H., Casper, H. H., & Tacke, B. K. (1994). Potato starch paste behavior as related to some physical/chemical properties. *Journal of Food Science, 59*, 644.

45. Zobel, H. F. (1988). Molecules to granules: A comprehensive starch review. *Starch, 40*(2), 44–50.

Chapter 12

1. Abdel-Aal, E. S. M., Hucl, P., Miller, S. S., Patterson, C. A., & Gray, D. (2011). Microstructure and nutrient composition of hairless canary seed and its potential as a blending flour for food use. *Food Chemistry, 125*(2), 410–416.

2. Abdel-Aal, E. S. M., Hucl, P., Miller, S. S., Patterson, C. A., & Gray, D. (2010). Fractionation of hairless canary seed (*Phalaris canariensi L.*) into starch, protein and oil. *Journal of Agricultural and Food Chemistry, 58*, 7046–7050.

3. Abdel-Aal, E. S., Huci, M., & Sosulski, P. (1997). Characteristics of canary seed starch. *Journal of Agricultural and Food Chemistry, 9*, 475–480.

4. Abdel-Aal, E. S., Huci, M., & Sosulski, P. (1997). Structural and compositional characteristics of canary seed

(*Phalaris canariensis*). *Journal of Agricultural and Food Chemistry, 45*, 3049–3055.

5. Anonymous. (2017). Flour production edges upward in early 2012; estimate for 2016 cut. *Milling & Baking News, 96*(5), 1, 35.

6. Anonymous. (2017). Whole grains fizzle under Trump administration. *Milling & Baking News, 96*(5), 2.

7. Anonymous. (2017). Perdue gives schools more flexibility in nutrition standards. *Milling & Baking News, 96*(5), 20.

8. Albertson, A. M., Affenito, S. G., Bauserman, R., Holschuh, N. M., Eledridge, A. L., & Barton, B. A. (2009). The relationship of ready-to-eat cereal consumption to nutrient intake, blood lipids, and body mass index of children as they age through adolescence. *Journal of the American Dietetic Association, 109*, 1557–1565.

9. Al-Babili S., & Beyer, P. (2005). Golden rice—Five years on the road—Five years to go? *Trends in Plant Science, 10*(12), 565–573.

10. Albrecht, J. A., Asp, E. H., & Buzzard, I. M. (1987). Cooked in unsalted or salted water1. *Cereal Chemistry, 64*(2), 106–109.

11. American Association of Family and Consumer Sciences. (2001). *Food: A handbook of terminology, purchasing, and preparation* (10th ed.). Alexandria, VA: Author.

12. American Dietetic Association. (2008). Position of the American Dietetic Association: Health implications of dietary fiber. *Journal of the American Dietetic Association, 108*, 1716–1731.

13. Avant, S. (2016). Sweet success for new rice-blend products. *Agricultural Research Magazine, 64*(6), 1.

14. Avant, S. (2016). Taking the gray of wheat products. *Agricultural Research Magazine, 64*(4), 1.

15. Avant, S. (2016). Making cookies with ancient grains and seeds. *Agricultural Research Magazine, 64*(3), 1.

16. Baik, B. K., Czuchajowska, Z., & Pomeraz, Y. (1995). Discoloration of dough for Oriental Noodles. *Cereal Chemistry, 72*(2), 198–205.

17. Bazile, D., Salcedo, S., & Santivañez, T. (2013). Conclusions: Challenges, opportunities and threats to quinoa in the face of global change. Ch 7.1 *In State of the art of quinoa in the World 2013*. Rome: FAO & CIRAD.

18. Behall, K. M., Scholfield, D. J., & Hallfrisch, J. (2006). Whole-grain diets reduce blood pressure in mildly hypercholesterolemic men and women. *Journal of the American Dietetic Association, 106*, 1445–1449.

19. Berat, D. E. M. İ., Bilgiç, N., Elgün, A., & Demi, M. K. (2010). Effects of chickpea flours and whole egg on selected properties of erişte, Turkish noodle. *Food Science and Technology Research, 16*(6), 557–564.

20. Best, D. (2009). Whole seed –Better than whole grain? *Cereal Foods World, 54*(5), 226–227.

21. Bhattacharya, M., Zee, S. Y., & Corke, H. (1999). Physicochemical properties related to quality of rice noodles. *Cereal Chemistry, 76*(6), 861–867.

22. Bilgiçli, N. (2008). Utilization of buckwheat flour in gluten-free egg noodle production. *Journal of Food Agriculture and Environment, 6*(2), 113.

23. Bliss, R. M. (2010). Whole-grain rice stakes out its claim. *Agricultural Research Magazine, 58*(4), 16–17.

24. Bond, J., Capehart, T., Allen, E., & Allen, E. (2015). Feed Outlook Special Article/FDS-15a-SA Boutoique Brews, Barley, and the Balance Sheet: Changes in malt barley industrial use require and updated forecasting approach. January 14. U.S. Department of Agriculture, Economic Research Service.

25. Buzby, J., Farah, H., & Vocke, G. (2005). Will 2005 be the year of the whole grain? *Amber Waves, 3*(3), 13–17.

26. Carroll, L. E. (1990). Functional properties and applications of stabilized rice bran in bakery products. *Food Technology, 44*(4), 74.

27. Chaisiricharoenkul, J., Tongta, S., & Intarapichet, K. O. (2011). Structure and chemical and physicochemical properties of Job's tear (Coix lacryma-jobi L.) kernels and flours. *Suranaree Journal of Science and Technology, 18*, 109–122.

28. Cohen, S. M., Arnold, L. L., Beck, B. D., Lewis, A. S., & Eldan, E. (2013). Evaluation of the carcinogenicity of inorganic arsenic. *Critical Reviews in Toxicology, 43*(9), 711–752.

29. Comis, D. (2002). Let them eat cake. *Agricultural Research Magazine, 50*(3), 1.

30. Core, J. (2002). New rice could benefit malnourished populations. *Agricultural Research Magazine, 50*(9), 14–15.

31. Demirbas, A. (2005). β-Glucan and mineral nutrient contents of cereals grown in Turkey. *Food Chemistry, 90*(4), 773–777.

32. Deshmukhh-Taskar, P. R., Nicklas, T. A., O'Neil, C. E., Keast, D. R., Radcliffe, J. D., & Cho, S. (2010). The relationship of breakfast skipping and type of breakfast consumption with nutrient intake and weight status in children and adolescents: The National Health and Nutrition Examination Survey 1999–2006. *Journal of the American Dietetic Association, 110*, 869–878.

33. Dziezak, J. D. (1991). Romancing the kernel: A salute to rice varieties. *Food Technology, 45*(6), 74.

34. Fast, R. B. (1990). Chapter 2: Manufacturing technology of ready-to-eat cereals. In Fast, R. B., & Caldwell, E. F. (Eds.), *Breakfast cereals and how they are made* (pp. 15–42).

35. Fu, B. X. (2008). Asian noodles: History, classification, raw materials, and processing. *Food Research International, 41*, 888–902.

36. Giese, J. H. (1992). Pasta: New twists on an old product. *Food Technology, 46*(2), 118.

37. Graf, B. L., Rojas-Silvas, P., Roho, L. E., Delatoree-Herrera, J., Baldeon, M. E., & Raskin, I. (2015). Innovations in health value and functional food development of quinoa (*Chenopodium quinoa* Willd.). *Comprehensive Reviews in Food Science and Food Safety, 14*, 431.

38. Harris, K. A., & Kris-Etherton, P. M. (2010). Effects of whole grains on coronary heart disease risk. *Current Atherosclerosis Reports, 12*(6), 368–376.

39. Ho, E., Marquart, L. F., & Camire, M. E. (2016). Whole grains and health: Empowering dietary change. *Food Technology, 70*(4), 47–51.

40. Hoseney, R. C. (1990). *Principles of cereal science and technology*. St. Paul, MN: The American Association of Cereal Chemist, Inc.

41. Hou, G. (2001). Oriental noodles. *Advances in Food and Nutrition Research, 43*, 142–194.

42. Hui, Y. H., Corke, H., De Leyn, I., Nip, W. K., & Cross, N. (Eds.). (2006). *Bakery products science and technology*. Ames, IA: Blackwell.

43. Jara, E. A., & Winter, C. K. (2014). Dietary exposure to total and inorganic arsenic in the United States, 2006-2008. *International Journal of Food Contamination, 1*, 3.

44. Jonnala, R. S., MacRitchie, F., Herald, T. J., Lafiandra, D., Margiotta, B., & Tilley, M. (2010). Protein and quality characterization of triticale translocation lines in breadmaking. *Cereal Chemistry, 87*(6), 546–552.

45. IARC. (2012). Agents Classified by the IARC Monographs, Volumes 1–109.

46. Jonnalagadda, S. S., Harnack, L., Liu, R. H., McKeown, N., Seal, C., Liu, S., & Fahey, G. C. (2011). Putting the whole grain puzzle together: Health benefits associated with wholegrains—Summary of American Society for Nutrition 2010 Satellite Symposium. *Journal of Nutrition, 141*, 1011S–1022S.

47. Kahn, C. B., & Penfield, M. P. (1983). Snack crackers containing whole-grain triticale flour: Crispness, taste, and acceptability. *Journal of Food Science, 48*, 266.

48. Khan, M. N., Des Rosiers, M. C., Rooney, L. W., Morgan, R. G., & Sweat, V. E. (1982). Corn tortillas: Evaluation of corn cooking procedures. *Cereal Chemistry, 59*, 279.

49. Kurtzweil, P. (1996). How folate can help prevent birth defects. *FDA Consumer, 30*(7), 7.

50. Labensky, S. R., Hause, A. M., Martel, P. A. (2015). *On Cooking* (5th ed.) (update). Upper Saddle River, NJ: Pearson Education.

51. Lawton, J. W. (2002). Zein: A history of processing and use. *Cereal Chemistry, 79*(1), 1–18.

52. Liu, L., Herald, T. J., Wang, D., Wilson, J. D., Bean, S. R., & Aramouni, F. M. (2012). Characterization of sorghum grain and evaluation of sorghum flour in a Chinese egg noodle system. *Journal of Cereal Science, 55*(1), 31–36.

53. Liu, J., Li, S., Zhang, A., Zhao, W., Liu, Y., & Zhang, Y. (2017). Volatile profiles of 13 foxtail millet commercial cultivars (*Setaria italic* Beauv.) from China. *Cereal Chemistry, 94*(2), 170–176.

54. Liu, K., & Barrows, F. T. (2017). Wet processing of barley grains into concentrates of proteins, beta-glucan and starch. *Cereal Chemistry, 94*(2), 161–169.

55. Lu, H., Yang, X., Ye, M., Lius, K. B., Xia, Z., Rem, X., Cai, L., Wu, N., Liu, T. S. (2005). Millet noodles in Late Neolithic China. *Nature, 437*(13), 967–968.

56. Marquart, L., & Cohen, E. A. (2005). Increasing whole grain consumption. *Food Technology, 59*(12), 24–32.

57. Medeiros, D., Vazquez-Araujo, L., & Chambers, E., IV. (2011). Sorghum: The forgotten grain. *Food Technology, 65*(6), 52–60.

58. Mermelstein, N. H. (2001). Processing pasta for ingredient use. *Food Technology, 55*(7), 72–75.

59. Murdock, G. P. (1960). Staple subsistence crops of Africa. *Geographical Review, 50*(4), 523–540.

60. Nachay, K. (2014). Reinventing rice. *Food Technology, 68*(4), 89–95.

61. Nicklas, T. A., Myers, L., & Berenson, G. S. (1994). Impact of ready-to-eat cereal consumption on total dietary intake of children: The Bogalusa Heart Study. *Journal of the American Dietetic Association, 94*, 316.

62. O'Brien, D., & Durham, S. (2015). Boosting Sorghum's growing range and yield. *Agricultural* Research Magazine, *63*(2), 4–5.

63. Ohr, L. M. (2009). Good-for-you grains. *Food Technology, 63*(1), 57–61.

64. Parlin, S. (1997). Rice flour makes its mark. *Food Processing, 58*(10), 60.

65. Pszczola, D. E. (1998). What's beyond the horizon? *Food Technology, 52*(9), 94.

66. Pszczola, D. E. (2000). A pasta for all paisans. *Food Technology, 54*(4), 84–92.

67. Pszczola, D. E. (2001). Rice: Not just for throwing. *Food Technology, 55*(2), 53–59.

68. Pszczola, D. E. (2005). Ingredients for bread meet changing needs. *Food Technology, 59*(1), 55–63.

69. Pszczola, D. E. (2005). Never say never: Emerging technologies solve familiar problems. *Food Technology, 59*(2), 53–67.

70. Pszczola, D. E. (2007). Formulators get to the (whole) grain. *Food Technology, 61*(8), 62–72.

71. Pszczola, D. E. (2008). The reawakening of breakfast foods. *Food Technology, 62*(1), 46–57.

72. Raloff, J. (1991). Beyond oat bran. *Food Technology, 45*(8), 62.

73. Rao, D. R., Patel, G., & Nishimuta, J. F. (1980). Comparison of protein quality of corn, triticale, and wheat. *Nutrition Reports International, 21*, 923.

74. Scherer, F. M. (1982). The breakfast food industry. *The Structure of American Industry, 5*,191–217.

75. Serna-Saldivar, S. O. (2010). *Cereal grains: Properties, processing, and nutritional attributes.* New York, NY: CRC Press.

76. Shoemaker, R., Johnson, D. D., & Golan, E. (2003). Consumers and the future of biotech foods in the United States. *Amber Waves, 1*(5), 30–36.

77. Slavin, J. (2004). Whole grains and human health. *Nutrition Research Reviews, 17*, 1–12.

78. Slavin, J., Jacobs, D., Marquart, L., & Wiemer, K. (2001). The role of whole grains in disease prevention. *Journal of the American Dietetic Association, 101*, 780–785.

79. Slavin, J., & Kritchevsky, D. (2002). Pass the whole-grain snack food, please. *Food Technology, 56*(5), 216.

80. Sloan, E. A. (2015). Predicting pasta's potential. *Food Technology, 69*(5), 17.

81. Smith Edge, M., Miller Jones, J., & Marquart, L. (2005). A new life for whole grains. *Journal of the American Dietetic Association, 105*, 1856–1860.

82. Sousa, V. M. C., & Farfán J. A. (2012). State of knowledge on amaranth grain: A comprehensive review. *Journal of Food Science, 77*(4), R93–R104.

83. Stone, G. D., & Glover, D. (2017). Disembedding grain: Golden rice, the green revolution, and heirloom seeds in the Philippines. *Agric Hum Values, 34*, 87–102.

84. Suszkiw, J. (2002). Rice, oh so nice. *Agricultural Research Magazine, 50*(5), 17.

85. Tang, G., Qin, J., Dolnikowski, G. G., Russell, R. M., & Grusak, M. A. (2009). Golden rice is an effective source of vitamin A. *American Journal of Clinical Nutrition, 89*, 1776–1783.

86. Teutonico, R. A., & Knorr, D. (1985). Amaranth: Composition, properties, and applications of a rediscovered food crop. *Food Technology, 39*(4), 49.

87. U.S. Department of Agriculture Economic Research Service. (2016). Administrative Publication Number 073. Selected Charts 2016 from Ag and Food Statistics: Charting the Essentials. USDA.

88. U.S. Department of Health and Human Services and U.S. Department of Agriculture. (2015). *2015–2020 Dietary guidelines for Americans* (8th ed.). U.S. Government Publishing Office.

89. U.S. Department of Agriculture. (2006, August). Genetically engineered rice. Fact Sheet Release No. 0306.06. USDA/U.S. Government Publishing Office.

90. U.S. Department of Agriculture, Animal and Plant Health Inspection Service. (2006, August). BRS Qs & As: Biotechnology regulatory services. USDA.

91. U.S. Department of Agriculture, Animal and Plant Health Inspection Service. (2007, November). Biotechnology. USDA.

92. U.S. Department of Agriculture, Economic Research Service. (2011). Adoption of genetically engineered crops in the U.S. USDA.

93. U.S. Department of Agriculture, Economic Research Service. (2013). Data sets. Food availability (per capita) data system. USDA.

94. U.S. Food and Drug Administration. (2006, February 16). FDA news: FDA provides guidance on "whole grain" for manufacturers.

95. U.S. Government Publishing Office & National Archives and Records Administration's Office of the Federal Register. (2017). U.S. Government Printing Office.

96. U.S. Government Publishing Office. (2010). What We Eat in America, NHANES 2007-2010 for average intakes by age-sex group. Healthy U.S.-Style Food Patterns, which vary based on age, sex, and activity level, for recommended intake ranges.

97. Vansevenant, P., & Soubry, J. (1996). Instant pasta: A short story. *Food Ingredients and Analysis International,* 17–18.

98. Viuda-Martos, M., López-Marcos, M. C., Fernández-López, J., Sendra, E., López-Vargas, J. H., & Pérez-Álvarez, J. A. (2010). Role of fiber in cardiovascular diseases: A review. *Comprehensive Reviews in Food Science and Food Safety, 9,* 240–258.

99. Wang, F., Huang, W., Kim, Y., Liu, R., & Tilley, M. (2011). Effects of transglutaminase on the rheological and noodle-making characteristics of oat dough containing vital wheat gluten or egg albumin. *Journal of Cereal Science, 54*(1), 53–59.

100. Wei, Y., Zhang, Y., Liu, R., Zhang, B., Li, M., & Jin, S. (2017). Origin and evolutions of Chinese noodles. *Cereal Foods World, 62*(2), 44–51.

101. Wójtowicz, A. (2005). Influence of some functional components addition on the microstructure of precooked pasta. *Polish Journal of Food and Nutrition Sciences, 14*(4), 417.

102. Winter, C. D., Jara, E. A., & Coughlin, J. R. (2015). Assessing and understanding arsenic exposure. *Food Technology, 69*(1), 44–48.

103. Wooten, S. (2016). An Indigenous Slow Food Revolution: Agriculture on the West African Savanna. *Dublin Gastronomy Symposium,* Dublin, Ireland.

104. Zhao, Y. H., Manthey, F. A., Chang, S. K. C., Hou, H. J., & Yuan, S. H. (2005). Quality characteristics of spaghetti as affected by green and yellow pea, lentil, and chickpea flours. *Journal of Food Science, 70*(6), S371–S376.

Chapter 13

1. Al-Mazeedi, H. M., Regenstein, J. M., & Riaz, M. N. (2013). The issue of undeclared ingredients in halal and kosher food production: A focus on processing aids. *Comprehensive Reviews of Food Science and Technology, 12,* 228–233.

2. Alvarez-Jubete, L., Auty, M., Arendt, E. K., & Gallagher, E. (2010). Baking properties and microstructure of pseudocereal flours in gluten-free bread formulations. *European Food Research and Technology, 230,* 437–445.

3. American Dietetic Association. (2005). Position of the American Dietetic Association: Fat replacers. *Journal of the American Dietetic Association, 105,* 266–275.

4. Barrera, G. N., Ribotaa, P. D. (2007). Influence of damaged starch on cookie and bread-making quality. *European Food Research and Technology, 225,* 1–7.

5. Brandolini, A., & Hidalgo, A. (2012). Wheat germ: Not only a by-product. *International Journal of Food Sciences and Nutrition, 63*(sup 1), 71–74.

6. Bowers, J. (1992). *Food theory and applications* (2nd ed.). New York, NY: MacMillan Publishing Company.

7. Bushuk, W. (1998). Wheat breeding for end product use. *Euphytica, 100,* 137–145.

8. Butaki, R. C., & Dronzek, B. (1979). Comparison of gluten properties of four wheat varieties. *Cereal Chemistry, 56,* 159.

9. Fermin, B. C., Hahm, T. S., Radinsky, J. A., Kratochvil, R. J., Hall, R. E., & Lo, M. Y. (2005). Effect of praline and glutamine on the functional properties of wheat dough in winter wheat varieties. *Journal of Food Science, 70*(4), E273–E278.

10. Figoni, P. (2008). *How baking works: Exploring the fundamentals of baking science* (2nd ed.). Hoboken, NJ: John Wiley & Sons.

11. Hansen, L., & Rose, M. S. (1996). Sensory acceptability is inversely related to development of fat rancidity in bread made from stored flour. *Journal of the American Dietetic Association, 96,* 792.

12. Hoseney, R. C. (1994). *Principles of cereal science and technology* (2nd ed.). St. Paul, MN: American Association of Cereal Chemists, Inc.

13. Il, B., Daun, H., & Gilbert, S. G. (1991). Water sorption of gliadin. *Journal of Food Science, 56,* 510.

14. Izydorczyk, M., Biliaderis, C. G., & Bushuk, W. (1991). Physical properties of water-soluble pentosans from different wheat varieties. *Cereal Chemistry, 68*(2), 145–150.

15. Jimenez Gonzalez, A. T., DiFonzo, N. (ed.), Kaan, F. (ed.), & Nachit, M. (ed.), (1995). Milling process of durum wheat. *Ciheam Options Méditerranéennes, 22,* 43–51.

16. Kendall, P. (2003). *High altitude baking.* Denver: 3D Press, Inc., Colorado State University Cooperative Extension.

17. Khan, K. (2006). Gluten. In Hui, Y. H., Corke, H., De Leyn, I., Nip, W. K., & Cross, N. (Eds.), *Bakery products science and technology* (pp. 97–108). Ames, IA: Blackwell.

18. Kiszonas, A. M., Fuerst, E. P., Luthria, D., & Morris, C. F. (2015). Tracking arabinoxylanes through the preparation of pancakes. *Cereal Chemistry, 92*(1), 37.

19. Labensky, S. R. Martel, P. A., & Van Damme, E. (2016). *On baking* (3rd ed. Update). Upper Saddle River, NJ: Pearson Education, Inc.

20. Lai, H. M., & Lin, T. C. (2006). Bakery products: Science and technology. In Hui, Y. H., Corke, H., De Leyn, I., Nip, W. K., & Cross, N. (Eds.), *Bakery products science and technology* (pp. 2–68). Ames, IA: Blackwell.

21. Lebovits, M. D., Schiffenbauer, B., Belsky, H. Y. (2009). The halachos of chodosh and yoshon. *Halachically Speaking*, 5(2), 1–10.

22. Létang, C., Piau, M., & Verdier, C. (1999). Characterization of wheat flour-water doughs. Part I: Rheometry and microstructure. *Journal of Food Engineering*, 41, 121–152.

23. Lorenz, K. (1972). Food uses of triticale. *Food Technology*, 26(11), 66.

24. Lorenz, K., & Pagenkopf, A. L. (1975). High altitude food preparation and processing. *Critical Reviews in Food Science and Nutrition*, 5(4), 403–441.

25. Lukow, O. M. (2006). Wheat flour classification. In Hui, Y. H., Corke, H., De Leyn, I., Nip, W. K., & Cross, N. (Eds.), *Bakery products science and technology* (pp. 69–86). Ames, IA: Blackwell.

26. Lutz, E., Wieser, H., & Koehler, P. (2012). Identification of disulfide bonds in wheat gluten proteins by means of mass spectrometry/electron transfer dissociation. *Journal of Agricultural and Food Chemistry*, 60, 3708–3716.

27. Ma, C., Oomah, B. D., & Holme, J. (1986). Effect of deamidation and succinylation on some physicochemical and baking properties of gluten. *Journal of Food Science*, 51, 99.

28. Mani, K., Tragardh, C., Eliasson, A. C., & Lindahl, L. (1992). Water content, water soluble fraction, and mixing affect fundamental rheological properties of wheat flour doughs. *Journal of Food Science*, 57, 1198.

29. Mermelstein, N. H. (2011). Testing for gluten in foods. *Food Technology*, 65(2), 74–80.

30. Myhre, D. V. (1970). The function of carbohydrates in baking. *Baker's Digest*, 44(3), 32.

31. Nachay, K. (2016). Grains: Bakery and beyond. *Food Technology*, 70(12), 53–64.

32. Nachay, K. (2017). Bolstering the bakery aisle. *Food Technology*, 71(2), 51–52.

33. Ngo, W., Hoseney, R. C., & Moore, W. R. (1985). Dynamic rheological properties of cake batters made from chlorine-treated and untreated flours. *Journal of Food Science*, 50, 1338.

34. Pomeranz, Y., & MacMasters, M. M. (1968). Structure and composition of the wheat kernel. *Baker's Digest*, 42(4), 24.

35. Pszczola, D. E. (2005). Ingredients for bread meet changing "kneads." *Food Technology*, 59(1), 55–63.

36. Pyler, E. J., & Gorton, L. A. (2008). *Baking science & technology Vol II: Formulations and production* (4th ed.). Kansas City, MO: Sosland Publishing Group.

37. Pyler, E. J., & Gorton L. A. (2008). *Baking science & technology Vol I: Fundamentals and ingredients* (4th ed.). Kansas City, MO: Sosland Publishing Group.

38. Regenstein, J. M., Chaudry, M. M., & Regenstein, C. E. (2003). The kosher and halal food laws. *Comprehensive Reviews in Food Science and Food Safety*, 2, 111–127.

39. Riaz, M. N. (2007). Halal food production for the cereal industry and the halal certification process. *Cereal Foods World*, 15(2), 192–195.

40. Riaz, M. N. (2009). Navigating halal. *Baking & Snack*, 31(5), 53–58.

41. Sanchez-Marroquin, A., Domingo, M. V., Maya, S., & Saldana, C. (1985). Amaranth flour blends and fractions for baking applications. *Journal of Food Science*, 50, 789.

42. Shewry, P. R., Halford, N. G., Belton, P. S., & Tatham, A. S. (2002). *Phil. Trans. R. Soc. Lond.* 357, 133–142.

43. Sosland, L. J. (2017). Stybel Ad Halom: Port city epicenter of rapidly changing company. *Milling & Baking News*, 95(26), 35–40.

44. Thanhaeuser, S. M., Wieser, H., & Koehler, P. (2014). Correlation of quality parameters with the baking performance of wheat flours. *Cereal Chemistry*, 91(4), 333–341.

45. Tickelmann, R. E., & Steele, R. E. (1991). Higher assay grade of calcium peroxide improves properties of dough. *Food Technology*, 45(1), 107–109.

46. Tilley, K. A., Benjamin, R. E., Bagorogoza, K. E., Okot-Kother, B. M., Parkash, O., & Kwen H. (2001). Tyrosine cross-links: Molecular basis of gluten structure and function. *Journal of Agricultural and Food Chemistry*, 48, 2627–2632.

47. Watson, C. A., Shuey, W. C., Crawford, R. D., & Gumbmann, M. R. (1977). Physical dough, baking, and nutritional qualities of straight-grade and extended-extraction flours. *Cereal Chemistry*, 54, 657.

48. Watanabe, A., Larsson, H., & Eliasson, A. C. (2002). Effect of physical state of nonpolar lipids on rheology and microstructures of gluten-starch and wheat flour doughs. *Cereal Chemistry*, 79(2), 203–209.

49. Webb, D. (2016). Ancient grains. *Today's Dietitian*, 18(8), 45–47.

50. Wieser, H. (2006). Chemistry of gluten proteins. *Food Microbiology*, 24, 115–119.

51. Lorenz, K. (1979). Ergot on cereal grains. *Critical Reviews in Food Science and Nutrition*, 114, 311–354.

Chapter 14

1. Bowers, J. (1992). *Food theory and applications* (2nd ed.). New York, NY: Macmillan Publishing Co.

2. Charley, H. (1971). *Food science* (2nd ed.). New York, NY: John Wiley & Sons.

3. Childs, J., Bertholle, L., & Beck, S. (2009). *Mastering the art of French cooking*. New York, NY: Alfred-A-Knopf.

4. Figoni, P. (2008). *How baking works: Exploring the fundamentals of baking science* (2nd ed.). Hoboken, NJ: John Wiley & Sons.

5. Fulton, L., & Hogbin, M. (1993). Eating quality of muffins, cake, and cookies prepared with reduced fat and sugar. *Journal of the American Dietetic Association*, 93, 1313.

6. Gisslen, W. (2005). *Professional baking* (4th ed.). Hoboken, NJ: John Wiley & Sons, Inc.

7. Hartman, L. R. (2017). New year, new formulations. *Food Processing*, 78(1), 33–35.

8. Hippleheuser, A. L., Landberg, L. A., & Turnak, F. L. (1995). A system approach to formulating a low-fat muffin. *Food Technology*, 92(3), 49.

9. Holt, S. D., McWatters, K. H., & Resurreccion, A. V. A. (1992). Validation of predicted baking performance of muffins containing mixtures of wheat, cowpea, peanut, sorghum, and cassava flours. *Journal of Food Science*, 57, 470.

10. Hoseney, R. C. (1996). *The principles of cereal science and technology*. St. Paul, MN: American Association of Cereal Chemists, Inc.

11. Huber, R., Kalas, G., & Schoenlechner, R. (2017). Waffle production: Influence of baking plate material on sticking of waffles. *Journal of Food Science, 82*(1), 61–68.

12. Labensky, S. R., Martel, P. A., Van Damme, E. (2016). *On baking* (3rd ed. Update). Upper Saddle River, NJ: Pearson.

13. Labensky, S. R., Hause, A. M., & Martel, P. A. (2011). *On cooking: A textbook of culinary fundamentals* (5th ed.). Upper Saddle River, NJ: Pearson Prentice Hall.

14. Matthews, R. H., Kirkpatrick, M. E., & Dawson, E. H. (1965). Performance of fats in muffins. *Journal of the American Dietetic Association, 47*, 201.

15. Petrak, L. (2017). Smart snacks. *Progressive Grocer, 3*(1), 22–26.

16. Petrak, L. (2017). Why millennials matter. *Progressive Grocer, 3*(1), 10–14.

17. Polizzotto, L. M., Tinsley, A. M., Weber, C. W., & Berry, J. W. (1983). Dietary fibers in muffins. *Journal of Food Science, 48*, 111.

18. Rombauer, I. S., Becker, M. R., & Becker, E. (2006). *Joy of cooking*. New York, NY: Scribner.

19. Sloan, A. E. (2017). Shoppers shift to fresh. *Food Technology, 17*(1), 29–37.

Chapter 15

1. Anonymous. (1996). A guide to dough conditioners. *Lallemand Baking Update, 1*(13), 1.

2. Avital, Y., Mannheim, C. H., & Miltz, J. (1990). Effect of carbon dioxide atmosphere on staling and water relations in bread. *Journal of Food Science, 55*, 413.

3. Baguena, R., Soriano, M. D., Martinez-Anaya, M. A., & Benedito de Barber, C., (1991). Viability and performance of pure yeast strains in frozen wheat dough. *Journal of Food Science, 56*, 1690.

4. Bath, D. E., & Hoseney, R. C. (1994). *Cereal Chemistry, 71*(5), 403–408.

5. Bekatorou, A., Psarianos, C., & Koutinas, A. (2006). Production of food grade yeasts. *Food Technology and Biotechnology, 44*(3), 407–415.

6. Burger, A. (1996). Patent No. US5514395. U.S. Patent and Trademark Office: USPTO.gov.

7. Claus, A., Mongili, M., Weisz, G., Schieber, A., Carle, R. (2008). Impact of formulation and technological factors on acrylamide content of wheat bread and bread rolls. *Journal of Cereal Science, 47*, 546–554.

8. Cleveland, L. E., Moshfegh, A. J., Albertson, A. M., & Goldman, J. D. (2000). Dietary intake of whole grains. *Journal of the American College of Nutrition, 19*(3), 331S–338S.

9. Collar, C., Mascaros, A. F., & Benedito de Barber, C. (1992). Amino acid metabolism by yeasts and lactic acid bacteria during bread dough fermentation. *Journal of Food Science, 57*, 1423.

10. Dresser, K. (2009, March/April). Discovering authentic ciabatta. *Cook's Illustrated, 97*, 22–24.

11. Dziezak, J. D. (1987). Yeasts and yeast derivatives: Definitions, characteristics, and processing. *Food Technology, 41*(2), 104.

12. Dziezak, J. D. (1991). Enzymes: Catalysts for food processes. *Food Technology, 45*(1), 78.

13. Figoni, P. (2008). *How baking works: Exploring the fundamentals of baking science*. Hoboken, NJ: John Wiley & Sons.

14. Gorton, L. (2016). Creative solutions. *Baking & Snack, 38*, 11, 49–56.

15. Gray, J. A., & BeMiller, J. N. (2003). Bread staling: Molecular basis and control. *Comprehensive Reviews in Food Science and Food Safety, 2*, 1–21.

16. Hallberg, L. M., & Chinachoti, P. (2002). A fresh perspective on staling: The significance of starch recrystallization on the firming of bread. *Journal of Food Science, 67*, 1092–1096.

17. Hoseney, R. C. (1994). *Principles of cereal science and technology* (2nd ed.). St. Paul, MN: American Association of Cereal Chemists, Inc.

18. Hoseney, R. C., Lineback, D. R., & Seib, P. A. (1978). Role of starch in baked foods. *Baker's Digest, 52*(4), 11.

19. Hui, Y. H. (Ed.), Corke, H., De Leyn, I., Nip, W. K., Cross, N. (Ass. Eds.). (2006). *Bakery products science and technology*. Ames, IA: Blackwell.

20. Janjigian, A. (2010, September/October). Better focaccia. *Cook's Illustrated, 106*, 21–23.

21. Janjigian, A. (2011, March/April). Whole-wheat sandwich bread. *Cook's Illustrated, 109*, 22–24.

22. Kelsey, C. (2008, November/December). Perfecting rustic dinner rolls. *Cook's Illustrated, 95*, 14–15.

23. Khan, K., & Nygard, G. (2006). Gluten. In Hui, Y. H., Corke, H., De Leyn, I., Nip, W. K., & Cross, N. (Eds.), *Bakery products science and technology* (pp. 97–106). Ames, IA: Blackwell.

24. Labensky, S. R., Hause, A. M., & Martel, P. A. (2015). *On cooking: A textbook of culinary fundamentals* (5th ed. Update). Upper Saddle River, NJ: Pearson Prentice Hall.

25. Labensky, S. R., Martel, P. A., & Van Damme, E. (2016). *On baking: A textbook of baking and pastry fundamentals* (3rd ed.). Upper Saddle River, NJ: Pearson Prentice Hall.

26. Lai, C. S., Hoseney, R. C., & Davis, A. B. (1989). Effects of wheat bran on breadmaking. *Cereal Chemistry, 66*(3), 217–219.

27. Lynch, E. J., Dal Bello, F., Sheehan, E. M., Cashman, K. D., & Arendt, E. K. (2009). Fundamental studies on the reduction of salt on dough and bread characteristics. *Food Research International, 42*, 885–891.

28. Marston, P. E., & Wannan, T. L. (1976). Bread baking. *Baker's Digest, 50*(4), 24.

29. Martin, M. L., Zeleznak, K. J., & Hoseney, R. C. (1991). A mechanism of bread firming. I. Role of starch swelling. *Cereal Chemistry, 68*, 498.

30. Meyers, D. K., Lawlor, D. T. M., & Attfield, P. V. (1997). Influence of invertase activity and glycerol syntheses retention on fermentation of media with a high sugar concentration by *Saccharomyces cerevisiae. Applied and Environmental Microbiology, 63*(1), 145–150.

31. Miller, R. A., Hoseney, R. C., Graf, E., & Soper, J. (1997). Garlic effects on dough properties. *Journal of Food Science, 62*, 1198–1201.

32. Molt, M. (2011). *Food for fifty* (13th ed.). Upper Saddle River, NJ: Pearson Prentice Hall.

33. Pomeranz, Y. (1980). Molecular approach to breadmaking–An update and new perspectives. *Baker's Digest, 54*(1), 26.

34. Pomeranz, Y., & Finney, K. F. (1975). Sugars in breadmaking. *Baker's Digest, 49*(1), 20.

35. Powers, E. M., & Berkowitz, D. (1990). Efficacy of an oxygen scavenger to modify the atmosphere and prevent mold growth on meal, ready-to-eat pouched bread. *Journal of Food Protection, 53*, 767.

36. Pszczola, D. E. (2002). Bakery ingredients: Past, present, and future directions. *Food Technology, 56*(1), 56–72.

37. Rajabzadeh, N., & Asadian Haj Aghaei, G. (2007). Study of the effect of inactive dry yeast on rheological properties of wheat flour dough. *Pajouhesh-Va Sazandegi.* (73 in Agronomy and Horticulture), *19*(4), 74–78.

38. Ranhotra, G., Gelroth, J., Novak, F., & Matthews, R. (1985). B vitamins in selected variety breads commercially produced in major U.S. cities. *Journal of Food Science, 50*, 1174.

39. Ranhotra, G., Gelroth, J., Novak, F., & Matthews, R. (1985). Minerals in selected variety breads commercially produced in four major U.S. cities. *Journal of Food Science, 50*, 365.

40. Rezaei, M. N., Dornez, E., Jacobs, P., Parsi, A., Verstreoebm, K. J., & Courtin, C. M. (2014). Harvesting yeast (*Saccharomyces cerevisiae*) at different physiological phases significantly affects its functionality in bread dough fermentation. *Food Microbiology, 39*, 108–115.

41. Roof, B., & Janjigian, A. (2010, May/June). Notes from readers: Does your bread sound done? *Cook's Illustrated, 104*, 2.

42. Shogren, M. D., Pomeranz, Y., & Finney, K. F. (1981). Counteracting the deleterious effects of fiber in bread making. *Cereal Chemistry, 58*, 142.

43. Sloan, A. E. (1999). The upper crust. *Food Technology, 53*(10), 26.

44. Sloan, A. E. (2001). Dietary fiber moves back into the mainstream. *Food Technology, 55*(7), 18.

45. Sluimer, P. (2005). *Principles of breadmaking: Functionality of raw materials and process steps.* St. Paul, MN: American Association of Cereal Chemists, Inc.

46. Sosland, J. (2016). Industry leaders seek "new normal" in sluggish U.S. bread. *Milling & Baking News, 95*(15), 1.

47. Stoica, A., Barascu, E., Iuja, L. (2013). The influence of ascorbic acid and l-cysteine combination on bread quality. *Annals of Food Science and Technology, 14*(1), 51–53.

48. Thiele, C., Gänzle, M. G., & Vogel, R. F. (2001). Contribution of sourdough lactobacilli, yeast, and cereal enzymes to the generation of amino acids in dough relevant for bread flavor. *Cereal Chemistry, 79*(1), 45–51.

49. Thompson, J. B. (1980). Patent No. US4216241 A. U.S. Patent and Trademark Office: USPTO.gov.

50. Tieckelmann, R. E., & Steele, R. E. (1991). Higher-assay grade of calcium peroxide improves properties of dough. *Food Technology, 45*(1), 106.

51. Trivedi, N. B., Cooper, E. J., & Bruinsma, B. L. (1984). Development and applications of quick-rising yeast. *Food Technology, 38*(6), 51.

52. Umbach, S. L., Davis, E. A., & Gordon, J. (1990). Effects of heat and water transport on the bagel making process: Conventional and microwave baking. *Cereal Chemistry, 67*(4), 355–360.

53. U.S. Department of Agriculture (8th ed.) Dietary Guidelines for Americans 2015-2020. Retrieved at https://health.gov/dietaryguidelines/2015/resources/2015-2020_Dietary_Guilines.pdf.

54. U.S. Department of Agriculture. Economic Research Service. (2016). Wheat's role in the U.S. diet: Wheat's role in the U.S. diet has changed over the decades. *Economic Research Service.* Retrieved at https://www.ers.usda.gov/topics/crops/wheat/wheats-role-in-the-us-diet/.

55. U.S. Government Publishing Office. (2017). Code of federal Regulations. *Title 21 Food and Drugs.* Retrieved from http://www.ecfr.gov.

56. Unrein, J. (2002). U.S. customers get serious about artisan bread. *Milling and Baking News, 81*(10), 28–91.

57. Wu, J. Y., Maningat, J. I., Ponte, J. G., Jr., & Hoseney, R. C. (1988). Short-time breadmaking systems. Effect of formulation, additives, temperature, and flour quality. *Journal of Food Science, 53*, 535.

58. Yang, C.-H. (2006). Fermentation. In Hui, Y. H., Corke, H., De Leyn, I., Nip, W. K., & Cross, N. (Eds.), *Bakery products science and technology* (pp. 261–271). Ames, IA: Blackwell.

Chapter 16

1. American Association of Family and Consumer Science (2001). *Food: A handbook of terminology, purchasing, and preparation* (10th ed.). Alexandria, VA: American Association of Family and Consumer Sciences.

2. Barmore, M. A. (1936). The influence of various factors including altitude in the production of angel food cake. Colorado State University Experiment Station Technical Bulletin No. 15.

3. Bean, M. M., Yamazaki, W. T., & Donelson, D. H. (1978). Wheat starch gelatinization in sugar solutions. II. Fructose, glucose, and sucrose: Cake performance. *Cereal Chemistry, 55*, 945.

4. Berglund, P. T., & Hertsgaard, D. M. (1986). Use of vegetable oils at reduced levels in cake, pie crust, cookies, and muffins. *Journal of Food Science, 51*, 640.

5. Berry, D. (2017). Racing pulses. *Baking News, 39*(3), 69–75.

6. Bowers, J. (1992). *Food theory and applications.* New York, NY: MacMillan Publishing Co.

7. Briant, A. M., & Willman, A. R. (1956). Whole-egg sponge cakes. *Journal of Home Economics, 48.*

8. Brooker, B. F. (1993). The Stabilisation of air in foods containing fat-A Review. *Food Structure, 12*, 115–122.

9. Brooker, B. F. (1993). The Stabilisation of air in cake batters: The role of fats. *Food Structure, 12*(3), 285–296H.

10. Bruce, E. (2004, March). The best classic brownies: Whatever happened to the chewy, not over-the-top, yet chocolaty brownie? *Cook's Illustrated,* 22–23.

11. Charley, H. (1956). Characteristics of shortened cake baked in a fast- and in a slow-baking pan at different oven temperatures. *Food Research, 21*, 302–305.

12. Charley, H. (1982). *Food science* (2nd ed.). New York, NY: John Wiley & Sons.

13. Lindley, M. G. (1982). Sucrose in baked products. *British Nutrition Bulletin, 12*(1), 41.

14. Conforti, F. D. (2006). Cake manufacture. In Hui, Y. H. (Ed.), Corke, H., Leyn, I. D., Nip, W. K., & Cross, N. (Ass. Eds.), *Bakery products: Science and technology*. Ames, IA: Blackwell Publishing.

15. Conforti, F. (2007). Fundamentals of cake: Ingredients and production. In Hui, Y. H. (Ed.), Chanan, R. C., Clark, S., Cross, N., Dobbs, J., Hurst, W. J., Nollet, L. M. L., Shimimoni, E., Sinha, N., Smith, E. B., Surapat, S., Tichenal, A., & Toldra (Ass. Eds.), *Handbook of food products manufacturing* (pp. 307–318). Hoboken, NJ: John Wiley & Sons.

16. Curley, L. P., & Hoseney, R. C. (1984). Effects of corn sweeteners on cookie quality. *Cereal Chemistry, 61*(4), 274–278.

17. Delcour, J. A., & Hoseney, R. C. (2010). *Principles of cereal science and technology* (3rd ed.). St. Paul, MN: AACC.

18. Donelson, J. R., Gaines, C. S., & Finney, P. L. (2000). Baking formula innovation to eliminate chlorine treatment of cake flour. *Cereal Chemistry, 77*(1), 53–578.

19. Ebeler, S. E., Breyer, L. M., & Walker, C. E. (1986). White layer cake batter emulsion characteristics: Effects of sucrose ester emulsifiers. *Journal of Food Science, 51*, 1276.

20. Elgidaily, D. A., Funk, K., & Zabik, M. E. (1969). Baking temperature and quality of angel cakes. *Journal of the American Dietetic Association, 54*, 401.

21. Faridi, H. (1980). Short-time saltine cracker. *Bakers Digest, 54*(3), 16–21.

22. Foegeding, E. A., Luck, P. J., & Davis, J. P. (2006). Factors determining the physical properties of protein foams. *Food Hydrocolloids, 20*, 284–292.

23. Franks, O. J., Zabik, M. E., & Funk, K. (1969). Angel cakes using frozen, foam-spray-dried, freeze-dried, and spray-dried albumen. *Cereal Chemistry, 46*, 349.

24. Fulton, L., & Hogbin, M. (1993). Eating quality of muffins, cake, and cookies prepared with reduced fat and sugar. *Journal of the American Dietetic Association, 93*, 1313.

25. Frye, A. M., & Setser, C. S. (1991). Optimizing texture of reduced-calorie yellow layer cakes. *Cereal Chemistry, 69*(3), 338–343.

26. Frye, A. M., & Setser, C. S. (1993). Bulking agents and fat substitutes. *Food Science and Technology*. New York, NY: Marcel Dekker.

27. Gaines, C. S., & Donelson, J. R. (1982). Contribution of chlorinated flour fractions to cake crumb stickiness. *Cereal Chemistry, 59*, 378.

28. Geary, A. (2010, November/December). Foolproof sugar cookies. *Cook's Illustrated, 107*, 24–25.

29. Gisslen, W. (2005). *Professional baking* (4th ed.). Hoboken, NJ: John Wiley & Sons, Inc.

30. Gonzales-Galan, A., Wang, S. H., Sgarbieri, V. C., & Moraes, M. A. C. (1991). Sensory and nutritional properties of cookies based on wheat-rice-soybean flours baked in a microwave oven. *Journal of Food Science, 56*, 1699.

31. Gough, B. M., & Greenwood, C. T. (1978). The role and function of chlorine in the preparation of high-ratio cake flour. *CRC Critical Reviews in Food Science and Nutrition, 10*(1), 91–110.

32. Grewe, E., & Child, A. M. (1930). The effect of acid potassium tartrate as an ingredient in angel cake. *Cereal Chemistry, 7*, 111–119.

33. Hoseney, R. C. (1990). *Principles of cereal science and technology*. St. Paul, MN: American Association of Cereal Chemists, Inc.

34. Hoseney, R. C. (1994). *Principles of cereal science and technology* (2nd ed.). St. Paul, MN: American Association of Cereal Chemists, Inc.

35. Kahlenberg, O. J. (1948). Preliminary studies on factors affecting egg white quality. *Bakers Digest, 22*, 117–119.

36. Kelsey, C. (2009, May/June). The perfect chocolate chip cookie. *Cook's Illustrated, 98*, 22–24.

37. Kim, C. S., & Walker, C. E. (1992). Changes in starch pasting properties due to sugars and emulsifiers as determined by viscosity measurement. *Journal of Food Science, 57*, 1009.

38. Kim, C. S. (1994). The role of ingredients and thermal setting in high-ratio layer cake systems. *Journal of Korean Soc. Food Nutrition, 23*(3), 520–529.

39. Knightly, W. H., & Lynch M. J. (1960). The role of surfactants in baked foods. *The Bakers Digest, 41*(2), 28–31.

40. Kweon, M., Slade, L., & Levine, H. (2011). Development of a benchtop method for chemically leavened crackers I, identification of a diagnostic formula and procedure. *Cereal Chemistry, 88*(1), 19–24.

41. Kweon, M., Slade, L., & Levine, H. (2011). Development of a benchtop method for chemically leavened crackers II. Validation of the method. *Cereal Chemistry, 88*(1), 25–30.

42. Labensky, S. R., Van Damme, E., Martel, P., Tenberben, K. (2005). *On baking*. Upper Saddle River, NJ: Pearson Prentice Hall.

43. Labensky, S. R., Martel, P. Van Damme, E. (2016). *On baking* (3rd ed update). Upper Saddle River, NJ: Pearson Prentice Hall.

44. Lawson, H. W. (1985). *Volume 5 of the series The L. J. minor food service standards series standards for fats & oils Ch 11*, Baking Technology. Westport: The Avi Publishing Co.

45. Manley, D. (2000). *Technology of biscuits, crackers and cookies* (3rd ed.). Cambridge, England: CRC Press, Woodhead Publishing Ltd.

46. Manley, D. (2001). *Biscuit, cracker and cookie recipes for the food industry*. Cambridge, England: CRC Press, Woodhead Publishing Ltd.

47. Marx, J. T., Marx, B. D., & Johnson, J. M. (1990). High-fructose corn syrup cakes made with all-purpose flour or cake flour. *Cereal Chemistry, 67*, 502–504.

48. Matthews, R. H., & Dawson, E. H. (1966). Performance of fats in white cake. *Cereal Chemistry, 43*, 538.

49. McCullough, M. A. P., Johnson, J. M., & Phillips, J. A. (1986). High fructose corn syrup replacement for sucrose in shortened cakes. *Journal of Food Science, 51*, 536.

50. Mizukoshi, M. (1985). Model studies of cake baking. VI. Effects of cake ingredients and cake formula on shear modulus of cake. *Cereal Chemistry, 62*(4), 247–251.

51. Mihaelos, M. (2014). Cracker Tech 101. *Baking & Snack, 36*(10), 81–89.

52. Moncrieff, J. (1970). Shortening and emulsifiers for cakes and icings. *The Bakers Digest, 44*(5), 60–65.

53. Ngo, W., Hoseney, R. C., & Moore, W. R. (1985). Dynamic rheological properties of cake batters made from chlorine-treated and untreated flours. *Journal of Food Science, 50*, 1338.

54. Paton, D., Larocque, G. M., & Holme, J. (1981). Development of cake structure: Influence of ingredients on the measurement of cohesive force during baking. *Cereal Chemistry, 58*, 527.

55. Pareyt, B., Talhaoui, F., Kerckhofs, G., Brijs, K., Goesaert, H., Weevers, M., & Delcour, J. A. (2009). The role of sugar and fat in sugar-snap cookies: Structural and textural properties. *Journal of Food Engineering, 90*, 400–408.

56. *Pillsbury Best Cookies Cookbook.* (1997). New York, NY: Clarkson Potter Publishers.

57. Pizzinatto, A., & Hoseney, R. C. (1980). Rheological changes in cracker sponges during fermentation. *Cereal Chemistry, 57*(3), 185–188.

58. Pyler, E. J., & Gorton, L. A. (2009). *Baking science & technology* Vol II (4th ed.). Kansas City, MO: Sosland Publishing Co.

59. Paton, D., Larocque, G. M., & Holme, J. (1981). Development of cake structure: Influence of ingredients on the measurement of cohesive force during baking. *Cereal Chemistry, 58*, 527.

60. Pizzinatto, A., & Hoseney, R. C. (1980). Rheological changes to cracker sponge during fermentation. *Cereal Chemistry, 7*(3), 185.

61. Rankin, L. L., & Bingham, M. (2000). Acceptability of oatmeal chocolate chip cookies prepared using puréed white beans as a fat ingredient substitute. *Journal of American Dietetic Association, 100*, 831–833.

62. Rogers, D. E., & Hoseney, R. C. (1989). Effects of fermentation in saltine cracker production. *Cereal Chemistry, 66*(1), 6–10.

63. Ruperti, Y. (2009, January/February). Chewy chocolate cookies. *Cook's Illustrated, 96*, 22–23.

64. Ruperti, Y. (2011, January/February). Overhauling gingerbread cake. *Cook's Illustrated, 108*, 24–25.

65. Sloan, E. A. (2017). Shoppers shift to fresh. *Food Technology, 71*(1), 28–29, 31–37.

66. Spencer, J. (2017). Breakfast sandwiches latest trend in breakfast battle. *Milling and Baking News, 96*(4), 22.

67. Swanson, R. B., & Musayac, L. J. (1999). Acceptability of fruit purées in peanut butter, oatmeal, and chocolate-chip reduced-fat cookies. *Journal of the American Dietetic Association, 99*, 343–345.

68. Trimbo, H. B., & Miller, B. S. (1973). The development of tunnels in cakes. *Bakers Digest, 47*(5), 24–26, 70–71.

69. Trimbo, H. B., & Miller, B. S. (1966). Batter flow and ring formation in cake baking. *Bakers Digest, 40*(1), 40–42, 44–45.

70. Shelke, K., Faubion, J. M., Hoseney, R. C. (1990). The dynamics of cake baking as studied by a combination of viscometry and electrical resistance oven heating. *Cereal Chemistry, 67*(6), 575–580.

71. Thomasson, C. A., Miller, R. A., & Hoseney, R. C. (1995). Replacement of chlorine treatment for cake flour. *Cereal Chemistry, 72*(6), 616–620.

72. Vega, C., & Sanghvi, A. (2012). Cooking literacy: Meringues as culinary scaffoldings. *Food Biophysics, 7*, 103–113.

73. Tom Vierhile. (2016). In and out. *Prepared Foods, 185*(3), 15–20.

74. Wilderjans, E., Luytus, A., Brijs, K., & Delcour, J. A. (2013). Ingredient functionality in batter type cake making. *Trends in Food Science & Technology, 30*, 6–15.

75. Wilderjans, E., Pareyt, B., Goesaert, H., Brijs, K., & Delcour, J. A. (2008). The role of gluten in a pound cake system: A model approach based on gluten-starch blends. *Food Chemistry, 110*, 909–915.

76. Wright, G. (2015). Rotary moulded biscuits. *Biscuit People Magazine. (online journal)* April 26. Retrieved at http://www.biscuitpeople.com/magazine/post/rotary-moulding.

77. Wright, G. (2015). The lamination process in fermented crackers. *Biscuit People Magazine (online journal)* January 12. Retrieved at http://www.biscuitpeople.com/magazine.

78. Zhou, J., Faubion, J. M., & Walker, C. E. (2011). Evaluation of different types of fats for use in high-ratio layer cakes. *LWT-Food Science and Technology, 44*, 1802–1808.

Chapter 17

1. Berglund, P. T., & Hertsgaard, D. M (1986). Use of vegetable oils at reduced levels in cake, pie crust, cookies, and muffins. *Journal of Food Science, 51*, 640.

2. Briant, A. M., & Snow, P. R (1957). Freezer storage of pie shells. *Journal of the American Dietetic Association, 33*, 796.

3. Chysirichote, T., Utaipatanacheep, A., & Varanyanond, W (2011). Effect of reducing fat and using fat replacers in the crust of flaky Chinese pastry. *Kasetsart J. (Natural Science), 45*, 120–127.

4. Hirahara, S., & Simpson, J. I (1961). Microscopic appearance of gluten in pastry dough and its relation to the tenderness of baked pastry. *Journal of Home Economics, 53*, 681.

5. Labensky, S. R., Hause, A. M., & Martel, P. A (2011). *On cooking: A textbook of culinary fundamentals* (5th ed.). Upper Saddle River, NJ: Pearson Prentice Hall.

6. Matthews, R. H., & Dawson, E. H (1963). Performance of fats and oils in pastry and biscuits. *Cereal Chemistry, 40*, 291.

7. Miller, B. S., & Trimbo, H. B (1970). Factors affecting the quality of pie dough and pie crust. *Baker's Digest, 44*(1), 46.

Chapter 18

1. Academy of Nutrition and Dietetics. (2015). Position of the Academy of Nutrition and Dietetics: Health implications of dietary fiber. *Journal of the Academy of Nutrition and Dietetics, 115*, 1861–1870. http://dx.doi.org/10.1016/j.jand.2015.09.003

2. Arnold, J. (2002). Watermelon packs a powerful lycopene punch. *Agricultural Research Magazine, 50*(6), 12–13.

3. Barrett, D. M. (2007). Maximizing the nutritional value of fruits and vegetables. *Food Technology, 61*(4), 40–44.

4. Bliss, R. M. (2006). Fresh-cuts are popular, any way you slice them. *Agricultural Research Magazine, 54*(7). Retrieved from http://www.ars.usda.gov/is/AR/archive/jul06/produce0706.htm

5. Bowman, F., Page, E., Remmenga, E. E., & Trump, D. (1971). Microwave vs. conventional cooking of vegetables at high altitude. *Journal of the American Dietetic Association*, *58*, 427.

6. Brody, A. L. (2005). What's fresh about fresh-cut? *Food Technology*, *59*(11), 74–77.

7. Buzby, J. C., Wells, H. F., Aukakh, J. (2014, June). Food loss—Questions about the amount and causes still remain. *Amber Waves*. Retrieved from https://www.ers.usda.gov/amber-waves/2014/june/food-loss-questions-about-the-amount-and-causes-still-remain/

8. Calvin, L., Avendaño, B., & Schwentesius, R. (2007). Outbreak linked to spinach forces reassessment of food safety practices. *Amber Waves*, *5*(3), 24–31. Retrieved from http://www.ers.usda.gov/AmberWaves/Scripts/print.asp?page=/June07/Features/Spinach.htm

9. Carlson, A., Dong, D., Stewart, H., & Frazão, E. (2015, September). Following dietary guidance need not cost more—but many Americans would need to re-allocate their food budgets. *Amber Waves*. Retrieved from https://www.ers.usda.gov/amber-waves/2015/september/following-dietary-guidance-need-not-cost-more-but-many-americans-would-need-to-re-allocate-their-food-budgets/

10. Carlson, A., & Stewart, H. (2011). A wide variety of fruits and vegetables are affordable for SNAP recipients. *Amber Waves*, *9*(4), 6–7. Retrieved from http://www.ers.usda.gov/AmberWaves/AllIssues

11. Carlson, B. L., & Tabacchi, M. H. (1988). Loss of vitamin C in vegetables during the foodservice cycle. *Journal of the American Dietetic Association*, *88*, 65.

12. Dangour, A. D., Lock, K., Hayter, A., Ailenhead, A., Allen, E., & Uauy, R. (2010). Nutrition-related health effects of organic foods: A systematic review. *American Journal of Clinical Nutrition*, *90*(3), 680–685.

13. Darmon, N., Darmon, M., Maillot, M., & Drewnowski, A. (2005). A nutrient density standard for vegetables and fruits: Nutrients per calorie and nutrients per unit cost. *Journal of the American Dietetic Association*, *105*, 1881–1887.

14. Eheart, M. S., & Odland, D. (1972). Storage of fresh broccoli and green beans. *Journal of the American Dietetic Association*, *60*, 402.

15. Fordham, J. R., Wells, C. E., & Chen, L. H. (1975). Sprouting of seeds and nutrient composition of seeds and sprouts. *Journal of Food Science*, *40*, 552.

16. Galgano, F., Favati, F., Caruso, M., Pietrafesa, A., & Natella, S. (2007). The influence of processing and preserving on the retention of health-promoting compounds in broccoli. *Journal of Food Science*, *72*(2), S130–S135.

17. Gnanasekharan, V., Shewfelt, R. L., & Chinnan, M. S. (1992). Detection of color changes in green vegetables. *Journal of Food Science*, *57*, 149.

18. Herbach, K. M., Stintzing, F. C., & Carle, R. (2006). Betalain stability and degradation—Structural and chromatic aspects. *Journal of Food Science*, *71*(4), R41–R50.

19. Herranz, J., Vidal-Valverde, C., & Rojas-Hidalgo, E. (1981). Cellulose, hemicellulose and lignin content of raw and cooked Spanish vegetables. *Journal of Food Science*, *46*, 1927.

20. Herranz, J., Vidal-Valverde, C., & Rojas-Hidalgo, E. (1983). Cellulose, hemicellulose and lignin content of raw and cooked processed vegetables. *Journal of Food Science*, *48*, 274.

21. Humphrey, A. M. (2004). Chlorophyll as a color and functional ingredient. *Journal of Food Science*, *69*(5), C422–C425.

22. Institute of Food Technologists' Expert Panel on Food Safety and Nutrition. (1989). Dietary fiber. *Food Technology*, *43*(10), 133.

23. Institute of Food Technologists' Expert Panel on Food Safety and Nutrition. (1990). Quality of fruits and vegetables. *Food Technology*, *44*(6), 99.

24. Institute of Food Technologists' Expert Report on Biotechnology and Foods. (2000). Human food safety evaluation of rDNA biotechnology-derived foods. *Food Technology*, *54*(9), 53–61.

25. Jarden Corporation. (2005). *Ball blue book of preserving*. Muncie, IN: Jarden Corporation.

26. Jiménz-Monreal, A. M., García-Diz, L., Martínez-Tomé, M., Mariscal, M., & Murcia, M. A. (2009). Influence of cooking methods on antioxidant activity of vegetables. *Journal of Food Science*, *74*(3), H97–H103. doi:10.1111/j.1750-3841.2009.01091.x

27. Labensky, S. R., Hause, A. M., & Martell, P. A. (2011). *On cooking: A textbook of culinary fundamentals* (5th ed.). Upper Saddle River, NJ: Pearson Prentice Hall.

28. Lazan, H., Ali, Z. M., Mohd, A., & Nahar, F. (1987). Water stress and quality during storage of tropical leafy vegetables. *Journal of Food Science*, *52*, 1286.

29. Liener, I. (1979). Significance for humans of biologically active factors in soybeans and other food legumes. *Journal of the American Oil Chemists' Society*, *56*, 121.

30. Lin, B. H., Morrison, R. (2016, July). A closer look at declining fruit and vegetable consumption using linked data sources. *Amber Waves*, Retrieved from https://www.ers.usda.gov/amber-waves/2016/july/a-closer-look-at-declining-fruit-and-vegetable-consumption-using-linked-data-sources/

31. MacLeod, A. J., & MacLeod, G. (1970). Effects of variations in cooking methods on the flavor volatiles of cabbage. *Journal of Food Science*, *35*, 744.

32. Matthee, V., & Appledorf, H. (1978). Effect of cooking on vegetable fiber. *Journal of Food Science*, *43*, 1344.

33. Maul, F., Sargent, S. A., Sims, C. A., Baldwin, E. A., Balaban, M. O., & Huber, D. J. (2000). Tomato flavor and aroma quality as affected by storage temperature. *Journal of Food Science*, *65*, 1228–1237.

34. Mayeaux, M., Xu, Z., King, J. M., & Prinyawiwatkul, W. (2006). Effects of cooking conditions on lycopene content in tomatoes. *Journal of Food Science*, *71*(8), C461–C464.

35. McComber, D. R., Osman, E. M., & Lohnes, R. A. (1988). Factors related to potato mealiness. *Journal of Food Science*, *53*, 1423.

36. McWatters, K. H., Chinnan, M. S., Walker, S. L., Doyle, M. P., & Lin, C. M. (2002). Consumer acceptance of fresh-cut iceberg lettuce treated with 2 percent hydrogen peroxide and mild heat. *Journal of Food Protection*, *65*, 1221–1226.

37. Molt, M. (2011). *Food for fifty* (13th ed.). Upper Saddle River, NJ: Prentice Hall.

38. Mook, K., Laraia, B. A., Oddo, V. M., & Jones-Smith, J. C. (2016). Food security status and barriers to fruit and vegetable consumption in two economically deprived communities of Oakland, California, 2013–2014. *Prevention Chronic Disease*, *13*(E21), 1–13. doi:http://dx.doi.org/10.5888/pcd13.150402

39. Murphy, M. M., Barrai, L. M., Herman, D., Bi, X., Cheatham, R., & Randolph, R. K. (2012). Phytonutrient intake by adults in the United States in relation to fruit and vegetable intake. *Journal of the Academy of Nutrition and Dietetics, 112*(2), 222–229. doi:10.1016/j.jada.2011.08.044

40. Oser, B. L., Melnick, D., & Oser, M. (1943). Influence of cooking procedure upon retention of vitamins and minerals in vegetables. *Journal of Food Science, 8*(2), 115–122. doi:10.1111/j.1365-2621.1943.tb16552.x

41. Papazian, R. (1996). Sulfites. *FDA Consumer, 30*(10), 10.

42. Prakash, A., Inthajak, P., Huibregtse, H., Caporaso, F., & Foley, D. M. (2000). Effects of low-dose irradiation and conventional treatments on shelf life and quality characteristics of diced celery. *Journal of Food Science, 65*, 1070–1075.

43. Produce Marketing Association. (2002). *The PMA fresh produce manual.* Newark, DE: Author.

44. Schwartz, S. J., & Von Elbe, J. H. (1983). Kinetics of chlorophyll degradation to pyropheophytin in vegetables. *Journal of Food Science, 48*, 1303.

45. Singh, B., Yang, C. C., Salunkhe, D. K., & Rahman, A. R. (1972). Controlled atmosphere storage of lettuce. 1. Effects on quality and the respiration rate of lettuce heads. *Journal of Food Science, 37*, 48.

46. Singh, R. P., Buelow, R. H., & Lund, D. B. (1973). Storage behavior of artificially waxed green snap beans. *Journal of Food Science, 38*, 542.

47. Smith-Edge, M., Kunkel, M. E., Schimdt, J., & Papoutsakis, C. (2018). 2015 evidence analysis library systemic review on advanced technology in food production. *Journal of the Academy of Nutrition and Dietetics, 118*, 1106–1127. https://doi.org/10.1016/j.jand.2017.08.005

48. Snyder, P. O., & Matthews, M. E. (1983). Percent retention of vitamin C in whipped potatoes after pre-service holding. *Journal of the American Dietetic Association, 83*, 454.

49. Steinmetz, K. A., & Potter, J. D. (1996). Vegetables, fruit, and cancer prevention: A review. *Journal of the American Dietetic Association, 96*, 1027.

50. Stewart, H. (2016, March). Fruit and vegetable recommendations can be met for $2.10 to $2.60 per day. *Amber Waves.* Retrieved from https://www.ers.usda.gov/amber-waves/2016/march/fruit-and-vegetable-recommendations-can-be-met-for-210-to-260-per-day/

51. Stone, M. B., & Young, C. M. (1985). Effects of cultivars, blanching techniques, and cooking methods on quality of frozen green beans as measured by physical and sensory attributes. *Journal of Food Quality, 7*, 255.

52. U.S. Centers for Disease Control and Prevention. (2018, March). Plan healthy meals. Retrieved from https://www.cdc.gov/features/nutritionmonth/index.html

53. U.S. Centers for Disease Control and Prevention. (n.d.). Eat a variety of fruits and vegetables every day: Fruit and vegetable benefits. Retrieved from http://www.fruitsandveggiesmatter.gov/benefits/nutrient_guide.html

54. U.S. Centers for Disease Control and Prevention. (n.d.). Fruit and vegetable of the month. Retrieved from http://www.fruitsandveggiesmatter.gov

55. U.S. Centers for Disease Control and Prevention. (n.d.). Nutrition, physical activity, and obesity: Data, trends, and maps: 2015 National. Retrieved from https://nccd.cdc.gov/dnpao_dtm/rdPage.aspx?rdReport=DNPAO_DTM.ExploreByLocation&rdRequestForwarding=Form

56. U.S. Department of Agriculture. (2018, January). Choose my plate: All about the vegetable group. Retrieved from https://www.choosemyplate.gov/

57. U.S. Department of Agriculture, Agricultural Marketing Service. (1994). *How to buy canned and frozen fruits.* Home and Garden Bulletin No. 261. Washington, D.C.: Author.

58. U.S. Department of Agriculture, Agricultural Marketing Service. (1994). *How to buy canned and frozen vegetables.* Home and Garden Bulletin No. 259. Washington, D.C.: Author.

59. U.S. Department of Agriculture, Agricultural Marketing Service. (1994). *How to buy fresh vegetables.* Home and Garden Bulletin No. 258. Washington, D.C.: Author.

60. U.S. Department of Agriculture, Agricultural Marketing Service. (1994). *How to buy potatoes.* Home and Garden Bulletin No. 262. Washington, D.C.: Author.

61. U.S. Department of Agriculture, Agricultural Marketing Service. (n.d.). Organic labeling. Retrieved from https://www.ams.usda.gov/rules-regulations/organic/labeling

62. U.S. Department of Agriculture, Service. (2002). USDA national nutrient database for standard reference, Release 15. Retrieved from http://www.ars.usda.gov/main/site_main.htm?modecode=12-35-45-00

63. U.S. Department of Agriculture, Economic Research Service. (2017, July). Interactive charts and highlights. Retrieved from https://www.ers.usda.gov/data-products/food-availability-per-capita-data-system/interactive-charts-and-highlights/#fruit

64. U.S. Department of Agriculture, Economic Research Service. (2017, September). Food availability and consumption. Retrieved from https://www.ers.usda.gov/data-products/ag-and-food-statistics-charting-the-essentials/food-availability-and-consumption.aspx

65. U.S. Department of Agriculture, Economic Research Service. (2018, January). Food availability (per capita) data system. Retrieved fromhttps://www.ers.usda.gov/data-products/food-availability-per-capita-data-system/

66. U.S. Department of Agriculture, National Agricultural Statistics Service. (2017, September). Potatoes: 2016 summary. Retrieved from http://usda.mannlib.cornell.edu/usda/current/Pota/Pota-09-14-2017.pdf

67. U.S. Department of Health and Human Services, & U.S. Department of Agriculture. (2015, December). 2015–2020 Dietary Guidelines for Americans (8th ed.). Retrieved from http://health.gov/dietaryguidelines/2015/guidelines/

68. U.S. Food and Drug Administration. (2003). Dietary guidance message about fruits and vegetables. Retrieved from http://www.fda.gov

69. U.S. Food and Drug Administration. (2007, March). FDA finalizes report on 2006 spinach outbreak. Retrieved from http://www.fda.gov/bbs/topics/NEWS/2007/NEW01593.html

70. U.S. Food and Drug Administration. (2017, May). Pesticide monitoring program: Fiscal year 2014 pesticide report. Retrieved from https://www.fda.gov/Food/FoodborneIllnessContaminants/Pesticides/ucm546327.htm

71. U.S. Food and Drug Administration, Center for Food Safety and Applied Nutrition. (1998). Guidance for industry: Guide to minimize microbial food safety hazards for fresh fruit and vegetables. Retrieved from http://www.fda.gov/Food/GuidanceComplianceRegulatoryInformation/GuidanceDocuments/ProduceandPlanProducts/ucm064574.htm

72. U.S. Food and Drug Administration, Center for Food Safety and Applied Nutrition. (2005, November). Safe handling of raw produce and fresh-squeezed fruit and vegetable juices. Retrieved from http://www.fda.gov

73. Van Buren, J. P., & Pitifer, L. A. (1992). Retarding vegetable softening by cold alkaline pectin deesterification before cooking. *Journal of Food Science, 57*, 1022.

74. Van Duyn, M. A. S., & Pivonka, E. (2000). Overview of the health benefits of fruit and vegetable consumption for the dietetics professional: Selected literature. *Journal of the American Dietetic Association, 100*, 1511–1521.

75. Von Elbe, J. H., Maing, I., & Amundson, C. H. (1974). Color stability of betanin. *Journal of Food Science, 39*, 334.

76. Watada, A. E., Abe, K., & Yamuchi, N. (1990). Physiological activities of partially processed fruits and vegetables. *Food Technology, 44*(5), 116.

77. Williams, P. G., Ross, H., & Miller, J. C. B. (1995). Ascorbic acid and 5-methyltetrahydrofolate losses in vegetables with cook/chill or cook/hot-hold foodservice systems. *Journal of Food Science, 60*, 541.

78. Winter, C. K. (2011). Filling my plate with fear. *Food Technology, 65*(11), 92.

79. Winter, C. K., & Davis, S. F. (2006). IFT: Scientific status summary: Organic foods. *Journal of Food Science, 71*(9), R117–R124.

80. Winter, C. K., & Katz, J. M. (2011). Dietary exposure to pesticide residues from commodities alleged to contain the highest contamination levels. *Journal of Toxicology*, 2011, 1–7. doi:10.1155/2011/589674

81. Wrolstad, R. E. (2004). Anthocyanin pigments—Bioactivity and coloring properties. *Journal of Food Science, 71*(5), C419–C421.

82. Zhao, X., Chambers, E., IV, Matta, Z., Loughin, T. M., & Carey, E. E. (2007). Consumer sensory analysis of organically and conventionally grown vegetables. *Journal of Food Science, 72*(2), S87–S91.

83. Zyren, J., Elkins, E. R., Dudek, J. A., & Hagen, R. E. (1983). Fiber contents of selected raw and processed vegetables, fruits and fruit juices as served. *Journal of Food Science, 48*, 600.

Chapter 19

1. Academy of Nutrition and Dietetics. (2016). Position of the Academy of Nutrition and Dietetics: Vegetarian diets. *Journal of the Academy of Nutrition and Dietetics, 116*, 1970–1980.

2. Bartelme, M. Z. (2016). Personalized granola; Drinking the sea; Beans for breakfast. *Food Technology, 70*(6), 19.

3. Boiling, B. W. (2017). Almond polyphenols: Methods of analysis, contribution to food quality, and health promotion. *Comprehensive Reviews in Food Science and Food Safety, 16*, 346–368. doi:10.1111/1541-4337.12260

4. Bond, J. K. (2017, February). Pulses production expanding as consumers cultivate a taste for U.S. lentils and chickpeas. *Amber Waves*. Retrieved from https://www.ers.usda.gov/amber-waves/2017/januaryfebruary/pulses-production-expanding-as-consumers-cultivate-a-taste-for-us-lentils-and-chickpeas/

5. Clark, J. P. (2002). Processing tree nuts. *Food Technology, 56*(6), 122.

6. Dawson, E. H., Lamb, J. C., Toepfer, E. W., & Warren, H. W. (1952). *Development of rapid methods of soaking and cooking dry beans*. Technical Bulletin No. 1051. Washington, D.C.: U.S. Department of Agriculture.

7. Despain, D. (2015). A plant-based paradigm shift for packaged food. *Food Technology, 69*(5), 32–45.

8. Doris, C. (2017). Plant-based eating evolves. *Food Technology, 70*(9), 27–37.

9. Doris, C. (2018). Mimicking meat, seafood, and dairy. *Food Technology, 72*(5), 22–35.

10. Dwyer, J. T., Goldin, B. R., Saul, N., Gualtieri, L., Barakat, S., & Adlercreutz, H. (1994). Tofu and soy drinks contain phytoestrogens. *Journal of the American Dietetic Association, 94*, 739.

11. Elbert, E. M., & Witt, R. L. (1968). Gelatinization of starch in the common dry bean, *Phaseolus vulgaris. Journal of Home Economics, 60*, 186.

12. Galloway, R. (2013). *Soyfood guide*. Chesterfield, Missouri: United Soybean Board.

13. Huis, A. V., Itterbeeck, J. V., Klunder, H., Mertens, E., Halloran, A., Muir, G., & Vantomme, P. (2013). *Edible insects: Future prospects for food and feed security*. Rome: Food and Agriculture Organization of the United Nations.

14. Loke, A., Baranda, L. C., Lezcano, S. C., & Jin, J. (2016). *Pulses: Nutritious seeds for a sustainable future*. Food and Agriculture Organization of the United Nations.

15. McHugh, T. (2016). How hummus is processed. *Food Technology, 70*(7), 91–94.

16. McHugh, T. (2016). How nut and seed butters are processed. *Food Technology, 70*(11), 70–73.

17. McHugh, T. (2016). How tofu is processed. *Food Technology, 70*(2), 72–74.

18. Mermelstein, N. H. (2013). Almonds and walnuts: Shaking out quality. *Food Technology, 67*(7), 91–94.

19. Mermelstein, N. H. (2015). Crickets, mealworms, and locusts, Oh my! *Food Technology, 69*(10), 69–73.

20. Mitchell, D. C., Lawrence, F. R., Hartman, T. J., & Curran, J. M. (2009). Consumption of dry beans, peas, and lentils could improve diet quality in the U.S. population. *Journal of the American Dietetic Association, 109*(5), 909–913. doi:10.1016/j.jada.2009.02.029

21. Nachay, K. (2015). Small ingredients offer big functional benefits. *Food Technology, 69*(8), 61–68.

22. Nachay, K. (2017). Ingredient development takes cues from research insights. *Food Technology, 71*(6), 83–98.

23. Nachay, K. (2017). The power of pulses. *Food Technology, 71*(3), 46–53.

24. Ohr, L. M. (2006). Health nuts. *Food Technology, 60*(12), 81–83.

25. Ohr, L. M. (2010). From beans to nuts. *Food Technology, 64*(4), 61–66.

26. Ohr, L. M. (2013). Wholesome nutrition. *Food Technology, 67*(5), 79–85.

27. Ohr, L. M. (2016). Wholly grains. *Food Technology, 70*(2), 63–66.

28. Palmer, S. (2017). Plant proteins. *Today's dietitian, 19*(2), 26.

29. Pszczola, D. E. (2012). Seeds of success. *Food Technology, 66*(11), 55–55.

30. Resurreccion, A. V. A., Sales, J. M., Potrebko, I., Francisco, M. L. L., & Hitchcock, H. L. (2009). Peanuts: Bioactive food in a shell. *Food Technology, 63*(12), 30–36.

31. Sloan, A. E. (2012). Nuts deliver nutrition, functionality, and taste. *Food Technology, 66*(12), 16.

32. Tarver, T. (2015). Oregon State puts more of the sea on the plate. *Food Technology, 69*(10), 18–20.

33. Tarver, T. (2015). Sea-ing a better way to feed the world. *Food Technology, 69*(8), 22–29.

34. Tarver, T. (2016). Increasing the "Maine" sources of U.S. aquaculture. *Food Technology, 70*(10), 17–21.

35. Tarver, T. (2016). Palatable proteins for complex palates. *Food Technology, 70*(3), 32–39.

36. Torres-Penaranda, A. V., Reitmeier, C. A., Wilson, L. A., Fehr, W. R., & Narvel, J. M. (1998). Sensory characteristics of soymilk and tofu made from lipoxygenase-free and normal soybeans. *Journal of Food Science, 63*(6), 1084–1087.

37. U.S.A. Dry Pea & Lentil Council. (2016). *U.S.A. Pulses: Processing information and technical manual.* Moscow, ID: USA Dry Pea & Lentil Council.

38. U.S. Department of Agriculture. (2017, May). Soybeans and oil crops: Background. Retrieved from https://www.ers.usda.gov/topics/crops/soybeans-oil-crops/background/

39. U.S. Department of Agriculture. (2017, November). Choose My Plate: All about the protein foods group. Retrieved from https://www.choosemyplate.gov/protein-foods

40. U.S. Department of Agriculture. (2018, March). Choose My Plate: Tips for vegetarians. Retrieved from https://www.choosemyplate.gov/tips-vegetarians

41. U.S. Department of Agriculture, Economic Research Service. (2018, January). Food availability (per capita) data system. Retrieved from https://www.ers.usda.gov/data-products/food-availability-per-capita-data-system/

42. U.S. Department of Health and Human Services, U.S. Department of Agriculture. (2015, December). 2015–2020 Dietary Guidelines for Americans. 8th Edition. Retrieved from http://health.gov/dietaryguidelines/2015/guidelines/

43. U.S. Food and Drug Administration. (2018, March). Food allergies: What you need to know. Retrieved from https://www.fda.gov/Food/ResourcesForYou/Consumers/ucm079311.htm

Chapter 20

1. Abe, K., & Watada, A. E. (1991). Ethylene absorbent to maintain quality of lightly processed fruits and vegetables. *Journal of Food Science, 56*, 1589.

2. Arnold, J. (2002). Watermelon packs a powerful lycopene punch. *Agricultural Research Magazine, 50*(6), 12–13.

3. Beveridge, T. (1999). Electron microscopic characterization of haze in apple juice. *Food Technology, 53*(1), 44–48.

4. Blue Goose Growers, Inc. (1986). *The buying guide for fresh fruits, vegetables, herbs, and nuts* (8th ed.). Shepherdstown, WV: Author.

5. Bourne, M. C. (1982). Effect of temperature on firmness of raw fruits and vegetables. *Journal of Food Science, 47*, 440.

6. Bouzari, A., Holstege, D., & Barrett, D. M. (2015). Vitamin retention in eight fruits and vegetables: A comparison of refrigerated and frozen storage. *Journal of Agricultural and Food Chemistry, 63*(3), 957–962.

7. Brody, A. L. (2005). What's fresh about fresh-cut. *Food Technology, 59*(11), 74–77.

8. Buzby, J. C., Wells, H. F., & Aulakh, J. (2014, June). Food loss – Questions about the amount and causes remain. *Amber Waves.* Retrieve from https://www.ers.usda.gov/amber-waves/2014/june/food-loss-questions-about-the-amount-and-causes-still-remain/

9. Carlson, A. (2016, May). Investigating retail price premiums for organic foods. *Amber Waves.* Retrieved from https://www.ers.usda.gov/amber-waves/2016/may/investigating-retail-price-premiums-for-organic-foods/

10. Chairote, G., Rodriguez, F., & Crouzet, J. (1981). Characterization of additional volatile flavor components of apricot. *Journal of Food Science, 46*, 1898.

11. Clark, J. P. (2002). Extending the shelf life of fruits and vegetables. *Food Technology, 56*(4), 98–100, 105.

12. Clark, J. P. (2003). Orange juice processing. *Food Technology, 57*(12), 50–51.

13. Clemens, R., & Pressman, P. (2011). Where would we be without honeybees? *Food Technology, 65*(11), 19.

14. Darmon, N., Darmon, M., Maillot, M., & Drewnowski, A. (2005). A nutrient density standard for vegetables and fruits: Nutrients per calorie and nutrients per unit cost. *Journal of the American Dietetic Association, 105*, 1881–1887.

15. Demetrakakes, P. (1996). Unconcentrated effort. *Food Processing, 57*(11), 77.

16. Faigh, J. G. (1995). Enzyme formulations for optimizing juice yields. *Food Technology, 49*(9), 79.

17. Frohlich, O., & Schreier, P. (1990). Volatile constituents of loquat (*Eriobotrya japonica* Lindl.) fruit. *Journal of Food Science, 55*, 176.

18. Greene, C., Ferreira, G., Carlson, A., Cooke, B., & Hitaj, C. (2017, February). Growing organic demand provides high-value opportunities for many types of producers. *Amber Waves.* Retrieved from https://www.ers.usda.gov/amber-waves/2017/januaryfebruary/growing-organic-demand-provides-high-value-opportunities-for-many-types-of-producers/

19. Knee, M. (1971). Ripening of apples during storage. III. Changes in chemical composition of Golden Delicious apples during the climacteric and under conditions simulating commercial storage practice. *Journal of the Science of Food and Agriculture, 22*, 371.

20. Labensky, S. R., Hause, A. M., & Martell, P. A. (2015). *On cooking: A textbook of culinary fundamentals* (5th ed.). Upper Saddle River, NJ: Pearson Prentice Hall.

21. Labuza, T. P. (1996). An introduction to active packaging for foods. *Food Technology, 50*(4), 68.

22. Lidster, P. D., Lightfoot, H. J., & McRae, K. B. (1983). Production and regeneration of principal volatiles in apples stored in modified atmospheres and air. *Journal of Food Science, 48*, 400.

23. Linshan, L., Pegg, R. B., Eitenmiller, R. R., Chuan, J-Y., & Kerrihard, A. L. (2017). Selected nutrient analysis of fresh, fresh-stored, and frozen fruits and vegetables. *Journal of Food Composition and Analysis, 59*, 8–17.

24. Minor, T., & Perez, A. (2018, April). Consumer demand for fresh fruit drives increases across sector. *Amber Waves.* Retrieved from https://www.ers.usda.gov/

amber-waves/2018/april/consumer-demand-for-fresh-fruit-drives-increases-across-sector/

25. Nachay, K. (2009). Commodities get COOL. *Food Technology, 63*(3), 42–46.

26. Noel, G. L., & Robberstad, M. T. (1963). Stability of vitamin C in canned apple juice and orange juice under refrigerated conditions. *Food Technology, 17,* 947.

27. Ohr, L. M. (2005). Brain foods. *Food Technology, 59*(7), 69–73.

28. Pratt, S. (1992). The "peachfuzz" plot. *Food Technology, 46*(8), 46.

29. Produce Marketing Association. (1995). *The foodservice guide to fresh produce.* Newark, DE: Author.

30. Produce Marketing Association. (2002). *The PMA fresh produce manual.* Newark, DE: Author.

31. Putnam, J. J., & Allshouse, J. (2001). Imports' share of U.S. diet rises in late 1990's. *Food Review, 24*(3), 15–22.

32. Segal, M. (1988). *Fruit.* U.S. Department of Health and Human Services Publication No. (FDA) 88-2226. Rockville, MD: U.S. Department of Health and Human Services.

33. Steinmetz, K. A., & Potter, J. D. (1996). Vegetables, fruit, and cancer prevention: A review. *Journal of the American Dietetic Association, 96,* 1027.

34. Stewart, H. (2016, March). Fruit and vegetable recommendations can be met for $2.10 to $2.60 per day. *Amber Waves.* Retrieved from https://www.ers.usda.gov/amber-waves/2016/march/fruit-and-vegetable-recommendations-can-be-met-for-210-to-260-per-day/

35. Stewart, H. (2018, March). Shopping at farmer's markets and roadside stands increases fruit and vegetable demand. *Amber Waves.* Retrieved from https://www.ers.usda.gov/amber-waves/2018/march/shopping-at-farmers-markets-and-roadside-stands-increases-fruit-and-vegetable-demand/

36. Sweeney, J. P., Chapman, V. J., & Hepner, P. A. (1970). Sugar, acid, and flavor in fresh fruits. *Journal of the American Dietetic Association, 57,* 432.

37. Talasila, P. C., Chau, K. V., & Brecht, J. K. (1995). Design of rigid modified atmosphere packages for fresh fruits and vegetables. *Journal of Food Science, 60,* 758.

38. U.S. Centers for Disease Control and Prevention. (2002, November 22). Multistate outbreaks of *Salmonella* serotype Poona infections associated with eating cantaloupe from Mexico—United States and Canada, 2000–2002. *Morbidity and Mortality Weekly Report, 51*(46), 1044–1047. Retrieved from http://www.cdc.gov/mmwr/preview/mmwrhtml/mm5146a2.htm

39. U.S. Centers for Disease Control and Prevention. (2005, December). Preventing health risks associated with drinking unpasteurized or untreated juice. Retrieved from http://www.cdc.gov

40. U.S. Centers for Disease Control and Prevention. (2011, October 7). Multistate outbreak of listeriosis associated with Jensen Farms Cantaloupe—United States, August–September 2011. *Morbidity and Mortality Weekly Report, 60*(39), 1357–1358. Retrieved from http://www.cdc.gov/mmwr/preview/mmwrhtml/mm6039a5.htm?s_cid=mm6039a5_w

41. U.S. Department of Agriculture, Agricultural Marketing Service. (2012, April 9). Country of origin labeling. Retrieved from http://www.ams.usda.gov

42. U.S. Department of Agriculture, Agricultural Marketing Service. (n.d.). Fruits: Grades and standards. Retrieved from https://www.ams.usda.gov/grades-standards/fruits

43. U.S. Department of Agriculture, Economic Research Service. (2011, February 1). Fruit and tree nuts: Trade. Retrieved from http://www.ers.usda.gov/Briefing/FruitandTreeNuts/trade.htm#frut

44. U.S. Department of Agriculture, Economic Research Service. (2017, July). Interactive charts and highlights. Retrieved from https://www.ers.usda.gov/data-products/food-availability-per-capita-data-system/interactive-charts-and-highlights/#fruit

45. U.S. Department of Agriculture, Economic Research Service. (2018, January). Food availability (per capita) data system. Retrieved fromhttps://www.ers.usda.gov/data-products/food-availability-per-capita-data-system/

46. U.S. Department of Health and Human Services, & U.S. Department of Agriculture. 2015–2020 Dietary Guidelines for Americans. 8th Edition. (2015, December). Retrieved from http://health.gov/dietaryguidelines/2015/guidelines/

47. U.S. Food and Drug Administration. (2003). Dietary guidance message about fruits and vegetables. Retrieved from http://www.fda.gov

48. U.S. Food and Drug Administration. (2017). 2016 food safety survey. Retrieved from https://www.fda.gov/downloads/food/foodscienceresearch/consumerbehaviorresearch/ucm529481.pdf

49. U.S. Food and Drug Administration, Center for Food Safety and Applied Nutrition. (1999, June). A food labeling guide. Chapter II—Name of food. Retrieved from http://www.fda.gov

50. U.S. Government Printing Office. (2001, April 1). Code of Federal Regulations: 21CFR102.33—Beverages that contain fruit or vegetable juice. Retrieved from http://ecfr.gpoaccess.gov/cgi/t/text/text-idx?c=ecfr&sid=8c-5344f04a8ae103e5b0ff5a17c7fa97&rgn=div8&view=text&node=21:2.0.1.1.3.2.1.5&idno=21

51. Van Duyn, M. A. S., & Pivonka, E. (2000). Overview of the health benefits of fruit and vegetable consumption for the dietetics professional: Selected literature. *Journal of the American Dietetic Association, 100,* 1511–1521.

52. Wiseman, J. J., & McDaniel, M. R. (1991). Modification of fruit flavors by aspartame and sucrose. *Journal of Food Science, 56,* 1668.

Chapter 21

1. Acikgoz, F. E., & Deveci, M. (2011). Comparative analysis of vitamin C, crude protein, elemental nitrogen and mineral content of canola greens (*Brassica napus* L.) and kale (*Brassica oleracea* var. *acephala*). *African Journal of Biotechnology, 10*(83), 19385–19391.

2. Anonymous. (2016). Olives a feature of Turkey since 4000 BC. *Olivae, 123,* 6–8.

3. Anonymous. (1950). *Betty Crocker's picture cookbook.* Minneapolis, MN: General Mills Inc & Macmillan Inc.

4. Arroyo-Lopez, F. N., Querol, A., Bautista-Gallego, J., & Garrido-Fernández, A. (2008). Role of yeast in table olive production. *International Journal of Food Microbiology, 128,* 189–196.

5. Aykın, E., Budak, N. H., & Güzel-Seydim, Z. B. (2015). Bioactive components of mother vinegar. *Journal of the American College of Nutrition, 34*(1), 80–89.

6. Bellatti, A. (2010). Good eats from around the globe. *Today's Dietitian, 12*(4), 38.

7. Bentley, J. (2017). *U.S. trends in food availability and a dietary assessment of loss-adjusted food availability*, 1970–2014. USDA Economic Research Service. Economic Information Bulletin No. (EIB-166) 38 pp, January 2017.

8. Bliss, M. (2008). Safe leafy greens before & after bagging. *Agriculture Research*, 56(6), 12–14.

9. Bond, J., & Minor, T. (2017). Vegetable and Pulses Outlook, VGS-358., U.S. Department of Agriculture, Economic Research Service. Washington, D.C.: U.S. Department of Agriculture.

10. Brenes, M., Romero, C., & Garcia-Garcia, P. (2017). Optimization of ripe olive processing with a single lye treatment. *Journal of Food Science*, 82(9), 2078–2084.

11. Bunning, M., & Kendall, P. (2007). Health benefits and safe handling of salad greens. Food and nutrition series. Health: Fact Sheet no. 9.373. Fort Collins, CO: The Colorado State University Extension.

12. Cantwell, M., Rovelo, J., Nie, X., & Rubatzky, V. (1996, September). Specialty salad greens: postharvest physiology and shelf-life. In III International Symposium Diversification of Vegetable Crops 467 (pp. 371–378).

13. California Department of Food and Agriculture. National Agricultural Statistics Service, Pacific Regional Office. (2017). 2017 California table olive probability survey report. Sacramento, CA: California Department of Food and Agriculture.

14. Charkowski, A. O. (2000). Safer sprouts. *Agriculture Research*, 48(8), 16–17.

15. Charley, H. (1971). *Food science* (2nd ed.). New York, NY: John Wiley & Sons.

16. Charoenprasert, S., Zweigenbaum, J. A., Zhang, C., & Mitchell, A. E. (2017). The influence of pH and sodium hydroxide exposure time on glucosamine and acrylamide levels in California-style black ripe olives. *Journal of Food Science*, 82(7), 1574–1581.

17. Chen, H., Chen, T., Giudici, P., & Chen, F. (2016). Vinegar functions on health: Constituents, sources, and formation mechanisms. *Comprehensive Reviews in Food Science and Food Safety*, 15, 1124–1138.

18. Clark, J. P. (2002). Extending the shelf life of fruits and vegetables. *Food Technology*, 56(4), 98.

19. Davis, R. M., Subbarao, K. V., Raid, R. N., & Kurtz, E. A. (eds.). (1997). *Compendium of lettuce diseases*. St. Paul, MN: APS Press.

20. Durham, S. (2015). 16 new lettuce lines. *Agriculture Research*, 63(5), 1.

21. Findki, M., Mutulu, E., & Bursa, M. (2016). What are natural olives? How are they produced? *Olivae*, 123, 23–26.

22. Food and Drug Administration. (2017). Title 7 Agriculture Part 944 Fruits, Import regulations 944.401 Olive Regulations. Washington, D.C.: U.S. Government Publishing Office.

23. Garcia, A., Mount, J. R., & Davidson, P. M. (2003). Ozone and chlorine treatment of minimally processed lettuce. *Journal of Food Science*, 68(9), 2747–2751.

24. Gelatin Manufacturers Institute of America. (2012). *Gelatin handbook*. New York, NY: Gelatin Manufacturers Institute of America.

25. Ghanbari, R., Anwar, F., Alkharfy, K. M., Gilani, A. H., & Saari, N. (2012). Valuable nutrients and functional bioactives in different parts of olives (Olea europaea L.)-A review. *International Journal of Medical Science*, 13, 3291–3340.

26. Gudmundsson, M. (2002). Rheological properties of fish gelatins. *Journal of Food Science*, 67(6), 2172–2176.

27. Heaney, R. P., & Weaver, C. M. (1990). Calcium absorption from kale. *The American Journal of Clinical Nutrition*, 51(4), 656–657.

28. Johnston, C. S., & Gaas, C. A. (2006). Vinegar: medicinal uses and antiglycemic effect. *Medscape General Medicine*, 8(2), 61.

29. Kaplan, K. (2015). Downy Mildew helps a bad hitchhiker in lettuce. *Ag Research Magazine*, 63, 7.

30. Kostyo, M. (2017). Expert insight: Salad consumption is up, but preferences are changing. Wellness Newsletter: February 21, 2017. Institute of Food Technologists.

31. Labensky, S. R., Hause, A. M., & Martel, P. A. (2015). *On cooking* (5th ed., update). Upper Saddle River, NJ: Pearson Education.

32. Lea, A. G. H. (1989). Cider vinegar. In Downing, D. L. (Ed.), *Processed apple products* (pp. 279–301). New York, NY: Van Nostrand Reinhold.

33. Li-Cohen, A. E., & Bruhn, C. M. (2002). Safety of consumer handling of fresh produce from the time of purchase to the plate: A comprehensive consumer survey. *Journal of Food Protection*, 65(8), 1287–1296.

34. Marchetti, R., Casadei, M. A., & Guerzoni, M. E. (1992). Microbial population dynamics in ready-to-use vegetable salads. *Italian Journal of Food Science (Italy)*, 2, 97–108.

35. Mas, A., Torija, M. J., García-Parrilla, M. D. C., & Troncoso, A. M. (2014). Acetic acid bacteria and the production and quality of wine vinegar. *The Scientific World Journal*, 2014, 394671. doi:10.1155/2014/394671

36. Mermelstein, N. H. (2017). Putting olives on the table. *Food Technology*, 71(2), 69–71.

37. Michelmore, R. W., & Ochoa, O. E. (2008). Breeding crisphead lettuce: Release of Downy mildew resistant breeding lines of crisphead lettuce. California Lettuce Research Program (Report April 1, 2007, through March 31, 2008). The Genome Center and the Department of Plant Science, University of California Davis.

38. Morales, M., & Janick, J. (2002). Arugula: A promising specialty leaf vegetable. In J. Janick and A. Whipkey (Eds.), *Trends in new crops and new uses* (pp. 481–423). Alexandria, VA: ASHS Press.

39. Nicholas, C., & Herrington, D. (2009). Fact Sheet Family and Consumer Science. HVG-53467-09. Columbus, OH: The Ohio State University Extension.

40. Oria, M. (2001). Report addresses safety of fruit and vegetables. *Food Technology*, 55(11), 22.

41. Pérez-López, U., Pinzino, C., Quartacci, M. F., Ranieri, A., & Sgherri, C. (2014). Phenolic composition and related antioxidant properties in differently colored lettuces: A study by electron paramagnetic resonance (EPR) kinetics. *Journal of Agricultural and Food Chemistry*, 62(49), 12001–12007. doi:10.1021/jf503260v

42. Rolls, B. J., Roe, L. S., & Meengs, J. S. (2004). Salad and satiety: Energy density and portion size of a first-course salad affect energy intake at lunch. *Journal of the American Dietetic Association*, 104, 1570–1576.

43. Rombauer, I. S., Becker, M. R., & Becker, E. (1997). *The joy of cooking*. New York, NY: Scribner.

44. Sibbett, G. S., Freeman, M. W., Ferguson, L., Welch, G., & Anderson, D. (1988). Timing Manzanillo olive harvest for maximum profit. *California Agriculture*, 40(11), 19–22.

45. Škevin, D., Rade, D., Štrucelj, D., Mokrovčak, Ž., Nederal, S., & Benčić, D. (2003). The influence of variety and harvest time on bitterness and phenolic compounds of olive oil. *European Journal of Lipid Science and Technology*, *105*, 536–541.

46. Su, L. J., & Arab, L. (2006). Salad and raw vegetable consumption and nutritional status in the adult U.S. population: Results from the Third National Health and Nutrition Examination Study. *Journal of the American Dietetic Association*, *106*, 1394–1404.

47. Tanaka, T. (1981). Gels. *Scientific American*, *244*(1), 124.

48. The FDA: Fresh leafy greens grown in the United States are safe. (2006). *FDA Consumer*, *40*(6), 11.

49. Thornsbury, S., Jerardo, A., & Wells, H. F. (2012). Vegetables and pulses outlook, VGS-351, U.S. Department of Agriculture, Economic Research Service.

50. United States Food and Drug Administration. (2017). CPG Sec. 525.825 Vinegar Definitions-Adulteration with Vinegar Eels. Washington, D.C.: U.S. Government Publishing Office.

51. U.S. Food and Drug Administration. (2017). CPG Sec. 562.100 Acetic Acid- Used in Foods-Labeling of Foods in Which Used. Washington, D.C.: U.S. Government Publishing Office.

52. U.S. Department of Health and Human Services Food and Drug Administration, Center for Food Safety and Applied Nutrition. (2017). *Draft guidance compliance with and recommendations for implementation of the standards for the growing, harvesting, packing, and holding of produce for human consumption for sprout operations: Guidance for industry*. Washington, D.C.: USHHS/FDA.

53. U.S. Department of Agriculture, Agricultural Marketing Service Fruit and Vegetable Programs Fresh Products Branch. (May 2004). Revised, May 2011, HU-155-12(a) Lettuce Shipping Point and Market Inspection Instructions. Washington, D.C.: U.S. Department of Agriculture.

54. United States Department of Agriculture, Agricultural Marketing Service Fruit and Vegetable Programs Fresh Products Branch. (April 2006). Spinach plants, spinach leaves, and bunched spinach shipping point and market inspection instructions. Washington, D.C.: U.S. Department of Agriculture.

55. United States Department of Agriculture, Agricultural Marketing Service Fruit and Vegetable Programs Fresh Products Branch. (April 2008). Revised, kale and greens (beet, broccoli, collard, dandelion, mustard, and turnip) shipping point and market inspection instructions. Washington, D.C.: U.S. Department of Agriculture.

56. Uylaser, V., & Yildiz, G. (2014). The historical development and nutritional importance of olive and olive oil constituted an important part of the Mediterranean diet. *Critical Reviews in Food Science and Nutrition*, *54*, 1092–1101.

57. Van Duyn, M. A. S., & Pivonka, E. (2000). Overview of the health benefits of fruit and vegetable consumption for the dietetics professional: Selected literature. *Journal of the American Dietetic Association*, *100*, 1511–1521.

58. Vegas, C., Mateo, E., González, Á., Jara, C., Guillamón, J. M., Polbet, M., Torija, M. J., & Mas, A. (2010). Population dynamics of acetic acid bacteria during traditional wine vinegar production. *International Journal of Microbiology*, *138*, 130–136.

59. Ward, A. G., & Courts, A. (Eds.). (1977). *The science and technology of gelatin*. New York, NY: Academic Press.

60. World Health Organization, Food and Agriculture Organization of the United Nations. Codex Alimentarius International Food Standards. (2013). Codex Standard for Table Olives Codex Stan 66-1981. Rome, Italy.

61. Wu, L., Velander, P., Liu, F., & Xu, B. (2017). Olive components oleuropein promotes cell insulin secretion and protects cells from amylin amyloid induced cytotoxicity. *Biochemistry* (Rapid Report 22 August 2017). doi:10.10102/acs.biochem.7b00199

62. Yada, S., Harris, L. J., York, G., & Vaughn, R. (2007). *Olives: Safe methods for home pickling*. Publication 8267. Davis, CA: University of California Division of Agriculture and Natural Resources.

63. Yetiman, A. E., & Kesmen, Z. (2015). Identification of acetic acid bacteria in traditionally produced vinegar and mother of vinegar by using different molecular techniques. *International Journal of Food Microbiology*, *204*, 9–16.

64. Zalkan, R. C., & Fabian, F. W. (1953). The influence of vinegar eels (*Anguillula aceti*) on vinegar production. *Food Technology*, *7*(11), 453–455.

65. Zhou, P., & Regenstein, J. M. (2007). Comparison of water gel desserts from fish skin and pork gelatins using instrumental measurements. *Journal of Food Science*, *72*(4), C196–C201.

Chapter 22

1. Abeni, F., Degano, L., Calza, F., Giangiacomo, R., & Pirlo, G. (2005). Milk quality and automatic milking: Fat globule size, natural creaming, and lipolysis. *Journal of Dairy Science*, *88*(10), 3519–3529.

2. American Cheese Society. (2016). State of the U.S. Artisan/Specialty Cheese Industry. Report of Key Findings as commissioned by University of Connecticut.

3. Anonymous. (2015). Transforming acid whey into valuable ingredients. *Food Technology*, *69*(4), 23.

4. Argov, N., Lemay, D. G., & German, J. B. (2008). Milk fat globule structure and function: Nanoscience comes to milk production. *Trends in Food Science & Technology*, *19*(12), 617–623.

5. Attaie, R., & Richter, R. L. (2000). Size distribution of fat globules in goat milk. *Journal of Dairy Science*, *83*(5), 940–944.

6. Augustin, M. A., & Clarke, P. T. (2008). Skim milk powders with enhanced foaming and steam-frothing properties. *Dairy Science and Technology*, *88*(1), 149–161.

7. Balthazar, C. F., Pimentel, T. C., Ferrão, L. L., Almada, C. N., Santillo, A., Albenzio, M., Mollakhalili, N., Mortazavian, A. M., Nascimento, J. S., Silva, M. C., Freitas, M. Q., Sant'Ana, A. S., Granato, D., & Cruz, A. G. (2017). Sheep milk: Physicochemical characteristics and relevance for functional food development. *Comprehensive Reviews in Food Science and Food Safety*, *16*(2), 247–262.

8. Barbano, D. (1995). *Cornell University: bST fact sheet*. Washington, D.C.: U.S. Food and Drug Administration [online].

9. Bauer, J. (1992). *Food theory and applications*. New York, NY: MacMillan Publishing Co.

10. Benjamin, R. M. (2010). From the surgeon general: Bone health: Preventing osteoporosis. *Journal of the American Dietetic Association, 110*(4), 498. doi:10.1016/j.jada.2010.02.018

11. Bermúdez-Aguirre, D., & Barbosa-Cánovas, G. V. (2010). Processing of soft Hispanic cheese (*"queso fresco"*) using thermo-sonicated milk: A study of physicochemical characteristics and storage life. *Journal of Food Science, 75*(8), S548–S554.

12. Blayney, D. P. (1994). Milk and biotechnology: Maintaining safe, adequate milk supplies. *Food Review, 17*(2), 27.

13. Bren, L. (2004). Got milk? Make sure it's pasteurized. *FDA Consumer Magazine, 38*(5), 29–31.

14. Brooker, B. E. (1985). Observations on the air-serum interface of milk foams. *Food Structure, 4*(2), 189–186.

15. Calvo, M. S., Whitting, S. J., & Barton, C. N. (2004). Vitamin D fortification in the United States and Canada: Current status and data needs. *American Journal of Clinical Nutrition, 80*(6), 1710S–1716S.

16. Chandan, R. (1997). *Dairy-based ingredients*. St. Paul, MN: Eagan Press.

17. Charley, H. (1982). *Food science* (2nd ed.). New York, NY: John Wiley& Sons, Inc.

18. Chavan, R. S., Chavan, S. R., Khedkar, C. D., & Jana, A. H. (2011). UHT milk processing and effect of plasmin activity on shelf life: A review. *Comprehensive Reviews in Food Science and Food Safety, 10*(5), 251–268.

19. Chia, J. S. J., McRae, J. L., Kukuljan, S., Woodford, K., Elliott, R. B., Swinburn, B., & Dwyer K. M. (2017). A1 beta-casein milk protein and other environmental predisposing factors for type 1 diabetes. *Nutrition & Diabetes, 7*, e274. doi:10.1038/nutd.2017.16

20. Costard, S., Espejo, L., Groenendaal, H., & Zagmutt, F. J. (2017). Outbreak-related disease burden associated with consumption of unpasteurized cow's milk and cheese, United States, 2009–2014. *Emerging Infectious Diseases, 23*(6), 957–964. dx.doi.org/10.3201/eid2306.151603.

21. Council on Foods and Nutrition. (1969). Substitutes for whole milk. *Journal of the American Medical Association, 208*, 58.

22. Couvreur, S., Hurtaud, C., Marnet, P. G., Faverdin, P., & Peyraud, J. L. (2007). Composition of milk fat from cows selected for milk fat globule size and offered either fresh pasture or a corn silage-based diet. *Journal of Dairy Science, 90*(1), 392–403.

23. Cranney, C., Horsely, T., O'Donnell, S., Weiler, H., Ooi, D., Atkinson, S., et al. (2007). Effectiveness and safety of vitamin D. Evidence Report/Technology Assessment No. 158 prepared by the University of Ottawa Evidence-based Practice Center under Contract No. 290-02.0021. AHRQ Publication No. 07-E013. Rockville, MD: Agency for Healthcare Research and Quality.

24. Curtis Steven, H., & O'Brien Nabors, L. (2009). Microbial food cultures: A regulatory update. *Food Technology. 63*(3), 36–41.

25. De Kruif, C. G., & Holt, C. (2003). Casein micelle structure, functions and interactions. In Fox, P. F., & McSweeney, P. L. H. (Eds.), *Advanced dairy chemistry volume 1: Proteins* (pp. 233–276). New York, NY: Kluwer Academic/Plenum Publishing.

26. Dennett, C. (2016). Organic milk and meat-are they healthier than their conventional counterparts? *Today's Dietitian, 18*(6), 28.

27. Di Domenico, M., Di Giuseppe, M., Wicochea Rodriguez, D. J. D., & Cammá, C. (2016). Validation of a fast real-time PCR method to detect fraud and mislabeling in milk and dairy products. *Journal of Dairy Science, 100*(1), 106–112.

28. Electronic Code of Federal Regulation. (2017). *Title 21 food and drug code*. Washington, D.C.: The U.S. Government Publishing Office.

29. Getz, L. (2011). A healthful dose of bacteria—yogurt is the best probiotic source, but clients do have other options. *Today's Dietitian, 13*(10), 46.

30. Goh, J., Kravchuk, O., & Deeth, H. C. (2009). Comparison of mechanical agitation, steam injection and air bubbling for foaming milk of different types. *Milchwissenschaft, 64*, 2.

31. Gupta, C. B., & Eskin, N. A. M. (1977). Potential use of vegetable rennet in the production of cheese. *Food Technology, 31*(5), 62.

32. Gwartney, E. A., Foegeding, E. A., & Larick, D. K. (2002). The texture of commercial full-fat and reduced-fat cheese. *Journal of Food Science, 67*, 812–816.

33. Hassan, A. N., Frank, J. F., Corredig, M. (2002). Microstructure of feta cheese made using different cultures as determined by confocal scanning laser microscopy. *Journal of Food Science, 67*(7), 2750–2753.

34. Hertzler, S. R., & Clancy, S. M. (2003). Kefir improves lactose digestion and tolerance for adults with lactose maldigestion. *Journal of the American Dietetic Association, 103*, 582–587.

35. Hill, A. (2017). Cheese making technology (ebook). In Goff, D. (Ed.), *Dairy science and technology e textbook. Guelph, Canada* [online University of Guelph, Canada].

36. Ho, S., Woodford, K., Kukuljan, S., & Pal, S. (2014). Comparative effects of A1 versus A2 beta-casein on gastrointestinal measures: A blinded randomised cross-over pilot study. *European Journal of Clinical Nutrition, 68*(9), 994–1000.

37. Habibi-Najafi, M. B., Lee, B. H., & Law, B. (1996). Bitterness in cheese: A review. *Critical Reviews in Food Science and Nutrition, 36*(5), 397–411.

38. Hensel, K. (2015). Kite hill: Balancing innovation and tradition. *Food Technology, 69*(5), 19.

39. Hoch, G. J. (1997). Whey to go. *Food Processing, 58*(3), 51.

40. Hollingsworth, P. (2001). Culture wars. *Food Technology, 55*(3), 43–46.

41. Holsinger, V. H., & Kligerman, A. E. (1991). Applications of lactase in dairy foods and other foods containing lactose. *Food Technology, 45*(1), 92.

42. Hoover, D. G. (1993). Bifidobacteria: Activity and potential benefits. *Food Technology, 47*(6), 120.

43. Hughes, D. B., & Hoover, D. G. (1991). Bifidobacteria: Their potential for use in American dairy products. *Food Technology, 45*(4), 74.

44. Hui, Y. H. (Ed.)., & Chandan, R. C., Clark, S., Cross, N., Dobbs, J., Hurst, W. J., Nollet, L. M. L., Shimoni, E., Sinha, N., Smith, E. B., Surapat, S., Titchenal, A., & Toldra, F.

(Associate. Eds.). (2007). *Handbook of food products manufacturing principles, bakery, beverages, cereals, cheese, confectionary, fats, fruits, and functional foods.* Hoboken, NJ: John Wiley & Sons, Inc.

45. Huffman, L. M. (1996). Processing whey protein for use as a food ingredient. *Food Technology, 50*(2), 49.

46. Huppertz, T. (2010). Foaming properties of milk: A review of the influence of composition and processing. *International Journal of Dairy Technology, 63*(4), 477–488.

47. Institute of Medicine, Food and Nutrition Board. (2010). *Dietary reference intakes for calcium and vitamin D.* Washington, D.C.: National Academy Press.

48. Jensen, R. G. (Ed.). (1995). *Handbook of milk composition.* New York, NY: Academic Press.

49. Jianqin, S., Leiming, X., Lu, X., Yelland, G. W., Ni, J., & Clarke, A. J. (2016). Effects of milk containing only A2 beta casein versus milk containing both A1 and A2 beta casein proteins on gastrointestinal physiology, symptoms of discomfort, and cognitive behavior of people with self-reported intolerance to traditional cows' milk. *Nutrition Journal, 15*(1), 35.

50. Jimenez-Junca, C. A., Gumy, J. C., Sher, A., & Niranjan, K. (2011). Rheology of milk foams produced by steam injection. *Journal of Food Science, 76*(9), E569–E575.

51. Joint FAO/WHO Working Group. (2002). *Guidelines for the evaluation of probiotics in food.* Ontario, Canada.

52. Kaffarnik, S., Kayademir, Y., Heid, C., Vetter, W. (2014). Concentrations of volatile 4-Alkyl-branched fatty acids in sheep and goat milk and dairy products. *Journal of Food Science, 79*(11), C2209–C2214.

53. Kamath, S., Huppertz, T., Houlihan, A. V., Deeth, H. C. (2008). The influence of temperature on foaming of milk. *International Dairy Journal, 18*(10–11), 994–1002.

54. Kanno, C., Shimomura, Y., & Takano, E. (1991). Physicochemical properties of milkfat emulsions stabilized with bovine milkfat globule membrane. *Journal of Food Science, 56*, 1219.

55. Kapoor, R., & Metzger, L. E. (2008). Process cheese: Scientific and technological aspects—A review. *Comprehensive Reviews in Food Science and Food Safety, 7*, 194–214.

56. Katz, F. (2001). Active cultures add function to yogurt and other foods. *Food Technology, 55*(3), 46–49.

57. Kinsella, J. E., & Morr, C. V. (1984). Milk proteins: Physicochemical and functional properties. *C R C Critical Reviews in Food Science and Nutrition, 21*(3), 197–262.

58. Koutchma, T., & Barnes, G. (2013). Shelf life enhancement of milk products. *Food Technology, 67*(10), 68–70.

59. Kroger, M., Kurmann, J. A., & Rasic, J. L. (1989). Fermented milks—Past, present, and future. *Food Technology, 43*(1), 92.

60. Kurtzweil, P. (1998). Skimming the milk label. *FDA Consumer, 32*(1), 22.

61. Labensky, S. R., & Hause, A. M. (2007). *On cooking: A textbook of culinary fundamentals* (4th ed.). Upper Saddle River, NJ: Pearson Prentice Hall.

62. La Comb, R. P., Sebastian, R. S., Enns, C. W., & Goldman, J. D. (2011). *Beverage choices of U.S. adults. What we eat in America* NHANES *2007-2998.* Food Surveys Research Group Dietary Data Brief No. 6. Beltsville, MD: United States Department of Agriculture, Agricultural Research Service.

63. Lavigne, C., Zee, J. A., Simard, R. E., & Béliveau, B. (1989). Effect of processing and storage conditions on the fate of vitamins B_1, vitamin B_2, and C and on the shelf life of goat's milk. *Journal of Food Science, 54*(1), 30–34.

64. Lee, S. Y., & Morr, C. V. (1993). Fixation staining methods for examining microstructure in whipped cream by electron microscopy. *Journal of Food Science, 58*, 124.

65. Light, A., Heymann, H., & Holt, D. L. (1992). Hedonic responses to dairy products: Effects of fat levels, label information, and risk perception. *Food Technology, 46*(7), 54.

66. Lindsay Ward, R., Kerth, C. R., & Pillai, S. (2017). Nutrient profiles and volatile odorous compounds of raw milk after exposure to electron beam pasteurizing doses. *Journal of Food Science, 82*(7), 1614–1621.

67. Lindmark Månsson, H. (2008). Fatty acids in bovine milk fat. *Food & Nutrition Research, 52*(1), 1821.

68. Linn, J. G. (1988). Factors Affecting the Composition of Milk from Dairy Cows. P 244. In National Research Council (US) Committee on Technological Options to Improve the Nutritional Attributes of Animal Products. *Designing Foods: Animal Product Options in the Marketplace.* Call, D.L. chairman. Washington, D.C.: National Academies Press (US).

69. Liu, J. R., & Lin, C. W. (2000). Production of kefir from soymilk with or without added glucose, lactose, or sucrose. *Journal of Food Science, 65*(4), 716–719.

70. Logan, A., Auldist, M., Greenwood, J., & Day, L. (2014). Natural variation of bovine milk fat globule size within a herd. *Journal of Dairy Science, 97*(7), 4072–4082.

71. Lopez, C. (2011). Milk fat globules enveloped by their biological membrane: Unique colloidal assemblies with a specific composition and structure. *Current Opinion in Colloid & Interface Science, 16*(5), 391–404.

72. Mangino, M. E. (1992). Gelation of whey protein concentrates. *Food Technology, 46*(1), 114.

73. McHugh, T. (2015). How yogurt is processed. *Food Technology, 69*(12), 70–72.

74. Mermelstein, N. H. (1997). Extending dairy product shelf life with carbon dioxide. *Food Technology, 51*(12), 72.

75. Michalski, M. C., Gassi, J. Y., Famelart, M. H., Leconte, N., Camier, B., Michel, F., & Briard, V. (2003). The size of native milk fat globules affects physico-chemical and sensory properties of Camembert cheese. *Le lait, 83*(2), 131–143.

76. Miller, G. D., Jarvis, J. K., & McBean, L. D. (2007). *Handbook of dairy foods and nutrition* (3rd ed.). Boca Raton, FL: CRC Press Taylor and Frances Group.

77. Mullan, W. M. A. (2001 revision October 2017). Microbiology of starter cultures. *Dairyscience.info.* [online].

78. Mullan, W. M. A. (2014). Starter cultures| importance of selected genera. In G. Smithers (Ed.), *Reference Module in Food Science, Encyclopedia of Food Microbiology (Second Edition) 3*, 515–521.

79. Mullan, W. M. A. (2017). Functions of starters in dairy fermentations and the relative importance and effectiveness of their antimicrobial mechanisms. *dairyscience.info.* [online].

80. Mulvihill, D. M., & Kinsella, J. E. (1987). Gelation characteristics of whey proteins and beta-lactoglobulin. *Food Technology, 41*(9), 102.

81. Murtaza, M. A., Ur-Rehman, S., Anjum, F. M., Huma, N., & Hafiz, I. (2014). Cheddar cheese ripening and

flavor characterization: A review. *Critical Reviews in Food Food Science and Nutrition, 54*, 1309–1321.

82. Nachay, K. (2017). Ingredients improve the art of cheesemaking. *Food Technology, 71*(10), 55–65.

83. National Restaurant Association Educational Foundation. (2006). *ServSafe coursebook* (4th ed.). Chicago: Author.

84. National Dairy Council. (1993). *Newer knowledge of milk*. Rosemont, IL: Author.

85. Neff, J. (1997). Fattening up a new dairy niche. *Food Processing, 58*(1), 45.

86. Ohr, L. M. (2002). Improving the gut feeling. *Food Technology, 56*(10), 67–70.

87. Palanuk, S. L., Warthesen, J. J., & Smith, D. E. (1988). Effect of agitation, sampling location, and protective films on light-induced riboflavin loss in skim milk. *Journal of Food Science, 53*, 436.

88. Park, Y. W., Jeanjulien, C., & Siddique, A. (2017). Factors affecting sensory quality of goat milk cheeses: A review. *Journal of Advanced Dairy Research, 5*(3), 1–9.

89. Patterson, K. Y., Phillips, K. M., Horst, R. L., Byrdwell, W. C., Exler, J., Lemar, J. M., & Holden, J. M. (2010). Vitamin D Content and variability in fluid milks from a Nationwide United States Department of Agriculture (USDA) Sampling to Update values in National Nutrient Data base for Standard Reference. *Journal of Dairy Science, 93*, 5082–5090.

90. Patterson, K. Y., Phillips, K. M., Horst, R. L. Byrdwell, W. C., Exler, J., Hamly, J. M., Lemar, L. E., Pehrsson, P. R., & Wolf, W. R. (2007). Variabiltiy in the Vitamin D$_3$ content of 2 percent milk from a nationwide United States Department of Agriculture (USDA) sampling. Beltsville, MD: USDA Beltsville Human Nutrition Research Center.

91. Potts, H. L., Amin, K. N., & Duncan, S. E. (2016). Retail lighting and packaging influence consumer acceptance of fluid milk. *Journal of Dairy Science, 100*, 146–156.

92. Pszczola, D. E. (2001). Say cheese with new ingredient developments. *Food Technology, 55*(12), 56–66.

93. Pszczola, D. E. (2010). Permissible indulgence in dairy. *Food Technology, 64*(2), 52–59.

94. Pszczola, D. E. (2013). Dairy in "Wheys" you've never seen before. *Food Technology, 67*(1), 46–57.

95. Rodavich, M. (2015). Probiotics may prevent and treat *Clostridium difficile. Today's Dietitian, 17*(11), 46.

96. Satin, M. (1996). *Food irradiation: A guidebook* (2nd ed.). Boca Raton, FL: CRC Press.

97. Schaeffer, J. (2014). Dairy's probiotic power—A review of the benefits of probiotics, the top sources, and what's new in the dairy case. *Today's Dietitian, 16*(8), 32.

98. Scruton, D. L., Fillman, F., Hinckley, L., Hylkema, C., Porter, J. (2006). Guidelines for the production and regulation of quality dairy goat milk DPC 59. *The Dairy Practices Council®*. Keyport, N.J. the Dairy Practices Council®.

99. Semo, E., Kesselman, E., Danino, D., & Livney, Y. D. (2007). Casein micelle as a natural nano-capsular vehicle for nutraceuticals. *Food Hydrocolloids, 21*(5), 936–942.

100. Shipe, W. F., Bassette, R., Deane, D. D., Dunkley, W. L., Hammond, E. G., Harper, W. J., et al. (1978). Off-flavors of milk: Nomenclature, standards, and bibliography. *Journal of Dairy Science, 61*, 855.

101. Shook, G. E., Ruegg, P. L., & Wendorff, W. L. (2003). Rethinking dairyland: milk composition, quality, and production efficiency: Where does Wisconsin stand? *Marketing and Policy Briefing Paper*, Paper No. 78E2.

102. Sloan, E. A. (2000). Say cheese! *Food Technology, 54*(6), 18–19.

103. Speck, M. L., Dobrogosz, W. J., & Casas, I. A. (1993). *Lactobacillus reuteri* in food supplementation. *Food Technology, 47*(7), 90.

104. Stanley, D. W., Goff, H. D., & Smith, A. K. (1996). Texture-structure relationships in foamed dairy emulsions. *Food Research International, 29*(1), 1–13.

105. Staff. (1989). Rennet containing 100 percent chymosin increases cheese quality and yield. *Food Technology, 43*(6), 84.

106. Swartzel, K. R. (1983). A method for predicting gelation of aseptically packaged steam inject UHT milk. *Journal of Food Science, 48*, 1376–1377.

107. Tamm, F., Sauer, G., Scampicchio, M., & Drusch, S. (2012). Pendant drop tensiometry for the evaluation of the foaming properties of milk-derived proteins. *Food Hydrocolloids, 27*(2), 371–377.

108. Tarver, T. (2016). A big fat dispute. *Food Technology, 79*(8), 22–35.

109. Tarver, T. (2017). Defining the humane treatment of food animals. *Food Technology, 71*(7), 17–25.

110. Thalheimer, J. C. (2017). Is A2 milk the game-changer for dairy intolerance? *Today's Dietitian, 19*(10), 26.

111. Tuinier, R., & De Kruif, C. G. (2002). Stability of casein micelles in milk. *The Journal of Chemical Physics, 117*(3), 1290–1295.

112. U.S. Department of Agriculture. Economic Research Service. Agricultural Handbook 697. (1992). *Weights, measures, and conversion factors for agricultural commodities and their products*. Washington, D.C.: Government Printing Office.

113. U.S. Department of Agriculture. (2016). *Dairy data*. Washington, D.C.: USDA Economic Research Service.

114. U.S. Service, Veterinary Services, National Animal Health Monitoring System. (2016). Dairy 2014, Dairy Cattle Management Practices in the United States, 2014 Report 1.

115. U.S. Department of Agriculture. (1974). *How to buy cheese*. Home and Garden Bulletin No. 193. Washington, D.C.: Author.

116. U.S. Department of Agriculture. (1995). *How to buy cheeses*. Home and Garden Bulletin No. 193. Washington, D.C.: Author.

117. U.S. Department of Agriculture. (1995). *How to buy dairy products*. Home and Garden Bulletin No. 255. Washington, D.C.: Author.

118. U.S. Department of Health and Human Services and U.S. Department of Agriculture. (2015). *2015–2020 Dietary Guidelines for Americans* (8th ed.). Washington, D.C.: U.S. Government Publishing Office.

119. U.S. Department of Agriculture. (2008). Commercial Item Description Cheese, Queso Blanco A-A-20347A. Commercial Item Description the United States Standards for Condition of Food Containers FSC 8910. Washington, D.C.: USDA.

120. U.S. Department of Health and Human Services, Public Health Service, Food and Drug Administration. (2015 revision). Grade A Pasteurized Milk Ordinance (Includes provisions from the Grade "A" Condensed and Dry Milk

Products and Condensed and Dry Whey–Supplement I to the Grade "A" PMO).

121. U.S. Department of Agriculture, Agricultural Marketing Service, Dairy Division. (August 2, 1991). *United States standards for grades of bulk American cheese*. Washington, D.C.: United States Department of Agriculture.

122. U.S. Department of Health and Human Services. (2004). *Bone health and osteoporosis: A report of the surgeon general*. Rockville, MD: USHHS.

123. U.S. Food and Drug Administration, Center for Food Safety and Applied Nutrition. (2006, April). Title 21—Food and Drugs, Subchapter B—Food for Human Consumption, Part 131—Milk and Cream. Washington, D.C.: U.S. Government Printing Office.

124. U.S. Department of Agriculture. (March 2012). U.S. Dairy Goat Operations Info Sheet. Animal and Plant Health Inspection Service, Veterinary Services Centers for Epidemiology and Animal Health.#639.0312. Fort Collins, CO: USDA-APHIS-VS-CEAH.

125. U.S. Department Agriculture. (1953). *Cheese varieties and descriptions the agriculture handbook No 54*. Washington, D.C.: U.S. Government Printing Office.

126. U.S. Department of Health and Human Services, Food and Drug Administration. (2017, August). Ultrafiltered milk in the production of standardized cheeses and related cheese products: Guidance for industry. College Park, MD: Office of Nutrition and Food Labeling Center for Food Safety and Applied Nutrition Food and Drug Administration.

127. Van Hekken, D. L. (2012). Quality aspects of raw milk cheese. *Food Technology, 66*(6), 66–78.

128. Van Hekken, D., & Farkye, N. Y. (2003). Hispanic cheeses: The quest for queso. *Food Technology, 57*(1), 32–38.

129. Wagner, R. D., & Johnson, S. J. (2017). Probiotic bacteria prevent Salmonella-induced suppression of lymphoproliferation in mice by an immunomodulatory mechanism. *BMC Microbiology, 17*(1), 77.

130. Weinberg, L. G., Berner, L. A., & Groves, J. E. (2004). Nutrient contributions of dairy foods in the United States, Continuing Survey of Food Intakes by Individuals, 1994–1996, 1998. *Journal of the American Dietetic Association, 104*, 895–902.

131. Welland, D. (2011). Make room for cheese—If incorporated wisely, it can be part of a healthful diet. *Today's Dietitian*, 13(2), 16.

132. Wijnen, M. E. (1997). *Instant foam physics. Formation and stability of aerosol whipped cream*. Wijnen. Thesis (doctoral)–Landbouwuniversiteit Wageningen.

133. Wikinga, L. Stagsted, J., Björck, L., & Nielsen, J. H. (2004). Milk fat globule size is affected by fat production in dairy cows. *International Dairy Journal, 14*(10), 909–913.

134. Ye, A., Cui, J., Dalgleish, D., & Singh, H. (2017). Effect of homogenization and heat treatment on the behavior of protein and fat globules during gastric digestion of milk. *Journal of Dairy Science, 100*(1), 36–47.

135. Yeager, D. (2016). What's trending in the dairy aisle? *Today's Dietitian*, 1892, 30.

136. Zhang, S., yung, R., Zhao, W., Hua, X., Zhang, W., & Zhang, Z. (2011). Influence of pulsed electric field treatments on the volatile compounds of milk in comparison with pasteurized processing. *Journal of Food Science, 76*(1), C127–C131.

Chapter 23

1. Agriculture Marketing Resource Center. (2017). *Egg profile*. Washington, D.C. and Ames, IA: USDA and Iowa State University.

2. Alexander, D. D., Miller, P. E., Vargas, A. J., Weed, D. L., & Cohen, S. S. (2016). Meta-analysis of egg consumption and risk of coronary heart disease and stroke. *Journal of the American College of Nutrition, 35*(8), 704–716.

3. American Egg Board. (2010). *Egg science and technology* (Vol. 2). Chicago, IL: Author.

4. American Egg Board. (2012). *Common production systems: Farmers offer choice*. Chicago, IL: American Egg Board.

5. American Egg Board. (2012). *Eggcyclopedia* (5th ed.). Chicago, IL: American Egg Board.

6. American Egg Board. (2012). *Safe food handling tips*. Chicago, IL: American Egg Board.

7. Ayadi M. A., Khemakhem, M., Belgith, H., & Attia, H. (2008). Effect of moderate spray drying conditions on functionality of dried egg white and whole egg. *Journal of Food Science, 73*(6), E281–E287. doi:10.1111/j.1750-3841.2008.00811.x

8. Baker, R. C., Darfler, J., & Lifshitz, A. (1967). Factors affecting the discoloration of hard-cooked egg yolks. *Poultry Science, 46*, 664.

9. Banerjee, P., & Keener, K. M. (2012). Maximizing carbon dioxide content of shell eggs by rapid cooling treatment and its effect on shell egg quality. *Poultry Science, 91*(6), 1444–1453.

10. Bartelme, M. Z. (2016). Edible films reduce food waste; Killing Salmonella in eggs. *Food Technology, 70*(4), 12.

11. Bowers, J. (1992). *Food theory and applications* (2nd ed.) New York, NY: Macmillan Publishing Co.

12. Code of Federal Regulations. (1997, January 7). *Inspection of eggs and egg products: Pasteurization of eggs*. 7CFR59.570. Washington, D.C.: U.S. Government Publishing Office.

13. Charley, H. (1982). *Food science* (2nd ed.). New York, NY: John Wiley & Sons.

14. Cremer, M. L. (1981). Microwave heating of scrambled eggs in a hospital foodservice system. *Journal of Food Science, 46*, 1573.

15. Egg Laying Cycle. (2017). *Eggs in schools*. Chicago, IL: American Egg Board.

16. Federal Register. (July 9, 2009). Part II Department of Health and Human Services, Food and Drug Administration 21 CFR Parts 16 and 118 Prevention of Salmonella enteritidis in shell eggs during production, storage and Transportation: Final Rule. Washington, D.C.: National Archives and Records Administration.

17. Gardner, F. A., Beck, M. L., & Denton, J. H. (1982). Functional quality comparison of whole egg and selected egg substitute products. *Poultry Science, 61*, 75.

18. Geveke, D. J., Bigley, A. B. W., & Brunkhorst, C. B. (2017). Pasteurization of shell eggs using radio frequency heating. *Journal of Food Engineering, 193*, 53–57.

19. Giese, J. (1994). Ultrapasteurized liquid whole eggs earn 1994 IFT Food Technology Industrial Achievement Award. *Food Technology, 48*(9), 94.

20. Gillis, J. N., & Fitch, N. K. (1956). Leakage of baked soft meringue topping. *Journal of Home Economics, 48*, 703.

21. Hanning, F. (1945). Effect of sugar or salt upon denaturation produced by beating and upon the ease of formation and the stability of egg white foams. *Iowa State College Journal of Science, 20*, 10.

22. Hester, E. E., & Personius, C. J. (1949). Factors affecting the beading and leaking of soft meringues. *Food Technology, 3*, 236.

23. Institute of Food Technologist. (2015). *U.S. egg farmers on road to recovery.* (online News August 31, 2015) Chicago, IL: Institute of Food Technologist.

24. Irmiter, T. F., Dawson, L. E., & Reagan, J. G. (1970). Methods of preparing hard cooked eggs. *Poultry Science, 49*, 1232.

25. Itoh, T., Miyazaki, J., Sugawara, H., & Adachi, S. (1987). Studies on the characterization of ovomucin and chalaza of the hen's egg. *Journal of Food Science, 52*, 1518.

26. Kanter, M. (2016). The new 2015 dietary guidelines and eggs. *Official Blog of the Egg Nutrition Center.* January 7, 2016. Chicago, IL: Egg Nutrition Center.

27. Kinner, J. A., & Moats, W. A. (1981). Effect of temperature, pH, and detergent on survival of bacteria associated with shell eggs. *Poultry Science, 60*, 761.

28. Kline, L., & Sugihara, T. F. (1966, August). Effects of pasteurization on egg products. *Baker's Digest, 40*, 40.

29. Kurisaki, J., Kaminogawa, S., & Yamauchi, K. (1980). Studies on freeze-thaw gelation of very low density lipoprotein from hen's yolk. *Journal of Food Science, 45*, 463.

30. Labensky, S. R., & Hause, A. M. (2015). *On cooking: A textbook of culinary fundamentals* (5th ed. update). Upper Saddle River, NJ: Pearson Education, Inc.

31. Lang, M. R., & Wells, J. W. (1987). A review of eggshell pigmentation. *World's Poultry Science Journal, 43*(3), 238–246.

32. Lau, K., & Dickinson, E. (2004). Structural and Rheological properties of aerated high sugar systems containing egg albumen. *Journal of Food Science, 69*(4), E232–E239.

33. Liang, Y., & Kristinsson, H. G. (2005). Influence of pH-induced unfolding and refolding of egg albumen on its foaming properties. *Journal of Food Science, 70*(3), C222–C230.

34. Macherey, L. N., Conforti, F. D., Eigel III, W., & O'Keefe, S. F. (2011). Use of *mucor miehei* lipase to improve functional properties of yolk-contaminated egg whites. *Journal of Food Science, 76*(4), C651–C655. doi:10.1111/j.1750-3841.2011.02138.x

35. Margoshes, B. A. (1990). Correlation of protein sulfhydryls with the strength of heat-formed egg white gels. *Journal of Food Science, 55*, 1753.

36. Matiella, J. E., & Hsieh, T. C. Y. (1991). Volatile compounds in scrambled eggs. *Journal of Food Science, 56*, 387.

37. Meehan, J. J., Sugihara, T. F., & Kline, L. (1962). Relationships between shell egg handling factors and egg product properties. *Poultry Science, 41*, 892.

38. Mermelstein, N. H. (2000). Cryogenic system rapidly cools eggs. *Food Technology, 54*(6), 100–103.

39. Mermelstein, N. H. (2001). Pasteurization of shell eggs. *Food Technology, 55*(12), 72–73, 79.

40. Mineki, M., & Kobayashi, M. (1997). Microstructure of yolk from fresh eggs by improved method. *Journal of Food Science, 62*, 757.

41. Mullally, C., & Lusk, J. L. (2018). The impact of farm animal housing restrictions on egg prices, consumer welfare, and production in California. *American Journal of Agricultural Economics, 100*(3), 649–669. aax049. doi:10.1093/ajae/aax049

42. Naderi, N., House, J. D., Pouliot, Y., & Doyen, A. (2017). Effects of high hydrostatic pressure processing on hen egg compounds and egg products. *Comprehensive Reviews in Food Science and Food Safety, 16*, 707–720. doi:10.1111/1541-4337.12273

43. Neff, J. (1998). The great egg breakthrough. *Food Processing, 59*(1), 25.

44. O' Brien, D. (2017). A New way to pasteurize eggs. *Ag Research Magazine, 65*(4), 1.

45. Parsons, A. H. (1982). Structure of the eggshell. *Poultry Science, 61*, 2013.

46. Pawne, W. D., & Nahai, S. (1985). Characteristics of edible fluids of animal origins: Eggs. In Fennema, O. (Ed.), *Food chemistry* (p. 842). New York, NY: Marcel Dekker.

47. Raeker, M. Ö., & Johnson L. A. (1995). Thermal and functional properties of bovine blood plasma and egg white proteins. *Journal of Food Science, 60*(4), 685–690. doi:10.1111/j.1365-2621.1995.tb06206.x

48. Roberts, J. R. (2004). Factors affecting egg internal quality and egg shell quality in laying hens. *The Journal of Poultry Science, 41*(3), 161–177.

49. Robinson, D. S., & King, N. R. (1970). The structure of the organic mammillary cores in soe weak egg shells. *British Poultry Science, 11*, 39–44.

50. Shan, Y., Ma, M., Huang, X., Guo, Y., Jin, G.,& Jin, Y. (2012). Simple pH treatment as an effective tool to improve the functional properties of ovomucin. *Journal of Food Science, 77*(7), C740–C745. doi:10.1111/j.1750-3841.2012.02761.x

51. Solomon, S. E. (2010). The eggshell: Strength, structure and function. *British Poultry Science, 51*(sup1), 52–59. doi:10.1080/00071668.2010.497296

52. Steele, L. (2017). Egg-cellent. *Duck, 101, 74–75.*

53. U.S. Department of Agriculture, Agriculture Market Service. (2000, July). *Egg grading manual.* Agriculture Handbook No. 75. Washington, D.C.: U.S. Government Publishing Office.

54. U.S. Department of Agriculture. (2012, July). USDA National Nutrient Database for Standard Reference, Release 24. Washington, D.C.: U.S. Government Publishing Office.

55. U.S. Department of Agriculture, Economic Research Service. (2012). Data sets. Food availability. Washington, D.C.: Economic Research Service and U.S. Government Publishing Office.

56. U.S. Department of Health and Human Services and U.S. Department of Agriculture. (2015). *2015–2020 Dietary Guidelines for Americans.* (8th ed.). Washington, D.C.: U.S. Government Publishing Office.

57. United States Department of Agriculture, Agricultural Research Service. (2017). USDA National Nutrient Database for Standard Reference Release 28 (online). Washington, D.C.: U.S. Government Publishing Office.

58. United States Department of Agriculture, Food Safety Inspection Service (2016). Biology of eggs. *Standard Egg Products Training Manual.* Washington, D.C.: United States Department of Agriculture.

59. United States Department of Agriculture, Marketing and Regulatory Programs, Agriculture Marketing Service

Poultry Programs (2000). *United States Standards, Grades and Weight Classes for Shell Eggs. AMS 56.* Washington, D.C.: U.S.D.A. Agriculture Marketing Service Poultry Programs.

60. U.S. Department of Agriculture. (2017). Egg Market News Report (ISSN 1520-6122) *Agricultural Marketing Service Livestock, Poultry, Grain Market News, 64*(42), 1–3.

61. U.S. Department of Agriculture. (2017). USDA National Retail Report Shell Egg and Egg Products Advertised Prices for Shell Eggs and Egg Products to Consumers at Major Retail Super market Outlets during the period of 10/20 to 10/26. Des Moines, IA: USDA Agricultural Marketing Service, Livestock, Poultry & See Market News.

62. United States Department of Agriculture, Agricultural Marketing Service. (2017, October). Monthly USDA Cage-Free Shell Egg Report. Des Moines, IA: USDA Livestock, Poultry, & Grain Market News.

63. United States Department of Agriculture, Agriculture Marketing Service Poultry Programs (2008). *Specifications for shell eggs A "How To" guide for food service suppliers and volume food buyers.* Washington, D.C.: USDA Agricultural Marketing Service.

64. Van Elswyk, M. E., Sams, A. R., & Hargis, P. S. (1992). Composition, functionality, and sensory evaluation of eggs from hens fed dietary menhaden oil. *Journal of Food Science, 57,* 342.

65. Wang, G., & Wang, T. (2009). Effects of yolk contamination, shearing, and heating on foaming properties of fresh egg white. *Journal of Food Science, 74*(2), C147–156. doi:10.1111/j.1750-3841.2009.01054.x

66. Wang, G., & Wang, T. (2009, October). Improving foaming properties of yolk-contaminated egg albumen by basic soy protein. *Journal of Food Science, 74*(8), C581–C587. doi:10.1111/j.1750-3841.2009.01306.x

67. Weaver, S. (2017). More than eggs. *Duck, 101,* 93–95.

68. Wild, N. (2008). Commercial news: shell e.g. pasteurization the facts. *Poultry Pluimvee Bulletin, 1,* 30–32.

69. Woodward, S. A., & Cotterill, O. J. (1986). Texture and microstructure of heat-formed egg white gels. *Journal of Food Science, 51,* 333.

70. Woodward, S. A., & Cotterill, O. J. (1987). Texture and microstructure of cooked whole egg yolks and heat-formed gels of stirred egg yolk. *Journal of Food Science, 52,* 63.

71. Wu, V. T., Brochetti, D., & Duncan, S. E. (1998). Sensory characteristics and acceptability of lactose-reduced baked custards made with an egg substitute. *Journal of the American Dietetic Association, 98,* 1467–1469.

72. Zhang, W., Zheng, J. X., & Xu, G. U. (2011). Toward better control of *Salmonella* contamination by taking advantage of the egg's self-defense system: A review. *Journal of Food Science, 76*(3), R76–R81. doi:10.1111/j.1750.3841. 2011.02053.x

73. Zhao, R., Xu, G. Y., Liu, Z. Z., Li, J. Y., & Yang, N. (2006). A study on eggshell pigmentation: biliverdin in blue-shelled chickens. *Poultry Science, 85*(3), 546–549.

Chapter 24

1. Akinwunmi, I., Thompson, L. D., & Ramsey, C. B. (1993). Marbling, fat trim, and doneness effects on sensory attributes, cooking loss, and composition of cooked beef steaks. *Journal of Food Science, 58,* 242.

2. Al-Obaidy, H. M., Khan, M. A., & Klein, B. P. (1984). Comparison between sensory quality of freshly prepared spaghetti with meat sauce before and after hot holding on a cafeteria counter. *Journal of Food Science, 49,* 1475.

3. Archer, D. L. (2000). *E. coli* 0157:H7—Searching for solutions. *Food Technology, 54*(10), 142.

4. Bouton, P. E., Harris, P. V., & Ratcliff, D. (1981). Effect of cooking temperature and time on the shear properties of meat. *Journal of Food Science, 46,* 1082.

5. Bowers, J. A., Craig, J. A., Kropf, D. H., & Tucker, T. J. (1987). Flavor, color, and other characteristics of beef longissimus muscle heated to seven internal temperatures between 55° and 85°C. *Journal of Food Science, 52,* 533.

6. Brody, A. L. (2002). The case for—or against—case-ready fresh red meat in the United States. *Food Technology, 54*(8), 153–156.

7. Brody, A. L. (2004). The case for case-ready meat. *Food Technology, 58*(8), 84–86.

8. Brody, A. L. (2007). Case-ready packaging for red meat. *Food Technology, 61*(3), 70–72.

9. Buchanan, R. L., & Doyle, M. P. (1997). Foodborne disease significance of *Escherichia coli* 0157:H7 and other enterohemorrhagic *E. coli. Food Technology, 51*(10), 69.

10. Buzby, J. C., & Crutchfield, S. R. (1997). USDA modernizes meat and poultry inspection. *Food Review, 20*(1), 14.

11. Campbell, R. E., Hunt, M. C., & Chambers, E., IV (2001). Dry-aging effects on palatability of beef longissimus muscle. *Journal of Food Science, 66*(2), 196–199.

12. Cassens, R. G. (1997). Residual nitrite in cured meat. *Food Technology, 51*(2), 53.

13. Costello, C. A., Penfield, M. P., & Riemann, M. J. (1985). Quality of restructured steaks: Effects of days on feed, fat level, and cooking method. *Journal of Food Science, 50,* 685.

14. Cover, S., & Hostetler, R. L. (1960). *Beef tenderness.* Texas Agricultural Experiment Station Bulletin No. 947. College Station: Texas Agricultural Experiment Station.

15. Cross, H. R., Berry, B. W., & Wells, L. H. (1980). Effects of fat level and source on the chemical, sensory, and cooking properties of ground beef patties. *Journal of Food Science, 45,* 791.

16. Dolezal, H. G., Smith, G. C., Savell, J. W., & Carpenter, Z. L. (1982). Comparison of subcutaneous fat thickness, marbling and quality grade for predicting palatability of beef. *Journal of Food Science, 47,* 397.

17. Egbert, W. R., & Cornforth, D. P. (1986). Factors influencing color of dark cutting beef muscle. *Journal of Food Science, 51,* 57.

18. Fabiansson, S., & Libelius, R. (1985). Structural changes in beef longissimus dorsi induced by postmortem low voltage electrical stimulation. *Journal of Food Science, 50,* 39.

19. Fan, X., Niemira, B. A., Rajkowski, K. T., Phillips, J., & Sommers, C. H. (2004). Sensory evaluation of irradiated ground beef patties for the National School Lunch Program. *Journal of Food Science, 69*(9), S384–S387.

20. Feiner, G. (2006). *Meat products handbook: Practical science and technology.* Boca Raton, FL: CRC Press.

21. Fogle, D. R., Plimpton, R. F., Ockerman, H. W., Jarenback, L., & Persson, T. (1982). Tenderization of beef: Effect of enzyme, enzyme level, and cooking method. *Journal of Food Science, 47,* 1113.

22. Gariepy, C., Amiot, J., Pommier, S. A., Flipot, P. M., & Girard, V. (1992). Electrical stimulation and 48 hours aging of bull and steer carcasses. *Journal of Food Science, 57,* 541.

23. Gerrier, S., & Bente, L. (2001). Food supply nutrients and dietary guidance, 1970–1999. *Food Review, 24*(3), 39–46.

24. Giese, J. H. (2001). It's a mad, mad, mad, mad cow test. *Food Technology, 55*(6), 60–62.

25. Giese, J. H. (2002). Washington news. *Food Technology, 56*(10), 22.

26. Hamm, R. (1982). Postmortem changes in muscle with regard to processing of hot-boned beef. *Food Technology, 36*(11), 105.

27. Hardin, B. (1999). Predicting tenderness in beefsteaks. *Agricultural Research Magazine, 47*(11), 10–11.

28. Howat, P. M., Sievert, L. M., Myers, P. J., Koonce, K. L., & Bidner, T. D. (1983). Effect of marination upon mineral content and tenderness of beef. *Journal of Food Science, 48,* 662.

29. Hueston, W., & Bryant, C. M. (2005). Transmissible spongiform encephalopathies. *Journal of Food Science, 70*(5), R77–R87.

30. Hunt, M. C., Sorheim, O., & Slinde, E. (1999). Color and heat denaturation of myoglobin forms. *Journal of Food Science, 60,* 1175–1196.

31. Hwang, I. H., Devine, C. E., & Hopkins, D. L. (2003). The biochemical and physical effects of electrical stimulation on beef and sheep tenderness. *Meat Science, 65*(2), 677–691.

32. Jacobs, D. K., & Sebranek, J. G. (1980). Use of prerigor beef for frozen ground beef patties. *Journal of Food Science, 45,* 648.

33. Jennings, T. G., Berry, B. W., & Joseph, A. L. (1978). Influence of fat thickness, marbling, and length of aging on beef palatability and shelf-life characteristics. *Journal of Animal Science, 46,* 658.

34. Johnston, M. B., & Baldwin, R. E. (1980). Influence of microwave reheating on selected quality factors of roast beef. *Journal of Food Science, 45,* 1460.

35. Killinger, K. M., Hunt, M. C., Campbell, R. E., & Kropf, D. H. (2000). Factors affecting premature browning during cooking of store-purchased ground beef. *Journal of Food Science, 65,* 585–587.

36. King, N. J., & White, R. (2006). Does it look cooked? A review of factors that influence cooked meat color. *Journal of Food Science, 71*(4), R31–R40.

37. Koohmaraie, M., Seideman, S. C., Schollmeyer, J. E., Dutson, T. R., & Babiker, A. S. (1988). Factors associated with the tenderness of three bovine muscles. *Journal of Food Science, 53,* 407.

38. Kukowshi, A. C., Wulf, D. M., Shanks, B. C., Page, J. K., & Maddock, R. J. (2003). Factors associated with surface iridescence in fresh beef. *Meat Science, 66,* 889–893.

39. Laakkonen, E., Wellington, G. H., & Sherbon, J. W. (1970). Low-temperature, long-time heating of bovine muscle. 1. Changes in tenderness, water-binding capacity, pH and amount of water-soluble components. *Journal of Food Science, 35,* 175.

40. Labensky, S. R., Hause, A. M., & Martel, P. A. (2011). *On cooking: A textbook of culinary fundamentals* (5th ed.). Upper Saddle River, NJ: Pearson Prentice Hall.

41. Leander, R. C., Hedrick, H. B., Brown, M. F., & White, J. A. (1980). Comparison of structural changes in bovine longissimus and semitendinosus muscles during cooking. *Journal of Food Science, 45,* 1.

42. Lin, J. C., & Kaufman, P. (1995). Food companies offer views of safe handling label for meat and poultry. *Food Review, 18*(3), 23.

43. Love, J. A., & Prusa, K. J. (1992). Nutrient composition and sensory attributes of cooked ground beef: Effects of fat content, cooking method, and water rinsing. *Journal of the American Dietetic Association, 92,* 1367.

44. Mandigo, R. W. (1986). Restructuring of muscle foods. *Food Technology, 40*(3), 85.

45. Maruri, J. L., & Larick, D. K. (1992). Volatile concentration and flavor of beef as influenced by diet. *Journal of Food Science, 57,* 1275.

46. McDowell, M. D., Harrison, D. L., Pacey, C., & Stone, M. B. (1982). Differences between conventionally cooked top round roasts and semimembranosus muscle strips cooked in a model system. *Journal of Food Science, 47,* 1603.

47. McIntosh, E. N. (1967). Effect of postmortem aging and enzyme tenderizers on mucoprotein of bovine skeletal muscle. *Journal of Food Science, 32,* 210.

48. McKeith, F. K., de Vol, D. L., Miles, R. S., Bechtel, P. J., & Carr, T. R. (1985). Chemical and sensory properties of thirteen major beef muscles. *Journal of Food Science, 50,* 869.

49. Mermelstein, N. H. (2018). Combating antibiotic resistance. *Food Technology, 72*(3), 62–65.

50. Mitchell, G. E., Reed, A. W., & Rogers, S. A. (1991). Influence of feeding regimen on the sensory qualities and fatty acid contents of beef steaks. *Journal of Food Science, 56,* 1102.

51. Moody, W. G. (1983). Beef flavor: A review. *Food Technology, 37*(5), 227.

52. Moore, L. J., Harrison, D. L., & Dayton, A. D. (1980). Differences among top round steaks cooked by dry or moist heat in a conventional or a microwave oven. *Journal of Food Science, 45,* 777.

53. Morris, C. (2011, October). New technology means increased consistency and efficiency in grading for beef industry. *United States Department of Agriculture.* Retrieved from https://www.usda.gov/media/blog/2011/10/19/new-technology-means-increased-consistency-and-efficiency-grading-beef

54. National Restaurant Association Educational Foundation. (2010). *ServSafe coursebook* (5th ed.). Chicago: Author.

55. Nielsen, M. M., & Hall, F. T. (1965). Dry-roasting of less tender beef cuts. *Journal of Home Economics, 57,* 353.

56. North American Meat Processors Association. (2007). *The meat buyer's guide.* Hoboken, NJ: John Wiley & Sons.

57. Olson, D. G., Caporaso, F., & Mandigo, R. W. (1980). Effects of serving temperature on sensory evaluation of beef steaks from different muscles and carcass maturities. *Journal of Food Science, 45,* 627.

58. Omaye, S. T. (2001). Preventing BSE in the U.S. *Food Technology, 55*(4), 26.

59. Omaye, S. T. (2001). Shiga-toxin–producing Escherichia coli: Another concern. *Food Technology, 55*(5), 26.

60. Oreskovich, D. C., Bechtel, P. J., McKeith, F. K., Novakofski, J., & Basgall, E. J. (1992). Marinade pH affects textural properties of beef. *Journal of Food Science, 57,* 305.

61. Peterson, R. J., & Chang, S. S. (1982). Identification of volatile flavor compounds of fresh, frozen beef stew and a comparison of these with those of canned beef stew. *Journal of Food Science, 47,* 1444.

62. Ralston, K., Starke, Y., Brent, P., & Riggins, T. (2000). Awareness of risks changing how hamburgers are cooked. *Food Review, 23*(2), 44–50.

63. Sanderson, M., & Vail, G. E. (1963). Fluid content and tenderness of three muscles of beef cooked to three internal temperatures. *Journal of Food Science, 28,* 590.

64. Savell, J. W., Branson, R. E., Cross, H. R., Stiffler, D. M., Wise, J. W., Griffin, D. B., et al. (1987). National consumer retail beef study: Palatability evaluations of beef loin steaks that differed in marbling. *Journal of Food Science, 52,* 517.

65. Sebranek, J. G., Hunt, M. C., Cornforth, D. P., & Brewer, M. S. (2006). Carbon monoxide packaging of fresh meat. *Food Technology, 60*(5), 184.

66. Shorthose, W. R., & Harris, P. V. (1990). Effect of animal age on the tenderness of selected beef muscles. *Journal of Food Science, 55,* 1.

67. Smith, G. C., Carpenter, Z. L., Cross, H. R., Murphey, C. E., Abraham, H. C., Savell, J. W., et al. (1984). Relationship of USDA marbling groups to palatability of cooked beef. *Journal of Food Quality, 7,* 289.

68. Tarver, T. (2017). Defining the humane treatment of food animals. *Food Technology, 71*(7), 16–25.

69. Tatum, J. D., Smith, G. C., & Carpenter, Z. L. (1982). Interrelationships between marbling, subcutaneous fat thickness and cooked beef palatability. *Journal of Animal Science, 54,* 777.

70. Troutt, E. S., Hunt, M. C., Johnson, D. E., Claus, J. R., Kastner, C. L., Kropf, D. H., et al. (1992). Chemical, physical, and sensory characterization of ground beef containing 5 to 30 percent fat. *Journal of Food Science, 57,* 25.

71. U.S. Centers for Disease Control and Prevention. (2011, June 10). Vital signs: Incidence and trends of infection with pathogens transmitted commonly through food—Foodborne diseases active surveillance network, 10 U.S. sites, 1996–2010. *Morbidity and Mortality Weekly Report, 60*(22), 749–755. Retrieved from http://www.cdc.gov/mmwr/preview/mmwrhtml/mm6022a5.htm

72. U.S. Centers for Disease Control and Prevention. (2018, March). FoodNet 2017 preliminary data. Retrieved from https://www.cdc.gov/foodnet/reports/prelim-data-intro-2017.html

73. U.S. Centers for Disease Control and Prevention. (2018, April). Reports of selected *E. coli* outbreak investigations. Retrieved from https://www.cdc.gov/ecoli/outbreaks.html

74. U.S. Centers for Disease Control and Prevention, Agency for Toxic Substances and Disease Registry. (2015, January). Public health statement for nitrate and nitrate. Retrieved from https://www.atsdr.cdc.gov/phs/phs.asp?id=1448&tid=258

75. U.S. Department of Agriculture. (2017, July). USDA detects a case of atypical bovine spongiform encephalopathy in Alabama. Retrieved from https://www.aphis.usda.gov/aphis/newsroom/stakeholder-info/sa_by_date/sa-2017/sa-07/bse-alabama

76. U.S. Department of Agriculture. (n.d.). BSE frequently asked questions. Retrieved from https://www.usda.gov/topics/animals/bse-surveillance-information-center/bse-frequently-asked-questions

77. U.S. Department of Agriculture, Agricultural Research Service, Nutrient Data Laboratory. (2018, April). USDA National Nutrient Database for Standard Reference, Legacy. Version Current: April 2018. Retrieved from https://www.ars.usda.gov/northeast-area/beltsville-md-bhnrc/beltsville-human-nutrition-research-center/nutrient-data-laboratory/docs/usda-national-nutrient-database-for-standard-reference/

78. U.S. Department of Agriculture, Economic Research Service. (2017, September). Food availability and consumption. Retrieved from https://www.ers.usda.gov/data-products/ag-and-food-statistics-charting-the-essentials/food-availability-and-consumption.aspx

79. U.S. Department of Agriculture, Food Safety and Inspection Service. (1998, March). Special survey on humane slaughter and ante-mortem inspection. Retrieved from http://www.fsis.usda.gov/oa/pubs/antemort.pdf

80. U.S. Department of Agriculture, Food Safety and Inspection Service. (2005, January). Livestock inspector training. Retrieved from http://www.fsis.usda.gov/PDF/LSIT_HumaneHandling.pdf

81. U.S. Department of Agriculture, Food Safety and Inspection Service. (2010, April). Fact sheets: Food labeling: Country of origin labeling for meat and chicken. Retrieved from http://www.fsis.usda.gov/Fact_Sheets/COOL_Meat_and_Chicken/index.asp

82. U.S. Department of Agriculture, Food Safety and Inspection Service. (2011, May). Ground beef and food safety. Retrieved from http://www.fsis.usda.gov/Fact_Sheets/Ground_Beef_and_Food_Safety/index.asp

83. U.S. Department of Agriculture, Food Safety and Inspection Service. (2012, April). Nutrition labeling information. Retrieved from https://www.fsis.usda.gov/wps/portal/fsis/topics/regulatory-compliance/labeling/labeling-policies/nutrition-labeling-policies/nutrition-labeling

84. U.S. Department of Agriculture, Food Safety and Inspection Service. (2013, June). Timeline of events related to *E. coli* 0157:H7. Retrieved from https://www.fsis.usda.gov/wps/portal/fsis/topics/regulatory-compliance/haccp/updates-and-memos/timeline-of-events-related-to-e-coli-o157h7/e-coli-timeline

85. U.S. Department of Agriculture, Food Safety and Inspection Service. (2013, August). Bison from farm to table. Retrieved from https://www.fsis.usda.gov/wps/portal/fsis/topics/food-safety-education/get-answers/food-safety-fact-sheets/meat-preparation/focus-on-bison/ct_index

86. U.S. Department of Agriculture, Food Safety and Inspection Service. (2013, August). Fresh pork from farm to table. Retrieved from https://www.fsis.usda.gov/wps/portal/fsis/topics/food-safety-education/get-answers/food-safety-fact-sheets/meat-preparation/fresh-pork-from-farm-to-table/ct_index

87. U.S. Department of Agriculture, Food Safety and Inspection Service. (2013, August). Key facts: Humane slaughter. Retrieved from https://www.fsis.usda.gov/wps/portal/fsis/topics/food-safety-education/get-answers/food-safety-fact-sheets/production-and-inspection/key-facts-humane-slaughter/key-facts-humane-slaughter

88. U.S. Department of Agriculture, Food Safety and Inspection Service. (2013, August). Lamb from farm to table. Retrieved from https://www.fsis.usda.gov/wps/portal/fsis/topics/food-safety-education/get-answers/food-safety-fact-sheets/meat-preparation/focus-on-lambfrom-farm-to-table/CT_Index

89. U.S. Department of Agriculture, Food Safety and Inspection Service. (2013, August). Slow cookers and food safety. Retrieved from https://www.fsis.usda.gov/wps/portal/fsis/topics/food-safety-education/get-answers/food-safety-fact-sheets/appliances-and-thermometers/slow-cookers-and-food-safety/ct_index

90. U.S. Department of Agriculture, Food Safety and Inspection Service. (2013, August). The color of meat and poultry. Retrieved from https://www.fsis.usda.gov/wps/portal/fsis/topics/food-safety-education/get-answers/food-safety-fact-sheets/meat-preparation/the-color-of-meat-and-poultry/the-color-of-meat-and-poultry/CT_Index

91. U.S. Department of Agriculture, Food Safety and Inspection Service. (2013, August). Veal from farm to table. Retrieved from https://www.fsis.usda.gov/wps/portal/fsis/topics/food-safety-education/get-answers/food-safety-fact-sheets/meat-preparation/veal-from-farm-to-table/CT_Index

92. U.S. Department of Agriculture, Food Safety and Inspection Service. (2013, August). Water in meat and poultry. Retrieved from https://www.fsis.usda.gov/wps/portal/fsis/topics/food-safety-education/get-answers/food-safety-fact-sheets/meat-preparation/water-in-meat-and-poultry/CT_Index

93. U.S. Department of Agriculture, Food Safety and Inspection Service. (2013, October). Bacon and food safety. Retrieved from https://www.fsis.usda.gov/wps/portal/fsis/topics/food-safety-education/get-answers/food-safety-fact-sheets/meat-preparation/bacon-and-food-safety/ct_index

94. U.S. Department of Agriculture, Food Safety and Inspection Service. (2015, March). Beef from farm to table. Retrieved from https://www.fsis.usda.gov/wps/portal/fsis/topics/food-safety-education/get-answers/food-safety-fact-sheets/meat-preparation/beef-from-farm-to-table/ct_index

95. U.S. Department of Agriculture, Food Safety and Inspection Service. (2016, January). Ham and food safety. Retrieved from https://www.fsis.usda.gov/wps/portal/fsis/topics/food-safety-education/get-answers/food-safety-fact-sheets/meat-preparation/ham-and-food-safety/CT_Index

96. U.S. Department of Health and Human Services, & U.S. Department of Agriculture. 2015–2020 Dietary Guidelines for Americans. 8th Edition. (2015, December). Retrieved from http://health.gov/dietaryguidelines/2015/guidelines/

97. Vickers, Z. M., & Wang, J. (2002). Liking of ground beef patties is not affected by irradiation. *Journal of Food Science, 67,* 380–383.

98. Warriss, P. D. (2000). *Meat science: An introductory text.* New York, NY: CABI Publishing.

99. Yu, L. P., & Lee, Y. B. (1986). Effects of postmortem pH and temperature on bovine muscle structure and meat tenderness. *Journal of Food Science, 51,* 774.

Chapter 25

1. Aleixo, J. A. G., Swaminathan, B., Jamesen, K. S., & Pratt, D. E. (1985). Destruction of pathogenic bacteria in turkeys roasted in microwave ovens. *Journal of Food Science, 50,* 873.

2. Bowman, M., Marshall, K. K., Kuchler, F., & Lynch, L. (2016). Raised without antibiotics: Lessons from voluntary labeling of antibiotic use practices in the broiler industry. *American Journal of Agricultural Economics, 98*(1), 622–642. doi.org/10.1093/ajae/aaw008

3. Cunningham, F. E., & Tiede, L. M. (1981). Influence of batter viscosity on breading of chicken drumsticks. *Journal of Food Science, 46,* 1950.

4. Deethardt, D., Burrill, L. M., Schneider, K., & Carlson, C. W. (1971). Foil-covered versus open-pan procedure for roasting turkey. *Journal of Food Science, 36,* 624.

5. Durham, S. (2002). It takes a tough scientist to make a tender (and juicy) chicken. *Agricultural Research Magazine, 50*(2), 14–15.

6. Hatch, V., & Stadelman, W. J. (1972). Bone darkening in frozen chicken broilers and ducklings. *Journal of Food Science, 37,* 850.

7. Hingley, A. (1999). *Campylobacter:* Low-profile bug is food poisoning leader. *FDA Consumer, 33*(5), 14–17.

8. Hoke, I. M., McGeary, B. K., & Kleve, M. K. (1967). Effect of internal and oven temperatures on eating quality of light and dark meat turkey roasts. *Food Technology, 21,* 773.

9. Holownia, K., Chinnan, M. S., & Reynolds, A. E. (2003). Pink color defect in poultry white meat as affected by endogenous conditions. *Journal of Food Science, 68*(3), 742–747.

10. Kattappan, V. A., Hargis, B. M., & Owens, C. M. (2016). White striping and woody breast myopathies in the modern poultry industry: A review. *Poultry Science, 95,* 2724–2733. http://dx.doi.org/10.3382/ps/pew216

11. Kuchler, F., Greene, C., Bowman, M., Marshall, K. K., Bovay, J., & Lynch, L. (2017). Federal nutrition and organic labels paved the way for single trait label claims. *Amber Waves.* Retrieved from https://www.ers.usda.gov/amber-waves/2017/november/federal-nutrition-and-organic-labels-paved-the-way-for-single-trait-label-claims/

12. Labensky, S. R., Hause, A. M., & Martel, P. A. (2014). *On cooking: A textbook of culinary fundamentals* (5th ed.). Upper Saddle River, NJ: Pearson Prentice Hall.

13. Lamuka, P. O., Sunki, G. R., Chawan, C. B., Rao, D. R., & Shackelford, L. A. (1992). Bacteriological quality of freshly processed broiler chickens as affected by carcass pretreatment and gamma irradiation. *Journal of Food Science, 57,* 330.

14. Lindsay, R. E., Krissinger, W. A., & Fields, B. F. (1986). Microwave vs. conventional oven cooking of chicken: Relationship of internal temperature to surface contamination by *Salmonella. Journal of the American Dietetic Association, 86,* 373.

15. Linonis, K. (2017, September). National chicken month: NASS counts chickens before—and after—they hatch. U.S. Department of Agriculture. Retrieved from https://www.usda.gov/media/blog/2017/09/27/national-chicken-month-nass-counts-chickens-and-after-they-hatch

16. MacDonald, J. M. (2014, August). Financial risks and incomes in contract broiler production. *Amber Waves.* Retrieved from https://www.ers.usda.gov/amber-waves/2014/august/financial-risks-and-incomes-in-contract-broiler-production/

17. Meiners, C., Crews, M. G., & Ritchey, S. J. (1982). Yield of chicken parts: Proximate composition and mineral content. *Journal of the American Dietetic Association, 81,* 435.

18. North American Meat Processors Association. (2007). *The meat buyer's guide.* Hoboken, NJ: John Wiley & Sons.

19. Proctor, V. A., & Cunningham, F. E. (1983). Composition of broiler meat as influenced by cooking methods and coating. *Journal of Food Science, 48,* 1696.

20. Sallam, K. I., & Samejima, K. (2004). Effects of trisodium phosphate and sodium chloride dipping on the microbial quality and shelf life of refrigerated tray-packaged chicken breasts. *Food Science Biotechnology, 13*(4), 425–429.

21. Smith, D. M., & Alvarez, V. B. (1988). Stability of vacuum cook-in-bag turkey breast rolls during refrigerated storage. *Journal of Food Science, 53*, 46.

22. Sneeringer, S. (2015, November). Restrictions on antibiotic use for production purposes in U.S. livestocks industries likely to have small effects on prices and quantities. *Amber Waves*. Retrieved from https://www.ers.usda.gov/amber-waves/2015/november/restrictions-on-antibiotic-use-for-production-purposes-in-us-livestock-industries-likely-to-have-small-effects-on-prices-and-quantities/

23. Suderman, D. R., & Cunningham, F. E. (1980). Factors affecting adhesion of coating to poultry skin, effect of age, method of chilling, and scald temperature on poultry skin ultrastructure. *Journal of Food Science, 45*, 444.

24. Tijare, V. V., Yang, F. L., Juttappan, V. A., Alvarado, C. Z., Coon, C. N., & Owens, C. M. (2016). Meat quality of broiler breast fillets with white striping and woody breast muscle myopathies. *Poultry Science, 95*, 2167–2173. http://dx.doi.org/10.3382/ps/pew129

25. U.S. Department of Agriculture, Agricultural Research Service, Nutrient Data Laboratory. (2018, April). USDA National Nutrient Database for Standard Reference, Legacy. Version Current: April 2018. Retrieved from https://www.ars.usda.gov/northeast-area/beltsville-md-bhnrc/beltsville-human-nutrition-research-center/nutrient-data-laboratory/docs/usda-national-nutrient-database-for-standard-reference/

26. U.S. Department of Agriculture, Economic Research Service. (2018, January). Food availability and consumption. Retrieved from https://www.ers.usda.gov/data-products/ag-and-food-statistics-charting-the-essentials/food-availability-and-consumption.aspx

27. U.S. Department of Agriculture, Food Safety and Inspection Service. (2013, July). Turkey: Alternate routes to the table. Retrieved from https://www.fsis.usda.gov/wps/portal/fsis/topics/food-safety-education/get-answers/food-safety-fact-sheets/poultry-preparation/turkey-alternate-routes-to-the-table/CT_Index

28. U.S. Department of Agriculture, Food Safety and Inspection Service. (2013, August). Duck and goose from farm to table. Retrieved from https://www.fsis.usda.gov/wps/portal/fsis/topics/food-safety-education/get-answers/food-safety-fact-sheets/poultry-preparation/duck-and-goosefrom-farm-to-table/ct_index

29. U.S. Department of Agriculture, Food Safety and Inspection Service. (2013, August). The poultry label says "fresh." Retrieved from https://www.fsis.usda.gov/wps/portal/fsis/topics/food-safety-education/get-answers/food-safety-fact-sheets/poultry-preparation/the-poultry-label-says-fresh/CT_Index

30. U.S. Department of Agriculture, Food Safety and Inspection Service. (2013, August). Turkey from farm to table. Retrieved from https://www.fsis.usda.gov/wps/portal/fsis/topics/food-safety-education/get-answers/food-safety-fact-sheets/poultry-preparation/food-safety-of-turkeyfrom-farm-to-table/CT_Index

31. U.S. Department of Agriculture, Food Safety and Inspection Service. (2013, August). Water in meat and poultry. Retrieved from https://www.fsis.usda.gov/wps/portal/fsis/topics/food-safety-education/get-answers/food-safety-fact-sheets/meat-preparation/water-in-meat-and-poultry/CT_Index

32. U.S. Department of Agriculture, Food Safety and Inspection Service. (2015, March). Chicken from farm to table. Retrieved from https://www.fsis.usda.gov/wps/portal/fsis/topics/food-safety-education/get-answers/food-safety-fact-sheets/poultry-preparation/chicken-from-farm-to-table/ct_index

33. U.S. Department of Agriculture, Food Safety and Inspection Service. (2015, August). Meat and poultry labeling terms. Retrieved from https://www.fsis.usda.gov/wps/portal/fsis/topics/food-safety-education/get-answers/food-safety-fact-sheets/food-labeling/meat-and-poultry-labeling-terms/meat-and-poultry-labeling-terms

34. U.S. Department of Agriculture, Food Safety and Inspection Service. (2015, September). Let's talk turkey—A consumer guide to safely roasting a turkey. Retrieved from https://www.fsis.usda.gov/wps/portal/fsis/topics/food-safety-education/get-answers/food-safety-fact-sheets/poultry-preparation/lets-talk-turkey/CT_Index

35. U.S. Department of Agriculture, Food Safety and Inspection Service. (2017, October). Nutrition labeling information. Retrieved from https://www.fsis.usda.gov/wps/portal/fsis/topics/regulatory-compliance/labeling/labeling-policies/nutrition-labeling-policies/nutrition-labeling

36. Woodburn, M. (1989). Myth: Wash poultry before cooking. *Diary, Food, and Environmental Sanitation, 9*, 65–67.

Chapter 26

1. Academy of Nutrition and Dietetics. (2014). Position of the Academy of Nutrition and Dietetics: Dietary fatty acids for healthy adults. *Journal of the Academy of Nutrition and Dietetics, 114*, 136–153. http://dx.doi.org/10.1016/j.jand.2013.11.001

2. Barber, K., & Takemura, H. (2002). *Sushi: Taste and technique*. London: Dorling Kindersley Ltd.

3. Brody, A. L. (2001). Is something fishy about packaging? *Food Technology, 55*(4), 97–98.

4. Cheung, L. K. Y., Tomita, H., Takemori, T. (2016). Mechanisms of docosahexaenoic and eicosapentaenoic acid loss from pacific saury and comparison of their retention rates after various cooking methods. *Journal of Food Science, 81*, C1899–C1907. doi:10.1111/1750-3841.13367

5. Educational Foundation of the National Restaurant Association. (2014). *ServSafe coursebook* (6th ed.). Chicago: Author.

6. Fish and Shellfish, 21 C.F.R. § 161.190 (2017).

7. Harris, M., Bruhn, C., Schor, D., Kapsak, W. R., & Blakistone, B. (2009). Communicating the net benefits of seafood consumption. *Food Technology, 63*(11), 39–44.

8. Hearn, T. L., Sgoutas, S. A., Hearn, J. A., & Sgoutas, D. S. (1987). Polyunsaturated fatty acids and fat in fish flesh for selecting species for health benefits. *Journal of Food Science, 52*, 1209.

9. Kantor, L. (2016, October). Americans' seafood consumption below recommendations. *Amber Waves*. Retrieved from https://www.ers.usda.gov/amber-waves/2016/october/americans-seafood-consumption-below-recommendations/

10. Labensky, S. R., Hause, A. M., & Martel, P. A. (2011). *On cooking: A textbook of culinary fundamentals* (5th ed.). Upper Saddle River, NJ: Pearson Prentice Hall.

11. Lee, C. M. (1984). Surimi process technology. *Food Technology, 38*(11), 69.

12. Lee, C. M., & Toledo, R. T. (1984). Comparison of shelf life and quality of mullet stored at zero and subzero temperature. *Journal of Food Science, 49,* 317.

13. MacDonald, G. A., & Lanier, T. (1991). Carbohydrates as cryoprotectants for meats and surimi. *Food Technology, 45*(3), 150.

14. Massachusetts Department of Public Health, Bureau of Environmental Health. (2013, April). Food protection program policies, procedures and guidelines: General guideline for the safe preparation of sushi. No: RF 3-2. Retrieved from https://www.mass.gov/lists/retail-food

15. Mermelstein, N. H. (2016). Product authenticity: Identifying species. *Food Technology, 70*(10), 60–62.

16. Mermelstein, N. H. (2017). Tracking traceability. *Food Technology, 71*(6), 111–114.

17. Morissey, M. T. (2006). Mercury in seafood: Facts and discrepancies. *Food Technology, 6*(8), 132.

18. Mozaffarian, D., Bryson, C. L., Lemaitre, R. N., Burke, G. L., & Siscovick, D. S. (2005). Fish intake and risk of incident heart failure. *Journal of the American College of Cardiology, 45*(12), 2015–2121.

19. Mozaffarian, D., & Rimm, E. B. (2006). Fish intake, contaminants, and human health: Evaluating the risks and benefits. *Journal of the American Medical Association, 296,* 1885–1899.

20. Omaye, S. T. (2001). Shark-fin soup and methylmercury: To eat or not to eat. *Food Technology, 55*(10), 26.

21. Regenstein, J. M. (2004). Total utilization of fish. *Food Technology, 58*(3), 28–30.

22. Seafood Business. (2005). *Seafood handbook*. Portland, ME: Diversified Business Communications.

23. University of Florida, IFAS Extension. (2004, January). Guide for processing sushi in retail operations. Document FSHN05-09. Printed by UF/IFAS Communications.

24. U.S. Department of Agriculture, Economic Research Service. (2012). Data sets. Food availability. Retrieved from http://www.ers.usda.gov/data-products/food-availability-(per-capita)-data-system.aspx

25. U.S. Department of Agriculture, Economic Research Service. (2018, January). Food availability and consumption. Retrieved from https://www.ers.usda.gov/data-products/ag-and-food-statistics-charting-the-essentials/food-availability-and-consumption.aspx

26. U.S. Department of Agriculture & U.S. Department Health and Human Services. (2010, December). *Dietary guidelines for Americans, 2010* (7th ed.). Washington, D.C.: U.S. Government Printing Office.

27. U.S. Department of Commerce, NOAA. (2016, January). NOAA expands opportunities for U.S. aquaculture. Retrieved from https://www.fisheries.noaa.gov/media-release/noaa-expands-opportunities-us-aquaculture

28. U.S. Department of Commerce, NOAA, National Marine Fisheries Service. (2017). Fisheries of the United States, 2016.Current Fishery Statistics No. 2016. Retrieved from https://www.st.nmfs.noaa.gov/commercial-fisheries/fus/fus16/index

29. U.S. Department of Health and Human Services, & U.S. Department of Agriculture. 2015–2020 Dietary Guidelines for Americans. 8th Edition. (2015, December). Retrieved from http://health.gov/dietaryguidelines/2015/guidelines/

30. U.S. Environmental Protection Agency. (2018, March). National listing of fish advisories: Advisories where you live map/search. Retrieved from https://fishadvisoryonline.epa.gov/General.aspx

31. U.S. Environmental Protection Agency. (n.d.). Choose fish and shellfish wisely: Fish and shellfish advisories and safe eating guidelines. Retrieved from https://www.epa.gov/choose-fish-and-shellfish-wisely/fish-and-shellfish-advisories-and-safe-eating-guidelines

32. U.S. Food and Drug Administration (2017, November). Aquaculture seafood. Retrieved from https://www.fda.gov/Food/GuidanceRegulation/GuidanceDocumentsRegulatoryInformation/Seafood/ucm518782.htm

33. U.S. Food and Drug Administration. (2017, November). Eating fish: What pregnant women and parents should know. Retrieved from https://www.fda.gov/Food/ResourcesForYou/Consumers/ucm393070.htm

34. U.S. Food and Drug Administration. (2017, November). What kind of fish is that? Retrieved from https://www.fda.gov/forconsumers/consumerupdates/ucm376473.htm

35. U.S. Food and Drug Administration. (2018). Guidance for industry: The seafoodlist. Retrieved from https://www.fda.gov/Food/GuidanceRegulation/GuidanceDocumentsRegulatoryInformation/ucm113260.htm

36. U.S. Food and Drug Administration. (2018). Regulatory fish encyclopedia (RFE). Retrieved from https://www.fda.gov/food/foodscienceresearch/rfe/default.htm

37. U.S. Food and Drug Administration. (2018, January). Enhanced aquaculture and seafood inspection – report to Congress. Retrieved from https://www.fda.gov/food/guidanceregulation/guidancedocumentsregulatoryinformation/seafood/ucm150954.htm

38. U.S. Food and Drug Administration. (2018, March). Seafood. Retrieved from https://www.fda.gov/food/populartopics/ucm341987.htm

39. U.S. National Oceanic and Atmospheric Administration, National Marine Fisheries Service. (n.d.). FishWatch: U.S. seafood facts. Retrieved from https://www.fishwatch.gov/

40. U.S. National Oceanic and Atmospheric Administration, National Marine Fisheries Service. (n.d.). FishWatch: U.S. seafood facts: Crab group. Retrieved from http://www.fishwatch.gov/seafood_profiles/species/crab/group_pages/index.htm

41. U.S. National Oceanic and Atmospheric Administration, National Marine Fisheries Service. (n.d.). Magnuson-Stevens Act. Retrieved from https://www.fisheries.noaa.gov/topic/laws-policies

42. U.S. National Oceanic and Atmospheric Administration, Seafood Inspection Program. (2018.). Seafood commerce and certification. Retrieved from https://www.fisheries.noaa.gov/topic/seafood-commerce-certification#eafood-inspection

43. Venugopal, V., & Gopakumar, K. (2017). Shellfish: Nutritive value, health benefits, and consumer safety. *Comprehensive Reviews in Food Science and Safety, 16,* 1219–1242. doi 10.111/1541-4337.12312

44. Wong, K., & Gill, T. A. (1987). Enzymatic determination of trimethylamine and its relationship to fish quality. *Journal of Food Science, 52,* 1.

Chapter 27

1. Aprotosoaie, A. C., Luca, S. V., & Miron, A. (2016). Flavor chemistry of cocoa and cocoa products—An overview. *Comprehensive Reviews in Food Science and Food Safety, 15,* 73–91. doi:10.1111/1541-4337.12180

2. Beverages. 21 C.F.R. § 165.10.

3. Beverages that contain fruit or vegetable juice, 21 C.F.R. § 102.33 (2011).

4. Bottled water beats soda for No. 1 U.S. beverage. (2017, March 20). *Food Technology.*

5. Breakfast cocoa. 21 C. F. R. § 163.112.

6. Bullers, A. C. (2002). Bottled water: Better than tap? *FDA Consumer Magazine, 36*(4), 14–18.

7. Bunker, M. L., & McWilliams, M. (1979). Caffeine content of common beverages. *Journal of the American Dietetic Association, 74,* 28.

8. Casa, D. J., Armstrong, L. E., Hillman, S. K., Montain, S. J., Reiff, R. V., Rich, B. S. E., et al. (2000). National athletic trainers' association position statement: Fluid replacement for athletes. *Journal of Athletic Training, 35*(2), 212–224.

9. Chen, T., Lui, C. K. F., & Smith, C. H. (1983). Folacin content of tea. *Journal of the American Dietetic Association, 82,* 627.

10. Chou, K. H., & Bell, L. N. (2007). Caffeine content of prepackaged national-brand and private-label carbonated beverages. *Journal of Food Science, 72*(6), C337–C342.

11. Clark, J. P. (2004). Ozone—Cure for some sanitation problems. *Food Technology, 58*(4), 75–76.

12. Clark, J. P. (2007). Lessons from chocolate processing. *Food Technology, 61*(12), 89–91.

13. Clemons, R., & Pressman, P. (2005). Chocolate and affairs of the heart. *Food Technology, 59*(9), 21.

14. Clydesdale, F. (2004). Functional foods: Opportunities and challenges. *Food Technology, 58*(12), 35–40.

15. Coleman, E. (1991). Sports drink research. *Food Technology, 45*(3), 104.

16. Craig, W. J., & Nguyen, T. T. (1984). Caffeine and theobromine levels in cocoa and carob products. *Journal of Food Science, 49,* 302.

17. Disler, P. B., Lynch, S. R., Charlton, R. W., Torrance, J. D., & Bothwell, T. H. (1975). The effect of tea on iron absorption. *Gut, 16,* 193.

18. Dziezak, J. S. (1989). Ingredients for sweet success. *Food Technology, 43*(10), 94.

19. Eckert, M., & Riker, P. (2007). Overcoming challenges in functional beverages. *Food Technology, 61*(3), 20–26.

20. Food Technology Staff. (2017). Asia leads coffee market growth. *Food Technology, 71*(4), 144.

21. Frederick, K. (2009). Booster shots for energy and health. *Food Technology, 63*(9), 26–34.

22. Giese, J. H. (1992). Hitting the spot: Beverages and beverage technology. *Food Technology, 46*(7), 70.

23. Grand, A. N., & Bell, L. N. (1997). Caffeine content of fountain and private-label store brand carbonated beverages. *Journal of the American Dietetic Association, 97,* 179.

24. Gunstone, F. D. (2002). Food applications of lipids. In C. A. Akoh & D. B. Min (Eds.), *Food lipids* (p. 742). New York: Marcel Dekker.

25. Hajiaghaalipour, F., Sanusi, J., & Kanthimathi, M. S. (2016). Temperature and time of steeping affect the antioxidant properties of white, green, and black tea infusions. *Journal of Food Science, 81,* H246–H254. doi: 10.111/1750-3341.13149

26. Heck, C. I., & DeMejia, E. G. (2007). Yerba mate tea (*Ilex paraguariensis*): A comprehensive review on chemistry, health implications, and technological considerations. *Journal of Food Science, 72,* R138–R151. doi:10.1111/j.1750-3841.2007.00535.x

27. Hensel, K. (2018). Making sustainable chocolate the norm. *Food Technology, 72*(1), 37–43.

28. Hollingsworth, P. (1997). Beverages: Redefining new age. *Food Technology, 51*(8), 44.

29. Hollingsworth, P. (2000). Functional beverage juggernaut faces tighter regulations. *Food Technology, 54*(11), 50–54.

30. Hollingsworth, P. (2002). Burgers or biscotti? The fast-food market is changing. *Food Technology, 56*(9), 20.

31. Hollingsworth, P. (2002). Profits pouring from bottled water. *Food Technology, 56*(5), 18.

32. Hughes, W. J., & Thorpe, T. M. (1987). Determination of organic acids and sucrose in roasted coffee by capillary gas chromatography. *Journal of Food Science, 52,* 1078.

33. Institute of Food Technologists' Expert Panel on Food Safety and Nutrition. (1987). Evaluation of caffeine safety. *Food Technology, 41*(6), 105.

34. Jayabalan, R., Malbaša, Lončar, E. S., Vitas, J. S., & Sathishkumar, M. (2014). A review on kombucha tea—Microbiology, composition, fermentation, beneficial effects, toxicity, and tea fungus. *Comprehensive Reviews in Food Science and Safety, 13,* 538–550. doi:10.1111/1541-4337.12073

35. Kanter, M. A. (2005). Energy drinks: A lot of "bull." *Food Technology, 59*(12), 104.

36. Kolpan, S., Smith, B. H., & Weiss, M. A. (2002). *Exploring wine: The Culinary Institute of America's complete guide to the wines of the world* (2nd ed.). New York: John Wiley & Sons.

37. Kuntz, L. A. (1996, July). Coffee and tea beverages. *Food Product Design.*

38. Labensky, S. R., Hause, A. M., & Martel, P. A. (2015). *On cooking: A textbook of culinary fundamentals* (5th ed.). Upper Saddle River, NJ: Pearson Prentice Hall.

39. Lal, G. G. (2007). Getting specific with functional. *Food Technology, 61*(12), 24–31.

40. McHugh, T. (2016). How dark chocolate is processed. *Food Technology, 70*(4), 134–136.

41. McHugh, T. (2017). How beer is processed. *Food Technology, 71*(11), 76–78.

42. McHugh, T. (2018). How tea is processed. *Food Technology, 72*(1), 65–67.

43. Nachey, K. (2016). Toasting ingredients in fermented and distilled beverages. *Food Technology, 70*(5), 50–58.

44. Nachey, K. (2017). Beyond the cup of coffee and tea. *Food Technology, 71*(1), 45–55.

45. Nelson, D. E., Rehm, J. D. W., Greenfield, T. K., Rey, G., Kerr, W. C., Miller, P., Shield, K. D., Ye., Y., & Naimi, T. S. (2013). Alcohol-attributable cancer deaths and years of potential life lost in the United States. *American Journal of Public Health, 103*(4), 641–648. doi:10.2105/AJPH.2012.301199

46. Ohr, L. M. (2004). All tea'd up. *Food Technology, 58*(7), 71–72.

47. Ohr, L. M. (2007). Energy boosters. *Food Technology*, *61*(4), 69–73.

48. Pandey, K. B., & Rizvi, S. I. (2009). Plant polyphenols as dietary antioxidants in human health and disease. *Oxidative Medicine and Cellular Longevity*, *2*(5), 270–278. doi:10.4161/oxim.25.9498

49. Pourshahidi, L. K., Navarini, L., Petracco, M., & Strain, J. J. (2016). A comprehensive overview of the risks and benefits of coffee consumption. *Comprehensive Reviews in Food Science and Food Safety*, *15*, 671–684. doi: 10.1111/1541-4337.12206

50. Pszczola, D. E. (1997). The bloom is off the chocolate. *Food Technology*, *51*(3), 28.

51. Pszczola, D. E. (1999). Sipping into the mainstream. *Food Technology*, *53*(11), 78–92.

52. Pszczola, D. E. (2001). How ingredients help solve beverage problems. *Food Technology*, *55*(10), 61–74.

53. Pszczola, D. E. (2006). Thinking outside the box (of chocolates). *Food Technology*, *60*(9), 50–61.

54. Reis, R., Charehsaz, M., Sipahi, H., Ekici, A. I. D., Macit, C., Akkaya, H., & Aydin, A. (2017). Energy drink induced lipid peroxidation and oxidative damage in rat liver and brain when used alone or combined with alcohol. *Journal of Food Science*, *82*, 1037–1043. doi:10.1111/1750-3841.13662

55. Rosinger, A., Herrick, K., Gahche, J., Park, S. (2017, January). Sugar-sweetened beverage consumption among U.S. adults, 2011–2014. NCHS data brief, No 270. Hyattsville, MD: National Center for Health Statistics. Retrieved from https://www.cdc.gov/nchs/products/databriefs/db270.htm

56. Rosinger, A., Herrick, K., Gahche, J., & Park, S. (2017, January). Sugar-sweetened beverage consumption among U.S. youth, 2011-2014. NCHS data brief, No 271. Hyattsville, MD: National Center for Health Statistics. Retrieved from https://www.cdc.gov/nchs/data/databriefs/db271.pdf

57. Sakano, T., Yamamura, K., Tamon, H., Miyahara, M., & Okazaki, M. (1996). Improvement of coffee aroma by removal of pungent volatiles using A-type zeolite. *Journal of Food Science, 61,* 473.

58. Schenker, S., Heinemann, C., Huber, M., Pompizzi, R., Perren, R., & Escher, F. (2002). Impact of roasting conditions on the formation of aroma compounds in coffee beans. *Journal of Food Science, 67,* 60–66.

59. Segal, M. (1996). Tea, a story of serendipity. *FDA Consumer*, *30*(2), 22.

60. Segall, S., Silver, C., & Bacino, S. (1970). The effect of reheating upon the organoleptic and analytical properties of beverage coffee. *Food Technology*, *24*(11), 54.

61. Sivetz, M. (1972). How acidity affects coffee flavor. *Food Technology*, *26*(5), 70.

62. Sloan, A. E. (2011). What's new in beverages. *Food Technology*, *65*(3), 19.

63. Tarver, T. (2007). Scientific status summary. "Just add water": Regulating and protecting the most common ingredient. *Journal of Food Science*, *73*(1), R1–R13.

64. Tarver, T. (2011). Healthy beverages: Back to the basics. *Food Technology*, *65*(1), 33–39.

65. U. S. Centers for Disease Control and Prevention. (2016, October). Drinking water: Water and nutrition. Retrieved from https://www.cdc.gov/healthywater/drinking/nutrition/index.html

66. U.S. Centers for Disease Control and Prevention. (2017, June). Fact sheets: Alcohol and caffeine. Retrieved from https://www.cdc.gov/alcohol/fact-sheets/caffeine-and-alcohol.htm

67. U.S. Department of Agriculture, Economic Research Service. (2018, January). Food availability (per capita) data system. Retrieved from https://www.ers.usda.gov/data-products/food-availability-per-capita-data-system/

68. U.S. Department of Health and Human Services, Food and Drug Administration, Center for Food Safety and Applied Nutrition. (2016, March). Guidance for industry: Acrylamide in foods. Retrieved from https://www.fda.gov/downloads/Food/GuidanceRegulation/GuidanceDocumentsRegulatoryInformation/ChemicalContaminantsMetalsNaturalToxinsPesticides/UCM374534.pdf

69. U.S. Department of Health and Human Services, & U.S. Department of Agriculture. 2015–2020 Dietary Guidelines for Americans. 8th Edition. (2015, December). Retrieved from http://health.gov/dietaryguidelines/2015/guidelines/

70. U.S. National Cancer Institute. (2013, June). Alcohol and cancer risk. Retrieved from https://www.cancer.gov/about-cancer/causes-prevention/risk/alcohol/alcohol-fact-sheet#r3

71. U.S. National Institute on Alcohol Abuse and Alcoholism. (2018, April). Surveillance report #110: Apparent per capita alcohol consumption: National, state, and regional trends, 1977-2016. Retrieved from https://pubs.niaaa.nih.gov/publications/surveillance110/CONS16.htm

72. Wallace, T. C., Wagner, M., Leveille, G., Keen, C. L., Woteki, C. E., Manley, C., et al. (2009). Unlocking the benefits of cocoa flavonols. *Food Technology*, *63*(10), 35–41.

73. West, R., & Rousseau, D. (2017). Understanding the chemistry and evolution of chocolate flavor. *Food Technology*, *71*(6), 70–81.

Chapter 28

1. Aloui, H., & Khwaldia, K. (2016). Natural antimicrobial edible coating for microbial safety and food quality enhancement. *Comprehensive Reviews in Food Science and Food Safety*, *15*, 1080–1103. doi:10.111/1541-4337.12226

2. Andress, E. L., & Harrison, J. A., (2006). *So easy to preserve* (6th ed.). Athens: Cooperative Extension Service, University of Georgia.

3. Bang, D. Y., Kyung, M., Kim, M. J., Jung, B. Y., Cho, M. C., Choi, S. M., … Lee, B. M. (2012). Human risk assessment of endocrine-disrupting chemicals derived from plastic food containers. *Comprehensive Reviews in Food Science and Food Safety*, *11*, 453–470. doi.org/10.1111/j.1541-4337.2012.00197.x

4. Barrett, D. M., & Theerakulkait, C. (1995). Quality indicators in blanched, frozen, stored vegetables. *Food Technology*, *49*(1) 62.

5. Brockgreinens, J., & Abbas, A. (2016). Responsive food packaging: Recent progress and technological prospects. *Comprehensive Reviews in Food Science and Safety*, *15*, 3–15. doi:10.111/154-4337.12174

6. Brody, A. L. (1996). Chills: A chronology of IFT's refrigerated and frozen foods division. *Food Technology*, *48*(12), 50.

7. Brody, A. L. (2000). Has the stand-up flexible pouch come of age? *Food Technology*, *54*(7), 94–95.

8. Brody, A. L. (2000). Smart packaging becomes Intellipac™. *Food Technology*, *54*(6), 104–107.

9. Brody, A. L. (2000). The when and why of aseptic packaging. *Food Technology*, *54*(9), 101–102.

10. Brody, A. L. (2002). Flavor scalping: Quality loss due to packaging. *Food Technology*, *56*(6), 124–125.

11. Brody, A. L. (2002). Food canning in the 21st century. *Food Technology*, *56*(3), 75–78.

12. Brody, A. L (2014). Take the heat off: Minimum heat processing and packaging. *Food Technology*, *68*(12), 86–87.

13. Brody. A. L. (2015). The trajectory of flexible packaging. *Food Technology*, *69*(1), 71–73.

14. Cabes, L. J., Jr. (1985). Plastic packaging used in retort processing: Control of key parameters. *Food Technology*, *39*(12), 57.

15. Clark, J. P. (2002). Drying still being actively researched. *Food Technology*, *56*(9), 97–101.

16. Clark, J. P. (2014). Putting on the pressure. *Food Technology*, *68*(1), 73–75.

17. Cooperative State Research, Education and Extension Service, & U.S. Department of Agriculture. (n.d.). National Center for Home Preservation. Retrieved from https://nchfp.uga.edu/index.html

18. Corcos, A. (1975). A note on the early life of Nicolas Appert. *Food Technology*, *29*(5), 114.

19. Cowell, N. D. (1995). Who introduced the tin can?—A new candidate. *Food Technology*, *49*(12), 61.

20. Cowell, N. D. (2007). More light on the dawn of canning. *Food Technology*, *61*(5), 40–45.

21. Delves-Broughton, J. (1990). Nisin and its uses as a food preservative. *Food Technology*, *44*(11), 100.

22. Dunn, T. (2015). The active, smart future of packaging. *Food Technology*, *69*(9), 118–121.

23. Gee, M., Farkas, D., & Rahman, A. R. (1977). Some concepts for the development of intermediate moisture foods. *Food Technology*, *31*(4), 58.

24. Giese, J. (1994). Antimicrobials: Assuring food safety. *Food Technology*, *48*(6), 102.

25. Goldblith, S. A. (1972). Controversy over the autoclave. *Food Technology*, *26*(12), 62.

26. Hintlian, C. B., & Hotchkiss, J. H. (1986). The safety of modified atmosphere packaging: A review. *Food Technology*, *40*(12), 70.

27. Institute of Food Technologists' Expert Panel on Food Safety and Nutrition. (1986). Effects of food processing on nutritive values. *Food Technology*, *40*(12), 109.

28. Institute of Food Technologists' Expert Panel on Food Safety and Nutrition. (1988). Migration of toxicants, flavors, and odor-active substances from flexible packaging materials to food. *Food Technology*, *42*(7), 95.

29. Ionizing radiation for the treatment of food, 21 C.F.R. § 179.26 (2017).

30. Ito, K. A., & Stevenson, K. E. (1984). Sterilization of packaging materials using aseptic systems. *Food Technology*, *38*(3), 60.

31. Jarden Home Brands. (2014). *Ball blue book guide to preserving* (37th ed.). Muncie, IN: Author.

32. Kester, J. J., & Fennema, O. R. (1986). Edible films and coatings: A review. *Food Technology*, *40*(12), 47.

33. Kimball, R. N., & Heyliger, T. L. (1990). Verifying the operation of steam retorts. *Food Technology*, *44*(12), 100.

34. Krochta, J. M., & De Mulder-Johnston, C. (1997). Edible and biodegradable polymer films: Challenges and opportunities. *Food Technology*, *51*(2), 61.

35. Lazaridis, H. N., & Sander, E. H. (1988). Home-canning of food: Effect of a higher process temperature (121°C) on the quality of low-acid foods. *Journal of Food Science*, *53*, 985.

36. Lisiecki, R., Spisak, A., Pawloski, C., & Stefanovic, S. (1990). Aseptic package addresses a variety of needs. *Food Technology*, *44*(6), 126.

37. McHugh, T. (2015). Ozone processing of foods and beverages. *Food Technology*, *69*(11), 72–74.

38. McHugh, T. (2016). Microwave processing heats up. *Food Technology*, *70*(10), 63–65.

39. McHugh, T. (2016). Putting ultrasound to use in food processing. *Food Technology*, *70*(12), 72–74.

40. McHugh, T. (2016). Radio frequency processing of food. *Food Technology*, *70*(8), 73–75.

41. McHugh, T. (2018). Freeze-drying fundamentals. *Food Technology*, *72*(2), 72–74.

42. McHugh, T., & Carswell, L. (2017). Illuminating e-beam processing. *Food Technology*, *71*(1), 64–66.

43. McHugh, T., & Milczarek, R. (2015). Solar thermal processing of foods for small operations. *Food Technology*, *69*(7), 102–104.

44. McHugh, T., & Pan, Z. (2015). Innovative infrared food processing. *Food Technology*, *69*(2), 79–81.

45. Marsh, K., & Bugusu, B. (2007). Food packaging—Roles, materials, and environmental issues. *Journal of Food Science*, *72*(3), R39–R55.

46. Marth, E. H. (1998). Extended shelf life refrigerated foods: Microbiological quality and safety. *Food Technology*, *52*(2), 57.

47. Mermelstein, N. H. (1999). Magnetic resonance imaging provides 100 percent inspection. *Food Technology*, *53*(11), 94–97.

48. Park, D. J., Cabes, L. J., Jr., & Collins, K. M. (1990). Determining temperature distribution in rotary, full-immersion, hot-water sterilizers. *Food Technology*, *44*(12), 113.

49. Poulsen, K. P. (1986). Optimization of vegetable blanching. *Food Technology*, *40*(6), 122.

50. Reid, D. S. (1990). Optimizing the quality of frozen foods. *Food Technology*, *44*(7), 78.

51. Robertson, G. L. (2014). Biobased but not biodegradable. *Food Technology*, *68*(6), 61–70.

52. Roos, Y. H., Karel, M., & Kokini, J. L. (1996). Glass transitions in low moisture and frozen foods: Effects on shelf life and quality. *Food Technology*, *50*(11), 95.

53. Sand, C. K. (2016). Modified atmospheric packaging expands, *Food Technology*, *70*(5), 72–74.

54. Sand, C. K. (2018). Packaging rules. *Food Technology*, *72*(4), 145–147.

55. Sand, C. K. (2018). The future of food packaging is personal. *Food Technology*, *72*(2), 75–77.

56. Sand, C. K., & Brody, A. L. (2015). Packaging that sells. *Food Technology*, *69*(8), 83–85.

57. Smith, J. P., Ramaswamy, H. S., & Simpson, B. K. (1990). Developments in food packaging technology. Part 1: Processing/cooking considerations. *Trends in Food Science and Technology, 1*(5), 107.

58. Smith, J. P., Ramaswamy, H. S., & Simpson, B. K. (1990). Developments in food packaging technology. Part 2: Storage aspects. *Trends in Food Science and Technology, 1*(5), 111.

59. Smith, J. S., & Pillai, S. (2004). Scientific status summary: Irradiation and food safety. *Food Technology, 58*(11), 48–55.

60. Tauxe, R. V. (2001). Food safety and irradiation: Protecting the public from foodborne infections. *Emerging Infectious Diseases, 7*(3), 516–521. Retrieved from http://www.cdc.gov/ncidod/eid/vol7no3_supp/tauxe.htm

61. Tuomy, J. M., & Young, R. (1982). Retort-pouch packaging of muscle foods for the Armed Forces. *Food Technology, 36*(2), 68.

62. U.S. Department of Agriculture. (2015). *Complete guide to home canning.* Agricultural Information Bulletin No. 539. Retrieved from https://nchfp.uga.edu/publications/publications_usda.html

63. U.S. Department of Agriculture. (2016, December). Irradiation and food safety answers to frequently asked questions. Retrieved from https://www.fsis.usda.gov/wps/portal/fsis/topics/food-safety-education/get-answers/food-safety-fact-sheets/production-and-inspection/irradiation-and-food-safety/irradiation-food-safety-faq

64. U.S. Environmental Protection Agency. (n.d.) Reducing wasted food & packaging: A guide for food services and restaurants. Document EPA-909-K14-002. Retrieved from https://www.epa.gov/sites/production/files/2015-08/documents/reducing_wasted_food_pkg_tool.pdf

65. U.S. National Oceanic Atmospheric Administration. (2017). Garbage patch fact sheet. Retrieved from https://marinedebris.noaa.gov/fact-sheet/garbage-patches-fact-sheet

66. U.S. National Oceanic Atmospheric Administration. (2018, July). Great Pacific Garbage Patch. Retrieved from eat hat are garbage patches? Retrieved from https://marinedebris.noaa.gov/info/patch.html

glossary

β-amylase an enzyme that hydrolyzes starch by breaking off two glucose units at a time, thus producing maltose.

5′-ribonucleotides compounds similar to the RNA found in all body cells; certain ones have been shown to act as flavor enhancers.

5-log reduction represents a reduction in organisms by a factor of 100,000-fold. This reduction represents a risk of less than one in 100,000. This reduction is accepted as making a product safe to eat when the pathogenic organism is one, such as salmonella, that requires a large number of microorganisms to cause illness.

acculturation the adaptation of a cultural group that has moved into a new area or country to the practices common in the new location.

adsorption the collection of a substance on the surface of a particle or globule without being taken in and incorporated into the globule.

aftertaste a taste that remains in the mouth after a food has been swallowed.

agglomerate to gather into a cluster, mass, or ball.

agglutination the sticking together, as with glue.

albumins simple proteins that are soluble in water.

alcohols chemical compounds characterized by an –OH group.

aldehydes chemical compounds characterized by a (–C–H) group.

alginate and carrageenan vegetable gums produced from seaweed.

amino acids small organic molecules, containing both an amino group (–NH$_2$) and an organic acid group (–COOH), that constitute the basic building blocks of proteins.

amino group a chemical group (–NH$_2$) characteristic of all amino acids.

amphiphilic liking or being attracted to both water and fat.

amylase an enzyme that breaks down or hydrolyzes starch to produce dextrins, maltose, and glucose.

amylopectin a fraction of starch with a highly branched and bushy type of molecular structure

amylose the long-chain or linear fraction of starch.

anaphylactic shock a multiple system reaction including the gastrointestinal tract, the skin, the respiratory tract, and the cardiovascular system that may be the result of a severe allergic reaction; severe hypotension and cardiovascular or respiratory collapse can occur within minutes, resulting in death.

anaphylactoid reactions generally involve several systems, including the gastrointestinal tract, the skin, the respiratory tract, and the cardiovascular system; death can occur within minutes of consuming an offending food.

antioxidant a substance that can stop the uptake of oxygen. For example, high-fat products develop off-flavors and off-odors due to the uptake of oxygen in a process called an oxidation reaction.

antioxidants a substance that retards or stops the development of oxidative rancidity; added to fatty foods in very small amounts.

appetite a desire or craving either for food in general or for some specific food.

aromatic having an aroma or fragrance; an ingredient added to enhance the natural aromas of food. Most herbs and spices, along with some vegetables, are aromatic.

aromatic compounds compounds that have an aroma or odor.

aseptic free from disease-producing microorganisms; filling a container that has been previously sterilized without recontaminating either product or container is an aseptic process.

aseptic canning a process in which the food material and the container are sterilized separately, and the container is filled without recontamination.

aseptic packaging a process that involves sterilizing the product and the package separately, filling the package without recontaminating the product, and sealing.

aspartame a high-intensity sweetener with the trade name Nutrasweet®.

astringency the puckering, drawing, or shrinking sensation produced by certain compounds in food.

atherogenic capable of contributing to the development of atherosclerosis (fatty deposits in the walls of the arteries).

atmospheric pressure downward pressure from the weight of the atmosphere (gas surrounding the earth); this pressure decreases at higher elevations.

adenosine triphosphate (ATP) adenosine triphosphate, a compound containing high-energy phosphate bonds in which the body cell traps energy from the metabolism of carbohydrate, fat, or protein; the energy in ATP is then used to do mechanical or chemical work in the body.

basted food moistened with pan drippings, melted fats, or other liquids during the cooking process.

beading the appearance of tiny droplets of syrup on the surface of a baked meringue as it stands.

biotechnology the use of biological systems and organisms to produce goods and services; may include biology, genetics, and biochemistry processes.

birefringence the ability of a substance to refract light in two directions; this produces a dark cross on each starch granule when viewed with a polarizing microscope.

blanch/blanched to heat for a few minutes by immersing in boiling water, surrounding with steam, or applying microwaves.

botulinum toxin a very potent toxin produced by *Clostridium botulinum* bacteria; in a low-acid environment, the high temperatures achieved in a pressure canner are required for complete destruction of the spores of this microbe.

botulism a serious illness resulting from consumption of a deadly toxin produced by the anaerobic bacterium *Clostridium botulinum*.

bound water water that is held so tightly by another molecule (usually a large molecule such as a protein) that it no longer has the properties of free water.

braise/braising to cook meat or poultry slowly in a small amount of liquid or in steam in a covered utensil after first browning.

brown roux equal parts, by weight, of flour and fat that are cooked together until a dark color and nutty aroma develop. A brown roux enhances the color and flavor of sauces and gravies.

buffer a substance that resists changes in pH.

bulking agents a substance used in relatively small amounts to affect the texture and body of some manufactured foods made without sugar or with reduced amounts; it compensates to some degree for the nonsweetening effects of sugar in a food product.

butyric acid a saturated fatty acid with four carbon atoms that is found in relatively large amounts in butter.

calorie a unit of heat measurement; in this chapter, we are referring to the small calorie used in chemistry; the kilocalorie (1 kilocalorie is equal to 1,000 small calories) is used in nutrition.

capon a male bird castrated when young.

caproic acid a saturated fatty acid with six carbon atoms; as a free fatty acid, it has an unpleasant odor.

caramelization the development of brown color and caramel flavor as dry sugar is heated to a high temperature; chemical decomposition occurs in the sugar.

carbonyl group a ketone $(C = O)$ or an aldehyde $(HC = O)$ group.

carcinogen/carcinogenic a cancer-causing substance.

carotenes yellow-orange, fat-soluble pigments.

carotenoid pigments fat-soluble, yellow-orange pigments that are produced by plants; may be stored in the fatty tissues of animals.

carotenoids yellow-orange-red, fat-soluble pigments found in some plant materials such as fruits and vegetables; for example beta-carotene.

casein a major protein found in milk.

catalyst a substance that changes the rate of a chemical reaction without being used up in the reaction; enzymes are catalysts.

catalyze/catalyzed to make a reaction occur at a more rapid rate by the addition of a substance, called a catalyst, which itself undergoes no permanent chemical change.

cellulase and hemicellulase enzymes that hydrolyze cellulose and hemicellulose, respectively.

certified colors synthetic colors tested on a batch-by-batch basis and certified by the FDA as having met set standards.

chelate to attach or bind a substance and hold it tightly so it does not react as usual; for example, to bind iron and copper atoms and hold them so they cannot act as pro-oxidants.

chicory a plant whose root is roasted and ground for use as a coffee substitute.

chlorogenic acid polyphenolic organic acid.

clarify/clarifying to make clear a cloudy liquid such as heated soup stock by adding raw egg white and/or egg shell; as the proteins coagulate, they trap tiny particles from the liquid that can then be strained out.

Clostridium botulinum a spore-forming, anaerobic bacterium that can produce a very potent toxin that causes botulism.

coagulate to produce a semisolid, firm mass or gel by denaturation of protein molecules followed by formation of new cross-links.

coagulation usually a change in proteins after denaturation, with new bonds being formed between protein chains, resulting in precipitation or gel formation; often accomplished by heating.

collagen a fibrous type of protein molecule found in the connective tissue of animals; produces gelatin when it is partially hydrolyzed.

colloidal usually refers to the state of subdivision of dispersed particles; intermediate between very small particles in true solution and large particles in suspension.

colloidal structure characterized by dispersed particles that are intermediate in size between very small particles in true solution and large particles in suspension. The particle size is generally 1 millimicron to 0.1 micron.

comminute/comminuted to reduce to small, fine particles.

complex carbohydrates carbohydrates made up of many small sugar units joined together, for example, starch and cellulose.

controlled atmosphere storage the monitoring and control of content of gases in the storage warehouse atmosphere; a low oxygen content slows down plant respiration and delays senescence (aging).

convenience foods foods that are partially or completely prepared by the food processor, with little or no additional food preparation required of the consumer.

covalent bonds a strong chemical bond that joins two atoms together.

cream of tartar potassium acid tartrate, the partial salt of tartaric acid, an organic acid.

critical control point any point in the process where loss of control may result in a health risk.

critical temperature the temperature above which a gas can exist only as a gas, regardless of the pressure, because the motion of the molecules is so violent.

cross-contamination contamination of one substance by another; for example, cooked chicken is contaminated with *Salmonella* organisms when it is cut on the same board used for cutting raw chicken.

cryoprotectants substances that offer protection to such sensitive molecules as proteins during freezing and frozen storage.

crystalline the aggregation of molecules of a substance in a set, ordered pattern, forming individual crystals.

crystallization the formation of crystals from the solidification of dispersed elements in a precise, orderly structure.

crystallize to form crystals, each of which consists of an orderly array of molecules in a pattern characteristic of that particular substance.

cuisine a style of cooking or manner of preparing food.

culture a way of life in which there are common customs for behavior and in which there is a common understanding among members of the group.

cytoplasm/cytoplasmic pertaining to the protoplasm of a cell, exclusive of the nucleus.

daily reference values (DRVs) refer to fat, carbohydrates (including fiber), protein, cholesterol, sodium, and potassium. These are listed on the Nutrition Facts label for 2,000- and 2,500-calorie intakes.

daily values nutrient standards used for labeling purposes; they include Daily Reference Values (DRVs) and Reference Daily Intakes (RDIs).

de-esterification the removal of the methyl ester groups from the galacturonic acid building blocks of the pectin molecule.

dehydrogenase an enzyme that catalyzes a chemical reaction in which hydrogen is removed, similar to an oxidation reaction.

demographic the statistical study of populations.

denaturation a change in a protein molecule, usually by unfolding of the amino acid chains, with a decrease in solubility.

density mass or weight per unit of volume.

desiccation the process of drying as moisture is lost.

dextrinization the process in which starch molecules are broken down into dextrins. Dextrins are polysaccharides composed of many glucose units, but are smaller than starch molecules.

dextrins polysaccharides, somewhat smaller in size than starch, resulting from the partial hydrolysis of starch; produced by dry roasting alone or with trace amounts of an acid catalyst.

diffusion the movement of a substance from an area of higher concentration to an area of lower concentration.

diglyceride glycerol combined with two fatty acids; usually present with monoglycerides in an emulsifier mixture.

disaccharide a sugar composed of two simple sugars or monosaccharides.

disappearance data data about food that "disappears" into the nation's food distribution system; quantities calculated from beginning inventories, annual production, imports, and exports.

disodium 5′-inosinate and disodium 5′-guanylate two of the 5′-ribonucleotides that appear to have the greatest strength as flavor enhancers.

disulfide linkages bonding through two sulfur atoms (–S–S–).

emulsifiers a substance that is active at the interface between two immiscible liquids, being attracted somewhat to each liquid; it acts as a bridge between them, allowing an emulsion to form.

emulsifying agents a substance that allows an emulsion to form because it has some characteristics of each of the two immiscible liquids and forms a bridge between them.

emulsions the dispersion of one substance within another with which it ordinarily does not mix (is immiscible). For example, oil and water or vinegar generally do not mix; however, in a product such as mayonnaise (containing oil and vinegar), an emulsion is formed.

encapsulate to enclose in a capsule; flavoring materials may be combined with substances such as gum acacia or modified starch to provide an encapsulation matrix and then spray-dried.

enriched enriched foods have had nutrients added so that the food meets the specified legal minimum or maximum levels of nutrients normally found in the food before processing. For example, flour and grain products are enriched to replace the nutrients lost when the bran and germ were removed to produce white flour.

enteropathogenic causing illness in the intestinal tract.

enzymatic oxidative browning the browning of cut surfaces of certain fruits and vegetables catalyzed by enzymes in the presence of oxygen. For example, sliced apples will brown even after a relatively brief period of air contact.

enzymatic reactions those that are *catalyzed* by enzymes, which are special proteins produced by living cells; a catalyst changes the rate of a reaction without itself undergoing permanent change.

enzymes protein molecules produced by living cells that act as organic catalysts and change the rate of a reaction without being used up in the process.

epidemiology/epidemiological the study of causes and control of diseases prevalent in human population groups.

espagnole sauce pronounced ess-span-yol, this is a classic brown sauce composed of brown stock, brown roux, mirepoix (diced onions, carrots, celery), and tomato purée.

essential oils concentrated flavoring oils extracted from food substances, such as oil of orange or oil of peppermint.

ester a type of chemical compound that results from combination of an organic acid (–COOH) with an alcohol (–OH).

ethnic pertains to basic divisions of humankind into groups that are distinguished by customs, characteristics, language, and so on.

ethylene a small gaseous molecule (C_2H_4) produced by fruits and vegetables as an initiator of the ripening process.

farm-value share the proportion of the retail price of food that is received by the farmer.

fatty acids a chemical molecule consisting of carbon and hydrogen atoms bonded in a chainlike structure; combined through its acid group (–COOH) with the alcohol glycerol to form triglycerides.

Federal Register provides citizens with official text of federal laws, presidential documents, and administrative regulations and notices. Also included are descriptions of federal organizations, programs, and activities. The *Federal Register* may be accessed on the Internet.

fermentation the transformation of organic molecules into smaller ones by the action of microorganisms; for example, yeast ferments glucose to carbon dioxide and alcohol.

ferric iron iron with a valence of 3^+ (Fe^{3+}).

ferrous containing iron.

fiber dietary fiber is nondigestible carbohydrates (including cellulose, hemicelluloses, and pectin) and lignin (a noncarbohydrate material found particularly in woody parts of plants) that are intrinsic and intact in plants; functional fiber consists of isolated nondigestible carbohydrates that have beneficial physiological effects in humans; and total fiber is the sum of dietary fiber and functional fiber.

flavonoid pigments a group of plant pigments with similar chemical structures; they include both anthoxanthins, which are white, and anthocyanins, which are red-blue.

flavor profile an outline of the major flavor components and their intensities that are blended to form the overall flavor sensation created by a food.

flocculated separated into small woolly or fluffy masses.

foam the dispersion of a gas in a liquid, such as a beaten egg-white mixture.

food additive a substance, other than usual ingredients, that is added to a food product for a specific purpose, such as flavoring, preserving, stabilizing, and thickening.

food allergy an abnormal immune response to components in food (usually proteins); symptoms can include gastrointestinal, cutaneous, and respiratory responses or other symptoms such as laryngeal edema, anaphylactic shock, or hypotension.

food infection illness produced by the presence and growth of pathogenic microorganisms in the gastrointestinal tract; they are often, but not necessarily, present in large numbers.

food intolerances abnormal responses to food that do not involve the immune system.

food intoxication illness produced by microbial toxin production in a food product that is consumed; the toxin produces the illness.

food safety a judgment of the acceptability of the risk involved in eating a food; if the risk is relatively low, a food substance may be considered safe.

food security access to enough nourishment, at all times, for an active, healthy life.

FoodNet the Foodborne Disease Active Surveillance Network, a project with the FDA, USDA, Centers for Disease Control and Prevention (CDC), and 10 states. Foodborne illness outbreaks are documented and tracked.

FORC-G Foodborne Outbreak Response Coordinating Group, a project with the USDA, FDA, and EPA.

fortified fortified foods have had ingredients, not normally found in the food, added to improve nutritional content. For example, orange juice is fortified with calcium because calcium is a nutrient not significantly found in oranges.

freeze-drying/freeze-dried a drying process that involves first freezing the product and then placing it in a vacuum chamber; the ice sublimes (goes from solid to vapor phase without going through the liquid phase); the dried food is more flavorful and fresher in appearance because it does not become hot in the drying process.

freezer burn characterized by grayish-brown or white leathery surfaces of meat that has been frozen and allowed air contact with the meat. Prevent by freezing in airtight packaging.

freezing mixtures mixtures of crushed ice and salt that become very cold, below the freezing point of plain water, because of the rapid melting of the ice by the salt and the attempt of the system to reach equilibrium; freezing mixtures are used to freeze ice creams in ice cream freezers.

functional foods any food that has a positive impact on an individual's health, physical performance, or state of mind in addition to its normal nutritive value; sometimes called *nutraceuticals*.

galacturonic acid a chemical molecule very similar to the sugar galactose and containing an organic acid (carboxyl) group in its chemical structure.

gamma rays one of three kinds of rays emitted by radioactive substances.

gastroenteritis inflammation of the gastrointestinal tract.

gel a colloidal dispersion that shows some rigidity and will, when unmolded, keep the shape of the container in which it had been placed.

gelatinization the sum of changes that occur in the first stages of heating starch granules in a moist environment; includes swelling of granules as water is absorbed and disruption of the organized granule structure.

gelatinization of starch the swelling of starch granules when heated in the presence of water.

Gelation is gel formation, as when a gel forms when starch paste cools, or when a gelatin dispersion thickens. It is characterized by a three-dimensional brush heap structure.

generic a class of packaged food products that do not carry a specific brand name.

genetic engineering the use of recombinant DNA or rDNA technology to modify plants and microorganisms genetically. Genetic engineering or modification allows for the efficient transfer of genetic material compared to traditional cross-breeding, which may require multiple generations.

germination the sprouting of a seed.

globulins simple proteins that are soluble in dilute salt solutions.

glucoamylase an enzyme that hydrolyzes starch by breaking off one glucose unit at a time, thus producing glucose immediately.

glucose a monosaccharide or simple sugar that is the basic building unit for starch.

glucose isomerase an enzyme that changes glucose to fructose.

gluten a protein found in wheat that gives structure to baked products.

glycemic response the rise in blood glucose after consumption of a food. The consumption of some foods (such as sugar or high sugar containing foods) results in a greater rise in blood glucose compared to other foods.

glycogen a complex carbohydrate—a polysaccharide—used for carbohydrate storage in the liver and muscles of the body; sometimes called *animal starch*.

glycoproteins proteins composed of amino acid chains with a carbohydrate moiety, such as a galactose derivative, attached at certain points.

goitrogen a substance that is capable of causing enlargement (goiter) of the thyroid gland in the neck area.

good manufacturing practices recommended rules for maintaining sanitation, safety, and quality assurance to be followed in a food-processing plant.

grade a symbol, such as Grade A or No. 1, that indicates that the food product carrying this label has met specified predetermined standards of quality.

grading the examining of food products and classifying them according to quality, such as Grade A, B, or C, based on defined standards.

GRAS the list of food additives that are "generally recognized as safe" by a panel of experts; this list is maintained and periodically reevaluated by the FDA.

guarana a South American berry with alleged aphrodisiac qualities; the seeds of the berry contain caffeine.

hazard a source of danger, long- or short-term, such as microbial food poisoning, cancer, birth defects, and so on.

headspace the volume above a liquid or solid in a container.

hedonic having to do with pleasure; a hedonic scale indicates how much a person likes or dislikes a food.

hedonic scale a rating scale indicating the degree of liking, usually involving a range from 1 for "dislike extremely" to 7 for "like extremely."

hemorrhagic colitis bleeding and inflammation of the colon or large intestine.

hepatitis inflammation of the liver.

hermetic/hermetically completely sealed so as to keep air or gas from getting in or out.

hermetic packaging packaging that is airtight.

hexose a simple sugar or monosaccharide with six carbon atoms.

high-risk or potentially hazardous foods these foods support the rapid growth of microorganisms. Potentially hazardous foods are generally moist, high in protein, and have a neutral or slightly acidic pH. Examples include milk and milk products, sliced melons, garlic and oil mixtures, poultry, meat, seafood, sprouts and raw seeds, baked or boiled potatoes, shell eggs, tofu, soy-protein foods, cooked rice, beans, or other heat-treated plant foods.

home meal replacement prepared foods purchased to be consumed at home that have similar characteristics to food that may be prepared in the home. Roasted chickens purchased in a food service establishment or a grocery store are an example of a home meal replacement food.

homogenization a process used to subdivide particles, usually fat globules, into very small, uniform-sized pieces. Milk is homogenized to prevent the separation of the cream from nonfat milk.

homogenization of whole milk a process in which whole milk is forced, under pressure, through very small openings, dividing the fat globules into very tiny particles

"hot" peppers peppers that contain a substance known as capsaicin, which gives them the highly pungent characteristic called "hot." This substance also stimulates the flow of saliva. "Hotter" peppers contain more capsaicin, concentrated mainly in the thin tissues or veins where the seeds are attached to the spongy central portion.

humectant a substance that can absorb moisture readily.

hydration capacity the ability of a substance, such as flour, to absorb water.

hydrocolloids large molecules, such as those that make up vegetable gums, that form colloidal dispersions, hold water, and often serve as thickeners and stabilizers in processed foods.

hydrogen bond the relatively weak chemical bond that forms between a hydrogen atom and another atom with a slight negative charge, such as an oxygen or a nitrogen atom; each atom in this case is already covalently bonded to other atoms in the molecule of which it is part.

hydrolysis the breaking of a chemical linkage between basic units of a more complex molecule to yield smaller molecules; water participates in the reaction and becomes part of the end products.

hygroscopic tending to attract or absorb moisture from the atmosphere.

idiosyncratic illnesses illnesses attributed to food although the mechanism for the illness is unknown; sulfite-induced asthma is a documented idiosyncratic illness.

immiscible describing substances that cannot be mixed or blended.

induction coil a coiled apparatus made up of two coupled circuits; interruptions in the direct current in one circuit produce an alternating current of high electrical potential in the other.

inspection the examining of food products or processes carefully and critically in order to assure proper sanitary practices, labeling, and/or safety for the consumer.

interesterification the hydrolysis of the ester bond between glycerol and the fatty acid. The ester bond is re-formed among the mixed free fatty acids and glycerol.

inulin a complex carbohydrate (a polysaccharide) found in the roots of some plants that yields fructose when broken down or hydrolyzed.

invert sugar composed of glucose and fructose; formed from sucrose heated in water, water and an acid, or with an enzyme called invertase (sucrase); desirable in food products because it resists crystallization and retains moisture.

invisible fat fat that occurs naturally in food products such as meats, dairy products, nuts, and seeds.

iodized salt table salt to which small amounts of a stabilized iodide compound have been added to increase dietary iodine and prevent goiter (enlargement of the thyroid gland); its use is encouraged particularly in areas where the soil is deficient in iodine.

ion an electrically charged atom or group of atoms; the electrical charge results when a neutral atom or group of atoms loses or gains one or more electrons; loss of electrons results in a positively charged ion.

irradiation the treatment of food by electron beams, gamma rays, or x-rays to reduce significantly bacteria, virus, or fungus contamination.

isomer a molecule that is chemically identical to another with a different structure and thus different properties.

isomerization a molecular change resulting in a molecule containing the same elements in the same proportions but having a slightly different structure and, hence, different properties; in carotenoids, heat causes a change in the position of the double bonds between carbon atoms.

jaundice a condition in which the skin and eyeballs become abnormally yellow due to the presence of bile pigments in the blood.

ketones chemical compounds characterized by a $\left(-\overset{\overset{\textstyle O}{\displaystyle\|}}{C}-\right)$ group.

kilocalorie one kilocalorie is equal to 1,000 small calories; the small calorie is used in chemistry, whereas the kilocalorie is used in nutrition.

kinetic motion the very rapid vibration and movement of tiny molecules or ions dispersed in true solution.

labile unstable.

lacquered tin an enamel coating on the inside of tin cans.

lacquered tin-coated cans an inner lacquer or enamel coating; the coating is of variable composition and overlies the basic tin-coated steel, protecting certain canned foods from discoloration.

lacto-ovo vegetarians those who consume milk, eggs, and products derived from them as well as vegetable foods.

latent heat the heat or energy required to change the state of a substance, that is, from liquid to gas, without changing the temperature of the substance.

LDL cholesterol cholesterol that is combined with low-density lipoproteins in the blood; sometimes called the "bad cholesterol," in contrast to the "good cholesterol" combined with blood high-density lipoproteins.

legume any of a large family of plants characterized by true pods enclosing seeds; dried beans and peas.

lignin a woody, fibrous, noncarbohydrate material produced in mature plants; component of the fiber complex.

linoleic acid a polyunsaturated fatty acid with 18 carbon atoms and two double bonds.

linolenic acid a polyunsaturated fatty acid with 18 carbon atoms and 3 double bonds between carbon atoms; omega-3 fatty acid.

lipase an enzyme that catalyzes the hydrolysis of triglycerides to yield glycerol and fatty acids.

lipids a broad group of fatlike substances with similar properties.

lipoprotein a lipid or fatty substance combined with a protein; egg yolk contains lipoproteins that combine phospholipids with protein.

lipoxygenase an enzyme that catalyzes the oxidation of unsaturated fatty acids.

lycopene a reddish, fat-soluble pigment of the carotenoid type.

Maillard reaction the carbonyl group of a sugar combines with the amino group of a protein, initiating a series of chemical reactions that result in a brown color and change in flavor; it may occur in relatively dry foods in long storage as well as in foods heated to high temperatures.

maltase an enzyme that hydrolyzes maltose to glucose.

maltodextrins a mixture of small molecules resulting from starch hydrolysis, having a dextrose equivalent (DE) of less than 20.

maltose a disaccharide or double sugar composed of two glucose units.

marbling the distribution of fat throughout the muscles of meat animals.

marinated to soak in a prepared liquid for a time, in this case for seasoning purposes.

mass the tendency of an object to remain at rest if it is stationary or to continue in motion if it is already moving; mass can be determined by measuring the force with which an object is attracted to the earth, i.e., by measuring its weight.

maturing agent a substance that brings about some oxidative changes in white flour and improves its baking properties.

mechanical separation meat separated from the bone by forcing the bones with the attached meat through a sieve. Mechanically separated meat will be a pastelike product. Mechanically separated beef is prohibited for human food use. Mechanically separated pork and poultry may be used for human food but must be listed on the label.

melting point the temperature at which a solid fat becomes a liquid oil.

meniscus the curved upper surface of a column of liquid.

mesophilic bacteria bacteria that grow best at moderate temperatures.

mesophilic microorganisms organisms that grow at moderate temperatures.

metabolic having to do with any of the chemical changes that occur in living cells.

metabolic food disorders the result of inherited defects in the ability to metabolize some components of a food or from a genetically determined enhanced sensitivity due to an altered metabolic pattern; lactose intolerance is an example of a metabolic food disorder.

methyl ester the chemical combination of methyl alcohol with an organic acid, such as galacturonic acid.

methyl ester of galacturonic acid ester is the chemical word used to describe the linkage between an organic acid group (–COOH) and an alcohol group (–OH); in this case, the alcohol is methanol (which contains only one carbon atom) and the acid is galacturonic acid.

micelles a colloidal particle.

microbiology the branch of biology that deals with microorganisms.

microencapsulation A coating is applied to very fine particles of a probiotic culture, which protects them until an appropriate time for their release in the gastrointestinal (GI) tract.

middlings the relatively fine wheat endosperm which must be further reduced by rollers to produce flour, also called *midds*.

mirepoix two parts diced onion, one part diced carrots, and one part diced celery. One cup of mirepoix would include ½ cup onion, ¼ cup carrots, ¼ cup celery. Mirepoix is used to flavor sauces and soups.

mitochondria sausage-shaped bodies in the cell cytoplasm that contain the enzymes necessary for energy metabolism.

modified atmosphere packaging the enclosure of food products in gas-barrier materials in which the gaseous environment has been changed or modified in order to extend shelf life.

moisture-/vapor-proof materials materials that are relatively impermeable to water vapor and other gases; they are desirable for wrapping frozen foods to minimize the loss of moisture, particularly from sublimation.

molecule the smallest particle of a substance that can exist separately and still preserve its characteristic properties. For example, a molecule of water (H_2O) still exhibits the chemical and physical properties of water. Molecules are composed of atoms bonded together. If the atoms are alike (as in oxygen formation, O_2) the resulting molecule is called a compound.

mollusks a type of shellfish characterized by a soft, unsegmented body enclosed in a shell of one or more pieces; examples are oysters and clams.

monoglyceride glycerol combined with one fatty acid; used as an emulsifier.

monosaccharide a simple sugar unit, such as glucose.

monounsaturated a fatty acid with one double bond between carbon atoms; capable of binding more hydrogen.

monounsaturated fatty acid a fatty acid with one double bond between carbon atoms.

mouthfeel how a food feels in the mouth (i.e. gritty, creamy, or lumpy).

mucoprotein a complex or conjugated protein containing a carbohydrate substance combined with a protein.

mycotoxins toxins produced by molds.

nitrogen base a molecule with a nitrogen-containing chemical group that makes the molecule alkaline.

noncariogenic not contributing to the development of caries in teeth.

nonenzymatic oxidation an oxidation reaction that occurs spontaneously and is not catalyzed by enzymes, for example, oxidation of fats that results in rancidity.

nonvolatile not able to vaporize or form a gas at ordinary temperatures.

nutrition labeling a special type of food labeling, in addition to basic requirements concerning net contents and manufacturer, that gives information about the nutrient and caloric content of the food on a per-serving basis.

objective evaluation having to do with a known object as distinguished from existing in the mind; in food science, measurement of the characteristics of food with a laboratory instrument such as a pH meter to indicate acidity or a viscometer to measure viscosity or consistency.

odor a smell, pleasant or unpleasant, perceived through stimulation of the olfactory center.

olfactory having to do with the sense of smell.

oligofructose an oligosaccharide; a carbohydrate molecule made up of a small number of fructose molecules linked together.

oligosaccharide the general term for sugars composed of a few—often between 3 and 10—simple sugars or monosaccharides.

omega-3 fatty acids polyunsaturated fatty acids that have the first double bond on the third carbon atom from the methyl ($-CH_3$) end of the carbon chain.

omega-3 PUFA a group of polyunsaturated fatty acids that have the first double bond on the third carbon atom from the end of the carbon chain; also called *n*-3 fatty acids.

omega-6 polyunsaturated fatty acids (PUFA) polyunsaturated fatty acids that have the first double bond on the sixth carbon atom from the methyl ($-CH_3$) end of the carbon chain.

organic acid an acid containing carbon atoms, for example, citric acid and acetic acid.

organic acids generally weak acids characterized by a

$$\overset{\overset{\textstyle O}{\|}}{\text{carboxyl} (-C-H)}\ \text{group.}$$

organic polymers large carbon-containing molecules made up of many small molecules linked together.

osmosis the movement of water through a semipermeable membrane; as ice crystals form extracellularly, the concentration of solute in this area is increased, and water then moves out of the cell in an attempt to equalize the solute concentration.

ovalbumin a major protein found in egg white.

ovary/ovaries part of the seed-bearing organ of a flower; an enlarged hollow part containing ovules that develop into seeds.

oven spring the rapid increase in volume in a loaf of bread during the first few minutes of baking.

oxalic acid an organic acid that forms an insoluble salt with calcium.

oxidase an enzyme that catalyzes an oxidation reaction.

oxidation a chemical reaction that involves the addition of oxygen.

oxidation reactions chemical reactions in which oxygen is added or hydrogen is removed or electrons are lost.

palatable pleasing to the taste.

papillae small, nipplelike projections of various shapes on the surface of the tongue.

pasteurization a mild heat treatment that destroys microorganisms that may cause disease but does not destroy all microorganisms in the product.

pasteurize to treat with mild heat to destroy pathogens—but not all microorganisms—present in a food product.

pathogenic microorganisms that cause disease may be called pathogens or pathogenic microorganisms.

pathogenic bacteria bacteria that can cause disease.

pathogenic microorganisms microbes capable of causing disease.

pearled a process that removes the outer hull, leaving a small, round, light "pearl" of grain.

pectin a complex carbohydrate (polysaccharide) composed of galacturonic acid subunits, partially esterified with methyl alcohol and capable of forming a gel.

pectin esterase an enzyme that catalyzes the hydrolysis of a methyl ester group from the large pectin molecule, producing pectic acid; pectic acid tends to form insoluble salts with such ions as calcium (Ca^{2+}); these insoluble salts cause the cloud in orange juice to become destabilized and settle.

pectinase an enzyme that hydrolyzes the linkages that hold the small building blocks of galacturonic acid together in the pectic substances, producing smaller molecules.

pentosans complex carbohydrates (polysaccharides) that yield five-carbon sugars (pentoses) when hydrolyzed.

pentose a simple sugar or monosaccharide with five carbon atoms.

peptide a chemical molecule composed of amino acids linked together.

peptide linkage linkage between two amino acids that connects the amino group of one and the acid (carboxyl) group of the other.

pH expression of the degree of acidity on a scale of 1 to 14, 1 being most acid, 7 neutral, and 14 most alkaline.

phenolic compound an organic compound that includes in its chemical structure an unsaturated ring with –OH groups on it; polyphenols have more than one –OH group.

phenylketonuria (PKU) a genetic disease characterized by an inborn error in the body's ability to metabolize the amino acid phenylalanine.

phospholipid a type of lipid characterized chemically by glycerol combined with two fatty acids, phosphoric acid, and a nitrogen-containing base, for example, lecithin.

phytochemicals biochemical substances, other than vitamins, of plant origin that appear to have a positive effect on health; they include phenolic compounds, terpenoids, pigments, and other antioxidants.

phytoestrogens substances found in plant foods, such as soybeans, that have an estrogenlike effect on the body when consumed in the diet.

plant exudates materials that ooze out of certain plants; some that ooze from certain tree trunks and branches are gums.

plastic able to be molded into various shapes without shattering as a force is applied; plastic fats can be mixed or creamed.

plastic fat a fat that can be molded or shaped, such as hydrogenated shortening, margarine, or butter.

plasticity the ability to be molded or shaped; in plastic fats, both solid crystals and liquid oil are present.

poach/poaching to cook in a hot liquid, carefully handling the food to retain its form.

polar having two opposite natures, such as both positive and negative charges.

polar materials chemical molecules that have electric charges (positive or negative) and tend to be soluble in water.

polarized light light that vibrates in one plane.

polydextrose a bulking agent made from an 89:10:1 mixture of glucose, sorbitol, and citric acid; in body metabolism, it yields one kilocalorie per gram.

polymer a large molecule formed by linking together many smaller molecules of a similar kind.

polymerization the formation of large molecules by combining smaller chemical units.

polymers molecules of relatively high molecular weight that are composed of many small molecules acting as building blocks.

polyol a sugar alcohol.

polyphenol a phenol compound with more than one –OH group attached to the unsaturated ring of carbon atoms; some produce bitterness in coffee and tea.

polysaccharide a complex carbohydrate made up of many simple sugar (monosaccharide) units linked together; in the case of starch, the simple sugars are all glucose.

polyunsaturated fats fats that contain a relatively high proportion of polyunsaturated fatty acids, which have two or more double bonds between carbon atoms; these fatty acids are shaped differently from saturated fatty acids because of the double bonds.

polyunsaturated fatty acids fatty acids that have two or more double bonds between carbon atoms; they could hold more hydrogen atoms if these bonds were broken.

pooled a term used to describe when several eggs are cracked out into a bowl. Several eggs "pooled" in one bowl increase contamination risk because one contaminated egg will contaminate the entire bowl of eggs.

potassium bromate an oxidizing substance often added to bread dough to strengthen the gluten of strong or high-protein flour.

prebiotics nondigestible foods that beneficially affect the host by selectively stimulating the growth and/or activity of one or more bacteria in the colon.

precipitate to become insoluble and separate out of a solution or dispersion.

precursor something that comes before; in flavor study, it is a compound that is nonflavorful but can be changed, usually by heat or enzymes, into a flavorful substance.

precursors a substance that "comes before"; a precursor of vitamin A is a substance out of which the body cells can make vitamin A.

probiotic live microorganism food ingredients that enhance human health by improving intestinal microbial balance.

proofing/proofed the last rising of bread dough after it is molded into a loaf and placed in the baking pan.

pro-oxidant a substance that encourages the development of oxidative rancidity.

protease an enzyme that hydrolyzes protein.

protein efficiency ratio a measure of protein quality assessed by determining the extent of weight gain in experimental animals when fed the test item.

proteinase an enzyme that hydrolyzes protein to smaller fragments, eventually producing amino acids.

protozoa one-celled animals.

P/S ratio the ratio of polyunsaturated to saturated fatty acids in a food, also sometimes calculated for a total diet; for example, a diet sometimes prescribed for certain individuals with high blood lipids may have a P/S ratio of 3:1 or 3.

psychrotrophic bacteria bacteria that grow best at cold temperatures (cold-loving bacteria).

psychrotropic microorganisms organisms that can grow at refrigerator temperatures.

PulseNet a national network of public health laboratories to "fingerprint" bacteria that may be foodborne, a project with the FDA, USDA, CDC, and all 50 states. Enables tracking of a foodborne illness outbreak to a single source or indicates more than one outbreak has occurred from multiple sources.

pungency a sharp, biting quality.

putrefactive fermentations decomposition of organic matter by microorganisms, producing foul-smelling end products.

quick service restaurants food services that provide limited, but fast, service. Menu selections are few and include foods that may be prepared and served quickly.

radioactive giving off radiant energy in the form of particles or rays, such as alpha, beta, and gamma rays, by the disintegration of atomic nuclei (the central part of atoms).

rancidity the deterioration of fats, usually by an oxidation process, resulting in objectionable flavors and odors.

raw starch flavor an undercooked starch in a sauce, gravy, or soup will reduce the flavor of the other ingredients and will provide a flat flavor. You can learn to identify this flavor by tasting a product shortly after the starch has been added, then by tasting it again as cooking proceeds. A fully cooked product should have no raw starch flavor.

reducing substance a molecule that has an effect opposite that of an oxidizing agent; hydrogen or electrons are gained in a reaction involving a reducing substance.

reducing substances chemical molecules that can supply hydrogen or electrons to prevent or reverse oxidation; the reduced state of iron is the ferrous form ($Fe2^+$).

reducing sugar a sugar with a free aldehyde or ketone group that has the ability to chemically "reduce" other chemical compounds and thus become oxidized itself; glucose, fructose, maltose, and lactose, but not sucrose, are reducing sugars.

reduction reactions chemical reactions in which there is a gain in hydrogen or in electrons.

reference daily intakes (RDIs) listed on the Nutrition Facts label for nutrients including vitamin A, vitamin C, calcium, and iron.

rehydrate to add water to replace that lost during drying.

respiration a metabolic process by which cells consume oxygen and give off carbon dioxide; continues after harvest.

reticulum a netlike sheath.

retort pressure canning equipment used in commercial canning operations to process low-acid foods at high temperatures.

retort pouch a flexible, laminated package made of special materials that withstands high-temperature processing in a commercial pressure canner called a retort.

retrogradation the process in which starch molecules, particularly the amylose fraction, reassociate or bond together in an ordered structure after disruption by gelatinization; ultimately, a crystalline order appears.

reverse osmosis a process of "dewatering" whereby ions and small molecules do not pass through a membrane but water does pass through.

risk a measure of the probability and severity of harm to human health.

roux a thickening agent made by heating a blend of fat and flour.

ruminant an animal with four stomachs; for example, cattle, sheep, goats, deer, and elk.

ruminant animal an animal with multiple stomachs, one of which is called a *rumen,* where bacterial action occurs on the food that has been eaten; the animal—for example, a cow—"chews its cud" (material regurgitated and chewed a second time).

salmonella bacteria, some strains of which can cause illness in humans; because the microorganisms themselves produce the gastrointestinal symptoms, the illness is called a food infection.

salmonellosis illness produced by ingestion of *Salmonella* organisms.

salt a chemical compound derived from an acid by replacement of the hydrogen (H^+), wholly or in part, with a metal or an electrically positive ion, for example, sodium citrate.

saturated fatty acid a fatty acid with no double bonds between carbon atoms; it holds all of the hydrogen that can be attached to the carbon atoms.

saturated solution a solution containing all of the solute that it can dissolve at that temperature.

Scoville heat units a measurement of chili pungency that was developed through taste testing of a trained sensory panel. High-performance liquid chromatography is now used to measure a chili's "heat."

secondary amines derivatives of ammonia (NH_3) in which two of the hydrogen atoms are replaced by other carbon-containing chemical groups.

senescing growing old or aging.

sensory having to do with the senses (sight, taste, smell, hearing, and touch); connected with receiving and transmitting sense impressions.

septicemia the presence of pathogenic microorganisms in the blood.

shear term used to describe various kinds of agitation or stirring that a starch mixture may be subjected to during cooking and processing. Excessive shear will damage the starch granule causing loss of viscosity.

shelf-stable foods foods that can be stored at room temperature.

shred the area on the sides of a loaf of bread, just above the pan, where the dough rises in the oven before the crust is formed; a desirable shred is even and unbroken.

slurry a thin mixture of water and a fine insoluble material such as flour.

smoke point the temperature at which smoke comes continuously from the surface of a fat heated under standardized conditions.

solute a dissolved or dispersed substance.

solution a mixture resulting from the dispersion of small molecules or ions (called the *solute*) in a liquid such as water (called the *solvent*).

solvent the liquid in which another substance is dissolved.

sorbitol a sugar alcohol similar to glucose in chemical structure but with an alcohol group (−C=OH) replacing the aldehyde group (H–CO5O) of glucose.

soy milk the liquid produced by cooking, mashing, and straining soybeans.

specifications a written description of the food or product that is desired. Generally used in food service purchasing. This written description must be thorough so that the desired characteristics, quality, and packaging of the item are clearly understood.

sponge the mixture of liquid, yeast, sugar, and part of the flour to make a thin batter that is held at a lukewarm temperature to allow yeast activity for a period before the remaining ingredients are added to form a dough.

spore an encapsulated, resistant form of a microorganism.

stabilizer a water-holding substance, such as a vegetable gum, that interferes with ice crystal formation and contributes to a smooth texture in frozen desserts.

standard of identity a standard set by the U.S. Food and Drug Administration to specifically describe a food; to be labeled as such, a food must meet these specifications.

standard operating procedures written instructions for performing a certain process; they must be followed exactly and a record kept of completion of the task.

starch gelatinization the swelling of starch granules when heated with water, often resulting in thickening.

starch granule a particle formed in the plant seed or root when starch is stored; composed of millions of starch molecules laid down in a very organized pattern; the shape of the granule is typical for each species.

steep/steeped to soak.

sterilization the complete destruction of microorganisms in a medium.

sterilize to destroy essentially all microorganisms.

sterol a type of fat or lipid molecule with a complex chemical structure, for example, cholesterol.

stew to simmer in a small to moderate quantity of liquid.

streams the various product flows in a mill which vary by particle size, ash content, and component of the wheat kernel.

sublimation a solid, such as ice, goes directly to the vapor state (water vapor) without going through the liquid state; in the freezer, sublimed water may collect as frost.

succulent having juicy tissues; not dry.

sulfhydryl compound a chemical substance that contains an –SH group.

surface activity the lowering of the surface tension of a liquid because of agents that tend to concentrate at the surface.

surface tension tension created over the surface of a liquid because of the greater attraction of the liquid molecules for each other than for the gaseous molecules in the air above the liquid.

syneresis separation or "weeping" of liquid from a gel.

synergism/synergistic an interaction in which the effect of the mixture is greater than the effect of the sum of component parts.

synthetic compounds those produced by chemically combining two or more simple compounds or elements in the laboratory.

tactile having to do with the sense of touch.

tallow is fat extracted from sheep or cattle. Tallow is highly saturated and is desirable for some purposes because of its meaty flavor.

taste sensations perceived through stimulation of taste buds on the tongue; primary tastes are sweet, salty, sour, and bitter.

taste buds a group of cells, including taste cells, supporting cells, and nerve fibers.

taste pore a tiny opening from the surface of the tongue into the taste bud.

taste receptor tiny ends of the taste cells that come in contact with the substance being tasted.

temper or tempering gradual warming of beaten eggs before adding to a hot liquid. If a recipe states to temper the eggs, when the mixture (usually milk and starch) is thoroughly hot, pour one-fourth or more of the hot mixture slowly into the beaten eggs while mixing. Complete the process by pouring this hot mixture containing eggs into the pan and finish cooking.

temperature danger zone a range of temperatures which allow rapid growth of bacteria and, in some cases, toxin production.

texture arrangement of the parts of a material showing the structure; the texture of baked flour products such as a slice of bread may be fine and even or coarse and open; the texture of a cream sauce may be smooth or lumpy.

toxin-mediated infections illness produced when a food containing pathogenic organisms is consumed; these organisms then produce illness-causing toxins in the intestines.

translucency partial transparency.

triglyceride glycerol combined with three fatty acids; most food fats are triglycerides.

trussed poultry tied with thread or butcher's twine into a more compact shape. The legs are tied together, then the string is pulled up across the leg and thigh joints up above the wings. Trussing a bird promotes even cooking and helps to retain moisture.

tuber a short, thickened, fleshy part of an underground stem, such as a potato; new plants develop from the buds or eyes.

ultrafiltration filtration through an extremely fine filter.

unsaturated fatty acid a general term used to refer to any fatty acid with one or more double bonds between carbon atoms; capable of binding more hydrogen at these points of unsaturation.

vacuum drying drying a product in a vacuum chamber in which water vaporizes at a lower temperature than at atmospheric pressure.

value added term used to describe a food to which value has been added, often by processing. Lettuce, for example, can be purchased as a head or chopped, washed, and ready to serve.

vapor pressure the pressure produced over the surface of a liquid as a result of a change in some of the molecules from a liquid to a vapor or gaseous state.

vegans those who exclude from their diet all products that are not of plant origin.

vegetable gums polysaccharide substances that are derived from plants, including seaweed and various shrubs or trees, have the ability to hold water, and often act as thickeners, stabilizers, or gelling agents in various food products; for example, algin, carrageenan, and gum arabic.

vegetable-fruit botanically, a fruit is the ovary and surrounding tissues, including the seeds, of a plant; a vegetable-fruit is the fruit part of a plant that is not sweet and is usually served with the main course of a meal, for example, squash, cucumbers, and tomatoes.

viscoelastic ability of a material to stretch, hold shape, and partially bounce back to original shape; a substance that is both viscous and elastic.

viscosity resistance to flow; thickness or consistency.

visible fats refined fats and oils used in food preparation, including edible oils, margarine, butter, lard, and shortenings.

warmed-over flavor describes the rapid onset of lipid oxidation that occurs in cooked meats during refrigerated storage; oxidized flavors are detectable after only 48 hours.

waxy maize a waxy variety of corn; the starch of this variety contains only the amylopectin fraction.

yeast autolysate the preparation of yeast in which the cells have been destroyed; contains many flavorful substances.

yeast fermentation a process in which enzymes produced by the yeast break down sugars to carbon dioxide and alcohol, and also produce some flavor substances.

index